CARSWELL

Environmental Law

Cases and Materials

Third Edition

by

Meinhard Doelle
BSc, LLB, LLM, JSD

Professor of Law, Dalhousie University,
Marine & Environmental Law Institute
Canadian Chair, Marine Environmental
Protection, World Maritime University

Chris Tollefson
BA (Hon.), LLB, LLM

Professor of Law, University of Victoria
Executive Director, Pacific Centre for
Environmental Law and Litigation

THOMSON REUTERS®

30835446

A cataloguing record for this publication is available from Library and Archives Canada

ISBN 978-0-7798-8968-6

Printed in the United States by Thomson Reuters.

 THOMSON REUTERS®

THOMSON REUTERS CANADA, A DIVISION OF THOMSON REUTERS CANADA LIMITED

One Corporate Plaza
2075 Kennedy Road
Toronto, Ontario
M1T 3V4

Customer Support
1-416-609-3800 (Toronto International)
1-800-387-5164 (Toll Free Canada U.S.)
Fax 1-416-298-5082 (Toronto)
Fax 1-877-750-9041 (Toll Free Canada Only)
Email CustomerSupport.LegalTaxCanada@TR.com

Preface

This, our third edition, goes to press as environmental law issues continue to take centre stage both domestically and internationally. Now more than ever, environmental law is a core practice area and an important realm of legal scholarship.

Just as our second edition was published after a flurry of environmental law reform at the federal level, so too is this third edition. When our second edition came out in 2013, the Harper government's controversial reforms to the *Canadian Environmental Assessment Act*, the *National Energy Board Act*, the *Fisheries Act*, and the *Navigable Waters Protection Act* had just come into force. One immediate effect was to change mid-stream the rules governing the Northern Gateway Pipeline project environmental assessment hearing. A key issue in that hearing was the project's impact on boreal caribou — an iconic and endangered species that we chose to adorn the cover of that edition.

The ultimate fate of these Harper era reforms remains uncertain. The Trudeau government pledged to restore the public trust in government's commitment to protect the environment, fight climate change, and recognize and respect Indigenous rights. This third edition chronicles and evaluates the extent to which the federal government is on track to fulfill those pledges. A key crucible in which to make that assessment is the saga of the Trans Mountain pipeline expansion project. This project — and its impacts and implications for species at risk (especially the Southern Resident Orca population), Canada's climate obligations, and Aboriginal rights and title — has already led to some precedent-setting environmental litigation, and will likely continue to do so. It is fitting, we think, that on the cover of this edition is featured a member of that Southern Resident Orca population.

This 2019 edition contains some substantial updates, changes and new material. Some chapters have been virtually rewritten. For example, in light of changes and developments in the areas of environmental assessment and climate law, the chapters addressing these topics (chapters 7 and 10) feature almost completely new content. We have included new material on the Paris Climate Agreement and its implications for Canada in Chapter 1. Likewise, our chapters on jurisdiction over the environment (Chapter 3), judicial review of environmental decision-making (Chapter 6) and species at risk (Chapter 9) have been restructured and contain substantial new content. Much of this new content is designed to provide updated and more in-depth coverage of Aboriginal and Indigenous rights perspectives and issues.

We have added some significant new cases casting light on and raising questions about the division of powers as it relates to environmental protection, and on the interpretation of the *Species at Risk Act*. In the judicial review context, we have expanded and updated our discussion of standard of review, judicial deference and "academies of science" concerns, and judicial reviews arising in relation to the duty to consult.

New content that integrates Aboriginal and Indigenous issues has also been added to chapters on the common law (Chapter 2) and parks and protected areas (Chapter 8). Finally, given the multi-faceted implications and dimensions of the Trans Mountain pipeline expansion controversy, we have developed case-study materials that will allow instructors to delve deeper into these issues either as part of an exploration of jurisdictional issues or as a stand-alone teaching module.

The primary focus of the third edition, as with its predecessors, is federal environmental law and practice. To provide comparative context, however, we integrate statutory and case law illustrations from provincial law and from other common law jurisdictions. We have also tried to ensure that the book exposes students to the interdisciplinary nature of environmental law, to the leading theoretical debates that animate environmental law, and to the complex ways environmental law intersects with international law, Aboriginal and Indigenous law, and natural resource law.

This edition owes much to our students — past, present and future. Significant research and editorial assistance was provided by interns who worked at the Pacific Centre for Environmental Law and Litigation ("CELL") under the supervision of Professor Tollefson during the summer of 2018: Amanda Spitzig (Osgoode Hall, 2019); Rory Shaw (Queen's Law, 2020); and Morgan McGinn (McGill Law, 2021). We likewise wish to thank Professor Doelle's research student William Wojcik (Schulich, 2021). The authors are also grateful for the input they have received from their environmental law students at the University of Victoria and Schulich School of Law. This input has provided important direction for this new edition. Deserving of special thanks are Andrew Mendelson, Sarah Robinson and Quinn Rochon (all UVic Law) who offered valuable editorial support at the galley stage.

Finally, deserving of special recognition is Anthony Ho, co-founding Associate at CELL. Anthony, who gained his introduction to environmental law from our first edition (2009), has been of tremendous editorial and creative assistance to us on both subsequent editions, for which we are truly grateful.

Much of the satisfaction we get from this ongoing book project springs from the hope that it will provoke, stimulate and equip a new generation of environmental lawyers to take up the pressing challenges that await them. It is to that next generation that we dedicate this edition.

MD and CT
April 2019

Table of Contents

Table of Cases

A case name appearing in boldface accompanied by an asterisked page number in boldface indicates a case that is reproduced in some material part.

Chapter 1

International Environmental Law

Introduction

This chapter explores the role of international environmental law in the development of Canadian environmental law. This is a relationship that has evolved significantly over time. Historically, developments in international law tended to follow developments in the domestic realm. Canadian governments generally tried to deal with environmental matters on their own, and pursued international cooperation only when domestic measures proved insufficient to address a problem. Over time, this has changed. In Canada, more and more of our domestic environmental measures have their origin in international commitments. Indeed, arguably, domestic action in the absence of some form of international commitment is becoming the exception rather than the rule.

The role of international law in our domestic legal system has also evolved. International law was historically seen as quite separate from domestic law in Canada. Some questioned whether international law was law at all. To the extent that international obligations were implemented, lawyers and courts focused on the interpretation of the domestic instrument of implementation, generally, without resorting to the international law instrument that represented the source of the obligation or commitment. Gradually, with the shift to more contextual interpretation of domestic law (certainly the interpretation of legislation), lawyers have more frequently relied on international instruments to advance interpretations of domestic law in the interests of their clients. Courts have thereby been challenged to consider whether and how international law influences domestic environmental law.

In Part I, we provide a brief overview of some of the key sources of international law. The three primary stages in the development of international environmental law are also introduced and summarized. Part II considers the principles Canadian courts have used when applying international law in the interpretation of domestic law, particularly in the environmental context. Building on these principles, Part III explores how the precautionary principle, which emerged as a soft law principle in the international law realm, is filtering into domestic law in Canada and elsewhere. Finally, in Part IV we provide an overview of some key international legal regimes — including the *Convention on Biological Diversity*, the *Basel Convention*, World Trade Organization agreements, international investment agreements, and the global climate change regime under the *United Nations Framework Convention on Climate Change* — that provide important context for, and in some cases may constrain, domestic initiatives to protect the environment.

Part I — Sources of International Law

Meinhard Doelle,
adapted and updated from *From Hot Air to Action? Climate Change,*
Compliance and the Future of International Environmental Law
(Toronto: Carswell, 2005)

International law consists of binding and non-binding principles, declarations, commitments, obligations and customs. Binding international law is generally referred to as hard law. The term used for non-binding components of international law is soft law. Hard law takes the form of either customary international law, or obligations set out in binding international agreements referred to as treaties. Customary law is generally binding on all States, whereas treaty obligations are binding only on States who ratify the treaty. Some soft law principles are included in otherwise binding treaties, while others stem from declarations and other forms of international agreements that are completely non-binding. Agreements with binding obligations are generally subject to ratification, whereas those without binding commitments are generally not subject to ratification. Ratification is the process by which States agree to be bound by a treaty or other agreement. Ratification is achieved through execution of a formal document/instrument that declares that the country will be and intends to be bound by the terms of the treaty. In some countries including Canada, the power to ratify international treaties rests with the executive. In other countries, such as the United States, this power rests with the legislative level of government.

Examples of obligations of customary international law include the principles of state sovereignty and the avoidance of trans-boundary harm. Soft law agreements dealing with environmental matters include the 1972 Stockholm Declaration, the 1992 Rio Declaration and the 2015 Sustainable Development Goals. Treaties have become the instrument of choice in the environmental law field, certainly for pressing global environmental challenges. Environmental issues that are addressed internationally through binding treaties include climate change, biodiversity, desertification, the management of toxic substances, ozone layer depletion, and wetland protection.

As discussed in more detail in Part II, these sources of international law can influence domestic environmental law in Canada in a variety of ways. Some hard and soft law will be implemented by Parliament or provincial legislatures through legislation. Some may be implemented by courts, especially through their role as the guardians of the development of the common law. International law, however, can also influence law enforcement, the exercise of discretion by administrative tribunals, and the actions of government officials. In short, international law can and does affect the full range of legal institutions and actors responsible for the development, interpretation and implementation of environmental law in Canada. Before we consider some of these influences in more detail, the following section offers some insights into the substance of international environmental law.

Evolving Substance of International Environmental Law

The birth of the modern environmental movement and with it the emergence of environmental law in North America is frequently traced back to the publication of *Silent Spring* by Rachel Carson in 1963. Its release eventually led to the creation of environmental agencies and departments and the enactment of environmental legislation in Canada and the United States. Concerns about the environmental impact of human activity were raised in Europe around the same time and similarly led to development of domestic environmental laws in Western European countries. While both the quantity and the nature of legal activity with respect to environmental issues has evolved significantly, domestically and internationally, since the publication of *Silent Spring*, the roots of international environmental law go back much further. The following is a brief overview of its evolution at the international level in three stages: international environmental law before the Stockholm Conference on the Human Environment in 1972, from Stockholm to Rio in 1992, and developments since the Rio Conference.

Pre-Stockholm

Before the beginning of the 20th century, there were relatively few international agreements on environmental issues in place, and those that dealt with the environment in some form were concerned with very specific and short term human benefits to be preserved or protected through limited international cooperation. These agreements, negotiated in most cases on a bilateral, sometimes regional basis, were entered into in the context of an acceptance of unrestrained national sovereignty over natural resources. Substantively, they tended to deal with shared waterways and other instances where Parties identified a need to protect national interests in certain natural resources of commercial importance. Examples include agreements dealing with the Rhine River, and bilateral resource management agreements. These agreements tended to address access to resources rather than concern about the protection of the resources from pollution or other human interference.

The 1930s and 1940s brought a gradual consideration of broader conservation issues in the context of the negotiation of international environmental agreements. This period saw the negotiation of agreements on the preservation of fauna and flora in their natural state, on nature and wildlife preservation, and more specific agreements such as the International Whaling Convention and other agreements on fisheries and land-based species.

The creation of the United Nations (UN) in 1945 marked a turning point in international law. The full impact of the United Nations on international environmental law, however, would not be felt for some time. The environment was not a focus of the United Nations during this period from 1945 until the late 1960s. At the same time, a number of organizations created under the UN umbrella did have some limited mandate to address environmental issues. They include the Food and Agriculture Organization (FAO), the United Nations Educational, Scientific and Cultural Organization (UNESCO), the World Health Organization (WHO), the International Maritime Organization (IMO) and the General Agreement on Tariffs and Trade (GATT).

The UN did hold its initial conference on the environment as early as 1949, even if only in the limited context of conservation and utilization of resources. This was followed by a conference, initiated by the UN General Assembly in 1954, on the Conservation of the Living Resources of the Sea leading to the 1958 Geneva Conventions. Other issues with environmental implications addressed through international treaties during this period included atomic energy, nuclear arms, and agreements on oil pollution, high seas fishing and wetlands.

The trend during this period of international environmental law was to react to specific issues of concern to individual (or groups of) nations. Efforts tended to be isolated, reactive, and lacking consistent structure and approach. There is little indication that the environmental issues addressed were considered in any broader context, be they linkages among environmental issues, trends that might suggest underlying problems in the direction taken by human kind, questions about overall limits to the ability of nature to absorb the impact of human activity, north-south equity issues, or intergenerational equity considerations.

From Stockholm to Rio

The year 1972 is generally recognized as the starting point for contemporary international environmental law. Not only was it the year of the United Nations Stockholm Conference on the Human Environment, but a number of issue-specific treaties were negotiated around the same time. More importantly, Stockholm marked the beginning of an explosion of international treaty making to address specific environmental issues for which international cooperation was deemed essential. Inspired by the birth of environmental movements in North America and Europe in the 1960s, and facilitated through the United Nations, the 1972 Conference on the Human Environment was the first global conference to consider environmental issues from a broader perspective.

The conference produced a number of non-binding instruments, and led to the creation of the United Nations Environment Programme (UNEP). It also provided the context for the negotiation of a number of binding multilateral treaties, such as the Convention on International Trade in Endangered Species (CITES), the London Ocean Dumping Convention, the World Heritage Convention, and the first regional seas convention. Most of the treaties between 1972 and 1992 were stand alone treaties. This period, however, did mark the beginning of the framework convention-protocol approach which has become dominant in international environmental law in the last two decades. The first such agreement was the Barcelona Convention for the Protection of the Mediterranean Sea Against Pollution, signed in 1976.

In addition to the sheer volume of international agreements dealing with environmental matters inspired by the Stockholm Conference, the 1972 conference is considered a turning point in the development of international environmental law in two other respects: the creation of an international structure to champion environmental issues in the form of UNEP, and the first attempt at an overall (non-binding) substantive context for the development of international environmental law. The substantive context was provided through the Stockholm Declaration in the form of 26 guiding principles and supplemented by an action plan with over 100 recommendations for international action on a range of environmental issues.

The focus of the 26 guiding principles is anthropocentric, and very much based on the primacy of state sovereignty over the use of nature within its borders, assuming that areas of incompatibility of state sovereignty and the obligation not to adversely affect other nations in the process will be limited and manageable through specific agreements on an issue by issue basis. Of particular note in this regard is Principle 21, perhaps the most commonly referenced part of the Stockholm Declaration, which provides as follows:

> States have, in accordance with the Charter of the United Nations and the principles of international law, the sovereign right to exploit their own resources pursuant to their own environmental policies, and the responsibility to ensure that activities within their jurisdiction or control do not cause damage to the environment of other states or of areas beyond the limits of national jurisdiction.

Principle 22 actually takes the issue of responsibility to other States one step further by recognizing, in general terms, the concept of liability and compensation for damage caused outside a State's border. The development of international law to deal with liability and compensation issues is identified for future negotiation. In hindsight, it seems that these two principles were negotiated with the expectation that human activities with extraterritorial environmental impact would be the exception rather than the rule, and that specific incidents of extra-territorial impact of human activity within the borders of a State could be dealt with either on a case-by-case basis through the development of issue-specific treaties, or through the development of general principles of liability and compensation. Clearly, these expectations have proven to be overly optimistic, and as a result, neither of the two options for dealing with environmental challenges internationally has proven to be realistic, or effective, to date.

At the same time, the declaration contains perhaps less well-known language that suggests in hindsight a surprisingly enlightened and visionary understanding of our relationship to nature. Paragraph 1 of the preamble, for example, reads as follows:

> Man [sic] is both creature and moulder of his environment, which gives him physical sustenance and affords him the opportunity for intellectual, moral, social and spiritual growth. In the long and tortuous evolution of the human race on this planet a stage has been reached when, through the rapid acceleration of science and technology, man has acquired the power to transform his environment in countless ways and on an unprecedented scale. Both aspects of man's environment, the natural and the man-made, are essential to his well being and the enjoyment of basic human rights — even the right to life itself.

Other provisions of the Stockholm Declaration suggest a recognition that a healthy natural environment is a precondition for human well-being, a recognition that quality of life and other goals of humanity depend upon cooperation with nature rather than a domination of nature. The declaration made repeated reference to the need to address the challenges ahead in a spirit of cooperation between developed and developing countries by addressing the inequities suffered by much of the human population living in developing countries. The concept of intergenerational equity was also introduced.

Another principle of particular note that was introduced in the Stockholm Declaration is the principle of integration. Principle 13 states:

> In order to achieve a more rational management of resources and thus to improve the environment, States should adopt an integrated and co-ordinated approach to their development planning so as to ensure that development is compatible with the need to protect and improve the environment for the benefit of their population.

The principle of integration was so new, and foreign to States, that it took 20 years for this principle to re-emerge in Rio and be taken seriously by the global community.

In fact, States are still struggling to implement the concept of integration in an effective manner. Domestically, one of the contributing factors to the failure to integrate effectively is, arguably, the creation of Environment Departments in many States. Ironically, the creation of these departments also goes back to the Stockholm Declaration, which urges States to institutionalize environmental protection. It was this reference to the need for domestic institutions that resulted in the establishment of Departments of the Environment in many States. The creation of those Departments has in turn made domestic integration more difficult by isolating environmental concerns from more mainstream concerns such as health, education, and economic development.

As mentioned, another development in 1972 that qualifies as a turning point in the evolution of international environmental law is the creation of the United Nations Environment Programme (UNEP). The establishment of UNEP by the General Assembly of the United Nations was in direct response to the recommendations contained in the action plan that accompanied the Stockholm Declaration. The initial mandate of UNEP was to oversee and guide the implementation of the action plan agreed to in Stockholm. UNEP was to do this by serving as a catalyst for international coordination of national action, but without any formal authority to implement the action plan in the absence of international consensus. This has been followed up with more specific mandates assigned to UNEP by the General Assembly from time to time. Structurally, UNEP is run by a governing council and an executive director, as well as a secretariat to carry out the instructions of the executive director. UNEP is funded mainly through direct voluntary payments from member States rather than through the UN general budget.

UNEP has played a key role in raising awareness about environmental issues in the international community since 1972, and was a driving force behind many of the multilateral environmental agreements entered into since then. While the influence of UNEP over the substance of these agreements is very much open to debate, it seems clear that UNEP was a catalyst for many of the agreements negotiated, and was instrumental in ensuring that the principles of the Stockholm Declaration were at least considered in the negotiation process.

In addition, this period from 1972 to 1992 saw the emergence of the international environmental community as an influential player in the development of international environmental law. In particular, international environmental non-governmental organizations (ENGOs) such as the IUCN, Greenpeace, the World Wildlife Fund, Friends of the Earth and others became active participants in international negotiations, both as observers and as advisors to State negotiators. Their influence can be traced through to Rio as well as individual Multi-Lateral Environmental Agreements (MEAs) such as the UNFCCC.

Substantively, the period from Stockholm in 1972 to Rio in 1992 saw an explosion in the number of international instruments dealing with environmental issues. Examples include the 1979 Convention on Long-Range Transboundary Air Pollution, the Law of the Sea Convention of 1982, the Vienna Convention on the Protection of the Ozone Layer, the Basel Convention on the Transboundary Movements of Hazardous Wastes and their Disposal, and the Protocol on Environmental Protection under the Antarctic Treaty, to name a few. These agreements demonstrated the complexity of the environmental issues facing the global community, the increasing number of environmental issues reaching a crisis level, and the unpreparedness of the international community to address these issues in a timely, effective, and coordinated manner in the absence of specific agreements on each environmental challenge discovered.

Almost without exception, the problems tackled in these agreements are still with us today. Furthermore, in the process of trying to address some of these problems, others have been created or exacerbated. Finally, most have been addressed without making any real progress on the fundamental issues raised, but not resolved, through the Stockholm Declaration, such as the conflict between state sovereignty and extraterritorial responsibility, the connection between environmental protection and equity, and the implication of the connections among economic development, quality of life, and protection of nature for the development and implementation of international environmental law.

At least some of these failures seem to have been recognized by UNEP and the world community in the years leading up to the 20th anniversary of Stockholm, resulting in the establishment of the Brundtland Commission, the publication of Our Common Future, and the follow-up negotiations leading up to the 1992 United Nations Conference on Environment and Development (UNCED) in Rio. In the next Section, the impact of the Rio Conference on international efforts to deal with these challenges will be briefly considered.

From Rio to the Present

The time leading up to UNCED in 1992 was marked by another flurry of multilateral environmental agreements, particularly on a number of global environmental challenges. Ozone Layer Depletion, Climate Change and Biodiversity are perhaps the most notable global environmental issues for which agreements were negotiated during this period. This time was also marked by efforts to reflect on the evolution of environmental law since Stockholm. The Brundtland Commission, with its publication of Our Common Future in 1987, is generally recognized as the most influential initiative in this regard. Brundtland provided the context for negotiations leading up to Rio, particularly with respect to the negotiations leading to the Rio Declaration and Agenda 21.

Given the efforts in the Brundtland report and elsewhere to reflect on the adequacy of global efforts to that point, the similarities between the Stockholm and Rio Declarations are surprising. A number of key principles from Stockholm, such as principles 21 and 22, are repeated, with minor changes, in Rio. The main change in the Rio Declaration is its attempt, following the approach advocated by the Brundtland Commission, to integrate environmental, equity, and economic issues. In the process, Rio arguably advocates, at least with respect to developing countries, for development as a precondition to addressing environmental issues.

In the process, the concept of sustainable development has, however, all too often become an excuse for the environmental impact of development, rather than a measuring stick to separate sustainable from unsustainable human activity.

Two additions to the Rio Declaration that possess the potential for positive contributions to the evolution of environmental law are the precautionary principle and the polluter pays principle. Both have been widely applied and their status under customary international law is being openly debated. Both have influenced the negotiation of specific instruments and the evolution of regimes since 1992, as have the concepts of sustainable development and integration.

After a flurry of activity leading up to and following UNCED in 1992, substantive developments in international environmental law have been modest. While issues such as Ozone Layer Depletion, for example, had caught the attention of the international community during this dynamic period leading up to UNCED, issues such as biodiversity and climate change have progressed at a much slower pace since the signing of the respective framework Conventions in 1992. The World Summit on Sustainable Development, held in 2002 in Johannesburg, and Rio + 20 in 2012 were by most accounts small steps forward at best. Both summits struggled to find any consensus on concrete new principles or institutions to move the agenda forward. As a result, the focus has been on discussions on how to more effectively implement what had been previously agreed to, rather than on new law.

There are a number of principles that have emerged from the evolution of international environmental law to date. First in time, but still very much a factor today in the development and implementation of international environmental law is the concept of state sovereignty over natural resources, modified by state responsibility for environmental impact outside its territory as set out in Principle 21 of the Stockholm Declaration. More recently, this principle has been supplemented with the concept of sustainable development, a key driving force behind the development of international environmental law since 1992. Still emerging to varying degrees, in terms of influence over the evolution of international environmental law, are: the precautionary principle, the polluter pays principle, and the concept of common but differentiated responsibility.

Other changes in international environmental law include the changing role of non-governmental actors in the development and implementation of international law, and the emergence of environmental impact assessment, economic instruments, monitoring, reporting, and verification as favoured implementation tools. As the stakes have become higher and the sheer number of obligations has increased, there has also been a renewed interest in the question of compliance. One crucial area identified in Stockholm, in which progress has been slow, is with respect to the development of international environmental law on liability and compensation for extraterritorial environmental damage. While some specific instruments may provide opportunities to establish liability and seek compensation, there is no overall framework for the establishment of liability and compensation as contemplated in Principle 22 of the Stockholm Declaration. In fact, Principle 13 of the Rio Declaration, at best, mirrors the expressed need to develop international law in this area, without demonstrating any tangible progress.

In 2007, the United Nations Declaration on the Rights of Indigenous Peoples (UNDRIP) was adopted by the UN General Assembly. It is a soft law instrument. Its implementation in Canada remains a work in progress. The current federal government, for the first time, has committed to its full implementation in Canada and has passed legislation to that effort in the form of the *United Nations Declaration on the Rights of Indigenous Peoples Act*. The following is a selection of key provisions of UNDRIP that are particularly relevant from an environmental law perspective:

Article 5

Indigenous peoples have the right to maintain and strengthen their distinct political, legal, economic, social and cultural institutions, while retaining their right to participate fully, if they so choose, in the political, economic, social and cultural life of the State.

Article 10

Indigenous peoples shall not be forcibly removed from their lands or territories. No relocation shall take place without the free, prior and informed consent of the indigenous peoples concerned and after agreement on just and fair compensation and, where possible, with the option of return.

Article 18

Indigenous peoples have the right to participate in decision-making in matters which would affect their rights, through representatives chosen by themselves in accordance with their own procedures, as well as to maintain and develop their own indigenous decision-making institutions.

Article 19

States shall consult and cooperate in good faith with the indigenous peoples concerned through their own representative institutions in order to obtain their free, prior and informed consent before adopting and implementing legislative or administrative measures that may affect them.

Article 26

1. Indigenous peoples have the right to the lands, territories and resources which they have traditionally owned, occupied or otherwise used or acquired.

Article 29

1. Indigenous peoples have the right to the conservation and protection of the environment and the productive capacity of their lands or territories and resources. States shall establish and implement assistance programmes for indigenous peoples for such conservation and protection, without discrimination.

Article 32

1. Indigenous peoples have the right to determine and develop priorities and strategies for the development or use of their lands or territories and other resources.

2. States shall consult and cooperate in good faith with the indigenous peoples concerned through their own representative institutions in order to obtain their free

and informed consent prior to the approval of any project affecting their lands or territories and other resources, particularly in connection with the development, utilization or exploitation of mineral, water or other resources.

More recently, the global community has agreed to another set of soft law principles in the form of the 2015 Agenda 2030 and its Sustainable Development Goals (SDGs). The SDGs are an attempt to set an integrated set of global goals for 2030 to address a broad range of global social, environmental and economic challenges. The product of this effort, titled "Transforming Our World: The 2030 Agenda for Sustainable Development," contains a preamble, a number of declarations, 17 goals and 169 targets, as well as provisions regarding means of implementation, and a framework for follow-up and review of implementation. The 17 SDGs cover health, economics, climate, oceans, urban development, peace and security, migrants, and intercultural understanding:

Sustainable Development Goals

Goal 1.   End poverty in all its forms everywhere.

Goal 2.   End hunger, achieve food security and improved nutrition and promote sustainable agriculture.

Goal 3.   Ensure healthy lives and promote well-being for all at all ages.

Goal 4.   Ensure inclusive and equitable quality education and promote lifelong learning opportunities for all.

Goal 5.   Achieve gender equality and empower all women and girls.

Goal 6.   Ensure availability and sustainable management of water and sanitation for all.

Goal 7.   Ensure access to affordable, reliable, sustainable and modern energy for all.

Goal 8.   Promote sustained, inclusive and sustainable economic growth, full and productive employment and decent work for all.

Goal 9.   Build resilient infrastructure, promote inclusive and sustainable industrialization and foster innovation.

Goal 10.   Reduce inequality within and among countries.

Goal 11.   Make cities and human settlements inclusive, safe, resilient and sustainable.

Goal 12.   Ensure sustainable consumption and production patterns.

Goal 13.   Take urgent action to combat climate change and its impacts.

Goal 14.   Conserve and sustainably use the oceans, seas and marine resources for sustainable development.

Goal 15.   Protect, restore and promote sustainable use of terrestrial ecosystems, sustainably manage forests, combat desertification, and halt and reverse land degradation and halt biodiversity loss.

Goal 16.   Promote peaceful and inclusive societies for sustainable development, provide access to justice for all and build effective, accountable and inclusive institutions at all levels.

Goal 17.   Strengthen the means of implementation and revitalize the global partnership for sustainable development.

Notes and Questions

1. Progress with respect to liability for transboundary harm in violation of customary law has been slow. In some rare cases, such as the Trail Smelter arbitration between Canada and the US (a case involving compensation for air pollution that moved from a Canadian smelter into the US), liability is settled through a mutually agreed upon process (See *Trail Smelter Arbitration United States v. Canada* (1931–1941), 3 RIAA 1905). More often, the issue is dealt with at a diplomatic level on a state-by-state basis, or left unresolved. One of the consequences has been that those affected have sought other recourse. An ongoing disagreement between the US and Canada over pollution of the Columbia River, resulting from the still operating Trail Smelter, resulted in enforcement action by the US Environmental Protection Agency directly against the Canadian company on the basis that it is polluting US territory. For a more detailed discussion of this case and its implications, see Neil Craik, "Trail Smelter Redux: Transboundary Pollution and Extraterritorial Jurisdiction" (2004) 14 J. Envtl. L. & Prac. 139 and Michael Robinson-Dorn, "The Trail Smelter: Is What's Past Prologue? EPA Blazes a New Trail for CERCLA" (2006) 14 NYU Envtl. L.J. 233.

2. In 2012, Rio hosted a global follow-up conference to UNCED commonly known as Rio+20 (Earth Negotiations Bulletin summary of Rio+20 is online: <http://www.iisd.ca/uncsd/rio20/enb/>). As was the case with Rio+10 in Johannesburg, the outcome from Rio+20 was modest when compared to UNCED. The results of Rio+20 continue to highlight on the one hand the global struggle to implement the path proposed in UNCED; on the other hand, it is an indication of the absence so far of a viable alternative path that has caught the imagination of the global community. As a result, both Rio+10 in Johannesburg and Rio+20 focused on specific implementation issues related to the direction set in UNCED, rather than on a new path forward.

3. A detailed exploration of the SDGs is not possible here. However, as they represent the global community's current effort to develop a comprehensive, integrated set of goals for 2030, it will be important to consider the relevance of the SDGs for any given environmental issue you explore. Consider, for example, how the 17 SDGs relate to the global environmental challenges of biodiversity loss, clean water, or climate change. Which of the 17 SDGs do you find to have relevance, and how might they guide the global effort to address these environmental challenges?

4. A key soft law instrument that has growing significance in Canada is the *United Nations Declaration on the Rights of Indigenous Peoples* (UNDRIP). What is its status in Canada? How do its key provisions relate to environmental law? How do they relate to section 35 of the *Constitution Act, 1982*? As you read the next section, consider how the provisions of UNDRIP excerpted above might be used by a court in dealing with Indigenous rights cases in Canada. We will return to this issue in Chapter 3.

Part II — Relevance and Application of International Law in the Canadian Environmental Law Context

In this Part, we consider how and to what extent, international norms, principles, commitments and obligations translate into Canadian domestic law. A key focus is the use of international law by Canadian courts. You will be challenged to think about the different ways international law has shaped, and has the potential to shape, the substance and implementation of domestic environmental law. As a starting point, consider the following survey of case law dealing with the role of international law in interpreting domestic law.

The following article considers three main issues: (1) the means by which international treaty obligations are translated into domestic law; (2) the use of international law as an aid in the interpretation of domestic legislation; and (3) the extent to which customary international law forms part of Canadian domestic law.

Elizabeth Brandon,
"Does International Law Mean Anything in Canadian Courts?"
(2001) 11 J. Envtl. L. & Prac. 399

Introduction

The number of international agreements related to the environment has grown rapidly in the past few decades, and the trend is set to continue. Canada is a party to many of these agreements, and promotes an 'environmentally friendly' image of itself abroad. However, international agreements are of little consequence unless they are implemented and enforced at the national level. Numerous international courts and legal mechanisms exist to resolve disputes between States and to monitor their implementation of certain agreements. However, these facilities generally do not provide a forum for individuals to take issue with their governments for a failure to enforce international obligations that have been implemented through national legislation, except in the area of human rights.

Although international monitoring agencies may apply political pressure to governments that are not conforming to their international legal obligations, these influences may not be sufficient to ensure enforcement. There is even less pressure on a government to conform where it is not involved in a dispute with another government, and therefore not subject to the jurisdiction of a court or dispute settlement body. Thus the responsibility of ensuring compliance with international law is often left to the government itself, or to individuals and pressure groups within the State. The enforcement of international law has become the most critical issue facing those who oversee its operation at the international level, and those who seek to rely upon it at the domestic level.

Implementation of international law may be achieved through legislative, regulatory and policy measures by governments, depending on the type of action required by each international agreement or legal principle. National courts also have a role in implementation, by interpreting and applying the laws enacted by governments to meet their international obligations. Courts may also play a more indirect part in implementation, by relying upon international legal principles and materials, and foreign judicial decisions, as a basis for their decisions. The various methods used by Canadian courts to apply international law will be discussed in this article. In addition, avenues that are often neglected in legal argument will be explored.

Until more recently, Canadian judges and litigators have made only limited use of international law in legal argument, particularly in the area of environmental litigation. [...] The slowness of the Canadian legal community to make use of international law, and particularly environmental treaties and principles, could derive partly from its lack of familiarity with them. It may also be attributed to the breadth of issues often covered by environmental treaties, and the general objectives that tend to be used in them instead of specific measures. However, the traditional legal stance — which viewed international law as existing outside of domestic law — may also, in a general sense, have discouraged litigators and judges from using international law. These factors mean that international law tends to be neglected in legal dialogue because it is often seen as irrelevant, imprecise or non-binding and therefore of little consequence. As a result, the judiciary is given few opportunities to develop skills in utilizing international law in decision-making.

Political and constitutional factors shape the way in which international law is accepted as part of domestic law. Until recently, the Canadian approach to treaties has been understood as firmly dualist, viewing them as distinct from domestic law until they have been implemented through government action. The approach to customary international law is less clear-cut. Although there is a belief that Canada is monist, in that customary legal principles apply directly to domestic law without needing specific implementation, the issue is far from settled. Some judicial decisions have required, expressly or implicitly, the transformation of customary law into domestic law. However, the recent decision of *Suresh v. Canada (Minister of Citizenship & Immigration)*, suggests that such 'transformation' is unnecessary and that customary law may be invoked at least indirectly. The *Suresh* decision arguably has the same significance for the status of treaties in domestic law.

International law is also treated with caution where it is perceived to jeopardize the distribution of powers between the federal and provincial governments. Moreover, the concept of parliamentary sovereignty may dissuade the courts from readily accepting the authority of international law. It is conceded that the Canadian constitutional framework poses a challenge to the widespread use of many types of international law. However, these factors need not, and should not, be obstacles to drawing from international environmental law in domestic courts. [...]

Implementation of Treaty Obligations

According to the view traditionally taken by Canadian courts and lawmakers, a treaty becomes legally binding within Canada only when the federal Executive has signed and ratified the treaty, and it has been implemented by the appropriate legislature through specific legislation. The dualist position holds that a treaty cannot be in any way relevant to Canadian law unless all of these steps have been taken. Therefore, without domestic action, the international commitments entered into by the Canadian government would be of no consequence within Canada and unenforceable in Canadian courts.

However, the traditional view conflicts with the long-standing rule of statutory interpretation that a legislature is presumed not to legislate in violation of international law. As a result of this presumption, it could be said that 'un-implemented' or 'unincorporated' treaties have also influenced Canadian law, even if they have not been recognized as directly applicable. This conclusion is supported by recent developments in Canadian judicial reasoning, marked by the important decisions of *Baker v. Canada (Minister of Citizenship & Immigration)*, [1999] 2 S.C.R. 817, *Suresh v. Canada (Minister of Citizenship & Immigration)*, [2002] 1 S.C.R. 3 and *Ahani v. Canada (Minister of Citizenship & Immigration)*, [2002] 1 S.C.R. 72.

Treaties Implemented Through Domestic Legislation

As noted above, the traditional approach to implementation of international law insists that specific implementing legislation is required for a treaty to have domestic effect. However, as van Ert observes, judicial thinking has now evolved to the point where an implementing statute need not make any mention at all of the treaty it implements. He contends that "the task of determining whether an act seeks to implement a treaty is no different than that of discerning the legislature's intent more generally". Thus a statute that does not rely directly on the text of the treaty but simply effects legal changes adequate to fulfill Canada's treaty obligations, would be acceptable.

Express Incorporation by Reference

Where there is legislation which sets out a treaty text in full or expressly refers to its implementation, and which has the specific purpose of implementing that treaty, the parliamentary intention seems sufficiently clear. While a treaty that has been set out in the schedule to a statute need not be accompanied by an express intention to implement, such intention should be discernable from the statutory provisions. The normal tools of statutory interpretation would be employed to assess the legislative intention, including presumptions of conformity with international law.

For a handful of environment-related treaties, the Canadian Parliament has enacted specific legislation which not only indicates an implementing purpose in its short title, but also gives an express approval of the treaty and even includes the full text of the treaty as a schedule (the *Convention on Salvage, Convention for Safe Containers, Comprehensive Nuclear Test Ban Treaty, Convention on Chemical Weapons*, and *Migratory Birds Convention*). [...]

Partial Incorporation

For domestic legislation which only partially incorporates a treaty, a similar argument to the above may be constructed on a smaller scale. The courts should view this method of implementation as importing at least some provisions of a treaty directly into Canadian law. In addition, the context of the treaty as a whole should inform the application of those provisions as part of the legislative regime. [...]

Limited References to a Treaty in the Statute

Where a statute contains only limited references to a particular treaty — for example, in its preamble, or in the definitions section — there may be sufficient grounds for establishing that Parliament in fact intended to implement the treaty as a whole. This approach was successful in *R. v. Crown Zellerbach Canada Ltd.*, in which the Supreme Court of Canada recognized the *Ocean Dumping Control Act* as directed to the implementation of Canada's obligations under the *London Convention on the Prevention of Marine Pollution by Dumping*. It reached this conclusion in the absence of an express legislative statement as to this purpose, relying instead upon several references to the Convention in the Act, provisions modeled closely on the Convention's annexes, and the Act's schedules which incorporated amendments to the Convention. While the majority did not directly apply the Convention text, it could arguably have done so on the basis that an intention to implement was established. [...]

Legislation Containing a General Power to Implement Treaties

Reliance by the government on a general implementation power contained in a statute to give effect to a particular treaty is evidence of an intention to implement that treaty. A general implementation power is commonly phrased as a power "to implement relevant international agreements," or a power to implement a particular treaty or type of treaty. While this type of legislation does not actually incorporate the treaty text, it provides a general power to implement the treaty and may also mirror its provisions. The implementing clause is usually located at the beginning of the statute.

An example of this practice is the legislative framework that has been put in place to meet Canada's obligations under the *Convention on International Trade in Endangered Species of Wild Fauna and Flora (CITES)*. The *Wild Animal and Plant Protection and Regulation of International and Interprovincial Trade Act (WAPPRIITA)* allows the Governor in Council to make regulations for carrying out the purposes of the Act, including regulations "generally to implement [CITES]". The purpose of the Act is "to protect certain species of animals and plants, particularly by implementing the Convention and regulating international and interprovincial trade in animals and plants". The text of the statute incorporates the permit requirements of the Convention. [...]

Patent Treaty Implementation by Legislation and/or Policy

A strong contention may be made that a treaty should be considered implemented because a combination of factors — the legislative and policy framework, together with representations from the Government — patently show that it is implemented. Where the legislative and regulatory measures taken by Government accord with the requirements of the treaty, and Government has expressed a belief that the treaty is 'implemented' or 'applicable,' there is a sufficient basis for this contention. An international legal perspective strongly supports taking a broad, flexible view of what constitutes implementation.

This contextual approach to determining whether implementation has occurred may be used for three scenarios. The first is where the Government has assessed its existing laws prior to ratification of a treaty, and deemed them adequate to meet the treaty commitments. This practice may be called 'passive incorporation'. The second scenario is where the Government takes positive steps to legislate and regulate in response to its treaty obligations, but stops short of expressly incorporating the treaty. Implementation is particularly patent in this situation, as an intention to implement is often easily discernable.

The third scenario would arise where the Government has only taken policy measures to comply with a treaty, but that treaty can nevertheless be considered implemented because its requirements have been met. In each of the above situations, evidence of implementation relies on the provisions of the individual treaty, the actions taken by the Government to comply with those provisions, and any expressions by the Government as to the status of the treaty in relation to Canada. If all three of these factors correlate, it must be assumed that the treaty is indeed implemented and therefore directly applicable to domestic law. [...]

Passive Incorporation

'Passive incorporation' may be said to occur when the government or legislature concludes that domestic law is already in line with the treaty and, therefore, no further measures are needed. This conclusion is generally reached prior to either signature or ratification of the treaty. It enables the Government to claim, before both its citizens and international treaty bodies, that Canada is bound by norms that are already implemented. This practice is common in relation to human rights treaties, which tend to be ratified on the basis that no new legislation is required. It is also becoming apparent for environmental treaties, particularly where federal Parliament may lack a solid jurisdictional basis for implementing the treaty through specific environmental legislation.

The phenomenon of passive incorporation is of particular relevance to Canada because it seems to be the preferred implementing technique of the Canadian Government for a number of environmental treaties. Canada has ratified a great number of international treaties, which are often ratified on the basis of existing conformity with the new treaty provisions. But ratification on this basis is problematic, as it inevitably leaves the courts with the difficult task of assessing Canada's compliance with international obligations in the absence of express implementing legislation.

Thus the courts need to look to other sources to confirm that the obligations are implemented — the existing legislative and policy framework, expressions of the government's intention to be bound by the relevant treaty, and the terms of the treaty itself. When a treaty to which Canada is a party enters into force, the Canadian Parliament (or, if appropriate, the provincial legislatures) must enact any legislation that may be necessary for the performance of the treaty obligations. Therefore, it is a common practice, although not a constitutional requirement, for the government to determine whether new legislation is necessary to fulfill Canada's treaty obligations.

In Canada, it is apparent that legislative action is generally not required for agreements concerning administrative or political matters, but is required for treaties which would impose financial burdens on the government, or "alter the law of the land". Although environment-related treaties tend to involve the taking of policy measures rather than the imposition of specific financial commitments, some treaties employ a range of tools to achieve their goals. They may involve large public expenditure together with changes to laws to prohibit certain activities or regulate resource use.

Given the common government practice of assessing Canada's legislative framework prior to signing a treaty, significance can be attached to legislative inaction by the government following signature. This inaction signals that the existing legislative or policy framework has been deemed adequate to fulfill the treaty obligations. The strong presumption that the Canadian government intends to comply with its international legal obligations should lead the courts' approach to a treaty in this situation. Absent any clear indications to the contrary, one must presume that the government intended to implement the treaty, thus making it relevant to the interpretation of domestic law.

One example of passive incorporation is the *Ramsar Convention on Wetlands of International Importance especially as Waterfowl Habitat*. Canada has ratified the Convention but, according to the Canadian Wildlife Service, it has not specifically incorporated it into domestic law. Although many federal and provincial policies exist for wetland preservation, they do not expressly address Canada's obligations under the Convention. However, according to the Federal Government, the Convention was deemed "self-implementing" and is used as a facilitating mechanism for domestic laws.

By early 2002, 36 sites within Canada had been designated for protection under the *Ramsar Convention*. Federal and provincial governments cooperate on site nominations and a procedure manual is used to interpret the *Ramsar Convention* guidelines for site designation. It appears that the federal and provincial governments already view the Convention as implemented without the need for legislation. Accordingly, the provisions of the *Ramsar Convention* may be considered relevant to the Canadian wetland management framework and to domestic law in general. [...]

Implementation by Positive Action

It may be evident from positive measures taken by the government that those measures were intended to fulfil Canada's treaty commitments. To determine whether a particular treaty has been implemented in this way, and where the relevant legislation does not have an express implementing purpose, a close examination of the legislative and regulatory framework is required. The specific requirements of the relevant treaty must be kept in mind during this analysis for comparative purposes.

Guidance for looking beyond the confines of a statute to ascertain parliamentary intention is found in the landmark English case of *Salomon v. Commissioners of Customs & Excise*. Diplock L.J. stated that if it is plain from extrinsic evidence that the enactment was intended to fulfil obligations under a particular treaty, no express reference to the treaty in the statute is needed. [...] A court may also be entitled to look at parliamentary reading speeches to identify the scope and purpose of a statute. [...]

The *Montreal Protocol on Substances that Deplete the Ozone Layer* provides a useful example of a treaty that has patently been implemented through positive measures taken by the Canadian Government. Canada has signed and ratified the *Montreal Protocol* and its amendments, committing itself to deadlines for the phasing-out of several substances. The position taken by the federal government is that, since signing the *Montreal Protocol* in 1987, "Canada has adopted adequate regulations to meet its *Montreal Protocol* commitments".

The clear targets and timelines set out by the Protocol make it easier to determine whether Canada's laws do in fact match up with its obligations. The legislative framework comprises the federal *Ozone-Depleting Substances Regulations* and the *Federal Halocarbon Regulations*, both made under the *Canadian Environmental Protection Act, 1999*. The regulations are supplemented by non-statutory initiatives such as national action plans and mandatory codes of practice. All of the provinces and one territory have pollution prevention regulations, and municipalities are also taking action. In addition, the regulatory impact analysis statement in support of the *ODS Regulations* clearly identified Canada's obligations under the *Montreal Protocol* as the central justification for the regulations. Evidently, the combination of regulations and policy addresses Canada's ozone protection commitments and future phase-out targets.

The close correlation between Canada's regulations and policies for phasing out ozone-depleting substances, and the provisions of the *Montreal Protocol*, provide sufficient evidence of Parliament's intention to implement those provisions. If further proof is needed, one need only look to the relevant regulatory impact analysis statements and government press releases. Domestically, Canada has kept up with the continual revisions of the *Montreal Protocol* timelines and, at least on paper, there are no regulatory gaps. Thus it should be possible to contend that the *Montreal Protocol* is in fact implemented into domestic law and should be taken into account by decision-makers where relevant.

Policy Measures

Environmental treaties are often distinctive for their lack of hard rules and their preference for policy measures and general principles, instead of legislation, to achieve the desired goals. Indeed, non-legislative measures may be the only feasible way of achieving certain treaty goals. 'Policy measures' could encompass measures for voluntary compliance, economic incentives, 'action plans', educational programs, allocation of financial resources, and environmental management plans.

A government may respond to its treaty obligations simply by assessing its policy framework and making any necessary changes. If a government takes policy measures in order to comply with its treaty obligations, thereby achieving the treaty goals, that treaty should be viewed as implemented. At the international level, and in the eyes of the government, these efforts are sufficient to carry out the treaty obligations. Thus the precise tools a government uses for implementation are irrelevant — the importance lies in the end result and the requisite government intention. From an international law viewpoint, the treaty is already deemed 'implemented' once its requirements are met, and it would be difficult for individual governments to refute this.

Thus a domestic policy that reflects or refers to the provisions of a treaty can be used as an implementing vehicle for that treaty. Conversely, a treaty can be of indirect legal effect if it is relevant to domestic policy and the exercise of statutory authority — regardless of whether Canada has signed the treaty. [...]

A prominent example of the notion that some provisions of a treaty can be implemented through non-legislative means is the *Convention on Biological Diversity*. The Canadian Government has ratified the Convention but has not specifically implemented it through legislation. However, an intention to implement the *Convention on Biological Diversity* through domestic policy and other measures is evident from government practice. The Government has used a range of non-statutory instruments to meet most of its obligations under the Convention, such as the Canadian Biodiversity Strategy and eight sectoral policies, and has repeatedly expressed its firm commitment to it. Such policy measures conform to the provisions of the Convention, which contain broad principles and focus on policy-making rather than legislation. Therefore it appears from an international and domestic perspective that the Convention is at least partially implemented, and thus relevant in Canada with respect to those implemented provisions.

At a minimum, courts should interpret domestic laws to conform as far as possible with Canada's commitments to the *Convention on Biological Diversity* even if it is deemed unimplemented as a whole. Some of the central principles in the Convention have been acknowledged in the preambles to federal and provincial legislation. Moreover, five provinces currently have specific endangered species legislation and the Federal Government is attempting to enact the same legislation. These legislative provisions provide sufficient grounds for the courts to refer to the *Convention on Biological Diversity* for elucidation when they engage in statutory interpretation.

The *Convention on Biological Diversity* is relevant not only as an interpretative aid, but to the exercise of statutory authority by government decision-makers. In particular, where policies exist that reflect the values and principles of the Convention, the responsible statutory authorities should ensure that these objectives are safeguarded. It is clear from *Baker* that the relevance of treaties does not begin and end with statutory interpretation, but reaches more widely to all areas in which government authority is exercised.

[Ed. Note: Much has happened in Canada with respect to species at risk and protected areas since this article was written. The current status of implementation of the *Convention of Biological Diversity* is covered in Chapters 8 and 9.]

International Law as an Interpretative Aid for Domestic Legislation

International law, including treaties, also becomes relevant to Canadian law in the interpretation of domestic statutes. Recognition of this source of law has grown rapidly in recent years. The role of international law is already evident where the statute involved is considered to implement the international principle or treaty. However, as mentioned above, it is now emerging that international law may be applied indirectly even where it cannot be considered already implemented through legislation or policy.

The interpretation of a statute is guided by the need for a contextual approach, which requires that domestic legislation be read in light of the conditions in which it was created, its purpose and object, any other relevant legal developments, and the social values of the present day. The ordinary rules of statutory interpretation dictate that the words of a statute must be interpreted in accordance with their 'total context'. Thus it is contended that the contextual approach should take into account relevant legal principles and materials — regardless of whether they originate within or outside of Canada — if they reflect Canadian values and aspirations. [...]

Despite recent judicial developments, there are no clear boundaries defining the use that may be made of international law as an aid to statutory interpretation. Even unratified and unsigned treaties have been considered by Canadian courts to be a useful interpretative aid. Likewise, courts have drawn freely from customary law, international tribunal decisions, and international declarations. This trend suggests that the courts will turn to international legal materials for clarification when the need arises, regardless of their binding status. Thus international law can be used as an interpretative aid wherever it is relevant and persuasive, because it expresses important principles and values. Arguably, Canadian laws must be presumed to comply with these international principles and values unless it has been made clear in each instance that Canada will be acting otherwise.

Implemented Treaties

As noted above, Canadian courts already use international law to interpret a treaty that has been implemented through domestic legislation. Based on the assumption that the statute is intended to implement the treaty, the latter may subsequently be used as a proper aid to interpretation. The courts have been prepared to refer to an underlying treaty (the subject of the implementing legislation) not only when the statute contains an ambiguity (either patent or latent), but before such an ambiguity is identified. [...]

Unimplemented Treaties

Until relatively recently, it was not clear whether unimplemented treaties could be considered as part of the 'total context' of domestic legislation. According to the prevailing view of international law, treaties would not become legally relevant unless specifically implemented. This view insists that the international and domestic legal spheres are separate and that international law must be 'transformed' or 'translated' into domestic law to have any effect.

It is submitted that the argument for 'transformation' ignores the influence already wielded by international law within Canada. This influence is recognized by Toope:

> The process of relating international law to domestic law is not a translation of norms from outside. Rather, Canadian voices join with foreign voices, weaving an increasingly rich and multi-textured narrative of international law.

The traditional insistence on implementing legislation has enabled Canada to "shield the executive from the consequences of its voluntary decision to enter into and therefore be bound by the [treaty]". There are signs that this ability to avoid the legal effects of ratifying a treaty is now being eroded. As Toope argues, recent cases such as *Baker* and other foreign jurisprudence pose "salutary challenges to governmental hypocrisy (or perhaps incompetence) in ratifying international treaties and failing to address the domestic law implications of those treaties".

The trend represented by the cases of *Baker*, *Suresh*, and *Ahani* demonstrates that an unimplemented treaty may indeed be highly relevant — albeit not directly applicable — to domestic legislation and decision-making. The Supreme Court of Canada in *Baker* widened the purview of the contextual approach to statutory interpretation. It concluded that the legal context should include any relevant values and principles expressed by the international community and reflected in Canadian legislation or policy. An unimplemented treaty could provide valuable guidance for the Court in seeking to clarify the provisions of the statute. [...]

The implication from *Baker* and *Suresh*, supported by other Canadian and foreign case law, is that the provisions of any treaty ratified by the government can be relevant in many ways to domestic laws and decision-making. As a result, arguably international principles and treaties need not be specifically implemented into domestic law to be relevant, and even instrumental, to the process of statutory interpretation. This development represents a sharp divergence from the traditional judicial approach, which asserts that treaties are of no domestic effect unless implemented through legislation.

Treaties Not Ratified by Canada

The notion of a 'total' legal context may be further extended to encompass treaties that have not been ratified or even signed by Canada. This extension would be consistent with the need expressed in *Baker*, *Suresh* and *Ahani* to take relevant international values and principles into account when engaging in statutory interpretation. Other cases add support because they specifically refer to the relevance of unratified and unsigned treaties to domestic law. [...]

Where Canada has signed a treaty but has not yet ratified it, it may nevertheless be obliged to act in accordance with the general purpose of that treaty. Article 18 of the *Vienna Convention on the Law of Treaties* imposes an obligation on signatory states not to defeat the object and purpose of a treaty prior to its entry into force. Thus a signatory state should refrain from acting to frustrate the objectives of a treaty until it has made clear its intention whether to ratify the treaty. For this reason, it should not be assumed that the act of signature is devoid of any effect. The act of signature has particular importance for states that engage in a rigorous constitutional check of domestic laws prior to signature. In Canada, the general government practice for some, but not all, treaties is to examine closely the draft treaty text, to consult the provinces if appropriate, and then to take any necessary legislative action to implement the treaty.

It has already been seen that the courts are prepared to look to ratified but unimplemented treaties when interpreting domestic legislation. There does not appear to be any reason why treaties signed but not ratified by the Canadian Government should be accorded less importance by the courts. The focus of the Supreme Court of Canada in *Baker* was not on the implemented status of the treaty, but the relevance of its values to Canadian society. Arguably, the values expressed in a treaty become relevant to Canadian law as soon as that treaty has been finalized by the signatories. This contention carries even more weight if the treaty is actually in force, and if Canada participated actively in its negotiation. The unratified treaty is no less an expression of international values and principles, and thus it must be taken into account by government decision-makers in their exercise of authority, and the courts when interpreting a statute.

Customary International Law as Part of Domestic Law

Customary international law provides a useful vehicle for a closer analysis of the relationship between international law and domestic law. Customary rules are clearly recognized as a source of international law by the *Statute of the International Court of Justice*. The precise legal relationship between customary international law — which is built upon these rules — and domestic Canadian law is a subject of some contention. Canadian case law to date has not produced a clear statement as to whether customary law may automatically be considered part of domestic law and thus directly applied. [...]

Arguably [...] foreign jurisprudence and recent Canadian case law support the direct application of norms of customary international law in the domestic sphere, in much the same manner domestic legislation is applied. Even where the precise status of a customary norm is unclear [...] an emerging or established norm may be highly relevant to domestic law. In fact, any attempt by a government to derogate from such a norm without reasonable justification should be actively discouraged by the courts.

A controversial and relatively recent development in international environmental law is the 'precautionary principle', also called the precautionary 'approach' or 'concept.' The principle has been described in many different ways, but generally it states that in cases where there are threats to human health and the environment the fact that there is no scientific uncertainty over those threats should not be used as the reason for not taking action to prevent harm.

The growth in popularity of the precautionary principle has led to extensive references to it in the texts of treaties and declarations. Thus it is arguable that, at a minimum, states have widely acknowledged its existence as a principle of international law. Sands ventures further in suggesting that evidence of state practice is now sufficient to demonstrate that the precautionary principle has customary law status. Foreign jurisprudence appears to support this conclusion, and Canadian courts are beginning to acknowledge its existence, as in the Supreme Court of Canada decision of *114957 Canada Ltée (Spray-Tech, Société d'arrosage) v. Hudson (Ville)*.

Even if customary international law is not directly applicable... the courts are entitled to use it as an aid to statutory interpretation. In *Baker*, the Supreme Court of Canada cited with approval the following passage from Driedger on the Construction of Statutes:

> [T]he legislature is presumed to respect the values and principles enshrined in international law, both customary and conventional. These constitute a part of the legal context in which legislation is enacted and read. In so far as possible, therefore, interpretations that reflect these values and principles are preferred. [...]

The endorsement in the *Baker* and *Spray-Tech* decisions of the use of international law as an interpretative aid means that the precautionary principle remains relevant even if it has not yet reached customary legal status. Given the presumption of conformity with international law, Canada's domestic laws must be interpreted in a broader legal context that takes into account both binding and non-binding international principles. Canada has ratified several treaties in which the precautionary approach or principle is mentioned. Many references to the principle have also been made in non-binding international documents. Based on the rationale in *Baker* and *Suresh*, these international legal principles may be considered relevant to domestic law because they reflect the values of the international community.

Conclusions

A gradual narrowing of the gap between the international and domestic legal spheres has led to a change in the concept of treaty implementation. This change is apparent in Canada, among other states, from an examination of developments in judicial reasoning. From an international legal viewpoint, a treaty may be considered implemented if the actions taken by individual states correspond with their treaty obligations. In Canada, from a domestic legal perspective, the focus has shifted from the question of whether a treaty has been specifically implemented through legislation, to whether government had an intention to implement the treaty.

It is contended that the method of implementation is less important than are indications of an intention to implement. An implementing intention that evidences a strong compliance with treaty requirements will clearly be the most persuasive indication that the treaty is of domestic effect. An intention to implement alone may be insufficient, and it should either be accompanied by positive measures by government or follow from an assessment of the existing regulatory framework. It must be possible to pinpoint a decision by the government to take implementing action or to accept the current framework as adequate. The more closely this positive action, or existing framework, corresponds to the terms of the treaty, the more accurately it may be viewed as actually implementing that treaty. [...]

The future direction of international law in Canada presents a challenge to all participants in the judicial process. In particular, the relationship between international and domestic law will inevitably be put to the test in environment-related litigation, as Canada ratifies growing numbers of environmental treaties. In the interval, and until the relationship between international and Canadian law is clarified, the legal community should draw widely from the international legal sources available to it. The large body of international law, encompassing treaties, declarations, international legal principles, and customary law, is a fertile source of legal argument to be used in domestic litigation. International environmental law offers a promising opportunity to bridge the gap between international obligations undertaken by Canada, and its domestic actions.

Notes and Questions

1. Governments may choose to implement their treaty obligations expressly, through direct incorporation in domestic legislation. According to Brandon, treaty obligations can also be deemed to be incorporated into domestic law in a number of ways. What are they?

2. It is well settled that Canadian courts may look to treaties that Canada has ratified and implemented as an aid to interpreting domestic legislation. Can they also rely on unimplemented or unratified treaties to this end? Is their use more limited? How?

3. What is customary international law? What determines whether a legal principle has achieved this status? According to Brandon, what domestic legal implications flow from a principle being recognized as customary international law? Can international norms that are yet to be recognized as customary international law still be used by courts as interpretive aids?

4. Since the Brandon article was first published in 2001, the federal government has enacted new legislation dealing with national parks (the *Canada National Parks Act*) and endangered species (the *Species at Risk Act*): see Chapters 8 and 9. When you review the materials on these federal statutes, consider whether they can be seen to be implementing the Convention on Biodiversity, in part or in whole, and what role various articles of the Convention could play in interpreting the provisions of these two statutes.

Since the Brandon article, there have been a number of cases decided by the Supreme Court of Canada that invoke or rely on international law. Below we include excerpts from one of these cases, *114957 Canada Ltée (Spray-tech, Société d'arrosage) v. Hudson (Town)*. In reviewing this case, consider carefully whether it sheds any further light on the domestic relevance of the various sources of international law (treaties, customary international law and international soft law), and on the principles relating to implementation of international treaty obligations.

114957 Canada Ltée (Spraytech, Société d'arrosage) v. Hudson (Town)
2001 SCC 40

[The majority reasons in *Spraytech* are notable in that they represent a particularly robust illustration of the use of international law in interpreting and, in the end, in upholding the validity of domestic legislation in the environmental context. Portions of this decision are reproduced elsewhere in this book (see Chapter 3). Here we excerpt extracts from the majority reasons of L'Heureux-Dubé J. bearing directly on the role of international law. The case arose as a result of a challenge to the validity of by-laws enacted by the Town of Hudson that restricted the use of pesticides. The challenge was brought by a group of land-scaping companies.]

L'HEUREUX-DUBÉ J.: — The context of this appeal includes the realization that our common future, that of every Canadian community, depends on a healthy environment. [...]

Regardless of whether pesticides are in fact an environmental threat, the Court is asked to decide the legal question of whether the Town of Hudson, Quebec, acted within its authority in enacting a by-law regulating and restricting pesticide use.

The case arises in an era in which matters of governance are often examined through the lens of the principle of subsidiarity. This is the proposition that law-making and implementation are often best achieved at a level of government that is not only effective, but also closest to the citizens affected and thus most responsive to their needs, to local distinctiveness, and to population diversity. La Forest J. wrote for the majority in *R. v. Hydro-Québec*, [1997] 3 S.C.R. 213 at p. 296, that the protection of the environment is a major challenge of our time. It is an international problem, one that requires action by governments at all levels (emphasis added). His reasons in that case also quoted with approval a passage from *Our Common Future*, the report produced in 1987 by the United Nations World Commission on the Environment and Development. The so-called Brundtland Commission recommended that local governments [should be] empowered to exceed, but not to lower, national norms" [...]

The appellants are landscaping and lawn care companies operating mostly in the region of greater Montreal, with both commercial and residential clients. They make regular use of pesticides approved by the federal *Pest Control Products Act*, R.S.C. 1985, c. P-9, in the course of their business activities and hold the requisite licences under Quebec's *Pesticides Act*, R.S.Q. c. P-9.3.

The respondent, the Town of Hudson, is a municipal corporation governed by the *Cities and Towns Act*, R.S.Q., c. C-19 (*C.T.A.*). It is located about 40 kilometres west of Montreal and has a population of approximately 5,400 people, some of whom are clients of the appellants. In 1991, the Town adopted By-law 270, restricting the use of pesticides within its perimeter to specified locations and for enumerated activities. The by-law responded to residents' concerns, repeatedly expressed since 1985. The residents submitted numerous letters and comments to the Towns Council. The definition of pesticides in By-law 270 replicates that of the *Pesticides Act*. [...]

[**Ed. Note:** After analyzing the statutory scheme to determine whether the Town had authority to enact the impugned by-law, the majority offered the following views on the relevance of the precautionary principle and international law.]

To conclude this section on statutory authority, I note that reading s. 410(1) to permit the Town to regulate pesticide use is consistent with principles of international law and policy. My reasons for the Court in *Baker v. Canada (Minister of Citizenship and Immigration)*, [1999] 2 S.C.R. 817 at p. 861, observed that the values reflected in international human rights law may help inform the contextual approach to statutory interpretation and judicial review. As stated in *Driedger on the Construction of Statutes, supra*, at p. 330:

> [T]he legislature is presumed to respect the values and principles enshrined in international law, both customary and conventional. These constitute a part of the legal context in which legislation is enacted and read. *In so far as possible, therefore, interpretations that reflect these values and principles are preferred.* [Emphasis added.]

The interpretation of By-law 270 contained in these reasons respects international law's precautionary principle, which is defined as follows at para. 7 of the *Bergen Ministerial Declaration on Sustainable Development* (1990): "In order to achieve sustainable development, policies must be based on the precautionary principle. Environmental measures must anticipate, prevent and attack the causes of environmental degradation. Where there are threats of serious or irreversible damage, lack of full scientific certainty should not be used as a reason for postponing measures to prevent environmental degradation".

Canada advocated inclusion of the precautionary principle during the Bergen Conference negotiations (D. VanderZwaag, CEPA Issue Elaboration Paper No. 18, *CEPA and the Precautionary Principle/Approach* (1995), at p. 8). The principle is codified in several items of domestic legislation: see for example the *Oceans Act*, S.C. 1996, c. 31, Preamble (para. 6); *Canadian Environmental Protection Act, 1999*, S.C. 1999, c. 33 (*CEPA*), s. 2(1)(a); *Endangered Species Act*, S.N.S. 1998, c. 11, ss. 2(1)(h) and 11(1).

Scholars have documented the precautionary principle's inclusion in virtually every recently adopted treaty and policy document related to the protection and preservation of the environment (D. Freestone and E. Hey, Origins and Development of the Precautionary Principle, in D. Freestone and E. Hey, eds., *The Precautionary Principle and International Law* (1996), at p. 41. As a result, there may be currently sufficient state practice to allow a good argument that the precautionary principle is a principle of customary international law (J. Cameron and J. Abouchar, The Status of the Precautionary Principle in International Law, in *ibid.*, at p. 52). See also O. McIntyre and T. Mosedale, The Precautionary Principle as a Norm of Customary International Law (1997), 9 J. Env. L. 221, at p. 241 (the precautionary principle has indeed crystallized into a norm of customary international law). The Supreme Court of India considers the precautionary principle to be part of the Customary International Law (*A.P. Pollution Control Board v. Nayudu*, 1999 S.O.L. Case No. 53 at p. 8). See also *Vellore Citizens Welfare Forum v. Union of India*, [1996] Supp. 5 S.C.R. 241. In the context of the precautionary principle's tenets, the Town's concerns about pesticides fit well under their rubric of preventive action. [...]

Disposition

I have found that By-law 270 was validly enacted [...]. For these reasons, I would dismiss the appeal with costs.

Notes and Questions

1. What sources of international law are invoked by L'Heureux-Dubé J. in the reasons above? How do these sources inform her conclusions with respect to the precautionary principle?
2. What does the case suggest is the appropriate role of international law in the interpretation of domestic legislation?

3. Did it matter in this case that the legislation was provincial, dealing with powers delegated to municipalities?

4. What difference did it make that the provision in question was a discretionary provision? What if a municipality refused to exercise its discretion in a precautionary manner?

5. Does the case tell us anything about the role of international law with respect to the common law? Could the precautionary principle be used to reverse the onus of proof in some torts dealing with environmental and human health risks? We return to consider this and other issues relating to the precautionary principle in Part III.

6. In *Gosselin c. Québec (Procureur général)*, 2002 SCC 84, the SCC considered the validity of a social assistance program in Quebec. Under the program, individuals entitled to social assistance were broken into two groups, those under and those over 30 years of age. For individuals under 30, the program established a base amount payable that was lower than the base amount for individuals over 30. In order to qualify for the higher base amount, individuals under thirty had to enroll in designated work activities or education programs. A key legal issue was whether the program violated section 45 of the *Quebec Charter* which provides that every person in need has a right to "measures of financial assistance and to social measures provided for by law, susceptible of ensuring such person an acceptable standard of living". In addressing this question, the SCC was split over the relevance of the *International Covenant on Economic, Social and Cultural Rights*, an international treaty which Canada has signed and ratified. However, both the majority and the dissent considered Canada's international human rights obligations in order to provide context for the interpretation of section 45 of the *Quebec Charter*. Where they disagreed was whether the *Quebec Charter* was intended to implement specific international human rights obligations. Thus, if the majority had agreed with L'Heureux-Dubé J. that section 45 was intended to implement international human rights obligations, it seems likely that it would have been prepared to read these international obligations into section 45. What difference does it make to the role of international law in interpreting section 45, whether the section was intended to implement the international treaty or not?

7. *Canadian Foundation for Children, Youth & the Law v. Canada (Attorney General)*, 2004 SCC 4, involves a *Charter* challenge to section 43 of the *Criminal Code*, which permits school teachers and parents to use minor corrective force in some circumstances without facing criminal sanction. It provides:

> Every schoolteacher, parent or person standing in the place of a parent is justified in using force by way of correction toward a pupil or child, as the case may be, who is under his care, if the force does not exceed what is *reasonable under the circumstances*. [Emphasis added.]

The Foundation sought a declaration that section 43 violated sections 7, 12, and 15 of the *Canadian Charter of Rights and Freedoms*. A key issue in the case was the meaning of the phrase "reasonable under the circumstances" in section 43. The Foundation contended that this phrase was unconstitutionally vague. In considering this argument, the SCC makes reference to various sources of international law.

Unlike *Gosselin*, whether the legislative provision at issue was an attempt to implement treaty obligations was not an issue in this case. In fact, it seems clear that section 43 of the *Criminal Code* is not intended to implement Canada's international obligations. Rather, the issue was whether the provision being challenged was consistent with Canada's international human rights obligations. Is the SCC's use of binding international human rights obligations in this case in keeping with the analysis in the Brandon article? Is the approach in this case consistent with the majority in *Gosselin*, which took the view that the provision at issue was not an attempt to implement treaty obligations?

8. Another SCC case dealing with the relationship between international and domestic law is *R. v. Hape*, 2007 SCC 26. In this case, the court approves an "adoptionist" approach to the reception of customary international law. In the words of LeBel J.:

> In my view, following the common law tradition, it appears that the doctrine of adoption operates in Canada such that prohibitive rules of customary international law should be incorporated into domestic law in the absence of conflicting legislation. The automatic incorporation of such rules is justified on the basis that international custom, as the law of nations, is also the law of Canada unless, in a valid exercise of its sovereignty, Canada declares that its law is to the contrary. Parliamentary sovereignty dictates that a legislature may violate international law, but that it must do so expressly. Absent an express derogation, the courts may look to prohibitive rules of customary international law to aid in the interpretation of Canadian law and the development of the common law.

Is the approach in *Hape* consistent with the analysis offered in the Brandon article? Can you think of a good reason not to apply the same approach to ratified treaties?

Part III — Domestic Application of the Precautionary Principle: A Case Study

In the previous Part, we examined the general principles that govern the application of international law in the domestic realm, particularly environmental law. To take this inquiry further, we now turn to a case study that focuses on the growing incorporation and influence of the precautionary principle in domestic law, of which the decision in *Spraytech* is but one illustration. The precautionary principle provides a useful vehicle for this case study for several reasons. First of all, it is a highly influential soft law principle in international law. Secondly, it has been incorporated into a number of binding international treaties, making it binding on member states in the context of those treaties. As well, as alluded to in *Spraytech*, there has been an ongoing debate about the status of the principle under customary international law. Thirdly, the principle has been incorporated into a variety of environmental statutes in Canada. And finally, the principle has been at the centre of ongoing debates about the adequacy of the common law in dealing with environmental cases, especially in response to scientific uncertainty and the burden of proof in tort cases involving risk of harm resulting from contamination.

As you review the excerpts from the following article, consider the opportunities to use international law to advance the application of the precautionary principle in Canada.

**Chris Tollefson,
"A Precautionary Tale: Trials and
Tribulations of the Precautionary Principle"**
in A. Ingelson, ed., *Environment in the Courtroom*
(Calgary: University of Calgary Press, 2019)

The rise to prominence of the precautionary principle both as a legal concept and public policy tool has prompted extraordinary attention and debate. Considered by many to be one of the foundational principles of modern environmental law, increasingly the principle is being incorporated into federal and provincial legislation, and invoked in litigation before domestic courts and tribunals.

This paper reflects on the challenges and opportunities associated with litigating the precautionary principle as a basis for seeking review of governmental action [...] a critical mass of domestic jurisprudence on the application and interpretation of the principle has continued to emerge. To date, however, within much of this jurisprudence, the principle continues to be adverted to as a discretionary consideration or background interpretive canon. Nevertheless, there is also growing evidence of a judicial appetite to engage with the principle in a more systematic doctrinal fashion: in the words of one leading jurist, to give it "some specific work to do". Whether and to what extent this aspiration can be realized depends on whether the precautionary principle can be rendered sufficiently coherent and predictable to serve as a basis for judicial decision-making.

In Part II, I offer some introductory thoughts on the principle and the challenges associated with its deployment as an adjudicative tool. Part III surveys the various avenues and legal theories through which litigants have sought to invoke the principle in domestic litigation. Part IV then considers the growing Canadian jurisprudence that has emerged out of these efforts, offering some views on overarching trends and themes. And, finally, in Part V, I return to the question of how and whether the principle can be given some specific work to do by exploring some recent Australian caselaw that has directly taken up this challenge.

The Precautionary Principle: An Overview

The origins and implications of the precautionary principle are the subject of a considerable and growing scholarly literature. Derivative of the maxim "better safe than sorry", at its core the principle seeks to formalize precaution as a regulatory obligation in the face of environmental threats and scientific uncertainty. In the domain of international law, the principle began to emerge in the early 1980s most notably in the *World Charter for Nature* (1982). Since that time, it has become a central feature of close to one hundred international agreements and has been incorporated into scores of domestic environmental and public health laws worldwide.

There are many differing formulations of the precautionary principle. The most widely-cited version of the precautionary principle is found in Principle 15 of the *Rio Declaration on Environment and Development* (1992):

> Where there are threats of serious or irreversible damage, lack of full scientific certainty shall not be used as a reason for postponing cost-effective measures to prevent environmental degradation.

This relatively permissive or "weak" version of the principle is frequently contrasted with a more rigorous version famously approved by environmental activists and scholars at the 1998 Wingspread Conference:

> When an activity raises threats to the environment or human health, precautionary measures should be taken, even if some cause-and-effect relationships are not fully established scientifically.

The chameleon-like nature of the principle has tended to undermine reasoned consideration and debate of its precise meaning and implications. In an effort to provide an operational taxonomy of the principle, Sandin argues that its various formulations can be usefully analyzed along four key dimensions: *threat*, *uncertainty*, *action* and *command*. Under Sandin's approach, *threat* refers to the nature of the imminent harm to the "state of the world" (particularly its seriousness and (ir)reversibility), while *uncertainty* connotes "our (lack of) knowledge as [to] whether and how this threat might materialize". Under most formulations of the principle, where both the threat and uncertainty meet defined thresholds, an *action* obligation is triggered e.g. to consider "cost effective measures to prevent environmental degradation", "preventative measures" or "regulatory steps". Finally, the *command* dimension prescribes the legal status of the action to be taken, which may be framed in either mandatory or permissive language "shall" or "may". According to Sandin, a key challenge to operationalizing the precautionary principle lies in the imprecision with which the dimensions of "threat", "uncertainty", "action" and "command" are typically framed. [...]

Sandin's work in the realm of risk assessment has parallels in the legal scholarship of Professor Applegate. Applegate argues that a "tamed" understanding of the precautionary principle is beginning to emerge. In particular, he argues that, through this taming, "the constituent elements of the precautionary principle have been altered over time to be less stringent or to narrow the scope of the principle." This emerging, tamed version of the principle has the potential to provide a procedural vehicle for decision-making in the face of uncertainty. Traditionally, where the principle has not been considered as part of a decision-making process, regulators have only taken a risk into account when it rises to a relatively high standard of certainty. In contrast, where the principle is part of the regulatory equation, a decision-maker is empowered (and, in some instances, obliged) to take it into account. However, this response must be proportional to the risk, and must adapt as knowledge of the risk becomes more certain.

If Applegate and other legal scholars are correct that a tamed version of the precautionary principle can offer decision makers the procedural means to take risk into account in a manner that is consistent with established administrative law principles, a host of important questions about the meaning and implications of the principle arise. These include:

- *when should the principle apply?* In other words, should it apply generically or only when certain threshold requirements relating to environmental damage and scientific uncertainty are met?
- *how should it apply?* Who should bear the burden of proof, should the burden shift at some juncture, what form of evidence should be considered, and what standard(s) of proof should apply?
- *what remedial consequences should flow from its application?* To what extent and how should an adjudicative body prescribe measures necessary to achieve compliance with the principle?

Enter Precaution: The Emergence of the Principle in Domestic Environmental Litigation

There are two distinct avenues for the precautionary principle to enter domestic litigation: through the domestic application of international law, or through its application as a principle of domestic law. Each of these categories may be further subdivided. International law may be applied directly, as binding in its own right; or it may apply indirectly, as an interpretive aid. Likewise, stand-alone principles of domestic law may be derived either from common law or statutory sources.

Application of International Law

To date, few courts have accepted that the precautionary principle, as a rule of international law, can be directly applied in domestic litigation. One prominent exception is the Supreme Court of India. In *Vellore Citizens Welfare Forum v. Union of India*, it held that the principle had become a part of customary international law and as such was binding domestic law.

An alternative way for international law to affect domestic litigation is for it to be applied indirectly as an interpretive aid. Generally, courts will be reluctant to apply the precautionary principle in this way if it is inconsistent with applicable domestic law. However, if domestic law is capable of being interpreted in a manner consistent with the principle, it may play a persuasive interpretive role.

The Supreme Court of Canada's decision in *Spraytech* is an illustration of the indirect application of international law. While the status of the principle in international law was not fully argued before the Court, the majority reasons cite scholarly opinion to the effect that "a good argument" could be made that it had become "a principle of customary international law". The majority went on to employ the principle as a relevant consideration in upholding the validity of a municipal ban on pesticide use. As such, the decision makes it clear that principles of international law — even those that are not binding on Canada — may be taken into account when interpreting domestic law.

In 2013, the Supreme Court of Canada [in *Castonguay Blasting Ltd. v Ontario (Environment)*] reinforced the views it expressed in *Spraytech*. In *Castonguay* the court relied on the principle to interpret a provision in the Ontario *Environmental Protection Act*, R.S.O. 1990 c. E.19 (EPA). The provision in question made it an offence to discharge a contaminant into the environment: see s. 15(1) EPA. Abella J., writing for the court, describes the EPA as "Ontario's principal environmental protection statute" concluding that "its status as remedial legislation entitles it to generous interpretation."

In support of the conclusion that a broad purposive approach should be given to the interpretation of s. 15(1) of the EPA, Abella J. specifically relies on the precautionary principle even though the EPA makes no specific mention of the principle. In the words of the Court:

> As the interveners Canadian Environmental Law Association and Lake Ontario Waterkeeper pointed out in their joint factum, s. 15(1) is also consistent with the precautionary principle. This emerging international law principle recognizes that since there are inherent limits in being able to determine and predict environmental impacts with scientific certainty, environmental policies must anticipate and prevent environmental degradation (O. McIntyre and T. Mosedale, "The Precautionary Principle as a Norm of Customary International Law" (1997), 9 *J. Envtl. L.* 221, at pp. 221-22; *114957 Canada Ltée (Spraytech, Société d'arrosage) v. Hudson (Town)*, 2001 SCC 40, [2001] 2 S.C.R. 241, at paras. 30-32)

The Common Law

The precautionary principle may also emerge as a principle of common law within a domestic legal system. This process can occur through the direct or indirect application of international law; or it can occur independently of international law. The jurisdiction that has been the most receptive to the notion that the principle has or is destined soon to achieve common law status is Australia where some scholars argue that this has already occurred.

One of the earliest and most oft-cited Australian decisions marshalled in support of this claim is *Leatch v. National Parks and Wildlife Service*. This case involved a review of a permit to kill endangered fauna issued to a local government in connection with a road-building project. The relevant legislation did not require the precautionary principle to be applied; as a result, the plaintiffs argued that the principle was binding by virtue of international law. Stein J., of the New South Wales Land and Environment Court, demurred:

> It seems to me unnecessary to enter into this debate. In my opinion the precautionary principle is a statement of common sense and has already been applied by decision-makers in appropriate circumstances prior to the principle being spelt out. It is directed towards the prevention of serious or irreversible harm to the environment in situations of scientific uncertainty. Its premise is that where uncertainty or ignorance exists concerning the nature or scope of environmental harm (whether this follows from policies, decisions or activities), decision makers should be cautious.

As a principle of "common sense" not excluded by the relevant legislation, he held that the precautionary principle should be taken into account when deciding whether the permit to take or kill should be issued.

Statutory Adoption

By far the most common way that the principle finds its way before domestic courts and tribunals is through its implicit or explicit adoption in domestic statutes. A growing number of jurisdictions have enacted legislation that explicitly incorporates the precautionary principle either as a substantive decisional criterion or in preambular language. In Canada, the principle is now found, in various iterations, in most federal environmental laws including the *Species at Risk Act* (*SARA*), the *Oceans Act*, the *Canadian Environmental Protection Act* (*CEPA*), the *Canadian Environmental Assessment Act* (*CEAA*) and the *Pest Control Products Act* (*PCPA*). It was also included in recently proposed amendments to the *Fisheries Act*.

Currently the principle appears in the preambles to *CEPA*, *SARA* and the *Oceans Act*, in the purposes section of *CEAA* (s. 4) and as a mandatory strategic management principle under the *Oceans Act* (s. 30). It is also expressed as a relevant consideration in the exercise of administrative duties vested in the Government of Canada and its agencies under *CEPA* and *CEAA*. Moreover, in several instances, as set out below, the principle operates as a substantive decisional criterion:

- When conducting various assessments of potentially toxic substances, federal Ministers shall "apply ... the precautionary principle": section 76.1, *CEPA*.

- In preparing a recovery strategy, action plan or management plan the competent minister shall "consider the principle that, if there are threats of serious or irreversible damage to the listed wildlife species, cost effective measures to prevent the reduction or loss of the species should not be postponed for lack of full scientific certainty": section 38, *SARA*.

- When conducting a re-evaluation or special review of a registered pesticide product, the Minister must take the precautionary principle "into account" when deciding whether "a situation ... endangers human health or safety or the environment": see subsections 20(1) and (2), *PCPA*.

It is also, somewhat more slowly, finding its way into provincial legislation. In this regard, Ontario has led the way, generating a growing caselaw discussed in Part IV. Here the principle has come to be incorporated in many of the Statements of Environmental Values (SEVs) that every provincial government ministry is obliged to develop and apply. For example, the Ontario Ministry of Environment's SEV commits it to "exercising a precautionary approach in its decision making". Where a Ministry's SEV contains language to this effect, public interest litigants have argued that a subsequent failure by Ministry officials to comply with the principle, in the issuance of a permit or the exercise of a regulation making power, provides a basis for seeking leave to appeal from a Ministry action under the *Environmental Bill of Rights*.

Endangered species legislation in Ontario provides for a more direct way to pursue judicial review invoking the principle. Under the *Endangered Species Act* (*ESA*), the principle must be considered in the development of species recovery strategy: see subsection 11(3), *ESA*. This provision is analogous to the requirement under section 38 of *SARA*.

The principle also appears in provincial environmental statutes in other jurisdictions. To date, however, such references are relatively rare and are typically restricted to preambular language: see section 2 of the Nova Scotia *Environment Act*, S.N.S. 1994-95, c. C-1; and section 2 of the New Brunswick *Clean Air Act*, S.N.B. 1997, c. C-52.

Trials and Tribulations: The Precautionary Principle Caselaw Post-Spraytech

[**Ed. Note:** The author then proceeds to examine the treatment of the precautionary principle in a number of Canadian cases. The detailed analysis is omitted; however, the key findings are summarized in the following section.]

Inside the Judicial Mindset

From these early cases, some themes are beginning to emerge. For one, there has been little patience for claims that the precautionary principle is a trump card that when played clinches the case. Courts and tribunals have, likewise, been unsympathetic to claims that the compliance with the principle requires decision-makers to defer approval for potentially harmful activities wherever any scientific uncertainty, no matter how remote or speculative, about the nature or extent of the harm exists. What level of scientific uncertainty is required, and what forms of scientific evidence can and should be relied in this assessment, is unclear. Where, however, there are diverging opinions within the "regulatory community" and especially amongst government's own scientific advisors as to the nature or extent of the harm, it would appear that the test is met. Likewise, adjudicators also seem clearly to want compelling evidence that a proposed action or standard poses a serious risk to human health or the environment before concluding that the principle applies. Moreover, what quantum of risk is necessary, once again, is unclear.

Secondly it would appear that, at least judicially, there is a growing appetite to consider the principle and give it work to do. This is certainly reflected in the Supreme Court of Canada (*Spraytech* and *Castonguay*) and, as well, in Federal Court jurisprudence (*Greater Sage Grouse*, *Nootsack Dace*, *Wier v. Canada (Health)* and *Morton*). And, of course, we can add to this list *Wier v. BC (EAB)* in the BCSC involving the same Dr. Wier. It is notable that, in three of these seven cases, courts have chosen to deploy the principle even where the principle itself has not been referenced in the legislation being interpreted.

Finally, however, both in cases where courts and tribunals have demurred from considering the principle and where they have chosen to engage with it, there is a very discernible sense that the "legal contours" of the principle remain uncertain. Can the principle become more than an interpretive "straw in the wind"; can it offer guidance as a decisional criterion? The Divisional Court in *Sierra Club* is illustrative, dismissing the idea that preambular language referring to the principle does anything more than serve "to introduce the ideas and concerns that inform the legislation that follows". Cases in which references to the principle in preambular and purpose provisions have been interpreted in a more robust light have tended, almost invariably, to be ones where the principle is also incorporated into a substantive decisional criterion within the same statutory regime. Yet, where the precautionary principle is framed as a substantive decisional criterion, what guidance can be relied upon to apply that criterion? In the next part, I discuss possible ways through which the principle can be applied.

Can the Principle Be Given Some "Specific Work To Do"?

> Although there has been very little judicial consideration of the precautionary approach or 'precautionary principle' ... the clear thread which emerges from what consideration has been given to the approach is that it does dictate caution, but it does not dictate inaction, and it will not generally dictate one specific course of action to the exclusion of others.

> — Justice Christine Wheeler,
> Court of Appeal of West Australia

I now propose to return to a question posed at th[e] beginning of this paper: assuming that courts or tribunals are inclined or required to apply the principle, to what extent can it be given specific work to do? As noted earlier, a variety of legal scholars have argued in favour of "taming" the principle, enabling it to provide useful guidance to decision-makers, rather than dictating to them. Whether this can occur — in effect, whether the principle can be rendered justiciable — depends heavily on the creativity and initiative of lawyers and courts alike. Five years ago, in the predecessor to this article, I profiled and critiqued a new decision of the Land and Environment Court of New South Wales which, in my view, represented an important step in this direction: *Telstra Corporation Ltd. v. Hornsby Shire Council*, [2006] NSWLEC 133. In the balance of this Part, I want to revisit *Telstra* and consider whether it has indeed given the principle something specific to do.

Telstra and its Progeny

The *Telstra* case arose out of a proposal to construct a mobile telephone base station in a suburb of Sydney, Australia. The Shire Council, in response to community fears about the health effects of radiofrequency electromagnetic energy, refused the development application for the base station despite the fact that the installation complied with a peer-reviewed, applicable national safety standard. The Council's decision was appealed to the Land and Environment Court of New South Wales, pursuant to the *Environmental Planning and Assessment Act*, 1979 (*EPAA*). The *EPAA* requires the principles of sustainable development, including the precautionary principle, to be taken into account when considering development applications.

Under the *Telstra* approach, determining whether and how to apply the precautionary principle in a particular case occurs in three discrete steps: (1) deciding whether the principle applies; (2) if so, reversing the onus of proof; and (3) identifying the appropriate governmental response.

An important feature of *Telstra* is its recognition of the importance of restricting the application of the principle to situations where it can add analytic value. As such, it holds that before the principle can be applied the Applicant must establish two conditions precedent: (1) the existence of a threat of serious or irreversible environmental damage *and* (2) the existence of scientific uncertainty as to the environmental damage. Whether these preconditions exist are questions of fact.

The first condition precedent requires that impending environmental damage must be *serious or irreversible*. This, according to *Telstra*, can be measured using a variety of factors including:

    (a) the spatial scale of the threat (eg local, regional, statewide, national, international);

    (b) the magnitude of possible impacts, on both natural and human systems;

    (c) the perceived value of the threatened environment;

    (d) the temporal scale of possible impacts, in terms of both the timing and the longevity (or persistence) of the impacts;

    (e) the complexity and connectivity of the possible impacts;

    (f) the manageability of possible impacts, having regard to the availability of means and the acceptability of means;

    (g) the level of public concern, and the rationality of and scientific or other evidentiary basis for the public concern; and

    (h) the reversibility of the possible impacts and, if reversible, the time frame for reversing the impacts, and the difficulty and expense of reversing the impacts.

Under this approach, the seriousness of the threat is primarily a "values" as opposed to a "science" question to be judged by consultations with a broad range of experts, stakeholders, and right-holders. This does not mean, however, that science is irrelevant at this stage of the inquiry: indeed, Preston C.J. specifically notes "the threat of environmental damage must be adequately sustained by scientific evidence."

The second condition precedent is that there be *a lack of full scientific certainty*. In assessing this question of fact, *Telstra* posits another menu of factors including:

    (a) the sufficiency of the evidence that there might be serious or irreversible environmental harm caused by the development plan, programme or project;

    (b) the level of uncertainty, including the kind of uncertainty (such as technical, methodological or epistemological uncertainty); and

    (c) the potential to reduce uncertainty having regard to what is possible in principle, economically and within a reasonable time frame.

Telstra leaves open the question of what constitutes a requisite level of scientific uncertainty sufficient to trigger application of the principle; in its view, this standard may differ depending upon the nature of the impending environmental damage. In a leading case that has recently applied *Telstra*, a standard of "substantial uncertainty" was adopted.

If these conditions precedent are met, the precautionary principle is then triggered. This means that the burden of proof shifts to the proponent to show that the threat of serious or irreversible environmental damage does not in fact exist or is negligible. If the proponent cannot do so, the government decision-maker must assume that serious or irreversible damage will occur.

In this situation, the decision-maker must respond in a manner that is consistent with the principle. The response that is required by the precautionary principle will depend on the outcome of a risk assessment. The overarching goal of the response is proportionality. The more significant and likely the threat, the greater the degree of precaution required. Where uncertainty exists, a margin of error should be left so that serious or irreversible harm is less likely to occur. This margin of error may be maintained through step-wise or adaptive management plans.

In the result, the carefully elaborated approach set out in *Telstra* was not put to the test on the facts of the case. Preston C.J. decided that the party seeking to rely upon the principle (in this case, the Shire Council) had failed to lead evidence capable of supporting the conclusion that the proposed cell tower presented a threat of serious or irreversible harm. As a result, the precautionary principle did not apply and it was unnecessary to proceed further with the analysis.

The *Telstra* approach has, however, been applied in a more fulsome fashion in several subsequent cases. Among these, the case that most faithfully applies the framework involves a familiar scenario, especially for those of us from the Canadian West Coast. The conflict here arose in a remote region in southern Australia, and was triggered by logging plans in an old growth Crown-owned forest that were said to threaten a variety of endangered species: see *Environment East Gippsland Inc. v. VicForests*, [2010] V.S.C. 335. It is instructive to reprise how Osborn J. for the Supreme Court of Victoria analyses this complex dispute employing the *Telstra* framework.

In this case, the plaintiff environmental group commenced an action seeking an injunction against proposed logging to be undertaken by the defendant, state-owned forest company. The defendant had secured timber-harvesting approvals for an area known as Brown Mountain, in the East Gippsland region of the state of Victoria, south-east of Melbourne. Surrounded by conservation reserve areas, Brown Mountain contains areas of old growth forest with high timber values and ecological significance. The area in contention was home to over a dozen threatened or endangered species including the Long-footed Potoroo, the Powerful Owl, and the Giant Burrowing Frog. Under a legally binding Code of Practice, the defendant was obliged to plan and undertake harvesting in accordance with the precautionary principle.

The case makes fascinating reading for Canadian environmental lawyers more accustomed to the highly constrained manner in which judicial supervision of natural resource decision-making occurs in Canada. Osborn J.'s careful reasons for judgment help, in my view, to dispel the notion that the principle can at best play a background or ancillary role in domestic adjudication.

The case arises in the context of what Osborn J. characterizes as a 'labyrinthine' maze of legislation and regulation. A central issue to be decided was whether and to what extent the precautionary principle applied to the defendant's tree harvesting plans, and what implications (in terms of injunctive relief) flow. The court heard evidence over the course of sixteen days. Ultimately, for five species — the Powerful Owl and the Spotted Owl, the Spot-tailed Quoll, the Giant Burrowing Frog and the Large Brown Tree Frog — the principle played a decisive role in the court's conclusion that logging should be enjoined pending further studies aimed at determining what measures were necessary to maintain species viability.

To provide a sense of how Osborn J. assessed the evidence in applying the *Telstra* test, it is worthwhile to reprise his analysis with respect to two of the species at issue: the Giant Burrowing Frog and the Large Brown Tree Frog. For these species, he concluded as follows:

(a) that the proposed logging presents a *real threat of serious or irreversible damage* to the environment (i.e. these two species) for a variety of reasons including their 'threatened' status and relevant expert evidence;

(b) that this damage is attended by a *lack of full scientific certainty* including evidence with respect to very significant uncertainties relating to their respective distribution, biology and conservation;

(c) the defendant has not demonstrated that the threat is *negligible* insofar as it led 'no evidence from an expert with specialist qualifications relating to the biology and conservation of frogs';

(d) the threat can be addressed through *adaptive management*, including 'management measures, which would significantly better inform a further judgment as to the relevant conservation values of the Brown Mountain ... [reducing] ... uncertainty with limited cost and within a reasonable timeframe';

(e) the 'measures proposed are *proportionate* to the threat in issue. They are limited operations. Further, they are capable of definition and ... controlling supervision ... In addition there is satisfactory evidence that postponement of timber harvesting pending the completion of such surveys would cause VicForests significant economic damage' (italics added).

While these excerpts may be not adequately convey the point, I would argue that this judgment grapples impressively with a dispute that is extraordinarily complex both in legal and scientific terms. And, I would argue, far from being a 'make-work' project for the precautionary principle, the judgment shows in convincing fashion that the principle — appropriately "tamed" — can indeed be a powerful tool for analyzing and resolving disputes of this kind. Among other reasons, I think that this is attributable to the care with which the Osborn J. applies the *Telstra* framework, particularly in relation to the conditions precedent to the principle, and the need to calibrate a judicial response that is proportionate to the risk.

As discussed at the end of Part II, turning the precautionary principle into a workable framework raises three important questions:

- *When should the principle apply?*
- *How should it apply?*
- *What remedial consequences should flow from its application?*

Telstra is a compelling illustration of how these three questions can be addressed in a manner that allows the principle to play a constructive role in a variety of administrative and adjudicative settings. The *Telstra* approach accomplishes this by responding to concerns about overbreadth by Professor Applegate and others: see Part II *supra*. It does this by injecting into the principle a proportionality mechanism that calibrates the precautionary measures required to the degree of risk that is present. Moreover, as knowledge of the risk grows more certain through adaptive management and learning, these precautionary measures can be fine-tuned.

Finally, the two conditions precedent under the *Telstra* approach offer another "taming" mechanism that clarifies and constrains what the precautionary principle is supposed to do. By requiring courts to first determine whether the principle applies in the first place, and then providing a framework for application where the principle is found to be applicable, the *Telstra* approach affirmatively answers Stein J.'s question on whether the principle can be given "specific work to do".

Notes and Questions

1. What difference does it make to its implementation in Canada whether the precautionary principle is customary international law?

2. Reflecting on the principles and cases covered in earlier parts of the chapter, do you agree with the author's assessment of the range of avenues available for the incorporation and application of the precautionary principle into environmental law in Canada?

3. Under what conditions do you think the principle should be applied in Canada? Why are some courts and tribunals reluctant to give the principle "work to do"? To what extent does *Telstra* respond to the concerns underpinning this reluctance? Do you think Canadian courts and tribunals will apply the *Telstra* approach?

4. One of the most common applications that has been advocated for the principle is to reverse the onus of proving harm. What are the implications of such an approach in cases of tort law? What about regulatory decisions about the use and release of substances? See further discussion in Chapter 2.

5. As discussed in this article, the Federal Court has been called upon on several occasions to interpret and apply the precautionary principle in Canadian law. Two important precedents are the Court's reasons in *Morton v. Canada (Fisheries and Oceans)*, 2015 FC 575 ("*Morton 2015*") and *Morton v. Canada (Fisheries and Oceans)*, 2019 FC 143 ("*Morton 2019*"). Both cases involved the interpretation of section 56 of the *Fishery (General) Regulations*, SOR/93-53 ("FGR") under the *Fisheries Act*, R.S.C. 1985, c. F-14, governing the release or transfer of fish. In particular, section 56(b) provides that the Minister may only issue a transfer licence "if the fish do not have any disease or disease agent that may be harmful to the protection and conservation of fish." In *Morton 2015*, Rennie J., as he then was, held that section 56(b) "properly construed, embodies the precautionary principle" and therefore licence conditions that derogate from the precautionary principle are inconsistent with section 56(b): at paras. 97-99. This case is important because neither the *Fisheries Act* nor the FGR explicitly mentions the precautionary principle; therefore, this case is one of the first times where a Canadian court has read the precautionary principle into a statute.

Justice Rennie's interpretation of the precautionary principle and section 56(b) was followed in the more recent Federal Court decision in *Morton 2019*. This case involved a challenge to a DFO policy under which the testing for PRV and HSMI is not required for the granting of a transfer licence. PRV and HSMI are infectious diseases associated with salmon aquaculture that have been found to infect wild salmon and impact wild salmon stocks. In that case, the applicants (an environmental activist and a First Nation) challenged, among other things, a decision by the Minister to maintain the DFO policy despite growing scientific evidence regarding the adverse impacts of PRV and HSMI on salmon.

In quashing the Minister's decision, Strickland J. held that decisions made pursuant to section 56 must adhere to, and not simply consider, the precautionary principle. A critical issue for the Court was the Minister's interpretation of "protection and conservation of fish" under section 56(b). Here, the Minister had unreasonably interpreted section 56(b) in a way that permits any transfer of fish having a disease or a disease agent "unless the transfer places genetic diversity, species or conservation units of fish at risk": at para. 125. By incorporating a level of harm at the species or conservation unit level, Strickland J. held that this interpretation "ascribes a level of harm that fails to embody and is inconsistent with the precautionary principle": at para. 165. Furthermore, Strickland J. held that, given the high degree of scientific uncertainty surrounding PRV and HSMI and the decline in wild salmon numbers, the Minister's failure to consider wild Pacific salmon health and status in deciding to continue the DFO policy under section 56 also fails to embody the precautionary principle: at para. 214.

Part IV — Key International Environmental Regimes to Watch

We conclude this chapter with a brief overview of five key international regimes with implications for domestic environmental law, to which we return in other chapters. The first of these regimes is the 1992 *Convention on Biological Diversity*. We discuss the implementation of aspects of this Convention in Chapter 8 (parks and wilderness protection) and Chapter 9 (species at risk). The second regime is the 1989 *Basel Convention* on the movement of hazardous waste. Implementation issues for this Convention are addressed in Chapter 4 (environmental regulation). We also consider the environmental implications of the *General Agreement on Tariffs and Trade* (GATT) and other environmental implications of the World Trade Organization; likewise, we consider the environmental implications of the *North American Free Trade Agreement* (NAFTA) and other international agreements governing foreign investment. Linkages between these international regimes and domestic environmental law are revisited in Chapter 4. Finally, a very brief introduction to the climate change regime is included. We look at the substance of the climate regime and domestic implications of Canada's obligations in Chapter 10.

Convention on Biological Diversity (CBD)

Elli Louka,
International Environmental Law,
Fairness, Effectiveness and World Order
(Cambridge: Cambridge University Press, 2006) at 299–303

The Biodiversity Convention is the first attempt to deal globally with biodiversity protection. The convention is a framework convention. It does not establish biodiversity protection standards but attempts to create the outline of a regime for biodiversity protection by focusing on *in situ* conservation and, marginally, on the restoration of deteriorated ecosystems and gene bank, management. Declaration of national sovereignty over natural resources, intellectual property rights, and technology transfers become the vehicles for the establishment of such a regime.

The convention emphasizes that states must preserve biodiversity "as far as possible and as appropriate" by undertaking measures that would protect biodiversity in nature or in gene banks. The convention clearly places biodiversity resources under national sovereignty. The convention places emphasis on national and bilateral action based on the presumption that biodiversity can be protected more effectively at the national/bilateral level.

Gene bank development is a supplemental goal in the overall scheme of biodiversity protection. The convention explicitly provides that states must adopt measures of gene bank development "for the purpose of complementing *in situ* measures". *Ex situ* conservation measures should preferably take place in the country of origin. Because most genetic resources are located in developing countries and gene banks are located in developed countries, the convention calls for an increase in the number of gene banks in the developing world. The convention also proposes that it is best for each country to have its own gene banks, an approach that is too limited and not very practicable. Given the possibilities presented by developing regional and even international gene banks, it is not cost-efficient for many developing countries to keep their own gene banks. In the area of gene bank development, self-sufficiency is costly, and collaboration is certainly a more cost-effective means to conserve germplasm.

The article on *in situ* conservation presents this type of conservation as the most fundamental method of protecting biodiversity. States must "as far as possible and as appropriate" establish a system of protected areas; develop guidelines for the selection and management of protected areas; regulate and manage biological resources both within and outside protected areas; promote "environmentally sound and sustainable development" in areas adjacent to protected areas; and adopt the necessary regulatory measures for the protection of endangered species. States must manage and control the risks associated with the release of bioengineered organisms and prevent the introduction of exotic species that may have adverse impacts on endemic species and habitats.

Overall, the article on *in situ* conservation seems intentionally vague so as to give states some latitude in designing their conservation programs. Because in practice *in situ* conservation often has meant total preservation of protected areas based on evictions of the people who inhabit those areas, it would have been desirable if the provisions on *in situ* conservation included a clause that ensured that *in situ* conservation will not be pursued by violating human dignity and human rights.

It must be acknowledged, however, that the Biodiversity Convention is one of the first international treaties to recognize the rights of indigenous peoples and local communities to their "knowledge", "innovations", and "practices". The Biodiversity Convention provides that the consent of indigenous peoples is needed to utilize their knowledge and that there should be equitable sharing of the benefits derived from such knowledge. The specifics of equitable sharing, however, still resist practical application. Parties must submit to the Conference of the Parties (COP) the measures taken to implement the convention. Parties must also submit an evaluation of the effectiveness of these measures in accomplishing the convention's objectives. Reporting on the effectiveness of measures to preserve biodiversity must be based on an accurate assessment of the existing biodiversity. Many attempts have been made to assess the world's biodiversity resources and to value these resources so that the goals of biodiversity protection become more concrete.

More than ten years have elapsed from the signing of the Biodiversity Convention, but not much has happened in terms of making the convention a functional instrument for the protection of biodiversity. Most of the debate on implementation focuses on the issue of access to genetic resources and equitable sharing of benefits derived from biotechnology that is based on such resources. Other issues that have preoccupied the Conference of the Parties include:

- the protection of coral reefs;
- the protection of agricultural biological diversity;
- conducting EIAs and SEAs;
- the global taxonomy initiative;
- the implementation of article 8(j) regarding the rights of indigenous peoples to their knowledge;
- the development of an ecosystem approach;
- the establishment of incentive measures for the protection of diversity by taking into account the distributional impacts of such measures;
- the integration of biodiversity protection into sectors of the economy;
- the protection of forest biodiversity; and
- the protection of coastal areas and integrated coastal zone management.

The Biodiversity Convention has [...] three objectives:

- the conservation of biological diversity;
- the sustainable use of its components; and
- and the fair and equitable sharing of benefits arising out of the utilization of genetic resources.

The convention affirms national sovereignty over biodiversity resources. The convention sidelines prior regimes that generated perceptions that biodiversity resources located under the Jurisdiction of a state can be freely accessed.

The convention provides that access to genetic resources must be subject to the prior informed consent of the country of origin. The convention requires state parties to develop legislative and administrative measures in order to share "in a fair and equitable way [...] the benefits arising from the commercial and other utilization of genetic resources" with state parties that provide genetic resources. Although the convention does not give the specifics of fair and equitable sharing, it provides that such sharing must occur on mutually agreed terms. The convention provides for access to and transfer of technology, such as biotechnology, to developing countries "under fair and most favourable terms". Article 19 provides that each party must take measures to provide for the participation in technological research activities by parties, especially developing countries, which provided the genetic resources for such research. State parties must take measures to advance priority access, on a fair and equitable basis, by developing countries, to benefits coming from technology. Such access is provided, however, if the technology is based on the genetic resources found in these developing countries.

The convention clarifies that new and additional financial resources are needed to enable developing countries to meet "the agreed full incremental costs" of implementing the convention. The extent to which developing countries are to implement the convention depends on developed countries executing their commitments with regard to the provision of financial resources and transfer of technology. In this context, the convention elucidates — in a spirit echoing concerns vocalized during the WSSD summit — that the implementation of the convention by developing countries "will take fully into account the fact that [...] development and eradication of poverty are the first and overriding priorities of the developing country Parties". A financial mechanism is to be established that would provide resources to developing countries.

The convention recognizes the rights of indigenous peoples in their knowledge and innovations. The convention provides that states must encourage the equitable sharing of benefits arising from the utilization of knowledge, innovations, and practices of indigenous peoples.

Notes and Questions

1. The Convention is intended both to protect biodiversity and to ensure an equitable sharing of the benefits arising from the use of genetic resources. How well does the CBD appear to balance these goals?

2. The major threats to biodiversity are generally recognized to be habitat loss, climate change, invasive species and pollution. How effectively are these threats recognized in the mandate of the CBD to protect biodiversity?

3. Canada has ratified the CBD. What legislation do you think is needed to comply with Canada's commitments under the Convention? Compare your answer with what steps Canada has actually taken on the biodiversity front as discussed in Chapters 8 and 9.

4. At the 10th Conference of the Parties to the convention in Japan in 2010, the parties reached an agreement on access and benefit sharing (ABS) with

respect to genetic material. For a summary of the agreement, see the Earth Negotiations Bulletin, online: <http://www.iisd.ca/biodiv/cop10/>.

5. Since 2010, the focus of the CBD has been on the implementation of existing commitments, something we will return to in the Canadian context in Chapters 8 and 9.

The Basel Convention

Ifeoma Onyerikam,
"Achieving Compliance with the Basel Convention on
Transboundary Movement of Hazardous Wastes"
(University of Alberta Faculty of Law, 2007) [unpublished]

Prior to 1989, transboundary movements of hazardous wastes were governed by the international law principle of "good neighborliness" or *sic utere tuo, ut alienum non laedas*. This simply means that States have an obligation to control activities within their jurisdiction and ensure that activities within their jurisdiction do not harm the resources of other States. As a general principle, the scope of its application was narrow and there was no enforcement mechanism to ensure compliance. Though this principle over time had developed into a rule of customary international law, the problems associated with the application of customary international law made it difficult for States to rely solely on this rule to regulate transboundary movement of hazardous waste. That was why, in 1981, the Governing Council of the United Nations Environmental Programme (UNEP) mandated a group of officials expert in environmental law to determine subject areas for increased global and regional co-operation for expansion of environmental law.

Toxic waste transport, handling and disposal were identified as one of the major subject areas for increased international co-operation. One reason for the identification of hazardous wastes as an area deserving international co-operation could be linked to the growing demand by industrialized nations for disposal sites in the developing States, especially in Africa, and the number of accidents from hazardous wastes transportation and disposal that occurred within that decade. The disappearance of landfill sites in the industrialized nations, the escalating disposal costs between the industrialized nations and the converse cheap disposal costs in the developing world and the difficulty of obtaining approval for incineration facilities contributed to the demand for waste disposal in developing States. [...]

The Conference of the Plenipotentiaries on the Global Convention on the Control of Transboundary Movements of Hazardous Wastes was thus convened in Basel from March 20–22, 1989 (hereinafter the Basel Conference). [...] 116 States were represented. The draft convention was considered and adopted by the parties on March 22, 1989. [...] 36 States signed the Convention on March 22, 1989.

The *Basel Convention* finally entered into force on May 5, 1992 upon the deposit of the 20th instrument of accession. The delay in the ratification by States could be attributed to several controversies raised during the negotiations. For instance, the African nations (supported by some non-governmental organizations like Greenpeace) were in favour of a complete ban of all transboundary waste shipment, whereas some of the developed nations advocated for regulation rather than a complete ban. Failing to meet their main objectives, the African nations nevertheless insisted on stringent measures, which were accepted by some of the industrialized nations, while others refused and deferred their signature.

The refusal by States to adopt a complete ban of transboundary movements of hazardous wastes did not deter the African nations from pursuing, and insisting on, a complete ban. Their efforts yielded fruits in March 1994 when the parties by Decision II/12 adopted the Basel Ban. The Basel Ban aims at banning the transport of hazardous wastes from OECD States to non-OECD States, whether for recycling or disposal. [...]

Although the Ban Amendment has been incorporated into the *Basel Convention* as Article 4A, it has not entered into force having not received the required number of ratifications. The delay in ratification may be attributed to the possible loss of economic gains from the transactions by the developing world, such as China, India, and the Philippines, that depend economically on the recyclable wastes. The developing countries are attracted by the foreign exchange to be earned from hazardous wastes transactions even though they often do not have the appropriate disposal or recycling facilities. [...]

The *Basel Convention* has undergone further amendments. The absence of provisions on liability and compensation in the Convention, coupled with the concerns expressed by developing countries of lack of funds and technology to combat accidental spills and illegal dumping, led to negotiations on a liability protocol. The necessity for such a liability protocol was based on the provisions of Article 13 of the *Rio Declaration* and the need to provide for third party liability. Negotiations were concluded and parties adopted the *Basel Protocol* on December 10, 1999 at the 5th Conference of the parties. The *Protocol* aims at providing a comprehensive regime of liability and compensation for damage resulting from transboundary movement of hazardous wastes and other wastes.

The *Basel Protocol* is not yet in force having not received the required number of ratifications to bring it into force. The delay in ratification could be linked to issues of implementation and costs.

Scope and Objectives

The Convention only applies to wastes that are "hazardous" and are subject to transboundary movement. A waste is hazardous if: it is listed in Annex I; it exhibits any of the characteristics in Annex III, such as flammability, explosivity, toxicity, and ecotoxicity; or it is defined as hazardous by the national laws of any State. Transboundary movement has been defined as "movement of hazardous wastes or other wastes from an area under the national jurisdiction of a State to or through an area under the national jurisdiction of another State provided two States are involved". This means that wastes not subject to transfrontier movement are not covered under the Convention. This definition is significant in that it covers not only obvious cases of transfrontier movement, for example, movement from the generating State to the disposing State, but also situations where the disposer and the generator are in the same State but during the course of the shipment the waste passes through another State. Radioactive wastes and wastes arising from the normal operations of a ship are excluded from the scope of the Convention. These types of wastes are excluded because other treaties or international instruments already cover them.

The key objectives of the *Basel Convention* are to minimize the generation of hazardous wastes in terms of quantity and dangerousness, dispose of hazardous wastes as close to the source of generation as possible, ensure an environmentally sound disposal of wastes, and as far as possible reduce the movement of hazardous wastes and the risks of accidents associated with such transportation.

Relevant Provisions of the Basel Convention

Generally, State parties are required *inter alia* to reduce the generation of hazardous wastes by adopting clean production methods, ensure that wastes generated are disposed of in an environmentally sound manner, refrain from exporting hazardous wastes to States that have banned the importation of the hazardous wastes, obtain the prior consent of the importing and transit States before exporting any waste from its territory, and comply with provisions of the Convention in the transboundary movement of the hazardous wastes and the international rules on packaging and labeling of products for shipment. [...]

The obligations imposed on the parties can be grouped into two: transportation obligations and disposal obligations. The Convention requires that exportation of hazardous wastes should only take place where the exporting State lacks the technical capacity and expertise to dispose of the wastes in an environmentally sound manner, or the waste is required as a raw material for recycling or recovery in the State of import. This requirement imposes two conditions that must be simultaneously satisfied before exportation can take place. Firstly, the exporting State must demonstrate lack of technical capacity and expertise to dispose of the wastes. Secondly, the importing State must have the technical expertise and appropriate disposal or recycling facilities to manage the hazardous wastes in an environmentally sound manner. Where both conditions are not satisfied, an exporting State is prohibited from exporting the hazardous wastes.

Environmentally sound management of wastes requires that there exist appropriate disposal facilities and precautionary measures for the management of hazardous wastes. It also involves addressing the issue of hazardous wastes through an "integrated life cycle approach" that involves strong controls from the generation of hazardous wastes to storage, transport, treatment, re-use, recycling, recovery and final disposal. The obligation to ensure that exported wastes are managed in an environmentally sound manner in the country of import has been imposed on the exporting State. There is evidence to show that States have on some occasions violated or ignored this obligation. For instance, the constant movement of hazardous wastes to developing States such as China, India and African States, where the wastes are disposed of in an unsound manner, is evidence of such non-compliance by States. A Greenpeace news report indicates that tones of hazardous wastes from computer and other metal scraps were continually dumped in China in 2005 and that the hazardous wastes were recycled manually. The Basel Action Network, a non-governmental organization, reports that about 500 containers filled with used electronic equipment are exported to Lagos, Nigeria every month where they are resold and the remainder dumped in landfills and later burnt, releasing dangerous substances into the environment.

Notes and Questions

1. The *Basel Convention* has been implemented in Canada through regulations under the *Canadian Environmental Protection Act*. Canadian government efforts ostensibly aimed at implementing the Convention gave rise to a lawsuit brought by SD Myers (a US-based hazardous waste disposal company) under the investor claim provisions of NAFTA chapter 11: see further discussion in Chapter 4 (Environmental Regulation).
2. Based on the article above, can you assess the effectiveness of this Convention in preventing the shipment of hazardous material to developing countries that lack the capacity to ensure proper disposal?
3. What, if any, improvement would you make to the Convention? Can you think of reasons why these improvements were not included?

World Trade Institutions

Elli Louka, *International Environmental Law, Fairness, Effectiveness and World Order*
(Cambridge: Cambridge University Press, 2006) at 383–394

The free movement of goods and services among states has been the exception rather than the norm in international trade. Countries have regulated international trade through a number of tariff and nontariff barriers. Every country has enacted its share of tariff and nontariff rules that put restrictions on foreign imports, thereby making foreign products more expensive than domestic products. These rules have acted as a barrier to international trade and have limited the choices available to the ultimate consumer.

Ideas of liberalism that free trade should be pursued for the benefit of the ultimate consumer, through the gradual elimination of tariff and nontariff barriers, launched the negotiations in 1946 for the development of an International Trade Organization. Eventually, countries agreed to adopt a milder version of a General Agreement on Tariffs and Trade (GATT). GATT acted as a legal agreement/quasi-legal institution for the regulation of international trade with the ultimate goal of bringing down the barriers to trade.

Since its inception in 1946, GATT has gone through several rounds of tariff reductions. In 1994, after seven years of negotiations, the World Trade Organization (WTO) emerged. The WTO manages a legal apparatus that includes the provisions of GATT as well as a General Agreement on Trade in

Services (GATS), an Agreement on Trade-Related Aspects of Intellectual Property Rights (TRIPs), an Agreement on Sanitary and Phytosanitary Measures (SPS), and an Understanding on Rules and Procedures Governing the Settlement of Disputes (DSU). These agreements were opened for signature at Marrakesh in 1994 and entered into force in 1995.

The WTO has become the institution through which all important trade matters are discussed, including conflicts between national policies and trade. As an international institution, the WTO presents a much-needed institutional framework alongside the International Monetary Fund (IMF) and the World Bank. The WTO has had already the opportunity to examine many matters that were previously reserved for national policy making. Such is the intrusion of the WTO into national and international policy making that some argue that the WTO is becoming a central lawmaking and adjudicative institution in international affairs. [...]

The Treaties

From its beginnings, GATT included provisions that were designed to reduce tariff and nontariff barriers. What has been called the "national treatment rule" included in article III of GATT provides that once goods have been imported from another member country they must be treated, by the laws of the importing country, no less favorably than goods produced domestically. Another rule that has been invoked frequently in international transactions is the "most favored nation" rule that provides that member states of the GATT must treat equally their trading partners by providing the same conditions to all of them for imports and exports of "like goods".

Article XX constitutes one of the most discussed articles of GATT because it provides general exceptions to the rules of GATT. Article XX allows for exceptions to free trade for the protection of natural resources and the environment. Article XX provides that:

> Subject to the requirement that such measures are not applied in a manner which would constitute a means of arbitrary or unjustifiable discrimination between countries where the same conditions prevail, or disguised restriction on international trade nothing in this Agreement shall be construed to prevent the adoption or enforcement by any contracting party of measures:
>
> [...] (b) necessary to protect human, animal or plant life or health;
>
> [...] (g) relating to the conservation of exhaustible natural resources if such measures are made effective in conjunction with restrictions on domestic production or consumption.

GATS contains a general exceptions clause in article XIV, which is similar to that included in article XX of GATT. One of the purposes of the new Committee on Trade and Environment (CTE), created under the auspices of WTO, is to examine the interconnection among trade, services, and the environment to determine whether article XIV requires any modification.

Another WTO agreement that goes to the heart of consumer protection involves the Sanitary and Phytosanitary Measures (SPS) Agreement. The SPS agreement provides that member states may adopt sanitary and phytosanitary measures for the purposes of food safety, human, animal, and plant health and safety. But it provides simultaneously that SPS measures must be based on science, should not create unnecessary obstacles to trade, should not arbitrarily discriminate between countries where the same conditions apply. Furthermore, SPS measures must be based on a risk assessment and must be transparent.

The TRIPs agreement provides that countries can recognize patents on most products and processes including pharmaceuticals, modified microorganisms, and microbiological processes (namely, biotechnology devices). Countries can protect plant varieties under patents or other *sui generis* systems, for instance, various versions of plant breeders' rights. The agreement gives countries some sort of discretion in deciding whether patents can be granted to "essentially biological processes for the production of plants and animals" (art. 27.3(b)). There also are exceptions to the provision of intellectual property rights if the refusal to grant such rights is done to protect public order, morality, human, animal, and plant life or health or to avoid adverse environmental effects (art. 27.2). However, the refusal to grant a patent cannot be based on an explanation that the national laws and regulations of a country have yet to approve the product or process. Thus, although this exception could be used occasionally to avert the assertion of intellectual property rights for environmental reasons, it is likely to be strictly interpreted and unlikely to be used lightly for granting derogations from the spirit of the agreement.

Dispute Settlement

The 1994 WTO agreement includes an Annex on "Understanding on Rules and Procedures Governing the Settlement of Disputes" (DSU). The DSU establishes the Dispute Settlement Body (DSB), ad hoc panels and the Appellate Body. The purpose of the DSB is to administer the dispute settlement proceedings. It is comprised of all members of the WTO and it is a political rather than a Judicial body. If members of the WTO face a dispute, they may refer the dispute to the DSB, which, in turn, would try to mediate the issue. If mediation or conciliation fails, the parties may ask the DSB to convene a panel. Unlike the recommendations of GATT panels, the recommendations of the WTO panels become binding when they are adopted by the DSB, an adoption that is deemed automatic within sixty days, unless a consensus is formed in the DSB against a panel's recommendation. Furthermore, unlike GATT proceedings, panel decisions can be appealed before the Appellate Body on legal grounds. Again, the report of the Appellate Body is deemed to be automatically adopted by the DSB unless there *is* a consensus against its adoption.

The DSU has increased the power of panels significantly. [As such] the decisions of the panels are not [...] vulnerable to the capriciousness of a member state. This dispute settlement procedure makes possible, for the first time, in the GATT/WTO system third-party adjudication. The general discontent with GATT dispute settlement arrangement, which led to the adoption of the DSU, is indicative of the quest in the international system for effective dispute resolution mechanisms.

Traditional public international law acts as a sort of constitutional law that provides a set of basic norms, and guidelines for their interpretation. The lack of a dispute resolution tribunal with mandatory jurisdiction in international law sets the DSU of the WTO as an enviable exception. [...]

1998 Shrimp-Turtle Case

The *Shrimp-Turtle* case involved the extraterritorial application of the U.S. endangered species legislation. According to this legislation, the United States required those who capture shrimp to use approved Turtle Excluder Devices (TEDS) at all times and in all areas (with certain exceptions) where there was the likelihood that shrimp harvesting would affect sea turtles.

Section 609(a) of the Act 31 required the Secretary of Commerce to initiate bilateral or multilateral agreements with foreign governments with regard to the adoption of similar conservation measures by other countries. Section 609(b) (1) imposed an import ban on shrimp harvested with technology that would adversely affect turtles. For shrimp to be imported, they would have to be certified. There are two types of certification that are required annually. The first certification would be issued to countries that have a fishing environment that does not pose a threat to the taking of turtles in the course of shrimp harvesting. The second certification would be granted to countries that provide documentation that they maintain a regulatory program similar to that of the United States. In addition, these countries would have to prove that the incidental taking of sea turtles is comparable to that of the United States. The program put in place by a foreign government had to be comparable to the U.S. program in terms of effectiveness and had to provide for credible enforcement. Countries in the Caribbean/western Atlantic region were exempted from certification for three years, during which time they had to phase in a regulatory program. [...]

Because the United States regulations were in accord with article XX(g), the question was whether they fulfilled the requirements of the chapeau of article XX. Legitimate measures adopted in accordance with article XX(g) must not be used

> in a manner which would constitute a means of arbitrary or unjustifiable discrimination between countries where the same conditions prevail, or a disguised restriction on international trade.

The Appellate Body elaborated further on the level of review required by the chapeau of article XX.

1. the measures adopted must not constitute arbitrary discrimination between countries where the same conditions prevail;
2. the measures adopted must not constitute *unjustifiable* discrimination between countries where the same conditions prevail;
3. the measures adopted must not constitute a *disguised* restriction on international trade.

According to the Appellate Body, the chapeau of article XX is an expression of the principle of good faith. The principle of good faith is a principle of general law and an international rule and it controls the exercise of rights of states.

The Appellate Body concluded that the U.S. measures were an "unjustifiable discrimination" because they imposed on an exporting WTO member the adoption of identical regulatory requirements to those applied by the United States. The Appellate Body claimed, thus, that the United States established "a rigid and unbending standard. The U.S. measures failed to take into account "different conditions" that may occur in the territory of other state members of WTO. The failure of the United States to use diplomacy, before engaging in the imposition of unilateral measures, and the failure to enter into negotiations with the affected states constituted the basis of discriminatory behavior". The Appellate Body mentioned the decision taken by the Ministers at Marrakesh to establish a Permanent Committee on Trade and Environment (CTE). In that decision, the ministers referred to the Rio Declaration and Agenda 21 that established the terms of reference of the CTE. The Appellate Body also referred to a number of international instruments and the importance of reaching consensus on the adoption of measures that deal with the global environment (e.g., article 5 of the Biodiversity Convention and the Convention on the Conservation of Migratory Species of Wild Animals). [...]

Because the Appellate Body therefore found that the U.S. regulations constituted an arbitrary and unjustifiable discrimination, it did not proceed further to examine the third standard provided for by the chapeau of article XX — that of "disguised restriction on international trade".

In making this final determination, the Appellate Body took pains to emphasize that its decision does not constitute an intrusion into the public policy matters of states:

> We have *not* decided that the protection and preservation of the environment is of no significance to the Members of the WTO. Clearly, it is. We have *not* decided that the sovereign nations that are Members of the WTO cannot adopt effective measures to protect endangered species, such as sea turtles. Clearly they can and should. And we have *not* decided that sovereign states should not act together bilaterally, plurilaterally or multilaterally, either within the WTO or in other international fora, to protect endangered species or to otherwise protect the environment. Clearly, they should and do [emphasis in the original].

2001 Shrimp-Turtle Case

After the conclusion of the 1998 *Shrimp-Turtle* case, the United States modified its regulations. According to the new regulations, a country may apply for certification even if it does not use TEDS. In such a case, the country has to prove that it is implementing and enforcing a "comparably effective" regulatory program. The United States also entered into multilateral negotiations with the states concerned, including Malaysia, so as to proceed with a multilateral agreement for protection of sea turtles in the course of shrimp harvesting. The negotiations were not fruitful; as a result, the United States resolved to ban the imports of shrimp from Malaysia. Malaysia claimed that the United States had an obligation, according to the 1998 decision of the Appellate Body, not only to enter into negotiations but also to conclude an agreement.

The panel viewed the obligation of the United States, as imposed by the 1998 *Shrimp-Turtle* decision, as an obligation to negotiate in good faith an international agreement rather than as an obligation to conclude an agreement, and ruled against Malaysia.

The Appellate Body agreed with the panel. The Appellate Body argued additionally that requiring the United States to conclude an agreement with

Malaysia in order to avoid a characterization of the turtle protective measure as arbitrary or discriminatory — would amount to giving Malaysia in effect a veto power over whether the United States can fulfill its obligations under the WTO. The Appellate Body concurred with the panel that the efforts of the United States regarding the negotiation of an agreement with Malaysia were serious and good faith efforts on the basis of "active participation and financial support to the negotiations". Thus, the Appellate Body concluded that a commitment to an, in principle, multi-lateral method would give ground to unilateral action when the multilateral approach fails to produce desirable results.

Asbestos Case

Another article of the GATT that has come under scrutiny is Article III(4), which includes the national treatment requirement. Article III(4) states:

> The products of the territory of any Member imported into the territory of any other Member shall be accorded treatment no less favorable than that accorded to *like products* of national origin in respect of all laws, regulations and requirements affecting their internal sale, offering for sale, purchase, transportation, distribution or use [...] [emphasis added].

The question that came before the panel was whether Canadian imports into France, such as asbestos fibers, are like certain other kinds of fibers. According to the French authorities, supported by the EU, asbestos fibers were not "like" other fibers because of the health risks associated with asbestos. Canada, by contrast, argued that health risks should not be taken into account when deciding on the likeness of products. The panel agreed with Canada by applying four criteria that had been applied unfailingly in prior cases when deciding the "likeness as below" of products:

1. the properties, nature, and quality of products;
2. the end-uses of products;
3. consumer's tastes and habits; and
4. the tariff classification of products.

The EU sought to reverse the panel's decision, claiming, *inter alia*, that the panel erred in its application of the concept of like products because it excluded from its consideration the health risks associated with asbestos fibers. The Appellate Body agreed with the EU and specified that the inquiry into the first criterion of physical properties of a product should include an analysis of the risks posed by the product on human health. The Appellate Body ruled that the carcinogenicity and toxicity of asbestos fibers are an aspect of their physical properties that separates them from other fibers. The Appellate Body ruled that the panel erred when it failed to take into account evidence relating to the consumers' tastes and habits in relation to asbestos fibers and other fibers.

Notes and Questions

1. What opportunities do you see for WTO/GATT trade rules to play a constructive role in addressing environmental issues internationally?

2. What threats do the WTO/GATT rules pose for the development of international environmental law?

3. How do you expect these international trade rules to affect environmental law and policy in Canada? Do you see them as a net positive or negative influence? Explain.

4. For a WTO decision dealing with an environmental issue that involves a dispute between Mexico and the US over "dolphin-safe" labeling of tuna products, see Panel Report, *US — Measures Concerning the Importation, Marketing and Sale of Tuna and Tuna Products*, WT/DS381/R (Sept. 15, 2011). For a commentary on this decision, see Elizabeth Trujillo, "The Tuna-Dolphin Encore — WTO Rules on Environmental Labeling" Insights 16:7, online: <http://www.asil.org/insights120307.cfm>.

   In this case, Mexico asked a WTO panel to assess the legality of a set of US measures relating to the labeling regime of tuna products. The US measures collectively establish the circumstances under which tuna products can be labeled as "dolphin-safe" in the US. Most importantly, the measures provide that tuna caught in the eastern tropical Pacific Ocean (ETP), with purse seine nets intentionally used to encircle dolphins, cannot be labeled "dolphin-safe", whereas the requirements to obtain the dolphin-safe label outside the ETP are more lenient. Most of the Mexican tuna is caught in the ETP, whereas most of the US tuna is not. The appellate body found that the US labeling regime was a technical regulation and that it violated Article 2.1 of the Agreement on Technical Barriers to Trade (TBT) because it essentially treated Mexican tuna differently than US tuna. The implication of the decision is that even voluntary labeling regimes can be considered technical regulations and therefore subject to WTO scrutiny.

5. More recently, a number of trade disputes have arisen that have challenged the efforts of jurisdictions to promote the manufacturing and use of renewable energy, such as wind and solar. See, for example, WTO Dispute DS412 between Japan and Canada — Certain Measures Affecting the Renewable Energy Generation Sector. The dispute centred around an Ontario feed-in tariff that included a local manufacturing requirement for solar PV. The case resulted in Ontario eliminating the local manufacturing requirement and soon thereafter discontinued the feed-in tariff. What does this case suggest about the compatibility of international environmental law and international trade law?

6. Since being elected in 2016, President Trump has been critical of existing global free trade arrangements. He has been particularly critical of NAFTA, and has preferred bilateral trade deals over regional or global trade agreements. Do you think Trump's approach may be an opportunity to better integrate trade and environment, or does his approach represent a further threat to environmental protection?

International Investment Agreements

Chris Tollefson & W.A.W. Neilson,
"Investor Rights and Sustainable Development"
in Kevin Gallagher, ed., *Handbook on Trade and the Environment*
(Northampton, MA: Edward Elgar, 2008)

Controversy surrounding the protection of investor rights through international investment agreements (IIAs) is of longstanding. This has been particularly so in the context of the relationship between developed countries (DCs) and their least developed country (LDC) counterparts. From an LDC perspective, such protections have traditionally been seen as a substantial derogation from state sovereignty; fettering not only the ability of a host state to determine domestic policy priorities (most notably with respect to resource management and development) but also, more generally, its ability to regulate the activities of transnational corporate (TNC) investors.

The constraining impact of IIAs on domestic policy space has also been a thorny issue within the more developed economies. Here the overriding concern has been the impact of IIAs on the ability of governments to enact measures to protect the environment and public health. Given these various concerns, it is perhaps not surprising that, over the last twenty years, three successive initiatives to broker broad-based multilateral investment treaties (under the auspices of the United Nations, the OECD and most recently the WTO) have ended in failure.

Yet despite this pervasive skepticism about and resistance to IIAs, the last two decades has nonetheless seen a dramatic consolidation of investor rights in the realm of international law that has been accompanied by an unprecedented expansion in global foreign direct investment (FDI). During this period, both FDI flows and FDI stock have expanded over fifteen-fold (UNCTD, 2006). In keeping with historical patterns, the predominant share (approximately 60%) of FDI has flowed from North to South. This dramatic growth in FDI has been paralleled by the emergence of highly complex and burgeoning international investment governance regime. This regime is comprised of a complex global network of well over 2500 IIAs over 1500 of which have been concluded within the last fifteen years. The vast majority of these IIAS are bilateral investment treaties (BITs) between DCs and LDCs although there are also a handful of regional investment treaties, most notably those contained in the 1994 North American Free Trade Agreement (NAFTA). The volume and magnitude of investor claims being submitted to arbitration has also risen sharply. As of June 2006, the total number of known investment-related arbitrations was 248, two-thirds of which were filed after 2001 the majority of which seek damages in the tens or hundreds of million dollars.

[Below we consider] the implications of this emerging IIA network for the ability (and indeed the appetite) of states to pursue domestic sustainable development policies. In framing our topic in this way, we have been mindful of the need to consider the relationship between IIAs and the capacity of governments to protect the environment and public health and likewise the relationship between IIAs and resource management and development. As it has evolved in international law scholarship, the concept of sustainable development not only embraces these concerns but emerging public participation, good governance and human rights norms. In what follows we reflect on the nature and extent of the tension between domestic sustainable development policy in this broad sense and investor rights under the emerging IIA regime.

The Tension Between Investor Rights and Sustainable Development

In the years following the watershed 1999 protests at the WTO trade meetings in Seattle, few issues have stirred more controversy within the broader globalization debate than investor rights. During this period, investor rights and their implications for domestic sustainable development initiatives have become front page news in jurisdictions around the world. Many of the most recent suits have targeted LDCs. Argentina has been particularly hard-hit facing close to thirty such suits, many arising out of its financial restructuring of 2002. Within the last two years alone, arbitral tribunals have ruled against it on four occasions. Other Latin American countries (including Ecuador, Bolivia, Peru and Mexico) have also faced or are facing investor suits as are several former Soviet Republics and African states.

Ongoing high profile claims include a suit brought by UK-based water TNC Biwater seeking damages from Tanzania for canceling a water and sewerage privatization deal; a suit by EU investors against South Africa seeking compensation for legislation aimed at bolstering black participation in the mining sector; a suit by the oil giant Occidental Petroleum against Ecuador in connection with the cancellation of oil leases due to allegations of environmental degradation and human rights abuses; and a suit by Texas farming interests claiming that the Mexico has infringed on their water rights. Frequently the damages sought, and in several recent cases awarded, have been in excess of a $100 million.

Developed states have also been increasingly been forced to defend themselves from analogous investor claims. Canada and the United States have each been sued close to a dozen times under NAFTA's investor rights provisions (Chapter 11) for various government measures in the realms of environmental protection, public health and resource management. In two of these cases, Canada has ended up paying compensation (one an out-of-court settlement of a claim arising out of ban on import of the fuel additive MMT; a second involving an arbitral ruling that a federal ban on the export of PCB waste violated NAFTA). To date, the United States has enjoyed more success most notably in its successful defence of a claim arising from a fuel additive ban in the *Methanex* litigation. However, several environmental protection-based claims are pending against both countries including a suit against Canada for banning the pesticide Lindane, and another against the United States targeting environmental measures imposed by the state of California on an open pit gold mining operation licenced to a Canadian mining company.

Environmental and social justice NGOs and scholars critical of the emerging IIA regime have voiced a variety of concerns with respect to both the substantive rules embedded in the regime and process by which these rules are enforced. They contend that the IIA regime represents a neo-liberal inspired Economic Bill of

Rights for TNCs that undermines the sovereignty of host countries (often LDCs desperate to attract FDI) to determine and implement key environmental and sustainable development priorities. It is also contended that IIAs are asymmetrical: conferring rights but imposing no correlative responsibilities on investors. Moreover, critics claim that the legal uncertainty surrounding the scope and ambit of investor rights combined with the economic risks and costs associated with defending potential claims has a chilling effect on governments' willingness to regulate in the public interest. Finally, it is argued that the arbitral processes and fora currently in place to adjudicate these cases (ICSID, UNCITRAL and other bodies originally constituted to deal with private international commercial disputes) are ill-suited to deal with what are fundamentally public policy matters.

Defenders of the current IIA regime typically reject the 'sovereignty critique' described above out of hand. While it is generally conceded that such agreements significantly strengthen the hand of TNCs when dealing with host states, most would strongly contend that entry into the regime is itself an exercise of sovereign will, reflecting a reasoned political judgment that the supposed costs of entry are outweighed by the benefits in terms of increased FDI. They also point out that accession into the IIA regime is not an all-or-nothing proposition since governments are allowed to reserve (exempt) from such agreements certain economic sectors or non-conforming measures. Further, although some regime defenders will concede that the IIA jurisprudence is inconsistent and unpredictable, and that many early investment treaties failed adequately to recognize the right of host states to regulate in the public interest, most strongly assert that it is premature to draw conclusions about what remains an embryonic regime. Indeed, it is claimed that tribunals 'get it right' most of the time, even in cases frequently cited by opponents as illustrations of where they have erred. Likewise, arguments about "regulatory chill" are characteristically dismissed as unproven and premature. And while there is some acceptance in these quarters of the need for procedural reform, most argue that the necessary changes can be incrementally accommodated within existing arbitral institutions.

Investor Protection Architecture and Procedures

Given the limitations of early treaties of 'Friendship, Commerce and Navigation' and the difficulties of securing multilateral investment treaty agreements, countries in recent decades have turned to IIAs to promote and protect foreign direct investment. It is estimated that by 2006 over 2500 IIAs will have been negotiated, convincing evidence of their primacy as the principal public international law instruments governing foreign investment. IIAs impose binding obligations on partner states with respect to their treatment of foreign investment as a major beneficial force for economic development. Enforcement of these protection and facilitation standards occurs through direct investor-state arbitration. Successful claims result in an award of damages in favour of the investor that are largely immune from meaningful appeal or review.

The great majority of the IIAs follow a standard pattern in detailing the obligations of the host state's treatment of an investment. The investor rights provisions found in NAFTA's Chapter 11 are illustrative. Under NAFTA, these rights (also known as disciplines) which when breached entitle an investor to sue a directly host state for damages, include: the right to national treatment and most favoured nation treatment (Articles 1102 and 1103); the right to international minimum standards of treatment (Article 1105); the right to be free from certain performance requirements (Article 1106); and the right to be compensated for expropriation of their investment (Article 1110).

Neither under the NAFTA nor in most other IIAs is the legal relationship between these private rights of action by aggrieved investors and the right of states to pursue sustainable development policies directly addressed. At the same time, such agreements typically provide a remarkably broad berth for investor rights. For example, under the NAFTA the range of governmental 'measures' that can trigger an investor claim includes 'any law, regulation, procedure, requirement or practice' emanating from any level of government (municipal, provincial or federal) or other arms of the state including the judiciary. Indeed, there is no requirement that the complained of "measure" have legal force or effect. Likewise, "investments" eligible for protection include not only direct investments but also debt security or loans to an enterprise or equity securities in an enterprise. A NAFTA tribunal has even held that a company's "market share" is a protected "investment".

Conferring upon investors a broad right to sue host states directly for damages in a legally binding, international adjudicative forum represents a seismic shift in international law. Prior to the emergence of IIAs, investors were forced to seek redress either by persuading their home state to champion their claim or to pursue litigation in the not always hospitable venue of the host state's domestic courts. Under provisions of modern day BITs, investors are transformed into 'private attorney generals' empowered to press their claims before arbitral tribunals organized under the auspices of variety of fora including: ICSID (International Centre for the Settlement of Investment Disputes), the ICC (International Chamber of Commerce), the SCC (Stockholm Chamber of Commerce) and UNCITRAL (UN Commission on International Trade Law).

Most IIAs set out a relatively standard set of procedures, including a notice of dispute to the host government, the selection of the particular tribunal, followed by the appointment of the panel of arbitrators and the conduct of the arguments by memorials, the exchange of evidence and the oral hearing itself in a non-public forum. Arbitrators tend to be trade law scholars, retired judges or members of the commercial arbitration bar. Each party to an arbitration proposes a list of acceptable arbitrators from which its counterpart must select. The two arbitrators selected in this fashion then confer with a view to selecting a Chair. Increasingly, critics have questioned whether this method of appointment adequately ensures arbitral independence.

(In)consistency Between the IIA Regime and Sustainable Development Goals

As a result of tribunal rulings under NAFTA's Chapter 11 as well as the growing torrent of litigation under various BITs, the emerging IIA regime has increasingly been characterized by critics as a serious impediment to sustainable development. A frequent point of departure for this critique is the asymmetric nature of the obligations IIAs respectively impose on host states, home states and foreign investors. While such agreements invariably impose on host states a broad range of legal responsibilities to investors, typically they contain no correlative obligations on investors. Moreover, they are generally silent with respect to obligations of the investor's home jurisdiction 'to ensure its nationals comply with standards of conduct in their operations abroad'.

It is also contended that the content and uncertainty surrounding the investor rights that IIAs enshrine is inconsistent with sustainable development norms. The controversy surrounding the content of these new rights is considered in more detail below. Regardless of the ostensible intent underlying these provisions, however, few would dispute that the ascendancy of the IIA regime has created considerable uncertainty with respect to the ability of host states to address serious health, consumer and environmental concerns without incurring liability to investors. This is underscored by the experience under NAFTA where tribunals have enunciated interpretations of its national treatment, international minimum standard of treatment, and expropriation provisions that are much broader (and hence more favourable to investors) than is generally accepted in international law. Whether and to what extent this uncertainty has created 'regulatory chill' — causing governments to resile from enacting measures aimed at promoting sustainable development — is a matter of considerable debate.

This uncertainty is compounded by the failure of most IIAs to address or define how investor rights are to be balanced against sustainable development considerations. A recent analysis of over seventy-one BITs confirms that references to sustainable development principles are the exception rather than the rule, even in non-binding, preambular language. Moreover, most IIAs, including NAFTA's Chapter 11, are silent with respect to the 'traditionally accepted prerogative of governments to protect public health and the environment', resulting in considerable controversy over how and whether competing private and public interests are to be balanced. This is in sharp contrast to the GATT where Article XX explicitly provides a justificatory basis for measures of this kind. A related source of uncertainty is whether host governments can invoke the precautionary principle to uphold legal measures against investors which it claims to have taken to protect legitimate public interests in health, consumer safety or environmental protection.

A third area of concern relates to the arbitral process itself. Here the critique is twofold: that the tribunals that have jurisdiction over such disputes are poorly equipped and ill-disposed to address the complex 'public' nature of issues raised; and that the prevailing arbitral processes lack transparency and openness in terms of access to documents, hearings and public participation. While some steps have recently been taken to alleviate this perceived 'democratic deficit', particularly in the NAFTA context, the tribunal competence and public participation remain key issues for many critics of the emerging IIA regime.

Notes and Questions

1.   A key issue of contention in this area is what the authors refer to as the "asymmetric" nature of obligations under IIAs. While such agreements spell out in detail the obligations of host states to foreign investors, they typically impose no correlative responsibilities on foreign investors with respect to the

management or operation of their investments nor do they normally impose any obligations on signatory states "to ensure [their] nationals comply with standards of conduct in their operations abroad". Are these issues that future IIAs should remedy? What steps could be taken to address these concerns, particularly as they relate to promoting sustainable development norms?

2. Should IIAs include a justificatory provision that would allow a host government to rely upon the precautionary principle to defend against claims made by investors? In light of the discussion of the principle earlier in this chapter, what challenges might present themselves in crafting a justificatory provision (akin to Article XX in the GATT) of this kind?

3. For an instructive illustration of how IIA-based rights can collide with domestic regulatory initiatives, consider the claim brought by SD Myers against the Canadian government in connection with the latter's decision to ban the export of PCB waste: see Chapter 4.

4. There has been a trend toward the inclusion of investor protection provisions in regional free trade agreements. Examples include the Trans Pacific Partnership, the EU–US free trade agreement, and the Comprehensive Economic and Trade Agreement (CETA) between Canada and the EU. Of these, only the Canada–EU agreement has survived the Trump Presidency.

5. A NAFTA Chapter 11 dispute that illustrates the risk of investor protection provisions to environmental laws is the case of Bilcon of Delaware and Canada (*Canada (Attorney General) v. Clayton*, 2018 FC 436). In this case, a NAFTA tribunal found that an independent environmental assessment panel struck under federal and provincial environmental assessment laws in Canada had violated the rights of a US investor. The case centred around the fact that the panel's approach to considering the social and economic consequences of the proposed project for local communities was a departure from the practice of previous panels. For a critique of the ruling, see, for example, Meinhard Doelle, "The Bilcon NAFTA Tribunal: A Clash of Investor Protection and Sustainability-Based Environmental Assessments", in Stanley Berger, ed., *Key Developments in Environmental Law 2017* (Thomson Reuters, 2017), 99–123.

6. At the time of writing, efforts by Mexico, Canada and the US to negotiate a successor to NAFTA were ongoing. See what you can find out about the status of these negotiations generally, and with respect to investor protection provisions more specifically. Compare investor protection provisions under the existing NAFTA, under CETA, under FIPA (discussed below), and, if available, under the successor to NAFTA. Which, if any, do you think strike an appropriate balance between investor protection and environmental protection?

The Canada/China Foreign Investment Protection Agreement (FIPA) is a controversial example of the types of agreements discussed in the Tollefson & Neilson piece, above. What follows are excerpts from a submission made by the Canadian Environmental Law Association to the Government of Canada with respect to a strategic environmental assessment of the proposed agreement (referred to in the submission below as "Final EA").

**Kyra Bell-Pasht, Counsel, Canadian Environmental Law Association
Submission to Government of Canada, regarding the
Final Strategic Environmental Assessment of the Canada-China FIPA**
(November 9th, 2012)

Dear Hon. Ed Fast and the Trade Agreements and NAFTA Secretariat,

Re: Commentary on the Final Strategic Environmental Assessment of the Canada-China FIPA

The Canadian Environmental Law Association (CELA) is pleased to provide the following comments in response to the Federal Government's Final Strategic Environmental Assessment of the Canada-China Foreign Investment Protection Agreement (FIPA) (the 'Agreement'). These comments will focus on the process of this EA and its failure to address potential environmental impacts.

CELA is a public interest law group founded in 1970 for the purposes of using and improving laws to protect public health and the environment. [...]

Environmental and Sustainable Development Impacts not Considered by the Final EA

The Final EA concludes,

> As new flows of investment from China into Canada (or Canada into China) cannot be directly attributed to the presence of FIPA, there can be no causal relationship found between the implementation of such a treaty and environmental impacts in Canada. It is for this reason that the claim made in the Initial EA, that no significant environmental impacts are expected based on the introduction of a Canada-China FIPA, is upheld.

However, environmental and sustainable development concerns from investment protection agreements, such as the Canada-China FIPA, include a *regulatory chill* on environmental protection measures as a result of the additional legal rights they grant to foreign investors in Canada, including the right to sue for indirect expropriation, as well as the Agreement's reliance on environmental exceptions and exemptions measures to protect the environment and sustainable development. These concerns will be examined in more detail below.

ISDS Mechanism

Under Article 20 of the Canada-China FIPA an investor's financial interests will be protected with new legal rights to sue the Canadian Government for measures, including legitimate environmental protection measures, that limit their reasonable expectation of profits. This mechanism is referred to as Investor-State Dispute Settlement (ISDS) [and] it is established in Article 20 of the Agreement,

Article 20. Claim by an Investor of a Contracting Party

1. An investor of a Contracting Party may submit to arbitration under this Part a claim that the other Contracting Party has breached an obligation [...]

The International Institute on Sustainable Development published a resource in 2012 which outlines the types of government public interest health, environmental and social equity measures that have been the subject of claims brought under ISDS mechanisms of investment treaties. They include:

[...] bans on harmful chemicals; bans on mining; environmental restrictions on the manner in which mining can take place; requirements for environmental impact assessments; regulations regarding transport and disposal of hazardous waste; regulations governing health insurance; measures aiming to reduce smoking; measures affecting the price and delivery of water; regulations aiming to improve the economic situation of minority populations; and measures aiming to increase revenues gained from production and export of natural resources.

The document further clarifies that "in addition to those actual claims, it is estimated that foreign investors often use the threat of such arbitrations to compel governments to alter or abandon regulations which may negatively impact an investor."

The threat of such claims and their substantial costs to defend as well as the substantial financial penalties that result if a Party is found to be in breach of an agreement, may reasonably place a regulatory chill on governments considering new or strengthened environmental regulations. We have outlined these concerns in several of our previous publications.

In comparison to Canada's judicial system, the international tribunals under the Canada-China FIPA lack transparency, consistency, and impartiality (see the September 29, 2012 Toronto Star article: *'Canada-China investment deal allows for confidential lawsuits against Canada'* by Gus Van Harten). By signing this agreement the parties (countries) contractually agree to terms which may require that they abide by decisions of tribunal arbitrators regardless of the Canadian court system and precedents. These hearings are held behind closed doors, the panels are ad hoc and their decisions, which are binding, are relatively unpredictable as arbitration panels are not bound by previous panel decisions, but rather consider them. Furthermore, provincial and local governments are not always provided the right to participate in order to defend their public interest measures subject to tribunal proceedings.

The practical effect of the new legal rights proposed by the Canada-China FIPA was aptly described by analyst Andrew Nikiforuk in an October 11th, 2012 article in the Tyee,

By November 1 [2012] three of China's national oil companies will have more power to shape Canada's energy markets as well as challenge the politics of this country than Canadians themselves.

Recommendation [...] Canada should follow suit with other countries such as Australia, India, and South Africa, and refuse to negotiate trade and or investment agreements including ISDS mechanisms. Such a stance would support Canada's commitment to sustainable development and environmental protection outlined in the *Cabinet Directive on the Environmental Assessment of*

Policy, Plan and Program Proposals, and the Treasury Board *Policy on Management of Real Property.*

Indirect Expropriation

Under Article 10 of the Agreement, China and Chinese investors are granted the right to sue Canada for direct or indirect expropriation except where expropriated for "a public purpose, under domestic due procedures of law, in a non-discriminatory manner and against compensation."

Indirect expropriation gives investors the right to sue for government measures that result in a reduction in reasonably expected profits. It is defined in Annex B. 10 of the Agreement.

Annex B.10. Expropriation

The Contracting Parties confirm their shared understanding that:

1. Indirect expropriation results from a measure or series of measures of a Contracting Party that has an effect equivalent to direct expropriation without formal transfer of title or outright seizure.

The Annex also includes some protection against a Party being sued on the basis of indirect expropriation on account of public interest measures.

Annex B.10. Expropriation

3. Except in rare circumstances, such as if a measure or series of measures is so severe in light of its purpose that it cannot be reasonably viewed as having been adopted and applied in good faith, a non-discriminatory measure or series of measures of a Contracting Party that is designed and applied to protect the legitimate public objectives for the well-being of citizens, such as health, safety and the environment, does not constitute indirect expropriation.

Recommendation [...] as CELA recommended in our report on the proposed Canada and European-Union Comprehensive and Economic and Trade Agreement (CETA),

[...] expropriation provisions would provide foreign investors with the right to compensation, at fair market value, in every case of direct or indirect expropriation. This right to compensation is a right that does not exist under Canadian law, where the right to determine compensation is reserved to parliaments and legislatures.

The threat of being sued for measures that limit the profits of foreign investors could reasonably deter a government from undertaking a wide array of legitimate environmental protection measures. As a result, the report recommends that even with a strict definition of indirect expropriation, as provided in the Annex B to this Agreement, the extraordinary rights and remedies provided are unnecessary and trade agreements should not give foreign investors rights greater than those of domestic investors in relation to expropriation.

Reliance on Environmental Exceptions

Environmental measures are protected to a limited extent by provisions included in the Agreement, namely:

Article 33. General Exceptions

2. Provided that such measures are not applied in an arbitrary or unjustifiable manner, or do not constitute a disguised restriction on international trade or investment, nothing in this Agreement shall be construed to prevent a Contracting Party from adopting or maintaining measures, including environmental measures:

(b) necessary to protect human, animal or plant life or health; or

(c) relating to the conservation of living or non-living exhaustible natural resources if such measures are made effective in conjunction with restrictions on domestic production or consumption.

These exceptions are a further basis for the Final EA's conclusion that the FIPA presents no environmental threats. However, these exceptions still provide room for environmental protection measures to be challenged by an individual investor as being 'unnecessary' or applied in an 'arbitrary or unjustifiable manner' and subsequently sue Canada for lost income. As we have outlined in our 2011 report on CETA, the necessity test has been interpreted by trade dispute bodies as an extremely difficult one to satisfy.

Conclusion

In short, we submit that the Final EA does not allow for effective public participation, nor does it appear to have any substantive impact on the text of the Agreement. In addition, we submit that [it] arrives at incorrect conclusions about the potential environmental impacts of the Canada-China FIPA.

Notes and Questions

1. The Canada-China FIPA has received more attention and stirred more controversy than any other agreement of its kind, at least since Canada entered into the *North American Free Trade Agreement*, which (in its Chapter 11) contains comparable investor protection rights. Why do you believe that this new deal has been so newsworthy and generated such opposition? The decision to enter into this agreement was challenged unsuccessfully by the Hupacasath First Nation based on a failure to consult. See *Hupacasath First Nation v. Canada (Minister of Foreign Affairs)*, 2015 FCA 4.

2. From the CELA critique set out above, can you discern any differences between this agreement and other investor agreements as set out in the Tollefson & Neilson article, including those into which Canada has entered on a bilateral or multilateral basis?

3. Should the federal government have the power to commit Canada to a deal such as this over other objections of provincial, territorial and local governments? If you do not think so, would your answer be the same with respect to a new global treaty to reduce greenhouse gas emissions?

4. Does the federal government under our current constitutional arrangement have the power to enter into this deal over the objections of provincial,

territorial and local governments? In this regard, is it relevant that currently, if there is an award of damages against Canada for violating such an agreement it is the Government of Canada that is liable to pay the award? Does this feature of such agreements make them less prone to constitutional challenge?

The Global Climate Change Regime

The origins of the international climate change regime can be traced back to a series of United Nations General Assembly resolutions adopted in the late 1980s. These resolutions resulted in the negotiation of the *United Nations Framework Convention on Climate Change* (UNFCCC), which was adopted at Rio de Janeiro in 1992 and entered into force in 1994, and established the architecture for subsequent climate change agreements. The General Assembly resolutions also resulted in the establishment of the Intergovernmental Panel on Climate Change (IPCC) to give scientific and technical advice to negotiators and policy makers. Since 1990, the IPCC has prepared five comprehensive assessment reports on the state of the science on climate change, each at critical junctures of the development of the climate change regime as well as, on request, more focused reports on issues ranging from land use change and forestry issues to carbon capture and storage. The most recent synthesis report was released in 2014 to inform the negotiation of the *Paris Agreement*.

The UNFCCC continues to serve as the foundation and provides important institutions, goals, and principles for the climate regime. The overall goal of the UNFCCC, described in Article 2, is to stabilize greenhouse gas (GHG) concentrations at levels that prevent dangerous human interference with the climate system, ensure that the rate of change allows nature to adapt, to not threaten food production and to allow sustainable development to take place. This overall goal is refined through additional principles set out in Article 3, including equity for present and future generations, common but differentiated responsibilities and respective capabilities (CBDR-RC), and the need to take precautionary measures to anticipate and mitigate, prevent or minimize the effects of climate change.

The first substantive agreement following the UNFCCC was the *Kyoto Protocol*, negotiated in 1997. While the key principles were accepted in 1997, the rules for implementation took much longer to develop. Most of these rules were finalized at the 7th Conference of the Parties (COP) in November 2001 in Marrakech. The package of rules required to implement the *Kyoto Protocol* was then formally adopted at the first meeting of the Parties to the Protocol in Montreal in 2005. Upon its entry into force in 2005, the *Kyoto Protocol* became the heart of the international climate change regime. It established the first binding emission reduction targets for each of the "developed countries" listed in Annex 1 of the UNFCCC for 2008 to 2012, the first commitment period.

At the core of the *Kyoto Protocol* are the GHG emission reduction targets for developed States. Each developed State was assigned a negotiated combined emission reduction target for the six gases covered in the Protocol. The target was expressed relative to emissions in that State in 1990 and presented in tons of carbon dioxide equivalent (CO_2e) emissions. This emission reduction target was then translated into emissions permits assigned to each State for the five years of the 2008 to 2012 commitment period. These permits are called assigned amount units (AAUs), and are the foundation of the emissions trading system under the Protocol.

The flexibility mechanisms established in the *Kyoto Protocol* are the Clean Development Mechanism (CDM), Emissions Trading (ET) and Joint Implementation. They were included in the *Kyoto Protocol*, at least in part, in recognition that the State-specific targets for developed countries provided only a crude tool for balancing the relative responsibility, capacity and potential of Parties to the *Protocol* to reduce emissions. In that respect, the mechanisms provide a degree of flexibility to ensure that if meeting one Party's target through reductions turned out to be disproportionately expensive or technically difficult to achieve, that Party had the option to delay reductions in its own country and instead support reductions in another country by using the flexibility mechanisms.

Informal efforts to start negotiating significant changes to the regime commenced once the rulebook for the implementation of the *Kyoto Protocol* was completed in 2001. By 2002 in New Delhi, the EU started to focus on these negotiations, with the initial focus on more ambitious targets for developed States and ways to engage developing States in the mitigation effort. However, the US was not willing to allow a formal negotiating process to be started and the developing world was unwilling to discuss emission reductions outside the developed world because in its view North America, Europe, Australia, New Zealand and Japan had failed to lead by example, and insufficient progress had been made on adaptation. Formal negotiations for the post-2012 regime did not get underway until the Conference of the Parties/Meeting of the Parties (COP/MOP) in December 2005 in Montreal. It ultimately took a decade for these negotiations to be concluded in Paris in December 2015.

The key elements of the *Paris Agreement* include its collective long-term goals, nationally determined mitigation efforts of each Party, five-year review cycles of progress in implementing individual efforts toward the collective goals, and a commitment to increase ambition as part of the five-year review cycles to ensure the collective long-term goals are met. The objective of the *Paris Agreement* is to keep global average temperature increases to "well below" 2°C and to make efforts to limit this increase to 1.5°C. The temperature goal is supplemented with a collective commitment to ensure emissions peak and decline as soon as possible, and to reach a balance of emissions and removals in the second half of the century. Arguably, 1.5°C has now become the ultimate standard against which the success of collective mitigation efforts under the UNFCCC will be measured. This ambitious set of long-term goals provides an important foundation for each State's future nationally determined contributions (NDCs), their justification on the grounds of equity, and the five-year cycles of NDC communication and the Global Stocktake.

Notes and Questions

1. In this section, we have briefly introduced the ongoing global effort to address the climate change challenge. For a more substantive discussion of climate change from a domestic law perspective, see Chapter 10. In particular, in Chapter 10, we will consider how the UN climate regime has interacted with domestic efforts in Canada, including the shifting roles of federal and provincial governments on this issue. Key steps in this include Canada's signing the Protocol in 1997, ratifying it in 2002, revoking its ratification in 2011, ratifying the *Paris Agreement* in 2016, and ongoing efforts to implement the *Paris Agreement*.

2. The climate change regime has been one of the most complex and slowly evolving global environmental regimes. The most recent round of negotiations initiated in 2012 in Durban and completed in Paris in 2015 was generally considered to be crucial for the future of the global effort to tackle climate change, perhaps a last hope for an effective global response. Since then, the US has indicated it intends to withdraw from the *Paris Agreement*, while the rest of the global community is negotiating the detailed rules to implement the agreement. The Conference of the Parties (COP) meets toward the end of every year, providing an opportunity to take stock of progress made. Try to follow media coverage on the negotiations and consider tracking progress through the Earth Negotiations Bulletin, online: <http://www.iisd.ca/process/climate_atm.htm>. In particular, try to determine what progress is being made, and the role Canada is playing in the negotiations.

References and Further Readings

Elizabeth Brandon, "Does International Law Mean Anything in Canadian Courts?" (2001) 11 J. Envtl. L. & Prac. 399

Meinhard Doelle, *From Hot Air to Action? Climate Change, Compliance and the Future of International Environmental Law* (Toronto: Thomson Carswell, 2005)

Tomilola Akanle Eni-ibukun, *et al.* "A Brief History of the UNFCCC and the Kyoto Protocol" (May 2012) Earth Negotiations Bulletin Vol. 12 No. 535, online: <http://www.iisd.ca/climate/sb36/>

Daniel Klein, Pia Carazo, Meinhard Doelle, Jane Bulmer, & Andrew Higham, eds, *The Paris Climate Agreement: Analysis and Commentary* (Oxford: Oxford University Press, 2017)

E. Louka, *International Environmental Law: Fairness, Effectiveness and World Order* (Cambridge: Cambridge University Press, 2006). Reprinted with the permission of Cambridge University Press.

Sharon Mascher, "Neglected Sovereignty: Filling Canada's Climate Change Gap with Unilateral Measures" (2016) 29 J. Envtl. L. & Prac. 362

Ifeoma Onyerikam, "Achieving Compliance with the Basel Convention on Transboundary Movement of Hazardous Wastes" (University of Alberta Faculty of Law, 2007) [unpublished]

Roxanne T. Ornelas, "Implementing the Policy of the U.N. Declaration on the Rights of Indigenous Peoples" (2014) 5 Int'l Indigenous Pol'y J. 1

Chris Tollefson, "A Precautionary Tale: the Trials and Tribulations of the Precautionary Principle" in A. Ingelson, ed., *Environment in the Courtroom* (Calgary: University of Calgary Press, 2019)

Chris Tollefson & W.A.W. Neilson, "Investor Rights and Sustainable Development" in Kevin Gallagher, ed., *Handbook on Trade and the Environment* (Northampton, MA: Edward Elgar, 2008)

Elizabeth Trujillo, "The Tuna-Dolphin Encore — WTO Rules on Environmental Labeling" Insights 16:7, online: <http://www.asil.org/insights120307.cfm>

Chapter 2

The Common Law

Introduction

The common law has been defined as "the system of jurisprudence, which originated in England and was later applied in Canada, that is based on judicial precedent rather than legislative enactments" (Canadian Law Dictionary, 1983). Elsewhere it has been described as "a few broad and comprehensive principles, founded on reason, natural justice, and enlightened public policy, modified and adapted to the circumstances of all of the particular cases which fall within it" (Shaw J., Mass S.C.). Among its defining features are its adaptability, its solicitude for individual rights (especially property rights) and the unique interpretive and law-making role that it assigns to the courts.

The three branches of the common law are property, contract and tort, which together comprise what is often referred to as the realm of private law. All three branches tend to involve the interpretation of individual rights in the context of bilateral relationships, with each playing a (somewhat) distinct role. Thus, property law addresses issues arising out of rights (including ownership and lesser interests) in personal and real property; contract law deals with bargained for (and sometimes un-bargained for) rights and obligations arising in the context of contractual relations; tort law provides principles for adjudicating claims arising from harms caused beyond the realm of contract.

Historically, what we would refer to today as "environmental harms" were addressed, if at all, within one or more of these three branches of the common law. Thus if an individual, for example, leased another's land and caused it to become contaminated, the landlord could potentially, depending on the relevant facts, rely on property, contract or tort law (or some combination of all three) to seek a remedy. Starting in the 1970s, in part as a reaction to perceived inadequacies of the common law, environmental legislation of various kinds began to be enacted. Over time, indeed, these new environmental laws came to be seen by many as superseding the common law as a means of responding to environmental harms. The nature and implications of these legislative initiatives are addressed in many of the other chapters of this book. Here, however, we focus on the present and future of the common law — most notably tort law — as a means of recognizing both private and public interests and rights to a clean and safe environment.

Part I of this chapter is an introduction to the application of tort law in the environmental context that focuses on four illustrative cases: *Palmer v. Stora Kopparbergs Bergslags AB* ("*Palmer*"), *Cambridge Water Co. v. Eastern Counties Leather Plc* ("*Cambridge Water*"), *Smith v. Inco Ltd.* ("*Inco*"), and *Thomas v. Rio Tinto Alcan Inc.*. Part II considers one of the key legal challenges for plaintiffs in cases of environmental harm: proof of causation. Part III considers the role of class action legislation in promoting access to justice, including in common law cases involving environmental harms. Part IV considers how, in some cases, the common law has been relied on as a means of deterring or discouraging public engagement in environmental decision making by means of Strategic Lawsuits Against Public Participation (also known as SLAPP suits). Finally, in Part V, we consider emerging developments in environmental tort law, including the potential recognition of the public trust doctrine and a new role for what might be termed public environmental rights, developments which have been given significant impetus by the Supreme Court of Canada's decision in *British Columbia v. Canadian Forest Products Ltd.*.

Part I — Applying Traditional Tort Law in Environmental Cases

Tort law affords plaintiffs the means of seeking a remedy for environmental harms by relying on several different causes of action. These include negligence, nuisance, the tort in *Rylands v. Fletcher* (1868), L.R. 3 H.L. 330 (U.K. H.L.), trespass, and battery. Plaintiffs will often plead multiple causes of action in a single case, as shown in the *Palmer*, *Cambridge Water*, and *Inco* cases. At the outset, it is worth reprising the requisite elements of these various torts.

Negligence has, over time, assumed a dominant role in common law litigation around environmental harms. To establish such a claim, a plaintiff must show that he or she was owed a duty of care, that the defendant breached the required standard of care, that he or she suffered damage, and that this damage was caused (factually and legally) by the defendant: see *Mustapha v. Culligan of Canada Ltd.*, 2008 SCC 27. The vexing nature of proving factual and legal causation (also known as remoteness) in negligence actions for personal injury is canvassed in depth in Part II.

The tort of nuisance takes two forms: private nuisance and public nuisance. A private nuisance claim alleges that the defendant unreasonably interfered with the plaintiff's use and enjoyment of an interest in land, causing foreseeable harm to the plaintiff. Private nuisance protects the quality of possession of land. Private nuisance, therefore, requires the plaintiff to have a sufficient property interest to be able to bring the claim. Key factors considered in determining whether an interference with possession of land is unreasonable include: whether there is physical damage to the land; the gravity and duration of the interference; the nature of the neighbourhood; the utility of the defendant's activities; and the sensitivity of the plaintiff. As we will see in *Inco*, courts have distinguished amenity nuisance from physical damage nuisance based on the first of these factors: whether the harm is based on physical harm to property. A key finding of the trial court in *Inco* in this regard is that the balancing of interests inherent in the other factors listed only applies in cases of amenity nuisance. Private nuisance is the most commonly used tort in environmental cases, and was pleaded by the plaintiffs in *Palmer*, *Cambridge Water*, and *Inco*.

The tort of public nuisance arises where there is an infringement of public as opposed to private rights. The ambit of what qualifies as "public" rights, as discussed in Part V, is the subject of some debate. Traditionally, such rights have been considered to include rights to access and use public waterways and highways as well as certain other public amenities. Because the Crown is considered to be the guardian of public rights, private citizens do not ordinarily have standing to sue for public nuisance, except with the consent of the Attorney General or where, as a result of the public nuisance, they have suffered special damage that is distinct from that suffered by members of the general public.

The tort of "strict liability" is commonly seen as originating in the case of *Rylands v. Fletcher*. It arises where the defendant brings a dangerous substance onto their land, which then escapes and causes injury to another. In this tort, liability is said to be strict in that whether the defendant acted negligently is legally irrelevant. A limiting requirement, however, in such cases, is that the plaintiff must show that the defendant's activity constituted a non-natural use of the land in question. A key issue in the *Cambridge Water* case concerned whether the damage suffered by the plaintiff in such an action must be reasonably foreseeable. This tort, as we shall see, was also pleaded in *Palmer* and in *Inco*.

Trespass to land involves the intentional and unjustifiable interference with another's possession of land. There is no need for physical damage or knowledge of ownership, as trespass protects the right of possession. Direct entry is a key element of trespass to land. This raises interesting legal issues with respect to activities that involve spraying, vibration and smells. As we shall see, trespass to land was pleaded both in *Palmer* and *Inco*. There has been a tendency in environmental cases to dismiss trespass to land summarily, and to focus the detailed analysis on nuisance and strict liability. As you study *Palmer* and *Inco*, consider whether they have fairly applied trespass to land. Trespass to the person, in the form of assault or battery, has, in rare circumstances, been used in cases of environmental harm causing personal injury. The potential for an expanded application of battery in case of serious human health risk is explored in Part II.

In considering how these principles have been applied, the balance of this chapter will explore several themes, including the role of the burden of proof, causation, and quantification of damage. It is also important to bear in mind the importance of remedial issues.

The standard remedy in tort law is monetary compensation, designed to make the plaintiff "whole". In other words, the focus of tort law is to award a successful plaintiff an amount of monetary damages that will restore him or her, as much as money can permit, to the position he or she would have been in had the tort not occurred. This approach means, in many cases, that environmental harm that cannot be assigned a market value will go uncompensated, that polluters will not be required to pay the full cost of the harm they have caused, and that the environment will not be restored to its prior condition.

A key area of environmental litigation is assessing damages in cases involving contaminated sites. The typical case involves historical contamination of a property from a neighbouring property that was engaged in a high-risk activity, such as the operation of a gas station. Most provinces have statutory laws that require the current owner of the site to undertake remediation. Usually, however, such laws only require remediation that eliminates ongoing risks to human health and the environment, rather than restoring the environment to its original condition. The common law is thus often the only resort for the innocent neighbour. Courts have struggled in these cases to agree on the appropriate basis for compensation. Some have favoured awarding damages on the basis of the cost of remediating the property to pre-contamination conditions. Others have focused on the effect of the residual contamination on the value of the property in combination with clean-up to the satisfaction of government officials. For two cases involving differing approaches, see *Tridan Developments Ltd. v. Shell Canada Products Ltd.* (2002), 57 O.R. (3d) 503 (Ont. C.A.), leave to appeal refused 2002 CarswellOnt 3960 (S.C.C.), and *Cousins v. McColl-Frontenac Inc.*, 2007 NBCA 83, leave to appeal allowed 2008 CarswellNB 174 (S.C.C.). The Supreme Court of Canada decision in *British Columbia v. Canadian Forest Products Ltd.* (see *infra*, Part V) also addresses the question of remedies in environmental cases.

One of the challenges governments can encounter when seeking to secure the remediation of a contaminated site is that the primary person responsible has limited resources or is in financial distress. Where the responsible person is insolvent, it is not always clear where his or her obligation to remediate the site ranks in priority to obligations owed to other creditors. This issue was considered by the Supreme Court of Canada in *AbitibiBowater Inc., Re*, 2012 SCC 67, and in *Orphan Well Assn. v. Grant Thornton Ltd.*, 2019 SCC 5. In these cases, the court was called upon to consider the status of a government remediation orders in bankruptcy proceeding and, in particular, how such a claim should be weighed against those of creditors. The implications of these decisions for the enforcement of environmental laws are discussed in Chapter 5.

The main alternative to monetary damages in tort law is injunctive relief. Injunctive relief can take the form of interim relief pending a final resolution of a legal dispute. It can also take the form of permanent injunctive relief as part of the final resolution of the dispute. As we will see in the *Palmer* case below, the availability of injunctive relief is discretionary and unpredictable. More often than not, courts are faced with balancing environmental harm against economic benefits.

The first of the four cases we consider in this Part arose as a result of concerns of residents of Cape Breton, Nova Scotia, about the use of herbicides by a forest company on adjacent forest lands pursuant to a provincially-issued permit. The legal basis for their claim is set out in the judgment extracted below. In this judgment, the court considers the residents' claim for permanent, *quia timet* injunction, a permanent order seeking to prevent anticipated damage before it occurs.

The case was brought at a time when there was an active and public debate about the health and environmental risks of some of the chemicals present in the herbicides to be sprayed; today, the harmful effects of these chemicals are well documented and undisputed. The case is, therefore, just as much about the ability of the common law to act in a preventative and precautionary manner as it is about the legal requirements of nuisance, trespass and strict liability, and the availability of injunctive relief to prevent environmental harm. Finally, it is worth pointing out that while the case involves a number of plaintiffs who stood to be adversely affected by the spraying program in very similar ways, the action was brought by way of a representative action and not a class action since class action legislation had not been enacted at that time. The most notable impact of this was that the issue of costs played a major role in the case, both in the way the plaintiffs were able to present their case, and in the way that the costs awarded against the plaintiffs essentially precluded an appeal. We will return to this issue in Part III.

Palmer v. Stora Kopparbergs Bergslags AB
(1983), (*sub nom. Palmer v. Nova Scotia Forest Industries*)
60 N.S.R. (2d) 271 (N.S. T.D.)

NUNN J.: — This is an application by the named plaintiffs in their individual capacities and as representatives of others for an injunction restraining the defendant, a company engaged in the forest industry in Nova Scotia, from spraying certain areas in the Province of Nova Scotia with phenoxy herbicides.

The action was originally brought in the late summer of 1982 when the plaintiffs obtained from this court per Burchell, J., an interim injunction restraining any spraying by the defendant pursuant to a license to spray during 1982 issued by the Nova Scotia Department of the Environment. The injunction was subsequently lifted by the Nova Scotia Court of Appeal in December, 1982 on the ground that no spraying could take place until the summer of 1983 and that there could be a full trial and hearing of the issues by that time.

The matter was then brought to trial in Sydney commencing May 2, 1983, with the relief claimed, in the statement of claim, to be a permanent injunction restraining the spraying of 2,4-D (Esteron 600), 2,4,5-T with its contaminant TCDD, and Esteron 3-3E, which is a mixture of 2,4-D and 2,4,5-T.

The trial commenced, by agreement of the parties, on the basis that although the defendant's license to spray was only for 1982, it was the defendant's intention, if spraying were permitted or not contested, to apply for a new license for 1983. It appeared that such a license would be granted if applied for in the absence of any restriction by this court. This was a troublesome matter, which I pointed out to the parties before and during the trial, as the court does not issue a useless injunction. Without a license there is nothing to enjoin. However, as I stated, it was in the interests of the parties, and the public generally, that this matter be heard and disposed of. It was on this basis, and by agreement, that the matter continued.

The trial consumed 21 days of taking evidence, 2 days of oral argument and further written briefs. The plaintiffs tendered 35 witnesses and the defendant 14. Aside from most of the named plaintiffs, all the rest of the witnesses with but a few exceptions were experts — highly educated in their various fields to which they gave evidence. There were approximately 150 filed exhibits which included 12 volumes of reports of the plaintiff's experts and 5 volumes of reports of the defendant's experts. Attached to the expert reports were literally hundreds of scientific articles and excerpts from scientific articles.

The subject of dioxins and chlorophenols has been widely disputed in many countries of the world both politically and before regulatory agencies. To my knowledge this is the first occasion where the dispute has reached the courts in Canada. [...]

John Dan MacIntyre, retired, of West Bay Road, plaintiff and a representative of others at or near site D — MacIntyre Mountain, owns a 100 acre farm which adjoins the site. His residence is two miles below the site. He uses the farm for growing vegetables and potatoes and for pasture for a horse and some cows, and his family pick blueberries and hunt in the area. [...] His family and some other neighbours live on the opposite side of the Trans Canada Highway from the site. He, his family and neighbours get their water from Rough Brook which adjoins his farm. He testified that this brook gets muddy after a rain storm which is indicative of some silting in this area. Rough Brook is actually on the site. His garden is located approximately one-half mile from the site. His concern was the possible harm the spray would create to his water and health. [...]

Brian GooGoo, a full-blooded MicMac Indian, lives on the Whycocomagh Reserve which is 1 1/2 miles from Site E — Skye Mountain and located at the base of the mountain. He was formerly a chief and has been delegated by the Whycocomagh Indian Band to represent the Band in a representative capacity in this action.

As part of life on the Reserve, the Indians hunt, fish, pick berries, medicinal bark, roots and herbs on the Reserve and on Crown lands. They fish eels, trout, salmon, flatfish, oysters and lobsters in the Bras D'Or Lakes into which a number of streams flow from Skye Mountain. The concern here is that their way of life is being threatened by the effect the spray program will have on the area and to their health through their water and food supply. This witness asserted such effects are an interference with his people's aboriginal rights to carry out their life-style activities as they have done for centuries. He suggested a greater interference with those aboriginal rights by the very fact that the defendant has come upon some of those Crown lands, by virtue of leases, cut the timber and destroyed wild life without any consultation with the Indians. This latter aspect may very well be beyond the scope of the matters involved in this action. [...]

Gerard MacLellan, a research assistant with the Nova Scotia Department of Environment, testified that he processed the applications for spray permits made by the defendant. In so doing he followed the usual procedure of sending copies of the application to four governmental bodies, namely, the Nova Scotia Departments of Health, Fisheries, Lands and Forests and Environment Canada. He flew over the sites by helicopter, wrote up the technical report which is attached to the permit and forwarded the information to his Minister who approved them and issued the licenses or permits to spray. His visitation to the sites was cursory, perhaps five minutes at each to oversee the area and checks for homes and water in or near the proposed spray area. His was not an environmental assessment. [...]

Finally, I now turn to [...] the main issue, whether or not the plaintiffs are entitled to injunctive relief. The relief claimed is set forth in the statement of claim as follows:

- a permanent injunction enjoining the defendant from spraying the phenoxy herbicides 2,4-D and 2,4,5-T at the sites,

- a declaration that the plaintiffs have the right to be free of exposure to the phenoxy herbicides 2,4-D and 2,4,5-T.
- the costs of this action,
- such other relief as this Honourable Court thinks just.

The legal causes of action on which the relief is claimed are alleged to arise from the proposed spraying by the defendant and fall within the following categories:

- private nuisance;
- trespass to land;
- the rule in *Rylands v. Fletcher*;
- the right of riparian owners to water undiminished in quality;
- the right of landowners to groundwater free of chemical contamination
- breach of the *Fisheries Act*, R.S.C. 1970, c. F-14 and particularly ss. 30, 31(1) and 32(2). [...]

The essence of private nuisance is explained by Salmond and Heuston on The Law of Torts (18th Ed.), at p. 48:

> The generic conception involved in private nuisance may really be found in the fact that liability in nuisance flows from an act or omission whereby a person is annoyed, prejudiced or disturbed in the enjoyment of land, whether by physical damage to the land or by interference with the enjoyment of the land or with his exercise of an easement, profit or other similar right or with his health, comfort or convenience as occupier of such land. [...]

The law is clear, however, that only some substantial interference with a person's enjoyment of property gives rise to an action in nuisance. Equally clear is the requirement that there must be proof of damage. In Halsbury's Laws of England (4th Ed.), vol. 34, p. 105 this proposition is put as follows:

> The damage need not consist of pecuniary loss but it must be material or substantial, that is, it must not be merely sentimental, speculative or trifling, or damage that is merely temporary, fleeting or evanescent [...]

In the present case the allegation is that these offending chemicals, if they get to the plaintiffs' land, will interfere with the health of the plaintiffs thereby interfering with their enjoyment of their lands. Clearly such an interference, if proved, would fall within the essence of nuisance. As a serious risk of health, if proved, there is no doubt that such an interference would be substantial. In other words, the grounds for the cause of action in nuisance exist here provided that the plaintiffs prove the defendant will actually cause it, i.e., that the chemicals will come to the plaintiffs' lands and that it will actually create a risk to their health.

Trespass to land, on the other hand, does not require proof of damage and is actionable per se. As stated in Salmond and Heuston on The Law of Torts, *supra*:

> It is a trespass [to land] to place anything upon the plaintiff's land, or to cause any physical object or noxious substance to cross the boundary of the plaintiff's land, or even simply to come into physical contact with the land. [...]

Again there is no doubt in my mind that, if it is proved that the defendant permits any of these substances on the plaintiffs' lands, it would constitute a trespass and be actionable [...] Again, entitlement to a remedy, will be based upon proof as to whether such substances will be deposited on the lands of the plaintiff. [...]

The rule in *Rylands v. Fletcher* (1868), L.R. 3 H.R. 330, is a simple one, of long standing in English jurisprudence. The rule is stated in Salmond and Heuston on The Law of Torts (18th Ed.), *supra*, at p. 297:

> This principle is one of the most important examples of absolute or strict liability recognized by our law — one of the chief instances in which a man acts at his peril and is responsible for accidental harm, independently of the existence of either wrongful intent or negligence. The rule may be formulated thus: The occupier of land who brings and keeps upon it anything likely to do damage if it escapes is bound at his peril to prevent its escape, and is liable for all the direct consequences of its escape, even if he has been guilty of no negligence.

No elaboration of the rule or applications of it are necessary. It is for the plaintiffs to prove the constituent elements — its likelihood to do damage, its escape and the direct consequences.

The complete burden of proof, of course, rests upon the plaintiffs throughout for all issues asserted by them. If the spraying had actually occurred, they would have to prove by a preponderance of probabilities the essential elements of either or all of the alleged causes of action as I have set them out. However, the spraying has not occurred and this application is for a "quia timet" injunction. This can be translated as "which he fears". In other words, a plaintiff does not have to wait until actual damage occurs. Where such damage is apprehended, an application for a "quia timet" injunction is an appropriate avenue to obtain a remedy which will prevent the occurrence of the harm. That remedy also, however, is not without its limitations.

In *Attorney General v. Corporation of Manchester*, [1893] 2 Ch. 87, Chitty, J., states at p. 92:

> The principle which I think may be properly and safely extracted from the quia timet authorities is, that the plaintiff must show a strong case of probability that the apprehended mischief will, in fact, arise.

This passage was approved by Anglin, J., in the Supreme Court of Canada in *Matthew v. Guardian Insurance Company* (1918), 58 S.C.R. 47, at p. 61 and is still the proper principle to consider in an application of this kind.

It was argued by the plaintiffs that the principle as expressed in Salmond and Heuston on The Law of Torts, *supra*, is more appropriate. At p. 555 they state as follows:

> In all cases, however, it seems necessary that there shall be a sufficient degree of probability that the injury will be substantial and will be continued, repeated, or committed at no remote period, and damages will not be a sufficient or adequate remedy.

It was suggested that this demonstrates that there is no set standard of proof that has to be met — simply that the risk that the plaintiff's right will be breached be significantly great in all the circumstances.

I fail to see the difference suggested. A "strong case of probability" and "a sufficient degree of probability" create only a semantic difference and not a difference in substance. I prefer the former as more clearly setting forth the proper principle. This does not impose an impossible burden nor does it deprive the court of its ability to consider the balance of convenience or inconvenience or hardship between the parties nor the size or amount of the injury or distress which might occur. All of these are factors which are woven into the fabric of "a strong probability" and are considered in determining whether the burden or proof has been met.

The plaintiffs must, however, prove the essential elements of a regular injunction, namely irreparable harm and that damages are not an adequate remedy as they are also essential elements of the "quia timet" injunction.

Finally, any injunction is a discretionary remedy and sufficient grounds must be established to warrant the exercise by the court of its discretion.

I am satisfied that a serious risk to health, if proved, would constitute irreparable harm and that damages would not be an adequate remedy. Further, recognizing the great width and elasticity of equitable principles, I would have no hesitation in deciding that such a situation would be one of the strongest which would warrant the exercise of the Court's discretion to restrain the activity which would create the risk.

This matter thus reduces itself now to the single question. Have the plaintiffs offered sufficient proof that there is a serious risk of health and that such serious risk of health will occur if the spraying of the substances here is permitted to take place? [...]

By way of background, the phenoxy herbicides are a group of herbicides which have been widely used in many parts of the world since the late 1940's and early 1950's. They are selective in that they affect only certain types of vegetation, namely broad-leaved plants, and have no, or little effect on conifers. They are a family of compounds having similar chemical and biological properties but each member compound differs in effect on individual plants. The two family members concerned here are 2,4-D (2,4-dichlorophenoxyacetic acid) and 2,4,5-T (2,4,5-trichlorophenoxyacetic acid).

2,4,5-T and all of its derivative herbicides contain a chemical contaminant formed in the manufacturing process, unavoidably to the present time and of no value, known as 2,3,7,8-tetrachlorodibenzo-p-dioxin and referred to as TCDD. Originally the quantity of TCDD in the manufactured product was in the range of 80 parts per billion but, over the years, improvements in manufacturing techniques have reduced this amount to less than 0.1 parts per million. In fact the present supply of 2,4,5-T held by the defendant has been formulated with a TCDD content indicated as "non-detectible" at 0.01 parts per million. The herbicide 2,4-D is free of any TCDD contamination.

Both herbicides have been widely used in Canada, and elsewhere, upon agricultural crops, forests, roadside and railroad rights-of-way in vast quantities and, only until recently, without too much precaution. In comparison to other uses, forestry has used only a small percentage of the total used.

Phenoxy herbicides are used to discriminate between the unwanted plants and those desired to be retained or encouraged. In a forestry site they are used to release the young conifers from competition. In Nova Scotia those competitors are the hardwoods, such as aspen, birch and maple, and raspberry. Their use is not designed to kill all competition but to permit light to reach the young conifers and decrease competition for soil nutrients and moisture. After a few years the young conifers will outgrow the competition and be permanently released. In Nova Scotia the evidence is, and I accept it, that the situation requires one treatment, and perhaps a second after 3 to 5 years, over a forty-year period. Treatment is usually applied in early summer when susceptibility is greatest but it can be applied in late summer or early fall. The benefits, of course, are a greater yield over a shorter period of time of the conifer forest.

The contaminant TCDD is one of the most toxic chemicals known to man. One witness described it as "exquisitely toxic". Much has been written on TCDD and its effects. It has been indicated that there are upwards of 40,000 different articles on the subject. A great number of those were submitted to the Court. It is not my intention to summarize those, nor is it necessary, as almost every scientific witness as well as the regulatory agencies have already done that. While there are opposing views, and the whole field is not without some uncertainty, there is no dearth of writings. So there can be no doubt that everything submitted was considered by me, I have read every article submitted to me, a formidable task in itself, and I now join the group who has reviewed all the relevant literature, although I am far from convinced that this volume of documents was necessary for this case.

Having mentioned regulatory agencies, it is appropriate to indicate that most countries, including Canada, have regulatory agencies, whose function it is to regulate and control the use of new chemical compounds before they are exposed to the environment. [...]

As to Canada and the United Kingdom, both have registered 2,4-D and 2,4,5-T for forestry use with a maximum TCDD level of 0.1 parts per million. Registration for use in Canada for 2,4-D was in 1947 and 2,4,5-T in 1952. In both jurisdictions reviews are made periodically after reviews of the literature and independent study by highly trained and competent scientists. The evidence indicates this to be an ongoing process. In both countries registration for use is still in effect and neither jurisdiction has accepted that there are valid studies which would cause them to cancel the registration. The provincial Department of Environment is also involved in this ongoing process as it relates to Nova Scotia and that department has not registered the use of these herbicides.

To some extent this case takes on the nature of an appeal from the decision of the regulatory agency and any such approach through the courts ought to be discouraged in its infancy. Opponents to a particular chemical ought to direct their activities towards the regulatory agencies or, indeed, to government itself where broad areas of social policy are involved. It is not for the courts to become a regulatory agency of this type. It has neither the training nor the staff to perform this function. Suffice it to say that this decision will relate to, and be limited to, the dispute between these parties [...] Having accepted Mr. Ross' testimony and accepting the evidence of Donald Freer and Exhibit D-70 that the defendant's supply of 2,4,5-T is formulated with a TCDD content of "non detectible" at 0.01 parts per million, it is obvious that the amount of TCDD to be sprayed in Nova Scotia by the defendant is infinitesimally small. After hearing Lt. Col. Thalken I do not accept Dr. Wulfman's suggestion that storage may affect the product in any way.

It is, therefore, in the light of this concentration of TCDD that I must consider whether the plaintiffs have met the burden of proof. [...]

A great deal of the evidence submitted related to animal studies where TCDD were reported to have caused various effects indicating it to be, among other things, fetotoxic, teratagenic, carcinogenic and to cause immunological deficiencies, enzymatic changes, liver problems and the like. Also it is alleged to bioaccumulate and be persistent both in soil and in tissue. I do not pretend to have included all of its effects, but those are the most major. I was asked to make findings of fact in all of these areas, but I decline to do so. Nothing would be added to the body of scientific fact by any such determination by this court. That TCDD has had all of these effects is undoubtedly true in the experiments described, but, in every case, the effect must be related to dose. In the animal studies the doses are extremely high and, in all cases, many, many thousands of times greater than any dose which could be received in Nova Scotia.

Human studies are a different matter because actual testing is not an acceptable process in our society. I do note that Dr. Newton, another of the defence witnesses, participated in some actual testing on himself and several others, without any apparent harmful result. The human information comes from a number of studies made in various countries of the world. Some resulted from industrial accidents, some from the Vietnam experiences and some from massive industrial exposure. It was in this area that a great deal of the evidence was directed. I am satisfied that in all these cases the exposure was massive, either through accident or industrial exposure or the Vietnam War.

[...] The evidence discloses that where particular health effects alleged to be caused by exposure were investigated, they were found not to be attributable to exposure. I refer particularly here to the evidence of Dr. Kilpatrick and the experience in the United Kingdom. While I am on this point, I must indicate something that has troubled me throughout this case. In the past 35 years these chemicals have had extremely high world-wide use and for most of those the TCDD content was many hundreds of times higher than that used today. It has been used in agriculture (widely used in the growth of rice), forestry, roadside and railway rights-of-way, etc., yet there is no evidence in the countries of use, except the Hardell results, already referred to, of proven injury to health from these uses with a few exceptions related to those actually spraying, i.e., massive personal occupationally-related exposure situations. Apparently those workers were unaware of possible harm with a corresponding lack of concern for care. 2,4-D itself has had extremely high use in agriculture throughout this time, again with no obvious ill effects. I find this dearth of evidence to be astonishing in view of the health effects alleged.

This brings me to the next suggestion by the plaintiffs which is that cancer, as a disease, has a long incubation period and the effects of dioxin cannot be known until time passes, approximately 40 years, so that it can be determined whether dioxin is indeed carcinogenic in humans. This again is not my function. I am to determine only if there is a probability of risk to health. To this point in time there is not sufficient acceptable evidence despite 35 years of use. One of the plaintiffs' witnesses, Dr. Daum, suggested that the only approach is to wait that period without permitting any further use. I cannot accept that. She is working from the premise that any substance should be proved absolutely safe before use but, as commendable as that may be, it is not practical nor is it in conformity with currently accepted determinations for use of many substances. I doubt very much if any substance can be proved absolutely safe.

If all substances which are carcinogenic or otherwise toxic were removed from use, we would have no air to breathe or potable water and many common everyday products, necessary to our life, would be removed. The key to the use of all these is dosage. Where it can be determined that there is a safe dosage, according to acceptable scientific standards, then a substance can be used. Our regulatory agencies and scientists around the world are daily involved in this very area.

As well, virtually all chemicals are toxic, but those in use generally are safe if used below the toxic levels, i.e., if the dose received is below the safety levels. Scientists also determine a "no observable effect level". That is a level of intake of any particular substance where no effect is observed. It is, in most cases, far below the safe level, at least several orders of magnitude (each order being a multiple of 10) lower. [...]

I am satisfied that the overwhelming currently accepted view of responsible scientists is that there is little evidence that, for humans either 2,4-D or 2, 4,5-T is mutagenic or carcinogenic and that TCDD is not an effective carcinogen, and further, that there are no-effect levels and safe levels for humans and wildlife for each of these substances [...]

Having reached this point it is appropriate to add that the evidence of risk assessments clearly indicates that any risk here in Nova Scotia, if, indeed, there is a risk at all, is infinitesimally small and many, many times less than one in a million which level, apparently, is regarded as a safe and acceptable risk by most of the world's regulatory agencies. Putting this in perspective, as indicated by Dr. Wilson in his evidence, the risk of cancer to a smoker is 1 in 800 and for a non-smoker continuously in the same room with smokers it is 1 in 100,000, while the risk to a person drinking two litres of water per day from a stream immediately after being sprayed (which will not happen with buffer zones) is 1 in 100,000 million or 100,000 times less than 1 in a million, which itself is regarded as a *de minimus* risk.

To my mind, after hearing all the evidence and reading all the exhibits, there is no doubt that the weight of current responsible scientific opinion does not support the allegations of the plaintiffs. I feel it is my responsibility, in view of the nature of this matter, to add that, while I do not doubt the zeal of many of the plaintiffs' scientific witnesses or their ability, some seemed at many times to be protagonists defending a position, thereby losing some of their objectivity. There was a noticeable selection of studies which supported their view and a refusal to accept any criticism of them or contrary studies. Where the study was by anyone remotely connected with industry there was a tendency to leap to the "fox in the chicken coop" philosophy, thereby ruling out the value of the study as biased. In my view a true scientific approach does not permit such self-serving selectivity, nor does it so readily decry a study on the basis of bias.

I had the opposite impression of the scientific witnesses offered by the defendant. I did not detect any sense of partisanship. They related their work, their involvement with the substances, the results of their studies and their considerations of other studies in a professional, scientific manner and I therefore found their opinions to be reliable and, indeed, I accepted them as such. [...]

Having made this finding, it is unnecessary for me to consider the matter of riparian rights or groundwater rights. Since I have accepted that no risk to health has been proved, I need not consider these areas. Were I required to do so, and perhaps to allay public fears, I will add that the strongest evidence indicates that these substances sprayed in the Nova Scotia environment will not get into or travel through the rivers or streams, nor will they travel via groundwater to any lands of the plaintiffs who are adjacent to or near the sites to be sprayed.

Further, if any did the amount would be so insignificant that there would be no risk.

I need not consider whether any particular area need be sprayed, whether other substances should be used, or whether manual release is a better approach. While considerable evidence was adduced in this regard, it is not the court's function to direct how the defendant should manage its affairs or carry out its activities. My only concern is whether or not the defendant should be restrained from the proposed activity. While those factors may have been considered in the wide discretionary area if an injunction were to be granted, they do not arise when the plaintiffs have not proved the grounds for an injunction.

There is, accordingly, no nuisance, real or probable. As to trespass, none has been proved as probable to occur. Possibilities do not constitute proof. Similarly, there has been no basis established for the application of the rule in *Rylands v. Fletcher*, as neither the danger of the substance nor the likelihood of its escape to the plaintiffs' lands has been proved.

Therefore, the answer to the single remaining question I posed earlier which has two parts — have the plaintiffs offered sufficient proof that there is a serious risk of health and that such serious risk of health will occur if the spraying of the substances here is permitted to take place — is, for each part, in the negative. [...] The plaintiffs, therefore, fail in this action and the defendant is entitled to its costs [...].

Notes and Questions

1. Consider carefully the "single question" identified by Nunn J. How does the question relate to the legal test for granting injunctive relief? What does it tell us about the Court's approach to nuisance, strict liability and trespass?

2. Can you differentiate, in Nunn J.'s reasoning, between the tests for the torts of nuisance, strict liability and trespass on the one hand, and the test for granting injunctive relief on the other?

3. In your view, based on Nunn J.'s findings of fact, were the tests for the torts of nuisance, trespass or strict liability made out?

4. What about negligence? Could a case in negligence have been made out based on the facts before the Court?

5. Nunn J. comments that this case almost takes the form of an appeal of the regulatory decisions to approve the use of herbicides in Canada, and to permit the spraying of the area in question. What role does this suggest for the common law with respect to the compensation of harm caused by

pollution permitted by an approval? Would a claim for monetary damages instead of injunctive and declaratory relief have been successful?

6. Nunn J. awarded costs against the plaintiffs despite the fact that the case had many hallmarks of "public interest" litigation. For many of the plaintiffs, this adverse costs award presented dire financial consequences. Ultimately, the plaintiffs agreed to abandon their appeal in return for the defendant agreeing to forego its entitlement to costs. In your view, had the case been appealed, what would have been the plaintiffs' strongest legal arguments for overturning Nunn J.'s judgment at trial? For further discussion of costs-related issues in public interest cases, see Chapter 6.

The next case is the landmark 1994 decision of the House of Lords concerning the ambit and nature of the rule in *Rylands v. Fletcher*. The *Cambridge Water Co v. Eastern Counties Leather Plc* case has been criticized by some as restricting the ambit of recovery in cases of historic pollution, particularly where the impugned conduct was consistent with prevailing industrial practices and scientific knowledge when the pollution occurred. It has been applauded by others for the same reason.

At trial, the plaintiff pleaded negligence, private nuisance and *Rylands v. Fletcher*. By the time the matter reached the House of Lords, the only live issue was whether the defendant should be liable under the third of these torts. In addressing this issue, two legal questions were central to the Court's decision: (1) whether the reasonable foreseeability of damage was an element of the tort; and (2) whether the defendant's storage and use of the chemical solvents constituted a "non-natural use of land" under the rule in *Rylands v. Fletcher*.

Cambridge Water Co. v. Eastern Counties Leather Plc
(1993), [1994] 2 A.C. 264 (U.K. H.L.)

LORD GOFF OF CHIEVELEY: — My Lords, this appeal is concerned with the question whether the appellant company, Eastern Counties Leather plc (ECL), is liable to the respondent company, Cambridge Water Co (CWC), in damages in respect of damage suffered by reason of the contamination of water available for abstraction at CWC's borehole at Sawston Mill near Cambridge. The contamination was caused by a solvent known as perchloroethene (PCE), used by ECL in the process of degreasing pelts at its tanning works in Sawston, about 173 miles away from CWC's borehole, the PCE having seeped into the ground beneath ECL's works and thence having been conveyed in percolating water in the direction of the borehole. CWC's claim against ECL was based on three alternative grounds, viz negligence, nuisance and the rule in *Rylands v. Fletcher* (1868), LR 3 HL 330.

The judge, Ian Kennedy J, dismissed CWC's claim on all three grounds — on the first two grounds, because (as I will explain hereafter) he held that ECL could not reasonably have foreseen that such damage would occur, and on the third ground because he held that the use of a solvent such as PCE in ECL's tanning business constituted, in the circumstances, a natural use of ECL's land. The Court of Appeal, however, allowed CWC's appeal from the decision of the judge, on the ground that ECL was strictly liable for the contamination of the water percolating under CWC's land, on the authority of *Ballard v. Tomlinson* (1885), 29 Ch D 115, and awarded damages against ECL in the sum assessed by the judge, viz £1,064,886 together with interest totalling £642,885, and costs. It is against that decision that ECL now appeals to your Lordships' House, with leave of this House. [...]

ECL was incorporated in 1879, and since that date has continued in uninterrupted business as a manufacturer of fine leather at Sawston. ECL employs about 100 people, all of whom live locally. Its present works are, as the judge found, in general modern and spacious, and admit of a good standard of housekeeping.

The tanning process requires that pelts shall be degreased; and ECL, in common with all other tanneries, has used solvents in that process since the early 1950s. It has used two types of chlorinated solvents — organochlorines known as TCE (trichloroethene) and PCE. Both solvents are cleaning and degreasing agents; and since 1950 PCE has increasingly been in common, widespread and everyday use in dry-cleaning, in general industrial use (e.g., as a machine cleaner or paint thinner), domestically (e.g., in 'Dab-it-off') and in tanneries. PCE is highly volatile, and so evaporates rapidly in air; but it is not readily soluble in water.

ECL began using TCE in the early 1950s and then changed over to PCE, probably sometime in the 1960s, and continued to use PCE until 1991. The amount so used varied between 50,000 and 100,000 litres per year. The solvent was introduced into what were (in effect) dry-cleaning machines. This was done in two different ways. First, from the commencement of use until 1976, the solvent was delivered in 40 gallon drums; as and when the solvent was needed, a drum was taken by forklift truck to the machine and tipped into a tank at the base of the machine. Second, from 1976 to 1991, the solvent was delivered in bulk and kept in a storage tank, from which it was piped directly to the machine.

There was no direct evidence of the actual manner in which PCE was spilled at ECL's premises. However, the judge found that the spillage took place during the period up to 1976, principally during the topping up process described above, during which there were regular spillages of relatively small amounts of PCE onto the concrete floor of the tannery. It is known that, over that period, the minimum amount which must have been spilled (or otherwise have entered the chalk aquifer below) was some 3,200 litres (1,000 gallons); it is not possible even to guess at the maximum. However, as the judge found, a reasonable supervisor at ECL would not have foreseen, in or before 1976, that such repeated spillages of small quantities of solvent would lead to any environmental hazard or damage — i.e., that the solvent would enter the aquifer or that, having done so, detectable quantities would be found down-catchment. Even if he had foreseen that solvent might enter the aquifer, he would not have foreseen that such quantities would produce any sensible effect upon water taken down-catchment, or would otherwise be material or deserve the description of pollution. I understand the position to have been that any spillage would have been expected to evaporate rapidly in the air, and would not have been expected to seep through the floor of the building into the soil below. The only harm that could have been foreseen from a spillage was that somebody might have been overcome by fumes from a spillage of a significant quantity.

I turn to CWC. CWC was created under its own Act of Parliament in 1853 (the Cambridge University and *Town Waterworks Act 1853* (16 & 17 Vict c xxiii), and is a licensed supplier of water following implementation of the *Water Act 1989*. Its function is to supply water to some 275,000 people in the Cambridge area. It takes all its water by borehole extraction from underground strata, mainly the middle and lower chalk prevalent in the area. Since 1945 public demand for water has multiplied many times, and new sources of supply have had to be found. In 1975 CWC identified the borehole at Sawston Mill as having the potential to meet a need for supply required to avert a prospective shortfall, and to form part of its long term provision for future demand. It purchased the borehole in September 1976. Before purchase, tests were carried out on the water from the borehole; these tests indicated that, from the aspect of chemical analysis, the water was a wholesome water suitable for public supply purposes. Similar results were obtained from tests carried out during the period 1979-83. At all events CWC, having obtained the requisite statutory authority to use the borehole for public sector supply, proceeded to build a new pumping station at a cost of »184,000; and Sawston Mill water entered the main supply system in June 1979.

Meanwhile, in the later 1970s concern began to be expressed in scientific circles about the presence of organic chemicals in drinking water, and their possible effects. Furthermore, the development of, inter alia, high-resolution gas chromatography during the 1970s enabled scientists to detect and measure organochlorine compounds (such as PCE) in water to the value of micrograms per litre (or parts per billion) expressed as μg/litre.

In 1984 the World Health Organisation (WHO) published a Report on Guidelines for Drinking Water Quality (vol 1: recommendations). Although not published until 1984, the Report was the product of discussion and consultation during several years previously, and its recommendations appear to have formed the basis of an earlier EEC Directive, as well as of later UK Regulations. Chapter 4 of the Report is concerned with 'Chemical and Physical Aspects', and Ch 4.3 deals with organic contaminants, three of which (including TCE and PCE) were assigned a 'Tentative Guideline Value'. The value so recommended for TCE was 30μg/litre, and for PCE 10μg/litre.

The EEC Directive relating to the Quality of Water intended for Human Consumption (80/778/EEC) was issued on 15 September 1980. Member states were required to bring in laws within two years of notification, and to achieve full compliance within five years. The Directive distinguished between 'Maximum Admissible Concentration' (MAC) values and 'Guide Level' (GL) values, the former being minimum standards which had to be achieved, and the latter being more stringent standards which it was desirable to achieve. TCE and PCE were assigned a GL value of only 1μg/litre, i.e., 30 times and 10 times respectively lower than the WHO Tentative Guideline Values.

The United Kingdom responded to the Directive by Department of the Environment circular 20/82 dated 15 August 1982. The effect was that, as from 18 July 1985, drinking water containing more than 1μg/litre of TCE or PCE would not be regarded as 'wholesome' water for the purpose of compliance by water authorities with their statutory obligations under the *Water Act 1973*. However, following a regulation made in 1989 (SI 1989/1147) the prescribed maximum concentration values for TCE and PCE have been respectively 30μg/litre and

10µg/litre, so that since 1 September 1989 the United Kingdom values have been brought back into harmony with the WHO Tentative Guideline Values. [...]

The conclusions reached by British Geological Society, and by the expert witnesses instructed by CWC and ECL in the present litigation, were as follows. Neat PCE had travelled down through the drift directly beneath ECL's premises, and then vertically downwards through the chalk aquifer until arrested by a relatively impermeable layer of chalk marl at a depth of about 50 metres. Thus arrested, the neat PCE had formed pools which were dissolving slowly in the groundwater and being carried down aquifer in the direction of Sawston Mill at the rate of about 8 metres per day, the travel time between pool and Sawston Mill being about 9 months, and the migration of the dissolved phase PCE being along a deep, comparatively narrow, pathway or 'plume'. On the balance of probabilities, this narrow plume had reached Sawston Mill and been at least materially responsible for the PCE concentrations found there. [...]

From the foregoing history, the following relevant facts may be selected as being of particular relevance:

(1) The spillage of PCE, and its seepage into the ground beneath the floor of the tannery at ECL's works, occurred during the period which ended in 1976, as a result of regular spillages of small quantities of PCE onto the floor of ECL's tannery.

(2) The escape of dissolved phase PCE, from the pools of neat PCE which collected at or towards the base of the chalk aquifers beneath ECL's works, into the chalk aquifers under the adjoining land and thence in the direction of Sawston Mill, must have begun at some unspecified date well before 1976 and be still continuing to the present day.

(3) As held by the judge, the seepage of the PCE beneath the floor of ECL's works down into the chalk aquifers below was not foreseeable by a reasonable supervisor employed by ECL, nor was it foreseeable by him that detectable quantities of PCE would be found down-catchment, so that he could not have foreseen, in or before 1976, that the repeated spillages would lead to any environmental hazard or damage. The only foreseeable damage from a spillage of PCE was that somebody might be overcome by fumes from a substantial spillage of PCE on the surface of the ground.

(4) The water so contaminated at Sawston Mill has never been held to be dangerous to health. But under criteria laid down in the UK Regulations, issued in response to the EEC Directive, the water so contaminated was not 'wholesome' and, since 1985, could not lawfully be supplied in this country as drinking water. [...]

Foreseeability of Damage in Nuisance

It is against this background that it is necessary to consider the question whether foreseeability of harm of the relevant type is an essential element of liability either in nuisance or under the rule in *Rylands v. Fletcher*. I shall take first the case of nuisance. In the present case, as I have said, this is not strictly speaking a live issue. Even so, I propose briefly to address it, as part of the analysis of the background to the present case.

We are concerned with the liability of a person where a nuisance has been created by one for whose actions he is responsible. Here, as I have said, it is still the law that the fact that the defendant has taken all reasonable care will not of itself exonerate him from liability, the relevant control mechanism being found within the principle of reasonable user. But it by no means follows that the defendant should be held liable for damage of a type which he could not reasonably foresee; and the development of the law of negligence in the past sixty years points strongly towards a requirement that such foreseeability should be a prerequisite of liability in damages for nuisance, as it is of liability in negligence. For if a plaintiff is in ordinary circumstances only able to claim damages in respect of personal injuries where he can prove such foreseeability on the part of the defendant, it is difficult to see why, in common justice, he should be in a stronger position to claim damages for interference with the enjoyment of his land where the defendant was unable to foresee such damage. Moreover, this appears to have been the conclusion of the Privy Council in *The Wagon Mound (No 2), Overseas Tankship (UK) Ltd v. Miller Steamship Co Pty Ltd*, [1966] 2 All ER 709, [1967] 1 AC 617. The facts of the case [arise] from a public nuisance caused by a spillage of oil in Sydney Harbour. [In concluding that in cases of this kind] foreseeability is an essential element, Lord Reid [stated]:

> It could not be right to discriminate between different cases of nuisance so as to make foreseeability a necessary element in determining damages in those cases where it is a necessary element in determining liability, but not in others. So the choice is between it being a necessary element in all cases of nuisance or in none. In their Lordships' judgment the similarities between nuisance and other forms of tort to which *The Wagon Mound (No. 1)*, [1961] 1 All ER 404, [1961] AC 388 applies far outweigh any differences, and they must therefore hold that the judgment appealed from is wrong on this branch of the case. It is not sufficient that the injury suffered by the respondents' vessels was the direct result of the nuisance if that injury was in the relevant sense unforeseeable.

It is widely accepted that this conclusion, although not essential to the decision of the particular case, has nevertheless settled the law to the effect that foreseeability of harm is indeed a prerequisite of the recovery of damages in private nuisance, as in the case of public nuisance. I refer in particular to the opinion expressed by Professor Fleming in his book on Torts (8th edn, 1992) pp 443-444. It is unnecessary in the present case to consider the precise nature of this principle; but it appears from Lord Reid's statement of the law that he regarded it essentially as one relating to remoteness of damage.

Foreseeability of Damage under the Rule in Rylands v. Fletcher

It is against this background that I turn to the submission advanced by ECL before your Lordships that there is a similar prerequisite of recovery of damages under the rule in *Rylands v. Fletcher* (1866), LR 1 Exch 265.

I start with the judgment of Blackburn J in *Fletcher v. Rylands* itself. His celebrated statement of the law is to be found where he said (at 279-280):

We think that the true rule of law is, that the person who for his own purposes brings on his lands and collects and keeps there anything likely to do mischief if it escapes, must keep it in at his peril, and, if he does not do so, is prima facie answerable for all the damage which is the natural consequence of its escape. He can excuse himself by showing that the escape was owing to the plaintiff's default; or perhaps that the escape was the consequence of vis major, or the act of God; but as nothing of this sort exists here, it is unnecessary to inquire what excuse would be sufficient. The general rule, as above stated, seems on principle just. The person whose grass or corn is eaten down by the escaping cattle of his neighbour, or whose mine is flooded by the water from his neighbour's reservoir, or whose cellar is invaded by the filth of his neighbour's privy, or whose habitation is made unhealthy by the fumes and noisome vapours of his neighbour's alkali works, is damnified without any fault of his own; and it seems but reasonable and just that the neighbour, who has brought something on his own property which was not naturally there, harmless to others so long as it is confined to his own property, but which he knows to be mischievous if it gets on his neighbour's, should be obliged to make good the damage which ensues if he does not succeed in confining it to his own property. But for his act in bringing it there no mischief could have accrued, and it seems but just that he should at his peril keep it there so that no mischief may accrue, or answer for the natural and anticipated consequences. And upon authority, this we think is established to be the law whether the things so brought be beasts, or water, or filth, or stenches.

In that passage Blackburn J spoke of 'anything likely to do mischief if it escapes'; and later he spoke of something 'which he knows to be mischievous if it gets on to his neighbour's [property]', and the liability to 'answer for the natural and anticipated consequences'. Furthermore, time and again he spoke of the strict liability imposed upon the defendant as being that he must keep the thing in at his peril; and, when referring to liability in actions for damage occasioned by animals, he referred (at 282) to the established principle 'that it is quite immaterial whether the escape is by negligence or not'. The general tenor of his statement of principle is therefore that knowledge, or at least foreseeability of the risk, is a prerequisite of the recovery of damages under the principle; but that the principle is one of strict liability in the sense that the defendant may be held liable notwithstanding that he has exercised all due care to prevent the escape from occurring. [...]

The point is one on which academic opinion appears to be divided: cf Salmond and Heuston on Torts (20th edn, 1992) pp 324-325, which favours the prerequisite of foreseeability, and Clerk and Lindsell on Torts (16th edn, 1989) para 25.09, which takes a different view. However, quite apart from the indications to be derived from the judgment of Blackburn J in *Fletcher v. Rylands*, LR 1 Exch 265 itself, the historical connection with the law of nuisance must now be regarded as pointing towards the conclusion that foreseeability of damage is a prerequisite of the recovery of damages under the rule. I have already referred to the fact that Blackburn J himself did not regard his statement of principle as having broken new ground; furthermore, Professor Newark has convincingly shown that the rule in *Rylands v. Fletcher* was essentially concerned with an extension of the law of nuisance to cases of isolated escape. Accordingly since, following the observations of Lord Reid when delivering the advice of the Privy Council in *The Wagon Mound (No 2)*, [1966] 2 All ER 709 at 717, [1967] 1 AC 617 at 640, the recovery of damages in private nuisance depends on foreseeability by the defendant of the relevant type of damage, it would appear logical to extend the same requirement to liability under the rule in *Rylands v. Fletcher*.

Even so, the question cannot be considered solely as a matter of history. It can be argued that the rule in *Rylands v. Fletcher* should not be regarded simply as an extension of the law of nuisance, but should rather be treated as a developing principle of strict liability from which can be derived a general rule of strict liability for damage caused by ultra-hazardous operations, on the basis of which persons conducting such operations may properly be held strictly liable for the extraordinary risk to others involved in such operations. As is pointed out in Fleming on Torts (8th edn, 1992) pp. 327-328, this would lead to the practical result that the cost of damage resulting from such operations would have to be absorbed as part of the overheads of the relevant business rather than be borne (where there is no negligence) by the injured person or his insurers, or even by the community at large. Such a development appears to have been taking place in the United States, as can be seen from the Restatement of Torts (2d) vol 3 (1977). The extent to which it has done so is not altogether clear; and I infer from para 519, and the comment on that paragraph, that the abnormally dangerous activities there referred to are such that their ability to cause harm would be obvious to any reasonable person who carried them on. [...]

Like the judge in the present case, I incline to the opinion that, as a general rule, it is more appropriate for strict liability in respect of operations of high risk to be imposed by Parliament, than by the courts. If such liability is imposed by statute, the relevant activities can be identified, and those concerned can know where they stand. Furthermore, statute can where appropriate lay down precise criteria establishing the incidence and scope of such liability.

It is of particular relevance that the present case is concerned with environmental pollution. The protection and preservation of the environment is now perceived as being of crucial importance to the future of mankind; and public bodies, both national and international, are taking significant steps towards the establishment of legislation which will promote the protection of the environment, and make the polluter pay for damage to the environment for which he is responsible — as can be seen from the WHO, EEC and national regulations to which I have previously referred. But it does not follow from these developments that a common law principle, such as the rule in *Rylands v. Fletcher*, should be developed or rendered more strict to provide for liability in respect of such pollution. On the contrary, given that so much well-informed and carefully structured legislation is now being put in place for this purpose, there is less need for the courts to develop a common law principle to achieve the same end, and indeed it may well be undesirable that they should do so.

[...] it appears to me to be appropriate now to take the view that foreseeability of damage of the relevant type should be regarded as a prerequisite of liability in damages under the rule. Such a conclusion can, as I have already stated, be derived from Blackburn J's original statement of the law; and I can see no good reason why this prerequisite should not be recognised under the rule, as it has been in the case of private nuisance. [...] It would moreover lead to a more coherent body of common law principles if the rule were to be regarded essentially as an extension of the law of nuisance to cases of isolated escapes from land, even though the rule as established is not limited to escapes which are in fact isolated. I wish to point out, however, that in truth the escape of the PCE from ECL's land, in the form of trace elements carried in percolating water, has not been an isolated escape, but a continuing escape resulting from a state of affairs which has come into existence at the base of the chalk aquifer underneath ECL's premises. Classically, this would have been regarded as a case of nuisance; and it would seem strange if, by characterising the case as one falling under the rule in *Rylands v. Fletcher*, the liability should thereby be rendered more strict in the circumstances of the present case.

The Facts of the Present Case

Turning to the facts of the present case, it is plain that, at the time when the PCE was brought onto ECL's land, and indeed when it was used in the tanning process there, nobody at ECL could reasonably have foreseen the resultant damage which occurred at CWC's borehole at Sawston.

However, there remains for consideration a point adumbrated in the course of argument, which is relevant to liability in nuisance as well as under the rule in *Rylands v. Fletcher*. It appears that, in the present case, pools of neat PCE are still in existence at the base of the chalk aquifer beneath ECL's premises, and the escape of dissolved phase PCE from ECL's land is continuing to the present day. On this basis it can be argued that, since it has become known that PCE, if it escapes, is capable of causing damage by rendering water available at boreholes unsaleable for domestic purposes, ECL could be held liable, in nuisance or under the rule in *Rylands v. Fletcher*, in respect of damage caused by the continuing escape of PCE from its land occurring at any time after such damage had become foreseeable by ECL.

For my part, I do not consider that such an argument is well founded. Here we are faced with a situation where the substance in question, PCE, has so travelled down through the drift and the chalk aquifer beneath ECL's premises that it has passed beyond the control of ECL. To impose strict liability on ECL in these circumstances, either as the creator of a nuisance or under the rule in *Rylands v. Fletcher*, on the ground that it has subsequently become reasonably foreseeable that the PCE may, if it escapes, cause damage, appears to me to go beyond the scope of the regimes imposed under either of these two related heads of liability. This is because when ECL created the conditions which have ultimately led to the present state of affairs — whether by bringing the PCE in question onto its land, or by retaining it there, or by using it in its tanning process — it could not possibly have foreseen that damage of the type now complained of might be caused thereby. Indeed, long before the relevant legislation came into force, the PCE had become irretrievably lost in the ground below. In such circumstances, I do not consider that ECL should be under any greater liability than that imposed for negligence. [...]

I wish to add that the present case may be regarded as one of what is nowadays called historic pollution, in the sense that the relevant occurrence (the seepage of PCE through the floor of ECL's premises) took place before the relevant legislation came into force; and it appears that, under the current philosophy, it is not envisaged that statutory liability should be imposed for historic pollution (see e.g. the Council of Europe's Draft Convention on Civil

Liability for Damages Resulting from Activities Dangerous to the Environment (Strasbourg, 29 January 1993) art 5.1, and para 48 of the Explanatory Report). If so, it would be strange if liability for such pollution were to arise under a principle of common law.

In the result, since those responsible at ECL could not at the relevant time reasonably have foreseen that the damage in question might occur, the claim of CWC for damages under the rule in *Rylands v. Fletcher* must fail.

Natural Use of Land

I turn to the question whether the use by ECL of its land in the present case constituted a natural use, with the result that ECL cannot be held liable under the rule in *Rylands v. Fletcher*. In view of my conclusion on the issue of foreseeability, I can deal with this point shortly.

The judge held that it was a natural use. He said:

> In my judgment, in considering whether the storage of organochlorines as an adjunct to a manufacturing process is a non-natural use of land, I must consider whether that storage created special risks for adjacent occupiers and whether the activity was for the general benefit of the community. It seems to me inevitable that I must consider the magnitude of the storage and the geographical area in which it takes place in answering the question. Sawston is properly described as an industrial village, and the creation of employment is clearly for the benefit of that community. I do not believe that I can enter upon an assessment of the point on a scale of desirability that the manufacture of wash leathers comes, and I content myself with holding that this storage in this place is a natural use of land.

It is a commonplace that this particular exception to liability under the rule has developed and changed over the years. It seems clear that in *Fletcher v. Rylands* (1866), LR 1 Ex 265 itself Blackburn J's statement of the law was limited to things which are brought by the defendant onto his land, and so did not apply to things that were naturally upon the land. Furthermore, it is doubtful whether in the House of Lords in the same case Lord Cairns, to whom we owe the expression 'non-natural use' of the land, was intending to expand the concept of natural use beyond that envisaged by Blackburn J. Even so, the law has long since departed from any such simple idea, redolent of a different age; and, at least since the advice of the Privy Council delivered by Lord Moulton in *Rickards v. Lothian*, [1913] AC 263 at 280, [1911-13] All ER Rep 71 at 80, natural use has been extended to embrace the ordinary use of land. [...]

Rickards v. Lothian itself was concerned with a use of a domestic kind, viz the overflow of water from a basin whose runaway had become blocked. But over the years the concept of natural use, in the sense of ordinary use, has been extended to embrace a wide variety of uses, including not only domestic uses but also recreational uses and even some industrial uses.

It is obvious that the expression 'ordinary use of the land' in Lord Moulton's statement of the law is one which is lacking in precision. There are some writers who welcome the flexibility which has thus been introduced into this branch of the law, on the ground that it enables judges to mould and adapt the principle of strict liability to the changing needs of society; whereas others regret the perceived absence of principle in so vague a concept, and fear that the whole idea of strict liability may as a result be undermined. A particular doubt is introduced by Lord Moulton's alternative criterion 'or such a use as is proper for the general benefit of the community'. If these words are understood to refer to a local community, they can be given some content as intended to refer to such matters as, for example, the provision of services; indeed the same idea can, without too much difficulty, be extended to, for example, the provision of services to industrial premises, as in a business park or an industrial estate. But if the words are extended to embrace the wider interests of the local community or the general benefit of the community at large, it is difficult to see how the exception can be kept within reasonable bounds. [...]

Fortunately, I do not think it is necessary for the purposes of the present case to attempt any redefinition of the concept of natural or ordinary use. This is because I am satisfied that the storage of chemicals in substantial quantities, and their use in the manner employed at ECL's premises, cannot fall within the exception. For the purpose of testing the point, let it be assumed that ECL was well aware of the possibility that PCE, if it escaped, could indeed cause damage, for example by contaminating any water with which it became mixed so as to render that water undrinkable by human beings. I cannot think that it would be right in such circumstances to exempt ECL from liability under the rule in *Rylands v. Fletcher* on the ground that the use was natural or ordinary. The mere fact that the use is common in the tanning industry cannot, in my opinion, be enough to bring the use within the exception, nor the fact that Sawston contains a small industrial community which is worthy of encouragement or support. Indeed I feel bound to say that the storage of substantial quantities of chemicals on industrial premises should be regarded as an almost classic case of non-natural use; and I find it very difficult to think that it should be thought objectionable to impose strict liability for damage caused in the event of their escape. It may well be that, now that it is recognised that foreseeability of harm of the relevant type is a prerequisite of liability in damages under the rule, the courts may feel less pressure to extend the concept of natural use to circumstances such as those in the present case; and in due course it may become easier to control this exception, and to ensure that it has a more recognisable basis of principle. For these reasons, I would not hold that ECL should be exempt from liability on the basis of the exception of natural use.

However, for the reasons I have already given, I would allow ECL's appeal with costs before your Lordships' House and in the courts below.

Notes and Questions

1. How do the trial judge and the House of Lords differ in their views of what constitutes a "non-natural use of land"? Which approach do you prefer? Explain.

2. Do you agree with the House of Lords that foreseeability of harm should be a precondition to recovery in private nuisance and the rule under *Rylands v. Fletcher*? Under this ruling, who is liable for unforeseeable harm resulting from an unnatural use of land? Recently, the Ontario Court of Appeal broke

away from English jurisprudence and held that foreseeability of harm is not an element of the tort of nuisance in Ontario: *Huang v. Fraser Hillary's Limited*, 2018 ONCA 527, leave to appeal refused 2019 CarswellOnt 5599 (S.C.C.). In this case, the defendant dry-cleaning business discharged solvents used in the dry-cleaning process into the ground in accordance with best practices of the time when the environmental impacts of the solvents were not known. The plaintiff sought damages for the cost of remediation for contamination on his property. The trial judge held that the defendant was liable under nuisance and section 99 of the Ontario *Environmental Protection Act*. A key issue on appeal was whether the trial judge erred in failing to consider reasonable foreseeability as part of his nuisance analysis. The Court of Appeal upheld the trial judge's decision. Writing for a unanimous Court, Hourigan J.A. held that the "addition of a foreseeability requirement blurs the distinction between negligence and nuisance" and that "the utility of the tort would be compromised" if such an element were required: para. 23. Whether reasonable foreseeability is an element of the rule in *Rylands v. Fletcher* in Canada remains an open question: see *Smith v. Inco Ltd.*, 2011 ONCA 628, leave to appeal refused [2012] 1 S.C.R. xii (note), reconsideration/rehearing refused 2014 CarswellOnt 12113 (S.C.C.), excerpted below.

3. What role does the House of Lords see for government in addressing the issue of harm resulting from environmental pollution?

4. Compare the House of Lords' comments on the role of government through legislation to Justice Nunn's comments on the federal and provincial regulatory process in place for the approval and application of herbicides.

5. Legislators have taken various steps to address the shortcomings of the common law with respect to historic pollution. In the context of contaminated sites, this has taken the form of site remediation requirements that facilitate recovery of remediation costs from historic polluters (often defined in broad terms as "persons responsible" deemed statutorily liable for historic on-site activities). A variety of issues have proven controversial including the definition of "persons responsible", retrospective/retroactive application of the legislation, and apportionment of liability: see *Workshop Holdings Ltd. v. CAE Machinery Ltd.*, 2003 BCCA 56. Is historic pollution a problem that should primarily be left to legislators? To what extent should the common law be relied upon in this setting?

6. The mix of common law and legislation dealing with many aspects of environmental harm raises many legal issues. One such issue is whether and under what circumstances a statutory authority or duty to act should exempt a public official from liability for engaging in conduct that would ordinarily constitute a tort under the common law. See *Mandrake Management Consultants Ltd. v. Toronto Transit Commission* (1993), 11 C.E.L.R. (N.S.) 100 (Ont. C.A.), for a discussion of this issue in the context of noise and vibration from the Toronto subway system. Leading cases from the SCC include *Tock v. St. John's (City) Metropolitan Area Board*, [1989] 2 S.C.R. 1181, and *Ryan v. Victoria (City)*, [1999] 1 S.C.R. 201.

7. Another key issue in understanding the relationship between the common law and legislation in the environmental field is the effect of legislative efforts to regulate human activity on the common law. The Court in *Palmer* was clearly influenced by regulatory decisions to allow the spraying of the herbicides in question. This issue is perhaps most apparent in the context of the duty of care under negligence. What if any effect should, for example, a regulatory approval for a certain concentration of a pollutant in effluent have on the duty of care imposed on the operator with respect to harm to neighbours?

8. It is important to be aware that special principles apply to the liability in negligence of public authorities. In this setting, courts draw a distinction between acts/omissions that are "operational" in nature as opposed to those that have occurred as the result of a deliberate "policy" decision: see *Just v. British Columbia*, [1989] 2 S.C.R. 1228. Where the alleged tort arises out of a policy decision, courts will often conclude that the government should be exempted from owing a duty of care to the plaintiff. On the other hand, where the harm arises out of an operational decision or activity, courts are more inclined to impose liability: see, for example, *Gauvin v. Ontario (Ministry of the Environment)* (1995), 22 C.E.L.R. (N.S.) 277 (Ont. Gen. Div.), affirmed (1997), 26 C.E.L.R. (N.S.) 325 (Ont. Div. Ct.), leave to appeal refused 1997 CarswellOnt 1309 (Ont. C.A.), and *Holland v. Saskatchewan (Minister of Agriculture, Food & Rural Revitalization)*, 2008 SCC 42.

The following case involves a class action suit brought by residents of the Ontario town of Port Colborne. As is common for class action suits, the consideration of the substance of the claim was preceded by a prolonged battle over the certification of the class. The final decision dealing with this aspect of the case is *Pearson v. Inco Ltd.* (2005), 20 C.E.L.R. (3d) 258 (Ont. C.A.), additional reasons 20 C.E.L.R. (3d) 292 (Ont. C.A.), leave to appeal refused 2006 CarswellOnt 4020 (S.C.C.). The challenges involved in using class action suits to address environmental harm are discussed in Part III, below. In the claim against Inco with respect to nickel contamination in Port Colborne, the end result of the battles over the certification of the class was that the claimants dropped their claim for human health impacts as a trade-off for achieving certification for the property claim that is the subject of this case. As you read the case, consider the impact the narrowing of the claim during the class certification process had on the ultimate outcome in this case.

Smith v. Inco Ltd.
2011 ONCA 628,
leave to appeal refused [2012] 1 S.C.R. xii (note),
reconsideration/rehearing refused 2014 CarswellOnt 12113 (S.C.C.)

DOHERTY J.A.: — Inco Limited ("Inco") appeals from a judgment rendered after a trial of common issues in a class proceeding. The trial judge found that the soil on the properties of the class members ("claimants"), as represented by the plaintiff, Ms. Ellen Smith, contained nickel particles placed in the soil as a result of emissions generated by Inco's nickel refinery in Port Colborne, Ontario over a 66-year period prior to 1985. The trial judge further held that beginning in 2000 concerns about the levels of nickel in the soil caused wide-spread public concern and adversely affected the appreciation in the value of the properties after September 2000. The trial judge held that Inco was liable in private nuisance and under strict liability imposed by the rule set down in *Rylands v. Fletcher* (1866), L.R. 1 Ex. 265, aff'd (1868), L.R. 3 H.L. 330 for that loss. He fixed damages at $36 million. He rejected a claim for punitive damages and there is no appeal from that part of his disposition.

Inco appeals, raising the following issues:

i.   Did the trial judge err in holding that the discharge of the nickel particles by Inco on to the property of the class members constituted an actionable nuisance?

ii.   Did the trial judge err in holding that Inco was liable for the discharge of the nickel particles under the rule established in *Rylands v. Fletcher*? [...]

Port Colborne is a small city located on the north shore of Lake Erie in southern Ontario. The Welland Canal linking Lake Erie and Lake Ontario cuts through the city. Inco opened a nickel refinery in Port Colborne in 1918. The refinery lies to the east of the Welland Canal. Inco was for many years the major employer in the Port Colborne area, employing as many as 2,000 people. The refinery closed in 1984.

Between 1918 and 1984, Inco emitted waste products including nickel, mostly in the form of nickel oxide, into the air from the 500-foot smoke stack located on its property. The vast majority of the nickel emissions occurred before 1960. None occurred after the closure of the refinery in 1984.

Nickel, consisting mostly of nickel oxide, has been found in widely varying amounts in the soil on many of the properties located within several miles around the Inco refinery. Inco accepts that its refinery is the source of the vast majority of the nickel found in the soil.

It was not alleged that Inco operated its refinery unlawfully or negligently at any time. To the contrary, the evidence indicated that Inco complied with the various environmental and other governmental regulatory schemes applicable to its refinery operation. There was no evidence that the emission levels from the refinery contravened any regulations. Nor did the claimants allege at trial that the presence of the nickel in the soil on their properties posed any immediate or long-term threat to human health.

The Ministry of the Environment ("MOE") has tested the soil on properties in the vicinity of the refinery for nickel and other metals from time to time since the 1970s. The early testing examined the effect of the nickel particles on some kinds of plant life. Many of the tests were conducted in response to complaints primarily from farmers about the effects the emissions had on certain particularly sensitive crops and trees. The early samples revealed widely varying levels of nickel in the soil. There was no suggestion of any threat to human health.

By the late 1990s, MOE had adopted a guideline of 200 parts per million (ppm) for nickel content in soil. That guideline, however, had no connection to any potential health risk posed by the nickel, and was based on levels at which nickel deposits in the soil could possibly adversely affect the most sensitive plant life (ecotoxicity).

In 1997 MOE carried out a Human Health Risk Assessment ("HHRA") based on soil samples taken in 1991. The HHRA Report was published in August 1998. The test results showed levels up to 9,750 ppm. MOE reported that it was unlikely that the nickel levels posed any risks to human health.

In January 2000, MOE released the results of a phytotoxicological study of soil samples taken from 89 different sites. The study showed nickel levels up to 5,000 ppm. The study also showed what were described as "two hot spots" where nickel levels were much higher. One was near the Smith property. MOE took samples from the Smith property and in September 2000, reported that nickel levels found on the property ranged from 4,300 ppm to 14,000 ppm.

The MOE decided that extensive testing should be done in the area immediately to the west of the Inco refinery and the east of the Welland Canal (referred to as the Rodney Street area ("RSA")).

In the fall of 2000 and the spring of 2001, MOE employees took some 2,000 samples from about 200 residential properties in the RSA. They tested for a variety of metals including nickel. In March 2002, MOE released an exhaustive and extensively peer reviewed report. Those test results revealed nickel levels that were higher than those reported in earlier testing. Other metals were also found in the soil at higher than anticipated levels.

Based on the findings in the 2002 report, MOE ordered Inco to remediate the 25 properties, among the 200 properties sampled, where one or more of the soil samples from the property had yielded nickel levels above 8,000 ppm. Remediation involved the removal of soil to a specified level and its replacement with new soil. In its 2002 report, MOE explained the selection of 8,000 ppm as the appropriate level for remediation in these words:

> In this Human Health Risk Assessment, the Ministry considered contaminant exposures from a variety of sources including: indoor and outdoor air; soil and dust; food from the supermarket and home gardens; and, the municipal drinking water supply. *To protect residents, and especially toddlers, the soil nickel intervention level was developed to ensure that all of these nickel exposures did not exceed a value that is well below any potential health risk.* [Emphasis added.]

Inco complied with the MOE order and, by the end of 2004, had remediated 24 of the 25 properties. Ms. Smith, the owner of the remaining property subject to the MOE order, would not allow Inco to remediate her property. As of the date of the trial, she and her family continued to live on the property in its unremediated state.

The class on whose behalf the action is brought consists of all persons who have, since September 2000, owned residential property within an area that takes up most of the city of Port Colborne. There are approximately 7,000 properties, most of which are in the urban part of Port Colborne, but some of which are in the rural area east of the Inco property.

The trial judge divided the class into three subsections based on the geographical location of their property [...]

This lawsuit was commenced in March 2001 shortly after public concerns about the nickel levels emerged. The claims initially advanced on behalf of the class included claims for personal injuries and adverse health effects based on the emission of a wide variety of pollutants including nickel particles. The claims were made against multiple defendants and set out numerous causes of action including negligence. In the months following the commencement of the lawsuit, many statements appeared in the press attributed to counsel for the claimants asserting that MOE studies had established conclusively that the nickel deposits in the soil were carcinogenic and exposed local residents to "serious health risks", including a risk of cancer "at least eight and possibly 40 times higher than the standards set by the Ontario government".

By the time the action reached trial, Inco was the only defendant and the only claim left related exclusively to property values. Allegations that the nickel deposits were carcinogenic or in any way harmful to the health of the residents had been abandoned.

The claimants alleged that their property values had not increased at the same rate as comparable property values in other small cities located nearby. The class contended that the failure to keep up with increases in comparable properties was caused by the reasonable, widespread public health concerns over the nickel deposits in the soil on their properties. According to the claimants, these concerns became prominent and widespread beginning in the fall of 2000 when soil samples taken from properties in the RSA revealed higher than expected levels of nickel in the soil. The claimants alleged that the facts gave rise to claims in nuisance, both public and private, trespass and under the strict liability doctrine in *Rylands v. Fletcher*.

The trial judge found against the claimants on the trespass claim and the public nuisance claim. There is no cross-appeal from those findings and we need not address those claims in these reasons.

It is important to emphasize the exact nature of the claim advanced at trial. It was not about contamination in the sense that it was alleged that the nickel emissions actually posed any threat to human health or otherwise adversely affected the claimants' use of their properties. The emissions had streamed from Inco's refinery for over 60 years. Everyone could see the smoke coming from the 500-foot stack on a daily basis. Common sense told everyone that nickel in some form must have been among the contaminants in the smoke. As Mrs. Smith testified, common sense would also tell anyone that some of the contaminants, including nickel, would eventually find their way into the soil of the properties around the refinery. On the claimants' case as it was ultimately presented, however, the emissions from the refinery did not give rise to any cause of action. The claims first arose long after the smoke stopped blowing from the Inco refinery.

On the claims as advanced at trial, it was concerns about the possible adverse health effects of the nickel in the soil that developed some 15 years after the refinery closed that gave rise to several causes of action against Inco. Ironically, those concerns that began with MOE's report of higher than previously recorded levels of nickel in the soil, were fuelled in part by the very serious, but subsequently abandoned, allegations made by the claimants' counsel in the months following the commencement of this lawsuit in March 2001. In those allegations, the nickel particles in the soil were said by counsel to have been shown by MOE to be carcinogenic and to pose serious health risks to the residents.

The claims rested on six assertions:

(1) The refinery emitted nickel particles for 66 years.

(2) Over the 66 years, nickel particles, primarily in the form of nickel oxide, made their way into the soil on the claimants' properties and became part of that soil. The vast majority of the nickel in the soil came from the refinery.

(3) Until 2000, while there were isolated complaints mostly about plant life contamination, there were no significant public health concerns associated with the nickel levels in the soil on the properties around the refinery.

(4) Beginning in early 2000 and continuing thereafter, as soil samplings revealed higher levels of nickel in the soil of many properties than had previously been recorded, widespread concerns about the potential health effects of those nickel deposits developed in the community and became a matter of widespread public concern and controversy.

(5) Those concerns caused a measurable negative effect on the value of properties owned by the claimants. After 2000, property values increased less than they would have but for the negative publicity surrounding the potential nickel contamination of the properties.

(6) The negative effect on the values of the properties could be quantified by comparing the increase in the property values on the claimants' properties with the larger increases in the values of similar properties in the nearby city of Welland during the same time period (1997–2008). [...]

Private Nuisance

People do not live in splendid isolation from one another. One person's lawful and reasonable use of his or her property may indirectly harm the property of another or interfere with that person's ability to fully use and enjoy his or her property. The common law of nuisance developed as a means by which those competing interests could be addressed, and one given legal priority over the other. Under the common law of nuisance, sometimes the person whose property suffered the adverse effects is expected to tolerate those effects as the price of membership in the larger community. Sometimes, however, the party causing the adverse effect can be compelled, even if his or her conduct is lawful and reasonable, to desist from engaging in that conduct and to compensate the other party for any harm caused to that person's property. In essence, the common law of nuisance decided which party's interest must give way. That determination is made by asking whether in all the circumstances the harm caused or the interference done to one person's property by the other person's use of his or her property is unreasonable: *Royal Anne Hotel Co. Ltd. v. Village of Ashcroft* (1979), 95 D.L.R. (3d) 756 (B.C.C.A.), at pp. 760-61.

The reasonableness inquiry focuses on the effect of the defendant's conduct on the property rights of the plaintiff. Nuisance, unlike negligence, does not focus on or characterize the defendant's conduct. The defendant's conduct may be reasonable and yet result in an unreasonable interference with the plaintiff's property rights. The characterization of the defendant's conduct is relevant only to the extent that it impacts on the proper characterization of the nature of the interference with the plaintiff's property rights: *Antrim Truck Centre Ltd. v. Ontario (Ministry of Transportation)* (2011), 106 O.R. (3d) 81 (C.A.), at para. 77; John Murphy, *Street on Torts*, 12th ed. (Oxford: Oxford University Press, 2007), at pp. 420, 431, 435.

In *St. Pierre v. Ontario (Minister of Transportation and Communication)*, [1987] 1 S.C.R. 906, at para. 10, McIntyre J. for the court, accepted as a working definition of private nuisance, the definition found in an earlier edition of *Street on Torts*:

> A person, then, may be said to have committed the tort of private nuisance when *he is held to be responsible for an act indirectly causing physical injury to land or substantially interfering with the use or enjoyment of land or of an interest in land, where, in the light of all the surrounding circumstances, this injury or interference is held to be unreasonable.* [Emphasis added.]

As evident from the definition relied on in *St. Pierre*, while all nuisance is a tort against land predicated on an indirect interference with the plaintiff's property rights, that interference can take two quite different forms. The interference may be in the nature of "physical injury to land" or it may take the form of substantial interference with the plaintiff's use or enjoyment of his or her land. The latter form of nuisance, sometimes described as "amenity nuisance" is not alleged here: see *Street on Torts* at p. 429; *The Law of Nuisance in Canada* at pp. 69-71; Conor Gearty, "The Place of Private Nuisance in a Modern Law of Torts" [1989] Cambridge L.J. 214.

The claimants do not argue that the nickel particles in the soil caused any interference with their use or enjoyment of their property. Instead, they claim that the nickel particles caused "physical injury" to their property. That physical injury was the product of the nickel particles becoming part of the soil and the subsequent adverse effect on the value of the property because of the public concerns over the potential health consequences of those particles being in the soil.

The courts have taken a somewhat different approach to nuisance claims predicated on physical damage to property and those claims based on amenity or nonphysical nuisance. Where amenity nuisance is alleged, the reasonableness of the interference with the plaintiff's property is measured by balancing certain competing factors, including the nature of the interference and the character of the locale in which that interference occurred. Where the nuisance is said to have produced physical damage to land, that damage is taken as an unreasonable interference without the balancing of competing factors. The distinction first appeared some 150 years ago in *St. Helen's Smelting Co. v. Tipping* (1865), 11 H.L.C. 642, at pp. 650-51:

> My Lords, in matters of this description it appears to me that it is a very desirable thing to mark the difference between an action brought for a nuisance upon the ground that the alleged nuisance produces material injury to the property, and an action brought for a nuisance on the ground that the thing alleged to be a nuisance is productive of sensible personal discomfort. *With regard to the latter, namely, the personal inconvenience and interference with one's enjoyment, one's quiet, one's personal freedom, anything that discomposes or injuriously affects the senses or the nerves, whether that may or may not be denominated a nuisance, must undoubtedly depend greatly on the circumstances of the place where the thing complained of*

actually occurs. If a man lives in a town, it is necessary that he should subject himself to the consequences of those operations of trade which may be carried on in his immediate locality, which are actually necessary for trade and commerce, and also for the enjoyment of property, and for the benefit of the inhabitants of the town and of the public at large. If a man lives in a street where there are numerous shops, and a shop is opened next door to him, which is carried on in a fair and reasonable way, he has no ground for complaint, because to himself individually there may arise much discomfort from the trade carried on in that shop. *But when an occupation is carried on by one person in a neighbourhood of another, and the result of that trade, or occupation, or business, is a material injury to property, then there unquestionably arises a very different consideration. I think, my Lords, that in a case of that description, the submission which is required from persons living in society to that amount of discomfort which may be necessary for the legitimate and free exercise of the trade of their neighbours, would not apply to circumstances the immediate result of which is sensible injury to the value of the property.* [Emphasis added.]

The distinction drawn in *St. Helen's Smelting Co.* perhaps reflects the real property origins of the tort of nuisance and the priority and status attached by the common law to land ownership and one's right to physical dominion over one's land: see John Murphy, "The Merits of *Rylands v. Fletcher*" (2004) 24 Oxford J. Legal Stud. 643, at p. 649. The give and take required between neighbours called for the balancing of potentially competing factors where the actions of one interfered with another's enjoyment of his or her property. The spirit of give and take could not, however, go so far as to require one to countenance actual and material physical harm to his or her property. [...]

There is, however, relatively recent *dicta* suggesting that there may be some role for the balancing of competing factors even where the nuisance takes the form of actual physical damage to land: see *Tock v. St. John's Metropolitan Area Board*, [1989] 2 S.C.R. 1181, at p. 1192; *Royal Anne Hotel Co. Ltd.* at p. 761. The difficulty that sometimes arises in distinguishing between what constitutes amenity nuisance and nuisance based on physical damage to land suggests that a uniform approach to nuisance claims allowing a court to balance competing factors, although perhaps weighing them differently depending on the nature of the interference alleged, may be preferable. We need not decide that issue. We approach this ground of appeal on the basis that the claimants are correct in contending that competing factors cannot be balanced where the nuisance involves actual physical damage to the claimants' lands. [...]

Material damage refers to damage that is substantial in the sense that it is more than trivial: *St. Lawrence Cement Inc. v. Barrette*, [2008] 3 S.C.R. 392, at para. 77. Actual damage refers to damage that has occurred and is not merely potential damage that may or may not occur at some future point: *Walker v. McKinnon Industries Ltd.* at pp. 558-59. Damage that is readily ascertainable refers to damage that can be observed or measured and is not so minimal or incremental as to be unnoticeable as it occurs. We do agree, however, with counsel for the claimants that the damage may be readily ascertainable even if it is not visible to the naked eye and does not produce some visibly noticeable change in the property. In our view, a change in the chemical composition of the soil measurable through established scientific techniques would constitute a readily ascertainable change in the soil: see *Gaunt v. Fynney* (1872), L.R. 8 Ch. App. 8. For the reasons we will develop below, the claimants' problem is not with the ascertainability of the change caused by the nickel particles, but with the characterization of that change as damage or harm to the property. [...]

With respect to the trial judge's reasons and Mr. Baert's submissions, we think the trial judge erred in finding that the nickel particles in the soil caused actual, substantial, physical damage to the claimants' lands. In our view, a mere chemical alteration in the content of soil, without more, does not amount to physical harm or damage to the property. For instance, many farmers add fertilizer to their soil each year for the purpose of changing, and enhancing, the chemical composition of the soil. To constitute physical harm or damage, a change in the chemical composition must be shown to have had some detrimental effect on the land itself or rights associated with the use of the land. For example, in *Russell Transport Limited*, the authority relied on by the claimants, it was not the mere emission of the iron oxide particles onto the plaintiff's property that constituted the nuisance. McRuer C.J.H.C. said, at pp. 625-26:

> The irresistible conclusion on the evidence is, and *I so find, that the defendant emits from its plant particles of iron and iron oxide together with other matters which settle on the plaintiffs' lands, rendering the plaintiffs' property unfit for the purpose for which it was purchased and developed.* The plaintiffs have therefore suffered and will continue to suffer material and substantial damage to their property unless the emission of injurious substances is abated. [Emphasis added.]

The Chief Justice's finding that the particles rendered "the plaintiffs' property unfit for the purpose for which it was purchased and developed" clearly distinguishes *Russell Transport Limited* from this case. The claimants cannot show, and indeed did not attempt to show, that the nickel particles in the soil had any impact on their ability to use their properties for any purpose.

Where the nuisance is said to flow from the physical harm to land caused by the contamination of that land, the claimants must show that the alleged contaminant in the soil had some detrimental effect on the land or its use by its owners. In this case, potential health concerns were the only basis upon which it could be said that the nickel particles harmed the land of the claimants. It was incumbent on the claimants to show that the nickel particles caused actual harm to the health of the claimants or at least posed some realistic risk of actual harm to their health and wellbeing. The authors of *The Law of Nuisance in Canada*, at p. 85, although in a somewhat different context, aptly describe the nature of the harm the claimants had to prove:

> It is true that private nuisance is predicated on harm to the plaintiff's property rights; but surely *one of those rights must be the right to occupy the property without harm to one's health or even at the risk of one's life.* This is particularly necessary for residential property, where the heart of the property interest stems from the desire to live on the property. *Private nuisance vindicates the bundle of rights associated with one's property, and the right to live on one's land without risk to life or health must be a right in that bundle.* Additionally, the 'health' aspect of the bundle of rights that are protected by nuisance law has been noted in several cases. [Emphasis added.]

The approach followed by the trial judge effectively removes any need to show that Inco's operation of its refinery caused any harm of any kind to the claimants' land. It extends the tort of private nuisance beyond claims based on substantial actual injury to another's land to claims based on concerns, no matter when they develop and no matter how valid, that there may have been substantial actual injury caused to another's land. On this approach, nuisance operates as an inchoate tort hanging over a property to become actionable, not by virtue of anything done to the property by the defendant, but because of public concerns generated many years after the relevant events about the possible effect of the defendant's conduct on the property.

In holding that actual, substantial, physical damage to the claimants' land required proof that the nickel particles posed at least some risk to the claimants' health and wellbeing, we do not mean that the trial judge was obliged to accept the MOE finding as to the level of nickel in the soil that required remediation as the applicable standard. The trial judge said, at para. 86:

> MOE did not set a standard for civil liability when it set the intervention level for nickel in the soil at 8,000 ppm.

We agree with this observation: see *Tridan Developments Ltd.* at paras. 10-12. However, the claimants had to show either that nickel at any level posed a risk, or that the nickel levels present in the soil were above levels at which there was a risk to human health and wellbeing. The MOE standard of 8,000 ppm said by MOE to be "well below any potential health risk" was the only post-2000 standard offered in the evidence.

The claimants did not join issue on the level at which nickel particles could be said to pose a risk to human health and wellbeing, but instead argued that concerns about potential risks were in and of themselves sufficient to make Inco's conduct an actionable nuisance if those concerns affected property values. This strategy no doubt reflected the reality that the level of nickel particles in the soil of the vast majority of the 7,000 properties covered by the class action were well below anything that could possibly be regarded as posing a health risk.

The extent to which the trial judge divorced actual, substantial, physical damage to the land from liability for nuisance is evident by considering a variation in the facts as actually found at trial. On the trial judge's analysis, even if the concerns which arose after 2000 were totally unfounded and were ultimately shown to be based on "junk science", Inco would still be liable in nuisance assuming those totally unfounded public concerns generated the same impact on property values.

The trial judge's analysis of nuisance raises a further anomaly. The primary *raison d'être* of nuisance is to equip a party who is suffering damage to his land or interference with his use of the land with a means of forcing the party causing that damage to stop doing so. However, on the trial judge's reasoning, the claimants would have had no basis upon which to gain any injunctive relief against Inco when it was operating the refinery up to 1985. As the trial judge analyzes the claim, a person seeking an injunction prior to 1985 would have no basis upon which to argue that Inco's actions caused any actual, substantial, physical damage to the land. It is inconsistent with the essential nature of nuisance as an interference with property to hold that Inco was not engaged in any interference with property when it operated the refinery and emitted the particles, but that it was engaged in an actionable nuisance 15 years after it stopped operating the refinery, when concerns were raised from a variety of sources about the potential health effects of the nickel in the soil and the property values were negatively affected as a result of those concerns.

This conceptual anomaly cannot be explained by reference to discoverability principles. The trial judge did not find that the nuisance occurred when the particles were deposited in the soil, but was only discovered when the claimants learned of the levels of nickel particles in the soil in 2000: *e.g.* see *Cambridge Water Co. v. Eastern Counties Leather Plc.*, [1994] 2 A.C. 264 (H.L.), at pp. 291-94. As outlined above, the levels of nickel deposits in the soil had nothing to do with the trial judge's finding that Inco was liable in nuisance. The trial judge made it clear that the significant damage to the claimants' properties relied on by him to establish the cause of action in nuisance did not occur until after 2000, and occurred then because of the public concerns about potential health issues that arose and not because of the actual levels of nickel in the soil. Discovery principles had nothing to do with the trial judge's finding that the claimants could rely on public concerns generated in 2000 and beyond to render substantial the physical damage to the property said to have occurred 15 years earlier when the particles worked their way into the claimants' lands. On his analysis, the material physical damage to the land was not merely discovered after 2000. It occurred after 2000.

Tridan Developments Ltd. does not assist the claimants. In *Tridan*, the defendants admitted liability for nuisance when a gas spill on their property contaminated the property of the neighbour. *Tridan* was about the quantification of the damages suffered by the plaintiff. Nothing in *Tridan* lends support to the trial judge's holding that public concerns about the potential harm done to the properties affecting the value of the properties could constitute substantial physical harm to the land for the purposes of a nuisance claim.

In our view, actual, substantial, physical damage to the land in the context of this case refers to nickel levels that at least posed some risk to the health or wellbeing of the residents of those properties. Evidence that the existence of the nickel particles in the soil generated concerns about potential health risks does not, in our view, amount to evidence that the presence of the particles in the soil caused actual, substantial harm or damage to the property. The claimants failed to establish actual, substantial, physical damage to their properties as a result of the nickel particles becoming part of the soil. Without actual, substantial, physical harm, the nuisance claim as framed by the claimants could not succeed.

Rylands v. Fletcher?

The rule in *Rylands v. Fletcher* imposes strict liability for damages caused to a plaintiff's property (and probably, in Canada, for personal damages) by the escape from the defendant's property of a substance "likely to cause mischief". The exact reach of the rule and the justification for its continued existence as a basis of liability apart from negligence, private nuisance and statutory liability have been matters of controversy in some jurisdictions: see *Transco plc v. Stockport Metropolitan Borough Council*, [2004] 2 A.C. 1 (H.L.); *Burnie Port Authority v. General Jones Pty. Ltd.* (1994), 179 C.L.R. 520 (Aust. H.C.); Murphy, "The Merits of *Rylands v. Fletcher*". In Canada, *Rylands v. Fletcher* has gone largely unnoticed in appellate courts in recent years. However, in 1989 in *Tock*, the Supreme Court of Canada unanimously recognized *Rylands v. Fletcher* as continuing to provide a basis for liability distinct from liability for private nuisance or negligence.

The language used by Mr. Justice Blackburn in *Rylands v. Fletcher* at pp. 279-80 (Ex. Ch.) suggested a broad basis for the imposition of strict liability. His Lordship spoke of strict liability for any damages caused as a result of the escape from the defendant's land of something brought on to that land by the defendant, for his or her own purposes, that was likely to do damage if it escaped from the defendant's property: see also the comments of Lord Cranworth at p. 340 (H.L.). Subsequent descriptions of the scope of the strict liability rule described in *Rylands v. Fletcher*, including that provided by Lord Cairns in *Rylands v. Fletcher* at p. 339 (H.L.), describe a narrower basis for the imposition of strict liability. Lord Cairns introduced the concept of "non-natural use" of property as a precondition to the imposition of strict liability. Later cases used words like "special", "unusual" or "extraordinary" to describe the use of the property: see *Transco plc v. Stockport Metropolitan Borough Council*, per Lord Bingham at para. 11, per Lord Hoffmann at paras. 44-45, per Lord Scott at paras. 81-85; *Rickards v. Lothian*, [1913] A.C. 263 (H.L.), at p. 280; Andrew Waite, "Deconstructing the Rule in *Rylands v. Fletcher*" (2006) 18 J. Envtl. L. 423.

The meaning of "non-natural use" of property has vexed lawyers and judges since the phrase was penned by Lord Cairns. Its uncertainty and vagueness led the High Court of Australia to abandon the rule entirely in favour of a negligence standard that took into account the dangerous nature of the activity in issue: *Burnie Port Authority v. General Jones Pty. Ltd.* at p. 540. In Canada, apart from some description of the "non-natural use" requirement found in *Tock*, appellate courts have paid no attention to the details of the rule much less the more fundamental question of the need for its continued existence. Inco does not suggest that the rule should be abrogated. It does, however, argue that it was misapplied in this case.

There are various formulations of the rule found in the case law and the academic commentary. The authors of *The Law of Nuisance in Canada* suggest different potential formulations, including one, at p. 113, that requires four prerequisites to the operation of the rule:

- the defendant made a "non-natural" or "special" use of his land;
- the defendant brought on to his land something that was likely to do mischief if it escaped;
- the substance in question in fact escaped; and
- damage was caused to the plaintiff's property as a result of the escape. [...]

The trial judge, at para. 65, [...] adopted a portion of the following passage from Allen M. Linden and Bruce Feldthusen, *Canadian Tort Law*, 8th ed. (Markham, Ont.: LexisNexis Butterworths, 2006), at pp. 540-41:

> Occasionally, language appears in a *Rylands v. Fletcher* decision that furnishes a glimpse of a *new basis of strict liability, free of the historic restraints of non-natural use, escape and mischief*. This emerging theory can be termed strict liability for abnormally dangerous activities. *Pursuant to this principle, there are a limited number of activities so fraught with abnormal risk for the community that the negligence standard is felt to provide insufficient protection against them.* Consequently, these

abnormally risky or extra-hazardous activities should be governed by a stricter form of liability that insists on compensation for all losses they generate, even when they are conducted with reasonable care. [...]

In other words, there are two general types of activities which are regulated by two different theories of tort liability. Firstly, there are ordinary pursuits that create normal risks, which are controlled by negligence law. Secondly, there are *other* *"types of conduct which, although they cannot be styled wrongful, are either so fraught* *with danger, or so unusual in a given community, that it is felt that the risk of loss* *should be shifted from the person injured to the person who merely by engaging in such* *conduct, created the risk which resulted in harm"*. [Emphasis added.]

The strict liability theory favoured by Linden and Feldthusen (and others, for example, see *Restatement of Torts* (2d), ss. 519, 520) is considerably broader than the strict liability rule under *Rylands v. Fletcher*. Under their theory, it is not necessary that the dangerous substance "escape" from the defendant's property or that the use of the defendant's land be characterized as "special" or "non-natural". Strict liability flows entirely from the nature of the activity conducted by the defendant. Linden and Feldthusen acknowledge that the theory of strict liability they present goes beyond *Rylands v. Fletcher*. According to them, support for their theory "lies hidden in the cases waiting to be openly embraced by Canadian courts": *Canadian Tort Law*, 9th ed. at p. 556.

We do not accept that strict liability based exclusively on the "extra hazardous" nature of the defendant's conduct is or should be part of the common law in this province. Before we explain why we reach that conclusion, we will, however, examine Inco's liability on the assumption that the trial judge was correct in viewing *Rylands v. Fletcher* as imposing strict liability for damages caused by "extra hazardous" activities. In our view, there is no basis in the evidence upon which Inco's refinery operations or its emissions of nickel particles could properly be described as "extra hazardous" or "fraught with danger".

The trial judge did not explain why he concluded that Inco's refinery operation fell within the category of "extra hazardous" activities that should attract strict liability. Nor did he explain why the nickel particle emissions posed "an abnormal risk of harm" to others' properties. The trial judge acknowledged that the nickel emissions were not *per se* dangerous (para. 54). On the evidence, the emissions posed no health risk to anyone (except perhaps in those relatively few instances where there was a small risk of harm to health before the soil was remediated). Nor did the nickel particles cause any damage to the soil or have any effect on the claimants' ability to use their properties. We see no evidence that Inco, in operating a refinery in accordance with the various regulatory regimes, presented an "abnormal risk" to its neighbours.

It may be that the trial judge inferred that the operation of the refinery presented "an abnormal risk of harm" because, in his view, that operation ultimately led to a diminution in property values. Putting the claimants' case at its highest, they alleged that the nickel particles placed in the soil up to 1984, combined with public health concerns, ultimately not validated, that arose in 2000 and beyond, caused a relatively small decrease in the appreciation of the value of the claimants' properties over a 10-year period beginning in 2000. Even if this harm is causally related to the refinery operation and the nickel particle emissions, it could not justify describing the refinery operation or the emissions as so inherently dangerous as to merit the imposition of strict liability based exclusively on the hazardous nature of the operation and the abnormal risk presented to others by that operation.

Even if strict liability for ultra hazardous activities, either as a freestanding basis for liability or a modification of *Rylands v. Fletcher,* were part of the law in Ontario, the claimants failed to prove that Inco's refinery constituted an "extra hazardous" activity.

Returning to the merits of the strict liability theory adopted by the trial judge, we begin by distinguishing the risk that is targeted by that theory from the risk targeted by the rule in *Rylands v. Fletcher.* Strict liability under *Rylands v. Fletcher* aims not at all risks associated with carrying out an activity, but rather with the risk associated with the accidental and unintended consequences of engaging in an activity. The *Rylands v. Fletcher* cases are about floods, gas leaks, chemical spills, sewage overflows, fires and the like. They hold that where the defendant engages in certain kinds of activities, the defendant will be held strictly liable for damages that flow from mishaps or misadventures that occur in the course of that activity. The escape requirement in *Rylands v. Fletcher* connotes something unintended and speaks to the nature of the risk to which the strict liability in *Rylands v. Fletcher* attaches: see *The Law of Nuisance in Canada* at pp. 132, 137.

The "extra hazardous" risk-based strict liability theory employed by the trial judge holds a defendant strictly liable for all damages associated with the activity. The defendant is liable for damages even if they are not the product of any accident or misadventure, but are instead the product of the intended consequences of the activity.

The two risks described above are quite different. The risk addressed in *Rylands v. Fletcher* is a more limited one, imposing strict liability for things that go wrong and produce unintended consequences that damage the property (or perhaps the person) of another. The trial judge overstated the rationale for *Rylands v. Fletcher* strict liability when he described it as applicable to damages caused by activities which create "an abnormal risk of harm".

There are, of course, policy arguments in favour of the imposition of strict liability where activities create "extra hazardous" risks. Examples of that kind of liability can be found in various statutes, such as the *Environmental Protection Act*, R.S.O. 1990, c. E.19, s. 99. The question is whether the courts, through a modification of the common law and in particular the rule in *Rylands v. Fletcher*, should impose that strict liability on all activities that are found to fit within a necessarily broad and generic description, or leave it to the various Legislatures to make that decision through appropriate statutory enactments applicable to specific activities.

The House of Lords has rejected any attempt to judicially extend *Rylands v. Fletcher* strict liability to all hazardous activities: see *Read v. J. Lyons and Co. Limited,* [1947] A.C. 156 (H.L.), per Lord Macmillan at pp. 172-73, per Lord Simonds at pp. 181-82; *Transco plc,* per Lord Bingham at para. 7; Donal Nolan, "The Distinctiveness of *Rylands v. Fletcher*" (2005) 121 Law Q. Rev. 421, at pp. 447-449.

In *Cambridge Water Co.* at p. 305, Lord Goff offered a compelling argument, which we accept, in favour of leaving to Parliament the decision to impose strict liability based exclusively on the nature of the activity:

Like the judge in the present case, I incline to the opinion that, *as a general rule, it is more appropriate for strict liability in respect of operations of high risk to be imposed by Parliament, than by the courts.* If such liability is imposed by statute, the relevant activities can be identified, and those concerned can know where they stand. Furthermore, statute can where appropriate lay down precise criteria establishing the incidents and scope of such liability.

It is of particular relevance that the present case is concerned with environmental pollution. The protection and preservation of the environment is now perceived as being of crucial importance to the future of mankind; and public bodies, both national and international, are taking significant steps toward the establishment of legislation which will promote the protection of the environment and make the polluter pay for damage to the environment for which he is responsible — as can be seen from the W.H.O., E.E.C. and national regulations to which I have previously referred. *But it does not follow from these developments that a common principle, such as the rule in Rylands v. Fletcher, should be developed or rendered more strict to provide for liability in respect of such pollution. On the contrary, given that so much well-informed and carefully structured legislation is now being put in place for this purpose, there is less need for the courts to develop a common law principle to achieve the same end, and indeed it may well be undesirable that they should do so.* [Emphasis added.]

More importantly, the expansion of strict liability under the banner of *Rylands v. Fletcher* to damages flowing from all hazardous activities is inconsistent with the description of the rule in *Rylands v. Fletcher* found in *Tock.* In *Tock*, a sewage system operated by the defendant failed after an exceptionally heavy rainfall. A large amount of water flooded the plaintiff's basement causing extensive damage. The flooding was caused by a blockage in the sewage system.

La Forest J., speaking for the entire court on this point, found that the operation of a sewage system under statutory authority was not a land use that could possibly give rise to strict liability for damages under *Rylands v. Fletcher.* Counsel for the claimants correctly point out that the *ratio* of *Tock* is narrow and does not assist Inco. Inco was not acting under any statutory authority. Nor was Inco engaged in an enterprise intended for the general benefit of the community.

However, Justice La Forest's description of the nature of the liability contemplated under *Rylands v. Fletcher* does assist Inco in that it forecloses any notion of strict liability based exclusively on whether the activity carried out by the defendant was abnormally hazardous. At para. 10 of *Tock,* La Forest J. adopted the language of Moulton L.J. in *Rickards v. Lothien* at p. 280:

It is not every use to which land is put that brings into play that principle [*Rylands v. Fletcher*]. It must be some special use bringing with it increased danger to others and must not merely be the ordinary use of the land or such a use as is proper for the general benefit of the community.

La Forest J. viewed the "non-natural user" component of the *Rylands v. Fletcher* rule as providing flexibility that would allow the rule to adjust to changing patterns in society. Those patterns were reflected in various levels of government regulation designed to control how and where various activities could be conducted: *Tock* at paras.11-12. *Tock* does not measure the reach of strict liability under *Rylands v. Fletcher* exclusively by reference to the risk presented by the activity. As La Forest J. said, at para. 13:

[T]he touchstone for the application of the rule in *Rylands v. Fletcher* is *to be damage occurring from a user inappropriate to the place where it is maintained* (Prosser cites the example of the pig in the parlour). [Emphasis added.]

The judgment in *Tock* forecloses treating strict liability under *Rylands v. Fletcher* as referable to all "ultra hazardous" activities. As explained in *Tock*, the rule is triggered by "a user inappropriate to the place". The appropriateness of a use depends on factors that include, but are not limited to, the risk posed by the use.

There are no doubt strong arguments for imposing strict liability on certain inherently dangerous activities. In our view, however, that is fundamentally a policy decision that is best introduced by legislative action and not judicial fiat. In declining to take the bold step advocated by Linden and Feldthusen, we observe that those who engage in dangerous activities are, of course, subject to negligence actions under which the dangerousness of the activity would be reflected in the standard of care required, nuisance actions, and in ever increasing situations, detailed and sometimes punitive statutory regimes.

Having concluded there is no common law rule imposing strict liability on those whose activities are said to be "ultra hazardous" and that even if there were, Inco's refinery was not shown to be an ultra hazardous activity, we turn to a measure of the claim against the specific criteria that have been developed in the *Rylands v. Fletcher* case law.

Inco operated a refinery on its property. The nickel emissions were part and parcel of that refinery operation and were not in any sense an independent use of the property. The use of the property to which the *Rylands v. Fletcher* inquiry must be directed is its use as a refinery. The nickel emissions are a feature or facet of the use of the property as a refinery. The question must be — was the operation of the refinery at the time and place and in the manner that it was operated a non-natural use of Inco's property?: see *Gertsen v. Municipality of Metropolitan Toronto* (1973), 2 O.R. (2d) 1 (H.C.), at pp. 19-20; David W. Williams, "Non-Natural Use of Land" (1973) 32 Cambridge L.J. 310, at pp. 314-21.

The trial judge found that Inco's use of the property was a non-natural use because it brought the nickel on to the property. If the characterization of a use as a non-natural one was ever tied solely to whether the substance was found naturally on the property, it has long since ceased to depend on the answer to that single question. It may be that something found naturally on the property cannot attract liability under *Rylands v. Fletcher*. It is not, however, the law that anything that is not found naturally on the property can be subject to strict liability under *Rylands v. Fletcher* if it escapes and causes damage. The disconnect between things found in nature on the property and the potential application of *Rylands v. Fletcher* is so complete that the House of Lords has abandoned the use of the phrase "non-natural use" as misleading in favour of the phrase "ordinary use": *Transco plc* at paras. 11-12.

The emphasis in *Tock* at para. 13 on a "user inappropriate to the place" and, at para. 10, to "changing patterns of existence" demonstrate that the distinction between natural and non-natural use cannot be made exclusively by reference to the origin of the substance in issue. To decide whether a use is a non-natural one, the court must have regard to the place where the use is made, the time when the use is made, and the manner of the use. Planning legislation and other government regulations controlling where, when and how activities can be carried out will be relevant considerations in assessing whether a particular use is a non-natural use in the sense that it is a use that is not ordinary.

The approach to non-natural user taken in *Tock* and in *Cambridge Water Co.* restricts those situations in which *Rylands v. Fletcher* applies. The non-natural use requirement of the *Rylands v. Fletcher* rule serves a similar role to the "give and take between neighbours" principle that is applied when determining whether one person's interference with another person's use and enjoyment of his property constitutes an actionable nuisance. Like the reasonable user inquiry in cases involving amenity nuisance, the non-natural user inquiry seeks to distinguish between those uses of property that the community as a whole should accept and tolerate and those uses where the burden associated with accidental and unintended consequences of the use should fall on the user. The nature and degree of the risk inherent in the use is obviously an important feature of this inquiry, but as *Tock* demonstrates, it is not the entire inquiry: see *Cambridge Water Co.* at pp. 299-300.

In addition to finding that Inco's use of the property was a non-natural use because it brought the nickel on to the property, the trial judge described the refinery "as bringing with it increased danger to others". He did not identify that danger. Finally, although the trial judge referred to Inco's argument that it complied with all environmental and zoning regulations, he dismissed that argument on the basis that a use could be reasonable and lawful and still not constitute a natural use.

We agree that compliance with various environmental and zoning regulations is not a defence to a *Rylands v. Fletcher* claim. In our view, however, compliance is an important consideration in light of the approach to non-natural user taken in *Tock*. The trial judge appears to have dismissed entirely Inco's compliance with the relevant regulations and zoning laws once he concluded that Inco's compliance was not determinative of the *Rylands v. Fletcher* claim in Inco's favour.

The claimants bore the onus of showing that the operation of the refinery was a non-natural use of the property in the sense that it was not an ordinary or usual use. In *Transco plc*, Lord Bingham, at para. 11, suggests the following inquiry:

> An occupier of land who can show that another occupier of land has brought or kept on his land an exceptionally dangerous or mischievous thing in extraordinary or unusual circumstances is in my opinion entitled to recover compensation from that occupier for any damage caused to his property interest by the escape of that thing subject to defences ...

Lord Bingham's inquiry is directed both at the degree of dangerousness posed by the activity and the circumstances surrounding the activity. We think that approach is consistent with the "user appropriate" approach in *Tock*.

Any industrial activity, and perhaps even more so a refinery, certainly carries with it the potential to do significant damage to surrounding properties if something goes awry. The claimants did not, however, in our view, demonstrate that Inco's operation of its refinery for over 60 years presented "an exceptionally dangerous or mischievous thing" or that the circumstances were "extraordinary or unusual". To the contrary, the evidence suggests that Inco operated a refinery in a heavily industrialized part of the city in a manner that was ordinary and usual and did not create risks beyond those incidental to virtually any industrial operation. In our view, the claimants failed to establish that Inco's operation of its refinery was a non-natural use of its property.

Although we have accepted Inco's submission that the refinery was not a non-natural use, we would not want to be taken as agreeing with its submission that the refinery operated "for the general benefit of the community" and could not, therefore, be subject to strict liability under *Rylands v. Fletcher*: see *Rickards v. Lothian* at p. 280. While Inco's refinery no doubt brought significant economic benefit to Port Colborne, Inco did not operate its refinery for the general benefit of the community. That phrase refers to entities, usually governmental ones, acting under statutory authority and engaged in activities that benefit the community or at least a significant segment of the community at large. The incidental benefit to the community flowing from the operation of the Inco refinery does not bring it within the phrase "for the general benefit of the community": see *Transco plc*, per Lord Bingham at para. 11.

Our conclusion that the trial judge erred in finding that Inco's operation of its refinery constituted a non-natural use of its property is sufficient to find in Inco's favour on this ground of appeal. We will, however, briefly consider two other issues that arise under the *Rylands v. Fletcher* claim.

The trial judge, at para. 58, observed:

> In England, unlike Ontario, the courts have added a foreseeability element to the rule in *Rylands v. Fletcher*. *Inco*, in its factum, asserts, albeit by way of a footnote only, that foreseeability is a requirement under *Rylands v. Fletcher*.

Neither the trial judge nor Inco explained what they meant by foreseeability in this context. The role, if any, of foreseeability of damages under the rule in *Rylands v. Fletcher* is an important jurisprudential question. To our knowledge, neither the Supreme Court of Canada nor any provincial appellate court has examined whether foreseeability of damages is an element of liability under *Rylands v. Fletcher*. We do not propose to decide the issue in the absence of full argument.

We will, however, make two observations that may be of assistance in future cases. First, foreseeability can refer to objective foreseeability of the escape from the defendant's land of the thing that causes damage or it can refer to objective foreseeability of the kind of damage said to have been caused. We see no reason to require foreseeability of the escape. To impose that requirement would all but merge the rule in *Rylands v. Fletcher* with liability in negligence.

There are, however, compelling reasons to require foreseeability of the kind of damages alleged to have been suffered by the plaintiffs. The arguments in favour of requiring foreseeability in that sense are fully articulated by Lord Goff in *Cambridge Water Co.* at pp. 301-306. If Lord Goff's views were applied to this case, the foreseeability of a diminution in the appreciation of the value of the claimants' properties some 15 years after the refinery closed, would be a live issue.

The second issue, which we will address briefly, concerns the escape component of the rule in *Rylands v. Fletcher*. That component raises two questions. First, we agree with the trial judge that *Rylands v. Fletcher* should not be limited to a single isolated escape. In some situations, the danger posed by the escape rests in the repeated and cumulative effect of the movement of a substance from the defendant's property to the property of others. The escape may go on for months or even years and the damage may not be caused until the accumulation of the escaping substance reaches certain destinations or accumulations. Assuming the other *Rylands v. Fletcher* requirements are established, we see no reason to distinguish between a one-time escape and continuous or multiple event escapes which produce the same kind of damages: see *Cambridge Water Co.* at p. 306.

The second issue pertaining to the escape requirement arises from the nature of the risk to which strict liability under *Rylands v. Fletcher* applies. As explained earlier (see paras. 83-84, 96-97), the *Rylands v. Fletcher* paradigm involves an unnatural use of the defendant's property and some kind of mishap or accident that results in damage. The application of *Rylands v. Fletcher* to consequences that are the intended result of the activity undertaken by the defendant has been doubted: *North York (City) v. Kert Chemical Industries Inc.* (1985), 33 C.C.L.T. 184 (Ont. H.C.); Lewis N. Klar, *Tort Law,* 4th ed. (Toronto: Carswell, 2008), at p. 628; *The Law of Nuisance in Canada* at pp. 132, 137.

We, too, doubt its application. It is one thing to impose strict liability for mishaps that occur in the course of the conduct of an unnatural or unusual activity. It is quite another to impose strict liability for the intended consequence of an activity that is carried out in a reasonable manner and in accordance with all applicable rules and regulations. [...]

The appeal is allowed. The judgment is set aside. Inco is entitled to judgment dismissing the action with costs of the appeal fixed at $100,000. Counsel may make further submissions as to the order that should be made with respect to the trial costs.

Notes and Questions

1. In parts of the decision not reproduced here, the Ontario Court of Appeal found that the claimants had failed to establish that property values in the affected area had, in fact, failed to keep up with comparable properties. In other words, leaving aside the question of nuisance and strict liability, the claimants had failed to establish that they had suffered the harm claimed, a reduction in the value of their properties.

2. The Court also found that the case raised limitation period concerns. The trial judge found that some members of the class of claimants had been aware that the nickel deposits would affect market values before the time for bringing the action expired. However, he held the action was not time-barred because most class members did not possess this knowledge at the relevant time. The Court of Appeal held that this was an error, as the trial judge should have addressed time limitations as an individual rather than a "common" issue.

3. The Court could have decided the case based on the limitation period issue or based on the failure to establish damages, but chose to focus its decision on the application of nuisance and strict liability. In the process, it rejected the trial judge's broad interpretation of strict liability, and his recognition of

the emerging principle of strict liability for abnormally dangerous activities as discussed in Note 8, below. Why do you think the Court took this approach to the case instead of rejecting the claim based on failure to prove damages? What does this do to the role of the common law and individual rights to environmental protection?

4. Recall that in *Cambridge*, the House of Lords concluded that the damages to the plaintiff's property were not foreseeable and that the strict liability claim failed on that basis alone. Could the Ontario Court of Appeal have decided the strict liability claim on the same basis? How does its approach to strict liability in *Inco* differ from that in *Cambridge*? What are the implications of the *Inco* approach for the application of strict liability to environmental cases?

5. It is clear from the class action certification process and from the trial judgment that the absence of a claim with respect to human health and environmental impacts resulting from the nickel contamination was a direct result of the class certification process, not of the absence of concern or evidence of human health or environmental risk associated with the contamination. Consider carefully how the absence of evidence on human health impacts is characterized in the decision. Was the Court fair in its treatment of this point?

6. A key difference between the trial decision and the decision on appeal is that the Court of Appeal found that the nickel contamination did not amount to damage to the plaintiff's property. Do you agree with the finding? What is needed in order to establish damage to property in the view of the Court of Appeal?

7. The Court of Appeal's approach to the traditional strict liability principle based on the rule in *Rylands v. Fletcher* differs in a number of important respects from that of the trial judge. Consider the Court's approach to the following issues and the implications they have for the effectiveness of the rule in *Rylands v. Fletcher* for environmental tort cases:

    a. The meaning of non-natural use of land, including:

        i.   its relation to zoning and regulatory compliance,
        ii. the role of "reasonable" use of land in establishing non-natural use,
        iii. the relevance of increased danger of the use to others,
        iv. the relevance of the substance not naturally being on the land,
        v.   whether the substance needs to be inherently dangerous for its use to constitute a non-natural use of land;

    b. Whether the rule applies only to isolated escapes or whether it also covers releases that are ongoing over time and not accidental;

    c. Where is the line between an accidental element in *Rylands v. Fletcher* and the "direct" requirement in trespass? If there is an accidental element to *Rylands v. Fletcher*, does this create a gap between it and trespass? Is there a good policy reason for such a gap? Does nuisance cover the gap?

    d. Is the House of Lords' foreseeability requirement for *Rylands v. Fletcher* as expressed in *Cambridge* now the law in Ontario? Consider the recent decision in *Huang v. Fraser Hillary's Limited*, 2018 ONCA 527, leave to appeal refused 2019 CarswellOnt 5599 (S.C.C.), in which the Ontario Court of Appeal broke away from English jurisprudence and held that reasonable foreseeability is not an element of the tort of nuisance in Canada. Does this decision help or hinder an argument that reasonable foreseeability is an element of the rule in *Rylands v. Fletcher* in Canada?

8. Consider the following excerpt from paragraph 60 of the trial decision in *Inco*:

> In my opinion, the fundamental principle in the *Rylands* decision is that a landowner who brings a non-natural substance onto his property that creates a potential danger for his neighbour will be strictly liable to his neighbour if that substance escapes from his property and causes damage. That same principle has also been applied to a landowner who undertakes abnormally dangerous activities on his property. In summary, he who creates an abnormal risk of harm to his neighbour will be responsible for any harm that actually occurs as a consequence of that risk. Given this principle, there is no logical reason to restrict the doctrine to circumstances of a single isolated escape from land.

How does this view differ from the approach taken by the Ontario Court of Appeal? Which approach to *Rylands v. Fletcher* do you prefer?

9. In paragraph 67 of the trial decision, the trial judge cites Linden & Feldthusen (8th ed., 2006) as summarizing the following emerging principle of strict liability for abnormally dangerous activities based on *Rylands v. Fletcher*:

> Pursuant to this principle, there are a limited number of activities so fraught with abnormal risk for the community that the negligence standard is felt to provide insufficient protection against them. Consequently, these extra-hazardous activities should be governed by a stricter form of liability that insists on compensation for all the losses they generate, even when they are conducted with reasonable care.

Why do you think the Court of Appeal rejected this emerging principle?

10. As was the case in *Palmer*, the trial judge in *Inco* rejected the claim in trespass rather summarily, relying on old English precedents on the basis that the claim failed to meet the direct entry requirement. What is interesting in both *Palmer* and *Inco* is that trespass offered a way out to the plaintiffs on foreseeability and proof of damages, as neither is a requirement for trespass to land. Was it reasonable for the trial judge to conclude that the deposit of nickel on the plaintiff's property does not constitute direct entry? Consider what a different approach to the requirement of direct entry would mean to the utility of the tort of trespass to land in environmental cases.

11. The case is binding in Ontario, but not in other provinces. Has it been adopted through subsequent case law in your province? Do you think the approach to nuisance and strict liability should be adopted in other provinces? If so, why should it? If not, what would be a better approach to nuisance and strict liability in Canada, and how would your suggested approach strike a more appropriate balance between legislative action to protect the environment and individual rights as expressed through the common law?

The final case in this Part involves a tort law claim brought by a First Nation in BC. As we have seen in previous cases, the plaintiffs pursue a number of torts in parallel. What is new in this case is that the property right that forms the basis of this claim is an asserted claim to aboriginal rights and title.

Thomas v. Rio Tinto Alcan Inc.
(*sub nom. Saik'uz First Nation v. Rio Tinto Alcan Inc.*) 2015 BCCA 154, leave to appeal refused 2015 CarswellBC 2965 (S.C.C.)

TYSOE J.: — The Kenney Dam was constructed in northwestern British Columbia in the early 1950s by the predecessor of the respondent, Rio Tinto Alcan (I will refer to Rio Tinto Alcan and its predecessors collectively as "Alcan"). The purpose of the Kenney Dam was to provide water for Alcan's power generation facility in Kemano so that the resulting electricity could be used in Alcan's aluminum smelter located in Kitimat. The smelter has now been in production for over 60 years. [...]

Each of the Saik'uz and Stellat'en First Nations (the "Nechako Nations") is an Aboriginal First Nation and a "band" within the meaning of the *Indian Act*, R.S.C. 1985, c. I-5. They are neighbouring Carrier First Nations and members of the Carrier Sekani Tribal Council, the unsuccessful party in one of the decisions of the Supreme Court of Canada dealing with the Crown's duty to consult with groups claiming Aboriginal title and other rights: *Rio Tinto Alcan Inc. v. Carrier Sekani Tribal Council*, 2010 SCC 43.

In September 2011, the Nechako Nations commenced the underlying action against Alcan. In brief terms, the Nechako Nations claimed against Alcan in nuisance and for breach of riparian rights as a result of the operations of the Kenney Dam. They sought relief in the form of interlocutory and permanent injunctions to restrain Alcan from committing the nuisance and interfering with their riparian rights (in their reply, the Nechako Nations claim damages in the alternative if one of Alcan's defences prevails).

Alcan brought an application seeking two orders and an award of costs. The first was for summary judgment under Rule 9-6 of the *Supreme Court Civil Rules* dismissing the claim on the basis the defence of statutory authority was a full defence to the claim; it also included a request for an order striking out a paragraph in the Nechako Nations' notice of civil claim and five paragraphs of the Nechako Nations' reply on the basis they constituted an impermissible collateral attack in connection with Alcan's defence of statutory authority. In the alternative, they sought an order under Rule 9-5(1)(a) of the *Supreme Court Civil Rules* striking out the whole of the notice of civil claim on the basis that it did not disclose a reasonable cause of action, and dismissing the action.

The chambers judge dismissed Alcan's application for summary judgment but he granted Alcan's application to strike out the notice of civil claim. As a result, the action was dismissed.

The Nechako Nations appeal the order striking out their notice of civil claim. Alcan cross appeals the dismissal of its application for summary judgment. [...]

Claims of the Nechako Nations

The Nechako Nations plead that they have used and exclusively occupied portions of the Central Carrier territory, including the Nechako River and the lands along the banks of the River, since the date at which British Sovereignty was asserted over British Columbia in 1846. They assert those lands and the bed of the Nechako River are subject to their Aboriginal title and rights, and claim proprietary interests in the waters and resources of the Nechako River. They also assert that at Sovereignty they used and exclusively occupied specific sites along the Nechako River and its tributaries for fishing purposes, and they claim proprietary rights to these fisheries. One of these fisheries was recognized as a fishing station in the 1916 Report of the Royal Commission on Indian Affairs for the Province of British Columbia. The Nechako Nations further plead that prior to and since first contact with Europeans they have harvested resources from the Nechako River system and carried out cultural and spiritual practices.

In addition, the Nechako Nations plead that they have reserves on the bank of the Nechako River system that were set aside as Indian Reserves and now fall under the *Indian Act*. Legal title to the reserves is held by the federal Crown on behalf of the Nechako Nations, which claim to be the owners and lawful occupiers of the reserves. The Nechako Nation claim their ownership of the reserves along the Nechako River system carries with it riparian rights at common law, including the right to the natural flow of water undiminished in quality and quantity.

The Nechako Nations say that the diversion of water by Alcan at the Kenney Dam has significant adverse impacts on the Nechako River, including alterations in the timing and quantity of water flow, impacts on water temperature, erosion of the banks, unnatural sedimentation in the river bed and interference with the surrounding ecological system. They allege these adverse impacts have negatively affected the fisheries resources of the Nechako River system, including a reduction in the fisheries resources (with a trend towards the extinction of the Nechako River Sturgeon as a result of their inability to spawn) and alteration of the health and demographics of the fish. They plead that they have suffered as a result of these adverse impacts, including interference with their ability to utilize fisheries resources, loss of use, enjoyment and value of the fisheries and lands subject to their Aboriginal title, and negative cultural impacts.

The Nechako Nations base their request for injunctive relief (and damages in the alternative) on private nuisance, public nuisance and breach of (or interference with) riparian rights.

As a result of defences pleaded by Alcan in its response to civil claim (including the defence of statutory authority), the Nechako Nations filed a reply that, among other things, pleaded that the statutory authority pleaded by Alcan is constitutionally inapplicable against the Nechako Nations' Aboriginal or proprietary rights. They plead in paras. 1 to 5 of the reply that the *Industrial Development Act*, the *Water Act*, R.S.B.C. 1996, c. 483, and its predecessors, the 1950 Agreement, the 1987 Settlement Agreement, the 1997 Settlement Agreement and the Final Water Licence are constitutionally inapplicable to their Aboriginal or proprietary rights to the extent that they purport to take away, diminish or extinguish those rights. In addition, para. 57 of the notice of civil claim had pleaded that the licences and agreements under which Alcan operates the Kenney

Dam are of no force or effect against the Nechako Nations' proprietary interests. A notice of constitutional question was served on the Province and the federal Crown, but neither has responded to it.

Decision of the Chambers Judge

In his reasons for judgment indexed as 2013 BCSC 2303, the chambers judge first dealt with Alcan's application for summary judgment on the basis of the defence of statutory authority. [...]

The judge then turned to Alcan's application to strike the Nechako Nations' notice of civil claim as not disclosing a reasonable cause of action. He reviewed the authorities with respect to applications under Rule 9-5(1)(a) (paras. 92 to 102), and he then referred to leading authorities dealing with Aboriginal titles and other rights and the Crown's duty to consult and accommodate pending proof of those titles and rights (paras. 103 to 111). He did not have the benefit of the Supreme Court of Canada's most recent decision on Aboriginal title and other rights, *Tsilhqot'in Nation v. British Columbia*, 2014 SCC 44. He also discussed the process of reserve creation (paras. 112 to 119).

The judge noted that the common law concept of riparian rights has been extinguished by legislation in British Columbia, including the current *Water Act*, R.S.B.C. 1996, c. 483, s. 2, and its predecessors (paras. 120 to 124). He then reviewed case authorities dealing with public and private nuisance, including some decisions involving First Nations (paras. 125 to 146).

The judge noted that the key problem with the intention of the Nechako Nations to prove their Aboriginal title and other rights in the underlying action was that their claim is against Alcan, not the Crown, and that the Crown is a key party and is the only party who can properly fulfill the role of adversary (paras. 158 to 162). He then concluded that a claim in private or public nuisance (or for breach of riparian rights) against Alcan, based on asserted but unproven claims to Aboriginal title and rights, had no reasonable chance of succeeding (para. 163 and 164).

The judge next considered whether the claims of the Nechako Nations to private nuisance or for breach of riparian rights could be supported by their interests in *Indian Act* reserves. The judge made some comments about private nuisance (paras. 171 to 176), and he then addressed the claim based on riparian rights. He observed that all water rights were vested in the Province prior to the creation of the Nechako Nations' reserves, and that those rights were not conveyed to the federal Crown when the lands were transferred to it for the purpose of creating the reserves (para. 177). He concluded that a claim in private nuisance, or for breach of riparian rights, based on a reserve interest, had no reasonable chance of succeeding (para. 178).

Discussion on Appeal

A pleading may be struck under Rule 9-5(1)(a) of the *Supreme Court Civil Rules* if it discloses no reasonable claim. The test for striking out claims under Rule 9-5(1)(a) is well known. It was most recently articulated by the Supreme Court of Canada in *R. v. Imperial Tobacco Canada Ltd.*, 2011 SCC 42 at para. 17:

"A claim will only be struck if it is plain and obvious, assuming the facts pleaded to be true, that the pleading discloses no reasonable cause of action" or "the claim has no reasonable prospect of success". As the pleaded facts are assumed to be true, no evidence is admissible: *Imperial Tobacco* at para. 22.

It is not determinative that the law has not yet recognized a particular claim; the court must err on the side of permitting a novel but arguable claim to proceed to trial: *Imperial Tobacco* at para. 21.

The Nechako Nations' notice of civil claim advances three claims: private nuisance, public nuisance and breach of riparian rights. I will set out the elements of the torts of private nuisance and public nuisance, and I will describe riparian rights and the effect of the *Water Act* upon them. I will also review the nature of Aboriginal title and other Aboriginal rights.

Private Nuisance

Mr. Justice Cromwell discussed the elements of the tort of private nuisance in the relatively recent decision in *Antrim Truck Centre Ltd. v. Ontario (Transportation)*, 2013 SCC 13:

> [19] The elements of a claim in private nuisance have often been expressed in terms of a two-part test of this nature: to support a claim in private nuisance the interference with the owner's use or enjoyment of land must be both *substantial* and *unreasonable*. A substantial interference with property is one that is non-trivial. Where this threshold is met, the inquiry proceeds to the reasonableness analysis, which is concerned with whether the non-trivial interference was also unreasonable in all of the circumstances.

The above passage refers to an owner's use or enjoyment of land. There is some uncertainty in Canadian law as to what occupiers of land other than owners have the ability to pursue a claim in private nuisance. In *Hunter v. Canary Wharf Ltd.*, [1997] A.C. 655 (H.L.), the House of Lords considered the issue of whether a licensee without exclusive possession of the land had the status to maintain a claim in private nuisance. On behalf of the majority, Lord Goff summarized the current state of the law at 692:

> It follows that, on the authorities as they stand, an action in private nuisance will only lie at the suit of a person who has a right to the land affected. Ordinarily, such a person can only sue if he has the right to exclusive possession of the land, such as a freeholder or tenant in possession, or even a licensee with exclusive possession. Exceptionally however, as *Foster v. Warblington Urban District Council* [[1906] 1 K.B. 648 (C.A.)] shows, this category may include a person in actual possession who has no right to be there; and in any event a reversioner can sue in so far his reversionary interest is affected. But a mere licensee on the land has no right to sue.

Lord Goff concluded that the law should not be developed to extend the category of persons who can sue in private nuisance to mere licensees, and he rejected the Court of Appeal's approach of expanding the category to all those who have a "substantial link" with the land.

The reason I say there is some uncertainty in Canadian law is that there is a Canadian appellate decision which held that a mere licensee could sue in private nuisance. In *Motherwell v. Motherwell* (1976), 73 D.L.R. (3d) 62 (Alta. S.C., App. Div.), the court held that the wife of the owner of the land had sufficient occupancy to found an action in private nuisance. In *Hunter*, Lord Goff considered *Motherwell* and concluded that the court in *Motherwell* had misunderstood *Foster v. Warblington Urban District Council* to hold that "occupancy of a substantial nature" was sufficient to enable the occupier to sue in private nuisance. In *Sutherland v. Canada (Attorney General)*, 2001 BCSC 1024, Mr. Justice Holmes preferred the narrower approach advocated in *Hunter*, and it remains to be seen whether other Canadian courts follow the *Hunter* approach or the broader *Motherwell* approach.

Public Nuisance

The Supreme Court of Canada discussed the doctrine of public nuisance in *Ryan v. Victoria (City)*, [1999] 1 S.C.R. 201, 168 D.L.R. (4th) 513. Mr. Justice Major accepted the following definition:

> [52] ... "A public nuisance has been defined as any activity which unreasonably interferes with the public's interest in questions of health, safety, morality, comfort or convenience": see *Klar*, [Lewis N. Klar, *Tort Law*, 2d ed. (Scarborough, Ont.: Carswell, 1996)] at p. 525. Essentially, "[t]he conduct complained of must amount to ... an attack upon the rights of the public generally to live their lives unaffected by inconvenience, discomfort or other forms of interference": See G.H.L. Fridman, *The Law of Torts in Canada*, vol. I (1989), at p. 168. An individual may bring a private action in public nuisance by pleading and proving special damage.

Whether an activity is a public nuisance is a question of fact, taking into account factors such as the inconvenience caused by the activity, the difficulty in lessening the risk and the character of the neighbourhood: *Ryan* at para. 53.

Riparian Rights

At common law, the owner of land adjoining water such as a river has riparian rights. Those rights include the right to access the water, the right of drainage, rights relating to the flow of water, rights relating to the quality of water, rights relating to the use of water and the right of accretion: see Gérard V. La Forest, *Water Law in Canada — The Atlantic Provinces* (Ottawa: Information Canada, 1973) at 200-201.

In the present case, the Nechako Nations claim riparian rights as being the owners of land adjoining the Nechako River and its tributaries. They claim ownership of the land based on their ownership of their reserves and on their Aboriginal title. Issues arise in respect of those claimed riparian rights because the Province has abolished common law riparian rights in British Columbia.

Shortly before the end of the 19th century, the Province enacted the *Water Privileges Act*, S.B.C. 1892, c. 47, which vested in the Province all water remaining unrecorded and unappropriated as of April 23, 1892. In *Cook v. Corporation of the City of Vancouver*, [1914] A.C. 1077, 18 D.L.R. 305, the Privy Council held that the effect of the Act was to take riparian rights away from land owners.

In 1925, the *Water Act Amendment Act, 1925*, S.B.C. 1925, c. 61, amended the *Water Act*, R.S.B.C. 1924, c. 271, to replace s. 4 with the following:

> 4. The property in and the right to the use of all the water at any time in any stream in the Province is for all purposes vested in the Crown in the right of the Province,

except only in so far as private rights therein have been established under special Acts or under licences is sued in pursuance of this or some former Act relating to the use of water. ...

Section 2 of the current version of the *Water Act* is to the same effect.

This extinguishment of common law riparian rights preceded the creation of the reserves of the Nechako Nations. The lands for the reserves were conveyed by the Province to the federal Crown by Order-in-Council 1036/1938 enacted by the Lieutenant-Governor in Council on July 29, 1938.

Nature of Aboriginal Title and Other Rights

The two leading authorities on Aboriginal title are *Tsilhqot'in Nation* and *Delgamuukw v. British Columbia*, [1997] 3 S.C.R. 1010, 153 D.L.R. (4th) 193.

Aboriginal title has been described as *sui generis* in order to distinguish it from fee simple proprietary interests and in order to understand it from both common law and Aboriginal perspectives: *Delgamuukw* at para. 112.

Briefly stated, the test for Aboriginal title is whether the land in question was exclusively occupied by the First Nation at the time of British sovereignty: *Delgamuukw* at para. 143; *Tsilhqot'in Nation* at para. 30. Aboriginal title extends to tracts of land regularly used for hunting or fishing if the First Nation exercised effective control of the tracts of land at the time of British sovereignty: *Tsilhqot'in Nation* at para. 50.

Aboriginal title is a beneficial interest in the land. It gives the First Nation the right to possess it, manage it, use it, enjoy it and profit from its economic development: *Tsilhqot'in Nation* at paras. 70 and 73.

Aboriginal title is the Aboriginal right that creates an interest in land. Other Aboriginal rights are typically activities such as fishing, hunting, trapping, harvesting of timber and berry gathering. In order to qualify as an Aboriginal right, the activity must be an element of a practice, custom or tradition integral to the distinctive culture of the First Nation: *R. v. Van der Peet*, [1996] 2 S.C.R. 507 at para. 46. In the present case, the Nechako Nations assert they have rights to fish and to a fishery, in addition to Aboriginal title.

Claims Relying on Aboriginal Title and Other Rights

The chambers judge struck the claims in private nuisance, public nuisance and breach of riparian rights, to the extent they were based on Aboriginal title and other Aboriginal rights, because the title and other rights were merely asserted and not yet proven. I will first consider whether, if it is assumed the facts alleged in the notice of civil claim are true, a reasonable cause of action in each of private nuisance, public nuisance and breach of riparian rights has been disclosed.

The Nechako Nations plead that they exclusively occupied portions of the Central Carrier territory, including the Nechako River and lands along its banks, at the time of British sovereignty. If this alleged fact is true, the Nechako Nations would have Aboriginal title to those lands. Although this is not ownership in fee simple, Aboriginal title would give the Nechako Nations the right to possess the lands. It is therefore not plain and obvious that the Nechako Nations do not have sufficient occupancy to found an action in private nuisance.

In addition, the Nechako Nations plead facts that support a claim for an Aboriginal right to harvest fish. The rights to harvest fish and trap animals have been likened to a *profit a prendre* and, on an application for an interim injunction, the right to trap has been held to be sufficient to found an argument that the holder of the right can maintain an action in private nuisance: *Bolton v. Forest Pest Management Institute* (1985), 21 D.L.R. (4th) 242, 66 B.C.L.R. 126 (C.A. Chambers).

The Nechako Nations plead the diversion of water by Alcan at the Kenney Dam has led to negative impacts on the fisheries resources of the Nechako River system. The alleged impacts are not trivial and are arguably unreasonable. Accordingly, on the basis of the pleaded facts, it is not plain and obvious that the Nechako Nations do not have a reasonable cause of action in private nuisance.

A public nuisance requires an activity that unreasonably interferes with the public's interest in such things as health, safety, morality, comfort or convenience. It is necessary in an action for public nuisance for the plaintiff to prove special damage. In my view, it is arguable that unreasonable interference with the public's interest in harvesting fish from the Nechako River system is a type of interference protected by the tort of public nuisance. The Aboriginal right to harvest fish pled by the Nechako Nations may be sufficient to demonstrate that they have suffered special damage as a result of the diversion of the Nechako River at the Kenney Dam. Hence, on the basis of the pleaded facts, it is not plain and obvious that the Nechako Nation do not have a reasonable cause of action in public nuisance.

The Nechako Nations base their claim to riparian rights on their interest in the lands adjacent to the Nechako River as a result of both their interest arising from Aboriginal title and their interest flowing from the creation of reserves for them. I will deal separately with the reserve interest in the next section of these reasons.

As I have stated, if the facts pled by the Nechako Nations are assumed to be true, they would have Aboriginal title to lands adjacent to the Nechako River. Although Aboriginal title is not the same as title in fee simple at common law, it is arguable that a similar kind of riparian rights associated with ownership in fee simple attach to Aboriginal title to lands adjacent to water. While the *Water Act* purports to vest all fresh water rights in the Province, it is arguable that, as asserted in the notice of constitutional question served by the Nechako Nations, this legislation is constitutionally inapplicable to the extent it purports to extinguish riparian rights held by them prior to the enactment of the *Water Privileges Act, 1892*. In my view, therefore, it is not plain and obvious that the pleading in connection with the claim for interference with riparian rights, to the extent it is based on Aboriginal title, discloses no reasonable cause of action. The constitutional question should be left for determination until it has been decided whether the Nechako Nations have riparian rights based on Aboriginal title to lands adjacent to the Nechako River.

Based on the above analysis, the claims of private nuisance, public nuisance and interference with riparian rights, to the extent they are based on Aboriginal title and other Aboriginal rights, should not have been struck because it is not plain and obvious that, assuming the facts pleaded to be true, the notice of civil claim discloses no reasonable cause of action in respect of those claims. However, the chambers judge did strike these claims because the assertions of Aboriginal title and other Aboriginal rights have not yet been proven (or accepted by the Crown). In my opinion, he was in error in doing so.

The effect of the ruling by the chambers judge is to create a unique prerequisite to the enforcement of Aboriginal title and other Aboriginal rights. Under this approach, these rights could only be enforced by an action if, prior to the commencement of the action, they have been declared by a court of competent jurisdiction or are accepted by the Crown. In my view, that would be justifiable only if Aboriginal title and other Aboriginal rights do not exist until they are so declared or recognized. However, the law is clear that they do exist prior to declaration or recognition. All that a court declaration or Crown acceptance does is to identify the exact nature and extent of the title or other rights.

The proposition that Aboriginal rights exist prior to a court declaration or Crown acceptance is embodied in s. 35(1) of the *Constitution Act, 1982* (being Schedule B to the *Canada Act 1982* (U.K.), 1982, c. 11):

> 35 (1) The *existing* aboriginal and treaty rights of the aboriginal peoples of Canada are hereby recognized and affirmed. [Emphasis added.]

The use of the words "recognized and affirmed" indicates that the Crown has already accepted the existing Aboriginal rights, and it is really just a matter of identifying what they are.

The Supreme Court of Canada has commented on s. 35 many times. In *Van der Peet*, the Court acknowledged that Aboriginal rights were not created by s. 35(1):

> [28] In identifying the basis for the recognition and affirmation of aboriginal rights, it must be remembered that s. 35(1) did not create the legal doctrine of aboriginal rights; aboriginal rights existed and were recognized under the common law: *Calder v. Attorney-General of British Columbia*, [1973] S.C.R. 313.

A similar comment was made in *Delgamuukw*:

> [133] Aboriginal title at common law is protected in its full form by s. 35(1). This conclusion flows from the express language of s. 35(1) itself, which states in full: "[t]he *existing* aboriginal and treaty rights of the aboriginal peoples of Canada are hereby recognized and affirmed" (emphasis [of Lamer C.J.C.]). On a plain reading of the provision, s. 35(1) did not create aboriginal rights; rather, it accorded constitutional status to those rights which were "existing" in 1982. The provision, at the very least, constitutionalized those rights which aboriginal peoples possessed at common law, since those rights existed at the time s. 35(1) came into force. Since aboriginal title was a common law right whose existence was recognized well before 1982 (e.g., *Calder, supra*), s. 35(1) has constitutionalized it in its full form. [Emphasis in original.]

In *Tsilhqot'in Nation*, the Court confirmed that the Aboriginal rights existed before the arrival of the first European settlers:

> [69] ... At the time of assertion of European sovereignty, the Crown acquired radical or underlying title to all the land in the province. This Crown title, however, was burdened by the pre-existing legal rights of Aboriginal people who occupied and used the land prior to European arrival. The doctrine of *terra nullius* (that no one owned the land prior to European assertion of sovereignty) never applied in Canada ...

As whatever Aboriginal rights the Nechako Nations may have are already in existence, it seems to me there is no reason in principle to require them to first obtain a court declaration in an action against the Province before they can maintain an action against another party seeking relief in reliance on their Aboriginal rights. As any other litigant, they should be permitted to prove in the action against another party the rights that are required to be proved in order to succeed in the claim against the other party.

As an example, assume that a lessee of land sued Alcan in private nuisance and that there was some issue with respect to the validity of the lessee's lease. In order to prove that it had sufficient occupancy to found an action in private nuisance, the plaintiff/lessee would have to prove the validity of its lease. The plaintiff/lessee would be entitled to prove the lease's validity in the action against Alcan, and no one would suggest that the plaintiff had no cause of action until it first sued the lessor and obtained a court declaration as to the validity of the lease. Nor would the lessor be required to be a party to the action, although it may be in the interests of the plaintiff/lessee to make the lessor a party so that the findings with respect to the validity of the lease would be binding on the lessor.

Aboriginal people are part of Canada's community, and they should not be treated disadvantageously in comparison to any other litigant asserting claims for nuisance and breach of riparian rights. Setting a separate standard for Aboriginal people before they can sue other parties in order to enforce their rights is not only lacking in principle but could also be argued to be inconsistent with the principle of equality under the *Charter of Rights and Freedoms*.

Alcan says it is unprecedented to allow "unrecognized" Aboriginal rights to ground common law claims in tort, and a change in the law to permit it would not be an incremental change of the nature that allows the courts to develop the common law. While it is true that there is no case where Aboriginal rights have founded a successful claim in tort, the real issue on this appeal is whether the Aboriginal rights have to be first "recognized" before the claim can be advanced.

There are examples of cases where an Aboriginal person has been permitted to attempt to prove an Aboriginal right founding a claim or defence in the action in which the claim or defence is being put forward. *R. v. Sparrow*, [1990] 1 S.C.R. 1075, 70 D.L.R. (4th) 385, and *Van der Peet* are examples of cases where Aboriginal persons were permitted to attempt to prove their Aboriginal fishing rights to defend charges of illegal fishing. In *R. v. Marshall; R. v. Bernard*, 2005 SCC 43, Aboriginal persons charged with illegal logging were allowed to pursue a defence based on Aboriginal title that had not been previously "recognized". While those cases did involve the Crown, it was not suggested there was no reasonable defence because the Aboriginal rights being relied upon had not been previously declared by the court or accepted by the Crown. Whether the Crown is party to the action should not be determinative of the issue whether the pleadings disclose a reasonable cause of action.

There are also cases not involving the Crown. In *Hunt v. Halcan Log Services Ltd.* (1986), 34 D.L.R. (4th) 504, 15 B.C.L.R. (2d) 165 (S.C. Chambers), the court granted an interlocutory injunction to a First Nation to restrain the owner of an island from logging the island. The First Nation claimed both Aboriginal and treaty rights to hunt on the island, to harvest fish from a fishery on and adjacent to the island and to harvest fruits and berries on the island. Alcan says this case is distinguishable because it involved treaty rights and was dealing with an interlocutory injunction, which is only designed to stop interim harm. It is distinguishable on those bases, but it contains a similar point of principle. The first leg of the three-part test for interlocutory injunctions is whether there is a serious or fair question to be tried. In *Hunt*, Mr. Justice Trainor found there was a fair question to be tried with respect to both Aboriginal rights and treaty rights. If Alcan were right in its assertion that Aboriginal rights have to be proven before an action against a private party can be maintained, then Trainor J. would have found there was no fair question to be tried with respect to Aboriginal rights because they had not yet been proven.

Another example is *Westar Timber Ltd. v. Gitksan Wet'suwet'en Tribal Council* (1989), 60 D.L.R. (4th) 453, 37 B.C.L.R. (2d) 352 (C.A.). In that case, this Court upheld, in large part, an interlocutory injunction restraining a logging company from building a bridge over a river and extending logging roads into an area claimed by the Gitksan First Nation to be subject to Aboriginal title in the *Delgamuukw* litigation. Although Mr. Justice Carrothers referred to the Aboriginal rights claimed by the Gitksan First Nation to be "speculative and prospective" (at 358, B.C.L.R.), it was not suggested there was no fair question to be tried because those rights remained unproven.

It should also be noted that another court has declined to follow the decision of the chambers judge in the present case. In *Uashaunnuat (Innus de Uashat et de Mani-Utenam) c. Compagnie minière IOC inc. (Iron Ore Company of Canada)*, 2014 QCCS 4403 (leave to appeal dismissed, 2015 QCCA 2), the First Nation sued the defendants, seeking recognition of Aboriginal title and other Aboriginal and treaty rights and a permanent injunction restraining mining and rail activity in the area in question. The defendants brought an application to dismiss the action on the basis that recognition of the Aboriginal title and rights binding on the Crown was a prerequisite to any other proceeding.

The Quebec Superior Court dismissed the application and permitted the action to proceed. Mr. Justice Blanchard considered the reasoning of the chambers judge in the present case and he declined to follow it (and, in particular, paras. 161 to 163 of the judge's reasons).

Alcan submits this decision is distinguishable because it involved Quebec civil law. However, it appears from para. 18 of the reasons of Blanchard J. ("[o]nly the clear and manifest absence of legal foundation allows an action to be dismissed pursuant to article 165(4) C.C.P.") that the test is similar to the test applicable to applications under Rule 9-5(1)(a) of the *Supreme Court Civil Rules*.

Alcan says one of the unmistakable characteristics of the s. 35 jurisprudence is that timing does matter. It cites *Haida Nation v. British Columbia (Minister of Forests)*, 2004 SCC 73, for the proposition that the Supreme Court of Canada disavowed the notion that third parties have any legal obligations to Aboriginal groups prior to proof of the rights in question. Alcan relies in this regard on the following passage:

> [53] It is suggested (*per* Lambert J.A. [in this Court's decision in *Haida Nation*, 2002 BCCA 147 and 2002 BCCA 462] that a third party's obligation to consult Aboriginal peoples may arise from the ability of the third party to rely on justification as a defence against infringement. However, the duty to consult and accommodate, as discussed above, flows from the Crown's assumption of

sovereignty over lands and resources formerly held by the Aboriginal group. This theory provides no support for an obligation on third parties to consult or accommodate. The Crown alone remains legally responsible for the consequences of its actions and interactions with third parties, that affect Aboriginal interests. ...

In my view, the above passage does not stand for the broad proposition advanced by Alcan. It simply stands for the proposition that the duty of consultation and accommodation that arises from the honour of the Crown pending proof of Aboriginal rights is not imposed on third parties. In *Haida*, Chief Justice McLachlin clarified (at para. 56) that while third parties cannot be held liable for failing to discharge the Crown's duty to consult and accommodate, that does not mean they can never be held liable for infringement of Aboriginal rights.

Alcan also submits that allowing a First Nation to sue a private party prior to recognition of its Aboriginal rights would be inconsistent with the reconciliation of Aboriginal rights with Crown sovereignty that has been advocated by the Supreme Court of Canada on numerous occasions. At para. 161 of his reasons, the chambers judge stated that "[c]onsultation, accommodation, and negotiation are without doubt the preferred routes of reconciliation of Aboriginal rights with the assertion of Crown sovereignty". One cannot argue with this sentiment, but parties cannot be forced to negotiate a settlement if one of them insists that the dispute be resolved by the court. More importantly, however, the goal of reconciliation cannot determine the issue of whether pleadings disclose a reasonable cause of action, which is a question of law.

In conclusion on this point, it is not plain and obvious, assuming the facts pleaded to be true, that the notice of civil claim discloses no reasonable cause of action in respect of the claims of private nuisance, public nuisance and interference with riparian rights, to the extent they are based on Aboriginal title and other Aboriginal rights. The chambers judge erred in holding that no reasonable causes of action existed until Aboriginal title and other Aboriginal rights were proven (or accepted by the Crown).

Claims Based on Reserve Interest

As I noted above, the Nechako Nations ground their claim to riparian rights on their interest in lands based on both Aboriginal title and their interest in reserve lands. As I have held in the previous section, their claim based on Aboriginal title should not have been struck. I will now deal with their claim for interference with riparian rights based on their interest in reserve lands. I will also deal with their claim in private nuisance based on their interest in reserve lands.

The reserves were created with land conveyed by the Province to the federal Crown in 1938. By that time, the Province had abolished riparian rights for land owners (except to the extent they were unrecorded and unappropriated). It follows that when the reserve lands were transferred to the federal Crown, riparian rights did not accompany the transfer of the lands.

The Nechako Nations say that the transfer of the lands in 1938 is not the determinative point in time because the lands had been set aside by provincial authorities in the 19th century, prior to the passage of the *Water Privileges Act, 1892*. They say the effect of the *Water Privileges Act, 1892* cannot be assessed in the absence of evidence of the reserve creation process, including evidence of the pre-existing rights of the Nechako Nations. However, there are no pleaded facts that would give the Nechako Nations an interest in the land supporting riparian rights prior to the 1938 Order-in-Council except for the pleaded facts giving rise to Aboriginal title. This section of the reasons deals only with riparian rights based on an interest in reserve lands, and is not addressing the issue of whether the Nechako Nations may have riparian rights on the basis of Aboriginal title.

The Nechako Nations point to *Burrard Power Co. v. The King*, [1911] A.C. 87 (P.C.), where it was held that, in the absence of a reservation of rights, the transfer of lands for the railway belt from the Province to the federal Crown included all the rights of the Province in the waters in the lakes and streams within the lands. They also point to the wording of Order-in-Council 1036/1938, which included the following provision:

> PROVIDED also that it shall be lawful for any person duly authorized in that behalf by Us, Our heirs and successors, to take and occupy such water privileges, and to have and enjoy such rights of carrying water over, through or under any parts of the hereditaments hereby granted, as may be reasonably required for mining or agricultural purposes is the vicinity of the said hereditaments, paying therefor a reasonable compensation.

The Nechako Nations say this wording would be unnecessary if no water rights were transferred by way of the Order-in-Council.

In my view, these submissions overlook the wording of s. 4 of the *Water Act*, R.S.B.C. 1924, c. 271, as amended by the *Water Act Amendment Act, 1925*. It provided that the water rights were vested in the Province except only those rights established by special Acts or water licences issued under the *Water Act*. The Order-in-Council does not fall within either of these exceptions and, thus, the Order-in-Council could not have conveyed any water rights to the federal Crown. The proviso contained in the Order-in-Council was necessary to enable the Province to transport water over the reserve lands for mining or agricultural purposes.

In my opinion, the chambers judge was correct in concluding that there was no reasonable prospect of success to the Nechako Nation's claim to entitlement to riparian rights based on their reserve rights. The notice of civil claim does not disclose a reasonable cause of action in respect of the claim for interference with riparian rights to the extent that those rights are said to arise from the Nechako Nations having an interest in the reserve lands.

While the chambers judge acknowledged the Nechako Nations were relying on their interest in the reserves to ground a claim of private nuisance, the only comment he made about it was: "The only tenuous support of a reserve interest providing sufficient standing for a claim of nuisance is found in the remarks *in obiter* by Nunn J. in *Palmer* [*Palmer v. Nova Scotia Forest Industries*, [1983] N.S.J. 534 (S.C.)] that a right arising out of reserve lands 'stands on the same footing' as other privately owned property (para. 509)" (para. 174). He then focused on the claim for riparian rights.

I referred above to *Hunter v. Canary Wharf Ltd.*, which held that a substantial link to the property is not sufficient to enable one to maintain an action in private nuisance and that the plaintiff must have the right of exclusive possession. This represents the narrower view, while the decision in *Motherwell* is support for a more relaxed criteria.

In my opinion, it is not plain and obvious that the Nechako Nations do not qualify as claimants in private nuisance under the narrower view. The term "reserve " is defined in s. 2 of the *Indian Act* to mean "a tract of land, the legal title to which is vested in Her Majesty, that has been set apart by Her Majesty for the use and benefit of a band". This would seem to give the band the right to exclusive possession of the reserve lands, which is sufficient to found a claim in private nuisance.

In *Joe v. Findlay* (1981), 122 D.L.R. (3d) 377, 26 B.C.L.R. 376 (C.A.), this Court upheld a finding of trespass on reserve lands. If the possession of reserve lands is sufficient to support a claim in trespass, it is not plain and obvious to me that it should not also be sufficient to support a claim in private nuisance. In my opinion, the chambers judge erred in striking the claim for private nuisance to the extent that it was based on the Nechako Nations having a right of possession to the reserve lands.

Conclusion on Appeal

I would set aside the portion of the order dated December 13, 2013 striking out the whole of the notice of civil claim and dismissing the action. I would dismiss Alcan's application under Rule 9-5(1)(a) except that I would strike the claim of the Nechako Nations for interference with riparian rights to the extent that those rights are alleged to arise from an interest in their reserves.

Notes and Questions

1. Consider the court's effort to fairly consider the claim while attempting to work within the parameters of the tort principles at play. Do you agree with the Court of Appeal that asserted aboriginal rights offer an adequate proprietary basis for tort claims based in nuisance or riparian rights?

2. Do you agree with the court's approach to the legislative provisions in BC that seek to extinguish riparian rights? How would the court's approach affect Indigenous riparian rights in your province? How do the current legislative provisions regarding riparian rights in your province compare to those in the BC legislation at the time of the events leading to this litigation? Would the provisions of the new BC *Water Sustainability Act*, S.B.C. 2014, c. 15, make a difference in the case? Does section 5 add anything new to the efforts to ensure all water rights are vested in the Crown? What about opportunities under section 40 for special rules for Indigenous communities?

Part II — Understanding the Limits of Traditional Torts

In Part I, we identified some of the challenges involved in using the tort system to prevent or compensate for harm to the environment. *Palmer*, *Cambridge Water*, *Inco* and *Rio Tinto Alcan* each illustrate vividly some of the difficulties faced by plaintiffs when seeking to establish liability in tort for environmental harms. Some of these are a direct function of scientific uncertainty; some are a function of legal rules, systemic barriers and judicial attitudes; and some are a function of the complex interplay between law and science. A compelling illustration of the lattermost phenomenon is the law of causation, which is the topic explored in this Part. The following article argues for a new approach to causation in environmental cases, and argues that the SCC has laid the foundation for such an approach in recent tort cases including *Snell v. Farrell*, [1990] 2 S.C.R. 311, *Hanke v. Resurfice Corp.*, 2007 SCC 7, and most recently *Clements (Litigation Guardian of) v. Clements*, 2012 SCC 32.

Lynda M. Collins,
"Material Contribution to Risk in the Canadian Law of Toxic Torts"
(2016) 91 Chi.-Kent. L. Rev. 567

Introduction

Common law approaches to causation have historically been based on the premise that if a defendant's negligence has caused a plaintiff's loss, she will probably be able to prove it. This assumption is untenable in our contemporary world of immense chemical complexity. In the toxic torts context, traditional approaches to causation have resulted in under-compensation of injured victims and under-deterrence of chemical wrongdoing. Indeed, writing extra-judicially in the late 1990s, the current Chief Justice of the Supreme Court of Canada noted that "[t]he all-or-nothing outcome of the [traditional] test [for causation] all too often results in a 'nothing,' inconsistent with modern expectations." Jurists and scholars have sought to soften the rigidity of the causation element by importing risk-based innovations into the causation analysis. This Article will introduce and analyze one such innovation: the test of "material contribution to risk" in the Canadian law of toxic torts.

Part II considers the unique challenges that arise in the causation analysis in toxic torts, with a particular focus on the problem of scientific uncertainty. Part III elucidates the stages of the causation inquiry in Canadian toxic tort law, including consideration of the standard of proof, the but-for test, and the new test of material contribution to risk. Part IV introduces proposals for risk-based reform in Canadian causation law, and Part V presents a brief conclusion. In order to do justice to toxic tort plaintiffs, and remain relevant in the twenty-first century, Canadian tort law needs to grapple with the new world of chemically-induced harm by adopting a broad test of material contribution to risk, complemented by stronger forms of risk-based liability.

Causation in the Chemical World

Scientific Uncertainty

In the decades since the 'chemical revolution' of the mid-twentieth century, thousands of synthetic chemicals and millions of chemical mixtures have entered the human environment. While some chemicals are harmless, others have caused untold human suffering. Toxic pollution and products cause tens of thousands of premature deaths each year in North America. In the middle ground between known innocuous and proven toxic substances is a vast grey area of profound and pervasive scientific uncertainty. Surprisingly, for many thousands of chemicals and millions of mixtures, rigorous toxicity data is simply lacking. The generation of chemical safety data has been frustrated by both legal and scientific factors. On the scientific side, the challenges are manifold. Environmental pollutants are difficult to trace once released and interact in complex and poorly understood ways with each other, environmental media and human bodies. Non-pharmaceutical chemicals cannot be tested directly on humans, leaving only animal testing, which is costly, time-consuming and ethically controversial. Thousands of new substances are invented every year and yet neither government nor academia has the capacity (in personnel, money or test animals) to subject this number of substances to thorough independent study. To summarize, our ability to invent and disseminate new chemical substances has far outpaced our ability to understand them.

On the legal side, outdated processes in both statutory environmental law and torts have strongly incentivized chemical producers to "choose ignorance" in order to limit liability. Statutory environmental law has presumed chemicals innocent until proven guilty, treating the absence of evidence of harm as evidence of an absence of harm, a fallacy that is soundly rejected by scientists. In a statutory system that requires data in order to justify regulatory limits, the rational manufacturer tends to under-study its products in order to limit the risk of adverse results. Tort law has similarly required the injured plaintiff to present evidence proving on a balance of probabilities that the defendant's substance caused her illness, even where the data to support or refute such a claim are unavailable. Carl Cranor summarizes the legal drivers of chemical uncertainty as follows:

> Because the regulation of suspect substances that enter the market without legally required testing will occur only if a governmental agency [shows] a risk of harm and a tort action will proceed only if a plaintiff shows [causation of] actual harm, firms have incentives to resist testing their products and monitoring them for adverse effects and often they have not.

Against this backdrop of massive (and sometimes intentional) chemical uncertainty, toxic tort plaintiffs have continued to bear the burden of proving causation, largely by reference to legal tests that long pre-date our current chemical reality.

Despite compelling scholarly calls for reform, causation remains a touchstone for tort liability in Canada. Indeed, the Supreme Court of Canada has described causation as "an expression of the relationship that must be found to exist between the tortious act of the wrongdoer and the injury to the victim in order to justify compensation of the latter out of the pocket of the former." Causation is an element of the negligence cause of action, without which there can be no recovery.

Even with respect to torts that are actionable without proof of injury (e.g., battery), the plaintiff must prove a causal link between the defendant's conduct and her injury in order to recover compensatory damages. A voluminous body of scholarship has attempted to resolve the dilemma of toxic causation, but causation remains the single biggest hurdle to recovery for the toxic tort plaintiff in Canada as elsewhere.

Legal Uncertainty in Toxic Causation

In toxic tort cases, the causation element can be broken down into two components: generic causation and specific causation. Generic causation refers to the capacity of the substance at issue to cause the kind of injury suffered by the plaintiff. It concerns the general characteristics of the substance, such as whether it has been shown in lab tests to cause a particular illness in test animals, or whether there is epidemiological evidence suggesting a substance-illness connection in human populations. If there is insufficient evidence that the defendant's substance is capable of causing the plaintiff's illness under any circumstances, then the causation inquiry is at an end. If, however, the plaintiff can prove generic causation, she must nonetheless show that the defendant's toxic substance actually caused her illness in the specific circumstances of her case. To assess specific causation, courts will consider factors such as the nature, duration and concentration of the plaintiff's exposure as well as other risk factors that might account for the plaintiff's illness.

Proof of both generic and specific causation frequently founders on the problem of scientific uncertainty discussed above (and thoroughly canvassed in the literature of toxic torts). In addition to the massive uncertainty surrounding the safety (or danger) of chemical substances, the illnesses at issue in many toxic tort actions are both multi-factorial and poorly understood, and the injurious encounter takes place at least partly on a microscopic level invisible to the naked eye. This constellation of factors has produced three discernible kinds of uncertainty in torts cases.

The first scenario involving the indeterminate plaintiff arises when a defendant increases the incidence of an illness that already occurs at background levels in a given population. Through epidemiological evidence, we know that the defendant has harmed some individuals within an exposed group, but there exists no individual plaintiff who can prove causation against the defendant. S.M. Waddams postulates the following hypothetical:

> The defendant pollutes the air and increases the risk to the whole population of Australia of contracting skin cancer, raising the risk, let us say, from 10 per 100,000 to 19 per 100,000. On these figures, no particular plaintiff with cancer can show that the defendant probably caused the disease: more probably than not the plaintiff would have contracted it in any case. Should the defendant be liable? If so, should the plaintiff recover full compensation, or only 9/19ths of it?

Population-based evidence is clearly sufficient where it establishes that more than 50% of the plaintiff's total risk factors emanate from the defendant's substance. However, questions arise where risk does not meet this threshold, as in the Waddams example above. In Canada, causation is a qualitative, logical and common sense inquiry rather than a mechanistic, scientific calculation; taking a "robust and pragmatic" common sense approach as instructed by the Supreme Court of Canada, proof of significant risk will often be sufficient to meet the but-for test in the absence of a convincing alternative explanation. Some claims in this category will fail due to scientific uncertainty, but in *Clements v. Clements*, the Supreme Court of Canada explicitly left open the possibility of causation reform in the indeterminate plaintiff scenario in a future case.

The second species of uncertainty identified in the toxic tort literature is that of indeterminate harm, or mere risk exposure. People who are exposed to toxic substances sometimes require medical monitoring, experience anxiety, or feel victimized by the defendant's conduct even if they have not yet contracted a disease (and might never do so). Canadian courts have thus far declined to answer repeated academic calls for the creation of a new tort of negligent creation of risk. There is currently no cause of action in Canada for the negligent infliction of risk alone, but the injury requirement may be met by psychiatric illness or relatively minor physical harm. Although there is no Supreme Court of Canada authority on point, a number of lower courts have also certified class actions for medical monitoring. Thus, there is some hope for Canadian plaintiffs in the indeterminate harm scenario.

The final species of uncertainty in toxic torts and perhaps the most notorious is that of defendant indeterminacy. In the indeterminate defendant scenario, a plaintiff can show that the particular substance at issue caused her illness, but it is impossible to determine which defendant is responsible for her exposure. Such cases occur where multiple defendants manufacture an identical defective drug or emit a hazardous pollutant that comingles with other identical discharges. In the indeterminate defendant scenario, the plaintiff can prove all elements of negligence except causation; she can demonstrate that each defendant breached a duty owed to her and that she sustained a proximate loss. Moreover, the plaintiff can show that the negligence of one or more in a group of identifiable defendants (e.g., a group of manufacturers of a particular drug) actually caused her illness. However, if she cannot point to the particular defendant or defendants responsible for her illness, then causation is not made out and, on a traditional analysis, she recovers nothing.

Courts in the United States have addressed the indeterminate defendant scenario in a wide variety of ways, from simple dismissal of plaintiffs' claims to the development of new forms of collective liability, most famously the doctrine of market share liability. As elaborated below, the Supreme Court of Canada has gone further, imposing joint and several liability on all defendants in the indeterminate defendant scenario.

These three varieties of uncertainty pose challenges at various stages of the causation inquiry in toxic torts. They complicate the court's assessment of evidence and drive choice-of-instrument decisions in the doctrinal analysis of causation.

Canadian Approaches to the Causation Problem in Toxic Torts

Standard of Proof

As in the United States, the standard of proof in Canadian tort actions is the balance of probabilities (also known as the preponderance of the evidence).

Although there is no doctrinal controversy on this point, judges in toxic tort actions run the risk of inadvertently adopting the scientific standard of proof as they receive and evaluate voluminous amounts of expert evidence from scientific witnesses. Unlike judges, pure research scientists operate on a limitless timeline and in a culture that places enormous value on causal skepticism. Since scientists do not consider a causal link to be established unless it is proven to a probability of 95% or greater, the importation of scientific standards of proof into torts cases is a serious error. In *Palmer v. Nova Scotia Forest Industries*, for example, the provincial court refused an application for an injunction against the spraying of a pesticide containing dioxin on the basis that there was "no scientifically acceptable proof of risk to health." The appropriate question whether there was legally acceptable proof of risk was never answered. In contrast, the court in *Ring v. The Queen* noted that while the representative plaintiff's proposed approach to proof of causation might not "'lead to a meaningful scientific answer with respect to a specific dose-response relationship,' it may lead to a meaningful legal answer regarding the creation of unreasonable risks for the general public."

Any amount of uncertainty may prevent a research scientist from concluding that substance X causes illness Y, but a civil court can make a finding of causation even in the presence of substantial doubt. In *Snell v. Farrell*, the Supreme Court of Canada suggested that apparent injustices resulting from the but-for test arose from rigidity in its application, and confirmed that causation need not be proved to a level of scientific precision. More recently, Chief Justice McLachlin in *Clements* reiterated that "[t]he 'but for' causation test must be applied in a robust common sense fashion. There is no need for scientific evidence of the precise contribution the defendant's negligence made to the injury." In other words, Canadian torts jurists need not search for the transcendent scientific "truth"; they are merely tasked with deciding whether a causal link is more likely than not.

Having adopted the appropriate standard of proof, courts adjudicating toxic tort actions in Canada are faced with a range of distinct approaches to the test for factual causation. First and foremost among causal tests in the Anglo-Canadian tradition is the but-for (sine qua non) approach.

The But-for Test

According to the traditional test for factual causation, a plaintiff must demonstrate that "but for" (i.e., in the absence of) the defendant's breach of the standard of care, she would not have sustained her loss. Thus, if a toxic tort plaintiff can prove a probability of 51% or greater that the defendant's negligence caused her illness or injury, then factual causation is treated as a certainty and the plaintiff is presumptively entitled to recover 100% of her past losses from the defendant. If the evidence falls short of a 51% probability of causation, the plaintiff has failed to discharge her burden of proof and recovers nothing. A rigid application of the but-for test produces manifest injustice where the defendant has exposed the plaintiff to an unreasonable risk of developing a particular illness that she does in fact contract, but causation is in doubt because of a lack of data concerning the substance in question. This injustice is particularly pronounced where the uncertainty stems from the defendant's own failure to investigate its substance. In his masterful book, *Toxic Torts: Science, Law and the Possibility of Justice*, Cranor explains:

[Given the] woeful ignorance that plagues much scientific and agency knowledge of the universe of chemical substances ... it is both possible and likely that some toxic tort cases are dismissed simply because of ignorance about a particular substance and its properties, leaving wrongfully injured plaintiffs without a remedy, and undermining the deterrence goal of tort law.

In many cases, recovery is possible on a but-for standard where courts adhere to the legal standard of proof, take a common sense perspective on causation, and apply the "robust and pragmatic" approach to evidence mandated by the Supreme Court of Canada. However, even when this flexible, contemporary approach to sine qua non is adopted, some meritorious plaintiffs will fail as a result of evidentiary gaps that result from a defendant's intentional choices.

Reverse Onus

Given the perverse incentive that exists when manufacturers benefit from a lack of data about their own substances, the idea of reversing the onus of proof would appear to make good sense in the toxic tort context. The House of Lords adopted a reverse onus on causation in the toxic tort case of *McGhee v. National Coal Board*. There, the plaintiff employee cleaned brick kilns for the defendant employer, resulting in the accumulation of dust on his skin. The defendant negligently failed to provide shower facilities for its employees resulting in the plaintiff being forced to bicycle home each day covered in layers of dust. The plaintiff subsequently developed dermatitis and sued the defendant for negligence. At trial, expert testimony established that the defendant's failure to provide showers materially increased the plaintiff's risk of developing dermatitis, but it was scientifically impossible to conclude (on a balance of probabilities) that it actually caused the dermatitis.

At the House of Lords, Lord Wilberforce developed a new test for causation to address this dilemma; he held that "where a person has, by breach of a duty of care, created a risk, and injury occurs within the area of that risk, the loss should be borne by him unless he shows that it had some other cause." A number of lower courts in Canada initially followed *McGhee*, adopting the reverse onus where there was proof of negligent creation of risk and injury within the ambit of that risk. Material contribution to risk survives in Canadian case law, but the reversal in burden of proof on causation was explicitly rejected in *Snell v. Farrell*, a rejection that was later confirmed in *Hanke v. Resurfice*.

The Material Contribution to Risk Test

In *Hanke v. Resurfice*, the Supreme Court of Canada returned to the material contribution to risk approach articulated in *McGhee*, but retained the traditional allocation of burden of proof. The plaintiff in *Hanke* was badly burned when he inadvertently placed a water hose into the gas tank of an ice-resurfacing machine, causing an explosion and fire. Hanke sued the manufacturer of the machine, alleging that the two tanks were designed and positioned in such a way that an operator was likely to make such a mistake and suffer injury. On the question of causation, Chief Justice McLachlin held as follows:

First, the basic test for determining causation remains the "but for" test. This applies to multi-cause injuries. The plaintiff bears the burden of showing that "but for" the negligent act or omission of each defendant, the injury would not have occurred. Having done this, contributory negligence may be apportioned, as permitted by statute.

This fundamental rule has never been displaced and remains the primary test for causation in negligence actions. As stated in *Athey v. Leonati*, at para. 14, per Major J., "[t]he general, but not conclusive, test for causation is the 'but for' test, which requires the plaintiff to show that the injury would not have occurred but for the negligence of the defendant." Similarly, as I noted in *Blackwater v. Plint*, at para. 78, "[t]he rules of causation consider generally whether 'but for' the defendant's acts, the plaintiff's damages would have been incurred on a balance of probabilities."

The "but for" test recognizes that compensation for negligent conduct should only be made "where a substantial connection between the injury and defendant's conduct" is present. It ensures that a defendant will not be held liable for the plaintiff's injuries where they "may very well be due to factors unconnected to the defendant and not the fault of anyone": *Snell v. Farrell*, at p. 327, per Sopinka J.

She went on to articulate an exception to the but-for test that subsequently generated a vigorous and contentious debate among advocates and legal scholars:

[I]n special circumstances, the law has recognized exceptions to the basic "but for" test, and applied a "material contribution" test. Broadly speaking, the cases in which the "material contribution" test is properly applied involve two requirements.

First, it must be impossible for the plaintiff to prove that the defendant's negligence caused the plaintiff's injury using the "but for" test. The impossibility must be due to factors that are outside of the plaintiff's control; for example, current limits of scientific knowledge. Second, it must be clear that the defendant breached a duty of care owed to the plaintiff, thereby exposing the plaintiff to an unreasonable risk of injury, and the plaintiff must have suffered that form of injury. In other words, the plaintiff's injury must fall within the ambit of the risk created by the defendant's breach. In those exceptional cases where these two requirements are satisfied, liability may be imposed, even though the "but for" test is not satisfied, because it would offend basic notions of fairness and justice to deny liability by applying a "but for" approach.

Although the phrase "material contribution" is left without object in *Hanke*, in *Clements*, the Supreme Court of Canada explicitly held that the test refers to material contribution to risk rather than injury. Indeed, Chief Justice McLachlin acknowledges that the material contribution test for causation is predicated on risk as the conceptual foundation for liability:

"[M]aterial contribution' as a substitute for the usual requirement of 'but for' causation . . . imposes liability not because the evidence establishes that the defendant's act caused the injury, but because the act contributed to the risk that injury would occur."

The plaintiff in *Clements* was severely injured when she was thrown from a motorcycle being driven by her husband, the defendant. The accident occurred when the vehicle ran over a nail that punctured the rear tire, causing it to rapidly deflate; Mr. Clements lost control of the vehicle and it ultimately crashed. The trial court found that the defendant negligently overloaded the vehicle and operated it at an excessive speed, but was not satisfied that the accident would not have occurred but for these factors.

The court concluded that the material contribution test set out in *Hanke* could be applied since it was scientifically impossible to determine at which speed and weight the motorcycle could have been brought under control after losing air pressure in the rear wheel.

Applying that test to the facts of the case, the trial judge imposed liability on Mr. Clements. The Court of Appeal reversed, holding that this was not an appropriate case for the application of material contribution.

Citing an article by Professor Erik Knutsen, the Court of Appeal held that material contribution may be used only in cases involving either "dependency causation" (the circumstance in which it is impossible to say what a third party would have done had the defendant exercised due care) or "circular causation" (the scenario in which it is clear that one in a group of tortfeasors caused the plaintiff's harm but it is impossible to identify which one). In contrast, the court held that material contribution could not be applied when causal uncertainty results from the fact that the science is "just not there yet."

The Supreme Court of Canada allowed the plaintiff's appeal in *Clements* but adopted a test that appears to be substantially similar to that employed by the Court of Appeal. After clarifying that the "material contribution" test does indeed refer to risk rather than injury, the Court articulated the following summary of causation:

> As a general rule, a plaintiff cannot succeed unless she shows as a matter of fact that she would not have suffered the loss "but for" the negligent act or acts of the defendant. A trial judge is to take a robust and pragmatic approach to determining if a plaintiff has established that the defendant's negligence caused her loss. Scientific proof of causation is not required.

> Exceptionally, a plaintiff may succeed by showing that the defendant's conduct materially contributed to risk of the plaintiff's injury, where (a) the plaintiff has established that her loss would not have occurred "but for" the negligence of two or more tortfeasors, each possibly in fact responsible for the loss; and (b) the plaintiff, through no fault of her own, is unable to show that any one of the possible tortfeasors in fact was the necessary or "but for" cause of her injury, because each can point to one another as the possible "but for" cause of the injury, defeating a finding of causation on a balance of probabilities against anyone.

As it did in *Hanke*, the Court emphasized that but-for remains the default test in cases involving multiple defendants:

> It is important to reaffirm that in the usual case of multiple agents or actors, the traditional "but for" test still applies. The question, as discussed earlier, is whether the plaintiff has shown that one or more of the defendants' negligence was a necessary cause of the injury. Degrees of fault are reflected in calculations made under contributory negligence legislation. By contrast, the material contribution to risk approach applies where "but for" causation cannot be proven against any of multiple defendants, all negligent in a manner that might have in fact caused the plaintiff's injury, because each can use a "point the finger" strategy to preclude a finding of causation on a balance of probabilities.

Thus, although the Court rejects the language of "circular causation" and "dependency causation," it has effectively limited material contribution to risk (for now) to the former scenario. The narrowing of material contribution in *Clements* poses a risk that plaintiffs who are negligently injured by chemical wrongdoing will be denied recovery as a result of uncertainty that is well beyond their control (and indeed, may have been intentional on the part of defendants). The requirement of multiple tortious causes precludes recovery in many cases and will produce absurd results in others.

In the famous case of *Cook v. Lewis*, for example, the Supreme Court of Canada imposed joint and several liability on two defendants who negligently shot in the direction of the plaintiff's face, simultaneously destroying the plaintiff's ability to identify which defendant caused the injury.

The *Clements* approach would inexplicably allow a defendant in the *Cook* scenario to "escape liability if he could show that, while he was negligent, the other shooter was not." Despite this anomaly, it does provide a remedy to plaintiffs who are injured by multiple negligent defendants and in this sense provides a meaningful response to the problem of the indeterminate defendant.

Moreover, the Supreme Court in *Clements* specifically left open the question of whether material contribution to risk might also apply in the indeterminate plaintiff scenario:

> This is not to say that new situations will not raise new considerations. I leave for another day, for example, the scenario that might arise in mass toxic tort litigation with multiple plaintiffs, where it is established statistically that the defendant's acts induced an injury on some members of the group, but it is impossible to know which ones.

Thus, although *Clements* undoubtedly represents a retreat from the broader, principled test of material contribution to risk set out in *Hanke*, it is nevertheless an improvement when compared to the traditional but-for approach.

Proposals for Risk-Based Reforms in Toxic Causation

Commentators have suggested a range of risk-based innovations, including the creation of a new tort of negligent creation of risk, the imposition of a reverse onus on proof of inadequate product testing, probabilistic proportional recovery, and the recognition of a cause of action in battery when plaintiffs are exposed to harmful or poorly understood chemicals.

The most likely starting point for the expansion of risk-based liability in Canada is through a resuscitation of the broad *Hanke* formulation of material contribution to risk as an alternative to but-for causation.

The Case for a Broad Conception of Material Contribution to Risk

The Supreme Court of Canada's decision in *Clements* is the first explicit articulation of risk-based liability in the Canadian law of causation. From this perspective, it can be seen as a significant step forward for toxic tort plaintiffs and environmental public policy. However, the decision clearly curtailed the broad innovation introduced in *Hanke*, while leaving the door open for future incremental reform in the indeterminate plaintiff scenario. The Supreme Court's back-and-forth dance in *Hanke* and *Clements* suggests some discomfort or even confusion in the court's approach to risk-based liability. From the perspective of tort law's traditional goals of compensation and deterrence, it would seem clear that a broad form of liability for material contribution to risk would improve tort law's ability to meet its objectives. More plaintiffs who are tortiously harmed by toxic wrongdoing would receive compensation, and the manufacturers and emitters of toxic substances would have an increased incentive to exercise care in the investigation and dissemination of chemical products and pollution.

Some critics have expressed a "floodgates" concern, suggesting that a broad test of material contribution to risk would eliminate the gate-keeping function of the causation element. Justice Brown, for example, wrote that on the *Hanke* approach, "if causation is the only obstacle, it is no obstacle at all," suggesting that the demonstration of risk at the causation stage would be redundant (and thus unnecessary) since the plaintiff already has to show unreasonable risk in order to establish a breach of the duty of care. While this proposition may hold true in some contexts, it does not apply to the toxic tort arena. The defendant who does not study its substance at all, for example, will undoubtedly be in breach of the duty of care, but will simultaneously make it impossible for the plaintiff to prove a material contribution to risk since there will be a complete lack of data. The demonstration of material contribution to risk requires a substantial body of reliable data as well as expert opinion by relevant scientists. In some cases, a rigorous data set may in fact demonstrate an absence of material risk. In other words, proof of generic causation under a broad conception of material contribution to risk would remain a formidable obstacle to recovery.

In addition to data demonstrating generic causation, plaintiffs seeking to prove a material contribution to risk would also have to adduce evidence concerning the nature of their exposure to the defendant's substance including concentrations, duration, etc. Thus, in many cases the principled risk-based test articulated in *Hanke* would defeat a claim for chemically induced damages; the gate-keeping function of causation remains intact under this approach.

Taking a broader, instrumentalist approach to tort doctrine, it seems clear that the expansion of risk-based liability in Canadian tort law would serve the public interest in environmental health protection. The post-*Clements*, narrow version of risk-based liability privileges defendants who release substances that increase the risk to a population of people but lack sufficient data to ground a finding of but-for causation in any individual case. The *Clements* test only applies in the rare case where the substance-illness connection is clear and the one remaining area of uncertainty is whose product or pollution harmed the plaintiff.

As explained above, with respect to many thousands of chemicals, there is inadequate data to prove causation of harm on a but-for test, even when it is clear that the defendant has exposed people to an unreasonable toxic risk. Defendants have the ability to test their substances, and profit from their production and dissemination; plaintiffs bear the risk of exposure and illness. In this context, there is a compelling argument that as between a negligent defendant and an innocent plaintiff, the former should bear the burden of risk.

Stronger Risk-based Reforms

Recognizing the profound vulnerability of individuals exposed to toxic substances and the converse informational advantage enjoyed by toxic defendants, it seems just to reverse the burden of proof of causation, once a plaintiff has demonstrated material increase in risk or a negligent failure to investigate. Reversing the burden of proof on causation is perhaps the single biggest contribution tort law could make to the generation of safety data on chemical substances. Currently, the rules of causation reward those defendants who produce minimal data, thus precluding a finding of toxicity. Even the broad test of material contribution to risk articulated in *Hanke* cannot be met if there is little or no safety data on the relevant substance.

One way to avoid this perverse incentive is to impose liability for a failure to discover and disseminate adequate information concerning a given product or substance, as proposed by Wendy Wagner and Margaret Berger.

Such liability may be framed in battery or in negligence. In a negligence action, the plaintiff should be required to prove that the defendant did not conduct adequate investigations and/or disclose relevant information, at which point the burden of proof on causation should be reversed. This formulation reverses the incentive structure inherent in the traditional approach by penalizing the manufacture of ignorance and aligning defendants' commercial interests with the societal interest in constraining the release of hazardous or poorly understood chemical substances.

In the battery formulation, liability is imposed based on the defendant knowingly exposing a particular population or individual plaintiff to "harmful or offensive contact" through a toxic or poorly understood substance. Involuntary touching by a toxic substance clearly meets the definition of "harmful or offensive contact" and touching by a substance that is not well understood may be viewed as involuntary experimentation — a recognized species of battery in Canada. Canadian torts jurisprudence has already recognized small-scale toxic battery actions. In one case the court imposed liability where striking workers introduced a chemical spray into the air system of a truck driven by a replacement worker. In another, the court held a landlord liable in "either negligence or battery" for knowingly supplying drinking water contaminated with arsenic to his tenants. Recognition of larger-scale pollution or provision of toxic products as forms of battery would vindicate the right of Canadian citizens to control their own bodies and would incentivize companies to choose safer products and minimize pollution.

Whether framed in negligence or battery, recovery for mere risk exposure (i.e., without present injury) raises questions as to timing and quantification of damages. Ariel Porat and Alex Stein argue that plaintiffs who are exposed to risk should be able to recover an amount proportional to the probability of their incurring the potential injury. They further suggest that plaintiffs should have the option of suing before or after the risk materializes; those who sue for risk alone would be foreclosed from returning to court if the illness ultimately does materialize. Probabilistic proportional recovery for risk alone would appear to be well beyond the conceptual grasp of current Canadian jurisprudence.

However, recovery in battery for involuntary chemical touching is a recognized cause of action in Canada, and a reversal in burden of proof on causation in negligence actions was at least entertained by the Supreme Court of Canada and lower courts in previous decades. It is possible that given the right set of facts, the Court might be willing to revisit this proposal.

Conclusion

There are moments in history when courts are faced with novel harms and must develop novel responses. In the decades following the industrial revolution, for example, society faced an unprecedented form of risk resulting from the new phenomenon of mass production. For the first time, consumers could be exposed to risks created by manufacturers who were far away and socially unaccountable to a person injured by their products. Courts responded with a groundbreaking innovation in the duty of care element of negligence, the articulation of a principled approach that broadened duty beyond the confines of historically recognized categories. Less than a century later, courts in Canada and elsewhere are beginning to recognize yet another unprecedented universe of risks resulting from the burgeoning production and dissemination of chemical products and pollution. Scholars and litigants are asking courts to rise to this challenge just as their predecessors did in response to industrialization.

The introduction of material contribution to risk as an alternative to but-for causation is a baby step in the evolution of Canadian toxic tort law. An expansion of risk-based liability through the broadening of material contribution (per *Hanke*), the imposition of a reverse onus on proof of inadequate testing, and the recognition of toxic battery would go further towards protecting the health of Canadian people and ecosystems. Given the dearth of chemical safety data, and the profound vulnerability of exposed populations, calls for these and other risk-based reforms are likely to persist until they are answered.

Notes and Questions

1. Based on the above article, identify the key deficiencies in current Canadian tort law with respect to causation in the toxic tort context.

2. Do you agree with the reforms advocated by the author with respect to reversing the onus of proof in material contribution situations? Do you support the author's proposal to allow claims for the creation of risk?

3. One of the key cases discussed in the article is *Hanke v. Resurfice Corp.*, 2007 SCC 7, a case in which the SCC addressed the issue of causation, confirming that the but-for test remains the default test for causation. The SCC makes an exception for situations in which, through no fault of the plaintiff, the but-for test causation cannot be established, for example, due to the limits of scientific knowledge. In this situation, it is open to the plaintiff to show causation by showing that: (1) the defendant(s) breached a duty of care in exposing the plaintiff to a material increase in the risk of harm, and (2) the plaintiff suffered from this harm. In these rare situations, the court may impose liability, even though the but-for test is not satisfied. A second, more recent SCC case to address causation is *Clements (Litigation Guardian of)*

v. Clements, 2012 SCC 32. How far does *Clements* advance the common law with respect to causation in environmental cases beyond the narrow exception in *Hanke*?

4.   Some commentators have suggested that the basic objectives of tort law are undermined by the causation issue in combination with the latency of harm in many environmental cases. Assuming that the three objectives of tort law are compensation, deterrence and corrective justice, do you agree? See Albert C. Lin, "Beyond Tort: Compensating Victims of Environmental Toxic Injury" (2004-2005) 78 S. Cal. L. Rev. 1439 at 1444-1453.

Part III — Class Action Suits and Environmental Tort Claims

While a long-standing part of American law, class actions are a relatively new phenomenon in Canada, yet one that is of growing importance. Class action legislation is now in force in nine provinces, with only PEI having yet to enact such a law. While there are some important differences amongst these various laws, all require a representative of the class to obtain certification before commencing a class action. This can be costly; lawyers specializing in the field report that securing certification can cost more than $1 million in legal and expert fees and disbursements. However, once an action is certified, under most class action regimes the plaintiffs are either immune from the spectre of being liable for adverse costs awards or qualify to have such costs paid out of a dedicated fund set aside for this purpose. As well, in many cases, certification will create powerful incentives for the defendant to agree to an out-of-court settlement of the claim.

When class actions first came to Canada, many commentators were optimistic about their potential to redress access to justice barriers in the environmental law context. For instance, Justice Rothman (formerly of the Quebec Court of Appeal) observed that class actions seem to be "a particularly useful remedy in appropriate cases of environmental damage", particularly where the numerous potential plaintiffs were similarly affected by air and water pollution, and would otherwise be deterred from seeking legal recourse by the cost and complexity of litigation.

It would appear, however, that with respect to environmental harms, class actions have yet to make a substantial difference in terms of promoting access to justice. According to Professor Heather McLeod-Kilmurray:

> Although class actions are designed to empower group litigation, environmental class actions are rarely permitted. This is partly because their claims for private law actions seeking monetary compensation cause courts to focus on individual aspects of the problem, and the collective harm caused by widespread environmental effects is overlooked. Because most environmental lawsuits are prohibitively complex and expensive for individuals to litigate, this results in a denial of justice. It also prevents courts from playing their institutional role in the struggle to craft appropriate legal responses [...] Greater focus on the role of groups and the collective nature of environmental harms would lead to different approaches to interpreting class action procedure. [see Heather McLeod-

Kilmurray, "*Hoffman v. Monsanto*: Courts, Class Actions, and Perceptions of the Problem of GM Drift" (2007) 27 *Bul Sci, Tech & Soc* 188]

Consider the following commentary, which offers a comparison of class action approaches in English Canada and Quebec. It concludes that the rest of Canada might be well served to look to Quebec for guidance on how to make class actions work in an environmental context. As you read this commentary, think back to the case of *Smith v. Inco Ltd.*, and in particular, the exclusion of human health impacts during the class certification process, and the impact this had on the claim in nuisance and strict liability based on diminution of property value.

Christie Kneteman,
"Revitalizing Environmental Class Actions:
Quebecois Lessons for English Canada"
(2010) 6 Can. Class Action Rev. 261

The Ontario Law Reform Commission (OLRC) has identified three main benefits of class actions: improving access to justice, encouraging behaviour modification, and serving judicial economy. Environmental class actions can generate these advantages when addressing the property and health effects of environmental torts. Environmental torts often affect large numbers of people, but their cost and complexity render individual actions non-viable. Facilitating the use of environmental class actions can help obtain compensation for affected individuals while deterring future environmental harm.

However, environmental class actions have been underutilized in English Canada since the Supreme Court's decision to refuse certification in *Hollick v. Toronto (City)*. [...] Environmental class actions have been generally unsuccessful in all provinces other than Quebec. As a result, many individuals in English Canada who have suffered harm to their health and property from environmental torts have been left without an avenue of redress. [...]

Access to Justice

Cost and complexity are the greatest barriers to individuals bringing actions for environmental harm. These impediments are especially problematic when one considers that many victims of environmental torts are members of vulnerable or marginalized communities. Class actions improve access to justice by consolidating individually non-viable claims and extending class coverage to individuals who would otherwise be unable to seek redress.

The costs of individual environmental actions often exceed their potential for recovery [...]. Class actions were intended to remedy exactly this kind of situation, "where complexity and expert scientific evidence make conflicting findings likely and individual litigation virtually impossible to afford." [...] [T]he number of potential claimants creates economies of scale for legal fees and makes it possible to attract counsel on a contingency basis.

In addition, environmentally harmful activities often occur in lower-income neighbourhoods, where the least enfranchised members of society live. [...] Environmental class action can provide financial and social support to individual

claimants. Class counsel can help educate the community about their legal rights.
[...]

Behaviour Modification

Environmental class action can directly or indirectly force polluters to modify their behaviour. Directly, class action can motivate corporate change by threatening large damage awards. Indirectly, they can stimulate the tightening of environmental regulations. [...] As explained by McLachlin C.J. in *Western Canadian Shopping Centres Inc. v. Dutton*, "[w]ithout class actions, those who cause wide-spread but individually minimal harm might not take into account the full costs of their conduct." [...] In modifying their behaviour or "internalizing" these costs, corporations become more aware of the potential for harm and quicker to act when there is even a small risk to their neighbours. [...]

Sometimes, however, companies may comply with existing environmental regulations but still cause unacceptable levels of harm. A class action can demonstrate to politicians the scope and extent of the harm caused by inadequate environmental standards. [...] An environmental class action can thereby be one of the most effective ways to instigate the tightening of lax regulations. [...]

Judicial Economy

By its nature, environmental harm often has widespread effects and impacts large groups of people. An environmental class action has the advantage of being able to reduce the total amount of litigation arising out of a single dispute, to resolve all common issues in one trial, and to prevent inconsistent outcomes across similar cases. [...]

For example, *Ring v. Canada (Attorney General)* involved the application of allegedly toxic herbicide over a large area and for a lengthy period of time. In this case, Barry J. noted that, "where a class consists of tens of thousands of people, access to justice would be promoted and judicial economy achieved by having the common issues resolved at a single hearing." He added that, "[f]urthermore, if the common issue [of general causation] is resolved in favour of the defendants and third parties, thousands of trials will probably be avoided."

[...] However, the goal of judicial economy has the potential to give perverse incentives against certifying non-individually viable claims. Professor Garry Watson notes this tension in his examination of Moldaver J.'s judgment in *Abdool v. Anaheim Management*: "[...] assuming that the plaintiffs will not proceed with their claims in the absence of a class action, judicial economy will always be served by denying certification." [...]

Comparing the Performance of Environmental Class Actions in English Canada and Quebec

In *Western Canadian Shopping Centres*, McLachlin C.J. emphasized that pollution cases may be especially suited to class proceedings because "[e]nvironmental pollution may have consequences for citizens all over the country." However, since *Hollick* there has been little success certifying environmental class actions in English Canada, especially when proposed actions include claims for personal injury. In contrast, Quebec has gained a reputation as Canada's "class action haven", particularly in the domain of environmental class actions. [...]

[T]here have been over two-and-a-half times as many environmental class actions in Quebec than in the rest of Canada combined. Of these, only four environmental class actions in English Canada (or 27 percent of the total) have been granted certification. In contrast, 68 percent of environmental class actions in Quebec were certified.

In addition, only one environmental class action has gone to trial in English Canada, while eleven of twenty-six — or 42 percent — of certified environmental class actions have gone to trial in Quebec. Of these Quebecois trails, 36 percent have found for the defendants.

Overall, it appears that courts in Quebec are more likely to certify environmental class actions — in order to "ensure a balance of power between the parties" [translation] — but they are also willing to find for the defendants on the merits of the case.

Treatment of Health-Related Claims

On a qualitative level, it is important to note the differential treatment of health-related environmental class actions in English Canada and Quebec. Most environmental class actions that have been granted certification in English Canada have focused on property value diminution and have excluded personal injury claims. In contrast, courts in Quebec have been willing to certify environmental class actions that involved personal injuries. [...]

In light of the goals of class action — especially that of improving access to justice — the trend in English Canadian courts to exclude claims for personal injuries in environmental class actions is worrisome and problematic. While damages to property are much easier to prove and calculate, class actions are intended to empower individuals to seek redress for harms that they could not bring individually. This objective is especially important for individuals who are already marginalized and unlikely to be able to bring actions on their own behalf. [...]

Differences in the Quebecois Approach to Environmental Class Actions

[...] First and foremost, the representative plaintiff in Quebec has the right to appeal a decision refusing certification, but a defendant has no right of appeal from a decision certifying a class action. In addition, there is no risk to class representatives or class counsel of heavy costs if certification is denied. In the case of a refusal, the representative plaintiff must simply pay $50 in court costs.

[...] [S]tautory causes of action are used more frequently in environmental class actions in Quebec. [...] In contrast, statutory causes of action are rarely relied upon in environmental class actions in English Canada. [...] According to Professor Ward Branch, statutory obligations and civil remedies for environmental damage reduce the individual issues in a class action. Branch believes that "class actions in environmental law will be easier to sustain as legislatures move toward the creation of statutory civil remedies for environmental damage." The mere existence of environmental protection statutes, however, appears to be insufficient to facilitate environmental class actions. Differences in quality and accessibility may account for the large discrepancy in the use of environmental statutory causes of actions in French and English Canada.

Precedents' Influence of Judicial Discretion

Class action certification proceedings place enormous power and discretion in the hands of judges. The exercise of this discretion is shaped by the personality of the individual judge and the influence of judicial precedents.

Alcan influenced a fairly liberal approach to environmental class actions in Quebec, but *Hollick* has served as a more conservative precedent in English Canada. Curiously, the Supreme Court's decision in *Barrette c. Ciment du St-Laurent inc.* has had little effect on liberalizing courts' treatment of environmental class actions in English Canada. [...]

Alcan's legacy permeates Quebec's liberal approach to environmental class actions. In this case, the plaintiff sought authorization on behalf of 2,400 residents of La Baie to recover damages caused by air pollution from Alcan's port operations. [...] At the Quebec Court of Appeal, Rothman J.A. held that class actions are appropriate and in fact well-suited to resolving environmental cases:

> The class action recourse seems to me a particularly useful remedy in appropriate cases of environmental damage. Air or water pollution rarely affects just one individual or one piece of property. They often cause harm to many individuals over a large geographic area. The issues involved may be similar in each claim, but they may be complex and expensive to litigate, while the amount involved in each case may be relatively modest. [...]

The plaintiff in *Hollick* sought class certification on behalf of 30,000 residents living near the Keele Valley landfill in Toronto. The plaintiff alleged that both physical and noise pollution were unlawfully emanating from the landfill and sought injunctive relief and compensatory and punitive damages.

The Supreme Court dismissed the action on the basis that a class proceeding was not the preferable procedure because, with respect to judicial economy, any common issues were negligible in relation to the individual issues. The judgment in *Hollick* gave the impression that environmental class actions were generally — or even inherently — undesirable due to their perceived overwhelmingly "individualized" nature. [...]

In refusing certification in *Hollick*, McLachlin C.J. took care to caution that "[w]hile the appellant has not met the certification requirements here, it does not follow that those requirements could never be met in an environmental tort case." However, McLachlin C.J.'s attempt to keep open the possibility of environmental class actions has proved less influential than *Hollick*'s overall conservative approach to environmental class action certification.

In contrast, courts in English Canada have taken little note of the Supreme Court's judgment in favour of the plaintiff class in *St-Laurent*. This inattention may be due to a perception that the case was only relevant to Quebec law. However, *St-Laurent* deserves more attention as the Supreme Court's first — and only — judgment on the merits of an environmental class action.

In *St-Laurent*, an environmental class action was brought against dust, odour, and noise pollution from a cement factory. Justices LeBel and Deschamps held that article 976 of the Civil Code of Quebec created a scheme of no-fault liability for neighbouring disturbances, so the company could be held liable even when no fault was proven and all applicable laws had been followed. The Court ultimately found for the plaintiff class [...]. [...] The Court also took pains to distinguish the case from *Hollick* and noted with approval that "the acceptance of no-fault liability furthers environmental protection objectives." [...]

Preferable Procedure

All English Canadian provinces with class action legislation have a similar requirement that a court shall only grant certification if "a class proceeding would be the preferable procedure for the resolution of the common issues." While the requirement for preferable procedure is not explicit in the Quebec legislation, it is present throughout Quebec jurisprudence on class actions.

However, courts in Quebec and English Canada have different approaches to determining whether a class action is a preferable procedure. English Canadian courts have favoured a predominance test — whether or not it is required by the province's legislation — which prioritizes concerns of judicial economy. In contrast, the Quebecois approach to preferability focuses on access to justice.

[...] In *Hollick*, the Supreme Court implicitly adopted a predominance test for preferable procedure, which has influenced subsequent jurisprudence in English Canada. In the case, the court held that "it would be impossible to determine whether the class action is preferable in the sense of being a 'fair, efficient and manageable method of advancing the claim' without looking at the common issues in their context." The court's contextual approach required a "cost-benefit analysis" of the impact of certification on the class, the defendants, and the justice system. [...]

Courts in English Canada generally ignore the question of whether there would be any realistic change of redress for plaintiffs with individually non-viable claims if a class action was not certified. However, judges are more likely to include this consideration in the preferability analysis in cases with particularly sympathetic plaintiffs, such as in *Rumley v. British Columbia* and *Cloud*. In *Cloud*, for example, the court held that "[t]he resolution of these common issues therefore takes the action framed in negligence, fiduciary duty and aboriginal rights up to the point where only harm, causation and individual defenses such as limitations remain for determination. This moves the action a long way." The Court's approach here is not easily reconciled with the decision in *Hollick* that individual causation and damage would overwhelm common issues of liability. [...]

In contract to English Canada's fixation on predominance and judicial economy, Quebec's preferable procedure analysis prioritizes access to justice. The purpose of the certification stage is "to filter cases which are manifestly unfounded or clearly frivolous." As long as there is a "serious colour of right," there is generally judicial consensus that a class action would be preferable and more practicable than a proliferation of individual actions. [...] For example, the court in *Curateur public c. Syndicat national des employés de l'Hôpital St-Ferdinand* found that "Québécois class action legislation has a social thrust and favours access to justice, particularly in cases where citizens have been physically or mentally harmed" [translation]. In practice, an environmental class action is generally certified if it lends itself adequately to a collective treatment of the defendant's liability. [...]

General Causation

Whether a class action is considered the preferable procedure in a particular case is often influenced by whether the court believes that resolving questions of general causation will significantly advance the action. Causation analysis requires two steps: establishing general causation — that a substance is capable of having a particular effect — and then establishing specific causation (that exposure led to this effect in a particular individual). General causation is a common issue to all class members, while specific causation is an individual issue that cannot be determined in a class action. One reason why Quebec courts have been more willing to certify environmental class actions is that they are more likely than courts in English Canada to consider resolution of questions of general causation to significantly advance a case. [...]

Courts in English Canada [however] often refuse to certify environmental class actions there they believe that determining the common issue of general causation will not be helpful in advancing the action overall. For example, in *Inco*, Nordheimer J. identified the question of general causation in the case as "at what level do the contaminants of concern pose a risk to the natural environment or to human health, or both?" However, he declared that all the common issues in the case, including that of general causation, were of "no more than theoretical interest" and their resolution would not significantly advance the action. [...]

Judicial Creativity

Finally, the certification of environmental class actions in Quebec is facilitated by the creativity of judges in establishing subgroups among class members. Creating subgroups, and assigning damage amounts to class members in each group, significantly decrease the number of individual issues in the case. [...] For example, in *St-Laurent* the Quebec Superior Court heard evidence from a representative sample of sixty-two class members regarding the degree of property damage and inconvenience they had suffered as a result of a cement plant's operation. Based on their testimony, Dutil J. created four subgroups or "zones." The judge determined the amount of damages to be awarded to each class member by calculating an average for each zone of the amount of injury suffered due to the defendant's misconduct. On appeal, the Supreme Court confirmed that Dutil J.'s approach was reasonable and appropriate, "given the trial judge's discretion and the difficulty of assessing environmental problems and annoyances." [...]

In light of the success of numerous Quebecois judges [...] in creating subgroups, where appropriate, to assess damages, it appears that the Supreme Court's concerns of "overwhelming" individual damage assessment in *Hollick* could have been easily addressed with a more creative judicial approach.

Conclusion

Environmental class actions can be useful tools to improve the health and well-being of Canadians and their environment, but their potential is being stifled in most provinces. English Canadian courts should look to Quebec for lessons on how to facilitate class actions on environmental issues. While certain discrepancies would require legislation to resolve, most could be addressed within the confines of judicial discretion.

In particular, courts in English Canada should be guided by precedents such as *St-Laurent*, *Alcan*, and *Inco*, which acknowledge how class actions are well-suited to resolving environmental problems. Courts should also place more weight on the goal of access to justice when determining whether a class action would be the preferable procedure in a particular case. In addition, judges should acknowledge that resolving questions of general causation can be helpful in moving cases forward, and they should feel empowered to create subgroups among the class when appropriate. [...]

Notes and Questions

1. What difference would it have made to the *Palmer* case if it had proceeded by way of a class action suit?

2. Having read this article, what, if any, changes would you make to the rules for certifying class action suits in your province? How would these changes improve the effectiveness of tort law in the environmental field? Should rules for class action certification be different for environmental cases than for other tort claims? Explain.

3. One of the challenges in English Canada has been the interaction between tort law and class certification rules under provincial legislation. Tort law has a tendency to require plaintiffs concerned about environmental harm to establish their claim in terms of the impact on human health and property rather than more directly based on the environmental harm of the defendant's conduct. Class action certification rules in English Canada tend to reject those very claims because the impact tends to be very individualistic. What solution do you see to this conundrum? Would you change the approach to class action certification, or would you broaden tort claims to include environmental harm independent from impact on human health or property?

4. There are some notable differences among the various provincial legislative class action regimes. In Ontario, for example, there is no immunity for adverse costs even after the class has been certified. This means that the representative plaintiff could potentially be liable for a significant adverse costs award if the action were ultimately unsuccessful. Recognizing the negative implications of this rule for access to justice, the Ontario legislation creates a fund of money, administered by the Law Foundation, that is available to provide indemnity for representative plaintiffs in certain cases. Representative plaintiffs must apply to the fund and persuade the committee that manages the fund *inter alia* that their case is meritorious and in the public interest. In *Smith v. Inco Ltd.*, 2012 ONSC 5094, affirmed 2013 ONCA 724, leave to appeal refused 2014 CarswellOnt 7503 (S.C.C.), the trial judge ordered costs against the unsuccessful plaintiffs, payable out of the fund, a decision that was upheld by the Court of Appeal. Other provinces, such as

BC, have opted to extend post-certification costs immunity to representative plaintiffs on the basis that this is a necessary measure to ensure access to justice. Along with the rules for certification, the issue of costs is often critical to plaintiffs in deciding whether to proceed with a class action. Consider the overall approach to costs in your province and its implications for environmental class actions. Can you find a more suitable approach in another province?

5. In early February 2009, a BC coastal First Nation filed the first class action based on Aboriginal rights alleging that the BC government should be held liable for damages as a result of licencing the operation of open-cage fish farms that it alleges has contributed to a steep decline in wild salmon stocks that its members have traditionally relied on for food and ceremonial purposes. In May 2012, the BC Court of Appeal rendered its decision on the certification in *Kwicksutaineuk/Ah-Kwa-Mish First Nation v. British Columbia (Minister of Agriculture and Lands)*, 2012 BCCA 193, leave to appeal refused 2012 CarswellBC 3565 (S.C.C.). The BC Court of Appeal overturned the trial judge, who had allowed the certification. It took the position that class proceedings in BC are limited to a group with individual rights, and cannot be applied to collective rights held by a group.

6. Nova Scotia was one of the last provinces to enact legislation in the form of the *Class Proceedings Act*, S.N.S. 2007, c. 28. The first environmental court case to apply the new Act relates to one of the most notorious contaminated sites in Canada, the Sydney Tar Ponds. In 2011, the Supreme Court of Nova Scotia certified a class action suit brought by the property owners and residents of an affected neighbourhood. See *MacQueen v. Sydney Steel Corp.*, 2011 NSSC 484, reversed 2013 NSCA 143, reconsideration/ rehearing refused *Canada (Attorney General) v. MacQueen*, 2014 NSCA 73, leave to appeal refused [2015] 1 S.C.R. ix (note), in which Justice Murphy classified two classes of claimants: property owners and residents. The Nova Scotia Court of Appeal allowed the appeal and struck the certification, and in the process has made environmental class actions under the current legislation in Nova Scotia very difficult. For a case comment, see Meinhard Doelle, "The Sydney Tar Ponds Case: Shutting the Door on Environmental Class Action Suits in Nova Scotia?" (2015) 27 J. Envtl. L. & Prac. 279.

Part IV — Tort Litigation Aimed at Deterring Public Participation

Tort litigation is not always a tool for environmental protection. It can also be harnessed to discourage public participation in environmental decision making and, more generally, in public debate surrounding environmental issues. The activities targeted in such suits include what many would consider to be at the core of a robust democracy: reporting health or environmental violations; filing complaints with government agencies; circulating petitions; information picketing; writing letters to government or the media; speaking at community, environmental or land use planning meetings; providing information to the media; and engaging in public information campaigns. Strategic Lawsuits Against Public Participation (SLAPP) suits characterize these ostensibly lawful activities as tortious: alleging defamation, inducing breach of contract, conspiracy and interference with contractual relations, and various other economic torts.

In the United States, SLAPP suits have reached epidemic proportions, prompting over 20 states to enact anti-SLAPP legislation. In addition to these statutory protections, defendants targeted in SLAPP suits filed in US courts can invoke the protection of the "right to petition" government as guaranteed by the First Amendment to the US Constitution. While the province of British Columbia became the first province to pass anti-SLAPP legislation (*Protection of Public Participation Act*, S.B.C. 2001, c. 19) in 2001, this law was later repealed following a change in government. Since then both Quebec and Ontario have enacted anti-SLAPP legislation, and the BC government has recently introduced legislation (modelled on the Ontario law) that would return anti-SLAPP protection in that province. The *Charter* has been interpreted as not applying in "private litigation" (see *Dolphin Delivery Ltd. v. R.W.D.S.U., Local 580*, [1986] 2 S.C.R. 573). Therefore, unlike their American counterparts, Canadian SLAPP targets are precluded from defending themselves by relying on *Charter* protections such as freedom of expression and association.

In Canada, SLAPP suits have been particularly prominent in the realm of environmental and land use decision making. According to one Canadian commentator, "SLAPPs directly threaten the core values of modern environmental law and policy: the right of citizens to participate in decision-making [...] [moreover] as public participation is enhanced both quantitatively and qualitatively so too will the incentive increase for powerful interests to respond by bringing [SLAPP suits]." See Chris Tollefson, "Strategic Lawsuits Against Public Participation: Developing a Canadian Response" (1994) 73 Can. Bar Rev. 200 at 201.

<hr>

Michaelin Scott & Chris Tollefson,
"Strategic Lawsuits Against Public Participation:
The British Columbia Experience"
(2010) 19 R.E.C.I.E.L. 45

An Overview of the SLAPP Phenomenon

SLAPPs are civil law suits that target citizens or citizen groups with a view to deterring their participation in public decision-making or policymaking processes, or undermining their efforts to influence public opinion. SLAPPs are often brought by corporations with an economic interest in the outcome of the issue at stake. Such suits are generally unmeritorious, and are aimed at thwarting or deterring otherwise legal behaviour such as demonstrating, boycotting, advocacy at public meetings, posting information on the Internet, signing or circulating petitions and so forth.

The power of a SLAPP comes not from the strength of the filer's legal position, but through the strategic use of the legal arena to intimidate the target and to exhaust its often limited resources. Eventually, despite being within their legal rights, SLAPP targets are often forced to abandon the advocacy work that has triggered the suit. Sometimes, the mere threat of being sued is sufficient to intimidate a target of a suit into submission.

While SLAPPs squander judicial resources and often represent an abuse of the judicial process, arguably their most detrimental impact is on democratic participation and dialogue. In many cases, winning the lawsuit is not the filer's principal goal. Instead, unlike typical plaintiffs, they use such suits for a variety of tangential purposes including silencing the target and draining its resources, discouraging future opposition, and offering a highly visible warning to others who might wish to express an opinion. As such, the harm associated with such suits is not only visited on their targets but also on the public at large.

In order to prevent SLAPPs, they first must be recognized and distinguished from conventional, *bona fide* tort lawsuits. Defining what constitutes a SLAPP is essential to developing a legislative fix. This can be surprisingly difficult. Among other things, determining which activities should be protected from legal action, and which should not, can involve complicated and competing policy priorities and considerations.

SLAPPs are usually framed using a wide variety of tort claims including defamation, conspiracy, trespass, interference with contractual relations, inducing breach of contract and nuisance. Given that SLAPPs will often closely resemble an ordinary tort lawsuit, identifying SLAPPs can be difficult. These definitional difficulties also present challenges for those who seek to quantify the pervasiveness of the SLAPP phenomenon; including the frequency with which such suits have been filed, and the magnitude of their impact in terms of squandered public and private resources.

Contributing to this quantification challenge is the fact that, much of the time, SLAPP cases do not proceed to trial. Given their limited resources, many targets are unable to mount a vigorous defence of their rights. As noted above, in many cases, victory over a potential SLAPP target is achieved without a suit being filed, with the mere threat of litigation dissuading the target from pursuing the battle any further.

In defining the scope of lawful democratic participation deserving of protection from SLAPPs, it is crucial to balance the right of the filer to access the justice system in order to protect its economic interests against the interest of the target in securing protection from suits brought for an improper purpose. As will be discussed, this is one of the most complex and contentious issues when developing a legislative response to SLAPPs.

Legal context is also important. In crafting a legislative response, reformers must be mindful of the context in which antecedent legislative anti-SLAPP responses have emerged. This is particularly true with respect to the US experience where, under American constitutional law, the right to petition government has been interpreted to lend broad constitutional protection to a wide variety of communications directed at government. This 'right to petition' is grounded in the First Amendment. Over time, this constitutional right has been relied on with considerable success by American SLAPP targets even in jurisdictions where there is no anti-SLAPP legislation. Because of the constitutionally protected right to petition, many US anti-SLAPP statutes do not incorporate a requirement that the suit be unmeritorious since, by definition, a lawsuit that targets constitutionally protected petitioning behaviour cannot succeed.

Currently, Canadian law does not extend protection to 'petitioning' activity that could be threatened by SLAPPs. Although the Canadian Charter of Rights and Freedoms (the Charter) guarantees the right to freedom of thought, belief, opinion and expression including freedom of the press, and freedom of peaceful assembly, it does not afford a constitutional defence to Canadians facing a SLAPP. This is because Canadian courts have interpreted the Charter to only apply to government action; as such, they have declined to extend Charter protection in disputes between private parties. This means that in Canada, SLAPP targets cannot invoke the protection of the Charter where they are being sued by another private party.

Despite this, there are compelling policy reasons for revisiting the bright line Canadian courts have drawn between State action and private litigation. An indication of an emerging judicial appetite to inject Charter values into the realm of tort law, with a view to promoting the public interest, is a recent decision of the Supreme Court of Canada that recognizes a new defence of 'responsible journalism' in defamation cases. This said, identifying and responding to SLAPPs remains a more complex and challenging task in Canadian jurisdictions than in the USA.

It must also be borne in mind that legal recognition of the rights of SLAPP targets — whether under a constitutional guise or some other legislative regime — is not a panacea. This is due to the chilling effect often associated with litigation of this kind. This chilling effect is, in turn, closely related to what is often a gross imbalance of economic power as between the parties, particularly once their dispute moves from the realm of politics into the courtroom. To be effective, therefore, a SLAPP remedy must be alive to and address this economic imbalance in ways that level the legal playing field; to do so requires reforming the law governing how legal 'costs' are allocated during and after the litigation. Achieving this goal will usually require either significant reforms to the rules governing civil procedure or the enactment of a stand-alone anti-SLAPP statute. As will be discussed, in recognition of the need for a comprehensive response to the phenomenon, after much debate in BC, it was ultimately decided that purpose-built, stand-alone anti-SLAPP legislation was necessary. [...]

Reducing the Cost of Defending a SLAPP

Much of the chilling effect of SLAPPs comes simply from anxiety surrounding the financial burden that defending a SLAPP almost inevitably entails. Reducing some of these costs by accelerating the hearing of a summary dismissal application is an important step towards reducing this burden. However, preparing for such an application requires a considerable amount of legal work, particularly because the defendant still bears the onus of proof.

Therefore, the PPPA also contained other mechanisms for decreasing the economic burden on the defendant of a SLAPP, particularly in relation to costs. As discussed above, in a typical BC law suit, the successful party is only awarded its 'party and party' costs, meaning that the unsuccessful party is obliged to pay an amount of money that typically represents approximately one half of its opponent's actual legal fees. In contrast, under the PPPA, if the defendant succeeded in her application for summary dismissal of the action, the court had discretion to order that the plaintiff pay 'all reasonable costs and expenses' incurred by the defendant. It should, however, be noted that such orders for full indemnification were not mandatory and, as such, whether and to what extent they would have relieved the financial burden on SLAPP targets remains somewhat speculative.

Thus, while this provision was a step in the right direction, many considered that it did not go far enough. This is because costs awards, both in ordinary civil litigation and under the PPPA, typically come at the end of trial. And because legal proceedings can take months, if not years, to be resolved, a target's legal bill can grow exponentially. SLAPP filers rely on this fact in the hopes of winning a war of attrition. As such, the prospect of an award of costs in the future may do little to 'relieve the more immediate day-to-day hardship felt by SLAPP targets'.

Disincentives to SLAPP Filers

The most effective way to provide protection to SLAPP targets is to prevent SLAPPs from being filed in the first place. If this goal is achieved, potential targets avoid expending their scarce funds defending meritless claims. Moreover, the chilling effect of such suits on public participation is prevented. Building disincentives against the filing of SLAPPs into a statutory regime is thus a key challenge for anti-SLAPP law drafters, and an area in which the PPPA deserves significant credit for innovation.

One area of innovation in this regard under the PPPA has already been discussed: the availability of cost awards to cover all 'reasonable costs and expenses' of the defendant. This represents an important financial deterrent to prospective SLAPP filers. Moreover, the PPPA broadened the discretion of courts to award punitive damages against a filer, either on its own motion or on the application of the defendant. The awarding of punitive or exemplary damages in a typical tort lawsuit is very rare; normally they are granted in only the most egregious of circumstances, where a party's actions offend community standards. By recognizing a broader judicial discretion to award punitive damages in SLAPP cases, the PPPA clearly underscored that the highhanded use of non-meritorious litigation to threaten and intimidate individuals exercising their democratic rights is unacceptable and not to be tolerated.

Another significant disincentive under the PPPA aimed at deterring SLAPP filers were its provisions relating to interim costs awards. If a defendant, on an application for dismissal, was unable to satisfy the court on a *balance of probabilities* that the action filed against them was a SLAPP (i.e. that the impugned conduct constituted public participation and that the proceeding was brought for an improper purpose), but was nonetheless able to prove that there was a *realistic possibility* that it was, the court could order that the plaintiff provide security in an amount considered sufficient to indemnify the defendant, and also an amount for punitive or exemplary damages to which the defendant may become entitled. This amount would be paid into court until the proceedings were completed, thus ensuring that these monies remained under judicial control for the duration of the trial process. This innovative provision created a powerful disincentive against delaying the case and against maintaining an action that had little prospect of succeeding.

Of course, there are some SLAPP filers whose economic power is so immense that this upfront expense would have little or no effect on their conduct of the case. Therefore, the PPPA empowered a court, where there was a realistic possibility that the suit was a SLAPP, to order that any settlement, discontinuance or abandonment of the action be approved by the court, on terms the court considered appropriate. This unusual form of judicial oversight afforded significant protection for a target who felt compelled to settle for terms inconsistent with the merits of their legal case. Under this provision, a court could examine the proposed settlement and make any changes that it felt necessary to ensure fairness in the circumstances. Furthermore, if the plaintiff decided to discontinue the action, perhaps because it had achieved its intended purpose of silencing the target, the court could impose terms on the plaintiff as a rebuke for its behaviour, despite not being able to render a decision on the actual case. This ongoing judicial supervision was intended to serve as a disincentive to those filers who did not have an honest belief that the action was necessary to enforce their legitimate rights. While an important innovation, this provision is by no means unique and indeed bears some resemblance to the broad supervisory powers given to courts in the oversight of class actions.

A final disincentive to SLAPP filers were provisions, discussed earlier, that shifted the onus of disproving improper purpose to a plaintiff once the defendant showed that there was a realistic possibility that the suit was a SLAPP. This onus-shifting provision was aimed at ensuring that a plaintiff could not file a tort claim and then bide its time while the defendant incurred the expenses associated with gathering the evidence necessary to refute its claim.

Although there were certainly some weaknesses and gaps in the PPPA, on balance, had it remained on the books, it would have significantly enhanced protection from SLAPPs in BC, and, in our view, measurably diminished their prevalence within the province. [...]

Notes and Questions

1. In *Daishowa Inc. v. Friends of the Lubicon* (1998), 27 C.E.L.R. (N.S.) 1 (Ont. Gen. Div.), the plaintiff, one of the world's largest pulp and paper companies, was targeted in a boycott campaign mounted by a small Toronto-based advocacy group known as the Friends of the Lubicon (FOL). The goal of the campaign was to secure Daishowa's agreement not to log on un-treated lands in northern Alberta, claimed by the Lubicon Cree, until the Lubicon's title claim had been resolved. The campaign consisted of various activities including information picketing at various retail locations where the company's paper products were in use, and efforts to persuade Daishowa wholesale purchasers not to renew their supply contracts. Daishowa alleged these actions constituted a tortuous conspiracy to injure its business, an interference with its contractual relations, and an inducement to its clients to

breach their contracts. Daishowa also alleged the FOL's use of the term "genocide" in its campaign literature was defamatory.

At the end of a 28-day trial, the trial judge dismissed the case against the defendants with the exception of the defamation claim, in respect of which it awarded damages of one dollar. Daishowa filed but later abandoned an appeal. Consider whether, in your view, the *Daishowa* case can, in all the circumstances, be considered as a SLAPP suit.

2. One of the first judicial considerations of SLAPPs in Canada was *Fraser v. Saanich (District)* (1999), 32 C.E.L.R. (N.S.) 143 (B.C. S.C.). In this case, a developer sued a group of residents who had campaigned against her attempt to rezone a property for development purposes. The lawsuit alleged conspiracy and a variety of other economic torts. The trial judge dismissed the action summarily, finding that it "not only contains an unreasonable claim, is meritless and devoid of any factual foundation, but also has been used as an attempt to stifle the democratic activities of the defendants, the neighbourhood residents. I find the plaintiffs' conduct reprehensible and deserving of censure by an award of special costs".

3. Since the first SLAPP legislation in Canada was repealed in BC in 2001, the issue of SLAPP suits has not disappeared in that province. One of the most interesting recent developments in BC is a case in which a local government employed SLAPP-style tactics against its critics. In this case, the City of Powell River (the City) threatened to sue three local residents who had objected to the City's decision to support a local harbour development. The City sent letters to the residents alleging that their public comments about the project were defamatory, and demanded a retraction and apology. The matter was brought before the BC Supreme Court, which held that it would be contrary to the *Charter of Rights and Freedoms* to allow a public body to bring a suit in these circumstances: *Dixon v. Powell River (City)*, 2009 BCSC 406. Special costs were also recently awarded by the BC Supreme Court against the filer of a claim that was summarily dismissed, on the basis that it constituted a SLAPP suit: *Scory v. Krannitz*, 2011 BCSC 936. This case, like many that in this area of law, arose out of a local land-use dispute. In 2018, the BC government again introduced anti-SLAPP legislation in the legislature. As of early 2019, the bill has only passed first reading.

4. In 2009, in the context of defamation, the SCC recognized a new defence of responsible communication on matters of public interest in *Grant v. Torstar Corp*, 2009 SCC 61, and *Cusson v. Quan*, 2009 SCC 62. The SCC applied a two-part test to determine whether the defence to defamation was made out:

- The defendant must establish that the communication related to a matter of "public interest" defined broadly to include matters ranging from science, the arts, environment, religion and morality.

- The Court looked to guiding factors to determine due diligence, i.e. seriousness of the allegation; public importance of the matter; urgency of the matter; status and reliability of the source; whether the plaintiff's side of the story was sought; whether inclusion of the defamatory statement was justifiable; and whether the defamatory statement lay in the fact it was made rather than its truth.

This new approach to defamation is encouraging in its recognition of the importance of public engagement in important matters of public interest. Does it offer effective protection against SLAPP suits?

5. In Ontario, anti-SLAPP protections came into effect in 2015 based on recommendations made in 2010 by an Anti-SLAPP Advisory Panel. These protections are set out in section 137.1 of the *Courts of Justice Act*, R.S.O. 1990, c. C.43. Below we provide extracts from section 137.1 and from *1704604 Ontario Ltd. v. Pointes Protection Association*, the first appellate case to interpret this new legislation.

Ontario Anti-SLAPP Legislation
Court of Justice Act, R.S.O. 1990, c. C.43

Prevention of Proceedings that Limit Freedom of Expression on Matters of Public Interest (Gag Proceedings)

Dismissal of proceeding that limits debate

Purposes

137.1 (1) The purposes of this section and sections 137.2 to 137.5 are,

(a) to encourage individuals to express themselves on matters of public interest;

(b) to promote broad participation in debates on matters of public interest;

(c) to discourage the use of litigation as a means of unduly limiting expression on matters of public interest; and

(d) to reduce the risk that participation by the public in debates on matters of public interest will be hampered by fear of legal action.

Definition, "expression"

(2) In this section,

"expression" means any communication, regardless of whether it is made verbally or non-verbally, whether it is made publicly or privately, and whether or not it is directed at a person or entity.

Order to dismiss

(3) On motion by a person against whom a proceeding is brought, a judge shall, subject to subsection (4), dismiss the proceeding against the person if the person satisfies the judge that the proceeding arises from an expression made by the person that relates to a matter of public interest.

No dismissal

(4) A judge shall not dismiss a proceeding under subsection (3) if the responding party satisfies the judge that,

(a) there are grounds to believe that,

(i) the proceeding has substantial merit, and

(ii) the moving party has no valid defence in the proceeding; and

(b) the harm likely to be or have been suffered by the responding party as a result of the moving party's expression is sufficiently serious that the public interest in permitting the proceeding to continue outweighs the public interest in protecting that expression.

No further steps in proceeding

(5) Once a motion under this section is made, no further steps may be taken in the proceeding by any party until the motion, including any appeal of the motion, has been finally disposed of.

No amendment to pleadings

(6) Unless a judge orders otherwise, the responding party shall not be permitted to amend his or her pleadings in the proceeding,

(a) in order to prevent or avoid an order under this section dismissing the proceeding; or
(b) if the proceeding is dismissed under this section, in order to continue the proceeding.

Costs on dismissal

(7) If a judge dismisses a proceeding under this section, the moving party is entitled to costs on the motion and in the proceeding on a full indemnity basis, unless the judge determines that such an award is not appropriate in the circumstances.

Costs if motion to dismiss denied

(8) If a judge does not dismiss a proceeding under this section, the responding party is not entitled to costs on the motion, unless the judge determines that such an award is appropriate in the circumstances.

Damages

(9) If, in dismissing a proceeding under this section, the judge finds that the responding party brought the proceeding in bad faith or for an improper purpose, the judge may award the moving party such damages as the judge considers appropriate.

Procedural matters

Commencement

137.2 (1) A motion to dismiss a proceeding under section 137.1 shall be made in accordance with the rules of court, subject to the rules set out in this section, and may be made at any time after the proceeding has commenced.

Motion to be heard within 60 days

(2) A motion under section 137.1 shall be heard no later than 60 days after notice of the motion is filed with the court.

The following is an excerpt from the leading case on the Ontario anti-SLAPP provisions. The decision includes a helpful overview of the new legislative provisions. It also grapples with some of the key elements of the SLAPP test set out in these provisions, including the public interest threshold for imposing the reversed onus, and the merit and public interest hurdles that follow.

1704604 Ontario Ltd. v. Pointes Protection Association
2018 ONCA 685,
additional reasons 2018 ONCA 853

DOHERTY J.A.: —

Introduction

Freedom of expression is a constitutionally-protected right in Canada. The free and open expression of divergent, competing, and strong viewpoints on matters of public interest is essential to personal liberty, self-fulfillment, the search for the truth, and the maintenance of a vibrant democracy.

From time to time, those who are the target of criticism resort to litigation, not to vindicate any genuine wrong done to them, but to silence, intimidate, and punish those who have spoken out. Litigation can be a potent weapon in the hands of the rich and powerful. The financial and personal costs associated with defending a lawsuit, particularly one brought by a deep-pocketed plaintiff determined to maximize the costs incurred in defending the litigation, can deter even the most committed and outspoken critic.

Lawsuits brought to silence and/or financially punish one's critics have come to be known as Strategic Lawsuits Against Public Participation ("SLAPP"). Defamation lawsuits, perhaps because of the relatively light burden the case law places on the plaintiff, have proved to be an ideal vehicle for SLAPPs.

SLAPPs have been part of the litigation landscape in North America for decades: Michaelin Scott & Chris Tollefson, "Strategic Lawsuits Against Public Participation: The British Columbia Experience" (2010) 19:1 R.E.C.I.E.L. 45, at 45. They have evoked various legislative responses sometimes referred to as Anti-SLAPP legislation. This appeal and the others heard with it require this court, for the first time, to interpret Ontario's Anti-SLAPP legislation.

The first Anti-SLAPP legislation in Ontario was introduced in December 2008 by way of a private member's bill. That Bill did not get past first reading: Bill 138, *Protection of Public Participation Act 2008*, 1st Sess., 39th Leg., Ontario, 2008. In 2010, Ontario struck an advisory panel to examine the SLAPP phenomenon and make recommendations as to the appropriate legislative response. In October 2010, that panel recommended Anti-SLAPP legislation: Anti-SLAPP Advisory Panel, *Report to the Attorney General* (Ontario: Ministry of the Attorney General, 2010). In November 2015, Bill 52, the *Protection of Public Participation Act, 2015*, came into force: S.O. 2015, c. 23 (the "Act"). The Act applied to any action commenced on or after December 1, 2014.

The Act amended various statutes, including the *Courts of Justice Act*, R.S.O. 1990, c. C.43 ("*CJA*"). Section 3 of the Act introduced ss. 137.1 to 137.5 to the

CJA. Those sections created a new pretrial procedure allowing defendants to move expeditiously and early in the litigation for an order dismissing claims arising out of expressions by defendants on matters of public interest. The sections are attached as Appendix A to these reasons.

Stripped to its essentials, s. 137.1 allows a defendant to move any time after a claim is commenced for an order dismissing that claim. The defendant must demonstrate that the litigation arises out of the defendant's expression on a matter relating to the public interest. If the defendant meets that onus, the onus shifts to the plaintiff to demonstrate that its lawsuit clears the merits-based hurdle in s. 137.1(4)(a) and the public interest hurdle in s. 137.1(4)(b). The details of the legislation are analyzed below.

The Section 137.1 Appeals Before the Court

In April 2016, the appellants, Pointes Protection Association ("Pointes") and individual members of its executive committee (referred to collectively as "Pointes" or "the defendants"), brought a motion under s. 137.1 of the *CJA* to dismiss an action that had been brought against them by 1704604 Ontario Ltd. ("170 Ontario") for breach of contract. In that lawsuit, 170 Ontario alleged that the defendants had breached the terms of a Settlement Agreement (the "Agreement") when one of the defendants gave evidence in a proceeding before the Ontario Municipal Board ("OMB"). 170 Ontario claimed that the terms of the Agreement prohibited the defendants from advancing, through the evidence of one of the defendants, the opinions offered before the OMB.

The motion judge dismissed the defendants' motion and ordered that the action proceed. The defendants appealed to this court pursuant to s. 6(1)(d) of the *CJA*. That section provides a right of appeal from "an order made under s. 137.1". [...]

The Legislation

[...]

Overview of the Legislation

The section of the Act that introduced ss. 137.1 to 137.5 into the *CJA* is entitled "*Prevention of Proceedings that Limit Freedom of Expression on Matters of Public Interest (Gag Proceedings)*". While the title of a legislative provision is far from determinative of its meaning, this title explicitly indicates that the purpose of the legislation is to prevent the use of litigation to "gag" those who would speak out or who have spoken out on matters of public interest.

Section 137.1(1) begins with a statement of the purposes of the provision:

   (a) to encourage individuals to express themselves on matters of public interest;
   (b) to promote broad participation in debates on matters of public interest;
   (c) to discourage the use of litigation as a means of unduly limiting expression on matters of public interest; and
   (d) to reduce the risk that participation by the public in debates on matters of public interest will be hampered by fear of legal action.

The purposes set down in s. 137.1(1) leave no doubt that the legislation was intended to promote free expression on matters of public interest by "discouraging" and "reducing the risk" that litigation would be used to "unduly" limit such expression.

To achieve the purposes set down in s. 137.1(1), s. 137.1(3) creates a new pretrial remedy. A defendant may move at any time after the proceeding is commenced for an order dismissing the proceeding: s. 137.2(1). Section 137.1(3) reads, in part:

> [A] judge shall, subject to subsection (4), dismiss the proceeding against the person if the person satisfies the judge that the proceeding arises from an expression made by the person that relates to a matter of public interest.

The word "expression" is defined broadly in s. 137.1(2) as:

> [A]ny communication, regardless of whether it is made verbally or non-verbally, whether it is made publicly or privately, and whether or not it is directed at a person or entity.

The phrase "a matter of public interest" in s. 137.1(3) is not defined in the legislation.

Standing alone, s. 137.1(3) would lead to the dismissal of many meritorious claims. To achieve the appropriate balance described by the Panel and the Attorney General at the time, subsection (3) is subject to subsection (4). That section provides that claims that would otherwise be dismissed under subsection (3) shall not be dismissed if the plaintiff (the responding party on the motion) satisfies the motion judge of two things. First, the plaintiff must clear a merits-based hurdle in s. 137.1(4)(a). That subsection requires that the plaintiff satisfy the motion judge that:

> [T]here are grounds to believe that,
>   (i) the proceeding has substantial merit, and
>   (ii) the moving party has no valid defence in the proceeding.

If the plaintiff clears the merits hurdle in s. 137.1(4)(a), it must also clear the public interest hurdle in s. 137.1(4)(b). That provision requires that the plaintiff satisfy the motion judge that:

> [T]he harm likely to be or have been suffered by the responding party [plaintiff] as a result of the moving party's [defendant's] expression is sufficiently serious that the public interest in permitting the proceeding to continue outweighs the public interest in protecting that expression.

Various provisions in s. 137.1 contain procedural rules intended to expedite the hearing of the s. 137.1 motion and reduce the costs associated with bringing the motion: see ss. 137.1(6), 137.2, and 137.3. Other provisions stay the action in which the motion is brought pending the outcome of the motion: see ss. 137.1(5) and 137.4. Still other provisions potentially impose significant cost consequences on plaintiffs whose claims are dismissed on a s. 137.1 motion, while at the same time providing that plaintiffs who successfully defeat s. 137.1 motions should not, in the normal course, receive their costs of the motion: see ss. 137.1(7) and 137.1(8).

Section 137.1(9) is a unique provision. It allows the motion judge to award damages to the defendant (moving party) if the defendant is successful in having the proceedings dismissed and satisfies the motion judge that the plaintiff brought the proceedings "in bad faith or for an improper purpose".

The purpose of s. 137.1 is crystal clear. Expression on matters of public interest is to be encouraged. Litigation of doubtful merit that unduly discourages and seeks to restrict free and open expression on matters of public interest should not be allowed to proceed beyond a preliminary stage. Plaintiffs who commence a claim alleging to have been wronged by a defendant's expression on a matter of public interest must be prepared from the commencement of the lawsuit to address the merits of the claim and demonstrate that the public interest in vindicating that claim outweighs the public interest in protecting the defendant's freedom of expression.

Significantly, the Act does not, except in a minor way, alter the substantive law as it relates to claims based on expressions on matters of public interest. There are no new defences created for those who speak out on matters of public interest. The law of defamation remains largely unchanged. Similarly, nothing in the Act affects the substantive law applicable to 170 Ontario's breach of contract claim.

Nor does s. 137.1 invoke the abuse of process model favoured in the now repealed British Columbia Anti-SLAPP legislation. Aside from the discretionary damages provision in s. 137.1(9), s. 137.1 does not fix on the plaintiff's purpose or motive in bringing the claim as the determining factor, but instead assesses the potential merits of the claim and the effects of permitting the claim to proceed on competing components of the public interest. The emphasis on the litigation's effect over its purpose is said to provide a more streamlined and accurate assessment of the legitimacy of the claims: Anti-SLAPP Advisory Panel, at paras. 32-35. That said, the purpose of the lawsuit can be an important consideration on a s. 137.1 motion. If the motion judge determines that the plaintiff's actual purpose in bringing in the lawsuit was to "gag" the target of the lawsuit on a matter of public interest, it seems highly unlikely that the lawsuit would clear the public interest hurdle in s. 137.1(4)(b).

Instead of creating new defences, removing or modifying existing causes of action, or providing for a more vigorous abuse of process remedy, s. 137.1 seeks to achieve the purposes stated in s. 137.1(1) by first, distinguishing between claims that arise from an expression that relates to a matter of public interest and other claims, and second, by providing for the early and inexpensive dismissal of claims based on expressions relating to matters of public interest, either because those claims lack sufficient merit to proceed, or because the public interest is, on balance, not served by allowing the action to proceed to an adjudication on the full merits.

While the purpose of s. 137.1 is clear, as is often the case, the devil is in the details of the procedure created by s. 137.1. I turn now to those details.

Section 137.1(3): The Threshold Requirement

For convenience, I repeat the section:

[A] judge shall, subject to subsection (4), dismiss the proceeding against the person if the person satisfies the judge that the proceeding arises from an expression made by the person that relates to a matter of public interest.

Section 137.1(3) puts the onus on the defendant (moving party) to satisfy the motion judge that: (i) the proceedings arise from an expression made by the defendant, and (ii) the expression relates to a matter of public interest. The word "satisfies" indicates that the defendant must establish both criteria on the balance of probabilities.

Expression, as defined in s. 137.1(2) (see above at para. 39), includes non-verbal communication and private communications. A legal proceeding arises from an expression if that expression grounds the plaintiff's claim in the litigation. A motion judge reviewing the claim should have little difficulty deciding whether the defendant has established that a claim arises from an expression made by the defendant. Only those claims are subject to s. 137.1.

If the claim arises from an "expression", the defendant must also show, on the balance of probabilities, that the expression "relates to a matter of public interest". That phrase is not defined.

The phrase "public interest" is used in two different ways in s. 137.1. In s. 137.1(4)(b), the phrase is used as a noun to refer to evaluations of the societal interests served by each of the defendant's expression and the plaintiff's claim. The phrase "public interest" as used in s. 137.1(3) (and s. 137.1(1)) has a different meaning. It modifies the word "matter", which refers to the subject matter of the expression giving rise to the claim. The subject matter of the expression must be one that is "of public interest". The "public interest" as referred to in s. 137.1(3) is determined by asking — what is the expression about, or what does it pertain to?

The phrase "public interest" in s. 137.1(3) is not qualified in any way. It does not require that the expression actually furthers the public interest. A qualitative assessment of the expression's impact on the issue to which it is directed is not part of the s. 137.1(3) inquiry. Nothing in the section justifies any distinction among expressions based on the quality, merits, or manner of the expression. An expression that relates to a matter of public interest remains so if the language used is intemperate or even harmful to the public interest. For example, a statement relating to a matter of public interest that is demonstrably false is nonetheless an expression relating to a matter of public interest: see Anti-SLAPP Advisory Panel, at paras. 28-31.

In reading s. 137.1(3) expansively to capture all expressions that relate to matters of public interest, one must bear in mind that the defendant who satisfies its onus under that subsection is not entitled to any relief. A finding in favour of the defendant under s. 137.1(3) only opens the claim to examination under both components of s. 137.1(4). That section provides the mechanism for separating claims arising from expressions on matters relating to public interest that should be allowed to proceed from those that should not. Nonetheless, passing the threshold requirement in s. 137.1(3) is significant in that it moves the burden of persuasion to the plaintiff (responding party) to satisfy the motion judge that the action should proceed.

A broad reading of the phrase "public interest" in s. 137.1(3) is consistent with the purposes described in s. 137.1(1). Any lawsuit that attacks a defendant's expression on a matter of public interest has the potential to unduly discourage public discourse on matters of public interest. Mitigating that risk is best achieved by allowing wide access to the pretrial remedy provided by s. 137.1. The ultimate availability of the remedy will depend on the proper application of s. 137.1(4).

What is "a matter of public interest"? Like virtually all of the motion judges who have wrestled with this issue, I find considerable assistance in the judgment of the Supreme Court of Canada in *Grant v. Torstar Corp.*, 2009 SCC 61, [2009] 3 S.C.R. 640. In that case, the court, following the path cut by this court in *Cusson v. Quan*, 2007 ONCA 771, 87 O.R. (3d) 241, at paras. 133-44, rev'd on other grounds, 2009 SCC 62, [2009] 3 S.C.R. 712, recognized a defence of responsible communication on matters of public interest. Chief Justice McLachlin's analysis of the meaning of "matters of public interest", at paras. 99-109, in the context of establishing the borders of the new defence, is properly applied to the interpretation of the phrase, "a matter of public interest" in s. 137.1(3).

There is no exhaustive list of topics that fall under the rubric "public interest". Some topics are inevitably matters of public interest. The conduct of governmental affairs and the operation of the courts come to mind. Other topics may or may not raise matters of public interest, depending on the specific circumstances: *Grant v. Torstar Corp.*, at paras. 103-106.

The context of a particular expression can be crucial in determining whether that expression relates to a matter of public interest. If the expression that gives rise to the lawsuit is part of a broader communication, the subject matter of the impugned expression is determined by reference to the communication as a whole: *Grant v. Torstar Corp.*, at para. 101. There is a distinction between statements or other expressions that make a reference to something of public interest and expressions that relate to a matter of public interest. Section 137.1(3) captures only the latter. A brief incidental reference to a topic capable of relating to a matter of public interest, in the course of a lengthy exchange of communications devoted to a purely private dispute between the parties, may not be regarded as an expression relating to a matter of public interest. However, the same comment in another context may be regarded as relating to a matter of public interest. The distinction lies in the answer to the question — what is the expression, when placed in its context and taken as a whole, about?

A matter of public interest must be distinguished from a matter about which the public is merely curious or has a prurient interest: *Grant v. Torstar Corp.*, at paras. 102, 105. Public people are entitled to private lives. Expressions that relate to private matters are not converted into matters relating to the public interest merely because those expressions concern individuals in whom the public have an interest or involve topics that may titillate and entertain.

An expression can relate to a matter of public interest without engaging the interest of the entire community, or even a substantial part of the community. It is enough that some segment of the community would have a genuine interest in the subject matter of the expression: *Grant v. Torstar Corp.*, at paras. 102 and 105.

Public interest does not turn on the size of the audience. Especially in today's world, communications on private matters can find very large audiences quickly. On the other hand, statements between two people can relate to matters that have a strong public interest component.

Finally, since the promotion of the open exchange of information and opinions on matters of public interest is one of the overarching purposes animating s. 137.1, the characterization of the expression as a matter of public interest will usually be made by reference to the circumstances as they existed when the expression was made.

In summary, the concept of "public interest" as it is used in s. 137.1(3) is a broad one that does not take into account the merits or manner of the expression, nor the motive of the author. The determination of whether an expression relates to a matter of public interest must be made objectively, having regard to the context in which the expression was made and the entirety of the relevant communication. An expression may relate to more than one matter. If one of those matters is a "matter of public interest", the defendant will have met its onus under s. 137.1(3).

When deciding whether an expression relates to a matter of "public interest", the motion judge will apply the legal principles from *Grant v. Torstar Corp.* to the relevant circumstances of the case as determined by the motion judge. The application of a legal standard to a set of facts raises a question of mixed fact and law. Absent the identification of an extricable error of law or a palpable and overriding factual error, an appellate court will defer to the motion judge's assessment: *Housen v. Nikolaisen*, 2002 SCC 33, [2002] 2 S.C.R. 235, at paras. 33-35; *Ledcor Construction Ltd. v. Northbridge Indemnity Insurance Co.*, 2016 SCC 37, [2016] 2 S.C.R. 23, per Wagner J., as he then was, at paras. 35-36, and per Cromwell J. (concurring), at paras. 100-101; *Benhaim v. St-Germain*, 2016 SCC 48, [2016] 2 S.C.R. 352, at paras. 36-39.

Section 137.1(4)(a): The Merits-Based Hurdle

If the defendant (moving party) clears s. 137.1(3), the inquiry moves on to s. 137.1(4)(a). That section reads:

> A judge shall not dismiss a proceeding under subsection (3) if the responding party satisfies the judge that,
> (a) there are grounds to believe that,
>   (i) the proceeding has substantial merit, and
>   (ii) the moving party has no valid defence in the proceedings.

The section puts the onus on the plaintiff (responding party). The word "satisfies" indicates that the balance of probabilities is the applicable standard of proof. The more difficult question is, what is it that the plaintiff must prove on the balance of probabilities? [...]

Broadly speaking, s. 137.1(4)(a) speaks to the potential merits of the lawsuit. Section 137.1(4)(a)(i) refers explicitly to the "merit" of the "proceeding", which I take to be the merits of the claim the plaintiff must prove to succeed in the litigation. Section 137.1(4)(a)(ii) addresses the absence of any "valid defence", which I take to mean any affirmative defence found in the statement of defence, if one has been filed, or specifically advanced in the material filed on the s. 137.1 motion by the defendant. I will explain this further below. [...]

Turning to the specific language of ss. 137.1(4)(a)(i) and (ii), the interpretation must begin by recognizing the purpose of s. 137.1. It provides a judicial screening or triage device designed to eliminate certain claims at an early stage of the litigation process. Sections 137.1(4)(a) and (b) identify the criteria to be used in that screening process. Section 137.1 does not provide an alternate means by which the merits of a claim can be tried, and it is not a form of summary judgment intended to allow defendants to obtain a quick and favourable resolution of the merits of allegations involving expressions on matters of public interest. Instead, the provision aims to remove from the litigation stream at an early stage those cases, which under the criteria set out in the section, should not proceed to trial for a determination on the merits.

Judicial screening of claims at a pretrial stage occurs in both criminal and civil litigation. The purpose of the screening process varies, as do the screening criteria. Judges engaged in pretrial screening generally do not make, however, findings of fact in relation to the issues on which the litigation turns, credibility determinations, or any ultimate assessment of the merits of a claim or a defence.

Put in the context of s. 137.1(4)(a), the motion judge must decide whether a trier could reasonably conclude that the plaintiff's claim has "substantial merit", and that the defendant has "no valid defence". If the motion judge decides that both fall within the range of conclusions reasonably available on the motion record, the plaintiff has met the onus under s. 137.1(4)(a). If the plaintiff does not meet that onus, its claim will be dismissed. [...]

Section 137.1(4)(b): The Public Interest Hurdle

For ease of reference, I repeat the section:

> A judge shall not dismiss a proceeding under subsection (3) if the responding party satisfies the judge that,...
>
> (b) the harm likely to be or have been suffered by the responding party as a result of the moving party's expression is sufficiently serious that the public interest in permitting the proceeding to continue outweighs the public interest in protecting that expression.

In some ways, s. 137.1(4)(b) is the heart of Ontario's Anti-SLAPP legislation. The section declares that some claims that target expression on matters of public interest are properly terminated on a s. 137.1 motion, even though they could succeed on their merits at trial. The "public interest" hurdle reflects the legislature's determination that the success of some claims that target expression on matters of public interest comes at too great a cost to the public interest in promoting and protecting freedom of expression. As explained by the Anti-SLAPP Advisory Panel, at para. 37 of its Report:

> If an action against expression on a matter of public interest is based on a technically valid cause of action but seeks a remedy for only insignificant harm to reputation, business or personal interests, the action's negative impact on freedom of expression may be clearly disproportionate to any valid purpose the litigation might serve. The value of public participation would make any remedy granted to the plaintiff an unwarranted incursion into the domain of protected expression. In such circumstances, the action may also be properly regarded as seeking an inappropriate expenditure of the public resources of the court system. Where these considerations clearly apply, the court should have the power to dismiss the action on this basis.

Under s. 137.1(4)(b), the plaintiff (responding party) has the persuasive burden. The plaintiff must satisfy the motion judge that the harm caused to it by the defendant's expression is "sufficiently serious" that the public interest engaged in allowing the plaintiff to proceed with the claim outweighs the public interest in protecting the defendant's freedom of expression.

The harm suffered or likely to be suffered by the plaintiff as a consequence of the defendant's expression will be measured primarily by the monetary damages suffered or likely to be suffered by the plaintiff as a consequence of the impugned expression. However, harm to the plaintiff can refer to non-monetary harm as well. The preservation of one's good reputation or one's personal privacy have inherent value beyond the monetary value of a claim. Both are tied to an individual's liberty and security interests and can, in the appropriate circumstances, be taken into account in assessing the harm caused to the plaintiff by the defendant's expression: *Hill v. Church of Scientology of Toronto*, [1995] 2 S.C.R. 1130, at paras. 117-21; *Blencoe v. British Columbia (Human Rights Commission)*, 2000 SCC 44, [2000] 2 S.C.R. 307, at paras. 79-80. [...]

On the s. 137.1 motion, the plaintiff must provide a basis upon which the motion judge can make some assessment of the harm done or likely to be done to it by the impugned expression. This will almost inevitably include material providing some quantification of the monetary damages. The plaintiff is not, however, expected to present a fully-developed damages brief. Assuming the plaintiff has cleared the merits hurdle in s. 137.1(4)(a), a common sense reading of the claim, supported by sufficient evidence to draw a causal connection between the challenged expression and damages that are more than nominal will often suffice.

The plaintiff cannot, however, rely on bald assertions in the statement of claim relating to damages, or on unsourced, unexplained damage claims contained in the pleadings or affidavits filed on the s. 137.1 motion. The motion judge must be able to make an informed assessment, at least at a general or "ballpark" level, about the nature and quantum of the damages suffered or likely to be suffered by the plaintiff: see *Able Translations Ltd. v. Express International Translations Inc.*, 2016 ONSC 6785, 410 D.L.R. (4th) 380, at paras. 85-95, aff'd 2018 ONCA 690; *Thompson v. Cohodes*, 2017 ONSC 2590, at paras. 33-38. [...]

Turning to the other side of the balancing exercise in s. 137.1(4)(b), the public interest in protecting the defendant's freedom of expression, the motion judge must assess the public interest in protecting the actual expression that is the subject matter of the lawsuit. On a general level, the importance of freedom of expression, especially on matters of public interest, both to the individual and to the community, is well understood: see *Grant v. Torstar Corp.*, at paras. 32-57. However, if the defendant asserts a public interest in protecting its expression beyond the generally applicable public interest, the evidentiary burden lies on the defendant to establish the specific facts said to give added importance in the specific circumstances to the exercise of freedom of expression.

Unlike the "public interest" inquiry in s. 137.1(3), in which the quality of the expression or the motivation of the speaker are irrelevant (see above at para. 65), both play an important role in measuring the extent to which there is a public interest in protecting that expression. Not all expression on matters of public interest serves the values underlying freedom of expression in the same way or to the same degree. For example, a statement that contains deliberate falsehoods, gratuitous personal attacks, or vulgar and offensive language may still be an expression that relates to a matter of public interest. However, the public interest in protecting that speech will be less than would have been the case had the same message been delivered without the lies, vitriol, and obscenities: *Able Translations Ltd.*, at paras. 82-84 and 96-103.

In addition to the quality of the expression and the defendant's motivation for making the expression, the consequences of the plaintiff's claim will figure into the weight to be given to the public interest in protecting that expression. Evidence of actual "libel chill" generated by the plaintiff's claim can be an important factor in the public interest evaluation required under s. 137.1(4)(b): *Able Translations Ltd.*, at para. 102.

The public interest evaluations required under s. 137.1(4)(b) cannot be reduced to an arithmetic-like calculation. It would be misleading to pretend they can be. The assessments are qualitative and, to some extent, subjective. Because the balancing of the competing public interests will often be determinative of the outcome of the s. 137.1 motion, and because the analysis contains an element of subjectivity, it is crucial that motion judges provide full reasons for their s. 137.1(4)(b) evaluations. [...]

In making the determination required under s. 137.1(4)(b), the motion judge will bear in mind that the plaintiff has the onus under the legislation. In applying that burden, however, the motion judge must appreciate the very significant consequences to the plaintiff if the motion is allowed under s. 137.1(4)(b). The courtroom door will be closed on the plaintiff even though the claim may have ultimately succeeded on the merits. The Anti-SLAPP Advisory Panel envisioned this result only if the plaintiff had a "technically valid cause of action" and had suffered "insignificant harm". The language of s. 137.1(4)(b) does not contain those limitations. However, I think the Panel's words do describe the kind of case that should be removed from the litigation process through s. 137.1(4)(b).

Notes and Questions

1. Doherty J.A.'s reasons in *170 Ontario* attempt to offer an interpretation of Ontario's anti-SLAPP law that provides balance and certainty both for plaintiffs and defendants in disputes (often defamation claims, although other torts and contractual claims may be pled) that involve freedom of expression issues. As explained in *170 Ontario*, whose guidance is then applied by the court in five companion cases, the legislation does not alter the substantive common law but rather is focused on offering new procedural means for the courts to respond to the SLAPP phenomenon. A key feature of the legislation is the reverse onus that arises where a defendant argues that the suit against them "arises from an expression made by the person that relates to a matter of public interest": subsection 137.1(3). This is what the court refers to as the "public interest threshold requirement". If the moving party satisfies this test, the responding party (typically the plaintiff) must overcome a series of hurdles or have their case

dismissed. The first hurdle has two elements: showing that there are reasonable grounds to believe that the case has "substantial merit" and that the defendant has no valid defences to the claim: subsection 137.1(4)(a). The responding party must also, however, satisfy what the court calls the "public interest hurdle": subsection 137.1(4)(b). To do this, it must be shown that on balance the harm to the responding party suffered as the result of the impugned expression is "sufficiently serious" to outweigh the public interest in protecting that expression by dismissing the claim.

2.   Do you think that the legislation as interpreted in *170 Ontario* strikes the right balance between competing interests? Is the reverse onus provision overly onerous on plaintiffs, especially given that they may be called upon to answer such a motion early on in the proceedings without the benefit of discovery? Do you think that the decision gives lower courts adequate guidance as to how to balance interests under the "public interest hurdle" set out in subsection 137.1(4)(b)?

Part V — Towards a Recognition of Common Law Public Rights in the Environmental Context

In the final Part, we reflect on what is both a newly emerging, as well as in some ways, an ancient feature of the common law: namely, the notion of public rights. While the common law is typically seen as being oriented towards protecting private/individual rights, especially those relating to property, closer scrutiny suggests that the common law has also recognized and loaned protection to collective/public rights. Likely the clearest illustration of this dimension is the tort of public nuisance. Another illustration, albeit one that remains inchoate in Canadian law, is the public trust doctrine. This doctrine, which is rooted in Roman law, has come to play a significant role in US environmental law as we will discuss in this Part and in Chapter 9. As a result of the recent Supreme Court of Canada decision in *British Columbia v. Canadian Forest Products Ltd.*, 2004 SCC 38 ("*Canfor*"), some commentators are predicting that in coming years the doctrine could have a similarly transformative impact on Canadian environmental law.

To consider the current and future role of common law-based public rights in Canadian environmental law, we offer first an article that provides a brief introduction to the public trust doctrine authored by Preston C.J., of the New South Wales Land and Environment Court. We then provide an excerpt from the SCC's much-discussed decision in *Canfor*, which offers some instructive observations on both the topic of the public trust doctrine and the tort of public nuisance. Finally, we include extracts from two commentaries on *Canfor* that chart its implications for Canadian environmental law.

Justice B.J. Preston,
The Role of the Judiciary in Promoting Sustainable Development:
The Experience of Asia and the Pacific
(University of Sydney Research Paper No. 08/46, 2008)

The concept of the "public trust" has its roots in Roman law, and was based on the idea that certain common resources such as the air, waterways and forests were held in trust by the State for the benefit and use of the general public. A broader conception of the public trust holds that the earth's natural resources are held in trust by the present generation for future generations. In this way, public trust law may be "the strongest contemporary expression of the idea that the legal rights of nature and of future generations are enforceable against contemporary users".

The essence of the public trust is that the State, as trustee, is under a fiduciary duty to deal with the trust property, being the common natural resources, in a manner that is in the interests of the general public. Hence, the State cannot alienate the trust property unless the public benefit that would result outweighs the loss of the public use or "social wealth" derived from the area. Although it was not until the early 1970s that the doctrine was explicitly applied as a mechanism for protecting the environment and managing resources, elements of it can be seen in much earlier cases.

In the Scottish case of *Lord Advocate v. Clyde Navigation Trustees*, the Lord Advocate, on behalf of the Crown, sought an order preventing a statutory body from dumping dredge waste in Loch Long. His claim was based on the idea that Loch Long was part of the kingdom, the Crown was the proprietor of the Loch, and thus the Crown had title to prevent interference with its rights unless they had been assigned to someone else. Referring to the existence of a trust and "trust subjects", the Court of Session granted the remedy sought by the Crown, stating clearly that "the Crown must use the property in the public interest".

In Australia, the concept of the doctrine of public trust can be traced back to an early dispute over a proposed coalmine in Sydney Harbour in the 1890s. A government authority granted a lease to a private company over an area of the northern foreshore. At issue was the effect this would have on the natural beauty of the area and "whether the people of Sydney and especially of St Leonards were to have the right to go over these water frontages". A young barrister objecting to the mine wrote to a newspaper declaring, "We in Sydney are the trustees for all Australia and of all time of that national heritage of beauty which gives to us our pride of place amongst the capitals of this continent and endows us with a reflected glory amongst the people of all nations who visit us".

When the case was heard in 1895, the New South Wales Land Appeal Court adopted public trust reasoning, holding that the Crown was under an obligation to use public land for the "health recreation, and enjoyment" of the people, and occupied "a position in relation to public lands something in the nature of a trustee under an obligation to dispose of, or alienate those lands, whether permanently or temporarily, only in the interest and for the benefit of the people of this Colony".

Professor Joseph Sax resurrected and expanded the concept of a public trust many decades later. In a famous article published in the *Michigan Law Review*,

Sax explored the extent to which the public trusteeship constrains the State, and concluded that three types of restrictions on government authority are imposed by a public trust. First, "the property subject to the trust must not only be used for a public purpose, but it must be held available for use by the general public". Secondly, the trust property may not be sold. And thirdly, "the property must be maintained for particular types of uses, such as navigation, recreation, or fishery". While realising that some elements of the public trust will inevitably be transferred into private ownership and control, Sax argued that the doctrine had "the breadth and substantive content which might make it useful as a tool of general application for citizens seeking to develop a comprehensive legal approach to resource management problems".

The public trust doctrine has, to differing extents, become part of the law of all countries with a common law heritage, and many maintain that it should play a principal part in sustainable resource allocation and decision-making. While traditionally applied primarily to waterways and rivers, the doctrine has now been extended to protect other natural resources from private use and harm as a tool of environmental conservation.

British Columbia v. Canadian Forest Products Ltd.
2004 SCC 38

BINNIE J.: — In the summer of 1992, a forest fire swept through the Stone Creek area of the Interior of British Columbia about 35 kilometres south of Prince George. Approximately 1,491 hectares were burned over, including areas where the appellant Canadian Forest Products Ltd. ("Canfor") and other tenure holders were licensed to log, areas of steep slopes where it was uneconomic to log, still other areas where the trees were too immature to log, and areas along watercourses subsequently declared by the Crown to have too much environmental value to permit logging at all. It is the assessment of compensation for the Crown's claim for environmental damage in these last-identified areas, called Environmentally Sensitive Areas ("ESAs"), that has created particular difficulty.

There is no longer any dispute about responsibility for the blaze. In the previous year, Canfor had carried out a controlled burn of its slashing and other logging waste, which failed to extinguish itself over the winter as expected. This fact went undetected because of the negligence of Canfor. The fire flared up again at the end of June 1992. The trial judge found that, while Canfor's negligence contributed to the failure to suppress the resurrection of the fire, the Crown's inadequate firefighting efforts also contributed to the loss ([1999] B.C.J. No. 1945 (QL)). He considered it impossible to apportion degrees of fault or blame-worthiness and thus divided responsibility evenly The Court of Appeal varied his decision by allocating 70 percent of the responsibility to Canfor and 30 percent to the Crown ((2002), 100 B.C.L.R. (3d) 114, 2002 BCCA 217). These findings are no longer in issue.

At trial, the Crown claimed damages for three categories of loss:

(1) Expenditures for suppression of the fire and restoration of the burned-over areas;

(2) Loss of stumpage revenue from trees that would have been harvested in the ordinary course (harvestable trees); and,

(3) Loss of trees set aside for various environmental reasons (non-harvestable or protected trees).

The trial judge awarded the Crown $3,575,000 under the first heading (which was an agreed figure), but otherwise dismissed the claim on the basis the Crown had failed to prove a compensable loss with respect either to harvestable or non-harvestable trees. [...]

The Court of Appeal dismissed the Crown's appeal on damages with respect to the harvestable trees, but awarded compensation for "diminution of the value" of the non-harvestable trees at a figure equivalent to one third of their commercial value. The task of assessing the commercial value of the non-harvestable trees, if the parties could not agree to it, was referred back to the trial court. This award is the subject matter of Canfor's appeal.

The Crown considers the award of compensation to be inadequate and in its cross-appeal claims the "auction value" of the standing timber in both harvestable and non-harvestable areas as of the date of the fire plus a premium over and above auction value for the degradation of the environment caused by destruction of the non-harvestable trees. In the alternative, it seeks an award of stumpage fees, plus the environmental premium on the non-harvestable trees. Canfor attacks the Crown's methodology and says that, on the evidence, the Crown has been overcompensated, not undercompensated, by the courts in British Columbia.

The question of compensation for environmental damage is of great importance. As the Court observed in *R. v. Hydro-Quebec*, [1997] 3 S.C.R. 213, ¶85, legal measures to protect the environment "relate to a public purpose of superordinate importance" In *Friends of the Oldman River Society v. Canada (Minister of Transport)*, [1992] 1 S.C.R. 3, the Court declared, at p. 16, that "[t]he protection of the environment has become one of the major challenges of our time". In *Ontario v. Canadian Pacific Ltd.*, [1995] 2 S.C.R. 1031, "stewardship of the natural environment" was described as a fundamental value. Still more recently, in *114957 Canada Ltée (Spraytech, Société d'arrosage) v. Hudson (Town)*, [2001] 2 S.C.R. 241, 2001 SCC 40, the Court reiterated, at para.1:

> [...] our common future, that of every Canadian community, depends on a healthy environment. [...] This Court has recognized that "(e)veryone is aware that individually and collectively, we are responsible for preserving the natural environment [...] environmental protection [has] emerged as a fundamental value in Canadian society" [...]

If justice is to be done to the environment, it will often fall to the Attorney General, invoking both statutory and common law remedies, to protect the public interest. In this case, the Attorney General has not resorted to statutory remedies (as under s. 161(1) of the *Forest Act*, R.S.B.C. 1979, c. 140 (now R.S.B.C. 1996, c. 157), for payment where timber is damaged or destroyed) but has sought damages at common law. The present appeal raises, therefore, the Attorney General's ability to recover damages for environmental loss, the requirement of proof of such loss and a principled approach to the assessment of environmental compensation at common law.

The Crown in right of British Columbia says it sues not only in its capacity as property owner but as the representative of the people of British Columbia, for whom the Crown seeks to maintain an unspoiled environment. Thus the claim for an environmental premium is made "in recognition of the fact that it [the Crown], and the public on whose behalf it owned the Protected Trees, valued them more highly as part of a protected ecosystem". The Crown frames the issue on appeal as the valuation of tort damages for a "publicly owned resource", and makes reference to the "worth to society" of the trees in their protected state. The Crown states that "[f]air compensation also requires that wrongdoers pay the public for damaging their ecosystems". In thus framing its claims, the Crown invokes its role as *parens patriae*.

The relationship between the Crown's status as property owner and the Crown as *parens patriae* is one of the issues presented for consideration, as is the Crown's hybrid role as regulator of the forest industry and at the same time recipient of a revenue stream established and limited by its own regulatory system. [...]

A claim for environmental loss, as in the case of any loss, must be put forward based on a coherent theory of damages, a methodology suitable for their assessment, and supporting evidence. No one doubts the need for environmental protection but, in this case, apart from the cost of reforestation, which was agreed to, the Crown claims only stumpage and "diminution of the value of the timber" within the burned-over area. The environment includes more than timber, but no allegations of loss were made in that regard. The pleadings, in other words, suggested a fairly narrow commercial focus and that is how the claim was defended.

The evidentiary record is also singularly thin on what precise environmental loss occurred, apart from damage to trees, and what value should be placed on it. The evidence of the Crown's own valuation experts, Deloitte & Touche, offered no support for the Crown's present expanded posture on environmental loss.

We cannot treat the Crown's argument as evidence; nor can we read into the record a theory of valuation that, rightly or wrongly, was supported by none of the experts. The Crown may have a more substantial environmental claim than is before us but she didn't prove it. Thus, while I would not interfere with the Court of Appeal's disposition of the claim in respect of the harvestable timber, in my opinion, with respect, the Crown did not establish its claim for compensation for environmental damage. I would therefore allow Canfor's appeal in that respect. The Crown's cross-appeal should be dismissed. [...]

Can the Crown also sue as a representative of the public to enforce the public interest in an unspoiled environment? If the Crown cannot do so, who (if anyone) can? Reference was made to *Prince Rupert (City) v. Pederson* (1994), 98 B.C.L.R. (2d) 84 (C.A.), where the court held that a municipal corporation cannot recover for the loss of "amenities" on behalf of its inhabitants arising from the destruction of trees.

In this Court, the Crown suggested that it was entitled to collect damages in negligence, "to effectively deter environmental harm and compensate the public for environmental damage". Canfor took the position that any such claim amounted to a "public law" remedy available only under special legislation such as the United States' *Comprehensive Environmental Responses, Compensation, and Liability Act of 1980*, 42 U.S.C. §§9601—9675 (1982 Supp. V 1987) (*"CERCLA"*), often called the "Superfund" law. Such losses are not, Canfor says, recoverable by a landowner in tort. The Crown's argument, Canfor implies, confuses distributive justice with corrective justice. Canfor was supported in this regard by the industry intervener, the Council of Forest Industries ("COFI") and others. Canfor and COFI took the view that when the Crown sues in tort, it is limited to the rights of a private party. It was conceded that there is an accepted role for the Attorney General as defender of the public interest in the law of public nuisance, but the remedy available in such cases is injunctive, not compensatory.

Historically, of course, the Attorney General, representing the Crown, has been the appropriate party to sue for abatement of a public nuisance. Recently, the Court adopted as correct the proposition that "any activity which unreasonably interferes with the public's interest in questions of health, safety, morality, comfort or convenience" is capable of constituting a public nuisance: *Ryan v. Victoria (City)*, [1999] 1 S.C.R. 201 at para. 52. It seems to me that the act of Canfor in burning down a public forest is capable of constituting a public nuisance. It was also negligence.

While a public nuisance may also be a crime (see *Criminal Code*, R.S.C. 1985, c. C-46, s. 180(1)), it is more often the subject of injunction proceedings brought by the Attorney General on behalf of the public. The usual objective is abatement. As put by McLachlin J. (as she then was) in *Stein v. Gonzales* (1984), 14 D.L.R. (4th) 263 (B.C. S.C.), "[p]ublic rights, including claims for public nuisance, can only be asserted in a civil action by the Attorney-General as the Crown officer representing the public" (p. 265). McLachlin J. went on to say that it is the "Attorney-General who is entrusted and charged with the duty of enforcing public rights" (p. 268). [...]

It is true that the role of the Attorney General has traditionally been to seek a stop to the activity that is interfering with the public's rights. This has led to a view that the only remedy available to the Attorney General is injunctive relief. Some commentators regard the injunction as the "public remedy" obtained by the Attorney General, while damages are a "private remedy" available to those private citizens who have suffered a special loss such as personal injury or damage to private property: see, e.g., P. H. Osborne, *The Law of Torts* (2nd ed. 2003), at p. 364. The reality, of course, is that it would be impractical in most of these environmental cases for individual members of the public to show sufficient "special damages" to mount a tort action having enough financial clout to serve the twin policy objectives of deterrence to wrongdoers and adequate compensation of their victims: *Bazley v. Curry*, [1999] 2 S.C.R. 534. Class actions will have a role to play but, as Professor Klar notes, "[w]hat has made public nuisance a particularly ineffective private law remedy is the special damages requirement" (L.N. Klar, *Tort Law* (3rd ed. 2003), at p. 647).

Canadian courts have not universally adhered to a narrow view of the Crown's available remedies in civil proceedings for public nuisance. In *The Queen v. The Ship Sun Diamond*, [1984] 1 F.C. 3 (T.D.), the federal Crown sought damages in relation to cleanup costs it had incurred to mitigate damage from an oil spill in the waters off Vancouver. Damages were awarded for the cost of the water cleanup activities, in addition to costs to clean Crown-owned beach and foreshore property. Walsh J. commented, "what was done was reasonable *and appears to be a good example of the parens patriae principle with the Crown [...] acting as what is referred to in civil law as 'bon pere de famille'*" (pp. 31-32 emphasis added)).

In *Attorney General for Ontario v. Fatehi*, [1984] 2 S.C.R. 536, the Province sought damages in relation to the cost of cleaning up a public highway following an accident. This Court held that Ontario was entitled to claim damages for harm to its property, like any other private property owner, and needed no statutory authority to bring such an action. [...]

The British Columbia Law Reform Commission in its *Report on Civil Litigation in the Public Interest, supra*, suggested that the reluctance of the courts to award damages against those who commit a public nuisance should be relaxed somewhat to provide an effective remedy (pp. 70-71). See also Ontario Law Reform Commission, *Report on Damages for Environmental Harm* (1990) ("*OLRC Report*"), at pp. 11–13.

In my view, Canfor takes too narrow a view of the entitlement of the Crown, represented by the Attorney General, to pursue compensation for environmental damage in a proper case.

Canadian courts have suggested that even municipalities have a role to play in defence of public rights. In *Scarborough v. R.E.F. Homes Ltd.* (1979), 9 M.P.L.R. 255 (Ont. C.A.), Lacourciere J.A., in an oral decision, said at p. 257 that:

> In our judgment, the municipality is, *in a broad general sense, a trustee of the environment* for the benefit of the residents in the area of the road allowance and, indeed, for the citizens of the community at large. [Emphasis added.]

This expression was referred to, without elaboration, by L'Heureux-Dubé J. in *114957 Canada, supra*, at para. 27.

The notion that there are public rights in the environment that reside in the Crown has deep roots in the common law: see, e.g., J.C. Maguire, "Fashioning an Equitable Vision for Public Resource Protection and Development in Canada: The Public Trust Doctrine Revisited and Reconceptualized" (1997), 7 J. Env. L. & Prac. 1. [...]

A similar notion persisted in European legal systems. According to the French *Civil Code*, art. 538, there was common property in navigable rivers and streams, beaches, ports, and harbours. A similar set of ideas was put forward by H. de Bracton in his treatise on English law in the mid-13th century (*Bracton on the Laws and Customs of England* (1968), vol. 2, at pp. 39-40):

> By natural law these are common to all: running water, air, the sea and the shores of the sea [...] No one therefore is forbidden access to the seashore [...]

> All rivers and ports are public, so that the right to fish therein is common to all persons. The use of river banks, as of the river itself, is also public by the *jus gentium* [...]

By legal convention, ownership of such public rights was vested in the Crown, as too did authority to enforce public rights of use. According to de Bracton, *supra*, at pp. 166-67:

(It is the lord king) himself who has ordinary jurisdiction and power over all who are within his realm. [...] He also has, in preference to all others in his realm, privileges by virtue of the *jus gentium*. (By the *jus gentium*) things are his [...] which by natural law ought to be common to all [...] Those concerned with jurisdiction and the peace [...] belong to no one save the crown alone and the royal dignity, nor can they be separated from the crown, since they constitute the crown.

Since the time of de Bracton it has been the case that public rights and jurisdiction over these cannot be separated from the Crown. This notion of the Crown as holder of inalienable "public rights" in the environment and certain common resources was accompanied by the procedural right of the Attorney General to sue for their protection representing the Crown as *parens patriae*. This is an important jurisdiction that should not be attenuated by a narrow judicial construction.

As stated, in the United States the *CERCLA* statute provides legislative authority for government actions in relation to the "public interest", including environmental damage, but this is not the only basis upon which claims in relation to the environment can be advanced by governments at the state and federal levels.

Under the common law in that country, it has long been accepted that the state has a common law *parens patriae* jurisdiction to represent the collective interests of the public. This jurisdiction has historically been successfully exercised in relation to environmental claims involving injunctive relief against interstate public nuisances: see, e.g., *North Dakota v. Minnesota*, 263 U.S. 365 at p. 374 (1923); *Missouri v. Illinois*, 180 U.S. 208 (1901); *Kansas v. Colorado*, 206 U.S. 46 (1907); *Georgia v. Tennessee Copper Co.*, 206 U.S. 230 (1907); and *New York v. New Jersey*, 256 U.S. 296 (1921). In *Tennessee Copper*, Holmes J. held for the Supreme Court of the United States, at p. 237, that, "the State has an *interest independent* of and behind the titles of its citizens, in all the earth and air within its domain" (emphasis added).

The American law has also developed the notion that the states hold a "public trust". Thus, in *Illinois Central Railroad Co. v. Illinois*, 146 U.S. 387 (1892), the Supreme Court of the United States upheld Illinois' claim to have a land grant declared invalid. The State had granted to the railroad in fee simple all land extending out one mile from Lake Michigan's shoreline, including one mile of shoreline through Chicago's central business district. It was held that this land was impressed with a public trust. The State's title to this land was

> different in character from that which the State holds in lands intended for sale. [...] It is a title held in trust for the people of the State that they may enjoy the navigation of the waters, carry on commerce over them, and have liberty of fishing therein freed from the obstruction or interference of private parties. [p. 452]

The deed to the railway was therefore set aside.

The *parens patriae* and "public trust" doctrines have led in the United States to successful claims for monetary compensation. Thus in *New Jersey, Department of Environmental Protection v. Jersey Central Power and Light Co.*, 336 A.2d 750 (N.J. Super. Ct. App. Div. 1975), the State sued a power plant operator for a fish kill in tidal waters caused by negligent pumping that caused a temperature variation in the fish habitat. The State sought compensatory damages for the harm to public resources. The court concluded that the State had the "right and the fiduciary duty to seek damages for the destruction of wildlife which are part of the public trust" in "compensation for any diminution in that [public] trust corpus" [...]

It seems to me there is no legal barrier to the Crown suing for compensation as well as injunctive relief in a proper case on account of public nuisance, or negligence causing environmental damage to public lands, and perhaps other torts such as trespass, but there are clearly important and novel policy questions raised by such actions. These include the Crown's potential liability for *inactivity* in the face of threats to the environment, the existence or non-existence of enforceable fiduciary duties owed to the public by the Crown in that regard, the limits to the role and function and remedies available to governments taking action on account of activity harmful to public enjoyment of public resources, and the spectre of imposing on private interests an indeterminate liability for an indeterminate amount of money for ecological or environmental damage.

This is not a proper appeal for the Court to embark on a consideration of these difficult issues. The Crown's own expert evidence treated the Crown as owner of Crown forests seeking compensation on the same basis as any other landowner for stumpage and "diminution of the value of the timber". Reliance was placed on s. 11(1) of the *Crown Proceeding Act*, R.S.B.C. 1996, c. 89, which provides that "the rights of the parties must, subject to this Act, be as nearly as possible the same as in a proceeding between persons". Of course it is perfectly open to the Crown to assert its private law rights as a property owner: *Fatehi*, *supra*, and *Toronto Transportation Commission v. The King*, [1949] S.C.R. 510. The groundwork for a claim on some broader "public" basis was not fully argued in the courts below. The Crown now suggests that it claimed "commercial value as a proxy" for environmental damage but, with respect, the pleadings suggest otherwise. It would be unfair to the other parties to inject such far-reaching issues into the proceedings at this late date.

I therefore proceed on the basis that the Crown's entitlement in this particular case is limited to entitlement in the role the Crown adopted in its statement of claim, namely that of the landowner of a tract of forest.

Notes and Questions

1. To what extent does *Canfor* open the door to the emergence of the public trust doctrine in Canada? What fact situations are most likely to provide a basis for expanding on and consolidating the status of the doctrine in Canadian law?

2. The first case following *Canfor* to rely on the public trust received a favourable response from the courts. In a case involving the province of Prince Edward Island and the federal Crown in 2006, PEI alleged that the federal government had violated its public trust obligations in its allocation of fishing licences. A motion to strike the statement of claim for failing to disclose a cause of action failed. The PEI Court of Appeal accepted in principle that a claim based on the public trust doctrine can succeed. See

Prince Edward Island v. Canada (Minister of Fisheries & Oceans), 2006 PESCAD 27, leave to appeal refused 2007 CarswellPEI 38 (S.C.C.).

3. The following commentary suggests a range of potential implications of the *Canfor* decision. As you learn about a number of developments in environmental law in Canada since 2005 throughout this book, consider which of the scenarios outlined in the article either appear most plausible or have come to fruition.

Jerry V. DeMarco, Marcia Valiante & Marie-Ann Bowden,
"Opening the Door for Common Law Environmental Protection in Canada:
The Decision in *British Columbia v. Canadian Forest Products Ltd.*"
(2005) 15 J. Envtl. L. & Prac. 233

The decision in *Canfor* is the latest in a series of Supreme Court of Canada cases to chart a positive future for environmental law in Canada. Most evident with the legacy of Mr. Justice LaForest, we have seen a Supreme Court with a heightened sense of environmental responsibility that has manifested itself in progressive decision-making. Be it an expanded role of municipalities in environmental protection, adoption of the polluter pays rule, or acceptance of the precautionary principle, the Court has actively engaged in the promotion of environmental protection as "a fundamental value in Canadian society."

Public Nuisance and Public Trust

[...] When commencing the action, British Columbia based its claim in negligence and identified the nature of the harm as damage to the Crown's property interest in the trees, which included harvestable and non-harvestable trees set aside for ecological purposes, plus the costs of fighting the fire and restoring the forest. In the B.C. courts, Canfor was held liable in negligence, contributing 70% to the fire that destroyed the trees. Because of the difficulty of valuing trees with no market value B.C.'s recovery was limited, as discussed above.

In the Supreme Court of Canada, British Columbia tried to recast its argument in support of recovery of damages for ecological harm. Supported by the interveners Sierra Club of Canada, David Suzuki Foundation, and the federal Attorney General, the provincial Crown argued that its interest in the trees goes beyond that of an ordinary property owner, that the Crown also holds public lands and resources on behalf of the people of the Province, as a guardian, and can therefore also recover damages to compensate the public for harm to their ecological interest in the forest. The implication of accepting this argument would be to entitle B.C. to recover damages to which a private landowner would not be entitled, and presumably, result in a larger award if proper evidence were to be provided.

Conceptually, then, the argument goes, this was not just the Crown's loss but also the public's. As representative of the public's rights in the forest, the Attorney General would be entitled to seek compensation on their behalf. The interveners argued that this compensation would then have to be put toward restoration and protection of the forest and not into general revenues.

Canfor and the forestry industry interveners argued that any claim on behalf of the public must be founded on a statutory scheme because such "public" damages are not recoverable in tort. In their view because there was no statutory scheme, there could be no recovery on this basis. Canfor did concede that the Crown is entitled to defend the public interest in the case of a public nuisance, but that injunction, not damages, is the only recognized remedy in such an action.

Binnie J. rejected Canfor's position as "too narrow a view of the entitlement of the Crown, represented by the Attorney General, to pursue compensation for environmental damage in a proper case". That this was not a proper case quickly became clear but Binnie J. went on to discuss his interpretation of this type of claim. He concluded that "there is no legal barrier to the Crown suing for compensation as well as injunctive relief in a proper case on account of public nuisance, or negligence causing environmental damage to public lands, and perhaps other torts such as trespass [...]". There are three elements to this conclusion with respect to public nuisance. First, the Attorney General representing the Crown is the proper party to sue to stop a public nuisance. "The notion that there are public rights in the environment that reside in the Crown has deep roots in the common law" and in civil law systems. These rights are vested in the Crown on behalf of the public and the Attorney General has the procedural right to sue for their protection under the Crown's parens patriae jurisdiction.

Second, the court should take a broad view of what constitutes a public nuisance. Quoting from the Supreme Court's decision in *Ryan v. Victoria (City)*, a public nuisance is "any activity which unreasonably interferes with the public's interest in questions of health, safety, morality, comfort or convenience". Here, Binnie J. concludes that "the act of Canfor in burning down a public forest is capable of constituting a public nuisance. It was also negligence".

Third, while the usual objective of a public nuisance action is abatement, injunction is not the only remedy available. The traditional view is that injunction is the only remedy because of its nature as a "public remedy" compared with the "private remedy" of damages. However, some Canadian courts have awarded damages in public nuisance actions, and this is supported by provincial law reform commissions. Binnie J.'s conclusion is that damages are not precluded. The key is to find an effective remedy in each case. In this case, injunction would not have been an effective remedy. [...]

On the substantive question of the basis of liability, Binnie J. referred to both the concepts of public nuisance and "public trust". Public trust came up because, in the Supreme Court in support of the Crown's entitlement to compensation for ecological harm, it was argued that the Crown is not simply the guardian of the public interest, but is a trustee, holding Crown resources on behalf of the public as beneficiaries. The argument built on statements made in previous cases that governments are, in a broad sense, trustees for the environment. This argument led Binnie J. into a discussion of the public trust doctrine, well-developed in the U.S., but so far not accepted in Canadian law despite its origins in common legal traditions.

In Canada, despite common legal foundations, the public trust doctrine has not developed. It appears that "there is no reported Canadian case wherein a common law public trust argument has been advanced". And, in the first case to argue a statutory trust, the concept was rejected. In *Green v. Ontario*, a researcher at Pollution Probe brought an action for breach of trust against the Crown for allowing a private company to excavate and remove sand dunes on public lands near Sandbanks Provincial Park. On preliminary motions, the Ontario High Court rejected the establishment of a trust arising under the *Provincial Parks Act* using traditional trust analysis. As well, the court held that the plaintiff had no standing to bring the action, having suffered no particular damage to himself. This decision apparently deterred further test cases in this area, though public trust has from time to time been argued.

[**Ed. Note:** The *Green* decision is excerpted in Chapter 8.]

While the majority does not accept that public trust is the basis for the Crown's entitlement to compensation in this case, by raising it, the Supreme Court has left it open for the Crown or public interest litigants to come forward in appropriate circumstances and argue a case on the basis of the public trust doctrine. It is not necessary, as was argued by Canfor, to look only to statutory compensation schemes, but the common law remains open. It is hard to reach firm conclusions based on the majority's comments on the public trust doctrine. However, given that the court made the effort to discuss the issue in some depth despite the fact that no party or intervener had canvassed U.S. public trust law in their arguments, it suggests a positive or sympathetic attitude that may manifest itself more fully in a future case (if pleaded properly and supported by evidence at trial). This will provide a spark of hope to those who have long "cast an envious eye south of the border" at the ability of U.S. groups to use the courts to hold state decision-makers accountable on this basis. [...]

Pulling these disparate strands together into a claim will be challenging, but the positive attitude of the Supreme Court in Canfor and other cases suggests it may at last bear fruit.

In summary, the majority of the Supreme Court could have dealt with the Crown's claim as a public nuisance and likely would have if the case had been pleaded differently. If it had done so, the only open issue would have been whether damages can be an appropriate remedy. Binnie J. makes it clear that he thinks so in this type of case, if there are proper pleadings and evidence. This likely resolves a key issue respecting the availability of damages in public nuisance claims. Binnie J. went on to discuss public trust concepts as well, thus opening the door to the further development of that area of the law in Canada. In doing so, Binnie J. signaled that the court might be sympathetic to future arguments based on a public trust analysis or similar approach. In particular, Binnie J.'s reference to novel questions relating to the "Crown's potential liability for inactivity in the face of threats to the environment" and "the existence or nonexistence of enforceable fiduciary duties owed to the public by the Crown in that regard" seems to be an invitation for test cases in these areas. This leaves the issue of standing for the public as one of the only remaining hurdles to the development of a more environmentally beneficial common law jurisprudence in Canada. This should provide encouragement to prospective public interest litigants who seek to demonstrate that government trustees not only have the option to protect public natural resources but the obligation to do so. This would be a welcome development.

Conclusion

Perhaps more than any other Supreme Court of Canada environmental law decision, the Canfor judgment raises more questions than it answers. Not surprisingly then, its ultimate significance will largely rest on how it is used and applied. Will the Court's recognition of oft-externalized values evolve into eventual compensation for them? If so, this could cause Canadian common law to yield an important societal benefit (as well as a more direct benefit to litigants seeking compensation in such cases). Will the Court's conclusion on remedies available in public nuisance cases encourage Attorneys-General to utilize this important tool? Will options for public interest litigants continue to expand in Canada such that they may have standing in public nuisance, public trust, or other cases that affect broad public interests? Will government entities be subject to further legal obligations (e.g. trusts, fiduciary obligations, and others) to protect the environment? By raising these important questions against a backdrop that emphasized the importance of environmental protection measures, Canfor has the potential to be a watershed in Canadian environmental law.

Notes and Questions

1. What are the implications of applying Canfor, which involved an action brought by the provincial Crown, to a tort claim between private litigants? Can the goal of compensating for environmental harms be achieved without a dramatic liberalization of the rules of standing (e.g. to non-human interests and future generations)?

2. As we move from considering the common law to legislative efforts to deal with the environmental impacts of human activities, keep in mind the question whether the common law or legislation is better suited to deal with specific aspects of the problem. What issues are better left to judges to decide, and what issues are better left to elected officials and administrative tribunals?

It is intriguing to compare the first public trust case to be decided by the Federal Court post-Canfor with the decision of the Court of Appeal in Prince Edward Island v. Canada (Minister of Fisheries & Oceans), 2006 PESCAD 27, leave to appeal refused 2007 CarswellPEI 38 (S.C.C.), discussed above. In this case, the Federal Court was called upon to consider a claim brought by the Burns Bog Conservation Society (excerpted below) that sought to invoke the public trust doctrine in an attempt to compel action by the Government of Canada to protect the bog. The Federal Court was not persuaded by the applicant's arguments and dismissed its claim summarily.

Burns Bog Conservation Society v. Canada (Attorney General)

2012 FC 1024,

affirmed 2014 FCA 170

RUSSELL J.: —

Background

This is a motion by the Defendants under section 215 of the *Federal Courts Rules* SOR/98-106 for summary judgment on the ground that there is no legal basis for the Plaintiff's claim.

Burns Bog, which is situated between the South Arm of the Fraser River and Boundary Bay, is one of the largest raised peat bogs in the world (Burns Bog or the Bog). The Burns Bog Conservation Society is a non-profit society registered in British Colombia under the *Society Act* RSBC 1996, c 433 and dedicated to preserving the Bog and raising public awareness of its ecological significance. [...]

In March 2004, the Bog Owners granted the Federal Crown a conservation covenant (Covenant) over the Bog under section 219 of the BC *Land Titles Act* RSBC 1996 c 250. The Covenant requires the Bog Owners to refrain from taking any action "that could reasonably be expected to destroy, impair, negatively affect, or alter" the Bog.

The Federal Government and the Bog Owners entered into the Burns Bog Management Agreement (Management Agreement) on 23 March 2004. The Management Agreement laid out the process by which the parties would develop a long-term management plan for the Bog in accordance with the Contribution Agreement. The Bog Owners collaborated with the Federal Government and, on 25 May 2007, they finalized the Burns Bog Ecological Conservancy Area Management Plan (Management Plan), which sets out policy direction and recommended actions to maintain the Bog's ecological integrity.

The South Fraser Perimeter Road

The South Fraser Perimeter Road (SFPR) is a component of the British Colombia Gateway Program, an effort by the government of British Colombia (Province) to improve bridge and road infrastructure throughout the Greater Vancouver area. Although no part of the SFPR will pass through Burns Bog itself, a stretch of it will run adjacent to the Bog.

On 3 September 2008, the Federal Government and the Province entered into an arrangement to fund the SFPR project. In total, the Federal government agreed to contribute $363 million to road construction. Notwithstanding its financial contribution, Canada did not assume any responsibility for construction or operation of the SFPR, which remains the Province's responsibility.

The Federal Government's monetary contribution, and the fact that the construction required permits under the *Fisheries Act* RSC 1985 c F-14 (Fisheries Act) and the *Navigable Waters Protection Act* RSC 1985 c N-22, triggered an environmental assessment under the *Canadian Environmental Assessment Act* SC 1992 c 37. The environmental assessment began on 11 December 2006. Environment Canada provided expert advice to Transport Canada (TC) and the Department of Fisheries and Oceans (DFO), who were responsible for completing the assessment. On 28 July 2008, TC and the DFO concluded that the SFPR was not likely to cause significant adverse environmental effects if certain mitigation measures were followed. These mitigation measures included the creation of a hydrology work plan and air quality work plan. [...]

Statement of Claim

The Plaintiff filed a Statement of Claim on 24 November 2010 by which it sought to compel the Defendants to protect Burns Bog. The Plaintiff claims the construction of the SFPR will negatively impact the hydrology of Burns Bog and says the Defendants owe the Canadian public a trust, fiduciary, or other legal duty to protect the Bog. The Plaintiff also claims that the Defendants are bound to protect Burns Bog under the Fisheries Act, the *Migratory Birds Convention Act* SC 1994 c 22 (MBCA), the *Canadian Environmental Protection Act* SC 1999 c 33 (CEPA) and the *Species at Risk Act* SC 2002 c 29 (SARA).

The Plaintiff also says that the Burns Bog Agreements created a duty on the Defendants to protect Burns Bog and asks the Court for an injunction halting construction of the SFPR or an order to reconsider the SFPR to protect the Bog. The Plaintiff also asks for a declaration that the Defendants are bound by the Burns Bog Agreements and a declaration that Burns Bog is subject to a public trust. [...]

Issues

The Defendants raise the following issues on this motion:

    a. Whether the Statement of Claim discloses a genuine issue for trial;
    b. Whether summary judgment is appropriate. [...]

Analysis

[...] Sections 213—215 of the Rules [*Federal Courts Rules* SOR/98-106] govern motions for summary judgment. The Rules permit an application for summary judgment on all or some of the issues raised in the pleadings. If the Court is satisfied there is no genuine issue for trial, the Court must grant summary judgment accordingly. [...]

In my view, this matter is appropriate for summary judgment. There are no contested facts on the matter at issue which need to be resolved in order to determine that the Plaintiff's claim has no chance of success and that it should not be allowed to proceed to trial.

As the Defendants correctly point out, the issue before me in this motion is not whether the construction of the SFPR by the Province may impact the ecology of Burns Bog. The issue is whether there is a genuine issue for trial over whether the Defendants owe to the Plaintiff any duty with respect to Burns Bog that compels any of the Defendants to intervene and ensure that the construction of the SFPR does not impact the ecological integrity of Burns Bog.

When it comes to arguing that there is a genuine issue for trial over whether Canada has such a duty or obligation, the Plaintiff relies heavily upon assertion but brings little to Court by way of evidence and authority. [...]

It is well-established that a summary judgment motion must be supported by specific evidence and the parties cannot simply rely upon their pleadings. (See

White v. Canada, [1998] FCJ No 981 (TD). Assertions in a statement of claim which are not supported by evidence will not be treated as proven facts (see *Kirkbi AG v. Ritvik Holdings Inc.*, [1998] FCJ No 912). A response to a motion for summary judgment cannot be based on conjecture as to what the evidence might be at a later stage in the proceedings. In fact, the Court is entitled to assume that the parties have put their best foot forward and that, if the case were to go to trial, no additional evidence would be presented. It is not sufficient for a responding party to say that more and better evidence will, or may, be available at trial. See *Rude Native Inc. v. Tyrone T. Resto Lounge* 2010 FC 1278.

In the present case, there is no specific evidence before me on the background concerns and the Plaintiff's assertion that the Defendants have allowed a game change to occur, and have reneged on the Covenant. In addition, there is no evidence at all before me that the Defendants have assumed some kind of legal obligation to take steps to prevent the Province from constructing the SFPR in a manner that might compromise the Bog's ecological integrity. The Plaintiff has simply asserted legal duties in the abstract and has made no effort to show the Court how such duties could arise on the facts of this case. The Plaintiff says that the environment is an important issue for Canadians and that Burns Bog needs to be protected, but there is no factual underpinning to show what the dangers to the Bog are or how the Defendants, given the facts of this case, are fixed with the legal duties and obligations asserted.

There is an obvious reason for this lack of evidence. The issue of Canada's obligations is almost entirely legal. We have before us all of the relevant agreements and principles required to answer the question of whether there is a genuine case for trial on this matter. There are no credibility concerns and no facts in dispute. This is the kind of question that the Court is well able to address and answer by way of summary judgment.

Having reviewed the record before me, the relevant agreements, and the principles and authorities put forward by both sides, it is my view that the Defendants have made their case for summary judgment. Generally speaking, I accept the Defendants' reasoning and authority on each point and adopt them for purposes of these reasons.

[**Ed. Note:** Discussion of covenant, management plan, and management agreement is omitted.]

No Trust Duty

The Plaintiff suggests that Canada owes a variety of trust obligations with respect to the Bog but does little to suggest how such obligations have arisen on the facts of this case. In particular, the Plaintiff alleges that Canada is in an "environmental and/or fiduciary an [*sic*]/or legal trust relationship" and that a "public and/or equitable or environment trust" was "created by the operation of Canadian environmental law." The Defendants and the Court are left to surmise how these obligations may have come about in the present case. The Defendants have taken the Court back to basic principles and have, in my view, clearly demonstrated that there is nothing to support such obligations in this case.

To begin with, a trust is a category of fiduciary relationship in which the trustee holds the title to property and manages it for the benefit of another, who has exclusive enjoyment of the property. As the Defendants point out, there are three essential characteristics of trusts, commonly referred to as the "three certainties":

> [...] first the language of the alleged settlor must be imperative; secondly, the subject matter or trust property must be certain; thirdly, the objects of the trust must be certain. This means that the alleged settlor, whether he is giving the property on the terms of a trust or is transferring the property on trust in exchange for consideration, must employ language which clearly shows his intention that the recipient should hold on trust. No trust exists if the recipient is to take absolutely, but he is merely put under a moral obligation as to what is to be done with the property. If such imperative language exists, it must secondly be shown that the settlor has so clearly described the property which is to be subject to the trust that it can be definitively ascertained. Thirdly, the objects of the trust must be equally clearly delineated. There must be no uncertainty as to whether a person is, in fact, a beneficiary. If any one of these three certainties does not exist, the trust falls to come into existence or, to put it differently, is void.

See *Scrimes*, above, at paragraph 16.

To establish a trust, it is also necessary to prove that the trust property is vested in the trustee. As established in *Scrimes*, above, at paragraph 17, there must be "an equitable interest based on a conscientious obligation which can be enforced against the legal owner" of the trust property, or no trust can exist.

This means that the Plaintiff must prove that Canada took ownership of specific trust property with the intention of holding that property in trust for the specified object.

The Plaintiff does not specifically identify the trust property in the Statement of Claim, but states that Canada is in a "trust relationship" with the Bog. The Plaintiff appears to allege that Canada holds the Bog subject to a trust.

However, Canada does not own the Bog. Ownership of the trust property by the trustee is an essential element of a trust. A trust is not perfected until the trust property is vested in the trustee. Accordingly, I agree with the Defendants that Canada is not a trustee of the Bog and does not owe to the Plaintiff, the Bog or the Canadian public any trust obligations respecting the Bog.

Despite the fact that Canada does not own the Bog, the Plaintiff alleges that a "public and/or equitable or environment trust" was created by agreement, statute and/or by an environmental trust doctrine. I agree with the Defendants that these allegations are bound to fail.

A review of the terms of the Covenant demonstrates that it does not create a trust relationship between Canada and the Bog.

The Covenant is a contract between Canada and the Bog Owners. The extent of Canada's interest in the Bog is defined by the Covenant. The Covenant does not give Canada title to the Bog. Further, it does not give Canada the ability to control the Bog.

Moreover, the Covenant expressly states that "no tort or fiduciary obligations or liabilities of any kind are created or exist between the parties in respect of this Agreement and nothing in the Agreement creates any duty of care or other duty on any of the parties to anyone else." [...]

No Public Trust

The Plaintiff also refers to a "public trust [...] created by operation of Canadian environmental law", and suggests that the Bog "is in a public trust and or equitable relationship with the Defendants." The Plaintiff suggests that the "public trust" requires Canada to take positive steps to protect land that is owned by other parties. This seems to me to be the Plaintiff's principal argument.

My review of the case law suggests that the Defendants are correct when they say that, to date, no Canadian courts have recognized a public trust duty requiring the Crown to take positive steps to protect the environment generally or a specific property.

In *Canfor*, above, Justice Binnie considered the possibility that there may be a place in Canadian law for a public trust doctrine, similar to the doctrine found in American law. After considering the American law, Justice Binnie concluded that it was not the proper case to embark upon a consideration of the issues involved because the issues were not fully addressed in the Court below.

In the US, the American Public Trust doctrine recognizes that a state's title to some lands may be held in trust for the public. The Public Trust Doctrine has been relied upon to permit the state to sue for damage to public resources and to restrain the state's own use of some public lands.

The key component of the American cases considered by Justice Binnie appears to be that they involved state obligations respecting public resources.

In *Canfor*, the province owned the land and sought a valuation of tort damages for the publicly owned resource. As the Defendants point out, this is a very different situation from the case at bar where the Bog is not owned by Canada. It is difficult to conceive of how a public trust duty could be imposed upon Canada concerning lands that it does not own. The Plaintiff is asserting some vague and undefined general concept that, in the end, amounts to saying that Canada has a general public trust duty to protect the environment in a way that the Plaintiff says it ought to be protected in this case. There is no legal support for such an assertion and, in my view, it is contrary to established principle and Canada's obligations to consider the best interests of all Canadians.

I think the Defendants are right to point out that the fact that Canada does not own the Bog presents a starkly different factual scenario than the one before the Supreme Court of Canada in *Canfor*. The Plaintiff is not suggesting that Canada must protect federally owned land. Rather, the Plaintiff seeks to impose upon Canada a trust duty to take steps to protect land that is owned by the Province, Vancouver and Delta. I agree that there is no basis in law or equity for the imposition of such a duty on Canada in this case. This aspect of the claim is bound to fail. [...]

Conclusions

The Plaintiff has chosen to respond to and resist this motion, not by addressing the Defendants' factual and legal arguments, but by appealing to the importance of the environment and an assertion that Canada should assume stewardship of the Bog so that the Plaintiff's concerns about the SFPR can be dealt with. The only evidence I have about those concerns comes from Ms. Olson, who tells me that the Plaintiff does not wish to block the SFPR, but wants to have the project reviewed and/or modified so that the Bog's raised area provides sufficient drainage, and so that the Bog is not dried out, leading to ecological harm and environmental damage.

These may well be worthwhile objectives and I can well appreciate the Plaintiff's concerns over the future of the Bog and its frustrations in trying to find an appropriate legal context in which to raise those concerns. But I have nothing before me that substantiates those concerns and, more importantly, I have nothing before me to suggest that the Defendants have a legal obligation — or the legal right — to step in and, on behalf of the Plaintiff, insist that the Province's SFPR project be reviewed and/or modified in ways that have not even been placed before me.

Notes and Questions

1. What are the key factual differences between the *Burns Bog* and the *Canfor* cases? Why did the judge place high importance on the ownership of the land in question?

2. The decision was appealed to the Federal Court of Appeal, which dismissed the appeal in a judgment that fully endorses the trial judge's reasoning. In light of this case, what are the prospects for the common law public trust doctrine in Canada today? Does this case change anything in your view? What are, in your view, the key reasons why the Court in *Burns Bog* was so decisive in its rejection of the public trust argument? Is this an example of bad facts making bad law?

3. In the 1983 *Mono Lake* case in California, the public trust doctrine was used successfully to require the state to protect a lake from water diversion projects. The Supreme Court of California held that Mono Lake had public trust values that must be protected, and that the state was under an obligation to enforce the maintenance of these values. The fact that the government did not own the property in question did not disqualify the application of the doctrine. Could the *Mono Lake* case have been used by the plaintiffs in the *Burns Bog* case?

The following article adopts a more ambitious and speculative approach to the significance of *Canfor* and the challenges ahead for public interest environmental law. In this article, Andrew Gage argues that *Canfor* should be seen as part of a broader paradigm shift in how we imagine and advocate for environmental rights.

Andrew Gage,
"Asserting the Public's Environmental Rights"
(BC Continuing Legal Education Society, 2008)

Public interest environmental lawyers have taken heart from statements of the Supreme Court of Canada about the fundamental importance of environmental protection to Canadians. However, despite such pronouncements and increased judicial sympathy, the law's approach to environmental protection remains largely unchanged from 30 years ago [...] I believe that environmental lawyers have failed to articulate a compelling story about the legal nature of environmental problems. [...]

We need to think outside the box in coming up with story-shifting arguments [...]. [...] in my view one of the most compelling and flexible arguments that we can use to shift the story involves turning to the very old idea of public rights. If the public has legal rights in respect of natural features this fact completely changes the relationship between the public and both industry and government.

The Nature of Public Environmental Rights

A public right is a legally enforceable right held not by an individual, or a community, but by the public at large. La Forest J., in his classic text on water law, explained:

> By public rights is not meant rights owned by government, whether federal, provincial or municipal. These bodies may own land and water rights [...] in the same way as private individuals, in which case they are, in a manner of speaking, public rights. But what is here called public rights are those vested in the public generally, rights that any member of the public may enjoy.

[...] The Supreme Court of Canada, in *Canfor*, adopted the phrase "public environmental rights" in relation to such rights, noting that: "The notion that there are public rights in the environment that reside in the Crown has deep roots in the common law". In particular, the court quoted several early authorities that spoke of public rights in respect of "running water, air, the sea and the shores of the sea".

Public environmental rights can play an important role in environmental law.

1. Public rights represent a direct counter-point to private rights that otherwise dominate legal analysis; in particular, they emphasizes public access to resources that are often privatized;

2. Public rights reflect how the environmental community often talks about air, water and land use issues.

3. Unlike *Charter* rights, the public's rights are not limited to claims involving human health, but apply to most issues where the public has an historic use of, or interest in, environmental features;

What Public Environmental Rights Exist?

Despite the Supreme Court's comments about the long roots of the idea of public environmental rights in the common law, the idea has not had a lot of recent attention, and lawyers, and judges, may be skeptical that they exist in Canadian law — other than the well established public rights to fish and to use waterways for navigation.

In fact, however, there is judicial and statutory authority in support of the existence of a wide range of public rights in respect of natural features and lands. These include rights to use air; fish and continued existence of fish habitat; use water for navigation, and likely for domestic purposes; use parkland and other lands dedicated for a public purpose; hunt wildlife in accordance with the law.

Jerry De Marco has recently suggested that the Supreme Court of Canada has recently indicated that a more general right to a safe environment exists. In addition to the court's statements in *Canfor*, he summarizes these authorities as follows:

> Taken together, the judgments in *Canadian Pacific*, *Hydro-Quebec* and *Imperial Oil*, as well as several provincial and territorial statutes, clearly recognize the existence of environmental rights. [These cases] provide further recognition of duties and entitlements that are similar to environmental rights. [...]

Public Rights and Conservation

Traditionally, public rights have been understood in terms of the public's right to make use of land or a resource. As such, they are a mixed blessing from an environmental point of view, since they are a consumptive right. Indeed, in the case of the public right to use water, the courts began emphasizing the unique private rights of riparian owners in part because of concerns about water conservation.

Although public rights have traditionally been conceived of as rights to use resources or land, there are several reasons to believe that they may also have a more general environmental protection or conservation aspect.

First, the Supreme Court in *Canfor* suggested as much. In that case Canadian Forest Products was held to be potentially liable for environmental harm for a negligently set forest fire in respect of non-harvestable timber. However, there was no suggestion that the public was likely to directly use that timber; nor was there evidence that the river, fish or wildlife likely to be impacted by the forest fire were used by the public. Rather, the public rights in question gave rise, in the court's view, to a general public interest in the ecological services provided by the forest.

Canfor suggests that the public may have a right to the conservation of environmental features, independently of any actual use of the resource. In some ways this may be one of the most significant aspects of *Canfor*.

Second, the public includes not just the user but also the community at large and even future generations. It is for this reason that Jerry DeMarco has suggested that the concept of environmental rights can help the law move away from a focus on the individual:

> Embracing environmental rights might, for example, put a priority on collective public rights, rather than just individual rights. Broader environmental rights may even allow us to question the human-centred ends that dominate human discourse and law making. [...] And the interrelated concepts of intergenerational equity, sustainability and public trust may help serve to end the discounting of the future.

Third, the case law concerning aboriginal rights of aboriginal people have emphasized the importance of conservation in respect of these resources. Thus the aboriginal rights cases have held that conservation is a valid legislative objective that can justify interference with the aboriginal rights. Similarly, aboriginal title cases emphasize the need to manage these commonly held lands in a way that recognizes the community's ongoing relationship with the land: see *Delgamuukw* (SCC, 1997).

Adopting the concept of "continuity of relationship" in relation to public rights, which, like aboriginal rights, are collectively held, could be an important step in reconciling aboriginal law with the wider common law.

Fourth, when legislation regulates the use of public environmental rights, it is natural for the courts to assume that it is ensuring conservation of the public right. Consequently, the use-focus of public rights is not so problematic when environmental rights are used to interpret environmental legislation. [...]

How Can We Use Public Environmental Rights?

In general, the conversation of how to assert public rights has begun and ended with the tort of public nuisance. This tort is both the most obvious way to raise public rights and one of the most difficult — due to the limitations of standing associated with the tort. However, there are other ways that public rights can be raised in environmental litigation. These include: as a means of interpreting environmental legislation; and as a basis for asserting a fiduciary duty owed by the Crown to protect such rights;

Standing in Public Nuisance Claims

The primary obstacle to asserting public rights through the tort of public nuisance has been the restrictive rules about who can bring such a claim. In general, only the Attorney General — or his or her designate — can bring a claim. In a modern era of environmental legislation, the government generally pursues environmental protection through statutory means, meaning that public nuisance claims as an environmental protection tool has at first glance been largely emasculated.

There is, of course, an exception to this rule of standing: an individual who has suffered "special harm" as a result of the public nuisance will have standing to bring a claim. Unfortunately, uncertainty about what this term means, and a small number of environmental cases which adopted an extremely restrictive definition of the term, has meant that few public nuisance cases are initiated by public interest litigants.

The most frequently cited case on the issue of public nuisance standing in an environmental context is *Hickey v. Electric Reduction Co.* Furlong, C. J., in *Hickey*, held that fishermen did not have standing to bring a claim in public nuisance for an oil spill because they had merely suffered a greater amount of harm from the impact of the spill on the public's right to fish and not a harm "peculiar" to themselves [...]

If public nuisance is to be used by public interest environmental lawyers to advance public environmental rights, this approach to public nuisance must be challenged. Fortunately there are multiple grounds for doing so.

First, *Hickey*, while often cited, is a trial court decision which has rarely been applied; the vast majority of public nuisance cases have held that individuals suffering direct financial loss as a result of interference with a public right do suffer "special harm". This principle has been applied to individuals who suffered a disproportionate degree of harm as a result of the obstruction of a public highway or a navigable river, or the contamination of a river.

[...] there are also a series of cases, primarily related to highways and other public spaces, in which community organizations or municipalities with a special interest in the nuisance complained of were granted such standing. These cases, which further emphasize a broad approach to standing, are difficult to reconcile with the "special harm" rule.

The apparent contradiction between these approaches has been noted by the courts and remains a live issue.

Second, the courts might consider abandoning the public nuisance standing rule altogether. The courts, since *Hickey*, have replaced this standing test with a new public interest standing test in constitutional and administrative law challenges. Academic criticism of the restrictions on standing in public nuisance cases, combined with over thirty years of experience with the more progressive public interest standing test, provide compelling reasons to modernize the public nuisance standing rule. [...]

Interpreting Environmental Laws

However, even without resorting to public nuisance claims, the argument that the public has rights in respect of the environment has the potential to transform how we understand environmental legislation. [...] This transformation begins with the well established principle that legislation should be interpreted, where possible, as not infringing existing legal rights. The principle is routinely applied in relation to private property rights and aboriginal rights, but few lawyers are aware of the body of case law applying the same principle to public rights. [...]

This presumption of interpretation started with cases concerning the Crown's prerogative powers and the question of whether the Crown can interfere with public rights absent authority from Parliament. Thus, a public right "can only be modified or extinguished by an authorizing statute, and as such a Crown grant of land of itself does not and cannot confer a right to interfere with navigation".

According to this principle, grants or licenses made by the Crown will not be interpreted, absent a clear intention to do so, as authorizing interference with public rights. [...]

This principle is also applicable to the interpretation of legislation [... and ...] it can even constrain the apparently unlimited discretion of a statutory decisionmaker, on the basis that if the legislature had intended the discretion to be used in a way inconsistent with the public right, it would have said so explicitly. [...]

Emphasizing public environmental rights as an important source of the interpretation of environmental legislation is particularly important in that it turns the mainstream legal story about the role of environmental legislation on its head. According to the mainstream view environmental law is a modern innovation. Prior to the modern era environmental concerns were minor or non-existent, and new laws were required after the industrial revolution to restrain the worst excesses of the market place and of private property rights. Environmental legislation is viewed as representing a departure from a previous era where private property owners were allowed to do whatever they wanted, provided there was no direct interference with other property owners.

By interpreting an environmental statute with reference to environmental rights and responsibilities that exist at common law, instead of ignoring that common law context, a very different understanding of environmental legislation emerges. According to this view, the common law has, since its inception, recognized public rights in respect of the environment. Environmental concerns may now have an unprecedented importance, but they have always been an important concern of the legal system. As a result, private property owners have acquired their property subject to a pre-existing common law duty not to negatively affect the rights of their neighbours, including public environmental rights; government regulation develops and expands upon the existing public rights in respect of a clean environment, adding additional remedies and powers to protect those rights.

Consider the differences in perspective:

The public's environmental interests are protected by statute alone	The public has common law rights in respect of Environment
Government's job is to balance private rights and environmental interests; where there is a conflict, the private rights, as the earlier of the two, should be favoured.	Government's job is to protect both public and private rights; where there is a conflict, the public rights, as the earlier of the two, should be favoured.
Until environmental legislation is enacted, the environment has no legal protection. New environmental laws, therefore, can be viewed as restricting or infringing on private rights.	At common law a violation of the public's environmental rights amounts to a public nuisance. Environmental legislation expands on the protections available to these public rights. Private land owners were already obliged to avoid infringing public rights, so environmental legislation generally will not create new liability or infringe on existing private rights.
Government has discretion to allow interference with the environment. If the Legislator intends to restrict that discretion it would do so in clear language.	If the Legislator intended to give government discretion to interfere with public environmental rights, it would do so in clear and unambiguous language.
The government owes procedural fairness to people directly affected by government decision, but not to the general public.	Public rights are as significant to government decisions as private ones; the government has a duty to consult the public, as holders of environmental rights, as well as people more directly affected by government decisions.

One major advantage to this paradigm shift is that it reflects the way, in the author's experience, that the public tends to understand their relationship to environmental values. While there is no single monolithic entity known as the public, many, probably most, members of the public believe that they have a right to clean air, and to clean water. They believe that the government will protect these rights. Consequently, the public environmental rights framework represents both a way to translate concerns of members of the public into legal language and, conversely, a way to explain environmental law in a way that may understandable to members of the public.

Conclusion

Public environmental rights are one of several story-changing arguments that have the potential to alter how public interest environmental lawyers argue cases. It allows us to better represent the views of public interest litigants, as well as presenting new arguments and legal tools. The Supreme Court of Canada has signaled that the common law can evolve to address fundamental values of environmental protection. However, we need to articulate a new — or perhaps an updated version of an old — vision of where and how the law can evolve. We cannot expect judges to supply a vision that we do not ourselves have. Public environmental rights are a critical piece of that vision.

Notes and Questions

1. In a 2015 book, David Boyd (the current UN special rapporteur on human rights and the environment) reports on the results of his research into the status of a human right to a clean environment around the world. He concludes that in at least twenty countries, the recognition of such a right was initiated through court action. Some form of right to a clean environment is now recognized in the constitution of over ninety countries. Canada does not explicitly recognize environmental rights in our constitution. See David Boyd, *Cleaner, Greener, Healthier: A Prescription for Stronger Canadian Environmental Laws and Policies* (Vancouver: University of British Columbia Press, 2015). Consider the roles of provisions such as section 35 of the *Constitution Act, 1982* and sections 7 or 15 of the *Charter* in bringing environmental rights into Canada's *Constitution*.

References and Further Readings

Peter Bowal, "Environmental Class Actions for Historical Contamination: *Smith v. Inco Limited*" (2013) 24 J. Envtl. L. & Prac. 295

David R. Boyd, *Cleaner, Greener, Healthier: A Prescription for Stronger Canadian Environmental Laws and Policies* (Vancouver: University of British Columbia Press, 2015)

David R. Boyd, "The Implicit Constitutional Right to Live in a Healthy Environment" (2011) 20 R.E.C.I.E.L. 171

W. Branch, *Class Actions in Canada* (Aurora: Canada Law Book, 2005)

Nathalie Chalifour, "Environmental Justice and the Charter: Do Environmental Injustices Infringe Sections 7 and 15 of the Charter?" (2015) 28 J. Envtl. L. & Prac. 89

Lynda Collins, "Material Contribution to Risk in the Canadian Law of Toxic Torts" (2016) 91:2 Chi.-Kent. L. Rev. 567

Lynda Collins & David Boyd, "Non-Regression and the Charter Right to a Healthy Environment" (2016) 29 J. Envtl. L. & Prac. 285

J. DeMarco, M. Valiante & M. Bowden, "Opening the Door for Common Law Environmental Protection in Canada: The Decision in *British Columbia v. Canadian Forest Products Ltd.*" (2005) 15 J. Envtl. L. & Prac. 233

Meinhard Doelle, "The Sydney Tar Ponds Case: Shutting the Door on Environmental Class Action Suits in Nova Scotia?" (2015) 27 J. Envtl. L. & Prac. 279

Monique Evans, "Parens Patriae and Public Trust: Litigating Environmental Harm Per Se" (2016) 12:1 McGill Int'l J. Sust. Dev. L. & Pol'y 3

Andrew Gage, "Asserting the Public's Environmental Rights" (BC Continuing Legal Education Society, 2008)

M. Good, "Access to Justice, Judicial Economy, and Behaviour Modification: Exploring the Goals of Canadian Class Actions" (2009) 47 Alta. L. Rev. 185

David Grinlinton, "The Continuing Relevance of Common Law Property Rights and Remedies in Addressing Environmental Challenges" (2017) 62:3 McGill L.J. 633

M. James, "*Susan Heyes Inc. (Hazel & Co.) v. South Coast B.C. Transportation Authority*, Case Comment" (2011) 23 J. Envtl. L. & Prac. 85

Scott Kidd, "Keeping Public Resources in Public Hands: Advancing the Public Trust Doctrine in Canada" (2006) 16 J. Envtl. L. & Prac. 187

C. Kneteman, "Revitalizing Environmental Class Actions: Quebecois Lessons for English Canada" (2010) 6 Can. Class Action Rev. 261

E.S. Knutsen, "Ambiguous Cause-In-Fact and Structured Causation: A Multi-Jurisdictional Approach" (2003) 38 Tex. Int'l. L.J. 249

P.B. Kutner, "The End of *Rylands v. Fletcher? Cambridge Water Co. v. Eastern Counties Leather Plc*" (1995-1996) 31 Tort & Ins. L.J. 73

A.C. Lin, "Beyond Tort: Compensating Victims of Environmental Toxic Injury" (2004-2005) 78 S. Cal. L. Rev. 1439

A.M. Linden & B. Feldthusen, *Canadian Tort Law,* 8th ed. (Markham: Lexis-Nexis Canada, 2006)

Anna Lund, "Canadian Approaches to America's Public Trust Doctrine: Classic Trusts, Fiduciary Duties & Substantive Review" (2012), 23 J. Envtl. L. & Prac. 105

K. Marron, "Cleaning the Air (*Smith v. Inco*, CA)" (2012) 36 Can. Law. 20

H. McLeod-Kilmurray, "*Hoffman v. Monsanto*: Courts, Class Actions, and Perceptions of the Problem of GM Drift" (2007) 27 Bull. Sci., Tech. & Soc. 188

H. McLeod-Kilmurray, "*Hollick* and Environmental Class Actions: Putting Substance into Class Action Procedures" (2002-2003) 34 Ottawa L. Rev. 263

T. Moran, N.M. Ries, & D. Castle, "A Cause of Action for Regulatory Negligence? The Regulatory Framework for Genetically Modified Crops in Canada and the Potential for Regulator Liability" (2009) 6 U.O.L.T.J. 1

B. Pardy, "Risk, Cause, and Toxic Torts: A Theory for a Standard of Proof" (1988-1989) 10 Advocates' Q. 277

B.H. Powell, "Cause for Concern: An Overview of Approaches to the Causation Problem in Toxic Tort Litigation" (1999) 9 J. Envtl. L. & Prac. 227

Justice B. J. Preston, *The Role of the Judiciary in Promoting Sustainable Development: The Experience of Asia and the Pacific* (University of Sydney Research Paper No. 08/46, 2008)

D. Saxe, "Government must combat SLAPPs, says panel" (2010) 30 Lawyers Weekly No. 21

M. Scott & C. Tollefson "Strategic Lawsuits Against Public Participation: The British Columbia Experience" (2010) 19 R.E.C.I.E.L. 45

Claire Seaborn, "How *Smith v. Inco* Failed: Recognizing the Category of 'Chemical Interference' in Private Nuisance Cases" (2013) 26 J. Envtl. L. & Prac. 59

C. Tollefson, "Strategic Lawsuits Against Public Participation: Developing A Canadian Response" (1994) 73 Can. Bar Rev. 200

B.H. Wildsmith, "Of Herbicides and Human Kind: Palmer's Common Law Lessons" (1986) 24 Osgoode Hall L.J. 161

H. Wilkins & R. Nadarajah, *Breaking the Silence: The Urgent Need for Anti-SLAPP Legislation in Ontario* (Toronto: Ecojustice; Canadian Environmental Law Association, 2010)

J.A. Yogis & S.H. Gifis, *Canadian Law Dictionary* (Woodbury, NY: Barron's Educational Series, 1983)

Chapter 3

Jurisdiction over the Environment

Introduction

This chapter considers the broad topic of jurisdiction over the environment. Often this topic is addressed solely in terms of the constitutional division of powers as it relates to matters of environmental law and policy. How the Canadian Constitution allocates jurisdiction over the environment and what the Supreme Court of Canada has said on this subject are clearly important. But in this chapter we also explore some other important jurisdictional questions and issues.

One question is the relationship between legal jurisdiction over the environment, and the actual dynamics and nature of Canadian environmental law and policy in practice. A critical question in this regard is whether, and to what extent, the jurisdictional uncertainty and conflict, reflected in much of the case law we will review, present a serious and enduring obstacle to grappling with the pressing environmental challenges we collectively confront.

We also believe it is important to explore the interplay between the division of powers, interpretive doctrine and related constitutional issues. These issues include the jurisdiction of local government over environmental matters, and intersection between jurisdiction over the environment and Aboriginal rights as guaranteed by section 35 of the *Constitution Act, 1982*.

In Part I we provide a basic overview of constitutional jurisdiction and interpretive doctrine. Part II considers a selection of leading decisions, arising in the division of powers context, which address jurisdiction over environmental law. Part III considers the extent to which these legal decisions have influenced the nature and dynamics of Canadian environmental law and policy, both in terms of policy and legal outcomes and the manner in which federal and provincial governments have interacted around environmental issues. In Part IV, we introduce some emerging environment-related jurisdictional issues — including Aboriginal rights and local government — to which we return later in this book. Finally, in Part V we consider the Trans Mountain Pipeline Expansion project as a case study profiling how the division of powers, Aboriginal rights, and political processes can come into conflict in practice.

Part I — Division of Powers and Interpretive Doctrine Relevant to Environment Cases

In this part, we offer an overview of the constitutional heads of power relevant to environmental law, and to the interpretive doctrine that courts apply when adjudicating division of powers cases.

Division of Powers Overview

Meinhard Doelle,
adapted and updated from the constitutional chapter in
The Federal Environmental Assessment Process: A Guide and Critique
(Markham: LexisNexis Butterworths, 2008) at 51–61

At the time of Confederation, neither level of government was assigned exclusive responsibility over environmental matters; indeed the concept of "environment" as a constitutional subject matter would not emerge until about a century later. Instead, both levels of government were granted responsibilities that have since been recognized to have implications for the protection and preservation of our natural environment. Analysis of the Canadian Constitution from the perspective of how it allocates responsibility for environmental protection began in earnest in the 1970s. In particular, articles written by Dale Gibson ("Constitutional Jurisdiction over Environmental Management in Canada" (1973) 23 U. Toronto L. J. 54) and Paul Emond ("The Case for a Greater Federal Role in the Environmental Protection Field: An Examination of the Pollution Problem and the Constitution" (1972) 10 Osgoode Hall L.J. 647) at this time started to consider the extent of federal jurisdiction before there were any serious efforts at the federal level to fully exercise these responsibilities.

The Supreme Court of Canada began to confront the tension between the division of powers and environmental protection in the early 1980s, in cases dealing with fisheries and marine pollution issues. The most important landmarks in its environmental law jurisprudence in the division of powers setting, that we shall be examining shortly in some detail, are *R. v. Crown Zellerbach Canada Ltd.*, [1988] 1 S.C.R. 401; *Friends of the Oldman River Society v. Canada (Minister of Transport)*, [1992] 1 S.C.R. 3 and *R. v. Hydro-Québec*, [1997] 3 S.C.R. 213.

Jurisdictional issues in the area of natural resources and the environment have been a source of considerable friction between federal and provincial governments for some time. In particular, battles between the federal government and Alberta over the control of energy production and consumption have featured prominently, especially in the period following the energy crisis of the 1970s. More recently, similar issues have been raised in the context of Canada's efforts to implement the Federal Carbon Tax, interprovincial pipelines, and the regulation of the aquaculture industry.

Relevant provisions of the Canadian Constitution include those in the original 1867 *British North America Act* and the 1982 *Constitution Act*. Identifying provincial jurisdiction over the environment is generally a straightforward matter. Of particular note is that since public lands in Canada (and, by extension the resources associated with these lands) are predominantly vested in the provincial Crown, the provinces wield significant proprietary rights as putative landowner. This state of affairs is subject to an important caveat, to which we will return in Part III. Emerging judicial authority suggests that provincial Crown title is subject to section 35 of the Constitution which, in turn, guarantees underlying existing Aboriginal rights, including Aboriginal title: see *Tsilhqot'in Nation v. British Columbia*, 2014 SCC 44. This, of course, has significant implications for provinces, such as British Columbia, where title to much of the landbase has yet to be resolved through treaty negotiations.

Courts have also traditionally conferred broad legislative authority upon the provinces, which is relevant in the environmental context. The primary constitutional basis for this jurisdiction is *property and civil rights* (subsection 92(13)). Provincial legislative authority also flows from other enumerated heads of power including: *matters of a merely local or private nature* (subsection 92(16)), and jurisdiction over *mines and minerals* (section 109), *non-renewable natural resources, forestry and electrical energy* (section 92A), *municipal institutions* (subsection 92(8)), and *local works and undertakings* (subsection 92(10)), except those under federal control. It is important to note that provincial heads of power are frequently subject to some limitations in light of either exclusive or concurrent federal jurisdiction over subject matters that overlap with these provincial heads of power. This will be canvassed in Part II. Furthermore, provincial jurisdiction is restricted to the territory of the province, the limits of which are an ongoing area of uncertainty in many coastal areas.

The territorial reach of federal jurisdiction extends to all of Canada, including all provinces and territories as well as Canada's territorial waters. However, since federal Crown land is relatively limited (except in the northern territories) federal jurisdiction depends primarily on legislative heads of power specifically enumerated in the Constitution. The list of relevant federal heads of power is therefore much longer. The result is a patchwork of federal powers superimposed on a carpet of provincial powers. In some cases, the federal powers restrict provincial powers; in other areas, both levels of government have concurrent jurisdiction. In many cases, the scope of the federal power with respect to environmental issues is still evolving, making it difficult to get a clear picture of the respective constitutional boundaries within which these two levels of government operate.

The key *federal* heads of power can be organized into two categories, *conceptual* powers and *functional* powers. This categorization goes back to the early 1970s. While the line between these two categories is not always perfectly clear, it has been broadly adopted by academics and courts alike, particularly in the environmental context. The conceptual/functional distinction is described by Prof. Emond as follows:

> The heads of power under the BNA Act that may support federal involvement in the environmental control field fall neatly into two distinct categories — conceptual powers and functional powers. The first provides general federal competence to legislate over a broad range of important activities, which by analogy include environmental quality; the second specifically gives Parliament control over certain

activities that are closely related to pollution in the sense that they may be adversely affected by, or may in fact contribute to the pollution problem.

Conceptual Powers

On the conceptual side, there are a number of federal powers that have the potential to be relevant in the environmental field. These include: the criminal law power (subsection 91(27)), the federal spending power, the federal taxation power (subsection 91(3)), the trade and commerce power (subsection 91(2)) and the residual power with respect to Peace, Order and Good Government (POGG) (section 91). With each of these conceptual powers, there are some applications in the environmental context that are relatively uncontroversial and others that are more controversial and uncertain.

Federal use of the *criminal law power* to implement prohibitions with stiff penalties to prevent harm to human health is well established. However, as the legislative scheme in question becomes more complex, and is more regulatory in nature, deployment of the criminal law power becomes more controversial. The 1997 SCC case of *R. v. Hydro-Québec* has resolved at least some of these issues, by confirming environmental protection as a legitimate purpose of the exercise of the criminal law power, and approving of the embedding of criminal law measures within a broader regulatory scheme. Limits and uncertainties, however, remain. For example, the more precautionary the regulatory approach and the less clear the evidence of harm, the greater the debate over the use of this head of power is likely to be. Most importantly, perhaps, the criminal law power is limited in the tools available to protect the environment to some form of prohibition or restriction with a penalty for non-compliance. As was pointed out by Emond in the 1970s, while the criminal law power may be broad insofar as allowing the federal government to weigh in on many environmental issues, it does not necessarily empower it to mount the most effective "multi-level attack on the problem that employs various regulatory and remedial tools".

The federal *spending power* complements the command and control approach authorized under the criminal law power. It can either be used directly to influence those engaged in activities, or support provincial environmental protection initiatives. It can be used to provide incentives to those engaged in harmful activities to reduce their environmental impact, and reward environmental innovation and superior performance. The potential of this power was described as far back as 1972 as allowing for the implementation of national environmental policies akin to the implementation of universal health care. The precise breadth of the spending power remains somewhat uncertain. However, its exercise does not involve compulsion of resistant or disinterested provinces; it is unlikely that the *bona fide* exercise of this power would be interpreted as being in conflict with provincial jurisdiction.

The federal *taxation power* similarly has the potential to supplement the command and control approach authorized under the criminal law power. This power can be used in two different ways to support federal efforts in the environmental field. One would be a non-targeted revenue generating approach, essentially to support the use of the federal spending power or to fund command and control efforts. The other lies in influencing behaviour by taxing undesirable behaviour and providing tax relief to more desirable alternatives. In many cases, both purposes can work in combination to help achieve an environmental objective. As with all federal powers, the taxation power cannot be used as a colourable device to invade provincial jurisdiction.

The *trade and commerce power* has generally been interpreted narrowly. This is due to judicial concerns about the potential for conflict between this power and the broad provincial jurisdiction over property and civil rights. In *Parsons v. Citizens' Insurance Co.* (1880), 4 S.C.R. 215, the trade and commerce power was limited to trade and commerce that crosses a provincial or international border. The case left open the possibility of general trade and commerce affecting the whole country also coming within this head of power. Given recent comments from the SCC, it is questionable whether the trade and commerce power significantly adds to the powers of the federal government to take measures to protect the natural environment from the effects of human activity. There may be circumstances, however, such as Canadian participation in an international emissions trading system, where the trade and commerce power will be applicable.

Federal jurisdiction to legislate with respect to *Peace, Order, and Good Government* (POGG) is a residual power, one that applies to subject matters not already assigned to the exclusive jurisdiction of either level of government. Two branches have emerged over time, an "emergency" branch and a "national concern" branch. The emergency power has been relatively uncontroversial. It has allowed Parliament to step in and legislate in areas otherwise beyond federal jurisdiction at times of war or during a similar national crisis. As certain environmental issues reach the status of a national crisis, this branch of POGG may very well be utilized by Parliament on a temporary basis. The national concern branch has extended the reach of POGG beyond emergencies to subject matters that either did not exist at Confederation, such as air or space travel, or to matters that have evolved from local issues to issues of national concern.

It is the national concern branch that has been the most relevant and controversial in the environmental context. Key environmental cases dealing with the application of the national concern branch of POGG include SCC rulings in *R. v. Crown Zellerbach Canada Ltd.*, [1988] 1 S.C.R. 401, *Ontario Hydro v. Ontario (Labour Relations Board)*, [1993] 3 S.C.R. 327 and *R. v. Hydro-Québec*, [1997] 3 S.C.R. 213. In addition to the general concept that a subject matter has become of national concern, the key elements of the test that have evolved for the national concern branch include the "singleness", "distinctiveness", and "indivisibility" of the subject matter. Finally, the court has to consider the extra-provincial impact of the failure of a province to adequately deal with the subject matter.

Functional Powers

For conceptual powers, the jurisdictional connection is generally between a given environmental issue and the response measure, be that taxation, spending, or a command and control response. The exception to this is the POGG power, which essentially provides a means for adding new functional heads of power. On the functional side, the jurisdictional connection is generally between the environment and a head of power that assigns jurisdiction over all, or some aspect, of a natural resource to the federal government.

Some functional heads of power grant federal jurisdiction directly over a component of the environment potentially threatened by human activities. Other functional heads of power grant federal jurisdiction over activities that pose a threat to the environment. Key functional heads of federal power include sea coast and inland fisheries, navigation and shipping, federal works and undertakings, and canals, harbours, rivers, and lake improvements.

Federal jurisdiction over *sea coast and inland fisheries* under subsection 91(12) is perhaps the functional power with the most obvious connection to environmental protection. On the surface, it may appear that this head of power grants exclusive rights over the fishing industry and the protection of fish and its habitat to the federal government. It is important to note, however, the reference to fisheries as opposed to fish. In practice, provinces have retained considerable jurisdiction under general heads of power such as property and civil rights, particularly with respect to activities such as fish processing.

Navigation and shipping, under subsection 91(10), have been treated as separate heads of power by the courts. With respect to navigation, the federal government has exclusive control over matters concerning navigation in all navigable waters, regardless of whether the title in a particular watercourse rests with a province or is in private hands. While provinces therefore cannot control navigation, they may still have other areas of jurisdiction with respect to the same watercourses. Examples of areas of overlapping jurisdiction and potential for conflict include dams for purposes of power production, flood control, or water resource control. While federal power over navigation has been interpreted broadly, jurisdiction over shipping has historically been interpreted more narrowly to be limited to interprovincial and international shipping.

Subsections 92(10) and 91(29) combine to grant federal jurisdiction over *certain works and undertakings*. Subsection 92(10) lists a number of specific works and undertakings dealing with a variety of modes of communication and transportation of an interprovincial nature. In addition, it provides authority for Parliament to declare other works to be for the advantage of two or more provinces and thereby declared to be federal works. As with other federal powers, the power to make a statutory declaration is limited in that it cannot be used as a colourable device to intrude into provincial jurisdiction. The power has been exercised with respect to works such as grain elevators, warehouses, an international bridge, and a local railway.

Jurisdiction over canals, harbours, rivers, and lake improvements complements other functional powers over fisheries, navigation and shipping, and federal works and undertakings. Federal jurisdiction over watercourses and a range of human activities associated with them is thereby solidified. The subsequent acceptance by the SCC of marine pollution as a new head of federal power under POGG in *Crown Zellerbach* further complements this jurisdiction.

As the foregoing illustrates, the task of identifying the boundaries between federal and provincial jurisdiction over environmental issues can be daunting. A comprehensive review of the interpretive tools and legal principles applied by the courts to resolve these issues in the context of a particular case are neither possible nor necessary, as they have been covered well elsewhere. A brief discussion of the following issues is nevertheless useful:

1. Exclusive versus concurrent jurisdiction
2. Limited power to delegate
3. Interjurisdictional immunity
4. Functional and conceptual powers
5. Role of territory and ownership
6. Treaty implementation

One of the critical issues in determining the jurisdictional boundaries between the federal and provincial levels of government in Canada is whether the jurisdiction granted to one level is concurrent or exclusive. In cases where one level of government has exclusive jurisdiction over a certain aspect of an activity, the other level of government cannot legislate the same aspect of that activity. However, there may be another aspect of the same activity that is within the jurisdiction of the other level of government. In case of concurrent or overlapping jurisdiction, both levels of government can legislate. If both legislate, federal legislation prevails in case of any inconsistencies.

The ability of one level of government to delegate (directly or impliedly) to another is limited. This means, among other things, that the failure of one level of government to exercise its exclusive jurisdiction does not empower the other level of government generally to step into the void. While legislative delegation is not permitted, administrative arrangements that have had the effect of delegating responsibility have been upheld.

A third issue worth noting is the concept of interjurisdictional immunity, which deals with the extent to which one level of government is bound to follow laws passed by another level of government. The general proposition is that there are constitutional limits on the ability of a province to bind the federal government to its environmental laws. The reverse (i.e. the ability of the federal government to bind the provincial crown to its environmental laws) is not a constitutional principle but remains an issue of legislative construction. Federal environmental laws, if validly enacted, and clear in their application to the provincial Crown, have generally been upheld.

For practical purposes, it is useful to distinguish between jurisdiction over a substantive issue and the jurisdiction to implement a particular response. This distinction is implicit in the functional/conceptual distinction between federal powers discussed above. Functional powers tend to limit the range of environmental issues to which the federal government can respond, whereas the conceptual powers tend to limit the availability of federal response measures. From a federal perspective, therefore, attention to this interaction between functional and conceptual powers becomes important when contemplating potential action on environmental issues.

Territory and ownership play a central role in any jurisdictional analysis. Territory is an important constraint on provincial jurisdiction in that provinces do not have jurisdiction to legislate in pith and substance outside the boundaries of their respective provinces. For example, a province cannot regulate activities in marine waters surrounding the province unless those waters form part of the territory of that province. Provincial legislation is permitted, however, to have incidental effects outside provincial borders. Ownership, on the other hand, is sometimes critical on the federal side, in that federal ownership of land or other property within the territory of a province allocates federal jurisdiction over matters that would otherwise be within the exclusive jurisdiction of the province.

A central issue in the environmental field has been the extent to which the federal government has the jurisdiction to implement international treaty obligations it accepts on Canada's behalf. With respect to some issues, such as marine pollution and migratory birds, there is unequivocal federal jurisdiction over the subject matter of the treaty. The federal government's role in negotiating environmental protection treaties is however not limited to environmental issues within a federal jurisdiction. When the federal government negotiates treaties and undertakes obligations to protect or enhance aspects of the environment that are within provincial jurisdiction (such as treaties designed to conserve non-renewable resources) this raises difficult implementation issues. We consider this question in relation to climate change in Chapter 10.

Interpretive Doctrine

Prior to delving into the case law regarding the division of powers and the environment, it is important to understand the constitutional doctrines that tend to inform judicial interpretations in this area of law. The doctrines described below are generally applicable in division of powers litigation. However, *how* they are applied by courts is often heavily influenced by considerations of cooperative federalism, including a judicial concern to encourage all levels of government to engage in efforts to take steps to protect the environment and manage our natural resources responsibly. This theme is emphasized in various SCC decisions including *Friends of the Oldman River Society v. Canada (Minister of Transport)*, [1992] 1 S.C.R. 3 (extracted *infra* this chapter).

The following decision reviews with admirable completeness and clarity the various interpretive doctrines that can come into play. It arises in a case in which a noted environmental activist challenged the authority of the province of British Columbia to regulate finfish aquaculture carried on in marine waters off BC's coast.

Morton v. British Columbia (Minister of Agriculture & Lands)
2009 BCSC 136,
affirmed 2009 BCCA 481, additional reasons 2010 BCSC 100

HINKSON J.: —

General Constitutional Principles

[...] the following constitutional principles are relevant to the questions raised by the petitioners, and must guide my analysis of the issues to be determined:

    a.   The presumption of constitutionality
    b.   The onus of proof of unconstitutionality
    c.   The interpretation that favours validity is to be preferred.

Laws passed by Parliament and the Legislatures are presumed to be within their respective spheres of constitutional jurisdiction. Courts should approach questions as to the validity of legislation based upon the assumption that the legislation was validly enacted: see *Nova Scotia Board of Censors v. McNeil*, [1978] 2 S.C.R. 662 at 687-688.

A party who challenges legislation must show that the legislation does not fall within the jurisdiction pursuant to which it was passed: see *Reference re Firearms Act (Can.)*, 2000 SCC 31, [2000] 1 S.C.R. 783 at para. 25 [*Firearms Reference*].

Where a challenged law is open to more than one interpretation, the court should prefer the interpretation that favours the validity of the legislation: see Peter W. Hogg, *Constitutional Law of Canada*, 5th ed. Supp., vol. 1 (Scarborough, ON: Thomson Canada Limited, 2007) at 15-23 [Hogg vol. 1].

Division of Powers

The respective powers of Parliament and the provincial legislatures are set out in ss. 91 and 92 of the *Constitution Act, 1867*. Neither Parliament nor a provincial legislature can expand its jurisdiction over the classes of subjects in ss. 91 or 92 by passing legislation which purports to do so.

In *Canadian Western Bank v. Alberta*, 2007 SCC 22, [2007] 2 S.C.R. 3 [*Canadian Western Bank*], the majority referred to co-operative federalism, also described as flexible federalism, at para. 42-43:

> ... A broad application [of the interjurisdictional immunity doctrine] also appears inconsistent, as stated, with the flexible federalism that the constitutional doctrines of pith and substance, double aspect and federal paramountcy are designed to promote. [...] It is these doctrines that have proved to be most consistent with contemporary views of Canadian federalism, which recognize that overlapping powers are unavoidable. Canadian federalism is not simply a matter of legalisms. The Constitution, though a legal document, serves as a framework for life and for political action within a federal state, in which the courts have rightly observed the importance of co-operation among government actors to ensure that federalism operates flexibly.
>
> Excessive reliance on the doctrine of interjurisdictional immunity would create serious uncertainty. It is based on the attribution to every legislative head of power of a "core" of indeterminate scope — difficult to define, except over time by means of judicial interpretations triggered serendipitously on a case-by-case basis. The requirement to develop an abstract definition of a "core" is not compatible, generally speaking, with the tradition of Canadian constitutional interpretation, which favours an incremental approach. While it is true that the enumerations of ss. 91 and 92 contain a number of powers that are precise and not really open to discussion, other powers are far less precise, such as those relating to the criminal law, trade and commerce and matters of a local or private nature in a province. Since the time of Confederation, courts have refrained from trying to define the possible scope of such powers in advance and for all time [...]

The interplay of these doctrines and principles to be applied to constitutional analysis was discussed at para. 22-24. Binnie and LeBel JJ., for the majority explained:

... federalism was the legal response of the framers of the Constitution to the political and cultural realities that existed at Confederation. It thus represented a legal recognition of the diversity of the original members. The division of powers, one of the basic components of federalism, was designed to uphold this diversity within a single nation. Broad powers were conferred on provincial legislatures, while at the same time Canada's unity was ensured by reserving to Parliament powers better exercised in relation to the country as a whole. Each head of power was assigned to the level of government best placed to exercise the power. The fundamental objectives of federalism were, and still are, to reconcile unity with diversity, promote democratic participation by reserving meaningful powers to the local or regional level and to foster co-operation among governments and legislatures for the common good. [...]

As the final arbiters of the division of powers, the courts have developed certain constitutional doctrines, which, like the interpretations of the powers to which they apply, are based on the guiding principles of our constitutional order. The constitutional doctrines permit an appropriate balance to be struck in the recognition and management of the inevitable overlaps in rules made at the two levels of legislative power, while recognizing the need to preserve sufficient predictability in the operation of the division of powers. The doctrines must also be designed to reconcile the legitimate diversity of regional experimentation with the need for national unity. Finally, they must include a recognition that the task of maintaining the balance of powers in practice falls primarily to governments, and constitutional doctrine must facilitate, not undermine what this Court has called "co-operative federalism" [citations omitted]....

The doctrines and principles include the pith and substance doctrine, the double aspect doctrine, the necessarily incidental or ancillary doctrine, the interjurisdictional immunity doctrine, the doctrine of paramountcy, and the doctrine of subsidiarity.

Constitutional Doctrines and Principles

Pith and Substance

It is upon this doctrine that the petitioners principally rely. The doctrine characterizes and classifies the challenged legislation in order to determine its dominant purpose. It requires a consideration of the essential character of the legislation that is impugned.

In *Canadian Western Bank*, Binnie and LeBel JJ. recognized that a constitutional analysis must begin with an analysis of the "pith and substance" of the impugned legislation, and at para. 26 to 27 commented:

This initial analysis consists of an inquiry into the true nature of the law in question for the purpose of identifying the "matter" to which it essentially relates. As Rand J. put it in *Saumur v. City of Quebec*, [1953] 2 S.C.R. 299, at p. 333:

... the courts must be able from its language and its relevant circumstances, to attribute an enactment to a matter *in relation to which* the legislature acting has been empowered to make laws. That principle inheres in the nature of federalism... . [Emphasis in original.]

If the pith and substance of the impugned legislation can be related to a matter that falls within the jurisdiction of the legislature that enacted it, the courts will declare it *intra vires*. If, however, the legislation can more properly be said to relate to a matter that is outside the jurisdiction of that legislature, it will be held to be invalid owing to this violation of the division of powers.

To determine the pith and substance, two aspects of the law must be examined: the purpose of the enacting body and the legal effect of the law (*Reference re Firearms Act*, at para. 16). To assess the purpose, the courts may consider both intrinsic evidence, such as the legislation's preamble or purpose clauses, and extrinsic evidence, such as Hansard or minutes of parliamentary debates. In so doing, they must nevertheless seek to ascertain the *true* purpose of the legislation, as opposed to its mere stated or apparent purpose (*Attorney-General for Ontario v. Reciprocal Insurers*, [1924] A.C. 328 (P.C.), at p. 337). Equally, the courts may take into account the effects of the legislation. For example, in *Attorney-General for Alberta v. Attorney-General for Canada*, [1939] A.C. 117 ("*Alberta Banks*"), the Privy Council held a provincial statute levying a tax on banks to be invalid on the basis that its effects on banks were so great that its true purpose could not be (as the province argued) the raising of money by levying a tax (in which case it would have been *intra vires*), but was rather the regulation of banking (which rendered it *ultra vires*, and thus invalid).

[...]

Double Aspect Doctrine

Gonthier J. for the Court discussed this doctrine in *Law Society of British Columbia v. Mangat*, 2001 SCC 67, [2001] 3 S.C.R. 113 at para. 48-50, and described it as first enunciated by the Privy Council in *Hodge v. The Queen* (1883), 9 App. Cas. 117 at 130 [*Hodge*] where Lord Fitzgerald stated that "subjects which in one aspect and for one purpose fall within sect. 92, may in another aspect and for another purpose fall within sect. 91".

[Gonthier J. then referred to the decision of Dickson J., as he then was, in *Multiple Access Ltd. v. McCutcheon*, [1982] 2 S.C.R. 161 at pp. 180-82 [*Multiple Access*]:

> Because "[t]he language of [ss. 91 and 92] and of the various heads which they contain obviously cannot be construed as having been intended to embody the exact disjunctions of a perfect logical scheme" ..., a statute may fall under several heads of either s. 91 or s. 92. For example, a provincial statute will often fall under both s. 92(13), property and civil rights and s. 92(16), a purely local matter, given the broad generality of the language. There is, of course, no constitutional difficulty in this. The constitutional difficulty arises, however, when a statute may be characterized, as often happens, as coming within a federal as well as a provincial head of power. "To put the same point in another way, our community life–social, economic, political, and cultural–is very complex and will not fit neatly into any scheme of categories or classes without considerable overlap and ambiguity occurring. There are inevitable difficulties arising from this that we must live with so long as we have a federal constitution"...
>
> ...
>
> But if the contrast between the relative importance of the two features is not so sharp, what then? Here we come upon the double-aspect theory of interpretation, which constitutes the second way in which the courts have dealt with inevitably overlapping categories. When the court considers that the federal and provincial features of the challenged rule are of roughly equivalent importance so that neither

should be ignored respecting the division of legislative powers, the decision is made that the challenged rule could be enacted by either the federal Parliament or provincial legislature. In the language of the Privy Council, "subjects which in one aspect and for one purpose fall within sect. 92, may in another aspect and for another purpose fall within sect. 91".

[Citations omitted.]

In *114957 Canada Ltée (Spraytech, Société d'arrosage) v. Hudson (Town)*, 2001 SCC 40, [2001] 2 S.C.R. 241 [*Spraytech*], the Supreme Court of Canada again considered the double aspect doctrine.[...] L'Heureux-Dubé J. stated at para. 39 that:

As a general principle, the mere existence of provincial (or federal) legislation in a given field does not oust municipal prerogatives to regulate the subject matter. As stated by the Quebec Court of Appeal in an informative environmental decision, *St-Michel-Archange (Municipalité de) v. 2419-6388 Québec Inc.*, [1992] R.J.Q. 875 (C.A.), at pp. 888-91:

[TRANSLATION] According to proponents of the unitary theory, although the provincial legislature has not said so clearly, it has nonetheless established a provincial scheme for managing waste disposal sites. It has therefore reserved exclusive jurisdiction in this matter for itself, and taken the right to pass by-laws concerning local waste management away from municipalities. The *Environment Quality Act* therefore operated to remove those powers from municipal authorities.

According to proponents of the pluralist theory, the provincial legislature very definitely did not intend to abolish the municipality's power to regulate; rather, it intended merely to better circumscribe that power, to ensure complementarity with the municipal management scheme ...

...

The pluralist theory accordingly concedes that the intention is to give priority to provincial statutory and regulatory provisions. However, it does not believe that it can be deduced from this that any complementary municipal provision in relation to planning and development that affects the quality of the environment is automatically invalid.

...

A thorough analysis of the provisions cited *supra* and a review of the environmental policy as a whole as it was apparently intended by the legislature leads to the conclusion that it is indeed the pluralist theory, or at least a pluralist theory, that the legislature seems to have taken as the basis for the statutory scheme.

Doctrines Requiring Validity of the Impugned Legislation

The necessarily incidental, interjurisdictional immunity and paramountcy doctrines all apply only where the impugned legislation is valid. However, the other criteria for each of these doctrines and their effects differ.

Necessarily Incidental or Ancillary Doctrine

This doctrine permits valid provincial legislation to encroach on the federal sphere of competence. In *Canadian Western Bank*, Binnie and LeBel JJ. explained the doctrine at para. 28:

> ... legislation whose pith and substance falls within the jurisdiction of the legislature that enacted it may, at least to a certain extent, affect matters beyond the legislature's jurisdiction without necessarily being unconstitutional. At this stage of the analysis of constitutionality, the "dominant purpose" of the legislation is still decisive. Its secondary objectives and effects have no impact on its constitutionality: "merely incidental effects will not disturb the constitutionality of an otherwise *intra vires* law" (*Global Securities Corp. v. British Columbia (Securities Commission)*, [2000] 1 S.C.R. 494, 2000 SCC 21, at para. 23). By "incidental" is meant effects that may be of significant practical importance but are collateral and secondary to the mandate of the enacting legislature: see: *British Columbia v. Imperial Tobacco Canada Ltd.*, [2005] 2 S.C.R. 473 , 2005 SCC 49, at para. 28. Such incidental intrusions into matters subject to the other level of government's authority are proper and to be expected [...]

This doctrine therefore recognizes that so long as the impact of provincial legislation on matters within federal jurisdiction is secondary or incidental to the law's most important aspect, the secondary or incidental impact is permissible. If this doctrine applies, then the effect of the doctrine is to confirm the validity of the provincial legislation.

Interjurisdictional Immunity Doctrine

This is an interpretive doctrine that confines provincial legislation to the Province's jurisdiction. It applies where the provincial law is valid with respect to most applications of the law, as set out in Hogg vol. 1 at 15-28, but in some applications impairs a vital or essential part of a federal undertaking, person, or thing: *Canadian Western Bank* at para. 42 and 48-49. Where interjurisdictional immunity applies, the result is that the impugned law is not held to be invalid, but simply inapplicable to the federal undertaking, person or thing, and is limited in application to matters within the jurisdiction of the Province by reading down the legislation: Hogg vol. 1 at 15-28.

In *Canadian Western Bank* the majority commented at para. 35-47 that the dominant tide of constitutional interpretation does not favour interjurisdictional immunity. Thus, although the doctrine has a proper part to play in appropriate circumstances, the Court neither encouraged an intensive reliance on the doctrine, nor accepted it as a doctrine of first recourse in a division of powers dispute.

Doctrine of Paramountcy

Paramountcy ensures that valid provincial legislation does not encroach too far into the federal sphere. It applies where there are two valid laws, one federal and one provincial, that are inconsistent with each other: Hogg vol. 1. at 16-2 to 16-3. The application of this doctrine was explained by Binnie and LeBel JJ. for the majority in *Canadian Western Bank* at para. 75:

> ... To sum up, the onus is on the party relying on the doctrine of federal paramountcy to demonstrate that the federal and provincial laws are in fact

incompatible by establishing either that it is impossible to comply with both laws or that to apply the provincial law would frustrate the purpose of the federal law.

If the doctrine is triggered, then the federal law prevails over the provincial law. The provincial law becomes inoperative and is held in abeyance unless and until Parliament repeals the federal law. The provincial law remains both valid and applicable, but does not operate while the federal law does: Hogg vol. 1 at 16-19 to 16-20. [...]

Analysis

Pith and Substance

[...] The petitioners assert that the pith and substance of the impugned legislation is the management of an ocean fishery, through licensing and regulation that controls all important aspects of the interaction between and impact of the farm fish and the wild ocean species and habitat including:

1) the number of ocean fish farms,
2) the location of the fish farms,
3) the size of the fish farms both in area and in the number of fish allowed in each facility,
4) the species of fish allowed, and
5) the management and operation of the fish farms.

The petitioners also argue that the Province's regulatory scheme grants property rights in the ocean fisheries and interferes with and restricts the public right to fish in the ocean. [...]

What is Finfish Aquaculture?

I am unable to conclude, as the respondents argue, that the activity of finfish aquaculture is an activity other than a fishery. The activity of fish farming involves the rearing of fish as the fish must reside in provincial waters until such time as they reach a sufficient age and size to be of commercial value. The farms vary in size, but on the evidence before me the cages containing the farm fish can occupy several hectares and hold several hundreds of thousands of fish. The farm fish are reared in areas previously frequented by "wild" fish. But for the finfish farms, the areas would still be frequented by "wild" fish, but the "wild" fish are prevented from doing so due to the presence of the cages in which the farm fish are reared.[...]

I am also unable to accept the provincial Crown's argument that the activity of finfish farming is at first instance within provincial jurisdiction. The management and preservation of the fisheries has been clearly held to be within the exclusive jurisdiction of Parliament: [...]

[Ed. Note: The Court then cites in support *Northwest Falling Contractors Ltd. v. the Queen*, [1980] 2 S.C.R. 292 at 301, and *R. v. Crown Zellerbach Canada, Ltd.*, [1988] 1 S.C.R. 401 at 422.]

The inclusion of fisheries in s. 91(12) of the *Constitution Act, 1867* was a recognition that fisheries, as a national resource, require uniformity of the legislation which affects and protects that national resource. Accepting that the management and preservation of the fisheries, including farmed fisheries, is within the jurisdiction of Parliament, the question then becomes whether the respondents can rely on ss. 92(5), 92(13), 92(16) or 95 of the *Constitution Act, 1867* to justify the impugned legislation.

Double Aspect Doctrine

I have concluded that the activity of fish farming falls under the jurisdiction of Parliament, pursuant to s. 91(12) of the *Constitution Act, 1867*. Yet the Province of British Columbia may enact legislation that affects the fisheries, so long as that legislation falls within a head which the *Constitution Act, 1867* has assigned to the jurisdiction of the Province.

The provincial Crown has asserted that it is entitled to legislate with respect to farm fishing based upon the legislative authority given to it pursuant to ss. 92(5) (management of lands), 92(13) (property and civil rights), 92(16) (matters of local or private nature in the Province), and 95 (agriculture) of the *Constitution Act, 1867*.

As stated above, pursuant to para. 25 of the *Firearms Reference* a party who challenges legislation must show that the legislation does not fall within the jurisdiction pursuant to which it was passed.

The provincial Crown has chosen to refer to fish farming under the rubric of "aquaculture". Ms. Morton says that "aquaculture" is the cultivation of marine plants and animals, or the natural produce of the marine environment. I accept Ms. Morton's definition of the term. [...]

[Ed. Note: The Court then dismisses BC's arguments that it is entitled to legislate under the authority of sections 92(5), 92(13), 92(16) or 95 on the basis of the double aspect doctrine. It therefore finds the impugned BC legislation to be *ultra vires*. In the alternative that this conclusion is incorrect, the Court then considers the applicability of the necessary incidental, interjurisdictional immunity and paramountcy doctrines, all doctrines that apply only if the impugned legislation is *intra vires*.]

Doctrines Assuming Validity of the Impugned Legislation

If I am wrong that the challenged provincial legislation [...] is *ultra vires* the Province, then does it meet the requirements of the necessarily incidental doctrine? For the reasons set out below, I find that it does not.

Necessarily Incidental/Ancillary Doctrine

I find that dominant purpose of the impugned provincial legislation [...] is to regulate aquaculture. Consequently its effects on the federal fisheries power are not incidental, and the scheme is constitutionally invalid.

Interjurisdictional Immunity Doctrine

As indicated above, this is not a doctrine of first recourse in a division of powers dispute, and the Supreme Court of Canada discouraged intensive reliance on this doctrine in *Canadian Western Bank*.

I find that the impugned legislation [...] involves the provincial Crown in the management and regulation of fisheries, and thus constitutes an interference with the core of a matter within the exclusive jurisdiction of Parliament: the management and regulation of fisheries.

As the jurisdiction of Parliament in issue is the management and preservation of the fisheries, confining the provincial legislation [...] to non-fisheries matters by reading it down leaves essentially only that part of the legislation that applies to marine plants. To conclude otherwise would be inconsistent with the broad federal jurisdiction pursuant to s. 91(12) of the *Constitution Act, 1867* as it has been interpreted by the courts.

Doctrine of Paramountcy

I have concluded above that the provincial Crown's attempt to save the legislation based on the double aspect doctrine fails and that the jurisdiction to regulate fish farms is exclusively federal. I therefore find that the doctrine of paramountcy does not apply because there can be no valid inconsistent provincial legislation where the jurisdiction is exclusively federal.

Notes and Questions

1. In *Morton*, in view of the Court's conclusion that impugned provincial legislation was *ultra vires* on both a pith and substance and double aspect analysis, strictly speaking it was unnecessary for it to consider the necessarily incidental, paramountcy and interjurisdictional immunity ("IJI") doctrines. Accordingly, the judgment does not opine in detail on the paramountcy and IJI doctrines.

2. A first point to note is that both the paramountcy (or "federal" paramountcy) and the IJI doctrines are typically used to challenge and render inoperative provincial laws. In the case of paramountcy-based challenges, it must be shown that the impugned provincial law conflicts (or is "inconsistent" with) the federal law. In the case of IJI-based challenges, it must be shown that the provincial law impairs the functioning of core or essential aspects of a federal head of power. If the paramountcy test is met, the impugned provincial law will be read down (declared inoperative) to the extent of the inconsistency. If the IJI test is met, the impugned provincial law will be declared inapplicable.

3. Assuming that otherwise *intra vires* federal and provincial laws are in conflict, a court must then consider whether the federal paramountcy doctrine is triggered. It can be triggered in two situations. The first arm of the paramountcy test asks whether it is impossible to comply with both the provincial and the federal laws. Even if dual compliance is possible, however, the provincial law may be rendered inoperative if it frustrates the purpose of the federal law. The scope of this second arm of the test is much broader and more policy driven than the first, and entails a consideration both of the nature of the federal purpose and of the nature of the allegedly harmful effects of the provincial law on that purpose: see *Alberta (Attorney General) v. Moloney*, 2015 SCC 51.

4. While the doctrine of paramountcy is an extraordinary one, to be deployed with care so as not to undermine cooperative federalism, the doctrine of IJI is generally considered to pose even greater potential risks to cooperative federalism. This is no doubt because it has the effect of rendering provincial laws inapplicable even where in pith and substance they are within provincial jurisdiction and do not offend the paramountcy doctrine. As such the application of IJI is restricted to the cores of federal works or undertakings, or federal legislative powers identified in the jurisprudence: *Quebec (Attorney General) v. Canadian Owners and Pilots Association,,* 2010 SCC 39 at para. 26. The manner in which the provincial law "trenches" on the federal core must also be demonstrably "serious". Recent SCC cases such as *Tsilhqot'in Nation v. British Columbia*, 2014 SCC 44 (extracted *infra* this chapter) and *PHS Community Services Society v. Canada (Attorney General)*, 2011 SCC 44, have continued to underscore the exceptional nature of the doctrine and its limited utility in an era of cooperative federalism.

5. At the end of this chapter we offer a case study of the Trans Mountain pipeline controversy, which presents a host of intriguing and unresolved division of powers interpretation issues. Among them is whether the province of British Columbia has jurisdiction under provincial environmental management laws to enact regulations that govern the transportation of hazardous substances, including heavy oils such as bitumen, through the province. The province has sketched out the basic elements of such a regime, which would apply to pipelines and railways alike, and referred the matter to the BC Court of Appeal. The regime would involve provincial statutory decision-makers issuing permits to pipeline and railway operators upon being satisfied that permit requirements relating to environmental and health protection had been met. It is conceded that there would be some overlap but no overt conflict between the applicable federal and provincial regulations.

6. In a recent paper Professor Olszynski argues that the BC government is unlikely to win the reference case, predicting that the BCCA will rule against it on both paramountcy and IJI grounds: see "Testing the Jurisdictional Waters: The Provincial Regulation of Interprovincial Pipelines" (2018) 23 Rev. Const. Stud. 91. Olszynski concedes that the proposed provincial law is likely *intra vires* the province in pith and substance.

However, he predicts the BCCA will find that the proposed BC law conflicts with federal law and will declare the BC law inoperative under the paramountcy doctrine. He concedes that it is not impossible to comply with both the new provincial law and the existing National Energy Board (NEB) regulations. However, in his view, the federal NEB regulatory regime is "comprehensive" in its coverage; accordingly, "it seems plain that legislation that second-guesses a substantial part of that regime (i.e. spill assessment, prevention, response, financial assurance, and liability) and purports to authorize a recalibration of the risk assessment made by the NEB frustrates Parliament's purpose": at pp. 24 and 25.

Further, he contends that the provincial law will likewise trigger application of the IJI doctrine. This is because, in his view, the various spills-related components of the BC law (spill assessment, prevention, response, financial assurance and liability) collectively recalibrate the "economics of a project" and accordingly "may be deemed to fall within the protected core of Parliament's jurisdiction over interjurisdictional pipelines": *ibid.* What do you think of Professor Olszynski's analysis?

Part II — Leading Cases on Federalism and the Environment

It was not until well over 100 years after Confederation that the Supreme Court began to grapple with the federalism implications of growing concern over the environment. Three cases, all decided in the 1980s, are generally regarded as the Court's initial forays into this new jurisprudential realm. The first two, *R. v. Fowler*, [1980] 2 S.C.R. 213, and *R. v. Northwest Falling Contractors Ltd.*, [1980] 2 S.C.R. 292, were decided based on existing functional powers. The third, *R. v. Crown Zellerbach Canada Ltd.*, [1988] 1 S.C.R. 401, considered the application of a number of conceptual powers to the environment.

All three cases dealt with federal legislation that was seeking to control the impact of private operations on marine ecosystems. In *Fowler*, the accused had deposited wood debris into a stream during forestry operations in violation of a provision of the *Fisheries Act* specifically dealing with the deposit of wood debris into a watercourse. This provision made it an offence to deposit waste *per se* without proof that the deposit adversely affected fish or fish habitat. Because of the lack of nexus between the prohibited action and harm to fish and fish habitat, the Supreme Court held that the relevant provision was *ultra vires* federal jurisdiction under subsection 91(12).

In *Northwest Falling*, the accused was charged under what is now subsection 36(3) of the *Fisheries Act* for depositing a deleterious substance into waters frequented by fish. In this case, the challenge to the legislation failed. For the Court, what was critical was that subsection 36(3), unlike the provision struck down in *Fowler*, contemplated a clear nexus between the prohibited act and federal jurisdiction to protect fish and fish habitat.

Of these three early cases, by far the most important to an understanding of the relationship between the division of powers and the environment is *Crown Zellerbach*. The facts in *Crown Zellerbach* are somewhat akin to those in *Fowler* and *Northwest Falling* in that all three involved charges arising out of forestry operations in British Columbia. In this case, however, the prosecution was pursued under the federal *Ocean Dumping Control Act* (OCDA). As there was no clear nexus between the charging provisions of the OCDA and the protection of fish and fish habitat, *Fowler* precluded the Crown from relying on subsection 91(12). As such, it sought to defend the impugned provisions on other grounds. To this end, it invoked the federal peace, order and good government power (POGG).

The majority, per Le Dain J., concluded that marine pollution had become a matter of national concern, and had a sufficient singleness, distinctiveness and indivisibility to come under the national concern branch of the POGG test. It also concluded that the impact on provincial jurisdiction of recognizing marine pollution as a new head of exclusive federal power could be justified in the circumstances. Justice La Forest, for the dissent, disagreed on a number of grounds. As we shall see, his reasons evince a deep concern about the implications of assigning to the federal government such a broad exclusive jurisdiction, a theme to which he returns in his reasons in *Friends of the Oldman River Society v. Canada (Minister of Transport)*, [1992] 1 S.C.R. 3, four years later.

Consider the following excerpts from the decision.

R. v. Crown Zellerbach Canada Ltd.
[1988] 1 S.C.R. 401

LE DAIN J.: — The question raised by this appeal is whether federal legislative jurisdiction to regulate the dumping of substances at sea, as a measure for the prevention of marine pollution, extends to the regulation of dumping in provincial marine waters. In issue is the validity of s. 4(1) of the *Ocean Dumping Control Act*, S.C. 1974-75-76, c. 55, which prohibits the dumping of any substance at sea except in accordance with the terms and conditions of a permit, the sea being defined for the purposes of the Act as including the internal waters of Canada other than fresh waters. [...]

The general purpose of the *Ocean Dumping Control Act* is to regulate the dumping of substances at sea in order to prevent various kinds of harm to the marine environment. The Act would appear to have been enacted in fulfilment of Canada's obligations under the *Convention on the Prevention of Marine Pollution by Dumping of Wastes and other Matter*, which was signed by Canada on December 29, 1972. [...]

The concerns of the Act are reflected in the nature of the prohibited and restricted substances in Schedules I and II and in the factors to be taken into account by the Minister of the Environment in granting permits to dump, which are set out in ss. 9 and 10 of the Act and in Schedule III. What these provisions indicate is that the Act is concerned with marine pollution and its effect on marine life, human health and the amenities of the marine environment. There is also reference to the effect of dumping on navigation and shipping and other legitimate uses of the sea.

Section 4(1) of the Act, with the contravention of which the respondent was charged, reads as follows:

4. (1) No person shall dump except in accordance with the terms and conditions of a permit.

The respondent carries on logging operations on Vancouver Island in connection with its forest products business in British Columbia and maintains a log dump on a water lot leased from the provincial Crown for the purpose of log booming and storage in Beaver Cove, off Johnstone Strait, on the northeast side of Vancouver Island. [...] At the relevant time the only permit held by the respondent under the Act was one issued on or about July 28, 1980, effective until July 25, 1981, to dump at a site in Johnstone Strait some 2.2 nautical miles from the place where the woodwaste was dumped. [...]

On the appeal to this Court the constitutional question was framed as follows: Is section 4(1) of the *Ocean Dumping Control Act*, S.C. 1974-75-76, c. 55, *ultra vires* of the Parliament of Canada, and, in particular, is it *ultra vires* of the Parliament of Canada in its application to the dumping of waste in the waters of Beaver Cove, an area within the province of British Columbia? [...]

Before considering the application of the federal peace, order and good government power it is necessary to express an opinion as to the effect of the judgments of this Court in *Fowler* and *Northwest Falling*, because of the particular reliance that was placed on them in the judgments below and in the argument of the respondent and the provincial Attorneys General in this Court. [...]

I agree with Schmidt Prov. Ct. J. and the British Columbia Court of Appeal that federal legislative jurisdiction with respect to seacoast and inland fisheries is not sufficient by itself to support the constitutional validity of s. 4(1) of the Act because that section, viewed in the context of the Act as a whole, fails to meet the test laid down in *Fowler* and *Northwest Falling*. While the effect on fisheries of marine pollution caused by the dumping of waste is clearly one of the concerns of the Act it is not the only effect of such pollution with which the Act is concerned. A basis for federal legislative jurisdiction to control marine pollution generally in provincial waters cannot be found in any of the specified heads of federal jurisdiction in s. 91 of the *Constitution Act, 1867*, whether taken individually or collectively.

It is necessary then to consider the national dimensions or national concern doctrine (as it is now generally referred to) of the federal peace, order and good government power as a possible basis for the constitutional validity of s. 4(1) of the Act, as applied to the control of dumping in provincial marine waters. [...]

From this survey of the opinion expressed in this Court concerning the national concern doctrine of the federal peace, order and good government power I draw the following conclusions as to what now appears to be firmly established:

1. The national concern doctrine is separate and distinct from the national emergency doctrine of the peace, order and good government power, which is chiefly distinguishable by the fact that it provides a constitutional basis for what is necessarily legislation of a temporary nature;

2. The national concern doctrine applies to both new matters which did not exist at Confederation and to matters which, although originally matters of a local or private nature in a province, have since, in the absence of national emergency, become matters of national concern;

3. For a matter to qualify as a matter of national concern in either sense it must have a singleness, distinctiveness and indivisibility that clearly distinguishes it from matters of provincial concern and a scale of impact on provincial jurisdiction that is reconcilable with the fundamental distribution of legislative power under the Constitution;

4. In determining whether a matter has attained the required degree of singleness, distinctiveness and indivisibility that clearly distinguishes it from matters of provincial concern it is relevant to consider what would be the effect on extra-provincial interests of a provincial failure to deal effectively with the control or regulation of the intra-provincial aspects of the matter.

This last factor, generally referred to as the "provincial inability" test and noted with apparent approval in this Court in *Labatt*, *Schneider* and *Wetmore*, was suggested, as Professor Hogg acknowledges, by Professor Gibson in his article, "Measuring 'National Dimensions'" (1976), 7 *Man.* L.J. 15, as the most satisfactory rationale of the cases in which the national concern doctrine of the peace, order and good government power has been applied as a basis of federal jurisdiction. As expounded by Professor Gibson, the test would appear to involve a limited or qualified application of federal jurisdiction. As put by Professor Gibson at pp. 34-35:

> By this approach, a national dimension would exist whenever a significant aspect of a problem is beyond provincial reach because it falls within the jurisdiction of another province or of the federal Parliament. It is important to emphasize however that the *entire* problem would not fall within federal competence in such circumstances. Only that aspect of the problem that is beyond provincial control would do so. Since the "P.O. & G.G." clause bestows only residual powers, the existence of a national dimension justifies no more federal legislation than is necessary to fill the gap in provincial powers. For example, federal jurisdiction to legislate for pollution of interprovincial waterways or to control "pollution price-wars" would (in the absence of other independent sources of federal competence) extend only to measures to reduce the risk that citizens of one province would be harmed by the non-cooperation of another province or provinces. [...]

This would appear to contemplate a concurrent or overlapping federal jurisdiction which, I must observe, is in conflict with what was emphasized by Beetz J. in the *Anti-Inflation Act* reference that where a matter falls within the national concern doctrine of the peace, order and good government power, as distinct from the emergency doctrine, Parliament has an exclusive jurisdiction of a plenary nature to legislate in relation to that matter, including its intra-provincial aspects. [...]

Marine pollution, because of its predominantly extra-provincial as well as international character and implications, is clearly a matter of concern to Canada as a whole. The question is whether the control of pollution by the dumping of substances in marine waters, including provincial marine waters, is a single, indivisible matter, distinct from the control of pollution by the dumping of substances in other provincial waters. The *Ocean Dumping Control Act* reflects a distinction between the pollution of salt water and the pollution of fresh water. The question, as I conceive it, is whether that distinction is sufficient to make the control of marine pollution by the dumping of substances a single, indivisible matter falling within the national concern doctrine of the peace, order and good government power.

Marine pollution by the dumping of substances is clearly treated by the *Convention on the Prevention of Marine Pollution by Dumping of Wastes and other Matter* as a distinct and separate form of water pollution having its own characteristics and scientific considerations. [...]

There remains the question whether the pollution of marine waters by the dumping of substances is sufficiently distinguishable from the pollution of fresh waters by such dumping to meet the requirement of singleness or indivisibility. In many cases the pollution of fresh waters will have a pollutant effect in the marine waters into which they flow, and this is noted by the U.N. Report, but that report, as I have suggested, emphasizes that marine pollution, because of the differences in the composition and action of marine waters and fresh waters, has its own characteristics and scientific considerations that distinguish it from fresh water pollution. Moreover, the distinction between salt water and fresh water as limiting the application of the *Ocean Dumping Control Act* meets the consideration emphasized by a majority of this Court in the *Anti-Inflation Act* reference — that in order for a matter to qualify as one of national concern falling within the federal peace, order and good government power it must have ascertainable and reasonable limits, in so far as its impact on provincial jurisdiction is concerned.

For these reasons I am of the opinion that s. 4(1) of the *Ocean Dumping Control Act* is constitutionally valid as enacted in relation to a matter falling within the national concern doctrine of the peace, order and good government power of the Parliament of Canada, and, in particular, that it is constitutional in its application to the dumping of waste in the waters of Beaver Cove. I would accordingly allow the appeal, set aside the judgments of the Court of Appeal and Schmidt Prov. Ct. J. and refer the matter back to the Provincial Court judge. The constitutional question should be answered as follows:

> Is section 4(1) of the *Ocean Dumping Control Act*, S.C. 1974-75-76, c. 55, *ultra vires* of the Parliament of Canada, and, in particular, is it *ultra vires* of the Parliament of Canada in its application to the dumping of waste in the waters of Beaver Cove, an area within the province of British Columbia?
> Answer: No.

LA FOREST J. (dissenting): — The issue raised in this appeal involves the extent to which the federal Parliament may constitutionally prohibit the disposal of substances not shown to have a pollutant effect in marine waters beyond the coast but within the limits of a province. [...]

I see no more merit in the submission, which appeared in the appellant's written submission, that the prohibition in s. 4(1) is justifiable as criminal law, and it is significant that counsel rather ignored this submission in his oral argument. It may be true that some of the items listed in the schedules to the Act could be harmful to human health if dumped in water, and it is also true that a prohibition properly directed at the protection of health might be justifiable as an exercise of the criminal law power; see *Reference re Validity of Section 5(a) of the Dairy Industry Act*, [1949] S.C.R. 1 at pp. 49-50. But it is difficult to see how the impugned provision preventing the dumping into marine waters of any substance, however innocuous, can be said to be aimed at the protection of health. [...]

There remains, then, the appellant's argument that s. 4(1) is valid as legislation respecting ocean pollution under the peace, order and good government clause. [...]

I start with the proposition that what is sought to be regulated in the present case is an activity wholly within the province, taking place on provincially owned land. Only local works and undertakings are involved, and there is no evidence that the substance made subject to the prohibition in s. 4(1) is either deleterious in any way or has any impact beyond the limits of the province. It is not difficult, on this basis, to conclude that the matter is one that falls within provincial legislative power unless it can somehow be established that it falls within Parliament's general power to legislate for the peace, order and good government of Canada.

Peace, Order and Good Government

There are several applications of the peace, order and good government power that may have relevance to the control of ocean pollution. One is its application in times of emergency. The federal Parliament clearly has power to deal with a grave emergency without regard to the ordinary division of legislative power under the Constitution. The most obvious manifestation of this power is in times of war or civil insurrection, but it has in recent years also been applied in peacetime to justify the control of rampant inflation; see *Re: Anti-Inflation Act*, *supra*. But while there can be no doubt that the control of ocean pollution poses a serious problem, no one has argued that it has reached such grave proportions as to require the displacement of the ordinary division of legislative power under the Constitution.

A second manner in which the power to legislate respecting peace, order and good government may be invoked in the present context is to control that area of the sea lying beyond the limits of the provinces. The federal government may not only regulate the territorial sea and other areas over which Canada exercises sovereignty, either under its power to legislate respecting its public property, or under the general power respecting peace, order and good government under s. 91 (*Reference re Offshore Mineral Rights of British Columbia*, [1967] S.C.R. 792) or under s. 4 of the *Constitution Act, 1871* (U.K.), 34 & 35 Vict., c. 28. I have no doubt that it may also, as an aspect of its international sovereignty, exercise legislative jurisdiction for the control of pollution beyond its borders; see *Reference re Newfoundland Continental Shelf*, [1984] 1 S.C.R. 86.

In legislating under its general power for the control of pollution in areas of the ocean falling outside provincial jurisdiction, the federal Parliament is not confined to regulating activities taking place within those areas. It may take steps to prevent activities in a province, such as dumping substances in provincial waters that pollute or have the potential to pollute the sea outside the province. Indeed, the exercise of such jurisdiction, it would seem to me, is not limited to coastal and internal waters but extends to the control of deposits in fresh water that have the effect of polluting outside a province. Reference may be made here to *Interprovincial Co-operatives Ltd. v. The Queen*, [1976] 1 S.C.R. 477, where a majority of this Court upheld the view that the federal Parliament had exclusive legislative jurisdiction to deal with a problem that resulted from the depositing of a pollutant in a river in one province that had injurious effects in another province. This is but an application of the doctrine of national dimensions triggering the operation of the peace, order and good government clause.

It should require no demonstration that water moves in hydrologic cycles and that effective pollution control requires regulating pollution at its source. That source may, in fact, be situated outside the waters themselves. It is significant that the provision of the *Fisheries Act* upheld by this Court in *Northwest Falling Contractors Ltd. v. The Queen*, *supra*, as a valid means of protecting the fisheries not only prohibited the depositing of a deleterious substance in water, but *in any place* where it might enter waters frequented by fish. Given the way substances seep into the ground and the movement of surface and ground waters into rivers and ultimately into the sea, this can potentially cover a very large area. Indeed, since the pollution of the ocean in an important measure results from aerial pollution rather than from substances deposited in waters, similar regulations could be made in respect of substances that so pollute the air as to cause damage to the ocean or generally outside the provinces. [...]

The power above described can be complemented by provisions made pursuant to the criminal law power. Thus specific provisions prohibiting the deposit of particular substances could be devised in a manner similar to the prohibitions in the *Food and Drugs Act*, R.S.C. 1970, c. F-27. The combination of the criminal law power with its power to control pollution that has extra-provincial dimensions gives the federal Parliament very wide scope to control ocean pollution. While it would not be proper for me to enter into the validity of the provisions of the *Clean Air Act*, S.C. 1970-71-72, c. 47, which were upheld in *Re Canada Metal Co. and The Queen* (1982), 144 D.L.R. (3d) 124 (Man. Q.B.), those provisions do indicate that a combination of the general federal legislative power and the criminal power could go a long way towards prohibiting the pollution of internal waters as well as those in territorial waters and the high seas.

In fact, as I see it, the potential breadth of federal power to control pollution by use of its general power is so great that, even without resort to the specific argument made by the appellant, the constitutional challenge in the end may be the development of judicial strategies to confine its ambit. It must be remembered that the peace, order and good government clause may comprise not only prohibitions, like criminal law, but regulation. Regulation to control pollution, which is incidentally only part of the even larger global problem of managing the environment, could arguably include not only emission standards but the control of the substances used in manufacture, as well as the techniques of production generally, in so far as these may have an impact on pollution. This has profound implications for the federal-provincial balance mandated by the Constitution. The challenge for the courts, as in the past, will be to allow the federal Parliament sufficient scope to acquit itself of its duties to deal with national and international problems while respecting the scheme of federalism provided by the Constitution.

However widely one interprets the federal power to control ocean pollution along the preceding line of analysis, it will not serve to support the provision impugned here, one that, as in the *Fowler* case, *supra*, is a blanket prohibition against depositing *any* substance in waters without regard to its nature or amount, and one moreover where there is, in Martland J.'s words, at p. 226 of that case, "no attempt to link the proscribed conduct to actual or potential harm" to what is sought to be protected; in *Fowler*, the fisheries, here, the ocean. As in *Fowler*, too, there is no evidence to indicate that the full range of activities caught by the provision cause the harm sought to be prevented. [...]

Why Parliament should have chosen to enact a prohibition in such broad terms is a matter upon which one is left to speculate. It may be that, in view of the lack of knowledge about the effects of various substances deposited in water, it may be necessary to monitor all such deposits. We have no evidence on the extent to which it is necessary to monitor all deposits into the sea to develop an effective regime for the prevention of ocean pollution. A system of monitoring that was necessarily incidental to an effective legislative scheme for the control of ocean pollution could constitutionally be justified. But here not only was no material advanced to establish the need for such a system, the Act goes much further and prohibits the deposit of any substance in the sea, including provincial internal waters. If such a provision were held valid, why would a federal provision prohibiting the emission of any substance in any quantity into the air, except as permitted by federal authorities, not be constitutionally justifiable as a measure for the control of ocean pollution, it now being known that deposits from the air are a serious source of ocean pollution? [...]

To allocate environmental pollution exclusively to the federal Parliament would, it seems to me, involve sacrificing the principles of federalism enshrined in the Constitution. As Professor William R. Lederman has indicated in his article, "Unity and Diversity in Canadian Federalism: Ideals and Methods of Moderation" (1975), 53 Can. Bar Rev. 597, at p. 610, environmental pollution "is no limited subject or theme, [it] is a sweeping subject or theme virtually all-pervasive in its legislative implications". If, he adds, it "were to be enfranchised as a new subject of federal power by virtue of the federal general power, then provincial power and autonomy would be on the way out over the whole range of local business, industry and commerce as established to date under the existing heads of provincial powers". And I would add to the legislative subjects that would be substantially eviscerated the control of the public domain and municipal government. Indeed as Beetz J. in *Re: Anti-Inflation Act, supra,* at p. 458, stated of the proposed power over inflation, there would not be much left of the distribution of power if Parliament had exclusive jurisdiction over this subject. For similar views that the protection of environmental pollution cannot be attributed to a single head of legislative power, see P. W. Hogg, *Constitutional Law of Canada* (2nd ed. 1985), at pp. 392 and 598; Gérald A. Beaudoin, "La protection de l'environnement et ses implications en droit constitutionnel" (1977), 23 McGill L.J. 207.

It is true, of course, that we are not invited to create a general environmental pollution power but one restricted to ocean pollution. But it seems to me that the same considerations apply. I shall, however, attempt to look at it in terms of the qualities or attributes that are said to mark the subjects that have been held to fall within the peace, order and good government clause as being matters of national concern. Such a subject, it has been said, must be marked by a singleness, distinctiveness and indivisibility that clearly distinguishes it from matters of provincial concern. In my view, ocean pollution fails to meet this test for a variety of reasons. In addition to those applicable to environmental pollution generally, the following specific difficulties may be noted. First of all, marine waters are not wholly bounded by the coast; in many areas, they extend upstream into rivers for many miles. The application of the Act appears to be restricted to waters beyond the mouths of rivers (and so intrude less on provincial powers), but this is not entirely clear, and if it is so restricted, it is not clear whether this distinction is based on convenience or constitutional imperative. Apart from this, the line between salt and fresh water cannot be demarcated clearly; it is different at different depths of water, changes with the season and shifts constantly; see U.N. Report, op. cit., at p. 12. In any event, it is not so much the waters, whether fresh or salt, with which we are concerned, but their pollution. And the pollution of marine water is contributed to by the vast amounts of effluents that are poured or seep into fresh waters everywhere (id., at p. 13). There is a constant intermixture of waters; fresh waters flow into the sea and marine waters penetrate deeply inland at high tide only to return to the sea laden with pollutants collected during their incursion inland. Nor is the pollution of the ocean confined to pollution emanating from substances deposited in water. In important respects, the pollution of the sea results from emissions into the air, which are then transported over many miles and deposited into the sea; see id., at p. 15; I.J.C. Report, op. cit., at p. 22. I cannot, therefore, see ocean pollution as a sufficiently discrete subject upon which to found the kind of legislative power sought here. It is an attempt to create a federal pollution control power on unclear geographical grounds and limited to part only of the causes of ocean pollution. Such a power then simply amounts to a truncated federal pollution control power only partially effective to meet its supposed necessary purpose, unless of course one is willing to extend it to pollution emanating from fresh water and the air, when for reasons already given such an extension could completely swallow up provincial power, no link being necessary to establish the federal purpose.

This leads me to another factor considered in identifying a subject as falling within the general federal power as a matter of national domain: its impact on provincial legislative power. Here, it must be remembered that in its supposed application within the province the provision virtually prevents a province from dealing with certain of its own public property without federal consent. A wide variety of activities along the coast or in the adjoining sea involves the deposit of some substances in the sea. In fact, where large cities like Vancouver are situated by the sea, this has substantial relevance to recreational, industrial and municipal concerns of all kinds. As a matter of fact, the most polluted areas of the sea adjoin the coast; see U.N. Report, op. cit., at pp. 3-4. Among the major causes of this are various types of construction, such as hotels and harbours, the development of mineral resources and recreational activities (id., at p. 3). These are matters of immediate concern to the province. They necessarily affect activities over which the provinces have exercised some kind of jurisdiction over the years. Whether or not the "newness" of the subject is a necessary criterion for inventing new areas of jurisdiction under the peace, order and good government clause, it is certainly a relevant consideration if it means removing from the provinces areas of jurisdiction which they previously exercised. As I mentioned, pollution, including coastal pollution, is no new phenomenon, and neither are many of the kinds of activities that result in pollution.

A further relevant matter, it is said, is the effect on extra-provincial interests of a provincial failure to deal effectively with the control of intra-provincial aspects of the matter. I have some difficulty following all the implications of this, but taking it at face value, we are dealing here with a situation where, as we saw earlier, Parliament has extensive powers to deal with conditions that lead to ocean pollution wherever they occur. The difficulty with the impugned provision is that it seeks to deal with activities that cannot be demonstrated either to pollute or to have a reasonable potential of polluting the ocean. The prohibition applies to an inert substance regarding which there is no proof that it either moves or pollutes. The prohibition in fact would apply to the moving of rock from one area of provincial property to another. I cannot accept that the federal Parliament has such wide legislative power over local matters having local import taking place on provincially owned property. The prohibition in essence constitutes an impermissible attempt to control activities on property held to be provincial in *Reference re Ownership of the Bed of the Strait of Georgia and Related Areas*, *supra*. It may well be that the motive for enacting the provision is to prevent ocean pollution, but as Beetz J. underlines in *Re: Anti-Inflation Act, supra,* Parliament cannot do this by attempting to regulate a local industry, although it can, of course, regulate the activities of such an industry that fall within federal power, whether such activities are expressly encompassed within a specific head of power, e.g., navigation, or affect areas of federal concern, e.g., health under the criminal law power, or cause pollution to those parts of the sea under federal jurisdiction. But here the provision simply overreaches. In its terms, it encompasses activities — depositing innocuous substances into provincial waters by local undertakings on provincial lands — that fall within the exclusive legislative jurisdiction of the province.

Finally, it was argued that the provision might be read down to apply to federal waters only, but I do not think this is possible. One need only look at the broad definition of "the sea" in s. 2(2) and (3) to appreciate the comprehensive reach of the Act. Besides, it is well known that many bays and other internal bodies of waters in Canada fall within the limits of the provinces. Many of the federal internal waters are located in the Arctic and have been expressly dealt with by the federal government.

Disposition

I would dismiss the appeal with costs and reply to the constitutional question in the affirmative.

Notes and Questions

1. What would have been the outcomes in *Fowler* and *Northwest Falling* if the Court had applied the POGG test as set out by the majority in *Crown Zellerbach*? Conversely, what would have been the outcome in *Crown Zellerbach* if the case had been decided purely on the basis of the federal government's functional powers over fisheries and navigation?

2. What is your sense of the importance placed on the role of the federal government in the field of environmental protection by the majority and the dissent?

3. What is at the heart of the disagreement between majority and dissent on the application of the POGG test to the *Ocean Dumping Control Act*?

4. What sources of marine pollution are covered by the new federal power established in this case? Are airborne sources of pollution, such as the acidification of the ocean from carbon dioxide, included in the federal power over marine pollution?

5. What impact does the use of POGG have on the role of the provinces? What would happen if these provisions were upheld based on the criminal law power instead of POGG?

6. What role does La Forest J.'s dissent suggest for the use of the criminal law power as the basis for establishing a federal role in the environmental protection field?

7. Do you find the functional/conceptual distinction to be a useful way to understand federal jurisdiction over the environment? Can you think of other ways to categorize the powers allocated?

Some four years after *Crown Zellerbach*, the Supreme Court of Canada was asked again to consider the scope of federal environmental jurisdiction. In *Oldman River*, the central issue was the basis and breadth of federal jurisdiction over environmental assessments carried out to help federal decision makers decide whether to approve or otherwise support proposed new initiatives.

Determining federal jurisdiction to conduct environmental assessments of proposed activities is a complex question with several dimensions. A threshold question is the nature of federal jurisdiction to engage in environmental assessment in the first place. However, this question cannot be answered fully in the abstract. To some extent, the answer will depend on the nature of the proposed activity to be assessed, and the scope of the assessment that is being contemplated: see Chapter 7 for further discussion of these issues. *Oldman River* does not resolve them all; however, it remains the seminal case on federal jurisdiction over environmental assessment. In the process, it offers key insights into the Supreme Court's view of the role of the federal government in environmental matters more generally.

The case arises out of a broader controversy with a rich history. The current case arose as an application for *certiorari* and *mandamus* respectively against the Ministers of Transport and Fisheries with respect to federal approval of a proposed dam along the Oldman River in Alberta. It was brought by Friends of the Oldman River Society in order to force both Ministers to complete an environmental assessment process under the EARP Guidelines Order before making a decision on whether to allow the proposed dam to proceed. The Minister of Transport had issued a permit under the NWPA without applying EARP, and the Minister of Fisheries had refused to apply either the *Fisheries Act* or the EARP process. At the Supreme Court, a number of intervenors were granted standing to address the critical issue in the case, whether the environmental assessment process established through the EARP Guidelines Order was a valid exercise of federal jurisdiction.

Consider the following excerpts from the decision.

Friends of the Oldman River Society v. Canada (Minister of Transport)
[1992] 1 S.C.R. 3

LA FOREST J.: — The protection of the environment has become one of the major challenges of our time. To respond to this challenge, governments and international organizations have been engaged in the creation of a wide variety of legislative schemes and administrative structures. In Canada, both the federal and provincial governments have established Departments of the Environment, which have been in place for about twenty years. More recently, however, it was realized that a department of the environment was one among many other departments, many of which pursued policies that came into conflict with its goals. Accordingly at the federal level steps were taken to give a central role to that department, and to expand the role of other government departments and agencies so as to ensure that they took account of environmental concerns in taking decisions that could have an environmental impact.

To that end, s. 6 of the *Department of the Environment Act*, R.S.C., 1985, c. E-10, empowered the Minister for the purposes of carrying out his duties relating to environmental quality, by order, with the approval of the Governor in Council, to establish guidelines for use by federal departments, agencies and regulatory bodies in carrying out their duties, functions and powers. Pursuant to this provision the *Environmental Assessment and Review Process Guidelines Order* ("*Guidelines Order*") was established and approved in June 1984, SOR/84-467. In general terms, these guidelines require all federal departments and agencies that have a decision-making authority for any proposal, i.e., any initiative, undertaking or activity that may have an environmental effect on an area of federal responsibility, to initially screen such proposal to determine whether it may give rise to any potentially adverse environmental effects. If a proposal could have a significant adverse effect on the environment, provision is made for public review by an environmental assessment panel whose members must be unbiased, free of political influence and possessed of special knowledge and experience relevant to the technical, environmental and social effects of the proposal.

The present case raises the constitutional and statutory validity of the *Guidelines Order* as well as its nature and applicability. These issues arise in a context where the respondent Society, an environmental group from Alberta, by applications for *certiorari* and mandamus, seeks to compel two federal departments, the Department of Transport and the Department of Fisheries and Oceans, to conduct a public environmental assessment pursuant to the *Guidelines Order* in respect of a dam constructed on the Oldman River by the Government of Alberta. That government had itself conducted extensive environmental studies which took into account public views. However, since the project affects navigable waters, fisheries, Indians and Indian lands, federal interests are involved. Specifically, the Society argues that the Minister of Transport must approve the project under the *Navigable Waters Protection Act*, R.S.C., 1985, c. N-22, and in doing so is required to provide for public assessment of the project pursuant to the *Guidelines Order*. It also argues that the Minister of Fisheries and Oceans has a similar duty in the performance of his functions under the *Fisheries Act*, R.S.C., 1985, c. F-14 [...]

I come now to a step of prime importance in this action. On March 10, 1986 the Alberta Department of the Environment applied to the federal Minister of Transport for approval of the work under s. 5 of the *Navigable Waters Protection Act*. That provision provides that no work is to be built in navigable waters without the prior approval of the Minister. In assessing the application, the Minister considered the project's effect on marine navigation and approved the application on September 18, 1987 subject to certain conditions relating to marine navigation. I underline, however, that he did not subject the application to an assessment under the *Guidelines Order*. As we shall see, whether he should have done so raises several of the major issues in this appeal. [...]

The constitutional question asks whether the *Guidelines Order* is so broad as to offend ss. 92 and 92A of the *Constitution Act, 1867*. However, no argument was made with respect to s. 92A for the apparent reason that the Oldman River Dam project does not, in the appellants' view, fall within the ambit of that provision. At all events, the matter is of no moment. The process of judicial review of legislation which is impugned as *ultra vires* Parliament was recently elaborated on in *Whitbread v. Walley, supra,* and does not bear repetition here, save to remark that if the *Guidelines Order* is found to be legislation that is in pith and substance in relation to matters within Parliament's exclusive jurisdiction, that is the end of the matter. It would be immaterial that it also affects matters of property and civil rights (*Whitbread,* at p. 1286). The analysis proceeds first by identifying whether in pith and substance the legislation falls within a matter assigned to one or more of the heads of legislative power.

While various expressions have been used to describe what is meant by the "pith and substance" of a legislative provision, in *Whitbread v. Walley* I expressed a preference for the description "the dominant or most important characteristic of the challenged law". Naturally, the parties have advanced quite different features of the *Guidelines Order* as representing its most important characteristic. For Alberta, it is the manner in which it is said to encroach on provincial rights, although no specific matter has been identified other than general references to the environment. Alberta argues that Parliament has no plenary jurisdiction over the environment, it being a matter of legislative jurisdiction shared by both levels of government, and that the *Guidelines Order* has crossed the line which circumscribes Parliament's authority over the environment. The appellant Ministers argue that in pith and substance the *Guidelines Order* is merely a process to facilitate federal decision-making on matters that fall within Parliament's jurisdiction — a proposition with which the respondent substantially agrees.

The substance of Alberta's argument is that the *Guidelines Order* purports to give the Government of Canada general authority over the environment in such a way as to trench on the province's exclusive legislative domain. Alberta argues that the *Guidelines Order* attempts to regulate the environmental effects of matters largely within the control of the province and, consequently, cannot constitutionally be a concern of Parliament. In particular, it is said that Parliament is incompetent to deal with the environmental effects of provincial works such as the Oldman River Dam.

I agree that the *Constitution Act, 1867* has not assigned the matter of "environment" *sui generis* to either the provinces or Parliament. The environment, as understood in its generic sense, encompasses the physical, economic and social environment touching several of the heads of power assigned to the respective levels of government. Professor Gibson put it succinctly several years ago in his article "Constitutional Jurisdiction over Environmental Management in Canada" (1973), 23 U.T.L.J. 54, at p. 85:

> [...] "environmental management" does not, under the existing situation, constitute a homogeneous constitutional unit. Instead, it cuts across many different areas of constitutional responsibility, some federal and some provincial. And it is no less obvious that "environmental management" could never be treated as a constitutional unit under one order of government in any constitution that claimed to be federal, because no system in which one government was so powerful would be federal.

I earlier referred to the environment as a diffuse subject, echoing what I said in *R. v. Crown Zellerbach Canada Ltd.*, *supra*, to the effect that environmental control, as a subject matter, does not have the requisite distinctiveness to meet the test under the "national concern" doctrine as articulated by Beetz J. in *Reference re Anti-Inflation Act*, *supra*. Although I was writing for the minority in *Crown Zellerbach*, this opinion was not contested by the majority. The majority simply decided that marine pollution was a matter of national concern because it was predominately extra-provincial and international in character and implications, and possessed sufficiently distinct and separate characteristics as to make it subject to Parliament's residual power.

It must be recognized that the environment is not an independent matter of legislation under the *Constitution Act, 1867* and that it is a constitutionally abstruse matter which does not comfortably fit within the existing division of powers without considerable overlap and uncertainty. A variety of analytical constructs have been developed to grapple with the problem, although no single method will be suitable in every instance. Some have taken a functional approach by describing specific environmental concerns and then allocating responsibility by reference to the different heads of power; see, for example, Gibson, *supra*. Others have looked at the problem from the perspective of testing the ambit of federal powers according to their general description as "conceptual" or "global" (e.g., criminal law, taxation, trade and commerce, spending and the general residuary power) as opposed to "functional" (e.g., navigation and fisheries); see P. Emond, "The Case for a Greater Federal Role in the Environmental Protection Field: An Examination of the Pollution Problem and the Constitution" (1972), 10 Osgoode Hall L.J. 647, and M. E. Hatherly, *Constitutional Jurisdiction in Relation to Environmental Law*, background paper prepared for the Protection of Life Project, Law Reform Commission of Canada (1984).

In my view the solution to this case can more readily be found by looking first at the catalogue of powers in the *Constitution Act, 1867* and considering how they may be employed to meet or avoid environmental concerns. When viewed in this manner it will be seen that in exercising their respective legislative powers, both levels of government may affect the environment, either by acting or not acting.[...]

It must be noted that the exercise of legislative power, as it affects concerns relating to the environment, must, as with other concerns, be linked to the appropriate head of power, and since the nature of the various heads of power under the *Constitution Act, 1867* differ, the extent to which environmental concerns may be taken into account in the exercise of a power may vary from one power to another. For example, a somewhat different environmental role can be played by Parliament in the exercise of its jurisdiction over fisheries than under its powers concerning railways or navigation since the former involves the management of a resource, the others activities. The foregoing observations may be demonstrated by reference to two cases involving fisheries. In *Fowler v. The Queen*, [1980] 2 S.C.R. 213, the Court found that s. 33(3) of the *Fisheries Act* was *ultra vires* Parliament because its broad prohibition enjoining the deposit of "slash, stumps or other debris" into water frequented by fish was not sufficiently linked to any actual or potential harm to fisheries. However, s. 33(2), prohibiting the deposit of deleterious substances *in any place* where they might enter waters frequented by fish, was found *intra vires* Parliament under s. 91(12) in *Northwest Falling Contractors Ltd. v. The Queen*, [1980] 2 S.C.R. 292.

The provinces may similarly act in relation to the environment under any legislative power in s. 92. Legislation in relation to local works or undertakings, for example, will often take into account environmental concerns. What is not particularly helpful in sorting out the respective levels of constitutional authority over a work such as the Oldman River dam, however, is the characterization of it as a "provincial project" or an undertaking "primarily subject to provincial regulation" as the appellant Alberta sought to do. That begs the question and posits an erroneous principle that seems to hold that there exists a general doctrine of interjurisdictional immunity to shield provincial works or undertakings from otherwise valid federal legislation. [...]

What is important is to determine whether either level of government may legislate. One may legislate in regard to provincial aspects, the other federal aspects. Although local projects will generally fall within provincial responsibility, federal participation will be required if the project impinges on an area of federal jurisdiction as is the case here.

There is, however, an even more fundamental fallacy in Alberta's argument, and that concerns the manner in which constitutional powers may be exercised. In legislating regarding a subject, it is sufficient that the legislative body legislate on that subject. The practical purpose that inspires the legislation and the implications that body must consider in making its decision are another thing. Absent a colourable purpose or a lack of *bona fides*, these considerations will not detract from the fundamental nature of the legislation. A railway line may be required to locate so as to avoid a nuisance resulting from smoke or noise in a municipality, but it is nonetheless railway regulation.

An Australian case, *Murphyores Incorporated Pty. Ltd. v. Commonwealth of Australia* (1976), 136 C.L.R. 1 (H.C.), illustrates the point well in a context similar to the present. There the plaintiffs carried on the business of mining for mineral sands from which they produced zircon and rutile concentrates. The export of those substances was regulated by the *Customs (Prohibited Exports) Regulations* (passed pursuant to the Commonwealth's trade and commerce power) and approval from the Minister of Minerals and Energy was required for their export. The issue in the case arose when an inquiry was directed to be made under the *Environment Protection (Impact of Proposals) Act*, 1974-1975 (Cth), into the environmental impact of mineral extraction from the area in which the plaintiffs had their mining leases. The Minister responsible informed the plaintiffs that the report of that inquiry would have to be considered before allowing any further export of concentrates.

The plaintiffs contended that the Minister could only consider matters relevant to "trading policy" within the scope of the Commonwealth's trade and commerce power, rather than the environmental concerns arising from the anterior mining activity which was predominantly a state interest. That argument was unanimously rejected, Stephen J. putting it as follows, at p. 12:

> The administrative decision whether or not to relax a prohibition against the export of goods will necessarily be made in the light of considerations affecting the mind of the administrator; but whatever their nature the consequence will necessarily be expressed in terms of trade and commerce, consisting of the approval or rejection of

an application to relax the prohibition on exports. It will therefore fall within constitutional power. The considerations in the light of which the decision is made may not themselves relate to matters of trade and commerce but that will not deprive the decision which they induce of its inherent constitutionality for the decision will be directly on the subject matter of exportation and the considerations actuating that decision will not detract from the character which its subject matter confers upon it.

I hasten to add that I do not mean to draw any parallels between the Commonwealth's trade and commerce power as framed in the Australian Constitution and that found in the Canadian Constitution. Obviously there are important differences in the two documents, but the general point made in *Murphyores* is nonetheless valid in the present case. The case points out the danger of falling into the conceptual trap of thinking of the environment as an extraneous matter in making legislative choices or administrative decisions. Clearly, this cannot be the case. Quite simply, the environment is comprised of all that is around us and as such must be a part of what actuates many decisions of any moment.

Environmental impact assessment is, in its simplest form, a planning tool that is now generally regarded as an integral component of sound decision-making. Its fundamental purpose is summarized by R. Cotton and D. P. Emond in "Environmental Impact Assessment", in J. Swaigen, ed., *Environmental Rights in Canada* (1981), 245, at p. 247:

> The basic concepts behind environmental assessment are simply stated: (1) early identification and evaluation of all potential environmental consequences of a proposed undertaking; (2) decision making that both guarantees the adequacy of this process and reconciles, to the greatest extent possible, the proponent's development desires with environmental protection and preservation.

As a planning tool it has both an information-gathering and a decision-making component which provide the decision maker with an objective basis for granting or denying approval for a proposed development; see M. I. Jeffery, *Environmental Approvals in Canada* (1989), at p. 1.2, {SS} 1.4; D. P. Emond, *Environmental Assessment Law in Canada* (1978), at p. 5. In short, environmental impact assessment is simply descriptive of a process of decision-making.

The *Guidelines Order* has merely added to the matters that federal decision makers should consider. If the Minister of Transport was specifically assigned the task of weighing concerns regarding fisheries in weighing applications to construct works in navigable waters, could there be any complaint that this was *ultra vires*? All that it would mean is that a decision maker charged with making one decision must also consider other matters that fall within federal power. I am not unmindful of what was said by counsel for the Attorney General for Saskatchewan who sought to characterize the *Guidelines Order* as a constitutional Trojan horse enabling the federal government, on the pretext of some narrow ground of federal jurisdiction, to conduct a far ranging inquiry into matters that are exclusively within provincial jurisdiction. However, on my reading of the *Guidelines Order* the "initiating department" assigned responsibility for conducting an initial assessment, and if required, the environmental review panel, are only given a mandate to examine matters directly related to the areas of federal responsibility affected. Thus, an initiating department or panel cannot use the *Guidelines Order* as a colourable device to invade areas of provincial jurisdiction which are unconnected to the relevant heads of federal power.

Because of its auxiliary nature, environmental impact assessment can only affect matters that are "truly in relation to an institution or activity that is otherwise within [federal] legislative jurisdiction"; see *Devine v. Quebec (Attorney General)*, [1988] 2 S.C.R. 790 at p. 808. Given the necessary element of proximity that must exist between the impact assessment process and the subject matter of federal jurisdiction involved, this legislation can, in my view, be supported by the particular head of federal power invoked in each instance. In particular, the *Guidelines Order* prescribes a close nexus between the social effects that may be examined and the environmental effects generally. [...]

I should make it clear, however, that the scope of assessment is not confined to the particular head of power under which the Government of Canada has a decision-making responsibility within the meaning of the term "proposal". Such a responsibility, as I stated earlier, is a necessary condition to engage the process, but once the initiating department has thus been given authority to embark on an assessment, that review must consider the environmental effect on all areas of federal jurisdiction. There is no constitutional obstacle preventing Parliament from enacting legislation under several heads of power at the same time; see *Jones v. Attorney General of New Brunswick*, [1975] 2 S.C.R. 182, and *Knox Contracting Ltd. v. Canada*, [1990] 2 S.C.R. 338 at p. 350. In the case of the *Guidelines Order*, Parliament has conferred upon one institution (the "initiating department") the responsibility, in the exercise of its decision-making authority, for assessing the environmental implications on all areas of federal jurisdiction potentially affected. Here, the Minister of Transport, in his capacity of decision maker under the *Navigable Waters Protection Act*, is directed to consider the environmental impact of the dam on such areas of federal responsibility as navigable waters, fisheries, Indians and Indian lands, to name those most obviously relevant in the circumstances here.

In essence, then, the *Guidelines Order* has two fundamental aspects. First, there is the substance of the *Guidelines Order* dealing with environmental impact assessment to facilitate decision-making under the federal head of power through which a proposal is regulated. As I mentioned earlier, this aspect of the *Guidelines Order* can be sustained on the basis that it is legislation in relation to the relevant subject matters enumerated in s. 91 of the *Constitution Act, 1867*. The second aspect of the legislation is its procedural or organizational element that coordinates the process of assessment, which can in any given case touch upon several areas of federal responsibility, under the auspices of a designated decision maker, or in the vernacular of the *Guidelines Order*, the "initiating department". This facet of the legislation has as its object the regulation of the institutions and agencies of the Government of Canada as to the manner in which they perform their administrative functions and duties. This, in my view, is unquestionably *intra vires* Parliament. It may be viewed either as an adjunct of the particular legislative powers involved, or, in any event, be justifiable under the residuary power in s. 91. [...]

The Court adopted a similar approach in the related situation that arose in *Jones v. Attorney General of New Brunswick, supra*. There this Court dealt with the constitutional validity, on a division of powers basis, of certain provisions of the *Official Languages Act*, R.S.C. 1970, c. O-2, the *Evidence Act* of New Brunswick, R.S.N.B. 1952, c. 74, and the *Official Languages of New Brunswick Act*, S.N.B. 1969, c. 14. The federal legislation made English and French the official languages of Canada, and the impugned provisions recognized both languages in the federal courts and in criminal proceedings. Laskin C.J. held, at p. 189:

> [...] I am in no doubt that it was open to the Parliament of Canada to enact the *Official Languages Act* (limited as it is to the purposes of the Parliament and Government of Canada and to the institutions of that Parliament and Government) as being a law "for the peace, order and good government of Canada in relation to [a matter] not coming within the classes of subjects [...] assigned exclusively to the Legislatures of the Provinces". The quoted words are in the opening paragraph of s. 91 of the *British North America Act*; and, in relying on them as constitutional support for the *Official Languages Act*, I do so on the basis of the purely residuary character of the legislative power thereby conferred. *No authority need be cited for the exclusive power of the Parliament of Canada to legislate in relation to the operation and administration of the institutions and agencies of the Parliament and Government of Canada.* Those institutions and agencies are clearly beyond provincial reach. [Emphasis added.]

The Court went on to uphold the federal legislation on the additional grounds that it was valid under Parliament's criminal jurisdiction (s. 91(27)) and federal power over federal courts (s. 101). Laskin C.J. also remarked that there was no constitutional impediment preventing Parliament from adding to the range of privileged or obligatory use of English and French in institutions or activities that are subject to federal control. For similar reasons, the provincial legislation providing for the use of both official languages in the courts of New Brunswick was upheld on the basis of its power over the administration of justice in the province (s. 92(14)).

In the end, I am satisfied that the *Guidelines Order* is in pith and substance nothing more than an instrument that regulates the manner in which federal institutions must administer their multifarious duties and functions. Consequently, it is nothing more than an adjunct of the federal legislative powers affected. In any event, it falls within the purely residuary aspect of the "Peace, Order, and Good Government" power under s. 91 of the *Constitution Act, 1867*. Any intrusion into provincial matters is merely incidental to the pith and substance of the legislation. It must also be remembered that what is involved is essentially an information gathering process in furtherance of a decision-making function within federal jurisdiction, and the recommendations made at the conclusion of the information gathering stage are not binding on the decision maker. Neither the initiating department nor the panel are given power to subpoena witnesses, as was the case in *Canadian National Railway Co. v. Courtois*, [1988] 1 S.C.R. 868, where the Court held that certain provisions of the *Act respecting occupational health and safety*, S.Q. 1979, c. 63, which, *inter alia*, allowed the province to investigate accidents and issue remedial orders, were inapplicable to an interprovincial railway undertaking. I should add that Alberta's extensive reliance on that decision is misplaced. It is wholly distinguishable from the present case on several grounds, most importantly that the impugned provincial legislation there was made compulsory against a federal undertaking and was interpreted by the Court as regulating the undertaking.

For the foregoing reasons I find that the *Guidelines Order* is *intra vires* Parliament and would thus answer the constitutional question in the negative. [...]

On the matter of costs, it is my view that this is a proper case for awarding costs on a solicitor-client basis to the respondent Society, given the Society's circumstances and the fact that the federal Ministers were joined as appellants even though they did not earlier seek leave to appeal to this Court.

Notes and Questions

1. With respect to environmental assessment, how does *Oldman River* affect the ability of either level of government to make integrated decisions about a project's contribution to long-term sustainability?

2. La Forest J., writing for a majority of eight to one, starts his judgment with a number of very broad statements on the importance of environmental issues and the implications this has for the Court's approach to the division of powers between the federal and provincial governments. What developments in the realm of international environmental law, emerging at the time of the decision, may have played a role in the Court's analysis? How relevant are these statements today?

3. The starting point for La Forest J.'s constitutional analysis is the recognition that both federal and provincial decision makers affect the environment, "either by acting or not acting". He illustrates the implications of this using a hypothetical interprovincial railway project, which would be subject to the exclusive jurisdiction of the federal government. What is the significance of this example? How does it differ from the narrower jurisdiction over the environmental impact of forest activity in *Fowler* and *Northwest Falling*?

4. In reviewing the decision, it is important to consider carefully whether a particular comment relates to the jurisdiction granted under the EARP Guidelines Order, or the limits imposed by the Constitution. Second, it is important to separate constitutional limits from practical limits. In other words, there may be sound, practical reasons in many cases for the federal decision maker not to exercise its power to the limits of its jurisdiction.

5. There are several questions to be considered in a comprehensive analysis of federal constitutional jurisdiction regarding an environmental assessment of a proposed activity. The first is whether there is jurisdiction to conduct a federal assessment of a proposal. Related to this is a consideration of constitutional limits on the scope of the proposal assessed. Next, are there constitutional limits on the scope of the assessment to be carried out? Finally, are there constitutional limits on the final decision, either in terms of whether the proposal can be rejected or in terms of conditions imposed? What does *Oldman River* say about each of these discrete questions?

6. Carefully consider the Court's comments to the effect that an assessment can consider environmental effects on all areas of federal jurisdiction. Can

you reconcile the Court's focus on the need for integrated assessments and decision-making with this statement? In light of the railway example, and the reference to *Murphyores Incorporated Pty. Ltd. v. Commonwealth of Australia* (1976), 136 C.L.R. 1 (H.C. Aust.), is the Court here indicating that environmental effects that are outside federal jurisdiction cannot be considered?

Chronologically, the next important Supreme Court of Canada case to address division of powers issues in the environmental context arose out of charges laid in the mid-1990s against Hydro-Québec under the newly proclaimed *Canadian Environmental Protection Act* (CEPA). This Act is discussed in more detail in Chapter 4. The charges related to an accidental discharge of PCB waste into a Quebec river. Hydro-Québec argued that the relevant CEPA provisions, upon which the charges were based, were unconstitutional. The Quebec courts called upon to hear this challenge all agreed that CEPA was *ultra vires* the federal government, setting the stage for what has become a landmark Supreme Court of Canada decision.

Consider the following excerpts from the decision.

Canada (Procureure générale) c. Hydro-Québec

(*sub nom. R. v. Hydro-Québec*) [1997] 3 S.C.R. 213

The CHIEF JUSTICE and IACOBUCCI J. (dissenting): —

The Pith and Substance of the Legislation

The manner of analysing matters involving division of powers is well established: see Hogg, *supra*, at p. 15-6. The law in question must first be characterized in relation to its "pith and substance", that is, its dominant or most important characteristic. One must then see if the law, seen in this light, can be successfully assigned to one of the government's heads of legislative power.

[**Ed. Note:** The dissenters interpret section 11 of the Act more broadly than the majority, describing the pith and substance as protection of the environment and human life and health from any and all harmful substances by regulation. As is discussed later by La Forest J., the majority views the pith and substance of the impugned provisions as allowing the Ministers of Health and the Environment to identify toxic substances, and to prohibit their introduction into the environment, except in accordance with certain terms.]

The Criminal Law Power

Parliament has been given broad and exclusive power to legislate in relation to criminal law by virtue of s. 91(27): *RJR-MacDonald Inc. v. Canada (Attorney General)*, [1995] 3 S.C.R. 199; *Scowby v. Glendinning*, [1986] 2 S.C.R. 226. This power has traditionally been construed generously. As La Forest J. noted in *RJR-MacDonald*, at p. 240, "[i]n developing a definition of the criminal law, this Court has been careful not to freeze the definition in time or confine it to a fixed domain of activity".

Nevertheless, the criminal law power has always been made subject to two requirements: laws purporting to be upheld under s. 91(27) must contain prohibitions backed by penalties; and they must be directed at a "legitimate public purpose" (*Scowby*, at p. 237). As Rand J. stated in the *Margarine Reference, supra,* at pp. 49-50:

> A crime is an act which the law, with appropriate penal sanctions, forbids; but as prohibitions are not enacted in a vacuum, we can properly look for some evil or injurious or undesirable effect upon the public against which the law is directed. That effect may be in relation to social, economic or political interests; and the legislature has had in mind to suppress the evil or to safeguard the interest threatened [...]. Is the prohibition then enacted with a view to a public purpose which can support it as being in relation to criminal law? Public peace, order, security, health, morality: these are the ordinary though not exclusive ends served by that law [...]

Criminal law under s. 91(27) must attempt to achieve a criminal public purpose through the imposition of prohibitions and penalties. Colourable attempts to invade areas of provincial jurisdiction under the guise of criminal legislation will be declared *ultra vires*. As La Forest J. wrote in *RJR-MacDonald*, at p. 246:

> The scope of the federal power to create criminal legislation with respect to health matters is broad, and is circumscribed only by the requirements that the legislation must contain a prohibition accompanied by a penal sanction and must be directed at a legitimate public health evil. *If a given piece of federal legislation contains these features, and if that legislation is not otherwise a "colourable" intrusion upon provincial jurisdiction, then it is valid as criminal law.* [...] [Emphasis added.] [...]

The next step is therefore to examine the impugned provisions and determine whether they meet these criteria. In our view, they fall short. While the protection of the environment is a legitimate public purpose which could support the enactment of criminal legislation, we believe the impugned provisions of the Act are more an attempt to regulate environmental pollution than to prohibit or proscribe it. As such, they extend beyond the purview of criminal law and cannot be justified under s. 91(27).

A Legitimate Public Purpose

The appellant and several interveners urged us to uphold the provisions as related to health, one of the criminal public purposes recognized in the *Margarine Reference, supra.* In this regard, they cited numerous studies outlining the hazardous effects of PCBs, which were the subject of the Interim Order that gave rise to this litigation. [...] With respect, the toxicity of PCBs, while clearly important to the environment itself, is not directly relevant to this appeal, since what is at issue is not simply the Interim Order, but the enabling provisions under which that order was enacted. That is, the question is not whether PCBs pose a danger to human health, which it appears they clearly do, but whether the Act purports to grant federal regulatory power over substances which may *not* pose such a danger.

In our view, there is no question but that the Act does so. [...] It is not necessary that a substance constitute a danger to human life or health for it to be labelled "toxic" and brought under federal control; under s. 11(a), it is enough that it may have a harmful effect on the environment. It is not even necessary to show that the aspect of the environment threatened be one upon which human life depends; this is made a separate category under s. 11(b), and should not, therefore, be read into s. 11(a). A substance which affected groundhogs, for example, but which had no effect on people could be labelled "toxic" under s. 11(a) and made subject to wholesale federal regulation.

By defining "toxic" in this way, Parliament has taken explicit steps to ensure that no risk to human life or health, direct or indirect, would have to be proven before regulatory control could be assumed over a given substance. As such, we cannot see how the provisions can be upheld as legislation relating to health. Their scope extends well beyond matters relating to human health into the realm of general ecological protection. Parliament's clear intention was to allow for federal intervention where the environment itself was at risk, whether or not the substances concerned posed a threat to human health and whether or not the aspect of the environment affected was one on which human life depended. Having specifically excluded both direct and indirect danger to human health as preconditions for the application of these provisions, Parliament cannot now say that they were enacted in order to guard against such dangers.

To the extent that La Forest J. suggests that this legislation is supportable as relating to health, therefore, we must respectfully disagree. We agree with him, however, that the protection of the environment is itself a legitimate criminal public purpose, analogous to those cited in the *Margarine Reference, supra*. We would not add to his lucid reasoning on this point, save to state explicitly that this purpose does not rely on any of the other traditional purposes of criminal law (health, security, public order, etc.). To the extent that Parliament wishes to deter environmental pollution specifically by punishing it with appropriate penal sanctions, it is free to do so, without having to show that these sanctions are ultimately aimed at achieving one of the "traditional" aims of criminal law. The protection of the environment is itself a legitimate basis for criminal legislation.

However, we still do not feel that the impugned provisions qualify as criminal law under s. 91(27). While they have a legitimate criminal purpose, they fail to meet the other half of the *Maragarine Reference* [sic] test. The structure of Part II of the Act indicates that they are not intended to prohibit environmental pollution, but simply to regulate it. As we will now explain in further detail, they are not, therefore, criminal law: see *Hauser, supra*, at p. 999.

Prohibitions Backed by Penalties

Ascertaining whether a particular statute is prohibitive or regulatory in nature is often more of an art than a science. As Cory J. acknowledged in *Knox Contracting, supra*, what constitutes criminal law is often "easier to recognize than define" (p. 347). Some guidelines have, however, emerged from previous jurisprudence.

The fact that a statute contains a prohibition and a penalty does not necessarily mean that statute is criminal in nature. Regulatory statutes commonly prohibit violations of their provisions or regulations promulgated under them and provide penal sanctions to be applied if violations do, in fact, occur. Any regulatory statute that lacked such prohibitions and penalties would be meaningless. However, as La Forest J. himself recognized in *Thomson Newspapers Ltd. v. Canada (Director of Investigation and Research, Restrictive Trade Practices Commission)*, [1990] 1 S.C.R. 425 at pp. 508—17, and in *R. v. McKinlay Transport Ltd.*, [1990] 1 S.C.R. 627 at p. 650, the penalties that are provided in a regulatory context serve a "pragmatic" or "instrumental" purpose and do not transform the legislation into criminal law. (Also see *Wetmore, supra, Scowby, supra,* and *Knox Contracting, supra*.) In environmental law, as in competition law or income tax law, compliance cannot always be ensured by the usual regulatory enforcement techniques, such as periodic or unannounced inspections. Hence, in order to ensure that legal standards are being met, a strong deterrent, the threat of penal sanctions, is necessary. [...]

At the same time, however, a criminal law does not have to consist solely of blanket prohibitions. It may, as La Forest J. noted in *RJR-MacDonald, supra,* at pp. 263-64, "validly contain exemptions for certain conduct without losing its status as criminal law". See also *Lord's Day Alliance of Canada v. Attorney General of British Columbia*, [1959] S.C.R. 497; *Morgentaler, supra*; *R. v. Furtney*, [1991] 3 S.C.R. 89. These exemptions may have the effect of establishing "regulatory" schemes which confer a measure of discretionary authority without changing the character of the law, as was the case in *RJR-MacDonald*.

Determining when a piece of legislation has crossed the line from criminal to regulatory involves, in our view, considering the nature and extent of the regulation it creates, as well as the context within which it purports to apply. A scheme which is fundamentally regulatory, for example, will not be saved by calling it an "exemption". As Professor Hogg suggests, *supra,* at p. 18-26, "the more elaborate [a] regulatory scheme, the more likely it is that the Court will classify the dispensation or exemption as being regulatory rather than criminal". At the same time, the subject matter of the impugned law may indicate the appropriate approach to take in characterizing the law as criminal or regulatory.

Having examined the legislation at issue in this case, we have no doubt that it is essentially regulatory in nature, and therefore outside the scope of s. 91(27). In order to have an "exemption", there must first be a prohibition in the legislation from which that exemption is derived. Thus, the *Tobacco Products Control Act*, S.C. 1988, c. 20, at issue in *RJR-MacDonald, supra,* contained broad prohibitions against the advertising and promotion of tobacco products in Canada. Section 4 of that Act provided that "[n]o person shall advertise any tobacco product offered for sale in Canada". It also provided a labelling requirement in the form of a prohibition, stating in s. 9 that it was illegal to sell tobacco products without printed health warnings. Any exemptions from these general prohibitions were just that — exceptions to a general rule.

In the legislation at issue in this appeal, on the other hand, no such prohibitions appear. [...] In fact, the only time the word "prohibition" appears in s. 34(1) [of CEPA] is in s. 34(1)(l), which provides that the Governor in Council *may*, at his or her discretion, prohibit the manufacture, import, use or sale of a given substance. Clearly, this is not analogous to the broad general prohibitions found in the statutes cited above.

The only other mentions of prohibition in relation to the impugned provisions are in ss. 113(f) and 113(i) of the Act, which provide that failure to comply with a regulation made under ss. 34 or 35 is an offence. The prohibitions, such as they are, are ancillary to the regulatory scheme, not the other way around. This strongly suggests that the focus of the legislation is regulation rather than prohibition. [...]

In this case, there *is* no offence until an administrative agency "intervenes". Sections 34 and 35 do not define an offence at all: which, if any, substances will be placed on the List of Toxic Substances, as well as the norms of conduct regarding these substances, are to be defined on an on-going basis by the Ministers of Health and the Environment. It would be an odd crime whose definition was made entirely dependent on the discretion of the Executive. This further suggests that the Act's true nature is regulatory, not criminal, and that the offences created by s. 113 are regulatory offences, not "true crimes": see *R. v. Wholesale Travel Group Inc.*, [1991] 3 S.C.R. 154, *per* Cory J. Our colleague, La Forest J., would hold that the scheme of the impugned Act is an effective means of avoiding unnecessarily broad prohibitions and carefully targeting specific toxic substances. The regulatory mechanism allows the schemes to be changed flexibly, as the need arises. Of course, simply because a scheme is effective and flexible does not mean it is *intra vires* the federal Parliament.

This is particularly true in light of the striking breadth of the impugned provisions. The 24 listed heads of authority in s. 34 allow for the regulation of every conceivable aspect of toxic substances; in fact, in case anything was left out, s. 34(1)(x) provides for regulations concerning "any other matter necessary to carry out the purposes of this Part". It is highly unlikely, in our opinion, that Parliament intended to leave the criminalization of such a sweeping area of behaviour to the discretion of the Ministers of Health and the Environment. [...]

The appellant relies on this Court's decision in *RJR-MacDonald*, *supra*, arguing that the statutory regime in this case is analogous to that upheld (on division of powers grounds) in *RJR-MacDonald*. We believe this reliance is, with respect, misplaced. As noted above, the legislation at issue in *RJR-MacDonald* contained broad prohibitions, tempered by certain exemptions. The impugned provisions in this case, on the other hand, involve no such general prohibition. In our view, they can only be characterized as a broad delegation of regulatory authority to the Governor in Council. The aim of these provisions is not to prohibit toxic substances or any aspect of their use, but simply to control the manner in which these substances will be allowed to interact with the environment.

RJR-MacDonald, may be further distinguished, in our view. The *Tobacco Products Control Act* addressed a narrow field of activity: the advertising and promotion of tobacco products. The impugned provisions here deal with a much broader area of concern: the release of substances into the environment. This Court has unanimously held that the environment is a subject matter of shared jurisdiction, that is, that the Constitution does not assign it exclusively to either the provinces or Parliament: *Oldman River*, *supra*, at p. 63; see also *Crown Zellerbach*, *supra*, at pp. 455-56, *per* La Forest J. A decision by the framers of the Constitution not to give one level of government exclusive control over a subject matter should, in our opinion, act as a signal that the two levels of government are meant to operate in tandem with regard to that subject matter. One level should not be allowed to take over the field so as to completely dwarf the presence of the other. This does not mean that *no* regulation will be permissible, but wholesale regulatory authority of the type envisaged by the Act is, in our view, inconsistent with the shared nature of jurisdiction over the environment. As La Forest J. noted in his dissenting reasons in *Crown Zellerbach*, at p. 455, "environmental pollution alone [i.e. as a subject matter of legislative authority] is itself all-pervasive. It is a by-product of everything we do. In man's relationship with his environment, waste is unavoidable".

We agree completely with this statement. Almost everything we do involves "polluting" the environment in some way. The impugned provisions purport to grant regulatory authority over all aspects of any substance whose release into the environment "ha[s] or [...] may have an immediate or long-term harmful effect on the environment" (s. 11(a)). One wonders just what, if any, role will be left for the provinces in dealing with environmental pollution if the federal government is given such total control over the release of these substances. Moreover, the countless spheres of human activity, both collective and individual, which could potentially fall under the ambit of the Act are apparent. Many of them fall within areas of jurisdiction granted to the provinces under s. 92. Granting Parliament the authority to regulate so completely the release of substances into the environment by determining whether or not they are "toxic" would not only inescapably preclude the possibility of shared environmental jurisdiction; it would also infringe severely on other heads of power assigned to the provinces. [...].

For all of the above reasons, we are unable to uphold the impugned provisions of the Act under the federal criminal law power. That being said, we wish to add that none of this should be read as foredooming future attempts by Parliament to create an effective national — or, indeed, international — strategy for the protection of the environment. We agree with La Forest J. that achieving such a strategy is a public purpose of extreme importance and one of the major challenges of our time. There are, in this regard, many measures open to Parliament which will not offend the division of powers set out by the Constitution, notably the creation of environmental crimes. Nothing, in our view, prevents Parliament from outlawing certain kinds of behaviour on the basis that they are harmful to the environment. But such legislation must actually seek to *outlaw* this behaviour, not merely regulate it [emphasis in original].

Other potential avenues include the power to address interprovincial or international environmental concerns under the peace, order and good government power, which is discussed below. Parliament is not without power to act in pursuit of national policies on environmental protection. But it must do so pursuant to the balance of powers assigned by ss. 91 and 92. Environmental protection must be achieved in accordance with the Constitution, not in spite of it. As Professor Bowden concludes in her case comment on *Oldman River, supra*, (1992), 56 Sask. L. Rev. 209, at pp. 219-20, "it is only through legislative and policy initiatives at and between both levels of government that satisfactory solutions may be attainable".

The impugned provisions are not justified under s. 91(27) of the *Constitution Act, 1867*. We will now consider the appellant's second argument, namely that the provisions may be upheld under the peace, order and good government power.

[Ed. Note: POGG and trade and commerce discussion is omitted.]

LA FOREST J.: — This Court has in recent years been increasingly called upon to consider the interplay between federal and provincial legislative powers as they relate to environmental protection. Whether viewed positively as strategies for maintaining a clean environment, or negatively as measures to combat the evils of pollution, there can be no doubt that these measures relate to a public purpose of superordinate importance, and one in which all levels of government and numerous organs of the international community have become increasingly engaged. In the opening passage of this Court's reasons in what is perhaps the leading case, *Friends of the Oldman River Society v. Canada (Minister of Transport)*, [1992] 1 S.C.R. 3 at pp. 16-17, the matter is succinctly put this way:

> The protection of the environment has become one of the major challenges of our time. To respond to this challenge, governments and international organizations have been engaged in the creation of a wide variety of legislative schemes and administrative structures.

The all-important duty of Parliament and the provincial legislatures to make full use of the legislative powers respectively assigned to them in protecting the environment has inevitably placed upon the courts the burden of progressively defining the extent to which these powers may be used to that end. In performing this task, it is incumbent on the courts to secure the basic balance between the two levels of government envisioned by the Constitution. However, in doing so, they must be mindful that the Constitution must be interpreted in a manner that is fully responsive to emerging realities and to the nature of the subject matter sought to be regulated. Given the pervasive and diffuse nature of the environment, this reality poses particular difficulties in this context.

This latest case in which this Court is required to define the nature of legislative powers over the environment is of major significance. The narrow issue raised is the extent to and manner in which the federal Parliament may control the amount of and conditions under which Chlorobiphenyls (PCBs) — substances well known to pose great dangers to humans and the environment generally — may enter into the environment. However, the attack on the federal power to secure this end is not really aimed at the specific provisions respecting PCBs. Rather, it puts into question the constitutional validity of its enabling statutory provisions. What is really at stake is whether Part II ("Toxic Substances") of the *Canadian Environmental Protection Act*, R.S.C., 1985, c. 16 (4th Supp.), which empowers the federal Ministers of Health and of the Environment to determine what substances are toxic and to prohibit the introduction of such substances into the environment except in accordance with specified terms and conditions, falls within the constitutional power of Parliament. [...]

In considering how the question of the constitutional validity of a legislative enactment relating to the environment should be approached, this Court in *Oldman River, supra*, made it clear that the environment is not, as such, a subject matter of legislation under the *Constitution Act, 1867*. As it was put there, "the *Constitution Act, 1867* has not assigned the matter of 'environment' *sui generis* to either the provinces or Parliament" (p. 63). Rather, it is a diffuse subject that cuts across many different areas of constitutional responsibility, some federal, some provincial (pp. 63-64). Thus Parliament or a provincial legislature can, in advancing the scheme or purpose of a statute, enact provisions minimizing or preventing the detrimental impact that statute may have on the environment, prohibit pollution, and the like. In assessing the constitutional validity of a provision relating to the environment, therefore, what must first be done is to look at the catalogue of legislative powers listed in the *Constitution Act, 1867* to see if the provision falls within one or more of the powers assigned to the body (whether Parliament or a provincial legislature) that enacted the legislation (*ibid.* at p. 65). If the provision in essence, in pith and substance, falls within the parameters of any such power, then it is constitutionally valid.

Though pith and substance may be described in different ways, the expressions "dominant purpose" or "true character" used in *R. v. Morgentaler*, [1993] 3 S.C.R. 463 at pp. 481-82, or "the dominant or most important characteristic of the challenged law" used in *Whitbread v. Walley*, [1990] 3 S.C.R. 1273 at p. 1286, and in *Oldman River, supra*, at p. 62, appropriately convey the meaning to be attached to the term. If a provision dealing with the environment is really aimed at promoting the dominant purpose of the statute or at addressing the impact of a statutory scheme, and the scheme itself is valid, then so is the provision.

In examining the validity of legislation in this way, it must be underlined that the nature of the relevant legislative powers must be examined. Different types of legislative powers may support different types of environmental provisions. The manner in which such provisions must be related to a legislative scheme was, by way of example, discussed in *Oldman River* in respect of railways, navigable waters and fisheries. An environmental provision may be validly aimed at curbing environmental damage, but in some cases the environmental damage may be directly related to the power itself. There is a considerable difference between regulating works and activities, like railways, and a resource like fisheries, and consequently the environmental provisions relating to each of these. Environmental provisions must be tied to the appropriate constitutional source.

Some heads of legislation may support a wholly different type of environmental provision than others. Notably under the general power to legislate for the peace, order and good government, Parliament may enact a wide variety of environmental legislation in dealing with an emergency of sufficient magnitude to warrant resort to the power. But the emergency would, of course, have to be established. So too with the "national concern" doctrine, which formed the major focus of the present case. A discrete area of environmental legislative power can fall within that doctrine, provided it meets the criteria first developed in *Reference re Anti-Inflation Act*, [1976] 2 S.C.R. 373, and thus set forth in *Crown Zellerbach, supra*, at p. 432:

> For a matter to qualify as a matter of national concern in either sense it must have a singleness, distinctiveness and indivisibility that clearly distinguishes it from matters of provincial concern and a scale of impact on provincial jurisdiction that is reconcilable with the fundamental distribution of legislative power under the Constitution;

Thus in the latter case, this Court held that marine pollution met those criteria and so fell within the exclusive legislative power of Parliament under the peace, order and good government clause. While the constitutional necessity of characterizing certain activities as beyond the scope of provincial legislation and falling within the national domain was accepted by all the members of the Court, the danger of too readily adopting this course was not lost on the minority. Determining that a particular subject matter is a matter of national concern involves the consequence that the matter falls within the exclusive and paramount power of Parliament and has obvious impact on the balance of Canadian federalism. In *Crown Zellerbach*, the minority (at p. 453) expressed the view that the subject of environmental protection was all-pervasive, and if accepted as falling within the general legislative domain of Parliament under the national concern doctrine, could radically alter the division of legislative power in Canada.

The minority position on this point (which was not addressed by the majority) was subsequently accepted by the whole Court in *Oldman River, supra*, at p. 64. The general thrust of that case is that the Constitution should be so interpreted as to afford both levels of government ample means to protect the environment while maintaining the general structure of the Constitution. This is hardly consistent with an enthusiastic adoption of the "national dimensions" doctrine. That doctrine can, it is true, be adopted where the criteria set forth in *Crown Zellerbach* are met so that the subject can appropriately be separated from areas of provincial competence.

I have gone on at this length to demonstrate the simple proposition that the validity of a legislative provision (including one relating to environmental protection) must be tested against the specific characteristics of the head of power under which it is proposed to justify it. For each constitutional head of power has its own particular characteristics and raises concerns peculiar to itself in assessing it in the balance of Canadian federalism. This may seem obvious, perhaps even trite, but it is all too easy (see *Fowler v. The Queen*, [1980] 2 S.C.R. 213) to overlook the characteristics of a particular power and overshoot the mark or, again, in assessing the applicability of one head of power to give effect to concerns appropriate to another head of power when this is neither appropriate nor consistent with the law laid down by this Court respecting the ambit and contours of that other power. In the present case, it seems to me, this was the case of certain propositions placed before us regarding the breadth and application of the criminal law power. There was a marked attempt to raise concerns appropriate to the national concern doctrine under the peace, order and good government clause to the criminal law power in a manner that, in my view, is wholly inconsistent with the nature and ambit of that power as set down by this Court from a very early period and continually reiterated since, notably in specific pronouncements in the most recent cases on the subject.

The Criminal Law Power

Section 91(27) of the *Constitution Act, 1867* confers the exclusive power to legislate in relation to criminal law on Parliament. The nature and ambit of this power has recently been the subject of a detailed analytical and historical examination in *RJR-MacDonald, supra*, where it was again described (p. 240), as it has for many years, as being "*plenary in nature*" (emphasis added). [...]

What appears from the analysis in *RJR-MacDonald* is that as early as 1903, the Privy Council, in *Attorney-General for Ontario v. Hamilton Street Railway Co.*, [1903] A.C. 524 at pp. 528-29, had made it clear that the power conferred on Parliament by s. 91(27) is "the criminal law in its *widest sense*" (emphasis added).

Consistently with this approach, the Privy Council in *Proprietary Articles Trade Association v. Attorney-General for Canada*, [1931] A.C. 310 (hereafter *PATA*), at p. 324, defined the criminal law power as including any prohibited act with penal consequences. As it put it, at p. 324: "The criminal quality of an act cannot be discerned [...] by reference to any standard but one: Is the act prohibited with penal consequences?" This approach has been consistently followed ever since and, as *RJR-MacDonald* relates, it has been applied by the courts in a wide variety of settings. Accordingly, it is entirely within the discretion of Parliament to determine what evil it wishes by penal prohibition to suppress and what threatened interest it thereby wishes to safeguard, to adopt the terminology of Rand J. in the *Margarine Reference*, *supra*, at p. 49, cited *infra*.

Contrary to the respondent's submission, under s. 91(27) of the *Constitution Act, 1867*, it is also within the discretion of Parliament to determine the extent of blameworthiness that it wishes to attach to a criminal prohibition. So it may determine the nature of the mental element pertaining to different crimes, such as a defence of due diligence like that which appears in s. 125(1) of the Act in issue. This flows from the fact that Parliament has been accorded plenary power to make criminal law in the widest sense. This power is, of course, subject to the "fundamental justice" requirements of s. 7 of the *Canadian Charter of Rights and Freedoms*, which may dictate a higher level of *mens rea* for serious or "true" crimes; cf. *R. v. Wholesale Travel Group Inc.*, [1991] 3 S.C.R. 154, and *R. v. Rube*, [1992] 3 S.C.R. 159, but that is not an issue here.

The *Charter* apart, only one qualification has been attached to Parliament's plenary power over criminal law. The power cannot be employed colourably. Like other legislative powers, it cannot, as Estey J. put it in *Scowby v. Glendinning*, [1986] 2 S.C.R. 226 at p. 237, "permit Parliament, simply by legislating in the proper form, to colourably invade areas of exclusively provincial legislative competence". To determine whether such an attempt is being made, it is, of course, appropriate to enquire into Parliament's purpose in enacting the legislation. As Estey J. noted in *Scowby*, at p. 237, since the *Margarine Reference*, it has been "accepted that some legitimate public purpose must underlie the prohibition". Estey J. then cited Rand J.'s words in the *Margarine Reference* (at p. 49) as follows:

> A crime is an act which the law, with appropriate penal sanctions, forbids; but as prohibitions are not enacted in a vacuum, we can properly look for some evil or injurious or undesirable effect upon the public against which the law is directed. That effect may be in relation to social, economic or political interests; and the legislature has had in mind to suppress the evil or to safeguard the interest threatened.

I simply add that the analysis in *Scowby* and the *Margarine Reference* was most recently applied by this Court in *RJR-MacDonald*, *supra*, at pp. 240-41.

In the *Margarine Reference*, *supra*, at p. 50, Rand J. helpfully set forth the more usual purposes of a criminal prohibition in the following passage:

> Is the prohibition [...] enacted with a view to a public purpose which can support it as being in relation to criminal law? Public peace, order, security, health, morality: these are the ordinary though not exclusive ends served by that law. [...] [Emphasis added.]

See also *Morgentaler, supra*, at p. 489; *RJR-MacDonald*, at p. 241. As the final clause in the passage just cited indicates, the listed purposes by no means exhaust the purposes that may legitimately support valid criminal legislation. Not only is this clear from this passage, but subsequent to the *Margarine Reference*, it is obvious from Rand J.'s remarks in *Lord's Day Alliance of Canada v. Attorney General of British Columbia*, [1959] S.C.R. 497 at pp. 508-9, that he was in no way departing from Lord Atkin's statement in the *PATA* case, *supra* (he cited the relevant passage with approval). His concern in the *Margarine Reference*, as he indicates in the *Lord's Day* case (at p. 509), was that "in a federal system distinctions must be made arising from the true object, purpose, nature or character of each particular enactment". In short, in a case like the present, all one is concerned with is colourability. Otherwise, one would, in effect, be reviving the discarded notion that there is a "domain" of criminal law, something Rand J., like Lord Atkin before him, was not prepared to do. All of this is, of course, consistent with the view, most recently reiterated in *RJR-MacDonald*, at pp. 259-61, that criminal law is not frozen in time.

During the argument in the present case, however, one sensed, at times, a tendency, even by the appellant and the supporting interveners, to seek justification solely for the purpose of the protection of health specifically identified by Rand J. Now I have no doubt that that purpose obviously will support a considerable measure of environmental legislation, as perhaps also the ground of security. But I entertain no doubt that the protection of a clean environment is a public purpose within Rand J.'s formulation in the *Margarine Reference*, cited *supra*, sufficient to support a criminal prohibition. It is surely an "interest threatened" which Parliament can legitimately "safeguard", or to put it another way, pollution is an "evil" that Parliament can legitimately seek to suppress. Indeed, as I indicated at the outset of these reasons, it is a public purpose of superordinate importance; it constitutes one of the major challenges of our time. It would be surprising indeed if Parliament could not exercise its plenary power over criminal law to protect this interest and to suppress the evils associated with it by appropriate penal prohibitions.

This approach is entirely consistent with the recent pronouncement of this Court in *Ontario v. Canadian Pacific Ltd.*, [1995] 2 S.C.R. 1031, where Gonthier J., speaking for the majority, had this to say, at para. 55:

> It is clear that over the past two decades, citizens have become acutely aware of the importance of environmental protection, and of the fact that penal consequences may flow from conduct which harms the environment. [...]

This is, of course, in line with the thinking of various international organisms. The World Commission on Environment and Development (the Brundtland Commission) in its report *Our Common Future* (1987) (see at pp. 219-20, and pp. 224-25) long ago recommended the adoption of appropriate legislation to protect the environment against toxic and chemical substances, including the creation of national standards that could be supplemented by local legislation. [...]

What the foregoing underlines is what I referred to at the outset, that the protection of the environment is a major challenge of our time. It is an international problem, one that requires action by governments at all levels. And, as is stated in the preamble to the Act under review, "Canada must be able to fulfil its international obligations in respect of the environment". I am confident that Canada can fulfil its international obligations, in so far as the toxic substances sought to be prohibited from entering into the environment under the Act are concerned, by use of the criminal law power. The purpose of the criminal law is to underline and protect our fundamental values. While many environmental issues could be criminally sanctioned in terms of protection of human life or health, I cannot accept that the criminal law is limited to that because "certain forms and degrees of environmental pollution can directly or indirectly, sooner or later, seriously harm or endanger human life and human health", as the paper approvingly cited by Gonthier J. in *Ontario v. Canadian Pacific*, *supra*, observes. But the stage at which this may be discovered is not easy to discern, and I agree with that paper that the stewardship of the environment is a fundamental value of our society and that Parliament may use its criminal law power to underline that value. The criminal law must be able to keep pace with and protect our emerging values.

In saying that Parliament may use its criminal law power in the interest of protecting the environment or preventing pollution, there again appears to have been confusion during the argument between the approach to the national concern doctrine and the criminal law power. The national concern doctrine operates by assigning full power to regulate an area to Parliament. Criminal law does not work that way. Rather it seeks by discrete prohibitions to prevent evils falling within a broad purpose, such as, for example, the protection of health. In the criminal law area, reference to such broad policy objectives is simply a means of ensuring that the prohibition is legitimately aimed at some public evil Parliament wishes to suppress and so is not a colourable attempt to deal with a matter falling exclusively within an area of provincial legislative jurisdiction.

The legitimate use of the criminal law I have just described in no way constitutes an encroachment on provincial legislative power, though it may affect matters falling within the latter's ambit. [...]

I conclude that Parliament may validly enact prohibitions under its criminal law power against specific acts for the purpose of preventing pollution or, to put it in other terms, causing the entry into the environment of certain toxic substances. I quite understand that a particular prohibition could be so broad or all-encompassing as to be found to be, in pith and substance, really aimed at regulating an area falling within the provincial domain and not exclusively at protecting the environment. A sweeping prohibition like this (and this would be equally true of one aimed generally at the protection of health) would, in any case, probably be unworkable. But the attack here ultimately is that the impugned provisions grant such a broad discretion to the Governor in Council as to permit orders that go beyond federal power. I can imagine very nice issues being raised concerning this matter under certain types of legislation, though in such a case one would tend to interpret the legislation narrowly if only to keep it within constitutional bounds. But one need not go so far here. For, it seems to me, as we shall see, when one carefully peruses the legislation, it becomes clear enough that Parliament has stayed well within its power.

Though I shall deal with this issue in more detail once I come to consider the legislation, it is well at this point to recall that the use of the federal criminal law power in no way precludes the provinces from exercising their extensive powers under s. 92 to regulate and control the pollution of the environment either independently or to supplement federal action. The situation is really no different from the situation regarding the protection of health where Parliament has for long exercised extensive control over such matters as food and drugs by prohibitions grounded in the criminal law power. This has not prevented the provinces from extensively regulating and prohibiting many activities relating to health. The two levels of government frequently work together to meet common concerns. The cooperative measures relating to the use of tobacco are fully related in *RJR-MacDonald, supra*. Nor, though it arises under a different technical basis, is the situation, in substance, different as regards federal prohibitions against polluting water for the purposes of protecting the fisheries. Here again there is a wide measure of cooperation between the federal and provincial authorities to effect common or complementary ends. It is also the case in many other areas. The fear that the legislation impugned here would distort the federal-provincial balance seems to me to be overstated.

One last matter requires comment. The specific provision impugned in this case, the Interim Order, would seem to me to be justified as a criminal prohibition for the protection of human life and health alone (a purpose upheld most recently in *RJR-MacDonald*). That would also at first sight appear to be true of many of the prohibited uses of the substances in the List of Toxic Substances in Schedule I. So if the protection of the environment does not amount to a valid public purpose to justify criminal sanctions, it would be simply a question of severing those portions of s. 11 of the Act that deal solely with the environment to ensure the validity of the Interim Order and the rest of the enabling provisions. After all, the protection of the environment, as we earlier saw, is closely integrated, directly or indirectly, with the protection of health. But for my part, I find this exercise wholly unnecessary. The protection of the environment, through prohibitions against toxic substances, seems to me to constitute a wholly legitimate public objective in the exercise of the criminal law power. Humanity's interest in the environment surely extends beyond its own life and health.

The Provisions Respecting Toxic Substances

The respondent, the *mis en cause* and their supporting interveners primarily attack ss. 34 and 35 of the Act as constituting an infringement on provincial regulatory powers conferred by the Constitution. This they do by submitting that the power to regulate a substance is so broad as to encroach upon provincial legislative jurisdiction. That is because of what they call the broad "definition" given to toxic substances under s. 11, and particularly para. (a), thereof which, it will be remembered, provides that:

> 11. For the purposes of this Part, a substance is toxic if it is entering or may enter the environment in a quantity or concentration or under conditions
>
> (a) having or that may have an immediate or long-term harmful effect on the environment;

This, along with the expansive definitions of "substance" and "environment" in s. 3(1), makes it possible, they say, in effect to regulate any substance that can in any way prove harmful to the environment.

I cannot agree with this submission. As I see it, the argument focusses too narrowly on a specific provision of the Act and for that matter only on certain aspects of it, and then applies that provision in a manner that I do not think is warranted by a consideration of the provisions of the Act as a whole and in light of its background and purpose. I shall deal with the latter first. Before doing so, however, I shall comment briefly on the concern expressed about the breadth of the phraseology of the Act. As Gonthier J. observed in *Ontario v. Canadian Pacific, supra,* this broad wording is unavoidable in environmental protection legislation because of the breadth and complexity of the subject and has to be kept in mind in interpreting the relevant legislation [...]. In light of this, he went on to hold that environmental protection legislation should not be approached with the same rigour as statutes dealing with less complex issues in applying the doctrine of vagueness developed under s. 7 of the *Charter.* The effect of requiring greater precision would be to frustrate the legislature in its attempt to protect the public against the dangers flowing from pollution. He thus summarized his view, at para. 58:

> In the environmental context, each one of us is vulnerable to the health and property damage caused by pollution. Where the legislature provides protection through regulatory statutes such as the EPA, it is appropriate for courts to take a more deferential approach to the *Charter* review of the offences contained in such statutes. [...]

I turn then to the background and purpose of the provisions under review. Part II does not deal with the protection of the environment generally. It deals simply with the control of toxic substances that may be released into the environment under certain restricted circumstances, and does so through a series of prohibitions to which penal sanctions are attached. It replaces the *Environmental Contaminants Act,* first enacted in 1975 (S.C. 1974-75-76, c. 72), which was intended to control substances entering or capable of entering into the environment in a quantity or concentration sufficient to constitute *a danger* to health or the environment; see s. 4. The continuity of policy is evident from the fact that the toxic substances controlled under the earlier legislation including PCBs were automatically included as Schedule I of the present legislation, entitled "List of Toxic Substances".

The underlying purpose for the enactment of the present Act, so far as toxic substances are concerned, is evident from a series of reports of studies made in the mid-1980s; see Environment Canada, *From Cradle to Grave: A Management Approach to Chemicals* (1986); Environment Canada and Health and Welfare Canada, *Final Report of the Environmental Contaminants Act Amendments Consultative Committee* (1986). What these reveal is that the earlier Act was clearly deficient in identifying substances that could be toxic and that what was really needed was a regime whereby the government could assess material that could be harmful to health and the environment before the substance was already in use. [...]

There was no intention that the Act should bar the use, importation or manufacture of all chemical products, but rather that it should affect only those substances that are dangerous to the environment, and then only if they are not regulated by law. The report recognized that "[a] great deal of our industrial strength and economic progress is based upon the use of chemicals" (p. 2), and that only a fraction of these were "believed to be hazardous but few have been assessed to make sure" (p. 2).

The manner of assessment traditionally employed — related as it was to the concern for "pollution that could be seen, touched, smelled or tasted" and "cleaning up a mess after it occurred" (p. 3) — was no longer adequate. As the report put it (at p. 3):

> Toxic chemical contamination cannot be handled in this way. Ordinary sense perception cannot identify chemical contamination because it is usually invisible until the damage, sometimes irreparable damage, has been done. *Since chemical pollution exists at the molecular level, it cannot usually be treated, contained or recovered from the environment. And since its effects are pervasive and long term, rather than local or immediate, quick-fix measures are not practical.* [Emphasis added.]

Not surprisingly, the report emphasized the need to improve the procedures for assessing whether chemical substances were hazardous; see e.g. pp. 10-11. The Act would operate through the listing of chemicals, including "a schedule of dangerous chemicals which are subject to regulation under the [Act]" (p. 15).

The impugned Act appears to me to respond closely to these objectives. The subject of toxic substances is dealt with principally in Part II of the Act. It begins, we saw, with s. 11, which has been described as a "definition" in argument. While the provision has some properties of a definition, to speak of it in this way is misleading and does not do full justice to its purpose and function. It should be observed that it does not purport to define a "toxic substance" in the manner in which s. 3 defines various concepts, e.g. "air contaminant", "air pollution", etc. which describes with finality what the defined concept means. Rather, it sets forth that a substance can only be toxic, for the purposes of Part II, if it is entering or may enter the environment in a quantity or concentration or under conditions that result in the detrimental effects on the environment, human life and human health described in paras. (a) to (c). [...]

I add that the determination of whether the various components of s. 11 are satisfied in respect of particular substances is by no means an easy task. Whether substances enter or may enter the environment in a quantity, concentration or conditions sufficient to have the effects set forth in that provision are not matters that are generally known. Rather these are matters that must be ascertained by assessments or tests set forth in s. 15, and in accordance with a procedure that requires consultation with the provinces, the informed community and the general public with a view to determining whether certain substances "are toxic or capable of becoming toxic", to use the expression employed in the provisions of Part II dealing with testing, beginning with the Ministers' weeding out most substances by establishing a priority list of substances to be tested. [...] In light of this, it is difficult to believe "toxic" is not given its ordinary meaning in the Act, and that s. 11 is, therefore, simply a drafting tool for the demarcation of those aspects of toxicity that are to be considered in the tests required in the sections that follow.

What the assessments described in Part II are aimed at is the selection of new items to add to the List of Toxic Substances set forth in Schedule I. Thus s. 11 is the first of a series of provisions respecting testing or assessment for toxicity. The first step in the process of assessment is s. 12, which requires the Ministers to compile a Priority Substances List in respect of substances to which the Ministers are satisfied priority should be given in assessing whether they are toxic or capable of becoming toxic; this list and any amendments to it are published in the *Canada Gazette*, and the provinces and other interested parties are informed (s. 12(2) and (3)). The process of testing is a detailed one and includes informing the provinces and other interested groups and the public at all stages; see, for example, s. 13. In performing their duties, the Ministers are given broad powers to collect data, conduct investigations and correlate and evaluate any data so obtained (see, for example, s. 15). The testing process culminates in a decision of the Ministers to recommend or not to recommend that a substance be added to the List of Toxic Substances in Schedule I of the Act, and, if a recommendation is made, what regulations should be made in respect of the substance under s. 34 [...].

In summary, as I see it, the broad purpose and effect of Part II is to provide a procedure for assessing whether out of the many substances that may conceivably fall within the ambit of s. 11, some should be added to the List of Toxic Substances in Schedule I and, when an order to this effect is made, whether to prohibit the use of the substance so added in the manner provided in the regulations made under s. 34(1) subject to a penalty. These listed substances, toxic in the ordinary sense, are those whose use in a manner contrary to the regulations the Act ultimately prohibits. This is a limited prohibition applicable to a restricted number of substances. The prohibition is enforced by a penal sanction and is undergirded by a valid criminal objective, and so is valid criminal legislation.

This, in my mind, is consistent with the terms of the statute, its purpose, and indeed common sense. It is precisely what one would expect of an environmental statute — a procedure to weed out from the vast number of substances potentially harmful to the environment or human life those only that pose significant risks of that type of harm. Specific targeting of toxic substances based on individual assessment avoids resort to unnecessarily broad prohibitions and their impact on the exercise of provincial powers. [...]

I turn now to a more detailed examination of the provisions of the Act impugned in the present case [...] s. 34 authorizes the Governor in Council to make regulations setting forth the restrictions imposed on those using or dealing with such substances. Failure to comply with any such restriction constitutes an offence and is punishable on summary conviction by a fine not exceeding three hundred thousand dollars or a term of imprisonment not exceeding six months, or both; or, on indictment, by a fine not exceeding one million dollars or a term of imprisonment not exceeding three years, or both (s. 113(f), (o) and (p)).

Without attempting to regurgitate the whole of s. 34, I shall simply give some flavour of the nature of the prohibitions created by the regulations made thereunder. Generally, s. 34 includes regulations providing for or imposing requirements respecting the quantity or concentration of a substance listed in Schedule I that may be released into the environment either alone or in combination with others from any source, the places where such substances may be released, the manufacturing or processing activities in the course of which the substance may be released, the manner and conditions of release, and so on. In short, s. 34 precisely defines situations where the use of a substance in the List of

Toxic Substances in Schedule I is prohibited, and these prohibitions are made subject to penal consequences. [...]

What Parliament is doing in s. 34 is making provision for carefully tailoring the prohibited action to specified substances used or dealt with in specific circumstances. This type of tailoring is obviously necessary in defining the scope of a criminal prohibition, and is, of course, within Parliament's power. As Laskin C.J. noted in *Morgentaler v. The Queen*, [1976] 1 S.C.R. 616 at p. 627: "I need cite no authority for the proposition that Parliament may determine what is not criminal as well as what is". [...]

In truth, there is a broad area of concurrency between federal and provincial powers in areas subjected to criminal prohibitions, and the courts have been alert to the need to permit adequate breathing room for the exercise of jurisdiction by both levels of government. [...]

This type of approach is essential in dealing with amorphous subjects like health and the environment. In my reasons for the minority in *Crown Zellerbach*, *supra*, (addressing an issue which the majority did not discuss), I had this to say about the matter as it relates to environmental pollution (at p. 455):

> [...] environmental pollution [...] is [...] all-pervasive. It is a by-product of everything we do. In man's relationship with his environment, waste is unavoidable. The problem is thus not new, although it is only recently that the vast amount of waste products emitted into the atmosphere or dumped in water has begun to exceed the ability of the atmosphere and water to absorb and assimilate it on a global scale. There is thus cause for concern and governments at every level have begun to deal with the many activities giving rise to problems of pollution. [...]

I observe that in enacting the legislation in issue here, Parliament was alive to the need for cooperation and coordination between the federal and provincial authorities. This is evident throughout the Act. In particular, under s. 34(2), (5) and (6), Parliament has made it clear that the provisions of this Part are not to apply where a matter is otherwise regulated under other equivalent federal or provincial legislation.

In *Crown Zellerbach*, I expressed concern with the possibility of allocating legislative power respecting environmental pollution exclusively to Parliament. I would be equally concerned with an interpretation of the Constitution that effectively allocated to the provinces, under general powers such as property and civil rights, control over the environment in a manner that prevented Parliament from exercising the leadership role expected of it by the international community and its role in protecting the basic values of Canadians regarding the environment through the instrumentality of the criminal law power. Great sensitivity is required in this area since, as Professor Lederman has rightly observed, environmental pollution "is no limited subject or theme, [it] is a sweeping subject or theme virtually all-pervasive in its legislative implications"; see W. R. Lederman, "Unity and Diversity in Canadian Federalism: Ideals and Methods of Moderation" (1975), 53 Can. Bar Rev. 597, at p. 610.

Turning then to s. 35, I mentioned that it is ancillary to s. 34. It deals with emergency situations. The provision, it seems to me, indicates even more clearly a criminal purpose, and throws further light on the intention of s. 34 and of the Act generally. It can only be brought into play when the Ministers believe a substance is not specified in the List in Schedule I or is listed but is not subjected to control under s. 34. In such a case, they may make an interim order in respect of the substance if they believe "immediate action is required to deal with a significant danger to the environment or to human life or health".

In sum, then, I am of the view that Part II of the Act, properly construed, simply provides a means to assess substances with a view to determining whether the substances are sufficiently toxic to be added to Schedule I of the Act (which contains a list of dangerous substances carried over from pre-existing legislation), and provides by regulations under s. 34 the terms and conditions under which they can be used, with provisions under s. 35 for by-passing the ordinary provisions for testing and regulation under Part II in cases where immediate action is required. I have reached this position independently of the legal presumption that a legislature intends to confine itself to matters within its competence; see *Reference re Farm Products Marketing Act*, [1957] S.C.R. 198 at p. 255; *Nova Scotia Board of Censors v. McNeil*, [1978] 2 S.C.R. 662 at p. 688. However, it follows that the position I have taken would by virtue of the presumption displace a possible reading of the Act that would render it unconstitutional.

Since I have found the empowering provisions, ss. 34 and 35, to be *intra vires*, the only attack that could be brought against any action taken under them would be that such action went beyond the authority granted by those provisions; in the present case, for example, such an attack might consist in the allegation that PCBs did not pose "a significant danger to the environment or to human life or health" justifying the making of the Interim Order. This would seem to me to be a tall order. The fact that PCBs are highly toxic substances should require no demonstration. This has become well known to the general public and is supported by an impressive array of scientific studies at both the national and international levels. [...]

From what appears in these studies, one can conclude that PCBs are not only highly toxic but long lasting and very slow to break down in water, air or soil. They do dissolve readily in fat tissues and other organic compounds, however, with the result that they move up the food chain through birds and other animals and eventually to humans. They pose significant risks of serious harm to both animals and humans. As well they are extremely mobile. They evaporate from soil and water and are transported great distances through the atmosphere. High levels of PCBs have been found in a variety of arctic animals living thousands of kilometres from any major source of PCBs. The extent of the dangers they pose is reflected in the fact that they were the first substance sought to be controlled in Canada under the *Environmental Contaminants Act*, the predecessor of the present legislation. They were also the first substance regulated in the United States under the *Toxic Substances Control Act*, 15 U.S.C. §2605(c). [...]

I conclude, therefore, that the Interim Order is also valid under s. 91(27) of the *Constitution Act, 1867*.

Appeal allowed with costs, LAMER C.J. *and* SOPINKA, IACOBUCCI *and* MAJOR JJ. *dissenting.*

Notes and Questions

1. What are the key differences in the approach to the criminal law power test taken by La Forest J. for the majority and by Lamer C.J. for the dissent?

2. What is the purpose of CEPA according to the majority and the dissent? Do you agree with the majority that it is appropriate to determine the purpose by relying on the implementation of the process and the regulations passed to date, or was the dissent correct in emphasizing the broad definition of "toxic"?

3. The majority seems confident that recognizing broad federal jurisdiction under the criminal law power will not adversely affect the ability of the provinces to regulate toxic substances. The dissent is of the view that by upholding CEPA under the criminal law power, the regulatory authority of the provinces will be undermined. Who is right?

4. Could CEPA have been upheld under other conceptual powers, such as POGG or trade and commerce? In light of the cases in this chapter, how likely do you think it is that the Court would have upheld CEPA under these heads of power, had the majority not found that the criminal law power was sufficient? What would have been the implication of such an approach? What potential do you see for the use of the emergency branch of POGG in the environmental field? The application of the emergency branch of POGG is discussed in Chapter 10 in the context of climate change.

Syncrude Canada Ltd. v. Canada (Attorney General)
2016 FCA 160

[Syncrude challenged the constitutionality of subsection 5(2) of the *Renewable Fuels Regulations*, SOR/2010-189 ("RFRs"), which require that 2% of diesel fuel be renewable, and create a market-based regulatory scheme allowing for the buying and selling of "compliance units" to meet this 2% requirement. Syncrude alleged that the subsection was not a valid exercise of Parliament's criminal law power under subsection 91(27) of the *Constitution Act, 1867* because it lacked a criminal law purpose and impermissibly trenched into provincial jurisdiction by regulating non-renewable natural resources. In the Federal Court, the judge relied on *Canada (Procureure générale) c. Hydro-Québec*, (*sub nom. R. v. Hydro-Québec*) [1997] 3 S.C.R. 213, and ruled that a valid criminal law purpose existed in the protection of the environment. The Federal Court of Appeal upheld this ruling.]

RENNIE J.A.: —

Characterization of Subsection 5(2) of the RFRs

There are two stages to the division of powers analysis. The first is an inquiry into the essential character of the law, or, as is often said, its pith and substance. The second is "to classify that essential character" by reference to the heads of power under the *Constitution Act, 1867: Reference re Firearms Act (Canada)*, 2000 SCC 31 at para. 15, [2000] 1 S.C.R. 783 [*Firearms Reference*].

The characterization exercise is informed by both the law's purpose and its effect. Purpose is gleaned first, from the law itself, as stated by Parliament, but also from extrinsic sources such as Hansard and government policy papers: see *Firearms Reference* at paragraph 17 for a discussion of the use of extrinsic evidence in the characterization exercise. The purpose can also be informed by reference to the mischief to which the law is directed.

Following identification of purpose, the inquiry turns to the legal effect of the law — how does the law operate and what effect does it have? At this stage, the court may consider both the legal and practical effect of the law. Having regard to Syncrude's argument, which is predicated on the ineffectiveness of a renewable fuel requirement, the language of the Supreme Court in *Firearms Reference*, at paragraph 18, is highly instructive:

> Determining the legal effects of a law involves considering how the law will operate and how it will affect Canadians. The Attorney General of Alberta states that the law will not actually achieve its purpose. Where the legislative scheme is relevant to a criminal law purpose, he says, it will be ineffective (e.g., criminals will not register their guns); where it is effective it will not advance the fight against crime (e.g., burdening rural farmers with pointless red tape). These are concerns that were properly directed to and considered by Parliament. Within its constitutional sphere, Parliament is the judge of whether a measure is likely to achieve its intended purposes; efficaciousness is not relevant to the Court's division of powers analysis: *Morgentaler, supra*, at pp. 487-88, and *Reference re Anti-Inflation Act*, [1976] 2 S.C.R. 373. Rather, the inquiry is directed to how the law sets out to achieve its purpose in order to better understand its "total meaning": W. R. Lederman, *Continuing Canadian Constitutional Dilemmas* (1981), at pp. 239-40. In some cases, the effects of the law may suggest a purpose other than that which is stated in the law: see *Morgentaler, supra*, at pp. 482-83; *Attorney-General for Alberta v. Attorney-General for Canada*, [1939] A.C. 117 (P.C.) *(Alberta Bank Taxation Reference)*; and *Texada Mines Ltd. v. Attorney-General of British Columbia*, [1960] S.C.R. 713; see generally P. W. Hogg, *Constitutional Law of Canada* (loose-leaf ed.), at pp. 15-14 to 15-16. In other words, a law may say that it intends to do one thing and actually do something else. Where the effects of the law diverge substantially from the stated aim, it is sometimes said to be "colourable".

The application of these principles to the regulation in issue leads to the conclusion that subsection 5(2) is directed to maintaining the health and safety of Canadians, as well as the natural environment upon which life depends. At the risk of repetition, the following points can be derived from the enabling statutory framework in support of this conclusion:

- The RFRs were enacted under subsection 140(2) of CEPA, which requires the Governor in Council be of the opinion that the regulation could make a significant contribution to the reduction of air pollution.

- Subsection 3(1) of CEPA defines "air pollution" as a condition of the air arising from any substance that directly or indirectly endangers health and safety.

- Six substances which comprise GHGs were added to Schedule 1 of CEPA in 2005. Section 64 of CEPA defines a toxic substance as one which may have an immediate or long-term harmful effect on the environment, or its diversity, or may constitute a danger to human life or health.

- Subsection 140(1) contemplates a wide range of regulations in respect of fuel, including "the concentrations or quantities of an element, component or additive in a fuel; the physical or chemical properties of a fuel; the characteristics of a fuel [...] related to [...] conditions of use; [and] the blending of fuels [...]."

- In imposing a 2% renewable fuel requirement subsection 5(2) is directed to the reduction of toxic substances in the atmosphere. The Order in Council promulgating subsection 5(2) stated that the regulation "would make a significant contribution to the prevention of, or reduction in, air pollution, resulting from, directly or indirectly, the presence of renewable fuel gasoline, diesel fuel or heating distillate oil."

The RFRs impose requirements respecting the concentration of renewable fuels and thus limit the extent to which GHGs that would otherwise arise from the combustion of fossil fuel are emitted. GHGs are listed as toxic substances under Schedule 1 of CEPA. By displacing the combustion of fossil fuels, the renewable fuel requirement reduces the amount of "air pollution" arising from the GHGs (toxic substance) which would otherwise enter the atmosphere. In sum, the purpose and effect of subsection 5(2) is unambiguous on the face of the legislative and regulatory scheme in which it is situated. It is directed to the protection of the health of Canadians and the protection of the natural environment. [...]

The purpose and effect of subsection 5(2) having been determined, the inquiry turns to the scope of the criminal law power and whether subsection 5(2) fits within its ambit.

Scope of the Criminal Law Power

In broad terms, the jurisprudence of the Supreme Court of Canada establishes a three-part test for a valid exercise of the criminal law power. A valid exercise of the criminal law power requires a) a prohibition, b) backed by a penalty, c) for a criminal purpose: *AHR*. Only the last of these is contested in the case at bar.

Supreme Court jurisprudence as far back as the *Reference re Validity of s. 5(a) of Dairy Industry Act (Canada), (Margarine Case)*, [1949] S.C.R. 1, [1949] 1 D.L.R. 433 [*Margarine Reference*] has described the nature of the criminal purpose requirement as a requirement that the law be aimed at suppressing or reducing an "evil." Put in more contemporary language, to have a valid criminal law purpose the law must address a public concern relating to peace, order, security, morality, health or some other purpose (*AHR* at para. 43), but it must stop short of pure economic regulation.

Protection of the environment is, unequivocally, a legitimate use of the criminal law purpose. The Supreme Court of Canada has held that "the protection of a clean environment is a public purpose [...] sufficient to support a criminal prohibition [...] to put it another way, pollution is an 'evil' that Parliament can legitimately seek to suppress": *Hydro-Québec* at para. 123. In dissent although not on this point, at paragraph 43, Chief Justice Lamer and Iaccobucci [*sic*] J. echoed La Forest J.'s view:

To the extent that La Forest J. suggests that this legislation is supportable as relating to health, therefore, we must respectfully disagree. We agree with him, however, that the protection of the environment is itself a legitimate criminal public purpose, analogous to those cited in the *Margarine Reference, supra*. We would not add to his lucid reasoning on this point, save to state explicitly that this purpose does not rely on any of the other traditional purposes of criminal law (health, security, public order, etc.). To the extent that Parliament wishes to deter environmental pollution specifically by punishing it with appropriate penal sanctions, it is free to do so, without having to show that these sanctions are ultimately aimed at achieving one of the "traditional" aims of criminal law. The protection of the environment is itself a legitimate basis for criminal legislation.

It is useful to recall that, in *Hydro-Québec* at paragraph 150, the disputed regulation was directed to "providing or imposing requirements respecting the quantity or concentration of a substance listed in Schedule 1 that may be released into the environment either alone or in combination with others from any source" and therefore was a valid use of the criminal law power. Subsection 5(2) of the RFRs operates in the same manner.

More recently, in AHR the Supreme Court observed that pollution was one of the "new realities" facing Canada, and that Parliament needed flexibility in making decisions as to the types of conduct or activity that required the sanction of criminal law: para. 235.

The Ineffectiveness of the RFRs

[Ed. Note: Syncrude argued that the RFRs were ineffective in achieving their purpose and that, in fact, the evidence showed that the practical effects of the scheme contradicted the suggestion that the dominant purpose was to reduce GHG emissions. In rejecting this argument, the Court explained pith and substance analysis.]

[...] The legal and practical effect of legislation is relevant for the purpose of determining the pith and substance of the law: *Global Securities Corp. v. British Columbia (Securities Commission)*, 2000 SCC 21 at para. 23, [2000] 1 S.C.R. 494 [*Global Securities Corp.*]. However, it is well established doctrine that "the wisdom or efficacy of the statute" is not relevant to determining its pith and substance: *R. v. Morgentaler*, [1993] 3 S.C.R. 463 at 487-488, 107 D.L.R. (4th) 537, citing P. W. Hogg, *Constitutional Law of Canada*, vol. 1, 3d ed. (Toronto: Carswell, 1992, loose-leaf) at 15-15, and more recently, in *Ward*, at para. 18.

Syncrude contends that the evidence (which, as noted, is not compelling) that the RFRs would not in fact reduce GHG emissions is relevant to the characterization of the dominant purpose because it addresses *the legal and practical* effect of the provision. It contends that the evidence that the RFRs will not be effective in reducing GHGs is not addressed to the question of whether the provision is *in fact* efficacious. It concedes, correctly, that whether the measure is worthwhile or useful is not germane to the characterization exercise.

This distinction simply seeks to circumvent the proposition, consistent since *Global Securities Corp.*at paragraph 22, and more recently iterated in *Ward* at paragraph 26, that the effectiveness of the legislation is irrelevant for the purposes of characterization. There is no doubt as to what the regulations seek to achieve, how they operate, and their practical effect. The argument that there may be a better, more efficacious way to reduce GHGs does not alter the conclusion. As noted in *Ward*, at paragraph 26 "the purpose of legislation cannot be challenged by proposing an alternative, allegedly better, method for achieving that purpose." Syncrude's argument that, because the RFRs are ineffective, an assertion which fails on the evidence, the dominant purpose must have been to establish a local market, fails.

The Regulation Is Not an Economic Measure

As noted, Syncrude contends that the dominant purpose of the RFRs was to create a market in renewable fuels. The RIAS reveals careful consideration of the refining industry, transportation to the consumer, and the effect of subsection 5(2) on agriculture. There is also evidence that the creation of long-term demand for renewable fuels was an integral part of the strategy to reduce GHGs.

It must be recalled that it is uncontroverted that GHGs are harmful to both health and the environment and as such, constitute an evil that justifies the exercise of the criminal law power. Syncrude concedes that GHGs are air pollution within the definition of CEPA. Nevertheless, Syncrude urges that subsection 5(2) is *ultra vires* because the government foresaw and hoped for the development of a market whereby more renewable fuels would be available for consumption, replacing the consumption of fossil fuels which produce the GHGs. It also contends that the RFRs do not in fact, achieve the goal of reducing air pollution, indeed, it says that the renewable fuel requirement would lead to a net increase in GHGs, arising from the GHG emissions associated with the planting, harvesting, transportation and refining of bio-fuel crops.

The Attorney General does not contest that Canada foresaw that the RFRs would have favourable economic consequences and that there would be market responses in agriculture to the increased demand for renewable fuel. The impact on various sectors of agriculture was negligible: *Canada Gazette, Part II*, Vol. 144, No. 18, (September 1, 2010), pp. 1708-1710). The overall cost of the RFRs would be borne by consumers, at an estimated cost of 1¢ per litre, and would be lost in day to day fluctuation of fuel prices: pp. 1746-1717. These effects were considered to be minimal.

However, these consequential effects cannot be considered in isolation. The reason the government hoped for the development of a renewable fuels market in Canada was because the availability of renewable fuels would lead to a long-term reduction of GHGs. The judge concluded that "these economic effects are *part of* a four-pronged Renewable Fuels Strategy" (emphasis in original).

Insofar as the effect on agriculture was concerned, the Minister of the Environment noted that the reason why the government hoped for the emergence of a renewable fuels market was "to provide the maximum opportunity for emissions reductions." When asked whether the RFRs would cause a net benefit for the environment, the Minister replied: "Yes. And that is why we brought these three components together. We can't do this framework without the three components of energy, environment and agriculture."

The environment and economy are intimately connected. Indeed, it is practically impossible to disassociate the two. This point was well-made in *Friends of the Oldman River Society v. Canada (Minister of Transport)*, [1992] 1 S.C.R. 3,

88 D.L.R. (4th) 1 where the Court said "it defies reason to assert that Parliament is constitutionally barred from weighing the broad environmental repercussions, including socio-economic concerns, when legislating with respect to decisions of this nature."

The existence of the economic incentives and government investments, while relevant to the characterization exercise, do not detract from the dominant purpose of what the RFRs do and why they do it. The inquiry does not end with proof of an incentive or market subsidy. Consistent with *Ward*, one must inquire as to the purpose and effect. For example, regulations under the *Firearms Act*, S.C. 1995, c. 39 could call for new, enhanced locking mechanisms. The fact that capital investments are made to assist the lock industry to transition to the new requirements would not detract from the dominate purpose being addressed to "peace, order, security, morality, health or some other purpose" (*AHR* at para. 43). Here, the RIAS (*Canada Gazette, Part I*, Vol. 145, No. 15, (July 20, 2011), p. 699) states the purpose of collateral investments in infrastructure costs related to the production of renewable fuels was "to generate greater environmental benefits in terms of GHG emission reductions."

The evidence demonstrates that part of the objective of the RFRs was to encourage next-generation renewable fuels production and to create opportunities for farmers in renewable fuels. However, the evidence also demonstrates that a market demand and a market supply for renewable fuels and advanced renewable fuels technologies had to be created to achieve the overall goal of greater GHG emissions reduction.

The criminal law power is not negated simply because Parliament hoped that the underlying sanction would encourage the consumption of renewable fuel and spur a demand for fuels that did not produce GHGs. All criminal law seeks to deter or modify behaviour, and it remains a valid use of the power if Parliament foresees behavioural responses, either in persons or in the economy.

To close on this point, the consequential shifts in agriculture and the market for fuel arising from the renewable fuel requirement is not inconsistent with the dominant purpose of subsection 5(2) being the reduction of GHGs, with their uncontroverted costs to the health of the human and natural environment; rather, it reinforces the dominant purpose.

The Absence of an Absolute Prohibition

Syncrude also argues that the RFRs cannot be a valid exercise of the criminal law power given certain exemptions in the RFR regime, and that in imposing a 2% renewable fuel requirement, they do not ban outright the presence of GHGs in fuel.

I note at the outset that this appears to be, in essence, an allegation that the "prohibition" requirement for a valid exercise of the criminal law power is unmet, not the "criminal law purpose" requirement. This gives me pause because, before the Federal Court, Syncrude conceded the presence of a prohibition. This is of no consequence, however, as constitutionality, as a matter of law, cannot be conceded. In any event, the judge found that the absence of a total prohibition on the use of non-renewable fuels (and the absence of a total prohibition on a given supplier using more than 98% non-renewable fuels at a given time) did not preclude subsection 5(2) from being a valid exercise of Parliament's criminal law power.

A prohibition need not be total, and it can admit exceptions: *Firearms Reference* at para. 39 and *RJR-Macdonald Inc. c. Canada (Procureur général)*, [1995] 3 S.C.R. 199 at paras. 52-57, 127 D.L.R. (4th) 1 [*RJR-MacDonald*]. Indeed, environmental regulations often set limits, or concentrations of listed substances; so too do regulations of the food industry. Recall that in *Hydro-Québec* the majority observed, at paragraph 150, that regulations imposing requirements prescribing *the manner and condition of release or the source of release* of substances listed in Schedule 1 to CEPA into the environment were a valid use of the criminal law power. Recall as well that paragraph 140(1)(a) of CEPA authorizes regulations respecting "the concentration or quantities of an element, component or additive in fuel."

Syncrude points to the fact that the regulation is, in some circumstances, suspended during the winter due to technical challenges in blending traditional and renewable fuels. There are two answers to this, one legal, the other pragmatic. It may be that a criminal law requires exceptions in circumstances where a total prohibition would either be unjust or contrary to other interests which Parliament is charged with safeguarding. Many uncontroversial exercises of the criminal law establish a regime whereby, if certain measures or steps are taken otherwise-prohibited conduct becomes permissible. The *Food and Drugs Act*, R.S.C. 1985, c. F-27, *Controlled Drugs and Substances Act*, S.C. 1996, c. 19, and *Firearms Act*, along with many others and their attendant regulations, require licenses in order to possess particular substances or items. Indeed, other regulations made pursuant to CEPA, such as the *Gasoline Regulations*, SOR/90-247, sections 4 and 6, prescribe a maximum amount of a harmful substance that is allowed in fuel without prohibiting that substance completely.

There is no constitutional threshold of harm that must be surpassed before the criminal law power is met, provided there is a reasonable apprehension of harm. Syncrude has no answer to the question of whether the RFRs become constitutional at a 10%, 25%, 50% or 100% renewable fuel requirement. There is no magic number. As the Supreme Court observed in *AHR* at paragraphs 55 to 56, "there is no constitutional threshold of harm."

Turning to the pragmatic answer; if the winter exemption is engaged, the RFRs require a greater than 2% utilization during the summer months. The regulatory obligation is met by purchasing compliance units from another user. On a national basis, the net effect is the same.

To conclude, Syncrude's argument that the regulation is invalid because it is not a blanket prohibition has no doctrinal support. Further, Syncrude concedes that other regulations, such as those limiting concentration of lead and sulphur in fuel are valid: *Sulphur in Diesel Fuel Regulations*, SOR/2002-254. Nothing distinguishes the prohibition of a certain amount of sulphur or lead in fuel from a positive requirement of a certain amount of renewable fuel in fuels. Both seek to prevent the emission of toxic substances, whether sulphur dioxide or GHGs, and both are addressed to the reduction of air pollution.

[Ed. Note: The Court upheld the ruling of the federal judge, finding that subsection 5(2) of the RFRs was *intra vires* both the *Constitution Act, 1867* and *CEPA*.]

Notes and Questions

1. In the wake of *Hydro-Québec* it was speculated by some that the majority's approach to the criminal law power was tenuous and unlikely to be sustained in subsequent decisions. *Syncrude*, however, tends strongly to confirm the majority's approach in *Hydro-Québec*. *Syncrude* also represents an attempt to recognize the complex realities of regulatory enforcement in relation to not only toxic substances, but also substances that are likely to have adverse climate impacts.

2. Does *Syncrude* clarify how the pith and substance approach should be applied where Parliament seeks to justify environmental regulation under the criminal law power?

3. How, and to what extent, does the decision in *Syncrude* depart from, or augment, the majority and dissenting judgments in *Hydro-Québec*? How persuasive do you find the arguments advanced on behalf of Syncrude? Could they have framed the arguments in a way that would have had a better chance of succeeding?

4. What implications, if any, flow from *Syncrude* for pending challenges to federal climate change legislation, in particular the constitutional challenge to the federal carbon pricing mechanism currently being mounted by the province of Saskatchewan?

Part III — The Politics and Practicalities of Jurisdiction over the Environment

You have now considered in detail some of the Supreme Court of Canada's leading constitutional cases in the environmental area. As you will discern, collectively they underscore the need for coordinated action on environmental issues and affirm the constitutional basis for federal leadership in this area. Yet, an ongoing theme to which we will return throughout this book — and which figures centrally in scholarly writing on Canadian environmental law and policy — is a sense that overall effective intergovernmental coordination and federal leadership around environmental issues has been lacking.

In the Introduction to this Chapter, one of the questions we posed was whether, and to what extent, the jurisdictional uncertainty and conflict, as reflected in many of the cases you have now read, is a serious and enduring obstacle to grappling with the pressing environmental challenges we collectively confront. Put another way, to what extent can we ascribe to the division of powers, as interpreted in these cases, responsibility for some of the shortcomings we observe in environmental law and policy outcomes? Your views on these questions may evolve as you read on in this book. Bearing this in mind, consider the following article that considers what Canadian academics from several disciplines have to say about this and related topics. A key thesis of this article is that understanding jurisdiction over the environment in the Canadian context requires more than simply a familiarity with the leading cases and sections 91 and 92 of the *Constitution Act, 1867*.

William R. MacKay,
"Canadian Federalism and the Environment: The Literature"
(2004) 17 Geo. Int'l. Envtl. L. Rev. 25

[...] Although political negotiation has been the dominant force in shaping environmental policy in Canada, the jurisprudence remains important. Historically, the courts have recognized the concurrent jurisdiction of the two levels of government and have discouraged federal unilateralism. Nevertheless, two court decisions have increased the potential scope of federal legislative power.

[**Ed. Note:** Discussion of *R. v. Crown Zellerbach* and *R. v. Hydro-Québec* omitted.]

Despite the importance of these decisions, a purely legalistic description of federal-provincial jurisdictions over environmental policy is misleading. Theories of intergovernmental relations tend to reveal more about environmental policy than a strict analysis of the constitutional powers. [...] recent [intergovernmental relations] literature on environmental policy-making [...] addresses three themes:

- Factors affecting the federal role in Canadian environmental policy
- The dominant pattern of intergovernmental relations in Canadian environmental policy
- The preferred model of intergovernmental relations with respect to environmental policy

Factors Affecting the Federal Role in Canadian Environmental Policy

[...] Overall, the literature in this field concludes that the federal government has been historically restrained in exercising authority in the environmental field. However, there were times when the federal government took a more active role in environmental policy. Initially, scholars explained federal involvement in the environmental field as reflective of the constitutional restraints placed on the federal government by the constitution. Gradually, however, as federal powers in this area were expanded by constitutional decisions, academics observed a shift in the basis of federal timidity from fear of constitutional toe stepping to a fear of provincial resistance. More recently, scholars have noted that the lack of federal action is based on the waxing and waning of external pressure on the federal government to take action. These three distinct explanations provide reasons for the historically weak federal role interspersed by periods of federal intervention. The three reasons, constitutional constraint, provincial resistance, and external pressure on the federal government will now be examined in more detail.

Constitutional Constraints

Many authors suggest that the federal government has been constrained by limited constitutional authority. These authors, writing primarily before the Supreme Court decision of *R. v. Crown Zellerbach*, generally agreed that the provinces had strong claims to jurisdiction over the environment within their borders. However, as its constitutional authority to intervene in the environment became wider as a result of Supreme Court decisions expanding the Criminal Law power and the "peace order and good government" (POGG) power, the federal government became more involved in environmental management. Many academics see the expansion of its constitutional mandate as the primary impetus for the federal government's eventual involvement in environmental management.

The federal government, following the expansion of its constitutional jurisdiction under the *Crown Zellerbach* decision, undertook several important legislative initiatives. Most importantly, the *Canadian Environmental Protection Act* (CEPA) was passed in 1988. CEPA consolidated a number of federal environmental acts, including the *Clean Air Act*, the *Environmental Contaminants Act*, and the *Ocean Dumping Control Act* (the impugned legislation of the *Crown Zellerbach* decision). More important, CEPA provided for federal authorities to regulate and control toxic substances, a domain until then predominantly controlled by the provinces. The federal *Pulp and Paper Effluent Regulations* were amended in 1990 to allow the federal Department of the Environment to issue separate pollution control permits rather than having federal control requirements incorporated into provincially issued permits. Federal officials therefore had more direct access to enforcement proceedings. The *Canadian Environment Assessment Act* (CEAA) was passed in 1992. The CEAA creates a statutory obligation for a compulsory federal environmental impact assessment for development projects that are financed by the federal government, sited on federal lands, or subject to federal legal authority. Finally, the federal "Green Plan" was initiated in 1990. The Green Plan is designed to promote and fund environmentally sustainable projects and programs across several government departments and in co-ordination with the private sector and the provinces. Starting with an initial federal commitment of three billion dollars Canadian in new spending, the Green Plan committed the government of Canada to reducing waste generation by fifty percent by the year 2000; developing new processes to ensure all federal policies are subject to prior environmental assessment; promoting the practice of applied sustainable development in the forestry, agricultural, and fisheries industries; and regulating up to forty-four priority toxic substances in five years.

Initially, therefore, the literature addressing federalism and the environment focused on the constitutional powers of the federal government as an explanation for the historically weak federal role in the field. Scholars point out that the court took action when the Supreme Court recognized the federal government's expanded environmental powers. However, scholars are also quick to point out that in the years following the Court's recognition of possible federal activism, the federal government was reluctant to use its newly granted power to effect environmental change. Literature in the field then sought new explanations for federal inactivity.

Legal scholars argue that the federal government has taken a surprisingly limited view of its own environmental powers despite its increased presence in the environmental field. Scholars note that even when the federal government was given a broader constitutional mandate from the *Crown Zellerbach* decision, it was reluctant to press for greater control over environmental policy-making due to provincial resistance. Robert Franson and Alastair Lucas suggest that "the excuse of constitutional difficulties is used as a smokescreen to hide a basic unwillingness on the part of those involved to take the actions that are necessary". Professor

Lucas attributes the federal timidity to an unwillingness to confront the provinces, which were highly protective of their jurisdiction over natural resources. Lucas states that much of the federal leadership is coloured by the implicit restraints in the "political constitution", which Lucas defines as the understood role of the federal and provincial governments in environmental policy-making, notwithstanding clear federal constitutional authority. These underlying restraints help to explain federal reluctance to "push its legal regulatory mandate [...] in the face of provincial opposition". [...]

Given the provincial Crowns' ownership of virtually all natural resources, these scholars believe a preferential role was given to locally dominant economic interests. The result is that provincial environmental policy often reflects the close links between provincial governments and industry. [...]

According to many scholars, the federal government has avoided unilateral action because of the conflict with the provinces it engenders. Indeed, the provinces continue to exercise the greater share of environmental authority. The federal government has asserted its authority in matters with extra-provincial or international implications but it is generally unwilling to press for a greater role. Instead, the federal government favoured a collaborative approach to interprovincial relations with respect to the environment. The main reason for this, according to many academics, is the fear that if the federal government were to take a leading, visible role in the environment, this strengthened presence would be perceived as federal interference provoking separatist sentiment in Québec and objections from provinces highly dependent on natural resource revenue.

External Pressures

Constitutional constraints and provincial opposition to federal control offer a limited explanation of the restricted role often taken by the federal government in environmental policy. Recently, academics have taken a broader approach to explaining intergovernmental relations with respect to environmental policy-making. Kathryn Harrison and others increasingly argue that the explanation for federal and provincial roles in environmental protection is not complete without considering governments' electoral incentives to extend or defend their jurisdiction over the environment in the first place. Other scholars point to international pressure as an important factor in the expansion of government jurisdiction (particularly federal) in the environmental area.

Harrison notes that environmental protection usually involves diffuse benefits and concentrated costs, and thus it offers few political benefits but significant political costs. According to Harrison, one can expect the opponents of environmental regulation to be better organized, informed, and funded than the supporters. Additionally, since environmental protection typically involves imposing costs on business, stronger environmental standards will often run counter to voters' concerns about the economy. Where environmental concerns in the general public are high, however, (for example, after a major environmental disaster) or when the economy is doing well and voters are less concerned about loss of jobs or deleterious economic effects, the benefits become less diffuse and the price imposed on industry less costly to the politicians. Governments will then respond with more environmental protection. Harrison concludes that this is a better explanation for infrequent federal action on the environment than the federal government's concerns about provincial resistance or constitutional restraints.

Instead, Kathryn Harrison argues, the real impetus to a larger federal role [in the years following *Crown Zellerbach*] was the greater importance of environmental protection to the electorate by the mid 1980s. The mid 1980s constitute an appropriate dividing line in analyzing Canadian environmental policy [...] air and water pollution control and depletion of natural resources dominated the first generation of environmental policy. The second generation of environmental policy (after the mid 1980s) is marked by more diverse global and local issues [...] Harrison [and others contend] that the federal government entered the field of environmental policy-making because it was faced with the interdependencies and externalities represented by pressure from both international coalitions and local environmental groups for higher and more consistent environmental standards. Grace Skogstad similarly notes:

> [S]trong international pressures for governments to formulate environmentally sustainable policies have created new incentives for governments at both levels to become actively involved in protecting the environment. [...]

Locally, environmentalists have played a role in pressuring the federal government to take on a greater role in the environment. Environmentalists have also challenged the appropriateness of the relatively closed process of policy-making. According to Neil Hawke, these activist positions were validated by legal decisions that legitimized a voice for citizen groups in resource development projects: see *Friends of the Oldman River v. Canada (Minister of Transport)* [...]

When scholars began discussing reasons for the lack of a strong federal role in the environmental field, the general consensus was that the federal government lacked the constitutional power to intervene and that it feared igniting provincial opposition. More recently most scholars point to public environmental concern, both domestic and international, as the impetus for federal involvement. The consensus among many academics today is that the close relationship between industry and government that determined environmental policy in the past has shifted to a broader consultative process with greater public involvement, especially from environmental groups (although industry, of course, is still an important player). As a result, the federal government has played a larger role in what was once an area of provincial constitutional jurisdiction with little federal involvement. Most scholars now view the principal explanation for this to be external pressure on the federal government, both domestic and international, rather than expanded federal constitutional power or provincial acquiescence to federal involvement. These conclusions provide a useful lesson to federal policy-makers. The development of environmentalism as a national political cause provides a powerful antidote to constitutional restraint and provincial resistance to national environmental standards.

The Dominant Pattern of Intergovernmental Relations in Canadian Environmental Policy

[...] Most academics conclude that [over time] the collaborative model [of Canadian environmental policy] has prevailed. Moreover, the ascendancy of the collaborative model came at the same time many warned of federal domination of the field in the wake of the *Crown Zellerbach* and *Hydro-Québec* decisions. Scholars see evidence of the pre-eminent role of the collaborative model in the use of equivalency agreements in federal legislation. Under an equivalency agreement the province's local laws apply if its environmental standards are equivalent to federal standards.

According to Steven Kennett, in most cases governments will favour a competitive model. Indeed, Kennett notes that unilateralism (competitive federalism) is the normal (or as Kennett says, the baseline) condition under which governments operate. According to Kennett, incentives to co-operate exist when unilateralism leads to direct costs or foregone benefits. Governments are therefore most likely to co-operate in two circumstances. The first is where cooperation gives a government greater control over domestic policy agendas than does unilateralism. Therefore, where there are significant interdependencies or externalities beyond the government's control, co-operation becomes necessary for effective policy. Co-operation may also allow for the best policy instruments to be used in light of expertise, constitutional powers, or regional (or national) concerns and to avoid duplication. Second, intergovernmental conflict may also impose political costs, and to reduce these costs governments will try to induce co-operation. Therefore, for Kennett, the collaborative approach is the natural one in an area such as the environment where the shared policy fields and many mobilized interests constitute externalities beyond either government's control, making collaboration necessary for effective policy.

Kennett's observations seem prophetic, as many scholars note (many with resignation) that the collaborative approach was largely institutionalized in the time between 1998 and 2000. Mark Winfield describes this period as being marked by "the most important developments in federalism and environmental policy in Canada of the past 30 years". This period was preceded by the *Statement on Interjurisdictional Co-operation*, signed by the provinces and the federal government in 1990. The statement committed the provinces and federal government to co-operate on environmental policy to avoid duplication and work toward harmonization of environmental standards. The immediate result was the establishment of the Canadian Council of Ministers of the Environment (CCME) in 1993. In 1995, after much consultation with stakeholders and provincial and federal officials, the *Environment Management Framework Agreement* (EMFA) was released. The document committed the provincial governments to conclude sub-agreements in different areas of environmental regulation that harmonize standards and reduce duplication. However, the provinces eventually rejected the EMFA.

The EMFA was in large part revived by the *Canada-Wide Accord on Environmental Harmonization*, signed by the Federal Environment Minister and her provincial counterparts (except Québec) on January 29, 1998. The *Accord* sets out the goals of the harmonization initiative and includes a framework for the contents of the substantive sub-agreements. Decisions pursuant to the *Accord* are to be "consensus based" and "driven by the commitment to achieve the highest level of environmental quality within the context of sustainable development". Three sub-agreements have been signed under the Accord's auspices — including the *Sub-Agreement on Inspections*, the *Sub-Agreement on Canada-Wide Standards*, and the *Sub-Agreement on Environmental Assessment*. All of these sub-agreements, like the Accord itself, emphasize the delivery of environmental protection by the government best situated to deliver the service. Indeed, there is an absolute bar on action by the level of government not charged with service delivery. In most cases this will be the provincial government.

There are several other federal-provincial agreements regarding environmental governance. Scholars point to such federal-provincial agreements as evidence of the importance of the political regime in environmental governance in Canada. F.L. Morton, specifically points to such bilateral agreements as proof that:

> The real centre of action in determining jurisdictional responsibilities has not been in the courts but at the administrative level of federal-provincial negotiation. To forget this is to misunderstand the Canadian reality. As a result of these developments, academics by and large conclude that the collaborative approach that has dominated intergovernmental relations towards the environment has become part of the core of the Canadian environmental policy regime.

[**Ed. Note:** A similar dynamic and approach was seen in the federal-provincial discussions surrounding development and drafting of the *Species at Risk Act*: see Chapter 9.]

The Preferred Model of Intergovernmental Relations with Respect to Environmental Policy

Much of the literature in the environment and federalism field focuses on the preferred model of intergovernmental relations. [This final] section of the paper will examine the arguments advanced by academics regarding intergovernmental relations models and environmental policy. First, [it]notes that the literature by and large concludes that although not the ideal pattern to facilitate effective national environmental policy, the collaborative model dominates in Canada. Second, despite the predominance of the collaborative model, it is also important to examine how choosing a particular model will determine whether environmental policy is based on enforceable legal obligations or non-enforceable guidelines. Third, the choice of model will promote either provincial or federal control of the environment.

Collaboration vs. Competition

Advocates of collaboration stress the advantages of joint action. With joint action, unnecessary duplication is avoided. Moreover, potential obstruction by provincial governments in implementing unilaterally imposed federal standards is reduced and intergovernmental conflict is reduced. Using environmental assessment as an example, Kennett notes that industry pressure on both levels of government for "one project, one assessment" has led to a demand for federal-provincial collaboration to avoid duplicate assessment requirements. Nevertheless, on the whole, academic opinion on intergovernmental relations and environmental policy generally disfavours the current model of collaborative federalism.

A major criticism of collaborative federalism, as it is practiced in the environmental field, is the "race to the bottom" that the current model engenders. Collaboration virtually precludes federal intervention absent provincial support.

The result of the provinces' power under the collaborative regime and the corollary impotence of the federal government is weak environmental standards and the creation of pollution havens. Advocates of competition, on the other hand, say unilateralism promotes healthy federal-provincial competition to satisfy voters. Moreover, competition facilitates oversight of each level of government by the other. [...] Winfield notes that the period of competitive federalism was characterized by upward competition between the federal government and the provinces to increase visibility and solidify their reputations as champions of the environment.

[But] the fact remains that the collaborative model is entrenched in the federal-provincial environmental regime and is generally favoured by the federal government in all fields where jurisdiction is shared. In that light, scholars generally take the view that the best means of maintaining the federalist peace achieved by collaboration is to ensure that the decision-making process is one that supports collaboration yet has significant legal force to prevent neglect of environmental issues. Of course, the same criticism could be made of the international institutional arrangements designed to address environmental concerns, which lack any formal dispute resolution agreements and are marked by collaborative relations among states zealously guarding their sovereignty.

Therefore, the choice of the intergovernmental relations model has important repercussions for scholars. Collaboration or competition lead to different legal instruments with different degrees of enforceability. Further, the choice of intergovernmental relations will affect which government is dominant in the environmental policy-making field.

Legal Enforceability

In many ways, however, the above criticisms are not of collaborative federalism generally but rather of the institutional structure established to implement environmental policy. Central to the dissatisfaction expressed by many academics of collaborative federalism as practiced in Canadian environmental policy is a condemnation of intergovernmental agreements and their lack of legal enforceability. Debora VanNijnatten notes that the elaborate intergovernmental policy-making system created in Germany is a collaborative model but is effective in reaching agreements on national standards, ensuring those standards are high, and supporting implementation and enforcement of the high standards. VanNijnatten points out that the chief reasons for this are the strict enforcement provisions the Länder provincial government) are subject to under the German intergovernmental regime. In contrast, under the CCME regime, a government found to have fallen below the standards set by the process must undergo six months of consultation with the other governments. If these consultations prove fruitless, the government may withdraw from the sub-agreement. VanNijnatten points out that all the agreements produced by the CCME process are outlines of what governments should do rather than uniform binding standards.

Alastair Lucas and Cheryl Sharvit address the legal force of the *Canada-Wide Accord on Environmental Harmonization*. The authors note that the Accord exemplifies the collaborative model of intergovernmental relations but the price paid for the federal peace is non-binding legal commitments. Lucas and Sharvit conclude that the intergovernmental agreements entered into with respect to environmental protection are generally unenforceable. The agreements, according to Lucas and Sharvit, do not meet the legal requirements of a binding contract and are merely ministerial decisions that cannot bind the governments in any substantial way. [...]

On the other hand, Steven Kennett is less pessimistic about the enforceability of inter-governmental agreements on the environment. Kennett applies the concepts of "hard" and "soft" law, which are central to the international law paradigm. [...] According to Kennett, diplomacy is used to advance from the formulation of general principles to the adoption of legally binding rules and formal intergovernmental arrangements. This is readily applicable to the federal structure in Canada. Kennett notes that although intergovernmental environmental agreements are soft law, soft law has been used as a means of encouraging the evolution of law in broad areas of environmental management. This is particularly true in situations that require global solutions. Kennett adds that the domestic adoption of soft law does not in itself portend a new division of environmental powers between national and sub-national governments. However, Kennett maintains that, at least in a Canadian context, the growing use of framework agreements and accords in federal-provincial co-operation on natural resources and environmental management bears some similarity to framework conventions in the context of international law. [...]

The disagreement over enforceability reflects the overall disagreement over which model of intergovernmental relations should prevail in environmental policy-making in Canada. Where collaboration generally produces federal-provincial agreements whose enforceability is unclear, the federal unilateralism made possible by competitive federalism produces legislation binding on Canadians in all provinces. The debate over enforceability thus mirrors the main disagreement among scholars over what level of government should have primary legislative power over the environment.

Federal vs. Provincial Control

Most of the literature criticizes the collaborative model because it seems to result in the devolution of legislative power to the provinces. Provincial control is considered to inevitably lead to deleterious effects on the environment.

As a result, many academics feel that the federal government should use its substantial powers to act unilaterally to impose national standards in the environment, as condoned by the Supreme Court in both *Hydro-Quebec* and *Crown Zellerbach*. Environmentalists have even charged in the federal court that the federal government has fettered its authority by entering into the *Accord on Environmental Harmonization*. Ultimately, the court did not accept this argument.

Advocates of federal responsibility emphasize economies of scale in studying environmental problems and developing technically complex standards. The scholars note that the federal government is better able to respond to interprovincial spillovers of environmental problems. They further note that the federal government can provide greater resistance to regionally dominant interests. Finally, the scholars note the importance of strong national standards to overcome a potential race to the bottom. [...]

Anthony Scott sees devolution of environmental powers as the inevitable abandonment of environmental management by both levels of government. Scott maintains that provincial governments receive even more advice and demands than the federal government, where the environment is a less important ministry. As a result, provinces lack both the resources and the political will to screen information from both environmentalists and client resource users in the same way that the federal government can. Consequently, many provinces download environmental management to crown corporations, local governments, and even private corporations that favour economic development over environmental protection.

At the same time, there are others that see benefits to significant provincial roles. Diverse provincial policies may be able to better satisfy geographically diverse citizen preferences concerning environmental protection. [...]

Experimentation could also be a benefit of an increased a provincial role. Both Steven Kennett and Grace Skogstad note that devolution may encourage policy experimentation. Different policies may be tested in different provinces and their effectiveness gauged without engaging the nation as a whole. [...]

Proponents of provincial control note that provincial governments have a more intimate knowledge of local environmental problems and can tailor solutions to local circumstances. [...] regional governments may have more detailed and first-hand knowledge of environmental problems and a greater attachment to the specific ecosystems. Steven Kennett summarizes the potential problems with uniform environmental standards as:

> The problem with process standardization is that it runs counter to the federal principle that regional diversity is to be respected. In fact, one would expect inter-provincial variation in EA (Environmental Assessment) regimes within a federal system where significant authority regarding resource use, industrial development and environmental protection is in provincial hands. These differences reflect variations in circumstances and political preferences across the country.

In the end, the environment is such a large and diverse field of legislative competence that most authors doubt either level of government could be completely divested of its respective power to manage the environment. As Dale Gibson notes:

> [...] environmental management could never be treated as a constitutional unit under one order of government in any constitution that claimed to be federal, because no system in which one government was so powerful would be federal.

Conclusion

Scholars generally conclude that collaborative federalism has in large part eclipsed the other models of intergovernmental relations in environmental policy-making in Canada. Scholars point to a general assumption that changes to the federal bargain cannot be achieved through formal constitutional change without great difficulty. Instead, the literature notes that governments now favour intergovernmental agreements. This is evident in a wide range of policy fields. It is especially true with the environment where collaborative federalism has become "the hallmark of environmental policy in Canada". The literature points to a number of explanations for this trend. First, collaborative federalism is now generally preferred in all shared policy fields, and this preference has naturally been extended to the environment. Second, the federal government has recently used its long dormant legislative power to enter the environmental arena in response to international and local pressure. Third, the federal government has consistently favoured a collaborative model in order to avoid offending the provinces, which have traditionally guarded their legislative powers in this area to protect vital natural resource industries.

Although many academics favour a strong federal role and less collaboration in policy-making, most conclude that no model of intergovernmental relations alone will likely be effective in advancing effective environmental policies. Different problems will inevitably call for different approaches. However, the federal government has in recent times been reluctant to act unilaterally or to compete with the provinces in delivering environmental services. Moreover, the collaborative model has been institutionalized [...] As a result of the institutionalization, the literature now questions the appropriateness of using the collaborative model to the exclusion of any other model in environmental policy and laments that the institutionalization of the process means it will likely be the rule in environmental policy-making for some time.

Notes and Questions

1. In this article, the author argued that the historical record reveals a general lack of federal leadership on environmental issues "interspersed by periods of federal intervention". What explanations does the author offer for this pattern? How compelling do you find these explanations?

2. Compare and contrast the competitive and collaborative models of environmental policy outlined in this article. What are the most salient distinctions between these models? Why has the collaborative model enjoyed such dominance?

3. The MacKay article was written in 2004, well before the federal government started to retreat from its historical role in many areas of environmental protection discussed throughout this volume. In light of this change in the federal role, how would you characterize the current federal/provincial dynamic with respect to jurisdiction over the environment? How has the political and economic situation changed since 2004? Is the cooperative model still dominant in Canada? What lessons may be drawn from the challenges the Trudeau government is facing in implementing its Pan-Canadian Climate Plan?

4. Reflecting on federal environmental law developments over the last decade, how helpful is the distinction between collaborative and competitive models of environmental policy? Would you characterize the Harper era reforms, culminating in the controversial 2012 omnibus bill, as being illustrative of a competitive or collaborative approach? The Trudeau era, commencing in 2015, is conventionally seen as a reaction to the Harper approach. Is the

Trudeau era an illustration of a more collaborative approach or a competitive one?

5. The most significant contemporary federal-provincial conflict in the realm of environmental and resource law concerns the Trans Mountain Pipeline Expansion project (discussed at length later in the chapter) which involves a proposal to expand an existing pipeline from Edmonton to Burnaby. This project underwent a federal environmental assessment by the National Energy Board that was broadly criticized for its scope and adequacy, including by the BC government. Nonetheless, ultimately the BC government (then led by Christy Clark) and a newly elected federal government gave the project the go-ahead. The election of a new BC government in 2017 raised questions about the future of the project and the province's jurisdiction to regulate the transportation of heavy oil by rail and pipeline within their borders. The nature and scope of a province's authority to regulate in this area are the subject of a reference case to be heard by the British Columbia Court of Appeal in 2019. Reflect on the political dynamics between the provinces and the federal government in this case. How do they align with MacKay's analysis? To what extent, within our current federal arrangements, can a provincial government insist that a federally regulated work or undertaking comply with provincial environmental laws? See *Canadian Western Bank v. Alberta*, 2007 SCC 22. Later in this chapter we discuss the doctrine of interjurisdictional immunity, which is a key legal issue in this setting, when we consider the decision in *Tsilhqot'in Nation v. British Columbia*, 2014 SCC 44.

In addition to the issue of "federal" pipelines, a variety of other interesting federal-provincial environmental law-related controversies have emerged since MacKay's article was published in 2004. Recently, there has been growing controversy over the pan-Canadian framework to fight climate change: see Chapter 10. A key issue is whether the federal government has constitutional jurisdiction to enact national carbon pricing legislation. In April 2018, Saskatchewan filed a constitutional challenge to the federal carbon pricing mechanism. Initially only Manitoba and Saskatchewan refused to sign the pan-Canadian framework. As of the fall of 2018, Ontario and Alberta are signaling that they may do likewise.

Jurisdictional issues and challenges of this kind are a persistent feature of Canadian environmental law and policy, and are further explored in the context of environmental assessment in Chapter 7, and species at risk in Chapter 9.

Part IV — Emerging Issues in Jurisdiction over the Environment

In this Part, we turn our attention to two themes that will undoubtedly figure prominently in environmental law and policy in the years ahead. The first concerns the relationship between environmental protection (and, more broadly the sustainable management of natural resources) and the constitutionally guaranteed rights of Canadian Aboriginal peoples. We return to this theme in many of the ensuing chapters in this book. For now our goal is to provide an introduction to the complex and fluid nature of this relationship, flagging some of the key questions and challenges that it presents for practitioners, policy and decision-makers and courts. A second theme canvassed in this Part is the increasingly significant role played by local governments in environmental protection in both hard law and soft law settings.

Aboriginal Rights and Jurisdiction over the Environment

Enacted in 1982, section 35 of the *Constitution Act, 1982* plays a central and defining role in any consideration of the relationship between jurisdiction over the environment and Aboriginal rights. It reads as follows:

> (1) The existing aboriginal and treaty rights of the aboriginal peoples of Canada are hereby recognized and affirmed.

> (2) In this Act, "aboriginal peoples of Canada" includes the Indian, Inuit and Métis peoples of Canada.

> (3) For greater certainty, in subsection (1) "treaty rights" includes rights that now exist by way of land claims agreements or may be so acquired [...]

At the outset it is important to clarify some terminology. In this text, we employ the following distinction between Aboriginal law and Indigenous law articulated by Jim Reynolds, a leading Aboriginal law practitioner, in his recently published treatise *Aboriginal Peoples and the Law* (UBC Press, 2018) at 3:

> Aboriginal law deals with the legal situation of the Aboriginal peoples of Canada under the laws of Canada; "Indigenous law" refers to the law of a particular Aboriginal group, developed and applying to that group.

To understand the significance of Aboriginal law and of section 35 of the *Constitution Act, 1982,* it is important to acknowledge the role of law, legislatures, and courts in supporting the colonization of Canada through the dispossession of Aboriginal peoples. Often, as the SCC underscored in *R. v. Sparrow*, [1990] 1 S.C.R. 1075, the Aboriginal interest in land and resources has simply been ignored. A key part of that process of colonization was the undermining of Indigenous law. Restoring those laws and seeking to reconcile them with Aboriginal law is a key priority for many legal scholars and Aboriginal communities.

Section 35 of the *Constitution Act, 1982* provides constitutional protection to Aboriginal rights existing as of 1982. These rights include those secured by past and future treaties as well as unextinguished customary rights that are found to exist by the courts. Where the Aboriginal right in question is once secured by treaty, the language of the treaty is scrutinized to give definition to the right in question: see *Mikisew Cree First Nation v. Canada (Minister of Canadian Heritage)*, 2005 SCC 69 (discussed in Chapter 8). Aboriginal rights may, however, also exist independent of treaty entitlements. Subsequent case law has established that there are two varieties of rights protected under section 35 that fall into this latter category.

The first are rights that protect activities which comprise an "element of a practice, custom or tradition integral to the distinctive culture of the aboriginal group claiming that right": see *R. v. Vanderpeet*, [1996] 2 S.C.R. 507, reconsideration / rehearing refused (January 16, 1997), Doc. 23803 (S.C.C.). This, for example, would include rights to hunt, gather, fish and use timber. The second form is Aboriginal title. Aboriginal title is a much broader entitlement that encompasses the right to exclusive use and occupation of land for a variety of purposes, which need not be aspects of those Aboriginal practices, customs and traditions which are integral to distinctive Aboriginal cultures: see *Delgamuukw v. British Columbia*, [1997] 3 S.C.R. 1010. Both of these forms of Aboriginal rights are unique (or *sui generis*) in that they are inalienable (i.e. they cannot be transferred, sold or surrendered to anyone other than the Crown). They are also distinct from other types of property rights in that they are held communally.

Canadian governments, whether acting in their regulatory or legislative capacities, are precluded by virtue of section 35 from infringing existing Aboriginal rights unless such action meets a justification test. The nature of this test differs depending on whether the affected right relates to a protected traditional activity, or to Aboriginal title.

Since 1982, a considerable body of jurisprudence has developed that elaborates on the nature and scope of the rights guaranteed under section 35. In many of the early cases, section 35 was relied upon to provide a defence from regulatory prosecutions, often under federal fisheries laws: see *R. v. Sparrow*, *supra*; *R. v. Vanderpeet*, *supra*; and *R. v. Gladstone*, [1996] 2 S.C.R. 723. In cases such as these, the Aboriginal defendants challenged the legislative authority under which charges were mounted as being inconsistent with section 35 Aboriginal rights. In many of these cases, courts have concluded that the impugned provision interferes with a constitutionally protected Aboriginal right. In this situation, courts must then determine whether the infringement can be justified on the basis that the impugned provision "minimally impairs" the asserted right and that it advances a legitimate overarching governmental concern for resource conservation. Where the Crown fails to meet this test, the case law underscores that priority must be given to Aboriginal food and ceremonial requirements.

More recently, section 35 has been deployed as a basis for seeking judicial review for resource development licensing and permitting decisions made by provincial or federal authorities: see *Haida Nation v. British Columbia (Minister of Forests)*, 2004 SCC 73; *Taku River Tlingit First Nation v. British Columbia (Project Assessment Director)*, (*sub nom. Taku River Tlingit First Nation v. Tulsequah Chief Mine Project (Project Assessment Director)*) 2004 SCC 74; *Mikisew Cree, supra*; *Dene Tha' First Nation v. Canada (Minister of Environment)*, 2006 FC 265; and *Tsleil-Waututh Nation v. Canada (Attorney General)*, 2018 FCA 153, additional reasons 2018 FCA 155 (both the *Dene Tha'* and *Tsleil-Waututh* cases are extracted in Chapter 6). Here the courts have developed an ever-burgeoning jurisprudence that seeks to define the Crown's duty to consult and accommodate Aboriginal rights prior to making decisions or taking actions that might undermine or impair Aboriginal rights. This case law establishes that even where Aboriginal rights or title claims remain unproven, the honour of the Crown may impose a procedural duty to consult with the affected Aboriginal group, and potentially take steps to accommodate their interests: see SCC decisions in *Haida, supra*, and *Tsilhqot'in Nation v. British Columbia*, 2014 SCC 44.

Jurisdictional issues have also arisen, albeit much more rarely, in the context of legal actions seeking to establish Aboriginal title. To date, only two such cases have gone to trial: see *Delgamuukw, supra*, and *Tsilhqot'in, supra*. Both of these cases arose in British Columbia where, unlike much of the rest of Canada, treaties between the Crown and First Nations have yet to be concluded over much of the landbase. In *Tsilhqot'in*, the SCC established that provincial laws of general application which trench into Aboriginal law are not *ultra vires*, and are valid insofar as they can be justified under the *Sparrow* approach. This ruling from the Court settled a long-standing jurisdictional uncertainty, making it clear that both the federal and provincial governments can validly enact laws affecting Aboriginal rights, title and treaties. In fact, *Tsilhqot'in* stated that the issue is not jurisdictional, "but rather how far the provincial government can go in regulating land that is subject to Aboriginal title or claims for Aboriginal rights". First Nations have also sought to rely on constitutional division of powers arguments as a means of ousting or constraining provincial regulation in the resource management context: see *Kitkatla Band v. British Columbia (Minister of Small Business, Tourism & Culture)*, 2002 SCC 31, and *Paul v. British Columbia (Forest Appeals Commission)*, 2003 SCC 55. In cases such as these, it has been argued that the impugned provincial laws tread on exclusive federal jurisdiction over "Indians and lands reserved for Indians" under subsection 91(24) of the *Constitution Act, 1867*. The *Tsilhqot'in* case, however, has put this argument to rest, as the SCC conclusively held that interjurisdictional immunity is supplanted by section 35, and the idea that Aboriginal rights are at the competence of federal power of "Indians" was rejected. Instead, it was recognized that Aboriginal rights are not a core competence of Parliament, but rather limit both federal and provincial jurisdiction. The tension, therefore, does not arise due to competition between provincial and federal power, but how the Aboriginal right holder seeks to use their land and how the province seeks to regulate it.

An emerging area in Aboriginal law litigation concerns the implications of treaty rights infringement. A key recent case is *Clyde River (Hamlet) v. Petroleum Geo-Services Inc.*, 2017 SCC 40. The applicant was a majority Inuit hamlet on Baffin Island, where the residents relied upon marine mammals for their food security as well as economic and cultural well-being. The proponents (respondents) applied to the NEB for permission to conduct seismic testing adjacent to the area where the Inuit have treaty rights for their harvest. After consultation and environmental assessment, the NEB found that environmental damage was not likely to result and granted permission. The claimants brought an application for judicial review and their case eventually came before the SCC, where the Court decided that the consultation had been inadequate, and accordingly the authorization granted was void. Moreover, the Court found that, where treaty rights were at stake, there was a strong duty to consult. This case has opened the door for a number of Aboriginal treaty rights cases, including

Yahey v. British Columbia, 2017 BCSC 899; *Restoule v. Canada (Attorney General),* 2018 ONSC 114; and *West Moberly First Nations v. British Columbia,* 2018 BCSC 1835. In these ongoing cases, the Indigenous claimants allege that their treaty rights have been, or will be, violated by government action. If the claimants are successful in these cases, it could potentially empower treaty-holding Indigenous groups to exercise greater control over natural resources and development over their treaty lands.

Tsilhqot'in Nation v. British Columbia
2014 SCC 44

[In the first part of the judgment, the Court clarified the test for determining Aboriginal title, and in applying the test to the facts of the case, determined that the Tsilhqot'in Nation have proven their claim. This is followed by a section where the Chief Justice explains the content of Aboriginal rights, echoing past case law insofar as characterizing it as *sui generis,* communal, and inalienable, as well as conferring the right to exclusive use and occupation. Moreover, the Court established that even where title has not yet been established, the Crown owes a duty to consult to the claimant Nation. The depth of consultation must be measured in relation to the *prima facie* strength of the claim. Below is an excerpt of the Court's discussion of the Crown's duty to consult and jurisdictional issues regarding Aboriginal title and rights.]

THE CHIEF JUSTICE: —

What Rights Does Aboriginal Title Confer?

[...]

Justification of Infringement

To justify overriding the Aboriginal title-holding group's wishes on the basis of the broader public good, the government must show: (1) that it discharged its procedural duty to consult and accommodate; (2) that its actions were backed by a compelling and substantial objective; and (3) that the governmental action is consistent with the Crown's fiduciary obligation to the group: *Sparrow.* [...]

As *Delgamuukw* explains, the process of reconciling Aboriginal interests with the broader interests of society as a whole is the *raison d'être* of the principle of justification. Aboriginals and non-Aboriginals are "all here to stay" and must of necessity move forward in a process of reconciliation (para. 186). To constitute a compelling and substantial objective, the broader public goal asserted by the government must further the goal of reconciliation, having regard to both the Aboriginal interest and the broader public objective.

What interests are potentially capable of justifying an incursion on Aboriginal title? In *Delgamuukw,* this Court, *per* Lamer C.J., offered this:

> In the wake of *Gladstone,* the range of legislative objectives that can justify the infringement of [A]boriginal title is fairly broad. Most of these objectives can be traced to the reconciliation of the prior occupation of North America by [A]boriginal peoples with the assertion of Crown sovereignty, which entails the

recognition that "distinctive [A]boriginal societies exist within, and are a part of, a broader social, political and economic community" (at para. 73). *In my opinion, the development of agriculture, forestry, mining, and hydroelectric power, the general economic development of the interior of British Columbia, protection of the environment or endangered species, the building of infrastructure and the settlement of foreign populations to support those aims, are the kinds of objectives that are consistent with this purpose and, in principle, can justify the infringement of [A]boriginal title.* Whether a particular measure or government act can be explained by reference to one of those objectives, however, is ultimately a question of fact that will have to be examined on a case-by-case basis. [Emphasis added; emphasis in original deleted; para. 165.]

If a compelling and substantial public purpose is established, the government must go on to show that the proposed incursion on the Aboriginal right is consistent with the Crown's fiduciary duty towards Aboriginal people.

The Crown's fiduciary duty in the context of justification merits further discussion. The Crown's underlying title in the land is held for the benefit of the Aboriginal group and constrained by the Crown's fiduciary or trust obligation to the group. This impacts the justification process in two ways.

First, the Crown's fiduciary duty means that the government must act in a way that respects the fact that Aboriginal title is a group interest that inheres in present and future generations. The beneficial interest in the land held by the Aboriginal group vests communally in the title-holding group. This means that incursions on Aboriginal title cannot be justified if they would substantially deprive future generations of the benefit of the land.

Second, the Crown's fiduciary duty infuses an obligation of proportionality into the justification process. Implicit in the Crown's fiduciary duty to the Aboriginal group is the requirement that the incursion is necessary to achieve the government's goal (rational connection); that the government go no further than necessary to achieve it (minimal impairment); and that the benefits that may be expected to flow from that goal are not outweighed by adverse effects on the Aboriginal interest (proportionality of impact). The requirement of proportionality is inherent in the *Delgamuukw* process of reconciliation and was echoed in *Haida*'s insistence that the Crown's duty to consult and accommodate at the claims stage "is proportionate to a preliminary assessment of the strength of the case supporting the existence of the right or title, and to the seriousness of the potentially adverse effect upon the right or title claimed" (para. 39).

In summary, Aboriginal title confers on the group that holds it the exclusive right to decide how the land is used and the right to benefit from those uses, subject to one carve-out — that the uses must be consistent with the group nature of the interest and the enjoyment of the land by future generations. Government incursions not consented to by the title-holding group must be undertaken in accordance with the Crown's procedural duty to consult and must also be justified on the basis of a compelling and substantial public interest, and must be consistent with the Crown's fiduciary duty to the Aboriginal group.

Remedies and Transition

Prior to establishment of title by court declaration or agreement, the Crown is required to consult in good faith with any Aboriginal groups asserting title to the land about proposed uses of the land and, if appropriate, accommodate the interests of such claimant groups. The level of consultation and accommodation required varies with the strength of the Aboriginal group's claim to the land and the seriousness of the potentially adverse effect upon the interest claimed. If the Crown fails to discharge its duty to consult, various remedies are available including injunctive relief, damages, or an order that consultation or accommodation be carried out: *Rio Tinto Alcan Inc. v. Carrier Sekani Tribal Council*, 2010 SCC 43, [2010] 2 S.C.R. 650, at para. 37.

After Aboriginal title to land has been established by court declaration or agreement, the Crown must seek the consent of the title-holding Aboriginal group to developments on the land. Absent consent, development of title land cannot proceed unless the Crown has discharged its duty to consult and can justify the intrusion on title under s. 35 of the *Constitution Act, 1982*. The usual remedies that lie for breach of interests in land are available, adapted as may be necessary to reflect the special nature of Aboriginal title and the fiduciary obligation owed by the Crown to the holders of Aboriginal title.

The practical result may be a spectrum of duties applicable over time in a particular case. At the claims stage, prior to establishment of Aboriginal title, the Crown owes a good faith duty to consult with the group concerned and, if appropriate, accommodate its interests. As the claim strength increases, the required level of consultation and accommodation correspondingly increases. Where a claim is particularly strong — for example, shortly before a court declaration of title — appropriate care must be taken to preserve the Aboriginal interest pending final resolution of the claim. Finally, once title is established, the Crown cannot proceed with development of title land not consented to by the title-holding group unless it has discharged its duty to consult and the development is justified pursuant to s. 35 of the *Constitution Act, 1982*.

Once title is established, it may be necessary for the Crown to reassess prior conduct in light of the new reality in order to faithfully discharge its fiduciary duty to the title-holding group going forward. For example, if the Crown begins a project without consent prior to Aboriginal title being established, it may be required to cancel the project upon establishment of the title if continuation of the project would be unjustifiably infringing. Similarly, if legislation was validly enacted before title was established, such legislation may be rendered inapplicable going forward to the extent that it unjustifiably infringes Aboriginal title.

What Duties Were Owed by the Crown at the Time of the Government Action?

Prior to the declaration of Aboriginal title, the Province had a duty to consult and accommodate the claimed Tsilhqot'in interest in the land. As the Tsilhqot'in had a strong *prima facie* claim to the land at the time of the impugned government action and the intrusion was significant, the duty to consult owed by the Crown fell at the high end of the spectrum described in *Haida* and required significant consultation and accommodation in order to preserve the Tsilhqot'in interest.

With the declaration of title, the Tsilhqot'in have now established Aboriginal title to the portion of the lands designated by the trial judge with the exception as set out in para. 9 of these reasons. This gives them the right to determine, subject to the inherent limits of group title held for future generations, the uses to which the land is put and to enjoy its economic fruits. As we have seen, this is not merely a right of first refusal with respect to Crown land management or usage plans. Rather, it is the right to proactively use and manage the land.

Breach of the Duty to Consult

The alleged breach in this case arises from the issuance by the Province of licences permitting third parties to conduct forestry activity and construct related infrastructure on the land in 1983 and onwards, before title was declared. During this time, the Tsilhqot'in held an interest in the land that was not yet legally recognized. The honour of the Crown required that the Province consult them on uses of the lands and accommodate their interests. The Province did neither and breached its duty owed to the Tsilhqot'in.

The Crown's duty to consult was breached when Crown officials engaged in the planning process for the removal of timber. The inclusion of timber on Aboriginal title land in a timber supply area, the approval of cut blocks on Aboriginal title land in a forest development plan, and the allocation of cutting permits all occurred without any meaningful consultation with the Tsilhqot'in. [...]

Provincial Laws and Aboriginal Title

As discussed, I have concluded that the Province breached its duty to consult and accommodate the Tsilhqot'in interest in the land. This is sufficient to dispose of the appeal.

However, the parties made extensive submissions on the application of the *Forest Act* to Aboriginal title land. This issue was dealt with by the courts below and is of pressing importance to the Tsilhqot'in people and other Aboriginal groups in British Columbia and elsewhere. It is therefore appropriate that we deal with it.

The following questions arise: (1) Do provincial laws of general application apply to land held under Aboriginal title and, if so, how? (2) Does the British Columbia *Forest Act* on its face apply to land held under Aboriginal title? and (3) If the *Forest Act* on its face applies, is its application ousted by the operation of the Constitution of Canada? I will discuss each of these questions in turn.

Do Provincial Laws of General Application Apply to Land Held Under Aboriginal Title?

Broadly put, provincial laws of general application apply to lands held under Aboriginal title. However, as we shall see, there are important constitutional limits on this proposition.

As a general proposition, provincial governments have the power to regulate land use within the province. This applies to all lands, whether held by the Crown, by private owners, or by the holders of Aboriginal title. The foundation for this power lies in s. 92(13) of the *Constitution Act, 1867*, which gives the provinces the power to legislate with respect to property and civil rights in the province.

Provincial power to regulate land held under Aboriginal title is constitutionally limited in two ways. First, it is limited by s. 35 of the *Constitution Act, 1982*. Section 35 requires any abridgment of the rights flowing from Aboriginal title to be backed by a compelling and substantial governmental objective and to be consistent with the Crown's fiduciary relationship with title holders. Second, a province's power to regulate lands under Aboriginal title may in some situations also be limited by the federal power over "Indians, and Lands reserved for the Indians" under s. 91(24) of the *Constitution Act, 1867.*

This Court suggested in *Sparrow* that the following factors will be relevant in determining whether a law of general application results in a meaningful diminution of an Aboriginal right, giving rise to breach: (1) whether the limitation imposed by the legislation is unreasonable; (2) whether the legislation imposes undue hardship; and (3) whether the legislation denies the holders of the right their preferred means of exercising the right (p. 1112). All three factors must be considered; for example, even if laws of general application are found to be reasonable or not to cause undue hardship, this does not mean that there can be no infringement of Aboriginal title. As stated in *Gladstone*:

> Simply because one of [the *Sparrow*] questions is answered in the negative will not prohibit a finding by a court that a *prima facie* infringement has taken place; it will just be one factor for a court to consider in its determination of whether there has been a *prima facie* infringement. [para. 43]

It may be predicted that laws and regulations of general application aimed at protecting the environment or assuring the continued health of the forests of British Columbia will usually be reasonable, not impose an undue hardship either directly or indirectly, and not interfere with the Aboriginal group's preferred method of exercising their right. And it is to be hoped that Aboriginal groups and the provincial government will work cooperatively to sustain the natural environment so important to them both. This said, when conflicts arise, the foregoing template serves to resolve them.

Subject to these constitutional constraints, provincial laws of general application apply to land held under Aboriginal title.

Does the Forest Act on its Face Apply to Aboriginal Title Land?

[...] I conclude that the legislature intended the *Forest Act* to apply to lands under claims for Aboriginal title, *up to the time title is confirmed by agreement or court order*. To hold otherwise would be to accept that the legislature intended the forests on such lands to be wholly unregulated, and would undercut the premise on which the duty to consult affirmed in *Haida* was based. Once Aboriginal title is confirmed, however, the lands are "vested" in the Aboriginal group and the lands are no longer Crown lands.

Applied to this case, this means that as a matter of statutory construction, the lands in question were "Crown land" under the *Forest Act* at the time the forestry licences were issued. Now that title has been established, however, the beneficial interest in the land vests in the Aboriginal group, not the Crown. The timber on it no longer falls within the definition of "Crown timber" and the *Forest Act* no longer applies. I add the obvious — it remains open to the legislature to amend the Act to cover lands held under Aboriginal title, provided it observes applicable constitutional restraints.

Is the Forest Act Ousted by the Constitution?

The next question is whether the provincial legislature lacks the constitutional power to legislate with respect to forests on Aboriginal title land. Currently, the *Forest Act* applies to lands under claim, but not to lands over which Aboriginal title has been confirmed. However, the provincial legislature could amend the Act so as to explicitly apply to lands over which title has been confirmed. This raises the question of whether provincial forestry legislation that on its face purports to apply to Aboriginal title lands is ousted by the Constitution.

Section 35 of the Constitution Act, 1982

Section 35 of the *Constitution Act, 1982* represents "the culmination of a long and difficult struggle in both the political forum and the courts for the constitutional recognition of [A]boriginal rights" (*Sparrow*, at p. 1105). It protects Aboriginal rights against provincial and federal legislative power and provides a framework to facilitate negotiations and reconciliation of Aboriginal interests with those of the broader public.

Section 35(1) states that existing Aboriginal rights are hereby "recognized and affirmed". In *Sparrow*, this Court held that these words must be construed in a liberal and purposive manner. Recognition and affirmation of Aboriginal rights constitutionally entrenches the Crown's fiduciary obligations towards Aboriginal peoples. While rights that are recognized and affirmed are not absolute, s. 35 requires the Crown to reconcile its power with its duty. "[T]he best way to achieve that reconciliation is to demand the justification of any government regulation that infringes upon or denies [A]boriginal rights" (*Sparrow*, at p. 1109). Dickson C.J. and La Forest J. elaborated on this purpose as follows, at p. 1110:

> The constitutional recognition afforded by the provision therefore gives a measure of control over government conduct and a strong check on legislative power. While it does not promise immunity from government regulation in a society that, in the twentieth century, is increasingly more complex, interdependent and sophisticated, and where exhaustible resources need protection and management, it does hold the Crown to a substantive promise. The government is required to bear the burden of justifying any legislation that has some negative effect on any [A]boriginal right protected under s. 35(1).

Where legislation affects an Aboriginal right protected by s. 35 of the *Constitution Act, 1982*, two inquiries are required. First, does the legislation interfere with or infringe the Aboriginal right (this was referred to as *prima facie* infringement in *Sparrow*)? Second, if so, can the infringement be justified?

A court must first examine the characteristics or incidents of the right at stake. In the case of Aboriginal title, three relevant incidents are: (1) the right to exclusive use and occupation of the land; (2) the right to determine the uses to which the land is put, subject to the ultimate limit that those uses cannot destroy the ability of the land to sustain future generations of Aboriginal peoples; and (3) the right to enjoy the economic fruits of the land (*Delgamuukw*, at para. 166).

Next, in order to determine whether the right is infringed by legislation, a court must ask whether the legislation results in a meaningful diminution of the right: *Gladstone*. As discussed, in *Sparrow*, the Court suggested that the following three factors will aid in determining whether such an infringement has occurred:

(1) whether the limitation imposed by the legislation is unreasonable; (2) whether the legislation imposes undue hardship; and (3) whether the legislation denies the holders of the right their preferred means of exercising the right (at p. 1112).

General regulatory legislation, such as legislation aimed at managing the forests in a way that deals with pest invasions or prevents forest fires, will often pass the *Sparrow* test as it will be reasonable, not impose undue hardship, and not deny the holders of the right their preferred means of exercising it. In such cases, no infringement will result.

General regulatory legislation, which may affect the manner in which the Aboriginal right can be exercised, differs from legislation that assigns Aboriginal property rights to third parties. The issuance of timber licences on Aboriginal title land for example — a direct transfer of Aboriginal property rights to a third party — will plainly be a meaningful diminution in the Aboriginal group's ownership right and will amount to an infringement that must be justified in cases where it is done without Aboriginal consent.

As discussed earlier, to justify an infringement, the Crown must demonstrate that: (1) it complied with its procedural duty to consult with the right holders and accommodate the right to an appropriate extent at the stage when infringement was contemplated; (2) the infringement is backed by a compelling and substantial legislative objective in the public interest; and (3) the benefit to the public is proportionate to any adverse effect on the Aboriginal interest. This framework permits a principled reconciliation of Aboriginal rights with the interests of all Canadians.

While unnecessary for the disposition of this appeal, the issue of whether British Columbia possessed a compelling and substantial legislative objective in issuing the cutting permits in this case was addressed by the courts below, and I offer the following comments for the benefit of all parties going forward. I agree with the courts below that no compelling and substantial objective existed in this case. The trial judge found the two objectives put forward by the Province — the economic benefits that would be realized as a result of logging in the claim area and the need to prevent the spread of a mountain pine beetle infestation — were not supported by the evidence. After considering the expert evidence before him, he concluded that the proposed cutting sites were not economically viable and that they were not directed at preventing the spread of the mountain pine beetle.

Before the Court of Appeal, the Province no longer argued that the forestry activities were undertaken to combat the mountain pine beetle, but maintained the position that the trial judge's findings on economic viability were unreasonable, because unless logging was economically viable, it would not have taken place. The Court of Appeal rejected this argument on two grounds: (1) levels of logging must sometimes be maintained for a tenure holder to keep logging rights, even if logging is not economically viable; and (2) the focus is the economic value of logging compared to the detrimental effects it would have on Tsilhqot'in Aboriginal rights, not the economic viability of logging from the sole perspective of the tenure holder. In short, the Court of Appeal found no error in the trial judge's reasoning on this point. I would agree. Granting rights to third parties to harvest timber on Tsilhqot'in land is a serious infringement that will not lightly be justified. Should the government wish to grant such harvesting rights in the future, it will be required to establish that a compelling and substantial objective is furthered by such harvesting, something that was not present in this case.

The Division of Powers

The starting point, as noted, is that, as a general matter, the regulation of forestry within the Province falls under its power over property and civil rights under s. 92(13) of the *Constitution Act, 1867.* To put it in constitutional terms, regulation of forestry is in "pith and substance" a provincial matter. Thus, the *Forest Act* is consistent with the division of powers unless it is ousted by a competing federal power, even though it may incidentally affect matters under federal jurisdiction.

"Indians, and Lands reserved for the Indians" falls under federal jurisdiction pursuant to s. 91(24) of the *Constitution Act, 1867.* As such, forestry on Aboriginal title land falls under both the provincial power over forestry in the province and the federal power over "Indians". Thus, for constitutional purposes, forestry on Aboriginal title land possesses a double aspect, with both levels of government enjoying concurrent jurisdiction. Normally, such concurrent legislative power creates no conflicts — federal and provincial governments cooperate productively in many areas of double aspect such as, for example, insolvency and child custody. However, in cases where jurisdictional disputes arise, two doctrines exist to resolve them.

First, the doctrine of paramountcy applies where there is conflict or inconsistency between provincial and federal law, in the sense of impossibility of dual compliance or frustration of federal purpose. In the case of such conflict or inconsistency, the federal law prevails. Therefore, if the application of valid provincial legislation, such as the *Forest Act*, conflicts with valid federal legislation enacted pursuant to Parliament's power over "Indians", the latter would trump the former. No such inconsistency is alleged in this case.

Second, the doctrine of interjurisdictional immunity applies where laws enacted by one level of government impair the protected core of jurisdiction possessed by the other level of government. Interjurisdictional immunity is premised on the idea that since federal and provincial legislative powers under ss. 91 and 92 of the *Constitution Act, 1867* are exclusive, each level of government enjoys a basic unassailable core of power on which the other level may not intrude. In considering whether provincial legislation such as the *Forest Act* is ousted pursuant to interjurisdictional immunity, the court must ask two questions. First, does the provincial legislation touch on a protected core of federal power? And second, would application of the provincial law significantly trammel or impair the federal power? (*Quebec (Attorney General) v. Canadian Owners and Pilots Association*, 2010 SCC 39, [2010] 2 S.C.R. 536 ("*COPA*").

The trial judge held that interjurisdictional immunity rendered the provisions of the *Forest Act* inapplicable to land held under Aboriginal title because provisions authorizing management, acquisition, removal and sale of timber on such lands affect the core of the federal power over "Indians". He placed considerable reliance on *R. v. Morris*, 2006 SCC 59, [2006] 2 S.C.R. 915, in which this Court held that only Parliament has the power to derogate from rights conferred by a treaty because treaty rights are within the core of the federal power over "Indians". It follows, the trial judge reasoned, that, since Aboriginal rights are akin to treaty rights, the Province has no power to legislate with respect to forests on Aboriginal title land.

The reasoning accepted by the trial judge is essentially as follows. Aboriginal rights fall at the core of federal jurisdiction under s. 91(24) of the *Constitution Act, 1867*. Interjurisdictional immunity applies to matters at the core of s. 91(24). Therefore, provincial governments are constitutionally prohibited from legislating in a way that limits Aboriginal rights. This reasoning leads to a number of difficulties.

The critical aspect of this reasoning is the proposition that Aboriginal rights fall at the core of federal regulatory jurisdiction under s. 91(24) of the *Constitution Act, 1867*.

The jurisprudence on whether s. 35 rights fall at the core of the federal power to legislate with respect to "Indians" under s. 91(24) is somewhat mixed. While no case has held that Aboriginal rights, such as Aboriginal title to land, fall at the core of the federal power under s. 91(24) , this has been stated in *obiter dicta*. However, this Court has also stated in *obiter dicta* that provincial governments are constitutionally permitted to infringe Aboriginal rights where such infringement is justified pursuant to s. 35 of the *Constitution Act, 1982* — this latter proposition being inconsistent with the reasoning accepted by the trial judge.

In *R. v. Marshall*, [1999] 3 S.C.R. 533, this Court suggested that interjurisdictional immunity did not apply where provincial legislation conflicted with treaty rights. Rather, the s. 35 *Sparrow* framework was the appropriate tool with which to resolve the conflict:

> [T]he federal and provincial governments [have the authority] within their respective legislative fields to regulate the exercise of the treaty right *subject to the constitutional requirement that restraints on the exercise of the treaty right have to be justified on the basis of conservation or other compelling and substantial public objectives* ... [para. 24]

More recently however, in *Morris*, this Court distinguished *Marshall* on the basis that the treaty right at issue in *Marshall* was a commercial right. The Court in *Morris* went on to hold that interjurisdictional immunity prohibited any provincial infringement of the non-commercial treaty right in that case, whether or not such an infringement could be justified under s. 35 of the *Constitution Act, 1982*.

Beyond this, the jurisprudence does not directly address the relationship between interjurisdictional immunity and s. 35 of the *Constitution Act, 1982*. The ambiguous state of the jurisprudence has created unpredictability. It is clear that where valid *federal* law interferes with an Aboriginal or treaty right, the s. 35 *Sparrow* framework governs the law's applicability [emphasis in original]. It is less clear, however, that it is so where valid *provincial* law interferes with an Aboriginal or treaty right. The jurisprudence leaves the following questions unanswered. Does interjurisdictional immunity prevent provincial governments from ever limiting Aboriginal rights even if a particular infringement would be justified under the *Sparrow* framework? Is provincial interference with Aboriginal rights treated differently than treaty rights? And, are commercial Aboriginal rights treated differently than non-commercial Aboriginal rights? No case has addressed these questions explicitly, as I propose to do now.

As discussed, s. 35 of the *Constitution Act, 1982* imposes limits on how both the federal and provincial governments can deal with land under Aboriginal title. Neither level of government is permitted to legislate in a way that results in a meaningful diminution of an Aboriginal or treaty right, unless such an infringement is justified in the broader public interest and is consistent with the Crown's fiduciary duty owed to the Aboriginal group. The result is to protect Aboriginal and treaty rights while also allowing the reconciliation of Aboriginal interests with those of the broader society.

What role then is left for the application of the doctrine of interjurisdictional immunity and the idea that Aboriginal rights are at the core of the federal power over "Indians" under s. 91(24) of the *Constitution Act, 1867*? The answer is none.

The doctrine of interjurisdictional immunity is directed to ensuring that the two levels of government are able to operate without interference in their core areas of exclusive jurisdiction. This goal is not implicated in cases such as this. Aboriginal rights are a limit on both federal and provincial jurisdiction.

The guarantee of Aboriginal rights in s. 35 of the *Constitution Act, 1982*, like the *Canadian Charter of Rights and Freedoms*, operates as a limit on federal and provincial legislative powers. The *Charter* forms Part I of the *Constitution Act, 1982*, and the guarantee of Aboriginal rights forms Part II. Parts I and II are sister provisions, both operating to limit governmental powers, whether federal or provincial. Part II Aboriginal rights, like Part I *Charter* rights, are held *against* government — they operate to *prohibit* certain types of regulation which governments could otherwise impose. These limits have nothing to do with whether something lies at the core of the federal government's powers.

An analogy with *Charter* jurisprudence may illustrate the point. Parliament enjoys exclusive jurisdiction over criminal law. However, its criminal law power is circumscribed by s. 11 of the *Charter* which guarantees the right to a fair criminal process. Just as Aboriginal rights are fundamental to Aboriginal law, the right to a fair criminal process is fundamental to criminal law. But we do not say that the right to a fair criminal process under s. 11 falls at the core of Parliament's criminal law jurisdiction. Rather, it is a *limit* on Parliament's criminal law jurisdiction. If s. 11 rights were held to be at the core of Parliament's criminal law jurisdiction such that interjurisdictional immunity applied, the result would be absurd: provincial breaches of s. 11 rights would be judged on a different standard than federal breaches, with only the latter capable of being saved under s. 1 of the *Charter*. This same absurdity would result if interjurisdictional immunity were applied to Aboriginal rights.

The doctrine of interjurisdictional immunity is designed to deal with conflicts between provincial powers and federal powers; it does so by carving out areas of exclusive jurisdiction for each level of government. But the problem in cases such as this is not competing provincial and federal powers, but rather tension between the right of the Aboriginal title holders to use their land as they choose and the province which seeks to regulate it, like all other land in the province.

Moreover, application of interjurisdictional immunity in this area would create serious practical difficulties.

First, application of interjurisdictional immunity would result in two different tests for assessing the constitutionality of provincial legislation affecting Aboriginal rights. Pursuant to *Sparrow*, provincial regulation is unconstitutional if it results in a meaningful diminution of an Aboriginal right that cannot be justified pursuant to s. 35 of the *Constitution Act, 1982*. Pursuant to interjurisdictional immunity, provincial regulation would be unconstitutional if it impaired an Aboriginal right, whether or not such limitation was reasonable or justifiable. The result would be dueling tests directed at answering the same question: How far can provincial governments go in regulating the exercise of s. 35 Aboriginal rights?

Second, in this case, applying the doctrine of interjurisdictional immunity to exclude provincial regulation of forests on Aboriginal title lands would produce uneven, undesirable results and may lead to legislative vacuums. The result would be patchwork regulation of forests — some areas of the province regulated under provincial legislation, and other areas under federal legislation or no legislation at all. This might make it difficult, if not impossible, to deal effectively with problems such as pests and fires, a situation desired by neither level of government.

Interjurisdictional immunity — premised on a notion that regulatory environments can be divided into watertight jurisdictional compartments — is often at odds with modern reality. Increasingly, as our society becomes more complex, effective regulation requires cooperation between interlocking federal and provincial schemes. The two levels of government possess differing tools, capacities, and expertise, and the more flexible double aspect and paramountcy doctrines are alive to this reality: under these doctrines, jurisdictional cooperation is encouraged up until the point when actual conflict arises and must be resolved. Interjurisdictional immunity, by contrast, may thwart such productive cooperation. In the case of forests on Aboriginal title land, courts would have to scrutinize provincial forestry legislation to ensure that it did not impair the core of federal jurisdiction over "Indians" and would also have to scrutinize any federal legislation to ensure that it did not impair the core of the province's power to manage the forests. It would be no answer that, as in this case, both levels of government agree that the laws at issue should remain in force.

This Court has recently stressed the limits of interjurisdictional immunity. "[C]onstitutional doctrine must facilitate, not undermine what this Court has called 'co-operative federalism'" and as such "a court should favour, where possible, the ordinary operation of statutes enacted by both levels of government" (*Canadian Western Bank v. Alberta*, 2007 SCC 22, [2007] 2 S.C.R. 3, at paras. 24 and 37 (emphasis deleted)). Because of this, interjurisdictional immunity is of "limited application" and should be applied "with restraint" (paras. 67 and 77). These propositions have been confirmed in more recent decisions: *Marine Services International Ltd. v. Ryan Estate*, 2013 SCC 44, [2013] 3 S.C.R. 53; *Canada (Attorney General) v. PHS Community Services Society*, 2011 SCC 44, [2011] 3 S.C.R. 134.

Morris, on which the trial judge relied, was decided prior to this Court's articulation of the modern approach to interjurisdictional immunity in *Canadian Western Bank* and *COPA*, and so is of limited precedential value on this subject as a result (see *Marine Services*, at para. 64). To the extent that *Morris* stands for the proposition that provincial governments are categorically barred from regulating the exercise of Aboriginal rights, it should no longer be followed. I find that, consistent with the statements in *Sparrow* and *Delgamuukw*, provincial regulation of general application will apply to exercises of Aboriginal rights, including

Aboriginal title land, subject to the s. 35 infringement and justification framework. This carefully calibrated test attempts to reconcile general legislation with Aboriginal rights in a sensitive way as required by s. 35 of the *Constitution Act, 1982* and is fairer and more practical from a policy perspective than the blanket inapplicability imposed by the doctrine of interjurisdictional immunity.

For these reasons, I conclude that the doctrine of interjurisdictional immunity should not be applied in cases where lands are held under Aboriginal title. Rather, the s. 35 *Sparrow* approach should govern. Provincial laws of general application, including the *Forest Act*, should apply unless they are unreasonable, impose a hardship or deny the title holders their preferred means of exercising their rights, and such restrictions cannot be justified pursuant to the justification framework outlined above. The result is a balance that preserves the Aboriginal right while permitting effective regulation of forests by the province, as required by s. 35 of the *Constitution Act, 1982.*

The s. 35 framework applies to exercises of both provincial and federal power: *Sparrow*; *Delgamuukw*. As such, it provides a complete and rational way of confining provincial legislation affecting Aboriginal title land within appropriate constitutional bounds. The issue in cases such as this is not at base one of conflict between the federal and provincial levels of government — an issue appropriately dealt with by the doctrines of paramountcy and interjurisdictional immunity where precedent supports this — but rather how far the provincial government can go in regulating land that is subject to Aboriginal title or claims for Aboriginal title. The appropriate constitutional lens through which to view the matter is s. 35 of the *Constitution Act, 1982* , which directly addresses the requirement that these interests must be respected by the government, unless the government can justify incursion on them for a compelling purpose and in conformity with its fiduciary duty to affected Aboriginal groups.

Conclusion

I would allow the appeal and grant a declaration of Aboriginal title over the area at issue, as requested by the Tsilhqot'in. I further declare that British Columbia breached its duty to consult owed to the Tsilhqot'in through its land use planning and forestry authorizations.

Notes and Questions

1. *Tsilhqot'in* offers potential for First Nations to have jurisdiction over their traditional territories judicially recognized through the court process where governments are reluctant to negotiate such recognition at the bargaining table. However, the costs of bringing title cases are immense. Likewise, the costs of litigating claims of treaty rights infringement can also be staggering. This has led to nations seeking to bring strategically focused title claims to smaller, more manageable territorial units.

2. In Chapter 6, we discuss the legal regime governing the judicial review of governmental decision-making, which often raises interesting and complex

jurisdictional issues. Consider the procedural and other differences between judicial review, on the one hand, and treaty and title rights claim litigation on the other. What factors might explain a First Nation's decision whether to judicially review governmental action or to bring a title or rights claim?

3. How does the *Tsilhqot'in* decision advance our understanding of the federal-provincial division of powers? In particular, what implications can be drawn from its discussion of IJI? Can, or should, its approach to IJI be extrapolated to litigation settings relating to issues other than section 35 of the *Constitution Act, 1982*?

Municipal Jurisdiction

The role of municipalities is only indirectly guided by constitutional considerations. Municipalities derive their powers from the provinces. Provinces are constitutionally empowered to pass on aspects of their own jurisdiction to municipalities. Most provinces have consolidated their legislative delegation of power in some form of *Municipal Government Act*. Such legislation tends to give municipalities power and responsibility over a range of local matters, many of which have environmental implications and connections.

A critical function of a municipality is to make land-use decisions within its boundaries. Available tools include zoning powers, development permits, and subdivision approval requirements. Through zoning by-laws, municipalities can control what range of activities are possible. Through zoning, a municipality can promote public and active transportation, restrict or control high risk industrial activities, encourage redevelopment of contaminated sites, and otherwise influence the environmental impact of human activities within its boundaries.

In many municipalities, development permits are required for major new developments. This provides a municipality with the ability to influence whether, and how, major developments within its boundaries are implemented. A subset of such developments is proposals for new subdivisions. Many municipalities have separate processes in place for the approval of subdivisions. The implications of new subdivisions for transportation, municipal services, and the loss of habitat are influencing how municipalities are exercising these powers. As with all municipal powers, the provinces also retain the ability to direct municipalities on how to make land-use decisions through provincial land-use policies or similar measures.

Examples of other powers often delegated by provinces to municipalities include: the power to pass by-laws dealing with noise and odour; the control of cosmetic pesticide use; and the collection and disposal of solid waste and litter within the boundaries of the municipality. Most legislation also includes some general provisions that allow municipalities to pass by-laws for the general health and welfare of its residents. In some cases, a subject matter may be completely delegated. Often, however, provinces set general rules on a subject matter through separate provincial legislation and then allow municipalities to decide on how to best implement them within their boundaries.

Many provinces have passed provincial laws dealing with solid waste management. Such laws may also establish what materials have to be re-processed, re-used or recycled. They may also set general rules for the handling and processing of various waste streams. Provincial regulations may also establish design criteria for landfills, composting facilities, tire storage facilities and facilities that incinerate medical waste. Municipalities, in turn, tend to be responsible for collection of material and for ensuring that the material is properly sorted and taken to approved facilities.

A key emerging jurisdictional concern is the relationship between a growing appetite on the part of local governments to use their regulatory powers to promote environmentally sustainable practices within their boundaries and analogous and potentially competing powers that are constitutionally vested provincially and federally. In *Friends of the Oldman River Society v. Canada (Minister of Transport)*, [1992] 1 S.C.R. 3, La Forest J. offered observations on the need for the courts to respect and promote the ability of both levels of government to tackle the mounting environmental challenges of the day. As citizens and community organizations increasingly turn to local governments as a readily accessible and available vehicle for translating their environmental values and preferences into regulation, should by extension the courts generously construe powers vested by provinces in their elected local officials and tribunals?

Earlier, in Chapter 1, we briefly considered the 2001 decision of the Supreme Court of Canada in *114957 Canada Ltée (Spraytech, Société d'arrosage) v. Hudson (Town)* in the context of the majority's invocation of the precautionary principle. As we saw, the majority invoked this principle to bolster its conclusion that a by-law restricting the use of pesticides enacted by the Town of Hudson was constitutional. We now return to this decision to explore more fully the Supreme Court's approach to the interesting and timely jurisdictional issues raised in the case.

114957 Canada Ltée (Spraytech, Société d'arrosage) v. Hudson (Town)

2001 SCC 40

L'HEUREUX-DUBÉ J.: — The context of this appeal includes the realization that our common future, that of every Canadian community, depends on a healthy environment. In the words of the Superior Court judge: "Twenty years ago there was very little concern over the effect of chemicals such as pesticides on the population. Today, we are more conscious of what type of an environment we wish to live in and what quality of life we wish to expose our children [to]". This Court has recognized that "[e]veryone is aware that individually and collectively, we are responsible for preserving the natural environment [...] environmental protection [has] emerged as a fundamental value in Canadian society": *R. v. Canadian Pacific Ltd.*, [1995] 2 S.C.R. 1031, at para. 55 (S.C.C.). See also *Friends of the Oldman River Society v. Canada (Minister of Transport)*, [1992] 1 S.C.R. 3 at pp. 16-17 (S.C.C.).

Regardless of whether pesticides are in fact an environmental threat, the Court is asked to decide the legal question of whether the Town of Hudson,

Quebec, acted within its authority in enacting a by-law regulating and restricting pesticide use.

The case arises in an era in which matters of governance are often examined through the lens of the principle of subsidiarity. This is the proposition that lawmaking and implementation are often best achieved at a level of government that is not only effective, but also closest to the citizens affected and thus most responsive to their needs, to local distinctiveness, and to population diversity. La Forest J. wrote for the majority in *Canada (Procureure générale) c. Hydro-Québec*, [1997] 3 S.C.R. 213 (S.C.C.), at p. 296, that "the protection of the environment is a major challenge of our time. It is an international problem, one that requires action by *governments at all levels*" (emphasis added). His reasons in that case also quoted with approval a passage from *Our Common Future*, the report produced in 1987 by the United Nations' World Commission on the Environment and Development. The so-called "Brundtland Commission" recommended that "local governments [should be] empowered to exceed, but not to lower, national norms" (p. 220).

There are now at least 37 Quebec municipalities with by-laws restricting pesticides: John Swaigen, "The Hudson Case: Municipal Powers to Regulate Pesticides Confirmed by Quebec Courts" (2000), 34 C.E.L.R. (N.S.) 162, at p. 174. Nevertheless, each level of government must be respectful of the division of powers that is the hallmark of our federal system; there is a fine line between laws that legitimately complement each other and those that invade another government's protected legislative sphere. Ours is a legal inquiry informed by the environmental policy context, not the reverse.

Facts

The appellants are landscaping and lawn care companies operating mostly in the region of greater Montreal, with both commercial and residential clients. They make regular use of pesticides approved by the federal *Pest Control Products Act*, R.S.C. 1985, c. P-9, in the course of their business activities and hold the requisite licences under Quebec's *Pesticides Act*, R.S.Q., c. P-9.3.

The respondent, the Town of Hudson ("the Town"), is a municipal corporation governed by the *Cities and Towns Act*, R.S.Q., c. C-19 ("*C.T.A.*"). It is located about 40 kilometres west of Montreal and has a population of approximately 5,400 people, some of whom are clients of the appellants. In 1991, the Town adopted By-law 270, restricting the use of pesticides within its perimeter to specified locations and for enumerated activities. The by-law responded to residents' concerns, repeatedly expressed since 1985. The residents submitted numerous letters and comments to the Town's Council. The definition of pesticides in By-law 270 replicates that of the *Pesticides Act*.

In November 1992, the appellants were served with a summons by the Town to appear before the Municipal Court and respond to charges of having used pesticides in violation of By-law 270. The appellants pled not guilty and obtained a suspension of proceedings in order to bring a motion for declaratory judgment before the Superior Court (under art. 453 of Quebec's *Code of Civil Procedure*). They asked that the court declare By-law 270 (as well as By-law 248, which is not part of this appeal) to be inoperative and *ultra vires* the Town's authority.

The Superior Court denied the motion for declaratory judgment, finding that the by-laws fell within the scope of the Town's powers under the *C.T.A.* This ruling was affirmed by a unanimous Quebec Court of Appeal. [...]

Issues

There are two issues raised by this appeal:

(1) Did the Town have the statutory authority to enact By-law 270?

(2) Even if the Town had authority to enact it, was By-law 270 rendered inoperative because of a conflict with federal or provincial legislation?

Did the Town Have the Statutory Authority to Enact By-law 270?

In *R. v. Sharma*, [1993] 1 S.C.R. 650 (S.C.C.), at p. 668, this Court recognized "the principle that, as statutory bodies, municipalities 'may exercise only those powers expressly conferred by statute, those powers necessarily or fairly implied by the expressed power in the statute, and those indispensable powers essential and not merely convenient to the effectuation of the purposes of the corporation' [...] Included in this authority are "general welfare" powers, conferred by provisions in provincial enabling legislation, on which municipalities can draw. As I.M. Rogers points out, "the legislature cannot possibly foresee all the powers that are necessary to the statutory equipment of its creatures [...] Undoubtedly the inclusion of 'general welfare' provisions was intended to circumvent, to some extent, the effect of the doctrine of *ultra vires* which puts the municipalities in the position of having to point to an express grant of authority to justify each corporate act" (Ian MacFee Rogers, *The Law of Canadian Municipal Corporations*, 2nd ed. (looseleaf, updated 2001, release 1), cum. supp. to vol. 1 (Toronto: Carswell: 1971), at p. 367).

Section 410 *C.T.A.* is an example of such a general welfare provision and supplements the specific grants of power in s. 412. More open-ended or "omnibus" provisions such as s. 410 allow municipalities to respond expeditiously to new challenges facing local communities, without requiring amendment of the provincial enabling legislation. There are analogous provisions in other provinces' and territories' municipal enabling legislation: see *Municipal Government Act*, S.A. 1994, c. M-26.1, ss. 3(c) and 7; *Local Government Act*, R.S.B.C. 1996, c. 323, s. 249; *Municipal Act*, S.M. 1996, c. 58, C.C.S.M., c. M225, ss. 232 and 233; *Municipalities Act*, R.S.N.B. 1973, c. M-22, s. 190(2), First Sched.; *Municipal Government Act*, S.N.S. 1998, c. 18, s. 172; *Cities, Towns and Villages Act*, R.S.N.W.T. 1988, c. C-8, ss. 54 and 102; *Municipal Act*, R.S.O. 1990, c. M.45, s. 102; *Municipal Act*, R.S.Y. 1986, c. 119, s. 271.

While enabling provisions that allow municipalities to regulate for the "general welfare" within their territory authorize the enactment of by-laws genuinely aimed at furthering goals, such as public health and safety, it is important to keep in mind that such open-ended provisions do not confer an unlimited power. Rather, courts faced with an impugned by-law enacted under an "omnibus" provision such as s. 410 *C.T.A.* must be vigilant in scrutinizing the true purpose of the by-law. In this way, a municipality will not be permitted to invoke the implicit power granted under a "general welfare" provision as a basis for enacting by-laws that are in fact related to ulterior objectives, whether mischievous or not. [...]

Within this framework, I turn now to the specifics of the appeal. As a preliminary matter, I agree with the courts below that By-law 270 was not enacted under s. 412(32) *C.T.A.* [...] As a result, since there is no specific provision in the provincial enabling legislation referring to pesticides, the by-law must fall within the purview of s. 410(1) *C.T.A.* The party challenging a by-law's validity bears the burden of proving that it is *ultra vires*: see *Kuchma v. Tache (Rural Municipality)*, [1945] S.C.R. 234 at p. 239 (S.C.C.), and *Fountainhead Fun Centre Ltd. v. Montréal (Ville)*, [1985] 1 S.C.R. 368 at p. 395 (S.C.C.).

Section 410(1) *C.T.A.* provides that councils may "make by-laws:

> (1) To secure peace, order, good government, health and general welfare in the territory of the municipality, provided such by-laws are not contrary to the laws of Canada, or of Québec, nor inconsistent with any special provision of this Act or of the *Charter*.

In *Nanaimo (City) v. Rascal Trucking Ltd.*, [2000] 1 S.C.R. 342, 2000 SCC 13 (S.C.C.), at para. 36, this Court quoted with approval the following statement by McLachlin J. (now Chief Justice) in *Shell Canada Products Ltd. v. Vancouver (City)*, [1994] 1 S.C.R. 231 (S.C.C.), at p. 244:

> Recent commentary suggests an emerging consensus that courts must respect the responsibility of elected municipal bodies to serve the people who elected them and exercise caution to avoid substituting their views of what is best for the citizens for those of municipal councils. *Barring clear demonstration that a municipal decision was beyond its powers, courts should not so hold.* In cases where powers are not expressly conferred but may be implied, courts must be prepared to adopt the "benevolent construction" which this Court referred to in *Greenbaum*, and confer the powers by reasonable implication. Whatever rules of construction are applied, they must not be used to usurp the legitimate role of municipal bodies as community representatives. [Emphasis added.]

The appellants argue that By-law 270 imposes an impermissible absolute ban on pesticide use. They focus on s. 2 of the by-law, which states that: "The spreading and use of a pesticide is prohibited throughout the territory of the Town". In my view, the by-law read as a whole does not impose such a prohibition. By-law 270's ss. 3 to 6 state locations and situations for pesticide use. As one commentary notes, "by-laws like Hudson's typically target non-essential uses of pesticides. That is, it is not a total prohibition, but rather permits the use of pesticides in certain situations where the use of pesticides is not purely an aesthetic pursuit (e.g. for the production of crops)": Swaigen, *supra*, at p. 178. [...]

In *Shell*, *supra*, at pp. 276-277, Sopinka J. for the majority quoted the following with approval from Rogers, *supra*, §64.1, at p. 387:

> In approaching a problem of construing a municipal enactment a court should endeavour firstly to interpret it so that the powers sought to be exercised are in consonance with the purposes of the corporation. The provision at hand should be construed with reference to the object of the municipality: to render services to a group of persons in a locality with a view to advancing their health, welfare, safety and good government.

In that case, Sopinka J. enunciated the test of whether the municipal enactment was "passed for a municipal purpose". Provisions such as s. 410(1) C.T.A., while benefiting from the generosity of interpretation discussed in *Nanaimo, supra*, must have a reasonable connection to the municipality's permissible objectives. As stated in *Greenbaum, supra*, at p. 689: "municipal by-laws are to be read to fit within the parameters of the empowering provincial statute where the by-laws are susceptible to more than one interpretation. However, courts must be vigilant in ensuring that municipalities do not impinge upon the civil or common law rights of citizens in passing *ultra vires* by-laws".

Whereas in *Shell*, the enactments' purpose was found to be "to affect matters beyond the boundaries of the City without any identifiable benefit to its inhabitants" (p. 280), that is not the case here. The Town's By-law 270 responded to concerns of its residents about alleged health risks caused by non-essential uses of pesticides within Town limits. Unlike *Shell*, in which the Court felt bound by the municipal enactments' "detailed recital of [...] purposes", the by-law at issue requires what Sopinka J. called the reading in of an implicit purpose. Based on the distinction between essential and non-essential uses of pesticides, it is reasonable to conclude that the Town by-law's purpose is to minimize the use of allegedly harmful pesticides in order to promote the health of its inhabitants. This purpose falls squarely within the "health" component of s. 410(1). As Ruth Sullivan appositely explains in a hypothetical example illustrating the purposive approach to statutory interpretation:

> Suppose, for example, that a municipality passed a by-law prohibiting the use of chemical pesticides on residential lawns. With no additional information, one might well conclude that the purpose of the by-law was to protect persons from health hazards contained in the chemical spray. This inference would be based on empirical beliefs about the harms chemical pesticides can cause and the risks of exposure created by their use on residential lawns. It would also be based on assumptions about the relative value of grass, insects and persons in society and the desirability of possible consequences of the by-law, such as putting people out of work, restricting the free use of property, interfering with the conduct of businesses and the like. These assumptions make it implausible to suppose that the municipal council was trying to promote the spread of plant-destroying insects or to put chemical workers out of work, but plausible to suppose that it was trying to suppress a health hazard. (*Driedger on the Construction of Statutes*, 3rd ed. (Toronto: Butterworths, 1994), at p. 53)

Kennedy J. correctly found that the Town Council, "faced with a situation involving health and the environment", "was addressing a need of their community". In this manner, the municipality is attempting to fulfil its role as what the Ontario Court of Appeal has called the "trustee of the environment" *Scarborough (Borough) v. R.E.F. Homes Ltd.* (1979), 9 M.P.L.R. 255 at p. 257 (Ont. C.A.).

The appellants claim that By-law 270 is discriminatory and therefore *ultra vires* because of what they identify as impermissible distinctions that affect their commercial activities. There is no specific authority in the *C.T.A.* for these distinctions. Writing for the Court in *Sharma, supra*, at p. 668, Iacobucci J. stated the principle that:

[...] in *Fountainhead Fun Centre Ltd. v. Montréal (Ville)*, *supra*, this Court recognized that discrimination in the municipal law sense was no more permissible between than within classes (at pp. 405-6). Further, the general reasonableness or rationality of the distinction is not at issue: discrimination can only occur where the enabling legislation specifically so provides *or where the discrimination is a necessary incident to exercising the power delegated by the province* (*Fountainhead Fun Centre Ltd. v. Montréal (Ville)*, *supra*, at pp. 404-6). [Emphasis added.] [...]

Without drawing distinctions, By-law 270 could not achieve its permissible goal of aiming to improve the health of the Town's inhabitants by banning non-essential pesticide use. If all pesticide uses and users were treated alike, the protection of health and welfare would be sub-optimal. For example, withdrawing the special status given to farmers under the by-law's s. 4 would work at cross-purposes with its salubrious intent. Section 4 thus justifiably furthers the objective of By-law 270. Having held that the Town can regulate the use of pesticides, I conclude that the distinctions impugned by the appellants for restricting their businesses are necessary incidents to the power delegated by the province under s. 410(1) *C.T.A.* They are "so absolutely necessary to the exercise of those powers that [authorization has] to be found in the enabling provisions, by necessary inference or implicit delegation". *Arcade Amusements*, *supra*, at p. 414, quoted in *Greenbaum*, *supra*, at p. 695.

To conclude this section on statutory authority, I note that reading s. 410(1) to permit the Town to regulate pesticide use is consistent with principles of international law and policy. My reasons for the Court in *Baker v. Canada (Minister of Citizenship & Immigration)*, [1999] 2 S.C.R. 817 (S.C.C.), at p. 861, observed that "the values reflected in international human rights law may help inform the contextual approach to statutory interpretation and judicial review. As stated in *Driedger on the Construction of Statutes*, *supra*, at p. 330:

> [T]he legislature is presumed to respect the values and principles enshrined in international law, both customary and conventional. These constitute a part of the legal context in which legislation is enacted and read. *In so far as possible, therefore, interpretations that reflect these values and principles are preferred.* [Emphasis added.]

The interpretation of By-law 270 contained in these reasons respects international law's "precautionary principle", which is defined as follows at para. 7 of the *Bergen Ministerial Declaration on Sustainable Development* (1990):

> In order to achieve sustainable development, policies must be based on the precautionary principle. Environmental measures must anticipate, prevent and attack the causes of environmental degradation. Where there are threats of serious or irreversible damage, lack of full scientific certainty should not be used as a reason for postponing measures to prevent environmental degradation.

Canada "advocated inclusion of the precautionary principle" during the Bergen Conference negotiations (David VanderZwaag, *CEPA Issue Elaboration Paper No. 18, CEPA and the Precautionary Principle/Approach* (Ottawa: Environment Canada, 1995), at p. 8). The principle is codified in several items of domestic legislation: see, for example, the *Oceans Act*, S.C. 1996, c. 31, Preamble (para. 6); *Canadian Environmental Protection Act, 1999*, S.C. 1999, c. 33 ("*CEPA*"), s. 2(1)(a); *Endangered Species Act*, S.N.S. 1998, c. 11, ss. 2(1)(h) and 11(1).

Scholars have documented the precautionary principle's inclusion "in virtually every recently adopted treaty and policy document related to the protection and preservation of the environment" (D. Freestone and E. Hey, "Origins and Development of the Precautionary Principle", in David Freestone and Ellen Hey, eds., *The Precautionary Principle and International Law* (The Hague: Kluwer Law International, 1996), at p. 41. As a result, there may be "currently sufficient state practice to allow a good argument that the precautionary principle is a principle of customary international law" (James Cameron and Juli Abouchar, "The Status of the Precautionary Principle in International Law", in *ibid.*, at p. 52). See also Owen McIntyre and Thomas Mosedale, "The Precautionary Principle as a Norm of Customary International Law" (1997), 9 *J. Env. L.* 221, at p. 241 ("the precautionary principle has indeed crystallized into a norm of customary international law"). The Supreme Court of India considers the precautionary principle to be "part of the Customary International Law" (*A.P. Pollution Control Board v. Nayudu*, 1999 S.O.L. Case No. 53 at p. 8). See also *Vellore Citizens Welfare Forum v. Union of India*, [1996] Supp. 5 S.C.R. 241. In the context of the precautionary principle's tenets, the Town's concerns about pesticides fit well under their rubric of preventive action.

Even If the Town Had Authority to Enact It, Was By-law 270 Rendered Inoperative Because of a Conflict with Federal or Provincial Legislation?

This Court stated in *Hydro-Québec, supra*, at p. 286, that *Oldman River, supra*, "made it clear that the environment is not, as such, a subject matter of legislation under the *Constitution Act, 1867*. As it was put there, 'the *Constitution Act, 1867* has not assigned the matter of "environment" *sui generis* to either the provinces or Parliament' (p. 63). Rather, it is a diffuse subject that cuts across many different areas of constitutional responsibility, some federal, some provincial (pp. 63-64)". As there is bijurisdictional responsibility for pesticide regulation, the appellants allege conflicts between By-law 270 and both federal and provincial legislation. These contentions will be examined in turn.

Federal Legislation

The appellants argue that ss. 4(1), 4(3) and 6(1)(j) of the *Pest Control Products Act* ("*PCPA*"), and s. 45 of the *Pest Control Products Regulations* allowed them to make use of the particular pesticide products they employed in their business practices. They allege a conflict between these legislative provisions and By-law 270. In *Multiple Access Ltd. v. McCutcheon*, [1982] 2 S.C.R. 161 (S.C.C.), at p. 187, Dickson J. (later Chief Justice) for the majority of the Court reviewed the "express contradiction test" of conflict between federal and provincial legislation. At p. 191, he explained that "there would seem to be no good reasons to speak of paramountcy and preclusion except where there is actual conflict in operation as where one enactment says 'yes' and the other says 'no'; 'the same citizens are being told to do inconsistent things'; compliance with one is defiance of the other". [...] By-law 270, as a product of provincial enabling legislation, is subject to this test.

Federal legislation relating to pesticides extends to the regulation and authorization of their import, export, sale, manufacture, registration, packaging, and labelling. The *PCPA* regulates which pesticides can be registered for manufacture and/or use in Canada. This legislation is permissive, rather than exhaustive, and there is no operational conflict with By-law 270. No one is placed in an impossible situation by the legal imperative of complying with both regulatory regimes. Analogies to motor vehicles or cigarettes that have been approved federally, but the use of which can nevertheless be restricted municipally, well illustrate this conclusion. There is, moreover, no concern in this case that application of By-law 270 displaces or frustrates "the legislative purpose of Parliament". See *Multiple Access*, *supra*, at p. 190; *Bank of Montreal*, *supra*, at pp. 151 and 154.

Provincial Legislation

Multiple Access also applies to the inquiry into whether there is a conflict between the by-law and provincial legislation, except for cases (unlike this one) in which the relevant provincial legislation specifies a different test. The *Multiple Access* test, namely "impossibility of dual compliance", [...] was foreshadowed for provincial-municipal conflicts in *dicta* contained in this Court's decision in *Arcade Amusements*, *supra*, at p. 404. There, Beetz J. wrote that "otherwise valid provincial statutes which are *directly contrary* to federal statutes are rendered inoperative by that conflict. Only the same type of conflict with provincial statutes can make by-laws inoperative: Ian M. Rogers, *The Law of Canadian Municipal Corporations*, vol. 1, 2nd ed., 1971, No. 63.16" (emphasis added). [...]

Some courts have already made use of the *Multiple Access* test to examine alleged provincial-municipal conflicts. For example, [see] [...] *British Columbia Lottery Corp. v. Vancouver (City)* (1999), 169 D.L.R. (4th) 141 (B.C. C.A.), at pp. 147-148, the British Columbia Court of Appeal [...] [in this case] the court summarized the applicable standard as follows: "A true and outright conflict can only be said to arise when one enactment compels what the other forbids".

As a general principle, the mere existence of provincial (or federal) legislation in a given field does not oust municipal prerogatives to regulate the subject matter: [see]. *St-Michel Archange (Municipalité) c. 2419-6388 Québec Inc.*, [1992] R.J.Q. 875 (Que. C.A.). [...]

In this case, there is no barrier to dual compliance with By-law 270 and the *Pesticides Act*, nor any plausible evidence that the legislature intended to preclude municipal regulation of pesticide use. The *Pesticides Act* establishes a permit and licensing system for vendors and commercial applicators of pesticides and thus complements the federal legislation's focus on the products themselves. Along with By-law 270, these laws establish a tri-level regulatory regime.

According to s. 102 of the *Pesticides Act*, as it was at the time By-law 270 was passed: "The provisions of the *Pesticide Management Code* and of the other regulations of this Act prevail over any inconsistent provision of any by-law passed by a municipality or an urban community". Evidently, the *Pesticides Act* envisions the existence of complementary municipal by-laws. As Duplessis and Hétu, *supra*, at p. 109, put it, [TRANSLATION] "the Quebec legislature gave the municipalities the right to regulate pesticides, provided that the by-law was not incompatible with the regulations and the *Management Code* enacted under the *Pesticides Act*". Since no *Pesticide Management Code* has been enacted by the province under s. 105, the lower courts in this case correctly found that the by-law and the *Pesticides Act* could co-exist. In the words of the Court of Appeal, at p. 16: [TRANSLATION] "The *Pesticides Act* thus itself contemplated the existence of municipal regulation of pesticides, since it took the trouble to impose restrictions". [...]

Disposition

I have found that By-law 270 was validly enacted under s. 410(1) *C.T.A.* Moreover, the by-law does not render dual compliance with its dictates and either federal or provincial legislation impossible. For these reasons, I would dismiss the appeal with costs.

Notes and Questions

1. *Spraytech* is notable for its judicial approval of two important environmental law concepts: the subsidiarity principle and the precautionary principle. To date, few courts have elaborated upon the subsidiarity principle. There has been more judicial discussion of the precautionary principle. Indeed, jurisprudence in the Federal Court has given the precautionary principle an increasingly robust and important role in judicial review of environmental decision-making. See further discussion of this case law in Chapter 1 as discussed in the article "Trials and Tribulations of the Precautionary Principle".

Spurred on by the SCC's *Spraytech* decision and the relative inaction of Canadian municipalities when compared to counterparts in other countries, the following article explores more generally the powers available to municipalities in Canada to deal with environmental issues.

Howard M. Epstein,
"Subsidiarity at Work — The Legal Context for Sustainability
Initiatives at the Local Government Level: How an Environmental
Agenda Could Be Advanced by Canadian Municipalities"
(2009) Municipal and Planning Law Reports (Articles) 4th series

Introduction

[...] [T]here is enormous potential to transform how we live our lives through exercise of the appropriate powers at the municipal level. In this context, transformation refers to adoption of a serious sustainability agenda. There are well-known examples in the world where municipal leadership has the effect of moving communities towards sustainability. In New York, taxis that have to be decommissioned are to be replaced by hybrids. In Lund, Sweden, a community of some 98,000 person population, approximately 85% of the apartment houses are connected to district heating, 30% of which is generated from geothermics. In the UK, London has had a Metropolitan Green Belt for almost 75 years, and has recently put in place special fees for cars entering the urban core. In Mexico City, a similar vehicle control programme exists, known as 'hoy no circula' or 'one day without a car'; only vehicles with license plates ending in the designated number are allowed on the various days. [...] In Berlin, the inner city is an 'environment zone' where only cars meeting certain emissions standards are allowed.

Even recognizing that distance may increase the apparent beauty of other's policies or laws, by way of contrast, Canadian municipalities have a relatively undistinguished record when it comes to sustainability initiatives. No significant sized population centre in Canada has a comprehensive range of programmes. The emphasis seems to be, where programmes do exist, on limiting them to municipally-owned property or on voluntary compliance by the private sector. To the extent that any similar initiatives exist, they tend to be established at the provincial level. Analysts have suggested that Canada's environmental footprint is really the equivalent of almost all of India's, a nation with some 30 to 40 times our population. Those are national figures. The municipal record is undistinguished in comparison not only with the possibilities demonstrated in other places to be achievable, but in comparison with the global need, in comparison with Canada's notorious wastefulness, and, as I hope to demonstrate, in comparison with what the law now lends itself to. [...]

For the most part, it is the two senior levels of government that have taken responsibility for environmental issues. In part this reflects the financial capacity to do so compared with municipalities, and in part it reflects the undoubted ambit of their jurisdiction over the environment. Is it technically feasible, then, for all matters relating to the environment to simply be left to the federal and provincial governments? Would such an arrangement make sense?

Clearly it is legally possible for the senior levels of government to take full and exclusive responsibility for all environmental matters. But if they did so it would bring into question the very rationale for local government at all. As a matter of basic Constitutional law there is nothing a municipality can do that the province creating it could not also do, since the municipalities are mere creatures of statute. And if the federal government were inclined to devise national land use policies for the purpose of dealing with environmental matters and want to administer them, it might be able to find a Constitutional basis for doing so, especially if it were to make out a case for a pressing national concern as it might for example be able to do over climate change on the basis of provincial inability to take appropriate measures. The federal government does already exercise significant land use and land use planning powers emanating from its Constitution-assigned heads of power; aeronautics, communications, the National Capital Commission, and harbour lands are all well-known examples. What has occurred, though, is that the senior levels of government have tended to address point sources of pollution and major projects, and have left it to local government to address non-point sources. To take an example: the federal government regulates effluent from pulp and paper mills, a matter of water quality. Provincial governments regulate emissions from electricity generating plants, a matter of air quality. But in their day-to-day decisions about land use planning, municipalities make decisions that affect the establishment of residential subdivisions and thus pressure on aquifers; they also make decisions that affect transportation use and thus of necessity emissions from vehicles; a municipality that allows sprawl thereby allows more vehicle traffic and thereby allows more air pollution and GHG emissions. [...]

The prevailing legal regulatory system for the environment in Canada remains tri-level. In 1997 La Forest J. wrote in *Canada c. Hydro-Québec* that "the protection of the environment is a major challenge of our time. It is an international problem, one that requires action by *governments at all levels*." This statement, with the emphasis added, was quoted by L'Heureux-Dube J. in *Spray-Tech*. But *Spray-Tech* has not settled all legal issues associated with local government powers over the environment. The subject is an entangled one and could evolve both in terms of statutory provisions and court decisions. My purpose here is to survey the current state-of-play over municipal powers. [...]

Land Use Law and Environmental Law

Primarily, municipal powers are powers over land use. How far does land use law overlap with environmental law? To what extent would environmentally beneficial initiatives such as those international examples just mentioned, have legal sanction if adopted by a Canadian municipality? In part, such questions are approached as a matter of statutory interpretation, i.e. whether the provincial government intended to grant the particular power to local governments, and in some instances as a matter of constitutional law, i.e. whether a particular power is exclusively federal rather than provincial and therefore able to be assigned through legislation to local government.

There is an active discussion of both the theoretical and practical interaction of land use law and environmental law. Some older Canadian cases have suggested that there is a limited power for local governments to address environmental issues, a view that has, in some instances, persisted; however, the predominant view is that there are certainly some relevant local government powers. The SCC has recognized a municipal concern for protecting natural resources as a legitimate purpose, thus making it highly unlikely that any attack on municipal sustainability measures on the basis of improper purpose or malice (along the lines of the principles of *Roncarelli v. Duplessis* could be made out on a philosophical basis alone, i.e. absent special circumstances. It is also the case that judicial recognition of local government jurisdiction over environmental matters involves a submerged Constitutional issue, that is, the placement of 'environment' as a head of power in a written constitution that did not contemplate it when first enacted in 1867. Thus, decisions such as *Spray-Tech* involve an assumption that the particular environmental matter being addressed by the municipality is a legitimate provincial power as a matter of Constitutional law. [...]

Is there a difference between land use law and environmental law, and if so is this an instance of a distinction without a difference or are any of the distinctions truly useful? Duplessis and Hetu say: "Il n'existe pas de distinction fondamentale entre le droit de l'environnement et le droit de l'amenagement du territoire, les deux domains etant intimement relies." It is not necessary here to go into a full analysis of the topic of environmental law. Suffice it to say that conceptually it is possible to think of the topic as dealing with three p's: preservation, projects, and pollution. Of course more, and extensive, elaboration is possible. Environmental Law is regulatory in that it sets standards. A crucial feature is its allowance for evaluation of proposed specific projects in advance of their start, i.e.

environmental assessment. It also embodies certain principles such as stewardship, ecosystem focus, the precautionary principle, and polluter pays. [...]

Planning and environmental law both proceed from a policy stance that overrides traditional conceptions of private property rights. That is, they both counter any notion that private ownership allows complete freedom of action on privately owned land. It is certainly the case that the common law has always recognized external limits, in the form of nuisance law or the rule in *Rylands v. Fletcher*, the result being that owners have to behave in ways that take into account that they are part of a community, that they have neighbours who may suffer the consequences of what may appear to be private decisions. The common law focus is on present relations among nearby landowners. But land use planning and environmental law go further, and explicitly take into account intergenerational equity. They both take the stance that it is not open to an owner to commit waste, broadly understood. Avoiding present transboundary environmental impacts is a minimum requirement; future impacts, both inside and outside the owner's metes and bounds demesne, form the focus of both schemes of regulation. Nonetheless, it often appears that land use law is more about the present than about the future, certainly in comparison with the full array of environmental law, which is just as firmly focused on the long-range as on the present. [...]

In sum, land use law and environmental law are historically intertwined through their origins in the common law of nuisance; they retain significant similar features such as a focus on planning for the future, avoidance of the juxtaposition of incompatible uses, and public involvement in their processes. At the same time municipalities are inherently more parochial in the geographic ambit of their authority than are the senior levels of government. So far as the necessity of making conceptual distinctions between the two, the question primarily arises in constitutional litigation which so far has been relatively sparse in Canada although it may prove more significant as energy regulation evolves; the view of the courts has been that there is no bright line distinction, so results of future disputes are extremely uncertain.

Overview of Municipal Environmental Powers

[...] It is my purpose to suggest that given the typical array of powers now granted by the provinces to their municipalities, what is required is the dedication of local government political officials to use those powers in ways that are designed to advance a sustainability objective. Little more. For no entirely clear reason, local governments have been slow to adapt their thinking. To take a very striking example, consider the topic of transportation.

Local governments are usually assigned powers that allow them to design transportation systems. Traditionally, this power has been used to build, maintain and expand road systems. What elected officials and their staff believe they have been doing is creating infrastructure to service the community. Undoubtedly, this is true. But if urban sprawl is a problem, then the very same powers that allow a municipality to construct a road system could be used not to expand that system, but, rather, to invest in public transit, to promote pedestrian activity, cycling, carpooling, and any other alternatives to the typical single-passenger private automobile. What is potentially particularly attractive about such a revised mode of thinking is that a municipality of even moderate size will likely have long-range plans for expansion of its road system over the coming decades, and cancelling such plans will free up the funds for any necessary investments in alternatives. Does the legal framework exist to allow such changes to take place? For a relatively explicit matter such as transportation, the answer is clearly 'yes', but as initiatives become less seen as connected with the usual range of local government matters, the legal aspects can become a bit more complicated.

Conclusion and Limitations

Our starting point was the observation that there are considerable powers available under existing legislation to enable local governments to move aggressively towards putting in place sustainability measures. I hope this has been demonstrated. At the same time, despite the wide ambit of local government powers, there are real limitations. Central to many of the cases on municipal jurisdiction is the problem of their interaction with the regulatory powers of other levels of government. It will not always be the case that local government powers can legally coexist with the regulatory powers of the province or the federal government, and in those instances will have to give way. The main limitations on municipal powers over environmental/sustainability matters tend to be on account of the Constitutional separation of powers, on account of direct conflicts with other valid legislation, or on account of explicit legislated exclusion of municipal jurisdiction. [...]

Leading by example, public education, formal studies, round tables, and varieties of political advocacy all have their place in any government's engagement with environmental issues. The advantage of regulation is that it goes forward through a public process that inherently involves research and education, and has the potential to have wide practical effect. But it is just one of a variety of available tools. [...]

In the planning of our communities, the overall situation is the same as with so many other areas of human activity such as agriculture, the fishery, forestry, mining, or energy: in virtually all instances we know a much better way of going about our business. [...] As with so many areas of human endeavour, the barriers to change are not the absence of knowledge of better ways to shape our lives; the barriers tend to be the self-imposed adherence to the status quo. It is time to let go of an outdated mode of thinking, and try to manage change before it is forced upon us by disastrous external forces. The legal tools are in place.

Notes and Questions

1. As part of the effort to reduce GHG emissions and diversify sources of energy, many jurisdictions in Canada have taken steps to promote the installation of wind turbines. Local opposition in some jurisdictions has led some municipalities to consider their ability to control whether, where and under what conditions wind turbines can be installed within the boundaries of their municipality. In light of the *Spraytech* case and the article above, take a look at relevant legislation in your province to consider the powers of

municipalities to control wind power installations. Be sure to consider both the powers specifically granted to municipalities and the extent to which your province is exercising direct regulatory control over this issue.

2. What are some other activities with associated environmental concerns in your province that municipalities might be interested in regulating? Air pollution from industrial activities, mining, shale gas developments and various farming activities are among the issues municipalities in Canada are interested in controlling to protect the interests of their residents and to protect the environment. Explore an issue that is currently being publicly debated in your province and consider the potential for municipalities to control or prevent the activity in question.

Part V — Case Study:
Trans Mountain Pipeline Expansion Project

Overview

Over the past several years, one of the most contentious and interesting jurisdictional disputes in Canada has centred on the proposed Trans Mountain pipeline expansion project ("TMX"). The original proponent of this project was Trans Mountain Pipeline ULC ("Trans Mountain"). Kinder Morgan Inc., a Texas-based oil company, was one of Trans Mountain's majority owners. In 2018, in an apparent attempt to quell uncertainties surrounding the project's future, the federal government purchased the project from its former owners for $4.5 billion.

The stated purpose of the project is to update and "twin" an existing pipeline from the Alberta oil sands to a coastal terminus in the City of Burnaby. The project would significantly increase the amount of heavy oil (bitumen) transported through the pipeline from 300,000 to 890,000 barrels per day and would increase the tanker traffic from the Burnaby terminal from 60 to more than 400 tankers per year. Trans Mountain claims that the project will allow for Alberta oil to be exposed to new markets in Asia, and command better prices than is currently possible. Project opponents have raised various concerns, including pipeline and tanker traffic safety, climate impacts, inadequacies and uncertainties associated with the federal assessment and approval process, and the potential that the project will infringe constitutionally protected Aboriginal rights and title.

Interprovincial pipelines are regulated by the National Energy Board ("NEB"). In December 2013, Trans Mountain applied to the NEB for regulatory approval. From the outset, the NEB process was highly controversial. Under new rules enacted by the Harper government, the NEB was given authority not only to provide regulatory approval under the *National Energy Board Act* ("NEB Act"), but also to conduct an environmental assessment under the *Canadian Environmental Assessment Act, 2012*. Numerous First Nations and BC municipalities criticized the scope and adequacy of the NEB's assessment, including its decision not to hold an oral hearing into the application or to allow cross-examination of evidence adduced by Trans Mountain.

During the federal election of 2015, the Trudeau Liberals were highly critical of the NEB process and promised reforms aimed at restoring public trust in major project approvals if elected. Despite this, based on the NEB's May 2016 recommendation that the project be approved, in late 2016 a newly elected Trudeau government gave the project the go-ahead. And, in January 2017, the British Columbia government of Christy Clark — relying on the NEB's assessment and recommendations — did likewise. This decision prompted a public outcry that led, at least in part, to the defeat of the Clark government at the polls in May 2017 and the election of an NDP government led by John Horgan. With the support of the Green Party, the NDP pledged to use "every tool in the toolbox" to oppose the TMX project which, despite having received the BC government's approval in principle, still required hundreds of construction and operating permits.

In the face of mounting controversy, Trans Mountain issued an ultimatum in April 2018, suspending all non-essential spending and warning that it would terminate the project unless a satisfactory resolution of outstanding regulatory issues was reached by May 31, 2018. On May 29, 2018, to appease the Alberta government upon which it was relying to implement its pan-Canadian climate agreement, the federal government agreed to purchase the pipeline from Kinder Morgan for $4.5 billion. Meanwhile, the BC government announced its intention to enact new regulations governing the transport of heavy oil and other hazardous goods within the province through amendments to BC's *Environmental Management Act*. To this end, it submitted a reference question to the BC Court of Appeal seeking clarification of its jurisdiction to pass such legislation. The governments of Alberta, Canada and various other intervenors have joined in this case, which is expected to be heard in 2019.

The most recent development in this fast-moving story is the decision of the Federal Court of Appeal in the consolidated appeal of close to a dozen separate challenges to the federal Cabinet's decision, based on the NEB's report and recommendations, to approve the TMX pipeline. Defying the predictions of many, the FCA struck down the approval on two grounds: *Tsleil-Waututh Nation v. Canada (Attorney General)*, 2018 FCA 153, additional reasons 2018 FCA 155. The first was that the NEB had erred in scoping marine traffic out of its environmental assessment of the project, causing it to fail to properly inquire into the impacts of the project on Southern Resident Orcas, and ultimately depriving Cabinet of the evidence it needed to decide the project's fate. The second flaw related to the so-called "Phase III" consultations undertaken by the federal government with affected Indigenous nations following receipt of the NEB report. The FCA concluded that government officials approached these consultations as "notetakers", who saw their task as simply recording First Nations' concerns and transmitting them to Cabinet. In the court's view, consultation required meaningful dialogue, something missing from the Phase III process.

In an ironic turn, the deal the federal government negotiated to buy the project formally closed the day after the FCA decision was released, having secured an over 99% approval from Kinder Morgan shareholders. Alberta's reaction to the FCA decision also followed swiftly. Less than 24 hours after the decision, Premier Notley declared the *Pan-Canadian Framework Agreement* "not worth the paper it was printed on" and gave notice that her province would be exiting the agreement effective immediately until such time as the federal government "got its act together".

_____

Scope of Municipal Jurisdiction

A key battleground in the fight over the pipeline has been at the municipal level. The City of Burnaby, the municipality where the terminus is located, strongly opposed the project from the beginning. This has caused friction, as Trans Mountain has required access to the City's property to complete the project. On August 19, 2014 the NEB issued Ruling No. 28, confirming Trans Mountain had power to enter Crown or privately owned lands, without the consent of the owner, to "make surveys, examinations or other necessary arrangement on the land for fixing the site of the pipeline". Later that month Trans Mountain began work on Burnaby Mountain Conservation Area. Burnaby alleged that this violated City bylaws, and on September 2, 2014 issued an Order to Cease Bylaw Contravention to Trans Mountain. In response, Trans Mountain applied for a ruling from the NEB confirming that the NEB had jurisdiction to find Burnaby's bylaws invalid, inapplicable or inoperative, and asked the NEB to make such a ruling on the facts. In Ruling No. 40, the NEB granted all orders sought by Trans Mountain.

On the question of jurisdiction, the NEB stated that it had "legal authority to consider constitutional questions relating to its own jurisdiction and this is such a question" (p. 7). The NEB then considered whether the impugned municipal bylaws were invalid, inapplicable or inoperative. To this end, it considered the status of the impugned bylaws under both the paramountcy and interjurisdictional immunity ("IJI") doctrines. The NEB stated that the impugned bylaws had the effect of frustrating or conflicting with the purpose or operation of the enabling federal statute. Specifically, the Board found that the impugned bylaws conflicted with powers given to Trans Mountain to collect information for the process of assessing the feasibility of proposed projects on City property. Burnaby's impugned bylaws, therefore, were inoperative insofar as they conflicted with the *NEB Act* by virtue of federal paramountcy.

The NEB also found that the bylaws were inapplicable by the interjurisdictional immunity doctrine. IJI is activated when an impugned law trenches into the core jurisdictional competence of another legislative body (thus far it has only been applied where provinces trench into federal jurisdiction). The NEB held that regulations relating to the location of interprovincial pipelines fell within the core competence of Parliament over interprovincial trade, a jurisdiction that Parliament vested in the NEB. Accordingly, the impugned municipal bylaws which impaired the NEB's ability to consider the appropriate routing of the pipeline impermissibly intruded into the core of federal jurisdiction.

Burnaby unsuccessfully sought leave to appeal Ruling No. 40 at the Federal Court of Appeal. Burnaby also challenged Ruling No. 40 in the BC Supreme

Court: *Burnaby (City) v. Trans Mountain Pipeline ULC*, 2015 BCSC 2140, affirmed 2017 BCCA 132 ("*Burnaby*").

At the BCSC, Burnaby argued that the NEB had improperly made a declaration of general invalidity *vis-à-vis* the impugned bylaws. Conversely, Trans Mountain asserted that the Court should refrain from exercising its jurisdiction, as the issue had previously been litigated in an appropriate arena and Burnaby had subsequently been denied leave to appeal. In the alternative, Trans Mountain argued that the NEB had only made a limited declaration of invalidity, and that such a ruling was within the jurisdiction of the NEB. While the Court agreed with Burnaby that only provincial and territorial superior courts can make general declarations of invalidity, it found that the NEB had only "made a *limited* declaration in relation to the matter before it, determining that the bylaws did not apply to Trans Mountain work" (para. 35, emphasis in original). Moreover, the Court was reluctant to relitigate the constitutional issues, stating that the result would be "likely chaotic" if the Court's judgment was inconsistent with that of the NEB (para. 44). In *obiter*, the Court noted that if it were necessary to make a ruling as to the validity of the impugned bylaws, it would have concurred with the NEB's use of paramountcy and interjurisdictional immunity. The Court stated that while co-operative federalism has increased in salience in recent jurisprudence, "one legal regime needs to prevail over the other where there is a conflict", and that "[o]ur law makes clear that it is the federal regime which is paramount" (para. 76).

In October 2017, Trans Mountain again petitioned the NEB, this time seeking relief from Certificate Condition 2, which stipulated that Trans Mountain must comply with all municipal bylaws throughout the expansion project. Trans Mountain sought an order that would relieve them of the requirement to follow the bylaws. The NEB granted the order sought. While it reiterated the views it expressed in Ruling No. 40, this time the NEB went further, finding that Burnaby had not been acting in good faith to issue the permits in a timely manner, and concluding that it was in the public interest to relieve Trans Mountain of its responsibilities under Certificate Condition 2. Both the Province and Burnaby sought to appeal this October 2017 NEB ruling, but were denied leave by the FCA on March 23, 2018.

Notes and Questions

1. Under the NEB's approach, what authority does Burnaby have to regulate in relation to the pipeline or within the pipeline corridor?

2. To what extent does *Burnaby* align with the approach adopted by the NEB in Ruling No. 40? To what extent does it differ from the NEB?

3. What are the key differences between NEB Ruling No. 40 and its October 2017 ruling?

4. Consider the use of paramountcy and IJI in *Burnaby*. Does it differ from the approach set out by the SCC in *Tsilhqot'in*?

5. Compare and contrast the approach to federalism set out in these rulings and cases with the approach set out in *Spraytech* by L'Heureux-Dubé J.

Judicial Review of Provincial Government Action

Kinder Morgan's Trans Mountain Expansion proposal has triggered significant litigation against both federal and provincial administrative and regulatory bodies. In the provincial arena, these judicial reviews have challenged the adequacy of the province's environmental assessment of the project and of the province's consultation with First Nations affected by the project.

The environment is an area of shared jurisdiction between federal and provincial governments. Under the principles of co-operative federalism, both levels of government are encouraged to collaborate in the regulation of undertakings affecting the environment. Environmental assessment is one such area. In BC, the enabling statute is the BC *Environmental Assessment Act* ("BCEAA"). The federal counterpart is the *Canadian Environmental Assessment Act, 2012* ("CEAA 2012"). Both statutes are validly enacted within the jurisdiction of their respective legislatures and empower provincial and federal Ministers to conduct environmental assessments prior to the issuance of project-specific permits or certificates.

On June 21, 2010 the Executive Director of the BC Environmental Assessment Office (EAO) entered into an Equivalency Agreement with the NEB regarding all reviewable projects requiring approval from both bodies. In the agreement, the EAO accepted that any NEB assessment of a project constitutes an equivalent assessment under the BCEAA, therefore eliminating any requirement for assessment by the EAO and the need for a provincial Environmental Assessment Certificate (EAC) to be granted.

In *Coastal First Nations - Great Bear Initiative Society v. British Columbia (Minister of Environment)*, 2016 BCSC 34, additional reasons 2016 BCSC 804 ("*CFN*"), Coastal First Nations (the petitioners) alleged that the decision of the Executive Director of the EAO to enter into the Equivalency Agreement was invalid on two grounds. First, they argued that while the BCEAA does provide the authority for co-operation to avoid duplication or redundancy, the *Act* does not allow for the province to abdicate its responsibility to make decisions regarding the issuance of EACs. Therefore, the Executive Director's decision not to make a determination was *ultra vires*. Second, they argued that there is a constitutional obligation on the part of the provincial Crown to consult with First Nations before engaging in any activity that may affect First Nations' rights. The CFN claimed that the Province had a duty to consult with First Nations prior to entering into the Agreement, as it allowed the Province to circumvent its obligation to make future determinations, thus avoiding any future consultation. In response, Northern Gateway Pipeline ("NGP"), which at the time was proposing to construct a pipeline that was subject to the Agreement, argued that the paramountcy and IJI doctrines should be applied in this case, citing *Burnaby* as clearly establishing interprovincial pipelines as federal undertakings. As a result, NGP claimed that any requirement to comply with a Provincial environment assessment process would be unconstitutional.

The Court sided with the petitioners. It ruled that it was premature to conclude that provincial EA requirements were unconstitutional absent actual project-specific regulations or approval conditions that were clearly beyond provincial jurisdiction. The only live constitutional issue, according to the Court, was whether section 17 of the BCEAA, which empowered the EAO to issue a project certificate upon completion of an assessment, is *ultra vires* the Province's jurisdiction over the environment. In this regard the Court dismissed NGP's IJI and paramountcy arguments, stating that "[t]he fact that s. 17 of the [BCEAA] affects a federal undertaking is not enough to demonstrate that the provision is unconstitutional; NGP must establish that the legislation's effects on federal powers render it inapplicable or inoperable", and "[t]o make out the doctrine of paramountcy the respondents must show either a conflict between the provincial and federal legislation such that 'compliance with one is defiance of the other', or, if dual compliance is possible, that provincial legislation frustrates the purpose of the federal statute" (para. 57).

The Court also concurred with the petitioners' claim that the Province had abdicated its responsibility to conduct environmental assessments, stating that the objective of the BCEAA is to protect the environment and advance the economic interests of British Columbia, and therefore that "it cannot be the intention of the legislators to allow the voice of British Columbia to be removed in this process for an unknown number of projects, when the purpose behind the [BCEAA] is to promote economic interest in this province, and to protect its land and environment" (para. 178). Finally, on the issue of duty to consult, the Court held that the Province did not have a duty to consult prior to entering into the agreement, as the link between entering into the agreement and the possibility of First Nations' rights being infringed by an unknown future project was not sufficient. The Court found, however, that the Province breached its duty to consult by failing to consult with the CFN prior to deciding not to terminate the Agreement, as this decision was tantamount to accepting the federal process wherein the CFN was not consulted.

Following this decision, the BC government did conduct its own, perfunctory EA which consisted of essentially reviewing and adopting the report of the NEB. It also carried out a consultation with First Nations, and then immediately re-approved the project. In response, the City of Vancouver and the Squamish Nation filed suits against the Province. Both were dismissed by the BC Supreme Court.

In *Squamish Nation v. British Columbia (Environment)*, 2018 BCSC 844, the petitioner alleged that the process of consultation undertaken by the Crown prior to issuance of an EAC to Trans Mountain was not sufficient to satisfy the honour of the Crown, and that the Crown could not have reasonably concluded, as it did, that its duty to consult and accommodate had been met. The Court rejected this claim, finding that the Crown had indeed met its duty to consult throughout the process. The Court pointed to inclusion of conditions to the EAC which had been raised by Squamish Nation as evidence of this process. Moreover, the Court stated that the Province did not necessarily have to accommodate all concerns of First Nations, and that the Province had explicitly acknowledged First Nations' concerns in its reasons for decision and explained why the EAC was issued with conditions despite such concerns.

In *Vancouver (City) v. British Columbia (Environment)*, 2018 BCSC 843, the petitioner alleged that the Province did not engage in sufficient public consultation, thus breaching the duty of procedural fairness and failing to follow the process set out in the BCEAA. Because of this failure, Vancouver alleged the Province did not conduct a proper assessment and failed to consider appropriate conditions. The Court dismissed the claims of procedural unfairness and found that the decision and the process fell within the scope of reasonable outcomes. This decision was largely informed by the constitutional jurisdiction of the province in the matter. In *CFN*, the Court found that because the pipeline is a federal undertaking, the Province does not have the power to say "no" through the EA process, but may say "yes, with some conditions". As a result, the Court found that the Province was tightly limited in the stringency of conditions that could be applied. Accordingly, the Minister's decision was found to be within the range of reasonable outcomes.

Notes and Questions

1. How broadly should the *ratio* in *CFN* be read? The BCSC held that the BC government erred by failing to make its own decision following the EA of the project. Does this mean that provinces must always reach their own independent decision following EAs within their jurisdiction?

2. The BC government did not appeal the decision in *CFN,* and instead took the Court's advice about making its own decision. In reaching this decision, the BC government relied entirely on the EA done by the NEB, a process that was widely considered to be highly deficient, including by the BC government itself. The approach followed by BC following *CFN* was challenged by Vancouver and Squamish Nation. What explains why both of these suits were unsuccessful? What were the key factors that explained the judge's decision in these cases? What does this tell us about the procedural rights and constitutional rights of citizens and First Nations seeking to overturn a discretionary government decision?

Challenges to Federal Pipeline Approval:
Pipelines and the Division of Powers Going Forward

Controversy surrounding the NEB's assessment process and the subsequent federal government project approval has also triggered significant litigation. In October 2017, fifteen distinct legal challenges to these federal approvals were argued before the FCA in a lengthy consolidated hearing.

A key theme of many of First Nations applicants' arguments was that each First Nation was owed a process of open-minded consultation with the Crown. Many contended that the fact that no NEB conditions were changed or added following the consultation process subsequent to the Board's recommendation was indicative of the fact that the Crown was paying lip service to this obligation.

The City of Burnaby argued that the process was unreasonable, that the NEB did not produce a valid report in compliance with the CEAA 2012 and the *NEB Act*, and therefore that Cabinet's decision made based on the report must be overturned. Burnaby cited the NEB's failure to consider alternative locations for the marine terminal and its decision to defer collection of information on certain risks until after Cabinet had issued its decision as indicative of the unreasonableness of the process. Moreover, Burnaby argued that the unreasonableness of the decision was exacerbated by procedural issues, including refusal to allow cross-examination of evidence, refusal to require Trans Mountain to address missing evidence, and failure to provide adequate reasons for the decision. Conversely, Canada argued that consultation with First Nations was indeed adequate, and that the factors outlined in *Gitxaala Nation v. Canada*, 2016 FCA 187, leave to appeal refused *R. v. Raincoast Conservation Foundation*, 2017 CarswellNat 263 (S.C.C.), which had rendered that process unconstitutional were not repeated in the TMX review process. Furthermore, Canada and Trans Mountain each argued that the process was robust and complete and that there was no basis on which to allege a lack of procedural fairness. Ultimately, as discussed elsewhere in this book (see Part V Overview, above, Chapter 6 (judicial review), and Chapter 9 (species at risk)), the Federal Court of Appeal upheld challenges to the project's Cabinet approval on two grounds. The first was that the NEB had erred in scoping marine traffic out of its environmental assessment of the project, causing it to fail to properly inquire into the impacts of the project on Southern Resident Orcas, and ultimately depriving Cabinet of the evidence it needed to decide the project's fate. The second flaw related to the so-called "Phase III" consultations undertaken by the federal government with affected Indigenous nations following receipt of the NEB report.

Meanwhile, TMX's opponents to the proposed project gained a powerful ally in June 2017, when the BC NDP formed government with the support of the Green Party, bringing Premier John Horgan into power. Both the NDP and Green Party had run campaigns opposing the Trans Mountain Expansion project and promised to use "every tool available" to halt it. In January 2018, the new government announced it would investigate regulating the pipeline. Soon after, it announced that it would file a reference question to the BC Court of Appeal seeking confirmation that it had jurisdiction to regulate the flow of heavy oils such as bitumen within the province.

The proposed amendments to the *Environmental Management Act* would empower the BC government to require companies or persons to secure permits before moving, shipping or possessing listed hazardous substances above a specified quantity. The draft bill applies not only to the TMX project, but to any carrier that is involved in the transportation of hazardous substances through the province of British Columbia by pipeline, rail or other means. It is unclear whether the legislation is intended to impose new construction or operational related safety requirements on new or existing pipelines, for instance, early spills detection equipment or spills shut-off valve requirements. BC Attorney General David Eby stated that "[o]ur goal from the beginning is to ensure that we are actually exercising the full extent of our jurisdiction, the full extent of our authority". The provincial governments of Alberta and Saskatchewan were granted intervenor status in the case, as well as the Government of Canada. The BC government referred the following three questions to the BC Court of Appeal:

1. Is it within the legislative authority of the Legislature of British Columbia to enact legislation substantially in the form set out [...]?

2. If the answer to question 1 is yes, would the attached legislation be applicable to hazardous substances brought into British Columbia by means of interprovincial undertakings?

3. If the answers to questions 1 and 2 are yes, would existing federal legislation render all or part of the attached legislation inoperative?

The Alberta government has been particularly agitated over the Horgan government's unwillingness to green-light the Trans Mountain Project as currently proposed. It has taken various steps to turn up the heat on BC, including banning the import of BC wines, and threatening to shut off the flow of Alberta oil products to BC. On May 29, 2018, in response to an ultimatum by Trans Mountain seeking immediate resolution of all outstanding issues, the federal government announced that it had negotiated a deal to buy the Trans Mountain Pipeline and TMX Project from Trans Mountain for $4.5 billion.

Notes and Questions

1. What are the key features of the proposed legislation that the BC government is relying on to support its jurisdiction over the pipeline?

2. Based on what you have learned in this chapter, what are the key constitutional arguments that are likely to be raised in support of the draft legislation, and what are likely to be mounted against it? How do you expect the BC Court of Appeal to rule? In what ways might the case ultimately augment or clarify the jurisprudence with respect to constitutional division of powers?

3. In a recent article noted earlier in this chapter, Professor Olszynski predicts that the reference will fail: see "Testing the Jurisdictional Waters: The Provincial Regulation of Interprovincial Pipelines" (2018) 23 Rev. Const. Stud. 91. While he concedes that the proposed provincial law is likely *intra vires* the province in pith and substance, he expects that the BCCA will find that the proposed BC law conflicts with federal law, and will declare the BC law inoperative under the paramountcy doctrine and inapplicable to interprovincial pipelines under the IJI doctrine.

   With respect to paramountcy, he concedes that it is not impossible to comply with both the new provincial law and the existing NEB regulations. However, in his view, the federal NEB regulatory regime is "comprehensive" in its coverage. Accordingly, "it seems plain that legislation that second-guesses a substantial part of that regime (i.e. spill assessment, prevention, response, financial assurance, and liability) and purports to authorize a recalibration of the risk assessment made by the NEB frustrates Parliament's purpose".

Likewise, he argues that the provincial law offends the IJI doctrine. This is because, in his view, the various spills-related components of the BC law (spill assessment, prevention, response, financial assurance and liability) collectively recalibrate the "economics of a project" and accordingly will "be deemed to fall within the protected core of Parliament's jurisdiction over interjurisdictional pipelines".

What does Professor Olszynski mean when he says that the BC law "second-guesses" the federal one? Does second-guess mean the same thing as "frustrate" for the purposes of the paramountcy doctrine? And when (if at all) do provincial measures that "recalibrate" or affect the economics of a federal work or undertaking constitute an impairment of an essential aspect of that work or undertaking sufficient to justify judicial invocation of the IJI doctrine?

References and Further Readings

N. Bankes, "Water Management Planning and the Crown's Duty to Consult and Accommodate: A Comment on *Tsuu T'ina First Nation v. Alberta*" (2008) 103 Resources 1

J. Benidickson, *Environmental Law*, 5th ed. (Toronto: Irwin Law, 2019)

S. Blackman, *et al.*, "The Evolution of Federal/Provincial Relations in Natural Resource Management" (1994) 32 Alta. L. Rev. 511

L. M. Collins & M. Murtha, "Indigenous Environmental Rights in Canada: The Right to Conservation Implicit in Treaty and Aboriginal Rights to Hunt, Fish, And Trap" (2010) 47 Alta. L. Rev. 959

D.C. Cole *et al.*, "Municipal bylaw to reduce cosmetic/non-essential pesticide use on household lawns — a policy implementation evaluation" (2011) 10 Environmental Health 1

S. Deimann, "*R. v. Hydro-Quebec*: Federal Environmental Regulation as Criminal Law" (1998) 43 McGill L.J. 923

M. Doelle, "CEAA, New Uncertainties, But a Step in the Right Direction" (1994) 4 J. Envtl. L. & Prac. 59

M. Doelle, *The Federal Environmental Assessment Process: A Guide and Critique* (Markham: LexisNexis Butterworths, 2008)

P. Emond, "The Case for a Greater Federal Role in the Environmental Protection Field: An Examination of the Pollution Problem and the Constitution" (1972) 10 Osgoode Hall L.J. 647

Howard M. Epstein, "Subsidiarity at Work — The Legal Context for Sustainability Initiatives at the Local Government Level: How an Environmental Agenda Could Be Advanced by Canadian Municipalities" (2009) Municipal and Planning Law Reports (Articles) 4th series

D. Gibson, "Constitutional Jurisdiction over Environmental Management in Canada" (1973) 23 U.T.L.J. 54

J. Hanebury, "Environmental Impact Assessment and the Constitution: The Never-Ending Story" (1999) 9 J. Envtl. L. & Prac. 169

K. Harrison, *Passing the Buck: Federalism and Canadian Environmental Policy* (Vancouver: UBC Press, 1996)

B. Hobby, *et al.*, eds., *Canadian Environmental Assessment Act: An Annotated Guide* (Aurora: Canada Law Book, 1995)

S.A. Kennett, "Federal Environmental Jurisdiction after *Oldman*" (1993) 38 McGill L.J. 180

A.W. MacKay, "The Supreme Court of Canada and Federalism: Does/ Should Anyone Care Anymore?" (2001) 80 Can. Bar Rev. 241

W.R. MacKay, "Canadian Federalism and the Environment: The Literature" (2004) 17 Geo. Int'l. Envtl. L. Rev. 25. Reprinted with permission of the publisher, Georgetown International Environmental Law Review: 2004

M. Olszynski, "Testing the Jurisdictional Waters: The Provincial Regulation of Interprovincial Pipelines" (2018) 23 Rev. Const. Stud. 91

J. Reynolds, *Aboriginal Peoples of Canada* (UBC Press, 2018)

M. Warkentin, "*Friends of the Oldman River Society v. Canada (Minister of Transport)*" (1992) 26 U.B.C. L. Rev. 313

Chapter 4

Environmental Regulation

Introduction

This chapter provides an overview and critical analysis of the topic of environmental regulation. The breadth and complexity of this topic makes it a daunting one for environmental law students and instructors alike. It is also an area in which, particularly in the realm of industrial pollution and climate change impacts, the public has a strong appetite to see governments play a more rigorous and effective regulatory role than they have to date. While there appears to be a consensus that governments need to do more to protect the environment, there is also a broad sense that regulatory approaches employed in the past need to be revisited. Indeed, as we discuss shortly, many scholars and policy-makers claim that we need to radically rethink how we regulate to achieve desired environmental outcomes.

Recent years have been tumultuous for Canadian environmental regulation, particularly at the federal level. In 2012, the Harper government introduced and ultimately secured passage of a package of sweeping reforms. The centrepiece of this reform package was Bill C-38. To a large extent, these reforms were motivated by a desire to reduce red tape and delays associated with the approvals of major new resource development projects with a view to getting oil and gas exports to new and more lucrative world markets. To this end, Bill C-38 repealed and replaced the *Canadian Environmental Assessment Act* ("CEAA 1995") with a far more discretionary and industry-friendly law: see Chapter 7. The reforms also dramatically reduced the protections for fish and fish habitat contained in the *Fisheries Act* and repealed the *Navigable Waters Protection Act*.

These reforms had an immediate and highly controversial impact on the process by which several major pipeline projects were assessed, including Trans Mountain (see Chapter 3) and Energy East. The adequacy and political independence of these assessment processes became a major issue in the 2015 federal election. The Trudeau government campaigned on promises of restoring public trust in these processes and ensuring that environmental protection was not compromised to expedite resource development. Legislative and policy initiatives aimed at fulfilling these promises are ongoing. Chapter 7 discusses in detail the nature of these initiatives in the environmental assessment area. There are also significant changes proposed to the *Fisheries Act*, discussed in this chapter, which would largely return the statute to its configuration prior to the Harper-era reforms.

The vigorous and unprecedented debate over the future of environmental regulation in this country triggered by the Harper-era reforms shows no signs of abating. It is a debate that is closely linked to many of the legal and political issues that we have canvassed in Chapter 2. This chapter seeks to build on those themes. It also seeks to provide context for this debate, and to introduce and elaborate on the concepts and principles that have and will play a central role in this debate. To this end, Part I offers some differing and at times competing perspectives on the historical development and future trajectory of Canadian environmental law; one perspective is penned from a more recent vantage point, while two others were written during the early years of the development of Canadian environmental law and policy. Part II provides an overview of environmental standard setting processes and the key concepts and terminology that pervade the current debate over the future of environmental regulation, including the distinction and relative merits of management-, technology- and performance-based forms of standard. Part III considers the current state of the debate over the future of environmental regulation and related issues, including the evolving role of government and the emergence of new regulatory tools and approaches. In Part IV we consider the relationship between environmental regulation and economic prosperity, exploring the so-called "Porter Hypothesis". Finally, in Part V we take a closer look at the architecture and operation of two of Canada's most important federal environmental laws: the *Fisheries Act* and the *Canadian Environmental Protection Act*.

Part I — Environmental Regulation in Canada: Some Context and Perspective

We commence our consideration of this topic with a series of excerpts designed to offer some historical as well as current-day context to the chapter that follows. The first two articles were both authored in the early 1990s, an important juncture in the history of Canadian environmental law; a time when Canada was, at least in some respects, playing a leading role in this area. The third piece, authored in 2010, chronicles developments in Canadian environmental law over the subsequent two decades, a period, the authors argue, during which Canada has become an "environmental law backwater".

D. Paul Emond,
"The Greening of Environmental Law"
(1991) 36 McGill L.J. 742

Environmental law has changed dramatically over the last twenty years since modern environmental protection statutes were first enacted in Canada. While the word "greening" is perhaps somewhat over-used, it does, in my view, describe the stages through which environmental law has "progressed" over this period, and the levels of consciousness or frustration through which environmental counsel have moved. This paper organize[s] the development of environmental law into three stages of consciousness. The labels that best describe each stage are: symbolic regulation; preventive regulation; and mutual or co-operative problem-solving.

While there are a variety of ways in which one might trace evolving perceptions of pollution and legal responses to those changing perceptions, I believe that both fit nicely into the three distinct stages noted above. Each stage is characterized by a unique perception or definition of the problem and that in turn has prompted a particular response. Furthermore, each response has encouraged a unique form of participation from the principal actors — the regulatory departments, the corporations and the public interest groups [...]. The stages are not mutually exclusive. All three overlap as one set of perceptions and definitions fades into another. Not all jurisdictions have adopted similar approaches to solving environmental problems, although I believe that all are moving slowly or will be forced to move towards the third, "greener", more enlightened and more effective approach to the issues of pollution and environmental degradation.

Stage One: Symbolic Regulation

[...] The focus at this point in the regulatory cycle is on the obvious — smoke — stacks spewing black smoke into the sky, or outfall pipes discharging fibrous sludge into lakes and rivers. Without trying to belittle these early regulatory efforts, this form of regulation follows a predictable pattern. First, the regulation usually responds to either an environmental "catastrophe" such as an Exxon Valdez or to recent revelations about consumption practices and impending environmental doom. The Club of Rome painted an especially vivid picture in 1972 of the environmental nightmare that lay ahead unless governments intervened to curb growth and promote conservation. Notwithstanding the rhetorical outrage of the public and crusading legislators, the regulatory legislation that followed was flawed. It invariably vested enormous discretion in the regulator and thus laid the foundation for a process in which the enthusiasm and zeal of the optimistic regulator could be converted into the comfortable working relationship of the cynical environmental manager. Dependent on the regulated for information and legitimacy, both the regulator and the regulated had no real option other than to strike a symbiotic balance in which each contributed to the political well being of the other.

Failures of Symbolic Regulation

The structural problems with these early approaches to pollution control can be summarized in the following way. First, the process is reactive rather than anticipatory. Like the courts, the regulatory mechanisms do not "kick in" until a problem has been identified. By then, most regulation comes too late to solve all but the simplest of problems. Secondly, the process generally lacks legitimacy. By assuming that "the government" speaks for the public; by excluding public interest participation, the process is perceived as being little more than symbolic reassurance for an apprehensive and increasingly cynical public. Environmental regulation has become a convenient phrase to describe a cosy relationship in which industry makes relatively minor reductions in their pollution in return for government approval of their activities. A third problem is that as site specific and technical regulation increases, liability begins to shift from the regulated to the regulator. Ultimately, industry is able to demand that government set the regulatory standards and write the specifications for the pollution control equipment. If those standards are met, the fault then lies with the standard and hence with those who set the standard, not with the polluter. The fourth problem is that the definition of the problem — market and technological failures destines the regulators to define success in terms of technological fixes and market adjustments. Neither definition, however, addresses the underlying social problems that have lead to pollution. Finally, knowledge about the problem is growing in more or less direct proportion to the level of regulatory effort, with the result that the problem is continually being redefined in response to increased regulatory effort. Regulatory solutions — usually expressed in terms of maximum permissable levels of pollutants — are obsolete almost as soon as the standard is announced. Finding a solution is like shooting at a moving target; with the trigger attached to the target. Each new regulatory initiative changes society's perception of the problem and the solution. The result? A strategy focused on solving yesterday's problems that is just not working.

Stage Two: Preventive Regulation

Both the pollution problem and its perceived causes change as society moves into a second level of environmental consciousness. The problem is no longer described as "gross pollution" — blackened skies and sludge-filled northern lakes — it is now more subtle and insidious, and less obvious. Perhaps the most frightening aspect of this new order of pollution relates to what has come to be described as "exquisite toxics" — odourless, colourless, tasteless and deadly substances, such as dioxins, P.C.B.s and furans. The problem is often described as one of "environmental risk" and surfaces as the deadly toll that is documented in epidemiological studies exposing birth defects, allergies and mutations. Many pollutants are bio-accumulative. Others are relatively harmless on their own but when released into the environment combine with other toxins to create a deadly synergy.

Another dimension of the problem centres around what has traditionally been called land use planning or resource allocation decisions. At one level, these planning problems are described by the neighbourhood battle cry of "Not in My Backyard" (N.I.M.B.Y.). At another level they are described by the persistent and unrelenting opposition to cutting last stands of old growth forests, to committing last wild rivers to hydro-electric development, or to despoiling significant natural landscape with transmission facilities. Both types of decisions are irreversible, at least in the short to medium term, and both involve long term impacts, with relatively little opportunity to remediate. [...]

Failures of Preventive Regulation

While preventive regulation is clearly an improvement over earlier regulatory efforts, this approach continues to suffer from many of the earlier problems. It continues to rely far too heavily on an adjudicative model of dispute resolution: adjudication is used to fashion environmental policy; adjudication is used to put policies, to the extent that they are ever expressed, into effect; and, of course, adjudication, in the form of prosecutions, is used to enforce policy. There is little opportunity for the parties to seek out creative, innovative solutions. In fact, given the uncertainty and unpredictability of the process, the incentives are all in the opposite direction. Proponents attempt to overwhelm opponents with enormous quantities of largely irrelevant information, and opponents cross-examine witnesses on every conceivable issue. One side hopes to win through exhaustion and attrition; the other, by stumbling across the "fatal flaw" in the proponent's case. The resources consumed in this "charade" are so great that environmental assessments are saved for the "mega project", leaving the vast majority of problems to be dealt with through the less comprehensive, and often ineffectual, approval process.

A further failure of the preventive approach is that because it loads up the approval process for new projects with elaborate assessment and hearing requirements, there is a built-in bias in favour of the status quo. In one sense, this is environmentally sound. Procedures that slow down the rush toward new activities by requiring a sober second thought cannot help but benefit the environment. On the other hand, to the extent that the process prefers old problems such as leaking toxic waste disposal sites, to new solutions, it imposes an enormous cost on the environment.

Finally, recent amendments to the traditional environmental protection statutes have done much to eliminate the last vestiges of the cozy relationship between the regulator and the regulated. While this is certainly to be applauded, there is now growing concern in corporate Canada that increased prosecutorial activity undermines any incentive to work cooperatively with government and the scientific community to solve environmental problems. Few still seek a "sweet deal" from governments. What responsible corporations now want is recognition that there are no simple solutions to pollution problems and that society's resources should be deployed to find solutions, not fight over alternatives.

Stage Three: Co-operative Problem-Solving

[...] Not much has worked very well in the environmental protection field up to this point. Granted there have been some notable successes, but the general consensus seems to be that we are slipping further and further behind. The problem is that the approach has generally been wrong. It has proceeded from an adversarial, competitive, rights-oriented model that was destined to siphon off creative energies in a contest of rights regulated only by the logic of justice and due process. The focus has been on defining rights and fine-tuning the dispute resolution process, rather than on solving environmental problems. What is needed is a new model that will redirect these energies toward practical solutions to real environmental problems. This model must be based on principles that emphasize interdependence, connectedness, respect, obligation, and cooperative approaches to problem-solving.

Problems and Prospects for Co-operative Problem-Solving

Any call for a new co-operative approach to solving environmental problems must address several problems or concerns. One concern relates to the danger that mediation, with its emphasis on accommodation and compromise, will deter large-scale structural changes in political and societal institutions, that only court adjudication can accomplish, and that it will thus serve the interests of the powerful against the disadvantaged?

A second concern might be expressed in terms of the relationship between process and result. Is it correct to assume, for example, that environmental disputes can be resolved through a focus on dispute resolution process(es)? Is the attempt to find a better process misplaced? At some point, one is bound to become sceptical about the ability of seemingly "fair" processes to sanction and legitimize "wrong" results. Related to the general question about the role of process in solving more specific environmental problems is the question about the role of negotiation and co-operative problem-solving. Negotiation presupposes compromise. And yet, as environmental issues are increasingly defined in terms of values and ethics — neither of which may be susceptible to compromise — there is some doubt about just how far negotiation can respond to the value demands of environmentalists.

Third, as has already been noted above, this approach to dispute resolution presupposes a group of practitioners with a different orientation from those who practice in the judicial system. The result of the lawyer's orientation and the litigation paradigm on which it is based is that "lawyers tend not to recognize mediation as a viable means of reaching a solution; and worse, they regard the kinds of unique solutions that mediation can produce as threatening to the best interests of their clients". Until lawyers accept a legitimate role for a cooperative approach to problem-solving, environmental regulation will not move forward to generate the creative, innovative solutions we so urgently need.

Notwithstanding these challenges, the prospects for this co-operative approach to solving environmental problems are very exciting indeed. Government, however, must take a far more creative and pro-active role in terms of facilitating such an approach to resolving environmental disputes — perhaps to the point of legislatively mandating negotiation and mediation.

Conclusion

By and large, this paper has focused on process. It has attempted to describe the correlation between a problem — or more precisely the way in which a problem is defined — and the process or processes for resolving that problem. Thus, regulation — initially symbolic regulation — describes a process response to the problem of market and technological failure. Similarly, environmental assessments and environmental audits are processes for anticipating irreversible environmental problems. Finally, negotiation and co-operative problem-solving are ways of addressing and solving highly complex, interdependent, multi-party environmental problems. The first two processes are largely, but not exclusively, adversarial in nature and assume that solutions will emerge from a clash of rights — that is, the right to participate in economic activity versus the right to a clean environment. The third, however, follows from the apparently novel premise that we are all in this mess together — that we are all part of the problem and thus we must all be part of the solution.

What is the role of law in all of this? Clearly, the plethora of new statutes and regulations suggests a key role. Laws, however, do not solve problems. Indeed, it sometimes seems that environmental problems are growing at more or less the same rate as new laws are being passed. Laws create a complex of rights, obligations, liabilities, incentives and disincentives — a framework within which parties can or cannot solve problems. What environmental laws must now do is:

(1) recognize the legitimacy of negotiation, mediation and other innovative means of problem-solving; (2) establish a regime of rights and obligations that ensures that all parties are able to participate effectively in the process; and (3) recognize the limits of co-operative problem-solving.

Notes and Questions

1. In the preceding piece, authored over 20 years ago, Emond envisages progress towards a model in which law facilitates cooperative problem-solving to tackle current and newly emerging environmental challenges. This chronological model progressively sees more sophisticated and effective forms of environmental regulation emerging over time. Do you agree with the main features and assumptions of his analysis? Are the challenges confronting environmental regulation essentially the same as when Emond's article was first published, or has the situation changed?

2. In an article published soon after Emond's piece, M'Gonigle *et al.* offer a contrasting view of the nature of and challenges confronting environmental law. They contend that existing environmental regulation in Canada for the most part is characterized by what they term "permissive regulation". Portraying this as a "paradigm in crisis", they argue for the need to take uncertainty seriously by transitioning to a model of regulation that focuses on "preventative design". As you read extracts from this piece, consider whether and to what extent we have moved in this direction. Consider also, whether and to what extent Emond and M'Gonigle *et al.* concur in either the diagnosis or prescription of what was ailing Canadian environmental law when these articles were written.

R. Michael M'Gonigle, *et al.*,
"Taking Uncertainty Seriously: From Permissive Regulation to
Preventative Design in Environmental Decision Making"
(1994) 32 Osgoode Hall L.J. 99

In the past decade, the growing scale and impact of the industrial use of hazardous substances have raised concerns in Canada and around the world. After decades of widespread usage, compounds once thought to be harmless, like polychlorinated biphenyls (PCBs), dioxins, and chloro-fluorocarbons (CFCs), have become household names because of increasing evidence of their serious and, in some cases, potentially catastrophic effects. Many industrial activities and by-products have followed a pattern of an initial judgement of safety, followed by uncertainty and circumstantial evidence of harm, acrimonious debate, and finally hard evidence of detrimental effects. With the dramatic increase in recent years in the use of artificial chemical substances, a regulatory approach that permits specific discharges of industrial by-products, subject to an "acceptable" limit that is based on uncertain scientific information, may no longer be adequate for assuring acceptable environmental quality.

[...] Of particular concern is the pattern of scientific inference and legal regulation that underlies our current control strategy for industrial pollution. This pattern has focused largely on what we know, rather than what we do not know; that is, it has emphasized cause-and-effect relationships that can be demonstrated between substances and the environment, and not relationships that may exist but which, despite extensive scientific testing, remain hidden. This pattern applies to more than just toxic substances. Failure to detect an effect when one exists is a common problem associated with the widely used, discharge-based regulatory approach in Canada, the approach that we call "permissive regulation". Although this problem also pervades other sectors, such as fisheries management and timber harvesting, it has been rarely acknowledged by scientists, legislators, environmental decision makers, or the judiciary in Canada. In contrast, a new regulatory approach oriented to the character of the whole industrial process, an approach that we call "preventative design", is being developed in other jurisdictions to deal with precisely this problem. [...]

Permissive Regulation: The Paradigm in Crisis

Underlying the legislation and common law described above is a way of thinking about the control of toxic pollution that is largely taken for granted. This is the "paradigm" of permissive regulation, which permits discharges into, or activities in, a receiving environment, some of which may occur only to a specified limit which purportedly reflects "safe" levels. The problems associated with the paradigm are evident in the common but ill-considered and incorrect assumptions about how the environment assimilates waste, how scientific research is done, how reliable the results of such research are, and how regulatory agencies operate. These problems undermine the paradigm on both theoretical and practical levels, and lead to growing criticism of permissive regulation worldwide.

The Assumption of Assimilative Capacity

The permissive regulation paradigm is based on the philosophy of what might be called the "assimilative capacity" theory of pollution control. Under this theory, "allowable" levels of polluting behaviours, or levels of discharge into the receiving environment, are permitted in accordance with the central assumption that the environment has an enduring capacity to assimilate these prescribed levels of pollutants without harm. With the increasing experience of the environmental "surprises" referred to above, this approach has, in recent years, come under mounting international criticism by governments, non-governmental organizations, and international regulatory bodies.

[...] Muldoon and Valiante have made a similar critique in the Canadian context and point to five structural changes needed in the regulatory framework. These changes require the shift from: (1) a medium-specific to cross-media approach, (2) a waste-management to a reduction-of toxic-use-at-the-source approach, (3) a focus on allowable concentrations to one on absolute load reductions, (4) point-source to non-point-source pollution control, and (5) interjurisdictional regulation to an ecosystem approach.

The Assumption of Scientific Knowledge

Underlying the assumption of assimilative capacity is a corresponding assumption that we are, in some way, basing our regulations and allowable limits on firm scientific knowledge. It is not necessary to review in detail the statistical and research problems discussed above, but it is useful here to consider how these problems restrict our ability to actually protect environmental quality on a scientific basis. Indeed, the range of problems are so great that the very character of the regulatory process as "scientific" must be called into question.

First, is the sheer scale of the regulatory problem. There are presently some 30,000 to 45,000 industrial emissions and effluents that remain unassessed with regard to toxicity, and between 500 and 1,000 new chemicals that are introduced each year. When regulation occurs on a substance-by-substance basis (as is common with the current permissive approach), a huge diversity of chemicals necessarily escapes regulation, including a large number of new substances introduced annually. This is so, at least partly, because the amount of testing required to determine whether a chemical is dangerous enough to regulate is prohibitively expensive and time-consuming.

In addition to the huge number of chemicals in use, it is difficult to set criteria for determining which of those substances require priority action. The generally accepted criteria are toxicity, persistence, and bioaccumulation. However, because of the concerns discussed earlier, these are rendered quite subjective as guides to identifying what to regulate and what thresholds of harm should be set.

Testing has historically focused on acute toxicity, rather than on sub-lethal, chronic, or cumulative effects, so that the database of scientific knowledge in the latter areas is extremely limited. Yet, as one critic noted in relation to Canadian regulations under the CEPA, for many highly toxic substances, "it is their chronic effects and their potential to cause severe damage over the longer term at sub-lethal levels of exposure that is cause for concern and serious regulatory prohibitions". At the final stages of the regulatory process, without such data on regulated substances, prosecutors trying to establish environmental damage must rely on the testimony of toxicological and epidemiological expert witnesses, whose testimony is based on a variety of scientific studies. Unfortunately, these studies deal with "issues of causality in terms of statistical probabilities [and] [t]raditionally, the courts have been reluctant to accept probabilistic evidence as showing causation".

It is in this realm of hidden relationships that surprising results are so often experienced, given the temporal and spatial latencies associated with so many cause-effect relationships. For example, in the case of carcinogenesis, the latency period between exposure to a cancer-causing substance and the appearance of a tumour may range between five and forty years. [...] Chronic effects that result from long-term, low-level exposure to toxic or hazardous substances often go undetected until considerable damage has been done. Even when the potential harm is large but subject to some uncertainty, or when the proximate sources of the damage are not easily established, or when the delay between exposure and effect is large, regulation may be delayed pending the availability of more conclusive evidence.

In this light, it is not surprising that the courts have often cited intervening causes, remoteness, and foreseeability as reasons to deny liability in such cases. This is especially a problem in industrialized areas, where several point sources of the same or different pollutants may contribute to the causation of the same disease. The denial of a claim on such bases may occur "even though it is generally accepted that excessive exposure to the pollutant is unhealthy". Whatever the obstacle, the courts' denial of liability in these terms points to the inherent difficulties of demonstrating causation when spatial and temporal latencies exist. [**Ed. Note:** See Chapter 2.]

The Assumption of Effective Regulation

The assumption of assimilative capacity when science is uncertain has led to serious practical problems for government agencies in the implementation of permissive regulatory strategies. For instance, the success of any regulatory system based on a substance-by-substance approach is dependent on access of the regulatory agency to high levels of funding, expert staffing, and sufficient research and enforcement facilities. The vast number of chemicals to be tested for toxicity and monitored in industrial effluents, in addition to the large number and types of individual industrial operations subject to regulation, create difficult practical problems for regulatory agencies. For example, in place of independent government testing and monitoring programmes, regulatory agencies often rely on industry research and even self-policing. This puts the government at a disadvantage because industry is then "uniquely well supplied with information on product and process characteristics, abatement technology and costs, production and effluent volumes, and numerous other variables". Even where industry testing is honestly undertaken, agencies may not have sufficient resources or access to the raw data to allow them to evaluate properly the experimental design and the statistical power of the results.

The combination of the above factors — the problematic assumption of assimilative capacity, the limited scientific understanding of environmental effects, and constrained agency resources — has created a situation in which the environment is effectively treated as a free good. This leads to externalization of the true costs of industrial production through the degradation of environmental quality and an increase in public health risks. Yet, in attempting to correct this after the fact, private citizens and public regulators may confront significant transaction costs, including the costs of litigation, negotiation, and regulation. Avoiding these costs leads to economically inefficient outcomes which may favour polluters. For example, where a Crown prosecutor weighs the costs of litigation against its potential benefits, pollution may not be penalized until the harm to individuals exceeds their transaction costs. In Canada, this situation has encouraged a strategy based on negotiated, rather than enforced, compliance between industry and government.

Negotiations between the stakeholders in environmental regulation (government, industry, and the public) as the basis for setting standards may be an effective approach, so long as all affected parties are involved in the process and the ability of government to force technological development is not compromised [...]. Negotiation as the basis for ensuring compliance is, however, even more problematic, as it may politicize what should be a predictable enforcement process, ultimately making compliance voluntary. This tends to be the case where a continuous negotiating process costs less for the industry than actually complying with existing regulations. In British Columbia, this strategy led to the widespread granting of exceptions to compliance. [...]

In conclusion, the regulatory paradigm underlying Canadian pollution legislation is critically weakened by a number of problems: its assumption of the environment's assimilative capacity, its failure to acknowledge the implications of scientific uncertainty, and its unrealistic expectations of regulatory agencies. In short, such a system of regulation does not ensure long-term environmental quality as it was designed to do but, instead, inefficiently employs agency resources to facilitate the externalization of the environmental and social costs of industrial production.

Precedents for Incremental Reform

In response to the difficulties experienced with permissive regulation, many national governments and international regulatory bodies have begun to shift from the control of pollution to varying degrees of pollution reduction. In addition to alternative approaches however, the potential exists for incremental reforms within the framework of permissive regulation itself.

Lowering the Standard of Proof

A number of precedents exist in common law tort actions where the standard of proof has been lowered to protect environmental values and public health. American courts have shown a particular willingness to accept uncertain scientific information as sufficient to establish a fact on "the preponderance of the evidence".

Creation of Risk as Evidence

Since many types of harm that have potentially severe consequences are also characterized as having a low probability of occurrence, application of the traditional standard of proof may lead to downplaying the likelihood and thus the potentially high costs of the defendant's actions on society. Lowering the standard of proof, by accepting evidence of "creation of risk", allows the courts to make decisions which minimize judicial subjectivity when confronted with uncertain proof of causation to avoid serious harm which may have only a small probability of occurrence; and, at the same time, to achieve broader societal values. [**Ed. Note:** See further discussion in Chapter 2.]

In effect, risk-benefit analysis alters what needs to be proven by relieving the plaintiff of demonstrating that the occurrence of harm is more probable than not. Instead, the plaintiff need only show both that there exists a mere risk of harm, and that the costs of that risk to the plaintiff outweigh the benefits to the defendant. Similarly, in enforcing regulatory standards, substituting a "risk-benefit analysis" approach for a damage-oriented, punitive approach could effectively lower the standard of proof by allowing the plaintiff to establish merely that the expected costs of potential environmental degradation that could be induced are greater than the expected benefits. A common approach to calculating the expected costs and benefits of proposed activities is to measure the possible cost of environmental degradation multiplied by the probability of occurrence, against the expected benefit of a new technology or development multiplied by the probability that there will be a benefit.

[Problems in implementing this approach include ...] estimating costs and benefits as many of the variables in a risk assessment are unquantifiable, and the probabilities of occurrence of different outcomes, as well as the range of possible outcomes, may not be known with any degree of certainty. In addition, treatment of intangible costs, intergenerational effects, and synergistic and cumulative effects assessment are difficult, given the uncertainties involved.

Despite these limitations, the risk-benefit approach has important implications for the Canadian environmental regulatory framework, which have not allowed for the "creation of risk" as adequate proof of an offence. For instance, causing harm to the receiving environment is not directly prohibited under the B.C. *Waste Management Act* [now the *Environmental Management Act*], even though this may be the intent of the Act. The focus instead is on preventing unauthorized discharges which cause pollution. In this regard, the prosecution must establish that the discharge fits the statutory definition of pollution — "the presence in the environment of substances or contaminants that substantially alter or impair the usefulness of the environment" — rather than just demonstrating the creation of a risk as sufficient proof of this element of the offence.

Similarly, for offences under sections 35(1) and 36(3) of the *Fisheries Act* the standard of proof would be lowered if it were sufficient to establish that an accused's activity put a fish habitat at risk. Indeed, the standard and burden of proof required to establish elements of an offence under the *Fisheries Act* have been somewhat relaxed through the use of inferences. It is yet to be seen whether risk of harm will be sufficient to regulate substances under CEPA, although the phrase "may have an immediate or long-term harmful effect on the environment" [...]

The Right to Environmental Quality

In the United States, a number of states have enacted legislation that specifically seeks to secure a right to environmental quality by lowering the standard of proof and, on some issues, by shifting the burden onto the defendant. Similar to the judicial acceptance of "creation of risk", acts like the *Michigan Environmental Protection Act* alter the standard and burden of proof rules. The plaintiff may establish a prima facie case by showing that the defendant's actions are merely likely to harm the environment. The burden of proof then shifts to the defendant, who must show that his or her conduct was reasonable "by way of an affirmative defence, that there is no feasible and prudent alternative [...] and that such conduct is consistent with the promotion of the public heath, safety and welfare in light of the state's paramount concern for the protection of its natural resources". The MEPA defines a violation as the "impairment" of a "natural resource", but the Act does not establish a threshold which must be met by the plaintiff, thus making it possible for the courts to apply the statute flexibly. The MEPA also allows the court to "determine the validity, applicability and reasonableness of the standard", and, if the court decides that a standard is deficient, it may "direct the adoption of a standard approved and specified by the court". [**Ed. Note:** See discussion of an analogous law reform proposal for Canada in Chapter 5.]

Establishing the affirmative defence may be onerous for the defendant. Abrams argues that "[i]f a low level of environmental harm satisfies the threshold, defendants will be forced to explore alternative courses of action in a greater range of cases". If so, this could be a significant step toward a more preventative and less legalistic approach to environmental protection. In assessing alternatives, economic criteria must not determine the outcome. Rather, it should be shown that there are unique non-economic problems which preclude the selection of other alternatives.

This single technique of emphasizing alternative processes encourages the courts to make innovative decisions in spite of scientific uncertainty about causal relationships, thus reducing the potential costs to society and to the environment [...]. Such an approach has not yet made an appearance in Canadian legislation.

Shifting the Burden of Proof

A few common law precedents exist in which the traditional allocation of the burden of proof has been reversed so that the defendant had to prove that he was not the cause of the injury. The theory of "alternate liability" applies in situations in which there is more than one possible defendant or cause of harm. As discussed above, the negligence of the two defendants had been established, but the plaintiff could not prove which one was at fault and, therefore, caused the injury. The court reversed the burden so as to require each defendant to absolve himself by showing on a balance of probabilities that he was not to be held responsible for the injury. In other words, the defendants were given the task of proving that their actions were not harmful.

The applicability of the alternative liability rule to environmental regulatory issues is, however, limited since it requires that harm already have occurred, that there is a proven and limited number of possible causes of the harm, and that the negligence of the defendants has been established. The overall burden on the prosecution is thus still high, especially in quasi-criminal regulatory environmental offences where the higher standard of proof beyond a reasonable doubt is still applied. In such cases, each defendant would only need to raise a doubt that points to one of the others as the cause of harm to make it difficult to convict any of the defendants.

Going beyond the alternative liability rule is the common law tort standard of strict liability where "[a]nyone having care or control of a substance likely to do harm [is] to be held strictly liable for the consequences should it escape". Strict liability, which does not reverse the burden of proof but removes the burden of establishing the defendant's negligence, has been explicitly recognized in some environmental protection acts in Canada. For instance, under the "*Ontario Spills Act*" the costs of clean-up are subject to absolute liability rules, and strict liability is applied to loss or damage from spills. Plaintiffs are not required to show that the defendant was at fault or was negligent in allowing the spill, but the "due diligence defence" is open to the defendant once the offence has been shown: see *R. v. Sault Ste. Marie* [...].

While the strict liability offence does shift some of the legal burden onto the polluter, the extensive investigation and the use of expert witnesses required to rebut the due diligence defence add to the expense and difficulty of prosecuting a strict liability offence. [Also] strict liability offences [are vulnerable to be] challenged under section 11(d) of the *Canadian Charter of Rights and Freedoms*, which provides the right "to be presumed innocent until proven guilty", and under section 7 of the *Charter*, the "right to life, liberty and security of the person [...] in accordance with the principles of fundamental justice". [**Ed. Note:** See further discussion in Chapter 5.]

Structural Reform Through Preventative Design

The lack of judicial innovation in Canada to overcome intractable problems of establishing causation is an example of the impediments to effective environmental protection within the existing regulatory and judicial framework. More important still are the technical and scientific problems that regulators who rely on "end-of-pipe" solutions face daily [...]. Thus, for example, the solution for improving local air quality, tall stacks, was a major source of acid rain. Similarly, technologies to remove heavy metals from effluent streams or particulate matter from tall stacks merely transferred the pollution to landfills in the form of sludges or fly-ash, which may then leach into the surrounding water table.

Overcoming both the inherent contradictions of permissive regulation and the escalating pollution problem requires a new regulatory approach which does not merely treat waste once it has been generated, but deals with it at its source through new production processes. A range of terms have been used to describe this new approach, such as waste minimization, waste reduction, toxics use reduction, best available technology, and clean production.

Several precedents exist for such structural reforms, and an examination of them provides us with a detailed model for a "preventative design" strategy. Such a strategy takes a "precautionary approach" [...] by creating a presumption of harm and translates this presumption into a comprehensive new procedure and administrative framework for regulation of the entire production process.

Precedents for Structural Reform

Historically, initial demands for a more precautionary approach arose from the deteriorating state of the shared rivers and enclosed seas of northern Europe. In the mid-1980s, new concepts such as "low waste/non-waste and low-emission/non-emission technologies" were being considered to deal with an emerging crisis. A number of national governments, notably those of Germany and the Netherlands, began to move toward a more preventative or "precautionary" approach with new legislation that sought to encourage waste prevention and clean technology. These goals have been promoted through licensing and siting requirements for waste management facilities, operational standards, and the wide use of economic incentives such as pollution charges and direct financial support for research, development, and implementation of so-called clean technologies.

[...] in the United States, early signs of a new approach were evident by the mid-1980s. The 1984 *Hazardous and Solid Waste Amendments to the Resource Conservation and Recovery Act* outlined a national policy on waste management, which stated that "wherever feasible, the generation of hazardous waste, is to be reduced or eliminated as expeditiously as possible". Included in the amendments were requirements that firms using or manufacturing toxics must report their efforts to reduce the volume and toxicity of waste prior to treatment [...].

This cause has been taken up most aggressively at the state, rather than the federal, level, with the 1989 Massachusetts *Toxic Use Reduction Act* setting the U.S. national standard. In response to substantial public interest pressure from the National Toxics Campaign, the new legislation establishes a statewide goal of reducing toxic waste generation by 50 per cent by 1997.

In October 1990, the American federal government passed the *Pollution Prevention Act* which also sets out a national policy on pollution prevention and source reduction. The Act is intended to improve Environmental Protection Agency (EPA) data collection systems and the dissemination of information regarding the reduction of toxic emissions in all media, and to assist the government in providing information on, and technical assistance for, source reduction. Under the *Pollution Prevention Act*, the Administrator of the EPA will establish an office that will develop and implement a strategy to promote source reduction; investigate methods of coordinating, streamlining, and improving public access to data collected under existing environmental statutes; develop an inventory of existing data; and consider developing consistent report formats, nomenclature and data storage and retrieval systems [...].

Both conceptually and in practice, Canadian legislative policy lags far behind these initiatives. Internationally, the International Joint Commission (of which Canada is a co-member with the United States) has, since 1978, articulated in its Great Lakes Water Quality Agreement the goal of "zero discharge" for persistent toxic pollutants. To help achieve this, in 1990, the Commission called for a reverse onus provision so that a chemical should be assumed to be harmful unless demonstrated otherwise. Nationally and provincially, however, despite the fact that 3.5 million tonnes of hazardous wastes are generated annually by Canadian industry, "there is neither an explicit national policy nor legislative provisions promoting source reduction". Meanwhile, many provincial governments remain within the old regulatory paradigm [...].

Conclusion

In contrast to the piecemeal [Canadian] approach to reforming the present paradigm of permissive regulation, the revolution in regulatory strategies, evident in a diverse number of multilateral agencies, state and national governments, points to a new paradigm which has gained wide international acceptance. Canadian legislation, regulatory action, and environmental decision making have yet to recognize this dramatic shift. To facilitate this transition in Canada, a new approach is needed.

This new approach is that of preventative design. The permissive model is no longer viable because it cannot work well in the face of the large uncertainties presently found. Its failure demands a comprehensive rethinking and restructuring of existing legislation, as well as a basic reorientation of judicial decision making. Standards must no longer be set without the recognition of uncertainty. Instead, the inescapable presence of uncertainty should lead to a shift of the regulatory burden onto those seeking to utilize, and profit from, our common environment's questionable assimilative capacity [...].

Rigorous science recognizes the need to account for uncertainty. The application of statistical power analysis to test design is a crucial step, and this formal recognition of uncertainty can become the foundation of the precautionary principle and the paradigm of preventative design. This model of regulation now has precedents to follow [...]. These precedents point to the importance of new management techniques (economic penalties are an essential tool) and agencies oriented to technology-forcing and industrial design. As the review of American legislation concludes, "[g]overnment action is needed to provide incentives and information to fundamentally change industry's focus on pollution control towards toxics use reduction". Similarly, the judiciary must be more cognizant of the implications of scientific uncertainty in order to respond realistically and imaginatively to problems of causation. Reallocating the burden of proof from the environmental management agencies or public to the polluter, and setting appropriate standards of proof, are important ways to begin.

Notes and Questions

1. The preceding article has been excerpted at some length due to the wide range of relevant issues it canvasses. M'Gonigle *et al.* make the case for both incremental and structural reforms. Many of the incremental reforms for which they advocate are aimed at remedying perceived weaknesses or defects in common law approaches to environmental regulation. Ultimately, however, they contend that the cause of structural reform must be championed through the enactment of national legislation that "tak[es] uncertainty seriously" through adoption of a precautionary approach to environmental protection. To what extent have we seen incremental or, indeed, structural reforms of the type for which they advocated? What factors (constitutional, institutional, ideological) account for the progress (or lack of it) that we have witnessed?

2. An important phenomenon that neither of the preceding articles anticipated or discussed, which took centre stage in environmental law debates during the mid-1990s and continues to hold considerable sway, concerns the role of market forces and civil society organizations in "governing" the environment. A key feature of this trend was a growing sense that enhancing environmental outcomes required new ways of thinking about the role of government. Increasingly, it was argued that traditional *government*-centred prescriptions (often termed "command and control" approaches) were less likely to succeed than *governance*-based ones premised on the idea that businesses, consumers, and civil society organizations were often better positioned to leverage change. The merits of this emerging governance model of environmental stewardship, it is argued, are especially compelling in terms of ensuring that environmental leadership and best practices are recognized and rewarded: on this theme, see Gunningham and Sinclair, *Leaders and Laggards* (2002). Later, in Part III we canvass the origins and

nature of this increasingly influential approach to environmental protection. In Part II, however, we lay the conceptual foundation for that discussion by introducing some key concepts and terminology relevant to environmental standard setting. In the meantime, consider the next article which chronicles nicely the many ways in which Canadian environmental law has changed over the last 20 years.

Stepan Wood, Georgia Tanner & Benjamin J. Richardson,
"Whatever Happened to Canadian Environmental Law?"
(2010) 37 Ecology Law Quarterly 981

An Environmental Law Backwater

Few would have predicted twenty years ago that Canada would become such an environmental laggard. The 1990s began with great promise, with the unveiling of the Green Plan, Canada's active international involvement, and the high public support expressed for environmentally responsible policies. Before evaluating the causes of this decline in Canada's environmental record, it is useful to examine some of its regulatory and policy symptoms and compare the Canadian experience with the direction other countries took.

One of the most significant symptoms of decline is that Canadian environmental law has increasingly lacked the cornucopia of policy instruments found in comparable jurisdictions. Many Canadian regulators have remained hinged to a simplistic conceptualization of policy instrument choice as a binary choice between "command-and-control" regulation and voluntary action. Other possibilities that have been adopted in many countries, such as ecological tax reform, extended producer responsibility, and tradable pollution allowances, have lingered on the fringes of policy making in Canada. Although there have some recent innovations at a provincial level, such as adoption of modest carbon taxes in Quebec and British Columbia in 2007 and 2008 respectively, these steps were inspired by foreign examples. Canada may be "innovating," but, to a greater extent than earlier periods, more of the inspiration comes from abroad.

The reticence of Canada's lawmakers to use economic instruments is one of the most notable lacunae in its environmental law. In many jurisdictions, especially in the European Union, such instruments have been deployed in diverse areas of environmental policy to create financial incentives for improved corporate behaviour. The OECD advised Canada as early as 1995 to be more ambitious with economic instruments. Some ad hoc initiatives have since occurred, such as an amendment of the Income Tax Act in 1996 to encourage landowners to donate ecologically significant land for conservation. Recent federal initiatives on climate change also dabble with economic incentives, but mainly in the form of subsidies for clean energy technology. More radical alternatives, such as ecological tax reform, as proposed in the 2008 federal election by the Liberals and Greens, have been shunned by the current Conservative government and were abandoned by the Liberals after losing the election.

Both the Liberals and Conservatives — Canada's two major national political parties — share blame for Canada's intransigence on climate change policy. The former Liberal governments of Jean Chrétien and Paul Martin, while publicly keen on the Kyoto Protocol, were very slow to develop climate change policies and failed to implement any significant measures before they lost office in 2006. The subsequent Conservative government of Stephen Harper has been overtly hostile to action on climate change. While it has introduced some soft measures, including the C$1 billion Green Infrastructure Fund to support projects such as public transit, the government effectively disavowed Kyoto. And [...] it has sought to avoid meaningful compliance with the Kyoto Protocol Implementation Act, 2007, sponsored by the Opposition Parties.

Although Canada has an international reputation for respecting human rights and promoting citizen participation in public affairs, even here some retreat is evident. One example is access to environmental information. The Aarhus Convention on Access to Information, Public Participation in Decision-making and Access to Justice in Environmental Matters, drafted by the UN Economic Commission for Europe in 1998, spawned the creation of pollutant emission inventory systems throughout much of Europe. Canada was once in the vanguard in this area, having established a National Pollutant Release Inventory in 1992, second only to the United States to do so. Today, Canada has declined to ratify the Aarhus Convention and its supplementary 2003 protocol on pollutant release registers.

In addition to legislative inaction, Canada's poor record also owes to its failure to implement existing laws. One instance is a landmark provision in the amended Canada National Parks Act which made ecological integrity the "first priority" in all decisions affecting park management. Despite this statutory mandate, subsequent parks management, dominated by the traditional "parks for people" ethos, has struggled to fulfill this goal. Parks Canada's practices have been challenged, but in virtually all cases the courts have deferred to its judgment. For example, in May 2001 the Minister of Canadian Heritage, on behalf of Parks Canada, authorized construction of a winter road through Wood Buffalo National Park. The Federal Court rejected the arguments of the Canadian Parks and Wilderness Society that the Minister had failed to comply with the Canada National Parks Act's ecological integrity requirement. Judge Gibson reasoned that the Act "requires a delicate balancing of conflicting interests which include the benefit and enjoyment of those living in, and in close proximity to, Wood Buffalo National Park [...] [and] does not require that ecological integrity be the 'determinative factor.'"

Meanwhile, other countries have embraced reform, in turn setting precedents to guide Canada — in contrast to earlier times when Canada pioneered some best practices. Over the past decade, California and Germany, for instance, have adopted various incentive measures and regulatory standards to promote energy efficiency and uptake of renewable energies. Ontario's recent "green energy" statutory reforms, including a feed-in tariff system to support renewable energy production, were inspired by these examples. Not all precedents have been positive, however. The United States, nearly always a significant influence on Canadian environmental regulation, is also setting the bar low on climate change policy: the Harper government insists that it will deal with climate change only in a manner consistent with American efforts.

Further evidence of Canada's trailing performance is in the area of pollution regulation. The U.S. Environmental Protection Agency's Project XL substituted traditional emission controls designed and mandated by government with a pollution control regime determined between government, the regulated entity, and other stakeholders. Its Performance Track program offered regulatory and other benefits to hundreds of companies and public sector facilities that had environmental management systems in place and adopted ambitious beyond-compliance environmental performance targets. Meanwhile, the Australian state of Victoria pioneered another approach to regulatory flexibility, allowing companies to prepare an "environmental improvement" plan as a partial alternative to environmental licensing systems. Some Canadian governments have begun to adopt their own schemes for regulatory flexibility, such as Ontario's Environmental Leaders Program, introduced in 2002. Some of these initiatives reflect the New Public Management model of administration. One example, cited by Professor Winfield, is the Ontario Ministry of Natural Resources' restructuring in the late 1990s of its compliance inspection system for forestry operations into a "partnership" with the logging industry. The majority of the Ministry's inspectors were retrenched, and replaced by a model of self-inspection by the logging companies. Similar arrangements were established in other natural resource sectors in the province, including for mining and fisheries management. Their effectiveness in identifying and reporting non-compliance has been questioned. The very notion of "regulatory flexibility" has attracted criticism as a return to a "bipartite bargaining" model of policy making, privileging the state and industry while marginalizing community involvement and public accountability.

Another example of the New Public Management model is the delegation of public service delivery to arms-length agencies. This trend, pioneered in the United Kingdom and New Zealand, was inspired by the idea that government should "steer," not "row." In practice, however, these agencies have limited accountability and are often run by the regulated industries themselves. "Rather than 'steering,'" wrote Professor Winfield and others of an Ontario example, "the government provided the boat, but largely left the authority to define its own course and speed." [...]

The financial economy is another domain where Canada is a legal backwater. A new international frontier of environmental law reform is socially responsible investment, which can provide a means of encouraging lenders and investors to discriminate among companies based on their sustainability performance. Since the early 2000s, several European countries and Australia have introduced regulations requiring pension funds and other types of financial institutions to disclose their policies for taking into account social, environmental, and ethical matters in investment decisions. Public sector pension funds in Norway, Sweden, and New Zealand have even been mandated by legislation to invest ethically and responsibly. Economic incentives to stimulate socially responsible investment (SRI) have also been adopted in some jurisdictions; the leading example, the Netherlands' Green Project Directive of 1995, has greatly spurred the Dutch SRI market.

Canada has largely shunned such ideas. Calls to reform the statutory mandate of the Canada Pension Plan have been rejected, and an opposition private member's bill in 2001, modeled on Britain's law providing for disclosure of SRI policies, failed to pass. Another example is the Ontario Securities Commission's rejection in January 2010 of proposed new regulations to enhance corporate environmental reporting. Even Canada's National Round Table on the Environment and Economy, often an advocate for innovation, recommended in its 2007 report on this subject that "we do not see the need for increased regulation, increased taxation, or increased interference in the normal value-creating activities of Canadian businesses." [...]

The foregoing is not a comprehensive account of Canada's slide into an environmental law backwater, but indicates a general trend. Although it has been shown that some comparable jurisdictions continue to pioneer environmental law reform, this should not imply that they have put their economies on a sustainable footing. Far from it; all countries are struggling to achieve effective legal and policy responses to worsening environmental conditions. However, even with that caveat, Canada has tended to perform worse.

Notes and Questions

1. Elsewhere in their article, Wood *et al.* offer some potential explanations for Canada's "slide into an environmental law backwater". What factors, in your view, have contributed to the decline? Is it a decline that Emond or M'Gonigle *et al.* would have anticipated?

2. What are the similarities and differences between these three notable contributions to the Canadian environmental law literature? Do the authors share any stated or unstated assumptions or values that might not be shared by others in legal academe, or Canadian society at large?

Part II — Environmental Standard Setting

Before attempting to assess the nature and relative merits of differing *forms* of standards, it is instructive to consider how standards are developed in general terms. To do this, we will consider how environmental protection standards, particularly those in the pollution-control context, are developed. Standard setting is typically conceived of as a four-stage chronological process that consists of: (1) setting an objective; (2) developing criteria; (3) establishing an ambient quality standard; and (4) defining an individualized operational standard. Ordinarily, as part of the final stage of the process, the government regulator will issue a licence or permit to a firm that will specify its compliance obligations. As we shall discuss shortly, the form of standard embedded in such licences or permits can vary. In the "command and control" terminology that is often employed in this area of law, the permit or licence supplies the legal "command" that the regulated party is bound to obey. In Chapter 5, we will consider in some detail the "control" measures upon which government can rely to monitor and secure compliance with these commands. Below, however, we turn first to a more detailed description of the process by which environmental standards are set.

Chris Tollefson, Fred Gale & David Haley,
Setting the Standard
(UBC Press, 2008) at 245-253

All standard-setting processes, whether undertaken by governments or private entities, should, in theory, proceed from a clear definition of the overarching outcome(s) that the regime exists to achieve. Defining these objectives is a quintessentially political choice, a judgment about values (Franson, Franson, and Lucas 1982). Typically, the objective will be stated in broad, categorical terms (i.e., securing safe drinking-water; protecting biodiversity). However, this is not always true. A case in point is the statement of objectives set out in the regulations recently enacted by the BC government to implement its new results-based forest practices legislation. For each of the different forest values (soils, timber, wildlife, biodiversity, and so on), the discrete objective is stated as being to conserve the value in question "without unduly reducing the supply of timber from BC forests" (see *Forest and Range Practices Act*, s. 510).

Where the standard takes the form of hard law, the articulation of these threshold objectives will sometimes occur in legislation or, more often, by means of a legally enforceable regulation (as is the case with recently passed regulations under British Columbia's new results-based *Forest and Range Practices Act*). Where the standard is being developed by a non-governmental entity, these outcomes will usually form part of an organizational mission statement or code of practice [...].

Having identified the objective that a standard exists to protect, the next task is to identify the criteria by which to gauge whether that objective is being achieved or compromised. This is typically a daunting scientific undertaking. Whether the objective is safeguarding potable water or protecting ungulate winter habitat, the range of potential threats, and the nature of the interaction amongst these threats, can be highly complex. Inevitably, therefore, there are knowledge gaps in the "dose-response" relationship [...]. As a result, a pragmatic approach is frequently adopted and criteria are formulated on the basis of a limited number of parameters (i.e., threats, risks, etc.) of greatest and/or most obvious concern [...].

The third generic step in the process is the formulation of ambient quality standards. This process has both a technical and a political dimension. It involves taking the data generated by the criteria-identification process and undertaking an evaluation that considers how, in light of this data, the objective(s) identified can best be achieved, taking account of the costs, benefits, and risk acceptability associated with setting the standard at different levels. Identification of the ambient standard is often thought of in terms of the receiving environment's carrying capacity. It can take various forms [...]. It may be expressed in the form of an upper limit on the mass or concentration of harmful substances in the receiving environment, or it may, alternatively, prescribe the lower limit of desired substances. When governments engage in this type of analysis (many Canadian governments do not), ambient standards are typically established informally in the form of policy.

The final stage in a standard-setting process involves moving from a statement of the desired ambient outcome to creating standards that define the permissible behaviour of the individual party the standard is purporting to regulate. In the context of point-source air and water pollution, this is typically referred to as a "discharge standard". Once again, this process is both scientific/ technical and political, requiring a complex assessment of both the incremental impact of the activity being regulated and the costs/benefits and compliance issues associated with different standard prescriptions. Governments frequently express standards of this kind in pollution permits adapted to suit the particular circumstances of the applicant and the airshed or watershed within which they are proposing to operate. In Canada, the prevailing practice with respect to air- and water-pollution permits has been to express discharge standards in terms of an upper limit for the mass or concentration of specified substances that the permit holder is entitled to release into the environment over a designated period of time. In contrast, the United States has adopted a distinctly different approach to permitting. There, in recognition of the difficulties associated with individually calibrating discharge standards in a manner that does not compromise ambient standards, the dominant legislative approach has been to issue technology-based permits. Under this approach, the permissible level of discharge is defined with reference to the level of environmental protection the permit holder could achieve using the best available technology (BAT) — in this case, the best available pollution-control technology.

Forms of Standard

Regulators use three main forms of standard to influence behaviour. Before discussing their relative merits, it is worth offering some ideal-type definitions. *Performance-based standards* are intended to be a specific and measurable indicator of a desired objective to be achieved; they leave broad discretion as to how to achieve this objective to the regulated firm. In contrast, in their pure form, *technology-based standards* are silent about desired outcomes; instead, they specify a particular technology, input, or mode of operation that is thought to optimally promote the overall objective of the standard. Finally, *management-based standards* (also known as process-based standards) eschew specification of both outcomes and means, opting instead to promote achievement of identified policy objectives by obliging operators to undertake specified management-planning activities.

[...] in regulating air and water pollution, Canadian governments have tended to employ performance-based standards; their American counterparts have elected to use technology-based ones. Over the last two decades, considerable research has been carried out to examine the experience of using both forms of standard in these and other jurisdictions. In contrast, both the experience with, and the literature considering the efficacy of, management-based standards has been much sparser. A helpful way to conceive of the relationship between these three forms of standard has recently been offered by Coglianese and Lazar. They argue that, in developing standards, regulators can choose to intervene at various stages of a firm's production process: the planning stage, the acting stage, or the output stage. The goal of such intervention is to correct market failure by seeking to promote the production of social-good outputs (i.e., environmental protection) without unduly fettering the production of the private-good outputs (i.e., timber). As the Table below illustrates, management-based standards represent an intervention in a firm's planning processes; technology-based standards can be seen as an intervention in the operational or "acting" stage; and performance-based standards constitute an intervention at the output stage, specifying what social outputs must (or must not) be attained.

Figure 1.

Stage of Production	Planning	Acting	Outputs
Form of Standard	Management-based	Technology-based	Performance-based

Source: Adapted from Coglianese and Lazar (2003).

Prescriptiveness and Standard Form

A key feature of the debate over the relative merits of these three forms of standard is the often-asserted proposition that performance- and management-based approaches are superior to technology-based standards because they are less prescriptive. This "prescriptiveness" critique is seldom fully elaborated, but it appears to refer to the extent to which a particular form of regulation constrains firm actions and decisions while imposing additional (and potentially unnecessary) production costs. The above schemata helps demonstrate the fallacy of this critique. When they are seen as reflecting different "moments" for intervention in the production process, all three forms of standard are potentially prescriptive in the relevant sense. How prescriptive depends, in turn, more on the content as opposed to the form of the standard in question.

Although technology-based standards are clearly prescriptive in terms of production methods, they are notably non-prescriptive in terms of management planning and, more significantly, outcomes or outputs. Similarly, the prescriptiveness of management-based standards can vary widely, from a simple exhortation that operators implement a generic environmental management system, to a standard that tightly specifies the nature of planning to be undertaken and requires government signoff before production activity can proceed.

Performance-based standards also vary considerably in their prescriptiveness, Depending on whether the standard in question is loosely or tightly specified. The specificity of a standard in this regard is often closely related to whether the standard is qualitative or quantitative in nature. To illustrate, assume that the standard's objective is maintaining slope stability and preventing soil erosion. A qualitative performance standard could be framed so that it turns this desired outcome into a mandatory obligation by implicitly adding the words "thou shalt" (i.e., thou shalt maintain slope stability and prevent soil erosion). Conversely, the same outcome could be sought through the use of a quantitative performance standard framed as follows: "No tree felling shall take place on slopes that exceed 35 degrees". This latter formulation — clearly a performance-based standard — is, on its face, highly prescriptive in that it purports to override the manager's discretion as to where and when to log.

Arguably, by foreclosing the potential for a manager to seek to achieve the expressed objective (maintaining slope stability and preventing soil erosion), the quantitative standard is more prescriptive than management- or technology-based standards that could be crafted to secure the same goal. Under a management-based standard, where the slope in question was greater than thirty-five degrees, a requirement that the manager conduct slope stability tests or third-party assessments prior to logging might be triggered. Under such an approach, if the tests confirmed that logging could occur without compromising the slope stability or creating soil erosion, the manager would be at liberty to proceed. It is also possible to posit a technology-based standard that preserves a relatively broad scope of managerial autonomy. For example, such a standard could stipulate that logging can take place on slopes of over thirty-five degrees, but only if a specified mode of low-impact harvesting (i.e., helicopter logging) were employed.

Private Autonomy versus Certainty

The corollary of the prescriptiveness critique discussed above is the assertion that performance standards, relative to other forms of standard, are superior in terms of preserving private autonomy. The preceding hypothetical situation shows that this generalization is misleading. Performance standards can sometimes preserve private autonomy; however, the extent to which they do so will depend on the congruency between the objective that the standard exists to advance and the form of standard itself. The greater the congruency, the more discretion the regulated party will enjoy in determining how to meet the standard. Thus a performance standard that transforms the desired objective (stable slopes) into a generic mandatory obligation ("thou shalt protect slope stability") preserves much greater private autonomy than one that specifies a narrower or subsidiary goal (prohibiting or restricting logging on slopes of greater than a specified steepness). As a general proposition, therefore, qualitative performance standards rate much higher than quantitative ones in terms of private autonomy.

Indeed, as we have argued, quantitative performance standards are often highly prescriptive. It is important to recognize that preserving private autonomy comes at a price in terms of certainty that the promulgated standard will achieve the policy objective it exists to serve. In other words, all other things being equal, it can be argued that the more generic and imprecise the formulation of a performance standard, the higher the risk the objective of the standard will be compromised. Whether, and in what circumstances, the risks inherent in performance-based standards are worth the potential benefits in terms of promoting other values (such as reducing industry regulatory costs, promoting innovative practices, etc.) is a question that must be assessed on a case-specific basis. Relevant to this determination will be the nature and importance of the objective the standard exists to promote and the pervasiveness, severity, (ir)reversibility, and probability of the risk that the regulated activity will compromise this objective. Also relevant will be the circumstances, and particularly the compliance history, of the party being regulated. Different strategies may be advisable depending on whether the regulator's goal is to create incentives for industry leaders or, alternatively, to police the activities of their laggard counterparts (Gunningham and Sinclair 2002).

Another set of issues relate to the "ownership of uncertainty" [...] Assuming we can assess who benefits and who loses from the uncertainty that some types of performance standard introduce, should the beneficiaries be called upon to bear a higher level of accountability in the event that an objective is compromised? In other words, should greater private accountability be the quid pro quo for greater private autonomy? Or should parties regulated under an open-ended performance standard be able to defend their failure to meet the standard by claiming "due diligence", as their counterparts regulated under more prescriptive regimes are able to do?

Protecting private autonomy by enacting a standard that confers broad managerial discretion to choose how compliance is to be achieved can also have a cost in terms of transparency and public participation. The move toward an approach under which managers are mandated to develop in-house strategies to meet the requirements of a pure performance standard inevitably leads to heavy reliance on complex, predictive models of performance. Even assuming members of the public are given access to this modelling information (which is by no means assured), their ability to effectively participate in regulatory decision making will decline as the complexity of the analysis increases. This professionalization of standard setting also has the potential to undermine the capacity for meaningful regulatory oversight by government or private standard-setting bodies, causing them to rely more heavily on third-party experts (e.g., academics, consultants, certifiers) or, alternatively, accepting on faith analyses provided by private managers.

Measuring, Evaluating, and Verifying Performance

It is broadly accepted that performance standards work best "when actual performance can be measured, evaluated and verified" [...] As we have noted, in standards where there is a close congruency between the objective to be achieved and the form of standard, uncertainty arises, with the result that measurement, evaluation, and verification of performance can be undermined.

To minimize this uncertainty (and enhance the potential for accurately measuring, evaluating, and verifying performance), one obvious option is to employ quantitative performance standards. This prospect raises its own questions. One set of questions concern what is being measured and to what extent it serves as a reliable indicator that the objective the standard exists to promote is being achieved. In theory, the most reliable quantitative indicator would be one that offers a direct measure of the condition of an ambient environmental value (i.e., ambient water or soil conditions; the continued viability of specified listed species in the area being logged). Because such ambient values are, by definition, affected by a variety of other natural and non-natural factors, however, quantitative performance standards are typically crafted so as to measure the incremental impact of the activity being regulated. They thus normally take the form of discharge or resource impact standards (i.e., they prescribe acceptable discharge limits or restrict logging to slopes of more than thirty-five degrees).

Even carefully crafted discharge standards do not, of course, eliminate uncertainty with respect to measuring whether the objective is being met. For instance, there will always be some uncertainty in what we referred to earlier as the dose-response relationship — in other words, the nature of the relationship between the behaviour the standard targets and the impact of that behaviour on the ambient environment. As well, because of the diversity of environments within which the activity being regulated occurs (of which forestry is a prime example), a generalized standard that may be consistent with the achievement of the objective in one context may not be appropriate in others. Indeed a one-size-fits-all quantitative performance standard can be under-protective of the desired objective in some contexts, and over-protective in others. Thus, under particularly sensitive soil conditions, logging on slopes of less than thirty-five degrees may well have significant environmental consequences. Conversely, where soil conditions are less sensitive, or if a low-impact logging method is used, it is plausible that harvesting could occur on slopes steeper than the standard prescribes without the objective of the standard being put in jeopardy.

There is also, in this context, the looming question of who is responsible for measuring, evaluating, and verifying performance. The logistical and resource challenges associated with these various tasks were a primary reason why, in first-generation environmental laws, the US government opted to employ a technology-based BAT approach. For similar reasons, many have been critical of the BC government's decision to replace the *Forest Practices Code* with results-based legislation, particularly given dramatic and ongoing budget cutbacks at the Ministry of Forests. The dilemma, of course, is that any potential gains in terms of the cost of regulatory oversight that might be achieved by moving toward a performance-based model are likely to be nullified if responsibility for measuring, evaluating, and verifying performance remains with the regulator. Indeed, many would argue that performance-based regulation, which offers the potential to reduce business costs, will actually lead to a significant increase in government administration costs if administered in a reasonably robust fashion. This is particularly so given the diversity of regulatory compliance arrangements that performance-based standards authorize.

Governments are, of course, not alone in expressing concerns on this front. To the extent that open-ended performance-based standards (as opposed to more easily auditable management- or technology-based standards) play a key role in voluntary codes, the task of certifiers is made more difficult. More importantly, however, unless there is broad confidence that the standards articulated are subject to rigorous and regular measurement, evaluation, and verification, their perceived legitimacy (and ultimately their viability) will be put in jeopardy.

Choosing the Optimal Form of Standard

A consensus appears to be emerging that choosing the best form of standard requires careful consideration of a variety of context-specific factors, including the logistics associated with measuring, evaluating, and verifying achievement of the objectives of the standard, as well as the nature of the "regulated community".

It is claimed, for example, that where it is a relatively straightforward matter to assess whether a standard's objective is being achieved (by means of measurable indicators or other well-correlated proxies, for example), and if it can be done at a relatively low cost, a preference should be given to performance-based standards. Alternatively, where it may be difficult or costly to monitor firm-level performance, and where the regulated sector is relatively homogenous, the best regulatory option may be one that is technology-based. This is especially likely to be true when the relationship between action and output is well understood and can be easily evaluated.

However, where the regulated community is composed of "heterogeneous enterprises facing heterogeneous conditions", there is emerging agreement that a strong theoretical justification exists for management-based standards, all other things being equal. Adopting this option, it is said, allows operators to deploy their informational resources and act on their private incentives insofar as they are not inconsistent with achieving the standard's broader public objectives. To make such a system work, however, two key considerations will be, first, whether to exhort or actively enforce management planning, implementation, or both; and, second, the degree of overlap between a firm's private interests and society's needs.

Notes and Questions

1. Do you agree with the authors' contention that the choice of what form of standard regulators should adopt should be entirely context-dependent? Should the default preference be for performance-based standards, as many in business would argue?

2. In selecting a form of standard, what should be the most decisive factors? What form(s) of standard are most suitable for regulating the environmental impacts of the following sectors and/or industries: nuclear technology, computer component manufacturing, drycleaners, auto-parts recyclers, mining, fisheries, forestry, airlines?

Part III — The Emerging Governance-based Approach to Environmental Regulation

Contemporary debate over the future of environmental regulation is influenced by a variety of factors. A common feature is an appetite for new approaches born, certainly at least in part, out of a sense that traditional regulatory approaches have failed (whether cast in M'Gonigle et al.'s terminology as "permissive regulation" or by business critics as prescriptive "command and control" regulation). Increasingly, there is a consensus that governments cannot and should not be expected to do it all; as it is often expressed, governments should "steer, not row". Thus, as several authors suggest below, while command and control should remain the preferred mode of regulation in some contexts, in others there are good reasons to experiment with new forms of regulation aimed at enlisting market forces and civil society in promoting more sustainable environmental outcomes. In short, this emerging literature on new or reconfigured environmental regulation argues for a new conception of both how we govern the environment and who the "we" includes.

However, before we introduce some of the leading proponents (and critics) of what might be termed "new governance-based" environmental regulation, we will first offer the following excerpt by Howlett that provides an overview of what for most of the last half of the twentieth century has been the prevailing approach to understanding policy instruments.

Michael Howlett,
"Policy Instruments, Policy Styles, and Policy Implementation:
National Approaches to Theories of Instrument Choice"
(1991) 19 Policy Studies Journal 1

Political scientists have studied policy instruments in order to better understand the linkages between policy formulation and policy implementation, and to gain insights into the public policy decision-making process. [...]

Grappling with the complexity of policy instrument choices poses an interesting set of problems for political scientists, who have responded by developing a number of categorization schemes and taxonomies in the effort to reduce or manage the complexity and systematically identify the key variables at work in such decisions. Interestingly enough, as shall be argued below, political scientists working in different countries have come up with a number of different schemes identifying different sets of key variables at work in policy instrument choices. [...]

Conceptualizing Policy Instruments: General Considerations

"Policy instruments" is the generic term provided to encompass the myriad techniques at the disposal of governments to implement their public policy objectives. Sometimes referred to as "governing instruments" or "tools of government," these techniques range in complexity and age, although most are well known to students and practitioners of public administration.

Most present day studies of policy instruments have their origins in the work of Theodore Lowi. Policy analysts in many countries were influenced by Lowi's early efforts to categorize the types of policies which governments could enact, and by his effort to differentiate policies according to the criterion of coerciveness [...].

Policy Instruments: The Canadian Literature

[A distinct] approach to the question of instrument choice exists in Canada, where debate among political scientists over the issue has taken the form of criticisms and reformulations of ideas initially developed by G Bruce Doern of Carleton University in collaboration with several other colleagues at Ontario universities. Doern and his colleagues were [...] influenced by the writings of Theodore Lowi, and especially by Lowi's observation that governments faced distinct choices in deciding how to implement their policies, choices which, to a certain extent, dictate the nature of future policies and policy decisions in the area concerned." In [...] monographs published in the late 1970s and early 1980s, Doern et al created a single continuum model of instrument choice, altering Lowi's matrix of policy choices into a continuum of instruments graded according to the "degrees of legitimate coercion" utilized [...] (see Figure 2).

At first Doern et al placed only self-regulation, exhortation, subsidies, and regulation on the scale [...] but later added categories for "taxation" and public enterprise [...] finally, [adding] an entire series of finer 'gradations" within each general category (Doern & Phidd, 1983). For Doern and his colleagues, this taxonomical exercise led to the hypothesis of a two-fold rationale of instrument choice, one that fit very well with the notion of a "continuum" of choices, and one which offered a great deal of explanatory power in the Canadian context. The Doern rationale was based on an appreciation of the ideological preferences of Canadian governments and on the "strength" of societal forces those governments wished to regulate. Assuming that all instruments were "substitutable" it was argued that in a liberal democratic society governments preferred to use the least coercive instruments available and would "move up the scale" as necessary to overcome societal resistance to effective regulation.

Figure 2.

Single Continuum of Instrument Choice				
Private Behavior	Exhortation	Expenditure	Regulation	Public Ownership
Self-Regulation	Speeches Conferences Advisory	Grants Subsidies Transfers Investigations	Taxes Tariffs Fines Imprison- ment	Crown-Corporations Mixed-Corporations
Minimum (Degrees of Legitimate Coercion) Maximum				

Source: Adapted from *Canadian Public Policy: Ideas, Structure & Process* by G.B. Doern and R.W. Phidd (1983).

The rationale behind the choice of instrument in the Doern model, then, is essentially ideological, with a good measure of contextual politics thrown in. That is, any instrument could "do the job", but governments will prefer less coercive instruments unless forced, by either recalcitrance on the part of the target group and/or continued social pressure for change, to utilize more coercive instruments.

Kathryn Harrison,
"Talking with the Donkey: Cooperative Approaches to Environmental Protection"
(1999) 2 Journal of Industrial Ecology 51

In the past decade, governments throughout the world have expressed growing interest in more flexible cooperative approaches to environmental protection. In the United States, this trend can be viewed as a reaction against the uniquely conflictual American approach to environmental regulation. This perspective is reflected in U.S. President Clinton's statement that

> The adversarial approach that has often characterized our environmental system precludes opportunities for creative solutions that a more collaborative system might encourage. When decision-making is shared, people can bridge differences, find common ground, and identify new solutions. To reinvent environmental protection, we must first build trust among traditional adversaries (Clinton and Gore 1995).

Interestingly, there is also renewed interest in cooperative policy instruments in countries such as the Netherlands, Canada, Australia, the United Kingdom, and Japan, where environmental regulation has traditionally been relatively cooperative. Thus, the European Union's Fifth Action Plan (EC 1996) states that

> Whereas previous environmental measures tended to be prescriptive in character with an emphasis on the "thou shalt not" approach, the new strategy leans more towards a "let's work together" approach. This reflects the growing realization in industry and in the business world that not only is industry a significant part of the (environmental) problem but it must also be part of the solution. The new approach implies, in particular, a reinforcement of the dialogue with industry and the encouragement, in appropriate circumstances, of voluntary agreements and other forms of self-regulation.

Cooperative approaches to environmental policy emphasize the valuable expertise residing in the business community and thus take seriously . . . the industrial firm as an "agent of change" rather than the "culprit" responsible for environmental degradation. Further, many policy instruments of particular interest to industrial ecology — covenants, extended producer responsibility, ecolabeling, and so on — rely to varying degrees on cooperation and voluntariness. Finally, some have speculated that voluntary approaches may be particularly amenable to forging collaborative networks across the product life cycle.

Clearly, the term "cooperative approaches" to environmental protection encompasses a wide variety of approaches, from more flexible enforcement of regulations to voluntary agreements, with much in-between. The first objective of this article is to provide a conceptual framework to distinguish among policy instruments predicated on cooperation between government and nongovernmental actors. The second is to focus on a subset of those approaches, voluntary agreements between government and business, and to examine theoretical arguments and empirical evidence concerning their effectiveness.

The article concludes that little empirical evidence exists concerning the environmental benefits of voluntary agreements. This is attributable, in part, to the recent nature of these policy reforms. However, the paucity of empirical evaluations also reflects more fundamental challenges in evaluating voluntary programs, which are characterized by self-selection and voluntary reporting and by an inadequate commitment to program evaluation by advocates of voluntary programs.

"Command and Control" versus Cooperation

As noted above, interest in cooperative approaches arises in large part from disenchantment with "command and control" regulation. The command and control model of uniform mandatory standards has been subject to a litany of criticisms. It has been argued that uniform standards are economically inefficient, that development and revision of formal regulations are unnecessarily slow, and that command and control regulation encourages end-of-pipe solutions rather than pollution prevention. Command and control regulation has also been criticized for specifying technologies rather than performance standards, thus stifling innovation and increasing costs to business; for failure to provide incentives for firms to go beyond compliance; and for a fragmented media-specific, pollutant-specific, and sector-specific approach. And finally, it is often argued that command and control regulation is unnecessarily adversarial and legalistic.

These are serious critiques indeed, although it should be noted that not all are uncontroversial. For instance, many argue that regulation is an important stimulus for, rather than impediment to, innovation. More importantly, analysts of environmental policy must be wary of the tendency to use the term "command and control" as a pejorative catchall for any and all criticisms of environmental regulation, because the term denies important differences among regulatory approaches and contexts. For instance, there is nothing inherent in the policy instrument of regulation (broadly defined as rules of behavior backed by sanctions legitimately available to government) that requires regulators to specify control techniques or to limit their focus to individual media, nor is the regulatory process in other countries as adversarial and litigious as in the United States. By the same token, one must resist the temptation to embrace equally diverse cooperative approaches as a panacea for all that ails regulation. As discussed below, many cooperative approaches that have been adopted in recent years are, in fact, regulatory. Moreover, cooperative approaches do not necessarily avoid media or technology specificity.

It is also important to acknowledge that to some degree interest in cooperative approaches may have little to do with the effectiveness of regulation in achieving environmental objectives. Governments routinely balance multiple policy objectives in choosing policy instruments. The choice of cooperative approaches thus may be driven more by concerns about the impacts of inflexible regulations on industrial competitiveness than by a desire to achieve a higher level of environmental protection. Alternatively, governments placing a high priority on deficit reduction may embrace voluntary cooperative approaches simply because they can no longer afford to pursue regulatory programs in the face of budgetary restraint. The evaluation of the effectiveness of voluntary approaches in the latter half of this article will thus consider multiple policy objectives of protecting the environment, cost effectiveness for both government and business, and democratic accountability and participation.

It is also noteworthy that the emphasis on cooperative approaches may in part reflect their political popularity rather than administrative effectiveness. Politicians may embrace cooperative nonregulatory approaches because they are unwilling to impose the costs of regulation on powerful business interests. The fact that cooperative approaches can be adopted for reasons that have little to do with environmental or other policy objectives (other than reelection) provides all the more reason to carefully evaluate the effectiveness of these new approaches to environmental protection.

Defining Cooperation

It is important to clarify at the outset just what is meant by "cooperation", because the term is likely to have different meaning from different perspectives. The Oxford Concise Dictionary defines cooperation as "working together to the same end". Several aspects of this definition warrant closer examination. First is the implicit question of just who is "working together". Many cooperative approaches that have emerged in recent years focus on partnerships between business and government, to the exclusion of other parties. Such approaches may enhance government cooperation with one group at the expense of conflict with others, such as environmentalists, who may resent exclusion or have substantive objections to agreements reached between government and business. One person's cooperation thus may be another's conflict. Consistent with recent policy developments, this article focuses on approaches that promote cooperation between business and government, although other parties may be involved as well.

A second element of the definition of cooperation concerns commonality of objectives. Cooperation is predicated on some measure of agreement or consent. However, when one is considering agreements between government and nongovernmental interests, the nature of that consent requires closer examination. This is because government, unlike private actors, has legitimate authority to coerce others (subject of course to constitutional limitations). This raises the question of whether business — government agreement with respect to environmental policy constitutes genuine cooperation, in the same way as one might question whether handing over one's wallet to an armed assailant constitutes cooperation. Bearing this in mind, one can envision various cooperative approaches situated along a continuum that varies in the extent of explicit or implied government coercion. From a practical perspective, the issue is that some approaches to public policy are *more cooperative* than others. The following section revisits this notion of a continuum in offering a simple typology of cooperative approaches.

The third element of the definition of cooperation is "working together". Government and business may collaborate in devising or implementing policies, or both. It is questionable, however, whether a government's choice not to intervene at all can be considered a form of business — government cooperation.

A Typology of Cooperative Approaches

One of the most straightforward typologies of policy instruments is that offered by Doern and Phidd (1992) who argue that governments choose among five broad classes of policy tools:

- Regulation (legal requirements backed by government sanctions);
- Government enterprise (direct provision of goods and services by either government agencies or government-owned enterprises);
- Expenditure;
- Exhortation;
- Inaction

In terms of the familiar analogy of how to get a donkey to pull a cart, these policy instruments correspond to using a stick to coerce the donkey (regulation), the driver pulling the cart herself (government enterprise), inducing the donkey to move with carrots (expenditure), encouraging the donkey through ear stroking and persuasion (exhortation), and leaving it up to whomever want the goods in the cart to work out their own arrangements with the donkey (government inaction).

These categories are, of course, not as simple as they seem. There is a broad range of tools within each category. Moreover, as noted above, there can also be a fine line between informal persuasion and formal regulation, because a donkey that has felt the stick in the past may respond to ear stroking less out of good will than fear. However, this typology nonetheless offers a useful starting point to distinguish among the variety of cooperative approaches to environmental protection that have emerged in recent years.

The vast majority of cooperative reforms fall into the three categories of regulation, exhortation, and government inaction. Assuming comparable policy objectives, these three classes of policy instruments can be placed along a continuum of coerciveness from regulation to exhortation to government inaction (Doern and Phidd 1992) [**Ed. Note:** discussed in preceding excerpt], although with considerable variation within each category. The following discussion reviews recent reforms in each of these categories, from most to least coercive.

Regulation: Kinder, Gentler Sticks

Compliance Support

Many cooperative reforms adopted in recent years are adaptations to traditional regulation. For instance, although mandatory compliance with regulations is still the norm, regulators in many jurisdictions are increasingly willing to assist regulated interests by clarifying requirements and providing technical advice on how to achieve compliance. Such programs are increasingly popular among the U.S. states, particularly as the reach of regulatory programs extends to increasingly small enterprises, which have fewer resources to devote to legal and environmental affairs.

Flexible Approaches to Compliance

A substantial body of literature argues that greater rates of compliance can be achieved by a cooperative and flexible approach to *enforcement* than an adversarial one. Proponents of cooperative enforcement argue that although frequent resort to the stick may compel greater compliance among firms inclined to evade the law, it risks destroying the good will of a much larger number of law-abiding firms, who resent being treated like criminals. Such firms may respond with perfunctory compliance with the narrow letter of the law rather than public-spirited efforts to comply with the intent of the law. At worst, a "culture of resistance" may emerge, in which firms help each other identify and exploit loopholes in regulations. Proponents of cooperative enforcement advocate a "tit for tat" strategy of initial forgiveness combined with increasingly stringent sanctions in the face of recalcitrant behavior.

A critical assumption underlying this argument is that there are more "good apples" than "bad apples". However, other scholars adopt an assumption consistent with public choice and neoclassical economic theory that virtually all firms are "bad apples" motivated exclusively by profits and thus inclined to comply with regulations only if anticipated sanctions outweigh the financial benefits of noncompliance. Quantitative comparisons of actual rates of compliance in response to different enforcement regimes are few and conflicting. Despite this, there has been growing attention to a variety of reforms to promote flexible and cooperative enforcement, including

- Reduced compliance monitoring for firms with certified environmental management systems;
- Guarantees of confidentiality for self-audits, with reduction or waiver of penalties in the event of voluntary disclosure and correction of noncompliance;
- Negotiated compliance agreements, which waive enforcement actions in exchange for a firm's commitment to a program to achieve compliance;
- Variances from regulatory requirements for firms pursuing innovative control strategies.

Cooperative Development of Regulatory Standards

The discussion thus far has concerned more cooperative ways to *implement* regulations. However, cooperation can also be extended to *development* of regulations in the first place. Cooperative standards development can take a variety of forms.

First, the number of participants in cooperative standard setting can vary. In Canada, Japan, and European countries with corporatist traditions of developing policies in concert with key interests, environmental standards have traditionally been set through bipartite negotiation with the regulated industry. Amid criticisms from excluded groups, some countries are now turning to multipartite processes. In Canada, "multistakeholder consultations" have become the norm in environmental standard setting at the federal level. The approach is similar to negotiated rulemaking in the United States. The U.S. Common Sense Initiative also attempted to achieve consensus among diverse interests on new approaches to environmental regulation. The number of participants in cooperative rulemaking thus can range from two to several dozen, with obvious implications for the speed, cost, and likelihood of agreement.

Mechanisms for public involvement in regulatory decision making also differ in the weight given to input from nongovernmental actors and the emphasis placed on consensus. When input is viewed as simply advisory to government decision makers, as in notice and comment rulemaking, there is no need for a single recommendation to emerge from nongovernmental participants. However, if there is a presumption that participants' recommendations will carry considerable weight, mechanisms to bring diverse societal interests together and to resolve their differences are more important. Regulatory negotiations often rely on a decision rule of consensus, although this has been criticized by some as overly resistant to change.

Exhortation: Talking with the Donkey

Governments can seek to persuade individuals or firms to change their behavior in a variety of ways. Although such approaches are nominally voluntary, in that no formal legal requirement is applied, they vary in degree of coerciveness. Closest to regulation along the spectrum of coercion are "voluntary agreements" between business and industry and government-sponsored codes of conduct. Voluntary agreements, such as the Dutch covenants discussed below, are characterized by strong expectations on the part of government that industry will comply. Such agreements are typically accompanied by an explicit or implied threat of regulation or other mandatory instruments should voluntary measures fail. Voluntary agreements or codes are usually negotiated by government and the private sector. Although many agreements take the form of nonbinding "gentlemen's agreements", others are legally binding contracts. Such contracts can still be considered voluntary, however, in the sense that the parties consent to assume certain obligations, in contrast to laws and regulations, which apply equally to all regardless of consent.

In contrast to voluntary agreements, governmental efforts to persuade target groups to change their behavior via "voluntary challenges" involve little or no arm-twisting in the form of threats of regulation or penalties for nonparticipation. Requirements of participation tend to be very flexible. Examples of these less coercive voluntary challenge programs include the U.S. Environmental Protection Agency's (EPA's) 33/50 program and Environment Canada's Accelerated Reduction/Elimination of Toxics program (ARET) . . . discussed below.

The least coercive approaches in this category are education and information dissemination programs, which may be directed at either the business community or consumers. Here, government does not explicitly encourage particular actions but does so implicitly by providing particular kinds of information to influence consumers' or firms' behavior. Examples of educational programs seeking to influence business include pollution prevention clearing-houses that provide information about pollution prevention techniques, while efforts to inform consumers include environmental awards for businesses and government-sponsored ecolabeling programs.

Government Inaction: Leaving the Donkey Alone

The final policy tool is for government to do nothing, leaving it to civil society to address a given environmental problem. Government coercion may still be a factor in this category, as when an implied threat of coercion causes actors to change their behavior in anticipation of government intervention, although in other cases the objectives of governmental and non-governmental actors may fortuitously coincide. Approaches in this category, including the Forest Stewardship Council, the Coalition for Environmentally Responsible Economies (CERES) Principles, Responsible Care, and International Standards Organization (ISO) 14000, essentially parallel the exhortation programs discussed above but with some entity other than government doing the educating or persuading. Programs in this category tend to rely on cooperation among nongovernmental actors rather than between government and business, and thus are not examined in detail in this article. [...]

Jody Freeman & Daniel Farber,
"Modular Environmental Regulation"
(2005) 54 Duke L.J. 795

Environmental law and natural resource management feature another important debate over the preferred tools of environmental regulation — a debate that pits traditional "command and control" regulation (referred to here as prescriptive regulation) against market mechanisms, which are thought to be more efficient. Emissions trading schemes are the most common form of market mechanism in environmental regulation thus far. The most familiar example is the acid rain program in the *Clean Air Act* (CAA). Emissions trading schemes allocate pollution rights within an industrial sector or geographic region based on the theory that firms that can reduce their emissions at a lower cost will be encouraged to do so by a market mechanism in which they can sell their excess allocation to firms for which such reductions would be more expensive. This presumably accomplishes the ultimate regulatory goal (which government still establishes) in the most efficient way.

In contrast, prescriptive regulation usually requires that all firms in a given industrial sector reduce emissions equally. Such an approach is too costly, the argument goes, because it fails to account for the marginal cost of compliance among differently situated firms. Uniform regulation is widely thought to be intrusive, interfering with the industrial process by mandating the adoption of particular technologies regardless of the peculiarities of different industrial processes. Another related criticism of prescriptive regulation, especially at the national level, is that it is too "centralized" and coarse grained to respond adequately to differences in local conditions, let alone to the diversity of local preferences regarding the degree of pollution control that is appropriate given its costs. Centralized top-down regulation is thought to inhibit the kind of policy and institutional innovations that come only from local knowledge and experience.

Prescriptive regulation is also widely believed to inhibit technological innovation because firms required to reduce emissions to the same level have no incentive to develop new technologies that could reduce emissions even further below the agency standard. Another more practical concern is that much of the information most relevant to prescriptive regulators is in the hands of industry, including information about the costs of controlling emissions, operational details about industrial processes, and rates of compliance. Unless ordered to do so, industry has little incentive to reveal this kind of information fully. Without this information, agencies will find implementation difficult. And prescriptive regulation requires procedures, such as rulemaking, that tend to be slow, cumbersome, conflict ridden, and, therefore, costly. The pace of rulemaking makes it difficult to respond to rapid changes in technology or new information.

In view of this critique, the standard advice of economists is to move toward a system of market-based incentives. Already, there are proposals to extend emissions trading to pollutants other than sulfur dioxide, as in the Bush administration's Clear Skies initiative, as well as to carbon, as recent legislation proposes. Other proposals go beyond the air context to address different settings and harms. Examples include watershed-based effluent trading and wetlands mitigation banking. Moving further in the direction of market approaches would also presumably require making greater use of a wider range of mechanisms, including effluent taxes, deposit-refund systems, and user fees such as those levied in "Pay-As-You-Throw" waste collection systems.

Advocates of prescriptive regulation argue two things in response to the critique just described: first, that many of the assumptions about the uniformity, inflexibility, and high cost of prescriptive regulation are either wrong or overstated; and second, that prescriptive regulation is still necessary as the backbone of the regulatory system because market mechanisms are risky and frequently do not deliver on their promise. Indeed, although some market experiments are reputed to be enormous successes (e.g., the *Clean Air Act*'s Acid Rain program), the empirical record on their performance is, in fact, mixed. Advocates of conventional prescriptive regulation argue that despite its imperfections, command and control has delivered significant environmental gains.

Even those favorably disposed to market mechanisms in theory will concede that significant problems of design and enforcement can in practice inhibit their ability to deliver environmental benefits. For example, political considerations tend to dominate the initial allocation of entitlements in market regimes (as was the case with allocation of units of sulfur dioxide pollution in the acid rain program), which can undermine their purported efficiency. Markets can be too narrowly or broadly drawn, and prices can be set inaccurately. To establish an effluent tax or design an emissions trading system, the government must establish a shadow price — a price that reflects the real costs of pollution — but the unavailability of a market benchmark makes this a difficult undertaking. This, of course, is the problem with public goods like the environment: the ostensible market justification for intervening in environmental regulation in the first place is that the market is unable to price environmental harms properly. In addition, the more the system is tailored to local conditions, whether by adjusting the effluent or emissions tax to account for variations in harm, or by establishing a system of "exchange rates" for permits, the more cumbersome the system becomes.

Trading schemes can falter because of difficulties both in valuing environmental commodities and ensuring that trades involve commensurate goods. It may be especially challenging to devise market approaches to natural resource management rather than pollution, because natural resources, like ecosystems, perform functions that may be enormously difficult to value and to trade. Markets can also create "hotspots" of concentrated pollution, which can disproportionately affect subpopulations, leading to claims of distributional inequity. Again, to the extent that the market regime is tailored to address such distributional concerns, some efficiencies may be lost.

Finally, market mechanisms generally require some easily monitored indicator that can be subject to trading or tax. This may be feasible for some pollution problems (as with sulfur dioxide, which is emitted by a fairly small number of power plants) but it is more difficult to implement in other contexts in which there are large numbers of sources or in which the emissions rates are hard or expensive to monitor. This is the case with the pollutants that contribute to ground level ozone.

And so the debate goes. Framing the debate between prescriptive versus market based regulation in either-or terms echoes the dichotomous nature of the federalism debate. In reality, both environmental law and natural resource management rely on a mix of mechanisms. Moreover, neither kind of instrument is as "pure" as the two poles of the debate would suggest: virtually every market mechanism of environmental regulation depends on some prescribed government limit, such as setting a cap, in the emissions trading context, beneath which trades occur. And in all of these regimes, the government — either Congress through legislation or agencies through regulation — plays a crucial role in monitoring and adjusting the rules to respond to new events or information.

Similarly, prescriptive regulations, such as technology-based standards, are not as uniform and rigid as some would suggest. Most standards are performance standards that firms can achieve in any way they choose (although admittedly, the easiest assurance of compliance is to adopt whatever technology the relevant agency used to set the standard). Most importantly, prescriptive regulation always relies to some extent on adjustments in light of economic realities — both in the initial phase of level setting, when the regulatory agency takes account of industrial processes and capacities in choosing the standard, and later, when agencies negotiate particular permits. There is also considerable flexibility in the enforcement process, when agencies must determine whether firms are out of compliance and what must be done in response. The so-called "command and control" system is infused with negotiation and accommodation. To label it "uniform", "rigid", and "centralized", although rhetorically powerful, is somewhat misleading. In practice, levels established by regulation frequently operate more like targets than like strict requirements. There are market-driven limits, in other words, to the extent to which government both "commands" and "controls" firm behavior.

The point is this: twenty years of experience suggests that it is impossible to declare a clear winner in this debate. Whether an instrument works optimally depends on a variety of factors, some of which are easier to predict and control than others. These include: the sophistication of the market participants; the size and diversity of the market; the vulnerability of the environmental "good" or "service" to accurate valuation; the vulnerability of the regime to political rigging in the allocation process; and the potential for gaming, shirking, and cheating by the regulated entities, among other things. The challenge now is to mix and match instruments in a way that is sensitive to the contexts — political, economic, geographical — in which they are deployed, and to remember that no matter how well-designed regulatory or management tools might be in theory, for their success they each require effective implementation and monitoring. [...]

Chris Tollefson, Fred Gale & David Haley,
Setting the Standard
(UBC Press, 2008) at 254–257

The critique of command-and-control-style regulation can, in many ways, be seen as the result of an ongoing, sometimes overtly ideological, battle over US environmental policy. Paradoxically, federal American environmental laws became a target for sustained critique not because they had failed, but in large measure because they had succeeded. Most of these laws — most notably the *Clean Air Act*, the *Clean Water Act*, and the *Resource Conservation and Recovery Act* — were enacted within a single decade, between 1970 and 1980.

Unlike other federal jurisdictions, where national governments, for various constitutional and political reasons, have tended to eschew taking a leadership role in tackling environmental issues, in the United States these laws reflected a broad consensus that the federal government not only had the legal authority (founded on the powerful Commerce Clause) to take leadership on environmental issues, but that it was also politically obliged (and, arguably, best situated) to do so.

The American approach was anomalous in terms of the scope of the federal role; it was also unique in terms of its reliance on a particular mode of regulation. Virtually all the federal environmental laws enacted in this period employed best available technology (BAT) standards. Under these standards, regulated facilities were obliged to install the most stringent pollution-control technology available, up to the point that the costs of doing so would cause them to shut down. For the most part, BAT standards were sector specific and were typically applied uniformly on a national basis. These American laws were also unique insofar as they provided legal means (known as "citizen suits") by which citizens could challenge permit holders and governments for failing to comply with or effectively enforce legal obligations prescribed by these permitting arrangements. [**Ed. Note: See further discussion of citizen suits as an enforcement mechanism in Chapter 5.**] The decision to adopt the BAT approach was justified on various grounds: among other benefits, they minimized government monitoring and enforcement costs, enhanced public scrutiny and participation in compliance efforts, reduced the potential for "regulatory capture" and other forms of political manipulation, and minimized inter-state competition that might arise from the potential for pollution havens.

By most accounts, over the ensuing quarter-century these laws, and the programs that were funded to implement them at the federal and state levels, brought about significant improvements in environmental quality. These improvements were particularly notable in relation to discharges from single point sources. Before long, however, these first-generation environmental laws came under sustained criticism.

Although the critics usually conceded that these first-generation laws had been successful in "picking the low-hanging fruit", they argued that the BAT model was in many ways highly inefficient. They claimed, for example, that one-size-fits-all approaches (such as BAT) ignore basic cost-benefit analysis by failing to take into account the social benefits of reducing pollution in a given setting (relative to the costs of securing those benefits) or the differential ability of firms within a given sector to meet the BAT standard. Critics also railed at the costs to business of the culture of legal adversarialism that, they claimed, the laws promoted. Moreover, they contended that, although a case could be made that BAT was an effective means of regulating industry laggards, it provided no incentive for more responsible firms to make research and development investments in new pollution-control technologies. For these reformers, the policy prescription was clear. Having combated the first-generation challenges of curbing the most serious and pressing major sources of pollution, the time had come to enact a second generation of laws that were capable of leveraging further pollution reductions in circumstances where the marginal cost of achieving progress was typically high, and that could also address discharges from small, non-point sources, including those in the consumer, services, and agricultural sectors.

The reformers' critique did not go unchallenged. Defenders of the prevailing legal regime pointed to its record of achievement in enhancing air and water quality, to the additional regulatory costs associated with requiring federal agencies to undertake additional cost-benefit and risk analyses, to the dangers of leaving to the market (through pollution-trading regimes and other less state-centric instruments favoured by reformers) determinations with respect to risk exposure at the local level, and, perhaps above all, to the state's obligation to actively engage in safeguarding environmental values as public goods.

Through much of the late 1980s and early 1990s, this debate was cast as a classic showdown between proponents of free markets and defenders of a strong, interventionist state. By the mid-1990s, with the arrival of the Clinton administration, a shift in the tenor of the debate began to emerge. At this point, it was becoming clear that the ambitious legislative aspirations of the reformers were unlikely to be realized in the short term, if at all. At the same time, their critique was having an impact in a more interstitial fashion. Starting in the early 1990s, the US Environmental Protection Agency drew on the reformers' arguments to initiate a variety of programs aimed at combating the perceived rigidities and inflexibilities associated with first-generation laws. Among them were programs that facilitated pollution credit trading and provided new incentives, including regulatory relief, for superior environmental performers. Existing legislative arrangements were left largely intact.

By the mid-1990s, a debate that had focused on US environmental law and been dominated by American legal scholars and economists began to expand outward. There was a growing sense that the regulatory questions being mooted in relation to the future of US environmental law were of much wider significance. The most important of the new contributions to the debate is an approach to regulatory reform that its Australian originators termed "smart regulation" (Gunningham and Grabosky 1998; Gunningham and Sinclair 2002).

The thesis promoted by Gunningham and his colleagues is deceptively simple: a pluralistic, flexible, context-specific approach should be taken to instrument choice in the realm of environmental policy and beyond. Drawing on case studies of regulatory innovation in North America, Europe, and Australia, the authors contend that framing the choice of instrument in ideological terms — state versus market — was unhelpful. Moreover, it is important not to underestimate the successes of, nor the continuing need for, command-and-control-style regulation. However, they argued that, in many cases, better environmental outcomes can be leveraged by deploying a mix of policy instruments tailored to the particular goals and circumstances of the regulatory context. Governments can also achieve better results (given static or declining budgets) if they harness resources from outside the public sector by engaging directly with regulated parties, communities, and civil society organizations. In this regard, governments should "steer not row" and should, where possible, "govern from a distance". To this end, they should be ready to engage in continuing governance experiments aimed at identifying and testing new ways to share governance responsibilities by empowering business and civil society through information, networks, and partnerships.

The debate over "smart regulation" has produced a remarkable outpouring of scholarly work. Many governments have adopted the term to provide intellectual justification for a wide range of public-sector regulatory reform initiatives. In the United States, for example, federal agencies are now directed by executive order (originally issued by President Clinton and later affirmed by President Bush) to specify performance objectives, rather than behaviour, whenever this is feasible as they craft new regulations. Many federal agencies, including the Environmental Protection Agency, the Nuclear Regulatory Commission, and the federal Highway Administration, to name a few, are piloting performance-based regulatory programs. The influence of the smart-regulation critique has also resonated in potentially sweeping law and policy reforms taking place in many other Western liberal democracies, including Canada, the United Kingdom, and Australia.

Neil Gunningham,
"Beyond Compliance: Next Generation Environmental Regulation"
(2002), online: < https://pdfs.semanticscholar.org/55d2/
db0bf9c9002feca23073d1d8dff27c47556c.pdf >

The environmental impact of industry, especially pollution, has been subject to regulation for at least three decades, under an approach that is somewhat unfairly called "command and control" regulation. This approach typically specifies standards, and sometimes technologies, with which the regulated must comply (the "command") or be penalized (the "control"). It commonly requires polluters to apply the best feasible techniques to minimize the environmental harm caused by their activities. Command and control has achieved some considerable successes, especially in terms of reducing air and water pollution. However, this "first generation" of environmental regulation has been widely criticized by economists for inhibiting innovation and for its high costs, inflexibility and diminishing returns.

The problems of command and control can be overstated and its considerable achievements too easily dismissed. At the same time, its limitations have led policymakers and regulators to recognize that it provides only a part of the policy solution, particularly in a rapidly changing, increasingly complex and interdependent world. However, regulatory reform must take place in an environment of shrinking regulatory resources, making it necessary in some contexts to design strategies capable of achieving results even in the absence of a credible enforcement regime (as when dealing with small and medium-sized enterprises), and in almost all circumstances to extract the "biggest bang" from a much diminished "regulatory buck" [...]

The crucial question is: where should one go next in terms of regulatory policy? The challenge is to find ways to overcome the inefficiencies of traditional regulation, to devise better ways of encouraging innovation and of achieving environmental protection at an acceptable economic and social cost. This will involve the design of a "second phase" of regulation: one that still involves government intervention, but selectively and in combination with a range of market and non-market solutions, and of public and private regulatory orderings.

In designing innovative regulation, it is crucial to remember that "one size does not fit all". Different sized organizations experience different challenges in complying with regulations, and very different regulatory strategies will be needed to address them (contrast the issues in regulating transnational corporations with those of regulating small and medium-sized enterprises). So, too, it is necessary to design different strategies for different industry sectors: what is appropriate for the chemical industry may be entirely inappropriate for regulating agriculture [...]

Broadly speaking, policy instruments can be located on a continuum from the least to the most interventionist. For example, the paradigm case of the latter is command and control regulation in the American mould: highly prescriptive and enforced coercively. At the other extreme are instruments such as pure voluntarism, education and some information-based approaches. In between (in escalating degrees of intervention) lie mechanisms such as self-regulation and economic instruments.

Self-regulation

Self-regulation is not a precise concept, but for present purposes it may be defined as a process whereby an organized group regulates the behaviour of its members. Most commonly it involves an industry-level organization (as opposed to the government or individual firms) setting rules and standards (codes of practice) relating to the conduct of firms in the industry.

Because standard-setting and identification of breaches are the responsibility of practitioners, with detailed knowledge of the industry, this will arguably lead to more practicable standards, more effectively policed. There is also the potential for utilizing peer pressure and for successfully internalizing responsibility for compliance. Moreover, because self-regulation contemplates ethical standards of conduct that extend beyond the letter of the law, it may significantly raise standards of behaviour and lead to a greater integration of environmental issues into the management process. Finally, and crucially, in some circumstances and forms, self-regulation holds out the possibility of encouraging dissemination of information about new technologies and of thereby facilitating their more rapid introduction.

Yet in practice, self-regulation often fails to fulfil its theoretical promise. The evidence suggests that self-regulation is rarely effective in achieving compliance (i.e., obedience by the target population/s with regulation/s) — at least if it is used as a "stand alone" strategy without sanctions. This is because self-regulatory standards are often weak, enforcement is commonly (although not invariably) ineffective, and punishment is secret and mild.

Voluntary Agreements

At a general level this category embraces agreements between governments and individual businesses or industry sectors, taking the form of "non-mandatory contracts between equal partners, one of which is government, in which incentives for action arise from mutual interests rather than from sanctions". However, the variety of such agreements makes precise classification difficult. The most common categories are (a) public voluntary agreements such as "challenge" programmes and (b) negotiated voluntary agreements between governments and industry. There is very little evidence to suggest the former has a positive impact on innovation and for present purposes we focus on the latter.

Negotiated agreements involve specific commitments to environmental protection elaborated through bargaining between industry and a public authority. In Europe they are usually entered into by an industry association and government against a backdrop of threatened legislation: the tacit bargain being that if the industry will commit to reach given environmental outcomes through its own initiatives, government will hold off on legislation it would otherwise contemplate enacting to address the problem.

Unfortunately, the empirical literature on negotiated agreements is very limited. Many existing agreements lack clear targets, and have inadequate reporting requirements and deadlines, making evaluation of their success extremely difficult. Indeed, one of the few things upon which almost all analysts of voluntary agreements seem to agree is that far too little attention has so far been given to evaluating either their economic or environmental benefits. However, preliminary assessments of the value of the early voluntary agreements are not encouraging.

Informational Regulation and Civic Environmentalism

An increasingly important alternative or supplement to conventional regulation is what is becoming known as "informational regulation". As the OECD (1994: 8) puts it: "People and businesses often care deeply about contributing responsibly to the public good (businesses also care about 'reputation'), and governments can use information, communication, encouragement, peer pressure, and education strategies to convince the public of the need for change". In contrast to command and control, informational regulation involves the state encouraging (as in corporate environmental reporting) or requiring (as with community right to know) information about environmental impacts but without directly requiring a change in those practices. Rather, this approach relies upon economic markets and public opinion as the mechanisms to bring about improved performance.

Informational regulation is growing rapidly, partly because of the success of some of the early initiatives, partly because it offers a cost effective and less interventionist alternative to command and control in a period of contracting regulatory resources, partly because of its capacity to empower communities and NGOs, and partly because changes in technology make the use of such strategies increasingly viable and cost-effective.

Probably the most successful and best known form of information regulation is the use of community right to know (CRTK) and pollution inventories.

Space precludes a discussion of other forms of informational regulation such as the use of corporate reporting on environmental (and on ethical and social) performance, and product labeling and certification. Suffice it to say that informational regulation strategies work better in some circumstances than others. The evidence suggests that they work best with respect to large companies and environmentally aware communities.

A related development is the growth of "civic regulation", whereby various manifestations of civil society act in a variety of ways to influence corporations, consumers and markets, often by-passing the state and rejecting political lobbying in favour of what they believe to be far more effective strategies [...] Market campaigning focusing on highly visible branded retailers is a particularly favoured strategy. Less so are campaigns that seek to provide a market premium for "environmentally preferred" produce, due largely to the unwillingness of consumers to support such a strategy. More recently, certification programmes such as the Forest Stewardship Council are "transforming traditional power relationships in the global arena. Linking together diverse and often antagonistic actors from the local, national and international levels [...] to govern firm behaviour in a global space that has eluded the control of states and international organizations".

[...] the evolving role of civic regulation has not taken place entirely divorced from state intervention. On the contrary, either in response to pressure from the institutions of civil society or in recognition of the limits of state regulation, governments are gradually providing greater roles for communities, environmental NGOs and the public more generally. Thus a number of second-generation policy instruments are geared to empower various institutions of civil society to play a more effective role in shaping business behaviour, thus facilitating civic regulation. These include not only the sort of CRTK legislation described above, but also a variety of other mechanisms that seek to empower third parties, for example, by giving environmental NGOs or communities a "seat at the table" (and enabling them to influence directly planning or licensing conditions), by providing them with the standing to bring a legal action, or the information with which to threaten the reputation capital of large corporations.

Notes and Questions

1. As Gunningham suggests, "policy instruments can be located on a continuum from the least to the most interventionist" as measured in terms of government involvement. At one end of the spectrum are what many would refer to as "command and control"-based approaches, which typically take the form of licences or permits that specify what technology a regulated party must employ or what environmental outcome they must achieve (specified either in terms of permissible discharges or resulting environ-mental quality). At the other end of the spectrum are approaches where government involvement is modest or absent altogether. Within this category are approaches in which industry (and sometimes civil society organiza-tions) take the lead, including voluntary codes of practice, educational programs, and some information- and certification-based approaches of the type Gunningham describes above. Towards the middle of this spectrum lie what are often referred to as market-based approaches, such as cap and trade regimes and environmental taxes. A defining feature of these approaches is that, while they are established and administered by government, firms retain considerable autonomy in terms of whether and how they participate in such regimes.

2. Historically, Canadian governments have been much more reluctant to employ emissions trading (often called "cap and trade") approaches to pollution control than their American counterparts. Cap and trade systems require government to establish a maximum "cap" on emissions/discharges into a specific air- or watershed. Firms are then each allocated an emission or discharge entitlement. This entitlement then becomes a tradeable

commodity. Depending on its needs, the firm can deploy its entitlement to meet its legal obligations, bank it for future use, or sell it on the open market. By pricing pollution in this way, the theory is that firms will have a strong incentive to reduce their environmental footprint. As Freeman and Farber describe, while a cap and trade regime established under the US *Clean Air Act* to combat acid rain has enjoyed some success, such regimes are by no means an environmental panacea. Bearing this in mind, it is intriguing to note that several Canadian provinces are in the process of establishing greenhouse gas (GHG) cap and trade regimes as a means of responding to climate change: see further discussion in Chapter 10.

Part IV — Environmental Regulation, Innovation and Economic Performance

Another important facet of the debate over environmental regulatory reform and governance is the nature of the relationship between environmental regulation and economic performance. Can governments, by careful deployment of well-crafted environmental regulation, simultaneously spur innovation and competitiveness? The conditions under which and means by which this could occur remain the subject of considerable debate. Likely the best-known proponent of the potential for this outcome to occur was Harvard economist Michael Porter. The next excerpt offers a retrospective view on the "Porter Hypothesis". It is followed by an excerpt from an article that considers a pioneering legislative experiment in Nova Scotia that builds on many of the principles of new governance we have been discussing, which aims to promote both enhanced environmental outcomes and economic prosperity.

Stefan Ambec, *et al.*,
"The Porter Hypothesis at 20: Can Environmental Regulation Enhance Innovation and Competitiveness?"

(Resources for the Future, 2011),
online: < http://ssrn.com/abstract = 1754674 >

Introduction

Twenty years ago, Harvard Business School economist and strategy professor Michael Porter stood conventional wisdom about the impact of environmental regulation on business on its head by declaring that well-designed regulation could actually enhance competitiveness. According to Porter (1991), "Strict environmental regulations do not inevitably hinder competitive advantage against rivals; indeed, they often enhance it." He went on to suggest various mechanisms by which environmental regulations might enhance competitiveness, such as reduction in the use of costly chemicals or lower waste disposal costs. The traditional view of environmental regulation held by virtually all economists until that time was that requiring firms to reduce an externality like pollution necessarily restricted their options and thus by definition reduced their profits.

After all, if profitable opportunities existed to reduce pollution, profit-maximizing firms would already be taking advantage of those opportunities.

Over the past 20 years, much has been written about what has since become known simply as the Porter Hypothesis (PH). Yet even today, we find conflicting evidence, alternative theories that might explain the PH, and oftentimes a misunderstanding of what the PH does and does not say. However, a careful examination of both the theory and evidence yields some important policy implications for design of regulatory instruments, as well as a rich research agenda to further understand what works, what does not, and why [...]

The Porter Hypothesis

The traditional view among economists and managers concerning environmental protection is that it comes at an additional cost imposed on firms, which may erode their global competitiveness. Environmental regulations (ER) such as technological standards, environmental taxes, or tradable emissions permits force firms to allocate some inputs (labor, capital) to pollution reduction, which is unproductive from a business perspective. Technological standards restrict the choice of technologies or inputs in the production process. Taxes and tradable permits charge firms for their emissions pollution, a by-product of the production process that was free before. These fees necessarily divert capital away from productive investments.

This traditional paradigm was challenged by a number of analysts, notably Professor Michael Porter (Porter 1991) and his coauthor Claas van der Linde (Porter and van der Linde 1995). Based on case studies, the authors suggest that pollution is often a waste of resources and that a reduction in pollution may lead to an improvement in the productivity with which resources are used. More stringent but properly designed environmental regulations (in particular, market-based instrument such as taxes or cap-and-trade emissions allowances) can "trigger innovation [broadly defined] that may partially or more than fully offset the costs of complying with them" in some instances (Porter and van der Linde 1995, 98) [...]

As Porter and van der Linde first described this relationship, if properly designed, environmental regulations can lead to "innovation offsets" that will not only improve environmental performance, but also partially—and sometimes more than fully—offset the additional cost of regulation.

Porter and van der Linde go on to explain that there are at least five reasons that properly crafted regulations may lead to these outcomes:

- First, regulation signals companies about likely resource inefficiencies and potential technological improvements.
- Second, regulation focused on information gathering can achieve major benefits by raising corporate awareness.
- Third, regulation reduces the uncertainty that investments to address the environment will be valuable.
- Fourth, regulation creates pressure that motivates innovation and progress.
- Fifth, regulation levels the transitional playing field.

Finally, they note, "We readily admit that innovation cannot always completely offset the cost of compliance, especially in the short term before learning can reduce the cost of innovation-based solutions" (Porter and van der Linde 1995, 100).

The Porter Hypothesis has met with great success in political debate, especially in the United States, because it contradicts the idea that environmental protection is always detrimental to economic growth. The PH has been invoked to persuade the business community to accept environmental regulations, as it may benefit from them in addition to other stakeholders. In a nutshell, well-designed environmental regulations might lead to a Pareto improvement or "win—win" situation in some cases, by not only protecting the environment, but also enhancing profits and competitiveness through the improvement of the products or their production process or through enhancement of product quality.

The PH has been criticized for being incompatible with the assumption of profit-maximizing firms (see Palmer et al. 1995). Indeed, the hypothesis rests on the idea that firms often ignore profitable opportunities. In other words, why would regulation actually be needed for firms to adopt profit-increasing innovations? In fact, Porter directly questions the view that firms are profit-maximizing entities: "The possibility that regulation might act as a spur to innovation arises because the world does not fit the Panglossian belief that firms always make optimal choices." As discussed below, firms might not appear to be making optimal choices for many reasons, such as imperfect information or organizational or market failures.

Moreover, even if systematically profitable business opportunities are missed ("low-hanging fruits"), the next question is, how could environmental regulations change that reality? Are regulators in a better position than managers to find these profitable business opportunities? Porter argues that environmental regulation may help firms identify inefficient uses of costly resources. They may also produce and disseminate new information (e.g., best-practice technologies) and help overcome organizational inertia.

There is much confusion in the literature about what the Porter Hypothesis actually says. As we note above, it does *not* say that all regulation leads to innovation—only that well-designed regulations do. This is consistent with the growing trend toward performance-based and/or market-based environmental regulations. Second, it does *not* state that this innovation necessarily offsets the cost of regulation—that is, it does not claim that regulation is *always* a free lunch. Instead, it does make the claim that in many instances, these innovations will more than offset the cost of regulation—in other words, there may be a free lunch in many cases...

Design of Policies to Enhance Competitiveness

It is clear from both the original Porter writings and empirical evidence to date that both innovation and competitiveness outcomes depend significantly on the context. The PH itself was premised on flexible, market-based regulation— not rigid command-and-control regulation. Beyond environmental regulations, other government policies can interact with the link between environmental regulation and innovation or competitiveness. In this section, we briefly explore the implications of policy design for the PH.

Environmental Policies

As mentioned by Porter, the type of regulatory instrument is an important premise of the PH. As Porter and van der Linde (1995, 110) argue:

> If environmental standards are to foster the innovation offsets that arise from new technologies and approaches to production, they should adhere to three principles. First, they must create the maximum opportunity for innovation, leaving the approach to innovation to industry and not the standard-setting agency. Second, regulations should foster continuous improvement, rather than locking in any particular technology. Third, the regulatory process should leave as little room as possible for uncertainty at every stage.

Market-based and flexible instruments such as emissions taxes or tradable allowances, or performance standards, are more favorable to innovation than technological standards, because they leave more freedom to firms on the technological solution to minimize compliance costs.

Some authors, like Jaffe and Palmer (1997), refer to that as the narrow version of the PH. In this vein, Burtraw (2000) provides evidence that the switch in environmental regulations for SO2 emissions in the United States from a technological standard with emissions caps to an allowance trading program in 1990 considerably reduced compliance cost (40% to 140% lower than projection)—although the net effect was still a net cost. However, the switch to an emissions cap enhanced innovation and fostered organizational change and competition on the upstream input market. The program left enough flexibility for the firm to select the best strategy for reducing emissions, including a switch to coal with lower sulfur content. The industry also experienced innovation in fuel blending and in the scrubber market. In addition, the switch from a technological standard to tradable emissions allowances led to a transfer of responsibility from engineers or chemists, typically in charge of environmental issues, to top executives such as financial vice presidents, who are trained to treat SO2 emissions allowances as financial assets [...]

Organizational or Governance Conditions

As noted, Porter argues that organizational inertia can be one reason why firms are missing profitable opportunities to both reduce pollution and increase profits. In the same vein, environmental regulations might help firms overcome their organizational inertia by forcing them to review the organization of production and their business model. This is more likely in firms with deficient governance structures, including asymmetric information with firms among divisions, lack of commitment by the hierarchy, costly communication, or contractual incompleteness. Such organizational or governance failures either constrain the ability of managers to pursue their objectives or distort incentives within the firm. The results from Burtraw (2000) showing how SO2 allowances were handled by financial officers instead of environmental managers is a good example, as financial officers presumably had more of an incentive to reduce pollution (which would either increase the value of allowance they could sell or reduce the need to buy allowances). Inspired by three case studies, Arjalies and Ponssard (2010) analyze the managerial dimension of the Porter Hypothesis in firms that face different forms of environmental regulations and pressures regarding climate change. They conclude that the ability to support the Porter Hypothesis depends on the stage of development of the firm.

Recent trends to increase corporate transparency and reporting (e.g., the Carbon Disclosure Project and Global Reporting Initiative), provide training on sustainability issues, hire corporate responsibility officers who often report directly to the Board of Directors, and appoint members of the Board of Directors with sustainability experience all point to actions that might reduce organizational inertia further [...]

Conclusions

Twenty years ago, by declaring that well-designed regulation could actually enhance competitiveness, Michael Porter certainly generated enormous interest among scholars, policymakers, businesses, and pressure groups. Indeed, much has been written about what has since become known simply as the Porter Hypothesis (PH).

This paper has provided an overview of the key theoretical and empirical insights on the PH to date. First, on the theoretical side, it turns out that the theoretical arguments that could justify the PH are now more solid than they appeared at first in the heated debate that took place in 1995 in the *Journal of Economic Perspectives* (Palmer et al. 1995). On the empirical side, on one hand, the evidence about the "weak" version of the hypothesis (stricter regulation leads to more innovation) is also fairly well established. On the other hand, the empirical evidence on the strong version (stricter regulation enhances business performance) is mixed, with more recent studies providing more supportive results.

The PH raises important questions for policymakers as to how to design and implement policies that will induce environmental innovation and how to protect and diffuse these innovations among firms. More research is certainly needed to better understand the different mechanisms at play.

William Lahey & Meinhard Doelle,
"Negotiating the Interface of Environmental and Economic Governance:
Nova Scotia's *Environmental Goals and Sustainable Prosperity Act*"
(2012) Dal. L.J. 3

Introduction

Nova Scotia's *Environmental Goals and Sustainable Prosperity Act* (*EGSPA*) came into force on 7 June 2007. In addition to setting a performance schedule and a process of accountability for the achievement of twenty-one discrete environmental goals, the *Act* proclaimed Nova Scotia's ambition to achieve two overarching goals by 2020: to "demonstrate international leadership by having one of the cleanest and most sustainable environments in the world" and to improve "the Province's economic performance to a level that is equal to or above the Canadian average." This combination of ambitions reflected the influence of a previously adopted provincial economic development strategy that linked environmental sustainability and economic growth through the concept of "sustainable prosperity."

[...] this paper evaluates the impact of the *Act* as an instrument of environmental and economic governance. While the analysis concentrates on the impact of *EGSPA* in the specific context of Nova Scotia and the conclusions focus on how *EGSPA* might be strengthened and improved, the analysis examines the broader question of what Nova Scotia's experience under *EGSPA* tells us more generally about the potential role of this kind of legislation in environmental and economic governance.

There are two core conclusions. The first is that *EGSPA* seems, in large measure, to have succeeded in improving the performance of the Nova Scotia government in implementation of environmental policy commitments, including those which require action by departments of government that are primarily responsible for other domains of public policy, and those that require continuity of effort by successive governments [...] The second core conclusion is that *EGSPA* has not yet succeeded in transforming Nova Scotia into a jurisdiction that achieves high environmental performance and higher economic performance through the integrated pursuit of ambitious environmental and economic objectives. While this conclusion suggests an inherent limitation to legislation as a policy instrument, it may also show that legislation which aspires to play a role in such a transformation must address its economic objectives more rigorously than has *EGSPA* during its first five years. Further, the implementation of legislation, including *EGSPA*, must pay more explicit attention to the distinct and overriding goal of integration and the mechanics to achieve this end. The paper concludes with suggestions for how *EGSPA*, and other "aspirational legislation," might be designed and administered to enhance its effectiveness in improving governmental policy performance at the interface of environmental and economic governance.

Overview of EGSPA

At the heart of the *Act* is the long-term objective of integrating environmental sustainability and economic prosperity, as articulated in section 4(1):

> 4. (1) The long-term environmental and economic objective of the Province is to fully integrate environmental sustainability and economic prosperity and to this end to (a) demonstrate international leadership by having one of the cleanest and most sustainable environments in the world by the year 2020; and (b) provide certainty to all sectors of the economy through the Government's economic development strategy entitled Opportunities for Sustainable Prosperity and establish clear environmental goals while improving the Province's economic performance to a level that is equal to or above the Canadian average by the year 2020.

To achieve this long-term objective, the *Act* enumerates twenty-one short and medium term goals, establishes a process to ensure the effective implementation of these goals, and creates authority for the adoption and implementation of additional measures necessary to meet the long-term objective. The twenty-one goals are set out in subsection 4(2) of the *Act* and are reproduced in full in the appendix to this paper. The goals cover a range of issues, from more substantive targets on greenhouse gas (GHG) emissions, air pollutants, energy, solid waste, protected areas, wastewater treatment, and drinking water, to process-related targets such as the requirement to develop strategies, policies, or regulations on resource management, wetlands, brownfield redevelopment, and government procurement [...]

The *Act* is, however, clearly concerned with both economic prosperity and environmental protection. The twenty-one environmental goals are explicitly linked to a single long-term objective: "to fully integrate environmental sustainability and economic prosperity." Furthermore, there are clear economic opportunities associated with a number of the goals. For example, the province had already created employment through solid waste reduction efforts. It is also generally recognized that there are economic opportunities associated with renewable energy production and with energy efficiency and conservation efforts.

The *Act* assigns responsibility for implementation of the goals to the government of Nova Scotia. It is, however, clear that some goals are more directly within the control of the government than others. The substantive goals, such as the reduction of GHG emissions, require action from other levels of government and other non-state actors, including Nova Scotia's privately owned power utility, major industries, and the general population. Other goals that focus on the development of policy rather than the meeting of a specific substantive target are more directly within the control of the provincial government, though many have involved extensive stakeholder consultations.

The powers granted in the *Act* are allocated to the Governor in Council, as opposed to any particular minister. These powers consist of broad agreements with other governments or non-state actors in order to achieve the goals of the *Act*. This approach makes sense, since integration of environmental and economic policy can only happen optimally if it happens on a government-wide, or at least multi-departmental, scale. But on the other hand, as mentioned already, the *Act* gives the responsibility for reporting to the House of Assembly on implementation of the *Act* to the Minister of Environment, while most of the specific goals established by the *Act* fall within the mandate of the same minister under Nova Scotia's *Environment Act*.

EGSPA's Uniqueness: Applying Law to the Policy-Making Process

[...] the *EGSPA*, however, is different from Nova Scotia's green plan and from its counterparts in other Canadian jurisdictions in one important respect: it explicitly mandates the government to follow through on its own environmental policy commitments. In other words, *EGSPA* is different from typical green plans because it is law. That said, *EGSPA* does not do what environmental law typically does: it does not regulate, or create authority to regulate, nongovernmental actors. At most, it sets the stage for regulation necessary for the achievement of its goals, primarily, but not exclusively under Nova Scotia's *Environment Act* [...] In *EGSPA*, twenty-one environmental goals and the specific schedule for their achievement between 2007 and 2020 are given the force of law. All of the prescribed goals are either ones that only government can make happen or that can only be achieved with significant action from government.

There is nothing in the *Act* to dictate the particular approach to environmental governance that government is to follow in implementing the legislation. Some of the goals seem to clearly imply new or elevated regulatory standards of a traditional sort. Meanwhile, a number of indications might all be taken to invite "new governance" approaches: the fact that a number of the goals relate to the adoption of non-legislative policy frameworks or strategies, the emphasis in the broader language of the *Act* on economic prosperity and partnerships, and the emphasis in the legislative process on the government's intention to work on implementation of the *Act* with diverse stakeholders. Neither traditional nor "new governance" approaches, however, can be said to be required by the *Act*.

That said, *EGSPA*, as law, does regulate the performance of government in making and implementing environmental policy. There are three key aspects to how it regulates government policy-making and implementation that warrant mention to set the stage for the subsequent evaluation of *EGSPA*'s performance.

First, *EGSPA* applies what is properly characterized as "soft" regulation to the policy-making process of government. As noted above, the main mechanism of accountability for implementation is an annual report from the Minister of Environment that is tabled in the House of Assembly [...]

Second, given the range of environmental policy goals within *EGSPA*, the *Act* applies a very wide-ranging regulatory framework to government's environmental policy-making process. In light of its goal of integrating environmental sustainability with economic prosperity, *EGSPA* casts a wider net as compared to many non-legislative environmental policy frameworks. One of the consequences of *EGSPA*'s breadth is that even though most of the goals fall wholly or largely within the mandate of the Minister of the Environment, a significant number fall under or have significant implications for the mandate of a number of other departments of the Nova Scotia government. These departments include those responsible for energy, natural resources, economic development, transportation, public works, and government services.

Third, the regulatory framework that *EGSPA* applies to the policymaking process is primarily directed at environmental policy. Although the *Act* connects the implementation of the twenty-one environmental policy commitments to the broader integration of Nova Scotia's stated policy objectives in environmental and economic governance, *EGSPA* contains little guidance or direction on the mechanics of this connection. *EGSPA* does say that Nova Scotia, a traditional "have not" province, will enjoy "economic performance" by 2020 at a "level that is equal to or above the Canadian average." The *Act* declares that "environmentally sustainable economic development that recognizes the economic value of the Province's environmental assets is essential to the long-term prosperity of the Province" and acknowledges that "a long-term approach to planning and decision-making is necessary to harmonize the Province's goals of economic prosperity and environmental sustainability."

In all of these ways, *EGSPA* implicates broad fields of economic policy. This justifies the conclusion that *EGSPA* aspires, at least rhetorically, to influence government decision-making so as to integrate environmental and economic policy-making. But the patent limitation of *EGSPA* in this regard is its silence on both specific goals for economic policy to match those it enumerates for environmental policy and on the mechanisms to be used to ensure the integration of environmental and economic objectives in policy-making in both policy fields. The deeper limitation is its failure to address how environmental goals are best selected and implemented to ensure economic prosperity and vice versa. Instead, it asserts and assumes a mutually beneficial connection between an assortment of mostly pre-existing environmental policy objectives and a vaguely defined future economic prosperity.

Implementation of EGSPA

How has *EGSPA* performed in ensuring that government implements the policy commitments that *EGSPA* enumerates? This question will be answered from two perspectives. First, an evaluation of the performance of the Nova Scotia government in meeting the twenty-one specific goals in accordance with the schedule set out in *EGSPA* is provided. Second, a broader evaluation is offered of whether the implementation of *EGSPA* has moved Nova Scotia's policy-making process forward in achieving integration of environmental and economic policy-making.

Performance in Meeting EGSPA's Specific Environmental Goals

[...] the (Nova Scotia) government is reporting, with Round Table validation, that it is meeting the majority of the goals that were scheduled for completion prior to 2012 [...] the quantitative track record is impressive by itself. Of the fifteen goals that were to be met before 2012, seven were achieved on time, one was achieved prior to the due date, and four were achieved late. In other words, twelve of fifteen goals (80%) have been achieved and slightly more than 50% have been achieved on time.

In short, none of the goals that have been missed have been ignored or abandoned, while the solid majority have been implemented either on time or only modestly behind schedule. It is disturbing that the unachieved goals relate to adoption of drinking water quality standards and the reduction of mercury emissions—two goals connected directly to human health and that address issues on which Nova Scotia lags behind other provinces. The municipal drinking water goal is, however, largely accomplished and the government has proposed to deal with the mercury reduction on a different timeline by pursuing a renewable energy target that goes well beyond the one set out in the *Act*.

A detailed and thorough comparison of *EGSPA*'s effectiveness with the effectiveness of non-legislative policy frameworks in other Canadian jurisdictions is beyond the scope of this paper. But it would appear that *EGSPA* has had more success in getting a defined program of environmental policy goals implemented in Nova Scotia than non-legislated environmental policy frameworks have generally had elsewhere. The evaluations of provincial government "green plans" (that are readily available) suggest that, like *EGSPA*, none have succeeded in transforming the policy-making process that they seek to guide or to direct.

[...] we suggest that it matters that *EGSPA*, unlike its non-legislated comparators, is rooted in legislation. The regulation of policy-making that *EGSPA* brings to bear may be "soft" and the accountability mechanism it prescribes may be basic, but *EGSPA*, unlike non-legislated alternatives, nevertheless makes action on policy commitments obligatory. The significance of this distinction comes through not only in the relatively high compliance rate that *EGSPA* has garnered, but also in the extent to which the obligatory force of the *Act* has been recognized by Nova Scotia's government when it has failed to meet goals on time or decided (in the case of mercury emissions) to delay compliance with a goal. More generally, the obligatory force of the *Act* has probably been reinforced and strengthened by the fact that it was taken seriously by the NDP government that came into office in 2009. Nova Scotia's experience shows, therefore, that a legislated green plan along the lines of *EGSPA* can influence policy priorities and change priorities of the party in power into priorities of the state.

Of course, legislation that seeks to direct governmental policy-making has its limits, unless the political process has the will and the means, as in a minority government situation, to enforce it against resistant governments. It is legislation that can be ignored with legal impunity. This is illustrated by the fate of the federal *Kyoto Protocol Implementation Act*. [...] many issues can divert the attention of governments from the implementation of a wide-ranging and multifaceted environmental policy agenda. The experience of Nova Scotia under *EGSPA* suggests that putting the agenda into law can keep that agenda in the forefront.

Performance in Integrating Environmental and Economic Policymaking

The question is: has the implementation of *EGSPA* produced greater integration of environmental and economic policy-making within the Nova Scotia government? Evaluating *EGSPA*'s impact in this sphere is more difficult than evaluating its impact in terms of the implementation of the twenty-one goals listed in subsection 4(2). In the context of its five-year review of the *Act*, the Round Table concluded that limited or uncertain progress has been made under *EGSPA* on integrating environmental and economic policy-making, either in respect of the implementation of the specific *EGSPA* goals or more broadly.

The contributions that *EGSPA* has made can be evaluated from at least two perspectives regardless of whether or not they are matters covered by *EGSPA*'s specific goals—first from the perspective of whether *EGSPA* can be said to have been administered with integration as an objective and second, from the perspective of *EGSPA*'s broader influence within government on matters that are relevant to *EGSPA*'s objective of policy integration [...].

From the perspective of how *EGSPA* has been administered, there is little evidence that policy integration has been aggressively pursued as an overarching objective. Judging by the four annual reviews that have been published, implementation of the *Act* has been overwhelmingly limited to the achievement of twenty-one discrete environmental goals. [...] The focus on discreet environmental goals in the implementation of *EGSPA* [...] reflects the emphasis that the *Act* places on the achievement of environmental goals.

As to whether *EGSPA* has had a broader influence on policy-making that is relevant to *EGSPA*'s objective of integration between environmental and economic policy-making, there is some evidence of this broader influence at play [...] At the same time, *EGSPA* has been unevenly invoked when major issues at the interface between environmental sustainability and economic prosperity have been addressed [...] facts suggest that the broad framework that the *Act* creates for the integration of environmental and economic policy has not been fully embraced either by the government that initiated *EGSPA* or the one that has overseen much of its implementation.

To be fair, and according to the bulk of public administration literature on the challenges that governments face in achieving optimal "horizontality," achieving integration between branches of policy that are allocated to different government departments is not easy. It is not as straightforward as implementing even a long and demanding list of discrete policy commitments that are largely severable among government departments. So, in a significant sense, it is not unexpected to find that *EGSPA* has had less success in this dimension of its regulatory task than it has had in the regulation of government's performance in implementing specific environmental policy commitments. But given the generality of *EGSPA* on integration and the absence from *EGSPA* of any institutional apparatus for making integration happen, this finding does not justify the conclusion that legislation such as *EGSPA* cannot be successful in moving environmental and economic policy towards greater and more comprehensive integration. It does, however, argue strongly in favour of the conclusion that if goal-setting legislation such as *EGPSA* is to be effective, it has to be much more specific than *EGSPA* is on what integration means and requires.

Improving the Regulation of Governmental Policy Performance at the Interface of Environmental and Economic Governance

The Round Table submitted its five-year review of *EGSPA* in March of 2012. The report endorsed the goal of integrating environmental leadership with economic prosperity, and suggested that more attention is necessary to ensure that the integration actually occurs. It also includes a number of recommendations that could, if adopted, help to make that integration happen [...].

Integration of environmental and economic policy within a legislative framework that gives equal weight to a clean environment and a productive economy can take place in at least two ways. First, the integration can come about through the mechanisms chosen to achieve specific policy goals, such as the twenty-one goals currently listed in *EGSPA*. For example, the manner in which a given GHG emission reduction target is met can have significant short, medium and long-term economic implications [...].

The second way that the integration of economic and environmental prosperity can manifest itself under *EGSPA* is through the development of additional goals. [...] *EGSPA* needs to be amended to ensure that it enables the establishment of economic and integration goals as well as additional environmental goals. Future goals could then more explicitly target the integration of the environment and the economy, such as setting benchmarks for green jobs or for specific green industries.

Both in relation to existing and newly established goals, the role of *EGSPA* in achieving economic prosperity could be more clearly stated. It is important to carefully consider the short, medium, and long-term connection between *EGSPA* and economic prosperity, particularly since some opportunities to integrate the environment and the economy come at a short-term economic cost. Setting unrealistic economic goals for the short and medium term, therefore, can serve to undermine integration efforts rather than support them [...].

Where there are clear opportunities for integration, future goals should be carefully designed to encourage the full exploration of these opportunities. For example, goals around solid waste, renewable energy, and energy efficiency and conservation could be associated with specific economic goals, such as the number of new jobs created or revenues retained in the province as a result of avoided imports of fossil fuels, or the direct connection of the goal to improvement in economic productivity. Similarly, goals that explore the relationship between environmental sustainability and economic prosperity could be developed on a range of issues not yet addressed in *EGSPA*. One example may be the recommendation of the Round Table for a new goal to increase Nova Scotia's energy productivity.

Conclusions

EGSPA has demonstrated the value of governance through legislative goal setting. The results are encouraging. Over a five-year period, not a single specific goal set in *EGSPA* was abandoned. The majority of the goals that were to be achieved before 2012 were met and met on time. Several of the goals that are to be met after 2012 have either already been met or are clearly part of the impetus for significant work that is going on to ensure that these goals are met in the future.

EGSPA has played an important role in concentrating and maintaining government's attention on a range of worthwhile environmental policy goals that have been addressed or gained momentum. In doing so, it has functioned as a meaningful counterweight to a range of forces that might easily have postponed or derailed these goals.

This suggests that *EGSPA* has largely achieved one of its core functions: to improve the performance of government in implementing its environmental policy commitments, including those which require sustained policy effort across the mandate of multiple governments. At the same time, *EGSPA* has not yet put Nova Scotia on a trajectory to be "one of the cleanest places on earth" with economic prosperity that is integrated with environmental stewardship. The *Act* has strengthened, but not transformed environmental governance in Nova Scotia. It has, so far, not transformed the making and implementation of government environmental policy in the province. Specifically, it has not yet achieved the integration of policy-making in the environmental and economic governance that it envisages.

Nonetheless, the legislative model represented by *EGSPA* should be continued in Nova Scotia and considered for adoption by other jurisdictions. The success it has enjoyed in meeting its more modest ambition, to improve the performance of government in implementing its environmental policy commitments, is itself a significant achievement. With a more careful and perhaps somewhat more modest articulation of the goal of integrating environmental sustainability with economic prosperity in combination with goals more directly designed to promote the integration, the loftier goals of *EGSPA* are not out of reach. As with the government's performance under the existing twenty-one goals, effective reporting and accountability for the integration of environmental sustainability and economic prosperity will be a key ingredient of success in this more ambitious endeavour.

Notes and Questions

1. Proponents of the Porter Hypothesis claim that only certain types of environmental regulation, namely "flexible, market-based regulation, not rigid command-and-control regulation", have the potential to promote innovation, growth and prosperity. Where does this leave other forms of regulation that employ more hands-on management-based or technology-based approaches? Is there a downside to the Porter Hypothesis' supposition that performance-based regulation is superior?

2. To what extent, in your view, has the Porter Hypothesis made inroads in political and legal discourse in Canada? Has it now become accepted as common sense, or is it still regarded by many as a radical idea? To what extent is it embedded at some level in the EGSPA initiative?

3. The EGSPA strikes many as an experiment that builds on considerable work done in the 1990s around environmental indicators: see Peter A. Victor, "Indicators for Sustainable Development: Some Lessons from Capital Theory" (1991) 4 Ecological Economics 191; A. Hammond *et al.*, *Environmental Indicators: A Systematic Approach to Measuring and Reporting on Environmental Performance in the Context of Sustainable Development* (WRI, 1995); H. Bossel, *Indicators for Sustainable Development: Theory, Method, Applications* (IISD, 1999). Yet despite being very much a logical extension of this work, it remains a unique initiative in Canada, if not North America. Why have governments seemingly been slow to embrace the approach to promoting environmental performance reflected in the EGSPA?

4. The EGSPA is an interesting amalgam of hard and soft law, and depends heavily if not exclusively for its efficacy on the power of transparency and spotlighting. Discuss.

Part V — An Overview of Canadian Regulatory Models

In this part, we focus on two of the most important federal environmental protection laws: the *Fisheries Act* and the *Canadian Environmental Protection Act* (CEPA). In keeping with the preceding discussion, these exemplars have been chosen as illustrations of "first generation" (*Fisheries Act*) and "second generation" (CEPA) approaches to environmental protection. They are also the two federal statutes that have generated the most attention to date in terms of compliance and enforcement, the topic to which we turn in Chapter 5. An in-depth examination of the *Canadian Environmental Assessment Act* (CEAA) and the *Species at Risk Act* (SARA) follows, respectively, in Chapters 7 and 9.

Fisheries Act

The *Fisheries Act* is one of Canada's oldest statutes, providing federal regulators with a range of powerful tools to protect the environment. *Fisheries Act* reform has been the subject of ongoing parliamentary review and debate since 2005. During these review processes, it has become readily apparent that there were widely divergent views on the efficacy of the legislation and the need for reform. While environmentalists were, for the most part, strong supporters of the Act, they nonetheless raised concerns about its efficacy in terms of compliance and enforcement. In contrast, many in the business community, particularly on the West Coast, have contended that the *Fisheries Act* impedes environmental resource development by imposing costly, inconsistent and unjustifiable burdens on businesses.

The two *Fisheries Act* sections that are most important in terms of environmental protection are subsection 35(1) (dealing with fish habitat protection) and section 36 (dealing with pollution prevention). In 2012, as part of its controversial Bill C-38 initiative, the Harper government made some very substantial changes to section 35. As discussed in the next section, these changes are being rolled back under legislation introduced in 2018 by the Trudeau government.

Habitat Protection: Subsection 35(1)

The provision of the *Fisheries Act* that most squarely addresses the protection of fish habitat has come to be known colloquially as "HADD", an acronym for the Act's broad prohibition on the "harmful alteration, disruption or destruction" of fish habitat. This provision was a key target in recent reforms introduced by the Harper government. Section 35 formerly stated:

> 35. (1) No person shall carry on any work or undertaking that results in the harmful alteration, disruption or destruction of fish habitat.

> (2) No person contravenes subsection (1) by causing the alteration, disruption or destruction of fish habitat by any means or under any conditions authorized by the Minister or under regulations made by the Governor in Council under this Act.

Formerly, violation of subsection 35(1) was an offence unless the HADD occurred under an authorization provided under subsection 35(2). In the terminology we have employed in this chapter, subsection 35(1) can be classified as a performance standard; it regulates the impact of firms on the environment by focusing on the "results" of their activities on the environment. As such, it does not tell firms how to achieve compliance (by specifying approved technologies or management systems). For firms interested in certainty and minimizing liability risk, therefore, there is a strong incentive to secure advance Department of Fisheries and Oceans (DFO) approval for proposed new works or undertakings.

The requirement for this HADD approval, which in turn formerly triggered an environmental assessment under the *Canadian Environmental Assessment Act* (CEAA), has long been a source of discontent within some parts of the business community. (Further discussion of how this ultimately led to the reform of CEAA is canvassed in Chapter 7.) It was also argued that the protections for fish and fish habitat were overbroad and impeded resource development.

The Harper-era changes to the *Fisheries Act* under Bill C-38 came into force in two distinct stages. Under the stage one changes, HADDs no longer automatically triggered a federal environmental assessment. These stage one changes also significantly broadened the range of activities that were exempt from DFO review and approval. Even more controversial, however, were the stage two amendments. Under these amendments, protection for fish under section 35 was reduced to situations where the harm was "serious", and where the species in question were "part of a commercial, recreational or Aboriginal fishery". The amendments defined "serious harm" as arising only where the activity in question actually caused fish to die, or where it caused "permanent" alteration or destruction of fish habitat.

In early 2018, the Trudeau government introduced legislation to restore the environmental protections that had been undermined by the Harper-era reforms. Under Bill C-68 (currently before the Senate), the *Fisheries Act* gains a new purpose provision which declares that its goal is to conserve and protect "all fish and fish habitat, including pollution prevention". The amendments also provide that decisions made under the *Fisheries Act* shall be guided by principles of sustainability, precaution and ecosystem management. The legislation also restores the broad language of the former HADD provisions and eliminates many of the exemptions to and restrictions on HADD protections brought in during the Harper era. The government has said it intends to enact regulations that will designate which projects require a federal assessment and permit. Certain types of works, undertakings or activities will be permitted to proceed without federal assessment or permits, but these will still have to comply with codes of practice established by regulation.

Pollution Prevention: Section 36

Provisions in the *Fisheries Act* concerning pollution prevention have likewise been the subject of academic and public controversy. Section 36 has been described by critics as overbroad, creating a "zero-tolerance" regime for marine pollution, even where the "deleterious substance" that has been discharged has caused no actual harm to the environment.

Subsection 36(3) provides that:

> subject to subsection (4), no person shall deposit or permit the deposit of a deleterious substance of any type in water frequented by fish or in any place under any conditions where the *deleterious substance* or any other deleterious substance that results from the deposit of the deleterious substance may enter any such water. [emphasis added]

Subsection 36(4) deals with deposits authorized by regulation. The term "deleterious substance" is defined in subsection 34(1) as including:

> (a) any substance that, if added to *any water*, would degrade or alter or form part of a process of degradation or alteration of the quality of that water so that it is rendered or is likely to be rendered deleterious to fish or fish habitat or to the use by man of fish that frequent that water [emphasis added]

Like subsection 35(1), subsection 36(3) takes the form of a performance-based standard, prescribing that firms shall not release into "any water" a substance that would affect the quality of that water to support fish or fish habitat. To avoid liability, however, a firm may rely on regulations that authorize such discharges. Subsection 36(5) of the Act enumerates the scope of these regulations that currently exempt certain substances (or classes of substances), as well as specific sites, works and undertakings. If, however, a project or activity being undertaken by a firm falls outside the scope of these regulations, it is by default subject to the requirements of subsection 36(3). This is the case even if the discharge is provincially permitted, though a defence of statutory authority may exist.

In this situation, courts — including two provincial Courts of Appeal — have been called upon in several leading cases to interpret what the reference to "any water" in the definition of "deleterious substance" in subsection 34(1) refers to. Both the British Columbia and Ontario Courts of Appeal have arrived at the same "zero-tolerance" conclusion. In their view, "any water" is not a reference to the water into which the discharge actually occurred but rather, literally, any water whatsoever, regardless of quantity or other characteristics, including whether it actually is frequented by fish. In the words of a critic, according to this approach, it therefore "does not matter whether the deposit actually disturbs any fish. All that counts is whether the substance itself is deleterious, meaning that, when added to any water in a laboratory, it makes that water deleterious". (On this topic see discussion in Richler, *infra*.)

R. v. MacMillan Bloedel (Alberni) Ltd.
(1979), 47 C.C.C. (2d) 118 (B.C. C.A.),
leave to appeal refused [1979] 1 S.C.R. xi (S.C.C.)

SEATON J.A.: — The appellant was charged that it did unlawfully deposit a deleterious substance in water frequented by fish, contrary to s. 33(2) of the *Fisheries Act* [now s. 36(3)]. It was acquitted in the Provincial Court but an appeal was taken to the County Court where the acquittal was set aside and a conviction entered. This appeal from conviction is restricted to a question of law alone.

The appellant says that the County Court judge erred in his interpretation of the phrase "water frequented by fish", in his interpretation of the phrase "deleterious substance", and in denying the appellant's application to reopen the case.

The charge arose out of a spill of about 170 gallons of bunker C oil during unloading at the appellant's deep sea dock at Alberni Inlet. A suction valve was not closed when it ought to have been and the oil spilled beneath the dock. The appellant was prepared for this sort of accident and the response was prompt. Very little oil spread beyond the dock and the cleanup was carried out relatively quickly. If an offence was committed when the oil was spilled, the containment of the oil and the prompt cleanup would be relevant to the sentence but not the conviction [...]

I turn now to what is meant by "deleterious substance". It is the appellant's submission that to prove this charge the Crown must show that after the spill the water was made deleterious.

[...] Section 33(2) prohibits the deposit of a deleterious substance, not the deposit of a substance that causes the water to become deleterious. The argument to the contrary is based on the definition of "deleterious substance" [...] in terms of this case, oil is a deleterious substance if, when added to any water, it would degrade or alter or form part of a process of degradation or alteration of the quality of that water so that that water is rendered deleterious to fish or to the use by man of fish that frequent that water. Applying that test to the findings of fact here, bunker C oil is a deleterious substance. Once it is determined that bunker C oil is a deleterious substance and that it has been deposited, the offence is complete without ascertaining whether the water itself was thereby rendered deleterious.

The appellant says that the purpose of this legislation is to prevent waters being rendered deleterious to fish and that if given the plain meaning of the words, an absurdity will result. It is said that if a teaspoon of oil was put in the Pacific ocean and oil was a deleterious substance, that would constitute an offence. In its submission that absurdity can be avoided by reading the Act to require that the water be made deleterious. There are some attractions to that reasoning, but I think that the result would be at least as unsatisfactory. Nothing could be done to prevent damage to the water that fell short of rendering the water deleterious. To prove that the damage had gone that far would be difficult indeed.

Had it been the intention of Parliament to prohibit the deposit of a substance in water so as to render that water deleterious to fish, that would have been easy to express. A different prohibition was decided upon. It is more strict. It seeks to exclude each part of the process of degradation. The thrust of the section is to prohibit certain things, called deleterious substances, being put in the water. That is the plain meaning of the words used and is the meaning that I feel bound to apply [...]

I would dismiss the appeal.

Fletcher v. Kingston (City)
(2004), 7 C.E.L.R. (3d) 198 (Ont. C.A.),
leave to appeal refused 2005 CarswellOnt 288 (S.C.C.)

[The City of Kingston operated a municipal dump site on the west shore of the Cataraqui River, adjacent to Belle Island, from the early 1950s to the early 1970s. The landfill was created in a marsh in the Cataraqui River and formed a peninsula of garbage. After its closure, the landfill site was transformed into a recreational area but little was done to address the possibility of leachate generation and migration. The charges in the instant case arise from alleged contaminants emanating from the landfill site and entering the Cataraqui River. Ms. Fletcher laid charges by means of a private citizen's information. The Ministry laid separate charges by means of its own information. Both the private prosecutor and the Ministry took and tested samples of leachate entering the Cataraqui River from the landfill site. See discussion of private prosecutions in Chapter 5.]

GILLESE J.A.: — All the experts at trial agreed that ammonia was the main toxicant rendering the samples acutely lethal. Ammonia is a naturally occurring substance which, at certain concentration levels, is necessary for life. Ammonia is composed of unionized ammonia (NH3) and ionized ammonia (NH4+). Unionized ammonia is much more toxic than ionized ammonia. [...] Some species of fish are more sensitive to unionized ammonia than others [...]

On an ordinary and plain reading of paragraph (a) [of section 34(1)], a substance is deleterious if, when added to *any water*, it would alter the quality of the water such that it is likely to render the water deleterious to fish, fish habitat or to the use by man of fish that frequent the water. There is no stipulation in paragraph (a) that the substance must be proven to be deleterious to the receiving water. There is no reference to the receiving water in paragraph (a). On the contrary, the language makes it clear that the substance is deleterious if, when added to any water, it degrades or alters the quality of the water to which it has been added. The "any water" referred to in paragraph (a) is not the receiving water. Rather, it is any water to which the impugned substance is added, after which it can be determined whether the quality of that water is rendered deleterious to fish, fish habitat or the use by man of fish that frequent that water.

[Approving the BCCA's approach in *MacMillan Bloedel*, the Ontario Court of Appeal went on to conclude that what subsection 36(3) prohibits is the deposit of a deleterious substance in water frequented by fish, not "the deposit of a substance that causes the receiving water to become deleterious".]

Notes and Questions

1. In the following article, Ian Richler argues that subsection 36(3) is constitutionally overbroad, contrary to section 7 of the *Canadian Charter of Rights and Freedoms*. Invoking *Reference re s. 94(2) of Motor Vehicle Act (British Columbia)*, [1985] 2 S.C.R. 486, he contends that this is because it risks criminalizing conduct that is not harmful. Thus, even though protection of fish and fish habitat is a worthy and pressing objective, "[i]f the state, in pursuing a legitimate objective, uses means which are broader than is necessary to accomplish that objective, the principles of fundamental justice will be violated because the individual's rights will have been limited for no reason". Richler then proceeds to consider a variety of counter-arguments to his contention.

Ian Richler,
"*R. v. Kingston* and the Criminalization of
Harmless Pollution", Case Comment

(2005) 15 J. Envtl. L. & Prac. 319

I anticipate several challenges to my argument that s. 36(3), as interpreted in *MacMillan Bloedel* and *Kingston*, is unconstitutionally overbroad. One is that my argument has already been rejected by the courts. [...] In *R. v. Leveque* the Ontario Superior Court held that s. 35(1) of the *Fisheries Act* [**Ed. Note:** the HADD provision considered above], which prohibits carrying on "any work or undertaking that results in the harmful alteration, disruption or destruction of fish habitat", is not overbroad [...]

That reasoning does not apply to s. 36(3) because the two provisions are very different. For one thing, s. 35(1) requires proof of harm to fish habitat, whereas s. 36(3) does not look at real-world effects. Also, the Court in *Leveque* held that s. 35(1) "does not attract [penal] consequences for trivial or minimal impacts on fish habitat". By contrast, *MacMillan Bloedel* made it clear that the extent of the injury to fisheries is of no consequence. Finally, unlike s. 36(3), s. 35(1) has a built-in pre-authorization process whereby anyone wishing to do something that might harm fish habitat may apply for permission. For the Court in *Leveque*, this process was another reason that s. 35(1) is not overbroad. [...]

The second challenge to my overbreadth argument is that it makes no sense to assess s. 36(3) based on its impact on what Peter Hogg calls the "most innocent possible offender". My response is that the Supreme Court has expressly endorsed the notion of using "reasonable hypotheticals" when determining whether a law is overbroad — after all, the B.C. Court of Appeal said that a conviction could result from a teaspoon of oil in the ocean. [...] Indeed there is no need to resort to imagining, because *Kingston* provides a perfect illustration of the problem. The Ontario Court of Appeal noted that ammonia is a natural substance that is actually beneficial to aquatic life in some circumstances. Should someone who deposits a demonstrably benign amount of ammonia face a conviction? Zero-tolerance for such substances is not only illogical, it may actually be counterproductive.

The third challenge is related to the second one. It says that s. 36(3) is not overbroad because prosecutors and environmental investigators have enough good sense never to charge people with trivial breaches of the provision. But this notion is directly at odds with [...] *R. v. Smith*, where the SCC held that a law cannot be saved just by showing that its unfair applications are in fact avoided due to the discretion of officials: even if no one is likely ever to be charged with depositing a minute amount of pollution, it is entirely conceivable that charges will be laid in situations where the actual or likely harm to fisheries is unclear. Indeed that is exactly what happened in *MacMillan Bloedel* and *Kingston*. It is also worth noting that *Kingston* started as a private prosecution. The discretion argument loses much of its force when any concerned citizen can investigate and prosecute an alleged offence.

The fourth challenge was raised by the B.C. Court of Appeal in *MacMillan Bloedel*: it would be too onerous for the Crown to have to prove that the deposit in question caused harm. My response is simply that it *should* be onerous for the Crown to make out a criminal or quasi-criminal conviction. It is true that regulatory offences are subject to a lower standard of *Charter* scrutiny than purely criminal ones. But the rationale for that lower standard does not fully apply to s. 36(3). In particular, it cannot be said that everyone charged under s. 36(3) made a conscious decision to enter a regulated arena: s. 36(3) applies in the same way to the recreational canoeist as it does to a chemicals manufacturer or to a municipality. Besides, the s. 7 rights of anyone charged with depositing a deleterious substance are reduced in other respects. That is, the Crown already gets a break. Most notably, there is no need for the Crown to prove *mens rea*. A lower standard of *Charter* scrutiny does not mean that the accused has no *Charter* rights at all. While requiring proof of harm would make prosecutions harder (and thus, presumably, rarer) than they are today, it should not be seen as being unduly harsh on the Crown. Such a requirement is, after all, imposed on the Crown when prosecuting several other environmental offences, including s. 35(1) of the *Fisheries Act* and s. 30(1) of the [*Ontario Water Resources Act*].

The fifth challenge to my overbreadth argument is that a broad law is necessary in order to deter pollution. This can easily be rebuffed. There is simply no value in deterring harmless pollution. An overbroad law will not deter harmful pollution any more effectively than a law that captures only harmful pollution. An overbroad law may even lead to disrespect and disregard for that law.

The sixth challenge is that s. 36(3) already has enough built-in safeguards for the accused. In particular, imprisonment is not available as a punishment for someone's first conviction under s. 36(3), but rather only for subsequent convictions. Also, the accused can always raise a defence of due diligence. That is, someone charged with spilling a deleterious substance could be acquitted if it were shown that he or she took all reasonable care to prevent the spill. The problem with this line of reasoning is that just because an offence is not as draconian as it could be does not mean that it is not draconian.

The seventh challenge is that the courts should not second-guess Parliament when it decides to enact broad laws [...] Drafting pollution laws is especially tricky because, as the Court held in *Canadian Pacific*, environmental protection "is not conducive to precise codification". The Court elaborated:

> Environmental protection is a legitimate concern of government, and as I have already observed, it is a very broad subject-matter which does not lend itself to precise codification. Where the legislature is pursuing the objective of environmental protection, it is justified in choosing equally broad legislative language in order to provide for a necessary degree of flexibility.

This challenge is not convincing because it presupposes that s. 36(3) means what *MacMillan Bloedel* and *Kingston* say it means. That is, it merely begs the question. But, as I will argue later on, s. 36(3) is open to another, better interpretation. A court that opted for that alternative interpretation would have at least as good a claim to judicial deference as the courts in *MacMillan Bloedel* and *Kingston*.

The eighth and strongest challenge to my argument is that s. 36(3) must be very broad because only then could it capture deposits that, though seemingly innocuous on their own, can lead to real harm when combined with similar deposits over time. As the Law Reform Commission of Canada noted 20 years ago when it examined the notion of adding a pollution offence to the *Criminal Code*, "A lake can finally lose the ability to cope with accumulated acid rain, and will die". The problem with this challenge is that its logic does not extend to all types of substances. While it may be true that even a tiny amount of a substance like PCBs — which is persistent and bio-accumulative — is harmful or forms part of a process of harm, the same does not hold for, say, ammonia, which dissipates quickly in water and is actually beneficial to aquatic life in some concentrations. It is simply irrational to adopt a zero-tolerance policy towards substances like ammonia. But that is precisely what *Kingston* has done.

One solution to this problem is the one devised in *Inco*: a distinction is drawn between "inherently toxic" substances, for which there is zero-tolerance, and all other substances, for which there is some tolerance based on the circumstances of the discharge [...] the Superior Court in *Kingston* adopted this solution only to be overturned by the Court of Appeal. This solution is sensible because it refocuses s. 36(3) on harm to the receiving water. That is, it draws a clear nexus between the prohibition and the objective.

Notes and Questions

1. Do you agree that *Fisheries Act* offences should be framed as performance-based? What are some of the reasons why subsection 35(1) and subsection 36(3) are drafted as they are?

2. When businesses lobby government for performance-based regulations that allow them to decide how they will comply with regulatory requirements, are these sections akin to what they have in mind? Why do you suppose that in Bill C-38 the Harper government targeted section 35 of the *Fisheries Act* for amendment but not subsection 36(3)?

3. Earlier, the originators of the Smart Regulation concept suggested that, where the regulated community is composed of "heterogeneous enterprises facing heterogeneous conditions", there is a strong theoretical justification for management-based standards, all other things being equal (Gunningham and Sinclair, 2002). How, if at all, does this conclusion apply to pollution prevention in the fisheries context?

4. Can it be said that subsection 35(1) (new and old) and subsection 36(3) are forms of prescriptive regulation? Consider, in this regard, the discussion of the concept of "prescriptiveness" *infra* in this chapter. Why or why not?

Canadian Environmental Protection Act (CEPA)

Meinhard Doelle,
adapted from *Canadian Environmental Protection Act and Commentary*
(Markham, Ont.: LexisNexis Butterworths, 2008)

While the *Fisheries Act* is Canada's oldest and arguably still Canada's most rigorous federal environmental law, the *Canadian Environmental Protection Act* (CEPA) is broadly seen as the cornerstone of federal environmental law and policy. Originally enacted in 1988, CEPA was the first serious attempt to provide a coordinated response to the growing range of environmental challenges confronting Canada at the national level.

A key feature of the CEPA, from its origins to date, is its focus on the classification, identification, and regulation of the thousands of chemical substances currently used, or proposed for use in Canada. While development of Toxic Substances List proceeded at a relatively slow (some might even say "leisurely") pace during CEPA's early years, in recent years (particularly after the Act was amended in 1999) additions to the "List" have accelerated.

However, CEPA's ambit extends far beyond the regulation of harmful substances. In recent years, it has become the implementation tool of choice for a variety of international obligations Canada has undertaken including ozone layer depletion (the *Montreal Protocol*), ocean dumping (the *London Convention*), and the movement of hazardous goods and substances (the *Basel Convention*). It also seems poised to serve as a key vehicle for implementing the Kyoto Protocol on Climate Change.

CEPA is divided into twelve parts. Key among these are its provisions relating to public participation (Part 3); information gathering (Part 4); pollution prevention (Part 4); toxic substance categorization and control (Part 5); biotechnology (Part 6); pollution control (Part 7); emergency orders and measures (Part 8); and enforcement (Part 10).

Various Parts of the Act are substantially integrated. For instance, the provisions on biotechnology in Part 6 mirror the categorization process set out in Part 5. And the pollution prevention provisions in Part 4 are likewise closely linked to the pollution control provisions found in Part 5.

Public participation plays a central role in CEPA's architecture. CEPA contains a variety of provisions aimed at keeping the public informed about administrative decisions made under its provisions. These include a variety of informational measures including mandating of a public registry and requirements on decision makers to provide "notice and comment" opportunities to the public. There are also several "action-forcing" provisions including a provision that allows for members of the public to trigger an investigation into violations of CEPA, and, in limited circumstances, to commence an environmental protection in their own right where the Minister has failed to conduct or report on an investigation. There is also a provision that entitles members of the public to commence an action for damages resulting from losses arising from violation of CEPA. However, no environmental protection actions or actions seeking damages for harm to the environment have been brought to date.

In many respects, the "heart and soul" of CEPA is Part 5 which focuses on the control of toxic substances. As set out in Chapter 3, federal jurisdiction in this area was confirmed in the well known SCC decision of *R. v. Hydro-Quebec*, [1997] 3 S.C.R. 213. In this case, albeit in a split decision, the Court upheld the validity of this aspect of CEPA under the "criminal law power" which it opined not only vested the federal Crown to regulate to protect public health (in this case by means of an interim order banning the release of PCBs) but also, more broadly, to protect the environment.

Part 5 contemplates a two-step procedure for regulating toxic substances. The first involves an assessment of the risks associated with the substance in question. If this analysis leads to a conclusion that a substance is "toxic", a second stage of analysis is triggered that involves consideration of potential means through which the risks identified can be managed, reduced or eliminated through regulation, alternative measures or a combination of both.

CEPA provides that all substances used or proposed to be used in Canada must initially be listed on either the Domestic Substances List or the Non-Domestic Substances List. The former category consists of some 23,000 substances being used domestically within Canada when CEPA was first enacted. Substances on the Domestic List were "grandfathered"; as such, they were not subject to CEPA regulation until such time as they could be appropriately reviewed and categorized. Substances on the Non-Domestic List are prohibited from import into or manufacture in Canada until they are approved under CEPA.

Given the large number of substances on the Domestic List, this review process has in many cases proceeded at a rate that has given rise to criticism. [**Ed. Note:** See, for example, the M'Gonigle *et al.* article, *supra*, this chapter.] This process of review can be convoluted, contested and time consuming. It commences with a classification stage; a screening level assessment; possible assessment for inclusion on the Priority Substances List (a list of substances identified as being priorities for listing due to their potential toxicity); control or virtual elimination of the substance by virtue of listing under the Toxic Substances List; or alternatively a confirmation that the substance should remain unregulated on the Domestic Substances List.

Once a substance has been identified as toxic under the Part 5 review process, the Ministers of Health and Environment are given two years to pass regulations controlling its import, manufacture and use. PCBs (polychlorinated biphenyls) were among the first substances designated for regulation under this process. Initially, this was done by means of an interim order that gave rise to the jurisdictional challenge in *R. v. Hydro Quebec*. Subsequently, the use, storage and export of PCBs have come under a variety of purpose-specific regulations enacted under CEPA including the Chlorobiphenyls Regulations, SOR/91-152 (governing permitted and prohibited uses); the Federal Mobile PCB Treatment and Destruction Regulations, SOR/90-5 (governing treatment and destruction of PCB waste on federal land); the Storage of PCB Material Regulations, SOR/92-507 (governing the storage of PCB waste awaiting destruction and disposal); and the PCB Export Regulations, SOR/97-109 (governing the export of PCB abroad). New regulations designed to update and consolidate existing regulations relating to PCB use and storage have been drafted and are expected to come into force in the near future.

One of the most controversial episodes in the history of Part 5 arose in 1995 when then Minister of the Environment Sheila Copps, acting under subsection 35(1) of CEPA, made an interim order banning the export of PCB waste from Canada. This order led to a claim under the investor protection provisions of NAFTA chapter 11 by S.D. Myers, an Ohio-based PCB disposal company.

Another key component of CEPA is the National Pollutants Release Inventory (NPRI) which the Minister of Environment is required to establish, maintain and publish under Part 4 of CEPA: see sections 48-50. The NPRI is intended to "daylight" information about pollutants that is in the possession of the federal government with a view to promoting research, developing best practices and guidelines for pollutant management, and enhancing public knowledge and participation around pollutant-related issues. While the requirement to establish and maintain the NPRI is mandatory under CEPA, there is considerable Ministerial discretion under Part 4 as to what kind of information is reported and in what circumstances. The following case, which was brought with a view to challenging the exercise of this discretion, confirms both the importance of Part 4 and the fact that this ministerial discretion must be exercised judicially.

Great Lakes United v. Canada (Minister of Environment)
2009 FC 408

[This was an application seeking judicial review of the Minister's failure under the *Canadian Environmental Protection Act* (CEPA) to require reporting by mining facilities of releases or transfers of pollutants to waste rock and tailings disposal areas. The applicants argued that CEPA required the Minister to publish data related to releases or transfers of pollutants to waste rock and tailings disposal areas through the National Pollutants Release Inventory (NPRI) by operation of sections 48 and 50 of CEPA. The NPRI is an annual inventory of industrial and commercial pollutants released into the environment. While the Minister has required NPRI reporting of pollutants that *exit* disposal areas, he has not required reporting of movements of substances *within* disposal areas. The principal issue was whether the Minister was required by CEPA to provide pollutant release information through the NPRI in relation to releases and transfers to mining tailings and waste rock disposal areas.]

RUSSELL J.: — The applicants say that the Minister has failed to discharge his duties under the CEPA to provide information to the public regarding onsite releases and transfers by mining facilities of pollutants to TIAs (tailings impoundment area) and WRSAs (waste rock storage areas) They say that this failure defeats the purpose of the CEPA which was brought into being to ensure public transparency and accountability in achieving pollution reductions.

The applicants take the view that, since 1993, when the NPRI was first established, the Minister has failed in this obligation and that such failure continues to the present time. They want the Court to intervene and declare the Minister to be in breach of the CEPA by his not requiring mining facilities to provide pollutant information for releases and transfers to TIAs and WRSAs in 2006 and subsequent years. They also want the Minister to publish the relevant information through the NPRI for 2006 and subsequent years. At the very least, the applicants want the Court to compel the Minister to make manifest to the public that he is, in effect, allowing an exemption to mining facilities in relation to this extremely important information on a major source of pollution in Canada.

The Present Impasse

The applicants say that the Minister's failure to ensure the reporting of the on-site release and transfer of pollutants is contrary to the fundamental purpose and objectives of the CEPA, which legislation compels the Minister (in accordance with section 2) to:

  (a) Encourage the participation of the people of Canada in the making of decisions that affect the environment;

  (b) Facilitate the protection of the environment by the people of Canada;

(c) Provide information to the people of Canada on the state of the Canadian environment;

(d) Endeavour to exercise his/her powers to require the provision of information in a coordinated manner; and

(e) Apply and enforce the CEPA in a fair, predictable and consistent manner.

In particular, the applicants point to Part 3 of the CEPA, which was brought into being in 1999, and which sets out the duties of the Minister to collect and publish pollutant release information through the NPRI (sections 44, 46-53) and to set objectives, guidelines and codes of practice to reduce pollution (sections 44, 54-55). The applicants' position is that sections 48 and 50 in Part 3 of the CEPA impose mandatory duties on the Minister to require reporting of major pollutant releases and to publish that information publicly to the NPRI in order to ensure that pollutant releases are reduced in Canada.

Section 48 of the CEPA reads as follows:

> 48. The Minister shall establish a national inventory of releases of pollutants using the information collected under section 46 and any other information to which the Minister has access, and may use any information to which the Minister has access to establish any other inventory of information.

Although section 46 of the CEPA indicates that the Minister may exercise a discretion in gathering information, the applicants say that section 46 cannot be used to thwart the duties of the Minister under section 48 and the entire purpose of the CEPA, as has occurred in this case, by exempting Canada's largest source of pollution from the information gathering and reporting process.

Section 46 of the CEPA reads as follows:

> 46. (1) The Minister may, for the purpose of conducting research, creating an inventory of data, formulating objectives and codes of practice, issuing guidelines or assessing or reporting on the state of the environment, publish in the *Canada Gazette* and in any other manner that the Minister considers appropriate a notice requiring any person described in the notice to provide the Minister with any information that may be in the possession of that person or to which the person may reasonably be expected to have access [...]

All in all, the applicants say that the Minister's conduct, as demonstrated in the 2006 notice, has frustrated the purpose and objects of the CEPA in the various ways set out in their written submissions in that the Minister has:

(a) Hidden the largest source of pollution in Canada;

(b) Distorted the information currently reported on the NPRI;

(c) Mischaracterized a major pollutant release;

(d) Failed to promote the "polluter pays" principle which is essential to the scheme under CEPA;

(e) Failed to ensure Canada–U.S. harmony on pollutant release reporting;

(f) Delayed in requiring the reporting in accordance with his statutory duties.

Behind all of this lies an extensive history of consultation and discussions between and among various public interest groups, industry and government departments, dating back to at least 1992, concerning how on-site transfers and releases by mining facilities to TIAs and WRSAs should be reported and made manifest to the public.

No resolution of this issue has been achieved to date. Before I come to the legalities, it seems to me that the applicants' frustration and sense of urgency which has prompted this application is perfectly understandable. After more than 16 years of consultation with stakeholders and interest groups, there is still no clear indication from the Minister as to how and when this important information is going to be gathered and provided to the Canadian public.

The Minister and the intervener appear to accept that all stakeholders now recognize the importance of reporting this information. The disagreement has arisen over the way it should be reported. The applicants feel it should appear in the NPRI, while the intervener and the industry it represents feel that a separate and different reporting system is required in order to avoid confusion and distortions *vis-à-vis* the information that appears in the NPRI.

In any event, the upshot is that the information from the mining industry on waste rock and tailings disposals on-site is not being gathered and reported by the Minister, even though other sectors are required to provide similar information that is reported through the NPRI.

The applicants say that this amounts to an exemption for the mining industry that the Minister is hiding from the public. The Minister's failure to act means that the default position is pretty well the position taken by the industry, and the public does not really know what is being done to record, report and discourage a major source of pollution in Canada. In other words, whatever the merits of the debate as to how information regarding the on-site releases and transfers of pollutants by mining facilities should be gathered and reported, the end result is a stalemate that thwarts the objectives of the CEPA and that denies the Canadian public its rights to know how it is threatened by a major source of pollution.

Generally speaking, the evidence shows that between 1993, the first NPRI reporting year, and 2005, the Minister, for various reasons, decided to exempt tailings and waste rock from reporting unless the pollutants were released from a disposal area.

The evidence shows that, since the creation of the NPRI, the processing of mined materials has always been reportable and that, since 2006, NPRI reporting has also been required for mining extraction activities. Also, NPRI reporting is required for substances that leave a TIA or WRSA.

What has not been reportable are the controlled movements of tailings and waste rock inside a mining facility to a TIA or WRSA. This issue has not been dealt with because there is, as yet, no consensus between stakeholders as to how such reporting should be done.

It was in 2006 that the Minister accepted the consensus reached on mining extraction and removed the reporting exemption for that activity so that both processing and extraction were reportable [...]

My review of the record leads me to conclude that there was no intention, when the mining exemption was removed in 2006, to include reporting substances in tailings and waste rock that remain inside a mining facility. The whole history of the discussion and consultative process shows that this issue has long been a problem and that, as yet, it has not been resolved through stakeholder consultation and consensus. The evidence also reveals that the applicants have taken part in the consultative process and are aware that no consensus exists on this issue and that the Minister has yet to make a decision on what form the reporting of these pollutants should take.

Whether the Canadian public is aware of this residual problem and is being misled by the exclusion of the pollutants found in on-site tailings and waste rock is a different issue. The lack of consensus over the issue has meant that the consultative process has broken down and the Minister is currently studying how the relevant information ought to be collected and reported publicly in a system other than the NPRI.

The end result is that all stakeholders appear to recognize that this information should be collected and reported, but cannot reach consensus on what form the reporting should take. There is no evidence as to how long it will take to devise a way of reporting this information to the public and, in the meantime, the information is not being reported through the NPRI system, and mining remains the only sector not required to report on-site disposals of pollutants identified in the CEPA to the NPRI.

Legalities aside, this is a very unsatisfactory situation, and the impasse amongst stakeholders does not serve the needs of the Canadian public. The Minister conceded at the hearing that this information is not yet reported but that this was not the result of guile, and that the Minister was merely looking for the right reporting vehicle. While not being reported as yet, the Minister assured the Court that it is not the intention of the Minister to exempt this information from being reported.

Notwithstanding these assurances, it is clearly unsatisfactory that such an important part of the pollution picture in Canada is not being reported to the public under the CEPA. The Minister and his predecessors have continued the incremental and consultative process envisaged under the CEPA, but the record shows that the debate concerning the need to report the information in question, and the form that such reporting should take in the mining sector, has been going on since at least 1992. At some point incremental becomes glacial, study becomes stasis, and stasis clearly favours those who are not required to report. The Canadian public is the loser and, without such information being readily accessible, cannot participate in the debate or gauge fully the environmental and health concerns that arise from the pollutants in on-site TIAs and WRSAs. At the time of the hearing of this application, there was no indication of when, or how, this information would be made available.

In view of this impasse, and its consequences for Canadians, the present application is entirely understandable. The question is, however, whether there is any legal basis upon which the Court should intervene and grant the declarative and mandatory relief sought by the applicants.

Legal Issues

The applicants say that they seek judicial review of the ongoing course of action of the Minister who has failed, since 1993 when the NPRI was first established, to require reporting by mining facilities of releases or transfers of pollutants to TIAs *and* WRSAs. Their argument is, in essence, that the CEPA requires the Minister to provide this pollutant release information to the public and he has failed to do so.

The applicants base their case upon the obligatory language found in sections 48 and 50 of the CEPA, as well as the general objects of the CEPA and its overall purpose, which is to protect the Canadian environment and human health from pollutants. [...]

The Relevant Statutory Provisions

To begin with, it seems clear to me that section 48 compels the Minister to "establish a national inventory of releases of pollutants". In doing this, he is compelled to use "the information collected under section 46 and any other information to which the Minister has access". In addition, section 48 allows the Minister, but does not compel him, to "use any information to which the Minister has access to establish any other inventory of information." It seems clear to me, then, that there has to be a "national inventory of releases of pollutants" that, subject to subsection 53(4), must be published in accordance with section 50.

In other words, the "any other inventory" that the Minister "may" establish under section 48 is in addition to, and not an alternative to, the "national inventory" that must be established. This interpretation would appear to accord with Environment Canada's understanding as expressed at the MSST meeting in October 2007 and its decision to establish a "national inventory" for the reporting of on-site tailings and waste rock pollutants.

It also seems to me that the "national inventory" established under section 48 must contain "releases of pollutants". So the next issue is whether the onsite releases and transfers by mining facilities to TIAs and WRSAs constitute "releases of pollutants". [...]

For these reasons, I think I must conclude that "releases of pollutants" in section 48 of the CEPA must, as a matter of statutory interpretation, include the releases and transfer of materials to TIAs and WRSAs that are the subject-matter of this application. This brings the Court to the meaning of section 46 and its relationship with sections 48 and 50 of the CEPA.

Section 46

The respondent points out that the Minister has always required the reporting of substances listed in the NPRI *Canada Gazette* notice that leave a facility's TIA or WRSA but the Minister has never required the reporting of these substances in tailings or waste inside a facility to a TIA or WRSA. The basic reason for this state of affairs offered by the respondent is that the CEPA grants the Minister a discretion under section 46 of the CEPA, which means that there is no legislative duty imposed on the Minister to either use the provisions of section 46 or to require specific data. It is important to read section 46 together with section 47 which compels the Minister to "issue guidelines respecting the use of the powers provided for by subsection 46(1)". Subsection 47(2) also compels the Minister to consult with various parties in carrying out his/her duties under subsection 47(1).

The respondent argues that the use of the word "may" in section 46 makes it clear that the section is wholly permissive, and the Minister's choice of the scope of information required under any notice sent out under section 46 is entirely the function of a policy decision formulated in accordance with section 47 [...]

If this interpretation were accepted, however, it would mean that, if the Minister chooses not to collect information under section 46 about any "releases of pollutants", either from a particular sector or otherwise, then any national inventory established under section 48 need not accurately or fully reveal to Canadians the environmental and health hazards they face.

This interpretation is very difficult to reconcile with the obligations imposed upon the Government of Canada under other sections of the CEPA and, in particular, section 2 which, among other things, obliges the Government of Canada to protect the environment and to provide information to the people of Canada on the state of the Canadian environment.

Simply put, I cannot see how the national inventory that must be established under section 48 can, when the full context of the CEPA is examined, be entirely governed by whatever information the Minister may, or may not, choose to collect under section 46.

The discretion allowed under section 46 must, in my view, be exercised in a way that meets the obligations of the Government of Canada, as those obligations are defined in the CEPA, and that allows the various tools necessary to fulfill the general scheme and objects of the CEPA to be assembled and used in a meaningful way. A national inventory of releases of pollutants can hardly play the role ascribed to it by the CEPA if the Minister decides, under section 46, not to collect information so that the people of Canada are not provided with a full and accurate picture of the releases of those pollutants that pose environmental and health risks.

In my view, then, section 46 cannot be used by the Minister to simply excuse or exempt any particular sector from providing information that, in the full context of the CEPA, as well as under specific provisions, is needed to allow Canadians to know what environment and health risks they are confronting.

In the present case, all stakeholders agree that the Canadian public should have the pollutant information in question and that it should be presented in some kind of national inventory. The Minister has simply used section 46 to exempt mining facilities from reporting such information for historical, economic and procedural reasons.

In my view, section 46 is a facilitating and enabling provision that gives the Minister wide powers to gather information required to carry out the Minister's obligations under other provisions of the CEPA.

I can see that, in certain instances, there could be a dispute as to whether information is significant enough or appropriate for inclusion in a national inventory. But in the present case no such dispute arises. All stakeholders agree that the information in question belongs in a national inventory. And from my reading of section 48, the Minister is obliged to establish "a national inventory of releases of pollutants" and that national inventory already exists under the NPRI system.

To read section 46 in the way the respondent invites the Court to read it would mean that the people of Canada will only, if ever, be informed in a national inventory about released pollutants including, in this case, pollutants that all stakeholders agree should appear in a national registry, as and when the Minister decides to collect and publish the relevant information. I cannot reconcile that position with the stated purpose and objectives of the CEPA and the obligations of the Government of Canada under the CEPA.

It seems to me that the reason the Minister has issued notices and guides under sections 46 and 47 telling mining facilities not to report such information is because, if it is reported, then the Minister is obliged to publish it under section 48 in the established NPRI. But this approach amounts to turning a blind eye to relevant information that all stakeholders agree should appear in a national inventory. I see nothing in section 46 or the general scheme of the CEPA that allows the Minister to do this.

Section 48 obliges the Minister to establish a national inventory of releases of pollutants using the information collected under section 46 "and any other information to which the Minister has access". The record shows that the Minister is well aware that information is readily available (indeed the Minister may already possess it) that should be collected and placed in a national inventory of releases of pollutants. Indeed, the only thing that would appear to be preventing this from occurring is that not all stakeholders want the relevant information to appear under the NPRI; some want a separate reporting and inventory system. Mr. Lavallée, for the respondent, opines that the "NPRI is not the appropriate tool to collect this information, and the Department would examine options to put in place this reporting through another mechanism. The mechanism to use for this reporting has not yet been decided by Environment Canada".

The Court is not told how and when it will be decided. Nor is there evidence to suggest some practical difficulty in using the NPRI. Meanwhile, the Canadian public is deprived of information concerning a significant source of pollution in Canada and concerning the environmental and health risks that releases of such pollutants pose for Canadians. I do not see how such an approach can be reconciled with the obligatory language of section 48 or with the general scheme and objectives of the CEPA. There is nothing before me to suggest that this situation will be resolved any time soon or that the people of Canada will be told in a national inventory just what pollutants have been released into the environment from this source. The Court is simply told that it cannot review and interfere with the ministerial powers granted under section 46 of the CEPA to gather information.

Availability of Judicial Review

Both the Minister and the intervener take the position that judicial review is not available to the applicants in the circumstances of this case. The Minister says that the imposition of reporting requirements and what may be included in the *Canada Gazette* notice under section 46 of the CEPA, 1999, is a discretionary decision in the nature of policy action and, as such, is not subject to judicial review. The Minister cites the usual authorities for this proposition, including the Supreme Court of Canada decision in *Maple Lodge Farms Ltd. v. Canada*, 1982 CanLII 24 (SCC), [1982] 2 S.C.R. 2. In the alternative, the Minister says that the decision to publish a notice in the *Canada Gazette*, requiring the reporting of certain data, is a legislative action and is not subject to judicial review. The Minister's position is that there is no legislative duty imposed on the Minister to either use the provisions of section 46 or to require specific data. This is because the word "may" is used in section 46, and there is nothing in the context that would give it any other than the permissive meaning ascribed to it in section 11 of the *Interpretation Act*.

I have already found that section 46 is an enabling provision that must be read in the full context of the CEPA. Part 3 of the CEPA imposes various duties upon the Minister that must be discharged under the terms of the CEPA. Section 44 is compulsory and has its own enabling provision under subsection 44(2). Likewise section 45, dealing with health issues, is compulsory and obliges the Minister to "distribute available information to inform the public about the effects of substances on human health."

Sections 46 to 53 of Part 3 deal with "Information Gathering" and make it obligatory for the Minister, under sections 48 and 50, to establish a national inventory of releases of pollutants and, subject to subsection 53(4), to "publish the national inventory of releases of pollutants." Under section 50 the Minister has a discretion regarding the manner of publication of the national inventory of releases but, subject to 53(4), the national inventory must be published and, under the NPRI, this is what has occurred. The applicants have brought this application pursuant to section 48 of the CEPA, which obliges the Minister to establish a national inventory of pollutants. In doing this, the Minister must use the information collected under section 46 "and any other information to which the Minister has access".

On the record before me, there is no doubt that, even if the Minister does not possess the information regarding tailings and waste rock disposal areas that are the subject of this application, the Minister certainly has access to that information. Section 46 gives the Minister all the access he needs. The Minister has simply chosen not to access the information by using sections 46 and 47 to exempt mining facilities from providing the information in question, and he has done so in a context where all stakeholders — including, to their credit, the mining sector represented by the intervener — agree that such information is available and ought to be reported in an inventory to the public.

I see nothing in the scheme of Part 3, or the CEPA as a whole, that gives the Minister a discretion to use sections 46 and 47 in this way [...]

The Minister has, in effect, taken the position that, in establishing a national inventory under section 48, he can choose not to include some releases of pollutants that he knows about and in relation to which, he can readily access information under section 46.

Section 50 makes it clear that the national inventory established under section 48 "shall" be published. The manner of publication is for the Minister's discretion. But nowhere do I read that a discretion concerning the manner of publication can be used to forestall or avoid the publication of a national inventory of released pollutants that includes information readily accessible to the

Minister under section 46. And that appears to be what has happened on the record placed before me.

The preamble to the CEPA makes it clear that the Government of Canada "recognizes that the risk of toxic substances in the environment is a matter of national concern and that toxic substances, once introduced into the environment, cannot always be contained within geographic boundaries", and the duties assumed by the Government of Canada under section 2 require the Government to "provide information to the people of Canada on the state of the Canadian environment" and to "apply and enforce this Act in a fair, predictable and consistent manner." Instead of adhering to these objectives and duties in the present case, the Minister has chosen not to publish information in a national inventory of releases of pollutants about mining facilities to which he has ready access while, at the same time, publishing similar information accessed from other sectors. The result is that the people of Canada do not have a national inventory of releases of pollutants that will allow them to assess the state of the Canadian environment and take whatever measures they feel are appropriate to protect the environment and facilitate the protection of human health.

Publishing the information in question under the NPRI will not inhibit the Minister from continuing to study and collaborate on the issue of whether this information might not also need its own inventory. The record suggests that the information is accessible to the Minister, yet the Minister has decided not to publish it through the NPRI and to explore other means to find an "appropriate tool". François Lavallée, on behalf of the Minister, opines as follows:

> General consensus was achieved on the need for a mandatory, periodic reporting system for information that would help characterize the hazards associated with mine tailings and waste rock.

All stakeholders agree on the need for reporting this information. The Minister can access the information. Yet the Minister has chosen not to access and report it because he wants to find a more "appropriate tool" than the NPRI. Meanwhile, the hazards associated with tailings and waste rock held on site go unreported. Reporting the information under section 48 will not prevent the Minister from finding a more "appropriate tool" that all stakeholders can accept.

The Minister's present approach is the equivalent of granting a sectorial exemption on the reporting of information that stakeholders agree should be reported to the Canadian public. This is not, in my view, reconcilable with the Minister's duties under section 48, or with the general scheme and purpose of the CEPA. Similarly, the Minister's position on section 46 is the equivalent of saying that the CEPA has left to the Minister, in his absolute discretion, the decision on whether or not to report to the Canadian public on environmental hazards that all stakeholders agree should be reported. Once again, I cannot reconcile such a position with the general scheme and purpose of the CEPA. In my view, this application does not ask the Court to interfere with the exercise of a statutory discretion granted under section 46 of the CEPA; it is concerned with the Minister's failure to carry out the mandatory obligations imposed on him under sections 2, 48 and 50 of the CEPA. My understanding is that judicial review is available to appropriate applicants in this kind of situation.

The respondent and the intervener are of the view that this application for judicial review challenges the scope of the information collected under section 46 of the CEPA for the purpose of creating an inventory of data. They believe that section 46 is permissive and imposes no legislative duty on the Minister to either use the provisions of section 46 or to require specific data.

If the decision in question is not policy action and so discretionary, then the respondent and the intervener say that it involves a determination of what ought to be published in the *Canada Gazette* notice ad, for this reason, is a legislative act that is not subjection to judicial review.

My view of this application, as I have made clear in my reasons, is that its focus is the Minister's statutory duty under sections 48 and 50 of the CEPA to establish a national inventory of releases of pollutants and to publish that national inventory. The Minister has declined to carry out the obligations imposed by statute in this regard, relying upon what he perceives to be a broad discretion in section 46 of the CEPA to gather information. My conclusion is that the discretion and power to gather information under section 46 cannot be used to abrogate mandatory obligations under sections 48 and 50 of the CEPA. Hence, I believe that the conduct of the Minister complained of by the applicants is subject to judicial review. See *Middlesex (County) v. Ontario (Minister of Municipal Affairs)* reflex, (1992), 10 O.R. (3d) 1 (Gen. Div.).

I agree with the respondent and the intervener that a purely ministerial decision, on grounds of public policy, or a decision that is the exercise of legislative function may not be amenable to judicial supervision. But that is not the case in this application where the Court has been asked to review the actions of the Minister taken in the exercise of a statutory power. See *Martineau v. Matsqui Institution Disciplinary Board*, 1979 CanLII 184 (SCC), [1980] 1 S.C.R. 602, at page 619; and *Sutcliffe v. Ontario (Minister of the Environment)* 2004 CanLII 31687 (ON CA), (2004), 72 O.R. (3d) 213 (C.A.), at paragraph 23.

Standard of Review

The Court's view is that this application involves the Minister's misinterpretation of, in particular, sections 46 and 48 of the CEPA resulting in the Minister's failure to discharge his obligations under section 48 of the CEPA to require the reporting of releases of pollutants to TIAs and WRSAs and publication to the NPRI.

The Court in *Nunavut Wildlife Management Board v. Canada (Minister of Fisheries and Oceans)*, 2009 FC 16 (CanLII), 2009 FC 16, [2009] 4 F.C.R. 544 held at paragraph 61 that, "[a] failure to comply with a statutory requirement is an error of law subject to a standard of correctness."

The applicant in *Environmental Resource Centre v. Canada (Minister of the Environment)* 2001 FCT 1423 (CanLII), 2001 FCT 1423, 40 Admin. L.R. (3d) 217 argued at paragraph 52 that, "[f]ailure to comply with a mandatory requirement is an error of law reviewable on the standard of correctness": *Alberta Wilderness Assn. v. Cardinal River Coals Ltd.*, 1999 CanLII 7908 (FC), [1999] 3 F.C. 425, at pages 440 and 442 and *Friends of the West Country Assn. v. Canada (Minister of Fisheries and Oceans)*, 1999 CanLII 9379 (FCA), [2000] 2 F.C. 263 (F.C.A.), affg 1998 CanLII 7113 (FC), [1998] 4 F.C. 340 (T.D.).

Therefore, based on the case law, I agree with the applicants that the standard of review on the failure to comply with the statutory requirement in this case is correctness.

Mandamus

For the reasons stated by the applicants, I believe that the conditions laid down in *Apotex Inc. v. Canada (Attorney General)*, 1993 CanLII 3004 (FCA), [1994] 1 F.C. 742 (C.A.), at paragraph 45, for the issuance of a writ of *mandamus* have been met in this case ...

JUDGMENT

THIS COURT ORDERS AND ADJUDGES that:

1. The Minister has erred in his interpretation of the CEPA as not requiring him to provide pollutant release information to the public through the NPRI in relation to releases and transfers to tailings and waste rock disposal areas by mining facilities in 2006 and subsequent years;

2. An order in the nature of *mandamus* is hereby issued and the Minister is directed to publish pollutant release information to the public through the NPRI in relation to releases and transfers to tailings and waste rock disposal areas by mining facilities for the 2006 and subsequent reporting years in accordance with sections 48 and 50 of the CEPA.

Notes and Questions

1. Transparency is a foundational principle of environmental law, making this case an important one in the development of Canadian environmental jurisprudence. What are the significant features of the decision in terms of elaborating and affirming this principle?

2. In his reasons, Russell J. finds as follows:

   [...] there was no intention, when the mining exemption was removed in 2006, to include reporting substances in tailings and waste rock that remain inside a mining facility. The whole history of the discussion and consultative process shows that this issue has long been a problem and that, as yet, it has not been resolved through stakeholder consultation and consensus. The evidence also reveals that the applicants have taken part in the consultative process and are aware that no consensus exists on this issue and that the Minister has yet to make a decision on what form the reporting of these pollutants should take. Whether the Canadian public is aware of this residual problem and is being misled by the exclusion of the pollutants found in on-site tailings and waste rock is a different issue. The lack of consensus over the issue has meant that the consultative process has broken down and the Minister is currently studying how the relevant information ought to be collected and reported publicly in a system other than the NPRI.

   Given these findings of fact, explain why he ultimately decided there was, in his words, a "legal basis upon which the Court should intervene and grant the declarative and mandatory relief sought by the applicants"? Are you surprised that he rejected the Crown's argument that "judicial review was not available" due to the discretionary, policy-based nature of the ministerial (in)action being challenged?

Parliamentary Review of CEPA

In the summer of 2017, after extensive hearings, the House of Commons Standing Committee on Environment and Sustainable Development tabled a report on the results of its review of CEPA, which by statute must be reviewed every five years. The Report, which contained 87 recommendations, identified a number of areas in which a majority of the Committee saw the need for substantial reform. A key set of recommendations concerned moving towards a more precautionary approach to the regulation of toxic chemicals, an issue that sparked considerable controversy during the Committee's hearings. To date, as set out in the news report below, the government's response to the Report has been somewhat noncommittal, indicating that it is still studying the implications of the recommendations and that reforms will need to await a future parliamentary session.

Jolson Lim,
"Feds Shy Away from Endorsing Regulatory Overhaul for
'High-Concern' Chemicals in CEPA Reform"
The Hill Times (July 9, 2018)

A bill reforming Canada's foremost environment law won't be tabled until a "later Parliament," McKenna said. The federal government is not moving away from its current approach toward regulating high-risk chemicals, despite strong calls from environmentalists to change the formula to require industry to prove to federal regulators that some substances are safe before they're used.

Environment Minister Catherine McKenna (Ottawa Centre, Ont.) responded to the 87 recommendations on June 29 that were put forward by the House Environment Committee in its 2017 review of the Canadian Environmental Protection Act (CEPA), a cornerstone environmental law that hasn't been updated since 1999. In a lengthy report released on June 29, the minister didn't endorse moving toward a hazard-based approach for regulating a series of chemicals categorized in the European Union as "of very high concern." Such an approach would mean some substances are prohibited until companies can prove they're safe or that there are not feasible substitutes.

These substances include ones that are carcinogenic, mutagenic, and harmful for reproduction, as well as persistent and bio-accumulative substances, and others of similar concern such as endocrine disruptors. The category includes some lead-based products. Instead, the report notes that CEPA currently provides "broad authority, including an extensive suite of risk management tools, to manage the risks posed by substances with these characteristics." However, it said it would "further consider" the committee's recommendation for changing the regime.

The issue divided environmentalists and industry, who, despite their differences, lobbied together on a set of other reforms around CEPA. Currently, Canada generally takes a "risk-based" approach towards regulating chemicals, where the regulator assumes a risk to safety but doesn't prohibit the substance, and then works with producers to find out if the chemical is safe. Those who want to restrict certain substances must prove their harm to humans or the environment to federal regulators. But environmentalists have strongly called for the burden to be reversed, and to get federal regulators to first err on the side of caution on whether to permit those chemicals to be used. Such a change would fundamentally shift the regulation of a small but significant subset of chemicals, and advocates believe such a move would better protect humans and the ecosystem. The system is used in the European Union, which has some of the world's toughest environmental protection laws.

Elaine MacDonald, a scientist with Ecojustice, said "we felt it was something the department was willing to move on, but industry wasn't really in agreement." She said Environment Canada provided a reverse onus proposal at stakeholder meetings but industry members had opposed it. Bob Masterson, president and CEO of the Chemistry Industry Association of Canada, said he was "most happy" to see the risk-based regulatory approach maintained, which he described as the foundation for CEPA and the Chemicals Management Plan (CMP), the central regulatory framework born out of the 1999 act. The industry association opposes a change because it would assume too many chemicals are unsafe without first conducting scientific studies. Mr. Masterson said there were a "number of opportunities for continued improvement but the foundation remains one of 'We're going to assess and manage our substances on the basis of where they pose risks to society and the environment.'"

"We need some kind of similar approach to the introduction of novel chemicals into human bodies and the environment as we have with pharmaceuticals," said Tim Gray, executive director of Environmental Defence. "You need to prove it's safe, not introduce it, and then after people get sick, you decide to look at it." Since 1994, federal regulators have taken a preventative approach with new chemical substances, not allowing them to enter into the marketplace without their approval. There are 23,000 chemical substances used in Canada, with about 4,300 watched by regulators through the CMP, and a smaller number actually managed. A reverse burden currently applies for chemicals under the "virtual elimination" regime, according to Ms. MacDonald, although an online list shows only two substances.

Often overlooked, CEPA is a sprawling, complex, yet critical piece of environmental legislation that establishes federal regulatory powers for restricting and managing the use of chemical substances, as well as setting strategies for fighting air pollution.

Other Issues in McKenna's Report

Vulnerable populations: The feds strongly signalled it would do more to protect "vulnerable populations" — such as children, pregnant women, the poor, and Indigenous communities — from harm caused by chemicals. The report stated support for the committee's recommendations, which include considering such groups in risk assessments. Ms. MacDonald cited vulnerable populations is a top issue that must be addressed in CEPA reforms.

Environmental rights: Ms. McKenna didn't endorse recognizing a right to a healthy environment, instead committing to further consultation. It was a proposal supported by both environmental advocates and industry, and a recommendation by the committee. At the party's April convention, the Liberals endorsed an environmental bill of rights as an official policy.

Increased transparency: The feds signalled it would generally improve public access to information and promote efforts to be more transparent with its regulatory effort. However, such a mov[e] raises a "yellow flag" for industry, Mr. Masterson said. He wants the government to balance a public right to know with protecting trade secrets in a capital-intensive sector.

Endocrine disruptors: The government also stated its support for considering endocrine disruption in its risk assessments and improve its ability to consider emerging science around it. Such substances, such as BPA and lead, play with human hormone behaviour and can harm a body's immune system.

Regulatory capacity: Mr. Gray said a "gaping hole" is any comment on how the feds would increase enforcement. He said Canada has a "terrible record" on enforcing existing laws, citing the fact Canada did not prosecute Volkswagen officials for its emissions cheating scandal. He had hoped there would be mention of hiring more staff for its regulatory regime and "take on a culture of enforcement instead of advisement."

Data and registries: The government rejected a proposal for daily, weekly, and monthly pollution data, stating that its national pollutant release inventory is intended for assessing trends. However, it supports lowering the threshold for pollutant reporting and for generally more thorough reporting requirements. The feds are also improving its environmental offenders registry. The feds indicated it would look further into substance's cumulative effects on the environment in its regulatory process. It would support reviewing its product labelling requirements.

No Legislative Update Until After Election

A pledge to update Canada's environmental protection law came with a caveat: it would have to occur in a "later Parliament."

While the federal Liberals can move on a number of regulatory fronts without legislation, it effectively means CEPA won't be updated until after the 2019 federal election, making it uncertain whether it'll even occur.

Ms. McKenna's press secretary, Caroline Thériault, affirmed that the Liberals are committed to introducing a bill "as soon as possible" in the next mandate, if elected. She cited CEPA as the legal tool the government used to ban asbestos and microbeads.

Mr. Gray said he was "disappointed but not surprised" that the Liberals decided it wouldn't update the act at this moment. He noted it wasn't a 2015 election promise, and that in his opinion, the only reasons why there is any political momentum is due to the substantiveness of the committee report, public concern, and collective efforts by environmentalists and industry to push Ottawa to act.

"We knew it was going to be tough one because of the heavy legislative agenda," added Ms. MacDonald, who said she hopes that the government's movement won't be a "false start." First enacted in 1988 and updated legislatively in 1999, stakeholders and all political parties say the bill is badly outdated. However, successive government[s] have sat on updating the law since 1999. While disappointed that Ms. McKenna didn't endorse several core recommendations, Mr. Gray was just happy to see a signal that a bill is promised. "The environment's always been important to people," he said, "but it isn't the main thing politicians campaign on and differentiating themselves on."

Notes and Questions

1. A key issue flagged in the above article is a recurring theme in environmental law: the tension between *risk-based* approaches to decision-making and *precautionary* ones. What do you understand to be the key differences between these two approaches?

2. In Chapter 1, we introduced this debate and described the *Telstra* decision of the New South Wales Land and Environment Court, which offers a test for determining *when* a precautionary approach to decision-making should apply, and a methodology that prescribes *how* such an approach could be operationalized by courts, tribunals and other decision-makers. This tension between the precautionary principle and its risk-based counterpart (sometimes referred to as "adaptive management") is also addressed in Chapter 5 (compliance and enforcement) and Chapter 7 (environmental assessment). In the article above, Tim Gray, executive director of the ENGO Environmental Defence, suggests that the prevailing precautionary approach to the regulation of pharmaceuticals should also be used in relation to regulating toxic chemicals under CEPA. Do you agree? Why or why not?

3. Along with many other CEPA reform issues, it appears that environmental rights will have to await "a later Parliament". What kinds of rights should CEPA recognize, and how should they be recognized and protected?

References and Further Readings

Stefan Ambec *et al.*, "The Porter Hypothesis at 20: Can Environmental Regulation Enhance Innovation and Competitiveness?" (Resources for the Future, 2011), online: <http://ssrn.com/abstract=1754674>

C. Coglianese & D. Lazar, "Management-based Regulation: Prescribing Private Management to Achieve Public Goals" (2003) 37 Law & Soc'y. Rev. 691

C. Coglianese, J. Nash & T. Olmstead, "Performance-based Regulation: Prospects and Limitations in Health, Safety and Environmental Protection" (2003) 55 Admin. L. Rev. 705

D. Paul Emond, "The Greening of Environmental Law" (1991) 36 McGill L.J. 742

M.A.H. Franson, R.T. Franson & A.R. Lucas, *Environmental Standards: A Comparative Study of Canadian Standards, Standard Setting Processes, and Enforcement* (Edmonton: Environmental Council of Alberta, 1982)

J. Freeman & D. Farber, "Modular Environmental Regulation" (2005) 54 Duke L.J. 795

N. Gunningham & P. Grabosky, *Smart Regulation Designing Environmental Policy* (Oxford: Oxford University Press, 1998)

N. Gunningham & D. Sinclair, *Leaders and Laggards: Next Generation Environmental Regulation* (Sheffield: Greenleaf, 2002)

K. Harrison, "Talking with the Donkey: Cooperative Approaches to Environmental Protection" (1999) 2 Journal of Industrial Ecology 51. Copyright 1999, Yale University.

M. Howlett, "Policy Instruments, Policy Styles, and Policy Implementation: National Approaches to Theories of Instrument Choice" (1991) 19 Policy Studies Journal 1

William Lahey & Meinhard Doelle, "Negotiating the Interface of Environmental and Economic Governance: Nova Scotia's *Environmental Goals and Sustainable Prosperity Act*" (2012) 35 Dal. L.J. 1

Jolson Lim, "Feds Shy Away from Endorsing Regulatory Overhaul for 'High-Concern' Chemicals in CEPA Reform", *The Hill Times* (July 9, 2018)

R.M. M'Gonigle *et al.*, "Taking Uncertainty Seriously: From Permissive Regulation to Preventative Design in Environmental Decision Making" (1994) 32 Osgoode Hall L.J. 99

I. Richler, "*R. v. Kingston* and the Criminalization of Harmless Pollution", Case Comment, (2005) 15 J.E.L.P. 319

C. Tollefson, "Games without Frontiers: Investor Claims and Citizen Suits under the NAFTA Regime" (2002) 27 Yale J. Int'l. L. 217

C. Tollefson, F. Gale & D. Haley, *Setting the Standard: Certification, Governance and the Forest Stewardship Council* (UBC Press, 2008). Reprinted with permission of the Publisher from *Setting the Standard: Certification, Governance and the Forest Stewardship Council* by Chris Tollefson, Fred Gale & David Haley, University of British Columbia Press 2008. All rights reserved by the Publisher.

Stepan Wood, Georgia Tanner & Benjamin J. Richardson, "Whatever Happened to Canadian Environmental Law?" (2010) 37 Ecology L.Q. 981

Chapter 5

Compliance and Enforcement

Introduction

A key measure of the effectiveness of environmental regulation is compliance by the regulated community. Where compliance is not forthcoming, regulators must respond by taking enforcement action or risk undermining the legitimacy and credibility of the regulatory regime. This chapter surveys a range of compliance and enforcement-related issues that arise in the environmental law context.

Part I provides definitions for some of the key concepts in this area, and reflects on the difficulties associated with assessing the efficacy of compliance and enforcement efforts. It also seeks to provide an overview of the current state of environmental compliance and enforcement "on the ground". In Part II, we consider the ongoing debate over the relative merits of cooperative versus adversarial approaches to environmental enforcement. Part III concerns the legal principles and leading cases in this area. It considers a variety of topics, including:

- The role of the *Criminal Code* in environmental prosecutions;
- The nature and role of the regulatory offence under federal and provincial legislation;
- The prosecution and defence of environmental charges;
- Directors' and officers' liability;
- Sentencing in environmental cases;
- Administrative monetary penalties (AMPs);
- The role of adaptive management; and
- The interplay between statutory remediation liability orders and bankruptcy/ insolvency law.

The chapter concludes in Part IV with reflections on the current and potential future role of citizens in environmental enforcement. This Part considers citizen suit provisions, avenues for citizen participation in enforcement actions under Environmental Bill of Rights (EBR) provisions, and private prosecutions.

Part I — Regulatory Compliance and Enforcement Strategies

Introduction

Joseph Castrilli,
"Canadian Policy and Practice with Indicators of
Effective Environmental Enforcement"

Annex 3 to Indicators of Effective Environmental Enforcement
Proceedings of a North American Dialogue (CEC, 1999),
online: < http://www.cec.org/ >

In recent years, international recognition of the importance of compliance and enforcement to environmental management has reinforced interest at the national and sub-national level in ensuring compliance and enforcement with domestic environmental laws. In Canada, at both the federal and provincial levels, the concepts of "compliance" and "enforcement" have been developed at the policy level in most of the jurisdictions under consideration. In general, "compliance" has been defined as "the state of conformity with the law". Measures that governments use to ensure compliance include written and verbal communication, consultation, monitoring, inspection, data review, and enforcement. In general, "enforcement" has been defined as "activities that compel offenders to comply with their legislative requirements". Enforcement activities are seen to include investigations of alleged violations, imposition of corrective measures, administrative responses to compel compliance, and prosecution.

Overview of Federal and Provincial Roles in Compliance Measurement

There are several characteristics of federal and provincial environmental legislation which have implications for developing performance measures of compliance. First, a key characteristic of federal law (CEPA and the *Fisheries Act*), is that compliance is considered primarily in relation to the regulations promulgated under both laws.

Second, in comparison to federal environmental law, a key characteristic of provincial law is that compliance must be measured to a substantial degree in relation to approvals, licenses and permits as well as prohibitions, administrative orders and regulations. This broad regulatory authority can be a greater challenge to provincial governments in developing measures of compliance performance in the large areas of responsibility encompassed by provincial law, particularly during a period of resource constraints and government cutbacks.

Third, differences in the place where compliance is to be measured under federal and provincial law can have implications on how performance measures of compliance, such as inspections and self-monitoring and reporting, will be employed in determining overall levels of compliance.

Fourth, whereas federal regulations, with some exceptions, tend to be either substance specific, without regard to medium or industrial sector, or substance-industrial sector-medium specific, provincial regulations may be substance-medium specific, without regard to industrial sector, or industrial sector-medium specific, without regard to substance. This divergence in regulation type has the potential to produce a different approach to measuring compliance, as well as the potential to produce different conclusions about the status of compliance at the same facility or class of facility.

These various differences in legislative and regulatory regimes, which may simply indicate a rich, if complex, framework in which to test compliance, also suggests the potential for a confusing, fragmented, and inconsistent approach to assessment of compliance performance. Moreover, these differences may take on greater significance in the future, either in terms of resolving or exacerbating potential inconsistencies, to the extent that federal-provincial agreements result in provincial responsibility for ensuring compliance with federal requirements or become a substitute for federal requirements.

Overview of Federal and Provincial Roles in Enforcement Measurement

One of the earliest policies in Canada on the subject of environmental enforcement was the 1988 Environment Canada enforcement and compliance policy developed in conjunction with the coming into force of *CEPA*. The policy had been preceded by concern expressed over the years by federal advisory bodies that there was "an inadequate level of enforcement of statutes and regulations which were designed to protect the quality of the environment". The policy established enforcement principles, identified enforcement personnel and their responsibilities, listed criteria for responding to violations, and set out the enforcement measures available for responding to violations. Similar policies, preceded by similar public concerns, have also been developed at the provincial level for defining enforcement, enforcement principles, and enforcement activities. Several characteristics of federal and provincial environmental legislation have implications for developing performance measures of enforcement.

First, a key characteristic of federal law (*CEPA* and the *Fisheries Act*) is that enforcement of environmental standards primarily involves the use of command and control statutory prohibitions or regulations, violations of which are prosecuted in the courts in virtually the same manner as criminal offences. This process is expensive, time-consuming, and requires intensive preparation and resources.

Second, in comparison to federal environmental law, a key characteristic of provincial law is that enforcement mechanisms for violations are more multifaceted and include, besides prosecutions: administrative orders, directives, minor offense ticketing, cancellation of permits or approvals and, in some provinces, administrative monetary penalties. This authority to respond to violations in a variety of ways gives the provinces more enforcement options, the ability to deal with less serious violations before they become more serious, and a wider variety of forums in which to proceed against offenders. These differences in legislative and regulatory regimes may take on greater significance in the future to the extent that federal-provincial agreements result in provincial responsibility for enforcing federal requirements, or where provincial requirements become a substitute for federal requirements.

Correlating Compliance and Enforcement Outcomes with Environmental Results

The ultimate goal of federal and provincial compliance and enforcement efforts is to achieve environmental goals and objectives. However, the ability of governments in Canada to measure the relationship between compliance and enforcement outputs and outcomes on the one hand, and the overall state of the environment on the other is still rudimentary. Environment Canada has noted, for example, in its compliance and enforcement report on six regulations under *CEPA* and the *Fisheries Act* that: "Care should be taken in drawing conclusions from the state of compliance information [...] even a 100 [percent] compliance level does not equate to a 100 [percent] protection of the environment. The reason for this is that regulations and their provisions do not necessarily consider every aspect of a regulated product, substance, or activity. Nor do regulations cover all aspects of environmental protection. Consequently, the [six regulations] report is not about describing the state of the environment".

This begs the question of whether government should attempt to determine the relationship between changes in the behavior of the regulated community and overall environmental quality. Moreover, in a period of reduced government resources, making this link would appear to be increasingly difficult, especially if government efforts to report on compliance rates and trends diminish.

Conclusions

Compliance and enforcement indicators may be a combination of: (1) outputs (2) outcomes and (3) resulting improvements in environmental quality. While initiatives are occurring with respect to some of these matters, the overall development of comprehensive environmental compliance and enforcement performance measures is still in its early stages in most jurisdictions in Canada. Moreover, as one moves along the spectrum from reporting outputs to measuring resulting environmental quality, the efforts of governments appear less developed and more fragmentary.

This is not surprising, but does indicate where greater governmental effort should be directed in future. Historically, federal and provincial governments have focused on reporting compliance and enforcement outputs such as numbers of inspections conducted, or prosecutions initiated. This traditional approach is itself not old in Canada, and is by no means uniformly undertaken at the federal and provincial levels, as some governments still do not regularly report this information, or have discontinued doing so. Moreover, such traditional reporting measures may be undergoing significant change arising from trends such as: (1) targeting "chronic offenders" for inspection; (2) requiring self-monitoring and reporting, as well as encouraging voluntary compliance by the regulated community; and (3) providing "single window" inspection and enforcement pursuant to emerging federal-provincial arrangements.

[...] it is difficult to correlate compliance and enforcement outcomes with environmental results. Efforts of governments in Canada to measure the relationship are in their infancy. The few government reports that discuss the issue are quick to disclaim a relationship between compliance performance and overall environmental quality [...]. Perhaps the single most important approach governments in Canada should undertake in this area is to establish performance objectives and measures and develop methods for evaluating their effectiveness for compliance and enforcement outputs, outcomes and environmental quality goals.

With respect to outcomes, these initiatives could include annual reporting of such matters as: compliance rates by permit, regulation, industrial sector, environmental media, geographic region, or a combination thereof; companies in significant non-compliance; progress in returning chronic and significant offenders to compliance as a result of compliance or enforcement efforts; rate of recidivism among significant or chronic offenders following compliance or enforcement efforts; compliance rates of companies employing voluntary compliance measures; and compliance rates of companies where public liaison committees exist. With respect to environmental quality goals, these initiatives could include annual reporting of such matters as: emission or discharge reductions by company, environmental media, permit category, regulation, substance, industrial sector, geographic region, or a combination thereof; and state of the environment by company, environmental media, regulated substance, industrial sector, geographic region, or combination thereof. The above does not constitute an exhaustive list of what might be included in such a program, but could contribute to a more systematic approach to evaluating compliance and enforcement measures than is currently used in Canada.

Notes and Questions

1. Castrilli draws and elaborates on the important distinction between "compliance" and "enforcement". What are some of the various activities undertaken by governments in these two realms? What differences exist between the federal and provincial levels in the type of compliance-related activities that are carried out? What differences are there in the way that federal and provincial regulators carry out their enforcement duties?

2. How do governments measure the efficacy of their compliance and enforcement activities? How should they? What measurement challenges exist?

Regulatory Enforcement: The Canadian Record

Jerry V. DeMarco & Toby Vigod,
"Smarter Regulation: The Case for Enforcement and Transparency"
(2007) 17 J. Envtl. L. & Prac. 85

Historically, there was a shift in the mid 20th century from a reliance on the common law to address environmental issues to increased involvement by governments in regulatory activities. This signified a shift from a focus on private rights between parties to a focus on public law. This was coupled with an understanding that the environment was a public resource worthy of protection. The increase in government regulation commenced in the 1950s and continued with the establishment of Departments and Ministries of the Environment and the coming into force of a considerable amount of environmental legislation in the 1970s and 1980s. However, regulatory activity did not necessarily mean that these regulations were aggressively enforced. In Ontario, for example, from the early 1970s to the mid 1980s, the focus shifted to the use of administrative tools, such as permits and orders to obtain compliance. There was some success in dealing with 'conventional' pollutants during this period, but the negotiation approach favoured during these years had limited effectiveness. During this period, fines were criticized as being too low, too few, and too uncertain. A 1984 study for the Law Reform Commission of Canada described the regulatory process of the 1970s as somewhere between "cautious" and "captured".

The period of the late 1980s to the early 1990s was a period of increased regulatory activism and concern about the environment at the federal level and in some provinces, notably Ontario. Beginning in 1985, there was a major change of focus in Ontario, with increasing emphasis on prosecution. A special branch of professional investigators was created, prosecutions staff increased, and higher fines provided for in legislation. As a result, by 1988-89, the number of prosecutions had increased 500 per cent, and fines had greatly increased. The World Commission on Environment and Development's publication of *Our Common Future* in 1987 led to the embracing of the need to move towards 'sustainable development', however ambiguous that concept has subsequently become. There was a new emphasis on the need to address greenhouse gasses and toxic pollutants that did not respect jurisdictional boundaries. The 1992 United Nations Conference on the Environment and Development (the Rio Earth Summit) was a highpoint of public concern for the environment. In Ontario, the period of emphasis on regulatory enforcement occurred from 1985-1994, while in British Columbia there was a period of regulatory activism in the mid-1990s.

In some jurisdictions toward the end of the 1980s, and increasingly during the 1990s, there was a considerable backlash against regulatory activity and aggressive enforcement. This was coupled with an increasingly prevalent view that governments were, first of all, too large, and second, too interventionist in the affairs of industry, resulting in a lack of competitiveness in an increasingly global economy. Former Prime Minister Brian Mulroney's infamous comment when he ran for office in 1984 that there would be "pink slips and running shoes" for bureaucrats may have been the start of a rash of politicians running on anti-government platforms, which culminated in former Ontario Premier Mike Harris's Common Sense Revolution in 1995. Deregulation and regulatory "reform" became key themes of election platforms and government agendas.

The shift in emphasis to more voluntary approaches usually occurs in jurisdictions where the governing party has been elected primarily on a platform of fiscal restraint and the need to reduce the size of government. These governments often adopt the view that government needs to be dramatically restructured and that it should not be actively competing with private business interests, or at least should develop partnerships with industry in order to encourage economic growth and cut its costs [...]

In Ontario, a Red Tape Review Commission was established and issued its Final Report in January 1997. Coupled with "deregulation" initiatives was the trend towards use of self-regulation as a means of attaining environmental protection. Self-regulation can include voluntarism, codes of practice and administrative agreements. Yet at the same time, there has been growing public concern about the failure of regulators to regulate properly, whether they be government or self-regulating entities, particularly in the areas of public health, safety and the environment. While Ontario had been the most aggressive with its deregulatory agenda, in 2001, the British Columbia government established a "Deregulation Framework" with the objective of cutting regulations by one-third within three years [...]

Obviously, not every environmental objective can be accomplished by a binding standard and a strong enforcement approach. Many situations are better suited to education or incentives, especially for motivating the good actors who want to lead, rather than deterring the bad actors seeking to take advantage of a situation. However, for those areas of environmental management that are predicated on a traditional approach of binding government-imposed standards, such as water pollution, and for which there is a risk of opportunistic behaviour by bad actors, a strong enforcement regime should be a key part of an effective compliance toolkit alongside other measures. If enforcement measures are unlikely to be used by regulators, bad actors or free riders may take advantage of the situation. For these actors, violating environmental standards may appear to be justified vis-a-vis the possible positive impact on the bottom line. An over-emphasis on voluntary measures without maintaining a strong enforcement system may thus compromise compliance efforts. Regulators, therefore, have a responsibility to make sure that enforcement measures are strong enough to ensure that pollution does not pay. A strong enforcement system can help implement the polluter pays principle, which is widely accepted in Canadian environmental law. Public disclosure of environmental performance creates an additional, strong incentive for pollution control.

Ecojustice Canada,
Environmental Enforcement by Canada's
Federal Government (The Essentials)
(2011)

[This] document outlines the highlights of [...] *Getting Tough on Environmental Crime* that can be downloaded from Ecojustice's website: ecojustice.ca/.

Chronic Under-Enforcement

The number of inspections, investigations, charges, and convictions under the *Fisheries Act* has declined consistently since 2002-03 and 2008-09, the most recent year for which data is available. The number of inspections and warnings under the *Canadian Environmental Protection Act* (CEPA) has declined since 2005-06, despite an increase in the number of enforcement officers. The number of CEPA investigations, prosecutions, and convictions has declined steadily since 2003-04.

Many Warnings, Few Prosecutions or Convictions

Warnings and inspections remain the most frequently used enforcement tools under both CEPA and the *Fisheries Act*. But while there are typically around 2,000 warnings and 5,000 inspections per year under CEPA, there are just over 20 prosecutions — and barely half of those end in convictions. Given that the threat of prosecution and conviction is crucial to deterring violations, the low absolute numbers of prosecutions and convictions cast doubt on the effectiveness of CEPA as a stick as opposed to a carrot.

Low Fines Do Little to Dissuade

Once a violation is confirmed and a conviction is obtained, the average fines measured across several environmental laws appear extremely low relative to the revenues and profits of most industrial actors. For the past three years, the average fine obtained under CEPA was $10,524, an amount that is unlikely to deter large industrial actors from committing violations.

A Hodgepodge of Incomplete Data

Enforcement data under different federal environmental laws is hard to access because it is gathered using inconsistent methods. This unnecessarily complicates the comparison and analysis of enforcement data, diminishing the public's ability to hold government accountable and to assess the risks to environmental and human health.

Or No Data at All

The *Canada Wildlife Act* and *Canada Shipping Act* contain no legal obligation to report enforcement activity, and no information is disclosed voluntarily. Industry compliance rates across all environmental laws are also not made public. These gaping holes in environmental enforcement data leave Canadians with almost no way to determine whether these laws are achieving their respective goals of conserving wildlife species and habitat and protecting the marine environment.

Making the Public Wait for Information

The public release of annual reports (containing environmental enforcement information) under different laws has been chronically late. On at least one occasion, this prompted environmental groups to launch a successful lawsuit for the federal government's failure to comply with annual reporting rules. The disclosure of timely and accurate information regarding enforcement has simply not been a priority for the federal government.

What Enforcement Is Happening Near You?

Very limited information identifying environmental offenders, incident location, and the exact nature of the violation (specific substance, quantities, etc.) is disclosed to the Canadian public. This information is needed if individuals and industry are to be held to account for breaking environmental laws.

Conclusion

Canadians should be concerned by the findings of this report. The levels of environmental enforcement activities are too low to deter violations, and the information disclosed about such activities is too limited to promote public participation. The lack of enforcement transparency distorts market investment decisions and property values, as risks of environmental harm associated with non-compliance rates are unknown regarding specific regulated entities in particular locations.

This situation will likely be exacerbated by the 700 job cuts announced in August 2011 at Environment Canada, whose primary mandate is to protect the environment and conserve the country's natural heritage. Meanwhile, future cuts are anticipated across all departments responsible for environmental protection, and these do not bode well for future enforcement trends.

Ecojustice calls on the federal government to deliver on the commitments made in the *Environmental Enforcement Act* by confronting the serious deficiencies in its enforcement efforts. The federal government must also follow through on its promise to get tough on environmental crime by enforcing our laws and by shining a bright light on its enforcement activities. We believe the Commissioner of Environment and Sustainable Development can play an important role in evaluating whether or not departments responsible for enforcing environmental laws are upholding their commitments, on the basis of our findings in this report.

Office of the Auditor General of Canada,
2011 December Report of the Commissioner of the
Environment and Sustainable Development
"Chapter 3: Enforcing the Canadian Environmental Protection Act, 1999"

Conclusion

Environment Canada has made a number of important improvements to the organization and administration of the enforcement program. These improvements include centralizing the management of the program under the direction of a Chief Enforcement Officer; establishing a methodical, risk-based enforcement planning process for determining enforcement priorities; and identifying aspects of the enforcement program that need improvement. Environment Canada has also developed an enforcement policy and management controls intended to ensure that enforcement officers apply the Act in a fair, predictable, and consistent manner across its regional offices.

However, the Environmental Enforcement Directorate does not have adequate information on whom it is regulating and who is not complying with the *Canadian Environmental Protection Act, 1999* (CEPA 1999) regulations. This information is needed to determine which regulatees and activities pose the greatest risks to human health or the environment as a result of non-compliance. Without a clear understanding of whom it is regulating and which regulatees pose the greatest threats, the Directorate cannot be sure that its National Enforcement Plan is targeting the highest risks to human health and the environment.

In addition, in many cases we found no evidence that the Directorate had applied key management controls intended to ensure that enforcement officers carry out their enforcement activities in a fair, predictable, and consistent manner as the Act and the enforcement policy require or that enforcement officers followed up on their enforcement actions to verify whether violators returned to compliance.

The Department does not know the extent to which its enforcement activities are improving compliance or minimizing environmental damage and threats to Canadians. In addition, Environment Canada has been slow to address significant shortcomings such as inadequate training and inadequate gathering and analysis of information to inform enforcement planning and targeting.

As a result, we concluded that the enforcement program was not well managed to adequately enforce compliance with the *Canadian Environmental Protection Act, 1999* and ensure that threats to Canadians and their environment from pollution are minimized.

Office of the Auditor General of Canada,
2018 Fall Reports of the Commissioner of the Environment and Sustainable Development
"Report 1: Toxic Substances"

Enforcement priorities. Environment and Climate Change Canada had an annual process, with input from regions and headquarters, to identify enforcement priorities. According to the Department, key areas for enforcement were selected on the basis of factors such as environmental and human health risk, compliance issues, and operational capacity.

For example, for the 2015-16 fiscal year, the Department selected regulations related to vehicles and engines, for which non-compliance could lead to smog and acid rain. For the same fiscal year, the Department selected the *PCB Regulations* to verify whether businesses had destroyed equipment containing polychlorinated biphenyls (PCBs) as required. Such equipment posed an increased risk of soil and groundwater contamination.

However, we found overall that risk to the environment and human health was not a key criterion in prioritizing most of Environment and Climate Change Canada's enforcement activities. According to the Department, it prioritized enforcement activities mainly on the basis of businesses' potential for non-compliance. Consequently, the Department did not know whether its targeted enforcement activities focused on businesses that posed the greatest risks to human health and the environment.

We found that most toxic substance regulations received few inspections and enforcement measures (Exhibit 1.4). The Department carried out 10,180 inspections in the 2014-15 to 2016-17 fiscal years. Of these, 2,231 (about 22%) focused on tetrachloroethylene, a single toxic substance used by dry cleaners. No documentation indicated that this substance, a toxic air pollutant, posed a higher risk to human health and the environment than other substances.

Department officials told us that Environment and Climate Change Canada prioritized tetrachloroethylene to respond to our 2011 audit recommendation to calculate compliance rates. Although the focus on this substance did result in higher compliance rates, given the seven years since our 2011 audit, we would have expected other substances to have been selected as priorities for enforcement, based on risk.

We found that the Department carried out fewer inspections for other regulations as compared with the tetrachloroethylene regulation. For example, a regulation prohibiting 26 toxic substances from being manufactured, used, sold, or imported in Canada (the *Prohibition of Certain Toxic Substances Regulations, 2012*) had no inspections.

Court actions. We found that there were more prosecutions under the *Canadian Environmental Protection Act, 1999* than in our previous audit, with most court actions related to the dry cleaning regulation.

In the 2010-11 fiscal year, there were 2 prosecutions and no convictions for all regulations. In the 2016-17 fiscal year, there were 21 prosecutions and 9 convictions for regulations related to toxic substances. During the 2014-15 to 2016-17 fiscal years, nearly 70% of convictions were related to the dry cleaning regulation.

Furthermore, we found that according to Environment and Climate Change Canada, the amounts of fines collected under the Act had increased. For example, in the 2016-17 fiscal year, convictions under the *PCB Regulations* led to $1.74 million in fines from two regulated businesses — the largest fines that had ever been imposed under the Act.

Recommendation. Environment and Climate Change Canada should ensure that risks to human health and the environment are taken into account when prioritizing its enforcement activities.

Notes and Questions

1. The Ecojustice report excerpted above makes reference to anticipated cutbacks at Environment Canada in 2011. Since this report was authored, the cutbacks — at Environment Canada and other enforcement agencies, including Fisheries and Oceans Canada and the Coast Guard — have been significant, reportedly involving the elimination of up to 700 positions nationwide: see M. Fitzpatrick, "Environment Canada job cuts cause concern", *CBC News* (4 August 2011), online: <http://www.cbc.ca/news/canada/story/2011/08/04/pol-environment-job-cuts.html>. The Liberal Government under Prime Minister Trudeau committed to restoring lost protections. Are you able to determine to what extent the enforcement capability of the federal government has been restored?

2. DeMarco and Vigod discuss in their article the relationship between environmental enforcement patterns and electoral politics. Does a similar relationship exist at the provincial level in your home province? Is there a disconnect between the political rhetoric on the need for strong enforcement

of environmental laws and actual enforcement practice? If so, what are the factors that foster or maintain this disconnect?

3. Concerns about the efficacy with which Canadian governments have enforced environmental laws have led to a number of citizen complaints under the *North American Agreement on Environmental Cooperation* (NAAEC), established under the umbrella of the *North American Free Trade Agreement* (NAFTA). Under the NAAEC, a citizen or NGO from any of the three Party countries (Canada, the US or Mexico) is entitled to file a submission with the NAAEC Secretariat alleging that a Party is "failing to effectively enforce its environmental laws". If the submission satisfies certain procedural requirements, the governing council of the NAAEC may decide to order the Secretariat to investigate and produce a "factual record". The main benefit of this unique citizen submission process is to serve a spotlighting function; factual records are neither adjudicative nor binding in nature. Moreover, they can only address failures to enforce existing environmental laws rather than gaps or deficiencies in a Party's environmental laws. Nonetheless, the process has been deployed with considerable frequency (and some success), particularly by Canadian and Mexican environmental organizations: see C. Tollefson, "Games without Frontiers: Investor Claims and Citizen Submissions under the NAFTA Regime" (2002) 27 Yale J. Int'l. L. 217 and David L. Markell & John H. Knox, eds., *Greening NAFTA: The North American Commission for Environmental Cooperation* (Stanford: Stanford University Press, 2003). At the time of writing in late 2018, the content and fate of the replacement agreement to NAFTA is still uncertain, though an agreement in principle in the form of the USMCA agreement had been announced. Did the citizen complaint process under NAFTA survive the 2018 negotiations?

Part II — Cooperative versus Adversarial Enforcement Approaches

A key tension in environmental enforcement is the challenge of defining the respective roles of adversarial approaches and more cooperative strategies. Most commentators concur that both "sticks" and "carrots" can be useful. Beyond this general consensus, however, views diverge over when and how to deploy these varying approaches.

Matthew D. Zinn,
"Policing Environmental Regulatory Enforcement: Cooperation, Capture and Citizen Suits"
(2002) 21 Stan. Envtl. L.J. 81

Advocates of adversarial enforcement emphasize the importance of general and specific deterrence: adversarial enforcement discourages targeted defendants and regulated entities at large from violating the law. They argue that only substantial, predictable, and public sanctions for noncompliance can achieve adequate compliance in the long run by making violation uneconomic: proper penalties make the expected cost of noncompliance higher than its expected economic benefit. The expected cost is equal to the probability that a penalty actually will be imposed multiplied by the dollar value of the penalty. The economic benefit from noncompliance is the avoided cost of attaining and maintaining compliance, including the capital and operating costs of pollution control equipment, the opportunity cost of reduced or less efficient production, and the transaction costs of compliance, such as ascertaining regulatory requirements or applying for a permit.

Deterrence advocates reject cooperative enforcement as insufficiently punitive and insufficiently certain. Cooperative enforcement often eschews penalties altogether, and where penalties are imposed, they may be small. As a result, violators face minimal material incentives to avoid noncompliance. Instead, the deterrent effect of cooperative enforcement is limited to the transaction costs of bargaining with the agency plus the expected costs of incremental compliance, which include the cost of reaching compliance over months or years and the amount of any minimal penalties imposed along the way (multiplied by their low risk), all discounted to present value. A firm may often be able to reduce the cost of incremental compliance by absorbing the cost of minor penalties along the way, allowing the firm to remain noncompliant for years.

A few values unrelated to deterrence also support adversarial, punitive enforcement. First, punishment may shore up the moral authority of the regulatory rule and the enforcement agency. For instance, formal, publicly visible enforcement actions validate the compliance decisions of voluntary compliers who might see failure to enforce vigorously against noncompliant firms as unfair. Failure to sanction violators publicly may delegitimize the rule violated and actually encourage noncompliance by others who would otherwise comply voluntarily. Second, penalties and formal administrative or judicial orders also simply express public disapprobation of polluting activity. Where enforcement is negotiated "under the table", the ethical message that polluting is "wrong" is not delivered. Finally, by forcing violators to disgorge the ill-gotten gains of noncompliance, penalties also prevent unjust enrichment. Regardless of the incentives created for future compliance, we might view profits derived from lawbreaking as "tainted" and demanding forfeiture.

Advocates of cooperative enforcement reject the unstated premise of deterrence theory that all regulated firms are "amoral calculators" that will consciously choose to violate where economically reasonable. Professors Robert Kagan and John Scholz argue that the "amoral calculator" model of firm behavior is inaccurate in many cases and that two other "types" of regulated firm are also common: the "political citizen" and the "incompetent". The citizen-firm will voluntarily comply with the subset of legal rules that the firm's decision makers view as legitimate, but will shirk compliance with rules that are considered "unreasonable". The incompetent firm, on the other hand, may be noncompliant due to ignorance of the rule, incapacity to comply (technical or fiscal), or failure of intra-organizational process.

Advocates of cooperative enforcement also advance a broader critique of adversarial enforcement, based on the ongoing relationship of regulator and regulatee inherent in much regulatory enforcement. Because pollution discharges will continue at one level or another as long as the polluting firm is in operation, the firm will necessarily interact repeatedly with the regulatory agency. In this kind of ongoing relationship, regulators must carefully assess the impact of their enforcement strategy on the agency's long-term relationship with regulated firms. Cooperative enforcement, advocates argue, is necessary to reduce (and thus avoid the costs of) the friction otherwise inherent in the regulatory process.

In this regard, cooperative enforcement may provide at least four distinct benefits in comparison to an adversarial approach. First, cooperative enforcement may lower an agency's administrative costs in each individual enforcement action, reducing transaction costs in the short run. In formal enforcement actions, agencies devote enormous resources to provide notice, develop evidence, and prosecute the enforcement action and judicial appeals. The agency can avoid these costs if it can secure voluntary compliance through informal action. The savings may be especially significant where small sources are involved: the administrative cost of adversarial enforcement may outweigh the benefits of compliance in such cases. Nevertheless, given the variation among "types" of violator discussed above, informal or negotiated enforcement might induce compliance from some firms but not others. Amoral calculators could feign compliance or withhold compliance, knowing that the costs of formal action make any threat of action merely a bluff. A general strategy of cooperation can actually undermine compliance by such firms.

Second, cooperative enforcement may also enable agencies to mitigate the perceived irrationality and unfairness of generally applicable regulations. Regulatory policy making frequently results in "overinclusiveness" — rules that are too general, stringent, and costly, if fully enforced. Faced with uniform rules, regulated firms may experience what Professors Bardach and Kagan call "site-level unreasonableness", in which the generic legal rule applies to factual settings that fail to advance the goal of the rule or do so with apparently unbalanced costs and benefits. Cooperative enforcement may mitigate this perceived unfairness and irrationality by encouraging regulators to exercise their broad discretion equitably. The regulator can withhold sanctions where the policy of the legal rule is not advanced by its application to a particular regulated firm. Avoiding irrationality and unfairness also carries significant utilitarian benefits by boosting the Agency's credibility and legitimacy. Unfairness may inspire recalcitrance in regulated firms that would otherwise comply voluntarily [...]. This resistance will raise the agency's transaction costs in the long run, as firms try to hide noncompliance or fight future enforcement efforts because of past unfairness. Cooperative enforcement may reduce these long-run transaction costs by legitimating the rule and agency in the eyes of some firms. Further, by reducing perceived unfairness, cooperative enforcement may dissuade regulated firms from making political attacks on the statutory regime or the agency's authority and budgets and may shore up general public support for the agency's regulatory mandate.

Third, the greater flexibility afforded by cooperative enforcement may help remove barriers to investment in environmentally beneficial new technologies. For instance, consider a manufacturing firm that falls within the terms of a rule — say, an end-of-pipe, pollution control technology specification standard — but which, because of the peculiarities of the firm's production process, would produce none of the pollution that the rule seeks to avoid. Application of the rule to this firm may make the process uneconomic, discouraging investment in an environmentally sound production process. Sanctioning noncompliance only where doing so in fact advances the rule's purpose might solve this problem but the flexibility that makes such enforcement attractive also makes it unreliable. The mere possibility that an enforcement officer down the line may withhold sanctions is unlikely to provide sufficient confidence to stimulate capital investment.

Finally, cooperative enforcement may allow "trades" in which an agency accepts under-compliance with a legal mandate in one area in exchange for a regulatee's commitment to over-compliance in another. In exchange for permission to reduce the level of compliance required in a regulatory area where marginal pollution control costs are high (call the area x), the regulated firm can offer to reduce pollution in an area in which the firm is already in compliance but where further pollution avoidance can be readily achieved (area y). In theory, the firm will make the trade where the marginal control costs associated with x are higher than those associated with y, and the agency will agree to the trade if the marginal pollution control benefits in area x are lower than in area y.

In practice, however, allowing regulators such broad discretion places great faith in their ability to recognize and represent public interests. The enforcer must determine that the benefits to the public from a reduction in area y are as great or greater than those accruing from a reduction in area x. We may have reason to question whether an enforcement official can adequately carry out the necessary informal cost-benefit analysis, or at least whether her analysis is better than that underlying the regulation as written. While an enforcer may be better placed than a rulemaker to understand the compliance costs of particular firms, that officer will likely have less information about the public costs of pollution: she will not have available the broad public input and time for reflection available in notice and comment rulemaking. To ask agencies to make such decisions on a case-by-case basis during enforcement may assume considerable capacity that the agency lacks and may leave the agency at the mercy of an industry's superior knowledge of its own processes.

Synthesis

The basic lesson of the debate between advocates of cooperative and adversarial enforcement is that neither strategy is completely satisfactory. Although adversarial enforcement is essential to ensure that strategic profit-maximizing firms internalize external costs, the process of deterrence may in some settings raise administrative costs and create simple injustice. To strike the proper balance, an agency's enforcement tactics should depend heavily on the particular violator involved and the agency's past interactions with it [...]. Agencies should cooperate with cooperators and punish evaders.

Many commentators have made the deceptively simple argument that regulators should treat different firms differently and like firms alike. The argument derives, in part, from firms' differing marginal-pollution-control-cost functions. Differences in control-cost functions may color the response of regulated firms to particular enforcement tools. That response may also vary with the less tangible, sociological variables of firm culture and the attitudes of management. In fact, not all firms with identical control-cost functions will respond to a legal rule in the same way. Some firms will always or nearly always comply with a legal rule regardless of cost, others will comply only where doing so is cost-effective, some will not comply simply out of ignorance or incapacity, and yet others will comply so long as managers consider the rule "reasonable". Accordingly, a uniform legal rule with uniform enforcement will not produce uniform results, and some flexible or "state-dependent" enforcement is justifiable.

The agency's enforcement approach should depend on where the agency and firm are in the enforcement process. Professor Scholz recommends this approach on the theory that regulatory enforcement involves the regulator and regulatee in an ongoing series of prisoner's dilemma games. Because the regulatory "game" is played repeatedly, the agency's optimal enforcement strategy is "tit-for-tat", in which the regulator chooses its action based on the regulatee's behavior in the prior round. If the regulatee has cooperated, the agency should cooperate, but if the regulatee "defects", the agency should punish until the regulatee again adopts a cooperative posture.

If a new violation is discovered, the agency should review the firm and agency's course of dealing, to determine whether the firm is in general an "incompetent", a "political citizen", or an "amoral calculator". The agency's choice of enforcement tools — cooperative or adversarial — should be based on the firm's history of reasonable cooperation with the agency, good faith, and patterns of compliance. The agency should forgive violations (and withhold penalties) if the regulatee has cooperated with the agency, such that the violation appears to have occurred notwithstanding the firm's best efforts. Where there are indicia of strategic behavior or knowing or negligent violation, however, the agency should apply punitive sanctions to each violation until the regulatee adopts a compliant strategy evidenced by continual compliance with agency orders. In other words, the agency must be willing to shift a firm from the category of "incompetent" or "political citizen" to "amoral calculator" until the firm shows a durable willingness to cooperate. When the firm returns to the fold, it may be treated again as something other than an amoral calculator.

After an individual enforcement interaction — informal negotiations or formal proceedings — has begun, the agency should be cognizant of the course of performance in that particular encounter. If the firm is dragging its feet in implementing a compliance bargain or administrative order, the agency should respond by imposing sanctions and escalating the formality of the enforcement action. Again, the severity of sanctions and the speed of their imposition should vary according to overall courses of performance and dealing.

To be sure, this approach is not perfect. Its greatest weakness is the substantial information it demands from agencies and firms. With adversarial enforcement, enforcers might reduce information costs by reducing monitoring while dramatically increasing penalties to raise the expected cost of noncompliance. Flexible enforcement, on the other hand, requires the agency to ascertain whether a penalty is justified based on more than the mere fact of a violation. Accordingly, agencies employing flexible enforcement must devote considerable resources to monitoring to learn of the regulatee's compliance status, efforts, and history, in circumstances of asymmetric information. To the extent that a flexible approach provides transaction-cost savings in individual enforcement actions and in the long run, those monitoring costs might be shouldered without substantial new resources. But in any event, agencies should impose strict monitoring and reporting terms in any negotiated compliance agreement and should remorselessly penalize all but entirely accidental violations of any such terms or statutory monitoring and reporting requirements.

The regulatee may also lack adequate information about the regulator's behavior. Because a firm will have little incentive to adopt a compliant strategy if it cannot be confident that the agency will also cooperate, the agency must broadcast its enforcement strategy. Dissemination of the agency's enforcement policy is also important to secure the legitimacy gains promised by cooperative enforcement: the agency must develop a reputation for cooperative enforcement to prove that it will not punish firms' good deeds and that good-faith compliers will not be competitively penalized by repeated violators' getting off scot-free.

Consequently, agencies should formalize their enforcement strategy in an enforcement policy and communicate that policy to firms. Although this raises the specter of inflexibility, the costs of that inflexibility must be weighed against the benefits of increased certainty that such a policy would provide. Given that this model strategy involves treating firms differently that are in many respects similarly situated, an enforcement policy may be necessary to describe to a firm why it and its competitors will be treated in particular ways.

Finally, this model of enforcement concededly does not in every case effectuate the "moral" or "expressive" function of regulation. Penalties will not be applied in every case to register societal moral outrage. Nevertheless, the tit-for-tat strategy calls for severe penalties where the violation is intentional or negligent. An agency should also impose penalties where the firm's polluting behavior causes significant effects on human health or environmental quality. Where those compelling circumstances are absent, however, the tit-for-tat strategy remains appropriate.

Notes and Questions

1. Empirically, the Zinn article draws heavily on the US experience with respect to environmental enforcement where the federal Environmental Protection Agency (EPA) has taken a strong leadership role in prosecuting environmental offences. As DeMarco and Vigod underscore, the Canadian experience differs significantly in several key respects. What, in your view, are the key differences?

2. Do you agree with Zinn that it is possible and desirable to develop an approach to enforcement that blends cooperative and adversarial elements? Are there parallels between the approach he advocates and the "Smart Regulation" approach advocated by Gunningham *et al.* outlined in Chapter 4?

3. In Chapter 4, there was considerable discussion about forms of standard; distinctions were drawn between technology-based, management-based and performance-based standards. To what extent is the discretionary approach to environmental law enforcement advocated for by Zinn constrained or influenced by the form of standard employed in the relevant law or regulation?

Part III — Selected Issues in Environmental Law Enforcement

In this Part, we canvass some of the key issues in environmental law enforcement including:

- The role of the criminal law as an enforcement tool;
- The role and nature of the regulatory offence;
- The prosecution and defence of environmental charges;
- Directors' and officers' liability;
- Sentencing in environmental cases;
- The emerging role of administrative monetary penalties (AMPs);
- The role of adaptive management in the assessment of new projects and the regulation of existing facilities; and
- The interplay between statutory remediation orders and bankruptcy/insolvency law.

The Role of the Criminal Law as an Enforcement Tool

In many cases where serious environmental harm has occurred, prosecutors have the option of proceeding by way of a *Criminal Code* prosecution or, alternatively, by way of prosecution under applicable federal (typically, CEPA or *Fisheries Act*) or provincial regulatory provisions. The *Criminal Code*, R.S.C. 1985, c. C-46, does not contain any specific environmental offences, although their inclusion has been advocated from time to time: see Law Reform Commission of Canada, "Crimes Against the Environment" (1985). As a result, criminal prosecutions for environmental harm must be framed in terms of more generic offences such as criminal negligence (section 219) or nuisance (section 180).

Stanley David Berger,
"The Future of Environmental Prosecutions in Ontario"
(2006) 19 C.E.L.R. (3d) 32

The *Criminal Code* will remain the "big-stick" when negligence or deliberation causes a major environmental event resulting in serious injury or the loss of life.

[**Ed. Note:** In offering this conclusion, the author acknowledges that, in many provinces, parallel regulatory provisions empower courts to impose multi-million dollar fines and jail terms of up to 5 years.]

Under the *Criminal Code*, if the Crown proceeds summarily, the maximum fine available against corporate organizations is $100,000 and only $2,000 for individuals. The maximum imprisonment is a paltry 6 months for summary conviction offences. Moreover, the fine is not specified to be daily, as it is for provincial offences. Federal prosecutors would have to proceed by indictment to achieve comparable fines and jail terms to those under the provincial regulatory regime, but this alone would not present any difficulty, since the offences of criminal negligence and common nuisance applicable to cases of death or bodily injury can be prosecuted only by indictment. Prosecution by indictment will, however, create additional delay and complexity in the proceedings, should the defence opt, as is its right, for a preliminary hearing and/or a jury. Regardless of whether the prosecution has the luxury of proceeding by summary conviction or indictment, the Crown bears the added burden of proving negligence, unlike traditional regulatory prosecutions before the courts where this burden is assumed by the defence. Finally, in the case of criminal negligence, the prosecution will need to meet the more exacting standard of a "marked and substantial" departure from the standard of a reasonable person.

Despite these drawbacks, prosecution under the *Criminal Code* will remain attractive for more serious offences [...]. There are two compelling reasons for this prosecution strategy. First, regulatory environmental prosecutions have not yet achieved the stigma of criminal prosecutions. When there is death, serious injury, or the real potential for either, the public expects government authorities to bring the full force of the law to bear on the perpetrators. Announcement of criminal charges demonstrates that the authorities have not shrunk from their responsibility, or have in any way been intimidated by events. The second reason is that the investigation in such serious cases is likely to be detailed and time-consuming. The short two-year limitation periods for laying regulatory charges will remain too confining to the authorities; when the Crown proceeds by indictment, there is no limitation period on bringing charges.

[**Ed. Note:** The author then discusses amendments to the Canadian *Criminal Code* (Bill C-45) that were proclaimed into force in 2004.]

These amendments dispensed with the identification theory of criminal liability, whereby a corporation could be found guilty of a criminal offence only if the offence could be proven against "a directing mind" of the corporation. The directing mind or minds of the corporation were those individuals within the corporation with decision-making authority over matters of corporate policy, as opposed to operational matters.

The amendments followed on the heels of the less-than-successful outcomes of the *Criminal Code* prosecutions of those responsible for the 1992 Westray Mining explosion in Nova Scotia, which had resulted in the deaths of 26 miners. The amendments now enable prosecutors to obtain criminal convictions against corporations, including partnerships, municipalities, trade unions and public bodies, for the acts or omissions of management; decision-making authority over corporate policy is no longer a prerequisite to corporate liability. Significantly, with respect to the criminal act, the law now acknowledges the compartmentalization of corporate functions, enabling the prosecutor to rely on the collective acts or omissions of one or more corporate representatives, including contractors, providing the prosecution can prove that the work that is alleged to have amounted to a crime was directed or negligently supervised by one or more senior officers. Thus, the amendments further create a positive legal duty on management to prevent bodily harm arising from supervised work. Finally, probation orders now apply to corporate defendants, including partnerships, municipalities, trade unions and public bodies, with creative conditions previously available only for regulatory offences such as restitution, the establishment of policies, standards and procedures, preventative or remedial orders, reporting requirements and public acknowledgement of responsibility.

[...] Criminal charges, primarily common nuisance, will become a more attractive enforcement tool with the passage of Bill C-45, as it has become easier to prove the criminal culpability of corporate organizations and as the legal duty of corporate managers has increased. When the investigation is time-consuming, regulatory limitation periods are compromised and the consequences of the offence are, or could be, grave, nothing less will do.

The Role and Nature of the Regulatory Offence

Most environmental prosecutions proceed on charges filed pursuant to regulatory offence provisions set out in federal and provincial statutes. In the context of regulatory offences, a key issue concerns what evidence of "fault" must be established, and who bears the burden of proof with respect to this issue. In this context, courts have been called upon to balance prosecutorial efficacy and protection of the public against competing concerns with respect to fairness to the accused.

John Swaigen,
"Absolute Liability Revisited: *Levis v. Tetrault***"**
in Stanley Berger and Dianne Saxe, eds., *Environmental Law:*
The Year in Review 2006 (Aurora: Canada Law Book, 2007)

The Development of Absolute and Strict Liability Offences

By the beginning of the 19th century it was "the accepted view" that the need for *mens rea* was a principle of natural justice, and few offences at that time were punishable without proof of fault. As a result of this recognition that punishing the morally innocent is wrong, it became a fundamental tenet of the common law that no one could be convicted of a crime without *mens rea*.

Yet, faced with the reality that regulatory offences are often committed unintentionally, and therefore, it is frequently impossible to establish intent, but it is still necessary to protect the public against harmful acts, the courts began to treat these offences as an exception to the general rule that *mens rea* is an essential element of an offence.

For regulatory offences, some courts held that *mens rea* was required, but permitted a defence of mistake of fact or reasonable care. However, others treated regulatory offences as a type of "crime" for which a conviction could be registered without any evidence of fault. This was most often referred to as "strict liability", but since *Sault Ste. Marie* liability without any fault, of course, is known as "absolute liability".

By the time regulatory offences began to proliferate in the mid-19th century, what we now call "absolute liability" had become widely recognized as unjust. Nevertheless, some advocated permitting a degree of injustice to enter the system on utilitarian grounds in relation to this particular kind of offence. They argued, in effect, that as long as absolute liability was limited to relatively minor offences, carrying a relatively small penalty, for which conviction carried little stigma, the injustice to the individual or company charged and convicted of a regulatory offence was outweighed by the potential injustice to victims of these offences and to the public at large from ineffective or inefficient enforcement that would result if proof of fault was required.

In 1978, in the seminal decision *R. v. City of Sault Ste. Marie*, a unanimous Supreme Court of Canada, speaking through Justice Dickson (as he then was), resolved to a great degree, [...] the question of whether regulatory offences are based on *mens rea* or are matters of absolute liability by recognizing three categories of offences — "true" crimes, requiring proof beyond a doubt of both the *actus reus* and subjective *mens rea*; strict liability offences, in which the prosecutor was required to prove the *actus reus* beyond a reasonable doubt but the accused could exonerate himself or herself by establishing on a balance of probabilities a defence of reasonable care; and absolute liability offences, for which neither *mens rea* nor negligence was required to obtain a conviction. For offences of absolute liability, it is not open to the accused to exculpate himself or herself by showing that he or she was free of fault. Moreover, the Court determined that there is a presumption that regulatory offences fall into the middle category, strict liability, unless the legislature has made it clear that it intended *mens rea* or absolute liability.

This new regime applies to all regulatory offences, but has been particularly important in the environmental area, largely because of the creation of many of new environmental offences in the 1980s and 1990s, the increased reliance on prosecution as a method of enforcing these laws, the heightened inducement to alleged polluters to fight charges resulting from stronger penalties, and the increasing stigma associated with conviction for environmental offences.

Notes and Questions

1. After *R. v. Sault Ste. Marie (City)*, [1978] 2 S.C.R. 1299, particularly outside the motor vehicle context, most regulatory offences came to be interpreted by courts as falling within the strict liability category. The trend became even more pronounced after enactment of the *Charter*: see *Reference re s. 94(2) of Motor Vehicle Act (British Columbia)*, [1985] 2 S.C.R. 486. Absolute liability as a form of regulatory liability continued to dwindle until 1995, when the SCC rendered its decision in *R. v. Pontes*, [1995] 3 S.C.R. 44. For a time, this case was seen by some as heralding a revival of absolute liability offences. In *Lévis (Ville) c. Tétreault*, 2006 SCC 12, however, the Court reaffirmed its commitment to the approach it adopted in *Sault Ste. Marie*.

Lévis (Ville) c. Tétreault

2006 SCC 12

LeBEL J.: —

Categories of Criminal Offences and Approach to Classification

The offences with which the respondents are charged belong to a vast category of offences known as regulatory offences. Legislatures enact such offences as incidental sanctions whose purpose is to enforce the performance of various duties, thereby safeguarding the general welfare of society (*Sault Ste. Marie*, at p. 1310, *per* Dickson J.). Establishing their legal framework gave rise to uncertainty because they are not always perfectly compatible with the fundamental principles of criminal law and because of the difficulty in defining the defences available to the accused. It was these problems that were addressed in *Sault Ste. Marie*.

Classifying the offence in one of the three categories now recognized in the case law thus becomes a question of statutory interpretation. Dickson J. noted that regulatory or public welfare offences usually fall into the category of strict liability offences rather than that of *mens rea* offences. As a general rule, in accordance with the common law rule that criminal liability ordinarily presupposes the existence of fault, they are presumed to belong to the intermediate category:

> Public welfare offences would *prima facie* be in the second category. They are not subject to the presumption of full *mens rea*. An offence of this type would fall in the first category only if such words as "wilfully", "with intent", "knowingly", or "intentionally" are contained in the statutory provision creating the offence. (*Sault Ste. Marie*, at p. 1326)

Absolute liability offences still exist, but they have become an exception requiring clear proof of legislative intent. This intent can be deduced from various factors, the most important of which would appear to be the wording of the statute itself:

> On the other hand, the principle that punishment should in general not be inflicted on those without fault applies. Offences of absolute liability would be those in respect of which the Legislature had made it clear that guilt would follow proof merely of the proscribed act. The overall regulatory pattern adopted by the Legislature, the subject matter of the legislation, the importance of the penalty, and the precision of the language used will be primary considerations [...]. (*Sault Ste. Marie*, at p. 1326)

The categories established by this Court were thus based on a presumption of statutory interpretation. Developments in constitutional law since the *Canadian Charter of Rights and Freedoms* came into force have reinforced their legal foundations. Without abolishing the category of absolute liability offences, the Court decided that imposing penal liability of this nature would violate the principles of fundamental justice protected by the *Charter* where a conviction would expose the accused to imprisonment (*Re B.C. Motor Vehicle Act*, [1985] 2 S.C.R. 486 at pp. 515-16; *R. v. Vaillancourt*, [1987] 2 S.C.R. 636 at p. 652, *per* Lamer J.).

This Court reconsidered the approach to classifying regulatory offences in *R. v. Pontes*, [1995] 3 S.C.R. 44. In that case, in which the Court had to decide whether a traffic offence was one of absolute liability, Cory J., writing for the majority, appeared to propose a two-stage test for determining whether an offence is an absolute liability offence. First, the analytical approach and presumptions of interpretation proposed by Dickson J. in *Sault Ste. Marie* would have to be considered (para. 27). However, it might also be determined whether the legislature intended to make a due diligence defence available (para. 28). This added refinement to the classification approach established in *Sault Ste. Marie* does not make it easier to apply. The objective of the interpretive approach adopted in *Sault Ste. Marie* is in fact to determine the nature of the defences available to the accused. To say that it is necessary to determine whether the accused can plead due diligence amounts simply to restating the very purpose of this juridical exercise. It would therefore be better to return to the clear analytical framework and classification approach adopted in *Sault Ste. Marie*.

The Prosecution and Defence of Environmental Charges

Corporate Regulatory Liability

In this section we consider one of the highest-profile environmental prosecutions to be mounted in Canada in recent years. The prosecution arose when, on a single day in the spring of 2008, approximately 1,600 migratory birds died as a result of landing on an oil sands tailing pond maintained by Syncrude Canada Ltd. As a result of public pressure, including a private prosecution brought by an environmentalist with the Sierra Club of Canada, ultimately federal and provincial prosecutors filed charges against the company in connection with the incident. Syncrude defended the charges vigorously, raising a multitude of arguments in its defence, as set out below. In the end, the company was convicted and in October 2010 was fined $3 million.

As with most environmental prosecutions, this case was brought in Provincial Court. Prosecutors pursued charges under both federal and provincial legislation; this is not unusual and avoids multiple proceedings and potential *res judicata* issues. Most of the judgment (excerpted below) on the merits at trial addresses numerous defences, including due diligence. Because of the clear and straightforward manner in which the trial judge lays out and applies the relevant law, we have excerpted from his reasons at some length. We have also excerpted from a commentary on the case by Professor Fluker.

R. v. Syncrude Canada Ltd.
2010 ABPC 229

TJOSVOLD J.: —

Introduction

On April 28, 2008, Todd Powell, a Senior Wildlife Biologist for the Province, received a telephone call at his Fort McMurray office from a concerned individual who wanted something done about a number of birds landing on Syncrude Canada Ltd.'s Aurora Settling Basin. The ensuing investigation revealed that several hundred waterfowl were trapped in bitumen on the surface of the Basin. All but a few of those birds died. The company was subsequently charged with failing to store a hazardous substance in a manner that ensured that it did not come into contact with any animals, contrary to s. 155 of Alberta's Environmental Protection and Enhancement Act, and with depositing a substance harmful to migratory birds in an area frequented by migratory birds, contrary to s. 5.1(1) of Canada's *Migratory Birds Convention Act*. This trial has been largely focussed on whether Syncrude did enough to deter birds from landing on the tailings pond but there are several other issues that must be considered.

Evidence

As part of its Aurora tar sands operation, Syncrude began depositing tailings in the Aurora Settling Basin in the Fort McMurray area in July of 2000. Tailings are deposited through large pipes into the Basin, located some distance from the extraction plant. The pond is contained within a berm. The area within the berm is approximately the size of 8.15 quarter sections or 640 football fields. The tailings include water, sand and bitumen. When deposited, the tailings still retain heat from the extraction process so ice on the Basin will melt before ice on nearby natural water bodies. Bitumen is found throughout the pond in strands or lumps. It is also found in a mat of the type that trapped the waterfowl on April 28, 2008. The mat was described as being several inches thick, viscous and cohesive with the consistency of a frothy roofing tar. It moves within the pond and eventually sinks, taking birds with it in this case. The mat found on April 28, 2008 covered a significant part of the pond.

Bird Migration and Behaviours

[...] The Fort McMurray area is found on the northern edge of the Boreal Plain, a region probably second only to the Prairie Parklands in importance for migratory birds during breeding season. The area lies beneath the Central and Mississippi Flyways for migratory waterfowl. Many birds, including ducks, geese, loons, grebes and other water birds, settle in the area and others stop on their northward migration in the spring. Most water birds migrating through the oil sands region are travelling to or from the Peace Athabasca Delta, 200 kilometres north. The Delta occupies a little more than 300,000 hectares in the southeast corner of Wood Buffalo National Park. It is described as the largest fresh water delta in the world and is an ideal staging area for migratory birds on their way to their final breeding grounds. It is globally significant and may become more so as ponds and marshes in the prairies continue to decline.

[...] Migratory birds travel north in time for the breeding season, leaving the wintering grounds in peak condition. Timing of migration is prompted partly by photo period but more strongly by spring temperatures rising high enough for species food to be produced along the route. For many species early arrival on the breeding grounds is critical to securing breeding territory. The birds are looking for habitat with the most food and greatest safety from predators. Early arrival also gives more time to raise chicks and allows the birds to find more food before competition arrives.

The travel time also depends on weather. Warm temperatures and following winds favour migration. Cold temperatures, northerly winds and especially precipitation slow migration speeds. In Northern Alberta, waterfowl spring migration is closely tied to the break-up of water bodies because most species of waterfowl depend on water for rest and foraging stopovers. Severe weather typically increases the length of stopovers. Waterfowl usually migrate in April and May. However, some research suggests that break-up in the oil sands region may occur as early as March 31 and migratory birds may appear as much as two weeks earlier than that.

Bird Deterrence

Since the 1970's tar sands operators have recognized the importance of deterring birds from landing on tailings ponds. The current state of technology requires the use of large tailings ponds containing the bitumen that cannot be extracted from the tar sand, despite the obvious financial motivation to do so. Since the mid-1970's, the two original oil sands operators, Syncrude and Suncor, have invested in research, protocols and equipment to deter birds from landing. Deterring birds from the tailings ponds presents many challenges for tar sands operators.

[**Ed. Note:** The Court then canvasses the evidence with respect to these challenges.]

[...] Migratory birds are able to stay in the air for some days. However, a combination of factors, including: travelling for many days without food, exhaustion, precipitation and the absence of other open water, may have forced waterfowl to land in the Aurora Settling Basin in this case. Although that is not certain, the probability of the birds landing on open water would be very high. Deterrent systems would be less effective in these conditions.

The most common deterrents are those used by Syncrude in 2008, sound cannons and effigies. Both of these deterrents can be effective. Although birds will habituate to effigies and sound cannons within days, some operators believe that habituation is unlikely in the short period during which the birds migrate through the area. Factors that counteract habituation are intensity of the stimulus (particularly with negative consequences), variation to the stimulus, time between stimuli, frequency of the presentation of the stimulus and pairing with another stimulus. Habituation to cannons occurs more rapidly when cannons are set to fire frequently, especially if set to fire in the same direction and from the same location.

Incident of April 28, 2008

[...] For the purpose of this decision, it is not necessary to summarize in any detail the incident of April 28, 2008 and its aftermath. An estimated 500 waterfowl were found trapped in the bitumen mat on the Aurora Settling Basin on that date and apparently sank with the bitumen. It is agreed between the Crown and defence that approximately 1600 birds died during the course of the incident. Despite efforts to recover and rehabilitate oiled birds, very few survived being oiled.

Analysis

[...] Syncrude is charged under s. 155 of Alberta's *Environmental Protection and Enhancement Act* which provides:

> A person who keeps, stores or transports a hazardous substance or pesticide shall do so in a manner that ensures that the hazardous substance or pesticide does not directly or indirectly come into contact with or contaminate any animals, plants, food or drink.

Syncrude is also charged in the same Information under s. 5.1(1) of the federal *Migratory Birds Convention Act*, which provides:

> No person or vessel shall deposit a substance that is harmful to migratory birds, or permit such a substance to be deposited, in waters or an area frequented by migratory birds or in a place from which the substance may enter such waters or such an area.

Characterizing the Offences

The offences here are regulatory. They fall within a very large category of offences meant to regulate conduct "[...] in the interests of health, convenience, safety and the general welfare of the public.": *R. v. Pierce Fisheries Ltd.*, [1971] S.C.R. 5 at p. 13; *R. v. Wholesale Travel Group Inc.*, [1991] 3 S.C.R. 154, paras. 121-137; *Lévis (City) v. Tétreault (City)*, [2006] 1 S.C.R. 420 at para. 13; Libman at pp. 2-4 to 2-7.

These specific offences are designed to protect animals and to prevent the harm that would be caused to our ecosystem without that protection. Regulatory offences are prima facie offences of strict liability unless there is language in the legislation which indicates the legislative intent to include mens rea: *R. v. Sault Ste. Marie (City)*, [1978] 2 S.C.R. 1299 at pp. 1325-26; *Levis (City) v. Tetreault (City)*, supra, at para. 16.

Onus and Standard of Proof

In strict liability cases the Crown still bears the onus of proving beyond a reasonable doubt that the accused committed the prohibited act. The defence must establish reasonable care on a balance of probabilities. The legislation places the onus on the accused to prove due diligence in s. 229 of the *Environmental Protection and Enhancement Act* and s. 13(1.8) of the *Migratory Birds Convention Act*. The defence found in the statute will be paramount but the legislation here does not suggest a legislative intent to create a defence which differs from the common law defence: *R. v. Consumers Distributing Co. Ltd.* (1980), 57 C.C.C. (2d)

317 (Ont. C.A.) at paras. 24-26; *R v. Edmonton (City)*, 2006 ABPC 56 at paras. 694-95.

Syncrude has raised a number of additional defences. Generally, once there is an air of reality to a defence, excuse or justification, the Crown bears the onus of disproving or negativing it by proof beyond reasonable doubt. Ewaschuk at 16:19005, 21:3100.

Swaigen suggests that Act of God, necessity and impossibility are subsumed in the defence of due diligence. It would follow that the defence should bear the onus of proving these defences: Swaigen, Regulatory Offences in Canada at pp. 193, 198-202.

In *R. v. British Columbia Hydro and Power Authority*, [1997] B.C.J. No. 1744 (B.C.S.C.) at para. 41, Lamperson, J. acknowledged that, in criminal cases, once a defence has an air of reality, the Crown must prove beyond reasonable doubt that it does not apply. He held, however, that, in respect of strict liability offences, the defence must establish all of its defences on a balance of probabilities.

On the other hand, in *R. v. Synergy Group of Canada Inc.*, 2006 ABPC 196 at paras. 27-33, Meagher, P.C.J. cited *R. v. Perka et al*, [1984] 2 S.C.R. 232 and concluded that the Crown bore the onus of disproving necessity in respect of a strict liability offence. In spite of my doubts on this point, I will proceed to determine, with the exception of due diligence, abuse of process, and officially induced error, whether the Crown has negatived the defences, excuses or justifications advanced by proof beyond reasonable doubt.

[**Ed. Note:** This is an interesting point of law regarding the onus in regulatory prosecutions, to which we will return in "Notes and Questions", *infra*. The Court goes on to discuss the applicable law and evidence, concluding that the Crown has established the facts necessary to prove the federal and provincial offences beyond a reasonable doubt.]

Due Diligence

The defence of due diligence will be available in a prosecution for a strict liability offence if the accused reasonably believed in a mistaken set of facts which, if true, would render the act or omission innocent; or if it took all reasonable steps to avoid the particular event. *R. v. Sault Ste. Marie (City)* at p. 1326.

The defence would apply if Syncrude established on a balance of probabilities that it could not have reasonably foreseen the contravention of the statutes. Syncrude's actions must be judged on the basis of the information available to it at the time of the alleged offence. *R. v. MacMillan Bloedel Ltd.*, 2002 BCCA 510 at paras. 44-49; *R. v. Starosielski*, 2001 ABPC 208 at para. 134; *R. v. Edmonton (City)* at para. 701.

There is no evidence of any mistake of fact here. Syncrude should have known that the proscribed conduct would occur. Bitumen would be deposited into the Aurora Settling Basin and Syncrude would not be able to ensure, i.e., make certain, that birds would not be contaminated by the bitumen in the Basin. It was reasonably foreseeable that those events could occur on April 28, 2008 at the Aurora Settling Basin.

The defence would also apply if Syncrude established that it took all reasonable care to avoid the contraventions. To meet the onus, Syncrude is not required to show that it took all possible or imaginable steps to avoid liability. It was not required to achieve a standard of perfection or show superhuman efforts. It is the existence of a "proper system" and "reasonable steps to ensure the effective operation of the system" that must be proved. The conduct of the accused is assessed against that of a reasonable person in similar circumstances. *Lévis (City) v. Tétreault, supra*, at para. 15 [...]

Various factors should be taken into account to determine whether the defence has established reasonable care. The defence applies in many different situations and so there can be no single comprehensive list of appropriate considerations for all cases. The decision must be based on the particular circumstances of the case. *R. v. Commander Business Furniture Inc.* (1992), C.E.L.R. (N.S.) 185 (Ont. C.J.) at p. 212 provides a lengthy list of factors that could bear on the defence:

1) the nature and gravity of the adverse effect;
2) the foreseeability of the effect, including abnormal sensitivities;
3) the alternative solutions available;
4) legislative or regulatory compliance;
5) industry standards;
6) the character of the neighbourhood;
7) what efforts have been made to address the problem;
8) over what period of time, and promptness of response;
9) matters beyond the control of the accused, including technological limitations;
10) skill levels expected of the accused;
11) complexities involved;
12) preventative systems;
13) economic considerations;
14) actions of officials.

The question then is whether Syncrude has established that it took all reasonable steps to ensure that waterfowl would not be contaminated in its tailings pond. Whether or not Syncrude could ensure against the contamination, it must still be determined whether it took all reasonable steps toward that end.

Although reasonable care to prevent the contamination of wildlife would not ordinarily be a defence to the federal charge, the federal Crown has conceded that, in the particular circumstances of this case, Syncrude should be acquitted of the federal charge if that reasonable care is proved.

[**Ed. Note:** The Court then proceeds to analyze the facts of the case, employing several of the factors listed in *R. v. Commander Business Furniture Inc.*, noted above.]

It may be reasonable that Syncrude did not anticipate the severity of the weather conditions or the total number of birds that would be killed but a reasonable person in Syncrude's place would have foreseen that Syncrude's acts and omissions leading up to the events of April 28, 2008 would cause an unacceptable hazard for waterfowl. Syncrude did not establish a proper system to ensure that wildlife would not be contaminated in the Aurora Settling Basin or take reasonable steps to ensure the effective operation of the system.

[Ed. Note: The Court next considers and rejects the defences of impossibility; Act of God; abuse of process; officially induced error; and *de minimus.*]

Impossibility

Syncrude maintains that it was impossible to "ensure", as required by s. 155 of the Environmental Protection Act, that waterfowl would not be contaminated in its tailings pond and the evidence supports that assertion. Impossibility appears to be available as an excuse where it is not physically or morally possible to comply with the law. *R. v. Royka*, [1980] O.J. No. 596 (C.A.) at paras. 29-30; *R. v. 605884 Saskatchewan Ltd.*, 2004 SKPC 16 at paras. 60-62; *R. v. Belman*, [2001] O.J. No. 2288 (Ont. C.J.) at paras. 40-42; Swaigen at pp. 194-200; Libman at pp. 8-13 to 8-15 [...] As I have already indicated, Syncrude could not "ensure" that waterfowl did not land on the Aurora Settling Basin on April 28, 2008 but it had a reasonable legal alternative. I am convinced beyond reasonable doubt that Syncrude could have acted lawfully by using due diligence to deter birds from the Basin, whether or not it was successful in its attempts at deterrence, and it did not do so.

Act of God

Syncrude argues that the defence of Act of God should apply. Swaigen describes the defence of Act of God in the following terms at p. 200-201:

> An Act of God is a natural event that is uncontrollable or unavoidable and causes harm completely independently of any contributing conduct or activity of man. An Act of God negates both negligence and causation, both because it is unforeseeable and because there is no human contribution.

> The defence of Act of God has three components: (1) foreseeability — if the occurrence could have been foreseen, then the defence does not lie; (2) the accused must have taken every precaution to avoid the occurrence, but could not avoid it; and (3) the forces of nature involved must act without any human contribution [...]

Here the convergence of adverse weather, an open tailings pond with natural water bodies frozen over and bird migration is an unavoidable natural event. The question is whether that convergence has all of the required components of the defence.

The evidence convinces me beyond reasonable doubt that Syncrude placed itself in a position where it was unable to take reasonable steps to deter birds from the Aurora Settling Basin on April 28, 2008. It could have set up its system to place deterrents sooner and more quickly, regardless of the weather that arrived in April of 2008. It was reasonable to take those precautions and Syncrude did not.

Abuse of Process

Syncrude argues that it has complied with all required approvals and that, consequently, it is an abuse of process for the Crown to proceed with either the federal or the provincial charge. It argues that, if it was to be sanctioned for a violation of the approvals, that should be done under s. 227 of the Environmental Protection and Enhancement Act. It denies any such violations.

The test for abuse of process is described in *R. v. Jewitt*, [1985] 2 S.C.R. 128 at pp. 136-37:

> I would adopt the conclusion of the Ontario Court of Appeal in *R. v. Young* [(1984), 40 C.R. (3d) 289], and affirm that "there is a residual discretion in a trial court judge to stay proceedings where compelling an accused to stand trial would violate those fundamental principles of justice which underlie the community's sense of fair play and decency and to prevent the abuse of a court's process through oppressive or vexatious proceedings". I would also adopt the caveat added by the Court in Young that this is a power which can be exercised only in the "clearest of cases".

Abuse of process has been found in a regulatory context where the accused reasonably believed, on the basis of representations by a senior government official, that if it took certain remedial action by a specified date there would be no prosecution and the accused then proceeded to take the remedial action. *Abitibi Paper Company Limited and the Queen* (1979), 24 O.R. (2d) 742 (Ont. C.A.).

Abuse of process was found on an application for *certiorari* stemming from a plain and unambiguous promise not to prosecute but the trial judge's decision to refuse a stay was not set aside. *Western Pulp Ltd. Partnership v. British Columbia*, [1988] B.C.J. No. 3127 (B.C.S.C.) at paras. 4, 22-23.

In *R. v. BHP Diamonds Inc.*, 2002 NWTSC 74 at paras. 203-204 an official threatened prosecution if the company did not take certain steps to remedy harm to the environment. The company did cooperate and carry out various improvements at considerable expense. It was held that the subsequent charges did not result in oppression or unfairness amounting to an abuse of the Court's process.

Laskin, J.A., speaking for the Ontario Court of Appeal in *R. v. Boise Cascade Canada Ltd.* (1995), 24 O.R. (3d) 483, held at para. 23 that the work permit to build roads and construct water crossings granted there did not provide a licence to pollute or grant immunity for poor construction that caused excessive sediment deposits. The failure to address the matter with appropriate regulations did not render the proceedings unfair or oppressive. (para. 27) If the company had complied with the permit it might have had a due diligence defence or been entitled to a stay for abuse of process. (para. 28)

The failure to prosecute for earlier violations has been held not to result in an abuse of process. *R. v. British Columbia Hydro and Power Authority*, [1997] B.C.J. No. 1744 at para. 51.

There is nothing in the evidence to suggest that Syncrude was promised that, even if it failed to take all reasonable steps to deter birds from its tailings ponds, it would not be prosecuted. Nor could Syncrude reasonably take from the provincial approval process any assurance that, if it simply complied with the approval process, its bird deterrent efforts would be viewed as due diligence. The evidence does not suggest that provincial officials would, through the approval process as it existed, have sufficient knowledge of the specific details of Syncrude's operations or procedures to make that judgment for Syncrude. I arrive at that conclusion without even considering the apparent errors in the 2007 Waterfowl Protection Plan.

It is conceivable that provincial officials could, through more intensive monitoring and regulation, become familiar enough with Syncrude's tailings operations to dictate in precise detail the deterrent system that would amount to reasonable steps to deter wildlife. Even if provincial officials did attempt that level of regulation, Syncrude's directing mind and will should still, given the complexity of its tailings operations and how they relate to wildlife hazards, be determining that it is taking all reasonable steps to deter birds from the tailings ponds; not simply relying on the fact that it has received approvals and is complying with them.

Although I have no direct evidence of it, Syncrude's employees might have convinced themselves that, so long as they had the requisite provincial approvals and implemented them, that would be the end of their obligations to comply with environmental legislation bearing on the deterrence of wildlife from its tailings ponds. Even if I was prepared to infer that to be the case, and I am not, it would not have been reasonable for the employees to come to that conclusion.

Section 227 of the Act creates offences for providing false information, failing to provide information and contravening the terms of an approval. Syncrude argues that the Crown should have proceeded with the offence of contravening a term of the approval if there was evidence of that offence. However, the Crown has a discretion as to which charges will be laid and the courts will show Crown discretion great deference, interfering only in a very narrow set of circumstances such as flagrant impropriety or malicious prosecution. I am satisfied that the Crown's decision to prosecute for the offence under s. 155 of the Act rather than restrict itself to prosecutions for violations of the approval does not call for such interference. *Krieger v. Law Society of Alberta*, [2002] 3 S.C.R. 37 at paras. 32, 42-49; *R. v. Nixon*, 2009 ABCA 269 at paras. 16-19, leave granted [2009] S.C.C.A. No. 514.

Dealing specifically with the federal count, had the federal Crown taken the position that a conviction should be entered regardless of due diligence to deter birds from the tailings pond, that might well have amounted to an abuse of process. However, it did not take that position and, consequently, Syncrude has not been mislead. On the contrary, federal officials made it clear that due diligence to deter birds from the tailings ponds was required.

There is no basis here for finding that the charges are a violation of the public's sense of decency and fair play amounting to an abuse of process.

Federal officials made representations that probably led Syncrude representatives to conclude that the company would not be prosecuted under the *Migratory Birds Convention Act* if it used due diligence to keep birds from landing on its tailings ponds. That is not sufficient for the defence of officially induced error to apply.

The accused must prove the following elements to have the benefit of the defence of due diligence:

1) that an error of law or of mixed law and fact was made;
2) that the person who committed the act considered the legal consequences of his or her actions;
3) that the advice obtained came from an appropriate official;
4) that the advice was reasonable;
5) that the advice was erroneous; and

6) that the person relied on the advice in committing the act. *Lévis (City) v. Tétreault; Lévis (City) v. 2629-4470 Québec Inc.*, [2006] 1 S.C.R. 420 at paras. 21-27; Libman, p. 8-115

Syncrude has not established that the advice it was given was erroneous advice on a question of law or mixed law and fact. The advice suggesting that prosecution would not occur, if Syncrude used due diligence to deter birds from the tailings ponds, is a statement of policy and that policy is being reflected in the position the Crown is now taking that a conviction should not be entered if such due diligence is established. It does not support the defence of officially induced error.

I find no communication by any provincial official in connection with the provincial charge that would have mislead Syncrude on a question of law or mixed law and fact.

De Minimis

Syncrude argues that I should apply the doctrine of *de minimis non curat lex* (the law does not concern itself with trifles) as a defence.

In *Ontario v. Canadian Pacific Ltd.*, [1995] 2 S.C.R. 1031 at para. 65, Gonthier, J., speaking for the majority and dealing with principles of statutory interpretation, cited the following explanation of de minimis by Sir William Scott in the case of The "Reward" (1818), 2 Dods. 265, 165 E.R. 1482, at pp. 269-70 and p. 1484:

> The Court is not bound to a strictness at once harsh and pedantic in the application of statutes. The law permits the qualification implied in the ancient maxim *De minimis non curat lex*. — Where there are irregularities of very slight consequence, it does not intend that the infliction of penalties should be inflexibly severe. If the deviation were a mere trifle, which, if continued in practice, would weigh little or nothing on the public interest, it might properly be overlooked.

Gonthier, J. also observed at para. 55:

> [...] It is clear that over the past two decades, citizens have become acutely aware of the importance of environmental protection, and of the fact that penal consequences may flow from conduct which harms the environment. [...] Everyone is aware that individually and collectively, we are responsible for preserving the natural environment.

The doctrine has been recognized as a defence in cases of strict liability. For example: *R. v. St. Paul (Town)*, [1993] A.J. No. 953 (Alta. Prov. Ct.); *R. v. Starosielski*, [2001] A.J. No. 1453 (Alta. Prov. Ct.); *R. v. G.(T.)*, [1990] A.J. No. 39 (Alta. Prov. Ct.). Other cases suggest that the doctrine should not apply in a regulatory context but I will proceed on the basis that the defence is available for strict liability offences.

On the facts as I have found them here, however, Syncrude's conduct in connection with the offences is not minimal or trivial. Unfortunately some waterfowl will die in the tar sands tailings ponds regardless of deterrent efforts. More birds will die without effective deterrents. I have no doubt that, in this context, the failure to take all reasonable steps to deter waterfowl from the Aurora Settling Basin was not at all trivial.

Conclusion

In light of the findings I have made, Syncrude Canada Ltd. is found guilty of both counts in the Information.

Shaun Fluker,
"*R. v. Syncrude Canada*: A Clash of Bitumen and Birds"
(2011) 49 Alta. L. Rev. 237

On 28 April 2008, approximately 1,600 migratory birds died when they landed on a tailings pond located on Syncrude Canada's Aurora North tar sands mine along the Athabasca River north of Fort McMurray. The Aurora mine, along with others in this region, falls under the pathway for migratory birds flying to and from breeding grounds in the Peace Athabasca freshwater delta in Wood Buffalo National Park. Weather or fatigue will influence migratory birds to rest along their route and a tailings pond located under the flyway is an attractive resting spot, particularly in early spring as the warm bitumen froth in the pond keeps its surface free of ice and snow. Unsuspecting birds who land on the pond risk being trapped in the sticky mat of toxic bitumen that floats on the surface before it sinks. The migratory birds who landed on the Aurora tailings pond that day were sentenced to certain death.

Bird deterrence programs have been a part of tar sands mining operations since their beginnings in the 1970s, and as one of the pioneer operators Syncrude Canada has decades of experience working to prevent tired birds from landing on its tailings ponds using techniques such as sound cannons. The bird deterrence systems used by Syncrude and other operators do not completely prevent birds from landing on tailings ponds, and in April 2008 an unusually large spring snowfall in the region elevated the appeal of the warm tailings pond and thereby attracted an unusually large number of migratory birds. Syncrude's bird deterrence system was not effective in these conditions.

None of this was likely to attract the attention of the Alberta justice system, but for the fact that Jeh Custer, a member of the Sierra Club of Canada, commenced a private prosecution in January 2009 alleging Syncrude had contravened the Migratory Birds Convention Act, 1994 for depositing substances harmful to migratory birds in its Aurora tailings pond. The Crown subsequently took control of this prosecution when Environment Canada and Alberta Environment laid their own charges against Syncrude under the MBCA and the Environmental Protection and Enhancement Act in relation to the death of the 1,600 migratory birds. In September 2009, Syncrude pled not guilty to the charges, and an eight-week trial ensued from March to May of 2010 at the Provincial Court in St. Albert with Justice Ken Tjosvold presiding. On 25 June 2010, Justice Tjosvold convicted Syncrude of both the federal and provincial charges. In late October 2010, Justice Tjosvold sentenced Syncrude to pay $3 million in fines.

There are a number of interesting storylines from which to assess this legal proceeding and Justice Tjosvold's decision to convict Syncrude [...] This comment is primarily focused on the argument that Syncrude was prosecuted for activity that has the regulatory approval of the Alberta government, and the implications of this conviction for the Alberta tar sands industry and migratory bird habitat in northern Alberta.

The Aurora Mine

Syncrude is the corporate front of a consortium of multinational energy companies. Although Suncor had established a small tar sands mine in 1967, Alberta officially entered the tar sands era in the early 1970s when the Peter Lougheed government came to terms with Syncrude on the development of the Mildred Lake mine. The Alberta government subsequently issued many more tar sands mining leases to various companies. Syncrude acquired several of these leases to acquire the right to develop the Aurora mine and replace the diminishing bitumen production from its original Mildred Lake mine. In June 1996, Syncrude applied to the Energy Resources Conservation Board (ERCB) under section 10 of the Oil Sands Conservation Act for approval to construct and operate the Aurora mine along the Athabasca river about 70 kilometres north of Fort McMurray. Syncrude provided Alberta Environment with its environmental impact assessment on the Aurora mine in compliance with terms of reference set by Alberta Environment pursuant to the EPEA in November 1995. The terms of reference called for an assessment of how wildlife use the proposed location for the Aurora mine. The Syncrude environmental impact assessment (EIA) report indicates that 81 species of waterfowl frequent the region, and notes that existing lakes are important stop-over zones for migratory birds. However, there is no discussion of any impact the Aurora mine tailings pond would have on migratory birds.

In response to the Syncrude environmental impact assessment report, Environment Canada recommended certain practices be implemented by Syncrude to address the potential for migratory birds to land on the Aurora tailings pond:

> To minimize the potential use of the tailings by migratory birds, Environment Canada recommends: Gradual filling of tailings ponds should be minimized to avoid the artificial creation of shoreline habitat and shallow edges suitable to shorebirds and waterfowl. Should the present bird deterrent procedures become ineffective, Environment Canada recommends that restraining booms and skimming devices be activated to minimize floating bitumen material. [...] Environment Canada recommends that the proponent plan to implement a comprehensive deterrent program throughout any new tailings ponds during the peak spring and fall migrations. The proponent is encouraged to investigate and use the best available technology for deterring devices.

In response to Environment Canada, Syncrude indicated the Aurora mine would implement the same bird deterrent program as employed at its Mildred Lake mine and furthermore that Syncrude recognizes "the need for particular diligence in operation of the bird deterrent program during peak migratory periods."

Nobody knows the full extent of social and environmental impacts of the Alberta tar sands. Nevertheless, both the Alberta and federal government approve tar sands projects on a case-by-case basis with faith in the industry assertions that project-specific and cumulative adverse socio-ecological impacts on the water, air, land, and the species that rely on each of these (humans or otherwise), are understood and will be mitigated. The evidence is not convincing, and continued government faith in these assurances is questionable at best.

The tailings ponds are perhaps the most significant problem facing development in the tar sands. The ponds contain a toxic mixture of water, sand, chemical, and bitumen, and are a byproduct of the extraction process to separate bitumen from sand. The extraction process collectively diverts approximately 650 million cubic metres of water annually to wash sand out of the bitumen. To industry, the bitumen that flows into a tailings pond represents lost profits. Evidence tendered at the Syncrude trial suggests anywhere from 3 to 10 percent of bitumen is not captured in the extraction process. For others, the tailings ponds are an environmental liability.

Nearly all of the massive quantity of water diverted from the Athabasca river for tar sands production ends up sitting in the tailings ponds mixed with toxins from the extraction process and the bitumen itself. The ponds are known to leak into the Athabasca river and the surrounding lands, thereby endangering nearby life and communities downstream. Even before commercial tar sands production really began in the 1970s, the tailings ponds were labeled as the "worst single ecological problem in the operation." In 1974 Environment Canada raised doubts on the extent to which Syncrude or the Alberta government had seriously addressed the environmental impact of the proposed tailings ponds. These doubts have been realized in the last decade as tar sands operations escalate to meet global demand for oil.

The Offences

Environment Canada charged Syncrude with contravening section 5.1 of the MBCA for depositing substances harmful to migratory birds in its Aurora tailings pond. Alberta Environment charged Syncrude with contravening section 155 of the EPEA by failing to keep or store a hazardous substance in a manner that ensures it does not come into contact with birds. The relevant federal and provincial statutory provisions read as follows:

> *Migratory Birds Convention Act*
>
> 5.1 (1) No person or vessel shall deposit a substance that is harmful to migratory birds, or permit such a substance to be deposited, in waters or an area frequented by migratory birds or in a place from which the substance may enter such waters or such an area.

> *Environmental Protection and Enhancement Act*
>
> 155 A person who keeps, stores or transports a hazardous substance or pesticide shall do so in a manner that ensures that the hazardous substance or pesticide does not directly or indirectly come into contact with or contaminate any animals, plants, food or drink.

Both statutes declare the contravention of these provisions to be an offence, and provide the accused with a due diligence defence. Justice Tjosvold deals with the elements of the provincial and federal offences in somewhat short order. In relation to the offence in section 155 of the EPEA, he rules the Crown proved beyond a reasonable doubt that Syncrude contravened the provision on the following evidence: (1) Syncrude stored bitumen in its Aurora tailings pond on 28 April; (2) bitumen is toxic to birds and thus falls under the legislated definition of a hazardous substance in section 1 of the legislation; and (3) bitumen came into contact with birds when they landed on the pond. Syncrude argued that the phrase "come into contact" in section 155 requires that the bitumen come to the birds, and therefore the section does not apply where the birds fly to the bitumen. Justice Tjosvold rejects this argument, ruling that the ordinary meaning of the phrase includes situations where birds come into contact with bitumen and that to rule otherwise would defeat the stated purposes of the EPEA to protect the environment, ensure environmentally responsible growth, and mitigate environmental impacts.

Justice Tjosvold rules the Crown also proved the elements of the offence in section 5.1 of the MBCA beyond a reasonable doubt on the following evidence: (1) Syncrude continuously deposits bitumen into its Aurora tailings pond as a necessary component of extracting bitumen from sand and thus deposited bitumen into the Aurora pond on 28 April; (2) bitumen is harmful to migratory birds; (3) bitumen initially sits on the surface of the pond; (4) the Aurora pond is located under two migration flyways and is approximately the size of 640 football fields making it an inviting landing spot, and (5) the pond is an area frequented by migratory birds.

Once the Crown established the actus reus of these two offences, the onus shifted to Syncrude to escape culpability with a defence. Syncrude raised a number of defences to the charges including due diligence, impossibility, Act of God, abuse of process, and de minimus. In my opinion, the due diligence and abuse of process arguments were Syncrude's primary grounds for a not guilty plea.

Due Diligence

Due diligence was Syncrude's most likely defence. The due diligence defence would allow Syncrude to avoid culpability for the death of the migratory birds by establishing on a balance of probabilities that the company took reasonable steps to avoid the action leading to the offence. The Supreme Court of Canada first established the availability of due diligence as a defence against a regulatory offence in *R. v. Sault Ste Marie* [...]

Much of the evidence tendered at trial focused on whether Syncrude took reasonable steps to prevent the death of the birds in April 2008, and likewise the majority of Justice Tjosvold's analysis focuses on this point. Justice Tjosvold canvasses the lengthy list of relevant factors in a due diligence defence, including: (1) efforts taken by Syncrude to prevent birds from landing on the pond; (2) industry standards in these deterrence efforts; (3) the complexity of the matter; (4) alternatives available to Syncrude in its deterrence initiatives; (4) economic considerations; (5) foreseeability of the circumstances that led to the deaths; and (6) the gravity of the offence. Convincing evidence for Justice Tjosvold here included expert testimony on what a minimum reasonable deterrent system would look like, statements from Syncrude employees documenting a decline in the company's resources dedicated to bird deterrence measures in recent years, and testimony that Syncrude's sound cannons were not operational on the Aurora tailings pond on the day of the incident.

Justice Tjosvold concludes that Syncrude did not have a proper system to prevent birds from landing on the Aurora pond or take reasonable measures to ensure the effectiveness of such a system. All of this evidence is particularly damning to Syncrude in light of its response to Environment Canada back in 1997 that the company recognized the need for extra care in bird deterrence during the spring migration period.

By and large this evidence was in relation to the provincial offence in section 155 of the EPEA. The federal Crown confirmed at trial that a due diligence defence to section 5.1 of the MBCA was not available to Syncrude on these facts because the purpose of the Aurora tailings pond is to store bitumen toxins. The offence occurs with the deposit of the toxins — an act contemplated by the very purpose of the tailings pond. It is nonsensical to argue Syncrude took reasonable care to avoid depositing toxic substances into a designated tailings pond whose very purpose is the storage of toxins. Efforts by Syncrude to deter birds from landing on the Aurora pond are not relevant evidence in relation to an offence under section 5.1 of the MBCA. Or at least they should not be relevant.

Surprisingly, the federal Crown indicated to the Court that should Syncrude establish a due diligence defence to the provincial charge by demonstrating reasonable efforts to deter the birds from landing on the Aurora pond, the federal Crown would not seek a conviction under the MBCA. This federal concession was important to Justice Tjosvold in his dismissal of Syncrude's argument that this prosecution constituted an abuse of process.

Abuse of Process

The Aurora tailings pond operates under licences and approvals issued pursuant to the OSCA, the EPEA, and joint federal-provincial environmental impact assessments that comply with the CEAA. As well, Syncrude and other tar sands producers purportedly rely on an Environment Canada policy that tar sands operators will not be liable under section 5.1 of the MBCA so long as they exercise due diligence to prevent migratory birds from landing on the tailings ponds. Syncrude argued at trial that any legal sanction for the death of the birds must rest on evidence that the company failed to comply with conditions in its regulatory license to operate the Aurora tailings pond. To hold otherwise amounts to an abuse of process because either (1) it is impossible for Syncrude to operate its Aurora mine and comply with the EPEA and the MBCA, or (2) Syncrude is being prosecuted by the Crown for conducting an activity authorized by the Alberta government under the OSCA.

The abuse of process doctrine is available to any court as a means to stay legal proceedings that would otherwise offend notions of justice or fairness towards an accused person. A common example where abuse of process might be invoked is unreasonable delay by the Crown in bringing proceedings forward. A closer example to the facts here would be the prosecution of an accused for an act that is induced by the representation from a government official. The doctrine is used sparingly by courts out of respect for the separation of powers between the judiciary and the executive.

Justice Tjosvold canvasses the applicable law and refuses to apply the abuse of process doctrine largely on the evidence that Syncrude failed to implement its bird deterrence system on the Aurora pond on 28 April. The evidence told a story of neglect on the part of Syncrude towards ensuring adequate resources and attention directed to bird deterrence. Moreover, bird deterrence was not substantively addressed in the 1996 regulatory approval process. In short, there was no evidence of government representations that regulatory approval of the tailings pond would preclude a subsequent prosecution, and in any event, Syncrude did not come to the court with clean hands.

Energy Development Versus Habitat Protection

This decision will have significant implications for the Alberta tar sands and its inevitable conflict with legislated habitat protection. The message to Syncrude and other tar sands operators is simply this: there are adverse environmental effects from bitumen recovery and the law does not expect you to completely eliminate them, however the law does require that you take reasonable measures to prevent them. Specifically in relation to migratory birds, this decision stands for the proposition that while birds will die in the tailings ponds, tar sands operators must pay special attention to bird deterrence. Empty promises, such as what Syncrude offered in its Aurora mines regulatory application, will not suffice to avoid legal liability. I suspect tar sands operators currently pay more attention to the effectiveness of their bird deterrence system, and that the ERCB and environmental impact assessments in forthcoming project applications will scrutinize migratory bird impacts more closely than in the past.

Environmentalists will, however, come to lament this decision in their battle against the Alberta tar sands, because it is precedent for a significant reading down from the literal or purposive interpretation of section 5.1 in the MBCA. Parliament added section 5.1 to the legislation in 2005 to comply with Canada's commitment under 1995 revisions to the *Migratory Birds Convention* that call for legal protection of migratory bird habitats. The very existence of a tailings pond contravenes the MBCA where the pond is frequented by migratory birds. A literal reading of section 5.1 provides no due diligence defence where the area frequented by migratory birds happens to be a tailings pond. This defence has nonetheless been read into the section by Environment Canada policy and was accepted as a necessary element by Justice Tjosvold when he rules that without this policy a prosecution under section 5.1 would likely have been an abuse of process [...]

There is one significant wrinkle in this case. The area frequented by migratory birds here is ironically not really bird habitat at all; it is rather a toxic soup. Perhaps if this case had involved some other body of water that truly was bird habitat, section 5.1 would not have been read down as such. Indeed, it is unlikely section 5.1 offences involving real bird habitats ever get to trial because the accused pleads guilty in the face of overwhelming evidence supporting a conviction. [...]

Postscript

Just days after Justice Tjosvold sentenced Syncrude to a $3 million fine in late October 2010, another 230 birds died in Syncrude's Mildred Lake tailings pond.

Notes and Questions

1. The federal Crown took the position that if Syncrude succeeded in establishing a due diligence defence to the provincial charges, it would not seek a conviction on the federal charges under section 5.1 of the *Migratory Birds Convention Act, 1994*, S.C. 1994, c. 22. Professor Fluker describes this decision as "surprising", yet later alludes to a potential reason the federal Crown took this position. Why do you think the federal Crown made this key concession? Do you agree with its decision?

2. Syncrude raised a plethora of defences in this case in addition to the defence of due diligence. It is settled law that the defendant has the burden on the balance of probabilities to establish the due diligence defence. However, as the trial judge notes, it is less clear whether the Crown or the defence has the burden of negativing/proving other defences for which there is an air of reality. In the end, Tjosvold J. states:

   > In spite of my doubts on this point, I will proceed to determine, with the exception of due diligence, abuse of process, and officially induced error, whether the Crown has negatived the defences, excuses or justifications advanced by proof beyond reasonable doubt.

   Why do you think he ultimately decided to proceed on this basis?

3. Defence counsel are under an obligation to fearlessly advance all plausible legal defences. Do you agree with the defence counsel's decision to argue the *de minimus* defence? Was there a downside to Syncrude relying on this defence?

4. A key issue in the case was whether lax enforcement in the past and negotiated understandings between government regulators and the defendant gave rise to a defence of abuse of process. The trial judge concluded that on the facts the defence was not established. What are the key reasons for this conclusion? Do you agree with the Court's decision?

Directors' and Officers' Liability

During the 1980s and 1990s, many Canadian jurisdictions broadened the ambit of legal liability for corporate directors and officers for corporate wrongdoing in the environmental context and beyond. The judgment below remains a leading articulation of the nature and scope of this still-evolving form of liability.

R. v. Bata Industries Ltd.
(1992), 7 C.E.L.R. (N.S.) 245 (Ont. Prov. Div.)

ORMISTON J.: — On August 1, 1989, two officers of the Ontario Ministry of the Environment attended at the shoe manufacturing facility of Bata Industries Limited (hereinafter Bata) located at Batawa, Ontario. They wanted to speak to the business officer in charge of the environment on an unrelated matter.

The plant was closed that day and its 700 workers were absent. They drove through an open gate looking for the business office. In the yard while turning around, they saw a large chemical waste barrel storage site. There were a large number of containers of various sizes and in varying stages of decay. Many were uncovered and exposed to the elements. Many were rusting. There was evidence of staining on the ground.

They entered the plant and spoke to the officer in charge. Eventually a series of charges were laid under the Ontario *Water Resources Act*, R.S.O. 1980, c. 361 (now R.S.O. 1990, c. O.40), as amended (hereinafter OWRA) and the *Environmental Protection Act*, R.S.O. 1980, c. 141 (now R.S.O. 1990, c. E.18), as amended (hereinafter EPA), and R.R.O. 1980, Reg. 309 under the EPA (hereinafter Reg. 309). [...]

In three separate informations, Keith Weston, the on-site director/general manager; Douglas Marchant, the president of Bata Industries Limited and a director; Thomas G. Bata, chief executive officer of Bata Shoe Organization (International), chairman of the board of Bata Industries Limited and a director were charged as directors with failing to take all reasonable care to prevent a discharge contrary to the [...] OWRA and the [...] EPA. [...]

The Legal Standard

There is very little Canadian judicial guidance on these sections at this time. The courts of the United States have had much more experience in dealing with the issue of directors' liability [...]

The parties in this action have asked the court to clarify a more exact legal standard by which corporate officers and directors may be held personally liable [...] A court under the circumstances before me should weigh the factors of the corporate individual's degree of authority in general and specific responsibility for health and safety practices, including hazardous waste disposal. These factors should be applied in order to answer the question of whether the individual [...] could have prevented or significantly abated the hazardous waste discharge that is the basis of the claim [...]

This court will look to evidence of an individual's authority to control, among other things, waste handling practices — evidence such as whether the individual holds the position of officer or director, especially where there is a co-existing management position: distribution of power within the corporation, including position in the corporate hierarchy and percentage of shares owned. Weighed along with the power factor will be evidence of responsibility undertaken for waste disposal practices, including evidence of responsibility undertaken and neglected, as well as affirmative attempts to prevent unlawful waste disposal. [...]

Both parts of this test boil down to corporate and societal responsibility — implicitly undertaken by the acquisition of increased power or authority within the corporation and responsibility explicitly undertaken by job description or agreement. Such a liability standard here will encourage increased responsibility as an individual's stake in the corporation increases [...] As power grows, the ability to control decisions about waste disposal increases, and second, as one's stake in the corporation increases, the potential for benefiting from less expensive (and less careful) waste disposal practices increases as well. [...]

This standard will encourage increased responsibility with increased authority within a corporation. I take this to be a positive result, and thus a better standard than one which measures only the most direct knowledge or involvement in waste disposal activity, because it encourages responsible conduct instead of causing high level corporate individuals "not to see" and "to avoid getting involved with waste disposal at their facilities" [...]

I ask myself the following questions in assessing the defence of due diligence:

(a) Did the board of directors establish a pollution prevention "system" as indicated in *R. v. Sault Ste. Marie*. i.e., was there supervision or inspection? was there improvement in business methods? did he exhort those he controlled or influenced?

(b) Did each director ensure that the corporate officers have been instructed to set up a system sufficient within the terms and practices of its industry of ensuring compliance with environmental laws, to ensure that the officers report back periodically to the board on the operation of the system, and to ensure that the officers are instructed to report any substantial non-compliance to the board in a timely manner?

I reminded myself that:

(c) The directors are responsible for reviewing the environmental compliance reports provided by the officers of the corporation, but are justified in placing reasonable reliance on reports provided to them by corporate officers, consultants, counsel or other informed parties.

(d) The directors should substantiate that the officers are promptly addressing environmental concerns brought to their attention by government agencies or other concerned parties including shareholders.

(e) The directors should be aware of the standards of their industry and other industries which deal with similar environmental pollutants or risks.

(f) The directors should immediately and personally react when they have notice the system has failed.

Within this general profile and dependent upon the nature and structure of the corporate activity, one would hope to find remedial and contingency plans for spills, a system of ongoing environmental audit, training programs, sufficient authority to act and other indices of a pro-active environmental policy.

The Bata Organization

The Bata Shoe Organization comprises some 80 companies around the world. Thomas G. Bata is the chief executive officer. The one company which is located in Canada and headquartered at Toronto is Bata Industries Limited. This company has four divisions. Each division operates autonomously under a general manager and each general manager is a vice-president and director of Bata Industries Limited. The president, also a director, of Bata Industries Limited during the material time, was Douglas Marchant. Thomas G. Bata, who functioned chiefly in an advisory capacity, was chairman of the board and a director of Bata Industries Limited.

The division of Bata Industries Limited that this case involves was the shoe manufacturing division located at Batawa, Ontario. The general manager/director/vice-president on site was Keith Weston.

The prosecution involves only three directors of Bata Industries Limited, namely, Thomas G. Bata, the chief executive officer, Douglas Marchant, the president, and Keith Weston, vice-president of Bata Manufacturing, a division of Bata Industries Limited located in Batawa, Ontario.

In my opinion, the principle of delegation in environmental matters is aptly summarized as follows: Delegation is a fact of life. The *Environmental Enforcement Amendment Act* is not intended to prevent a reasonable degree of delegation. However, the Legislature has clearly declared that environmental protection is too important to delegate entirely to the lower levels of a corporation. Although the Legislature does not expect the Board of Directors or the officers of the Corporations to make all environmental decisions, it is not acceptable for them to insulate themselves from all responsibility for environmental violations by delegating all aspects of compliance to subordinates.

Re Thomas G. Bata

Thomas G. Bata was the director with least personal contact with the plant at Batawa. His responsibilities were primarily directed at the global level of the Bata Shoe Organization. It was established in the evidence that TAC 298, the environmental alert, had been distributed to his companies throughout the world.

He attended on site in Batawa once or twice a year to review the operation and performance goals of the facility. He was a walk-around director while on the site. The evidence of Mr. Riden establishes that the plant managers could not orchestrate a visit for Mr. Bata: "You never knew where Mr. Bata was going to go, believe me. He had a habit of trying to outguess where you wanted him to go". There is no evidence that he was aware of an environmental problem.

Mr. Riden also established that when the Bata Engineering chemical storage problem was brought to Mr. Bata's attention, he immediately directed the appropriate resources ($20,000) to minimize the effect on the environment. The evidence also establishes that when a water problem was identified and funds were required to construct the water treatment plant for the town of Batawa, he (the family) authorized the expenditure of $250,000.

In short, he was aware of his environmental responsibilities and had written directions to that effect in TAC 298. He did personally review the operation when he was on site and did not allow himself to be wilfully blind or orchestrated in his movements. He responded to the matters that were brought to his attention promptly and appropriately. He had placed an experienced director on site and was entitled in the circumstances to assume that Mr. Weston was addressing the environmental concerns. He was entitled to assume that his on-site manager/director would bring to his attention any problem as Mr. Riden had done. He was entitled to rely upon his system as evidenced by TAC 298 unless he became aware the system was defective.

Bata Industries Limited is a privately held Ontario corporation. It complied with the minimal statutory requirements. However, unlike a public company, much of the business done at directors' meetings or between the board and the divisions was informal with no record kept. It is very difficult in the ordinary course for a director to establish due diligence if there is no contemporary written record.

Although the burden of establishing due diligence was onerous in the absence of more recorded corporate documentation, he has done so in my opinion and is not guilty of the offences charged.

Re Douglas Marchant

Mr. Marchant presents another variation in directors' liability. His responsibility is more than Mr. Bata, but less than Mr. Weston's. This "doctrine of responsible share" is well accepted in American jurisprudence (*United States v. Park*, supra) and is applicable in this case.

He was appointed to the Board as president on January 26, 1988. Mr. Richer testified that Mr. Marchant was "down in Batawa once a month" and these visits included a tour of the plant. Mr. Richer brought the storage problem to his personal attention around February 15, 1989.

The evidence, therefore, establishes that for at least the last six months of the time alleged in the charges (February 15, 1989 to August 31, 1989), he had personal knowledge. There is no evidence that he took any steps after having knowledge to view the site and assess the problem. There is no evidence that the system of storage was made safer or temporary steps were taken for containment until such time as removal could be affected.

The evidence establishes that $100,000 had been reserved for disposal in March 1988. On January 25, 1989, Mr. De Bruyn wrote to Tricel requesting quotes for disposal. By April 14, 1989, all the quotes were received. There was still no action until August 11 when the Ministry officials were on site, Tricel was contacted and told "to get the waste out as soon as possible".

In the circumstances, it is my opinion that due diligence requires him to exercise a degree of supervision and control that "demonstrate that he was exhorting those whom he may be normally expected to influence or control to an accepted standard of behaviour": *R. v. Sault Ste. Marie*, supra, and *R. v. Southdown Builders Ltd.* (1981), 57 C.P.R. (2d) 56 (Ont. G.S.P.), p. 59.

He had a responsibility not only to give instruction but also to see to it that those instructions were carried out in order to minimize the damage. The delay in clean-up showed a lack of due diligence: *R. v. Canadian Cellulose Co.* (1979), 2 F.P.R. 256 (B.C. Co. Ct.) and *R. v. Genge* (1983), 44 Nfld. & P.E.I.R. 109 (Nfld. T.D.). There is no corporate documentation between February 15, 1989 and

August 31, 1989 to assist him in his defence of due diligence. In my opinion, he has not established the defence of due diligence on the balance of probabilities and is therefore guilty as charged.

There will be a conviction registered pursuant to s. 75(1) of the OWRA. The charges under s. 147(a) of the EPA are stayed for reasons previously given.

Re Keith Weston

I have considered the fact that during Mr. Weston's tenure at Batawa, the company committed $250,000 to the building of a water treatment system for the village. This would seem inconsistent with the commission of the environment offence on the site of the plant. However, I note from the evidence that in this circumstance, Mr. Weston advised the Bata family of the village's needs. The Bata family agreed to donate the land, then established further financial limits for assistance over the period of five years. Why Mr. Weston did not pursue this course of action with the environmental problem on site has not been explained. The evidence establishes that Mr. Riden had no difficulty receiving such approval from Mr. Bata.

In my opinion, this evidence is not evidence of Mr. Weston's personal attention to environmental concerns, but rather an example of the personal and sentimental attachment that the Bata family had to the area.

Keith Weston's responsibilities as an "on-site" director make him much more vulnerable to prosecution. He demanded the authority to control his work environment before he took the job. He had experience in the production side and was aware toxic chemicals were used in the process. He was reminded of his environmental responsibilities by TAC 298. In my opinion, Keith Weston has failed to establish that he took all reasonable care to prevent unlawful discharge.

In addition to the evidence previously related in respect to the due diligence of Bata Industries, it is my opinion, red flags should have been raised in his environmental consciousness when the first quote of $58,000 was obtained. Instead of simply dismissing it out of hand, he should have inquired why it was so high and investigated the problem. I find that he had no qualms about accepting the second quote of $28,000 and he had no further information other than it was cheaper. This was not an informed business judgment, and he cannot rely upon the business judgment rule, which at its core recognized that a business corporation is profit-oriented and that an honest error of judgment should not impose liability provided the requisite standard of care is met.

I find confirmation in this opinion by the fact that when he was transferred in November, he allotted $100,000 to waste disposal, again without any further knowledge. One cannot help but wonder if his diminished incentive package was a motivating factor in the allotment of $100,000 at this time. This expense would only affect him personally to the amount of $500 because the company was now in a profit position and his salary incentive based on reducing losses was minimal.

It is my finding that Keith Weston cannot shelter behind the advice he received from Mr. De Bruyn. As Bata was "cut to the bone" by Mr. Weston, the additional responsibilities fell upon Mr. De Bruyn and grossly overloaded him. The problem was aggravated by the inference from the evidence that Mr. De Bruyn was not given the authority to expend the $58,000 or $28,000 on his own.

He required the approval of Mr. Weston. In my opinion the failings of Mr. De Bruyn fall on the shoulders of Mr. Weston who stands in sad comparison to Mr. Riden who occupied the same position and responsibilities at the plant next door.

As the "on-site" director Mr. Weston had a responsibility in this type of industry to personally inspect on a regular basis, i.e., "walk-about". To simply look at the site "not too closely" 20 times over his four-year tenure does not meet the mark. He had an obligation if he decided to delegate responsibility to ensure that the delegate received the training necessary for the job and to receive detailed reports from that delegate.

There will be a conviction registered pursuant to s. 75(1) of the OWRA. The charges under s. 147(a) of the EPA will be stayed for reasons previously given.

Notes and Questions

1. The trial judge fined Bata Industries $120,000 and imposed fines of $12,000 each on Marchant and Weston as corporate directors. In addition, the trial judge ordered that Bata Industries be prohibited from indemnifying the directors for their fines. An initial sentencing appeal resulted in the fines being reduced to $90,000 and $6,000 respectively, although the order prohibiting indemnification of Marchant and Weston was affirmed. On a further appeal to the Ontario Court of Appeal, the decision to reduce the fines was affirmed while the order prohibiting indemnification of the directors was vacated.

Sentencing in Environmental Cases

The following case remains a leading decision with respect to the principles of sentencing in cases of environmental harm involving corporate accused. At the same time, it contains some intriguing observations about the limitations of prosecutions that solely target a corporate accused, and the correlative need to explore new ways to achieve corporate behaviour modification. In this section, we first consider an early and still-influential corporate sentencing decision. We then review some recent research into "creative sentencing" in environmental cases.

R. v. United Keno Hill Mines Ltd.
(1980), 10 C.E.L.R. 43 (Y.T. Terr. Ct.)

[United Keno Hill Mines Limited ("Keno") pled guilty to depositing waste in Yukon waters on May 1, 1979 in excess of the waste discharge limits prescribed by a water licence and thereby contravening the *Northern Inland Waters Act*. Keno operated a combined open pit and underground mine. During the period of the infraction, the accused was operating under a licence that specified a maximum allowable concentration of contaminants in the effluent discharged by the accused into Flat Creek.]

STUART C.J.: — Before considering what sentence is appropriate, some preliminary questions should be addressed. Are there unique considerations to bear in mind in sentencing for environmental offences? Are there sentencing principles peculiar to sentencing a corporation as opposed to an individual offender?

Based on a review of American and Canadian authorities, I submit the answer to both questions is clearly — yes. In sentencing corporations and in dealing with environmental offences courts on both sides of the border have evolved a body of sentencing law that is a special application of common sentencing principles. *In R. v. Kenaston Drilling (Arctic) Ltd.* (1973), 12 C.C.C. (2d) 383, the Court explicitly acknowledges a "special approach" is required in sentencing corporate environmental offenders. What is this special approach? Why is there a need for a special approach in the case of corporate offenders committing breaches of environmental laws?

Special Considerations — Nature of Environmental Damage

In sentencing assault cases the courts consider the nature of the victim (relative ability to defend, provocation) and the degree of injury (permanent or temporary disability, etc.). Similarly, in environmental cases, the courts do and should vary the severity of punishment in accord with the nature of the environment affected and the extent of damage inflicted.

Nature of Environment

A unique ecological area supporting rare flora and fauna, a high-use recreational watershed, or an essential wildlife habitat, are environments calling upon users to exercise special care. Any injury to such areas must be more severely condemned than environmental damage to less sensitive areas.

Extent of Injury

Penalties should reflect the degree of damage inflicted. The resiliency of the environment or the capacity to repair the damage is a crucial consideration. If the damage is irreparable, extensive, persistent or has numerous consequential adverse effects, the penalty must be severe. In some instances not only the actual damage caused but the potential damage that might have emanated from the polluter's activities must be considered.

As in assault offences the more severe the beating the greater the condemnation expressed in sentencing. Similarly, evidence of injury should be tendered in environmental cases. Thus the Crown should place before the Court any evidence touching upon the special nature of the environment affected, the degree of damage inflicted, the consequential or peripheral adverse impacts, the prospects and cost of repairing the damage, the duration of the damage, and the potential damage that might have been caused if the actions of the offenders had been allowed to continue.

Courts have taken and should take judicial notice to the seriousness of environmental damage, but appropriate sentencing distinctions cannot be made in the absence of Crown evidence depicting the specific damage in issue. In the absence of Crown evidence the estimates of damage presented by the offender are persuasive and to a great extent restrict any severity of sentence prompted by judicial notice. ... Most sentencing dispositions in environmental cases necessitate expert and technical evidence to describe the extent of environmental harm caused by the offence.

The Offender — Corporations

The size, wealth, nature of operations and power of a corporation necessitate a special approach in sentencing. The activities of one corporation can reach into the lives of people and communities in many parts of the world. The scope of corporate activities has a multiplier effect on the extent and severity of risk potential flowing from corporate action.

Considerations in Sentencing of Corporations for Environmental Offences

Criminality of Conduct

The severity of punishment should be directly related to the degree of criminality inherent in the manner of committing the offence. Accidents, innocent mistakes, and not reasonably foreseen events are less damnable than wilful surreptitious violations. If a corporation surreptitiously dumps toxic waste in wilful disregard of regulations, a harsh sanction is required. Similarly, if a corporation is aware of the environmental damage being caused by their operations and does nothing to rectify or abate the problem, the Court is justified in accrediting such corporate conduct with a high degree of criminality.

Extent of Attempts to Comply

A corporation should not be harshly punished if evidence indicates diligent attempts to comply with government regulations. The diligence of a corporation can be measured by the duration of non-compliant operation, the cost of compliance contrasted with corporate profits, the general co-operative and frank nature of communication with responsible government agencies, and the actual investment of resources, time, and money in seeking to achieve compliance. If the responsible government agency is not pressing for compliance, or its actually encouraging non-compliance through tacit or explicit agreements to permit non-compliant operations, the corporation cannot be severely faulted.

Remorse

Talk is cheap, action speaks much clearer to the courts about the degree of corporate contrition than the smoothest of apologies enunciated by counsel. The actions underlying genuine contrition can take three principal forms.

Speed and efficiency of corporate action to rectify the problem or clean up the pollution is the clearest indication of corporate remorse.

Voluntarily reporting the violation to authorities indicates a genuine desire to act responsibly. The bulk of environmental regulation depends upon the integrity of corporations to provide full disclosure of the impact of their operation on the environment. Voluntarily reporting breaches must be acknowledged as a mitigating circumstance by the courts in sentencing. Pleas of guilty are not of any significance if detection and conviction were inevitable.

The personal appearance of corporate executives in Court and their personal statement outlining the company's genuine regret and stating future plans to avoid repetitions of such offences is another indication of genuine corporate contrition. Too often corporations appear solely by agents, through their lawyer, or through a lesser functionary of the company. This practice suggests the lack of significance the company accords the offence. If the Court is to properly assess the degree of sanctions required to effect the full rehabilitation of the offending corporation, the governing or guiding mind, in the person of senior executive officers, should be present and give evidence.

Size of Corporation

Courts take judicial notice to the size and wealth of a corporation. The larger the corporation, the larger the fine. Conversely, smaller operations are not fined as severely for similar offences. This approach is principally motivated by the desire to ensure the fine imposed in the case of large corporations is not readily absorbed as a simple cost of doing business, or as a mere slap on the wrist. In the case of smaller corporations, the courts attempt to avoid destroying the economic viability of the corporation by imposing a crippling fine. Large corporations cannot avoid large fines by establishing a network of small corporations as courts seem prepared to hear evidence of corporate connections or simply to take judicial notice of such corporate relationships.

[...] What amount will be an effective deterrent? To fairly determine a deterrent fine, the capacity of each corporate offender to deflect or absorb a fine should be assessed. Thereby such matters as profits, assets, current financial status, and characteristics of the relevant market must be before the Court.

Profits Realized by Offence

Courts attempt to ascertain the amount of profit or savings realized by the corporation as a consequence of the offence. Thus the amount of illegally realized windfall should establish in almost every case, in the absence of other outstanding mitigating circumstances, the minimum fine. Other matters considered should increase the amount of the fine. Establishing the quantum of illegal gains should reside with the defendant corporation as they are privy to the information and to the processes appropriate for determining the quantum of illegal gains. In the absence of conclusive evidence from the corporation the Court may rely on any reasonable estimate the Crown submits.

The assessment of a fine based on illegally obtained gains is essential to ensure that non-complying corporations do not acquire an economic advantage over complying competitors. It may be appropriate for the courts to hear evidence from complying competitors on the extent of economic advantages the offending corporation derived from non-compliance.

[...] In most cases restitution is a better means of attacking illegal gains than a fine. Restitution might embrace losses to corporate competitors, damage to public and private property, and the cost of prosecution. Restitution orders are best suited to compensate victims of criminal conduct; fines are more appropriately employed to sanction criminal conduct.

Criminal Record

A prior criminal record is especially important in sentencing corporations. Similar recidivistic conduct raises an assumption that the corporation is more concerned about profit than compliance.

Moral opprobrium and public censure of corporations arising from criminal prosecutions has questionable potential in promoting effective deterrence. Public censure directed at corporate criminality is diluted by the dispersal of responsibility throughout the hierarchy of the corporation and by the anonymity afforded by acting in the corporate name. Any corporation whose operations involve little or no direct contact through sales with the general public is probably only peripherally concerned about a public image. In such cases and particularly if the offence is a subsequent similar offence, the fine should be severe.

Evaluation of Sentencing Tools

In recent years the courts have relied upon substantial fines as the principal means of sanctioning corporations. This tactic assumes if the fine is significantly harsh, compliance will be assured. I disagree. Fines alone will not mould law abiding corporate behaviour. Fines are only one part of a necessary sentencing arsenal to foster responsible corporate behaviour. A greater spectrum of sentencing options is required to ensure effective deterrence and prevent illegal economic advantages accruing to corporations willing to risk apprehension and swallow harsh fines as operating costs.

Fines are inadequate principally because they are easily displaced and rarely affect the source of illegal behaviour. Usually fines can be ultimately passed on in the form of higher prices to either the consumer or the taxpayer. Sentencing, to be effective, must reach the guiding mind — the corporate managers: be they directors or supervisors. They are the instigators of the illegality either through wilfullness, wilful blindness, or incompetent supervisory practices.

Fining corporations leaves the upper echelon policy makers relatively unscathed. Fining corporate policy makers reduces somewhat the impotency of levying fines against corporate assets [...] People who value their standing in the community are likely to be extremely sensitive to the stigma emanating from criminal conviction. In the United States the imposition of criminal sanctions against corporate officials has been an effective deterrent. [...]

The American courts have partially resolved the problem of determining individual fault for corporate activities by laying the blame at the top of the corporate hierarchy. As a result, the courts imposed a duty upon upper echelon corporate officials to discover and control all corporate activities. After a few corporate presidents are prosecuted, it is likely senior executives will make it their business to know what all subordinates are doing and effective policies and checks against illegal activities will be implemented.

Upper echelon corporate officials should first prove the existence of a reasonable system of control before liability can be passed to a subordinate. This may impose hardships on some senior executives, but they are in the best position to act in protecting the public interest. The subordinate may deny liability if the matter is either outside his actual authority or was not a consequence of his lack of reasonable care. By placing the onus on senior corporate officials to identify the author of the illegal act the propensity may arise to affix responsibility to a "fall guy" or middle level manager who is stuck with the dilemma of losing his job by denying responsibility of ultimately facing criminal prosecution for activities he was powerless to oppose. Only time will take the real measure of this problem, but a court that begins with assuming corporate executives are liable will be sceptical of any evidence seeking to shift blame to lower management levels. In some cases, the answer may be a finding of joint responsibility.

Society is abruptly learning of the potentially dire consequences of some environmental regulatory violations. The authors of such environmental catastrophes, if criminally responsible, should be prosecuted with the full force of the law. A corporate veil should never afford the slightest measure of special protection to anyone for criminal conduct. By diverting corporate criminal conduct into conciliatory processes or by ignoring the criminality of responsible corporate officers, the criminal law process is offering concessions to one class of offender not afforded to others. This practice can only engender a public perception of bias and unjustifiable discrimination.

The imposition of personal responsibility necessitates an ability to identify the culpable corporate official. To do so, the Court must have power to require complete access to internal corporate allocations of responsibility.

I do not intend to suggest that fining or incarcerating corporate officials will ensure compliance; it will simply enhance the prospects of a positive criminal law contribution to the regulation of corporate activities. There must be further development of sentencing options and the use of non-criminal government tools to cope with the multifaceted requirements of corporate regulation.

The use of criminal sanctions for resource management can promote cooperation but will never by itself resolve the polycentric conflicts in resource use. Effective criminal sanctions can provide leverage for prompt and universal cooperation in negotiating, implementing and operating comprehensive resource use management schemes. In the United States, reliance on criminal sanctions encouraged voluntary compliance with pollution abatement programs and "halted the pattern of delay which was commonplace".

Elaine L. Hughes & Larry A. Reynolds,
"Creative Sentencing and Environmental Protection"

(2008) 19 J. Envtl. L. & Prac. 105

An Overview of Sentencing Alternatives

[...] early pollution control statutes often employed a fine as the primary sentencing option (with imprisonment also being often available but rarely used). The size of the fine was then crafted to attempt to achieve deterrence, taking into account such factors as the gravity of the offence (risk of harm versus cost of taking precautions, degree and magnitude of risk, actual damage and the nature of the environment) and the degree of responsibility of the offender ("criminality" or degree of disrespect for the law). Aggravating and mitigating factors that could be considered included: prior record of environmental misconduct; profits realized by the offence; the size, wealth and nature of the offender; pollution control and compliance efforts; remedial efforts; and degree of demonstrated remorse. Some modern statutes specifically require sentencing courts to take such factors into account. The availability of a solution (technology), and the need for a degree of uniformity in sentences (precedents) may also be considered by sentencing courts.

Despite the availability of prosecutions and traditional sentences (fines and imprisonment) in even the earliest pollution control statutes, routine enforcement and compliance was rarely achieved. Strict enforcement via the criminal process was often avoided in favour of negotiation, in part due to the expense and time commitment involved in court actions and in part due to problems associated with regulatory legislation. Other deficiencies in the early legislation, such as the ability of persons to hide behind the corporate veil or insolvency proceedings, were identified. A debate developed over the relative merits of amending and improving administrative compliance mechanisms, versus reforming quasi-criminal strict enforcement mechanisms.

In the result, by the late 1980s a variety of improvements were made to *both* administrative and quasi-criminal compliance mechanisms. On the quasi-criminal side, sentencing options in particular were broadened in two ways. First, the traditional option of a fine was revamped to include higher maximum fines, daily offence provisions, and profit-stripping fines. Imprisonment was either added as an option to deal with deliberate and flagrant offenders, or made more flexible via hybrid offence provisions and the ability to pursue directors and officers as parties to corporate offences. When coupled with a more vigorous prosecution policy, there is some evidence that compliance did improve.

Second, the so-called "creative" options or "non-fine measures" were added to the statutes. These include: licence revocation; forfeiture of property; restitution; prohibition, remedial and prevention orders; modifications to business operations; research orders; notification and publication orders; information orders; community service; probation; compensation; and performance bonds. Most recently, a third option — diversion processes — has also been added, such as absolute and conditional discharges, the use of restorative justice techniques (*e.g.* sentencing circles) and so-called "alternative measures" or EPAMS — a process by which sentencing is avoided if a negotiated compliance agreement is fulfilled.

Despite these modern additions, by all reports fines are still used more frequently than any other sentence for environmental offences. Courts continue to apply "the classical ["economics"] theory of non-compliance behaviour choice as a balancing act between benefits gained through noncompliance versus costs of being caught," in which "fines alone are said to be sufficient to achieve compliance." Yet, lack of rigorous enforcement continues to be a problem, and penalties have often been low. Numerous authors have concluded that "fines are only one part of a necessary sentencing arsenal." While lack of familiarity with regulatory regimes by judges is sometimes blamed for the failure to use creative sentencing more frequently, lack of prosecutional expertise and resources may also be a contributing factor. In addition, it is unclear whether creative sentencing will actually produce better environmental outcomes than traditional fines...

Existing Legislation: Creative Sentencing Options

[...] a wide variety of environmental legislation now contains some form of creative sentencing provision. However, the survey also indicated there is no real uniformity in federal and provincial regulatory schemes. In the federal sphere, the most comprehensive creative sentencing provisions are found in the *Fisheries Act* and the *Canadian Environmental Protection Act, 1999*. Most provinces have incorporated at least some creative sentencing options into their core environmental legislation as well. At the outset, it is worth noting that creative sentences are generally available "in addition to any other punishment that may be imposed," subject to the limits implied by the totality principle. Normally they are still combined with a fine. In brief, the following options are amongst those most frequently available in Canadian statutes:

(a) Removal of Benefits

Statutes may contain provisions which either confiscate the profits realized by commission of the offence (i.e., a "profit-stripping" fine), or authorize the forfeiture of property used in its commission. The latter can be used in cases such as wildlife infractions, to decrease the likelihood of repetition of the offence (*e.g.* seizure of traps, firearms) or to remove potential profits (*e.g.* poached wildlife parts).

(b) Restitution as Compensation

Property losses that result from the commission of an offence may result in a sentencing order for payment of compensation. Additionally, the Crown can usually be compensated for any costs incurred by it during its cleanup or remediation. A sentencing order for restitution is unlikely to be used very often, as administrative mechanisms to order it usually precede prosecutions, and are taken into account simply as mitigation measures during sentencing. Compensation for personal injury is generally recoverable only via civil (tort) actions.

(c) Licence Revocations and Prohibition Orders

Most statutes give the sentencing court the ability to order an offender to stop any action that may result in the continuation or repetition of the offence. Again, however, administrative orders to the same effect would generally have preceded prosecution. If an offender has been fined, some provincial statutes authorize licence suspensions until the fine is paid.

(d) Trust Funds, Research Orders and the EDF

Some statutes permit the sentencing court to impose a financial penalty on an offender either to conduct ecological research, or to pay the funds into some particular trust fund with conservation goals. Federally, the government has established the Environmental Damages Fund (EDF) for this purpose. The EDF is a special holding or trust account administered by Environment Canada. It is designed to take money from either civil judgments or regulatory sentences, and expend those funds on environmental repair in the location where the damage occurred, often in partnership with eligible non-governmental organizations. In addition to environmental restoration, the funds can be used for research or for education (*e.g.* funding scholarships). This type of penalty is particularly useful if technical solutions to environmental problems need additional development, or where supervision and administration of the Court order requires expertise that could be provided by an NGO partner. However, there is also a danger of "further research" producing no real benefit, and thus such orders can amount to simply retaining the *status quo*.

(e) Remedial and Prevention Orders

As an alternative to paying money into some type of restoration project, most environmental statutes permit the sentencing judge to require the offender either to take direct action to remedy any harm or, where it is clear what steps need to be taken to prevent future harm, to order the defendant to take such steps. The two types of order generally emerge from a single statutory provision, and thus will be discussed together. The time and expense involved in remedial orders or orders to conduct "beneficial environmental projects" can vary greatly. As a general rule, the undertaking ordered will be "reasonably related to the organization's criminal conduct and achievement of at least one...of the objectives of sentencing." It is a desirable form of sentence in theory as it requires offenders to take direct responsibility for the consequences of their actions and to direct their resources to environmental protection *per se*, although in practice, as was the case with prohibition or restitution orders, most often remedial action is ordered using administrative powers prior to engagement of the criminal process. Thus, the Crown normally treats the remedial action as a minimum expectation, while resort to prosecution and sentencing is a subsequent, super-added, punishment.

(f) Community Service Orders

In a similar vein, statutes frequently authorize courts to order community service. This is particularly useful if cleanup or direct remediation is either impossible, or beyond the defendants' means, yet the offenders' expertise could result in a related environmental or public benefit. Ideally, there should be some "nexus" between the offence and the community project [...]

(g) Notification, Publication and Information Orders

Another option in many environmental statutes is the ability of the court to require the offender to provide data to affected individuals, the community at large, or to the Crown. A notification order can ensure that affected persons receive information about pollution in a timely manner so that medical advice or compensation can be pursued. It also has an educative function, increasing awareness of environmental rules. Publication orders, on the other hand, are intended to achieve a deterrent effect via adverse publicity [...]

Information orders occupy a slightly different role, as they are generally not made at the time of sentencing. Rather, they allow the Crown to do supervision and follow-up, collecting information post-conviction, to check for any repetition of the offence or failure to comply with the terms of a sentence. These cause a practical difficulty for many enforcement agencies as they are often not equipped to maintain a watch on the convicted party for an extended period following sentencing. Court orders can also be drafted to grant leave to return for directions, if conditions set forth cannot be satisfied.

(h) Performance Bonds or Guarantees

Under some enactments, offenders may be required to post a performance bond, pay monies into court, or provide an irrevocable letter of guarantee. These funds help secure compliance with other aspects of the sentence, as they are forfeited if non-compliance occurs. Funds can also be put into lawyers' trust accounts when a creative sentence is negotiated, to ensure compliance with the order (if accepted by the Court).

(i) Suspended Sentences and "Probation"

Some Acts permit the Court to suspend sentences of fines or imprisonment, and make a sentencing order alone. The court is also given a general power to order an offender "to comply with such other reasonable conditions as the Court considers appropriate and just in the circumstances for securing the offender's good conduct and for preventing the offender from repeating the same offence or committing other offences." The effect of such an order is equivalent to placing an offender on probation and is potentially broad enough to require a corporation to even change its business practices. If the "probation" order is breached, the Court may revoke the sentence and impose an alternative. "Probation" could be used in cases where rehabilitation of the offender is the main goal (e.g. with first offenders).

(j) Ticketing and Diversion Processes

In addition to traditional sentences (fines, imprisonment) and creative sentences, there are various sentencing diversion processes available in some Acts. The three main options are ticketing, absolute and conditional discharges and EPAMs. These form part of the available enforcement ladder but are not to be confused with creative sentences, which result in a criminal record of conviction, and accordingly do not form part of the present study.

Application of Current Legislation: Process and Policies

Given the availability of a wide range of creative sentencing options, a number of interesting issues arise. These include: a) how often are creative sentences used? b) for what type of offence or offender will the Crown consider a creative sentencing option? c) what process is used? d) what policies or objectives does the Crown seek to achieve? e) what types of creative sentences are actually being imposed? and perhaps most importantly, f) what outcomes are being achieved that could not be reached using traditional sentences such as fines?

[...] federal Acts such as CEPA and the Fisheries Act are accompanied by general enforcement and compliance policies. In practice [...] the federal enforcement and compliance policies place considerable reliance on prosecutorial discretion. First, there is a preference to direct the creative sentence toward a project of direct environmental benefit to the general locale where the offence took place.

Second, it is seen as desirable that the creative sentence have a logical nexus to the nature of the offence. For example, it is desirable for an offence of "[...] harmfully altering, disrupting or destroying fish habitat [...]" pursuant to s. 35(1) of the *Fisheries Act* to generate a creative sentence which is directly connected to fish habitat. Alternatives might include restoration of previously harmed habitat or the creation of new habitat.

Third, whenever possible process should directly involve the offender. Specifically, the offender (or a highly placed executive if the offender is a corporation) should be personally engaged in creative sentencing discussions with the federal Crown. Finally, as noted previously, the creative sentence portion of the total monetary penalty in federal cases has tended to be as much as 90 per cent.

Assessment and Future Directions

What can be said about the use of creative sentencing in Canada to date? To reiterate the earlier discussion, in theory the main goal is to achieve compliance with environmental standards through specific and general deterrence measures. Specific deterrence could be achieved through remedial and prevention orders, prohibition orders, and measures that remove any benefits from offenders; in practice we see various prevention orders used that direct the offenders to improve their internal management systems (environmental management systems, employee training) as well as prohibition orders. In addition, community service is sometimes ordered, although unfortunately without any clear nexus to the environmental offence in some cases. General deterrence seems most readily touched by publication orders. In practice not only have publication orders been used to good effect but various orders related to educational funding also seem to have potential as part of creating a compliance culture.

Interestingly however, the largest group of potential orders set out in the statutes and used in practice, are orders to conduct specific projects of direct environmental benefit (whether remedial or preventive), usually by funding NGO's or government departments, and orders of a somewhat uncertain benefit to conduct research (again, often with educational NGO partners). While the offender may not undertake the actual project — these orders often simply provide funding to NGO's who then manage the enterprise — when properly constructed there is arguably considerable specific deterrent effect beyond that of a similarly-sized fine, in that many such projects are the result of substantial direct consultation between the Crown and the offender. This personal engagement of the offender in the sentencing process is perceived by prosecutors as providing specific deterrence effects which would not be achievable through a simple fine. (On the other hand, if the workload is being passed over and the offender need not develop any expertise nor devote personnel to the task at hand, there is always a danger an offender could try to evade responsibility via such an order.)

Significantly, however, creative sentencing is moving beyond traditional sentencing objectives by providing a direct environmental benefit (which may well extend beyond simply remediation at a minimum standard, and instead require improvements or enhancements) i.e., the sentence takes us beyond just "deterrence." If we think of the environment as "the victim" of the crime, we can perhaps see some parallels with modern victim's rights objectives that seek to have victim impacts taken into account in the sentencing process. Certainly, the actual and potential environmental damage and the uniqueness and sensitivity of the impacted ecosystem are all relevant aggravating factors.

What, then, of the modern movement in criminal sentencing toward restorative justice? Is this a concept which can or should extend to environmental "victims"? Restorative justice has been defined as:

> [...] an approach to accountability for crime based on the restoration of balanced social relations and repatriation of criminal harm that is rooted in values of equality, mutual respect and concern, and that uses deliberative processes involving crime victims, offenders, their respective supporters and representatives of the broader community under the guidance of authorized and skilled facilitators.

It is a voluntary process in which an offender accepts responsibility for wrongdoing, and it has arguably reduced recidivism rates while achieving "high rates of offender compliance with sanctions as well as high rates of satisfaction for victims." Thus, restorative sanctions are "intended to reconcile and repair the harm caused by an offence."

In environmental statutes, measures such as discharges and "alternative measures" have been added in order to provide the ability to divert offenders from the sentencing process. To move in this direction would clearly go beyond the realm of creative sentences, as it removes the offender from the criminal process entirely, "to another forum where they are not convicted or found guilty, and are not sentenced." However, in the environmental realm, it is unclear that restorative techniques will be of particular interest due at least in part to the deep distrust of industry that environmental representatives maintain; problems such as agency capture, the dominance of economic and industrial interests in policy development, and lack of true public participation mechanisms in environmental law create enormous obstacles to creating the type of volunteer community that is needed for restorative justice techniques to succeed. If experiments with environmental mediation can offer any insights, it is clear that bringing environmental offenders and "victims" to the same table may do nothing except reveal exactly how far apart their views are. It is also unclear whether "the environment" as victim would have any needs that parallel the benefits of a restorative approach to a human victim (*e.g.* the emotional need to forgive). If environmental restoration can be completed by a creative sentence, there seems to be no "victim benefit" to be derived by moving further to a restorative approach, unless personal injuries to present or future human victims are also part of the circumstances of individual cases.

Is the Crown justified in taking a more active approach to the care of environmental "victims"? Certainly, the Courts seem open to such developments. In *Hydro Quebec* the Supreme Court of Canada held that environmental stewardship, even in the absence of harm to human health, is a "fundamental value" in our society and a proper subject of the criminal law *per se*. Numerous other SCC cases have reiterated this notion that environmental protection is a fundamental value within Canada [...]

Indeed, in the civil context, the Crown's role toward environmental protection has been recently described as part of its *parens patriae* jurisdiction; it may act as a representative of the public to enforce the public interest in an unspoiled environment. At a minimum, therefore, the Courts seem prepared to recognize that the Crown is the "holder of inalienable 'public rights' in the environment and certain common resources...accompanied by the procedural right of the Attorney General to give for their protection ... as *parens patriae*"; and have recognized that this raises a number of important issues, including *inter alia* the potential liability of the Crown if it *fails* to act, and the enforceability of any fiduciary obligations involved. Coupled with its comments in the regulatory context, it seems clear the Supreme Court is open to entertaining the idea of an expanded fiduciary role for the Crown in environmental cases.

The legislatures have moved toward creative sentencing and the Courts have moved towards its use in fulfillment of the traditional sentencing goals of specific and general deterrence. The potential is there, however, to use creative sentencing for larger goals of direct environmental benefit where the "polluter pays," and in so doing to take steps toward fulfilling an expanded role for the Crown to act as *parens patriae*, or to enlarge its fiduciary role toward the protection of the public interest.

One might, in closing, add one further observation. The directions suggested by the SCC are all founded in existing statutory and common law concepts, and to date are based on a deliberate expansion of those concepts in a step-by-step fashion. Thus, they are a far cry from more radical theoretical concepts such as environmental rights. Will they be enough? Can we use this expanded potential to reach the root causes of environmental degradation? While increasing the effectiveness of the Courts in environmental litigation is arguably a positive and necessary step, it is unclear that reforms such as creative sentencing can truly reach some key causes of environmental degradation, such as overpopulation and excessive consumption. Nevertheless, by reaching beyond the traditional goal of "mere compliance," the Crown and Courts are moving in a positive direction where, at a minimum, restoration of environmental quality helps prevent the foreclosure of future options, one community at a time.

Notes and Questions

1. Almost 30 years separate the *United Keno Hill Mines* decision and the Hughes & Reynolds article on "creative sentencing". What have we learned in that period of time about deterring and punishing corporate wrongdoing, and how is that experience and knowledge reflected in the latter article?

2. Hughes & Reynolds discuss the growing trend of recognizing and giving voice to "victims" in the criminal and regulatory sentencing processes. Traditionally, this was an interest that was deemed to be exclusively represented by the Crown. In response to a variety of factors, this has changed. Many environmental crimes do not have readily identifiable victims, at least not victims that can readily appear and deliver "victim impact statements". Who, in your view, should have standing to give victim impact statements on behalf of the environment?

3. In the first-ever prosecution under subsection 32(1) of the *Species at Risk Act*, S.C. 2002, c. 29 (SARA), the defendant was found guilty of harassing a listed species by repeatedly approaching a pod of Orcas at high speed in his

motorboat. Crown counsel in the case was Larry Reynolds, co-author of the above article. In the end, the defendant was fined $7,500 (to be paid into Environment Canada's Environmental Damages Fund) and ordered to write an article for the local newspaper taking responsibility for his actions and discussing why they were wrong: see Chapter 9. Is this, in your view, a fit sentence? What principles and concepts from the Hughes & Reynolds article does it reflect or not reflect?

4. Compare the sentencing principles in *United Keno Hill Mines* to more recent cases, such as *R. v. Terroco Industries Limited*, 2005 ABCA 141. Can you detect any significant changes in the principles applied?

The Emerging Role of
Administrative Monetary Penalties (AMPs)

The *Bata* case underscores that criminal and regulatory prosecutions can be costly, time-consuming and unpredictable. As government budgets for environmental enforcement were cut back in Canada, the US and the UK starting in the 1990s, regulators began to explore alternative enforcement mechanisms.

Stepan Wood & Lynn Johannson,
"Six Principles for Smart Regulation"
(2008) 46 Osgoode Hall L.J. 345

Ontario borrowed the idea of environmental penalties from the United States, where similar tools have been available since the 1970s, usually under the name "administrative penalties" (APs). APs were introduced to allow government officials to issue relatively modest financial penalties for minor environmental violations without incurring the time and expense of a full-blown investigation, prosecution, and trial. Before APs, environmental law enforcement boiled down to a choice between voluntary industry compliance or the blunt instrument of criminal or quasi-criminal prosecution, with the latter reserved only for the most egregious cases. Investigations and prosecutions would often drag out for years before reaching a final conclusion. As a result, many violations were not investigated or prosecuted at all.

APs were one of several innovative enforcement tools introduced to get away from this often unsatisfactory binary choice. APs do away with the need for formal court proceedings altogether. In theory, this may reduce enforcement costs for governments, regulated firms, and interested third parties alike, and increase the level of enforcement of environmental laws. Research indicates that APs have a credible deterrent effect at very modest administrative cost. For these reasons many governments embraced APs enthusiastically.

Regulated industries, on the other hand, dislike them. One concern is absolute liability: the government may impose APs without proving the elements of the offence. Another concern is double jeopardy: in some jurisdictions, payment of an AP may not bar prosecution for the same offence. Industry also objects to the relative lack of judicial scrutiny of AP determinations, the high level of administrative discretion over some APs, and the one-size-fits all approach of others. Some environmental non-governmental organizations (ENGOs) have embraced APs, but others have condemned them as trivializing what should properly be considered crimes. These concerns notwithstanding, APs have proliferated in the US and have been introduced in several other countries. They are one of the US Environmental Protection Agency's favourite enforcement tools, increasing dramatically in the last few years.

Notes and Questions

1. Following the lead of many US jurisdictions, several Canadian provinces have now implemented AMP regimes. The first province to do so was Alberta, which incorporates an AMP regime into its *Environmental Protection and Enhancement Act*. AMPs also play a key role in British Columbia legislation governing forest practices. Ontario has joined the AMP bandwagon through amendments in 2004 to its *Environmental Protection Act* (Bill 133). In 2010, the federal government did likewise under provisions of what is often referred to as the "Environmental Enforcement Bill" (Bill C-16, introduced in March 2009). Bill C-16 set the stage for enactment of the *Environmental Violations Administrative Monetary Penalties Act*, S.C. 2009, c. 14, s. 126 (MPA). Under the MPA, the Governor in Council would be empowered to pass regulations to create AMPs under nine federal statutes including CEPA, the *Canada National Parks Act*, the *Migratory Birds Convention Act, 1994* and the *Canada National Marine Conservation Areas Act*. While the MPA came into force on December 10, 2010, the regulations necessary to give it practical effect did not come into force until 2017.

2. A detailed survey into current research into AMPs in the environmental law context concludes that:

   > Studies done on use of administrative penalties indicate that they can result in greater efficiencies for governments. These studies reveal that regulators are more likely to take enforcement action when administrative sanctions are available as opposed to when prosecution is the only enforcement tool. The lower standard of proof and the less stringent evidentiary rules under the administrative process means that enforcement action can be taken more readily and at lower cost than when criminal prosecution is the only option. There is also evidence that utilizing administrative sanctions has been effective in promoting regulatory compliance.

   > Ramani Nadarajah, "Environmental Penalties: New Enforcement Tool or the Demise of Environmental Prosecutions?", in Stanley Berger and Dianne Saxe, eds., *Environmental Law: The Year in Review 2007* (Aurora: Canada Law Book, 2008)

   While empirical evidence documenting the impact of implementing AMPs on compliance is surprisingly sparse, Nadarajah notes that, since the Canadian Food Inspection Agency introduced AMPs, industry compliance has risen from between 60-70% to over 90%.

3. One key benefit of AMPs is that they can encourage regulators to undertake enforcement action in instances where — due to resource constraints as well as standard of proof and evidentiary requirements — they might otherwise shy away from mounting a criminal prosecution. This, in turn, can have a positive deterrent effect on the behaviour of individuals and firms being regulated. Research done by Professor Brown suggests that certainty of punishment is the most significant single factor in promoting compliance: see R. Brown, "Administrative and Criminal Penalties in the Enforcement of Occupational Health and Safety Legislation" (1992) 3 Osgoode Hall L.J. 691.

4. Commentators warn, however, of the need to ensure that, for serious offences, criminal prosecution remains the preferred enforcement instrument. A key design issue, therefore, when establishing an AMP system is to determine which offences should be enforceable via AMPs alone, which should potentially be enforceable via AMPs or criminal prosecution, and which should be enforceable exclusively by way of criminal prosecution. In this vein, Chris Rolfe argues that

    ... for many offences such as willful dumping, interference with enforcement officials, falsifying records etc. the criminal court system is the only appropriate remedy. These are true crimes. The solemnity and stigma of the criminal court system are appropriate for these offences: see "Administrative Monetary Penalties: A Tool for Ensuring Compliance" (unpublished: West Coast Environmental Law Association, 1997).

    To reduce the potential that regulators will gravitate towards over-reliance on AMPs in appropriately serious cases, Professor Brown thus recommends a two-track system that clearly specifies a list of offences for which criminal prosecution is the only available enforcement option.

5. A final consideration is the relationship between AMP regimes and rights guaranteed under the *Charter of Rights and Freedoms*. Some commentators predict that AMP regimes, particularly those which incorporate substantial fines and rely on reverse onus or absolute liability, will be challenged under the *Charter*: see Berger (2006), *supra*, this chapter. Whether such challenges will succeed will depend heavily on the specifics of the regime in question and upon whether the Court concludes the penalty in question is "administrative" or "criminal" in nature: see *R. v. Wigglesworth*, [1987] 2 S.C.R. 541, and S. Berger, *The Prosecution and Defence of Environmental Offences* (Aurora: Canada Law Book, 2006).

The Role of Adaptive Management in Compliance and Enforcement

A key issue in compliance and enforcement is the role to be played by "adaptive management". The popularity of adaptive management, particularly in business and governmental circles, has grown remarkably in recent years. Once thought of as having relatively narrow application to a restricted set of natural resource management problems, it is now being championed as a means of addressing uncertainties in the context of environmental assessment (see *Pembina Institute for Appropriate Development v. Canada (Attorney General)*, 2008 FC 302) and as a way of managing the human health uncertainties and impacts associated with the issuance of an industrial air pollution permit (see *Toews v. British Columbia (Director, Environmental Management Act)*, 2015 CarswellBC 3804, BC Environmental Appeal Board Decision Nos. 2013-EMA-007(g) and 2013-EMA-010(g)).

The basic concept behind adaptive management is that adverse impacts of human activities can be mitigated through changes to the management and regulation of existing facilities as problems are identified through monitoring and scientific research during the operation. The implications of the concept of adaptive management are somewhat different during the course of an environmental assessment process than they are for the regulation of existing facilities. In the environmental assessment process, the key question is how the promise of adaptive management during the operation of a facility affects predictions of impacts of the proposed activity, mitigation measures imposed, and terms and conditions for approval. At the regulatory stage for existing facilities, key issues include the adequacy of monitoring and research into the actual impacts, the availability of appropriate action to address undesired impacts, and the actual imposition of terms and conditions to address undesired impacts. On the one hand, the promise of adaptive management is touted by proponents as a solution to unexpected, unforeseen, uncertain, and unknown impacts in environmental assessment and regulatory processes. On the other hand, there is concern that the adaptability of facilities and other activities is often assumed rather than studied, that monitoring of the actual effects of approved facilities is lacking, and that changes to the management and regulation of these facilities are sometimes not possible, and other times not implemented and enforced.

Defining what role adaptive management should play in environmental law is an important challenge for a variety of reasons. For one thing, unless kept in check, as Phelan J. points out in *Taseko Mines Limited v. Canada (Environment)*, 2017 FC 1099, an overly broad approach to adaptive management can overwhelm and undermine what many consider to be its corollary: the precautionary principle. Can adaptive management be reconciled with the precautionary principle? What kinds of risks (human health, animal health, ecosystem health) can or should be managed using an adaptive management approach?

In what follows, Professor Olszynski offers a somewhat skeptical assessment of the enthusiasm with which adaptive management has been embraced by environmental practitioners and decision-makers. We then offer an extract from the Federal Court's recent judgment in *Taseko Mines*.

Martin Z.P. Olszynski,
"Failed Experiments: An Empirical Assessment of
Adaptive Management in Alberta's Energy Resources Sector"
(2017) 50:3 U.B.C. L. Rev. 697

Background and Context

Adaptive Management

Most historical accounts on the origins of adaptive management begin with the publication, in the late 1970s, of *Adaptive Environmental Assessment and Management* by Canadian ecologists C.S. Holling and Carl J. Walters. Since that time, adaptive management has undergone considerable evolution and is now commonly applied to a wide variety of resource issues. Unfortunately, and perhaps the inevitable result of this evolution and variety of application, adaptive management has also become "a highly malleable term. It has been defined and applied in a variety of ways, ranging from highly detailed and rigorous to nearly vacuous."

Nevertheless, most scholars agree on certain core principles: adaptive management is supposed to be a structured or systemic process through which decisions are made and modified as a result of what is known and learned about the effect of previous decisions. Most scholars also agree that adaptive management should not to be confused or conflated with "trial and error" approaches (examples of which are discussed in Part IV). Current policy guidance from both the U.S. Department of the Interior and the Canadian Environmental Assessment Agency appear to capture the essence of adaptive management adequately: the former defines adaptive management as "a systematic approach for improving resource management by learning from management outcomes," the latter as "a planned and systematic process for continuously improving environmental management practices by learning about their outcomes."

Adaptive management is also generally associated with a six step cycle (see Figure 1), although the number of steps varies as some steps are combined while others are separated. In their recent article examining the administrative law barriers to the implementation of adaptive management in the U.S., Professors Robin Craig and J.B. Ruhl set out the following basic elements of what they refer to as a "structured, multistep protocol: (1) definition of the problem, (2) determination of goals and objectives for management, (3) determination of the baseline, (4) development of conceptual models, (5) selection of future actions [(1)-(5) constituting Steps 1 and 2 in Figure 1], (6) implementation of management actions, (7) monitoring, and (8) evaluation and return to step (1)."

Figure 1: The Adaptive Management Cycle

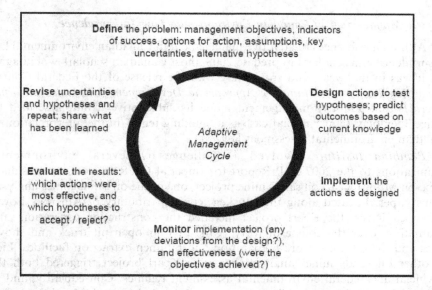

Define the problem: management objectives, indicators of success, options for action, assumptions, key uncertainties, alternative hypotheses

Revise uncertainties and hypotheses and repeat; share what has been learned

Design actions to test hypotheses; predict outcomes based on current knowledge

Adaptive Management Cycle

Evaluate the results: which actions were most effective, and which hypotheses to accept / reject?

Implement the actions as designed

Monitor implementation (any deviations from the design?), and effectiveness (were the objectives achieved?)

Adaptive management practitioners and scholars distinguish between two kinds of adaptive management: active and passive. As explained by Professor Brad Karkkainen, "'Active' adaptive management ... consists of conscious generation and testing of specific scientific hypotheses through narrowly tailored, scientifically designed management experiments. 'Passive' adaptive management ... involves heightened monitoring of key indicators and adjustment of policies in response ... while foregoing the conscious experimental hypothesis-testing of the 'active' mode."

While a detailed discussion about the theory of adaptive management is beyond the scope of this paper, a few additional comments are warranted. First and perhaps most importantly, adaptive management is not "fail-safe": "no form of adaptive management, no matter how rigorous, can guarantee successful resource protection ... Adaptive management can help us recognize management mistakes and limit the damage they cause ... But it does not prevent mistakes, nor does it guarantee that the mistakes we make will be reversible." Second, adaptive management is not a *panacea*: there are environmental problems for which adaptive management is not suitable. In fact, most U.S. scholars now suggest that it is probably not appropriate for most environmental problems. Ideal conditions for adaptive management have been described as those where the "management-problem context presents a dynamic system for which uncertainty and controllability are high and risk is low." Finally, in order to be effective adaptive management must be fully and rigorously implemented: "If the management actions are implemented in a way that strays from the design, if the experimental design does not isolate the signal of interest from background noise (through spatial/temporal contrasts, replicates and controls), or if monitoring focuses on the wrong variables, scale or frequency, it will be difficult if not impossible to learn anything meaningful." As will be seen, almost all of the actual and proposed applications of adaptive management considered in this paper do not reflect any of these limitations. [...]

Adaptive Management in Canadian Environmental Law Jurisprudence

Although references to adaptive management in Canadian environmental law jurisprudence and scholarship predate 2008, most Canadian scholars would agree that it was in that year, and specifically with the release of the Federal Court's decision in *Pembina Institute for Appropriate Development v Canada (Attorney General)*, that adaptive management made its substantive debut, described by Justice Tremblay-Lamer in that case as a "guiding tenet" in the interpretation of Canadian environmental assessment law.

Pembina Institute involved a challenge by several environmental organizations to the 2007 JRP Report for Imperial Oil Resources' (a subsidiary of Exxon Mobil) Kearl oil sands mine project, one of the oil sands mines analysed in this paper. Located along the Muskeg River, a tributary of Alberta's Lower Athabasca River, the Kearl project included the construction, operation, and reclamation, over the course of forty years, of four open pit truck and shovel mines and three trains of ore preparation and bitumen extraction facilities. Like the other oil sands mines analysed here, the Kearl project triggered both the provincial and federal environmental assessment regimes. Consequently, and as has been the practice since, Alberta and Canada agreed to establish a joint review panel to conduct a single environmental assessment. Following several months of hearings, the Kearl JRP Report concluded that the project was "not likely to result in significant adverse environmental effects" and was "in the public interest."

Adaptive management's role in Canadian environmental assessment law arose in response to the environmental groups' challenges to the joint review panel's treatment of end-pit lakes and peatland restoration. The Court in *Pembina Institute* described adaptive management as countering "the potentially paralyzing effects of the precautionary principle" by "permit[ing] projects with uncertain, yet potentially adverse environmental impacts to proceed based on flexible management strategies capable of adjusting to new information regarding adverse environmental impacts where sufficient information regarding those impacts and potential mitigation measures already exists." Applying this approach to the Panel's treatment of end-pit lakes, which the oil sands industry admits pose several additional challenges as compared to the coalmining context, the Court accepted that there was "some uncertainty with respect to end-pit lake technology," but it was not such that it should "paralyze the entire project." With respect to peatlands, the restoration of which the applicants argued was "not even known in general terms," the Court held that "while uncertainties ... remained, they could be addressed through adaptive management given the existence of generally known replacement measures contained in Imperial Oil's mine closure plan."

The *Pembina Institute* decision was quickly and widely criticized. Professor Arlene Kwasniak argued that the Court's approach "[ran] contrary to the *CEAA [1995]* for numerous reasons," including the explicit and relatively minor role for adaptive management envisioned by the legislation at that time. Professor Nathalie Chalifour pointed out that the Court's approach rendered "virtually meaningless" the statutory requirement that, to be considered, mitigation measures must be "technically and economically feasible." She also expressed doubts about its consistency with the statutory requirement to apply the precautionary principle: "A precautionary approach would place the onus on Imperial Oil to demonstrate that the reclamation technology relating to end pit lakes and peatlands was sufficient to ensure that they would not cause serious environmental impacts." Reflecting on the absence of any detailed discussion surrounding the proposed application of adaptive management by the panel (*e.g.* objectives, indicators, alternative actions, monitoring plans), this author suggested that in such instances "there would be little to no basis for concluding that the uncertainty associated with proposed mitigation measures will actually be reduced, let alone that these measures will prove effective ..." [...]

Since (and arguably because of) *Pembina Institute*, reliance on adaptive management has only increased. In addition to those developments described in the introduction to this paper, there are now twenty-five judicial decisions referring to adaptive management, sixty percent of which post-date that decision. There are also over eighty administrative decisions by various boards and tribunals that refer to adaptive management. But while tribunal understanding of adaptive management, especially the requisite conditions for actual learning, appears to have improved (as further discussed in Parts IV and V), judicial misunderstanding remains unchanged. In *Sierra Club Canada v. Ontario (Ministry of Natural Resources)*, the Ontario Superior Court limited its understanding of adaptive management to "require[ing] those engaged in the construction of [a road project] to continue to monitor how best to protect [certain] species and to adapt its management until the best answer is found." In *Greenpeace Canada v. Canada (AG)*, government respondents argued that Canadian courts "have endorsed 'adaptive management' as a necessary counterbalance [to the precautionary principle] to ensure that socially and economically desirable projects can come to fruition." Thus, a *quasi*-common law of adaptive management appears to have emerged that fails to reflect any of the principles and limitations of genuine adaptive management, *i.e.*, that it is not fail-safe, that it is not a panacea, and that it must be rigorously implemented. [...]

Discussion

If adaptive management is to play a useful role in Canadian environmental and natural resources management, this paper further affirms the need to right the course of its implementation. Below are several recommendations for law reform. Many of these recommendations have been previously made by other scholars in other contexts and take the form of a series of provisions that could be inserted into virtually any provincial or federal environmental or natural resources law in Canada. While some of what follows could perhaps be implemented as a matter of policy, and some regulators have demonstrated a willingness to require genuine adaptive management, the reality is that there is now in Canada a *quasi*-common law of "maladaptive management" that proponents can understandably be expected to cling to until it is modified by the judiciary or superseded by legislation. Bearing in mind adaptive management's technical nature and the

Canadian judiciary's reluctance to engage such issues, the prospects for judicial correction appear limited.

Defining Adaptive Management

Reflecting on the confusion surrounding what adaptive management is and what it requires, a first and obvious step would be to clearly distinguish adaptive management from its lesser cousins (*i.e.* a/m-lite, adaptive mitigation, compliance monitoring). One way to accomplish this would be to legislate a definition of adaptive management that reflects the necessary elements of structured learning. For example:

> "Adaptive management" means a planned and systematic process that enables the improvement of environmental management practices by learning about their outcomes, and includes the six step cycle of (i) problem identification, (ii) plan design, (iii) plan implementation, (iv) plan monitoring, (v) evaluation of implementation, and (vi) adjustment based on monitoring results as per the plan and further repetition of the cycle as required.

The term "enables" in the first line is deliberate and is intended to distinguish this definition from those that erroneously cast adaptive management as "fail-safe": improved management practices are the goal, but they are not "ensured." That being said, even this definition would not have necessarily prevented the occurrence of the kind of "adaptive management strategies" and frameworks encountered in this paper (*e.g.* Teck's Cheviot Grizzly Bear Plan, Grand Cache Coal's Selenium Management Program, or the mitigation objective frameworks found in *in situ* reports). In the interest of clarity, it may be necessary to go further and explicitly define what adaptive management is not, *e.g.* "For greater certainty, adaptive management is not th[e] same as compliance monitoring or contingency planning ...."

Requiring Discrete, Enforceable, and Peer-reviewed Adaptive Management Plans

In addition to defining adaptive management, legislative provisions should also require government departments or proponents (whichever party is actually going to be carrying out adaptive management) to prepare and submit adaptive management plans that address the key steps and sub-steps, and these should be peer-reviewed. Reflecting on the examples considered in this paper, one strong indicator of real adaptive management is the identification of the right kind of uncertainty. Merely being unable to predict the precise effect of a mitigation measure in a given context, which is tantamount to not being able to predict the future, is not sufficient and is suggestive of adaptive mitigation at best, *ad hoc* contingency planning at worst. Rather, the uncertainty should be of a conceptual nature, which is also more consistent with the existence of the hypothesis stage. At the design stage, and as suggested by Professors Schultz and Nye and confirmed by the Grand Cache Coal and *in situ* projects, triggers or thresholds must be clear, objective, and enforceable. Finally, all elements — including monitoring plans — should be bounded together; interested parties and other stakeholders should not have to scour reports for monitoring plans and data that may or may not be relevant to the adaptive management plan.

Requirements for an adaptive management plan should also include a section setting out the rationale for why adaptive management is appropriate in the given context. This will have both scientific and socio-legal dimensions. The former speaks to the limits of experimentation in the natural world and will overlap with the contents of the adaptive management plan itself. The latter speaks to resources, stakeholder commitment, and the ability to adjust decisions over time.

Adapting the Surrounding Legislative Context

Depending on the context, adaptive management may or may not come up against other legislative imperatives. For example, and as currently written at least, there would seem to be no obstacle preventing the Minister of Fisheries and Oceans from incorporating adaptive management into a section 35 *Fisheries Act* authorization for impacts to fish habitat. While he or she is supposed to consider fisheries management objectives and the sustainability and ongoing productivity of commercial, recreational and Aboriginal fisheries, this is essentially a "public interest" determination. The same applies under Alberta's *EPEA* and *Water Act*, which do not impose any substantive limits or set any legislated benchmarks for government decision-makers to meet when authorizing various activities and their associated environmental harms. In such instances, adaptive management may be considered in the public interest as a sort of *quid pro quo*: some risk of environmental harm now in exchange for learning and better decision-making in the future, bearing in mind always that this does not necessarily mean positive environmental outcomes but rather having a basis for saying "this management action or mitigation measure works" or "this action does not work and should be discontinued."

Conversely, and as in the U.S., adaptive management would seem inconsistent with Canada's "incidental take" regime under its endangered species legislation, pursuant to which the relevant Minister must form the opinion that the activity in question "will not jeopardize the survival or recovery of the species." Most Canadian environmental law scholars would also agree that adaptive management does not fit comfortably within the context of the current federal environmental assessment regime, the *Pembina Institute* decision and its progeny notwithstanding. Setting aside the fact that the singular reference to adaptive management was removed from the Act in 2012, as noted by Professor Chalifour there is the requirement that mitigation measures relied upon be "technically and economically feasible" and the imperative that government agencies "exercise their powers in a manner that ... applies the precautionary principle." While some scholars and courts have suggested that adaptive management is consistent with or even a response to the precautionary principle, I agree with Professor Chalifour that adaptive management is not a general substitute for precaution. At the very least, the matter should be understood as one of degree: the more uncertain a management action or mitigation measure is, the less precautionary a decision to proceed with potentially serious and/or irreversible environmental effects will be.

If adaptive management is going to be available in such contexts, the surrounding legislation should be amended to set out the relationship between it and those other legislative imperatives. For example, under *CEAA, 2012* (or any successor), Parliament could clarify that adaptive management cannot be relied upon for the environmental effects determination where uncertainty with respect to mitigation effectiveness is moderate to high; it might also require adaptive management for such measures should the project ultimately be approved anyway. This is essentially the approach that the joint review panel for the Lower Churchill Hydroelectric project took back in 2011. Similarly, *SARA*'s incidental take regime could be amended to allow reliance on adaptive management where the value of the potential learning is significant and the overall risks are low.

Public Registries for Adaptive Management Plans and Monitoring Results

Finally, in order to address concerns about transparency and accountability, provisions should be included to facilitate public participation in all aspects of the adaptive management cycle. Just as interested parties and other stakeholders should not have to scour reports for monitoring plans and data, they should also not be required to rely on freedom of information processes to get access to those plans and reports in the first place. Thus, inclusion of adaptive management into any environmental or natural resources statutes should be accompanied with provisions for a public registry that would contain the relevant plans and monitoring data. In some cases, such as *CEAA, 2012* and *SARA*, such registries already exist and would need only to be amended for this purpose. Alberta Environment and Parks also hosts several public registries online, including the EIS registry that was used for the purposes of this paper. In other cases, such as under the *Fisheries Act*, no public registry currently exists such that one would have to be created.

The role of adaptive management in the environmental assessment of proposed new projects was the subject of a court challenge by Taseko Mines Limited of the government's decision not to approve its mine following an environmental assessment of its project. A key question for the court was the relationship between adaptive management and precaution. Specifically, the court was asked to consider whether it was reasonable for the Panel and the Minister to conclude that certain impacts would be significant in the face of commitments from the proponent to apply an adaptive management approach to minimize any impact. As you read this case, keep in mind that we will return to the issue of environmental assessment processes in Chapter 7. We also consider a decision in this same litigation in Chapter 6 where we consider applicable principles of judicial review.

Taseko Mines Limited v. Canada (Environment)
2017 FC 1099

PHELAN J.: —

Introduction

This is an application for judicial review of a Review Panel Report [respectively Panel and Report] concerning the proposed New Prosperity Gold-Copper Mine that was made pursuant to the *Canadian Environmental Assessment*

Act, 2012, SC 2012, c 19, s 52 [*CEAA 2012*]. In this case, the judicial review centers on findings in the Report with respect to water seepage and impact on water quality in Fish Lake (Teztan Biny) and the surrounding area. [...]

The key dispute is the Panel's conclusion that toxic water seepage will be greater than Taseko Mines Limited [Taseko] estimated. This conclusion ultimately led to decisions not approving the proposed mine. [...]

Background Facts

The New Prosperity Gold-Copper Mine [the Project] is a proposed open pit gold and copper mine in British Columbia, 125 km southwest of Williams Lake (in the traditional territories of the Tsilhqot'in peoples). The $1.5 billion Project is said to provide a number of jobs as well as (allegedly) a $340 million contribution to British Columbia's gross domestic product.

The Project is the successor to another proposed mine, Prosperity, that was rejected by the GIC in 2010 following a federal environmental assessment. The original design of the mine would have necessitated draining the lake Teztan Biny.

In this second Project, Teztan Biny would not be drained because the proposal relocates the tailings storage facility [TSF] and introduces a lake recirculation water management scheme.

On November 7, 2011, the Minister stated that the Project would undergo a federal environmental assessment under the *Canadian Environmental Assessment Act*, SC 1992, c 37 [*CEAA*] (later continued according to the transition provisions of the *CEAA 2012*). [...]

Taseko submitted an EIS [Environmental Impact Statement] on September 27, 2012, purporting to deal with the deficiencies in the initial Prosperity project proposal.

The Panel then engaged in discussions with respect to the technical merits and adequacy of the EIS with "federal departments, the BC Ministry of Energy and Mines ('BC MEM'), aboriginal groups, including the Tsilhqot'in National Government ('TNG'), and Taseko."

Taseko's EIS described features of the proposed TSF and predicted seepage using two computer models: a 3-dimensional model representing the TSF as a horizontal plane, and 2-dimensional model representing the TSF as a vertical plane.

Natural Resources Canada [NRCan] identified significant concerns with the EIS including "deficiencies with both of Taseko's models, the data upon which they were based, Taseko's proposal to rely on adding estimates from both models, and Taseko's proposed mitigation measures."

As a result of these concerns, NRCan recommended the Panel request that Taseko provide a more comprehensive model of 3D numerical groundwater flow, which would address the deficiencies in the models provided in the EIS. [...]

In a letter dated May 24, 2013, Taseko sought to postpone dealing with the deficiencies. [...]

Taseko therefore declined to develop the 3D numerical groundwater flow model requested by the Panel.

On June 14, 2013, NRCan indicated that it was "in the process of developing a numerical groundwater flow model to assess seepage from the base of the tailings storage facility, similar to that requested by the Panel in SIR 12/14(A-a)" and offered to make the findings of this study available to the Panel.

The Panel accepted this offer in a letter dated June 21, 2013. At this time, the Panel also indicated that this information would be made publicly available (online) by way of the project registry. [...]

On July 4, 2013, NRCan provided the Panel with its 3D numerical model. On July 19, 2013, NRCan provided the Panel with written submissions. In its July 2013 submissions, NRCan stated that "[s]eepage from the TSF was estimated at 8650 m³/d (100 L/s) which is more than an order of magnitude greater than the proponent's 3D model prediction [of 9 L/s]."

Taseko disputes the accuracy of this seepage estimate characterization. [...]

The Panel issued its Report on October 31, 2013. It is the NRCan Technical Memorandum on seepage and the Panel's reliance on these submissions in concluding that the seepage of toxic water from the TSF would be greater than estimated by Taseko that lie at the heart of this judicial review. [...]

Issues

Each of the parties phrased their issues slightly differently but in the end the issues the Court considers that must be addressed are:

1. Did the Panel fail to observe principles of procedural fairness by accepting and relying upon the Technical Memorandum without giving Taseko a fair opportunity to respond?

2. Was the Panel's determination that Taseko underestimated the volume of tailings pore water seepage leaving the TSF unreasonable?

3. Was the Panel's decision to accept NRCan's upper bound estimate as the expected seepage rate from the TSF unreasonable?

4. Was the Panel's conclusion that the concentration of water quality variables in Fish Lake (Teztan Biny) and Wasp Lake would likely be a significant adverse environmental effect unreasonable?

[...]

Analysis

[...]

Issue 4: Was the Panel's conclusion that the concentration of water quality variables in Fish Lake (Teztan Biny) and Wasp Lake would likely be a significant adverse environmental effect unreasonable?

Taseko submits that the findings with respect to seepage, discussed above, "permeated" the Report. In a section on the water quality of Fish Lake (Teztan Biny), the Report stated:

> The Panel also notes that the *seepage* from the tailings storage facility expected by Natural Resources Canada is *considerably greater than estimated* by Taseko. On balance, the Panel concludes, as did most presenters on this subject, that there

would be higher concentrations of water quality contaminants of concern in Fish Lake than modelled by Taseko.

[Emphasis added]

Taseko argues the impugned seepage finding was directly responsible for the Panel's conclusion that the Project would lead to significant adverse environmental effects on the water quality of Fish Lake (Teztan Biny) and Wasp Lake. The water quality finding relies on the unreasonable seepage finding; therefore, it cannot stand and is inconsistent with the requirements under the Amended Terms of Reference.

The Panel's conclusion that the concentration of water quality variables in Fish Lake (Teztan Biny) and Wasp Lake would likely be a significant adverse environmental effect was reasonable. As discussed above, the impugned seepage findings were also reasonable; therefore, the Panel's reliance on these findings in reaching a conclusion on water quality was reasonable.

Furthermore, the water quality findings were supported by additional evidence, including Taseko's own admission that the water quality would not be in line with guidelines for the protection of aquatic life. The likely effectiveness of Taseko's water treatment mitigation measures were questioned by presenters for the TNG ("details on the effectiveness of the treatment were not provided or modelled"), the British Columbia Ministry of Environment ("unproven technology over the long term [and] potentially costly"), and the British Columbia Ministry of Energy, Mines, and Petroleum Resources ("[w]ater treatment for the Project did not provide confirmation that the proposed water quality objectives for Fish Lake (Teztan Biny) were likely to be either technically or financially achievable").

Therefore, it was open to the Panel to reject the "unproven and unprecedented" proposals put forward by Taseko.

The Panel stated:

> Based on the evidence, the Panel finds it is unable to accept Taseko's conclusion that the water treatment options proposed would effectively mitigate the adverse effects of the Project on Fish Lake (Teztan Biny) water quality. The Panel concludes that the proposed recirculation scheme, the adaptive management plan and the water treatment options are unlikely to work effectively in the long-term. On this basis, the Panel concludes the "proof of concept" test proposed by Taseko for the environmental assessment has failed.

The Panel therefore did not rely solely on the impugned seepage findings in reaching its conclusions on water quality.

With respect to the precautionary principle, there does not appear to be any dispute between the parties that the Panel was required to assess the proposal in a precautionary manner. The purpose section of the *CEAA 2012* states:

> 4 (1) The purposes of this Act are [...]
>
>> (b) to ensure that designated projects that require the exercise of a power or performance of a duty or function by a federal authority under any Act of Parliament other than this Act to be carried out, are considered in a careful and precautionary manner to avoid significant adverse environmental effects; [...]

(g) to ensure that projects, as defined in section 66, that are to be carried out on federal lands, or those that are outside Canada and that are to be carried out or financially supported by a federal authority, <u>are considered in a careful and precautionary manner to avoid significant adverse environmental effects</u>; [...]

(2) The Government of Canada, the Minister, the Agency, federal authorities and responsible authorities, in the administration of this Act, <u>must exercise their powers in a manner that protects the environment and human health and applies the precautionary principle.</u>

(Court's underlining)

However, there is clearly a conflict between the parties as to what this entails. Taseko's proposal relied on adaptive management; that is, Taseko proposed that environmental risks and mitigation measures could be dealt with during further stages of development. Other parties considered this an inadequate approach, and sought more information on the risks and feasibility of mitigation.

The Panel recognized the possibility of adaptive management, but found that it could not defer important decisions to the next stage of the process. In the Report, the Panel referenced the requirement that it act in a precautionary manner and stated, with respect to water quality in particular:

Taseko declined to provide some materials requested by the Panel and by other participants (e.g., description of water quality model for Fish Lake). To deal with the resulting uncertainties, the Panel considered various risk management strategies, including adaptive management in some circumstances. *However, when the Panel concluded the potential adverse environmental effects were potentially "significant", it did not agree that deferring decisions on the approach to manage the risk to subsequent regulatory processes is appropriate.* It is necessary at the environmental assessment stage for the Panel to determine if a significant adverse effect is likely and to consider if and how the risk can be managed to acceptable levels.

If, after reviewing the record of information for the review, the Panel decided that there were serious uncertainties about a potential adverse environmental effect and the ability to manage that effect and the risk of serious or irreversible environmental harm was high, then the Panel adopted a precautionary approach.

[Emphasis added]

It was reasonable for the Panel not to accept Taseko's "vague assurances" that it would engage in adaptive management in order to deal with adverse environmental effects. The Panel sought information on environmental effects and mitigation measures, and Taseko refused to provide this information. It was entirely reasonable, and in line with the Panel's (reasonable) interpretation of the precautionary principle, for the Panel to conclude that the concentration of water quality variables in Fish Lake (Teztan Biny) and Wasp Lake would likely be a significant adverse environmental effect.

Indeed, acceptance of vague adaptive management schemes in circumstances such as these would, in my view, tend to call into question the value of the entire review panel process — if all such decisions could be left to a later stage, then the review panel process would simply be for the sake of appearances.

Conclusion

[...] Therefore, this judicial review will be dismissed with costs to the Respondents.

Notes and Questions

1. What are some of the factors that explain the remarkable popularity adaptive management has gained as an environmental law concept? What interests have the most to gain from the concept? What interests have the most to lose?

2. What steps can be taken to better define and constrain the concept?

3. Define adaptive management and distinguish it from the precautionary principle (see discussion in Chapter 1). Can the two concepts be reconciled? If so, how?

4. Are there any risks or potential harms that it would be unethical or unconstitutional for governments to regulate using an adaptive management approach?

5. What role do you see for adaptive management in environmental assessment processes? What role do you see for it in the regulation of existing facilities? How can legislation ensure that adaptive management is used as a tool to minimize undesired impacts rather than avoid regulatory rigour?

The Interplay between Statutory Remediation Orders and Bankruptcy/Insolvency Law

An area of growing interest in the case law concerns the interplay between provincial environmental remediation regimes and federal laws governing corporate bankruptcy and insolvency. In most provinces, provincial regulators have broad statutory powers to issue remediation orders against individuals and corporate entities that, in the language typically used in such statutes, are "responsible persons". Typically, under provincial contaminated sites legislation, this is defined to include past and present owners and occupiers of the site in question.

Whether and against whom these remediation orders are issued is highly discretionary. Moreover, the case law suggests that, in making such orders, regulators cannot be fettered by private contractual arrangements that various "responsible persons" may have made to allocate remediation liability amongst themselves. For example, the fact that the former owner of a contaminated site may have contracted with a subsequent purchaser under an arrangement that the latter assumed full liability for remediation costs provides no protection for the former owner against a statutory remediation order. Indeed, if, in this scenario, the subsequent purchaser finds itself in financial distress or bankruptcy, the provincial regulator will in all likelihood target the most solvent "responsible person" with the cleanup order: see, for example, *Superior Fine Papers v. Director, Ministry of Environment*, Case No. 09-076/09-090/09-091.

Sometimes, however, there will be no obvious and solvent "responsible person". This situation can arise when the corporate entity responsible for the on-site contamination has encountered financial difficulties and is under federal creditor protection or facing bankruptcy. In such cases, the debtor company will likely have many creditors. Where this is the case, what is the legal status of the province's claim under applicable environmental laws to compel the company to clean up the site or pay for the costs of remediation? Is this claim akin to the rights of other creditors, and thus to being "compromised" in the bankruptcy or corporate restructuring process? Or does the "polluter pays principle" militate in favour of the conclusion that such claims are distinct and continue to bind the company even after it emerges from bankruptcy or restructuring? The Supreme Court of Canada addressed these issues in a high-profile case arising out of the corporate restructuring of pulp and paper giant AbitibiBowater Inc.

AbitibiBowater Inc., Re
2012 SCC 67

[AbitibiBowater (the "Company") carried on operations at five industrial sites in Newfoundland and Labrador (the "Province"). Under financial distress, it ceased operations in the Province, filed for insolvency protection in the United States and obtained a stay of proceedings under the *Companies' Creditors Arrangement Act*, R.S.C. 1985, c. C-36 ("*CCAA*"). The Province issued orders under the *Environmental Protection Act*, S.N.L. 2002, c. E-14.2, requiring the Company to undertake remediation at the five industrial sites it had occupied (three of which had been expropriated by the Province). The Province also applied for a judicial declaration that a claims procedure order issued under the *CCAA* in relation to the Company's proposed reorganization did not bar the Province from enforcing its remediation orders. It contended that these orders were not "claims" under the *CCAA* and therefore could not be stayed by a *CCAA* Court. It further argued that Parliament had no constitutional competence to stay orders that were validly made in the exercise of a provincial power. The Company opposed that application, arguing that the orders were monetary in nature and hence fell within the definition of the word "claim" under the *CCAA*. The *CCAA* court dismissed the Province's motion. The Quebec Court of Appeal denied the Province leave to appeal. We first reproduce the reasons of Deschamps J. for the majority, followed by the two dissenting reasons of Chief Justice and LeBel J.]

DESCHAMPS J.: — The question in this appeal is whether orders issued by a regulatory body with respect to environmental remediation work can be treated as monetary claims under the *Companies' Creditors Arrangement Act*, R.S.C. 1985, c. C-36 ("*CCAA*").

Regulatory bodies may become involved in reorganization proceedings when they order the debtor to comply with statutory rules. As a matter of principle, reorganization does not amount to a licence to disregard rules. Yet there are circumstances in which valid and enforceable orders will be subject to an arrangement under the *CCAA*. One such circumstance is where a regulatory body makes an environmental order that explicitly asserts a monetary claim.

In other circumstances, it is less clear whether an order can be treated as a monetary claim. The appellant and a number of interveners posit that an order issued by an environmental body is not a claim under the *CCAA* if the order does not require the debtor to make a payment. I agree that not all orders issued by regulatory bodies are monetary in nature and thus provable claims in an insolvency proceeding, but some may be, even if the amounts involved are not quantified at the outset of the proceeding. In the environmental context, the *CCAA* court must determine whether there are sufficient facts indicating the existence of an environmental duty that will ripen into a financial liability owed to the regulatory body that issued the order. In such a case, the relevant question is not simply whether the body has formally exercised its power to claim a debt. A *CCAA* court does not assess claims — or orders — on the basis of form alone. If the order is not framed in monetary terms, the court must determine, in light of the factual matrix and the applicable statutory framework, whether it is a claim that will be subject to the claims process.

The case at bar concerns contamination that occurred, prior to the *CCAA* proceedings, on property that is largely no longer under the debtor's possession and control. The *CCAA* court found on the facts of this case that the orders issued by Her Majesty the Queen in right of the Province of Newfoundland and Labrador ("Province") were simply a first step towards remediating the contaminated property and asserting a claim for the resulting costs. In the words of the *CCAA* court, "the intended, practical and realistic effect of the *EPA* Orders was to establish a basis for the Province to recover amounts of money to be eventually used for the remediation of the properties in question" (2010 QCCS 1261, 68 C.B.R. (5th) 1, at para. 211). As a result, the *CCAA* court found that the orders were clearly monetary in nature. I see no error of law and no reason to interfere with this finding of fact. I would dismiss the appeal with costs.

Constitutional Questions

At the Province's request, the Chief Justice stated the following constitutional questions:

1. Is the definition of "claim" in s. 2(1) of the *Companies' Creditors Arrangement Act*, R.S.C. 1985, c. C-36, *ultra vires* the Parliament of Canada or constitutionally inapplicable to the extent this definition includes statutory duties to which the debtor is subject pursuant to s. 99 of the *Environmental Protection Act*, S.N.L. 2002, c. E-14.2?

2. Is s. 11 of the *Companies' Creditors Arrangement Act*, R.S.C. 1985, c. C-36, *ultra vires* the Parliament of Canada or constitutionally inapplicable to the extent this section gives courts jurisdiction to bar or extinguish statutory duties to which the debtor is subject pursuant to s. 99 of the *Environmental Protection Act*, S.N.L. 2002, c. E-14.2?

3. Is s. 11 of the *Companies' Creditors Arrangement Act*, R.S.C. 1985, c. C-36, *ultra vires* the Parliament of Canada or constitutionally inapplicable to the extent this section gives courts jurisdiction to review the exercise of

ministerial discretion under s. 99 of the *Environmental Protection Act*, S.N.L. 2002, c. E-14.2?

I note that the question whether a *CCAA* court has constitutional jurisdiction to stay a provincial order that is *not* a monetary claim does not arise here, because the stay order in this case did not affect non-monetary orders. However, the question may arise in other cases. In 2007, Parliament expressly gave *CCAA* courts the power to stay regulatory orders that are not monetary claims ... Thus, future cases may give courts the opportunity to consider the question raised by the Province in an appropriate factual context. The only constitutional question that needs to be answered in this case concerns the jurisdiction of a *CCAA* court to determine whether an environmental order that is not framed in monetary terms is in fact a monetary claim.

Processing creditors' claims against an insolvent debtor in an equitable and orderly manner is at the heart of insolvency legislation, which falls under a head of power attributed to Parliament. Rules concerning the assessment of creditors' claims, such as the determination of whether a creditor has a monetary claim, relate directly to the equitable and orderly treatment of creditors in an insolvency process. There is no need to perform a detailed analysis of the pith and substance of the provisions on the assessment of claims in insolvency matters to conclude that the federal legislation governing the characterization of an order as a monetary claim is valid. Because the provisions relate directly to Parliament's jurisdiction, the ancillary powers doctrine is not relevant to this case. I also find that the interjurisdictional immunity doctrine is not applicable. A finding that a claim of an environmental creditor is monetary in nature does not interfere in any way with the creditor's activities. Its claim is simply subjected to the insolvency process.

What the Province is actually arguing is that courts should consider the form of an order rather than its substance. I see no reason why the Province's choice of order should not be scrutinized to determine whether the form chosen is consistent with the order's true purpose as revealed by the Province's own actions. If the Province's actions indicate that, in substance, it is asserting a provable claim within the meaning of federal legislation, then that claim can be subjected to the insolvency process.

Environmental claims do not have a higher priority than is provided for in the *CCAA*. Considering substance over form prevents a regulatory body from artificially creating a priority higher than the one conferred on the claim by federal legislation. This Court recognized long ago that a province cannot disturb the priority scheme established by the federal insolvency legislation: *Husky Oil Operations Ltd. v. Minister of National Revenue*, [1995] 3 S.C.R. 453. Environmental claims are given a specific, and limited, priority under the *CCAA*. To exempt orders which are in fact monetary claims from the *CCAA* proceedings would amount to conferring upon provinces a priority higher than the one provided for in the *CCAA*.

Claims under the CCAA

[...] One of the central features of the *CCAA* scheme is the single proceeding model, which ensures that most claims against a debtor are entertained in a single forum. Under this model, the court can stay the enforcement of most claims against the debtor's assets in order to maintain the *status quo* during negotiations with the creditors. When such negotiations are successful, the creditors typically accept less than the full amounts of their claims. Claims have not necessarily accrued or been liquidated at the outset of the insolvency proceeding, and they sometimes have to be assessed in order to determine the monetary value that will be subject to compromise.

These provisions [**Ed. Note:** referring to applicable provisions of the CCAA and the *Bankruptcy and Insolvency Act* (BIA)] [...] highlight three requirements that are relevant to the case at bar.

First, there must be a debt, a liability or an obligation to a *creditor*. Second, the debt, liability or obligation must be incurred *before the debtor becomes bankrupt*. Third, it must be possible to attach a *monetary value* to the debt, liability or obligation. I will examine each of these requirements in turn.

The *BIA*'s definition of a provable claim, which is incorporated by reference into the *CCAA*, requires the identification of a creditor. Environmental statutes generally provide for the creation of regulatory bodies that are empowered to enforce the obligations the statutes impose. Most environmental regulatory bodies can be creditors in respect of monetary or non-monetary obligations imposed by the relevant statutes. At this first stage of determining whether the regulatory body is a creditor, the question whether the obligation can be translated into monetary terms is not yet relevant. This issue will be broached later. The only determination that has to be made at this point is whether the regulatory body has exercised its enforcement power against a debtor. When it does so, it identifies itself as a creditor, and the requirement of this stage of the analysis is satisfied.

The enquiry into the second requirement is based on s. 121(1) of the *BIA*, which imposes a time limit on claims. A claim must be founded on an obligation that was "incurred before the day on which the bankrupt becomes bankrupt". Because the date when environmental damage occurs is often difficult to ascertain, s. 11.8(9) of the *CCAA* provides more temporal flexibility for environmental claims...

With respect to the third requirement, that it be possible to attach a monetary value to the obligation, the question is whether orders that are not expressed in monetary terms can be translated into such terms. I note that when a regulatory body claims an amount that is owed at the relevant date, that is, when it frames its order in monetary terms, the court does not need to make this determination, because what is being claimed is an "indebtedness" and therefore clearly falls within the meaning of "claim" as defined in s. 12(1) of the *CCAA*.

However, orders, which are used to address various types of environmental challenges, may come in many forms, including stop, control, preventative, and clean-up orders (D. Saxe, "Trustees' and Receivers' Environmental Liability Update" (1997), 49 C.B.R. (3d) 138, at p. 141). When considering an order that is not framed in monetary terms, courts must look at its substance and apply the rules for the assessment of claims.

Parliament recognized that regulatory bodies sometimes have to perform remediation work (see House of Commons, *Standing Committee on Industry*, No. 16, 2nd Sess., 35th Parl., June 11, 1996). When one does so, its claim with respect to remediation costs is subject to the insolvency process, but the claim is secured by a charge on the contaminated real property and certain other related property and benefits from a priority (s. 11.8(8) *CCAA*). Thus, Parliament struck a balance between the public's interest in enforcing environmental regulations and the interest of third-party creditors in being treated equitably. If Parliament had intended that the debtor always satisfy all remediation costs, it would have granted the Crown a priority with respect to the totality of the debtor's assets. In light of the legislative history and the purpose of the reorganization process, the fact that the Crown's priority under s. 11.8(8) *CCAA* is limited to the contaminated property and certain related property leads me to conclude that to exempt environmental orders would be inconsistent with the insolvency legislation. As deferential as courts may be to regulatory bodies' actions, they must apply the general rules [...].

The reason the *BIA* and the *CCAA* include a broad range of claims is to ensure fairness between creditors and finality in the insolvency proceeding for the debtor. In a corporate liquidation process, it is more equitable to allow as many creditors as possible to participate in the process and share in the liquidation proceeds. This makes it possible to include creditors whose claims have not yet matured when the corporate debtor files for bankruptcy, and thus avert a situation in which they would be faced with an inactive debtor that cannot satisfy a judgment. The rationale is slightly different in the context of a corporate proposal or reorganization. In such cases, the broad approach serves not only to ensure fairness between creditors, but also to allow the debtor to make as fresh a start as possible after a proposal or an arrangement is approved. The criterion used by courts to determine whether a contingent claim will be included in the insolvency process is whether the event that has not yet occurred is too remote or speculative: *Confederation Treasury Services Ltd. (Bankrupt), Re* (1997), 96 O.A.C. 75.

In the context of an environmental order, this means that there must be sufficient indications that the regulatory body that triggered the enforcement mechanism will ultimately perform remediation work and assert a monetary claim to have its costs reimbursed. If there is sufficient certainty in this regard, the court will conclude that the order can be subjected to the insolvency process.

The exercise by the *CCAA* court of its jurisdiction to determine whether an order is a provable claim entails a certain scrutiny of the regulatory body's actions. This scrutiny is in some ways similar to judicial review. There is a distinction, however, and it lies in the object of the assessment that the *CCAA* court must make. The *CCAA* court does not review the regulatory body's exercise of discretion. Rather, it inquires into whether the facts indicate that the conditions for inclusion in the claims process are met. For example, if activities at issue are ongoing, the *CCAA* court may well conclude that the order cannot be included in the insolvency process because the activities and resulting damages will continue after the reorganization is completed and hence exceed the time limit for a claim.

If, on the other hand, the regulatory body, having no realistic alternative but to perform the remediation work itself, simply delays framing the order as a claim in order to improve its position in relation to other creditors, the *CCAA* court may conclude that this course of action is inconsistent with the insolvency scheme and decide that the order has to be subject to the claims process. Similarly, if the property is not under the debtor's control and the debtor does not, and realistically will not, have the means to perform the remediation work, the *CCAA* court may conclude that it is sufficiently certain that the regulatory body will have to perform the work. Certain indicators can thus be identified from the text and the context of the provisions to guide the *CCAA* court in determining whether an order is a provable claim, including whether the activities are ongoing, whether the debtor is in control of the property, and whether the debtor has the means to comply with the order. The *CCAA* court may also consider the effect that requiring the debtor to comply with the order would have on the insolvency process. Since the appropriate analysis is grounded in the facts of each case, these indicators need not all apply, and others may also be relevant.

Having highlighted three requirements for finding a claim to be provable in a *CCAA* process that need to be considered in the case at bar, I must now discuss certain policy arguments raised by the Province and some of the interveners.

These parties argue that treating a regulatory order as a claim in an insolvency proceeding extinguishes the debtor's environmental obligations, thereby undermining the polluter-pay principle discussed by this Court in *Imperial Oil Ltd. v. Quebec (Minister of the Environment)*, 2003 SCC 58, [2003] 2 S.C.R. 624 (para. 24). This objection demonstrates a misunderstanding of the nature of insolvency proceedings. Subjecting an order to the claims process does not extinguish the debtor's environmental obligations any more than subjecting any creditor's claim to that process extinguishes the debtor's obligation to pay its debts. It merely ensures that the creditor's claim will be paid in accordance with insolvency legislation. Moreover, full compliance with orders that are found to be monetary in nature would shift the costs of remediation to third-party creditors, including involuntary creditors, such as those whose claims lie in tort or in the law of extra-contractual liability. In the insolvency context, the Province's position would result not only in a super-priority, but in the acceptance of a "third party-pay" principle in place of the polluter-pay principle.

Nor does subjecting the orders to the insolvency process amount to issuing a licence to pollute, since insolvency proceedings do not concern the debtor's future conduct. A debtor that is reorganized must comply with all environmental regulations going forward in the same way as any other person. To quote the colourful analogy of two American scholars, "Debtors in bankruptcy have — and should have — no greater license to pollute in violation of a statute than they have to sell cocaine in violation of a statute" (D. G. Baird and T. H. Jackson, "Comment: *Kovacs* and Toxic Wastes in Bankruptcy" (1984), 36 *Stan. L. Rev.* 1199, at p. 1200). Furthermore, corporations may engage in activities that carry risks. No matter what risks are at issue, reorganization made necessary by insolvency is hardly ever a deliberate choice. When the risks materialize, the dire costs are borne by almost all stakeholders. To subject orders to the claims process is not to invite corporations to restructure in order to rid themselves of their environmental liabilities.

And the power to determine whether an order is a provable claim does not mean that the court will necessarily conclude that the order before it will be subject to the *CCAA* process. In fact, the *CCAA* court in the case at bar recognized that orders relating to the environment may or may not be considered provable claims. It stayed only those orders that were monetary in nature.

Application

I now turn to the application of the principles discussed above to the case at bar. This case does not turn on whether the Province is the creditor of an obligation or whether damage had occurred as of the relevant date. Those requirements are easily satisfied, since the Province had identified itself as a creditor by resorting to *EPA* enforcement mechanisms and since the damage had occurred before the time of the *CCAA* proceedings. Rather, the issue centres on the third requirement: that the orders meet the criterion for admission as a pecuniary claim. The claim was contingent to the extent that the Province had not yet formally exercised its power to ask for the payment of money. The question is whether it was sufficiently certain that the orders would eventually result in a monetary claim. To the *CCAA* judge, there was no doubt that the answer was yes.

The Province's exercise of its legislative powers in enacting the *Abitibi Act* created a unique set of facts that led to the orders being issued. The seizure of Abitibi's assets by the Province, the cancellation of all outstanding water and hydroelectric contracts between Abitibi and the Province, the cancellation of pending legal proceedings by Abitibi in which it sought the reimbursement of several hundreds of thousands of dollars, and the denial of any compensation for the seized assets and of legal redress are inescapable background facts in the judge's review of the *EPA* Orders.

The *CCAA* judge did not elaborate on whether it was sufficiently certain that the Minister would perform the remediation work and therefore make a monetary claim. However, most of his findings clearly rest on a positive answer to this question. For example, his finding that "[i]n all likelihood, the pith and substance of the EPA Orders is an attempt by the Province to lay the groundwork for monetary claims against Abitibi, to be used most probably as an offset in connection with Abitibi's own NAFTA claims for compensation" (para. 178), is necessarily based on the premise that the Province would most likely perform the remediation work. Indeed, since monetary claims must, both at common law and in civil law, be mutual for set-off or compensation to operate, the Province had to have incurred costs in doing the work in order to have a claim that could be set off against Abitibi's claims.

That the judge relied on an implicit finding that the Province would most likely perform the work and make a claim to offset its costs is also shown by the confirmation he found in the declaration by the Minister that the Province was attempting to assess the cost of doing remediation work Abitibi had allegedly left undone and that in the Province's assessment, "at this point in time, there would not be a net payment to Abitibi".

The *CCAA* judge's reasons not only rest on an implicit finding that the Province would most likely perform the work, but refer explicitly to facts that support this finding. To reach his conclusion that the *EPA* Orders were monetary in nature, the *CCAA* judge relied on the fact that Abitibi's operations were funded through debtor-in-possession financing and its access to funds was limited to ongoing operations. Given that the *EPA* Orders targeted sites that were, for the most part, no longer in Abitibi's possession, this meant that Abitibi had no means to perform the remediation work during the reorganization process.

In addition, because Abitibi lacked funds and no longer controlled the properties, the timetable set by the Province in the *EPA* Orders suggested that the Province never truly intended that Abitibi was to perform the remediation work required by the orders. The timetable was also unrealistic. For example, the orders were issued on November 12, 2009 and set a deadline of January 15, 2010 to perform a particular act, but the evidence revealed that compliance with this requirement would have taken close to a year.

Furthermore, the judge relied on the fact that Abitibi was not simply designated a "person responsible" under the *EPA*, but was intentionally targeted by the Province. The finding that the Province had targeted Abitibi was drawn not only from the timing of the *EPA* Orders, but also from the fact that Abitibi was the only person designated in them, whereas others also appeared to be responsible — in some cases, primarily responsible — for the contamination. For example, Abitibi was ordered to do remediation work on a site it had surrendered more than 50 years before the orders were issued; the expert report upon which the orders were based made no distinction between Abitibi's activities on the property, on which its source of power had been horse power, and subsequent activities by others who had used fuel-powered vehicles there. In the judge's opinion, this finding of fact went to the Province's intent to establish a basis for performing the work itself and asserting a claim against Abitibi.

These reasons — and others — led the *CCAA* judge to conclude that the Province had not expected Abitibi to perform the remediation work and that the "intended, practical and realistic effect of the EPA Orders was to establish a basis for the Province to recover amounts of money to be eventually used for the remediation of the properties in question". He found that the Province appeared to have in fact taken some steps to liquidate the claims arising out of the *EPA* Orders [...]. In sum, although the analytical framework used by Gascon J. was driven by the facts of the case, he reviewed all the legal principles and facts that needed to be considered in order to make the determination in the case at bar. He did at times rely on indicators that are unique and that do not appear in the analytical framework I propose above, but he did so because of the exceptional facts of this case. Yet, had he formulated the question in the same way as I have, his conclusion, based on his objective findings of fact, would have been the same. Earmarking money may be a strong indicator that a province will perform remediation work, and actually commencing the work is the first step towards the creation of a debt, but these are not the only considerations that can lead to a finding that a creditor has a monetary claim. The *CCAA* judge's assessment of the facts, particularly his finding that the *EPA* Orders were the first step towards performance of the remediation work by the Province, leads to no conclusion other than that it was sufficiently certain that the Province would perform remediation work and therefore fall within the definition of a creditor with a monetary claim.

Conclusion

In sum, I agree with the Chief Justice that, as a general proposition, an environmental order issued by a regulatory body can be treated as a contingent claim, and that such a claim can be included in the claims process if it is sufficiently certain that the regulatory body will make a monetary claim against the debtor. Our difference of views lies mainly in the applicable threshold for including contingent claims and in our understanding of the *CCAA* judge's findings of fact.

With respect to the law, the Chief Justice would craft a standard specific to the context of environmental orders by requiring a "likelihood approaching certainty" that the regulatory body will perform the remediation work. She finds that this threshold is justified because "remediation may cost a great deal of money". I acknowledge that remediating pollution is often costly, but I am of the view that Parliament has borne this consideration in mind in enacting provisions specific to environmental claims. Moreover, I recall that in this case, the Premier announced that the remediation work would be performed at no net cost to the Province. It was clear to him that the *Abitibi Act* would make it possible to offset all the related costs.

Thus, I prefer to take the approach generally taken for all contingent claims. In my view, the *CCAA* court is entitled to take all relevant facts into consideration in making the relevant determination. Under this approach, the contingency to be assessed in a case such as this is whether it is sufficiently certain that the regulatory body will perform remediation work and be in a position to assert a monetary claim.

Finally, the Chief Justice would review the *CCAA* court's findings of fact. I would instead defer to them. On those findings, applying any legal standard, be it the one proposed by the Chief Justice or the one I propose, the Province's claim is monetary in nature and its motion for a declaration exempting the *EPA* Orders from the claims procedure order was properly dismissed.

THE CHIEF JUSTICE: —

Overview

The issue in this case is whether orders made under the Environmental Protection Act, S.N.L. 2002, c. E-14.2 ("*EPA*") by the Newfoundland and Labrador Minister of Environment and Conservation (the "Minister") requiring a polluter to clean up sites (the "*EPA* Orders") are monetary claims that can be compromised in corporate restructuring under the *Companies' Creditors Arrangement Act*, R.S.C. 1985, c. C-36 ("*CCAA*"). If they are not claims that can be compromised in restructuring, the Abitibi respondents ("Abitibi") will still have a legal obligation to clean up the sites following their emergence from restructuring. If they are such claims, Abitibi will have emerged from restructuring free of the obligation, able to recommence business without remediating the properties it polluted, the cost of which will fall on the Newfoundland and Labrador public.

Remediation orders made under a province's environmental protection legislation impose ongoing regulatory obligations on the corporation required to clean up the pollution. They are not monetary claims. In narrow circumstances, specified by the *CCAA*, these ongoing regulatory obligations may be reduced to monetary claims, which can be compromised under *CCAA* proceedings. This occurs where a province has done the work, or where it is "sufficiently certain" that it will do the work. In these circumstances, the regulatory obligation would be extinguished and the province would have a monetary claim for the cost of remediation in the *CCAA* proceedings. Otherwise, the regulatory obligation survives the restructuring.

In my view, the orders for remediation in this case, with a minor exception, are not claims that can be compromised in restructuring. On one of the properties, the Minister did emergency remedial work and put other work out to tender. These costs can be claimed in the *CCAA* proceedings. However, with respect to the other properties, on the evidence before us, the Minister has neither done the clean-up work, nor is it sufficiently certain that he or she will do so. The Province of Newfoundland and Labrador (the "Province") retained a number of options, including requiring Abitibi to perform the remediation if it successfully emerged from the *CCAA* restructuring.

I would therefore allow the appeal and grant the Province the declaration it seeks that Abitibi is still subject to its obligations under the *EPA* following its emergence from restructuring, except for work done or tendered for on the Buchans site.

The Proceedings Below

The *CCAA* judge took the view that the Province issued the *EPA* Orders, not in order to make Abitibi remediate, but as part of a money grab. He therefore concluded that the orders were monetary and financial in nature and should be considered claims that could be compromised under the *CCAA* (2010 QCCS 1261, 68 C.B.R. (5th) 1). The Quebec Court of Appeal denied leave to appeal on the ground that this "factual" conclusion could not be disturbed (2010 QCCA 965, 68 C.B.R. (5th) 57).

The *CCAA* judge's stark view that an *EPA* obligation can be considered a monetary claim capable of being compromised simply because (as he saw it) the Province's motive was money, is no longer pressed. Whether an *EPA* order is a claim under the *CCAA* depends on whether it meets the requirements for a claim under that statute. That is the only issue to be resolved. Insofar as this determination touches on the division of powers, I am in substantial agreement with my colleague Deschamps J.

The Distinction Between Regulatory Obligations and Claims under the CCAA

Orders to clean up polluted property under provincial environmental protection legislation are regulatory orders. They remain in effect until the property has been cleaned up or the matter otherwise resolved. It is not unusual for corporations seeking to restructure under the *CCAA* to be subject to a variety of ongoing regulatory orders arising from statutory schemes governing matters like employment, energy conservation and the environment.

The corporation remains subject to these obligations as it continues to carry on business during the restructuring period, and remains subject to them when it emerges from restructuring unless they have been compromised or liquidated. The *CCAA*, like the Bankruptcy and Insolvency Act, R.S.C. 1985, c. B-3 ("*BIA*") draws a fundamental distinction between ongoing regulatory obligations owed to the public, which generally survive the restructuring, and monetary claims that can be compromised. This distinction is also recognized in the jurisprudence, which has held that regulatory duties owed to the public are not "claims" under the *BIA*, nor, by extension, under the *CCAA*. The distinction between regulatory obligations under the general law aimed at the protection of the public and monetary claims that can be compromised in *CCAA* restructuring or bankruptcy is a fundamental plank of Canadian corporate law.

When Does a Regulatory Obligation Become a Claim under the CCAA?

This brings us to the heart of the question before us: when does a regulatory obligation imposed on a corporation under environmental protection legislation become a "claim" provable and compromisable under the *CCAA*?

Regulatory obligations are, as a general proposition, not compromisable claims. Only financial or monetary claims provable by a "creditor" fall within the definition of "claim" under the *CCAA*. "Creditor" is defined as "a person having a claim [...]" (*BIA* s. 2). Thus, the identification of a "creditor" hangs on the existence of a "claim". Section 12(1) of the *CCAA* defines "claim" as "any indebtedness, liability or obligation [...] that [...] would be a debt provable in bankruptcy", which is accepted as confined to obligations of a financial or monetary nature.

The *CCAA* does not depart from the proposition that a claim must be financial or monetary. However, it contains a scheme to deal with disputes over whether an obligation is a monetary obligation as opposed to some other kind of obligation.

Such a dispute may arise with respect to environmental obligations of the corporation. The *CCAA* recognizes three situations that may arise when a corporation enters restructuring. The first situation is where the remedial work has not been done (and there is no "sufficient certainty" that the work will be done, unlike the third situation described below). In this situation, the government cannot claim the cost of remediation: see s. 102(3) of the *EPA*. The obligation of compliance falls in principle on the monitor who takes over the corporation's assets and operations. If the monitor remediates the property, he can claim the costs as costs of administration. If he does not wish to do so, he may obtain a court order staying the remediation obligation or abandon the property: s. 11.8(5) *CCAA* (in which case costs of remediation shall not rank as costs of administration: s. 11.8(7)). In this situation, the obligation cannot be compromised.

The second situation is where the government that has issued the environmental protection order moves to clean up the pollution, as the legislation entitles it to do. In this situation, the government has a claim for the cost of remediation that is compromisable in the *CCAA* proceedings. This is because the government, by moving to clean up the pollution, has changed the outstanding regulatory obligation owed to the public into a financial or monetary obligation owed by the corporation to the government. Section 11.8(9), already discussed, makes it clear that this applies to damage after the *CCAA* proceedings commenced, which might otherwise not be claimable as a matter of timing.

A third situation may arise: the government has not yet performed the remediation at the time of restructuring, but there is "sufficient certainty" that it will do so. This situation is regulated by the provisions of the *CCAA* for contingent or future claims. Under the *CCAA*, a debt or liability that is contingent on a future event may be compromised.

It is clear that a mere possibility that work will be done does not suffice to make a regulatory obligation a contingent claim under the *CCAA*. Rather, there must be "sufficient certainty" that the obligation will be converted into a financial or monetary claim to permit this. The impact of the obligation on the insolvency process is irrelevant to the analysis of contingency. The future liabilities must not be "so remote and speculative in nature that they could not properly be considered contingent claims": *Confederation Treasury Services Ltd. (Bankrupt) Re* (1997), 96 O.A.C. 75 (para. 4).

Where environmental obligations are concerned, courts to date have relied on a high degree of probability verging on certainty that the government will in fact step in and remediate the property. In *Anvil Range Mining Corp., Re* (2001), 25 C.B.R. (4th) 1 (Ont. S.C.J.), Farley J. concluded that a contingent claim was established where the money had already been earmarked in the budget for the remediation project. He observed that "there appears to be *every likelihood to a certainty* that every dollar in the budget for the year ending March 31, 2002 earmarked for reclamation will be spent" (para. 15 (emphasis added)). Similarly, in *Shirley (Re)*, Kennedy J. relied on the fact that the Ontario Minister of Environment had already entered the property at issue and commenced remediation activities to conclude that "[a]ny doubt about the resolve of the MOE's intent to realize upon its authority ended when it began to incur expense from operations".

There is good reason why "sufficient certainty" should be interpreted as requiring "likelihood approaching certainty" when the issue is whether ongoing environmental obligations owed to the public should be converted to contingent claims that can be expunged or compromised in the restructuring process. Courts should not overlook the obstacles governments may encounter in deciding to remediate environmental damage a corporation has caused. To begin with, the government's decision is discretionary and may be influenced by any number of competing political and social considerations. Furthermore, remediation may cost a great deal of money. For example, in this case, the *CCAA* court found that at a minimum the remediation would cost in the "mid-to-high eight figures" (at para. 81), and could indeed cost several times that. In concrete terms, the remediation at issue in this case may be expected to meet or exceed the entire budget of the Minister ($65 million) for 2009. Not only would this be a massive expenditure, but it would also likely require the specific approval of the Legislature and thereby be subject to political uncertainties. To assess these factors and determine whether all this will occur would embroil the *CCAA* judge in social, economic and political considerations — matters which are not normally subject to judicial consideration: *R. v. Imperial Tobacco Canada Ltd.*, 2011 SCC 42, [2011] 3 S.C.R. 45, at para. 74. It is small wonder, then, that courts assessing whether it is "sufficiently certain" that a government will clean up pollution created by a corporation have insisted on proof of likelihood approaching certainty.

In this case, as will be seen, apart from the Buchans property, the record is devoid of any evidence capable of establishing that it is "sufficiently certain" that the Province will itself remediate the properties. Even on a more relaxed standard than the one adopted in similar cases to date, the evidence in this case would fail to establish that remediation is "sufficiently certain".

The Result in This Case

I would allow the appeal and issue a declaration that Abitibi's remediation obligations under the *EPA* Orders do not constitute claims compromisable under the *CCAA*, except for work done or tendered for on the Buchans site.

LeBEL J.: — I have read the reasons of the Chief Justice and Deschamps J. They agree that a court overseeing a proposed arrangement under the *Companies' Creditors Arrangement Act*, R.S.C. 1985, c. C-36 ("*CCAA*"), cannot relieve debtors of their regulatory obligations. The only regulatory orders that can be subject to compromise are those which are monetary in nature. My colleagues also accept that contingent environmental claims can be liquidated and compromised if it is established that the regulatory body would remediate the environmental contamination itself, and hence turn the regulatory order into a monetary claim.

At this point, my colleagues disagree on the proper evidentiary test with respect to whether the government would remediate the contamination. In the Chief Justice's opinion, the evidence must show that there is a "likelihood approaching certainty" that the province would remediate the contamination itself (para. 22). In my respectful opinion, this is not the established test for determining where and how a contingent claim can be liquidated in bankruptcy and insolvency law. The test of "sufficient certainty" described by Deschamps J., which does not look very different from the general civil standard of probability, better reflects how both the common law and the civil law view and deal with contingent claims. On the basis of the test Deschamps J. proposes, I must agree with the Chief Justice and would allow the appeal.

First, no matter how I read the *CCAA* court's judgment (2010 QCCS 1261, 68 C.B.R. (5th) 1), I find no support for a conclusion that it is consistent with the principle that the *CCAA* does not apply to purely regulatory obligations, or that the court had evidence that would satisfy the test of "sufficient certainty" that the province of Newfoundland and Labrador (the "Province") would perform the remedial work itself.

In my view, the *CCAA* court was concerned that the arrangement would fail if the Abitibi respondents ("Abitibi") were not released from their regulatory obligations in respect of pollution. The *CCAA* court wanted to eliminate the uncertainty that would have clouded the reorganized corporations' future. Moreover, its decision appears to have been driven by an opinion that the Province had acted in bad faith in its dealings with Abitibi both during and after the termination of its operations in the Province. I agree with the Chief Justice that there is no evidence that the Province intends to perform the remedial work itself. In the absence of any other evidence, an off-hand comment made in the legislature by a member of the government hardly satisfies the "sufficient certainty" test. Even if the evidentiary test proposed by my colleague Deschamps J. is applied, this Court can legitimately disregard the *CCAA* court's finding as the Chief Justice proposes, since it did not rest on a sufficient factual foundation. For these reasons, I would concur with the disposition proposed by the Chief Justice.

Notes and Questions

1. In this case, the difference between the judgment of the majority (*per* Deschamps J.) and that of the Chief Justice is described by LeBel J. as turning on the "proper evidentiary test with respect to whether the government would remediate the contamination". What is the legal significance of this factual issue? Do you agree with LeBel J. that this is the main difference between the judgments of the Chief Justice and Deschamps J.?

2. Both the Chief Justice and Deschamps J. make reference to policy considerations in the course of their respective reasons. For the Chief Justice, a central concern is ensuring the polluter and not the public-at-large ends up paying to clean up the on-site pollution. For Deschamps J., other policy considerations are given prominence. What are the policy considerations that drive Deschamps J.'s decision?

3. Should provincial environmental remediation claims made by government, whether monetary or non-monetary, be exempt from compromise under federal bankruptcy and insolvency laws? Why or why not? In the present case, the SCC decided it was largely unnecessary to delve into the division of powers issue lurking in this area. These division of powers issues have returned in a closely watched Alberta case heard by the SCC in early 2018 and decided in January 2019: *Orphan Well Assn. v. Grant Thornton Ltd.*, 2017 ABCA 124, reversed 2019 SCC 5. The Court of Appeal had approved an approach which would have allowed trustees in bankruptcy to disclaim abandoned wells while selling productive ones, returning the proceeds to creditors. This approach left considerable uncertainty about how and if the remediation of abandoned wells would be funded. In a split decision, the SCC allowed the appeal. Writing for majority, the Chief Justice held that there was no conflict between applicable federal and provincial legislation, and that the Alberta Energy Regulator's orders were not a claim provable in bankruptcy applying the *Abitibi* test. Writing in dissent, Côté J. concluded that the federal bankruptcy law was paramount and inconsistent with the provincial power to order remediation and that, in any event, the orders in question were claims provable in bankruptcy applying *Abitibi*. Which judgment do you find more persuasive and why? How does *Orphan Well* change, if at all, the applicable law as set out in *Abitibi*?

Part IV — Citizen Enforcement

Some would argue that vesting in governments an exclusive monopoly over environmental law enforcement is short-sighted and doomed to fail. As we have seen, there are a variety of reasons why governments may elect not to pursue a rigorous enforcement policy. These can range from budgetary constraints (costs and availability of prosecutorial resources) and political factors (including "protecting jobs", maintaining a positive investment climate, and avoiding intergovernmental conflict) to legal considerations (including the apparent strength of the case and likelihood of conviction). Historically, the notion that the Crown, and in particular the office of the Attorney General, should have broad discretion to make enforcement decisions has rested on a variety of rationales (as described by Ferguson's article below). Perhaps paramount among these is the idea that the Attorney General is in the best position to assess whether the "public interest" will be served by mounting a prosecution.

Critics argue, however, there are many "public interests" and that both democracy and the rule of law are well served by promoting more competition in the business of law enforcement: see, for example, K. Roach & M. Trebilcock, "Private Enforcement of Competition Laws" (1996) 34 Osgoode Hall L.J. 461. It is largely on this basis that the US Congress has incorporated "citizen suit" provisions in many federal environmental statutes. These provisions provide citizens with standing to bring enforcement actions as a "private attorney-general". Where such actions succeed, the citizen is rewarded by a requirement that they be indemnified for the costs of the action.

Canadian legislators have been extremely reluctant to follow the US lead by enacting analogous provisions. For example, unlike its US federal counterpart, the Canadian *Species at Risk Act* has no citizen provisions, despite concerted lobbying efforts by environmental organizations to have them included in the legislation (see further discussion in Chapter 9). And while some Canadian laws have environmental rights provisions (CEPA, the Ontario *Environmental Bill of Rights* and analogous provisions in Yukon and NWT legislation) that allow citizens to trigger investigations into environmental wrongdoing, and in some instances commence suit for environmental damages, to date these laws have been extremely circumscribed in both scope and application.

To remedy this, environmental groups have recently drafted a Canadian Environmental Bill of Rights, which would substantially enhance the role of citizens in environmental law enforcement. Until such a statute is enacted, however, the principal means for citizens to prosecute environmental offences remains the private prosecution. In some Canadian jurisdictions (most notably Ontario), this vehicle has proven in recent years to have significant value. Elsewhere, however, most notably in BC and Alberta, government policies have effectively precluded citizens from having access to this important enforcement tool.

In this Part, we provide a brief overview of the state of the law with respect to citizen environmental rights in Canada and emerging law reform proposals, along with a snapshot of parallel US provisions. We then turn to a more detailed exploration of the current status and future prospects of the private prosecution as an environmental law enforcement tool.

Citizen Suits and Environmental Bills of Rights

South of the border, there has been a long tradition of rights-based approaches to environmental protection. Many states have enacted Environmental Bills of Rights (EBRs) explicitly designed to allow citizens to litigate environmental protection issues. An early illustration is the Michigan EBR discussed in the preceding chapter: see M'Gonigle, *et al.*, in Chapter 4. These laws have provided the inspiration for a variety of successors including the proposed new Canadian Environmental Bill of Rights that we shall examine shortly. Of even greater systemic importance in terms of environmental law enforcement in the United States, however, has been the prevalence, particularly at the federal level, of the citizen suit. This article discusses the rise and role of citizen suit-based law enforcement in the United States, contrasting this with the approach that has prevailed in the area in Canada.

**Chris Tollefson, Jerry DeMarco & Darlene Gilliland,
"Towards a Costs Jurisprudence in Public Interest Litigation"**

(2004) 83 Can. Bar Rev. 473

Recognition of the benefits associated with encouraging private litigants to enforce public rights has been a central feature of the American legal tradition since at least the New Deal era. Over sixty years ago, Judge Jerome Frank is said to have coined the term "private Attorney General" to describe the mantle taken on by citizens who are statutorily empowered to initiate enforcement action. The private attorney general mechanism has emerged, over the last quarter century, as a primary instrument for securing compliance with federal law. It plays a key role in a variety of important U.S. laws including: all (but one) of the major anti-pollution laws enacted by Congress since 1970; virtually all modern civil rights statutes; most anti-trust and securities laws; and in the *Equal Access to Justice Act* (which governs non-tort suits brought against federal government departments and agencies if there is no other "fee shifting" statute applicable).

Private attorney general provisions allow citizens and public interest groups to commence enforcement actions against any person alleged to be in violation of one or more specified provisions of a designated statute or regulation or to sue governments alleged to have failed to perform nondiscretionary duties. Where such enforcement proceedings culminate in judgment for the plaintiff or otherwise prevail as reflected in a negotiated settlement of the action, courts are empowered to order that the defendant(s) reimburse the citizen attorney-general for their litigation costs including "reasonable" attorney fees. If a public interest attorney with conduct of the matter has been acting *pro bono*, courts have held that they should be compensated at the rate their services would have been billed in a private law firm.

A key design feature of the private attorney-general model is its adoption of a one-way costs rule (also known as fee-shifting) [...] this represents a fundamental departure from the common law-based, no-way American costs rule that ordinarily governs judicial costs allocation. In its place is substituted a regime under which a private attorney-general pursues enforcement actions on the expectation of being rewarded if they succeed, without risk of costs liability if they do not.

In the environmental law context, these so-called "citizen suits" have been hailed as "a defining theme of the modern environmental era". According to one commentator, the existence of environmental citizen suits has "brought competition, with its attendant virtues, to the business of environmental enforcement". As a result, the robustness and quality of environmental law enforcement has been significantly enhanced. The spectre of private enforcement has reportedly had a salutary effect in terms of governmental accountability for prosecutorial policy and compliance with environmental regulations by public and private bodies. It has also been credited with promoting broader democratic values including facilitating citizen involvement in environmental policy making, influencing judicial interpretation of key environmental provisions, and enhancing the legitimacy of environmental laws and law-making processes.

Not all commentators are as unequivocally supportive of private attorney general suits as a policy instrument. Some argue, for instance, that state enforcement is more efficient and that private enforcement can disrupt or conflict with state compliance strategies. However, [...] Roach and Trebilcock conclude that, on balance, the benefits of the American private attorney general model outweigh its drawbacks. In their view, many of the putative disadvantages identified with the model can be largely addressed or mitigated through design measures [...]

Although from time to time there have been legislative initiatives [mounted in the US] aimed at curtailing or eliminating the citizen suits and private attorney general provisions, these have almost invariably failed. In part, this result may in part be attributable to the fact that such provisions have a strong appeal to a variety of political constituencies:

> Liberals promote the private attorney general, in part, as an antidote to what they view as a conservative administration's reluctance to aggressively enforce various regulatory laws. Conservatives find virtue in the private attorney general concept because of its function in 'privatizing' law enforcement pursuant to the ideals of economic efficiency.

[**Ed. Note:** The authors then go on to examine the Canadian approach to citizen enforcement, which departs markedly from the American experience.]

Canadian governments [...] have also been relatively timid in pursuing legislative reforms [that support citizen environmental law enforcement] [...] To date, no Canadian laws contain "private attorney-general" or "citizen-suit" provisions modeled on those prevalent in American law. Federally, while the *Canadian Environmental Protection Act* contemplates the right of a citizen to commence an environmental protection action, due to the limited and constrained nature of this right it has never been used. Likewise, while in some provincial jurisdictions similar statutory causes of action exist, these provisions have been used only rarely. The same is true with respect to private prosecutions of environmental laws despite the existence, in some jurisdictions, of provisions allowing courts to award legal fees to successful citizen-prosecutors.

In Ontario, for example, under the *Environmental Bill of Rights, 1993* S.O.1993, c. 28 citizens are given statutory standing to enforce environmental laws under two distinct procedures. Section 84 gives a private citizen the right to commence an action to protect a public resource in Ontario from harm caused by a violation of environmental legislation. This provision, however, has only been used twice in the past ten years. One of those actions is still at the discovery stage, and the other was dismissed without costs when the plaintiffs discontinued their action. Likewise, section 103 gives an individual the right to bring an action on the basis of having suffered individual harm caused by a public nuisance. Only six actions have been brought under section 103; most of these have been class actions that have not made it past the certification stage [...] In assessing costs with respect to actions brought under either of these provisions, courts are given discretion to consider "any special circumstance", including whether or not a case is a test case or raises a novel point of law: see s. 100 of the *EBR*. Similar citizen suit provisions with analogous costs provisions are also in place in the Northwest Territories (*Environmental Rights Act*, R.S.N.W.T. 1988 c. 83 (Supp.), s. 5) and the Yukon (*Environment Act*, S.Y. 1991, c. 5, s. 1). To date, however, neither of the provisions has been utilized.

The paucity of citizen-led private prosecutions is likely the result of a cluster of factors. Private prosecutors in Canada must establish guilt beyond reasonable doubt whereas American citizen suits are governed by a civil standard of proof. Private prosecutions frequently also impose much more daunting legal and scientific challenges than do citizen suits, in part due to the differing burden of proof and the strictness with which American courts have interpreted many of the obligations citizen suits exist to enforce. Finally, in several provinces, the potential to pursue private prosecutions has effectively been nullified by the government policies that oblige the Attorney General, as a matter of course, to assume conduct of all such cases; a practice that almost invariably culminates in the prosecution being stayed.

Notes and Questions

1. What accounts for the differing national approaches to citizen law enforcement in Canada and the United States? As the above article notes, these differences prevail across a wide range of areas of legal regulation. To what extent is resistance to the notion of citizen enforcement more generally related to notions about citizen participation?

2. Recently, as part of a broader advocacy campaign, environmental organizations have drafted a model federal citizen rights-based EBR for consideration by Parliament: see *An Act to Establish a Canadian Environmental Bill of Rights*. This legislation was tabled in the House of Commons in 2009 by Linda Duncan, MP, as a Private Member's Bill C-469. Its stated purpose (section 6) is to:

   (a) safeguard the rights of present and future Canadians to a healthy and ecologically balanced environment;

   (b) confirm the Government of Canada's public trust duty to protect the environment under its jurisdiction; and

   (c) ensure all Canadians have access to:
      i.   adequate environmental information;
      ii. justice in an environmental context; and
      iii. effective mechanisms for participating in environmental decision-making.

Under the proposed law, the EBR "must be interpreted consistently with existing and emerging principles of environmental law", including the precautionary principle, the polluters principle, and the principles of sustainable development and intergenerational equity (section 3). A key feature is statutory recognition that "every Canadian has a right to a healthy and ecologically balanced environment" and that the Government of Canada is legally obligated to protect this right (section 9). The Government of Canada is also declared to be the "trustee of Canada's environment" and is obliged to "conserve it in accordance with the public trust for the benefit of present and future generations (subsection 9(3)).

The model bill incorporates a variety of substantive and procedural citizen rights to promote compliance with its requirements. These include the right to sue the federal Crown for failing to enforce the public trust or violating the right to a "healthy and ecologically balanced environment". It also creates a right to sue private parties where, due to a past or impending violation of federal law, "significant environmental harm" has or is likely to result: see generally section 23. And it broadens the ambit of judicial review of environmental decision-making by eliminating standing and other constraints on the review of governmental decisions that "arise in the context of environmental protection" (section 22).

It also proposes to enshrine a variety of procedural citizen rights, including the right to seek Ministerial review of any current federal law, regulation or policy (section 13); the right to trigger an investigation of violations of federal law or regulations (sections 14-15); the right to access environmental information (section 10); the right to participate in environmental decision-making (sections 11-12); and the right to be protected from federal employer reprisals (also known as whistleblower protection) where the employee has exercised rights protected by the model bill (section 25).

3. Are there any citizen rights that this model bill has omitted? We discuss the concept of the public trust elsewhere in the context of our chapters on the common law (Chapter 2) and parks and protected areas (Chapter 8). To what extent do the provisions in this model bill build on existing common law and statutory public trust concepts? For an extensive overview of the state of environmental rights worldwide, see D.R. Boyd, *The Environmental Rights Revolution* (UBC Press, 2012). Professor Boyd has also written a companion book that makes the case for constitutional recognition of environmental rights (and responsibilities) in Canada: *The Right to a Healthy Environment* (UBC Press, 2012).

Private Prosecutions

While the jurisprudence and debate surrounding EBRs remain very much in their infancy, private prosecutions are another matter. Here, the legal tool is ancient in origin, and one that in many jurisdictions has been constrained by both governmental policy and judicial precedent. In this section, we provide a critical account of the history and competing rationales relating to the role of private prosecutions in the environmental context, followed by excerpts from *Kostuch v. Alberta*, one of the leading appellate decisions in this area of the law.

Keith Ferguson,
"Challenging the Intervention and Stay of an
Environmental Private Prosecution"
(2004) 13 J. Envtl. L. & Prac. 153

Starting around the thirteenth century in England, private prosecutions played a prominent role in the enforcement of public wrongs. In fact "it was not only the privilege but the duty of the private citizen to preserve the King's Peace and bring offenders to justice". When English law came to Canada, similar rights to conduct private prosecutions came with it. Such rights and duties began to change, however, in the nineteenth century in response to the profound societal shifts resulting from the industrial revolution. A centralized bureaucracy was gradually formed to administer and enforce a broad new range of social regulation. Thus the dominance of the private prosecution began to wane, and there has been an ongoing "process of gradual and incremental erosion of private prosecutorial authority". Indeed, in recent years assessments have been undertaken to determine whether private prosecutions should be kept at all.

Although there are significant practical difficulties in bringing a private prosecution, especially in a technical arena such as environmental law enforcement, private prosecutions retain important roles to play. These include:

- Providing a cure to the "working entente" that "too often" evolves between "an over-worked bureaucracy" and "the persons subject to their regulation"

- Providing an "important safeguard in our society against real or perceived corruption in Crown prosecution decisions"

- Avoiding laws being rendered "nugatory" or becoming "paper tigers" due to government non-enforcement

- Providing reassurance to those who do comply with the law that their competitors will not benefit by non-compliance

- Providing "an important civil liberty" in a participatory democracy.

Despite these benefits, once a private prosecution has been brought, the Attorney General's office will often intervene and stay the prosecution. Indeed, in some provinces there is a policy to always intervene, such as in Alberta where, according to Duncan (in discussing environmental private prosecutions), it "has been the experience of private informants that regardless of the legal basis for their case or the strength of the evidence collected on their own accord, the Crown has intervened to stay the proceedings". In addition to being highly frustrating for a private prosecutor, this can raise suspicions that partisan politics have improperly interfered with the workings of law enforcement. Although the private prosecutor may attempt to seek judicial review of such an intervention and stay, courts have given the Attorney General's office a very high degree of deference, resulting in such attempts being "spectacularly unsuccessful".

[A key] rationale for the limited review of prosecutorial discretion is protection of the public interest and the accused. As noted by the Alberta Court of Appeal in *Kostuch* (1995) (in upholding the stay of a private prosecution):

> The criminal process is not the preserve of the private individual. The fundamental consideration in any decision regarding prosecutions must be the public interest [...]. In deciding whether to prosecute, the Attorney General must have regard not only to the interest of the person laying the charges, but also to the rights of the person charged with an offence, and to the public interest [...]. He or she is answerable to the Legislature and finally to the electorate, for decisions made. [see case excerpt below]

Avoiding frivolous, malicious or hopeless private prosecutions is an important part of the rationale for the Attorney General to be able to intervene and stay private prosecutions.

However, the public interest requires a balance be struck between avoiding the legal system being used for improper purposes by private prosecutors (such as "for personal gratification, private gain or malice"), termed "*zealousness error*" by Thompson, and avoiding under enforcement, termed "*leniency error*". (emphasis added). Judicial hesitancy to review a Crown counsel decision to stay a private prosecution certainly recognizes the important function of the Attorney General's office to oversee private prosecutions in order to avoid zealousness error, but appears to give little weight to the equally compelling public interest in avoiding leniency error.

Avoiding zealousness error is of course important, but this need not entail a blanket high standard of review that results in acceptance of unreasonable and even patently unreasonable decisions of the Attorney General to stay private prosecutions (and thus increasing leniency error). Given the time and expense to bring a private prosecution and the need to convince a judge or designated justice to first issue process or to give a written order for an indictment, the scale of zealousness error should first be questioned. If Crown counsel believes a private prosecution has been brought for improper motives, there should be little difficulty for them to provide a reasonable justification for their intervention and stay. If zealousness error remains a problem, punitive costs awards would appear the obvious solution.

Another important public interest factor is the democratic value of private prosecutions. In the U.S., for example, citizens have been given the right to enforce environmental laws through statutory citizen suits. Thompson suggests that:

> If citizen suits were not permitted, individual members of society would be placed in a position subservient to government enforcement officials, undermining the horizontal power structure of particular value to an effective democracy.

Such subservience well describes the current situation in Canada. Although courts have occasionally noted the important citizenship right to bring a private prosecution, they have ruled, for example, that the stay of a private prosecution does not generally violate *Charter* rights, and even if it did it would be saved by s. 1 (*i.e.* it would be "demonstrably justified in a free and democratic society") due to the added objectivity Crown counsel can bring. However, it makes little sense to allow unreasonable or patently unreasonable stays of private prosecutions if enhanced objectivity and democracy is part of the rationale. As Tingle put it:

> "The courts have simply not allowed the field of prosecutorial discretion to be 'democratised'."

Allowing such democratic citizenship rights to be frustrated can have adverse consequences against the public interest. As noted by the Law Reform Commission for Canada, "individuals, frustrated by the law, may seek to accommodate themselves by unlawful means", and "the form of retribution which is exacted by the citizen's resort to legal processes is clearly preferable to other unregulated forms of citizen self-help".

Courts have countered such democratic arguments with the idea that the Attorney General is accountable to the legislature and the electorate. However, this too is fraught with difficulties. For example, as noted by Tingle:

> One defect in this argument is that most decisions of the Attorney General are virtually invisible and, while they may dramatically affect the accused, they have a negligible impact on the voting public. The obscurity and political unimportance of prosecutorial discretion makes the legislature an ineffective oversight mechanism [...] [especially] when the people who benefited from the Attorney General's exercise of his discretion are the leaders of the current government.

Kostuch v. Alberta (Attorney General)
(1995), 128 D.L.R. (4th) 440 (Alta. C.A.),
leave to appeal refused (1996), 40 Alta. L.R. (3d) xxxi (note) (S.C.C.)

[The dispute at the centre of this litigation related to construction of the Oldman River Dam, a controversy which was previously considered in another context in Chapter 3. This case arises as an appeal from the dismissal of the appellant's application for an order setting aside the entry of a stay of proceedings by the Attorney General of Alberta ("AG") with respect to a private prosecution she had filed. Kostuch alleged that the provincial Crown and others involved in the construction of the Oldman River dam were in violation of subsections 35(1) and 40(b) of the *Fisheries Act*, R.S.C. 1985, c. F-14. She claimed further that the AG's decision to intervene and stay her prosecution constituted a violation of section 7 of the *Charter*. She also submitted that the power of the court to review the exercise of prosecutorial discretion by the Attorney General was not limited to cases of flagrant impropriety.]

HETHERINGTON, MCFADYEN & RUSSELL JJ.A.: — This matter involves the construction of the Oldman River Dam by the Province of Alberta. The information in question was the last in a series of eight informations sworn by Dr. Martha Kostuch against those involved in the construction of this dam. [...] each of the informations alleged that either the Government of Alberta, its ministers, or the Crown in Right of Alberta and various construction companies breached the *Fisheries Act* by constructing and operating river diversion channels at the dam site which interfered with fish habitat, without the required authorization of the Federal Minister of Fisheries and Oceans. The first of these informations had been sworn by the appellant on August 2, 1988. The first seven informations were stayed by the Attorney General or were otherwise disposed of by the Courts for a variety of reasons, none of which have any relevance here.

Following the laying of the first information, the Attorney General intervened. On his instructions, the R.C.M.P. commenced an investigation. Inspector Duncan was responsible for this investigation. In referring the matter to the R.C.M.P., the Attorney General's department, being concerned about conflicts of interest, advised the R.C.M.P. to seek instructions regarding the investigation and prosecution from the Federal Department of Justice.

The prosecution policy established by the Attorney General of Alberta contains a two-fold test: (1) the evidence must be such that there is a reasonable likelihood of conviction when the evidence as a whole is considered; and (2) whether the public interest requires prosecution [...]

In the course of the investigation, Inspector Duncan interviewed the appellant on at least two occasions, and obtained from her a statement of facts, as well as a summary of her position on the matter. Dr. Kostuch advised Duncan that she believed that the dam construction interfered with fish habitat, that the construction had never been approved by the Minister of Fisheries, and that any delegation of administrative authority under the *Fisheries Act* to the Province of Alberta was unconstitutional. The prosecution was one of many legal avenues being pursued by the group called the Friends of the Oldman River Society in its efforts to stop the construction of the Oldman River Dam.

Following an initial investigation, Duncan concluded that while it appeared that the construction of the dam had interfered or would interfere with fish habitat, serious questions of the availability of a defence under s. 35(2) of the *Fisheries Act* also had to be addressed. [**Ed. Note:** Ultimately, agents for the AG Alberta concluded that there was no reasonable likelihood of conviction and stayed the prosecution.]

By Notice of Motion dated March 22, 1993, the appellant brought an application for an order setting aside the intervention and the stay of proceedings of the Attorney General and prohibiting the Attorney General from again intervening in the prosecution. The application was dismissed and the appellant appeals to this court.

The learned Chambers Judge reviewed the agreements between federal and provincial departments, correspondence between departments responsible for fisheries and the environment, and statements by federal ministers in correspondence with others regarding the transfer of jurisdiction to the Province of Alberta. He concluded: "From the statement contained in the letter of the Minister, one could conclude that the Minister authorized the project under s. 35(2) of the *Fisheries Act*".

The learned Chambers Judge found that the Provincial officials had carried out a complete investigation of the effect of the dam on fish habitat, and they were satisfied that adequate plans had been put in place to protect fish. Therefore no net loss of fish would result from the project. In 1977/78, the Federal Minister of Fisheries and Oceans and the Minister of the Environment confirmed their understanding that Alberta had authority to deal with matters involving fish habitat in Alberta. The Province of Alberta and the Government of Canada entered into another agreement in 1987, confirming Alberta's assumption of responsibility for enforcement of the *Fisheries Act*. Alberta did not thereafter seek permission from the Federal Minister with respect to projects located in this province. Federal officials were aware of the plans for the Oldman River Dam, the investigations by the Provincial authorities and the plans which had been put into place to protect fish and the environment, and voiced no objections to the construction of the dam. Federal Ministers of Fisheries and Oceans, had expressly declined to intervene, and the Agents of the Federal Department of Justice refused to prosecute.

The learned Chambers Judge found that the Alberta Government had acted in good faith in approving the construction of the dam. On this ground, the Crown in the Right of Alberta and the corporate defendants who acted on the authorization had a complete defence to any prosecution. These findings were supported by the evidence.

Section 7 of the Charter

The appellant claims that her rights under s. 7 of the *Charter* have been breached in that "she has not been able to have a court adjudicate on a matter of concern to her" thus causing her emotional stress.

In other words, the appellant claims that she has a right to prosecute another person, that s. 7 of the *Charter* protects that right, and that the Attorney General cannot interfere with a private prosecution without according the informant an opportunity of examining the reports on the investigation conducted, and giving her an opportunity to address those facts before an impartial person.

Section 7 of the *Charter* provides: "Everyone has the right to life, liberty and security of the person and the right not to be deprived thereof except in accordance with the principles of fundamental justice".

In *Reference re s. 94(2) of Motor Vehicle Act* the Supreme Court of Canada established a two-stage test for the application of s. 7. First, the appellant must demonstrate a deprivation of her right to life, liberty and security of the person; and secondly, she must demonstrate this deprivation occurred in a manner not consistent with principles of fundamental justice.

However broadly the right to "liberty and security of the person" in s. 7 of the *Charter* may come to be interpreted, it is my view that it will not and cannot include the unrestricted right on the part of a private prosecutor to continue a criminal prosecution in the face of an intervention by the Attorney General. The criminal process is not the preserve of the private individual. The fundamental consideration in any decision regarding prosecutions must be the public interest. The function of protecting the public interest in prosecution matters has been granted by Parliament to the Attorney General of a province, and in some cases to the Federal Minister of Justice.

In deciding whether to prosecute, the Attorney General must have regard not only to the interests of the person laying the charges, but also to the rights of the person charged with an offence, and to the public interest. By the provisions of the *Criminal Code*, the Attorney General is given a discretionary power to intervene in private prosecutions. The Attorney General of a province is a member of the Executive who is charged with responsibility for the administration of justice in the province. He or she is answerable to the Legislature and finally to the electorate, for decisions made. The courts have understandably been very hesitant to intervene in the exercise of that discretion.

The right, if any, of a private prosecutor to prosecute another person is very limited and is clearly restricted by the provisions of the *Criminal Code* to cases where the Attorney General opts not to intervene.

The Extent of the Power of Review

Assuming that the court has power to review prosecutorial discretion, that power will be exercised only in cases where there has been flagrant impropriety in the exercise of the prosecutorial discretion. This rule has been clearly established by the Courts, and we accept it as correct. In *R. v. Balderstone et al.* (1983), 8 C.C.C (3d) 532 at 539 (Man. C.A.); leave to appeal refused [1983] 2 S.C.R. v, Monnin C.J.M. stated as follows:

> The judicial and executive must not mix. These are two separate and distinct functions. The accusatorial officers lay informations or in some cases prefer indictments. Courts or the curia listen to cases brought to their attention and decide them on their merits or on meritorious preliminary matters. If a judge should attempt to review the actions or conduct of the Attorney General — barring flagrant impropriety — he could be falling into a field which is not his and interfering with the administrative and accusatorial function of the Attorney General or his officers. That a judge must not do.

[In our view] [...] flagrant impropriety can only be established by proof of misconduct bordering on corruption, violation of the law, bias against or for a particular individual or offence. The test for review of prosecutorial discretion remains that of flagrant impropriety, and is not unreasonableness as suggested by counsel for the appellant.

Flagrant Impropriety

The appellant [...] alleges improper interference in the investigation by the Federal Department of Justice. She asks this Court to infer that the Department so directed the investigation as to predetermine the result, referring to such action as an abuse of power. There is no evidence to support any such suggestion. The appellant asks that an inference of impropriety be drawn from the fact that after the submission of the initial report, the investigation changed direction and focused on issues of mitigation and due diligence. The appellant appears to suggest that the police investigation and the prosecutors' concerns must be limited to evidence supporting the charge, and the possibilities of valid defences ought not to be explored by the investigator or the prosecutors in arriving at their decision. Needless to say, this argument is rejected as completely unfounded in law and on the evidence.

The appellant also suggests that the Attorney General was guilty of flagrant impropriety in deciding to intervene in a case in which the Province had an interest, prior to the receipt of the opinion from the independent prosecutors. For reasons more fully stated in the analysis of the argument on bias, we agree with the finding of the learned Chambers Judge that the Attorney General for Alberta acted appropriately in this case.

Bias

Faced with possible allegations of conflict of interest, the Attorney General of Alberta instructed that the file be directed to the Federal Department of Justice, in the event that Department wished to exercise its discretion and take over the prosecution. He also directed that the file be referred to the Manitoba Attorney General's Department for decision. The Manitoba Attorney General's Department had authority to decide whether to prosecute or to stay proceedings. Counsel for the appellant suggests that the Alberta Attorney General should have waited for the decision of the Manitoba Attorney General's Department before deciding to intervene in the prosecution, and alternatively that the decision by the Manitoba Department is tainted because of its association with the Attorney General of Alberta.

The Attorney General of Alberta acted appropriately in referring the decision on the prosecution to experienced prosecutors from another province. There is no suggestion that those prosecutors were influenced in any manner by the Attorney General of Alberta or by his agents in this province. In fact, such a suggestion would be contrary to the clear indication by Mr. Dangerfield, as an officer of the Court, that he and another prosecutor from Manitoba had reviewed the file and formed their own opinions.

Further, the appellant does not suggest that the authorization and approval by the Alberta Fish and Wildlife officials was granted otherwise than in good faith. The appellant merely suggests that the delegation of authority to the province is unconstitutional. The overwhelming evidence presented which establishes that over a period of time commencing with the agreement in 1930, correspondence in 1977-78 and ending with the agreement in 1987, the Federal Minister of Fisheries and Oceans and the Minister of the Environment were consistent in the position that jurisdiction for enforcement of the *Fisheries Act* had been transferred to the province. It is difficult to see how one could conclude otherwise than that Alberta acted in good faith in authorizing the construction in question. Flagrant impropriety has not been established.

The appeal is dismissed.

Notes and Questions

1. While in British Columbia and Alberta the Attorney General will almost invariably intervene in, take over and often stay (*i.e.*, terminate) private prosecutions brought by citizens in environmental cases, this is not the case in other Canadian provinces. In Ontario, for example, private prosecutors have worked alongside Crown prosecutors on several high-profile cases that originated as private prosecutions, including the pollution case involving the City of Kingston excerpted in Chapter 4.

2. The test employed by the Crown to determine whether a prosecution should be allowed to proceed is substantially the same in BC and Alberta (as set out in the preceding case). It has two elements: (1) whether there is a reasonable likelihood of conviction when the evidence as a whole is

considered; and (2) whether the public interest requires prosecution. Should this same test be applied to all cases where charge approval is required, or do different considerations apply where the case originates as a private prosecution? Should the Crown have unlimited discretion to intervene in and stay any and all private prosecutions?

References and Further Readings

Stanley David Berger, "The Future of Environmental Prosecutions in Ontario" (2006) 19 C.E.L.R. (3d) 32

Joseph Castrilli, "Canadian Policy and Practice with Indicators of Effective Environmental Enforcement" in Annex 3 to *Indicators of Effective Environmental Enforcement Proceedings of A North American Dialogue* (CEC, 1999), online: <http://www.cec.org/>

Jerry V. DeMarco & Toby Vigod, "Smarter Regulation: The Case for Enforcement and Transparency" (2007) 17 J. Envtl. L. & Prac. 85

Ecojustice Canada, *Environmental Enforcement by Canada's Federal Government (The Essentials)* (Ecojustice, 2011)

Keith Ferguson, "Challenging the Intervention and Stay of an Environmental Private Prosecution" (2004) 13 J. Envtl. L. & Prac. 153

Shaun Fluker, "*R. v. Syncrude Canada*: A Clash of Bitumen and Birds" (2011) 49 Alta. L. Rev. 237

Elaine L. Hughes & Larry A. Reynolds, "Creative Sentencing and Environmental Protection" (2008) 19 J. Envtl. L. & Prac. 105

David L. Markell & John H Knox, eds., *Greening NAFTA: The North American Commission for Environmental Cooperation* (Stanford: Stanford University Press, 2003)

Ramani Nadarajah, "Environmental Penalties: New Enforcement Tool or the Demise of Environmental Prosecutions?" in Stanley Berger and Dianne Saxe, eds., *Environmental Law: The Year in Review 2007* (Aurora: Canada Law Book, 2008)

Office of the Auditor General of Canada, "Chapter 3: Enforcing the Canadian Environmental Protection Act, 1999", *2011 December Report of the Commissioner of the Environment and Sustainable Development*

Office of the Auditor General of Canada, "Report 1: Toxic Substances", *2018 Fall Reports of the Commissioner of the Environment and Sustainable Development*

John Swaigen, "Absolute Liability Revisited: *Lévis v Tetrault*" in Stanley Berger and Dianne Saxe, eds., *Environmental Law: The Year in Review 2006* (Aurora: Canada Law Book, 2007)

C. Tollefson, "Games without Frontiers: Investor Claims and Citizen Submissions under the NAFTA Regime" (2002) 27 Yale J. Int'l. L. 217

Chris Tollefson, Jerry DeMarco & Darlene Gilliland, "Towards a Costs Jurisprudence in Public Interest Litigation" (2004) 83 Can. Bar Rev. 473

Stepan Wood & Lynn Johannson, "How Not to Incorporate Voluntary Standards into Smart Regulation: ISO 14001 and Ontario's *Environmental Penalties Regulations*", CLPE Research Paper 07/2008, Vol. 04, No. 02

Matthew D. Zinn, "Policing Environmental Regulatory Enforcement: Cooperation, Capture and Citizen Suits" (2002) 21 Stan. Envtl. L.J. 81

Chapter 6

Judicial Review of Environmental Decision-making

Introduction

This chapter provides an overview of the nature and role of judicial review in the environmental law context. Judicial review challenges courts to balance their role as protectors of the rule of law against the need to show appropriate deference to decisions that emerge through the operation of the democratic process. The inherent tension between these competing imperatives and, at times, the confusing and conflicting jurisprudence that it has generated has prompted Binnie J. to opine that, "Judicial review is an idea that has lately become unduly burdened with law office metaphysics": *Dunsmuir v. New Brunswick*, 2008 SCC 9, at para. 122. As discussed in this chapter, *Dunsmuir* would appear to have done little to quell debate over the nature and role of judicial review, whether at the level of metaphysics or practicalities. Indeed, another respected jurist has recently claimed that the judicial review case law post-*Dunsmuir* is increasingly incoherent and inconsistent: see Stratas J.A., excerpted *infra* this chapter in Parts I and III.

This chapter contains six Parts. Part I considers the role of administrative law and the relationship between courts and administrative decision-makers in a modern regulatory state.

Part II focuses on the key concept of "standard of review", a term that refers to the test used by courts to determine the level of scrutiny they will employ in reviewing a challenged administrative decision. To explore the meaning and significance of standard of review in the environmental context, we analyze *Dunsmuir* as well as a variety of other decisions arising in the environmental law context. Then, in Part III, we provide an overview of the legal grounds upon which judicial review may be sought, using illustrations from the environmental law jurisprudence.

Finally, we consider the growing impact on this jurisprudence of cases championed by public interest environmental organizations. In recent decades, cases of this kind have raised intriguing questions about access to justice and the rules and principles that have traditionally governed judicial review of administrative decision-making. One area that has seen significant developments is the law of public interest standing, reviewed in Part IV. Public interest environmental litigants have also pressed the courts to revisit and renovate the law governing injunctions (Part V) and costs (Part VI) that applies in judicial review proceedings.

Part I — Administrative Decision-making and Judicial Review in the Environmental Law Context

Administrative Decision-making, Appeals and Architecture

Administrative law is a body of law that is concerned with defining and governing the relationship between citizens and the state. As is underscored in *Dunsmuir*, administrative law is thus "intimately connected" with the rule of law: it is the notion that the state derives its power to make decisions that affect individual rights through law, and as such is legally accountable for the exercise of that power.

The range of state actors and actions governed by administrative law is impressively broad. All state actors that derive their power to act from statute (*statutory decision-makers*) exercise these powers subject to the principles of administrative law. Therefore, whether the statutory decision-maker is a Cabinet minister, a civil servant, a tribunal or a municipal council, in all instances the power in question must be exercised in a manner consistent with applicable administrative law principles. Likewise, administrative law principles govern a far-reaching range of forms of state action. In other words, administrative law governs not only specific decisions, but also the delegated power *to make regulations* that are of more general application. In the environmental context, for example, this means that administrative law defines and governs the exercise of powers to grant project- or firm-specific licences, permits and other approvals, and the power (usually vested in Cabinet) to enact regulations that address broader subject matters including generally applicable rules with respect to air, land and water protection.

As with many other areas of law, administrative law is an evolving amalgam of common law and legislation. As such, both the common law and applicable statutes define the procedures that statutory decision-makers must follow in the exercise of their powers, the means through which affected parties may seek to have input into and ultimately challenge the exercise of these powers, and the type of remedies that are available where a court determines that a decision-maker has acted unlawfully.

A key feature of modern regulation is that responsibility for making key decisions and enacting regulations is delegated by statute. As with other areas of regulation, this is an inevitable function of the complexity and scope of the state's mandate to protect the environment. The power to enact regulations is typically vested in the Minister of the Environment or other Cabinet-level official. On the other hand, the power to grant permitting, licencing or other environmental-related approvals is normally vested in a civil servant designated by statute and employed by the ministry responsible for regulating the activity in question. Most statutes provide for an internal process of appeal from decisions made at this level, either to a more senior decision-maker within the ministry or to an environmental or resource appeal tribunal.

All such decision-makers must comply with legally mandated procedures when exercising their statutory powers. Usually, these procedures are set out in some detail in the statute from which they derive their powers. However, their actions are also governed by the common law principles of *procedural fairness*. What these principles require in any particular case depends on three main factors: the nature of the decision being made, the relationship between the decision-maker and the party affected, and the effect of the decision on the rights of the party in question. Generally, procedural fairness at common law will require, at a minimum, that the affected party be given notice of the impending decision and an opportunity to comment; this is a dual requirement commonly referred to as *notice and comment*.

The rapid expansion of environmental law since the 1970s — and in many jurisdictions its increasing interconnections with municipal, transportation, energy and resource law — has given rise to a complex and at times bewildering architecture of administrative bodies and tribunals. While there are significant cross-jurisdictional differences in this architecture, there are also some common themes and challenges. One set of threshold questions concerns whether responsibility for hearing appeals from administrative decisions should be vested in a specialized environmental tribunal or in an "environmental court", or alternatively, whether dissatisfied parties should simply proceed directly to judicial review. If it is decided that an environmental tribunal or court shall be established, there are a host of other questions that arise, including what standing rules and participation rights should apply, and what mandate and powers it should possess. The following excerpt canvasses these and related questions, drawing upon research from a variety of Canadian and foreign jurisdictions.

Mark Haddock,
Environmental Tribunals in British Columbia
(UVic Environmental Law Centre, 2011)

The creation of specialized environmental courts and tribunals has become a common way for nations, states and even cities to address the need for accountability and fairness in the administration of environmental laws. Some jurisdictions (e.g. New Zealand and three Australian states) have established specialized courts with a judiciary dedicated to hearing environmental cases, while others follow tribunal models similar to [those that exist in most Canadian jurisdictions]. Where specialized courts do not exist, some jurisdictions have opted to have a "green bench" of judges dedicated to hearing environmental cases [...]. Although there clearly has been an increase in these tribunals over the last two decades, this trend began almost a century ago. Denmark established a Nature Protection Board as early as 1917, and Sweden's Water Court was created in 1918. Environmental tribunals are becoming common not just in wealthy nations but in the developing world as well, many of which have very progressive mandates and rules.

A recent study published by the World Resources Institute surveyed over 80 such tribunals in 35 countries, and identified the following as the most common reasons for establishing environmental courts and tribunals:

1. *Efficiency*: Reduce decisional time.

2. *Economy*: Reduce costs for all concerned with more efficient handling of cases, aggressive case management, more efficient use of experts, and use of ADR.

3. *Expertise*: Increase decisional quality with judges who have more expertise and experience with complex environmental laws, technical-economic questions, and value-laden issues than general jurisdiction judges.

4. *Uniformity*: Increase consistency in the interpretation and application of environmental law across the jurisdiction and discourage forum shopping.

5. *Access to Justice*: Improve access to justice for business, government, and the public by having an open, identified forum to handle environmental complaints.

6. *Case Processing*: Improve case processing and reduce backlog of undecided cases in the general court system.

7. *Commitment*: Demonstrate government's commitment to protection of the environment, sustainable development, compliance with international treaties and agreements, etc., by creating a visible court symbolic of that commitment.

8. *Problem-Solving*: Open up more flexible ways to solve environmental problems than the traditional adversary process — including alternative dispute resolution (ADR), collaborative planning and decision-making, hybrid civil-criminal prosecution, creative sentencing and enforcement options, court appointed special commissions, and facilitated settlement agreements. The "problem solving approach" (as opposed to the strict legalistic adjudication) can work better in some environmental cases, allowing judges to craft innovative solutions, focus on outcomes rather than outputs, take account of what is best for whole communities or the environment rather than just individual parties.

9. *Public Participation*: Encourage greater public participation and support for the decision-making process through more open standing, use of community expert committees, etc.

10. *Public Confidence*: Increase public confidence in the government's environmental and sustainable development efforts by having a transparent, effective, expert decisional body.

11. *Accountability*: Potential review by an independent body encourages government agencies to be more thorough, fair, and transparent in their decision-making.

12. *Prevent Marginalization*: Ensure that judicial resources will be dedicated to resolving environmental conflicts and that they will not be marginalized or pushed aside in favor of cases which are less time consuming and less complex.

There are many different approaches to standing: in Denmark, specific rights of complaint or appeal are granted to non-profit organizations named in legislation, in addition to "any party having an individual, significant interest in the case." In Sweden, third party appeals may be brought by any non-profit organization that has nature protection or environmental protection in their purposes, have been active for 3 years, and have at least 2000 members. In Spain, open standing rules allow anyone who wants to take part in a public inquiry about planning or environment problems to do so without restriction.

Moving to Commonwealth jurisdictions, New Zealand's legislation grants standing to any person who has an interest in the proceedings that is greater than the public generally, or anyone who is representing a relevant aspect of the public interest, or who made a submission in an earlier proceeding on the same matter. In Australia, New South Wales, Queensland and South Australia all have broad third party rights of appeal. Developing countries with relatively recent environmental tribunals also have broad standing rules.

In Ontario, the Environmental Review Tribunal has three levels of participation for members of the public: 1) a *presenter* may testify and present evidence [...] but may not cross-examine witnesses or make submissions; 2) a *participant* may make oral and written submissions to the tribunal, and 3) a *party* has the fullest range of rights and responsibilities.

Participant Funding and Costs

[...] the challenges of providing for participant funding for public interest appellants remain significant in most jurisdictions. [...]This is a major and vexing problem for public interest environmental litigation, because cases are typically very complex and require expert evidence. Public interest parties typically have no economic advantage to gain from their participation. As Justice Toohey of the Australian Federal Court stated 20 years ago: "Relaxing the traditional requirements for standing may be of little significance unless other procedural reforms are made. Particularly is this so in the area of funding of environmental litigation and the awarding of costs. There is little point in opening the doors to the courts if litigants cannot afford to come in."

Legal aid is available in many countries, but is typically underfunded and is used or available for criminal, family and poverty rather than environmental matters. One alternative model that has been adopted successfully for over 20 years in Australia is state government funding of non-profit Environmental Defenders Offices (EDOs), which represent public interest litigants. The adequacy and continuity of that funding is frequently an issue that limits the EDO's ability to carry out this service.

In Europe, 43 countries have committed to "consider the establishment of appropriate assistance mechanisms to remove or reduce financial and other barriers to access to justice" by ratifying the *Aarhus Convention on Access to Information, Public Participation in Decision-making and Access to Justice in Environmental Matters*. The state that appears to be delivering the most progress on this is Spain, which in 2006 adopted legislation to bring it into compliance with this provision. [**Ed. Note:** The *Aarhus Convention* has been used by UK litigants to leverage reforms to the law of costs in public interest cases in the United Kingdom: see *infra* this chapter in Part VI.]

It would appear then, that the best practices to enable the "*effective* access to judicial and administrative proceedings" called for the Rio Convention (which was ratified by Canada and endorsed by British Columbia) are to be found in the rules of the Alberta Environmental Appeals Board (which allows participant costs in advance) and the system of Environmental Defenders Offices in Australia. Canada's federal environmental assessment process also provides up-front participant funding from time to time, and requires the Minister "to establish a participant funding program to facilitate the participation of the public in comprehensive studies, mediations and assessments by review panels."

For costs after the fact of participation, the BC Utilities Commission and Ontario Environmental Review Tribunal provide models that are helpful but may limit the ability to participate fully with expert evidence because of the "gamble" that costs will not be awarded ultimately.

Tribunal Powers and Procedures

Investigative / Inquiry Powers

[...] Traditionally there has been a major fork in the road when it comes to how tribunals do their fact-finding, which is tied to the powers they are given. Purely adjudicative boards, like courts, will consider only the evidence put before them by the parties and will not carry out their own investigation so as not to taint the proceeding or open the door to potential allegations of bias or unfairness. At the same time, however, adjudicative tribunals typically have more relaxed evidentiary rules than courts, and tribunal members will often engage in the evidence in a more direct way than judges. Tribunals that primarily exercise investigative powers are, of course, far more active in their fact-finding, and may on their own initiative interview employees, government workers, witnesses and experts in order to arrive at the "truth of the matter." Traditionally, however, these tribunals (or commissioners of inquiry) make findings of fact followed by recommendations, rather than deciding rights.

One question that should be asked is whether these functions are necessarily mutually exclusive, and whether the complexity of environmental issues justifies a hybrid approach from time to time. Some jurisdictions endow their adjudicative tribunals with investigative/inquiry type powers. For example, the Alberta Environmental Appeals Board has "all the powers of a commissioner under the *Public Inquiries Act*." Many environmental tribunals, including the BC Environmental Appeal Board, Alberta EAB, Ontario ERT, European, Australasian and African tribunals, have the authority to invite witnesses to appear before them to assist the tribunal in its fact-finding. However, in our review of the literature to date, it appears that this authority is seldom used.

Some jurisdictions appoint environmental commissioners with investigative/ inquiry powers to receive and investigate complaints, and to undertake investigations on their own initiative or at the request of government. New Zealand was the first jurisdiction in the world to appoint a Commissioner of Environment in 1986. Ontario has an Environmental Commissioner, as does Canada federally, and Australia. Like Auditors General, these officers report directly to the Legislature or Parliament, rather than the Minister of Environment or Cabinet, in order to have greater independence from the political or executive branch of government.

Experts

Environmental disputes are often largely dependent on expert evidence, and this raises several issues for tribunals and public interest parties. Qualified experts are often necessary or important to the outcome of a hearing, yet many public interest parties cannot afford to retain them. Tribunals tend to deal with expert evidence in a similar fashion as courts, and there are many decisions in which citizen appellants failed to meet their burden of proof, or were unable to effectively counter an industry party's expert witness, because of a lack of either qualifications to provide opinion evidence or money to retain an expert. Even if they can afford an expert initially, there is often little control over the final cost, as they do not know how long the expert will be cross-examined, what counterevidence the industry or government party will call [...]

Environmental courts and tribunals in some jurisdictions have attempted to mitigate concerns about "hired gun" experts with a view to ensuring decision-making and adjudicative processes possess the best available scientific evidence. Australian courts adopted new expert rules in 2004 to address the adversarial process's "voracious appetite for the consumption of public and private resources." One strategy has been to try to get all parties to agree to a single expert witness. Another has been to have court-appointed experts following consultation with the parties. Although initially resisted by the legal profession, the "consistent comment from judges and legal practitioners had been that evidence from persons appointed as Court experts reflected a more thorough and balanced consideration of the issues than was previously the case." Yet another strategy is to engage expert panels who affirm their neutrality, duty to the tribunal, and provide evidence as a panel so each can respond to the other as appropriate.

The New Zealand Environment Court has a Code of Conduct for expert witnesses that requires a pledge of duty to the court acknowledging that they are not an advocate for the party who engages the witness, and that they have an "overriding duty to assist the Court impartially." Experts must follow the set of rules set out in the court's Practice Notes...

Alternative Dispute Resolution

Many environmental courts and tribunals in jurisdictions outside of Canada appear to use mediation and other ADR techniques quite extensively. It is a common practice for mediation to be carried out by those tribunal members, staff or officials who will not be involved if the matter proceeds to adjudication. For example, some jurisdictions like New Zealand have full-time judges who are lawyers, as well as full or part-time non-lawyer commissioners who administer pre-hearing settlement processes in addition to other duties such as advising the court or tribunal on technical matters.

[...] There are some differences among jurisdictions regarding whether ADR is always a voluntary exercise or whether a tribunal's practice is to try to actively promote or prod the parties into finding a resolution. In New Zealand mediation is voluntary, but a judge reviewing a newly filed appeal will "only rarely ...

conclude that an appeal is not suitable for mediation, and [the parties] will almost always be referred to a Commissioner for mediation to be arranged." Administrative Law judges in the US Environmental Protection Agency appeal process offer ADR in "essentially every environmental case filed" for a 60-day period [...]

Decision Deadlines

Several jurisdictions have legal or policy requirements and expectations respecting the time for decision following conclusion of a hearing. In Ontario, environmental statutes will sometimes specify a decision deadline. Some decisions, such as leave to appeal applications, require a decision within 30 days of the application unless extended by the Environmental Review Tribunal. In Sweden, judgments must be issued within two months of the conclusion of the main hearing. In Ireland, the Planning Appeals Board has a policy objective to dispose of appeals within four months, and must inform parties of the reasons for delay, and state when it intends to make the decision if this is not possible [...]

Environment Courts

One innovation is the establishment of environment courts, such as those now in place in Sweden, New Zealand, and the three Australian states of New South Wales, Queensland and South Australia. These courts may have jurisdiction over criminal (enforcement proceedings) and civil matters, as well as appeals and judicial review of approvals or authorizations granted by government agencies. Judges have tenure and are appointed until retirement. They may be dedicated to the environment court, or also sit on other civil or criminal courts at the same level. The New Zealand Environment Court also appoints commissioners who are typically non-lawyer technical experts for terms up to 5 years: commissioners may sit on panels chaired by a judge (but are excluded from some matters such as criminal) and carry out pre-hearing mediation.

[...] these courts essentially combine the appellate jurisdiction of [provincial environmental tribunals], the judicial review and real property jurisdiction of [provincial Superior Courts], and the criminal jurisdiction of Provincial Courts [...]

The establishment of environmental courts has been under consideration in many jurisdictions. In 1991, Lord Woolf of the Court of Appeal for England and Wales advocated "a multi-faceted and multi-skilled body which would combine the services provided in existing Courts, Tribunals and Inspectorate in the environmental field. It would be a 'one stop shop' which should lead to faster, cheaper and the more effective resolution of disputes in the environmental area." They would have "power to instruct independent counsel on behalf of the Tribunal or members of the public; [and] resources for direct investigation by the Tribunal itself." This proposal was followed up by numerous studies and academic articles in the UK since 2000 [...]

In the United States, [...] environmental administrative appeal tribunals exist in the federal system, and environmental courts have been established at the state, county and city levels.

Notes and Questions

1. A wide variety of tribunals with decision-making authority in relation to environmental and resource law issues exist across Canada at the federal, provincial and territorial levels. At the federal level, these include tribunals that are vested with authority under various statutes, including the *National Energy Board Act* (NEBA) and the *Canadian Environmental Assessment Act* (CEAA). Indeed for some projects, such as the Northern Gateway Pipeline proposal, tribunal panels were appointed with mandates under both the NEBA and CEAA (see further discussion in Chapter 7). At the provincial and territorial levels, "environmental" tribunals are typically endowed with jurisdiction to hear appeals from a variety of administrative decisions in various areas including land use and development, air and water discharges, contaminated site remediation, pesticide permitting, and wildlife management. There is also a wide range of tribunals that hear administrative appeals from decisions concerning natural resource allocation and use. These tribunals have jurisdiction to hear cases involving permits or licences for a range of activities including mineral exploration and development, oil and gas exploration and development, energy and hydro projects, forestry, and aquaculture. For the authoritative text on practice and procedure before environmental tribunals in Canada, see J. DeMarco & P. Muldoon, *Environmental Boards and Tribunals in Canada — A Practical Guide* (LexisNexis Canada, 2011).

2. How many tribunals with environmental or resource law jurisdiction exist in your province? What do you know about the nature of their mandate and powers? Have there been discussions about tribunal consolidation or reform? What are the main issues or decisions in your province that are tasked to such tribunals? Does the public perceive that these tribunals are doing an adequate job? Why or why not?

Judicial Review

Background and Overview

Ultimate responsibility for supervising administrative action lies with superior and federal courts. This function is referred to as *judicial review*. A key challenge for the courts is to determine how rigorously they should scrutinize administrative actions, whether in the form of the exercise of a regulation-making power or the exercise of a statutory power of decision. This judicial calculation is often referred to in terms of assessing the level of judicial *deference* that should be accorded to the decision under review. A key threshold question, therefore, is to determine what standard of review ("SOR") should govern the review. This continues to be a vexed question even after the SCC's effort to clarify the applicable law in its 2008 decision in *Dunsmuir*. Currently, the dominant SOR, as we discuss shortly in Part II, is one of "reasonableness"; although in a limited range of cases, including those where procedural fairness is at issue, courts still employ a "correctness" SOR.

The rules with respect to how and when an aggrieved party may seek judicial review (including standing requirements, forms of pleading, time limitations and available remedies) are, for the most part, set out in federal and provincial statutes that have been enacted for this purpose. Judicial review of decision-makers falling under federal jurisdiction (including decisions taken and regulations enacted under the *Canadian Environmental Protection Act* (CEPA), CEAA, the *Fisheries Act* and the *Species at Risk Act* (SARA)) is governed by the *Federal Courts Act* and proceeds in the Federal Court. Judicial review in most other cases falls under analogous provincial statutes and takes place in provincial superior courts.

In undertaking judicial review, courts frequently emphasize that their task is to review the legality of administrative action, not its merits. In Part III of this chapter, we provide illustrations of some of the common grounds upon which judicial review is sought, employing, where possible, cases arising in the environmental law context. These grounds include:

- Substantive *ultra vires* (administrative action that is beyond the jurisdiction of a statutory decision-maker, as discussed above);
- Failure to take account of relevant considerations (or consideration of irrelevant ones);
- Unlawful fettering of statutory discretion;
- Unlawful delegation of a statutory decision-making power;
- Real or apprehended bias;
- Exercising statutory discretion for an improper or discriminatory purpose or in bad faith; and
- Breach of procedural fairness.

Even where the aggrieved party establishes that there are legitimate grounds for questioning administrative action on one or more of these grounds, this will not necessarily entitle them to a remedy. Whether a remedy will be granted remains in the discretion of the reviewing court. In deciding whether to grant a remedy, courts will consider a variety of factors including equitable ones (has the aggrieved party come with "clean hands") and the appropriateness of the remedy sought (including whether the dispute is now moot). Another remedial consideration is the form of remedy sought. The main forms of remedy in the judicial review context are: (1) orders quashing administrative action (relief known historically as *certiorari*); (2) orders requiring the authority to act (relief in the nature of *mandamus*); (3) orders prohibiting the authority from acting (relief in the nature of *prohibition*); and (4) orders seeking a judicial declaration of existing rights, duties or powers (*declaratory relief*).

In many cases, an important and closely related procedural issue concerns whether, pending the hearing of their application for judicial review, aggrieved parties should be entitled to interim injunctive relief. As we shall see later in this chapter, for a variety of reasons, it can be difficult for public interest litigants to secure a remedy of this kind even where continuation of the *status quo* pending hearing may cause irreparable harm to the subject matter of the litigation.

Below we include a short excerpt from the leading Supreme Court of Canada case in this area. We then consider a recent Federal Court of Appeal decision in the environmental context (to which we return later in Chapter 9) that offers some further reflections on the role of judicial review in defining the relationship between democracy and the rule of law.

Dunsmuir v. New Brunswick

2008 SCC 9 (paras. 27-31)

BASTARACHE and LeBEL JJ. (for the majority): —

Judicial Review

As a matter of constitutional law, judicial review is intimately connected with the preservation of the rule of law. It is essentially that constitutional foundation which explains the purpose of judicial review and guides its function and operation. Judicial review seeks to address an underlying tension between the rule of law and the foundational democratic principle, which finds an expression in the initiatives of Parliament and legislatures to create various administrative bodies and endow them with broad powers. Courts, while exercising their constitutional functions of judicial review, must be sensitive not only to the need to uphold the rule of law, but also to the necessity of avoiding undue interference with the discharge of administrative functions in respect of the matters delegated to administrative bodies by Parliament and legislatures.

By virtue of the rule of law principle, all exercises of public authority must find their source in law. All decision-making powers have legal limits, derived from the enabling statute itself, the common or civil law or the Constitution. Judicial review is the means by which the courts supervise those who exercise statutory powers, to ensure that they do not overstep their legal authority. The function of judicial review is therefore to ensure the legality, the reasonableness and the fairness of the administrative process and its outcomes.

Administrative powers are exercised by decision-makers according to statutory regimes that they are themselves confined. A decision-maker may not exercise authority not specifically assigned to him or her. By acting in the absence of legal authority, the decision-maker transgresses the principle of the rule of law. Thus, when a reviewing court considers the scope of a decision-making power or the jurisdiction conferred by a statute, the standard of review analysis strives to determine what authority was intended to be given to the body in relation to the subject matter. This is done within the context of the courts' constitutional duty to ensure that public authorities do not overreach their lawful powers [...]

In addition to the role judicial review plays in upholding the rule of law, it also performs an important constitutional function in maintaining legislative supremacy [...]. In essence, the rule of law is maintained because the courts have the last word on jurisdiction, and legislative supremacy is assured because determining the applicable standard of review is accomplished by establishing legislative intent.

The legislative branch of government cannot remove the judiciary's power to review actions and decisions of administrative bodies for compliance with the constitutional capacities of the government. Even a privative clause, which provides a strong indication of legislative intent, cannot be determinative in this respect (*Executors of the Woodward Estate v. Minister of Finance*, [1973] S.C.R. 120 at p. 127). The inherent power of superior courts to review administrative action and ensure that it does not exceed its jurisdiction stems from the judicature provisions in ss. 96 to 101 of the *Constitution Act, 1867* [...].

Georgia Strait Alliance v. Canada (Minister of Fisheries & Oceans)

2012 FCA 40

MAINVILLE J.A.: —

Historical and Constitutional Foundations of Judicial Review

It is useful to set out briefly the foundations of judicial review in Canada. The two guiding principles of the British constitution — on which the constitution of Canada is modelled — are the sovereignty of Parliament and the rule of law. These constitutional principles were largely developed as a result of the English Civil War of the 17th Century and its aftermath. This long, difficult and often bloody struggle between the Crown and Parliament culminated in the victory of the Parliamentarians in the so-called "Glorious Revolution", which ensured the accession to the throne of William and Mary and led to the adoption of the *Bill of Rights* of 1689, later followed by the *Act of Settlement* of 1701.

Through these historical events, the Crown's powers were made subject to the laws of Parliament. Prior to the *Bill of Rights* of 1689, the Crown had asserted that it could "assum[e] and exercis[e] a power of dispensing with and suspending of laws and the execution of laws without the consent of Parliament": Preamble to the *Bill of Rights* of 1689. While the *Bill of Rights* of 1689 firmly consecrated the principle of Parliamentary sovereignty, it also implicitly empowered the courts, and particularly the common law courts, to both interpret Parliament's laws and censure unlawful behaviour on the part of Crown officials. This was further entrenched by the subsequent *Act of Settlement* of 1701 which recognized the independence of the judiciary.

The *Bill of Rights* of 1689, the *Act of Settlement* of 1701, and the constitutional principles flowing from those documents thus ensured that the Crown and its officials would be thereafter bound by Parliament's laws as interpreted by the independent common law courts: see Dussault and Borgeat, "Administrative Law — A Treatise" second edition, volume 4, Carswell, 1990 at pages 12-13 and 27 to 31; A. L. Goodhart and R. E. Megarry, "Judicial Review and the Rule of Law: Historical Origins" (1956), 72 L.Q.R. 345 at p. 362; Lord Hailsham of St. Marylebone, "Democracy and Judicial Independence" (1979), 28 N.B.L.J. 7 at page 9.

The principles of Parliamentary sovereignty and of the rule of law are still today at the heart of judicial review: *Dunsmuir* at paras. 27 to 30.

With the expansion of state intervention in the first part of the 20th Century, Parliament set up numerous intricate legislative schemes seeking to achieve complex economic and social goals. It delegated more and more powers to various administrative bodies entrusted with the authority to implement these schemes. Parliament also created numerous administrative tribunals to adjudicate the disputes resulting from these complex schemes. In some cases, Parliament sought to protect these administrative bodies and tribunals from interference by the courts. This was principally achieved by the inclusion of various privative clauses in the legislation enabling these administrative bodies and tribunals to carry out their functions.

Though the courts throughout the Commonwealth fiercely resisted these curtailments of their authority, they eventually relented in deference to the principle of Parliamentary sovereignty. However, the courts always maintained a right — albeit limited — to control administrative decisions on the ground that the rule of law required it in certain appropriate circumstances, notably in cases of excess of jurisdiction, abuse of power or failure to comply with principles of natural justice.

Part II — Standard of Review: *Dunsmuir* and the Environmental Case Law

Introduction

A threshold question that a court must determine when embarking on judicial review is what *standard of review* it should employ when assessing administrative action. As discussed above, this determination turns to a large degree on how much deference the reviewing court considers the decision under review should be accorded. This is a vexed and difficult contextual question that the Supreme Court in *Dunsmuir* seeks to clarify, as set out in the excerpt that follows. As we shall see, there is considerable debate as to whether the aspirations of *Dunsmuir* have been achieved, and growing calls for the SCC to revisit and renovate the *Dunsmuir* framework.

Dunsmuir v. New Brunswick
2008 SCC 9 (paras. 34-64)

BASTARACHE and LeBEL JJ. (for the majority): —

Reconsidering the Standards of Judicial Review

The current approach to judicial review involves three standards of review, which range from correctness, where no deference is shown, to patent unreasonableness, which is most deferential to the decision-maker, the standard of reasonableness *simpliciter* lying, theoretically, in the middle. In our view, it is necessary to reconsider both the number and definitions of the various standards of review, and the analytical process employed to determine which standard applies in a given situation. We conclude that there ought to be two standards of review — correctness and reasonableness. [...]

The operation of three standards of review has not been without practical and theoretical difficulties, neither has it been free of criticism. One major problem lies in distinguishing between the patent unreasonableness standard and the reasonableness *simpliciter* standard. The difficulty in distinguishing between those standards contributes to the problem of choosing the right standard of review. An even greater problem lies in the application of the patent unreasonableness standard, which at times seems to require parties to accept an unreasonable decision. [...]

Two Standards of Review

[...]

Defining the Concepts of Reasonableness and Correctness

[...] We therefore conclude that the two variants of reasonableness review should be collapsed into a single form of "reasonableness" review. The result is a system of judicial review comprising two standards — correctness and reasonableness. But the revised system cannot be expected to be simpler and more workable unless the concepts it employs are clearly defined. [...]

Reasonableness is a deferential standard animated by the principle that underlies the development of the two previous standards of reasonableness: certain questions that come before administrative tribunals do not lend themselves to one specific, particular result. Instead, they may give rise to a number of possible, reasonable conclusions. Tribunals have a margin of appreciation within the range of acceptable and rational solutions. A court conducting a review for reasonableness inquires into the qualities that make a decision reasonable, referring both to the process of articulating the reasons and to outcomes. In judicial review, reasonableness is concerned mostly with the existence of justification, transparency and intelligibility within the decision-making process. But it is also concerned with whether the decision falls within a range of possible, acceptable outcomes which are defensible in respect of the facts and law.

The move towards a single reasonableness standard does not pave the way for a more intrusive review by courts [...]

Deference in the context of the reasonableness standard therefore implies that courts will give due consideration to the determinations of decision-makers [...]. In short, deference requires respect for the legislative choices to leave some matters in the hands of administrative decision-makers, for the processes and determinations that draw on particular expertise and experiences, and for the different roles of the courts and administrative bodies within the Canadian constitutional system.

As important as it is that courts have a proper understanding of reasonableness review as a deferential standard, it is also without question that the standard of correctness must be maintained in respect of jurisdictional and some other questions of law. This promotes just decisions and avoids inconsistent and unauthorized application of law. When applying the correctness standard, a reviewing court will not show deference to the decision-maker's reasoning process; it will rather undertake its own analysis of the question. The analysis will bring the court to decide whether it agrees with the determination of the decision-maker; if not, the court will substitute its own view and provide the correct answer. From the outset, the court must ask whether the tribunal's decision was correct.

Determining the Appropriate Standard of Review

[...] An exhaustive review is not required in every case to determine the proper standard of review. Here again, existing jurisprudence may be helpful in identifying some of the questions that generally fall to be determined according to the correctness standard (*Cartaway Resources Corp. (Re)*, [2004] 1 S.C.R. 672, 2004 SCC 26). This simply means that the analysis required is already deemed to have been performed and need not be repeated.

For example, correctness review has been found to apply to constitutional questions regarding the division of powers between Parliament and the provinces in the *Constitution Act, 1867* [...]

Administrative bodies must also be correct in their determinations of true questions of jurisdiction or *vires*. [...] "Jurisdiction" is intended in the narrow sense of whether or not the tribunal had the authority to make the inquiry. In other words, true jurisdiction questions arise where the tribunal must explicitly determine whether its statutory grant of power gives it the authority to decide a particular matter. [...]

As mentioned earlier, courts must also continue to substitute their own view of the correct answer where the question at issue is one of general law "that is both of central importance to the legal system as a whole and outside the adjudicator's specialized area of expertise" (*Toronto (City) v. C.U.P.E.*, at para. 62, *per* LeBel J.). Because of their impact on the administration of justice as a whole, such questions require uniform and consistent answers. [...]

In summary, the process of judicial review involves two steps. First, courts ascertain whether the jurisprudence has already determined in a satisfactory manner the degree of deference to be accorded with regard to a particular category of question. Second, where the first inquiry proves unfruitful, courts must proceed to an analysis of the factors making it possible to identify the proper standard of review. [...]

The analysis must be contextual. As mentioned above, it is dependent on the application of a number of relevant factors, including: (1) the presence or absence of a privative clause; (2) the purpose of the tribunal as determined by interpretation of enabling legislation; (3) the nature of the question at issue, and; (4) the expertise of the tribunal. In many cases, it will not be necessary to consider all of the factors, as some of them may be determinative in the application of the reasonableness standard in a specific case.

Justice David Stratas,
"The Canadian Law of Judicial Review:
A Plea for Doctrinal Coherence and Consistency"
(2016), online: <https://papers.ssrn.com/sol3/papers.cfm?abstract_id=2733751> (pp. 1-8)

Doctrinal incoherence and inconsistency plague the Canadian law of judicial review. This must stop.

Professor Emeritus David Mullan — the dean of the Canadian administrative law academy — has identified at least fifteen fundamental, unresolved problems in the law of judicial review. For some time now, these have festered, and remain unaddressed. Other academic commentators highlight the growing pile of unanswered questions and doctrinal confusion. One rising member of the academy opines that only a couple of Supreme Court cases in the last eight years contribute to the doctrine while the rest — tens of cases — do not and are best ignored.

For a while now, judges attending judicial education conferences regularly have been expressing frustration. Some are now articulating it in their reasons.

These judges are not alone. Now, even judges on the Supreme Court are openly registering dissatisfaction about the current state of administrative law and the manner in which their Court applies it.

The administrative law of most other major Commonwealth countries does not seem to be in such turmoil. But ours is — and has been for far too long.

Our administrative law is a never-ending construction site where one crew builds structures and then a later crew tears them down to build anew, seemingly without an overall plan. Roughly forty years ago, the Supreme Court told us to categorize decisions as judicial, quasi-judicial or administrative. Then, largely comprised of different members, the Court told us to follow a "pragmatic and functional" test. Then, with further changes in its composition, it added another category of review, reasonableness, to join patent unreasonableness and correctness. Then, with more turnover of judges, it told us to follow the principles and methodology in *Dunsmuir*. Now it appears that we may be on the brink of another revision: as we shall see, the Supreme Court — mysteriously — is often not deciding cases in accordance with the principles in *Dunsmuir* and other cases decided under it.

Administrative law matters. Resting at its heart is the standard of review, the body of law that tells us when the judiciary can legitimately interfere with decision-making by the executive — a matter fundamental to democratic order and good governance, a matter where objectivity, consistency and predictability is essential.

Interference with the executive by the non-elected judiciary can be controversial, particularly in the many politically-sensitive matters that arise. If the standard of review is well-defined and applied objectively in accordance with stable law, much of the controversy disappears. The appearance, and of course the reality, is that the judiciary is not playing politics; it is dispassionately and neutrally applying objective doctrine worked out years before. The executive is measured up against known legal rules, not something made up or manipulated by the judiciary on the fly. Predictability is maximized: governments can know their powers and limits and everyone can knowledgeably plan their affairs.

Right now, we are far from realizing these objectives. Confusion and uncertainty surround so many fundamental questions in administrative law, at least as far as Supreme Court cases are concerned.

Why this article? I have to work with this jurisprudence every day. I may soon be faced with another reconstruction of this area of law. I have worked for clarity, consistency, unity, and simplicity in this crucial area of law for much of my life. As well, as I have recently explained elsewhere, growing inattention to doctrine in public law on the part of the judiciary, the legal profession and the academy threatens our ability to address possible abuses by government in the future. We must pay more attention now to the settlement of the doctrine in this area of law before it is too late.

To these ends and for these reasons, I have written this article. I identify some of the unresolved fundamental questions in the Canadian law of judicial review arising from Supreme Court jurisprudence. Then I offer some constructive suggestions for consideration.

Fundamental Questions

[...]

How Do We Conduct Reasonableness Review? What Does "Reasonableness" Mean?

The main effect of *Dunsmuir* has been to subject most administrative decisions to reasonableness review rather than correctness review. Thus, the proper methodology of reasonableness review and the meaning of reasonableness is very much the core of judicial review and must be doctrinally settled. Unfortunately, the core is a mash of inconsistency and incoherence.

- I -

The reasonableness standard of review means entirely different things in different cases but we know not why.

Often the Supreme Court purports to engage in reasonableness review — a "deferential standard" — but acts non-deferentially, imposing its own view of the facts or the law or both over the view of the administrative decision-maker, without explanation.

There are sometimes exceptions where the Supreme Court defers to administrative decision-making quite consistently with the words of *Dunsmuir*. Why deference prevails in these cases but not in so many others has never been explained. [...]

What does the reasonableness standard mean and how should it be applied? Reading the decisions of the Supreme Court, many are baffled.

- II -

Reasonableness review requires us to start with the administrative decision and "[inquire] into the qualities that make [it] reasonable." This makes sense: the legislator has chosen the administrative decision-maker to decide the merits and so reviewing courts should respect that choice by beginning with a careful examination of what the administrator decided.

But repeatedly reasonableness review has been conducted without starting with the administrative decision. Often the Supreme Court does its own analysis of the merits (supposedly under reasonableness review) and finds the administrative decision to be wrong, offering only cursory words; seldom is an administrative decision analyzed in any depth. Sometimes the fact that an administrative decision was made is not even mentioned.

On judicial review, the reviewing court is to review the administrative decision. This must especially be so in the case of reasonableness review. What are we to make of the fact that the administrative decision is often ignored or even unmentioned?

- III -

When conducting reasonableness review, reviewing courts are to pay "respectful attention" to the administrative decision-maker's reasons and "be cautious about substituting their own view of the proper outcome by designating certain omissions in the reasons to be fateful." In other words, reviewing courts should not embark on a "line-by-line treasure hunt for error."

But here too, chaos reigns, with administrators' reasons being closely parsed in some cases and barely looked at in others, all purportedly under the reasonableness standard of review.

Notes and Questions

1. The inconsistent and sometimes incoherent way courts apply the reasonableness standard has not only caused angst among the administrative law fraternity, but also prompted an increasingly spirited debate at the Supreme Court of Canada. A prime example is *Wilson v. Atomic Energy of Canada Ltd. Wilson* spotlights some fairly profound differences of opinion within the court. Justice Abella (writing for herself) as well as the dissenters (Côté J. writing for Brown and Moldaver JJ.) all explicitly express concern about *Dunsmuir's* impact on administrative law, though Abella J. and the dissenters clearly do not agree on how these concerns should be remedied.

2. As you read the extracts from *Wilson* below, bear in mind that the SCC has signalled that it wants to revisit the nature and scope of judicial review of administrative action, as addressed in *Dunsmuir* and other cases. It intends to do so in a trilogy of cases scheduled to be heard in December 2018: *National Football League v. Attorney General of Canada* (Doc. 37897); *Bell Canada v. Attorney General of Canada* (Doc. 37896); and *Minister of Citizenship and Immigration v. Vavilov* (Doc. 37748).

Wilson v. Atomic Energy of Canada Ltd.
2016 SCC 29

ABELLA J.: —

Analysis

The parties before this Court, as they had in all the prior judicial proceedings, accepted that the standard of review was reasonableness. I agree. The decisions of labour adjudicators or arbitrators interpreting statutes or agreements within their expertise attract a reasonableness standard: *Dunsmuir v. New Brunswick*, [2008] 1 S.C.R. 190, at para. 68 [...]

But while it is true that the standard of review in this case falls easily into our jurisprudence, it seems to me that some general comments about standard of review are worth airing, albeit in *obiter*. There are undoubtedly many models that would help simplify the standard of review labyrinth we currently find ourselves in. I offer the following proposal as an option only, for purposes of starting the conversation about the way forward. Because it is only the beginning of the conversation, which will benefit over time from submissions from counsel, this proposal is not intended in any way to be comprehensive, definitive, or binding.

A substantial portion of the parties' factums and the decisions of the lower courts in this case were occupied with what the applicable standard of review should be. This, in my respectful view, is insupportable, and directs us institutionally to think about whether this obstacle course is necessary or whether there is a principled way to simplify the path to reviewing the merits.

For a start, it would be useful to go back to the basic principles set out in *Dunsmuir*, under which two approaches were enunciated for reviewing administrative decisions. The first is deferential, and applies when there is a range of reasonable outcomes defensible on the facts and law. This is by far the largest group of cases. Deference is succinctly explained in *Dunsmuir* as follows:

> It does not mean that courts are subservient to the determinations of decision makers, or that courts must show blind reverence to their interpretations, or that they may be content to pay lip service to the concept of reasonableness review while in fact imposing their own view. Rather, deference imports respect for the decision-making process of adjudicative bodies with regard to both the facts and the law. [para. 48]

The reason for the wide range is, as Justice John M. Evans explained, because "[d]eference ... assumes that there is no uniquely correct answer to the question": "Triumph of Reasonableness: But How Much Does It Really Matter?" (2014), 27 *C.J.A.L.P.* 101, at p. 108. The range will necessarily vary. As Chief Justice McLachlin noted, reasonableness "must be assessed in the context of the particular type of decision making involved and all relevant factors" and "takes its colour from the context": *Catalyst Paper Corp. v. North Cowichan (District)*, [2012] 1 S.C.R. 5, at paras. 18 and 23, citing with approval *Canada (Citizenship and Immigration) v. Khosa*, [2009] 1 S.C.R. 339, at para. 59.

The other approach, called correctness, was applied when only a single defensible answer is available. As set out in *Dunsmuir*, this applied to constitutional questions regarding the division of powers (para. 58), "true questions of jurisdiction or *vires*" (para. 59), questions of general law that are "both of central importance to the legal system as a whole and outside the adjudicator's specialized area of expertise" (para. 60), and "questions regarding the jurisdictional lines between two or more competing specialized tribunals" (para. 61).

Most of the confusion in our jurisprudence has been over what to call the category of review in a particular case. Perhaps it is worth thinking about whether it is really necessary to engage in rhetorical debates about what to call our conclusions at the end of the review. Are we not saying essentially the same thing when we conclude that there is only a single "reasonable" answer available and when we say it is "correct"? And this leads to whether we need two different names for our approaches to judicial review, or whether both approaches can live comfortably under a more broadly conceived understanding of reasonableness.

It may be helpful to review briefly how we got here. In *Dunsmuir*, this Court sought to provide "a principled framework that is more coherent and workable" for the judicial review of administrative decisions (para. 32). As a result, the three existing standards of review were replaced by two. The aim was to simplify judicial review. But collapsing three into two has not proven to be the runway to simplicity the Court had hoped it would be. In fact, the terminological battles over which of the three standards of review should apply have been replaced by those over the application of the remaining two. And so we still find the merits waiting in the wings for their chance to be seen and reviewed. [...]

Dunsmuir had pointed out that courts were struggling with the "conceptual distinction" between two of the standards — patent unreasonableness and reasonableness *simpliciter* — and were finding that "any actual difference between them in terms of their operation appears to be illusory" (paras. 39-41). An argument can be made, as Prof. David Mullan has, that this Court too has blurred the conceptual distinctions in a number of cases, this time between correctness and reasonableness standards of review, and has sometimes engaged in "disguised correctness" review while ostensibly conducting a reasonableness review. Others too have expressed concerns about inconsistency and confusion in how the standards have been applied. The question then is whether there is a way to move forward that respects the underlying principles of judicial review which were so elegantly and definitively explained in *Dunsmuir*, while redesigning their implementation in a way that makes them easier to apply.

The most obvious and frequently proposed reform of the current system is a single reviewing standard of reasonableness. Before accepting it, it is important to remember the rule of law imperatives of judicial review. [...]

Nothing *Dunsmuir* says about the rule of law suggests that constitutional compliance dictates how many standards of review are required. The only requirement, in fact, is that there *be* judicial review in order to ensure, in particular, that decision-makers do not exercise authority they do not have. I see nothing in its elaboration of rule of law principles that precludes the adoption of a single standard of review, so long as it accommodates the ability to continue to protect both deference *and* the possibility of a single answer where the rule of law demands it, as in the four categories singled out for correctness review in *Dunsmuir*.

A single standard of reasonableness still invites the approach outlined in *Dunsmuir*, namely:

> ... reasonableness is concerned ... with whether the decision falls within a range of possible, acceptable outcomes which are defensible in respect of the facts and law. [para. 47]

Approaching the analysis from the perspective of whether the outcome falls within a range of defensible outcomes has the advantage of being able to embrace comfortably the animating principles of both former categories of judicial review. Courts can apply a wider range for those kinds of issues and decision-makers traditionally given a measure of deference, and a narrow one of only one "defensible" outcome for those which formerly attracted a correctness review. Most decisions will continue to attract deference, as they did in *Dunsmuir*, which means, as Justice Evans noted

> [that] a court may be more likely to conclude that a range of reasonable interpretative choices exists, and that deference is meaningful, when the tribunal's authority is conferred in broad terms. If, for example, a tribunal is authorized to

make a decision on the basis of the public interest, a reviewing court may well decide that the tribunal has a range of choices in selecting the factors it will consider in making its decision. At this point, questions of law shade imperceptibly into questions of discretion. Reasonableness review permits the court to determine whether the factors considered by the tribunal are rationally related to the generally multiple statutory objectives. It is not the court's role to identify the factors to be considered by the tribunal, let alone to reweigh them. [Footnote omitted; p. 110.]

Even in statutory interpretation, the interpretive exercise will usually attract a wide range of reasonable outcomes. [...]

But there may be rare occasions where only one "defensible" outcome exists. In *Mowat*, for example, this Court found that the ordinary tools of statutory interpretation made it clear that the administrative body under review did not have the authority to award costs in a specific context. In the particular circumstances of that case, no other result fell within the range of reasonable outcomes. Similarly, this Court has set aside decisions when they fundamentally contradicted the purpose or policy underlying the statutory scheme: *Halifax*.

The four categories, however, which were identified as attracting correctness under *Dunsmuir* based on rule of law principles, always yield only one reasonable outcome.

I acknowledge that no attempt to simplify the review process will necessarily guarantee consistent outcomes. Even under the current *Dunsmuir* model, there have been cases in this Court where judges applied the same standard, yet came to different conclusions about the decisional effect of applying the standard. But the goal is not to address all possible variables, it is to build on the theories developed in *Dunsmuir* and to apply them in a way that eliminates the need to sort cases into artificial categories.

Even if, however, there proves to be little appetite for collapsing the two remaining standards of review, it would, I think, still be beneficial if the template so compellingly developed in *Dunsmuir*, were adhered to, including by applying the residual "correctness" standard only in those four circumstances *Dunsmuir* articulated.

But as previously noted, in this case we need not do more than apply our usual approach to reasonableness. [...]

MCLACHLIN C.J.C. and KARAKATSANIS, WAGER and GASCON JJ. (concurring): — We agree with Justice Abella that, under the current framework, the standard of review is reasonableness. [...] We appreciate Justice Abella's efforts to stimulate a discussion on how to clarify or simplify our standard of review jurisprudence to better promote certainty and predictability. However, as it is unnecessary to do so in order to resolve this case, we are not prepared to endorse any particular proposal to redraw our current standard of review framework at this time.

CROMWELL J. (concurring): — I agree with Justice Abella, for the reasons she gives at paras. 15-18 and 38-40, that the standard of review is reasonableness. I also agree, for the reasons she gives at paras. 41-69, that the adjudicator's decision was reasonable. I therefore agree that the appeal should be allowed with costs throughout and that the decision of the adjudicator should be restored. I write separately only to indicate two things.

The first is that, in my respectful view, our standard of review jurisprudence does not need yet another overhaul and that, as a result, I respectfully disagree with the approach that Justice Abella develops in *obiter*. In my view, *Dunsmuir v. New Brunswick*, 2008 SCC 9, [2008] 1 S.C.R. 190, sets out the appropriate framework for addressing the standard of judicial review. No doubt, that framework can and will be refined so that the applicable standard of review may be identified more easily and more consistently. But the basic *Dunsmuir* framework is sound and does not require fundamental re-thinking.

The second and related point is to underline my agreement with para. 18 of Justice Abella's reasons in which she rejects the Federal Court of Appeal's approach of attempting "to calibrate reasonableness by applying a potentially indeterminate number of varying degrees of deference". Of course, reasonableness, while "a single standard" nonetheless "takes its colour from the context": see, e.g., *Canada (Citizenship and Immigration) v. Khosa*, 2009 SCC 12, [2009] 1 S.C.R. 339, at para. 59; *Catalyst Paper Corp. v. North Cowichan (District)*, 2012 SCC 2, [2012] 1 S.C.R. 5, at para. 18; *Communications, Energy and Paperworkers Union of Canada, Local 30 v. Irving Pulp & Paper, Ltd.*, 2013 SCC 34, [2013] 2 S.C.R. 458, at para. 74. Reasonableness must, therefore, "be assessed in the context of the particular type of decision making involved and all relevant factors": *Catalyst Paper Corp.*, at para. 18. However, in my opinion, developing new and apparently unlimited numbers of gradations of reasonableness review — the margins of appreciation approach created by the Federal Court of Appeal — is not an appropriate development of the standard of review jurisprudence.

CÔTÉ and BROWN JJ. (MOLDAVER J. concurring) (dissenting): —

[...]

Standard of Review

For the reasons we set out below, we would apply a correctness review to the narrow and distilled legal issue in this case.

The parties before this Court agreed that the standard of review is reasonableness. However, the determination of the standard of review that applies in any case is a question of law, and "agreement between the parties cannot be determinative of the matter": *Monsanto Canada Inc. v. Ontario (Superintendent of Financial Services)*, 2004 SCC 54, [2004] 3 S.C.R. 152, at para. 6. Our colleague Abella J. stated this point succinctly in *Celgene Corp. v. Canada (Attorney General)*, 2011 SCC 1, [2011] 1 S.C.R. 3, at para. 33, when she observed that "the parties should not be able, by agreement, to *contract out* of the appropriate standard of review" (emphasis in original).

We note Abella J.'s proposed revisions to the standard of review, expressly made in *obiter dicta*. While we appreciate the constructive spirit in which they are proposed, and while we harbour concerns about their merits, we prefer to confine any statement regarding what is already the subject of a peripatetic body of jurisprudence to a judicial pronouncement.

Rule of Law Concerns Justify Correctness Review in This Case

In our view, this case exposes a serious concern for the rule of law posed by presumptively deferential review of a decision-maker's interpretation of its home statute. In the specific context of this case, correctness review is justified. To conclude otherwise would abandon rule of law values in favour of indiscriminate deference to the administrative state.

This Court has recognized that, where deference is owed, a decision-maker's interpretation of the law will be reasonable if it falls within a range of intelligible, defensible outcomes: *Dunsmuir v. New Brunswick*, 2008 SCC 9, [2008] 1 S.C.R. 190, at para. 47. As a general proposition, we agree.

However, deferring in this way on matters of statutory interpretation opens up the possibility that different decision-makers may each reach opposing interpretations of the same provision, thereby creating "needless uncertainty in the law [in the sense that] individuals' rights [are] dependent on the identity of the decision-maker, not the law": J. M. Evans, "Triumph of Reasonableness: But How Much Does It Really Matter?" (2014), 27 *C.J.A.L.P.* 101, at p. 105. This concern was raised forcefully by Stratas J.A. at the Federal Court of Appeal in the present case, and has been expressed elsewhere: see, e.g., *Altus Group Ltd. v. Calgary (City)*, 2015 ABCA 86, 599 A.R. 223, at paras. 31-33; *Abdoulrab v. Ontario Labour Relations Board*, 2009 ONCA 491, 95 O.R. (3d) 641, at para. 48; *Taub v. Investment Dealers Assn. of Canada*, 2009 ONCA 628, 98 O.R. (3d) 169, at paras. 65-67. [**Ed. Note:** As we have seen, Stratas J.A. has also stated his views on this topic extra-judicially.]

In theory, these disagreements can last forever. Administrative decision-makers are not bound by the principle of *stare decisis*, and many decision-makers — like the labour adjudicators in the present case — lack an institutional umbrella under which issues can be debated openly and a consensus position can emerge.

This is precisely what has occurred in the present case. For decades, labour adjudicators across the country have come to conflicting interpretations of the unjust dismissal provisions of Part III of the *Code*. These conflicting interpretations go to the heart of the federal employment law regime: Is an employer ever permitted to dismiss a non-unionized employee without cause? Some adjudicators say yes. Some say no. Lower courts have found both interpretations to be reasonable: see, e.g., Federal Court reasons and *Pierre v. Roseau River Tribal Council*, [1993] 3 F.C. 756 (T.D.).

The rule of law and the promise of orderly governance suffer as a result. When reasonableness review insulates conflicting interpretations from judicial resolution, the identity of the decision-maker determines the outcome of individual complaints, not the law itself. And when this is the case, we allow the caprice of the administrative state to take precedence over the "general principle of normative order": *British Columbia (Attorney General) v. Christie*, 2007 SCC 21, [2007] 1 S.C.R. 873, at para. 20; *Reference re Secession of Quebec*, [1998] 2 S.C.R. 217, at para. 71; *Reference re Manitoba Language Rights*, [1985] 1 S.C.R. 721, at pp. 747-52.

More troubling still, such a situation calls into question our legal system's foundational premise that there is "one law for all" (*Reference re Secession of Quebec*, at para. 71), since, realistically, what the law means depends on whether one's case is decided by one decision-maker or another. It goes without saying that the rule of law, upon which our Constitution is expressly founded, requires something closer to universal application.

The cardinal values of certainty and predictability — which are themselves core principles of the rule of law (T. Bingham, *The Rule of Law* (2010), at p. 37) — are also compromised. [...]

The conflicting adjudicative jurisprudence has done more than just create general uncertainty. It creates the risk that the *very same* federally regulated employer might be subjected to conflicting legal interpretations, such that it may be told in one case that it *can* dismiss an employee without cause, while being told in another case that it *cannot*. As Rothstein J. stated in his concurring opinion in *Canada (Citizenship and Immigration) v. Khosa*, 2009 SCC 12, [2009] 1 S.C.R. 339, at para. 90, "[d]ivergent applications of legal rules undermine the integrity of the rule of law." [...]

Finally, the existence of lingering disagreements amongst decision-makers undermines the very basis for deference. It makes little sense to defer to the interpretation of one decision-maker when it is clear that other similarly situated decision-makers — whose decisions are equally entitled to deference — have reached a different result. To accord deference in these circumstances privileges the expertise of the decision-maker whose decision is currently subject to judicial review over the expertise of other similarly situated decision-makers without any compelling reason for doing so.

We believe, therefore, that where there is lingering disagreement on a matter of statutory interpretation between administrative decision-makers, and where it is clear that the legislature could only have intended the statute to bear one meaning, correctness review is appropriate. This lingering disagreement presupposes that both interpretations are reasonable, since, of course, a contradictory but unreasonable decision will be quashed on judicial review and no lingering disagreement can result. But we wish to make one point clear: it does not matter whether one or one hundred decisions have been rendered that conflict with the "consensus" interpretation identified by the majority. As long as there is one conflicting but reasonable decision, its very existence undermines the rule of law: L. J. Wihak, "Wither the correctness standard of review? *Dunsmuir*, six years later" (2014), 27 *C.J.A.L.P.* 173, at p. 197.

Such a lingering disagreement exists in this case. While the majority says that "almost all" of the adjudicators have adopted the interpretation of the legislative scheme that was accepted by the adjudicator in this case (para. 46), there is a significant line of cases adopting the opposite interpretation [...].

This is not an exhaustive list, but serves merely to illustrate that discord exists in the adjudicative jurisprudence on the issue of whether the *Code* permits an employer to dismiss an employee without cause. It is the existence of this discord that undermines the rule of law and justifies correctness review in this case. Further, this is a matter of general importance, defining the basis of the employment relationship for thousands of Canadians. We would also add that questions regarding the dismissal of federal employees do not fall exclusively within the jurisdiction of labour adjudicators. As we will explain below, civil courts also possess jurisdiction over some of these matters. The narrow and distilled question of law raised by this case goes to the very heart of the federal employment relationship. Consistency in defining the nature of this relationship is therefore required.

Notes and Questions

1. Below is an extract from a blog penned by Professor Sossin shortly after the SCC's *Dunsmuir* decision. Have developments over the last decade been consistent with his prediction?

   Dunsmuir is a step in the right direction. From the overly formalistic pragmatic and functional approach, we have now entered an era of what I would characterize as the contextual and transparent approach. The sometimes necessary but never tenable distinction between patent unreasonableness and reasonableness *simpliciter* has been happily abandoned. The dilemmas of complexity and inconsistency which plagued the standard of review analysis, however, likely have not been resolved. Courts will now puzzle over different degrees of deference *within* each standard and in what circumstances more or less exhaustive applications of the standard of review analysis might be appropriate.

   (L. Sossin, "*Dunsmuir* — Plus ca change" Blog, 2008)

2. Describe the nature and implications of the apparent disagreement within the Court over how to provide guidance with respect to the standard of review issue. How far apart are Abella J. and the dissenters in *Wilson*?

3. In an article extracted above, Stratas J.A. offers a plea for the "doctrinal incoherence and inconsistency", which he claims characterizes Canadian administrative law, to stop. What, in particular, does he find incoherent and inconsistent in the way courts employ reasonableness review? Does a more rational approach await?

4. The standard of review question is not only important, at the level of principle, to the rule of law and the relationship between the judiciary and the administrative state, it is often decisive to the outcome in environmental law cases. As you read the cases in the following section, reflect on the implications of jettisoning or tinkering with the *Dunsmuir* framework.

Standard of Review in the Environmental Law Context

Grand Riverkeeper, Labrador Inc. v. Canada (Attorney General)
2012 FC 1520

NEAR J.: —

Standard of Review

Dunsmuir v New Brunswick, 2008 SCC 9, [2008] SCJ No 9 requires that the Court first assess whether the existing jurisprudence has satisfactorily determined the degree of deference to be afforded to the category of question at issue (at para 62; see also *Canada (Canadian Human Rights Commission) v Canada (Attorney General)*, 2011 SCC 53, [2011] SCJ No 53 at paras 16-17). Should the jurisprudence be found wanting, the Court must then assess the factors set out by the Supreme Court in *Dunsmuir*, above, including: (1) the existence of a privative clause; (2) the purpose of the tribunal as determined by interpreting the enabling legislation; (3) the expertise of the tribunal; and (4) the nature of the question at issue (*Dunsmuir*, above, at para 64). In light of the recent trend in Canadian jurisprudence on the standard of review, I find that, while instructive, cases that pre-date *Dunsmuir*, above, such as *Alberta Wilderness Association v Express Pipelines Ltd*, [1996] FCJ No 1016 (*Express Pipelines*), *Alberta Wilderness Association v Cardinal River Coals, Ltd*, [1999] FCJ No 441, [1999] 3 FC 425 (*Cheviot*), are not determinative. As such, an analysis of the *Dunsmuir* factors is required.

Privative Clause

While there is no privative clause in CEAA, the presence or absence of a privative clause is no longer determinative of whether a particular body will be afforded deference (*Canadian Human Rights Commission*, above, at para 17; *Canada (Minister of Citizenship and Immigration) v Khosa*, 2009 SCC 12, [2009] SCJ No 12 at para 25; *Dunsmuir*, above, at para 52). The remaining factors will be weighed more heavily in accordance with this pronunciation by the Supreme Court.

Panel's Purpose and Expertise

A JRP is established to fulfill an information gathering and recommending function under CEAA (section 34 of CEAA; *Express Pipelines*, above, at para 14). The Panel does not render any final decisions with respect to the Project, nor does it make absolutely binding recommendations. Rather, its primary goal is to assist the RAs — the ultimate decision-makers — in obtaining the information they need to make environmentally informed decisions. It is one piece of the decision-making process mandated by CEAA.

As the courts found in both *Cheviot* and *Express Pipelines*, above, it is expected that a joint review panel boast a "high degree of expertise in environmental matters" (*Cheviot*, above, at para 24; *Express Pipelines*, above, at para 10). The JRP in this case was no exception, featuring five highly qualified members. The Panel was co-chaired by Ms. Lesley Griffiths, co-principal of a consulting firm that provides services in environmental impact assessment, among other things, and Mr. Herbert Clarke, who has experience with aboriginal affairs and impacts and benefits agreements, and who has been involved with fisheries resource conservation. The other Panel members were: Dr. Meinhard Doelle, an environmental law professor at Dalhousie University and environmental Counsel to a private Atlantic Canada firm; Ms. Catherine Jong, a consultant in the health care and education sectors, based in Happy Valley-Goose Bay; and Mr. James Igloliorte, a former judge at the Provincial Court of Newfoundland and Labrador.

The Panel's information gathering and recommending functions, along with its expertise in the matters before it, point towards a reasonableness standard of review.

Nature of the Question at Issue

The parties' contest as to what constitutes the appropriate standard of review stems primarily from their disagreement about the proper characterization of the issues raised in the application. The Applicants posit that the Panel's alleged failure to comply with the duties mandated by CEAA constitutes an error of law or a question of jurisdiction, both relating to the Panel's interpretation of CEAA. As such, they argue, they are reviewable on the standard of correctness.

The Proponent, for its part, prefers to frame the issues raised by the Applicants as attacks on the quality of the evidence before the Panel and on the correctness of its consequent conclusions, and thus reviewable on the standard of reasonableness.

The federal Respondents propose that the question of whether the Panel was required to make firm conclusions with respect to the need for, and alternatives to, the Project is a question of law, reviewable on the standard of correctness. All other issues, they assert, should be reviewed on the standard of reasonableness, as put forth by the Proponent.

This dispute over the nature of the question is not a new one. This Court and the Federal Court of Appeal have both held, consistent with the contentions of the parties, that "it is important to appropriately characterize a perceived failure to comply as a question of law or merely an attack on the 'quality' of the evidence and, therefore, the 'correctness' of the conclusions drawn on that evidence" (*Cheviot*, above, at para 24; *Express Pipelines*, above, at para 10). The former characterization attracts review on the correctness standard, while the latter "must not lightly be interfered with" (see *Cheviot*, above, at para 24).

In the case at hand, the Applicants do not challenge the Panel's determinations on the sufficiency of the evidence before it; in fact, they agree with the Panel's statements that there was inadequate information on the need for, alternatives to, and cumulative effects of the Project. The heart of the Applicants' challenge lies instead in their disagreement with the recommendations made pursuant to such determinations. They argue that the Panel ought to have taken a different course of action when faced with the information — or purported lack thereof — before it. This is evidence that the Applicants challenge the "correctness" of the conclusions drawn on the evidence before the Panel, and not a failure to exercise its jurisdiction.

This characterization of the issues is particularly apt given the recent trend in the jurisprudence. As Justice David Stratas highlighted in *Fort McKay First Nation Chief and Council v Mike Orr*, 2012 FCA 269, [2012] FCJ No 1353 at para 10, the Supreme Court has both suggested that characterizing a legislative provision as "jurisdictional" for the purposes of judicial review should be avoided (see *Halifax (Regional Municipality) v Nova Scotia (Human Rights Commission)*, 2012 SCC 10, [2012] SCJ No 10 at para 34) and questioned the very existence of "true questions of jurisdiction" (see *Alberta (Information and Privacy Commissioner) v Alberta Teachers' Association*, 2011 SCC 61, [2011] SCJ No 61 at para 34). The Federal Court of Appeal followed suit in *Fort McKay*, above, and so should this Court.

Furthermore, the Applicants' arguments that the JRP failed to provide a rationale for its conclusions must be read in conjunction with *Dunsmuir*, above, and *Newfoundland and Labrador Nurses' Union v Newfoundland and Labrador (Treasury Board)*, 2011 SCC 62, [2011] SCJ No 62. In that case, the Supreme Court opined that *Dunsmuir* does not stand "for the proposition that the 'adequacy' of reasons is a stand-alone basis for quashing a decision, or as advocating that a reviewing court undertake two discrete analyses — one for the reasons and a separate one for the result ... It is a more organic exercise — the reasons must be read together with the outcome and serve the purpose of showing whether the result falls within a range of possible outcomes" (para 14). The Supreme Court further cemented its view on this point in *Construction Labour Relations v Driver Iron Inc*, 2012 SCC 65, [2012] SCJ No 65:

> The Board did not have to explicitly address all shades of meaning of these provisions. This Court has strongly emphasized that administrative tribunals do not have to consider and comment upon every issue raised by the parties in their reasons. For reviewing courts, the issue remains whether the decision, viewed as a whole in the context of the record, is reasonable. [...]

While the JRP is not a judicial or quasi-judicial body, I find that such a decision maker's "reasons" are akin to the "rationale" requirements imposed on the JRP by CEAA and its Terms of Reference, and are thus owed deference.

Conclusions

Thus, in accordance with the recent jurisprudence, and given the purpose and expertise of the JRP, and the nature of the questions before it, I am satisfied that the entirety of issue (B) should be reviewed on the standard of reasonableness.

The Federal Court of Appeal noted in *Iverhuron & District Ratepayers' Association v Canada (Minister of the Environment)*, 2001 FCA 203, [2001] FCJ No 1008 at para 40 that a reasonableness review requires merely that the Court be able to perceive a rational basis for the Panel's conclusions. This Court elaborated on the point in *Pembina Institute for Appropriate Development v Canada (Attorney General)*, 2008 FC 302, [2008] FCJ No 324 (*Pembina*), stating that "deference to expertise is based on the cogent articulation of the rationale [*sic*] basis for conclusions reached" (para 75). This view is consistent with *Dunsmuir*, above, in which the Supreme Court held that reasonableness is concerned "mostly with the existence of justification, transparency and intelligibility within the decision-making process. But it is also concerned with whether the decision falls within a range of possible, acceptable outcomes which are defensible in respect of the facts and law" (at para 47).

Finally, it is well-established that questions of procedural fairness are to be assessed on the standard of correctness (*Khosa*, above, at para 43). NunatuKavut's arguments related to their right to be heard will thus be assessed on this standard.

Notes and Questions

1. *Grand Riverkeeper* arrives at the same conclusion that is now typically reached in most environmental law-related judicial reviews post-*Dunsmuir*: that the applicable standard of review is one of reasonableness. That said,

the case is especially interesting in that it underscores that reasonableness review must entail a careful consideration of whether the impugned decision is accompanied by a *"cogent articulation of the rationale for conclusions reached"*. It borrows this turn of phrase from *Pembina Institute for Appropriate Development v. Canada (Attorney General)*, 2008 FC 302, a case about whether the reasons offered by a tribunal met the *Dunsmuir* reasonableness standard that we consider later in this chapter in Part III. According to *Grand Riverkeeper*, the "cogent articulation" requirement set out in *Pembina* flows directly from *Dunsmuir's* observation that reasonableness review is concerned both with the "justification, transparency and intelligibility" of a decision and with whether the decision falls within "a range of possible, acceptable [and defensible] outcomes".

2. In light of the foregoing, consider the implications of the FCA's decision in *Ontario Power Generation v. Greenpeace* (*"OPG"*). By the time this matter arrived at the FCA, all parties agreed that the reasonableness standard of review governed, so the appeal turned on how this reasonableness test should be applied. In *OPG*, the applicable statute (the *Canadian Environmental Assessment Act* or "CEAA") required the reviewing panel (the "Panel") to "consider" a list of enumerated environmental effects in its report. Where the majority and dissent parted ways was over what kind of "consideration" could pass muster applying a reasonableness standard. Ultimately the majority concluded that a failure of the Panel to consider mandatory environmental effects under CEAA could only be proven under a reasonableness analysis if the challenger demonstrated that "the Panel gave no consideration at all to those environmental effects".

Greenpeace Canada v. Canada (Attorney General)
(*sub nom. Ontario Power Generation Inc. v. Greenpeace Canada*)
2015 FCA 186

[This was an appeal from a decision of Russell J. to grant an application for judicial review seeking to set aside an environmental assessment report and recommendations made by a Joint Review Panel (JRP) in relation to a proposal by OPG to build new nuclear generating facilities at Darlington, Ontario. Applying a reasonableness standard of review, Russell J. found that the JRP's report was deficient in several respects. OPG appealed.]

RENNIE J.A. (dissenting): —

Analysis

Standard of Review on Appeal

The parties agree that on appeal of an order issued in an application for judicial review, the task of this Court is to determine whether the Judge below identified the appropriate standard of review and applied it correctly: *Agraira v Canada (Minister of Public Safety and Emergency Preparedness)*, [2013] 2 S.C.R. 559, 2013 SCC 36; put otherwise, the appeal court itself reviews the tribunal decision on the standard of review.

As previously stated, the Judge characterized the issues before him as questions of mixed fact and law, and as such he concluded that the Panel's findings in the EA Report were subject to review on the reasonableness standard.

The parties agree that the Judge chose the appropriate standard of review. They disagree as to its application.

Generally speaking, the three parties appealing the Judge's decision (OPG, CNCS, and the Attorney General of Canada) submit that the Judge failed to show, in relation to the three matters, deference to the Panel's assessment of the nature and sufficiency of the evidence required by the reasonableness standard of review, and instead, he substituted his own view of the evidence on those issues.

The respondents, on the other hand, contend that the essence of the appellants' complaint is that the Judge, while deferential, was not sufficiently deferential. They noted that the Judge did not re-weigh the evidence before the Panel; rather, the essence of the Judge's decision is that the Panel did not do what it was required to do under the Act. [...]

[**Ed. Note:** Rennie J.A. then analyzes the Judge's reasons and concludes that Russell J.'s review of the tribunal's decision to grant the judicial review application should be upheld.]

TRUDEL and RYER JJ.A.: —

Standard of Review

Since the decision of the Supreme Court of Canada in *Dunsmuir v. New Brunswick*, 2008 SCC 9, [2008] 1 S.C.R. 190 [*Dunsmuir*], there are only two standards of review: correctness and reasonableness. When a question is reviewed on the correctness standard, the reviewing court is free to substitute its judgment on the question for that of the tribunal whose decision with respect to that question is under review. When the question is reviewed on the reasonableness standard, the reviewing court may not intervene by simply substituting its opinion for that of the tribunal. Rather, the reviewing court can only intervene if the decision is not reasonable.

Dunsmuir informs that the nature of the question under review will be the starting point in the determination of the applicable standard of review in respect of that question. Questions of law are sometimes reviewed on the standard of correctness, while questions of mixed fact and law are reviewed on the standard of reasonableness, absent readily extricable questions of law.

Discussion

Did the Judge Select the Correct Standard of Review?

The Judge selected reasonableness as the standard of review with respect to the question of whether the Panel considered or failed to consider the environmental effects of HSEs [Hazardous Substance Emissions] from the Project and their significance, as required by paragraphs 16(1)(*a*) and (*b*) of the Act. We are of the view that this is a question of mixed fact and law in respect of which we can discern no readily extricable legal issue. Accordingly, we agree with the Judge that this question must be reviewed on the standard of review of reasonableness.

Did the Judge Correctly Apply the Reasonableness Standard?

In the circumstances, the Panel made no specific finding that it had complied with the consideration requirements in paragraphs 16(1)(*a*) and (*b*) of the Act. However, it is our view that in conducting the EA and preparing the EA Report, the Panel must be taken to have implicitly satisfied itself that it was in compliance with those statutory requirements. In applying the reasonableness standard to this question, we must consider the Panel's decision as a whole, in the context of the underlying record, to determine whether the Panel's implicit conclusion that it had complied with the consideration requirements is reasonable (see *Agraira* at paragraph 53).

The Consideration Requirements

The consideration requirements in paragraphs 16(1)(*a*) and (*b*) of the Act have been interpreted by the Courts.

In *Friends of the West Country Assn. v. Canada (Minister of Fisheries and Oceans)*, [2000] 2 F.C. 263, 248 N.R. 25 (CA) [*Friends of the West Country Assn*], Justice Rothstein stated at paragraph 26:

> The use of the word "shall" in subsection 16(1) indicates that *some consideration* of each factor is mandatory. [Emphasis added]

We also endorse the finding of Justice Pelletier at paragraph 71 of *Inverhuron & District Ratepayers' Assn. v. Canada (Minister of the Environment)*, 191 F.T.R. 20, [2000] F.C.J. No. 682 (QL) [*Inverhuron*], as follows:

> It is worth noting again that the function of the Court in judicial review is not to act as an "academy of science" or a "legislative upper chamber". In dealing with any of the statutory criteria, the range of factual possibilities is practically unlimited. No matter how many scenarios are considered, it is possible to conceive of one which has not been. The nature of science is such that reasonable people can disagree about relevance and significance. *In disposing of these issues, the Court's function is not to assure comprehensiveness but to assess, in a formal rather than substantive sense, whether there has been some consideration of those factors in which the Act requires the comprehensive study to address. If there has been some consideration, it is irrelevant that there could have been further and better consideration.* [Emphasis added]

Having regard to this jurisprudence, and in the absence of any specific stipulation to the contrary in the Panel Agreement, Terms of Reference and EIS Guidelines, it is apparent that the Panel was at liberty to determine the type and level of consideration that it was required to give to the HSE environmental effects in conducting the EA and in preparing the EA Report.

The Judge appears to have reached the same conclusion with respect to the level or type of the consideration requirements in subsections 16(1) and (2) of the Act. He acknowledged that the "form and extent" of any such consideration was not stipulated in the Act and that the Panel is "required to use its expertise to gauge the extent and form of 'consideration' required in each particular case" (Reasons at paragraph 195).

In addition, at paragraph 198 of the Reasons, the Judge confirmed that it is not the role of the Court to assess and reweigh the methodology and conclusions of an expert panel, stating:

> In attacking the EA Report as inadequate, the Applicants are to a considerable extent asking the Court to assess and reweigh the methodology and conclusions of an expert panel. This is not the role of the Court. It is true that s. 16(1) and (2) of the CEAA mandate the "consideration" of certain factors, *but the way this is done and the weight to be ascribed to each factor is left to the expert Panel to be assessed in accordance with the purposes of the Act*. [Emphasis added]

It has not been asserted by any party to the appeals that the Panel Agreement, Terms of Reference or EIS Guidelines required, or the Panel itself stipulated, any particular type or level of consideration that it would give to the HSE environmental effects. Thus, in our view, the type or level of consideration that the Panel was required to give to those effects was simply that which is mandated in *Friends of the West Country Assn and Inverhuron*, namely, "some consideration." It follows, in our view, that a failure of the Panel to consider the HSE environmental effects can only be established if it is demonstrated that the Panel gave no consideration at all to those environmental effects.

Did the Panel Consider the HSE Environmental Effects?

[...] In conclusion, it is our view that the EA Report, the record before the Court, and indeed the Reasons themselves, demonstrate that in conducting the EA and preparing the EA Report, the Panel considered the HSE environmental effects as required by paragraphs 16(1)(*a*) and (*b*) of the Act. Accordingly, we are of the view that in concluding that the Panel failed to give consideration to the environmental effects of HSE, as required by paragraphs 16(1)(*a*) and (*b*) of the Act, the Judge misapplied the reasonableness standard of review.

Notes and Questions

1. The majority's suggestion in *OPG* that judicial scrutiny of whether a tribunal met its obligation to consider a mandatory statutory factor is limited to considering whether the tribunal gave any consideration whatsoever to the factor in question is novel and, to some, a troubling restriction on the judicial role. Notably, the *OPG* "some consideration" test has not been relied on or even mentioned in subsequent FCA or FC cases: see, for example, *Gitxaala Nation v. Canada*, 2016 FCA 187, leave to appeal refused *R. v. Raincoast Conservation Foundation*, 2017 CarswellNat 263 (S.C.C.), or *Tsleil-Waututh Nation v. Canada (Attorney General)*, 2017 FCA 128.

2. The *OPG* case has also been criticized for endorsing the idea that courts should avoid becoming "academies of science", as a basis for adopting a highly deferential posture on judicial review. As Olszynski and Doelle point out, the lineage of this "academies of science" concept is not well understood and does not necessarily tilt in favour of judicial deference: see online <https://blogs.dal.ca/melaw/2015/09/22/ontario-power-generation-

inc-v-greenpeace-canada-form-over-substance-leads-to-a-low-threshold-
for-federal-environmental-assessment/>. Moreover, it is a concept that has
been rejected in the Federal Court as a basis for constraining the judicial
role in environmental cases: see, for example, the reasons of Zinn J. in
Alberta Wilderness Assn. v. Canada (Minister of Environment), 2009 FC
710, additional reasons 2009 FC 882 (extracted in Chapter 9).

Jason MacLean & Chris Tollefson,
"Climate-Proofing Judicial Review after Paris:
Judicial Competence and Courage"
(2018) 31 J. Envtl. L. & Prac. 245

Introduction: Climate Change, Judicial Review and the Rule of Law

We are at a critical juncture in our efforts to mitigate climate change and
accelerate the transition towards sustainability. According to a recent report on
global greenhouse gas (GHG) emissions, if emissions continue to rise — or even
remain level — beyond the year 2020, the climate stabilization goals established in
the 2015 Paris climate change agreement will become almost assuredly
unattainable. Moreover, the UN Sustainable Development Goals (SDGs), also
established in 2015, will be similarly jeopardized. To meet its domestic and
international commitments, Canada must adopt comprehensive domestic policies
and regulations capable of reducing GHG emissions and promoting sustainability
as soon as possible.

It is in this urgent public policy context that the federal government
conducted a review of its environmental and regulatory assessment processes [...]

[...] While the environmental assessment law reform piece has received and
will continue to receive considerable critical attention, much less attention has
been paid so far to the equally crucial judicial review piece. The aim of this paper is
to begin to fill this gap by discussing how robust judicial review of environmental
assessments (EAs) is a critical component of Canada's ability to meet its climate
change and sustainability goals.

There are significant obstacles, however, impeding the adoption of such an
approach. The foremost obstacle to robust judicial review facilitating Canada's
compliance with the *Paris Agreement* and its contribution to the UN's SDGs is the
excessive deference reviewing courts tend to give to administrative agencies and
the government in respect of EAs. The high-water mark of this form and extent of
judicial deference is the Federal Court of Appeal's decision in *Ontario Power
Generation*, quoted above. In *Ontario Power Generation*, the majority of the court
established the "some consideration" threshold of judicial review — so long as the
administrative agency gives some consideration, for example as long as it does not
fail to give any consideration at all, to the potential environmental effects of a
proposed project, reviewing courts will defer to the agency's assessment.

While *Ontario Power Generation* may be the height — or perhaps nadir — of
judicial deference, many other cases may be cited as examples of Canadian courts'
categorical deference to the government regarding EAs. In *Gitxaala Nation v.
Canada*, for instance, Stratas J.A. for a unanimous Federal Court of Appeal noted

that "[i]n conducting its assessment [of the Northern Gateway oil pipeline project], the Governor in Council has to balance a broad variety of matters, *most of which are more properly within the realm of the executive, such as economic, social, cultural, environmental and political matters.*" According to Stratas J.A., "[t]he standard of review for decisions such as this — discretionary decisions founded upon the widest considerations of policy and public interest — is reasonableness".

A further case in point is the Federal Court of Appeal's decision in *Forest Ethics Advocacy Assn. v. National Energy Board.* Forest Ethics (now Stand.earth) challenged the National Energy Board's decision that it would "not consider the environmental or socio-economic effects associated with the upstream activities, the development of oil sands, or the downstream use of the oil transported by the [Enbridge Line 9B] pipeline." Notwithstanding the court's finding that the National Energy Board was "the main guardian of the public interest in this regulatory area," the court ruled that because the relevant provision of the *National Energy Board Act* (s. 52) is vague, the Board's own interpretation of it should be granted considerable deference:

> The words "to it," the imprecise meaning of the words "directly," "related" and "relevant" [...] and the highly factual and policy nature of relevant determinations, taken together, *widen the margin of appreciation that this Court should afford the Board.*

Judicial review of environmental decision-making in Canada tends to be shaded in a colour decidedly other than green.

Categorical, presumptive, and ultimately excessive judicial deference to executive and administrative decision-making of this kind risks undermining not only the efficacy of our environmental assessment laws but also the rule of law more generally. Indeed, the two are intimately intertwined. In *Wilson v. Atomic Energy of Canada Ltd.*, for instance, the Supreme Court of Canada's conflicting reasons for decision highlight this tension. Writing for the majority of the court, Abella J. proposed — in remarks made expressly in *obiter dicta* — a single judicial review standard of reasonableness. In their dissenting reasons, however, Coté and Brown JJ. (joined by Moldaver J.) observed that "this case exposes a serious concern for the rule of law posed by presumptively deferential review of a decision-maker's interpretation of its home statute." In particular, the dissenting justices in *Atomic Energy* argued that "deferring in this way on matters of statutory interpretation opens up the possibility that different decision-makers may each reach opposing interpretations of the same provision [...] This concern was raised forcefully by Stratas J.A. at the Federal Court of Appeal in the present case".

Not only does this concern potentially undermine the rule-of-law principle that "all exercises of public authority must find their source in law", but it also runs counter to the laudatory principles guiding the federal government's review of environmental assessment processes noted above, particularly the first principle of "fair, predictable and transparent environmental assessment processes", and the equally crucial principle that EAs embody "evidence based decisions reflecting the best available science and Indigenous knowledge." These are very much rule-of-law principles, and their implementation in administrative and executive decision-making merits robust judicial review.

In the sections that follow, we attempt to unpack the concerns at the core of categorical judicial deference toward government and administrative agency EAs and project decisions. These concerns vary by decision-maker and statutory context, and while sometimes made explicit, they are often left unarticulated and unexamined. We hope to show that categorically deferential judicial review of EAs is a significant obstacle to Canada meetings its climate change mitigation and sustainability commitments, particularly when based upon broad statutory language. We contend, however, that Canadian courts are nonetheless quite capable of adopting a more robust supervisory approach. Moreover, we argue that robust judicial review of EAs having climate change and sustainability implications can play an important role both in helping Canada move towards its climate and sustainability targets, and potentially in diminishing the frequency with which EAs are litigated on judicial review. Indeed, we argue that a robust judicial review regime is a critical precondition to the timely and efficient operation of EA processes, and to charting legal pathways to deep decarbonization and scalable renewable energy generation pursuant to the *Paris Agreement* and the UN's SDGs.

Academies of Science, Legislative Upper Chambers and Judicial Competence

In *Ontario Power Generation*, the majority of the Federal Court of Appeal endorsed an earlier Federal Court decision noting that the role of the court in a judicial review "is not to act as an 'academy of science' or a 'legislative upper chamber.'" The rest of the court's concern is worth quoting in full:

> In dealing with any of the statutory criteria, the range of factual possibilities is practically unlimited. No matter how many scenarios are considered, it is possible to conceive of one which has not been. The nature of science is such that reasonable people can disagree about relevance and significance. *In disposing of these issues, the Court's function is not to assure comprehensiveness but to assess, in a formal rather than substantive sense, whether there has been some consideration of those factors in which the Act requires the comprehensive study to address. If there has been some consideration, it is irrelevant that there could have been further and better consideration.*

We are mindful of Olszynski and Doelle's argument that the term "academy of science" must be understood as the product of a peculiar procedural context; we also agree with their assessment that it is a "strong turn of phrase." Indeed, it seems to have taken on a near mytho-legal status whereby it is ritually incanted by counsel seeking to limit reviewing courts' substantive inquiry into governmental and administrative decision-making in respect of environmental matters, which by definition involve complex hybrid issues of scientific and technical expertise interwoven with questions of law and public policy. Given the stakes, more robust judicial review is warranted in such cases. As some of the leading commentators on administrative law more generally observe,

> [w]hile reviewing courts should normally show a measure of deference to a specialist agency's interpretation of its enabling statute, it is appropriate to scrutinize more closely those decisions that seem contrary to the interests of those intended beneficiaries of the legislation or to that aspect of the public interest that the legislation was enacted to protect. Examples include [...] the protection offered by various statutory programs to members of the public in their capacity as [...]

breathers of air and drinkers of water. In this way, courts can provide a counterweight to the pressure that private economic interests often bring to bear on public agencies to sidestep their regulatory responsibilities.

The critical question then becomes what does this closer kind of scrutiny look like, and are courts even capable of providing it? Recall, for instance, Justice Stratas' admonition in the Federal Court of Appeal's decision in *Gitxaala* that the government's balancing of economic, cultural, and environmental considerations — including its access to scientific expertise — involves *"matters very much outside of the ken of the courts."* With Justice Binnie (quoted above), however, we argue that it is very much within the ken of the courts to carefully scrutinize technical and scientific evidence in relation to issues of law and public policy. Indeed, the most compelling evidence of this judicial competency, and the best description available of what such competence actually looks like in practice, may be found in judicial decisions themselves across a number of areas of law primarily under the jurisdiction of the federal courts.

Notes and Questions

1. The majority in *OPG* opines that, under a reasonableness standard of review, if there is any evidence whatsoever that the decision-maker turned its mind to the statutory factors that it was required to consider, a judicial review of the decision in question must necessarily fail. What judicial philosophy and assumptions likely underpin such a deferential approach? What would the dissenters in *Wilson* say about the majority decision in *OPG*?

2. To what extent does the majority legitimately worry about courts becoming "academies of science"? What is an academy of science and why is it thought that this is a compelling argument for judicial restraint? Note that this evocative turn of phrase is invoked by government lawyers in *Alberta Wilderness Assn. v. Canada (Minister of Environment)*, 2009 FC 710, additional reasons 2009 FC 882 (also known as *Greater Sage-Grouse*) as a reason why the court ought not to engage in careful scrutiny of the reasonableness of administrative action. Justice Zinn, the reviewing judge, took a different view: see Chapter 9.

3. Increasingly, in the wake of the Supreme Court's landmark decisions in *Haida Nation v. British Columbia (Minister of Forests)*, 2004 SCC 73, and *Taku River Tlingit First Nation v. British Columbia (Project Assessment Director)*, (*sub nom. Taku River Tlingit First Nation v. Tulsequah Chief Mine Project (Project Assessment Director)*) 2004 SCC 74, judicial review of government decisions is brought on the ground that the Crown has failed to comply with its duty to consult as guaranteed under section 35 of the *Constitution Act, 1982*: see Chapter 3. This has prompted significant judicial reflection on how cases framed in this fashion should be analyzed in terms of standard of review.

PART II — STANDARD OF REVIEW 529

Dene Tha' First Nation v. Canada (Minister of Environment)
2006 FC 1354,
affirmed 2008 FCA 20

[The applicant challenged the federal Crown, alleging a breach of the duty to consult in relation to its exclusion from discussions and decisions regarding the design of the regulatory and environmental review processes related to the Mackenzie Gas Pipeline ("MGP"). The proposed pipeline was to originate in Inuvik in the far north of the Northwest Territories and terminate just south of the Northwest Territories-Alberta border, traversing through the applicant's traditional territory.]

PHELAN J.: — The Ministers identified as the theme of its submissions the overall reasonableness of the Crown's behavior, asserting that this was the appropriate standard of review for the Court to adopt on this judicial review.

The Ministers further used the language of deference, imposing the pragmatic and functional approach from *Dr. Q v. College of Physicians and Surgeons of British Columbia*, [2003] 1 S.C.R. 226 that dominates administrative law onto the case at hand. This approach is not particularly helpful in this case where the core issue is whether there was a duty to consult and when did it arise.

The pragmatic and functional approach and the language of deference are tools most often used by courts to establish jurisdictional respect vis-a-vis statutorily created boards and tribunals. The law of aboriginal consultation thus far has no statutory source other than the constitutional one of s. 35. Therefore, to talk of deference and/or impose a test, the goal of which is to determine the level of deference, is inappropriate in this context.

In respect of the Ministers' "theme" of reasonableness, comments by the Chief Justice in *Haida* are illuminating. At paragraphs 60–63 of her judgment in *Haida Nation*, McLachlin C.J.C. concisely addresses the issue of administrative review of government decisions vis-à-vis first nations:

- Where the government's conduct is challenged on the basis of allegations that it failed to discharge its duty to consult and accommodate pending claims resolution, the matter may go to the courts for review. To date, the Province has established no process for this purpose. The question of what standard of review the court should apply in judging the adequacy of the government's efforts cannot be answered in the absence of such a process. General principles of administrative law, however, suggest the following.

- On questions of law, a decision-maker must generally be correct: for example, *Paul v. British Columbia (Forest Appeals Commission)*, [2003] 2 S.C.R. 585, 2003 SCC 55. On questions of fact or mixed fact and law, on the other hand, a reviewing body may owe a degree of deference to the decision-maker. The existence or extent of the duty to consult or accommodate is a legal question in the sense that it defines a legal duty. However, it is typically premised on an assessment of the facts. It follows that a degree of deference to the findings of fact of the initial adjudicator may be appropriate. The need for deference and its degree will depend on the nature of the question the tribunal was addressing and the extent to which the facts were within the expertise of the tribunal: *Law Society of New Brunswick v. Ryan*, [2003] 1 S.C.R. 247, 2003 SCC 20; *Paul, supra*. Absent error on legal issues, the tribunal may be in a better position to evaluate the issue than the reviewing court, and some degree of deference may be required. In such a case, the standard of review is likely to be reasonableness. To the extent that the issue is one of pure law, and can be isolated from the issues of fact, the standard is correctness. However, where the two are inextricably entwined, the standard will likely be reasonableness: *Canada (Director of Investigation and Research) v. Southam Inc.*, [1997] 1 S.C.R. 748.

- The process itself would likely fall to be examined on a standard of reasonableness. Perfect satisfaction is not required; the question is whether the regulatory scheme or government action "viewed as a whole, accommodates the collective aboriginal right in question": *Gladstone, supra*, [1996] 2 S.C.R. 723, at para. 170. What is required is not perfection, but reasonableness. As stated in *Nikal, supra*, [1996] 1 S.C.R. 1013, at para. 110, "in [...] information and consultation the concept of reasonableness must come into play [...]. So long as every reasonable effort is made to inform and to consult, such efforts would suffice". The government is required to make reasonable efforts to inform and consult. This suffices to discharge the duty.

- Should the government misconceive the seriousness of the claim or impact of the infringement, this question of law would likely be judged by correctness. Where the government is correct on these matters and acts on the appropriate standard, the decision will be set aside only if the government's process is unreasonable. The focus, as discussed above, is not on the outcome, but on the process of consultation and accommodation.

It thus follows that as the question as to the existence of a duty to consult and or accommodate is one of law, then the appropriate standard of review is correctness. Often, however, the duty to consult or accommodate is premised on factual findings. When these factual findings cannot be extricated from the legal question of consultation, more deference is warranted and the standard should be reasonableness.

These two standards of review dovetail onto the questions of whether there is a duty to consult and if so, what is its scope. The further question of whether the duty to consult has been met attracts a different analysis. From McLachlin C.J.C.'s reasons, it is clear that the standard of review for this latter question is reasonableness. To put that matter in slightly different terms, the government's burden is to demonstrate that the process it adopted concerning consultation with First Nations was reasonable. In other words, the process does not have to be perfect.

In this case, all parties agree that there is a duty to consult and accommodate the Dene Tha'. The disagreement centers on when this duty arose and whether the government's failure to consult the Dene Tha' on issues of design of the consultation process constituted a breach. The federal government's efforts made after the determination as to the scope and existence of the duty to consult may be reviewed on the reasonableness standard. The issue of when the duty to consult arose is, however, one that goes to the definition of the scope of this duty, as such, as it is considered a question of law, it would attract the correctness standard of review.

In my view, the question posed by the Dene Tha' is whether the duty to consult arose at the stage of process design — that is, from late 2000 to early 2002. The questions of fact involved in this issue — what the precise Aboriginal interests of the Dene Tha' are and what are the adverse effects of this failure to consult — are better contemplated in determining the content of the duty to consult, not its bare existence. As the question posed by Dene Tha' is a question of law focused on whether the duty to consult extends to a time period prior to any decision-making as to land use, the appropriate standard of review for this inquiry is correctness.

Whether or not the government's actions/efforts after the duty to consult arose complied with this duty, however, would be judged on a reasonableness standard, assuming that it actually engaged in consultation. The issue would be whether it had engaged in reasonable consultation or made reasonable efforts to do so.

Notes and Questions

1. Do you agree with Phelan J.'s conclusion that the standards of review in duty to consult cases should turn on whether the issue pertains to the "existence" of the duty versus its "content"? Insofar as the rights in question are constitutionally guaranteed, is there not an argument that, regardless of whether the government has erred in either respect, the standard of review should be correctness?

2. Phelan J. quotes the Chief Justice in *Haida* as follows:

   Should the government misconceive the seriousness of the claim or impact of the infringement, this question of law would likely be judged by correctness. Where the government is correct on these matters and acts on the appropriate standard, the decision will be set aside only if the government's process is unreasonable.

   Is Phelan J.'s proposed approach, which turns on the distinction between the "existence" as opposed to the "content" of the duty to consult, consistent with the Chief Justice's words? Why or why not? For further reflections on the relationship between the standard of review and the duty to consult see *Ktunaxa Nation v. British Columbia (Forests, Lands and Natural Resource Operations)*, 2017 SCC 54.

Part III — Grounds for Judicial Review

As described in Part I, applications for judicial review must specify the grounds upon which relief is being sought. The applicant must also identify the administrative action or decision for which review is being sought, the responsible decision-maker, and the form(s) of remedy being sought. In this

Part, we canvass a series of cases selected to illustrate frequently invoked grounds for judicial review in environmental cases. It should be borne in mind that many of these cases were decided prior to the SCC's landmark decision in *Dunsmuir* that, as discussed in Part II, establishes a reasonableness-focused inquiry as the default standard of review. Accordingly, it should not be assumed that the following cases would have been decided the same way post-*Dunsmuir*. That said, the various grounds for review profiled in the cases that follow will continue to be highly relevant to judicial reviews in the environmental law context going forward.

We commence with two cases where the applicant argued that the impugned decision was defective due to a reliance on irrelevant considerations: *Wimpey Western Ltd. v. Alberta (Department of the Environment)* and *Imperial Oil Ltd. v. British Columbia (Ministry of Water, Land & Air Protection)*. The latter case also illustrates that decision-makers are precluded from delegating (directly or by implication) their power to decide without clear statutory authority. Next we consider the principles governing challenges based on allegations of discrimination: *Moresby Explorers Ltd. v. Canada (Attorney General)*. We then reflect on the challenges based on procedural fairness: *Chameau Exploration Ltd. v. Nova Scotia (Attorney General)* and *Taseko Mines Limited v. Canada (Environment)*. We then consider whether, and to what extent, administrative decisions may be impugned on the basis of a failure to give adequate (or any) reasons: *Pembina Institute for Appropriate Development v. Canada (Attorney General)* and *Newfoundland & Labrador Nurses' Union v. Newfoundland & Labrador (Treasury Board)*. Finally, we consider the evolving case law where the ground for review is an alleged failure by the Crown to discharge its duty to consult and accommodate. To this end, we look at the FCA's recent decision *Tsleil-Waututh Nation v. Canada (Attorney General)*.

Reliance on Irrelevant Considerations / Fettering Discretion

Wimpey Western Ltd. v. Alberta (Department of the Environment)
(1983), 2 D.L.R. (4th) 309 (Alta. C.A.)

[The appellants sought a declaration compelling the Director of the Division of Standards and Approvals of the Department of the Environment to issue a permit for the construction of a wastewater treatment facility. The appellants owned a property in the Municipal District of Sturgeon. After obtaining subdivision approval to develop the land in stages as an industrial park, their application for a permit to construct a waste water treatment facility under the *Clean Water Act* was rejected. Their application for judicial review was dismissed by the Alberta Court of Queen's Bench, from which decision this appeal was brought.]

HARRADENCE J.A.: — The issues on this appeal are:

1. Whether the Director of the Standards and Approvals Division of the Department of the Environment (the "Director"), in exercising his discretion to grant a permit to construct a waste water treatment facility under the *Clean Water Act*, may consider the Minister's policy of not granting permits for major facilities until a "long-term servicing option" is operational.

2. Whether the Director fettered or refused to exercise his discretion in applying this policy to the appellant's application [...]

The appellants contend that the Director exceeded his jurisdiction by taking into account an irrelevant consideration, namely, the Minister's policy of deferring individual water treatment facilities in favour of larger Regional facilities. They argue that the Director's discretion is limited by the *Clean Water Act* to consideration of technical matters such as amounts, concentrations and rates of discharge of contaminants from waste water treatment facilities.

In determining the scope of the Director's discretion, one must start with the Act granting it — the *Clean Water Act*. Section 3(4) gives the Director a broad discretion as follows:

> The Director of Standards and Approvals may issue or refuse to issue a permit or may require a change in location of the water facility or a change in the plans and specifications as a condition precedent to giving a permit under this section.

The Act places no limitation on the Director's power to refuse to issue a permit. This does not mean, however, that his discretion is unfettered. As was stated by Lord Reid in *Padfield v. Minister of Agriculture, Fisheries & Food*, [1968] A.C. 997 (H.L.), at 1030:

> Parliament must have conferred the discretion with the intention that it should be used to promote the policy and objects of the Act; the policy and objects of the Act must be determined by construing the Act as a whole and construction is always a matter of law for the court.

While the Act does not set out the criteria which the Director must consider in making his decision, it is implicit that he may consider those items set out in subsections (2), (4) and (5) of section 3. The Act does not, however, require the Director to issue a permit once he is satisfied as to those items. It is reasonable to conclude that the Legislature intended that the Director have a discretion to refuse to issue a permit notwithstanding such satisfaction.

In de Smith, *Judicial Review of Administrative Action* (4th Ed.) at p. 340-341, it states:

> In determining what factors may or must be taken into account by the competent authority, the courts are faced with problems of statutory interpretation [...]. If relevant factors are specified in the enabling Act it is for the courts to determine whether they are factors to which the authority is compelled to have regard and, if so, whether they are to be construed as being exhaustive. If the relevant factors are not specified [...] it is for the courts to determine whether the permissible considerations are impliedly restricted, and, if so, to what extent [...]

The factors which are relevant need not be limited to those implicit in the enabling Act. The test is whether the consideration in question is within the intent and purpose of the Act.

It is clear that the purpose of this enactment is to create an effective and focal means of controlling and eliminating the problems created by exploitation or misuse of the environment. The Minister is given far-reaching powers and in my view it is within the scope of these powers to devise policies aimed at limiting the number of points of discharge of contaminants into Alberta's waterways for ease of monitoring. It is relevant for the Director to consider the policies of the Minister keeping in mind that he must neither act under dictation nor fetter his discretion.

Imperial Oil Ltd. v. British Columbia (Ministry of Water, Land & Air Protection)
2002 BCSC 219,
additional reasons 2002 BCSC 954

ROSS J.: — These proceedings arise from the attempts by the petitioner, Imperial Oil Limited ("Imperial"), to obtain an approval from the Ministry of Water, Land and Air Protection (the "Ministry") of a proposal to remediate certain lands in Salmo, British Columbia which have become contaminated with hydrocarbons.

Imperial alleges that the settlement of the civil claims was the sole reason that the respondent withheld the AIP and that this was an irrelevant consideration. Therefore, Imperial seeks an order of mandamus requiring the respondent to issue the AIP (approval-in-principle).

Imperial submits that, in this case, the only reason for the decision-maker's failure to issue the approval is one which is an improper consideration under the enabling legislation; namely, the consideration of the settlement of the civil claims of the Owners [of the contaminated lands]. In such cases, it submits, an order for mandamus is appropriate [...]

[**Ed. Note:** Review of applicable BC *Waste Management Act* provisions is omitted.]

These provisions do not confer jurisdiction upon the respondent with respect to tort claims, nor with respect to compensation for anything other than costs of remediation. The claims in question of the Owners were tort claims and not claims for the costs of remediation.

Under the [*Waste Management*] *Act* the respondent does not have the authority to order compensation to be paid with respect to such claims, nor is he empowered under the Act to adjudicate such claims. It follows that he cannot do indirectly what he is not entitled to do directly. Compensation for third parties, other than compensation for the costs of remediation, is therefore not a relevant factor for the respondent to consider in the exercise of his discretion with respect to an application for an AIP. Where he does so, he has exceeded his jurisdiction.

Further, where, as in this case, the irrelevant consideration is stated to be the only reason for the failure to issue the AIP, mandamus is appropriate, see *McKeown v. Port Moody (City)*, [2000] B.C.J. No. 185, per Skipp J. It is not, in my view, an appropriate or adequate remedy in this case to send Imperial back to repeat some or all of the process with another decision-maker.

Counsel for the respondent has argued that mandamus is not appropriate in this case even if the consideration of compensation for the civil claims of the Owners was an irrelevant consideration because there must be further consultation with the Owners prior to an AIP being issued. That submission, however, ignores the respondent's position, which was that he was prepared to issue the AIP, subject only to the settlement of the civil claims. In other words, he had come to a decision and was satisfied that there had been sufficient consultation with the concerned parties with respect to the content of the AIP.

There is a further problem. The respondent decided to issue the AIP upon confirmation from the Owners and the Village of Salmo that they had an acceptable agreement with Imperial. This effectively put the Owners and the Village in control of the decision to issue or withhold the AIP. In my view, this constituted an improper delegation of the Deputy Director's discretion and an improper fettering of his discretion, see *Vic Restaurant Inc. v. The City of Montreal*, [1959] S.C.R. 58 at 82, per Locke J.

Counsel for the Owners opposes the application for mandamus. Much of his submission was directed to matters that may well be appropriate considerations were this hearing to be an appeal or a hearing *de novo* with respect to the merits of the AIP. This, however, is not such a hearing.

[**Ed. Note:** In the result, the court made the order for *mandamus* sought by Imperial. The other relief sought by Imperial was denied because it was moot and had no practical application on the parties' rights.]

Notes and Questions

1. In both cases, the courts are quite unequivocal in their conclusions on the law. Are the cases that different? Why in the *Wimpey* case did the court conclude that the decision-maker acted within his discretion, while in the *Imperial* case the court reached the opposite conclusion?

2. Much of the discussion in both cases turns on the question of what is legally relevant to decision-makers when they are deciding an issue that affects individual rights. What tools or principles should courts use to determine "relevancy" in this setting?

Discrimination in the Exercise of Regulation-making Power

Moresby Explorers Ltd. v. Canada (Attorney General)
2007 FCA 273,
leave to appeal refused 2008 CarswellNat 388 (S.C.C.)

PELLETIER J.A. (for the court): —

Facts

This dispute arises out of the management of the Gwaii Haanas National Park Reserve (the Park) by the Archipelago Management Board (the AMB). The AMB is a structure adopted to permit the Government of Canada and the Council of the Haida Nation to collaborate in the management of the Park without prejudice to either's position in the negotiation of the Haida land claim over a territory which includes the Park. For the details of the AMB's structure and its legal underpinnings, see *Moresby Explorers Ltd. v. Canada (Attorney General)*, 2001 FCT 780, [2001] 4 F.C. 591 (T.D.) at paragraph 67.

In the exercise of its mandate, the AMB has adopted a group of policies limiting access to the Park with a view to protecting its natural and cultural resources. The starting point for those policies was the determination that the Park's carrying capacity was 33,000 user-day/nights per year. The AMB then allocated those user-day/nights equally between three groups, namely, independent users, Haida tour operators, and non-Haida tour operators. As a result, a maximum allocation of 11,000 user-day/nights was available to each group. The AMB also adopted a "Business caps" policy to limit the maximum number of user-day/nights available to any tour operator: 22 client-days per day, and 2,500 user-day/nights per year. This policy is designed to prevent any single operator from monopolizing Park resources.

The difficulty with the policies adopted by the AMB is that there are no Haida tour operators, while the non-Haida quota of user-day/nights is oversubscribed. Moresby alleges that the 11,000 user-day/nights limitation on non-Haida tour operators is unlawfully restricting the growth of its business.

Moresby's Submissions

Moresby attacks the Haida Allocation Policy and the Business caps on the ground of administrative discrimination, that is "delegated powers exercised by a subordinate authority (*e.g.* a National Parks superintendent) must be exercised strictly within the ambit of the empowering legislation, particularly where they restrict employment or the right to work".: Moresby's Memorandum, at para. 27.

This argument is succinctly summarized at paragraph 31 of Moresby's Memorandum where the following appears:

> There is nothing in either the *Canada National Parks Act* or *Businesses Regulations* that remotely authorizes a power to discriminate based on race or business size. The *Act*, in s. 4, expressly refers to *all* the people of Canada. The *Businesses Regulations*, ss. 4.1 and 5, proscribe the licensing discretion in relatively restrictive terms. All statutory provisions focus on the Park and none on the personal characteristics of

the licensee. The most that can be said is that a subordinate licensing authority may, by necessary implication, assess the merits and qualifications of individual licence applicants with respect to their competence to carry out the purposes of the legislation. However, the legislation nowhere indicates an intention to allow the Superintendent to fence out or restrict a whole class of applicants on the basis of their race or the size of their businesses. This is not within the ambit of this legislation. [...]

Analysis

[...] The only question remaining is whether the Superintendent has the legislative authority to distinguish between, or to create, different classes of businesses. An analogous issue was raised in *Sunshine Village Corp. v. Canada (Parks) (F.C.A.)*, 2004 FCA 166, [2004] 3 F.C.R. 600 (*Sunshine Village Corp.*), where Sunshine Village argued that setting building permit fees in Banff and Jasper National Parks at a higher rate than in other national parks was unlawful discrimination as it was *ultra vires* the Governor in Council. The Trial Division of the Federal Court of Canada (as it then was) accepted Sunshine Village's argument and held that the differential setting of business fees was discriminatory (in the administrative law sense) and was not authorized expressly or by necessary implication by the governing legislation: see *Sunshine Village Corp. v. Canada (Parks) (T.D.)*, 2003 FCT 546, [2003] 4 F.C. 459.

This Court allowed the Crown's appeal on the basis that the legislation authorizing the making of the Regulations which were allegedly discriminatory was broad enough to permit the Governor in Council to draw distinctions between users of different national parks. The Court distinguished the situation before it from the usual rule in municipal law cases, where discriminatory bylaws are prohibited, as follows:

> Unlike the historic practice of the provinces granting specific powers to municipalities, these words, on their face, confer broad authority on the Governor in Council. There is no indication that they are subject to any limitation. The Court must take the statute as it finds it. In the absence of limiting words in the statute, the Court will not read in limitations.
>
> ...
>
> The courts have historically required express or necessarily implied authorization in municipalities' governing statutes before the municipalities will be allowed to enact discriminatory by-laws. Conversely, when Parliament confers regulation-making authority on the Governor in Council in general terms, in respect of fees for Crown services, the courts approach the review of such regulations in a deferential manner. That is simply a matter of interpreting, in context, the words Parliament has used in accordance with their ordinary and grammatical meaning.

[*Sunshine Village Corp. v. Canada (Parks) (F.C.A.)*, at para. 18 and 22.]

Since there was no limitation in the governing legislation restricting the Governor in Council's power to set different scales for building fees in different parks, the Court was not prepared to read them in. The situation is therefore the exact opposite of that which prevails in municipal law where discrimination is prohibited unless it is expressly allowed. In the context of legislation conferring broad regulation making power on the Governor in Council, discrimination (in the administrative law sense) is permitted unless it is expressly prohibited. [...]

In this case, we are not dealing with a challenge to the Governor in Council's regulation making power, but rather with the exercise of the power conferred upon the Superintendent by those Regulations. The respondent alleges [...] that because the object of Moresby's challenge is a policy adopted pursuant to the Regulations rather than the Regulations themselves, the application cannot succeed, since mere policies (as opposed to decisions based on policies) are not subject to review.

The grounds on which a policy may be challenged are limited. Policies are normally afforded much deference; one cannot, for example, mount a judicial challenge against the wisdom or soundness of a government policy *Maple Lodge Farms Ltd. v. Canada*, [1982] 2 S.C.R. 2, at 7-8. This does not, however, preclude the court from making a determination as to the legality of a given policy *Canada (Attorney General) v. Inuit Tapirisat of Canada*, [1980] 2 S.C.R. 735 at 751-752; *Roncarelli v. Duplessis*, S.C.R. 121, at 140. Because illegality goes to the validity of a policy rather than to its application, an illegal policy can be challenged at any time; the claimant need not wait till the policy has been applied to his or her specific case (*Krause v. Canada (C.A.)*, [1999] 2 F.C. 476, at para. 16). [...]

The regulation making power found in the *Canada National Parks Act* contains no limitation which would prohibit the drawing of distinctions between various classes of businesses. The Regulations promulgated pursuant to that power deal with the regulation of business by means of the licensing power. That power is very broad. The Regulations do not contain any explicit limitation on the Superintendent's power to distinguish between classes of businesses. In fact, subsection 5(3) permits the Superintendent to impose conditions on a business license which depend upon the type of business. Those conditions include matters related to "the preservation, control and management of the park". I have no difficulty concluding that the legislation and the regulations are sufficiently broad to permit the Superintendent to impose conditions on business licenses which vary with the kind of business.

Moresby's argument is that it is one thing to distinguish between a hardware store and a restaurant but quite another to distinguish between a Haida owned business and a non-Haida owned business. The nature of the business being regulated may require special conditions to be imposed; the personal characteristics of the owner of the business do not impose a similar requirement. In fact, given human rights legislation and the equality provisions of the *Charter*, conditions or limitations based on race are generally contrary to public policy.

In my view, the question of administrative discrimination resolves itself as follows. The regulation making power conferred upon the Governor in Council by the *Canada National Parks Act* is not limited so as to prohibit discrimination between classes of business. Thus the Governor in Council is competent to promulgate regulations which authorize discrimination (in the administrative law sense) between individuals and businesses. This, in itself, sets the present case apart from the municipal law cases relied upon by Moresby where the delegated authority, the municipal council, lacks the power to discriminate unless it is specifically conferred by the legislation.

The Regulations passed by the Governor in Council contemplate distinctions being drawn between businesses, but not, says Moresby, the type of distinction being drawn in this case. As noted earlier, administrative law discrimination deals with drawing distinctions, as opposed to the basis on which such distinctions are drawn. Unless the distinction drawn by the Superintendent can be shown to be contrary to public policy, there is nothing in the Regulations which would preclude the type of distinction being drawn here. In the end the question is whether the allocation of access to the Park between Haida and non-Haida tour operators is contrary to public policy.

Public policy takes its color from the context in which it is invoked. Discrimination on the basis of race is contrary to public policy when the discrimination simply reinforces stereotypical conceptions of the target group. However, there is legislative support for the proposition that discrimination designed to ameliorate the condition of a historically disadvantaged group is acceptable. See, for example, section 16 of the *Canadian Human Rights Act*, R.S.C. 1985, c. H-6, where Parliament authorizes the adoption of special programs designed to prevent or reduce disadvantages suffered by groups when those disadvantages are based on prohibited grounds of discrimination. See also the *Employment Equity Act*, S.C. 1995, c. 44, which mandates programs designed to increase the representation of visible and other minorities in the workplace. Even the *Charter of Rights and Freedoms* contains a reservation at subsection 15(2) to the effect that the constitutional guarantee of equality "does not preclude any law, program or activity that has as its object the amelioration of conditions of disadvantaged individuals or groups". Consequently, the proposition that discrimination based on race is contrary to public policy is too broad. Discriminatory provisions designed to ameliorate the condition of the historically disadvantaged are not contrary to public policy.

[**Ed. Note:** Discussion of the remedial nature of the policy is omitted.]

In the end result, I conclude that the Regulations authorize the Superintendent to discriminate between classes of businesses and that the distinction drawn on the racial or ethnic origin of the owners of commercial tour businesses is not a distinction which is void on public policy grounds.

It follows from this that Moresby's argument with respect to administrative discrimination fails. As a result, I would dismiss Moresby's appeal.

Conclusion

In conclusion, I am of the view that the distinction drawn by the Superintendent, acting through the AMB, between Haida and non-Haida tour operators is not *ultra vires* the Superintendent on the basis that it results in discrimination between classes of businesses which is not authorized by the governing legislation. In my view, the Regulations are wide enough to include the power to draw such distinctions or, following this Court's decision in *Sunshine Village Corp.*, there is nothing in the Act or the Regulations which would prohibit such a distinction.

Notes and Questions

1. In this case, Pelletier J.A. points out that "discriminatory" policies are presumed to be illegal if enacted in by-law form at the local government level. In contrast, he observes that "in the context of legislation conferring broad regulation making power on the Governor in Council, discrimination (in the administrative law sense) is permitted unless it is expressly prohibited". What rationale(s) supports this distinction? Do you agree with it?

2. Here the Court concludes that the applicable regulations are those that empower the parks superintendent to issue business licences based on matters related to "the preservation, control and management of the park". This, in turn, means that the superintendent is entitled to "discriminate" between different kinds of businesses as long as this is not done in a manner that offends public policy. Do you agree with this line of reasoning? Do you agree with the result?

Procedural Fairness

In the administrative law context, courts have long prided themselves as defenders of procedural fairness. Illustrative of the judicial perception of this role are the following comments of Binnie J. in *Dunsmuir*:

> [...] a fair procedure is said to be the handmaiden of justice. Accordingly, procedural limits are placed on administrative bodies by statute and the common law. These include the requirements of "procedural fairness", which will vary with the type of decision-maker and the type of decision under review. On such matters, as well, the courts have the final say. The need for such procedural safeguards is obvious. Nobody should have his or her rights, interests or privileges adversely dealt with by an unjust process. Nor is such an unjust intent to be attributed easily to legislators. Hansard is full of expressions of concern by Ministers and Members of Parliament regarding the fairness of proposed legislative provisions. There is a dated hauteur about judicial pronouncements such as that the "justice of the common law will supply the omission of the legislature" (*Cooper v. Wandsworth Board of Works* (1863), 14 C.B. (N.S.) 180, 143 E.R. 414 at p. 420 (Eng. C.P.)). Generally speaking, legislators and judges in this country are working with a common set of basic legal and constitutional values. They share a belief in the rule of law. Constitutional considerations aside, however, statutory protections can nevertheless be repealed and common law protections can be modified by statute [...]

Bearing these sentiments in mind, consider the following case.

Chameau Exploration Ltd. v. Nova Scotia (Attorney General)
2007 NSSC 386

[The applicant, a company engaged in exploring and recovering artifacts from shipwrecks off the coast of Nova Scotia, sought an order quashing the decision of the Executive Director of the Nova Scotia Museum to deny a permit pursuant to the *Special Places Protection Act*, R.S.N.S. 1989, c. 438, and an order in the nature of *mandamus* to compel the Director to issue the permit. The applicant also alleged that the Director acted in excess of jurisdiction and erred in law by determining that the government of the United Kingdom owned a wreck thought to be in the area covered by the permit. In the alternative, it argued that the Director breached the rules of natural justice and procedural fairness by denying the applicant the opportunity to be heard with respect to the claim to ownership of the wreck asserted by the government of the United Kingdom.]

MacADAM J.: — The Applicant is of the view that the *Special Places Protection Act* and the *Treasure Trove Act* do not permit the Director to determine ownership of a vessel or artifact purportedly lying in an area covered by a treasure trove license. It says both statutes imply that the Province of Nova Scotia owns cultural and heritage property. It appears, however, from the correspondence noted above, that the director accepted the British claim of ownership. If there are other laws that are relevant to heritage and cultural property, over which the province claims constitutional jurisdiction, these determinations should be made in a proper forum, according to the Applicant.

The Applicant also says the Director failed to observe the rules of natural justice and procedural fairness in deciding not to issue the requested permit. An administrative decisionmaker has a duty of procedural fairness, including an obligation to give a party who will be affected by the decision an opportunity to put forward their views.

Existence of a Duty of Procedural Fairness

The existence of a common law duty of procedural fairness has long been recognized and in *Real Cardinal and Eric Oswald and Director of Kent Institution*, [1985] 2 S.C.R. 643, Le Dain, J. in delivering the judgment of the Court, at p. 653, stated:

> This Court has affirmed that there is, as a general common law principle, a duty of procedural fairness lying on every public authority making an administrative decision which is not of a legislative nature and which affects the rights, privileges or interests of an individual: [...]

Here the decision of the Director was an administrative decision, not of a legislative nature, that affected the "rights, privileges or interests" of the Applicants.

Scope and Conduct of the Duty

L'Heureux-Dube J. reviewed several factors relevant to determining the content of the duty of procedural fairness in *Baker v. Canada (Minister of Citizenship and Immigration)*, [1999] 2 S.C.R. 817:

> Although the duty of fairness is flexible and variable, and depends on an appreciation of the context of the particular statute and the rights affected, it is helpful to review the criteria that should be used in determining what procedural rights the duty of fairness requires in a given set of circumstances. I emphasize that underlying all these factors is the notion that the purpose of the participatory rights contained within the duty of procedural fairness is to ensure that administrative

decisions are made using a fair and open procedure, appropriate to the decision being made and its statutory, institutional, and social context, with an opportunity for those affected by the decision to put forward their views and evidence fully and have them considered by the decision-maker.

Several factors have been recognized in the jurisprudence as relevant to determining what is required by the common law duty of procedural fairness in a given set of circumstances. One important consideration is the nature of the decision being made and the process followed in making it [...]. The more the process provided for, the function of the tribunal, the nature of the decision-making body, and the determinations that must be made to reach a decision resemble judicial decision-making, the more likely it is that procedural protections closer to the trial model will be required by the duty of fairness [...]

A second factor is the nature of the statutory scheme and the "terms of the statute pursuant to which the body operates" [...] The role of the particular decision within the statutory scheme and other surrounding indications in the statute help determine the content of the duty of fairness owed when a particular administrative decision is made. Greater procedural protections, for example, will be required when no appeal procedure is provided within the statute, or when the decision is determinative of the issue and further requests cannot be submitted.

A third factor in determining the nature and extent of the duty of fairness owed is the importance of the decision to the individual or individuals affected. The more important the decision is to the lives of those affected and the greater its impact on that person or those persons, the more stringent the procedural protections that will be mandated.

Fourth, the legitimate expectations of the person challenging the decision may also determine what procedures the duty of fairness requires in given circumstances. Our Court has held that, in Canada, this doctrine is part of the doctrine of fairness or natural justice, and that it does not create substantive rights: [...] [it] is based on the principle that the 'circumstances' affecting procedural fairness take into account the promises or regular practices of administrative decision-makers, and that it will generally be unfair for them to act in contravention of representations as to procedure, or to backtrack on substantive promises without according significant procedural rights.

Fifth, the analysis of what procedures the duty of fairness requires should also take into account and respect the choices of procedure made by the agency itself, particularly when the statute leaves to the decision-maker the ability to choose its own procedures, or when the agency has an expertise in determining what procedures are appropriate in the circumstances.

The Applicant notes the Director did not inform it that it was in receipt of the British Diplomatic Note or the correspondence from the Department of Foreign Affairs, and says it had no opportunity to respond to any competing ownership claim before its application for the Heritage Research Permit was rejected [...] The Applicant had a legitimate expectation that the Director would consider and decide this administrative question issue according to the standard procedures set out in the legislation, and according to the principles of natural justice and procedural fairness. The Applicant had a significant interest in having the Permit issued.

Conclusion

The issue on this judicial review application is not the merits of the decision made by the Director, but rather the matter of procedural fairness. In reviewing the procedure used by a decision-maker, it is not the Court's role to substitute its own decision for that of the decision-maker. The Court's role is to determine whether the decision-maker accorded procedural fairness.

I am satisfied that an order in nature of certiorari is appropriate here. The Applicant was denied the opportunity to make submissions on the legal claim to ownership of the wreck of the Fantome, even though this claim was precisely the basis upon which the Applicant was denied a Heritage Research Permit. Regardless of the merits of the British claim, it was a fundamental error for the Director to accept it, without question, and without allowing the Applicant an opportunity to be heard.

Taseko Mines Limited v. Canada (Environment)

2017 FC 1100

[This judicial review alleged that the Minister of Environment improperly met with and considered submissions from the Tsilhqot'in National Government ("TNG") after the conclusion of a CEAA 2012 assessment with respect to a mine proposed by Taseko to be located on TNG traditional territory. The impugned meeting with the Minister occurred prior to her deciding whether to find that the project was likely to cause significant adverse environmental effects on the basis of the assessment report prepared by the CEAA panel.]

PHELAN J.: —

Standard of Review

It is well established and not argued here that the standard of review with respect to procedural fairness is correctness: *Canada (Citizenship and Immigration) v Khosa*, 2009 SCC 12, [2009] 1 SCR 339; *Arsenault v Canada (Attorney General)*, 2016 FCA 179, 486 NR 268.

The standard of review for constitutional issues is also correctness: *Dunsmuir v New Brunswick*, 2008 SCC 9, [2008] 1 SCR 190.

Analysis

Issue 1: Was Taseko afforded a fair process during the Minister's decision making process?

Procedural Fairness

The parties agree that there was a duty of procedural fairness owed to Taseko in this process. Contrary to Taseko's assertions, the Respondents are not arguing that the duty to consult ousts the duty of fairness owed to a proponent.

However, the parties are sharply divided as to the content of the duty of fairness owed to Taseko at this stage of the process.

The Respondents argue that Taseko was owed a high degree of procedural fairness at the Panel stage and a minimal degree of procedural fairness at the

Minister's decision making stage (Taseko calls this an "asymmetrical process") particularly as it afforded the TNG greater access to decision makers. Taseko argues that it was owed a high degree of procedural fairness at all stages of the process (and, essentially, that it was owed the *same* process as the TNG — i.e., a symmetrical process).

In my view, Taseko was owed a duty of procedural fairness throughout the whole process, but it was not owed a high degree of procedural fairness at this stage of the environmental review process. When the environmental assessment scheme at issue is understood as a whole, it is clear that the Panel process is the venue through which the parties are to be afforded a high degree of procedural fairness. That process involves oral hearings, the submission of evidence (including expert evidence) by interested persons, cross-examination, fact finding, and a number of other trappings associated with a quasi-judicial process.

The Minister's decision making process, by contrast, did not involve any elements that would indicate that Taseko was owed a high degree of procedural fairness.

I conclude that Taseko was owed a duty of procedural fairness in this environmental approval process but that the degree and type of procedural fairness varies at different stages of the whole process. The "process" encompasses from application through to the GIC decision.

A review of the *Baker v Canada (Minister of Citizenship and Immigration)*, [1999] 2 SCR 817, 174 DLR (4th) 193 [*Baker*] factors supports the finding that Taseko was owed a minimal degree of procedural fairness at this stage of the process:

- The Minister's decision making process did not resemble judicial decision making (i.e., the process was not established to be adversarial, and the Minister was not required to receive submissions). The Minister was making findings of fact (as argued by Taseko), but these findings were based on the findings in the Report during the stage of the process in which Taseko had been afforded a high degree of procedural fairness. Therefore, as discussed in *Jada Fishing Co v Canada (Minister of Fisheries and Oceans)*, 2002 FCA 103, 288 NR 237 [*Jada Fishing*], the duty of fairness in this case was not as rigorous as it would have been in an adversarial, judicial, or quasi-judicial process. As discussed below, and in line with *Pacific Booker Minerals Inc v British Columbia (Minister of the Environment)*, 2013 BCSC 2258, 82 CELR (3d) 195 [*Pacific Booker*], Taseko may have had additional rights if the Minister had decided not to follow the recommendations in the Report — but this is not the circumstance in the instant case.

- Furthermore, the statutory scheme indicates that the proponent would only provide submissions if requested to do so by the Minister (s 47(2)). This indicates that the proponent does not have a right to provide such submissions, and it is entirely at the Minister's discretion whether such submissions are warranted in the circumstances.

- The importance of the decision, indicated by Taseko's investment in the Project, was reflected in the extensive process provided in front of the Panel. Further, in my view, the importance of the decision does not require that each step of the process take on a quasi-judicial character, particularly when a party's procedural rights have been comprehensively addressed at an earlier stage of the process.

- In addition, Taseko's claim that it had legitimate expectations with respect to the Minister's decision making process must be rejected. It was explicitly informed that its own post-Panel submissions would not be posted on the online registry (and that reasoning could easily be extended to cover any other submissions) and the CEAA's silence in response to Taseko's queries does not justify its assumptions with respect to process as silence does not constitute "established practices, conduct or representations that can be characterized as clear, unambiguous and unqualified" per *Mount Sinai Hospital Center v Quebec (Minister of Health and Social Services)*, 2001 SCC 41 at para 29, [2001] 2 SCR 281.

Nonetheless, even if Taseko *were* owed a significant degree of procedural fairness, the record in this case indicated that Taseko was in fact afforded that degree of procedural fairness. Taseko made submissions on the Report in November of 2013, and then provided clarifications of its positions; the evidence indicates that this was forwarded to the Minister's office. The material that was before the Minister (i.e. the Hallman Memo) included discussions of the main contention raised in Taseko's post-Report submissions, particularly the memorandum on the "wrong project design" claim and the TNG's responses to Taseko's submissions.

Therefore, the Minister went "above and beyond" the procedural fairness requirements in this case. The facts indicate that both Taseko and the TNG were working hard to ensure that their views were considered by the relevant decision makers and they were.

Adequacy of Reasons

Failure of an administrative decision-maker to provide adequate (or any) reasons for its decision is a rarely invoked and even more rarely successful ground for judicial review. Indeed, some decision-makers (Cabinet Ministers, for example) are under no duty at common law to provide reasons. Nor is it entirely clear in what circumstances civil servants are bound by this duty. And, of course, the absence of such a duty can present serious evidentiary problems for a party seeking to challenge a decision on other administrative law grounds.

On the other hand, quasi-judicial entities such as tribunals are under a duty to provide reasons, as are their judicial cousins. The precise origin of this duty can sometimes be murky. Certainly it can be argued that it is an incident of procedural fairness. It may also, as in the case that follows, flow from a consideration of the legislative scheme within which the decision takes place.

Pembina Institute for Appropriate Development v.
Canada (Attorney General)
2008 FC 302

[The applicant sought judicial review with respect to an environmental assessment by a Joint Review Panel (the "Panel") of the Kearl Oil Sands Project. The Panel recommended to the responsible federal authority, the Department of Fisheries and Oceans (DFO), that the Project be authorized to proceed. The applicant submitted that the environmental assessment conducted by the Panel did not comply with the mandatory steps in the *Canadian Environmental Assessment Act* and in the Panel's Terms of Reference.]

TREMBLAY-LAMER J.: —

Greenhouse Gas Emissions

The applicants submit that the Panel erred by failing to provide a cogent rationale for its conclusion that the adverse environmental effects of the greenhouse gas emissions of the Project would be insignificant, and by failing to comment on the effectiveness of intensity-based "mitigation". According to Imperial Oil's EIA, the Project will be responsible for average emissions of 3.7 million tonnes of carbon dioxide equivalent per year, which equals the annual greenhouse gas emissions of 800,000 passenger vehicles in Canada, and will contribute 0.51% and 1.7% respectively, of Canada and Alberta's annual greenhouse gas emissions (based on 2002 data).

The respondent, Imperial Oil, argues that the EIA that was before the Panel set out the annual greenhouse gas emissions, as well as the intensity of greenhouse gas emissions on a per barrel basis for the Project during the operating period. Further, the Project Application sets out Imperial Oil's approach to greenhouse gas management including the requirement that the most energy efficient, commercially proven and economic technology be selected to minimize emissions. There is no evidence to suggest that the Panel failed to consider all the evidence that was before it, and while it did not comment specifically on the effects of the greenhouse gas emissions [...] the EARPGO (predecessor to the CEAA) does not specify a particular form for the report and thus, it is not the role of this Court to insist on a particular form in the present case. At the hearing, Imperial Oil's counsel added that for the Panel to comment on the proposed intensity based mitigation measures would shift its role into the realm of policy recommendation.

While I agree that the Panel is not to engage in policy recommendation, nevertheless, it is tasked with conducting a science and fact-based assessment of the potential adverse environmental effects of a proposed project. In the absence of this fact-based approach, the political determinations made by final decision-makers are left to occur in a vacuum.

I recognize that placing an administrative burden on the Panel to provide an in-depth explanation of the scientific data for all of its conclusions and recommendations would be disproportionately high. However, given that the Report is to serve as an objective basis for a final decision, the Panel must, in my opinion, explain in a general way why the potential environmental effects, either with or without the implementation of mitigation measures, will be insignificant.

Should the Panel determine that the proposed mitigation measures are incapable of reducing the potential adverse environmental effects of a project to insignificance, it has a duty to say so as well. The assessment of the environmental effects of a project and of the proposed mitigation measures occur outside the realm of government policy debate, which by its very nature must take into account a wide array of viewpoints and additional factors that are necessarily excluded by the Panel's focus on project related environmental impacts. In contrast, the responsible authority is authorized, pursuant to s. 37(1)(a)(ii), to permit the project to be carried out in whole or in part even where the project is likely to cause significant adverse environmental effects if those effects "can be justified in the circumstances". Therefore, it is the final decision-maker that is mandated to take into account the wider public policy factors in granting project approval.

I am fully aware of the level of expertise possessed by the Panel. The record shows that they had ample material before them relating to the issue of greenhouse gas emissions and climate change, and thus any articulated conclusions drawn from the evidence should be accorded a high measure of deference. However, this deference to expertise is only triggered when those conclusions are articulated. Instructively, in *Canada (Director of Investigation and Research, Competition Act) v. Southam Inc.*, [1997] 1 S.C.R. 748, [1996] S.C.J. No. 116 (QL), at para. 62, Iacobucci J. cited with approval the following excerpt from Kerans, R. P., Standards of Review Employed by Appellate Courts (Edmonton: Juriliber, 1994) [...]:

> Experts, in our society, are called that precisely because they can arrive at well-informed and rational conclusions. If that is so, they should be able to explain, to a fair-minded but less well-informed observer, the reasons for their conclusions. If they cannot, they are not very expert. If something is worth knowing and relying upon, it is worth telling. Expertise commands deference only when the expert is coherent. Expertise loses a right to deference when it is not defensible. That said, it seems obvious that [appellate courts] manifestly must give great weight to cogent views thus articulated.

Thus, deference to expertise is based on the cogent articulation of the rational basis for conclusions reached. The evidence shows that intensity-based targets place limits on the amount of greenhouse gas emissions per barrel of bitumen produced. The absolute amount of greenhouse gas pollution from oil sands development will continue to rise under intensity-based targets because of the planned increase in total production of bitumen. The Panel dismissed as insignificant the greenhouse gas emissions without any rationale as to why the intensity-based mitigation would be effective to reduce the greenhouse gas emissions, equivalent to 800,000 passenger vehicles, to a level of insignificance. Without this vital link, the clear and cogent articulation of the reasons behind the Panel's conclusion, the deference accorded to its expertise is not triggered.

While I agree that the Panel is not required to comment specifically on each and every detail of the Project, given the amount of greenhouse gases that will be emitted to the atmosphere and given the evidence presented that the intensity based targets will not address the problem of greenhouse gas emissions, it was incumbent upon the Panel to provide a justification for its recommendation on this particular issue. By its silence, the Panel short circuits the two step decision-making process envisioned by the CEAA which calls for an informed decision by a responsible authority. For the decision to be informed it must be nourished by a robust understanding of Project effects. Accordingly, given the absence of an explanation or rationale, I am of the view that the Panel erred in law by failing to provide reasoned basis for its conclusion as mandated by s. 34(c)(i) of the CEAA.

As this error relates solely to one of the many issues that the Panel was mandated to consider, I find that it would be inappropriate and ineffective to require the entire Panel review to be conducted a second time [...]. Accordingly, the application for judicial review is allowed in part. The matter is remitted back to the same Panel with the direction to provide a rationale for its conclusion that the proposed mitigation measures will reduce the potentially adverse effects of the Project's greenhouse gas emissions to a level of insignificance.

Newfoundland & Labrador Nurses' Union v.
Newfoundland & Labrador (Treasury Board)
2011 SCC 62

ABELLA J.: — [...] Read as a whole, I do not see *Dunsmuir* as standing for the proposition that the "adequacy" of reasons is a stand-alone basis for quashing a decision, or as advocating that a reviewing court undertake two discrete analyses — one for the reasons and a separate one for the result (Donald J. M. Brown and John M. Evans, *Judicial Review of Administrative Action in Canada* (loose-leaf), at §12:5330 and 12:5510). It is a more organic exercise — the reasons must be read together with the outcome and serve the purpose of showing whether the result falls within a range of possible outcomes. This, it seems to me, is what the Court was saying in Dunsmuir when it told reviewing courts to look at "the qualities that make a decision reasonable, referring both to the process of articulating the reasons and to outcomes" (para. 47).

In assessing whether the decision is reasonable in light of the outcome and the reasons, courts must show "respect for the decision-making process of adjudicative bodies with regard to both the facts and the law" (*Dunsmuir*, at para. 48). This means that courts should not substitute their own reasons, but they may, if they find it necessary, look to the record for the purpose of assessing the reasonableness of the outcome.

Reasons may not include all the arguments, statutory provisions, jurisprudence or other details the reviewing judge would have preferred, but that does not impugn the validity of either the reasons or the result under a reasonableness analysis. A decision-maker is not required to make an explicit finding on each constituent element, however subordinate, leading to its final conclusion (*Service Employees' International Union, Local No. 333 v. Nipawin District Staff Nurses Assn.*, [1975] 1 S.C.R. 382, at p. 391). In other words, if the reasons allow the reviewing court to understand why the tribunal made its decision and permit it to determine whether the conclusion is within the range of acceptable outcomes, the *Dunsmuir* criteria are met.

Justice David Stratas,
"The Canadian Law of Judicial Review:
A Plea for Doctrinal Coherence and Consistency"

(2016), online: < https://papers.ssrn.com/sol3/papers.cfm?abstract_id = 2733751 >
(pp. 19-20)

Appreciating the Role of Reasons

Reasons are, as the Supreme Court says in *Newfoundland Nurses*, to be viewed organically in light of the record. But some read *Newfoundland Nurses* as suggesting that administrative decision-makers need only show that they were alive to the matters before them.

Applying this low standard to all administrative decision-makers in all contexts — the monolithic approach — is at odds with administrative law principles. Further, it fails to take into account how reasons can affect the outcome of reasonableness review. I think that can happen in at last three ways.

First, the more an administrative decision-maker explains its decision and invokes expertise and specialized understandings in explicit reasons, the more the reviewing court is likely to find the administrative decision-maker acted within its margin of appreciation. An administrative decision-maker that does not explain its conclusion leaves it open to the reviewing court — baffled by how the administrator reached its conclusion — to find the conclusion wanting or to wonder whether the administrator even did the job it was supposed to do under its governing legislation. In short, good reasons can be an admission ticket to deference.

Take, for example, the dog licensing board, mentioned above. Suppose it acts under a legislative provision that allows it to grant licences to any "dog." Someone walks into the board's offices and wants a licence for a coyote dog. Is a coyote dog a "dog" within the meaning of the legislative provision? If the board says "yes" and invokes its licensing experience along with expert evidence about whether coyote dogs are part of the genus canine, a reviewing court may give the board a broader margin of appreciation. It is dealing with a subject-matter beyond the court's ken. But if the board says "yes" and offers no reasons, the court will be more likely to second-guess. In fact, it may conclude from the absence of reasons that the board failed to consider the matter before it at all, and quash its decision.

Administrators' reasons can be important in the reviewing process in another way. If insufficient reasons are given or if the record in conjunction with the reasons is too sparse, the reviewing court may not be able to understand enough about the case in order to conduct reasonableness review. Reasons must also be sufficient to allow the reviewing court to discharge its reviewing task.

Finally, in some cases, particularly where much turns on the matter, administrative decision-makers must provide a proper, transparent account of themselves and their decision-making to both the parties and the public at large. It must not be forgotten that administrative decision-makers form part of government and must be held accountable to the public they serve.

Notes and Questions

1. In *Pembina Institute*, what is the source and scope of the duty to provide reasons that Tremblay-Lamer J. found was violated?

2. In light of the SCC's subsequent *Newfoundland Nurses* decision and the observations on this topic by Stratas J.A., is *Pembina Institute* still good law? Why or why not? In this regard, consider the following passage from the *Grand Riverkeeper* case extracted earlier:

   > Furthermore, the Applicants' arguments that the JRP failed to provide a rationale for its conclusions must be read in conjunction with *Dunsmuir*, above, and *Newfoundland and Labrador Nurses' Union v Newfoundland and Labrador (Treasury Board)*, 2011 SCC 62, [2011] SCJ No 62. In that case, the Supreme Court opined that *Dunsmuir* does not stand "for the proposition that the 'adequacy' of reasons is a stand-alone basis for quashing a decision, or as advocating that a reviewing court undertake two discrete analyses — one for the reasons and a separate one for the result ... It is a more organic exercise — the reasons must be read together with the outcome and serve the purpose of showing whether the result falls within a range of possible outcomes" (para 14). The Supreme Court further cemented its view on this point in *Construction Labour Relations v Driver Iron Inc*, 2012 SCC 65, [2012] SCJ No 65:
   >
   > > "The Board did not have to explicitly address all shades of meaning of these provisions. This Court has strongly emphasized that administrative tribunals do not have to consider and comment upon every issue raised by the parties in their reasons. For reviewing courts, the issue remains whether the decision, viewed as a whole in the context of the record, is reasonable."

3. Assume that Tremblay-Lamer J.'s judgment in *Pembina Institute* was rendered in a case handed down today. Based on the current law, what would the key points of an appeal brief from her decision be? How would a respondent seek to have her decision upheld? Consider, in this regard, the decision of Crampton J. in *Adam v. Canada (Minister of the Environment)*, 2011 FC 962, excerpted in Chapter 9.

Failure to Discharge the Duty to Consult

In many environmental cases that go to judicial review, the outcome turns on the question of whether the challenger can establish that the Crown breached its constitutional duty to consult. As discussed in Chapter 3, this is a constitutional duty that flows from section 35 of the *Constitution Act, 1982* and is articulated in such cases as *Haida Nation v. British Columbia (Minister of Forests)*, 2004 SCC 73. While the constitutional nature of the duty distinguishes these kind of cases from their administrative law counterparts, there are many similarities between these two types of judicial review. For instance, both kinds of arguments can arise and need to be decided in the same case. As well, both can involve the court in quite fact-driven inquiries. Where the judicial review turns on the legality of administrative action under public law principles, normally this factual inquiry takes place based upon the evidentiary record before the original decision-maker: see *Newfoundland & Labrador Nurses' Union v. Newfoundland & Labrador (Treasury Board)*, 2011 SCC 62 at para. 59; see also *Judicial Review Procedure Act*, R.S.B.C. 1996, c. 241, s. 1 "record of the proceeding". Courts adopt a less restrictive approach to parties adducing evidence that was not before the decision-maker in duty to consult litigation. This is in part due to the fact that such evidence can often help the court understand and make a judgment about the lawfulness of the Crown's course of conduct over time, which is typically the issue in duty to consult cases.

The next excerpt is from the Federal Court of Appeal's recent decision in *Tsleil-Waututh v. Canada (Attorney General)*. This is a judgment to which we make reference at various points in this book (see chapters 3, 6, 7 and 9). Earlier in this chapter, we discussed the relationship between the standard of review and the duty to consult; in particular, we noted that the courts have applied a *correctness* standard to whether a duty to consult exists, and a *reasonableness* standard to the adequacy of the consultation: see *Dene Tha' First Nation v. Canada (Minister of Environment)*, 2006 FC 1354, affirmed 2008 FCA 20, extracted *supra* in Part II. In the extract that follows, the FCA lays out some principles governing how courts should approach the task of assessing the adequacy of Crown consultation; it then applies these principles to the "Phase III" consultation undertaken by the Government of Canada after the Governor in Council received the NEB's report on its assessment of the Trans Mountain pipeline expansion project and prior to the Governor in Council deciding whether to approve the project.

***

Tsleil-Waututh Nation v. Canada (Attorney General)
2018 FCA 153,
additional reasons 2018 FCA 155

[This decision arises in a consolidated proceeding involving challenges to the Cabinet approval of the Trans Mountain pipeline expansion project. We discuss other elements of this decision in Chapter 3 (jurisdiction) and Chapter 9 (species at risk). In this portion of the judgment, the court outlines the applicable principles governing judicial reviews alleging failures in the discharge of the duty to consult].

DAWSON J.A.: —

Canada's Consultation Process

The first step in the consultation process was determining the Indigenous groups whose rights and interests might be adversely impacted by the Project. In order to do this, a number of federal departments and the National Energy Board coordinated research and analysis on the proximity of Indigenous groups' traditional territories to elements of the Project, including the proposed pipeline right-of-way, the marine terminal expansion, and the designated shipping lanes. Approximately 130 Indigenous groups were identified, including all of the Indigenous applicants.

On August 12, 2013, the National Energy Board wrote to the identified Indigenous groups to advise that Trans Mountain had filed a Project description on May 23, 2013, and to provide preliminary information about the upcoming review process. This letter also attached a letter from the Major Projects Management Office of Natural Resources Canada. The Major Projects Management Office's letter advised that Canada would rely on the National Energy Board's public hearing process:

> to the extent possible, to fulfil any Crown duty to consult Aboriginal groups for the proposed Project. Through the [National Energy Board] process, the [Board] will consider issues and concerns raised by Aboriginal groups. The Crown will utilise the [National Energy Board] process to identify, consider and address the potential adverse impacts of the proposed Project on established or potential Aboriginal and treaty rights.

In subsequent letters sent to Indigenous groups between August 2013 and February 19, 2016, the Major Projects Management Office directed Indigenous groups that could be impacted by the Project to participate in and communicate their concerns through the National Energy Board public hearings. Additionally, Indigenous groups were advised that Canada viewed the consultation process to be as follows:

i.   Canada would rely, to the extent possible, on the Board's process to fulfil its duty to consult Indigenous peoples about the Project;

ii. There would be four phases of Crown consultation:

    a. "Phase I": early engagement, from the submission of the Project description to the start of the National Energy Board hearing;

    b. "Phase II": the National Energy Board hearing, commencing with the start of the Board hearing and continuing until the close of the hearing record;

    c. "Phase III": consideration by the Governor in Council, commencing with the close of the hearing record and continuing until the Governor in Council rendered its decision in relation to the Project; and

    d. "Phase IV": regulatory authorization should the Project be approved, commencing with the decision of the Governor in Council and continuing until the issuance of department regulatory approvals, if required.

iii. Natural Resources Canada's Major Projects Management Office would serve as the Crown Consultation Coordinator for the Project.

iv. Following Phase III consultations, an adequacy of consultation assessment would be prepared by the Crown. The assessment would be based upon the depth of consultation owed to each Indigenous group. The depth of consultation owed would in turn be based upon the Project's potential impact on each group and the strength of the group's claim to potential or established Aboriginal or treaty rights.

On May 25, 2015, towards the end of Phase II, the Major Projects Management Office wrote to Indigenous groups, including the applicants, to provide additional information on the scope and timing of Phase III Crown consultation. Indigenous groups were advised that:

i. Canada intended to submit summaries of the concerns and issues Indigenous groups had brought forward to date and to seek feedback on the completeness and accuracy of the summaries. The summaries would be issued in the form of Information Requests, a Board hearing process explained below. Canada would also seek Indigenous groups' views on adverse impacts not yet addressed by Trans Mountain's mitigation measures. The Crown would use the information provided by Indigenous groups to "refine our current understanding of the potential impacts of the project on asserted or established Aboriginal or treaty rights."

ii. Phase III consultation would focus on two questions:

   a. Are there outstanding concerns with respect to Project-related impacts to potential or established Aboriginal or treaty rights?

   b. Are there incremental accommodation measures that should be considered by the Crown to address any outstanding concerns?

iii. Information made available to the Crown throughout each phase of the consultation process would be consolidated into a "Crown Consultation Report". "This report will summarize both the procedural aspects of consultations undertaken and substantive issues raised by Aboriginal groups, as well as how these issues may be addressed in the process". The section of the Crown Consultation Report dealing with each Indigenous group would be provided to the group for review and comment before the report was placed before the Governor in Council.

iv. If Indigenous groups identified outstanding concerns there were a number of options which might "be considered and potentially acted upon." The options were described to be:

> The Governor in Council has the option of asking the [National Energy Board] to reconsider its recommendation and conditions. Federal and provincial governments could undertake additional consultations prior to issuing additional permits and/or authorizations. Finally, federal and provincial governments can also use existing or new policy and program measures to address outstanding concerns. (underlining added) [...]

The Applicable Legal Principles

Before commencing the analysis, it is helpful to discuss briefly the principles that have emerged from the jurisprudence which has considered the scope and content of the duty to consult. As explained in the opening paragraphs of these reasons, the applicable principles are not in dispute; what is in dispute is whether, on the facts of this case (which are largely agreed), Canada fulfilled its constitutional duty to consult.

The duty to consult is grounded in the honour of the Crown and the protection provided for "existing aboriginal and treaty rights" in subsection 35(1) of the *Constitution Act, 1982.* The duties of consultation and, if required, accommodation form part of the process of reconciliation and fair dealing (*Haida Nation*, paragraph 32).

The duty arises when the Crown has actual or constructive knowledge of the potential existence of Indigenous rights or title and contemplates conduct that might adversely affect those rights or title (*Haida Nation*, paragraph 35). The duty reflects the need to avoid the impairment of asserted or recognized rights caused by the implementation of a specific project.

The extent or content of the duty of consultation is fact specific. The depth or richness of the required consultation increases with the strength of the *prima facie* Indigenous claim and the seriousness of the potentially adverse effect upon the claimed right or title (*Haida Nation*, paragraph 39; *Rio Tinto Alcan Inc. v. Carrier Sekani Tribal Council*, 2010 SCC 43, [2010] 2 S.C.R. 650, paragraph 36).

When the claim to title is weak, the Indigenous interest is limited or the potential infringement is minor, the duty of consultation lies at the low end of the consultation spectrum. In such a case, the Crown may be required only to give notice of the contemplated conduct, disclose relevant information and discuss any issues raised in response to the notice (*Haida Nation*, paragraph 43). When a strong *prima facie* case for the claim is established, the right and potential infringement is of high significance to Indigenous peoples, and the risk of non-compensable damage is high, the duty of consultation lies at the high end of the spectrum. While the precise requirements will vary with the circumstances, a deep consultative process might entail: the opportunity to make submissions; formal participation in the decision-making process; and, the provision of written reasons to show that Indigenous concerns were considered and how those concerns were factored into the decision (*Haida Nation*, paragraph 44).

Parliament may choose to delegate procedural aspects of the duty to consult to a tribunal.

The Supreme Court has found the Board to possess both the procedural powers necessary to implement consultation and the remedial powers to accommodate, where necessary, affected Indigenous claims and Indigenous and treaty rights. The Board's process can, therefore, be relied on by the Crown to fulfil, in whole or in part, the Crown's duty to consult (*Clyde River (Hamlet) v. Petroleum Geo-Services Inc.*, 2017 SCC 40, [2017] 1 S.C.R. 1069, paragraph 34).

[...] the Supreme Court has described the Board as having considerable institutional expertise both in conducting consultations and in assessing the environmental impacts of proposed projects. Where the effects of a proposed project on Indigenous or treaty rights substantially overlap with the project's potential environmental impact, the Board "is well situated to oversee consultations which seek to address these effects, and to use its technical expertise to assess what forms of accommodation might be available" (*Clyde River*, paragraph 33).

When the Crown relies on a regulatory or environmental assessment process to fulfil the duty to consult, such reliance is not delegation of the Crown's ultimate responsibility to ensure consultation is adequate. Rather, it is a means by which the Crown can be satisfied that Indigenous concerns have been heard and, where appropriate, accommodated (*Haida Nation*, paragraph 53).

The consultation process does not dictate a particular substantive outcome. Thus, the consultation process does not give Indigenous groups a veto over what can be done with land pending final proof of their claim. What is required is a process of balancing interests — a process of give and take. Nor does consultation equate to a duty to agree; rather, what is required is a commitment to a meaningful process of consultation (*Haida Nation*, paragraphs 42, 48 and 62).

Good faith consultation may reveal a duty to accommodate. Where there is a strong *prima facie* case establishing the claim and the consequence of proposed conduct may adversely affect the claim in a significant way, the honour of the Crown may require steps to avoid irreparable harm or to minimize the effects of infringement (*Haida Nation*, paragraph 47).

Good faith is required on both sides in the consultative process: "The common thread on the Crown's part must be 'the intention of substantially addressing [Aboriginal] concerns' as they are raised [...] through a meaningful process of consultation" (*Haida Nation*, paragraph 42). The "controlling question in all situations is what is required to maintain the honour of the Crown and to effect reconciliation between the Crown and the Aboriginal peoples with respect to the interests at stake" (*Haida Nation*, paragraph 45).

At the same time, Indigenous claimants must not frustrate the Crown's reasonable good faith attempts, nor should they take unreasonable positions to thwart the government from making decisions or acting in cases where, despite meaningful consultation, agreement is not reached (*Haida Nation*, paragraph 42).

In the present case, much turns on what constitutes a meaningful process of consultation.

Meaningful consultation is not intended simply to allow Indigenous peoples "to blow off steam" before the Crown proceeds to do what it always intended to do. Consultation is meaningless when it excludes from the outset any form of accommodation (*Mikisew Cree First Nation v. Canada (Minister of Canadian Heritage)*, 2005 SCC 69, [2005] 3 S.C.R. 388, paragraph 54).

The duty is not fulfilled by simply providing a process for exchanging and discussing information. There must be a substantive dimension to the duty. Consultation is talking together for mutual understanding (*Clyde River*, paragraph 49).

As the Supreme Court observed in *Haida Nation* at paragraph 46, meaningful consultation is not just a process of exchanging information. Meaningful consultation "entails testing and being prepared to amend policy proposals in the light of information received, and providing feedback." Where deep consultation is required, a dialogue must ensue that leads to a demonstrably serious consideration of accommodation. This serious consideration may be demonstrated in the Crown's consultation-related duty to provide written reasons for the Crown's decision.

Where, as in this case, the Crown must balance multiple interests, a safeguard requiring the Crown to explain in written reasons the impacts of Indigenous concerns on decision-making becomes more important. In the absence of this safeguard, other issues may overshadow or displace the issue of impacts on Indigenous rights (*Gitxaala*, paragraph 315).

Further, the Crown is obliged to inform itself of the impact the proposed project will have on an affected First Nation, and, if appropriate in the circumstances, communicate its findings to the First Nation and attempt to substantially address the concerns of the First Nation (*Mikisew Cree First Nation*, paragraph 55).

Consultation must focus on rights. In *Clyde River*, the Board had concluded that significant environmental effects to marine mammals were not likely and effects on traditional resource use could be addressed through mitigation measures. The Supreme Court held that the Board's inquiry was misdirected for the purpose of consultation. The Board was required to focus on the Inuit's treaty rights; the "consultative inquiry is not properly into environmental effects *per se*. Rather, it inquires into the impact on the *right*" (emphasis in original) (*Clyde River*, paragraph 45). Mitigation measures must provide a reasonable assurance that constitutionally protected rights were considered as rights in themselves — not just as an afterthought to the assessment of environmental concerns (*Clyde River*, paragraph 51).

When consulting on a project's potential impacts the Crown must consider existing limitations on Indigenous rights. Therefore, the cumulative effects and historical context may inform the scope of the duty to consult (*Chippewas of the Thames*, paragraph 42).

Two final points. First, where the Crown knows, or ought to know, that its conduct may adversely affect the Indigenous right or title of more than one First Nation, each First Nation is entitled to consultation based upon the unique facts and circumstances pertinent to it (*Gitxaala*, paragraph 236).

Second, it is important to understand that the public interest and the duty to consult do not operate in conflict. As a constitutional imperative, the duty to consult gives rise to a special public interest that supersedes other concerns commonly considered by tribunals tasked with assessing the public interest. In the case of the Board, a project authorization that breaches the constitutionally protected rights of Indigenous peoples cannot serve the public interest (*Clyde River*, paragraph 40). [...]

Conclusion on the Mandate of the Crown Consultation Team

As this review of the evidence shows, members of the Crown consultation team advised the Indigenous applicants on a number of occasions throughout the consultation process that they were there to listen and to understand the applicants' concerns, to record those concerns accurately in the Crown Consultation Report, and to pass the report to the Governor in Council. The meeting notes show the Crown consultation team acted in accordance with this role when discussing the Project, its impact on the Indigenous applicants and their concerns about the Project. The meeting notes show little or no meaningful responses from the Crown consultation team to the concerns of the Indigenous applicants. Instead, too often Canada's response was to acknowledge the concerns and to provide assurance the concerns would be communicated to the decision-makers.

As this Court explained in *Gitxaala* at paragraph 279, Canada was required to engage, dialogue and grapple with the concerns expressed to it in good faith by the Indigenous groups impacted by the Project. Meaningful dialogue required someone representing Canada empowered to do more than take notes — someone able to respond meaningfully to the applicants' concerns at some point in time.

The exchanges with the applicants demonstrate that this was missing from the consultation process. The exchanges show little to facilitate consultation and show how the Phase III consultation fell short of the mark.

The consultation process fell short of the required mark at least in part because the consultation team's implementation of its mandate precluded the meaningful, two-way dialogue which was both promised by Canada and required by the principles underpinning the duty to consult.

Canada's Reluctance to Depart from the Board's Findings and Recommended Conditions and Genuinely Engage the Concerns of the Indigenous Applicants

During Phase III each Indigenous applicant expressed concerns about the suitability of the Board's regulatory review and environmental assessment. These concerns were summarized and reported in the appendix to the Crown Consultation Report maintained for each Indigenous applicant (Tsleil-Waututh appendix, pages 7-8; Squamish appendix, page 4; Coldwater appendix, pages 4-5; Stó:lō appendix, pages 12-14; Upper Nicola appendix, pages 5-6; SSN appendix, page 4). These concerns related to both the Board's hearing process and its findings and recommended conditions. The concerns expressed by the Indigenous applicants included:

- The exclusion of Project-related shipping from the definition of the "designated project" which was to be assessed under the *Canadian Environmental Assessment Act, 2012.*

- The inability to cross-examine Trans Mountain's witnesses, coupled with what were viewed to be inadequate responses by Trans Mountain to Information Requests.

- The Board's recommended terms and conditions were said to be deficient for a number of reasons, including their lack of specificity and their failure to impose additional conditions (for example, a condition that sacred sites be protected).

- The Board's findings were generic, thus negatively impacting Indigenous groups' ability to assess the potential impact of the Project on their title and rights.

- The Board's legislated timelines were extremely restrictive and afforded insufficient time to review the Project application and to participate meaningfully in the review process.

- The Board hearing process was an inappropriate forum for assessing impacts to Indigenous rights, and the Board's methods and conclusions regarding the significance and duration of the Project's impacts on Indigenous rights were flawed.

However, missing from both the Crown Consultation Report and the individual appendices is any substantive and meaningful response to these concerns. Nor does a review of the correspondence exchanged in Phase III disclose sufficient meaningful response to, or dialogue about, the various concerns raised by the Indigenous applicants. Indeed, a review of the record of the consultation process discloses that Canada displayed a closed-mindedness when concerns were expressed about the Board's report and was reluctant to depart from the findings and recommendations of the Board. With rare exceptions Canada did not dialogue meaningfully with the Indigenous applicants about their concerns about the Board's review. Instead, Canada's representatives were focused on transmitting concerns of the Indigenous applicants to the decision-makers, and nothing more. Canada was obliged to do more than passively hear and receive the real concerns of the Indigenous applicants. [...]

Conclusion on Canada's Execution of the Consultation Process

[...] the consultation framework selected by Canada was reasonable and sufficient. If Canada properly executed it, Canada would have discharged its duty to consult.

However, based on the totality of the evidence I conclude that Canada failed in Phase III to engage, dialogue meaningfully and grapple with the concerns expressed to it in good faith by the Indigenous applicants so as to explore possible accommodation of these concerns.

Certainly Canada's consultation team worked in good faith and assiduously to understand and document the concerns of the Indigenous applicants and to report those concerns to the Governor in Council in the Crown Consultation Report. That part of the Phase III consultation was reasonable.

However, as the above review shows, missing was a genuine and sustained effort to pursue meaningful, two-way dialogue. Very few responses were provided by Canada's representatives in the consultation meetings. When a response was provided it was brief, and did not further two-way dialogue. Too often the response was that the consultation team would put the concerns before the decision-makers for consideration.

Where responses were provided in writing, either in letters or in the Crown Consultation Report or its appendices, the responses were generic. There was no indication that serious consideration was given to whether any of the Board's findings were unreasonable or wrong. Nor was there any indication that serious consideration was given to amending or supplementing the Board's recommended conditions.

Canada acknowledged it owed a duty of deep consultation to each Indigenous applicant. More was required of Canada.

The inadequacies of the consultation process flowed from the limited execution of the mandate of the Crown consultation team. Missing was someone representing Canada who could engage interactively. Someone with the confidence of Cabinet who could discuss, at least in principle, required accommodation measures, possible flaws in the Board's process, findings and recommendations and how those flaws could be addressed.

The inadequacies of the consultation process also flowed from Canada's unwillingness to meaningfully discuss and consider possible flaws in the Board's findings and recommendations and its erroneous view that it could not supplement or impose additional conditions on Trans Mountain.

These three systemic limitations were then exacerbated by Canada's late disclosure of its assessment that the Project did not have a high level of impact on the exercise of the applicants' "Aboriginal Interests" and its related failure to provide more time to respond so that all Indigenous groups could contribute detailed comments on the second draft of the Crown Consultation Report.

Canada is not to be held to a standard of perfection in fulfilling its duty to consult. However, the flaws discussed above thwarted meaningful, two-way dialogue. The result was an unreasonable consultation process that fell well short of the required mark.

The Project is large and presented genuine challenges to Canada's effort to fulfil its duty to consult. The evaluation of Canada's fulfillment of its duty must take this into account. However, in largest part the concerns of the Indigenous applicants were quite specific and focussed and thus quite easy to discuss, grapple with and respond to. Had Canada's representatives met with each of the Indigenous applicants immediately following the release of the Board's report, and had Canada's representatives executed a mandate to engage and dialogue meaningfully, Canada could well have fulfilled the duty to consult by the mandated December 19, 2016 deadline.

Notes and Questions

1. In this case, the FCA's conclusion that the consultation was not meaningful formed one of two separate grounds upon which it decided that the challengers' applications for judicial review of the Governor in Council's decision should be granted. Accordingly, the FCA quashed the project certificate, and ordered the matter to be remitted back to the NEB with a direction that the Phase III consultation be redone once the NEB had submitted a new report, taking into account the FCA's judgment, to the Governor in Council.

2. Do you consider that the FCA's reasons for judgment provide those delegated to carry out Crown consultations with adequate direction as to how this should be done? Is it ever adequate, under a reasonableness standard, for those carrying out Crown consultation to simply take notes and report to their superiors?

3. The Supreme Court of Canada (Abella and Martin JJ. in dissent) has recently rejected the argument that the Crown is under a duty to consult with respect to proposed legislative changes that might adversely affect Aboriginal rights and title under section 35: see *Mikisew Cree First Nation v. Canada (Governor General in Council)*, 2018 SCC 40. A key reason for this conclusion was concerns about respecting Parliamentary sovereignty and the separation of powers. While the target of the litigation was executive action (by Cabinet through its various Ministers), the SCC characterized the impugned actions as being legislative in nature and thus beyond judicial scrutiny. This litigation had originally been commenced in response to the omnibus legislation enacted in 2012 by the Harper government, rolling back environmental protections contained in the *Fisheries Act*, the *Navigable Waters Protection Act*, and the *Canadian Environmental Assessment Act*.

Part IV — Public Interest Standing and Judicial Review

Introduction

As a prelude to our consideration of public interest standing, it is worthwhile to reflect upon the reasons why public participation is generally seen as a public good. The article excerpted below is an important early articulation of the case for public participation in environmental decision-making.

Raj Anand & Ian Scott,
"Financing Public Participation in Environmental Decision-Making"
(1982) 60 Can. Bar Rev. 81

Access to Justice

The objection that encouraging public participation would have the effect of stirring up unmeritorious litigation is only one aspect of a wider attack on "public interest" advocacy that is commonly mounted by critics who argue that conflict resolution is the sole legitimate purpose of civil actions. Another aspect of this approach is the assumption that when claims are not enforced through litigation, it is because they are unimportant to the affected individuals [...]

It is clear that the failure to advance a particular cause in a given piece of litigation often results from barriers to legal redress that have nothing to do with the merit of the cause or the relative importance of the harm that is perceived by the "victim". Economic barriers to participation in decision-making are well documented in all forms of litigation, and apply most severely to those who suffer in addition from social, psychological and cultural impediments to the redressing of their grievances.

Additional barriers present themselves in the case of public interest groups. Professor Michael Trebilcock, in a 1975 critique of the modern regulatory system and its effects on consumer interests, has identified three such barriers that have analogous effects on environmental groups. Firstly, the environmental concerns of the average citizen are spread across a great range of projects, issues and locations. On the other hand, a business interest that is concerned with the particular project, issue or location has "a sufficiently concentrated stake in any prospective regulation of it to make [its] views known very forcefully to government" [...]

Secondly, unlike highly concentrated producer interests, environmental interests are not generally homogeneous. Most environmentalists are also both consumers and producers of goods and services, and in these roles will often see things different [...].

The third barrier — is commonly known as the "free rider" phenomenon. Olson, for example, argues that unless the membership in a public interest group is small, or unless some special incentive is provided to encourage individuals to act in the common interests of the group, rational and self-interested individuals will not act to achieve their common or group interests. Olson cites the nation state as an extreme example of a large group that cannot survive on voluntary contributions but must resort to coercive taxes.

In the result, public interest groups never achieve the strength that their number of potential beneficiaries would indicate, since many of the possible contributors of money, time and expertise either require or are permitted to take a "free ride" at the expense of existing members. It is by overcoming these "barriers to litigation" that the encouragement of public participation achieves the significant benefit of obtaining confidence in our system of civil justice. A significant "process" value is attached by the community to enhanced public involvement in collective decision-making.

Private Enforcement of Public Rights

A common response to the argument for increased citizen involvement in environmental decision-making is the assertion that intervenors have no useful purpose to serve, given that the public agencies such as administrative tribunals and courts have been entrusted with the dual roles of regulators of industry and representatives of the public interest. Yet, enforcement of public policies can be achieved by private individuals by supplementing the work of the various tribunals or by "energizing the agencies" [...]

Professor Gellhorn has identified three principal factors which combine to produce what has become known as agency "capture" by regulated interests. Firstly, the limited resources that are allocated to administrative agencies, considered in relation to the sheer mass of activity that is required to monitor and test proposals and applications, necessitates close cooperation between the regulator and the regulated industry. Administrative boards thus become dependent upon industry as providers of information. A second cause of industry orientation is the dependence of regulatory agencies on the regulated interests for political support. Independent tribunals cannot rely upon the government to protect them from legislative attack and must therefore develop their own constituencies that are capable of generating support in the legislatures. In this regard, a natural ally can often be found in the regulated interests.

Most importantly, two other characteristics of the administrative process have combined to form a third source of agency deference to industry positions. At the very least, even if the interests of the regulated industry and the adjudicator do not fully coincide, it is clear that the "public interest" which is the theoretical mandate of the decision-maker is not unitary. It has diverse and indeed countervailing components, and so the environmental tribunal or court cannot be expected to become its guardian with unqualified success. Public intervention "softens the artificial two-sidedness which is often a by-product of the adversarial adjudicative process".

Improvement of the Administrative and Judicial Processes

Four distinct benefits accrue to the investigative and adjudicative processes as a result of increased public participation. Firstly, public participation provides decision-makers with a greater range of ideas and information on which to base their decisions. This input has important implications for what is essentially a decentralized, pluralistic system of adjudication by courts and tribunals; that is, one that, by delegation, performs the legislative function of balancing the concerns of competing interest groups. [...] The second element of substantive contribution is the presentation of a viewpoint or perspective that is not otherwise available to the decision-maker. Intervenors are often able to put forward a legal or factual argument which places a unique emphasis or interpretation upon existing issues or causes the tribunal to examine a new issue [...]

The second major benefit is that public participation can enhance public acceptance of judicial and administrative decisions . . . Public acceptability, in turn, can be expected to ease the implementation and enforcement of judicial and administrative decisions that rely upon public co-operation [...]

Third, problems of agency dependence on industry for political support may be alleviated by the broad participation of other parties. Such participation may promote the actual autonomy of the agency, both by giving it a broader perspective from which to view its own role, and by providing alternative potential bases of political support.

Fourth, the presentation of alternative viewpoints at the board or lower court level is said to induce these decision-makers to be more thorough in their analyses and to articulate more clearly and precisely the reasons for their decisions. These improvements may in turn contribute to the building of a record on which a reviewing or appellate court might reverse the initial decision.

Kirsten Mikadze,
"Pipelines and the Changing Face of Public Participation"
(2016) 29 J. Envtl. L. & Prac. 83

The Relationship Between Environmental Justice and Public Participation in Environmental Decision Making

Environmental justice as praxis first came to favour in the US in the 1970s, inspired by growing local protests to land uses. It has, in the intervening decades, been subject to varying definitions and understandings. These oscillations aside, an enduring feature of environmental justice has been its focus upon distributive justice and fairness — that is, the patterns through which environmental benefits and burdens are distributed across society and the processes through which these patterns are determined. Environmental justice has, in particular, sought to interrogate the impacts of environmental policy upon poor, marginalized, racialized, or otherwise underrepresented groups and their involvement in environmental decision making.

Central to these debates has been the role of participatory procedure in shaping and determining environmental justice. Indeed, some accounts of environmental justice, particularly those propounded by lawyers, have been based almost entirely on the notion of access to justice. However, to be responsive and engender transformation, processes for public involvement in environmental decision making must invite *meaningful* participation. Indeed, opportunities for participation must "challenge the interests of decision-making and environmental elites who have traditionally not included the more excluded communities or individuals."

Beyond its role in environmental justice, public participation in has long been considered an important element in environmental decision-making. It is a principle of particular importance in international environmental law and is enshrined as a tri-fold principle (the right to participate in environmental decision-making processes, the right to information concerning the environment and activities affecting it, and the right of access to justice) in the 1992 *Rio Declaration*.

Participation is often seen as beneficial for decision making in a number of ways. Under a liberal-democratic model in particular, public participation can prove profitable for decision- and policy-makers, for example, by enhancing the democratic legitimacy of environmental decisions. Increased public involvement can mean greater legitimacy in the environmental regulation process, which, in turn, smooths the processes of implementation and enforcement. Further, it can provide a means of managing social conflict and can minimize the frequency and magnitude of conflicts that do arise over the course of a project. It can also lead to greater accountability and effectiveness in governmental decision making.

Particularly in the context of environmental reviews, Sinclair and Diduck have underscored the value of participation in the environmental assessment process as providing an opportunity for "mutual learning" between state, citizenry, and proponent. In particular, participation can be the best — and indeed only — means through which local concerns, values, and context is brought to the attention of decision makers.

The availability of entry points for public participation in environmental review can also be essential towards empowering otherwise disenfranchised actors in the process of weighing of environmental, social, and economic interests in development activities. This, in turn, can contribute to a more equitable distribution of environmental benefits and burdens. Participation can provide for opening within existing economic structures and processes and provide mobilized citizenry with the opportunity to create a counter[vail]ing force against extant profit-seeking interests. In essence, participation can bring forward perspectives that interrogate "given" understandings of acceptable environmental tradeoffs and economic gains and invite the re-organization of these arrangements.

That said, public participation is not, in and of itself, a panacea. In fact, poorly designed or implemented efforts at public participation can, in some cases, have unintended or even harmful consequences. Under such circumstances, public participation can become an exercise in determining who has the "sharpest elbows." Depending upon the methods employed, it can foster antagonism, discourage thoughtful participation from genuinely concerned citizens, and create ambivalence among decision makers in hearing from the public. It can become a competition of resources and influence, where the ultimate aim of participants — and, indeed, the outcome of their participation — is less to reorganize benefit/burden patterns along more just lines than it is to see those burdens simply displaced elsewhere. This might have particular relevance in the context of resource development, where, as Fluker notes, the questions of who may participate and what issues may be brought forward "seem most contentious when persons without a property or economic interest at stake in the process seek to participate."

Even actors seeking, through participation, a more equitable redistribution of environmental benefits and burdens can fall victim to the very patterns and imbalances they seek to overcome. Critics in the field of resource management have long suggested that participation is limited by existing modes of power and can work both to legitimize unequal power relationships and to neutralize resistance through the generation of "buy-in." Put another way, the practice of participation will tend not only to be shaped by dynamics that favour the interests of the more powerful over the more marginalized, but it may also lend legitimacy to these power imbalances by creating support for projects and processes that reflect and further solidify these dynamics, while diminishing the impact of resistance by making available a public outlet for the expression of dissatisfaction.

Many commentators have observed that participatory mechanisms have a role to play in determining the effectiveness of participation. Richardson and Razzaque, for instance, note that under the currently dominant liberal-democratic model of participation, the kinds of participatory mechanisms that invite public input in environmental decisionmaking processes leave the power and authority that resides in existing institutions intact. As a result, participation in environmental decision making does not necessarily pave the way towards more ecologically sound approaches to development.

In essence, while participation is a vital and important component to the environmental decision-making process, to be effective — to occasion interrogation into and transformation of existing patterns of distribution — participation must be genuine, not merely superficially consultative or outright co-optive. And in its function as gatekeeper over questions of *who* may participate and *what* is open to debate, the procedural aspects of participation are crucial towards determining whether, and the extent to which, participation is genuine and capable of engendering environmental justice.

Notes and Questions

1. If some public participation is a good thing, is more public participation always a better thing? What critiques of public participation are particularly compelling? Does this depend on the nature of the forum?

2. Courts sometimes justify taking a more restrictive approach to standing and other procedural rights on the basis that it is the job of administrative tribunals and the administrative process generally to ensure robust public participation, not the courts. Do you think there is merit in this premise? Should participatory rights decrease as a matter proceeds up the judicial hierarchy? To what extent should courts be entitled to consider whether a party participated in an antecedent administrative process when deciding whether they should be granted standing or other rights (including remedies) in the context of a subsequent judicial review? Consider, in this regard, *MiningWatch Canada v. Canada (Minister of Fisheries & Oceans)*, 2010 SCC 2, at para. 50.

Public Interest Standing

During the 1970s and 1980s, the rules of public interest standing were liberalized as courts became increasingly mindful of the benefits associated with public interest litigation. Students of constitutional law will be familiar with the SCC's public interest standing trilogy from this period of *Thorson*, *McNeil* and *Borowski*. Also important to this development was the enactment of the *Canadian Charter of Rights and Freedoms* in 1982, and the SCC's extension of public interest standing to non-constitutional cases in *Finlay* in 1986. The *Finlay* test for public interest standing has three elements:

1. Is there a justiciable and serious issue to be tried?
2. Does the applicant have a genuine interest in the subject matter?
3. Is there another reasonable and effective manner for the case to be brought forward?

Affirming the need to ensure that the *Finlay* test is applied in a manner that promotes access to justice, in 2012 the Supreme Court of Canada approved a reformulation of the third arm of the test:

> I conclude that the third factor in the public interest standing analysis should be expressed as: whether the proposed suit is, in all of the circumstances, a reasonable and effective means of bringing the matter before the court. This factor, like the other two, must be assessed in a flexible and purposive manner and weighed in light of the other factors.

(*Canada (Attorney General) v. Downtown Eastside Sex Workers United Against Violence Society*, 2012 SCC 45, at para. 52, *per* Cromwell J.)

The SCC's decision in *Downtown Eastside* has now become the leading authority on public interest standing and offers a compelling critique of the concerns expressed by some that a flood of public interest cases would accompany liberalization of the standing rules. Nonetheless, while standing is not the barrier to public interest litigation that it once was, it is by no means irrelevant in environmental cases and other public interest spheres. In this vein is often cited the Court's 1992 decision in *Canadian Council of Churches* where this admonition was offered:

> [...] I would stress that the recognition of the need to grant public interest standing in some circumstances does not amount to a blanket approval to grant standing to all who wish to litigate an issue. It is essential that a balance be struck between ensuring access to justice and preserving judicial resources. It would be disastrous if the courts were allowed to become hopelessly overburdened as a result of the unnecessary proliferation of marginal or redundant suits brought by well-meaning organizations pursuing their own particular cases certain in the knowledge that their cause is all-important [...].

(*Canadian Council of Churches v. Canada (Minister of Employment and Immigration)*, [1992] 1 S.C.R. 236 *per* Cory J.)

It should also be noted that the authority to grant public interest standing is one that is exclusive to superior courts. The power of other decision-makers, such as regulatory tribunals, to grant standing is governed by the statutory authority under which they are constituted and operate. In British Columbia, for example, to gain standing before the Environmental Appeal Board (EAB), a party must show they are a "person aggrieved": see section 100 of the *Environmental Management Act*, S.B.C. 2003, c. 53. To date, the EAB has resisted invitations to interpret these words in light of the liberalizing approach to standing enunciated in cases such *Downtown Eastside*: see *Gagne v. British Columbia (Director, Environmental Management Act)*, 2014 BCSC 2077, additional reasons 2015 BCSC 154.

In the following section, we canvass several cases selected to illustrate some competing judicial approaches to public interest standing in the environmental context.

Shiell v. Canada (Atomic Energy Control Board)
(1995), 17 C.E.L.R. (N.S.) 286 (Fed. T.D.)

[This was an application for judicial review of a decision by the Atomic Energy Control Board approving an amendment to an operating licence and for *mandamus* to review a waste management plan. The corporate respondent operated a uranium mine and mill. An environmental impact study had been done. The corporate respondent questioned the applicant's standing. She lived in the province several hundred miles from the mine and had participated in a number of hearings and inquiries concerning the uranium industry. She had previously been denied standing in injunction proceedings in a related matter based on lack of a direct personal interest in the subject matter at issue.]

HEALD D.J.: — The respondent, Cameco, raises a number of issues. The first [...] [is] whether the applicant has standing to bring this application for judicial review.

The applicant was born in England and married a Canadian soldier in 1946. She came to Canada with her husband and son. The family farmed near Govan Saskatchewan for many years. The applicant moved to Nipawin Saskatchewan in 1994. Since 1976, the applicant has been interested in the various proposals for developing Saskatchewan's high-grade uranium. In 1977, she participated in the Cluff Lake Inquiry. In 1980, she fully participated in the Key Lake Inquiry. In 1981, she participated in hearings concerning a uranium mine at Rabbit Lake. As noted supra, she has been very interested in the proposed changes at Key Lake involving the respondent, Cameco.

Cameco submits that the applicant is in the same position on this application as she was in the case of *Shiell v. Amok Ltd. et al.*. In that case, this same applicant sought an injunction preventing the respondent Amok from reprocessing leach tails produced by a uranium mining operation pursuant to a Ministerial decision authorizing such processing. After a careful review of the relative jurisprudence, Barclay J. stated (page 14):

> I am satisfied that the plaintiff does not have a direct personal interest in the alleged improper granting of the ministerial approval under section 16 of the *Environmental Assessment Act*. If it was sufficient for the plaintiff to be interested in the sense that she is concerned about the environment and environmental issues, then it is difficult to conceive of cases where this criteria would not be met. In my respectful view, to

be afforded standing the plaintiff must be affected in the sense that the issue has some direct impact on her. This is clearly distinguishable from the Finlay case in which the respondent had a direct personal interest in the issue as deductions were being made from his cheques.

As in *Amok*, the applicant does not have a direct personal interest in these proceedings and, accordingly, the decision in *Finlay v. Canada (Minister of Finance)* has no relevance. She lives at Nipawin Saskatchewan, several hundred miles from the respondent's Key Lake operation. Her interest is neither direct nor personal. The decision a quo will not affect her in any way different from that felt by any other member of the general public. In *Finlay*, Le Dain J. stated:

> The judicial concern about the allocation of scarce judicial resources and the need to screen out the mere busybody is addressed by the requirements affirmed in *Borowski* that there be a serious issue raised and that a citizen have a genuine interest in the issue.

This concern expressed by the Supreme Court of Canada has been repeated in the more recent decision in *Canadian Council of Churches v. The Queen*, where Cory J. stated:

> I would stress that the recognition of the need to grant public interest standing in some circumstances does not amount to a blanket approval to grant standing to all who wish to litigate an issue. It is essential that a balance be struck between ensuring access to the Courts and preserving judicial resources; It would be disastrous if the Courts were allowed to become hopelessly overburdened as a result of the unnecessary proliferation of marginal or redundant suits brought by well-meaning organizations pursuing their own particular cases certain in the knowledge that their cause is all important. It would be detrimental, if not devastating, to our system of justice and unfair to private litigants.

On the basis of the jurisprudence cited *supra*, I have reluctantly come to the conclusion that this applicant does not enjoy the necessary standing to make this application for judicial review. I say "reluctantly" because I have no doubt about the applicant's *bona fide* interest and concern relative to the issues raised by this application. However, that interest and that concern do not *per se*, confer the requisite "standing" entitling her to continue with this application. For these reasons, the application for judicial review is dismissed.

The approach adopted by the Court in *Shiell* is arguably inconsistent with the more liberal posture adopted by most other courts. The next two cases are illustrative of a more liberal approach to standing. As you read them, consider whether they can be factually or legally distinguished from *Shiell*.

Algonquin Wildlands League v. Ontario (Minister of Natural Resources)
(1996), 21 C.E.L.R. (N.S.) 102 (Ont. Div. Ct.)

SAUNDERS J.: — The application is brought by Algonquin Wildlands League and the Friends of Temagami. As can be seen, they are asserting a public right or interest by the institution of proceedings for declaratory or injunctive relief. That is generally done by the Attorney General. These applicants have no standing as of right to apply for the relief sought as there is no evidence that they fall within the recognized exceptions to the general rule. They may however, in the discretion of the court, be granted standing as public interest applicants. See: *Minister of Finance of Canada v. Finlay* (1986), 33 D.L.R. (4th) 321.

It is uncontradicted that both applicants are nonprofit public interest environment organizations with a history of responsible involvement in forest and land use planning issues in the Temagami area. The issues raised by the applicants are justiciable and in my opinion there is no other reasonable or effective manner in which the issues are likely to be brought before the court. It was suggested that the Minister of the Environment might attack the decisions but that seems to me to be highly unlikely. It was also suggested that members of the community could have brought the matter before the court and had not done so. It is also uncontradicted that the members of the applicants include many persons, who either live in Temagami or frequent the area for pleasure or business. It is clear from the material that there is considerable controversy in the area and that many members of the community support or at least do not oppose the government actions. As I have said it seems to me that unless someone, like the applicants, bring these issues to the court, the court will not be asked to address them. Accordingly if the applicant can overcome the hurdle that these are serious issues to be tried, I would be prepared to grant them standing to bring the application.

[**Ed. Note:** In the result, Saunders J. granted standing. The decision, excerpted again later, is also notable for its discussion of injunction law: see Part V, *infra* this chapter.]

MiningWatch Canada v. Canada (Minister of Fisheries & Oceans)
2007 FC 955,
reversed on other grounds 2008 FCA 209,
reversed on other grounds 2010 SCC 2

MARTINEAU J.: —

Standing

Proponent's Submissions

With respect to standing, the Proponent contends that the Applicant has not raised a serious issue, that it does not have a genuine interest in the subject matter and that there are other directly affected parties who chose not to come forth with an application for judicial review.

The Proponent submits in this regard that the Applicant has not challenged the substantive outcome of the Course of Action Decision and that the issues raised by the Applicant have already been decided by this Court and the Federal Court of Appeal in the *True North* case, above. The Proponent notes that the Applicant is an advocacy group headquartered in Ottawa who does not represent any group of local citizens or interest groups directly affected by the Project. First Nations groups who are directly affected by the Project have not made an application for judicial review. Moreover, the Proponent stresses that the Applicant has chosen not to participate in the cooperative environment assessment process. Indeed, the Applicant has not made any submissions on the merits of the Project [prior to bringing this petition].

Tri-part Test

The jurisprudence of the Supreme Court of Canada establishes that standing will be granted to a public interest group who wishes to challenge the exercise of administrative authority, as well as legislation, where the following tri-part test is met: a serious issue is raised; the Applicant shows a genuine interest; and there is no other reasonable and effective manner in which the issue may be brought to the Court (*Thorson v. Attorney General of Canada et al.*, [1975] 1 S.C.R. 138; *Minister of Justice of Canada v. Borowski*, [[1981] 2 S.C.R. 575] at pages 339-340; *Canadian Council of Churches v. Canada*, [1992] 1 S.C.R. 236, at para. 33 and following).

In applying this tri-part test, this Court has consistently rejected the proposition that the words "directly affected" used in subsection 18.1(1) of the FCA should be given a restricted meaning. Indeed, it has been decided in the past that an applicant who satisfies the requirements of discretionary public interest standing may seek relief under subsection 18.1(1) of the FCA even though not "directly affected", when the Court is otherwise convinced that the particular circumstances of the case and the type of interest which the applicant hold justify status being granted [...]

Exercise of the Court's Discretion to Allow Standing

I accept the arguments submitted in writing and orally at the hearing on behalf of the Applicant. In the exercise of my discretion, I have considered all three factors of the tri-part test, as well as the purpose of the CEAA and the particular circumstances of this case.

The fundamental purpose of the CEAA is to ensure that projects requiring an EA are considered in a careful and precautionary manner before federal authorities take action in connection with them, in order to ensure that such projects do not cause "significant adverse environmental effects" (paragraph 4(a) of the CEAA). Another underlying purpose is to ensure that there are opportunities for *timely* and *meaningful public participation* throughout the environmental assessment process (paragraph 4(d) of the CEAA) [emphasis added]. Therefore, operational provisions found in the CEAA and its regulations must be interpreted and applied in a manner consistent with these purposes.

For the purpose of facilitating public access to records related to environmental assessments and providing notice in a timely manner of the assessments, there is a registry called the Canadian Environmental Assessment Registry (the Registry), consisting of an Internet Site and projects files (subsection 55(1) of the CEAA). Within fourteen days after the commencement of an EA under the CEAA, notice of its commencement must be posted on the Agency's Internet site (paragraph 55.1(2)(a) of the CEAA). The notice shall include a description of the scope of the project in relation to which an EA is to be conducted, as determined under section 15 of the CEAA (see paragraph 55.1(2)(c) of the CEAA). In the preceding section (see IV — Factual Background, particularly subsection B. Federal Assessment), I have examined the measures taken by the RAs and/or the Agency to inform the general public.

In addition to any requirement to notify the public or opportunities for public participation flowing from the provisions of the CEAA, an obligation on the Crown (though not on private companies or individuals) to consult First Nations exists where aboriginal rights may be affected by a project (see *Taku River Tlingit First Nation v. British Columbia (Project Assessment Director)*, [2004] S.C.J. No. 69; *Haida Nation v. British Columbia (Minister of Forests)*, [2004] S.C.J. No. 70). [...]

A serious issue is raised by the Applicant with respect to the legality of the Course of Action Decision which is a final decision for the purpose of the present judicial review. In this instance, the Applicant is contesting that the impugned decision represents a departure from a positive duty to consult the public. To this effect, the issue of public participation is of import, not just in this case, but for future projects across Canada. Comprehensive studies as stated, mandate public consultation.

Section 21 of the CEAA which the Applicant alleges to be applicable in the case at bar, has been amended substantially in 2003. The current and enhanced version of this provision was introduced by section 12 of the *Act to amend the Canadian Environmental Assessment Act*, S.C. 2003, c.9 (the Bill C-9 amendments). The former text of section 21 of the CEAA is also reproduced at the end of the present reasons for order (see Appendix "A"). The Bill C-9 amendments came into effect on October 30, 2003 and apply to the Project.

The True North decisions invoked by the Respondents to sustain the legality of the impugned actions or decisions are based on the law as it read prior to the Bill C-9 amendments.

Section 21 of the CEAA now makes *public consultation mandatory* when conducting an EA by means of a comprehensive study. Specifically, the new provision provides that "[w]here a *project* is described in the comprehensive study list, the RA shall ensure public consultation with respect to the *proposed scope of the project* for the purposes of the environmental assessment, the factors proposed to be considered in its assessment, *the proposed scope of those factors* and the ability of the comprehensive study to address issues relating to *the project*" [emphasis added]. [...]

A duty to consult the public at an early stage on key aspects of the environment assessment process is, therefore, one fundamental aspect introduced by the Bill C-9 amendments. Another one is participant funding. Previous subsection 58(1.1) required the Minister to establish a participant funding program to facilitate the public's participation in mediations and assessment by a review panel. The Bill C-9 amendments expand this program by extending participant funding to comprehensive studies and also clarifies that the participant funding program applies to joint assessment by a review panel as well. [...]

The Notice of Commencement which was posted on the Registry on May 23, 2004, announced that DFO would conduct a comprehensive study *commencing* on May 19, 2004. It can seriously be argued by the Applicant that this created a legitimate expectation that the general public would be consulted in accordance with section 21 of the CEAA. Moreover, at the time that the RAs changed "track" and chose to proceed by way of a screening, the documentation on file shows that the public consultation process under the provincial EA was well underway.

Indeed, it was completed prior to the announcement made on the Registry of the Scoping Decision of March 2005.

In the end result, there was no public consultation with respect to the screening report prepared in 2006 under the purported authority of section 18 of the CEAA. This contrasts sharply with the evidence on file that the public has been consulted by the RAs with respect to the comprehensive study prepared in the case of the Galore Creek Gold–Silver–Copper mine, which is also located in the area where the Red Chris property is situated. [...]

I defer to the reasoning of Justice Cory in *Canadian Council of Churches v. Canada*, [1992] 1 S.C.R. 236, at para. 38 wherein it was elucidated that the issues of standing and of whether there is a reasonable cause of action are closely related and indeed tend to merge. In the case at bar, compliance with the CEAA raises a serious and justiciable question of law.

The Applicant also shows a genuine interest in the issues raised in this application for judicial review. More than a mere *bona fide* interest and concern about social and environmental issues is necessary to obtain public interest standing. In *Citizens' Mining*, above, at para. 30, this Court determined that an applicant seeking public interest standing must demonstrate: "... a longstanding reputation and it must do significant work on the subject-matter of the challenge, and its interest must be greater than that possessed by a member of the general public".

Based on the evidence before me, MiningWatch clearly satisfies this requirement. It is a federally-registered non-profit society that functions as a coalition of environmental, social justice, aboriginal and labour organizations from across Canada. By focusing on federal aspects of mining development, the Applicant enjoys the highest possible reputation and has demonstrated a real and continuing interest in the problems associated with mine development. Indeed, MiningWatch has made submissions before the House Committee on Bill C-19, the predecessor of the 2003 amendments to the CEAA, and has published studies critical of failed mitigation plans in relation to mine development.

The Applicant's lack of participation in the provincial environment assessment process is not a barrier to the granting of standing in this judicial review as the provincial forum would not have been to appropriate place for the Applicant to raise its concerns about the conduct of the RAs, all of whom are federal departments. Further, this Court has ruled that the lack of participation in an assessment does not preclude an interested party from seeking standing: *Sierra Club*, above, at para. 68. Finally, I am also of the view that since Ms. Kuyek raised the Applicant's concerns with various delegates or employees of the Ministry of Environment, DFO and the Agency throughout 2005, this suggests an involvement with the Project that prevents the striking out of the application on the ground of lack of standing.

Although the Applicant raises a serious issue and has a genuine interest in the subject matter of this application, public interest standing may still be denied if there are other persons who are more directly affected than the Applicant, and are reasonably likely to institute proceedings to challenge the administrative action in question. The rationale for this final requirement is that those most directly affected by administrative action are often in the best position to bring to the court the information necessary for an appropriate resolution of the dispute.

It is obvious that members of the general public as well as aboriginal groups/individuals living geographically proximal to the Project may have an interest in this judicial review. However, given the complexities and interconnectedness of modern society (as discussed by the Supreme Court in *Canadian Council of Churches*, above, at para. 29), I am not persuaded that geographical proximity ought to be the determinative factor when assessing public interest standing.

Instead, I import the reasoning of Justice Mackay in *Citizens' Mining* that public interest standing should be accorded "where the applicant has a genuine interest and there is no evidence of another or others with a genuine interest that could reasonably be expected to bring a challenge". I disagree that that just because others might share the Applicant's concerns, but have not commenced legal action, the Applicant should be denied standing. In the case at bar, there is no evidence to suggest that others might raise the important issue raised by the Applicant concerning both the scope of section 21 of the CEAA, as amended by Bill C-9, and its application in relation to the Project.

In sum, MiningWatch represents a coalition of approximately twenty groups that express a communal concern and seek to challenge a decision that might otherwise be essentially beyond review. In my view, the Applicant is the only one to demonstrate sufficient interest or the means to launch this judicial review.

Therefore, standing is accorded to the Applicant under the doctrine of public interest.

Notes and Questions

1. Can *Shiell* be reconciled with *Algonquin Wildlands League* and *MiningWatch*? To what extent, if at all, can the outcome of these cases be explained on the basis of differing statutory language or other contextual factors?

Part V — Interim Injunctive Relief

Introduction

At stake in many environmental cases are apprehended harms that cannot be readily compensated for, if at all, by monetary damages. As such, the spectre of "irreparable harm" plays an especially prominent role in this area of the law. As Professor McLeod-Kilmurray has argued:

> Interlocutory injunctions are not merely procedural motions at the periphery of the main litigation. In many environmental cases, they *are* the litigation [...] Doctrinally, injunctions can affect the substantive law [...] Granting an injunction, even an interlocutory one, reveals the value placed on the protected interest, and that the interest is important enough to prevent, rather than compensate, harm to it.

(*The Process of Judging the Environment*: Ph.D. thesis, 2007.)

Of course, the corollary to McLeod-Kilmurray's point is that, where interim injunctive relief is denied, this likewise speaks powerfully as to how we value competing interests.

Chris Tollefson,
"Advancing an Agenda: Reflections on Recent Developments in
Public Interest Environmental Litigation"
(2002) 51 U.N.B.L.J. 175

A common stumbling block faced by environmental and other organizations that have sought recourse to the courts to protect natural areas from development has been their inability to obtain interlocutory injunctive relief. Even where courts have acknowledged that their legal claims have significant merit, judicial application of the prevailing test with respect to the availability of injunctions under *RJR-MacDonald Inc. v. Canada (Attorney General)* has frequently led to a denial of interim relief sought. *RJR-MacDonald* established a threefold test: (1) is there a serious issue to be tried?; (2) would the applicants suffer irreparable harm if the injunction were refused? and (3) does the balance of convenience between the parties to the application justify the relief sought? In addition, courts have traditionally deemed it necessary for the applicant to undertake to indemnify the respondent for damages in the event that the claim is ultimately dismissed [...]

The two primary difficulties environmental groups have encountered in securing interlocutory relief have related to this undertaking requirement, and judicial interpretation of the "irreparable harm" arm of the test under *RJR-MacDonald.* Many if not most such groups lack the financial resources to make an undertaking as to damages. As such, it seems appropriate that courts employ the undertaking requirement flexibly to ensure that the right to a remedy is not dictated solely by economic considerations. This is especially so insofar as one of the traditional reasons for imposing the undertaking requirement is to ensure that an applicant who secures interim relief is not unjustly enriched at the expense of the party against whom the relief has been granted, a rationale that seemingly has little application in the context of public interest litigation.

American courts have been alive to this concern and have been generally unwilling "to close the courthouse door in public interest litigation by imposing burdensome security requirement(s)". As such the usual practice in the United States has been to require public interest litigants seeking injunctive relief to post a nominal bond [...]

Recent Canadian authority suggests that our courts are beginning to reevaluate the appropriateness of invariably imposing an undertaking requirement on public interest litigants. For example in *Friends of Stanley Park et al. v. Vancouver Parks and Recreation Board*, Davies J. observed that

> If an applicant who applies for injunctive relief in a matter concerning serious public interests is able to establish a serious question to be tried, and that the balance of convenience, including the public interest, favours the granting of injunctive relief, such relief should not generally, at the interlocutory stage, be rendered ineffectual by reason of the fact that the applicant may not have the financial wherewithal to provide a viable undertaking as to damages.

Davies J. went to state that had the applicant succeeded in meeting the test to obtain an interim injunction, he would have issued the injunction without an undertaking as to damages. The decision in this case appears to accord with emerging authority.

[Ed. Note: See, for example, *Friends of Stanley Park v. Vancouver (City) Board of Parks & Recreation*, 2000 BCSC 372.]

The other barrier faced by public interest environmental litigants in securing interim injunctive relief has been the judicial treatment of the second arm of the *RJR-MacDonald* test: the requirement that the applicant demonstrate that they will suffer irreparable harm if relief is not granted. In private litigation, this inquiry has traditionally focused on the risk to the applicant of physical injury or economic loss. Where the applicant has been granted standing as a public interest litigant this risk is, by definition, absent; instead, in such cases, it has been argued that the relevant "irreparable harm" is harm to the environment.

The meaning of "irreparable harm" has been considered in a variety of cases that have sought to challenge the legality of proposed logging on public lands, often in old growth areas. In several cases, despite evidence that it can take hundreds of years for trees to reach mature (old growth) status, courts have concluded that the logging of old growth does not constitute irreparable harm. In *Wilderness Society v. Banff*, the court concluded that "irreparable harm" would not result from clear-cut logging of three hundred year old trees in Banff National Park, despite expert evidence that logging would have precisely this effect [...]

Recent cases have been more responsive to the argument that natural resource extraction, in particular clear-cut logging, can constitute "irreparable harm". Indeed, the Supreme Court's decision in *RJR MacDonald*, rendered in 1994, tends to support this view. There the Court relied on a case where logging was enjoined on an island claimed by First Nations to illustrate the meaning of irreparable harm. In its words, "irreparable" refers to the nature of the harm, not its magnitude: examples include where a permanent loss of natural resources will be the result when a challenged activity is not enjoined".

Over time, American courts have come to conclude that harm to the environment will almost always be "irreparable". In the words of the U.S. Supreme Court: "Environmental injury, by its nature, can seldom be adequately remedied by money damages and is often permanent or at least of long duration, i.e. irreparable. If such injury is sufficiently likely, therefore, the balance of harms will usually favour the issuance of an injunction to protect the environment".

Three recent decisions involving interim applications to enjoin logging activities in or near parklands suggest that Canadian courts may be coming to a similar realization. In 1998, Monnin J.A. (in chambers) upheld an interim injunction prohibiting construction of a road through a provincial park noting that "damages will not compensate for a destroyed forest", and observing that failure to grant the relief sought would "trigger a non-reversible process". In a similar vein, Lamek J. concluded that "absent an injunction, the clearing of the road will proceed and the trees will be gone, if not forever, at least for decades". Most recently, the Federal Court Trial Division held that because the proposed logging would result in the loss of trees that "could not be replaced in a person's lifetime" this meant that nature of the harm "could not be quantified in monetary terms".

Injunction Case Law in the Environmental Context

Our first illustrative injunction case arises in the *Algonquin Wildlands* litigation discussed earlier in this chapter in connection with public interest standing.

Algonquin Wildlands League v. Ontario (Minister of Natural Resources)
(1996), 21 C.E.L.R. (N.S.) 102 (Ont. Div. Ct.)

SAUNDERS J.: — The stay order sought is analogous to an injunction. There is no dispute as to the general nature of the test to be applied. It is the test set out in *RJR-MacDonald Inc. v. The Attorney General of Canada* (1994), 111 D.L.R. (4th) 385. It is a threefold test:

(i) Is there a serious issue to be tried?;

(ii) Would the applicants suffer irreparable harm if the stay were refused?; and

(iii) What is the balance of convenience? That is which of the parties would suffer the greater harm from the granting or refusing the interim relief.

Serious Issue to Be Tried

Initially this is the test with the lowest threshold. As stated in *RJR-MacDonald* at p. 411 unless the case on the merits is frivolous or vexatious or is a pure question of law, the judge as a general rule should go on to the next stage. The nature of the issues may be revisited at the end of the day when reaching a conclusion on the balance of convenience test. In dealing with this issue, the court should do no more at this stage than make a preliminary investigation of the merits. Indeed it is undesirable to go into the merits in any detail, having regard for the fact that they will be fully canvassed by the panel.

The applicant's attack on the municipal action is based on a noncompliance with the *Crown Forest Sustainability Act*, S.O. 1994, c. 25 and the conditions imposed by the Environmental Assessment Board. In my opinion the applicants have raised issues of statutory interpretation and ministerial conduct which are not frivolous and which require consideration before they can be determined. It is accordingly appropriate to pass to the second stage.

Irreparable Harm

The applicants allege irreparable harm, in effect, on the simple straightforward position, that once you cut down a tree you cannot put it back. The extent or even the existence of the harm is disputed by the respondents. Furthermore the Minister submits that even if there were to be harm demonstrated, there has been no harm to these applicants, which the Minister submits is a necessary element of the test. In support of this proposition the Minister relies on a passage from Beetz J. in the Supreme Court of Canada in *Metropolitan Stores (MTS) Ltd. v. Manitoba Food & Commercial Workers, Local 832* (1987), 38 D.L.R. (4th) 321 which is quoted in the *RJR-MacDonald* at p. 405 to the effect that only the harm to the applicant should be considered at this stage and the harm to the respondents and to the public interest, should be considered at the third or balance of convenience stage.

The cases suggest that the three tests should be considered in order and that if the applicant fails at any stage, that should be the end of the matter. It is important to note that neither the applicants in *Metropolitan Stores* nor the applicants in *RJR-MacDonald* were public interest applicants. The cases cited by the Minister in support of the submission that the irreparable harm must be suffered by the applicants either involved the issue of standing or were not binding on this court. It would be a rare case where a public interest applicant such as the organizations which are making this application would directly suffer irreparable harm. It would be illogical to grant these applicants standing and then turn around and deny them relief because they had not suffered harm. It would seem to me that a better approach would be to consider the public interest harm alleged by the applicants along with the harm to the respondents at the third stage of the inquiry. In my opinion there is nothing in the passage of Mr. Justice Beetz that would be inconsistent with that approach, bearing in mind that in *Metropolitan Stores* there was no public interest applicants. In short, in this situation, we should skip stage two and move to stage three.

The Balance of Convenience Stage

The third stage is the balance of convenience or as it is sometimes called the balance of inconvenience. The factors to be considered vary from case to case. In this case the public interest is very much involved. The applicants say there would be irreparable harm to the public interest if this stay is not grated. Conversely the respondents say there would be irreparable harm to the public interest if the stay were to be granted.

As I have said the applicants take the simple and straightforward position that if you cut down the trees you cannot put them back. The respondents dispute there will be any significant harm or indeed any harm at all. There is considerable conflicting evidence on this point and it is not possible to make any meaningful determination. For the purpose of this motion, I am prepared to assume there will be some irreparable harm to the natural growth and wildlife in the area in spite of the efforts to keep it to a minimum.

The harm to the respondents is of a different nature. The Crown will be hampered in pursuing its policy for the use of Crown lands. Crown revenue will be at least deferred and perhaps lost. It is uncontradicted that needed wood supply will be unavailable and the Goulard mill will not be able to operate at full capacity. It is also uncontradicted that if this occurs there will be loss of employment which will have a ripple effect in the community. Again it is hard to quantify the extent of the harm, but it must be assumed that there will be some harm.

What is going on here is part of a worldwide controversy or debate carried on in an effort to achieve a sustainable environment. In assessing the balance of convenience it is suggested in *RJR-MacDonald* that the court in determining whether to grant or withhold interlocutory relief should have regard not only to the harm which the parties contend they will suffer, but also to the nature of the relief sought, the nature of the legislation which is under attack, and where the public interest lies. To this I would add the nature of the authority of the Ministry which is under attack [...]

For a number of years the Ministry and interested segments of the public have been struggling with the issue of forest management. It is the obvious goal of all to achieve and maintain a sustainable environment while balancing the interests of the various segments. It is a complicated, ongoing and developing process. The details are set out in the material filed. In the course of argument it was not suggested that there had been anything other than good faith on the part of all parties to this application. The cutting of the forest at Owain Lake is clearly part of a comprehensive government policy with respect to the use of its land carried out in accordance with the principles I have tried to describe. While the applicants raised serious issues with respect to the compliance with the legislation and with the Environmental Assessment Board conditions they have not, as submitted by the respondents for the industry, demonstrated anything that is substantially inconsistent with the draft manual or any connection between the alleged deficiencies and the alleged harm. The government action has been consistent with its declared policy.

In all of the circumstances I considered the balance favours the respondents. In my opinion it would be inappropriate to interfere with the action of the government, even for a short time. The motion therefore will be dismissed.

Notes and Questions

1. Ultimately, the applicants prevailed at trial, a decision that underscored the strength of their claim for injunctive relief: *Algonquin Wildlands League v. Ontario (Minister of Natural Resources)* (1998), 26 C.E.L.R. (N.S.) 163 (Ont. Div. Ct.), additional reasons 27 C.E.L.R. (N.S.) 218 (Ont. Div. Ct.), reversed in part on unrelated grounds 29 C.E.L.R. (N.S.) 29 (Ont. C.A.), additional reasons 32 C.E.L.R. (N.S.) 233 (Ont. C.A.). They also received a substantial award of costs. If on these facts interim relief is unavailable, what does this suggest generally about the prospects of securing such relief in environmental cases? For further ruminations on this theme, see Stewart Elgie, "Injunctions, Ancient Forests and Irreparable Harm", (1991) 25 U.B.C.L.R. 387.

2. Another recent decision that applies the *RJR-MacDonald* framework is *West Moberly First Nations v. British Columbia*, 2018 BCSC 1835. In this case, the plaintiffs were seeking to enjoin construction of the massive "Site C" dam project by BC Hydro. The plaintiffs had previously unsuccessfully challenged the adequacy of EAs that had been done in connection with the project. In this suit, they claimed that the project would violate their constitutionally protected treaty rights to the land in question, and sought an injunction to protect specific critical areas pending trial. The BCSC rejected the interim injunction application on balance of convenience grounds, noting that West Moberly had delayed bringing the treaty claim forward, that there was no clear "path to success" on the main action, and that the plaintiffs had not offered an undertaking as to damages.

The next case arises in litigation with respect to the environmental assessment of the Kearl Oil Sands Project, discussed previously in Part III of this chapter.

Imperial Oil Resources Ventures Ltd. v.
Canada (Minister of Fisheries & Oceans)
2008 FC 382

de MONTIGNY J.: — This is an application for a stay of application or, alternatively, for an injunction prohibiting the Minister from revoking an authorization given under subsection 35(2) of the *Fisheries Act,* R.S.C. 1985, c. F-14 (the "Authorization") to Imperial Oil allowing work to be done as part of the Kearl Oil Sands (KOS) Project. [...]

Facts

The course of events leading to the present motion can be briefly summarized. Imperial Oil wishes to construct the KOS Project, an oil sands mine, in a location approximately 70 kilometres north of Fort McMurray, Alberta, on the east side of the Athabasca River. This is a huge project, consisting of four open pit truck and shovel mines providing for an average of 24,750 tonnes per hour mining capacity, corresponding ore preparation and bitumen separation facilities, a cogeneration plant, a bitumen froth processing plant, a terminal to deliver the oil sands products to a pipeline system, and utilities and off-site facilities to support the mining and processing operations. The operations at the KOS Project are expected to continue until approximately 2060 and will be followed by final reclamation of the KOS Project site. The total project is designed to produce a maximum capacity of 55,000 cubic meters of partially deasphalted bitumen per day for a period of 50 years.

The Project is subject primarily to regulation established by Alberta Environment pursuant to the *Environmental Protection and Enhancement Act,* R.S.A. 2000, c. E-12 and by the Alberta Energy & Utilities Board pursuant to the *Oil Sands Conservation Act,* R.S.A. 2000, c. O-7. It also falls within federal jurisdiction as a result of the need for Imperial Oil to obtain an authorization from the federal Minister of Fisheries and Oceans pursuant to sub-section 35(2) of the *Fisheries Act.* Accordingly, the Project was subject to the environmental assessment processes of both the Governments of Alberta and Canada. [...]

On January 18, 2006, the Department of Fisheries and Oceans, after consulting with other federal departments and agencies, recommended to the Minister of Environment that the KOS Project be assessed under the *Canadian Environmental Assessment Act,* S.C. 1992, c. 37 (the CEAA). More specifically, it was to be referred to a review panel due to the potential for the proposed project to cause significant adverse environmental effects. On July 14, 2006, Canada entered into an agreement with the government of Alberta to conduct a joint review panel.

> [...] the Joint Panel concluded that the proposed Project was not likely to result in significant adverse environmental effects, provided that the proposed mitigation measures and the recommendations of the Joint Panel were implemented (7).

Subsequent to the issuance of the Joint Panel Report, the Alberta Department of Environment and the Alberta Energy & Utilities Board issued the approvals required in connection with the KOS Project to Imperial Oil. On August 14, 2007, the Government of Canada issued a response to the Joint Panel Report, stating that it accepts all the conclusions and recommendations of the Joint Panel as presented in its Report.

On March 29, 2007, an application for leave and judicial review was filed by various non-profit organizations concerned about the environmental effects of the KOS Project (File T-535-07). They submitted that the environmental assessment conducted by the Joint Panel did not comply with the mandatory steps in the CEAA and in the Panel's Terms of Reference. The hearing took place from January 15 to 17, 2008.

Despite this challenge to the Joint Panel's Report, the Minister of Fisheries and Oceans issued Imperial Oil an authorization under subsection 35(2) of the *Fisheries Act* on February 8, 2008. On the basis of that authorization, Imperial Oil immediately commenced its work on the Project.

Madam Justice Tremblay-Lamer issued her Reasons and Order on March 5, 2008 (*Pembina Institute for Appropriate Development v. Canada (Attorney General)*, [2008] F.C.J. No. 324, 2008 FC 302). She allowed the application for judicial review in part, and remitted the matter back to the same Panel with the direction to provide a rationale for its conclusion that the proposed mitigation measures will reduce the potentially adverse effects of the Project's greenhouse gas emissions to a level of insignificance. She refrained, however, from requiring the entire Panel review to be conducted a second time, as the error related solely to one of many issues that the Panel was mandated to consider [...]

On March 11, 2008, the Chief Executive Officer for Imperial Oil wrote to the Minister of Fisheries and Oceans, articulating concerns over the impact of the Judgment on the Project work then underway, and on the Authorization issued on February 12, 2008, pursuant to subsection 35(2) of the *Fisheries Act*.

On March 13, 2008, two of the Applicants in the judicial review of the Joint Panel's Report initiated a new judicial review application (File T-418-08). Imperial Oil is named as a Respondent, as is the Minister of Fisheries and Oceans. This new judicial review application is directed to the Authorization issued on February 12, 2008, pursuant to subsection 35(2) of the *Fisheries Act*. It seeks relief which included an Order quashing the Authorization, and interlocutory injunctive relief enjoining all or part of the KOS Project until the final resolution of the issues raised.

On March 20, 2008, the Department of Fisheries and Oceans delivered a letter to Imperial Oil, stating their opinion that the Authorization had been rendered a nullity as a result of the decision of Madame Justice Tremblay-Lamer. On the same day, Imperial Oil filed Judicial Review Application T-460-08 which underlies the present motion for a stay of the Minister's decision to revoke the Authorization given on February 8, 2008.

Analysis

The test for issuing a stay of proceedings is well known, and has been set out by the Supreme Court of Canada in *RJR-MacDonald Inc. v. Canada (Attorney*

General), [1994] 1 S.C.R. 311. The applicant must establish a) a serious issue to be tried, b) that it will suffer irreparable harm if the stay is not granted, and c) that the balance of convenience favours the applicant.

In this case, I think it is beyond dispute that a serious issue to be tried has been established. Briefly stated, the arguments of the parties can be summarized in the following way. The applicant contends there is nothing in the *Fisheries Act* allowing the Minister to revoke the subsection 35(2) authorization or revisit his decision to grant the authorization. As to the argument that the authorization has been rendered a nullity as a legal consequence of the judgment of Madam Justice Tremblay-Lamer, the applicant further argues, first of all, that the Joint Panel's Report was not quashed or set aside, but was merely sent back for the Panel to better explain its recommendations with respect to the problem of greenhouse gas emissions and to provide a basis for its conclusion on this particular issue. In any event, counsel for the applicant submits that section 37 of the CEAA directs the Minister to take into account the Panel Report, not to rely solely on its rationale. While it was conceded that the result might be different if the Court had quashed the Report, it is argued that the authorization cannot fall merely because the reasoning of the Panel was found defective on one aspect of its findings.

The respondents, on the other hand, take the view that the Minister has not revoked the Authorization, but that it has become void as a legal consequence of the decision made by Madam Justice Tremblay-Lamer. If one is to follow their argument, the regulatory regime put in place in the CEAA emphasizes that environmental assessment is a process in which environmental assessment precedes and informs regulatory decision-making. Since there has been a material flaw in the environmental assessment process which, to use Madam Tremblay-Lamer's words, "short-circuits" this sequence, the Authorization is a nullity. In other words, the CEAA makes it clear that the Minister cannot proceed until a completed environmental assessment is over, one that meets all the requirements of the CEAA, and a report that as described in section 34 has been submitted to the Minister. Since the Court found a material error in the Panel's Report, it nullifies the Authorization as a condition precedent to the exercise of the authority has not been fulfilled. The responsible authority could not proceed because it could not make an informed decision.

It would be inappropriate, at this stage, to go any further into the arguments presented by counsel from each side. They are better left to the judge who will be seized of the underlying Application for Judicial Review, who will be in a much better position to rule on this legal issue after having considered a full record and more comprehensive written and oral arguments. Suffice it to say that, for the purposes of this Motion for a stay of application, I am satisfied the applicant has a case which deserves to be heard by the Court.

I am not convinced, however, that the applicant will suffer irreparable harm if the stay is not granted, especially if the Application for Judicial review is heard on an expedited basis. Indeed, counsel for the applicant conceded that much during his oral submission by teleconference. In his affidavit, Mr. Christopher Douglas Allard, Senior Project Manager for the KOS Project, stated that if work is to be stopped, there will be a domino effect on the time-line set for the work to be completed by 2012. While this is no doubt true, I also note that there is some vagueness in that schedule. For example, the ditching work will continue through "the first quarter or half of 2008" (para. 40 of the affidavit). Dewatering would then commence, and Imperial Oil "believes" it must start in the summer of 2008, as there are many different factors that can impact the pace of dewatering (para. 41 of the affidavit). If the ditching stops and dewatering cannot occur as planned, "that may extend the Project out one or more years" (para. 44 of the affidavit).

In light of these crude estimates, and in the absence of any cross-examination on the affidavits, it is difficult to assess with any degree of certainty the damage that would result from a long term stay. Imperial Oil also argued that if it wishes to commence operation of the KOS Project on schedule, it must order certain equipment, execute an engineering procurement and construction management contract and execute an earthworks construction contract. Many equipment items must be ordered 3 to 4 years prior to delivery, and the cost and availability of this equipment could change during this time. Moreover, the hundreds of engineers that have been mobilized for this project would likely be redeployed to other projects, and it would be impossible to say how many would be able to rejoin the KOS Project upon recommencement.

These are no doubt costs to be taken into consideration, but the amount of which is difficult to assess. How much of these costs would Imperial Oil be able to recoup is also difficult to foresee. What appears to be clear, however, is that a short term delay will most likely not be a major impediment in the overall schedule of the project. Moreover, Imperial Oil stands to lose a lot more if they were to do more work and expand further capital investment, only to see their Application for Judicial Review dismissed by the Court in a year or so.

It is true that from a compensation standpoint, Imperial Oil has committed to a No Net Loss Plan under the subsection 35(2) authorization such that any fish habitat that is altered, disrupted or destroyed must be replaced on a ratio of 2 to 1. I am also mindful of the undertaking given by the applicant as to damages that may be caused as a result of the granting of a stay. But these are only some of the considerations that must be taken into account. Of far more significance, it seems to me, is the crucial importance to resolve all the uncertainties, legal and otherwise, before embarking upon such an important project. This can only be done when the issues will have been fully canvassed, and when all the interested parties will have had an opportunity to be heard.

For all these reasons, the application for interim relief shall be denied.

Notes and Questions

1. Would the decision in the preceding case have been different had the company been able to quantify its potential loss more precisely? Did the company bear the risk of uncertainties here? How much turns on the Court's conclusion that a "short term delay will most likely not be a major impediment"?

2. Often, in environmental disputes, the project proponent and environmental protestors will both be seeking injunctions: the former in order to disperse the protestors, the latter to enjoin construction activities at the site. For an interesting decision that arose in this situation, see *Guelph (City) v. Soltys*

(2009), 45 C.E.L.R. (3d) 26 (Ont. S.C.J.) (excerpted in Chapter 9). This case arose in response to protests over a proposed subdivision slated to be built at a location that provided habitat for an endangered salamander. In a carefully reasoned judgment, the Court decided to enjoin both the protesters and the proposed construction (the latter for a period of 30 days to allow government to take appropriate protective action if desired).

Part VI — Costs in Judicial Review Proceedings

Judicial review can be a risky proposition for any litigant due to the potential for adverse costs liability. Public interest environmental litigants are especially at risk by virtue of the fact that if they are unsuccessful, they may be liable for not only the costs of the governmental agency whose decision was challenged, but also the costs of any private parties that may have joined (or been granted permission to be joined) in the litigation to uphold the decision in question. A recent survey of public interest environmental practitioners has revealed that the spectre of adverse costs liability is the most pressing access to justice issue confronted in their practice area: see C. Tollefson, "Costs and the Public Interest Litigant: *Okanagan Indian Band* and Beyond", (2006) 40 C.J.A.L.P. 39 at 49. What follows are excerpts from two articles canvassing recent developments in the law of costs relating to public interest litigants.

Chris Tollefson,
"Costs in Public Interest Litigation:
Recent Developments and Future Directions"
(2009) 35 Advocates' Q. 181

When counseling public interest clients on the prospect of pursuing litigation, the spectre of adverse costs liability invariably looms large. Even where the case is strong, has compelling public interest features and adequate legal resources are available to mount the claim, a litigator is duty-bound to ensure that their client is fully mindful of and reflects carefully on the risks of proceeding in terms of costs liability. These risks are significantly enhanced if the contemplated litigation, as it often does in environmental cases, involves government as well as other private parties, either at the outset or potentially down the road.

Across the Commonwealth world, it is broadly recognized that the application of traditional costs rules presents a formidable barrier to access to justice. Indeed, as Lord Justice Brooke has observed in a recent lecture on public interest environmental litigation, costs rules "[...] above all, the risk of having to pay one's opponent's costs if one loses, and the uncertainty at the outset of litigation as to how large those costs will be" are arguably the most substantial barrier to access to justice. This conclusion is one that has equal force in the Canadian setting, as a recent study of access to justice in public interest litigation tends to confirm.

In Canada, the allocation of costs, although governed by statute, remains largely a matter of judicial discretion. The breadth of this discretion has, in public interest cases, created a costs jurisprudence that has been characterized by what one trial judge has described as yielding "erratic and unpredictable results". Given the central role of costs in promoting access to justice, academics have argued that establishing a more coherent and predictable public interest costs jurisprudence is "the most critical variable affecting the long-term health of public interest litigation".

While progress towards this goal has been slow, there are some hopeful signs on the horizon. Overall, it would appear that courts are becoming increasingly attuned to costs as an access to justice issue. Moreover, appellate level decisions both in Canada and England suggest at least a modest appetite for renovating the law of costs in public interest cases. But transforming this rhetorical appreciation of the importance of access to justice into legal principles that measurably reduce the risks (real and perceived) associated with pursuing public interest litigation has been hobbled by a variety of judicial concerns. These include difficulties associated with developing a workable definition of "public interest"; concerns about the "fairness" implications of special public interest costs rules in litigation involving private parties; and a general apprehensiveness about eroding the historically broad judicial discretion that has existed in this realm.

The Costs Landscape in Public Interest Cases: Trends and Terminology

In general, the law of costs in Canada, both common law and statutory, establishes a presumption that costs will ordinarily "follow the event" on a partial indemnity basis. The entitlement of the victor to costs rests on a variety of rationales including compensation (ensuring that the prevailing party is compensated for defending the suit), deterrence (as a measure to deter wrongful conduct) and spoils (the notion that entitlement to costs accompanies victory *per se*). Courts also possess a broad discretion to depart from this practice in special circumstances. Thus, the victor may be denied its costs on equitable grounds, for example, to discipline bad faith or sharp conduct. Alternatively, a court may refuse to award costs in recognition of the public benefits associated with the litigation (for example, where the case involves consideration of a novel legal point or an issue of public significance) or on an access to justice rationale (where an adverse award would visit undue hardship on a responsible public interest litigant). In contrast, public interest intervenors are conventionally regarded as being outside normal costs rules, although there are exceptions to this general practice [...]

In other Commonwealth jurisdictions, costs law follows these same basic contours and reflects analogous policy considerations. There is, however, one material difference that distinguishes Canadian costs law from that prevailing in England and some other Commonwealth jurisdictions. While in Canada the victor is presumptively entitled to be compensated on a partial indemnity basis (that may, depending on the jurisdiction, cover only half of their actual legal costs), in England the prevailing judicial policy is that the victor should be fully indemnified. This, of course, makes the stakes even higher for unsuccessful public interest litigants seeking relief from adverse costs liability.

In the academic literature, the Commonwealth approach to costs is typically referred to as a "two-way" costs regime. This terminology refers to the fact that at the conclusion of litigation costs can flow in two distinct directions, with a litigant either receiving or being liable for costs depending on which party has prevailed on the merits. This is in contrast to prevailing common law practice in the United States where the default position is a "no-way" regime in which parties bear their own legal costs regardless of the outcome. But while unsuccessful American litigants are not normally liable for adverse costs, this no-way model has been statutorily modified to allow for the recovery of costs in successful citizen suit actions. Thus, where a party (typically a public interest litigant) has been granted standing as a "private attorney general" to enforce a legal obligation against government (including under many federal environmental and civil rights laws) they are entitled to recover their costs on a full indemnity basis if their suit ultimately succeeds. This form of costs regime is known as a "one-way" model; an approach under which public interest litigants are shielded from adverse costs liability if they lose but are compensated for their costs if they prevail.

Understandably, many in the Canadian public interest bar are somewhat envious of the American one-way costs model, an approach that has not only served to sustain public interest law as a robust practice area but is also reported to have significantly enhanced the efficacy of federal law enforcement under legislation containing citizen suit provisions. North of the border, however, efforts to secure comparable citizen suit laws have met with political resistance. As a result, and perhaps to some extent by default, the principal venue for advocacy with respect to costs law reform in Canada has been the courts.

In this setting, reformers have argued for judicial recognition of a "public interest costs exception" that would serve to shield responsible public interest litigants from adverse costs liability where they have unsuccessfully litigated an issue of public importance. Recognition of this exception would, in effect, institute a one-way costs model for Canadian public interest litigation. To date, Canadian courts have been reluctant to carve out a judicial exception to the prevailing two-way model for public interest litigation, preferring to deal with such cases under the ambit of their general discretion to afford relief from adverse costs liability in appropriate cases.

Chris Tollefson,
"Costs in Public Interest Litigation Revisited"
(2011) 39 Advocates' Q. 197

To date, the Canadian costs case law in the context of public interest litigation has dealt with three main scenarios:

- *ex post* applications for special costs;
- *ex post* applications for relief/immunization from adverse costs liability; and
- *ex ante* applications advance/interim costs

A fourth form of public interest costs order, which has in recent years come to play an important role in Australian and especially U.K. jurisprudence, is the protective costs order (PCO). Like the advance costs order, the PCO is, by definition, an *ex ante* order. In the remainder of this [article], I will consider the case law on special costs and costs immunity, then turn to the advance costs case law, and conclude with a discussion of the PCO jurisprudence.

Ex Post Claims for Special Costs and Relief from Adverse Costs Liability

In relation to applications by public interest litigants for special costs and relief from adverse costs, Canadian courts are increasingly applying a set of principles derived from what has proven to be a highly influential report authored by the Ontario Law Reform Commission (OLRC). In its 1989 *Report on the Law of Standing*, the OLRC bluntly observed that "costs rules [...] pose a formidable deterrent to litigation of the kind that our proposals [on standing] are intended to facilitate, and thus may fatally undermine our recommendations for the law of standing". The report went on to set out a series of five criteria for determining whether a special public interest costs award is warranted:

- The proceeding involves issues the importance of which extends beyond the immediate interests of the parties involved.

- The person has no personal, proprietary or pecuniary interest in the outcome of the proceeding, or, if he or she has an interest, it clearly does not justify the proceeding economically.

- The issues have not been previously determined by a court in a proceeding against the same defendant.

- The defendant has a clearly superior capacity to bear the costs of the proceeding.

- The plaintiff has not engaged in vexatious, frivolous or abusive conduct.

These five factors have been approved by various trial and appellate courts including the B.C. Court of Appeal and the Federal Court. The most sustained judicial consideration of the OLRC test is *Victoria (City) v. Adams*. In this case, the court noted that several years previously in its *Guide Outfitters Association* decision, it had approved use of the OLRC test to determine whether a party claiming to be a public interest litigant should be excused from adverse costs liability. In the present case, it dealt with the opposite situation, one in which a successful public interest litigant was seeking an order for special costs.

Despite this difference, however, the court concluded that in principle the two cases were not all that dissimilar. Both in *Guide Outfitters* and this case, the court was being asked to derogate from the normal rule as to costs. However, "not all forms of departure" from the normal rule "are of equal magnitude". Conceived as a spectrum of potential costs awards, an award of advance (or interim costs) or an award of costs to an unsuccessful party are significantly more exceptional orders and would thus require the claimant to mount a more compelling justification. Here, the court concluded, a lesser form of justification might well suffice.

In the result, therefore, the B.C.C.A. in *Victoria (City) v. Adams* concluded that a similar (or even identical), slightly modified test can be applied in all cases where the court is being asked to depart "from the normal rule" as to costs. The extent of the justification, in its view, will depend on the "magnitude of derogation from the usual cost structure of the award being considered". Its modified and distilled version of the OLRC test has four elements:

- the case involves matters of public importance that transcend the immediate interests of the named parties, and which have not been previously resolved;

- the [claimant] has no personal, proprietary or pecuniary interest in the outcome of the litigation that would justify the proceeding economically;
- [the party opposing the claimant] has a superior capacity to bear the costs of the proceeding; and
- [the claimant] has not conducted the litigation in an abusive, vexatious or frivolous manner.

It would appear based on the case law that a claimant in a public interest case seeking to either recover special costs or be relieved of adverse costs liability must satisfy all four elements of this "bundled" test. And, of course, a claimant's prospects for success will be significantly enhanced if, in addition to satisfying the above test, there are other factors in the litigation that tend to favour the order they are seeking.

A good illustration of this is a recent judgment of Russell J. in Georgia *Strait Alliance v. Minister of Fisheries and Oceans* [also known as the Consolidated Orcas). In this case, a complicated piece of litigation under the *Species at Risk Act* involving two petitions that were ultimately heard together, the applicant prevailed on the merits and later sought its solicitor-and-client costs. Applying the OLRC test, as approved by the Federal Court in *Harris v. Canada*, Russell J. concluded that public interest considerations militated in favour of the order sought. In addition, however, he concluded that such an order was justified as the result of the "unjustifiably evasive and obstructive approach" undertaken by the respondents that "unnecessarily lengthened and complicated the proceedings".

What I have termed the "bundled" approach to assessing *ex post* costs claims made by public interest litigants (inspired by the OLRC, applied in the *Harris*, *Georgia Strait Alliance* and *Guide Outfitters* decisions, and most recently distilled by the B.C.C.A. in *Victoria (City) v. Adams* as discussed above) has much to commend it. Through this bundling, three key aspects or rationales for exercising a judicial discretion to make a costs order designed to take account of the special realities of public interest litigation are each given expression. The first element of the test is a metric of the public benefit associated with the case being litigated; the second and third elements address access to justice considerations at play in the litigation; the final element recognizes the residual judicial discretion to consider other factors relating to the carriage of the litigation, including the applicant's own conduct.

While B.C. and federal courts are supportive of this bundled approach, in other jurisdictions somewhat different tests have evolved. In Ontario, for example, in answering the question of whether a litigant should be relieved from adverse costs liability, courts have tended to distill the inquiry into a single question: namely, whether the applicant seeking relief is a "genuine" public interest litigant: see *Incredible Electronics Inc. v. Canada (Attorney General)* 2006 CanLII 17939 (ON SC).

Ex Ante Claims for Advance Costs

The form of public interest costs order that has prompted the most judicial and academic musings over the last decade is also the most exotic; a species of judicial order that, at least in the public interest setting, would appear to be unique to Canada. The genesis of this form of order is *Okanagan Indian Band*, a 2003 decision of the Supreme Court of Canada. In this landmark case, the court expounded at length on the role of costs as a vehicle in public interest litigation. In this setting, according to Lebel J. for the majority, "the more usual purposes of costs awards are often superceded by other policy objectives" notably ensuring access to justice for ordinary citizens. To safeguard this goal, it holds that in exceptional cases courts should be prepared to order the opposing side to pay its public interest opponent's costs in advance and in any event in the cause.

To secure an advance costs order under *Okanagan* an applicant must initially satisfy the following three requirements:

1. The party seeking interim costs genuinely cannot afford to pay for the litigation, and no other realistic option exists for bringing the issues to trial — in short, the litigation would be unable to proceed if the order were not made.

2. The claim to be adjudicated is prima facie meritorious; that is, the claim is at least of sufficient merit that it is contrary to the interests of justice for the opportunity to pursue the case to be forfeited just because the litigant lacks financial means.

3. The issues raised transcend the individual interests of the particular litigant, are of public importance, and have not been resolved in previous cases.

The applicant must then establish that the case is "sufficiently special" such that it would be contrary to interests of justice to deny the application. In *Little Sisters*, writing for the majority, Bastarache and Lebel JJ. elaborated on this requirement. In their view this requires the applicant inter alia to show that if the advance order is not made, an "injustice" to the public at large is possible; that they have exhausted all other funding sources; and that there is no prospect of settling or resolving the matter without such an order.

The Supreme Court of Canada has addressed the question of advance costs in public interest litigation on three occasions. In two cases — *Okanagan* (2003) and *Caron* (2011) — it upheld funding orders made by courts below; in the third case — *Little Sisters No. 2* (2007) — it held that the funding order had been made in error. In absolute terms, the number of advance costs funding applications in public interest cases that have been made since 2003 is relatively small; my research suggests that only three or four such applications are made each year in Canadian courts. In addition to *Okanagan* and *Caron*, successful applications have been made in several aboriginal law cases.

Ex Ante Protective Costs Orders

While advance costs orders have generated considerable judicial and academic attention in Canada, the same cannot be said of protective costs orders. This is surprising given the prominent role they have come to play in U.K. and Commonwealth public interest litigation. It is also surprising given comments made by the majority in *Little Sisters No. 2*. There, in discussing the judicial approach to considering costs applications in the public interest context, Bastarache and Lebel JJ. state that

[...] different kinds of costs mechanisms, like adverse costs immunity, should also be considered. In doing so, courts must be careful not to assume that a creative costs award is merited in every case; such an award is an exceptional one, to be granted in special circumstances. Courts should remain mindful of all options when they are called upon to craft appropriate orders in such circumstances. Also, they should not assume that the litigants who qualify for these awards must benefit from them absolutely. In the United Kingdom, where costs immunity (or "protective orders") can be ordered in specified circumstances, the order may be given with the caveat that the successful applicant cannot collect anything more than modest costs from the other party at the end of the trial: see *R. (Corner House Research) v. Secretary of State for Trade and Industry*, [2005] 1 WLR 2600, [2005] EWCA Civ 192, at para. 76. We agree with this nuanced approach (para 40).

[Above] I briefly discussed the recognition under U.K. law of the power to order PCOs. The leading case remains *Corner House Research* though its principles must now be read in light of later cases that expand, particularly in environment cases, the availability of such orders: see *Morgan v. Hinton Organics (Wessex) Ltd. and R. (on the application of Garner) v. Elmbridge BC* [the *Morgan* and *Garner* cases].

The Court of Appeal in *Corner House* affirmed the existence of a discretion to order a PCO where:

(1) the issues were of general public importance;

(2) the public interest required resolution of these issues;

(3) the applicant had no private interest in the outcome of the case;

(4) having regard to the financial resources of the parties and the amount of costs likely to be involved, it was fair and just to make the order; and

(5) if the order was not made, the applicant would likely discontinue proceedings and, in so doing, be acting reasonably.

Where a trial judge decided to make such an order, Corner House stipulated two further requirements. First, that where the order allowed the applicant to recover its costs if successful, it should be limited to "solicitor's fees and a fee for a single advocate of junior counsel status". As well, the decision required, as a *quid pro quo* in all cases except where a "no way" costs order is made, that the order contain a "cap" on recoverable costs consistent with the previous requirement.

While applauded for its recognition of the need to respond to growing access to justice concerns (especially prominent under a full indemnification costs model such as exists in the U.K.), *Corner House* also had its share of critics. It has been argued that its requirement that the applicant possess no private interest in the subject-matter of the litigation is unrealistic and unfair (particularly in environmental and land use disputes); that it places applicants in an untenable situation of having to depose that they will terminate extant litigation if not funded; that its capping rules (especially its restrictions with respect to funding at a junior counsel level) do little to level a highly uneven legal playing field; and that in many cases the PCO application process has "ended up in satellite litigation, with witness statements and submissions flying around, costs racked up and the substantive proceedings delayed".

Of late, public interest lawyers have sought to renovate the *Corner House* principles by arguing that they are inconsistent with the U.K.'s obligations under the *Aarhus Convention on Access to Information, Public Participation in Decision-making and Access to Justice in Environmental Matters* (known as the *Aarhus Convention* after the Danish town where it was negotiated). The Convention was entered into in 1998 by various parties (including the U.K.), and ratified by the U.K. and the European Commission (E.C.) in 2005.

For domestic law purposes, the Convention has the status of an unincorporated international treaty. As such, it is not binding on domestic courts except to the extent that it has been implemented by an E.C. Directive. Several such directives have now been issued in the environmental assessment context. As such, the U.K. is bound, among other things, to ensure that its procedures for the review of environmental decision-making "provide adequate and effective remedies [that are] fair, equitable, timely and not prohibitively expensive". As a result of the *Morgan* and *Garner* cases [**Ed. Note:** cited *infra* in which the *Aarhus Convention* has been raised as an interpretive principle] it is generally considered that little remains of the *Corner House* principles in litigation arising in relation to environmental assessment matters [...]

Notes and Questions

1. As noted above, English public interest lawyers have succeeded in using the *Aarhus Convention* to encourage courts to refashion common law costs law principles. While the *Morgan* and *Garner* cases have succeeded in further liberalizing the availability of protective costs orders (PCOs) initially affirmed in the landmark *Corner House* case, Canadian case law has evolved somewhat more slowly and hesitantly. Thus, while *British Columbia (Minister of Forests) v. Okanagan Indian Band*, 2003 SCC 71, is still celebrated as a powerful affirmation of the need to promote access to justice through the jurisprudence on costs, subsequent decisions both at the Supreme Court of Canada and in lower courts have been cautious. Notably, as Wood *et al.* lament in Chapter 4, Canada is not a signatory to the *Aarhus Convention*.

2. Since the articles excerpted above were published, there has been an important new Canadian case on PCOs. It arose in the context of a lawsuit that was before the Ontario Superior Court, which sought to establish recognition under the *Charter* for a right to a clean environment. This litigation is not currently active. The public interest plaintiffs are members of Aamjiwnaang First Nation who claim that the Ontario Ministry of the Environment's (MOE) ongoing practice of granting air pollution approvals to companies operating in the heavily polluted airshed near Sarnia (known by some as "Chemical Valley") violates their rights under sections 7 and 15 of the *Canadian Charter of Rights and Freedoms*. The lawsuit also targets Suncor Energy Products Inc., the holder of the specific approval at issue in the case. In early 2012, the plaintiffs applied for a PCO "insulating them, absent improper conduct during this litigation, from adverse costs if the application for judicial review is ultimately unsuccessful". The application

was opposed by the Ministry and Suncor. Harvison Young J. dismissed the application on the basis of three principal considerations: (1) that the plaintiffs have *pro bono* representation; (2) that the case was not "of sufficient public importance to justify such an exceptional costs order"; and (3) that the consequences of the order sought would be to "force Suncor, a private party, to bear a large part of the costs of this litigation" which, in her view, was not appropriate given that there was no allegation the company was at fault and no relief was being sought from it: see *Lockridge v. Ontario (Director, Ministry of the Environment)*, 2012 ONSC 2316 (Ont. Div. Ct.).

3. As the decision in *Lockridge* illustrates, courts are reluctant to grant costs orders that affect the rights of companies, as private parties, to recover their litigation costs if successful, even where the case has compelling public interest features. Governments, which as in *Lockridge* are typically involved in environmental or resource cases by virtue of having issued the permit or approval at issue, tend to be regarded in a different light. Often, in public interest cases that are ultimately unsuccessful but are perceived as being of public importance, governments will refrain from seeking (or will be judicially denied) costs. In this situation, however, the corporate permit or approval holder invariably seeks its costs, and the judicial tendency has been to grant the award: see for example *Sierra Club of Western Canada v. British Columbia (Attorney General)* (1991), 83 D.L.R. (4th) 708 (B.C. S.C.), affirmed 1992 CarswellBC 2416 (B.C. C.A.). In *Incredible Electronics Inc. v. Canada (Attorney General)* (2006), 80 O.R. (3d) 723 (Ont. S.C.J.), the assumption that corporations should be routinely entitled to costs when they prevail in a lawsuit that concerns their entitlement to enjoy state-conferred entitlements (including access to public resources) is criticized by Justice Perell. Moreover, in his view, the access to justice implications of awarding costs to corporations in this situation can be profound. As he puts it, "... from the perspective of a public interest litigant, not having to pay costs to the Attorney General, but having to pay costs to [a private corporation in this context] would be similar to avoiding a car only to be hit by a train".

4. To what extent is the reluctance of courts to depart from the traditional approach to costs allocation in public interest cases a function of their discomfort with the malleability of the concept of the "public interest"? Does this depend upon one's confidence in whether one assumes that the role of the office of the Attorney General is to represent the public interest?

References and Further Readings

Raj Anand & Ian Scott, "Financing Public Participation in Environmental Decision Making" (1982) 60 Can. Bar Rev. 81

David Phillip Jones & Anne S. de Villars, *Principles of Administrative Law*, 4th ed. (Toronto: Thomson Carswell, 2004)

Kirsten Mikadze, "Pipelines and the Changing Face of Public Participation" (2016) 29 J. Envtl. L. & Prac. 83

David J. Mullan, *Administrative Law* (Toronto: Irwin Law, 2001)

L. Sossin, *"Dunsmuir — Plus, ca change"* (Blog: March 17, 2008), online: <http://www.thecourt.ca/2008/03/17/dunsmuir-%E2%80%93-plus-ca-change/>

David Stratas J.A., "The Canadian Law of Judicial Review: A Plea for Doctrinal Coherence and Consistency" (2016), online: <https://papers.ssrn.com/sol3/papers.cfm?abstract_id=2733751>

C. Tollefson, "Costs and the Public Interest Litigant: *Okanagan Indian Band and Beyond*" (2006) 40 Can. J. Admin. L. & Prac. 39

C. Tollefson, "Costs in Public Interest Litigation: Recent Developments and Future Directions" (2009) 35 Advocates' Q. 181

C. Tollefson, "Costs in Public Interest Litigation Revisited (2011) 39 Advocates' Q. 197

C. Tollefson, "When the 'Public Interest' Loses: The Liability of Public Interest Litigants for Adverse Costs Awards" (1995) U.B.C.L. Rev. 303

C. Tollefson, D. Gilliland & J. DeMarco, "Towards a Costs Jurisprudence in Public Interest Litigation" (2004) 83 Can. Bar Rev. 607

Chapter 7

The Federal Environmental Assessment Process

Introduction

Environmental assessment processes (EAs) differ from environmental regulatory processes in that they seek to anticipate, prevent or reduce environmental impacts of proposed new activities rather than try to manage the impacts of existing activities. A good EA process does this by engaging government officials and members of the public in the project planning and design process. The ability to anticipate potential environmental effects and influence decision-makers to take steps to avoid them by either imposing conditions for approval or not approving the proposed activity has been the great promise of environmental assessment and, at the same time, its greatest challenge. After over 40 years of experience with various forms of EA, it still remains to be seen whether environmental assessment can deliver on its promise of ensuring a sustainable development path. In fact, concern over the efficiency of the EA process has led some jurisdictions, including the federal government in 2012, to significantly scale back its EA process.

Of course, EA is not the only information-gathering and decision-making process that seeks to anticipate and prevent adverse consequences of new developments before decisions are made about whether and under what conditions to approve new human activities. Municipalities have perhaps the most and longest experience with this through various planning processes for new developments. Changes in land use within municipalities in particular have attracted various forms of planning processes in jurisdictions across Canada for a long time.

In addition to EAs and municipal planning processes, all levels of government have, from time to time, utilized largely ad hoc processes to gather information and views of stakeholders to assist in the process of developing policy on a range of issues, many of which have environmental implications. The EA process, which is the focus of this chapter, should be seen as a prominent example rather than the only process utilized by governments in Canada to engage non-state actors in the process of gathering information and making decisions about proposed new human activities.

Most of Canada's environmental assessment laws are of fairly recent vintage. While Canada's first EAs were carried out in the early 1970s, it was not until the 1990s that most Canadian jurisdictions enacted mandatory EA legislation. The original *Canadian Environmental Assessment Act*, S.C. 1992, c. 37 ("CEAA 1995"), is a case in point, coming into force in 1995. Many provinces passed EA legislation in the 1980s and 1990s. Some provinces' processes have remained more or less unchanged, while others have undergone significant changes over time.

Due to the diversity of provincial EA regimes across Canada, we focus in this chapter on federal environmental assessments. The federal process under CEAA 1995 remained fundamentally the same from the entry into force in 1995 until 2012, when a new CEAA was passed by Parliament as part of an omnibus budget bill with minimal opportunity for public input. The *Canadian Environmental Assessment Act, 2012*, S.C. 2012, c. 19, s. 52 ("CEAA 2012"), drastically reduced the number of federal assessments carried out, limited the scope and process options, and imposed strict timelines. More recently, the federal assessment process was reviewed again, leading to the introduction of Bill C-69, which included the new federal *Impact Assessment Act* ("IAA"). At the time of writing, IAA had been passed by the House of Commons, but had not entered into force. In this chapter, we track the evolution of federal assessment processes and in particular contrast the approaches taken under CEAA 1995, CEAA 2012, and IAA.

At this time of transition from CEAA 2012 to IAA, it is important to understand each of the three major federal EA processes and the scale and nature of the change that has taken place over the past ten years. By introducing you to all three processes, we will give you the opportunity to make up your own mind on how the processes compare in their effectiveness, efficiency and fairness. Furthermore, CEAA 1995 and CEAA 2012 will continue to have relevance for lawyers for years to come even after the entry into force of IAA. Many of the important court cases on EA in Canada were fought over the implementation of CEAA 1995, making an understanding of that Act critical to the understanding of these cases and their application today. Finally, a contextual interpretation of IAA will inevitably draw upon CEAA 1995, CEAA 2012, and the intention of Parliament in its most recent overhaul of the federal EA process.

To this end, we start in Part I with a short history of EA at the federal level, followed in Part II by a brief overview of the first federal EA statute in the form of CEAA 1995. In Part III we then turn to CEAA 2012 and provide an overview of the key changes it introduced, followed in Part IV by a summary of the key elements of IAA. In Part V we then offer a summary of an academic perspective on the key elements of good EA to give you a basis on which to assess the relative strengths and weaknesses of each of the three legislative approaches to federal assessments in Canada covered in this chapter. Finally, in Part VI we have included a selection of court cases that highlight some law and policy issues that persist in spite of the many changes to the federal assessment process.

Part I — Introducing Federal EA

Environmental assessment has been an important environmental policy tool since the early 1970s. One of the earliest illustrations of EA becoming a legally regulated requirement was under the 1969 *National Environmental Policy Act*

(NEPA) in the US. Between the mid-1980s and the mid-1990s, the federal and most provincial EA processes in Canada gradually moved in this direction, evolving from their discretionary roots towards a more legalized form. In some jurisdictions in Canada, the focus during this time period also shifted from pollution control to a more proactive and comprehensive consideration of proposed activities and alternatives in light of the overall risks and benefits. Many statutory processes developed during this time tended to focus on physical projects, while some have since started to include policies, plans and programs.

Approaches to environmental assessments proposed in Canadian EA literature have also evolved over time. The characteristics of a sound EA process are now generally recognized to include several key features explored in more detail in Part V of this chapter. A strong legislative foundation helps to ensure clarity, certainty, fairness and consistency. Procedures, in order to be suitable, have to be able to adapt to the needs of a particular project or activity to be assessed. At the same time, the procedures have to be true to basic principles of fairness and openness, and they have to be as consistent and predictable as possible to facilitate public engagement. Public involvement is recognized as an important principle, both in terms of access to the process and the opportunity to influence the decision. All of this suggests that EA processes should be orientated toward problem solving, and that there should be a clear link between the process and decision-making. The importance of monitoring and feedback capabilities, to ensure compliance and to evaluate the process and the project, are also increasingly recognized in the literature.

In moving from these principles to the design and implementation of EA processes, there are a number of key issues to be explored. The first is *what human activities are to be covered* by the process. Most EA processes in Canada focus on project-based assessments. Projects to be assessed can be listed, they can be identified through a threshold test, or they can be determined through the exercise of either professional or political judgment. However decided, some EA processes are limited to government projects, but most include private developments. Some have focused on large-scale projects, whereas others have included smaller projects. A few have gone beyond projects to provide for assessments of policies, plans and programs.

Closely related to the question of coverage is *the nature of the EA process*. Where the process only applies to large-scale government projects, it may be reasonable to design a "one size fits all" process. Where it includes a broader range of projects, and perhaps even policies, plans and programs, designing processes that are sufficiently flexible to accommodate the range of activities to be assessed while remaining true to the fundamental principles of a sound EA process becomes important. A key challenge is to design processes that identify appropriate roles for the proponent, the public, non-governmental organizations, regulators, other departments within the level of government initiating the assessment, governments other than the level initiating the process, proponents of alternatives, and Indigenous communities.

Another critical issue in the design and implementation of EA processes is the *scope of the assessment* to be carried out. Scope in this context refers to the substance of the assessment. As a starting point, this involves often difficult decisions about the scope of the project, policy, plan or program to be assessed. Does the assessment include the whole activity proposed, or just one component? Does it include only what is proposed by one particular proponent, or does it extend to other activities made possible by allowing a particular proposed activity to proceed? The scope of the assessment also refers to the issues to be addressed. Does the EA focus on biophysical impacts, or include economic, social, health and cultural effects? What is the role of values, ethical considerations, traditional and Indigenous knowledge in the assessment?

Another key issue in the design and implementation of EA processes is the *nature and implications of the final outcome*. Some EA processes result in binding decisions on the activities assessed, with the decision made by the tribunal responsible for the EA process. At the other end of the spectrum, the EA process can be an information-gathering process that is completely separate from the decision-making process. Under such a process, the information gathered by and the results of the EA are simply made available to the decision-maker, who may be under an obligation to simply consider such information and results when making a final decision.

Federal efforts to carry out environmental assessments predate federal legislation by almost two decades. The federal Cabinet decided in the early 1970s to establish the Federal Environmental Assessment Review Office to oversee the newly established non-legislative EA process. The focus was on a screening process to identify proposed federal projects that had the potential to cause unacceptable pollution. Proposed projects identified through the screening process as warranting further assessment were expected to go through a more thorough environmental assessment process.

The initial Cabinet decision was followed with a broader Cabinet policy directive in 1973 to carry out an environmental assessment of significant new proposals. The main implication of the 1973 directive was to broaden the application of EAs from federal projects to private projects with federal involvement in the form of federal financial support, land, or regulatory oversight. Federal EAs continued to be non-legislative. The determination of whether a full assessment was needed, as well as the design and implementation of the EA process, was left in the hands of those responsible for the ultimate project decision. This has generally been referred to as a self-assessment approach in the federal EA process.

It was the period from 1974 to 1980 that brought about the first evolution of federal EAs in Canada. A catalyst for this evolution was the Berger Inquiry on the proposed Mackenzie Valley Pipeline, which took place between 1974 and 1977. In many respects, the Berger Inquiry process looks very familiar to anyone who has followed federal EA panel reviews over the past two decades, though it was in fact broader in scope than most panel reviews carried out today.

In parallel with the Berger Inquiry from 1974 to 1977, the federal EA process was gradually strengthened and formalized as the Environmental Assessment and Review Process (EARP). Some of the changes included encouraging earlier public consultations and improving the independence of review panels by not including federal decision-makers on review panels if they were involved in proposing the activity to be assessed. Nevertheless, it was still common for major projects to be approved before the environmental assessment was completed or without any assessment.

In the early 1980s, further events influenced the evolution of federal EA. First among these was a proposed new approach to environmental impact assessment published by Beanlands and Duinker in 1983. It has become the most cited, if not always followed, methodology for predicting the biophysical impacts of proposed activities in Canada. Around the same time, Liberal Member of Parliament Charles Caccia became the federal Minister of the Environment and convinced his Cabinet to formalize the EARP process as a guidelines order issued by Cabinet. The guidelines order was drafted in mandatory language. However, federal departments did not consider themselves bound until a series of court cases confirmed the binding nature of the EARP Guidelines Order in the early 1990s.

The EARP Guidelines Order was passed in 1984, following both an internal and external review. The guidelines order applied to proposals that were "initiatives, undertakings, and activities" for which the federal government has a "decision-making responsibility." During the implementation of the EARP Guidelines Order, it became clear that proposals included not only physical projects and activities, but also policies, plans and programs. At the same time, the requirement that there had to be a "decision-making responsibility" for something to be considered a proposal was interpreted narrowly, to mean a legal duty. This duty, for EARP purposes, could relate to the federal government as either proponent, financial contributor, landowner, or regulator.

In response to ongoing criticism of the federal EA process under the EARP Guidelines Order and the growing number of successful court challenges involving the EARP process, the government introduced a bill in 1990 to entrench the federal EA process in legislation in the form of the *Canadian Environmental Assessment Act* (CEAA). The Act was passed in 1992 by the Conservative Government, but proclamation was delayed pending the development of key regulations. A change in government in 1993 resulted in some changes by the new Liberal Government and led to proclamation of CEAA in January 1995. We therefore refer to it as "CEAA 1995".

Part II — The Original Canadian Environmental Assessment Act (CEAA 1995)[1]

Introduction

In this section, we provide a brief overview of CEAA 1995. CEAA 1995 differed from the EARP Guidelines Order in a number of important ways. The most obvious distinction is that the federal EA process was now, for the first time, set out in legislation. This made the process less susceptible to interference by government without the approval of Parliament, but also more difficult to update in light of changing circumstances. However, CEAA 1995 was limited in its

---

[1] This overview of CEAA 1995 is adapted from Meinhard Doelle, *The Federal Environmental Assessment Process* (Toronto: LexisNexis, 2008).

application to physical projects, whereas the EARP Guidelines Order had included the assessment of policies, plans and programs. The assessment of policies, plans and programs was left to a separate process under a Cabinet Directive on Strategic Environmental Assessments (SEA).

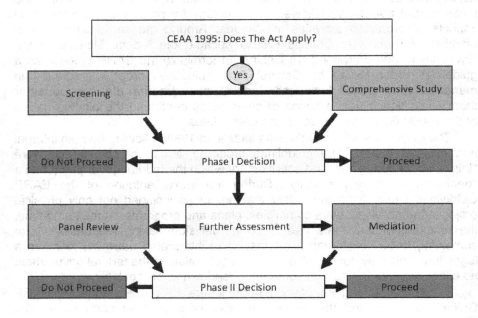

When Did the Act Apply?

For many EA processes at the provincial level in Canada, activities which trigger the process are identified through a project list or are left to the discretion of a Minister. A combination of the two is also common. The application of CEAA 1995, however, was determined through a more complex but legally clear combination of definitions and project lists. There were three principal reasons for the approach taken in CEAA 1995.

The dominant influence on the approach was constitutional. It was thought to be difficult to come up with a list of all projects, or all types of projects, that warrant an environmental assessment and for which there was a sufficient federal role to justify an assessment at the federal level. The second was a concern that a list would tend to exclude unanticipated and new types of projects, which are sometimes the projects most in need of environmental assessment. The third consideration was to ensure a consistent and predictable application of the process, rather than a discretionary one influenced by political considerations.

The definition of "project" was central to determining whether the CEAA 1995 process applied. If a proposed activity did not meet the definition of "project" in section 2 of the Act, the process did not apply. If the proposed activity did meet the definition, the process applied only if additional requirements discussed below were met. The definition of "project" had two branches, one for undertakings in relation to a physical work, and one for physical activities not in relation to a physical work.

Projects that were not excluded required an assessment before a federal authority, as defined in section 2, made a decision under section 5 of the Act. The requirements of section 5 were central to the application of the CEAA 1995 process. They identified the federal decisions that triggered an assessment under the Act. They also set an expectation that the EA process be carried out early, before federal project decisions were made. If no section 5 decision was required, the project did not trigger an assessment under CEAA 1995.

The requirements of section 5 created practical difficulties in cases where it was unclear for one reason or another whether a section 5 decision would be required. For example, section 35 of the *Fisheries Act*, R.S.C. 1985, c. F-14, required an approval in cases of harmful alteration of fish habitat. Whether a project would cause a sufficient alteration of fish habitat may not be known for certain until the late design stages of the project, much later than an EA process should ideally be initiated.

Scoping Basics

The term "scoping" refers to the process of deciding what will be included in, and excluded from, an environmental assessment. Scoping involves determining the scope of the activity to be assessed and the scope of the assessment to be carried out. In other words, scoping requires decision-makers to determine exactly what is to be assessed, and what questions are to be answered through the assessment.

Decisions on scope are critical to any environmental assessment process. They determine how the project is defined for purposes of the assessment, what issues can be raised, and what impacts will be considered. As a result, scoping can have a fundamental impact on the assessment process and on the final decision. The narrower a project is scoped, the narrower will be the range of environmental impacts considered. For example, the environmental impacts of an entire forestry operation will be far broader than the environmental impacts of only a stream crossing. The broader the scope, the more time and resources will likely be required to complete the assessment.

Scoping was the subject of much litigation over CEAA between 1995 and 2012. In particular, these cases explored the limits of the discretion of federal decision-makers in determining the scope of the project to be assessed, the factors to be considered in the assessment and the scope of those factors.

Process Options

There were four process options under CEAA 1995. Assessments were carried out by way of a screening, a comprehensive study, a panel review, mediation, or some combination of these four processes. Screenings and comprehensive studies were generally regarded as alternative forms of self-assessment (by the federal decision-maker responsible for deciding whether to approve, fund, or otherwise support the project), whereas mediation and panel reviews were more independent forms of assessment to be carried out by independent panels or mediators.

More than 99% of all projects that triggered the EA process under CEAA 1995 underwent a screening-level assessment only. The screening process was designed to impose minimal process and substantive requirements, thereby offering maximum flexibility to federal decision-makers responsible for the EA process of a particular project. At any time before, during or after a screening of a project, a responsible authority or the Minister of the Environment could decide that a panel review was the more appropriate process option and refer the project to a panel. Screening-level assessments could be further streamlined through the use of model and replacement class screening options.

Key mandatory steps in the screening process included public notice of commencement of the assessment, determination of the scope of project and assessment, preparation of the screening report, and the final project decision. Coordination among federal decision-makers and with other jurisdictions depended on the nature and extent of the involvement of multiple decision-makers and jurisdictions. Transparency and public engagement obligations were limited to certain notice requirements and minimum waiting periods before decision-making. Active public engagement in scoping, the preparation of the screening report and the final decision was discretionary.

Follow-up was also within the discretion of federal decision-makers on a project-by-project basis. Process and final project decisions were made by responsible authorities, the federal decision-makers with section 5 responsibilities for the project being assessed. Responsible authorities were required to make final decisions in light of the outcome of the EA process. A fundamental question in this process was whether the project was likely to cause significant adverse environmental effects. Depending on the answer to this question, responsible authorities had different options to exercise their powers, duties or functions, to refuse to do so, or to impose conditions.

About five to ten comprehensive studies a year were carried out under CEAA 1995. Comprehensive studies were required as the minimum level of assessment for all project types listed in the comprehensive study regulations. A comprehensive study, while still considered a form of self-assessment, was really a hybrid between a screening and a panel review. It was similar to a screening in the sense that the responsible authorities retained control over much of the process and the final project decision. It was similar to a panel review in that it included mandatory public engagement at all critical steps in the process, as well as a participant funding program. The minimum standard for the scope of the assessment of a comprehensive study was also the same as for a panel review.

Key mandatory steps in the comprehensive study included and built on those required for a screening. After the notice of commencement of the EA, a comprehensive study included mandatory public engagement at the scoping stage, during the preparation of the environmental assessment report and before the project decision. In addition, a comprehensive study involved a final track decision. This meant that, contrary to the screening process, a formal decision was made early in the comprehensive study process to either continue with the comprehensive study or refer the project to a review panel. The decision was usually made in conjunction with the scoping decision. The public had to be given an opportunity to comment before the decision was made, and the decision, once made, was final.

The Minister of the Environment, who was not involved in screenings other than to decide whether a panel review was warranted, played an oversight role in the comprehensive study process. Most notably, the Minister was required to review the comprehensive study report, seek public input, and essentially give the green light for responsible authorities to make final project decisions. Responsible authorities were then required to make final decisions in light of the outcomes of the EA process; in particular, in light of whether the project was likely to cause significant adverse environmental effects. As was the case for screenings, responsible authorities had different options to exercise their powers, duties or functions, to refuse to do so, or to impose conditions. Follow-up was mandatory for all comprehensive studies.

Panel reviews made up between one and five assessments initiated under the Act in a given year. Key differences between comprehensive studies and panel reviews included the following:

- The process was taken out of the hands of responsible authorities and placed in the hands of independent panel members;
- Panel reviews, as a matter of practice, always involved public hearings, while public hearings were optional for comprehensive studies;
- Panel reviews involved an enhanced role for the Minister of the Environment, most notably with respect to scoping; and
- The final project decision in the case of a panel review was subject to Cabinet approval.

The key process decisions in a panel review were made by the Minister, while the implementation of the process was left to an independent panel. Once the decision to refer a project to a panel was made, the Minister determined the scope of the project and the scope of the assessment, set the terms of reference for the panel, and appointed panel members. In practice, the panel was often involved in the scoping process, and frequently held scoping hearings. Once the scope determinations were made, the review panel took control over the process in accordance with the terms of reference issued by the Minister. It established procedures, held hearings, reviewed oral and written submissions, and prepared recommendations for decision-makers. Section 34 of CEAA 1995 outlined the key responsibilities of the panel:

- Ensure that the required information is obtained and made available to the public;
- Hold hearings in a manner that offers the public an opportunity to participate in the assessment;
- Prepare a report that includes conclusions, recommendations and a summary of comments received from the public; and
- Submit the report to the Minister and the responsible authority.

A review panel had the power to summon any person to appear as a witness to give evidence and produce documents considered necessary for the assessment. The panel had the same powers as a court of record, and its orders could be enforced in the Federal Court.

At the conclusion of the EA process, the panel prepared a final report on the results of the environmental assessment. The report usually identified whether the project was likely to cause significant adverse environmental effects, and whether it should be allowed to proceed. If the panel recommended that the project be permitted to proceed, it would usually propose conditions and make other recommendations on how to minimize any adverse effect and maximize expected benefits. Panels, commonly, also commented on the contribution the project was expected to make to sustainable development.

The Minister had the responsibility to make the panel report available to the public. The report was then used by the responsible authority, with the approval of the Governor in Council, to determine whether to exercise its powers, duties and functions to allow the project to proceed. The determination that the project could proceed could be made either on the basis that the project was not likely to cause significant adverse environmental effects, or that significant effects were justified in the circumstances. If the Governor in Council decided that the project could proceed based on the environmental assessment carried out by the panel, responsible authorities still had discretion to decide whether to exercise their powers, duties and functions under section 5. The panel's recommendations beyond the "likely significant" were generally intended to assist responsible authorities in making determinations consistent with the purposes of the Act, such as the promotion of sustainable development.

Public participation is a key feature of panel reviews. The importance of public participation is reflected in part in the additional transparency measures incorporated in CEAA 1995. Included in the concept of transparency were public notices of important steps in the process, direct access to the panel through hearings, and access to relevant information and documentation through the electronic and paper registries. Intervenor funding and the ability to adjust the nature of the hearing to the cultural norms or preferences of those interested in participating were other strengths of the public participation process for panel reviews under CEAA 1995.

In addition to the standard panel review process, CEAA 1995 provided for joint panel reviews with other jurisdictions and for panel substitutions. A joint panel process allowed for cooperation between the federal government and other jurisdictions, such as provinces. It generally involved each jurisdiction appointing some of the panel members and an agreement on how the joint process would meet the legal requirements of all the jurisdictions involved. Issues covered in such agreements for joint panel reviews commonly included the scope of the assessment, timelines, intervenor funding, and other procedural issues. These agreements most commonly took the form of project-specific memorandums of understanding.

Mediation is available informally in most EA processes. Its function in those circumstances is to complement rather than replace the formal process. Most EA processes can accommodate a mediation process as part of the traditional EA process. In CEAA 1995, for example, there was nothing in the Act to prevent a responsible authority in the context of a screening or a comprehensive study, or a panel in case of a panel review, from appointing a mediator to resolve a particular issue. In addition to this informal use of mediation, CEAA 1995 also provided for mediation as a separate process option. In such cases, mediation could replace any other process requirements and the mediation report would be used like any other EA report by the responsible authority to make its final project decision. The discretion to refer a project to mediation rested with the Minister of the Environment. The Minister could exercise this discretion if the interested parties had been identified and were willing to participate in the mediation.

Notes and Questions

1. Assuming you have to operate within the existing constitutional structure, is there a better way to decide which projects will trigger the process than the approach in CEAA 1995? As you read on to consider the CEAA 2012 process and IAA, consider whether the triggering process for determining whether CEAA 1995 applies is more or less effective than the trigger in CEAA 2012 and IAA.

2. Assuming that screenings are intended for small and routine projects, comprehensive studies for medium-size projects and panel reviews for large and controversial projects, how could each process be improved to achieve greater efficiency, greater effectiveness, greater fairness, or all three? As you read on, consider the strengths and weaknesses of the four process options under CEAA 1995 and compare them to the process options under CEAA 2012 and IAA.

3. When do you think mediation should be used in EA? How could its use be encouraged?

Part III — The Revised Canadian Environmental Assessment Act (CEAA 2012)[2]

Introduction

CEAA 2012 fundamentally changed the way the assessment process was triggered. It abandoned the legal test involving the definition of "project", the law list and various exclusions in favour of a project list combined with broad discretion. Among the other key changes in CEAA 2012 was the elimination of two EA process options. Screenings and comprehensive studies were combined into a one-size-fits-all EA process that is much narrower in scope than either the screening or comprehensive study process under CEAA 1995. Another process option, mediation, was eliminated. Panel reviews were retained, but operate under different rules. The scope of some federal assessments was significantly narrowed, from a generally inclusive approach that tried to look at a broad range

---

[2] This overview of CEAA 2012 is adapted from Meinhard Doelle, "CEAA 2012: The End of Federal EA As We Know It?" (2012) 24 J. Envtl. L. & Prac. 1.

of adverse environmental effects of proposed projects to one that is focused on a few issues within the direct regulatory authority of the federal government. In short, there are many fewer federal EAs under CEAA 2012, with a much narrower scope of assessment. For projects assessed by the federal government alone, the federal process is only required to consider certain specific issues, such as the impact of the project on fisheries, aquatic endangered species, migratory birds, and affected Indigenous communities. In the following sections, some of the key features of CEAA 2012 are considered.

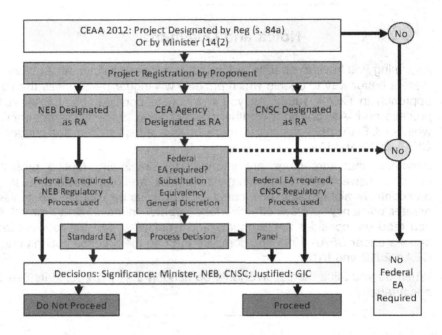

Who Is Responsible for Federal EAs?

CEAA 1995 was designed around the basic idea that all federal decision-makers, in principle, should consider the environmental implications of decisions they are asked to make about proposed new projects. To encourage federal decision-makers to seriously consider the environmental implications of their decisions, CEAA 1995 utilized a flexible screening process that was imposed directly on federal decision-makers. This screening process in CEAA 1995 applied to over 99% of the assessments carried out and could involve one or multiple federal decision-makers for a given project.

Under CEAA 2012, the number of federal decision-makers involved in the EA process was drastically reduced. The focus is now on three agencies, the National Energy Board (NEB), the Canadian Nuclear Safety Commission (CNSC) and the Canadian Environmental Assessment Agency (CEA Agency). The NEB and the CNSC utilize their own regulatory process to carry out assessments of projects under their regulatory control. All other EAs are carried out centrally by the CEA Agency.

This shift in responsibility largely spelled the end of the self-assessment experiment that was inherent in CEAA 1995. Self-assessment, in this context, refers to the idea that the federal decision-maker itself is asked to oversee the gathering of information about the broader environmental implications of its decision, and the evaluation of the information gathered, rather than have this work carried out by a more independent agency. To be fair, this experiment had been controversial from the start, and it had been questioned throughout the life of CEAA 1995, including in the parliamentary review in 2000.

Many federal decision-makers, such as the Department of Fisheries and Oceans, never fully accepted the idea that they should go beyond their core mandate and consider the broader environmental implications of the project decisions they were asked to make. What is less clear is to what extent the failure of the self-assessment process is a result of internal power struggles within the federal bureaucracies, inadequate resources made available to responsible departments, or a more fundamental problem with the concept that decision-makers should be encouraged to look beyond their core mandate to consider the broader implications of decisions they are required to make.

It is interesting, in this regard, that while the CEA Agency took over the EA process for most federal decision-makers, two federal decision-makers were shielded from this shift — the NEB and the CNSC. These two agencies continued under CEAA 2012 to operate on a self-assessment basis.

This raises a related issue, which is whether agencies responsible for regulatory processes, such as the NEB and the CNSC, are well positioned to carry out environmental assessment processes. Experience over the years has tended to show that regulatory agencies are more focused on technical issues, and less interested in the big picture planning issues so fundamental to effective EA. There are also legitimate concerns that some regulators may be captured by the industries they regulate, making it difficult for them to consider whether the sector offers the most sustainable long-term solution to the societal needs or benefits expected from the proposed project.

Furthermore, the perception of capture tends to undermine the credibility of the EA process to the general public. It is curious, then, that while CEAA 2012 generally signalled an abandonment of the self-assessment experiment, which clearly had been unsuccessful under CEAA 1995, it allowed the NEB and the CNSC to continue to play a self-assessment role.

Triggering Process

Under CEAA 2012 there is no longer a legal test for whether a project requires an assessment under the Act, but a definition of "designated project", which refers to a regulation that lists projects that require registration, governs what types of projects are subject to the Act. Once registered, however, designated projects, other than those under the control of the NEB or the CNSC, are not automatically assessed. Instead, the CEA Agency is given broad discretion to determine whether a federal EA is required for a designated project. The Act offers no clear direction on how this discretion is to be exercised. The preamble, the purpose section, and some general factors to be considered by the Agency offer the only guidance in this regard. The main limitation imposed on the CEA Agency is that it must consider the information provided by the proponent and the comments received by members of the public.

For projects not listed as designated projects, the Minister has discretion to require an EA under subsection 14(2). The Minister can exercise this discretion on the basis of the expected adverse environmental effects of the project or on the basis of public concern, but is not required to exercise this power. To date, this power has not been exercised.

Projects on federal lands and outside Canada are addressed in sections 67 and 68 of CEAA 2012. These provisions are fundamentally different from the transboundary provisions of CEAA 1995. First, sections 67 and 68 do not apply to projects with interprovincial effects, whereas the transboundary provisions in CEAA 1995 did. More fundamentally, sections 67 and 68 do not require federal decision-makers to carry out an EA process at all; they only require a determination as to whether the project is likely to cause significant adverse environmental effects, and, if so, whether those effects are justified in the circumstances. There is no requirement to follow the EA process set out in CEAA 2012 or any EA process before making these determinations.

In summary, whether a federal environmental assessment is required of a designated project listed in regulations is largely left to the discretion of the CEA Agency. Whether a federal environmental assessment is required of a project not listed as a designated project in regulations is left to the discretion of the Minister. The result is a triggering process with considerable uncertainty and a federal EA process that has been applied to only a small percentage of the number of projects triggered under CEAA 1995.

Process Options and Features

CEAA 1995 involved four basic process options: screenings, comprehensive studies, mediation, and panel reviews. Screenings and comprehensive studies were alternative forms of self-assessment, whereas mediation and panel reviews could either replace or follow the screening or comprehensive study process. Under CEAA 2012, there are two process options: one is referred to as a standard "environmental assessment", the other is the "panel review" process. In essence, comprehensive studies and mediation have been eliminated as process options under CEAA 2012, leaving a generic EA process and the option to refer EAs to a panel review.

The "Standard" EA Process

The "standard process" under CEAA 2012 is to proceed as follows. The process is initiated when the proponent of a designated project registers its project with the CEA Agency. The information required to be included with the registration of the project is set out in regulations. The proponent of a designated project is not permitted to take measures to implement the project that may cause any environmental effects listed in section 5 of the Act until either the CEA Agency has decided that no EA under CEAA 2012 is required or the proponent complies with the conditions imposed at the conclusion of the completed EA process.

The timelines from registration to the triggering decision are tight. The CEA Agency, on receiving the registration documents from the proponent, has 10 days to decide if it requires more information from the proponent. The CEA Agency has to post notices to the public on an electronic registry, allow 20 days for public comments, and make its decision within 45 days. The CEA Agency is also empowered to seek input from expert federal departments to inform its decision. A notice of the CEA Agency's decision at the end of this 45-day period is required to be posted on the electronic registry.

If a decision is made to require an environmental assessment of the project under the Act, a notice of commencement has to be posted on the electronic registry. The responsible authority takes over at this stage. For projects regulated by the NEB or the CNSC, the regulatory agency is responsible for the EA process. For projects without a regulatory agency designated as responsible for the EA process, the CEA Agency is the responsible authority for purposes of the EA process.

The EA process to be followed is not set out in any detail. Legislative provisions focus on the ability to delegate or coordinate with other jurisdictions, and the power to request additional information from the proponent and from expert federal departments, not on the actual process requirements of an environmental assessment under CEAA 2012. The scope of the EA to be carried out is set out in section 19 and is discussed below. The main process parameters in the Act are the public notice requirements already discussed and the timelines for completing the process.

Under section 27, the responsible authority is given 365 days to complete the standard environmental assessment. Time spent by the proponent to fulfill its obligations in the process does not count toward the 365 days, nor are timelines imposed on the proponent. The Minister may grant an extension of up to three months. Process requirements for EAs carried out by the NEB and the CNSC are tailored to their respective regulatory processes.

Panel Reviews

Review panels are the only process alternative to the standard assessment under CEAA 2012. There is limited guidance in the Act on the panel review process. The key legislative provisions for panel reviews are now briefly reviewed.

The Minister has sixty days from the notice of commencement of the EA process under CEAA 2012 to decide whether to refer an environmental assessment to a panel review. This is a significant departure, as the Minister previously had the discretion to refer any project to a panel review anytime during the EA process. Sixty days is a short time frame for the public to gain sufficient understanding of the proposed project to formulate and communicate its views, and for the Minister to make a final process decision.

No panel reviews are permitted for projects for which the NEB or the CNSC are identified as responsible authorities. This is consistent with the general approach in CEAA 2012 that deems the regulatory processes of the NEB and the CNSC, which include public hearings, sufficient to meet the objectives of CEAA 2012.

The Minister is specifically authorized under the new Act to seek further information from the proponent after reviewing the panel report and before making a final project decision. While this could allow the Minister to fill in information gaps left at the conclusion of a panel review, this new Ministerial power takes the intervenors and the panel out of the critical final stage of the EA process. The Minister will not have the benefit of those broader perspectives in evaluating the information provided by the proponent at this crucial stage. In the end, it is therefore an ineffective solution to a problem created by the timelines set in the new Act. A more appropriate approach would have been to give the panel the power and time to ensure there are no information gaps in its final report, rather than to require panels, as is common practice today, to meet strict timelines for the hearings, closure of the record and the preparation of the final report.

CEAA 2012 imposes an overall timeline of two years for panel reviews. As with the timeline for the standard EA process, time spent by the proponent to provide information requested by the panel does not count toward the two-year limit. The time limit can be extended for up to three months by the federal project decision-maker, or by the Governor in Council (GIC) on recommendation from the Minister. The Minister is required to specify time limits for individual steps in the panel review process that collectively do not exceed the two-year timeline. In cases where the panel does not conclude its work within the required timeline, the process is to be terminated by the Minister. In this case, the EA will be completed by the CEA Agency, which is then required to file a final report with the Minister in place of the panel report.

Many of the other features of panel reviews, such as the requirement for public hearings, access to relevant documents, notice and publication of the panel report, and final project decision, are retained in CEAA 2012. At the same time, federal review panels will be unrecognizable to anyone familiar with panel reviews under CEAA 1995, mainly due to the narrow scope of EA under CEAA 2012.

The power to establish a joint review panel with another jurisdiction is retained in CEAA 2012. This joint panel review option is the mechanism through which an environmental assessment under CEAA 2012 could still be sufficiently comprehensive to serve as a planning tool and as a basis for determining whether the proposed project can reasonably be expected to make a contribution to sustainable development. All other process options under CEAA 2012, including federal panel reviews, are too limited in scope to serve anything close to the function that panel reviews served under CEAA 1995.

Decision-making

There are important changes in CEAA 2012 to the way project decisions are made. The basic approach is that responsible authorities determine whether a project is likely to cause significant adverse environmental effects (SAEE) as defined in subsections 5(1) and (2). Where the responsible authority is the CEA Agency, that decision is made by the Minister. In case of a panel review, the SAEE determination is also made by the Minister. If the project is found to result in SAEEs under section 5, the GIC then determines whether those effects are justified in the circumstances.

If it is determined that the effects are justified, the responsible authority or Minister in charge of the EA process determines the conditions for approval of the project, not the GIC. Conditions are to be limited to those that are "directly linked or necessarily incidental to the exercise of a power or performance of a duty or function by a federal authority". The decision statement, which has to include conditions regarding mitigation measures and follow-up programs, is required under section 54 to be made public. The statement is to include the decision regarding significance, the decision on whether significant effects are justified and the conditions for approval.

CEAA 2012 introduces the concept of equivalency into the federal EA process. The basic concept is that in cases where a provincial process is found to be equivalent to the federal process, the federal process does not apply. In case of an equivalency finding under section 37 with respect to a provincial EA process, there would therefore be no federal process. There is no clear legislative requirement to consider the results of the equivalent provincial EA process, and no federal EA decision, though there could still be federal regulatory decisions with respect to the project. What is not clear is whether federal decision-makers responsible for regulatory decisions, in the case of a project subject to a provincial EA process declared to be equivalent, would have to consider the results of the provincial EA process in making their regulatory decisions.

Scope of EA

Along with the reduction of the number of EAs to be carried out and the discretion introduced into the triggering process, the changes to the scope of federal EAs was among the most significant changes to the federal process under CEAA 2012. The Act narrows the scope of the project, the definition of "environmental effect", and the factors to be considered. The combined effect of these changes is to turn the federal EA process into a rather narrow information-gathering process that largely duplicates existing federal decision-making responsibilities for the project.

The scope of the project to be assessed, which had been determined by the SCC in the 2010 Red Chris decision (*MiningWatch Canada v. Canada (Minister of Fisheries & Oceans)*, 2010 SCC 2) to be quite broad under CEAA 1995, was significantly narrowed in CEAA 2012. The definition of "designated project" includes "any physical activities incidental" to the physical activity that triggered the EA. A key difference between CEAA 1995 and CEAA 2012 in this regard is that CEAA 1995, as interpreted by the SCC in *Red Chris*, required that the scope of the project be at least the full project as proposed by the proponent. CEAA 2012 allows projects to be scoped much more narrowly.

Under CEAA 2012, depending on the interpretation of "incidental", the scope of the project can be limited to the specific component of the project listed on the designated project list. In other words, CEAA 2012 is legally a step back to the situation in the *TrueNorth* decision (*Prairie Acid Rain Coalition v. Canada (Minister of Fisheries & Oceans)*, 2004 FC 1265, affirmed 2006 FCA 31, leave to appeal refused 2006 CarswellNat 1981 (S.C.C.)), where an oil sands development was scoped as a river destruction project, because it was the destruction of the river that triggered the federal EA. The only specific provision regarding the scoping of a project in CEAA 2012, other than the definition of a designated project, is section 16, which provides for coordination in the case of two related designated projects.

The definition of "environmental effect" to be considered for some assessments was severely narrowed, making it the most drastic of the various changes to the scope of assessment under the new Act. Under CEAA 1995, environmental effects included any effect a project had on the biophysical environment, and it included the social, economic and cultural effects of those biophysical changes. Under CEAA 2012, the definition of "environmental effect" for some assessments is limited to a small number of environmental components specifically listed in subsection 5(1). Given the critical importance of the definition of "environmental effect" for the scope of EA, a summary of the components included in subsection 5(1) is included here:

- a change to the following components within the legislative control of Parliament:
    - fish and fish habitat as defined in the *Fisheries Act*,
    - aquatic species as defined in the *Species at Risk Act*,
    - migratory birds as defined in the *Migratory Birds Convention Act*,
    - any other component in Schedule 2 (which can be amended by the GIC);
- a change that may be caused to the environment that would occur:
    - on federal lands,
    - across a provincial boundary,
    - outside Canada;
- with respect to Aboriginal peoples, an effect of any change that may be caused to the environment on:
    - health and socio-economic conditions,
    - physical and cultural heritage,
    - the current use of lands and resources for traditional purposes, or
    - any structure, site or thing that is of historical, archaeological, paleontological or architectural significance.

In the case of an existing federal regulatory decision for the project assessed, subsection 5(2) provides for some requirement to consider other effects directly linked to the regulatory responsibility to be exercised, and to consider social, economic and cultural implications of the environmental effects included in subsection 5(1).

The factors to be assessed are set out in section 19, replacing section 16 of CEAA 1995. The changes to the factors are more subtle than the change to the definition of "environmental effect", but they signal a further erosion of the federal EA process. Most notably, the references to alternatives to the project and to the need for the project have been taken out. To be fair, these references in CEAA 1995 were not mandatory, but they had become standard for comprehensive studies and panel reviews. An assessment of the effect of the project on the capacity of renewable resources is also no longer required. On a positive note, the result of regional studies carried out under sections 73 and 74 are included in the list of factors to be taken into account. Unfortunately, there is no requirement to carry out such studies, and none have been carried out to date.

The end result of these fundamental changes to the scope of project and scope of assessment is to turn the federal EA process into a regulatory information-gathering process, with a focus on components of projects that are under direct regulatory control of the federal government and with a scope of assessment that is based only on selected functional jurisdiction over issues such as fisheries, aquatic species, migratory birds and Aboriginal peoples. Broader federal powers and responsibilities, as articulated by the SCC in cases such as *Oldman River* (*Friends of the Oldman River Society v. Canada (Minister of Transport)*, [1992] 1 S.C.R. 3) and *Red Chris*, will not be exercised in the application of CEAA 2012.

Harmonization with Provincial EAs

CEAA 2012 represents a rejection of the concept that harmonization is best achieved through interjurisdictional cooperation leading to one comprehensive EA process that provides the basis for decisions at all levels of government. Indeed, CEAA 2012 makes extraordinary efforts to ensure that the federal process will not apply whenever there is a concern about overlap with a provincial or other process. The approach in CEAA 2012 involves picking one jurisdiction to carry out an EA process, with no direct involvement by the other level of government and few other safeguards to ensure that the EA will provide a solid basis for decision-making at all relevant levels of government.

The discretion to decide on a case-by-case basis whether a designated project should undergo a federal EA under CEAA 2012, and whether the EA should take the form of a standard EA process or a panel review, already is a powerful tool to limit the application of the federal EA process and to avoid any actual or perceived duplication with provincial EA processes. The narrow scope of the federal EA process and the harmonization of the EA process with federal regulatory processes further reduces any risk of duplication with provincial EAs, as the nature of the federal process has shifted from an environmental assessment process to a process of gathering information already needed for regulatory decision-making. If there is duplication, it is duplication with federal regulatory processes, not with EA processes carried out by other jurisdictions. In short, when applied, the federal process under CEAA 2012 looks very different from any EA process carried out at a provincial level.

To add further opportunities for harmonization, CEAA 2012 includes provisions for substitution and equivalency. Substitution to provincial EA processes is framed in mandatory language and linked to a request by a province, while substitution to federal and Aboriginal processes is framed in more permissive language. In both cases, however, the substitution is dependent on the Minister forming an opinion that the process in question "would be an appropriate substitute". In the absence of an exclusive list of substantive criteria, this language, in the end, still leaves any substitution in the discretion of the Minister. Substitution can be approved for an individual designated project or a class of designated projects. Substitution is not an option for panel reviews or for EAs carried out by the NEB or the CNSC. Once a substitution is approved, the approved process is deemed to meet the EA requirements under CEAA 2012. The responsible authority or the Minister, as appropriate, must still make a project decision based on the final report prepared at the conclusion of the substitute process.

Equivalency takes the substitution process one step further by permitting the Governor in Council to fully exempt a designated project or class of designated projects from the application of CEAA 2012. The power for this complete exemption is limited to approved provincial substitution processes. The only two additional requirements currently identified in section 37 are that the provincial process must identify significant adverse effects and that it must ensure the implementation of mitigation measures. The section makes provision for the Minister to add additional conditions. It is unclear in the Act whether, in the case of an equivalency finding, federal decision-makers have to take the results of the provincial EA into account in making federal project decisions, such as funding decisions or permitting decisions.

In summary, when it comes to harmonization, CEAA 2012 represents a shift from a cooperative approach designed to encourage one comprehensive environmental assessment process, involving all jurisdictions with decision-making responsibilities, to one that sees delegation to the provinces and narrowing of federal EAs as the primary tools for avoiding duplication among jurisdictions involved in project EAs. The result is a federal process that is largely about gathering information already required for existing federal regulatory decisions, such as decisions under the *Fisheries Act*, the *Species at Risk Act* and the *Migratory Birds Convention Act*. As a result, CEAA 2012 placed significant new burdens on provincial and other EA processes in Canada, such as those carried out under Aboriginal self-government agreements, to ensure a comprehensive consideration of the environmental, social and economic implications of proposed new developments.

Public Engagement in the Process

The approach to public engagement in CEAA 2012 is a step backward in the effort to actively engage members of the public in the planning stage of project development, and to provide meaningful opportunities for mutual learning. As a starting point, the standard EA process in CEAA 2012 has few legislative requirements regarding public participation when compared to the comprehensive study process under CEAA 1995. Strict timelines tend to put members of the public at a disadvantage. Most importantly, fewer federal EAs mean fewer opportunities for members of the public to have input into project planning or decision-making.

The new concept of "interested party" may further reduce public engagement. CEAA 2012 has created two classes of the public, those with a direct interest who will be full participants, and those who do not qualify as having a direct interest who are excluded from parts of the federal EA process. To appreciate this concern, it is perhaps helpful to start with the definition of "interested party" in subsection 2(1). This definition is linked to designated projects. The determination of who is an interested party is not resolved in the definition, but is rather left to the discretion of the NEB or the review panel under subsection 2(2).

The implication is that for review panels and for EAs carried out by the NEB, it matters whether a member of the public is considered to be an "interested party". Paragraph 19(1)(c) uses the term "interested party", reinforcing the idea that two classes of members of the public are created. Everyone will get notice and will be able to participate in the standard EA process; however, only interested parties will have the right to fully participate in EAs carried out by the NEB and EAs referred to review panels.

Section 43 is particularly troubling in this regard. It requires a review panel to hold hearings in a manner that provides an opportunity to participate only to interested parties. This suggests members of the public that do not meet the definition of "interested party" can be excluded from the EA process. Given that under subsection 2(2) it is the panel that determines who is an interested party, CEAA 2012 clearly puts panels in a position of determining who will be permitted to participate in hearings and who will not. This may seem harmless given the independence of panels; however, when taken in combination with strict timelines offered to panels in their terms of reference, it is clear that this puts panels in a position of having to limit participation in order to meet the timelines imposed, or face having the panel review process terminated and completed by the CEA Agency.

Notes and Questions

1. Good EA can be thought of as EA that is effective, efficient and fair. How do you think CEAA 1995 and CEAA 2012 measure up against each of these three goals of Good EA?

2. Much of the debate leading up to the enactment of CEAA 2012 was about the choice between efficiency and effectiveness. How did CEAA 2012 do in striking a balance between efficiency and effectiveness? Can an EA process be both efficient and effective? Can it be all efficient, effective and fair?

3. In *Tsleil-Waututh Nation v. Canada (Attorney General)*, 2018 FCA 153, additional reasons 2018 FCA 155, the Federal Court of Appeal in its decision regarding Kinder Morgan's Trans Mountain Pipeline approval determined that the NEB was wrong to exclude increased tanker traffic as part of the project. It reached its decision on the basis that the increased tanker traffic was incidental to the proposed expansion of the existing pipeline. The NEB had excluded the increased tanker traffic from the project while acknowledging the significant adverse effect of the increase on killer whales, a listed species under SARA. In light of the provisions of CEAA 2012 regarding the scope of projects to be assessed, what insights does the decision offer on the discretion of the responsible authority to determine the scope?

4. As you read the following section on IAA, consider whether it has either struck a better balance between efficiency, effectiveness and fairness, or, even better, whether it has found ways to achieve all three, rather than compromise one for another.

Part IV — The New Federal Impact Assessment Act (IAA)[3]

Introduction

Having been elected on the promise to reform the federal EA process to restore public trust, the Liberal Government under Prime Minister Justin Trudeau started a multi-year review process of a number of federal statutes, including CEAA 2012, that resulted in the introduction of Bill C-69 in February 2018. Bill C-69 included a proposed new *Impact Assessment Act* to replace CEAA 2012. At the time of writing, IAA has been passed by the House of Commons, but has not been passed by the Senate, and has not entered into force. The following is an overview of the key elements of the assessment process under IAA as passed by the House of Commons in June 2018, and its key differences to CEAA 2012.

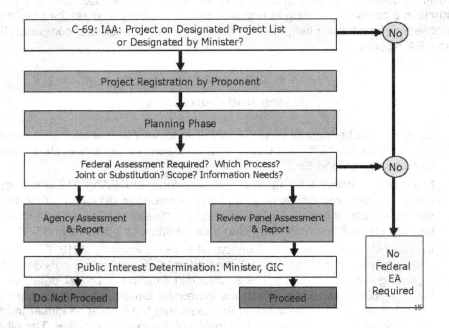

Triggers, Application of the Assessment Process

The triggering process for projects under IAA has not changed significantly from CEAA 2012. The starting point in both processes is a designated project list. There is a discussion document on the designated project list regulation available on the federal government website (<https://www.impactassessment

---

[3] This overview of the IAA is adapted from M. Doelle & John Sinclair, Environmental Impact Assessment Review (forthcoming).

regulations.ca/>). An overall assessment of the application of IAA will only be possible once the project list regulation is completed.

The Minister can, on request or on her own, require a project to be assessed that is not on the list. There is no power under IAA to require an assessment of a non-designated project that has substantially begun, or that has already received federal approvals. This is a new provision.

There are no triggers for strategic or regional assessments (just an opportunity to petition for an assessment under section 97), nor any criteria for when a regional or strategic assessment may be warranted. The initiation of any regional or strategic assessment is left to the discretion of the Minister. The Minister is to receive advice on priorities from a Minister's Advisory Council to be established under IAA. Strategic assessments appear limited to the implication of policies, plans and programs for project EAs, rather than broader questions about the environmental or sustainability implications of policies, plans or programs. The future of the Cabinet Directive on Strategic Environmental Assessment is not addressed in the Bill. Given that assessments under the Directive are not covered under the proposed *Impact Assessment Act*, the expectation is that it will continue as the main vehicle for strategic assessments of federal policies, plans and programs. There is no established link between project assessments and regional or strategic assessments (sometimes referred to as a strategic assessment off-ramp).

The Assessment Planning Process

The assessment planning phase is a new phase introduced in Bill C-69. It starts with an initial project description prepared by the proponent in accordance with regulations. The goal is clearly to initiate the process early, but it is uncertain whether this goal will be realized. In fact, the timelines may discourage a proponent from initiating the process until fairly late in its own planning process, and there are no legislative provisions to motivate an earlier start to the process. Ultimately, the timing of the initiation is left to the discretion of the proponent.

Under section 11, the public will have an opportunity to participate in the planning process, which will be led by the Impact Assessment Agency. It would appear that the purposes of the early planning process are to inform decisions on whether to carry out an assessment, whether and how to cooperate and coordinate with other jurisdictions, what the scope of the assessment will be, and whether to subject the project to a standard assessment or a panel review. The decision whether to require an assessment is to be made within 180 days, a time limit that can be extended by up to 90 days.

Determination of the scope of the assessment (other than the scope of the project itself) seems to be intended to start during the planning process, though it is not clear in IAA whether scoping is concluded at the planning phase or continues into the assessment phase. The process starts with the Agency proposing a list of issues, based on input from the public and any jurisdiction the Agency has consulted with. The proponent then responds with an indication of the information it intends to provide in response to the issues that have been identified.

A key change to scoping includes the addition of a number of factors to be assessed in section 22 when compared to the elements in section 19 of

CEAA 2012. Among the notable additions to section 22 are the need to consider impacts on Indigenous communities, impacts on Indigenous rights, the need and purpose of the projects, alternative means and some alternatives to the project, the project's contribution to sustainability, the results of regional and strategic assessments, impacts on the intersection of sex and gender with other identify factors, and the impact of the project on environmental obligations including climate change commitments. The scope of these factors is to be determined by the Minister for panel reviews, and the Agency for standard assessments. The public is to be involved in scoping.

The Agency determines whether it has enough information to decide whether to proceed with an assessment. This is one place where the existence and results of a regional or strategic assessment can be considered, suggesting that strategic and regional assessments could lead to fewer project assessments. The decision whether to refer the project to a panel review is a separate decision made by the Minister. The Minister can also decide at this stage that the project will be rejected without an EA. Finally, the Agency can decide that the project can proceed without an EA. The resulting process options at the end of the planning process are essentially the following:

1. No process (with either approval or rejection of the project);
2. Standard EA process (potentially with delegation);
3. Substitution to an Indigenous process or a provincial process;
4. A review panel.

The Standard (Agency) Assessment Process

The standard assessment process has not changed fundamentally from CEAA 2012. The Agency still runs the process, and the basic elements are similar. Of course, as discussed above, the scope has been broadened significantly under section 22. Timelines for the assessment phase are shorter than under CEAA 2012, though this is perhaps compensated by additional time for the planning phase, and a three-year window for the provision of information by the proponent before the start of the assessment process. The general impression left in Bill C-69 is that the Agency will be more front and centre in the assessment, and the proponent will play more of a supportive role of providing information rather than carrying out the assessment, as has been the case to date in the form of proponents' Environmental Impact Statements. Bill C-69 does not use the term "impact statement". It appears from the government IA Handbook that the proponent may still be expected to prepare some version of an impact statement under section 19. The IA Handbook is available in PDF format through the following link: <https://www.canada.ca/content/dam/themes/environment/conservation/environmental-reviews/ia-handbook-e.pdf>.

IAA, beyond the proponent's responsibility to provide information under section 19, and a general responsibility for federal authorities with expertise to assist, does not delineate the allocation of responsibility for the gathering of the information needed, particularly in light of the much broader scope of the assessment. Nor is IAA clear about the impact of information gathering (beyond the preparation of the impact statement) on the time limits for the assessment phase. Much of the scope of a particular assessment may now be outside the expertise of proponents. It remains to be seen who else will have responsibilities for ensuring adequate information is available on issues such as alternatives, impacts on Indigenous communities and rights, and social, economic and health impacts of proposed projects, and how this information will be gathered within the time frames permitted. Much of this information could be gathered in parallel with the proponent's gathering of information under section 19. However, this is not clear from the provisions of IAA, and the need for some of this work may arise out of the review of the information during the course of the assessment.

The Panel Review Process

Similar to the standard assessment, IAA continues the recent trend toward strict timelines to decide whether to proceed with a panel review, and to carry out such a review. Decisions to refer a project to a review panel are to be made within 45 days of the commencement of the assessment. The decision is to be made based on the potential for adverse effects on areas of federal jurisdiction, public concern, opportunities for collaboration with other jurisdictions, and any impact on the rights of Indigenous peoples.

The timeline for completing the panel review process has been shortened from two years to 600 days (and as short as 300 days for projects involving energy regulators). Time taken up by the proponent in responding to information requests after the impact statement is filed will no longer automatically be subtracted from the panel's time (assuming the panel continues to have the opportunity to seek additional information from the proponent), making the total time for panel reviews potentially significantly shorter than under CEAA 2012. The discretion to suspend time rests with the Minister, not the Panel.

As indicated, there is no legislative clarity on what happens if a panel, in carrying out its work after the impact statement is completed, determines that additional information is required either from the proponent, a federal agency, or some other source (though there is discretion to suspend time through regulations). There are opportunities to suspend time, and to extend the timelines, but the Minister's powers in this regard are limited, and the panel itself has no powers to extend time. The Cabinet has broader powers to extend the timelines during the course of a panel review, but this may not be a practical option for a panel faced with delays in getting the information it needs.

Section 56 allows the Minister to seek additional information from the proponent at the conclusion of the panel review process to inform her conclusion on whether the project is in the public interest. It is unclear why the proponent would be asked to feed into the public interest determination at this late stage. Furthermore, any information gathered at this stage in the process would not be available to the independent review panel, and would not be subject to the same level of public scrutiny.

Harmonization

The general approach to harmonization with other jurisdictions is one of cooperation, but with flexibility to harmonize through delegation or substitution at the discretion of the Minister. The key difference between cooperative assessments and delegation or substitution is that, through delegation and substitution, the assessment or parts of it are done by another jurisdiction and the results are then used for federal decision-making. Delegation and substitution are available for standard assessments, not for panel reviews. Under section 33(3), substitution can be approved after the completion of the process to be substituted. Substitution decisions under IAA appear to be made on a project-by-project basis.

Compared to CEAA 2012, there is a notable difference in tone and preference in favour of cooperation under IAA, but the main substantive change is the elimination of equivalency. Otherwise, the shift from delegation to cooperation, while reflected in the purposes, is dependent largely on the exercise of Ministerial discretion. Most notably, there are no clear provisions to support or encourage cooperation over other forms of harmonization. The elimination of equivalency means the federal government now clearly retains decision-making responsibility, but project decisions can in some cases be made based on information gathering and assessment carried out by another jurisdiction. It is important to note that the shift to broader sustainability considerations adds much more value judgment to the assessment process, raising even more serious questions about the appropriateness of federal decision-makers relying on provincial assessment and analysis than under CEAA 2012.

Of course, the Agency's discretion at the planning stage of the process not to require an assessment at all can also be used as a tool to avoid any federal assessment in situations where other jurisdictions are carrying out their own assessment. In such a case, there would not be a federal assessment decision at all, similar to the effect of the equivalency provisions under CEAA 2012.

The two fundamental concerns with a substitution and delegation approach to harmonization are:

1. that it does not ensure a fair and thorough information base and, perhaps even more importantly, an objective, unbiased assessment and analysis of the information gathered to adequately inform federal decisions, and

2. that federal decision-makers will not have adequate appreciation for the underlying value judgements of an assessment, and for the inevitable complexities of sustainability-based decision-making without having the federal government actively involved in the process of analyzing and assessing the information.

The discretion to delegate appears unlimited, whereas the discretion to substitute is subject to certain limitations under section 33(1).

For panel reviews, the approach to harmonization is focused on joint assessments. This includes the continuation of the long tradition of carrying out joint assessments with the provinces, a process that has generally worked well in the past. IAA includes a new variation on the long-standing effort to identify an appropriate role for energy regulators in the assessment process. The focus is on the new Canadian Energy Regulator (the CER, to replace the NEB), as well as the Canada Nuclear Safety Commission (CNSC) and the Nova Scotia and Newfoundland & Labrador offshore petroleum boards, all energy regulators.

Formal joint assessments are not to be carried out with these energy regulators, though they are expected to support the impact assessment process and will be directly involved in it. Most importantly, at least some but not a majority of the panel members are to be appointed from these energy regulators when the project is one that they regulate. The panel, at least in the case of some of the regulators, is authorized to exercise powers of the energy regulator, suggesting that the panel will have a dual regulatory and assessment function, similar to joint CEAA/NEB panels of the past.

Interestingly, all projects on the designated project list that are regulated by one of these energy regulators have to be assessed by way of a review panel (assuming the projects are assessed at all). What is unclear is what effect these provisions will have on which of the regulated projects will be listed on the designated project list. It would be fair to assume that smaller projects that do not warrant a panel review may be taken off the list, or the Agency will be under pressure to exercise its discretion not to require a federal assessment.

IAA includes amendments that would treat the Nova Scotia and Newfoundland & Labrador offshore petroleum boards in a manner similar to the CER and the CNSC. The main difference is that, in cases of panel reviews involving the offshore petroleum boards, the panels are to consist of five panel members, at least two of which are to be appointed from a roster from the offshore boards. The effect appears similar: to carry out a panel review that has a significant but not majority presence from the regulator. The ultimate question is what effect these alterations to the panel review process involving energy regulators will have on the quality and focus of the process and its ability to provide an appropriate impartial basis for the "public interest" determination.

Strategic and Regional Assessments

IAA allows the Minister to initiate regional and strategic assessments. Neither is defined, and neither is required. Regional assessment can either be entirely on federal lands, or outside. If partly or completely outside federal lands, a cooperative approach is clearly preferred under section 93, but a "federal only" regional assessment is identified as an option. The assessments are to be carried out by the Agency or through a committee, with terms of reference to be established (or approved) by the Minister. Similarly, strategic assessments are to be conducted by the Agency or through a committee. The focus of strategic assessments is on federal policies, plans and programs (and their impact on project assessments), and classes of designated projects.

The public is to have an opportunity to participate in the regional or strategic assessment, and to have access to relevant information. No further details are provided in IAA on the process or the outcome of a regional or strategic assessment. The final assessment report is to be filed with the Minister, but there is no provision for decision-making, and no guidance on how the results of a regional or strategic assessment are to be used in future project decisions.

Project Assessment Decision-making

For project assessments, the ultimate decision to be made is whether "a proposed project is in the public interest" in light of the project's effect on areas of federal jurisdiction. This is a departure from CEAA 2012, which broke the decision-making process into two somewhat different steps. Step 1 was the focus of the assessment, and resulted in a determination whether the project was likely to cause significant adverse environmental effects. If so, Step 2 resulted in a determination whether the likely adverse environmental effects were justified in the circumstances. The new decision-making process replaces Step 1 with an identification of effects on areas of federal jurisdiction, and then jumps straight to whether the project is in the public interest in light of the factors set out in section 63. The Minister either makes the decision or makes a recommendation to Cabinet, with Cabinet making the ultimate decision on whether a project is in the public interest in the case of panel reviews.

The end result is a focus on the "public interest" determinations, but along with an articulation of which areas of federal jurisdiction are impacted by the project. To achieve this, impacts on areas of federal jurisdiction initially need to be separated from other, broader impacts and benefits. The broader impacts and benefits are only to be taken into account in deciding whether to accept the effects on federal jurisdiction as being in the public interest in light of the broader effects. This step of identifying effects on areas of federal jurisdiction therefore appears designed not to replace the significance finding under CEAA 2012, but rather to clarify the basis for federal jurisdiction to make a project decision. In short, it seems not intended, as the previous significance test was, as a threshold finding leading to a presumption against approving a project that can only be overcome with a finding of other overriding benefits. Missing is an indication of the scale of the impact on an area of federal jurisdiction that will enable consideration of the public interest and the broader effects of the project.

Section 63 provides a list of factors to be considered in determining whether a project is in the public interest. Many but not all factors are also included in section 22 as factors to be considered in the assessment. Included in section 63 are the following:

- The extent to which the project contributes to sustainability;
- The extent to which effects on areas of federal responsibility are adverse;
- The implementation of mitigation measures (defined to include compensation);
- Impacts on Indigenous communities and Indigenous rights;
- Impacts on Canada's environmental obligations and climate commitments.

The decision-maker, whether it is the Minister or Cabinet, has to give reasons for the decision that demonstrate that the decision is based on the assessment report by the Panel or Agency (which in turn has to consider the factors in section 22). The reasons have to demonstrate that the factors in section 63 were considered in making the public interest determination. There is no clarity on the level of detail to be provided in the reasons, or the underlying analysis for determining, for example, whether a project makes a net contribution to sustainability, or whether it helps with or hinders Canada's climate commitments. There is no legislative opportunity to appeal or otherwise review the decision or its basis, leaving judicial review as the most likely avenue.

The final project decision must be published in the form of a decision statement. The statement can be amended, but not the underlying decision. There is no explicit link to monitoring and follow-up, such as the ability to adjust terms and conditions if mitigation measures turn out to be ineffective, or predictions made during the course of the assessment turn out to be wrong (thought that may very well be the intention). The decision (assuming approval) has to include a time period within which the proponent has to commence with the project, after which the approval expires.

Notes and Questions

1. The following table seeks to highlight some of the key differences between the three legislative versions of the federal assessment process. What do you think the key strengths and weaknesses of each are?

Issue	CEAA 1995	CEAA 2012	IAA
Number of Projects	1000s per year	Less than 100 per year	Unclear, depends on project list regulation
Triggering Process	Legislated through definition of project and exclusion regulations; all in unless excluded	Starting point is a project list, but final decision on whether an EA is required is ultimately discretionary, through review of registration, substitution and equivalency	Similar to CEAA 2012
Federal Decision-makers Involved	In principle all federal authorities with decision-making responsibility for a project were involved in the EA process	Federal authorities involved generally limited to NEB, CNSC, and CEA Agency	The role of the NEB and CNSC has been somewhat reduced, while the role of the offshore petroleum boards has been increased.
Scope of Project	Generally had to include everything a proponent proposed; see the SCC *Red Chris* decision	Discretionary, but generally limited to components of project subject to federal legislative control	The scope of project is unclear

Issue	CEAA 1995	CEAA 2012	IAA
Scope of EA	Broad on biophysical and Aboriginal impacts, limited on socio-economic impacts	Narrowly focused on selected areas of federal legislative control, limited biophysical, broad Aboriginal and general socio-economic impacts	The scope of the federal assessment process has been significantly broadened to include the full range of impacts and benefits of proposed projects. One exception to this broader scope are projects on federal land and outside Canada.
Process Options	Four process options: screenings, comprehensive studies, panel reviews and mediation	Two process options: standard EA or panel review	Similar to CEAA 2012
Public Participation	Discretionary for screenings, mandatory for other process options	Discretionary for standard EA, mandatory for panel review	Similar to CEAA 2012, though stronger language and more open
Harmonization with Provincial EA	General approach was one that encouraged cooperation and joint EAs, rather than one or the other	General approach is to only do a federal EA when there is no provincial EA that is looking into impacts on key areas of federal legislative control	Preference for cooperative harmonization, but largely discretionary, with all options on the table
Final Decision	Combination of legal test of "likely significant adverse environmental effect" and discretion inherent in "justified in the circumstances". Reasonably transparent, as recommendations and reasons for not following them had to be made public.	Discretionary, not transparent	Final decision remains discretionary, but some level of accountability through the need to base decision on assessment report, consider factors in section 63, and give reasons for decision.

2. Which of the three versions of the federal assessment process comes closest to meeting the three goals of being efficient, effective and fair?

3. If you had the opportunity to design the ideal federal assessment process, which elements would you take from each of the three versions?

Part V — Next Generation EA

Robert B. Gibson, Meinhard Doelle & John Sinclair,
"Fulfilling the Promise: Basic Components of Next Generation
Environmental Assessment"
(2016) 29 J. Envtl. L. & Prac. 257

Introduction

Canada has been practicing environmental assessment for over 40 years. You might think we would be good at it by now. But we are not. The history of Canadian environmental assessment has been a race between accomplishment and disappointment. Today, assessment deliberations are characterized by tensions between needs for improvement and pressures for faster, easier and cheaper approvals.

Probably that was predictable. From the outset, environmental assessment laws demanded change and stirred resistance. They required proponents of major undertakings to incorporate environmental factors (variously defined) alongside financial, technical and political considerations in their planning because many proponents were not motivated to do so voluntarily. Moreover, given Canadian constitutional arrangements, the laws needed to be designed and applied cooperatively by the many Canadian jurisdictions (federal, provincial, territorial and Aboriginal) with environmental responsibilities — evidently also something for which existing motivations would prove to be insufficient.

Canada's first generation environmental assessment regimes have made important contributions. They have won greater attention to environmental considerations. They have opened some significant decision making to public scrutiny. In their brightest moments, they have been instrumental in forcing re-examination of prevailing priorities and practices. But environmental assessment laws and practices in Canada have not achieved the initially desired transformation in proponent and associated decision-maker culture to integrate habitual attention to environmental concerns. And they have not yet moved effectively to take on new understandings and imperatives — especially growing recognition of complex interactions in socio-ecological systems and increasingly pressing needs to ensure progress towards sustainability.

Centred on applications for project approvals and focused on mitigation of adverse effects, Canadian assessment processes have usually aimed for less bad projects rather than best service to the public interest. Focused on the effects of individual projects, they have been poorly equipped to deal with cumulative and strategic effects and broad alternatives. No two Canadian assessment regimes are the same and none represents a consistently high standard. And with modest exceptions, assessment has not evolved well to address changing global and domestic conditions. Mostly, environmental assessment in Canada has struggled to be much more than a slightly earlier, more open and better integrated process for environmental licensing of conventional projects, and even then it has been criticized for slowing approvals.

Next generation environmental assessment will have to aim higher. Five main transitions are involved:

(i) In contrast to the prevailing focus on mitigating significant adverse effects, next generation environmental assessment would expect proposals to represent the best option for delivery of lasting wellbeing, preferably through multiple, mutually reinforcing and fairly distributed benefits, while also avoiding adverse effects.

(ii) In contrast to the common notion that economic, ecological and social objectives are inherently in conflict, can be addressed separately and will be accommodated through trade-offs that are "acceptable in the circumstances," next generation environmental assessment would recognize that sustainability-enhancing economic, ecological and social objectives are interdependent. While some trade-offs will be unavoidable, they will acceptable only in the last resort and under clearly delineated rules.

(iii) In contrast to the assumption that effectiveness, efficiency and fairness are competing objectives, next generation environmental assessment would see that they too are logically and practically interdependent. Efficiencies would be sought by emphasizing assessment requirements where they can be most effective, especially through assessment in the development of policies, programmes and plans that are best suited to addressing cumulative effects and broad alternatives and to providing efficient guidance for projects and other more specific initiatives, and by fostering upward harmonization of the disparate assessment regimes (and associated regulatory permitting and post-approval monitoring) across Canada to compatible versions of a high next generation standard.

(iv) In contrast to environmental assessment being one, unusually open contribution to the broader set of largely inaccessible decision-making processes affecting individual projects, next generation environmental assessment would be the main public vehicle for deliberations and decisions on significant undertakings. It would adopt comprehensive sustainability-based purposes and their elaboration in criteria and it would apply to strategic level policies, plans and programmes as well as projects. In effect, environmental assessment would evolve into a tiered and integrated sustainability governance process.

(v) In contrast to treating assessment as hoops for proponents to jump through to gain project approval, next generation environmental assessment would be centred on learning, building a culture of sustainability and serving the long as well as short term public interest.

The following sections sketch out an initial framework of interrelated next generation components for environmental assessment regimes in Canada at the federal, provincial and territorial levels. The substance may be largely relevant to federal jurisdictions beyond Canada and to Canadian assessment regimes established through Aboriginal land claim agreements. There is no assumption here that a next generation regime would rely entirely on environmental assessment law. Useful roles are, for example, likely for strategic processes in regional planning, sectoral policy and regulation, and municipal decision making. Insofar as Canadian jurisdictions may be persuaded to adopt the basic assessment regime components presented here (with adjustments for their own circumstances), the results should deliver beneficial upward harmonization of environmental assessment in Canada.

Components of a Framework for Next Generation Environmental Assessment

The basic components proposed for next generation environmental assessment are outlined below in categories that reflect the conventional steps of environmental assessment deliberations from purposes and application rules to follow-up monitoring and enforcement, plus design considerations that affect the whole process.

1. The Purpose of Environmental Assessment

The core purpose of next generation environmental assessment is to ensure that deliberations and decision making on new and renewed undertakings at the project and strategic (policies, plans and programmes) levels foster proposal development, approvals and implementation that deliver the strongest feasible positive contributions to lasting wellbeing while avoiding significant adverse effects. More generally, the objective is to protect and enhance the resilience of desirable biophysical, socio-ecological and human systems and to foster and facilitate creative innovation and just transitions to more sustainable practices.

Serving this core purpose would entail adoption of corollary purposes concerning process and substantive requirements. Because transition to sustainable structures, cultures and behaviour is a long-term venture, next generation assessment must aim to establish deliberative decision-making processes that foster mutual learning among all interested participants to build understanding and capacities for effective engagement in governance for lasting wellbeing. To do that, it would need to facilitate collaboration with other authorities and meaningful public engagement from the conception through to the end of potential effects from undertakings that may have significant implications for progress towards sustainability.

For very practical purposes, assessment regimes would need to be structured to strengthen consistency and efficiency in decision making — from policy making, planning and programme design to post-approval project implementation and monitoring — through process linking and application of a common set of fundamental requirements. They would also need to favour flexibility and decentralization by respecting uncertainty and context, work iteratively with relevant stakeholders, and emphasize capacity to adapt to different ecosystems and communities, new understandings, and emerging challenges and opportunities.

Entrenchment of these purposes in next generation assessment law would begin with an explicit overall legislated objective tied to seeking progress towards sustainability. But the purposes would also need to be incorporated in the substance of all legislated provisions. Crucial components would include requirements for

- development and application of broad but comprehensive sustainability-based criteria for evaluations and decisions (see next section);
- emphasis on comprehensive and integrated attention to all factors affecting the long term as well as immediate desirability and durability of effects;
- comparative evaluation of potentially reasonable alternatives to identify best options for each undertaking, to move cumulatively to more sustainable practice; and
- application of case-specified sustainability-based purposes and criteria as the main structure for deliberations and decisions at all process stages for subject undertakings from initial identification of appropriate purposes and options (alternatives) to final deliberations on renewal, closure, decommissioning and continued management.

2. Sustainability-based Criteria for Evaluations and Decision Making

In next generation environmental assessment, explicit sustainability-based criteria play several crucial roles. They provide a comprehensive, credible and explicit base for choices and decisions throughout the assessment process, enhancing the transparency and accountability of the deliberations. In the public interest, they ensure a focus on achieving maximum gains for sustainability by aiming for the selection of the best option, rather than attempting to judge the "acceptability" of proposed undertakings. They encourage enhancement of multiple, mutually reinforcing, fairly distributed and lasting benefits in addition to avoidance or mitigation of significant negative effects. And they motivate innovation in creating options that eliminate or minimize invidious trade-offs.

The legislation would need to establish the generic criteria for assessment decision making and provide for specification of these criteria for application to particular cases and contexts. The generic criteria would cover all core requirements for progress towards sustainability and their interactions. Specifying the criteria for individual applications would be through informed choices by authorities and stakeholders, without compromising any of the generic requirements. In particular cases, the criteria could evolve as new considerations and understandings arise, but they would provide the essential framework for evaluations and decisions through all stages of the assessment process.

In addition, next generation assessment law should establish explicit rules for evaluating trade-offs, and provide for case and context-specific elaboration of them. Trade-off rules would provide guidance on expectations for net sustainability gains, avoidance of significant adverse effects, allocation of the burden of argument, protection of unrepresented future generations, explicit justification, and open process.

This emphasis on specified criteria and trade-off rules is meant to ensure attention to all key considerations for lasting wellbeing, including openings for multiple, mutually reinforcing benefits. But it also facilitates more open discussion of the otherwise often hidden, obscure and/or confused grounds for important decisions. Because such criteria will have significant influence, their adoption and case specification may become a focus for controversy and conflict. Such tensions are common in assessment processes now and are inevitable in any process of transition. Centring the tensions on explicit grounds for decision making seems to be a sensible option. Moreover, the difficulties should be accompanied and slowly mitigated by incremental learning and gradual enhancement of capacities for discursive problem solving. Nevertheless, the potential for discord adds to reasons for insistence on fair process.

Key additional needs associated with sustainability-based criteria include requirements for

- defining the public interest purpose of each assessed undertaking;
- identifying and comparing alternatives with selection of the most desirable option in light of the criteria;
- providing reasons based on application of the criteria for all assessment decisions;
- explicit identification and justification of trade-offs in light of explicit trade-off criteria; and
- precautionary recognition of uncertainties, with preference for low risk options and adaptive design as well as implementation.

3. Application Rules

A fundamental aim of the assessment regime is to ensure sustainability-based assessments are carried out for all proposed undertakings — including policies, programmes and plans as well as capital projects and physical activities — that might have significant effects on prospects for sustainability in and beyond the legislating jurisdiction. This includes undertakings that have potential for significant adverse effects, on their own and cumulatively. It also includes proposed undertakings that could foreclose other initiatives that would make a more positive contribution, and undertakings that warrant careful consideration of the manner in which the undertaking should be carried out to maximize benefits and minimize harm.

Meeting this aim requires, as much as possible, the anticipation and pre-identification of categories or characteristics of undertakings that are, or are likely to be, subject to assessment requirements. This will allow proponents and other potential participants to begin deliberations knowing their obligations and incorporating them from the outset.

Application decisions, which determine what undertakings are subject to formal assessment requirements and the particular streams of assessment required, will be critical for the success of a next generation regime. To be predictable and accountable, all application decisions will need to be guided by the legislated purposes, principles and criteria, and to be fully transparent. Decisions need to be justified in written reasons demonstrating consistency with the general purposes of the process and the specific principles, rules and criteria developed for application decisions, in combination with an opportunity to challenge decisions that are not. At the same time, flexibility is needed to recognize unanticipated cases and exceptional situations.

The general scope of application should respect three core considerations. First, the process should apply to undertakings at the project and strategic levels with appropriate streams for different categories of undertakings. Second, it should apply to new undertakings as well as continuing undertakings that merit periodic review, or that are to be revised, renewed or replaced. And third, it should apply to undertakings that are not in active development but have been identified as desirable, such as a new strategic initiative to address a pressing or anticipated issue raised in a project level assessment.

Specific rules of application should be designed to ensure the following:

- automatic application to undertakings in pre-identified categories set out in regulations made under the law to ensure early recognition of assessment obligations on the part of proponents and other interests;

- effective mechanisms to ensure early application to other undertakings with potentially significant effects, with clear rules, principles and criteria to maximize clarity and accountability;

- application to significant policies, programmes and plans that require ministerial approval, again with clear rules, principles and criteria to maximize clarity and accountability;

- application to new strategic level initiatives where the need for strategic level clarification has been identified in the course of a project level assessment;

- application in other cases where the government chooses to require an assessment in response to public concern, through a transparent and accountable petition process set out in legislation, or on its own initiative in recognition of issues of significance for sustainability; and

- ability to make adjustments to application requirements in accordance with clearly established rules, principles and criteria and in a transparent and accountable manner.

4. Assessment Streams

To be effective, efficient, and fair, assessment processes must be suitable for the size and nature of the undertaking, the potential magnitude of adverse effects and benefits, and the level of public interest and concern. To this end, each type of undertaking should be clearly allocated to an appropriate assessment stream. The assessment process therefore needs to provide a range of specified streams. The number and particular characteristics of these streams might vary considerably among jurisdictions, but would include at least

- a demanding stream with detailed substantive evaluation and rigorous public and institutional review for the most significant undertakings with the greatest implications for ensuring and enhancing contributions to sustainability; and

- a more expeditious assessment stream for less significant undertakings.

While particular requirements for the scope of the assessment and the extent of public engagement will vary from stream to stream, all streams must meet a minimum standard of assessment. Each stream needs to apply the full set of sustainability criteria and trade-off rules, and include timely public notice and opportunities for public comment. Each stream must also meet the minimum scope requirements set out below, except where a narrower scope is established in the conclusions of a higher tier assessment. Each stream will have to include a mechanism for shifting exceptional cases to a more appropriate stream with clear rules, transparency and accountability for streaming decisions.

5. Linked Tiers

Tiers in assessment processes recognize that the design, approval and implementation of most undertakings that have important socio-economic and ecological implications are influenced by decisions at different levels, ranging from broad policy making to regulatory licensing, and that much can be gained by linking the decision making at all of these levels.

The main tiering idea links the project and strategic levels and has two parts — to use law-based strategic assessments for policies, plans and programmes to address big issues and opportunities, broad alternatives and cumulative effects that cannot be covered as effectively and efficiently at the project level, and to use the strategic level findings as authoritative guidance for project planning and assessment. Examples of strategic undertakings that would likely produce useful guidance for subsequent project planning and assessment include planning initiatives that explore desirable and feasible futures for a region, and policy development efforts that examine the characteristics and potential cumulative effects of alternative ways of meeting a societal need.

Policies, plans and programmes that have been subjected to or are based on sustainability-based next generation assessments may guide specific scoping, stream selection and other process decisions for assessments at the project level. They may help to focus the lower level assessment on a more limited range of alternatives than would be required in the absence of the broader level assessment. Findings at the strategic level about potential cumulative effects and their implications, and about appropriate means of avoiding adverse cumulative effects and enhancing positive ones, should also make project level assessments more efficient, effective and fair. In turn, project level assessments may often identify strategic assessment needs, opportunities, issues and options.

To facilitate such tiering, next generation assessment law would need to ensure application of assessment requirements to strategic level undertakings (see the discussion of application rules, above), provide for authoritative guidance from the strategic to project level and clarify the extent of, and limits to, this authority (e.g. through sunset provisions and renewal requirements). Legislative provisions would also establish equivalency rules for other sustainability-based and participative processes that develop and assess policies, plans or programmes that could provide legitimately authoritative guidance for projects planning and assessment.

For tiering links from the project to strategic level, next generation law should establish a mechanism for project level assessment processes to identify needs for strategic level consideration and response. Normally, resulting strategic level assessments would be carried out concurrently with the continuing project assessment, but some cases may require suspension of the project assessment to ensure the strategic assessment findings can be integrated fully into the project assessment. The law could provide for earlier consideration of requests for amendments to existing policies, plans or programmes in light of problems or opportunities at the project level, but only through open processes applying specified, sustainability-based criteria. Parties seeking an amendment would have to justify it on the grounds of exceptional circumstances or recent changes in important factors.

Tiering links that identify, clarify and coordinate the relationship between project assessments and regulatory licensing have similarly great potential. Next generation assessment legislative provisions as well as administrative changes will be needed for example to clarify the level of detail required at each level, enhance the compatibility of requirements (e.g. documentation expectations and effects prediction methodologies), establish procedures for reconsideration of assessment findings in light of new information at the regulatory licensing level, and integrate assessment monitoring and follow-up into the regulatory process.

6. Scope of Assessment Requirements

The overriding driver of scope determinations should be to allow environmental assessments to serve the sustainability-based purposes set out above. That entails ensuring the scope of all assessments covers the full suite of considerations that affect the potential for progress towards sustainability and facilitates identification of options, designs and implementation practices that deliver the best, most feasible undertakings in the long-term public interest. Efficiencies are gained by addressing appropriate issues at higher assessment tiers and using the results to shape project level decisions, not by artificially or arbitrarily limiting the scope of any assessment.

The assessment process should provide for a core legislated scope for all assessments (project and strategic levels) requiring attention to

- the purposes of and need for the undertaking (with both purposes and need related to the lasting public interest);
- potential reasonable alternatives;
- the full set of sustainability-related considerations and effects — biophysical and socio-economic (and their interactions), positive and negative, indirect and direct, interactive/cumulative and individual, lasting and immediate;
- the full life of options (alternatives to and alternative means of pursuing the preferred alternative), including the upstream and downstream life cycle plus legacy effects;
- cumulative effects;
- enhancement of positive effects as well as mitigation/avoidance of adverse effects;
- uncertainties and means of accommodating surprise; and
- monitoring of effects and compliance, and response to the findings.

The process should ensure application of the core scope to all levels and streams of assessment and to requirements for equivalency in tiering links with undertakings prepared and assessed under other processes and regimes. It should clearly set out the more specific scope requirements for different applications, including assessments at different levels and in different streams, as well as ways to adjust and finalize the scope for individual assessments.

7. Effects Assessment

Next generation assessment regimes need to be carefully designed to ensure reliable effects assessment. The prediction and evaluation of effects is a central process component. It is crucial to understanding the prospects for positive and adverse sustainability effects, illuminating the comparison of alternatives, identifying best means of enhancing positive effects and avoiding or minimizing adverse effects, and evaluating potential trade-offs. It also provides the basis for decision making concerning approvals or rejections, conditions of approval, and monitoring requirements.

To minimize process uncertainties and delays, effects assessment requirements should be pre-defined to the extent possible, so that all participants in the assessment process know the expectations and their obligations and openings to contribute. The key general requirement is that all effects assessment is to be guided by application of the sustainability criteria specified for the case, and must recognize and document uncertainties (in study design as well as in effects prediction). Consequently, the requirements for effects assessment must be tied directly to application of the legislated purposes, the more specific decision making rules and the sustainability-based criteria. In addition to requirements discussed elsewhere, the mandatory obligations in law should include application of the sustainability criteria in all steps of effects assessment, including selecting alternatives to be compared; identifying most valued ecological, social and socio-ecological systems, characteristics and services to be examined most closely; choosing methodologies and setting priorities for effects predictions and monitoring; and evaluating the significance of individual and cumulative effects and uncertainties (at the prediction and monitoring stages).

The assessment process should provide for early and open engagement of authorities, including Aboriginal governments, and stakeholders in criteria specification and application in the effects assessment steps above. Such engagement is also needed in discussions to clarify effects assessment scope and priorities (including identification of valued components), to review proposed methods, and to develop other case-specific guidance for design and implementation of effects studies and assessments. A final key topic for early and open engagement is the selection of consultants, which needs to be done in a way that will reduce conflicts associated with consultant dependency on and ties to proponent interest.

Beyond individual cases, it will be important to offer advanced general guidance materials on key aspects of sustainability-based effects assessment, including attention to positive sustainability effects and their enhancement, long term and legacy effects, and interactive and cumulative effects. General guidance should be complemented with more specific sectoral, regional and other guidance for assessment work relevant to categories of anticipated undertakings. In some cases, strategic level assessments will serve to develop such guidance.

Finally, effects assessment requirements need to ensure an emphasis on cumulative effects, and fully utilize the critical role of strategic level assessments for effective and efficient attention to cumulative effects predictions, implications and response options.

8. Participation

Participatory processes in next generation assessment regimes need to incorporate the insights of deliberative democracy, collaborative rationality and environmental justice. By participation we mean encouraging and facilitating the active involvement of members of the public, stakeholders, relevant authorities and proponents in environmental assessment with the aim to enhance the quality and credibility of assessment decision making and to ensure associated learning and capacity building benefits are captured. To ensure the basic legitimacy of next generation assessment, participatory processes also need to be meaningful by incorporating the basic components of participation into environmental assessment.

The basic components of meaningful participation have been well documented in the literature. They include provisions to ensure adequate public notice, timely and convenient access to information, participant assistance, opportunities for public comment, public hearings, deliberative forums and early and ongoing participation throughout the process stages, including

- early deliberations on purposes/needs and alternatives, criteria specification, main consultant selection, and determination of effects assessment priorities and design of effects studies;
- review of initial effects findings and conclusions concerning the relative merits of alternatives;
- formal review of submitted proposals for approval, including environmental impact statements (or the equivalent in sustainability-based assessments), as appropriate draft review recommendations and decisions by the responsible authorities; and
- design of and participation in monitoring programmes and review of findings and response plans.

While each of these basic components enjoys some recognition in assessment practice in Canada, special and renewed attention needs to be given to providing the capacity and funding necessary to enable representation of important interests and considerations not otherwise effectively included (for example, disadvantaged populations, future generations, broader socio-ecological relations). This will be a significant step given that only two jurisdictions in Canada currently offer some level of support to participants. Provisions for public hearings on cases of particular public interest and significance for sustainability will also have to include explicit detailed criteria for determining when public hearings are necessary and the establishment of an arm's-length body for advising on contested cases.

Initiating deliberative forums as an integral component of participation also requires new attention. Proponents, who most often lead participatory activities, frequently use open houses (and similar consultation methods), while government officials occasionally convene hearings, with the result that dialogic participation techniques are rarely used in Canadian assessment processes. As Sinclair and

Diduck have noted, effective techniques for assessment participation use vehicles such as multi-stakeholder advisory committees and task forces, mediation and non-adversarial negotiation, and community boards to facilitate ongoing dialogue and communication among project proponents, environmental assessment officials, and civic organizations, and serve important mutual learning, relationship building, and conflict resolution functions. Such approaches also anticipate the re-engagement of public officials and experts as well as stakeholders and members of the public in the participatory process.

Beyond specific provisions for involvement, next generation assessment also requires the establishment of a multi-stakeholder advisory body for open deliberations on issues and options for regulatory attention and other key matters of process implementation.

Also needed are mandatory requirements for regular and open public reviews of assessment regime performance, including consideration of potential improvements to participatory processes.

9. Review and Decision-making Processes

Thorough review of environment assessment documentation through credible and transparent decision-making processes is another essential component of next generation assessment. A basic aim in this regard is to ensure consistent efforts to serve the objectives of assessment to advance prospects for lasting wellbeing in all key decision making — not only about proponent assessments, but also about proposed assessment policies, guidance and other matters concerning regime implementation. Next generation assessment must also enhance the quality and credibility of assessment decision making, including by guarding against bias in public proceedings where the more narrowly motivated proponent leads proposal development and assessment.

As outlined above, more credible decision making will require mandatory development and application of explicit sustainability-based criteria, specified for the context of the case at hand. Evaluations of effects predictions, comparison of options and other key assessment review matters need to be based on the application of the explicit sustainability-based criteria developed. The review process also must be transparent and open to effective government, stakeholder and public engagement from the beginning of the deliberations. Regulation must allow the extent, nature and formality of requirements scaled to the significance of opportunities to avoid adverse effects and/or enhance positive ones, the level or potential for public concern and the potential for conflict or consensus.

Ensuring rigorous and open reviews will require multiple review process options that recognize differences among assessment streams, between strategic and project level undertakings, between single and multi-jurisdictional cases, and between cases promising conflict or consensus. Potentially desirable options include

- semi-formal public discussions with impartial facilitation where feasible and reasonable;
- reviews led by a credible government review body receiving open comments, and issuing draft findings, conclusions and recommendations for public review before finalization;

- informal hearings by an independent panel with members appointed in light of explicit selection criteria;
- opportunities for negotiation, arbitration or mediation (perhaps only on certain elements of a review);
- formal hearings, including consolidated hearings of two or more agencies and/or jurisdictions; and
- reviews with public deliberations led by independent experts with public review experience, such as those by the Royal Society and OEER Association.

10. Decisions

While the decision to approve a proposed undertaking attracts most attention, influential decisions are made at all stages of assessment processes. Many key decisions are made by or for the private or public sector proponents of undertakings subject to assessment requirements. Much of assessment law is aimed at guiding these proponent decisions, both directly by setting out assessment requirements and indirectly by establishing review, approval and other tests to ensure the requirements are met. Next generation environmental assessment must aim to ensure that all of these decisions are credible and sustainability-enhancing.

To be aligned with the purposes of next generation assessment, all decisions should aim to expand understanding and illuminate application of the "contribution to sustainability" test to the proposal and alternatives at hand. Approval decisions, in particular, play the gatekeeping role of ensuring that the earlier studies, deliberations and choices have delivered a proposed undertaking that represents the best option in the public interest, will deliver multiple mutually reinforcing gains and avoid significant adverse effects. Each approval decision must be supported by persuasive evidence reflecting application of the context-specified sustainability criteria. The main uncertainties must be identified. And where trade-offs are unavoidable, approval decisions must be accompanied by reasons based on the sustainability criteria and following explicit trade-off rules.

Next generation assessment law will also need provisions to ensure that decisions and conditions of approval (which may include meeting commitments made by the proponent in the proceedings) are practically enforceable. This will entail specification of enforcement and penalty powers; expectations for clear delineation of commitments and conditions of approval; and explicit allocation and provision of resources for, compliance monitoring and enforcement responsibilities.

Throughout all assessment decision making, the preference is for participative and, to the extent possible, consensus-based approaches, subject to adherence to the sustainability-based criteria. Over time, key next generation features, including insistence on public interest purposes and results, should increase prospects for consensus in assessment processes. Significant conflicts in aims and interests are, however, likely to characterize many future assessment cases. While integration of conflict management capacities in assessment deliberations may mitigate some tensions, assessment processes must continue to emphasize provisions not only for effective engagement (see "participation," above) but also for fair adjudication.

Consequently, decision-making responsibility and authority must be vested in credible and accountable hands. Credibility is most likely for impartial decision makers who have been closely engaged in the deliberations and evidence and accountability is most likely for elected officials. In these circumstances, the best option is likely to be reliant on approval decision making initially by the impartial government authority (in government but at arms length from particular departmental mandates or partisan pressures) that considered the evidence, with ultimate ministerial/Cabinet(s) authority within a specified period following the initial ruling to reverse, revise, or require reconsideration or new review. These arrangements would need to be accompanied by provisions for quasi-judicial appeals of the initial decision and judicial review of the ultimate political decision. The appeal should be based on a standard of correctness, whereas the judicial review could be based on reasonableness. Both avenues would consider whether the decision was adequately justified, based on and consistent with the sustainability-based criteria, and whether the decision-making process was fair.

11. Monitoring of Effects and Compliance, and Response to Findings

Sound environmental assessment requires follow-up, yet it is most often done poorly, when it is done at all. Follow-up properly includes monitoring, response to monitoring findings in environmental management, communication, and learning. Monitoring programmes must aim to identify unanticipated positive and adverse effects, as well as other unpredicted pressures, opportunities and changes that may require interventions to correct or pursue. Monitoring also needs to provide an information base for ensuring that the terms and conditions of approvals are met, and commitments are fulfilled. Throughout implementation and after completion of an undertaking, those responsible for environmental management must be able to act adaptively to address problems and new opportunities identified by monitoring work. There must also be communication with regulators and the interested public and commitment to learn from the experience to enable better predictions, more reliable assessments, and better decision making in the future.

Achieving these aims will depend on provisions for mandatory effects and compliance monitoring, scaled to the potential significance of the effects and contraventions, integrated into the regulatory framework of next generation assessment processes. The regulatory framework should also include powers to set requirements for

- specific commitments and conditions of approval (in part to facilitate effective monitoring of effects and compliance);
- anticipatory arrangements, and assignments of responsibility including for funding and public reporting, for monitoring of effects and compliance and for timely response to emerging problems and opportunities; and
- public reporting of effects monitoring findings, with particular efforts to foster application of insights from monitoring in future assessments.

Regime design should anticipate monitoring and response needs by recognizing adaptive capacity as a criterion for design of approvable undertakings and implementation plans, acknowledging that effective adaptive management depends on adaptive capacity including adaptable design. Best practice in effects monitoring implementation will entail emphasis on the engagement of local residents, who are often most motivated to undertake effective monitoring, best placed to do so regularly and efficiently and most likely to gain from the learning opportunity. Best practice expectations also affect monitoring priorities. In particular, they suggest a focus on debatable predictions, untried mitigation and enhancement measures, as well as potential effects on vulnerable people, communities, species, and ecological relationships. And they encourage particular efforts in early identification of emerging problems and opportunities and response options. These monitoring and response obligations need to be treated as costs of the undertaking and not paid for from the public purse.

Compliance monitoring needs should also be anticipated in regime design. Effective compliance monitoring and response depends on ensuring that approval conditions and commitments are clear and specific enough to be monitored and that repercussions of non-compliance are well known. Rather than treating compliance monitoring findings as confidential business information, transparent public reporting should be emphasized. The findings could reward responsible proponents, shame non-compliers and contribute to monitoring of overall progress towards sustainability.

12. Learning

At least since 1995, participation in environmental assessment has been recognized as a means to broad-based individual and social learning that could enable the transition to sustainability. Relying on assessment case evidence, Sinclair et al. developed a conceptual framework related to learning about and through environmental assessment. The framework establishes the potential for individual and collective capacity building and other learning, including about how to maintain and strengthen prospects for lasting ecological, social and economic wellbeing. In this regard, next generation assessment must build understandings, capacities and motivations in all sectors and among all players. Assessment would be a useful venue for increased research and practice aimed at shedding light on the factors and implications of learning-oriented approaches to participation.

To capture the potential for learning, next generation assessment will need to establish contributions to mutual learning as a responsibility for all assessment participants. Relevant responsibilities include providing opportunities for and facilitation of deliberative multi-stakeholder collaboration using the full range of methods in the participation toolbox — including more deliberative forums that include scenario building and visioning, increased attention to alternative dispute resolution and increased advocacy for sustainability assessment by public interest interveners. Where possible, contributions to mutual learning should occur in overall regime deliberations (for example, concerning regulation and policy development and revision) as well as in individual cases (for example, in specifying terms of reference, elaboration of sustainability-based evaluation and decision criteria for particular applications, and design and application of assessment methodologies, including in post-approval monitoring).

Especially important are strong linkages between improving the provisions, opportunities and support for public participation in next generation assessment development, review and monitoring, as outlined above, and the increased potential for mutual learning outcomes this will avail. Mandatory monitoring and public reporting of effects in comparison with effects predictions, and of the effectiveness of responses to emerging problems and opportunities, will be essential to encouraging learning outcomes that are lasting and applicable beyond a single case. In this regard, an important facilitating step will be the establishment of an easily accessed, well-organized and searchable electronic library (or linked set of libraries) of environmental assessment case materials, including documentation of impact predictions and monitoring findings, records of decisions and justifications, and associated cases in law. If made available to all, such a resource could be used by all parties in the assessment community to improve future project and strategic level assessments and decisions over time and to identify needs and opening for improvements to assessment law, regulation and policy. Regularly updating and upgrading guidance material and reviews of individual regime performance and progress towards upward harmonization within and across jurisdictions will also be required. [...]

16. Effectiveness, Efficiency and Fairness Considerations

The perceived trade-off between effectiveness and efficiency, at the expense of fairness, has dominated the implementation of environmental assessment since its inception. In next generation sustainability-centred assessment applications, effectiveness, efficiency and fairness are recognized to be interdependent and not candidates for trading off one for the other. In this context, effectiveness is centred on success in serving the purposes of sustainability-based environmental assessment (see above), while efficiency is the achievement of maximum benefit from the use of resources to deliver effectiveness. Fairness includes substantive fairness (enhancement of equity in the distribution of the positive and adverse effects of decisions, within and among generations) and process fairness (fairness in effective opportunity for able and influential engagement in deliberations and impartiality in decision making).

Within a sustainability-based assessment regime, effectiveness, efficiency and fairness in the delivery of positive contributions to sustainability are most likely to be enhanced by: clear generic rules, maintained beyond discretionary avoidance or compromise; early application; consistent guidance (e.g. from the strategic level to project planning); flexibility to recognize key contextual factors; and, by placing assessment at the centre of decision making on assessed undertakings. Within a jurisdiction, application of these enhancements will most likely be improved further with a strong commitment to progress towards sustainability, that includes collaboration and linking of associated policy, planning/assessment regulatory licensing and monitoring processes. This will require agencies within a jurisdiction to have shared sustainability-based purposes, shared information and expertise, equivalency of scope in policy, planning and assessment, equivalency of opportunity for effective public engagement, provisions for tiered guidance (for example, through law and policy to guide broad planning, in turn to guide project planning) and a focus on the collaborative implementation of associated policy, planning and regulatory licensing processes.

Across jurisdictions (federal/provincial/territorial/Aboriginal), effectiveness, efficiency and fairness in the delivery of positive contributions to sustainability are most likely to be enhanced by upward harmonization of assessment law and process to ensure equivalency in the key process components (purposes, scope, participative opportunities, etc.) as a foundation for linking associated policy, planning/assessment regulatory licensing and monitoring processes, and by sharing information and expertise. Such action should be guided by general law and process harmonization principles that include

- acceptance of process diversity within equivalency of fundamental process components;
- emphasis on broad engagement, sharing of expertise and learning (especially as governments reduce their in-house expertise in key areas of environmental assessment issues and applications); and,
- recognition that the greatest efficiency gains may require broader system changes that strengthen or expand motivations to incorporate attention to sustainability-related considerations (through carbon taxes, transparency in corporate reporting, requirements for free, prior and informed consent from affected communities, etc.).

Environmental assessment has always been about changing entrenched practices and next generation environmental assessment pushes this further. The transition to decision making that seeks positive contributions to sustainability, rather than only mitigation of significant adverse effects, is meant to bring lasting benefits and substantive fairness in relation to the distribution of the positive and adverse effects of decisions. Inevitably, however, this will cause disruptions and, despite best efforts, will involve trade-offs. In all change, risks are greatest for the sociologically and ecologically vulnerable. Next generation assessment must ensure consistent and committed attention to reduction of risks to the most vulnerable and fair distribution of the benefits. The likelihood of achieving this transition will be enhanced with provisions that at least ensure procedural fairness.

Notes and Questions

1. Based on what you have learned so far, you are now in a position to consider how IAA measures up. Where do you think IAA falls short of these standards? Can you think of reasons why it falls short? Do you think IAA comes closer to the standard set in the article than CEAA 1995 or CEAA 2012? Explain. The following questions explore a number of key areas more directly.

2. How do the purposes of IAA compare to those proposed in the article? Do the differences suggest a different overall approach to the assessment process?

3. Under IAA, assessments are to be carried out for projects listed in the designated project list regulation. The requirement for regional and strategic assessments is left to the discretion of the Minister. How does this approach

to the application of the assessment processes under IAA compare to the application rules explored in section 3 of the article?

4. How does the approach to sustainability in IAA (including the factors in sections 22 and 63) compare to the approach explored in section 2 of the article, including the need for legislative generic sustainability criteria, the requirement to develop project-specific criteria based on these generic criteria, and the need for strict trade-off rules to encourage integrated solutions over trade-offs between economic benefits and environmental harm?

5. Are the two assessment streams in IAA adequate in light of the points made in section 4 of the article? Do the two streams (standard assessment by the Agency and independent panel reviews) strike an appropriate balance between mandatory requirements and flexibility? Are they appropriate for the range of scale and complexity of projects to be assessed under the federal assessment process?

6. Does IAA offer appropriate links among regional assessments, strategic assessments, project assessments and regulatory processes? Are there any key elements explored in section 5 of the article missing in IAA?

7. To what extent to you see the elements of effective participation explored in section 8 of the article reflected in IAA? How important is the new planning phase to ensuring effective participation? What about participation after project approval during the follow-up phase of the assessment process?

8. Does the review and decision-making process under IAA stand up to the expectations explored in sections 9 and 10 of the article? How likely is it that the conclusions and recommendations or the project decisions at the end of the process will be reviewable by the courts? What objective standards are set out in IAA against which courts can assess the work of the Panel, the Agency, the Minister and Cabinet?

Part VI — Selected Court Cases

As part of the effort to understand the federal assessment process in its historical context, this section introduces you to a selection of court challenges that have been fought over the interpretation and implementation of the various iterations of the federal assessment process. You will have noted that the federal assessment process has a rich history of litigation. There are cases dealing with aspects of the assessment process in various chapters in this textbook on issues ranging from constitutional issues in Chapter 3 and adaptive management in Chapter 5 to judicial review in Chapter 6 and climate change in Chapter 10. The following cases were selected because they each explore an aspect of the federal assessment process that continues to have resonance in the face of major changes to the legislation over time. The first case, *Alberta Wilderness Association*, was one of the first court cases to deal with CEAA 1995. It still offers one of the best overviews of panel reviews, a process that has survived more or less intact through the various changes to the federal assessment process. The second case, *Grand Riverkeeper*, explores a number of specific issues respecting the duties of a review panel that also still have resonance today. The third case, *Greenpeace*, further explores the roles of the panel and political decision-makers at the conclusion of an assessment. Finally, the *Clyde River* case is the most recent SCC case dealing with the relationship between the duty to consult with Aboriginal communities and the environmental assessment process.

Alberta Wilderness Assn. v. Cardinal River Coals Ltd.
(1999), 30 C.E.L.R. (N.S.) 175 (Fed. T.D.)

[This litigation, often referred to as the "*Cheviot Mine*" case, gave rise to one of the earliest decisions under CEAA 1995. In this case, the Alberta Wilderness Association (AWA) challenged the adequacy of an environmental assessment carried out by one of the first-ever review panels to be established under CEAA 1995. The proposed Cheviot Coal Project was an open pit coal mine that the proponent, Cardinal River Coals Ltd., planned to construct and operate near the eastern boundary of Jasper National Park. The mine's lifespan was projected to be 20 years. As such, the AWA argued it would have significant ongoing environmental effects on the surrounding environment. The main issues presented by the case were the duties of a (joint) review panel, and requirements under section 16 to consider the cumulative effects of the proposed mine and alternative means of carrying out the project.]

CAMPBELL J.: — In March 1996, Cardinal River Coals Ltd. ("CRC") submitted applications to obtain Alberta regulatory approvals and a Federal Department of Fisheries and Oceans ("DFO") authorization to construct a 23 km long and 3.5 km wide open pit coal mine in its mine permit area located 2.8 km east of the Jasper National Park boundary.

The applicants have voiced substantial concerns about the Cheviot Coal Project ("the Project"), and commenced this judicial review to challenge the DFO authorization ("the Authorization") issued which allows work to begin on the Project. The challenge attacks the Authorization itself, and the environmental assessment which is a pre-condition to its issuance, with the intention of having the public environmental assessment process re-opened to address environmental concerns which, they argue, were not properly considered.

Factual Background and Issues

The Project involves excavating a series of 30 or more open pits, and the construction of associated infrastructure which includes roads, rail lines and the installation of a new transmission line for the supply of electricity. The undertaking will generate millions of tonnes of waste rock which will be deposited on site in stream valleys and other areas. The Project, being undertaken on the Eastern Slopes of the Rocky Mountains close to the eastern boundary of Jasper National Park, is located in an environmentally rich area that is home to a variety of wildlife. It is argued that the construction and operation of the Project, which is expected to be in operation for 20 years, will have a dramatic impact on the immediate and surrounding environment.

Section 35(2) of the federal *Fisheries Act* requires that an authorization be obtained from the Minister prior to the alteration, disruption, or destruction of fish habitat. In May 1996, CRC applied to DFO for the appropriate authorizations required under the *Fisheries Act*, in connection with the Project. However, before the Minister of Fisheries and Oceans (the "Minister") may issue an authorization for a project in compliance with the *Fisheries Act*, an environmental assessment must be conducted pursuant to s. 5(1)(d) of the *Canadian Environmental Assessment Act (CEAA)*. Accordingly, the Minister became the responsible authority for the project pursuant to s. 11(1) of *CEAA*.

A comprehensive study was commenced but, before it was completed, the Minister concluded that the Project may potentially result in significant adverse environmental effects and, therefore, should be referred to a panel under *CEAA*. Since an environmental review was also required under Alberta legislation, the federal Minister of Environment and the Alberta Energy and Utilities Board ("EUB") agreed to hold a joint federal and provincial review as is provided for under *CEAA*, and, to that end, signed the "Agreement for the Cheviot Coal Project", dated October 24, 1996 ("Joint Panel Agreement").

The Joint Panel Agreement set out the terms of reference for the EUB-*CEAA* Joint Review Panel ("the Joint Review Panel"), including the factors that they were required to consider in conducting the environmental assessment.

The Project was referred to the Joint Review Panel in the fall of 1996 and hearings were conducted from January 13, 1997 to February 20, 1997, with an additional hearing date on April 10, 1997.

On June 17, 1997, the Joint Review Panel issued its report and recommendations entitled "*Report of the EUB-CEAA Joint Review Panel: Cheviot Coal Project, Mountain Park Area, Alberta*" ("the Joint Review Panel Report") which recommended that the Minister approve the Project by providing CRC with the necessary regulatory authorizations under the *Fisheries Act*. [...]

On August 17, 1998, the Minister, pursuant to s. 35(2) of the *Fisheries Act*, issued the Authorization, which is the first of a series of authorizations required for the Project. The Authorization allowed CRC to begin construction of the access corridor for the Project. [...]

[**Ed. Note**: The AWA then brought this application for judicial review. Its main argument was that the Joint Review Panel (JRP) erred in failing to comply with its obligations under section 16 of CEAA 1995 and with the Joint Panel Agreement. In the following excerpt, the trial judge addresses this argument first by considering the nature of the duties vested in the JRP, and secondly by considering whether the JRP had complied with those duties.]

Legal Context

The Provisions of CEAA

An overview of duties under *CEAA* is conveniently expressed as follows:

- **Information-gathering**: the review panel must ensure that all information required for an assessment is obtained and made available (s. 34(a)) and hold hearings to foster public participation (s. 34(b)).

- **Considerations**: the panel must conduct an environmental assessment (EA) of the project which includes, *inter alia*, an assessment of all related operations and undertakings (s. 15), and consideration of cumulative environmental effects and their significance (ss. 16(1)(a) and (b)), mitigation measures (s. 16(1)(d)), the need for and alternatives to the project (s. 16(1)(e)), alternative means of carrying out the project and the environmental effects of those alternatives (s. 16(2)(b)), and the capacity of affected renewable resources to be sustained (s. 16(2)(d)).

- **Report**: the panel must prepare a report which includes the rationale, conclusions, and recommendations of the panel regarding the matters considered in the EA, and a summary of any public comments (s. 34(c)).

- **Decision**: the responsible authority (RA) must respond to the report, with the approval of the Governor in Council (s. 37(1)(a)). Then, the RA (in this case the Minister of Fisheries and Oceans) may take a course of action under s. 37(1), i.e. make a decision. If the project is likely to cause significant adverse environmental effects, the RA may approve the project only if its effects "can be justified in the circumstances" (s. 37(1)(a)). [...]

Precedent Interpreting the Provisions of CEAA

Two decisions clearly define the legal importance of the environmental assessment and the standard to be applied respecting its sufficiency.

The Appeal Division Decision in A-430-98 Respecting T-2354-97

Adapted to the present application, the points that emerge from Sexton J.A.'s decision are these: the environmental assessment carried out by the Joint Review Panel in accordance with *CEAA* is a pre-condition to the issuance of the Authorization; the assessment must be conducted in accordance with the *CEAA*, including the requirements of s. 16; and a "proper" assessment is one conducted in accordance with *CEAA*. I take this last statement to mean that an assessment which is not conducted in accordance with *CEAA* is one conducted in error of law.

Alberta Wilderness Assn. v. Express Pipelines Ltd.

The principle that an environmental assessment can be challenged and found not to be in accordance with *CEAA* on an error in law was previously established in *Alberta Wilderness Assn. v. Express Pipelines Ltd.* Adapted to the present application, the points that emerge from Hugessen J.A.'s decision are these: the Joint Review Panel's failure to comply with a requirement of s. 16 of *CEAA* can constitute an error of law; it is important to appropriately characterize a perceived failure to comply as a question of law or merely an attack on the "quality" of the evidence and, therefore, the "correctness" of the conclusions drawn on that evidence; if a perceived failure is in the latter category, no question of law arises and, therefore, the conclusions of the Joint Review Panel stemming from an uncontested high degree of expertise in environmental matters, must not lightly be interfered with; determining the "significance" of an environmental effect under s. 16(1)(b) of *CEAA* involves a subjective determination by the Joint Review Panel and does not involve an interpretation leading to possible error in law; the "alternative means" to be considered under s. 16(2)(b) are circumscribed by the scope of the environmental assessment set by the Joint Panel Agreement; and mitigation measures and environmental effects are properly considered together.

It is important to note that, in *Alberta Wilderness Assn. v. Express Pipelines Ltd.* the Appeal Division found that the joint review panel in that case conducted a "full and thorough environmental assessment". This is, therefore, a qualitative finding which, as a practical matter, contributed to arguments on the sufficiency of the panel report to be rejected. In effect, the Appeal Division found that the panel in that case met its statutory duties of information gathering and reporting.

Therefore, the primary question is whether the Joint Review Panel in the present case has met its statutory information gathering and reporting duties. If a duty is found to be breached, as a misinterpretation of a legal requirement, it is an error of law. It is uncontested that if such a finding is made, the standard of review of the error is correctness.

The Joint Review Panel: Duties

Section 35(2) of the Fisheries Act requires that an authorization be obtained from the Minister of Fisheries and Oceans prior to the alteration, disruption, or destruction of fish habitat. Under the CEA Act, prior to issuing such an authorization, an environmental assessment of the project must be undertaken. Following notification by CRC as to its intention to apply for the above authorization, the DFO, as a Responsible Authority under the CEA Act, initiated a review of the proposed project. In a letter dated 26 August 1996 to the Minister of the Environment, the Minister of Fisheries and Oceans stated that, following a review of CRC's environmental information, the DFO had determined that the project may potentially result in significant adverse environmental effects. In order to expedite the review process, the Minister of Fisheries and Oceans recommended that the Cheviot Coal Project should be referred by the Minister of the Environment for review by a panel and further recommended, in the spirit of the 1993 Canada/Alberta Harmonization Agreement for Environmental Assessment, that the CEAA attempt to integrate this panel review through a Joint Review Panel, with any hearing process required by the EUB.

Sections 40 and 41 of the CEA Act provide for the establishment and appointment of a Joint Review Panel and for the factors to be considered by a Joint Review Panel.

Decision-making and Recommendation Duty

As can be seen, the two distinct Alberta and Federal regulatory processes set different obligations for the Joint Review Panel to meet. The difference between the two is clearly set out in the following passage from the Joint Review Panel Report:

> There are significant differences worth noting in the role of the Panel in a combined provincial and federal decision-making process. Under the Alberta provincial statutes, the Panel is charged with determining whether a proposed energy development is in the public interest. In making its determination as to whether a project is in the public interest, the Panel is required to consider a range of factors, including resource conservation, safety, economic and social impacts of the project,

and effects on the environment. Its decision, including reasons, is documented in a Decision Report.

Under the CEA Act, the Panel is required to submit to the Minister of the Environment and to the Responsible Authority (in this case DFO) a report which provides its rationale, conclusions, and recommendations relating to the environmental assessment of the project, including any mitigation measures and follow-up programs. No decision on federal issues is made by the Panel. Section 37 of the CEA Act authorizes the Responsible Authority to exercise its power to allow a project to proceed if, taking into account the report submitted by a review panel and any mitigation measures, its adverse environmental effects are deemed to be insignificant or, if they are significant, felt to be justified in the circumstances.

As per the agreement between the EUB and CEAA, the Panel intends to issue a single Decision Report designed to meet the requirements of both levels of government.

Therefore, in the present case, the Joint Review Panel has two roles to fulfill: Alberta decision-making, and Federal recommending. The statutory schemes leading to the review reflects this difference. The Alberta scheme has the Joint Review Panel decision as the last step in a process which has first tested for deficiencies in the Environmental Impact Assessment (EIA) produced by CRC, whereas the Federal process has the Joint Review Panel recommendation as the first step in the decision-making to be conducted thereafter. Under *CEAA*, apart from the determination that the project may result in significant adverse environmental effects, prior to the Joint Review Panel's review activities, no pre-determination of sufficiency had occurred.

Therefore, the essential point is that, to satisfy the Minister's concern about the Project, the *CEAA* information gathering investigation can reasonably be expected to go farther than that necessary to meet Alberta requirements.

Consideration, Information Gathering, and Reporting Duties under CEAA and the Joint Panel Agreement

Consideration Duty

The general duty set out in s. 16(1) and s. 16(2) is as follows:

16. (1) Every screening or comprehensive study of a project and every mediation or assessment by a review panel *shall include a consideration* of the following factors: [...]

s. 16. (2) In addition to the factors set out in subsection (1), every comprehensive study of a project and every mediation or assessment by a review panel *shall include a consideration* of the following factors:[...] [Emphasis added]

Section 41 of *CEAA* requires that a joint panel agreement include the factors required to be considered under s. 16(1) and (2), and also provides that additional "requirements" can be set out. [...]

With regard to the scope of the consideration to be undertaken by the Joint Review Panel, s. 41(c) of *CEAA* requires that the Minister "shall fix or approve the terms of reference for the panel". Schedule 1 to the Joint Panel Agreement in the present case, named "Terms of Reference for the Panel of the Cheviot Coal

Project", sets out the terms of reference for consideration of the Project, and requires that: The Panel will include in its review of the Cheviot Coal Project consideration of the factors identified in Appendix 1. The Joint Review Panel's consideration of the factors listed in Appendix 1 shall be reflected in the Final Report.

With regard to the s. 16 *CEAA* factors to be considered by the Joint Review Panel, it is not contested that, in somewhat different wording, Appendix 1 to Schedule 1 of the Joint Panel Agreement requires that the factors listed in the following sections of *CEAA* are to be considered by the Joint Review Panel: s. 16(1)(a): environmental effects, including cumulative effects; s. 16(1)(b): significance of the effects; s. 16(1)(c): public comments; s. 16(1)(d): mitigating measures; s. 16(1)(e): need for the project and alternatives to the project; and s. 16(2)(b): alternative means of carrying out the project.

In addition, the opening words of Appendix 1 to the Joint Panel Agreement require as follows:

> For the purposes of the EUB, the Panel shall determine whether the Cheviot Coal Project is in the public interest, having regard to the social and economic effects of the project and the effects of the project on the environment and shall consider but not be limited to the factors itemized below. These factors will also be considered by the Panel in developing and substantiating conclusions and recommendations for federal decision-makers: [...]

I find that in the present case, given the Minister's conclusion that "the project may potentially result in significant adverse environmental effects", and the just identified need for information to be gathered to meet *CEAA* requirements as opposed to Alberta requirements, to meet the "consideration" duty in s. 16 of *CEAA* the Joint Review Panel is required to perform to a high standard of care.

Information Gathering Duty

A mandatory requirement of a *CEAA* environmental assessment is set out in s. 34(a) as follows:

> s. 34. A review panel shall, in accordance with any regulations made for that purpose and with its term of reference,
>
> (a) ensure that *the information required for an assessment by a review panel is obtained* and made available to the public; [...] [Emphasis added]

However, Schedule 1 of the Joint Panel Agreement states:

> 4. The Panel will ensure that *all information required for the conduct of its review is obtained* and made available to the public, which will include, but is not necessarily limited to:
>
> a) existing technical, environmental or other information relevant to the review, including documents filed in connection with applications No. 960313, and 960314 to the EUB and comments and critique on these documents,
>
> b) supplementary information including a description of any public consultation program, its nature and scope, issues identified, commitments made, and outstanding issues,

c) the terms of reference for the EIA, dated January 23, 1995, for the Cheviot Coal Project and documentation generated by the proponent, and other interested parties, in response to these terms of reference,

d) *any other available information that is required to assess the significance of the Environmental Effects.* [Emphasis added]

I find that the italicized words of paragraph 4 of Schedule 1 have an amplifying effect on the requirements of s. 34(a) of *CEAA* and create a clear and onerous evidence gathering duty on the Joint Review Panel in the present case, being the duty to obtain *all available information* that is required to conduct the environmental assessment.

Respecting the use of the phrase "all information required" in paragraph 4, with respect to the *CEAA* aspect of the Joint Review Panel's duty, I find that what is "required" is that which will meet the just found high standard of care respecting consideration of the s. 16 factors, and the onerous evidence gathering duty on the Joint Review Panel.

I also find that the information gathering duty of the Joint Review Panel does not depend on the Project proponent CRC's information gathering success, nor does it depend on that of any intervenor or interested party. The duty is the Joint Review Panel's to meet.

The Joint Review Panel is provided with ample powers to compel the production of evidence [...] [under] section 35 of *CEAA*.

[**Ed. Note:** Recitation of section 35 omitted.]

Reporting Duty

The opening words of Appendix 1 to the Joint Panel Agreement quoted above require that "[the factors listed in Appendix 1] will also be considered by the [Joint Review] Panel in developing and *substantiating conclusions* and recommendations for federal decision-makers". Therefore, by these words, I find it is reasonable to conclude that the Joint Review Panel is required to substantiate the recommendations made for the purposes of *CEAA*. [...]

Obviously, the Joint Review Panel Report has a multifaceted advisory purpose. First, the public has a right to know the basis for recommendations made in order to know how to respond legally or politically; similarly, federal decision-makers must know the evidentiary basis for any recommendation made in order to assign it weight in formulating an appropriate response.

Granted, there might be gaps in the evidence about cumulative environmental effects. Where such is the case, the *Canadian Environmental Assessment Act Responsible Authority Guide* properly suggests that the professional expertise of the panel members can be applied to fill the gaps.

However, in my opinion, the suggestion that gaps in the evidence can be filled by expert opinion only applies where the evidence is not available; that is, where either it does not exist or is inaccessible.

By the provisions of s. 35 of *CEAA*, which provide production of evidence powers, including confidential evidence, I find that the Joint Review Panel has a duty to use these powers to the full extent necessary to, in the words of paragraph 4 of Schedule 1, obtain and make available "all information required for the conduct of its review".

I find that to meet this duty it is incumbent on the Joint Review Panel to require the production of information which it knows exists, and which is apparently relevant to one or more of the s.16 factors. In my opinion, it is not sufficient to withdraw from this duty to fill a gap in the evidence with subjective, albeit, expert opinion, when actual information is known to be available. [...]

I find that to meet its reporting obligations, the Joint Review Panel must clearly state its recommendations in the Joint Review Panel Report, including the evidence it has relied upon in reaching each recommendation. I also find that if the Joint Review Panel decides to fill a gap in the evidence with its own expert opinion, it must clearly state this to be the case and give an explanation for why doing so is necessary. In this way, the *CEAA* decision-maker, and the public, will be able to decide the weight to be placed on each recommendation reached. [...]

The Joint Review Panel: Breach of Duty?: Cumulative Effects

Extent of the Duty to Consider Cumulative Effects

CEAA and Joint Panel Agreement requirements

The duty set under *CEAA* is contained in s. 16(1)(a) as follows:

16. (1) Every screening or comprehensive study of a project and every mediation or assessment by a review panel shall include a consideration of the following factors:

    (a) the environmental effects of the project, including the environmental effects of malfunctions or accidents that may occur in connection with the project and any cumulative environmental effects that are likely to result from the project in combination with other projects or activities that have been or *will be carried out*; [...] [Emphasis added]

In addition, paragraph 3 of Appendix 1 of the Joint Panel Agreement reads as follows:

The Environmental Effects of the Cheviot Coal Project including the Environmental Effects of malfunctions or accidents that may occur in connection with the Cheviot Coal Project and any cumulative Environmental Effects that are likely to result from the Cheviot Coal Project in combination with other projects or activities that have been or *are likely to be carried out*. [Emphasis added]

By comparing the above two provisions it can be seen that the requirements of *CEAA* are amplified by the Joint Panel Agreement: that is, in the former, the cumulative effects that are likely to result from the Project are to be considered in combination with others that "have been or *will be carried out*", while in the latter, cumulative effects are to be considered in combination with others that "have been or *are likely to be carried out*". Thus, the Joint Panel Agreement requires that certain projects which have not yet been approved are to be considered.

Federal Concerns

In its submission to the Joint Review Panel, the DFO clearly stated that one of its concerns relating to the Project is "the loss/degradation of stream habitat due to mine development which in conjunction with creation of multiple pit lakes in the area may affect the function and integrity of the aquatic ecosystems involved". In particular, DFO cited as an effect of loss/alteration of stream habitat the cumulative impacts of "multiple developments (e.g., the proposed mine development and forestry)".

The Joint Review Panel Report acknowledges that Parks Canada expressed concern that "the Cheviot Coal Project, as proposed, clearly has the potential to adversely impact the ecological integrity of Jasper National Park". In this respect Parks Canada recommended that "the cumulative effects/core area assessment should be expanded to include other planned or foreseeable human activities (e.g. timber harvesting, mineral and oil and gas exploration and development, recreation, etc.) in the larger analysis area [...]".

Therefore, the Joint Review Panel was certainly on notice that consideration of cumulative effects should include forestry and other mining development. On the basis of the above analysis of the requirements of *CEAA* in combination with the Joint Panel Agreement, I find that the Joint Review Panel had a duty to obtain all available information about likely forestry and mining in the vicinity of the Project, to consider this information with respect to cumulative environmental effects, to reach conclusions and make recommendations about this factor, and to substantiate these conclusions and recommendations in the Joint Review Panel Report.

Meeting the Duty

Forestry

Respecting forestry activities in the vicinity of the Project, the Joint Review Panel made the following statement:

> The Panel also notes that CRC, in attempting to carry out an assessment of potential cumulative effects (CEA), stated that it was unable to obtain the necessary information from other industry sources, particularly forestry. The Panel can appreciate the difficulty that this creates for an applicant. Given that a CEA is a requirement of both the provincial and federal EIA process, the Panel believes that the government has a responsibility for ensuring either that needed data can be collected or alternatively, that the current legislation is amended to recognize the limitations that lack of cooperation between industry sectors or companies within a sector can create for a CEA. In this particular case, the Panel notes that CRC was able to use data from the Tri-Creeks watershed as a surrogate measure of the likely effects of modern forestry practices on both discharge rates and water quality, and found little evidence of impact. Therefore, the Panel does not expect the cumulative effects of coal mining and forestry at present/predicted levels to have a significant impact on regional fisheries resources, or reduce their capacity as renewable resources, to meet either present or future needs.

I find that this statement proves two facts: the Joint Review Panel did not obtain "necessary information", and the Joint Review Panel determined that it was not its obligation to obtain the information.

In fact, information respecting likely future forestry activities in the vicinity of the Project site is available. Subsequent to the judicial review hearing of T-2354-97 before McKeown J., the Appeal Division allowed the filing of new evidence to prove this point. The same evidence has been filed in the present application. The evidence conclusively proves that extensive logging and road building activities are likely to the northeast, east and southeast of the mine site over at least the next seven years. [...] it is evident that the Joint Review Panel, while displaying concern about ungulate habitat in the mine area, operated on the apparently erroneous assumption that forest cover would be maintained in that area.

Therefore, I find that the Joint Review Panel breached its duty to obtain all available information about likely forestry in the vicinity of the Project, to consider this information with respect to cumulative environmental effects, to reach conclusions and make recommendations about this factor, and to substantiate these conclusions and recommendations in the Joint Panel Report.

Mining

Of primary concern in this application is the cumulative environmental effects of coal mining on carnivores. The geographic area about which concern exists is called the "Coal Branch" planning area, which is a large area on the eastern slopes of the Rocky Mountains which contains the Project's "Carnivore Cumulative Effects Assessment" area, which in turn contains the Project mine site.

Alberta government information describes coal mining in the Coal Branch as follows:

> Coal — Coal development in the Coal Branch dated back to the turn of the century and increased until the 1950's when railways converted to diesel fuel. Major coal development then occurred, as the demand for both metallurgical and thermal coal grew in the late 60's and 70's. Coal production in 1984 was just under eight million tonnes (about half metallurgical coal and half thermal). The extent of existing coal deposits presently proven in the planning area contains a total of nearly three billion tonnes of coal. Much of the coal rights are under disposition. Today, there are three, coal-mines operating in the Coal Branch. Two other projects have been issued mine permits and are awaiting growth and stabilization of both world and domestic coal markets. Preliminary disclosures of six coal projects have been recognized by the government as being consistent with government policies or intentions for these areas. With exploration, the more promising coal deposits are proven and reserves are increased.

The Coal Branch area is important for the development of high quality coals because of geology and the existing infrastructure.

[Ed. Note: The applicants led evidence that the Government of Alberta had granted approvals in principle to five other coal mining operations in the same planning area. They asked the Joint Review Panel to compel disclosure from the government of the nature of these proposed operations so that this information could be incorporated into the EA.]

About the application to compel the "approvals in principle", the Joint Review Panel said this:

> The AWA Coalition requested that the Panel require the Government of Alberta to produce copies of the preliminary disclosure documents, prepared under the requirements of the Coal Development Policy of Alberta, for a number of other surface coal mines which had been proposed in the region. The Government of Alberta advised the Panel that those documents had, in its view, been submitted in confidence and so could not be released, except perhaps under a request under the Freedom of Information and Protection of Privacy Act. The Government also noted

that the documents were dated, with some being submitted in the mid-1970's, and that without someone to speak to them, it would not be possible to determine if the various proposals remained relevant.

The Panel determined that, given the expectation of the parties that the documents were submitted in confidence and, more importantly, the inability of anyone, including the applicant, to test the relevance of the documents, it was not prepared to attempt to compel that the documents be submitted to the hearing.

I find that this statement proves that the Joint Review Panel failed to compel the production of the mining information because it misconstrued its power to do so, and it misconceived that it has the obligation to decide on its relevance once produced.

Therefore, with respect to the two projects for which permits have been granted and the five projects which have received approvals in principle, I find that the Joint Review Panel breached its duty to obtain all available information about likely mining in the vicinity of the Project, to consider this information with respect to cumulative environmental effects, to reach conclusions and make recommendations about this factor, and to substantiate these conclusions and recommendations in the Joint Review Panel Report.

The Joint Review Panel: Breach of Duty?: Alternate Means

Extent of the Duty to Consider Alternate Means

Section 16(2)(b) provides as follows:

s. 16.(2) In addition to the factors set out in subsection (1), every comprehensive study of a project and every mediation or assessment by a review panel shall include a consideration of the following factors: [...]

(b) alternative means of carrying out the project that are technically and economically feasible and the environmental effects of any such alternative means; [...]

In the present case, with respect to the method of mining, I find that the requirements of this section are properly restricted to the alternate means to open pit mining being underground mining.

With respect to alternative means, the [...] the Joint Review Panel limited its consideration because of CRC's practical and economic concerns [in particular, the CRC's reticence to seriously consider underground mining techniques] and, consequently, the terms of its proposal. As noted above, CRC applied for Alberta regulatory approval for an open pit coal mine, and the scope of its Environmental Impact Assessment (EIA) was limited accordingly. It appears that, as a result of this limitation, the Joint Review Panel's consideration was similarly limited.

While the alternative means of underground mining is generally considered in the Joint Review Panel Report, the effects of this alternative means, as compared to the effects of open pit mining, are not considered in any meaningful way. I agree with the applicant's argument that simply identifying potential "alternative means" without discussing their comparative environmental effects fails to provide any useful information to decision-makers, and fails to meet the requirements of s. 16(2)(b) of *CEAA*.

While it is true that, as the Joint Review Panel asserts, CRC has the right to carry out the extraction of the coal resources within the applied for mine permit boundary, I find that it does not have the right to do it by open pit mine.

Thus, I find that a comparative analysis between open pit mining and underground mining at the Project site is required to comply with the provisions of s. 16(2)(b).

During the course of the hearing, counsel for CRC tactfully pointed out that, prior to the Joint Review Panel's consideration of the Project under *CEAA*, all detailed Alberta regulatory approvals leading to a final decision had been given. The point made was that, in the face of these approvals, the Minister's concern and, therefore, the requirements of *CEAA* are incidental to this almost completed process. My response to this assertion is that *CEAA*, as well as Alberta resource and environmental protection legislation, serves the interests of Albertans, and consequently, its terms must be met as framed.

Conclusion

[...] during the course of argument, I expressed the opinion that, if the environmental assessment conducted by the Joint Review Panel is found not to be in compliance with the requirements of *CEAA*, the least intrusive approach to reaching compliance would be adopted.[...]

In view of my findings [...] it is clear that the Project cannot proceed until the Joint Review Panel's environmental assessment is conducted in compliance with *CEAA*. Therefore [...] in my opinion the Minister has authority and responsibility to direct the Joint Review Panel to reconvene and, having regard to my findings, direct that it do what is necessary to make adjustments to the Joint Review Panel Report so that the environmental assessment conducted can be found in compliance with *CEAA*. For this result to occur, in my opinion, the following directions must be met:

(1) Obtain all available information about likely forestry in the vicinity of the Project, consider this information with respect to cumulative environmental effects, and, accordingly, reach conclusions and make recommendations about this factor, and substantiate these conclusions and recommendations in the Joint Review Panel Report;

(2) Obtain all available information about likely mining in the vicinity of the Project, consider this information with respect to cumulative environmental effects, and, accordingly, reach conclusions and make recommendations about this factor, and substantiate these conclusions and recommendations in the Joint Review Panel Report;

(3) With respect to alternative means, do a comparative analysis between open pit mining and underground mining at the Project site to determine the comparative technical and economic feasibility and comparative environmental effects of each, consider this information, reach conclusions and make recommendations about this factor, and substantiate these conclusions and recommendations in the Joint Review Panel Report.

Notes and Questions

1. What are the information-gathering duties of a review panel under CEAA 1995?
2. What are the reporting obligations of a review panel?
3. Under what circumstances can a review panel apply its own expertise and judgment to fill information gaps?
4. In the case of *Sharp v. Canada (Transportation Agency)* (1999), 31 C.E.L.R. (N.S.) 1 (Fed. C.A.), leave to appeal refused (1999), 252 N.R. 391 (note) (S.C.C.), the Federal Court of Appeal dealt with the issue of alternatives to a project in the context of a railway line. The Transportation Agency was asked to consider approving a railway line. The decision triggered CEAA 1995 under paragraph 5(1)(d), a licensing provision on the Law List. The Transportation Agency made a decision to consider needs and alternatives under paragraph 16(1)(e), but was restricted under its own licensing provisions regarding the extent to which it was to consider needs and alternatives. The Court challenge was initiated to require the Transportation Agency to study in detail the need for, and alternatives to, the line under CEAA 1995. The Court decided that the Transportation Agency should strive to exercise its discretion under CEAA 1995 in a manner consistent with regulatory decisions that trigger EA, and should only consider needs and alternatives if the proposed project has serious adverse environmental effects. How does this decision fit with the *Cheviot Mine* decision of the Federal Court Trial Division? What is the role of alternatives under CEAA 2012?
5. The following two cases that were before the Federal Court, *Grand Riverkeeper* and *Greenpeace*, are more recent examples of judicial reviews in which the court grappled with issues surrounding the role of a review panel and the adequacy of the report that it completes.

Grand Riverkeeper, Labrador Inc. v. Canada (Attorney General)
2012 FC 1520

[This case was initiated by NunatuKavut, Grand Riverkeeper and Sierra Club to challenge the approval of the Muskrat Falls hydroelectric dam following a joint panel review involving the federal government and the province of Newfoundland and Labrador. Among the many conclusions and recommendations of the Joint Review Panel (JRP) were two conclusions and associated Panel recommendations that were at the centre of the dispute. The Panel concluded that it had inadequate information on the economic viability of the project and alternative ways to provide energy to the island of Newfoundland. The Panel chose to recommend independent studies to address these information gaps before project decisions were made. The plaintiffs challenged this aspect of the Panel report on the basis that the Panel should have carried out this work before finalizing its report.]

NEAR J.: —

Background

The Parties

[...] The Proponent, Nalcor, is a Crown Corporation incorporated pursuant to the *Energy Corporation Act*, SNL 2007, c E-11.01. It is wholly owned by the Government of Newfoundland and Labrador ("the Province"), and was created to "engage in and carry out activities pertaining to the Province's energy resources, including hydro-electric generation" (Application Record of the Respondent Nalcor Energy, vol 1, page 3). Nalcor is mandated to implement the Province's energy policy, and is governed in this regard by: the *Energy Corporation Act*, above; the Province's long-term energy policy, *Focusing Our Energy* ("the Energy Plan"); and the *Electrical Power Control Act, 1994*, SNL 1994, c E-5.1.

The Project

Nalcor's proposed Project involves the construction and operation of two hydroelectric generation facilities on the lower section of Churchill River in Labrador — one at Gull Island and the other at Muskrat Falls. The Project further proposes the construction of transmission lines and access roads connecting the two sites to each other, and to the existing Labrador electricity grid.

The Gull Island facility would have a generation capacity of 2,250 MW, necessitating the creation of a dam, a 232 km-long reservoir, and the flooding of an 85 km^2 area. The Muskrat Falls facility would have a generation capacity of 824 MW, with a dam, a 60 km-long reservoir, and a 41 km^2 flooded area. [...]

The CEAA Environmental Assessment Process

The Supreme Court recently described CEAA as "a detailed set of procedures that federal authorities must follow before projects that may adversely affect the environment are permitted to proceed" (*Mining Watch Canada v Canada (Fisheries and Oceans)*, 2010 SCC 2, [2010] SCJ No 2 at para 1). The basic framework for EAs under CEAA involves four broad components. First, the RAs determine whether CEAA applies to the project and what type of assessment it will conduct. There are three main types of assessment: screening, comprehensive study, and panel review. While panel reviews are the most involved, screenings and comprehensive studies are the most common types employed by RAs. Second, the assessment itself is conducted — in this case, by the JRP — according to the parameters set by the appropriate authority under CEAA. Third, the RAs determine whether, based on the assessment, the project should proceed. Fourth and finally is the post-decision phase, in which notice is given to the public about the RAs' decisions, mitigation measures are monitored and potential follow-up programs are carried out.

As previously mentioned, the Project in this case was registered with the federal authorities late in 2006. In February 2007, TC and DFO determined that an environmental assessment was required pursuant to CEAA. The Minister of the Environment subsequently referred the assessment to a review panel under the federal legislation in June 2007 and, as the Province concurrently determined that a public hearing was required for provincial environmental approvals, the two Governments established the JRP. To this effect, the "Agreement for the Establishment of a Panel for the Environmental Assessment of the Lower Churchill Hydroelectric Generation Project" ("the JRP Agreement") was concluded in January 2009, and the five-member panel was jointly appointed by the provincial Ministers of Environment and Conservation and Intergovernmental Affairs, and the federal Minister of the Environment.

The JRP Agreement set out the Terms of Reference for the Panel's EA, which provided, in part, as follows (see Application Record of the Applicants Sierra Club Canada and Grand Riverkeeper, Labrador, Inc, vol 5, tab 7, page 1488):

> The Panel shall consider the following factors in the EA of the Project/Undertaking as outlined in Sections 16(1) and 16(2) of the CEAA and Sections 57 and 69 of the EPA:
>
> 1. Purpose of the Project/Undertaking;
> 2. Need for the Project/Undertaking;
> 3. Rationale for the Project/Undertaking;
> ...
> 5. Alternatives to the Project/Undertaking;
> ...
> 10. Any cumulative Environmental Effects that are likely to result from the Project/Undertaking in combination with other projects or activities that have been or will be carried out;
> 11. The significance of the Environmental Effects as described in items 9 and 10;
> ...

[...] The JRP held thirty days of hearings in various communities between March 3 and April 15, 2011. Some of the hearings were issue-specific, while others were general sessions, in which the Panel invited participants to share their overall views and conclusions on the Project. Still others were community hearings, in which participants were invited to share their views on the impacts the Project might have on their specific communities. After the final hearing on April 15, the Panel declared the proceedings closed, determining that no further information would be considered. It issued the Report on August 23, 2011.

The Applicants filed this application for judicial review on December 20, 2011. [...]

The Impugned Report

The Panel's Report sets out the Proponent's and the public participants' views on a range of subjects, and gives over 80 recommendations. Overall, the Panel determined that the Project was likely to have significant adverse effects in the areas of fish habitat and fish assemblage; terrestrial, wetland and riparian habitat; the Red Wine Mountain caribou herd; fishing and seal hunting in Lake Melville should consumption advisories be required; and culture and heritage (the "loss of the river") (Report at page 269). It further identified that there was a range of potential benefits stemming from the Project. The Panel, in the final chapter of its Report, gave its thoughts on whether the proposed Project would create net benefits in a range of areas, including economics, social and cultural benefits, and benefits to future generations, to the Province, and to areas beyond the Province.

The portions of the Report in dispute are those recommendations related to the: (i) need for (Recommendation 4.1), (ii) alternatives to (Recommendation 4.2), and (iii) cumulative effects of (Recommendations 16.1 and 16.2, though the cumulative effects of specific components were considered throughout the Report) the Project.

Need

With respect to the need for the Project, the Panel came to two conclusions at page 25 of the Report:

> The Panel concludes that, in light of the uncertainties associated with transmission for export markets from Gull Island, Nalcor has not demonstrated the justification of the Project as a whole in energy and economic terms.

> The Panel further concludes that there are outstanding questions for each of Muskrat Falls and Gull Island regarding their ability to deliver the projected long-term financial benefits to the Province, even if other sanctioning requirements were met.

In response to these conclusions, the JRP recommended that, if the Project were to be approved by the RAs, the Province undertake a "separate and formal review of the projected cash flow" of the relevant Project component to confirm whether it would, in fact, provide "significant long-term financial returns to the Government for the benefit of the people of the Province" (Recommendation 4.1).

Alternatives

The Panel determined that Nalcor's analysis showing that the Muskrat Falls component of the Project was the best and least cost option for meeting domestic energy demands was "inadequate." As such, it recommended that an "independent analysis of economic, energy and broad-based environmental considerations of alternatives" be carried out (Recommendation 4.2, at page 34 of the Report). The Panel outlined what it thought would be appropriate parameters for such an independent study, suggesting that the following question be analysed:

> What would be the best way to meet domestic demand under the "No Project" option, including the possibility of a Labrador-Island interconnection no later than 2041 to access Churchill Falls power at that time, or earlier, based on available recall?

Cumulative Effects

Finally, the Panel allotted a chapter to the discussion of the cumulative effects of the Project. As previously stated, other chapters addressed the cumulative effects related to "specific valued ecosystem components and key indicators of the biophysical and socio-economic environments" (see Report at page 265). The Panel defined "cumulative effects" in Chapter 16 as "changes to the environment due to the Project where those overlap, combine or interact with the environmental effects of other existing, past or reasonably foreseeable projects or activities" (Report at page 265).

The JRP concluded that Nalcor's approach to cumulative effects was "less than comprehensive" and that public participants "raised valid concerns that contributed to a broader understanding of the potential cumulative effects of the Project" (Report at page 267). It further noted that the Proponent's approach "illustrates the limitation of project-specific cumulative effects" (Report at page 267). The Panel gave the following recommendation on this point (Recommendation 16.1, Report at page 268):

> The Panel recommends that, if the Project is approved, the provincial Department of Environment and Conservation, in collaboration with the provincial Department of Labrador and Aboriginal Affairs and other relevant departments, identify regional mechanisms to assess and mitigate the cumulative effects of current and future development in Labrador.

Issues

The principal issues raised in this application can be framed as follows:

A. What is the applicable standard of review?
B. Did the JRP fulfill its mandate with respect to the:

    i.   need for and alternatives to the Project; and
    ii. cumulative effects of the Project?

NunatuKavut also claims that the JRP breached principles of procedural fairness or violated its right to be heard.

Analysis

[**Ed. Note:** The section regarding the applicable standard of review is omitted. The court concludes that the appropriate standard is "reasonableness".]

The JRP's Mandate

Purpose and Role of the JRP in the EA Process

The basic goals of the EA process writ large are to ensure "(1) early identification and evaluation of all potential environmental consequences of a proposed undertaking; [and] (2) decision making that both guarantees the adequacy of this process and reconciles, to the greatest extent possible, the proponent's development desires with environmental protection and preservation" (*Friends of the Oldman River Society v Canada (Minister of Transport)*, [1992] SCJ No 1, [1992] 1 SCR 3 at para 95). [...]

[**Ed. Note:** The court's overview of key provisions of CEAA 1995 is omitted.]

This Court has held that, in order for the JRP to fulfill its "consideration" requirement pursuant to section 16 of CEAA, it must "perform to a high standard of care" (*Cheviot*, above, at para 36).

The JRP's information gathering function was also laid out in *Cheviot*, above. Justice Douglas Campbell underlined that the Terms of Reference in that particular case amplified the requirement under section 34(a) of CEAA, obligating the panel "to obtain all available information that is required to conduct the environmental assessment" (at para 39). He went on to determine that "required information" is that which will meet the high standard of care owed by the JRP with respect to its consideration requirements. Justice Campbell also determined that the JRP must make use of the production of evidence powers accorded to it under section 35 of CEAA to the full extent necessary to obtain and make available all information required for the conduct of its review (at para 48). It is important to note that in *Cheviot*, above, the applicable Alberta legislation that formed part of that panel's mandate required it to determine whether a proposed energy development was in the public interest — in other words, to determine whether it was justified (see *Cheviot*, above, at para 28). There is no equivalent requirement in the JRP's mandate in this case.

Finally, the JRP's reporting obligations require it to state its recommendations clearly, including the evidence it has relied upon in reaching each recommendation (see *Cheviot*, above, at paras 43-51). In other words, the JRP must substantiate the recommendations it makes for the purposes of CEAA. This substantiation allows the public, government decision-makers, and courts to identify the rational basis upon which the Panel must make its recommendations (see *Iverhuron*, above, at para 40).

The parties' main dispute in the case at hand is about the extent to which the JRP was mandated to consider and reach conclusions with respect to each of the factors listed in section 16 of CEAA and in its Terms of Reference. The general requirements for panel review set out in *Cheviot*, above, offer an instructive framework with which to assess the Panel's Report. As such, I will address three main issues with respect to each of (i) the need for and alternatives to the Project, and (ii) its cumulative effects, namely whether the Panel reasonably fulfilled its mandate to: (a) consider; (b) gather information; and (c) report.

As a preliminary note, there is no dispute between the parties about the scope of the JRP's mandate to make findings on justification. They agree that the Panel was not required to make such findings. Additionally, I do not find it necessary to rule definitively on the question of the weight to be afforded to the affidavit of Mr. Stephen Chapman in these proceedings.

"Need for" and "Alternatives to" the Project

The Respondents propose that the Panel's requirement to consider should be informed by the ordinary meaning of that word. They cite the Oxford English Dictionary definition of "consider" as "to contemplate mentally, fix the mind upon; to think over, meditate or reflect on, bestow attentive thought upon, give heed to, take note of" (Factum of the Respondent, Nalcor Energy at para 65). The federal Respondents frame the requirement as meaning that the JRP "simply had to turn its mind to these issues without reaching hard conclusions" (federal Respondents' Memorandum of Fact and Law at para 66). Additionally, they posit that, once the Panel met the minimum requirement to turn its mind to the issues before it, it then had the discretion to determine the parameters of the consideration required.

While the Applicants champion a more purposive conception, arguing that the Panel's failure to assess need and alternatives properly impeded its ability to reach conclusions on whether the Project was justified, I agree with the Respondents' position. It is clear that the JRP turned its mind to the issues of need and alternatives. These questions were at the center of at least one issue-specific public hearing, and were included in numerous information requests and responses throughout the EA process. Indeed, the extent to which the Panel requested further information was a matter for its judgment, judgment with which this Court is loath to interfere. It does not appear to me that the Panel misconceived of its responsibilities relating to need and alternatives. I find that the Panel considered the need and alternatives questions in a manner that is transparent, justifiable and intelligible. As such, it falls within an acceptable range of outcomes and is reasonable.

There are two parts to the parties' contentions relating to the Panel's information gathering requirement: (1) whether the JRP's determination that there was "insufficient evidence" meant insufficient evidence for the purposes of its EA or for the ultimate decision maker's purposes; and (2) whether the JRP's referral of additional "information gathering" to (i) the Province and (ii) an independent study panel was reasonable.

On the first part, the Applicants agree with the Panel's determination that there was insufficient evidence on need and alternatives, but posit that, given the paucity of evidence, it should have both obtained, through the use of its subpoena powers, and then assessed the requisite information. However, there is no evidence provided by the Applicants that such information existed for the Panel to obtain and utilize.

Further, I agree with the federal Respondents' argument that the Panel's subpoena power cannot be used to compel the creation of new information. In essence, the Applicants contend that the Panel must use the subpoena power to engage in a fishing exercise for further information that may exist. However, as I already mentioned, there is no evidence in this matter that such information did, in fact, exist during the Panel's deliberations. Otherwise, the Applicants submit that the subpoena power is to be used to compel, in an ongoing fashion, the creation of new information prior to the Panel concluding its Report. In my view, neither of these arguments have merit. There is no evidence that information was withheld from the Panel during its deliberations. Further, the Panel clearly drew upon its expertise to conclude that the information it had on hand was sufficient to fulfill its mandate. Such a conclusion should not lightly be interfered with by the Court.

It then follows that the Proponent's characterization of the JRP's conclusions with respect to the further information to be collected in accordance with Recommendations 4.1 and 4.2 is correct. Rather than relating to the sufficiency of the evidence for the purposes of completing the EA, these conclusions were items the Panel thought the government decision-makers might find useful in determining whether the Project should proceed.

Thus, to address the second part of the issue, it was entirely reasonable for the Panel to recommend that the Province and an independent study panel augment at a later time the information gathered with respect to the questions of need and alternatives. Indeed, this is expected behaviour from the Panel given the "ongoing and dynamic" nature of these large projects (*Pembina*, above, at para 24; *Union of*

Nova Scotia Indians v Canada (Minister of Fisheries and Oceans), [1996] FCJ No 1373 at para 65). As this Court held in *Pembina*, above, environmental assessment is "not to be conceptualized as a single, discrete event" (at para 24).

This is particularly so given the uncertainty of the process and the early phase in the process at which the EA occurs. Subparagraph 5(2)(b)(i) of CEAA states that RAs "shall ensure that an environmental assessment of the project is conducted as early as is practicable in the planning stages of the project and before irrevocable decisions are made."

The Federal Court of Appeal explored this point in *Express Pipelines*, above:

> Finally, we were asked to find that the panel had improperly delegated some of its functions when it recommended that certain further studies and ongoing reports to the National Energy Board should be made before, during and after construction. This argument misconceives the panel's function which is simply one of information gathering and recommending. The panel's view that the evidence before it was adequate to allow it to complete that function "as early as practicable in the planning stages ... and before irrevocable decisions are made" (see section 11(1)) is one with which we will not lightly interfere. By its nature the panel's exercise is predictive and it is not surprising that the statute specifically envisages the possibility of "follow up" programmes. Indeed, given the nature of the task we suspect that finality and certainty in environmental assessment can never be achieved.

I am in accord with the Federal Court of Appeal's analysis in *Express Pipelines*, above, and find that the Panel reasonably fulfilled its information gathering mandate in this case.

Finally, I am satisfied that the Panel adequately substantiated its conclusion that further study was needed in two areas. It explained in its conclusions on the need for the Project that there was insufficient information on the long-term financial viability of the Project, and, as such, that further study was recommended. Similarly, insufficient information was the reason cited as the basis for the Panel's recommendation that further study be conducted with respect to potential alternatives to the Project. These explanations each provide the rational basis that fulfills the Panel's reporting requirements for these items.

Cumulative Effects

The Applicants allege that, apart from an evaluation of the cumulative effects stemming from the Project on the Red Wine caribou, the Panel failed to conduct any cumulative effects assessment. It is clear, however, in looking at the Report that the JRP turned its mind to the question. There is an entire chapter dedicated to the Proponent's approach to cumulative effects, and the notion is built into many other chapters dealing with more specific issues. The Panel requested further information specifically relating to cumulative effects from the Proponent on at least two occasions, and gathered information on this point from public participants. It stated specifically that public participants had "raised valid concerns that contributed to a broader understanding of the potential cumulative effects of the Project" (Report at page 267). I am thus satisfied that the Panel met its consideration and information gathering requirements with respect to cumulative effects.

The main issue with respect to cumulative effects is the reporting requirement, more specifically the requirement to state conclusions clearly and substantiate them with evidence. The Applicants posit that the Panel's reliance on future regional processes within the control of provincial agencies in Recommendation 16.1 constitutes a failure to state a conclusion with respect to this specific Project. I disagree. The Panel dealt with cumulative effects in various parts of their Report. It also clearly considered and concluded in the Report that further future works were required with respect to cumulative effects. The Panel recommended a possible mechanism for this work to proceed, which, in my view, was entirely reasonable given the ongoing and dynamic nature of this large Project (see *Pembina*, above, at para 24). It is not logical to expect that the Panel would have finalized all informational aspects of possible cumulative effects prior to reporting to the RAs. Its conclusions on cumulative effects are grounded in a rational basis and, as such, I find that the Panel reasonably fulfilled its reporting mandate with respect to cumulative effects.

NunatuKavut: Procedural Fairness and the Right to Be Heard

NunatuKavut argues that the Panel's failure to consider the need for, alternatives to , and cumulative effects of the Project effectively denied it its right to be heard. As I have already found that the Panel fulfilled its section 16 mandate to consider, this argument must be rejected.

I must also reject NunatuKavut's arguments based on the Panel's purported duty to consult the group on all matters, and to compel evidence from them on all three issues in dispute in these proceedings. The Panel's mandate was not as expansive as NunatuKavut posits. Its Terms of Reference stated as follows:

> The Panel will have the mandate to invite information from Aboriginal persons or groups related to the nature and scope of potential or established Aboriginal rights or title in the area of the Project, as well as information on the potential adverse impacts or potential infringement that the Project/Undertaking will have on asserted or established Aboriginal rights or title (see Terms of Reference, Schedule 1 to JRP Agreement).

The mandate to invite information cannot be said to include a mandate to compel evidence.

Moreover, the Panel fulfilled its mandate by inviting, and accepting, on several occasions written submissions from NunatuKavut. In addition, the Panel heard from the group in the General Hearing Sessions it held in Happy Valley-Goose Bay and in St. John's. Indeed, the group received over $130,000 through the Participant Funding Program to participate in the EA process. NunatuKavut's choice not to participate in a portion of the hearings by virtue of its injunction proceedings, regardless of how good the group's intentions, cannot impose a duty on the Panel to compel evidence from it.

For all of these reasons, I find that there was no infringement of NunatuKavut's right to be heard or of any other principle of procedural fairness with respect to the group's participation in the EA process.

Conclusion

In light of my findings that the Panel reasonably fulfilled its mandate to consider, gather information, and report on the need for, alternatives to, and cumulative effects of the Project, the Applicants' prayer for relief is denied. Given the nature of the subject matter and the questions at issue, there will be no award as to costs.

Notes and Questions

1. Do you agree with the Court that it was appropriate for the JRP to recommend independent studies to determine the economic viability of the project, or do you think the Panel should have carried out this analysis before concluding its work? Have a look at media coverage about the Muskrat Falls project since its approval. It has turned out to be a financial disaster for the province and for the proponent. It is clear that the Panel was concerned about the economic viability of the project, and that it did not trust the proponent's economic analysis. What changes do you think need to be made to the federal assessment process to reduce the risk of bad projects being approved?

2. The Environmental Impact Statement (EIS) guidelines issued to the proponent allowed the proponent to assess alternatives based on its purpose and rationale for the project. The proponent identified the purpose and rationale of the project as maximizing the hydro potential of the Churchill river, and as a result, did not offer a detailed assessment of some alternative ways to meet the energy need of the province, such as energy conservation, efficiency, and wind power. In light of this, was it appropriate for the JRP to recommend an independent alternatives analysis, or should the panel have carried out this work before filing its report? What tools did the JRP have at its disposal to get credible information about alternatives, their economic viability, and their environmental impacts?

3. The JRP was operating under timelines imposed on it in the Terms of Reference developed by the federal and provincial Ministers of the Environment. If the Panel faced a choice between meeting the timelines set in its terms of reference, or carrying out an independent analysis of alternatives, what legal advice would you have given to the Panel?

Greenpeace Canada v. Canada (Attorney General)

2014 FC 463,

reversed 2015 FCA 186,

leave to appeal refused 2016 CarswellNat 1347 (S.C.C.)

[This case involves an application for judicial review in relation to the Darlington New Nuclear Power Plant Project proposed by Ontario Power Generation (OPG). The application challenges the adequacy of the federal environmental assessment conducted by a joint review panel established under a March 2009 agreement between the federal Minister of the Environment and the CNSC and the project approval that was based on the report. The governing statute at the time was CEAA 1995. At the heart of the case was a decision by the proponent not to select a specific nuclear reactor technology before the conclusion of the assessment, but rather to predict the environmental effects of a range of technologies. The Panel accepted this approach and concluded that the project was not likely to cause significant adverse effects. The project approval that followed resulted in the judicial review application. At trial, the Federal Court concluded that the Panel report, by failing to require the proponent to offer detailed design information about the major components of the project and to assess the environmental effects of these specific components, did not provide an adequate basis for the project approval, as it did not include adequate consideration of certain environmental effects of the project. A successful appeal was brought to the Federal Court of Appeal. However, the following excerpt from the decision of Russell J. was not addressed by the Federal Court of Appeal and remains a helpful articulation of the respective roles of the review panel and the ultimate decision-maker in a federal EA.]

RUSSELL J.: —

Links to the Issue of Improper Delegation

[...] In my view, Parliament's intention in allocating certain roles and decisions to expert bodies, and others to democratic bodies such as the federal Cabinet, must be considered and respected.

The most important role for a review panel is to provide an evidentiary basis for decisions that must be taken by Cabinet and responsible authorities. The jurisprudence establishes that gathering, disclosing, and holding hearings to assemble and assess this evidentiary foundation is an independent duty of a review panel, and failure to discharge it undermines the ability of the Cabinet and responsible authorities to discharge their own duties under the Act.

In *Pembina Institute*, above, Justice Tremblay-Lamer discussed the interconnection between the role of a review panel, which is charged with conducting a fact-based assessment, and that of political decision-makers, who are "mandated to take into account the wider public policy factors in granting project approval":

> The CEAA establishes a two-step decision-making process. The first step is an environmental assessment where potentially adverse environmental effects of a project are analysed (s. 5). The second step involves decision-making and follow-up where a federal authority decides, taking into consideration that assessment, if a particular project should be authorized and what follow-up measures, if any, are required to verify the accuracy of the assessment and the effectiveness of mitigation measures (ss. 37 and 38). [...]

> Specifically, the general duties that a review panel is mandated to fulfill are four-fold (s. 34). First, it must ensure that the information required for an assessment is obtained and made available to the public (s. 34(a)). Second, the panel is required to hold hearings in a manner that offers the public an opportunity to participate in the assessment (s. 34(b)). Third, the panel is charged with fulfilling a reporting function whereby it must prepare a report setting out "the rationale, conclusions and recommendations of the panel relating to the environmental assessment of the

project, including any mitigation measures and follow-up program" as well as a summary of public comments received (s. 34(c)). Finally, it must submit that report to the Minister and the responsible authority (s. 34(d)). [...]

While I agree that *the Panel* is not to engage in policy recommendation, nevertheless, it *is tasked with conducting a science and fact-based assessment of the potential adverse environmental effects of a proposed project. In the absence of this fact-based approach, the political determinations made by final decision-makers are left to occur in a vacuum.*

I recognize that placing an administrative burden on the Panel to provide an in-depth explanation of the scientific data for all of its conclusions and recommendations would be disproportionately high. However, *given that the Report is to serve as an objective basis for a final decision, the Panel must, in my opinion, explain in a general way why the potential environmental effects, either with or without the implementation of mitigation measures, will be insignificant.*

Should the Panel determine that the proposed mitigation measures are incapable of reducing the potential adverse environmental effects of a project to insignificance, it has a duty to say so as well. *The assessment of the environmental effects of a project and of the proposed mitigation measures occur outside the realm of government policy debate, which by its very nature must take into account a wide array of viewpoints and additional factors that are necessarily excluded by the Panel's focus on project related environmental impacts.* In contrast, the responsible authority is authorized, pursuant to s. 37(1)(a)(ii), to permit the project to be carried out in whole or in part even where the project is likely to cause significant adverse environmental effects if those effects "can be justified in the circumstances". Therefore, *it is the final decision-maker that is mandated to take into account the wider public policy factors in granting project approval.*

[emphasis added]

In short, Parliament has designed a decision-making process under the CEAA that is, when it functions properly, both evidence-based and democratically accountable. The CNSC, in considering future licensing decisions, will be in a fundamentally different position from the Panel that has conducted the EA. The CNSC will be the final authority making the decision, not merely an expert panel. Although the CNSC approaches this role with considerable expertise, it does not have the same democratic legitimacy and responsibility as the federal Cabinet.

This distinction is particularly relevant, in my view, where issues require reference not simply to scientific evidence, but to societal values and associated public policy choices. For example, the document intended to provide federal decision-makers with guidance on how to apply the precautionary principle set out in s. 4(2) of the CEAA makes repeated reference to the need to consider and make decisions in light of "society's chosen level of protection against risk" (see Privy Council Office, A Framework for the Application of Precaution in Science-based Decision Making About Risk (Government of Canada, 2003)). This is conspicuously the type of consideration that elected representatives, rather than expert bodies, seem well-placed to evaluate.

Choices by the Panel that could diminish the Cabinet's ability to consider and decide such matters, deferring them instead for consideration at a future date by an expert body, could signal a departure from Parliament's intention regarding the structure of decision-making under the CEAA. The issue is not timing so much as Parliament's intention as to who should decide what.

In some cases, what is left for the future will be verification that actual performance will conform to the accepted standard of environmental or health protection (see EA Report at p. 45). If this were the only purpose of environmental assessment, presumably it could be left entirely to expert bodies. However, when it is the appropriate standard itself that is at issue, or no standards exist, such an approach can become problematic.

This does not mean that future regulatory processes have no role to play in managing and mitigating a project's environmental effects, or that they should not factor into a review panel's analysis. Several examples in the present case illustrate this point and are discussed later in these reasons.

The key substantive point with respect to the decision-making structure of the CEAA is, in my view, that it is the role of s. 37 decision-makers to decide what is an acceptable level of environmental impact or risk. This decision-making component of the Act is not its *only* important feature, but the language of s. 37, the structure of the Act, and more than two decades' experience with its implementation make it undeniable that it is *an* important feature (see *Pembina Institute*, above, at para 15 applying *Oldman River*, above, at para 103). We cannot simply read it out of the Act, and the courts and those charged with its implementation must seek to maintain the integrity of the decision-making structure that Parliament has put in place.

At the same time, one cannot ignore the reality that many projects are subject to regulation by specialized bodies with a public interest mandate that includes managing and controlling the project's environmental and health impacts. Indeed, over the life of a project such as the one under consideration here, these other bodies may well have the greatest effect in minimizing a project's adverse effects if it does gain Cabinet approval. Determining when these processes are a reliable indicator that a project will not have significant adverse environmental effects is not a simple matter. It may be necessary to consider the nature of a regulatory regime itself, as regimes will vary widely in purpose and effect.

Notes and Questions

1. According to Russell J., there is a division of labour between a responsible authority (here the JRP) and the ultimate decision-maker. The integrity of the decision-making structure relied upon the responsible authority providing a proper evidentiary basis for the ultimate decision-maker. Do you agree with Russell J.'s articulation of the division of labour in federal EA? What relevance, if any, do you think this division of labour has on the level of deference that a reviewing court should give in a judicial review?

2. The following case is one in a long line of cases on the complex relationship between environmental assessment processes and the constitutional duty to consult Indigenous communities affected by proposed projects. The basic options are to try to integrate consultation into the assessment process, or to carry out the assessment and consultation separately. As you read the

judgment by the SCC in this case, consider the implications of this basic choice. What would happen if there was a clear and separate process of consultation, and Indigenous communities were invited to participate in the environmental assessment process without fear that their participation would affect their right to be consulted? Why do you think governments instead try to integrate assessment processes with consultation?

Clyde River (Hamlet) v. Petroleum Geo-Services Inc.
2017 SCC 40

KARAKATSANIS and BROWN JJ.: —

Introduction

This Court has on several occasions affirmed the role of the duty to consult in fostering reconciliation between Canada's Indigenous peoples and the Crown. In this appeal, and its companion *Chippewas of the Thames First Nation v. Enbridge Pipelines Inc.*, 2017 SCC 41, we consider the Crown's duty to consult with Indigenous peoples before an independent regulatory agency authorizes a project which could impact upon their rights. The Court's jurisprudence shows that the substance of the duty does not change when a regulatory agency holds final decision-making authority in respect of a project. While the Crown always owes the duty to consult, regulatory processes can partially or completely fulfill this duty.

The Hamlet of Clyde River lies on the northeast coast of Baffin Island, in Nunavut. The community is situated on a flood plain between Patricia Bay and the Arctic Cordillera. Most residents of Clyde River are Inuit, who rely on marine mammals for food and for their economic, cultural, and spiritual well-being. They have harvested marine mammals for generations. The bowhead whale, the narwhal, the ringed, bearded, and harp seals, and the polar bear are of particular importance to them. Under the *Nunavut Land Claims Agreement* (1993), the Inuit of Clyde River ceded all Aboriginal claims, rights, title, and interests in the Nunavut Settlement Area, including Clyde River, in exchange for defined treaty rights, including the right to harvest marine mammals.

In 2011, the respondents TGS-NOPEC Geophysical Company ASA, Multi Klient Invest As and Petroleum Geo-Services Inc. (the proponents) applied to the National Energy Board (NEB) to conduct offshore seismic testing for oil and gas resources. It is undisputed that this testing could negatively affect the harvesting rights of the Inuit of Clyde River. After a period of consultation among the project proponents, the NEB, and affected Inuit communities, the NEB granted the requested authorization.

While the Crown may rely on the NEB's process to fulfill its duty to consult, considering the importance of the established treaty rights at stake and the potential impact of the seismic testing on those rights, we agree with the appellants that the consultation and accommodation efforts in this case were inadequate. For the reasons set out below, we would therefore allow the appeal and quash the NEB's authorization.

Background

Legislative Framework

The *Canada Oil and Gas Operations Act*, R.S.C. 1985, c. O-7 (*COGOA*), aims, in part, to promote responsible exploration for and exploitation of oil and gas resources (s. 2.1). It applies to exploration and drilling for the production, conservation, processing, and transportation of oil and gas in certain designated areas, including Nunavut (s. 3). Engaging in such activities is prohibited without an operating licence under s. 5(1)(a) or an authorization under s. 5(1)(b).

The NEB is a federal administrative tribunal and regulatory agency established by the *National Energy Board Act*, R.S.C. 1985, c. N-7 (*NEB Act*). In this case, it is the final decision maker for issuing an authorization under s. 5(1)(b) of *COGOA*. The NEB has broad discretion to impose requirements for authorization under s. 5(4), and can ask parties to provide any information it deems necessary to comply with its statutory mandate (s. 5.31).

The Seismic Testing Authorization

In May 2011, the proponents applied to the NEB for an authorization under s. 5(1)(b) of *COGOA* to conduct seismic testing in Baffin Bay and Davis Strait, adjacent to the area where the Inuit have treaty rights to harvest marine mammals. The proposed testing contemplated towing airguns by ship through a project area. These airguns produce underwater sound waves, which are intended to find and measure underwater geological resources such as petroleum. The testing was to run from July through November, for five successive years.

The NEB launched an environmental assessment of the project.

Clyde River opposed the seismic testing, and filed a petition against it with the NEB in May 2011. In 2012, the proponents responded to requests for further information from the NEB. They held meetings in communities that would be affected by the testing, including Clyde River.

In April and May 2013, the NEB held meetings in Pond Inlet, Clyde River, Qikiqtarjuaq, and Iqaluit to collect comments from the public on the project. Representatives of the proponents attended these meetings. Community members asked basic questions about the effects of the survey on marine mammals in the region, but the proponents were unable to answer many of them. For example, in Pond Inlet, a community member asked the proponents which marine mammals would be affected by the survey. The proponents answered: "That's a very difficult question to answer because we're not the core experts" (A.R., vol. III, at p. 541). Similarly, in Clyde River, a community member asked how the testing would affect marine mammals. The proponents answered:

> . . . a lot of work has been done with seismic surveys in other places and a lot of that information is used in doing the environmental assessment, the document that has been submitted by the companies to the National Energy Board for the approval process. It has a section on, you know, marine mammals and the effects on marine mammals.

(A.R., vol. III, at p. 651)

These are but two examples of multiple instances of the proponents' failure to offer substantive answers to basic questions about the impacts of the proposed seismic testing. That failure led the NEB, in May 2013, to suspend its assessment. In August 2013, the proponents filed a 3,926-page document with the NEB, purporting to answer those questions. This document was posted on the NEB website and delivered to the hamlet offices. The vast majority of this document was not translated into Inuktitut. No further efforts were made to determine whether this document was accessible to the communities, and whether their questions were answered. After this document was filed, the NEB resumed its assessment.

Throughout the environmental assessment process, Clyde River and various Inuit organizations filed letters of comment with the NEB, noting the inadequacy of consultation and expressing concerns about the testing.

In April 2014, organizations representing the appellants and Inuit in other communities wrote to the Minister of Aboriginal Affairs and Northern Development and to the NEB, stating their view that the duty to consult had not been fulfilled in relation to the testing. This could be remedied, they said, by completing a strategic environmental assessment before authorizing any seismic testing. In May, the Nunavut Marine Council also wrote to the NEB, with a copy to the Minister, asking that any regulatory decisions affecting the Nunavut Settlement Area's marine environment be postponed until completion of the strategic environmental assessment. This assessment was necessary, in the Council's view, to understand the baseline conditions in the marine environment and to ensure that seismic tests are properly regulated.

In June 2014, the Minister responded to both letters, "disagree[ing] with the view that seismic exploration of the region should be put on hold until the completion of a strategic environmental assessment" (A.R., vol. IV, at p. 967). A Geophysical Operations Authorization letter from the NEB soon followed, advising that the environmental assessment report was completed and that the authorization had been granted.

In its environmental assessment report, the NEB discussed consultation with, and the participation of, Aboriginal groups in the NEB process. It concluded that the proponents "made sufficient efforts to consult with potentially-impacted Aboriginal groups and to address concerns raised" and that "Aboriginal groups had an adequate opportunity to participate in the NEB's [environmental assessment] process" (A.R., vol. I, at p. 24). It also determined that the testing could change the migration routes of marine mammals and increase their risk of mortality, thereby affecting traditional harvesting of marine mammals including bowhead whales and narwhals, which are both identified as being of "Special Concern" by the Committee on the Status of Endangered Wildlife in Canada (COSEWIC). The NEB concluded, however, that the testing was unlikely to cause significant adverse environmental effects given the mitigation measures that the proponents would implement.

The Judicial Review Proceedings

Clyde River applied to the Federal Court of Appeal for judicial review of the NEB's decision to grant the authorization. Dawson J.A. (Nadon and Boivin JJ.A.

concurring) found that the duty to consult had been triggered because the NEB could not grant the authorization without the minister's approval (or waiver of the requirement for approval) of a benefits plan for the project, pursuant to s. 5.2(2) of *COGOA* (2015 FCA 179, [2016] 3 F.C.R. 167). The Federal Court of Appeal characterized the degree of consultation owed in the circumstances as deep, as that concept was discussed in *Haida Nation v. British Columbia (Minister of Forests)*, 2004 SCC 73, [2004] 3 S.C.R. 511, at para. 44, and found that the Crown was entitled to rely on the NEB to undertake such consultation.

The Court of Appeal also concluded that the Crown's duty to consult had been satisfied by the nature and scope of the NEB's processes. The conditions upon which the authorization had been granted showed that the interests of the Inuit had been sufficiently considered and that further consultation would be expected to occur were the proposed testing to be followed by further development activities. In the circumstances, a strategic environmental assessment report was not required.

Analysis

The following issues arise in this appeal:

1. Can an NEB approval process trigger the duty to consult?
2. Can the Crown rely on the NEB's process to fulfill the duty to consult?
3. What is the NEB's role in considering Crown consultation before approval?
4. Was the consultation adequate in this case?

The Duty to Consult — General Principles

The duty to consult seeks to protect Aboriginal and treaty rights while furthering reconciliation between Indigenous peoples and the Crown (*Rio Tinto Alcan Inc. v. Carrier Sekani Tribal Council*, 2010 SCC 43, [2010] 2 S.C.R. 650, at para. 34). It has both a constitutional and a legal dimension (*R. v. Kapp*, 2008 SCC 41, [2008] 2 S.C.R. 483, at para. 6; *Carrier Sekani*, at para. 34). Its constitutional dimension is grounded in the honour of the Crown (*Kapp*, at para. 6). This principle is in turn enshrined in s. 35(1) of the *Constitution Act, 1982*, which recognizes and affirms existing Aboriginal and treaty rights (*Taku River Tlingit First Nation v. British Columbia (Project Assessment Director)*, 2004 SCC 74, [2004] 3 S.C.R. 550, at para. 24). And, as a legal obligation, it is based in the Crown's assumption of sovereignty over lands and resources formerly held by Indigenous peoples (*Haida*, at para. 53).

The content of the duty, once triggered, falls along a spectrum ranging from limited to deep consultation, depending upon the strength of the Aboriginal claim, and the seriousness of the potential impact on the right. Each case must be considered individually. Flexibility is required, as the depth of consultation required may change as the process advances and new information comes to light (*Haida*, at paras. 39 and 43-45).

This Court has affirmed that it is open to legislatures to empower regulatory bodies to play a role in fulfilling the Crown's duty to consult (*Carrier Sekani*, at para. 56; *Haida*, at para. 51). The appellants argue that a regulatory process alone cannot fulfill the duty to consult because at least some direct engagement between "the Crown" and the affected Indigenous community is necessary.

In our view, while the Crown may rely on steps undertaken by a regulatory agency to fulfill its duty to consult in whole or in part and, where appropriate, accommodate, the Crown always holds ultimate responsibility for ensuring consultation is adequate. Practically speaking, this does not mean that a minister of the Crown must give explicit consideration in every case to whether the duty to consult has been satisfied, or must directly participate in the process of consultation. Where the regulatory process being relied upon does not achieve adequate consultation or accommodation, the Crown must take further measures to meet its duty. This might entail filling any gaps on a case-by-case basis or more systemically through legislative or regulatory amendments (see e.g. *Ross River Dena Council v. Yukon*, 2012 YKCA 14, 358 D.L.R. (4th) 100). Or, it might require making submissions to the regulatory body, requesting reconsideration of a decision, or seeking a postponement in order to carry out further consultation in a separate process before the decision is rendered. And, if an affected Indigenous group is (like the Inuit of Nunavut) a party to a modern treaty and perceives the process to be deficient, it should, as it did here, request such direct Crown engagement in a timely manner (since parties to treaties are obliged to act diligently to advance their respective interests) (*Beckman v. Little Salmon/ Carmacks First Nation*, 2010 SCC 53, [2010] 3 S.C.R. 103, at para. 12).

Further, because the honour of the Crown requires a meaningful, good faith consultation process (*Haida*, at para. 41), where the Crown relies on the processes of a regulatory body to fulfill its duty in whole or in part, it should be made clear to affected Indigenous groups that the Crown is so relying. Guidance about the form of the consultation process should be provided so that Indigenous peoples know how consultation will be carried out to allow for their effective participation and, if necessary, to permit them to raise concerns with the proposed form of the consultations in a timely manner.

Above all, and irrespective of the process by which consultation is undertaken, any decision affecting Aboriginal or treaty rights made on the basis of inadequate consultation will not be in compliance with the duty to consult, which is a constitutional imperative. Where challenged, it should be quashed on judicial review. That said, judicial review is no substitute for adequate consultation. True reconciliation is rarely, if ever, achieved in courtrooms. Judicial remedies may seek to undo past infringements of Aboriginal and treaty rights, but adequate Crown consultation *before* project approval is always preferable to after-the-fact judicial remonstration following an adversarial process. Consultation is, after all, "[c]oncerned with an ethic of ongoing relationships" (*Carrier Sekani*, at para. 38, quoting D. G. Newman, *The Duty to Consult: New Relationships with Aboriginal Peoples* (2009), at p. 21). As the Court noted in *Haida*, "[w]hile Aboriginal claims can be and are pursued through litigation, negotiation is a preferable way of reconciling state and Aboriginal interests" (para. 14). No one benefits — not project proponents, not Indigenous peoples, and not non-Indigenous members of affected communities — when projects are prematurely approved only to be subjected to litigation.

Can an NEB Approval Process Trigger the Duty to Consult?

The duty to consult is triggered when the Crown has actual or constructive knowledge of a potential Aboriginal claim or Aboriginal or treaty rights that might be adversely affected by Crown conduct (*Haida*, at para. 35; *Carrier Sekani*, at para. 31). Crown conduct which would trigger the duty is not restricted to the exercise by or on behalf of the Crown of statutory powers or of the royal prerogative, nor is it limited to decisions that have an immediate impact on lands and resources. The concern is for adverse impacts, however made, upon Aboriginal and treaty rights and, indeed, a goal of consultation is to identify, minimize and address adverse impacts where possible (*Carrier Sekani*, at paras. 45-46).

In this appeal, all parties agreed that the Crown's duty to consult was triggered, although agreement on *just what* Crown conduct triggered the duty has proven elusive. The Federal Court of Appeal saw the trigger in *COGOA*'s requirement for ministerial approval (or waiver of the requirement for approval) of a benefits plan for the testing. In the companion appeal of *Chippewas of the Thames*, the majority of the Federal Court of Appeal concluded that it was not necessary to decide whether the duty to consult was triggered since the Crown was not a party before the NEB, but suggested the only Crown action involved might have been the 1959 enactment of the *NEB Act* (*Chippewas of the Thames First Nation v. Enbridge Pipelines Inc.*, 2015 FCA 222, [2016] 3 F.C.R. 96). In short, the Federal Court of Appeal in both cases was of the view that only action by a minister of the Crown or a government department, or a Crown corporation, can constitute Crown conduct triggering the duty to consult. And, before this Court in *Chippewas of the Thames*, the Attorney General of Canada argued that the duty was triggered by the NEB's approval of the pipeline project, because it was state action with the potential to affect Aboriginal or treaty rights.

Contrary to the Federal Court of Appeal's conclusions on this point, we agree that the NEB's approval process, in this case, as in *Chippewas of the Thames*, triggered the duty to consult.

It bears reiterating that the duty to consult is owed by the Crown. In one sense, the "Crown" refers to the personification in Her Majesty of the Canadian state in exercising the prerogatives and privileges reserved to it. The Crown also, however, denotes the sovereign in the exercise of her formal legislative role (in assenting, refusing assent to, or reserving legislative or parliamentary bills), and as the head of executive authority (*McAteer v. Canada (Attorney General)*, 2014 ONCA 578, 121 O.R. (3d) 1, at para. 51; P. W. Hogg, P. J. Monahan and W. K. Wright, *Liability of the Crown* (4th ed. 2011), at pp. 11-12; but see *Carrier Sekani*, at para. 44). For this reason, the term "Crown" is commonly used to symbolize and denote executive power. This was described by Lord Simon of Glaisdale in *Town Investments Ltd. v. Department of the Environment*, [1978] A.C. 359 (H.L.), at p. 397:

> The crown as an object is a piece of jewelled headgear under guard at the Tower of London. But it symbolises the powers of government which were formerly wielded by the wearer of the crown; so that by the 13th century crimes were committed not only against the king's peace but also against "his crown and dignity": *Pollock and Maitland, History of English Law*, 2nd ed. (1898), vol. I, p. 525. The term "the Crown" is therefore used in constitutional law to denote the collection of such of

those powers as remain extant (the royal prerogative), together with such other powers as have been expressly conferred by statute on "the Crown."

By this understanding, the NEB is not, strictly speaking, "the Crown". Nor is it, strictly speaking, an agent of the Crown, since — as the NEB operates independently of the Crown's ministers — no relationship of control exists between them (Hogg, Monahan and Wright, at p. 465). As a statutory body holding responsibility under s. 5(1)(b) of *COGOA*, however, the NEB acts on behalf of the Crown when making a final decision on a project application. Put plainly, once it is accepted that a regulatory agency exists to exercise executive power as authorized by legislatures, any distinction between its actions and Crown action quickly falls away. In this context, the NEB is the vehicle through which the Crown acts. Hence this Court's interchangeable references in *Carrier Sekani* to "government action" and "Crown conduct" (paras. 42-44). It therefore does not matter whether the final decision maker on a resource project is Cabinet or the NEB. In either case, the decision constitutes Crown action that may trigger the duty to consult. As Rennie J.A. said in dissent at the Federal Court of Appeal in *Chippewas of the Thames*, "[t]he duty, like the honour of the Crown, does not evaporate simply because a final decision has been made by a tribunal established by Parliament, as opposed to Cabinet" (para. 105). The action of the NEB, taken in furtherance of its statutory powers under s. 5(1)(b) of *COGOA* to make final decisions respecting such testing as was proposed here, clearly constitutes Crown action.

Can the Crown Rely on the NEB's Process to Fulfill the Duty to Consult?

As we have said, while ultimate responsibility for ensuring the adequacy of consultation remains with the Crown, the Crown may rely on steps undertaken by a regulatory agency to fulfill the duty to consult. Whether, however, the Crown is capable of doing so, in whole or in part, depends on whether the agency's statutory duties and powers enable it to do what the duty requires in the particular circumstances (*Carrier Sekani*, at paras. 55 and 60). In the NEB's case, therefore, the question is whether the NEB is able, to the extent it is being relied on, to provide an appropriate level of consultation and, where necessary, accommodation to the Inuit of Clyde River in respect of the proposed testing.

We note that the NEB and *COGOA* each predate judicial recognition of the duty to consult. However, given the flexible nature of the duty, a process that was originally designed for a different purpose may be relied on by the Crown so long as it affords an appropriate level of consultation to the affected Indigenous group (*Beckman*, at para. 39; *Taku River*, at para. 22). Under *COGOA*, the NEB has a significant array of powers that permit extensive consultation. It may conduct hearings, and has broad discretion to make orders or elicit information in furtherance of *COGOA* and the public interest (ss. 5.331, 5.31(1) and 5.32). It can also require studies to be undertaken and impose preconditions to approval (s. 5(4)). In the case of designated projects, it can also (as here) conduct environmental assessments, and establish participant funding programs to facilitate public participation (s. 5.002).

COGOA also grants the NEB broad powers to accommodate the concerns of Indigenous groups where necessary. The NEB can attach any terms and conditions it sees fit to an authorization issued under s. 5(1)(b), and can make such authorization contingent on their performance (ss. 5(4) and 5.36(1)). Most importantly, the NEB may require accommodation by exercising its discretion to deny an authorization or by reserving its decision pending further proceedings (ss. 5(1)(b), 5(5) and 5.36(2)).

The NEB has also developed considerable institutional expertise, both in conducting consultations and in assessing the environmental impacts of proposed projects. Where the effects of a proposed project on Aboriginal or treaty rights substantially overlap with the project's potential environmental impact, the NEB is well situated to oversee consultations which seek to address these effects, and to use its technical expertise to assess what forms of accommodation might be available.

In sum, the NEB has (1) the procedural powers necessary to implement consultation; and (2) the remedial powers to, where necessary, accommodate affected Aboriginal claims, or Aboriginal and treaty rights. Its process can therefore be relied on by the Crown to completely or partially fulfill the Crown's duty to consult. Whether the NEB's process did so in this case, we consider below.

What Is the NEB's Role in Considering Crown Consultation Before Approval?

The appellants argue that, as a tribunal empowered to decide questions of law, the NEB *must* exercise its decision-making authority in accordance with s. 35(1) of the *Constitution Act, 1982* by evaluating the adequacy of consultation before issuing an authorization for seismic testing. In contrast, the proponents submit that there is no basis in this Court's jurisprudence for imposing this obligation on the NEB. Although the Attorney General of Canada agrees with the appellants that the NEB has the legal capacity to decide constitutional questions when doing so is necessary to its decision-making powers, she argues that the NEB's environmental assessment decision in this case appropriately considered the adequacy of the proponents' consultation efforts.

Generally, a tribunal empowered to consider questions of law must determine whether such consultation was constitutionally sufficient if the issue is properly raised. The power of a tribunal "to decide questions of law implies a power to decide constitutional issues that are properly before it, absent a clear demonstration that the legislature intended to exclude such jurisdiction from the tribunal's power" (*Carrier Sekani*, at para. 69). Regulatory agencies with the authority to decide questions of law have both the duty and authority to apply the Constitution, unless the authority to decide the constitutional issue has been clearly withdrawn (*R. v. Conway*, 2010 SCC 22, [2010] 1 S.C.R. 765, at para. 77). It follows that they must ensure their decisions comply with s. 35 of the *Constitution Act, 1982* (*Carrier Sekani*, at para. 72).

The NEB has broad powers under both the *NEB Act* and *COGOA* to hear and determine all relevant matters of fact and law (*NEB Act*, s. 12(2); *COGOA*, s. 5.31(2)). No provision in either statute suggests an intention to withhold from the NEB the power to decide the adequacy of consultation. And, in *Quebec (Attorney General) v. Canada (National Energy Board)*, [1994] 1 S.C.R. 159, this Court concluded that NEB decisions must conform to s. 35(1) of the *Constitution*

Act, 1982. It follows that the NEB can determine whether the Crown's duty to consult has been fulfilled.

We note that the majority at the Federal Court of Appeal in *Chippewas of the Thames* considered that this issue was not properly before the NEB. It distinguished *Carrier Sekani* on the basis that the Crown was not a party to the NEB hearing in *Chippewas of the Thames,* while the Crown (in the form of BC Hydro, a Crown corporation) was a party in the utilities commission proceedings in *Carrier Sekani.* Based on the authority of *Standing Buffalo Dakota First Nation v. Enbridge Pipelines Inc.,* 2009 FCA 308, [2010] 4 F.C.R. 500, the majority of the Federal Court of Appeal in *Chippewas of the Thames* reasoned that the NEB is not required to evaluate whether the Crown's duty to consult had been triggered (or whether it was satisfied) before granting a resource project authorization, except where the Crown is a party before the NEB.

The difficulty with this view, however, is that — as we have explained — action taken by the NEB in furtherance of its powers under s. 5(1)(b) of *COGOA* to make final decisions is *itself* Crown conduct which triggers the duty to consult. Nor, respectfully, can we agree with the majority of the Federal Court of Appeal in *Chippewas of the Thames* that an NEB decision will comply with s. 35(1) of the *Constitution Act, 1982* so long as the NEB ensures the proponents engage in a "dialogue" with potentially affected Indigenous groups (para. 62). If the Crown's duty to consult has been triggered, a decision maker may only proceed to approve a project if Crown consultation is adequate. Although in many cases the Crown will be able to rely on the NEB's processes as meeting the duty to consult, because the NEB is the final decision maker, the key question is whether the duty is fulfilled prior to project approval (*Haida,* at para. 67). Accordingly, where the Crown's duty to consult an affected Indigenous group with respect to a project under *COGOA* remains unfulfilled, the NEB must withhold project approval. And, where the NEB fails to do so, its approval decision should (as we have already said) be quashed on judicial review, since the duty to consult must be fulfilled prior to the action that could adversely affect the right in question (*Tsilhqot'in Nation v. British Columbia,* 2014 SCC 44, [2014] 2 S.C.R. 257, at para. 78).

Some commentators have suggested that the NEB, in view of its mandate to decide issues in the public interest, cannot effectively account for Aboriginal and treaty rights and assess the Crown's duty to consult (see R. Freedman and S. Hansen, "Aboriginal Rights vs. The Public Interest", prepared for Pacific Business & Law Institute Conference, Vancouver, B.C. (February 26-27, 2009) (online), at pp. 4 and 14). We do not, however, see the public interest and the duty to consult as operating in conflict. As this Court explained in *Carrier Sekani,* the duty to consult, being a constitutional imperative, gives rise to a special public interest that supersedes other concerns typically considered by tribunals tasked with assessing the public interest (para. 70). A project authorization that breaches the constitutionally protected rights of Indigenous peoples cannot serve the public interest (*ibid.*).

This leaves the question of what a regulatory agency must do where the adequacy of Crown consultation is raised before it. When affected Indigenous groups have squarely raised concerns about Crown consultation with the NEB, the NEB must usually address those concerns in reasons, particularly in respect of project applications requiring deep consultation. Engagement of the honour of the Crown does not predispose a certain outcome, but promotes reconciliation by imposing obligations on the manner and approach of government (*Haida*, at paras. 49 and 63). Written reasons foster reconciliation by showing affected Indigenous peoples that their rights were considered and addressed (*Haida*, at para. 44). Reasons are "a sign of respect [which] displays the requisite comity and courtesy becoming the Crown as Sovereign toward a prior occupying nation" (*Kainaiwa/Blood Tribe v. Alberta (Energy)*, 2017 ABQB 107, at para. 117 (CanLII)). Written reasons also promote better decision making (*Baker v. Canada (Minister of Citizenship and Immigration)*, [1999] 2 S.C.R. 817, at para. 39).

This does not mean, however, that the NEB is always required to review the adequacy of Crown consultation by applying a formulaic "*Haida* analysis", as the appellants suggest. Nor will explicit reasons be required in every case. The degree of consideration that is appropriate will depend on the circumstances of each case. But where deep consultation is required and the affected Indigenous peoples have made their concerns known, the honour of the Crown will usually oblige the NEB, where its approval process triggers the duty to consult, to explain how it considered and addressed these concerns.

Was the Consultation Adequate in This Case?

The Crown acknowledges that deep consultation was required in this case, and we agree. As this Court explained in *Haida*, deep consultation is required "where a strong *prima facie* case for the claim is established, the right and potential infringement is of high significance to the Aboriginal peoples, and the risk of non-compensable damage is high" (para. 44). Here, the appellants had *established treaty rights* to hunt and harvest marine mammals. These rights were acknowledged at the Federal Court of Appeal as being extremely important to the appellants for their economic, cultural, and spiritual well-being (para. 2). Jerry Natanine, the former mayor of Clyde River, explained that hunting marine mammals "provides us with nutritious food; enables us to take part in practices we have maintained for generations; and enables us to maintain close relationships with each other through the sharing of what we call 'country food'" (A.R., vol. II, at p. 197). The importance of these rights was also recently recognized by the Nunavut Court of Justice:

> The Inuit right which is of concern in this matter is the right to harvest marine mammals. Many Inuit in Nunavut rely on country food for the majority of their diet. Food costs are very high and many would be unable to purchase food to replace country food if country food were unavailable. Country food is recognized as being of higher nutritional value than purchased food. But the inability to harvest marine mammals would impact more than ... just the diet of Inuit. The cultural tradition of sharing country food with others in the community would be lost. The opportunity to make traditional clothing would be impacted. The opportunity to participate in the hunt, an activity which is fundamental to being Inuk, would be lost. The Inuit right which is at stake is of high significance. This suggests a significant level of consultation and accommodation is required.

> (*Qikiqtani Inuit Assn. v. Canada (Minister of Natural Resources)*, 2010 NUCJ 12, 54 C.E.L.R. (3d) 263, at para. 25)

The risks posed by the proposed testing to these treaty rights were also high. The NEB's environmental assessment concluded that the project could increase the mortality risk of marine mammals, cause permanent hearing damage, and change their migration routes, thereby affecting traditional resource use. Given the importance of the rights at stake, the significance of the potential impact, and the risk of non-compensable damage, the duty owed in this case falls at the highest end of the spectrum.

Bearing this in mind, the consultation that occurred here fell short in several respects. First, the inquiry was misdirected. While the NEB found that the proposed testing was not likely to cause significant adverse environmental effects, and that any effects on traditional resource use could be addressed by mitigation measures, the consultative inquiry is not properly into environmental effects *per se*. Rather, it inquires into the impact on the *right*. No consideration was given in the NEB's environmental assessment to the source — in a treaty — of the appellants' rights to harvest marine mammals, nor to the impact of the proposed testing on those rights.

Furthermore, although the Crown relies on the processes of the NEB as fulfilling its duty to consult, that was not made clear to the Inuit. The significance of the process was not adequately explained to them.

Finally, and most importantly, the process provided by the NEB did not fulfill the Crown's duty to conduct deep consultation. Deep consultation "may entail the opportunity to make submissions for consideration, formal participation in the decision-making process, and provision of written reasons to show that Aboriginal concerns were considered and to reveal the impact they had on the decision" (*Haida*, at para. 44). Despite the NEB's broad powers under *COGOA* to afford those advantages, limited opportunities for participation and consultation were made available to the appellants. Unlike many NEB proceedings, including the proceedings in *Chippewas of the Thames*, there were no oral hearings. Although the appellants submitted scientific evidence to the NEB, this was done without participant funding. Again, this stands in contrast to *Chippewas of the Thames*, where the consultation process was far more robust. In that case, the NEB held oral hearings, the appellants received funding to participate in the hearings, and they had the opportunity to present evidence and a final argument. While these procedural protections are characteristic of an adversarial process, they may be required for meaningful consultation (*Haida*, at para. 41) and do not transform its underlying objective: fostering reconciliation by promoting an ongoing relationship (*Carrier Sekani*, at para. 38).

The consultation in this case also stands in contrast to *Taku River* where, despite its entitlement to consultation falling only at the midrange of the spectrum (para. 32), the Taku River Tlingit First Nation, with financial assistance (para. 37), fully participated in the assessment process as a member of the project committee, which was "the primary engine driving the assessment process" (paras. 3, 8 and 40).

While these procedural safeguards are not always necessary, their absence in this case significantly impaired the quality of consultation. Although the appellants had the opportunity to question the proponents about the project during the NEB meetings in the spring of 2013, the proponents were unable to answer many questions, including basic questions about the effect of the proposed testing on marine mammals. The proponents did eventually respond to these questions; however, they did so in a 3,926 page document which they submitted to the NEB. This document was posted on the NEB website and delivered to the hamlet offices in Pond Inlet, Clyde River, Qikiqtajuak and Iqaluit. Internet speed is slow in Nunavut, however, and bandwidth is expensive. The former mayor of Clyde River deposed that he was unable to download this document because it was too large. Furthermore, only a fraction of this enormous document was translated into Inuktitut. To put it mildly, furnishing answers to questions that went to the heart of the treaty rights at stake in the form of a practically inaccessible document dump months after the questions were initially asked in person is not true consultation. " '[C]onsultation' in its least technical definition is talking together for mutual understanding" (T. Isaac and A. Knox, "The Crown's Duty to Consult Aboriginal People" (2003), 41 *Alta. L. Rev.* 49, at p. 61). No mutual understanding on the core issues — the potential impact on treaty rights, and possible accommodations — could possibly have emerged from what occurred here.

The fruits of the Inuit's limited participation in the assessment process here are plain in considering the accommodations recorded by the NEB's environmental assessment report. It noted changes made to the project as a result of consultation, such as a commitment to ongoing consultation, the placement of community liaison officers in affected communities, and the design of an Inuit Qaujimajatuqangit (Inuit traditional knowledge) study. The proponents also committed to installing passive acoustic monitoring on the ship to be used in the proposed testing to avoid collisions with marine mammals.

These changes were, however, insignificant concessions in light of the potential impairment of the Inuit's treaty rights. Further, passive acoustic monitoring was no concession at all, since it is a requirement of the Statement of Canadian Practice With Respect to the Mitigation of Seismic Sound in the Marine Environment which provides "minimum standards, which will apply in all non-ice covered marine waters in Canada" (A.R., vol. I, at p. 40), and which would be included in virtually all seismic testing projects. None of these putative concessions, nor the NEB's reasons themselves, gave the Inuit any reasonable assurance that their constitutionally protected treaty rights were considered as *rights*, rather than as an afterthought to the assessment of environmental concerns.

The consultation process here was, in view of the Inuit's established treaty rights and the risk posed by the proposed testing to those rights, significantly flawed. Had the appellants had the resources to submit their own scientific evidence, and the opportunity to test the evidence of the proponents, the result of the environmental assessment could have been very different. Nor were the Inuit given meaningful responses to their questions regarding the impact of the testing on marine life. While the NEB considered potential impacts of the project on marine mammals and on Inuit traditional resource use, its report does not acknowledge, or even mention, the Inuit treaty rights to harvest wildlife in the Nunavut Settlement Area, or that deep consultation was required.

Conclusion

For the foregoing reasons, we conclude that the Crown breached its duty to consult the appellants in respect of the proposed testing. We would allow the appeal with costs to the appellants, and quash the NEB's authorization.

Notes and Questions

1. There has been an ongoing debate about the relationship between the duty to consult and environmental assessment processes. Among the issues that have informed this debate are the constitutional rights of Indigenous communities, their rights under the *United Nations Declaration on the Rights of Indigenous Peoples* (UNDRIP), the value that affected Indigenous communities bring to the assessment process, language and capacity barriers to their effective participation, a disconnect between traditional knowledge and western science, and a desire to improve the efficiency of assessment and regulatory processes for new projects and activities.

2. Among the options for an appropriate relationship between the assessment process, the regulatory process, and the duty to consult are the following: (i) integrating Indigenous consultations into the assessment process; (ii) a sequential approach that places the consultations after the assessment is completed but before the project decision is made; and (iii) a parallel process whereby consultations are carried out separate from but in parallel to the assessment process. Which approach would be most likely to avoid the issues that led to this court case? Which would lead to the most efficient process for approving new projects? Which would be most effective and fair to affected Indigenous communities?

3. In Chapter 3, in *Tsleil-Waututh Nation v. Canada (Attorney General)*, 2018 FCA 153, additional reasons 2018 FCA 155, we considered the approach of the Federal Court of Appeal to the duty to consult. How does the Federal Court of Appeal's approach to the relationship between EA and the duty to consult compare to the approach taken by the Supreme Court in *Clyde River*?

References and Further Readings

Neil Craik, "Process and Reconciliation: Integrating the Duty to Consult with Environmental Assessment" (2016) 53:2 Osgoode Hall L.J. 632

Jerry DeMarco, "Developments in Environmental Law: The 2009-2010 Term — Two Decisions on Environmental Assessment" (2010) 52:2 S.C.L.R. 247

Meinhard Doelle & Rebecca Critchley, "The Role of Strategic Environmental Assessments in Improving the Governance of Emerging New Industries: A Case Study of Wind Developments in Nova Scotia" (2015) 11:1 McGill Intl. J. Sustainable Development L. & Policy 87

Shaun Fluker & Nitin Kumar Srivastava, "Public Participation in Federal Environmental Assessment under the Canadian Environmental Assessment Act 2012: Assessing the Impact of 'Directly Affected'" (2016) 29 J. Envtl. L. & Prac. 65

Robert Gibson, Meinhard Doelle & John Sinclair, "Fulfilling the Promise: Basic Components of Next Generation Environmental Assessment" (2016) 29 J. Envtl. L. & Prac. 257

Anna Johnston, "Imagining EA 2.0: Outcomes of the 2016 Federal Environmental Assessment Reform Summit" (2016) 30 J. Envtl. L. & Prac. 1

Jason MacLean, "Striking at the Root Problem of Canadian Environmental Law: Identifying and Escaping Regulatory Capture" (2016) 29 J. Envtl. L. & Prac. 111

Rod Northey, "Fading Role of Alternatives in Federal Environmental Assessment" (2016) 29 J. Envtl. L. & Prac. 41

Martin Olszynski, "Environmental Assessment as Planning and Disclosure Tool: Greenpeace Canada v. Canada (A.G.)" (2015) 38 Dalhousie L.J. 207

Martin Olszynski, "Environmental Monitoring and Ecosystem Management in the Oil Sands: Spaceship Earth or Escort Tugboat?" (2014) 10:1 McGill Intl. J. Sustainable Development L. & Policy

Jocelyn Stacey, "The Environmental, Democratic, and Rule-of-Law Implications of Harper's Environmental Assessment Legacy" (2016) 2:21 Rev. Const. Stud. 165

Chapter 8

Parks and Protected Areas

Introduction

Parks and protected areas play both a central and a rapidly evolving role in Canadian environmental law and policy. Canadians are deservedly proud of their parks system that, especially over the last half century, has grown and evolved significantly. At the same time, Canadian parks and broader networks of protected areas are under growing pressure to deliver an ever-broadening range of values as species loss, climate change and environmental degradation across the broader landscape escalate. As a result, it is increasingly recognized that greater attention needs to be given to the role of parks and protected areas in mitigating wider landscape-level changes. This is especially true, as we will see, in the marine environment. Another critical challenge is to identify strategies to protect the marine and terrestrial environments that are consistent with the constitutional imperative to recognize and respect First Nations rights and title; in the past, this goal has been seldom achieved or even fully appreciated.

This chapter is in four Parts. In Part I, we offer a snapshot of developments in, and current status of, parks and protected areas in Canada. We then consider, in Part II, the values that parks and protected areas promote, how those values may be quantified or conceptualized, and the respective roles of the provincial and federal governments as parks stewards. In Part III, we address four key issues in protected areas law and policy that are of particular interest from a legal perspective. These include:

- The challenges associated with fulfilling Canada's international commitments to complete a marine protected area system;
- Legal and policy issues relating to the need for greater integration within our protected areas network to, among other things, enhance species protection;
- The unresolved tension between competing "use" and "preservation" mandates under the *Canada National Parks Act* (CNPA) and the role of "ecological integrity" in Parks Canada decision-making; and
- The implications of recognizing and respecting Indigenous rights and interests for the management and expansion of parks and protected areas.

Finally, in Part IV, we reflect on two more "prospective" issues of relevance to protected areas law and policy moving forward: the potential role of the public trust doctrine as a means of enhancing protection outcomes within our parks system and the possibilities for law reform that may exist, drawing on new parks legislation recently enacted by the province of Ontario.

Part I — History and Overview of
Parks and Protected Areas in Canada

Canadian Parks Council,
Canadian Protected Areas Status Report 2000–2005
Executive Summary,
online: < http://www.parks-parcs.ca/english/cpc/status.php >

Since Canada's first park was created in 1872, almost 100 million hectares of terrestrial protected areas have been set aside, an amount equal to 10% of this country's total land mass. Over 3 million hectares or 0.5% of Canada's oceans have been secured as marine protected areas. These protected areas play a central role in preserving our country's greatest asset — our natural capital. They also provide a variety of social and economic benefits to Canadians by creating both direct and tourism-based employment opportunities for many communities. In addition, protected areas offer world-class opportunities for nature appreciation, learning, research, spiritual enrichment and outdoor recreation, with resulting benefits to personal health and national identity. Protected areas are an important means of demonstrating Canada's commitment to a sustainable environment, society and economy. Finally, maintaining a healthy and dynamic protected areas system responds to recent polling which consistently indicates that Canadians rank protection of the environment next to health and education as priority issues.

Canadians can be proud of the progress that has been achieved over the last five years to preserve and manage the wealth of natural capital within the country's protected areas networks. Canada's protected areas family has grown by roughly 19% since Parks Ministers last gathered in Iqaluit in 2000. All governments have contributed to this progress, and have strengthened their respective protected areas programs. Over the last five years progress has included:

- developing and implementing protected areas strategies;
- increasing management effectiveness of protected areas;
- updating protected areas legislation; and
- allocating increased resources to protected areas programs.

Also since 2000, five important policy advances and shifts in industry practice promise to provide significant new opportunities to safeguard Canada's natural capital:

- Integrated landscape and oceans management is emerging in Canada as a means of ensuring that resource allocation decisions are made in concert with conservation planning.

- Leading resource industries are increasingly becoming partners and advocates for innovative conservation solutions as a proactive means to enhance competitiveness and demonstrate corporate social responsibility, while providing greater investment certainty.

- Land claim settlements and other cooperative agreements are providing means to preserve lands of ecological and cultural importance, that in turn provide economic and social benefits to Aboriginal communities.

- The federal government has initiated the Oceans Action Plan, a roadmap to integrated management for five Large Oceans Management Areas, and has adopted a government wide strategy to establish a federal marine protected area network.

- Canada has committed to the Convention on Biological Diversity's Programme of Work on Protected Areas, with an overall international objective of completing comprehensive global networks of terrestrial and marine protected areas by 2010 and 2012 respectively.

Philip Dearden,
"Progress and Problems in Canada's Protected Areas:
Overview of Progress, Chronic Issues and Emerging
Challenges in the Early 21st Century"
Paper commissioned for the Canadian Parks for Tomorrow:
40th Anniversary Conference, University of Calgary,
May 8 to 11, 2008, online: < http://parkscanadahistory.
com/publications/2008-conference/dearden.pdf >

[...] in 1992 Canada's federal, provincial and territorial Ministers of Environment, Parks and Wildlife signed *A Statement of Commitment to Complete Canada's Network of Protected Areas.* Terrestrial systems were to be completed by 2000 whereas marine designation was to be "accelerated". Despite impressive growth, Canada is still far from meeting these commitments. [...] In terms of overall protection of Canada's ecoregions, 29% are provided a high level of protection (ie over 12% of their area), 12.4% moderate protection (6 to 12%), 41.9% low protection (< 6%) and 16.6% have no protected areas (Environment Canada 2006).

Parks Canada's performance targets for creating and expanding new parks were to increase the number of represented terrestrial regions from 25 in March 2003 to 34 by March 2008, and increase the number of represented marine regions from two in March 2003 to eight by March 2008 (Parks Canada 2007). Neither of these were met and currently 28 terrestrial regions are represented by national parks. Progress was made on several candidate national parks but funding limitations and the complicated nature of the park establishment process resulted in a reduction of performance expectation for representation to 30 terrestrial regions represented by March 2008.

The marine target was also not met. Currently 2 of 29 marine regions are represented, but these are from existing areas and not new acquisitions protected under the NMCA Act. As a result, the goal was reduced to 4 of 29 in the 2007/ 2008 Corporate Plan, but as yet no areas have been designated, although progress is being made on several areas. Under 0.5% of Canada's marine area is set aside in protective designation and Canada ranks 70th globally in terms of the percentage of oceans protected (Environment Canada 2006). Projections suggest that Canada will optimistically achieve perhaps 33% of its international target goal by 2012 (Roff and Dearden 2007). [...]

There have also been major increases at the provincial level. In 1968, Ontario had 90 regulated protected areas totalling 1.6% of the province by area. Currently, Ontario has 632 protected areas totalling over 9.4 million ha, 8.7% of the province (Davis, pers com). Nova Scotia in 2007 passed the *Environmental Goals and Sustainable Prosperity Act* requiring the province to protect 12% of its terrestrial area by 2015 (Government of Nova Scotia 2007). In BC the area of parkland doubled between 1977 and 2005 and now totals over 12 million ha. BC is the only jurisdiction to accomplish the 12% target set by the WCED (1987). However, no provincial government has completed the 1992 Statement of Commitment to complete a representative network of protected areas (Environment Canada 2006).

To date, about 10% of Canada's terrestrial area has been awarded protective designation, well short of the average 14.6% protected by OECD countries (Environment Canada 2006). However, 95% of Canada's terrestrial protected areas fall within IUCN categories I–IV and hence have a strong protective mandate. Amongst OECD countries Canada ranks 16th out of 30 in terms of the proportion of land protected (the US, for example protects almost 25% compared with our 10%), yet ranks 4th in terms of proportion of land with strong protection (IUCN I–IV). Furthermore, Canada has some two-thirds of its protected area within a small number of sites that are in excess of 300,000 ha in size. Few countries have the ability to preserve such large intact landscapes.

The question of progress in terms of establishing a greater extent of protected area in Canada is clearly answered in the affirmative. The protected area system has grown enormously within the last forty years. Parks Canada is inching towards completion of the system plan and many provincial jurisdictions have set aside significant areas under their jurisdiction as PAs. However, much remains to be done. Canada is signatory to the UN Convention on Biological Diversity which calls for "the establishment and maintenance by 2010 for terrestrial and by 2012 for marine areas of comprehensive, effectively managed, and ecologically representative national and regional systems of protected areas [...]". Canada will not be able to meet these international commitments for quite some time after the target dates. The marine system is in its infancy and getting off to a very slow and underfunded start. A significant number of the ecoregions of Canada still remain unprotected. Canada is not a world leader in term of the proportion of area set aside, yet we have some of the largest and wildest PAs on Earth. Progress has undoubtedly been made, but much remains to be done.

Part II — The Role of Parks and Protected Areas

Philip Dearden & Rick Rollins,
"Parks and Protected Areas in Canada"

in P. Dearden & R. Rollins, eds., *Parks and Protected Areas in Canada:
Planning and Management*, 3rd ed. (Oxford University Press, 2009)

Protected Area Values

We expect protected areas to play a variety of roles in the landscape. These roles represent the values that we wish to see maintained within the landscape that, without protection, would not be able to withstand market forces. That is why they are protected. These values [may be] depict[ed] as [...] different locations and institutions in a city. The purpose of [this metaphor] [...] is to illustrate that PAs are not 'single use' areas, any more than all the functions of specific urban locations could be united into one, and to illustrate the diversity of values represented in PAs.

- *Art gallery*: Just as people visit an art gallery for aesthetic reasons, many parks were designated for their scenic beauty. When Banff was first established, Canadian Pacific Railway President, William Van Horne declared that 'since we can't export the scenery we shall have to import the tourists' and appreciation of scenery is still a major reason why people visit parks.

- *Zoo*: Parks are usually easy places to watch wildlife in relatively natural surroundings. Park wildlife, at least in the national parks, is protected from hunting, and not, therefore, as shy of humans as wildlife outside parks.

- *Playground*: Parks provide excellent recreational settings for many outdoor pursuits and provision of recreational opportunities has been one of the main functions of parks over the years. However, in keeping with the quote from the first Commissioner of National Parks, J.B. Harkin, park recreation should be thought of in a more profound sense of 're-creation' of self, rather than merely playing games.

- *Movie theatre*: Like a movie, parks are able to transport us into a different setting from our everyday existence. We go there to do different things than we would normally do. This is one of the arguments against having golf courses in our parks. Golf might be a fine recreational pursuit but it is not dependent upon being in a park to play it and, furthermore, it introduces everyday activities into the park environment at the cost of discovering new activities that are dependent upon a park environment. An excellent treatise on this topic, is *Mountains Without Handrails*, (Sax, 1980)

- *Cathedral*: Many people derive spiritual fulfillment from nature, just as others go to human-built structures, such as churches, temples, and mosques. Such sites, irrespective of denomination, help us appreciate the existence of forces more powerful than ourselves and remind us that humility is a virtue.

- *Factory*: The first national parks in Canada were designated with the idea of generating income through tourism. Since these early beginnings, the economic role of parks has been recognized, although it is a controversial one due to the potential conflict with other roles. A study by Eagles et al. (2000) on national parks, wildlife areas and provincial parks in Canada calculated total daily economic impact of between $120.47 to $187.69 per park visitor. Overall the economic impact was between $13.9 and $21.6 billion dollars for the year. Although these totals are high, of perhaps greater significance is the distribution of the benefits. As Walton and Simon (2003) point out in poor, northern, Aboriginal communities, income potential is extremely limited and the factory role of parks takes on great significance, perhaps requiring a different perspective on park policies than those extant in the south.

- *Museum*: Parks protect the landscape as it might have been when European colonists first arrived in North America. As such, parks act as museums to remind us of these conditions. Nash (1967), in his well-known history of the wilderness movement, describes this as a main reason behind the early growth of the parks' movement in the US, although it is certainly a less prominent motivation now. These museums also serve a valuable ecological function as they provide important areas against which to measure ecological change in the rest of the landscape, often known as the *benchmark* role. Davis et al. (2006) provide a review of this role and a Canadian example of a comparative monitoring system, Environment Canada's Ecological Monitoring and Assessment Network (EMAN) is described in more detail by Craig *et al.* (2003).

- *Bank*: Parks are places in which we store and protect our ecological capital, including threatened and endangered species. From these accounts we can use the interest to repopulate areas with species that have disappeared. Examples include the muskoxen from the Thelon Game sanctuary that have recolonized terrain outside the Sanctuary, and the elk and bison from Elk Island National Park outside Edmonton that have been used to start herds elsewhere.

- *Hospital*: Ecosystems are not static and isolated phenomena but are linked all over the planet. Protected areas constitute some of the few places where these processes still operate in a relatively natural manner. As such, they may be considered ecosystem 'hospitals' that help to maintain processes that may be damaged and not working effectively elsewhere. Much attention, for example, is now focused on the carbon cycle as imbalances caused by the burning of fossil fuels contribute to global warming. Forests are major carbon 'sinks' where carbon dioxide is taken in from the atmosphere and stored in organic form. Thus forests that are protected play a major role in maintaining some balance in the carbon cycle. Kulshreshtha and Johnston (2003), for example, calculate that Canada's national parks have sequestered 4.43 gigatonnes of carbon that would cost society between $72–$78 billion to replace. In a more modest but also interesting example of the *hospital role* Knowler et al. (2003) calculate the value to salmon of protecting freshwater habitat in protected areas on Canada's west coast. Although the hospital function is a commonly overlooked role of protected areas, it is becoming one of increasing interest to scientists.

- *Laboratory*: As relatively natural landscapes, parks provide outside laboratories for scientists to unravel the mysteries of nature. For example, Killarney Provincial Park in Ontario provided an important laboratory for early research on acid precipitation in Canada.

- *Schoolroom*: Parks can play a major role in education as outdoor classrooms. Direct physical contact with the complexities of the natural environment help inspire awe, humility, and respect. This function can also play a key role in helping influence visitors to change behaviours to more environmentally benign practices in their everyday lives.

It is useful to bear this full range of values in mind as the emphasis amongst them can change over time. As already mentioned, when Canada's national parks were inaugurated there was an overwhelming emphasis on the playground and factory roles. As the rest of the landscape became dominated by market forces for forestry, agriculture and urban uses, the ecological roles became increasingly recognized. For many years, Parks Canada legislation and policies laboured under what was known as the 'dual mandate' which required making full use of the parks for the enjoyment and benefit of the people while ensuring that they were unimpaired for future generations. Various administrators interpreted this balance in differing ways, but finally, in 1988 the *National Park Act* was amended to clear priority to protection of ecological integrity over human use, and this has been further emphasized in more recent policy and legislation [...]

Similar changes are evident at provincial levels as the need for more protection becomes evident. For example, the oldest and one of the most significant provincial parks in the country, Algonquin, some 260 km northeast from Toronto has been subject to extensive logging activity over the years and contains over 8,000 km of logging roads. The Ontario Parks Board recommended in 2007 that the area protected from logging needed to be raised from 22 per cent to 54 per cent of the park in order to increase protection for park ecosystems. There are also further nuances regarding changes in role priority. For example, historically within the ecological context most emphasis was placed on the *bank role*. Recently increasing interest has been shown in the *hospital role* and the value of ecosystem services provided by PAs. This interest reflects greater scientific understanding of ecosystem linkages and heightened public and political awareness of environmental degradation in general [...]

Notes and Questions

1. How would you rank in importance the various roles that the authors above ascribe to parks? Is ranking possible without embarking on an economic valuation of the various functions that parks can potentially perform?

2. For a more skeptical approach to the rationale for parks, which raises these and related questions, consider the following article.

Robert W. Turner,
"Market Failures and the Rationale for National Parks"
(2002) 33 J. Econ. Educ. 347

The most fundamental question is whether the government should provide things like national parks or, said another way, if private markets would provide them efficiently. If there is a case for national parks, the next question is whether the current size of the national park system is appropriate. Answering either question requires the identification of market failures that would justify national parks. After describing the market failures that may provide a rationale for national parks, I summarize what evidence is needed to make a strong case for a national park system. A large body of evidence arising from Krutilla's (1967) analysis of conservation relates to the conservation or preservation of nature or wilderness in general and in specific areas, sometimes including national parks. Nonetheless, the justification for national parks is based largely on assertions that, although reasonable, cannot be supported strongly by existing empirical evidence. This article is related to a large body of economic literature about "the amenities associated with unspoiled natural environments", to use the words of Krutila (1967, 778), which many consider the seminal article on the subject. Most of this literature concerns the recreational value of parks and other natural areas. My main focus in this article is on the existence of national parks, whereas most of the literature either uses national parks as examples of a broader class of natural areas or considers changes in particular attributes of specific national parks; I emphasize the importance of the non-recreational aspects of parks. [...]

The clearest rationale for government provision of national parks is the case of pure public goods. Pure public goods are both non-rival (some economists use the terms non-depletable or indivisible) and non-excludable. Non-rival refers to the property that the same unit of the good can be consumed by more than one person whereas non-excludable refers to the inability to prevent anyone from consuming the good once it is produced. National defense is the quintessential textbook example of a pure public good, and public health and safety examples are also common. Non-excludability leads to free (or easy) riding, where individuals refuse to pay (or understate their willingness to pay) for the good because they know that they can consume the good even if they do not pay (fully) for it. This provides the usual justification for government provision; because of the free rider problem, no company could profitably produce and sell the good [...]

National parks are not themselves pure public goods, however. Most national parks, at least the parts of them most heavily visited, are clearly excludable, as shown by the existence of entrance gates where visitors are asked to pay a fee. Club goods are excludable goods that are non-rival except for congestion. The provision of club goods is characterized by two decisions. First, the membership of the club is determined. Membership might be restricted or it might be open to the entire public; there may or may not be a membership fee. Second, when members visit the club, goods or services are provided; these goods or services are non-rival except for congestion.

National parks are more than recreational areas, however. They are also places where natural and historic resources are conserved for future generations. If the purpose of this conservation is to allow future visitors to enjoy the resources, this is viewed better as a club good than as a pure public good. If private owners know that future generations will want to visit the parks, they will conserve the parks' resources accordingly, just as the owner of any nonrenewable resource saves some of it to sell in the future. [...]

Park advocates maintain that national parks provide large benefits in addition to the recreational benefits received by present and future visitors. These benefits can be described as various kinds of non-use or existence values of the parks. National parks have non-use values if people get satisfaction from knowing that parks exist, even if they have never visited them and never plan to visit them. By their nature, goods with non-use values are pure public goods: There is no way to exclude individuals from getting non-use values, and one individual's value is unaffected by the fact that others are also getting nonuse values from the same resource. [...]

To the extent that the park system provides pure public goods, its existence may be justified on that basis. But a benefit-cost analysis is still required: The public goods provided by the parks must create enough benefits to offset the associated costs. These costs include the direct operating costs of the park system plus the opportunity costs of using land for this purpose. In addition, a case needs to be made that direct government provision is more effective than private provision with government subsidies or regulation. [...]

Another possible reason that private markets would not provide the efficient amount of places like national parks is that some visitors to the national parks create spillover effects on other people; that is, there are externalities. Students of economics are used to thinking of negative externalities, such as pollution, when market activities create direct harmful effects on third parties. Negative externalities certainly exist in national parks: One person's use of the park creates congestion externalities; alternative uses in parks conflict; and some uses harm the resources of the park, reducing the enjoyment of future park visitation and also reducing the non-use values associated with the resources. None of these provide a justification for government provision of parks, however; except for the effects on non-use values, all of these externalities would be taken into account by a private owner of a club good. [...]

Another possible argument for positive externalities is that national parks act as natural laboratories for scientific research of various kinds. Like other forms of research, the research activities may benefit society as a whole in addition to creating private benefits for the researchers. [...]

Another way in which externalities might justify government provision of national parks is that government provision may be an efficient response to external threats. Most national park units are threatened by negative externalities created by activities outside the parks. Mining, drilling, and electricity generation outside the parks can lead to water and air pollution in the parks, reducing visibility and creating health hazards to visitors as well as degradation of the ecosystem; the operations have also been known to cause seismic disturbances that threaten park ecosystems. Logging on adjacent lands can impair a park's scenic attractiveness and its ecosystem. [...]

National parks may potentially be justified on the basis of several market failures, but none of the possible explanations is compelling without some sense of the magnitude of the associated market failure. In the context of public-good provision, the magnitude of existence values for the resources conserved in national parks needs to be estimated and compared with the economic costs of conservation, including the opportunity cost of using the land for this purpose. To know if the park system as currently configured is justified, existence values and costs for the specific resources conserved in each park are needed, or else the existence values and costs must be related to the overall size of the park system so that marginal benefits can be compared with marginal costs. If positive spillover effects of visitation are to be used as the rationale for national parks, an estimate of their magnitude is required and a convincing argument must be made that government provision is administratively the best form of government intervention, rather than, for instance, government subsidies. [...]

Theoretical arguments can, in principle, justify some level of public provision of parks. More evidence needs to be marshalled, however, before the size and scope of the U.S. national park system can be clearly supported on economic grounds. Although this evidence will be difficult to obtain, it is hard to give an economic rationale for national parks without it.

Notes and Questions

1. How persuasive do you find the analysis in the preceding article as a rationale for the "public provision of parks"? If you disagree with the author's approach, are there nonetheless elements of his analysis that are worthy of consideration? To what extent, in your view, do (or should) governments make parks creation decisions employing the rationales set out in this article?

2. In federal states, both national and sub-national levels of government play a role in parks creation and maintenance. This complicates the task of parks and protected areas management, as it does in many other areas of environmental management. The following excerpt highlights some of the key differences between provincial and national parks.

Chris Malcolm,
"Protected Areas: The Provincial Story"

in P. Dearden & R. Rollins, eds., *Parks and Protected Areas in Canada:
Planning and Management*, 3rd ed. (Oxford University Press, 2009)

Provincial versus National Parks

What is the difference between a provincial and national park? At first glance, they both protect habitat and often provide recreational opportunities, including vehicle camping. Many people may not realize that they are in one type or the other. However, at the most fundamental level, national parks protect landscape of national significance. That being said, because of the vast size of Canada there are many provincial parks that are also of national significance. National parks are established by Parks Canada, a federal government agency within the Ministry of the Environment, through the *National Parks Act*. National Parks are placed on federal Crown land and can be in any province or territory of Canada. Parks Canada has developed a National Parks System Plan (Parks Canada, 1997), in which National Parks are organized into 39 terrestrial natural regions. As mentioned above, the provincial governments own most of the land in Canada's 10 provinces. This means that in order to establish a national park, the federal government usually has to negotiate with the provincial government to obtain the land; this can often be a tedious and expensive process.

Provincial parks are established and managed by the provincial governments in which the parks are situated. Similar to the federal natural region classification, all provinces have divided their lands into regions based on natural features. However, the method by which the classifications are determined may differ from province to province. Some of the first provincial parks in Canada were established based on similar reasoning to the first national parks, mainly as tourism destinations for economic profit. It is easy to understand, then, why provinces historically have been and can be reluctant to cede land to the federal government, as they lose potential long-term economic revenue. Sometimes, a better option for the provincial governments is to retain the land and create a provincial park. In doing so the province retains tourism revenue, as well as options for resource extraction, such as logging or mining, in the future. income from these activities can be put towards operating the provincial park system.

There are advantages and disadvantages, beyond economics, to development of provincial park systems. Some of the advantages may include:

- The provinces assess their landscapes at a smaller scale than does the federal government and, consequently, identify more 'natural regions' within their boundaries. As a result the provinces can identify a greater number of representative areas in which to place protective areas. As such, provincial protected area systems may be more ecologically diverse and therefore more resilient.

- Local management (provincial government), as opposed to federal management, based in Ottawa, can mean that local concerns are more likely to be taken into account, and local communities may be more able to take part in management issues.

There are potential disadvantages as well:

- There can be less emphasis on ecological conservation within provincial systems than is the case for national parks. Some provincial governments have weak conservation mandates and, therefore, provincial park systems are often less prone to protect against recreation and extraction activities (which can counteract the first advantage above).

- Multiple protected area agencies (e.g., Parks Canada, Environment Canada, Fisheries and Oceans Canada, as well as provincial government agencies) may cause inefficiencies in protected area establishment and management on a national scale, due to lack of communication, duplication of protected area types, and diverse conservation goals.

- The general public may not be aware whether they are visiting a national or provincial protected area. This can weaken the conservation message.
- National parks have very strong legislation, policy, management capability, and accountability mechanisms. Provincial parks often find themselves at the whim of provincial politicians and may lack adequate resources for effective protection.

Part III — Current Issues and Challenges

In this Part, we consider four challenges currently at the forefront of parks and protected areas law and policy reform. These are:

- Fulfilling Canada's international commitments to complete its marine protected area system;
- Promoting greater integration and coordination within our protected areas network to, among other things, enhance species protection;
- Grappling with the unresolved tension between competing "use" and "preservation" mandates under the *Canada National Parks Act* (CNPA) and operationalizing the concept of "ecological integrity" in Parks Canada decision-making; and
- Recognizing and respecting Aboriginal rights and title in the management and expansion of our parks and protected areas system.

Marine Conservation and Protected Areas

As discussed in Part I, in 1992 Canada's federal, provincial and territorial Ministers of Environment, Parks and Wildlife signed *A Statement of Commitment to Complete Canada's Network of Protected Areas*. Under this agreement, the Ministers committed to completing the terrestrial park system by 2000, and to "accelerating" the marine designation process. While significant progress has been achieved on the terrestrial front, less headway has occurred with respect to marine designations.

Philip Dearden & Rosaline Canessa, "Marine Protected Areas"

in P. Dearden & R. Rollins, eds., *Parks and Protected Areas in Canada: Planning and Management*, 3rd ed. (Oxford University Press, 2009)

Internationally, marine protected areas are defined as 'any area of intertidal or subtidal terrain, together with its overlying waters and associated flora, fauna, historical and cultural features, which has been reserved by legislation or other effective means to protect part or all of the enclosed environment' (Kelleher and Rechia, 1998). The potential contributions of MPAs include:

- protection of marine biodiversity, representative ecosystems and special natural features (Sobel, 1993);
- support rebuilding of depleted fish stocks, particularly groundfish, by protecting spawning and nursery grounds (e.g., see Wallace *et al.*, 1998);
- insurance against current inadequate management of marine resources;
- provision of benchmark sites against which to evaluate human impacts elsewhere and undertake scientific research;
- recognition of cultural links of coastal communities to biodiversity;
- provision of opportunities for recreation and education.

The effectiveness of marine reserves in providing for these benefits is largely conditional on size, how they are linked to other reserves, the kinds of activities allowed within the borders, the co-operation of local communities in supporting the reserve, the vulnerability to polluting influences from outside, and the ability to mitigate these negative impacts.

The Canadian Context

Canada has the longest coastline of any country in the world along three oceans and the second largest area of continental shelf. For over 30 years Canada has sought to gradually extend its jurisdiction over these waters and was a significant contributor to the UN Law of the Sea Convention (UNCLOS) between 1974 and 1982. Nevertheless, it was not until 2003 that Canada ratified UNCLOS. Ratification allows Canada to extend its sovereign rights over the seabed to the edge of the continental shelf, where it extends beyond the 200 nautical mile (370.4 km) exclusive economic zone (EEZ) thus adding 1,750,000 km2 (an area equivalent to the size of Canada's three prairie provinces). Once declared, Canada's jurisdiction will cover approximately 7 million km2, some 2 per cent of the world's oceans. This vast area and diversity of habitats give rise to a spectacular marine life wherein all major groups of marine organisms are represented. There are some 1,100 species of fish and globally important populations of many marine mammals, including gray, bowhead, right, beluga, minke, humpback and killer whales. Unfortunately several of these species are also on Canada's endangered and threatened lists including northern abalone, leatherback sea turtle, some salmon populations, Atlantic cod, and the beluga, bowhead, right and Georgia Strait killer whales (COSEWIC, 2007).

These pressures on marine species, at least in part, are a result of the high proportion of the Canadian population living in the coastal zone. Manson (2005) suggests that almost 40 per cent of Canada's population lives within 20 km of a coast (including the Great Lakes) and this will increase by 5 million people by 2015.

Canada's biophysical diversity is paralleled by its jurisdictional complexity. The federal government, for example, is empowered to deal with navigation, fisheries and general law-making and has a raft of legislation (e.g., the *Fisheries Act*, the Canada *Shipping Act*, the *Canadian Environmental Protection Act*, the *Coastal Fisheries Protection Act*), to enable it to do so. However, coastal provinces can also have considerable influence and have jurisdiction over activities such as aquaculture, fish processing and marketing, and ocean bed mining and drilling. In offshore areas the seabed is under federal jurisdiction, but in 'internal' waters, it is provincial. A 'federal' gray whale can enter a provincial marine park, and while still federal in the water column it may disturb the provincial substrate and eat a provincially protected amphipod that spent a short time as a free-swimming federally controlled larva, that subsists on federally supplied detritus from the water column. In subsequent years gray whales can enter a biosphere reserve in Mexico, a port authority in California, cross federal and state marine protected areas, become a target for Makah traditional fisheries, or even become a member of the International Whaling Committee sanctioned hunt in the Chuckchi Sea. Or wash up in a municipality on southern Vancouver Island and confound authorities as to who exactly is responsible for disposing of this once great and wonderful animal.

Speed of Establishment

The most fundamental problem besetting MPAs in Canada is that given such a vast and rich marine area within its jurisdiction, only 0.4 per cent of this area is designated for marine protection. The federal government has made commitments at both the international level (at the World Summit on Sustainable Development in Johannesburg in 2002 and under the Convention in 2004) and at the national level (in the throne speech of October 2004) to complete a network of MPAs by 2012. Clearly, we will be a long way from meeting these commitments. It is over 20 years since the MPA initiative began at the federal level. Although progress is occurring, the quality of the marine environment continues to deteriorate. It was more than 15 years ago when the Canadian Council of Ministers of the Environment, Canadian Parks Ministers Council of Canada and Wildlife Ministers' Council of Canada signed the Tri-Council Statement of Commitment to 'accelerate the protection of areas representative of Canada's marine natural regions'. Fisheries and Oceans Canada, Parks Canada and Environment Canada all have struggled since the mid-1990s to designate protected areas on the water. The Commissioner of the Environment and Sustainable Development was critical of the speed of progress by DFO in establishing MPAs. DFO did not meet its commitment to establish five MPAs by 2002. In fact, not one MPA had been designated by that time. The Commissioner's report noted that the MPA evaluation process alone was taking five to seven years (Office of the Auditor General of Canada, 2005). The report questioned the effectiveness of inter-departmental committees and the challenges DFO faces in shifting its focus from fisheries management to oceans management as mandated by the *Oceans Act*. It also cited the lack of performance expectations and accountability for the Oceans Action Plan and an anticipated higher level of funding by DFO to meet its goals. DFO is not alone. Parks Canada's proposed NMCAs and Environment Canada's proposed MWAs have similarly long gestation periods. This lack of performance puts into question the political will to create effective MPAs. Unfortunately the second phase of the Oceans Action Plan once again received minimal support in the 2007 budget emphasizing the lack of political support.

Level of Protection

Current levels of protection in existing MPAs are inadequate to ensure ecological integrity. MPAs are only effective in protecting ecological integrity insofar as the species and habitats are protected from destructive and disturbing activities. Large-scale habitat disturbance such as that caused by dredging, mining, oil or gas drilling, dumping, bottom trawling, dragging, finfish aquaculture or other extractive activities have to be excluded if MPAs are to achieve minimum standards of protection. Watling and Norse (1998), for example, compare the impacts of bottom trawling with that of clear-cutting and conclude that it is both more destructive and more widespread.

It is hard to generalize on the level of protection afforded to MPAs since this depends on individual regulations and site-specific planning for each MPA. Most of the sites held either provincially or by the CWS have little legal protection from destructive activities. The Canadian and BC governments, as part of the Marine Protected Areas Strategy for the Pacific coast of Canada, have set minimum protection standards for all sites within their jurisdictions, including the prohibition of ocean dumping, oil and gas exploration and development, and dredging. This strategy does not, however, have any legal basis and has remained under discussion since it was prepared in 1998. These restrictions are also applied to Parks Canada's NMCAs. Removal of living marine organisms and mineral resources in DFO's MPAs are only permitted as part of a formal research plan to better conserve, protect and understand the area. Prohibiting commercial fishing is a particularly contentious issue for MPAs and is usually accommodated with the trend towards zoned multiple-used MPAs.

Aboriginal Interests

[...] the obligations of the government of Canada in taking into account the needs and aspirations of Aboriginal peoples [...] [needs to] be particularly emphasized with respect to coastal peoples whose cultures and sustenance have been dependent upon the sea for thousands of years. In many cases governments have failed to consult meaningfully with Aboriginal people or have altered agreements after consultations had been held. The proposed Race Rocks MPA was to be announced as Canada's first under the *Oceans Act*, but was withdrawn after it was revealed First Nations no longer supported the proposal following changes that had been made after they had given their initial approval (Leroy et al., 2003).

Aboriginal peoples often have different perspectives on conservation principles and mechanisms (Ayers, 2005), and it is essential that governments are open to addressing these different world views through meaningful consultation. However there are also examples where Aboriginal interests seem to have been incorporated in a genuinely collaborative fashion. The Montagnais Essipit Band, for example is a strong supporter of the Saguenay-St Lawrence Marine Park and a member of the park co-ordinating committee. In Gwaii Hanaas National Park Reserve, there is successful co-management between the Haida and the federal government, and it is anticipated that a similar structure will be put in place for the proposed NMCA. Aboriginal peoples are more than another stakeholder group, and present a major challenge to governments in trying to establish MPAs. However, without their consent any MPAs that did result would be functionally meaningless.

Stakeholder Involvement

The level of protection is often a function of local wishes. Globally, protected area agencies are falling over backwards to 'include the local community'. It has become, and deservedly so, the mantra of the new century. Many parks were created in the days of Big Government when local populations had little say in their establishment and often contributed subsequently to making the park as ineffective as possible (Kessler, 2004). Those times are gone. Today stakeholder involvement is viewed as a necessary condition for a successful MPA [...] There is a difference, however, in paying due heed to local stakeholders and in compromising the fundamental goals of protected area establishment as a commons resource for the good of all of society both now and in the future. In their efforts to appease local stakeholders, protected agencies are now reluctant to emphasize their responsibilities to a broader range of stakeholders. As a result, often MPAs are stymied, such as the attempts by Parks Canada to establish them in the West Isles in New Brunswick and also in Bonavista/Notre Dame Bay in Newfoundland, due to objections from local resource extractors. On this basis it is doubtful whether scarcely a terrestrial park, would have been created anywhere in the country, as some segment of society is almost always involved with resource extraction in the area. Indeed, Yellowstone, the world's first national park, would never have been established had the government of the US listened to the local stakeholders who were there to slaughter the last of the mighty plains bison.

Even where MPA establishment might run the gauntlet of local opposition, all legislation allows such flexibility in terms of regulations, that actual protection might be nominal. When the Memorandum of Understanding was signed to establish Pacific Rim National Park Reserve, for example, crab fishing was allowed to continue, and has now grown to an extractive industry of over five times its original size. This kind of situation might in fact be more damaging than not having a park established. [...]

The foregoing is not to argue against local input by resource extractors into MPA designation and management. It is to point out that there are also broader societal responsibilities of protected area agencies and that the latter should not be uniformly sacrificed to the former as is currently the case. This situation is not unique to Canada, nor MPAs. As Ray and McCormick-Ray (1995: 37) point out: 'Unfortunately, there is an expedient tendency to speak to the lowest common denominator in proposing MEPAs (marine and estuarine protected areas) and their management, resulting from consensus-based participatory processes. This is self-defeating in the end, perhaps sooner than later'. However, it should be emphasized that the optimal situation is to establish MPAs that are ecologically viable and yet enjoy strong support from local communities. A case-sensitive approach is called for, but one that holds strong to conservation principles, one that invests in conservation education and actively tries to develop sustainable alternative futures for communities whose economic livelihoods are threatened.

"Networking" Our Parks and Protected Areas System

A current challenge faced by many countries is the need to secure greater integration of their parks and protected areas. As development pressures continue to encroach on these areas, their ability to provide ecological services is undermined. This is particularly true with respect to the provision of habitat and range for species at risk, a phenomenon that speaks to the need for better coordination between policy-making and implementation in the realms of parks and endangered species protection. Below we provide an excerpt from an article by Dearden and Dempsey that provides an overview of this increasingly important issue. We return to this topic in Chapter 9, where we profile research on this question recently completed by Deguise and Kerr.

Philip Dearden & Jessica Dempsey,
"Protected Areas in Canada: Decade of Change"

(2004) 48 Canadian Geographer 225

Habitat fragmentation and isolation of parks as 'islands' is an ongoing problem. Banff is flanked to the east by Canmore, which is outside the legislative power of Parks Canada and whose population doubled between 1988 and 1998, with estimates as high as 30,000 by 2015 (Bachusky 1998). Applications for seismic lines and mining are being considered near Nahanni National Park in NWT by the local resource board. Over the last few years, the rapid pace of development in the NWT is creeping closer to the park, with 12 applications for the development of mines, oil and gas activities around the park and near streams that flow into the park. In Waterton National Park, proposed housing developments on park boundaries threaten to fragment previously contiguous landscapes (Parks Canada Agency 2000a). These external developments are widely recognised as major impacts on park integrity. Recent research by Landry et al. (2001) shows that virtually all protected areas are too small to maintain ecological integrity on their own. In the 1997 State of the Parks survey, 24 of 36 parks reported major or severe impacts from external sources.

The need to think of protected areas as networks is widely recognised in parks' literature. Networks allow for wildlife movement beyond the boundaries of parks, most of which are too small to maintain viable populations over the long term. The Greater Yellowstone initiative, or Yellowstone to Yukon, which aims to build a contiguous area of land for the Rocky Mountain ecosystem across borders, is one example of such a connected system. In addition to building networks of protected habitat for wildlife, limiting fragmentation and the 'island effect' through sustainable land management and ecosystem-based management outside parks is central to these networks. However widely recognised these approaches are, the co-ordination across borders (internationally, national-provincial and private-public) has been difficult, if not impossible, to obtain.

Many external threats stem from jurisdictional problems between the provinces and the federal government, or between departments within governments. Provinces have jurisdiction over much of the land base outside the parks, control resource tenure on them and gain taxation revenue from development activities on them and are therefore reluctant to limit development anywhere in their boundaries, including near parks. This is a political problem embedded in Canada's federal system and therefore requires solutions beyond what Parks Canada itself can provide. Even more broadly, at the centre of this problem are land use and resource-extraction practices outside parks driven by a type of economic development that fails to recognise the value of ecological health. This is a problem that is obviously not going to be solved by Parks Canada alone. There are signs of hope that ecosystem-based management may materialise in small steps. Pending resources, Parks Canada Agency supports recommendations made by the First Minister's Roundtable on Parks Canada to support greater ecosystem management, advance regional partnerships in at least three national parks and advance a strategy to manage at least one contiguous network of protected areas. However, these partnerships and networks are still considered lower-priority needs for Parks Canada and "will be further evaluated as opportunities to pursue these approaches arise at a later date".

Conflicting Mandates? Use, Preservation and Ecological Integrity in Our National Parks

Throughout the 1990s, there was growing concern about development and visitor use impacts on the ecological health of Canada's national parks. In 1998, this prompted the federal government to appoint an expert panel to provide recommendations on conserving ecological integrity throughout the national parks system. The Panel concluded that, in light of growing stresses on the system, Parks Canada should "ensure ecological integrity is the first priority in all aspects of park management". This key recommendation was implemented through amendments to the *Canada National Parks Act*, S.C. 2000, c. 32 (CNPA), which came into force in early in 2001.

At the time of the Panel's report, the relevant legislation (then the *National Parks Act*, R.S.C. 1985, c. N-14 (NPA)) provided that maintenance of ecological integrity was first priority only "in relation to park zoning and visitor use" (subsection 5(1.2) NPA). The 2001 amendments broadened this mandate to require that the "[m]aintenance or restoration of ecological integrity, through the protection of natural resources and natural processes, shall be the first priority of the Minister *when considering all aspects of the management of parks*" (subsection 8(2) CNPA, emphasis added). In addition, the CNPA added a new definition of the term "ecological integrity", namely, "[...] a condition that is determined to be characteristic of its natural region and likely to persist, including abiotic components and the composition and abundance of native species and biological communities, rates of change and supporting processes" (subsection 2(1) CNPA).

Unaltered was the provision that is commonly known as the CNPA's "dedication" clause. This provision directs that "[t]he national parks of Canada are hereby dedicated to the people of Canada for their benefit, education and enjoyment [...] and the parks shall be maintained and made use of so as to leave them unimpaired for the enjoyment of generations" (section 4 CNPA). A key question, therefore, was how these "ecological integrity" amendments would be reconciled with the tension, inherent in this dedication language, between "use" versus "preservation". Shortly after the 2001 amendments came into force, the Federal Court was called upon to offer its views on this question. As we shall see, in the *CPAWS* case, excerpted below, environmentalists argued that the new CNPA's "ecological integrity" provisions imposed important new fetters on the exercise of ministerial discretion over parks policy and management. The facts of the case also gave rise to a legal challenge brought by the Mikisew Cree, discussed later in this chapter.

Canadian Parks & Wilderness Society v.
Canada (Minister of Canadian Heritage)

2003 FCA 197

[At trial, CPAWS's challenge was dismissed: see *Canadian Parks & Wilderness Society v. Canada (Minister of Canadian Heritage)*, 2001 FCT 1123, *per* Gibson J. On appeal, CPAWS framed one of its principal grounds of appeal as follows:

> [...] in approving the construction of the road, the Minister failed to discharge the statutory duty imposed by subsection 8(2) of the CNPA to make the "maintenance or restoration of ecological integrity [...] the first priority of the Minister when considering all aspects of the management of parks". In her reasons for decision, the Minister did not expressly take into account the maintenance of ecological integrity as the first priority, but referred only to the absence of significant adverse environmental effects. The Minister thus erred in law in the exercise of her discretion by failing to take into consideration a relevant factor or, in the alternative, the decision was unreasonable in light of the material before her.

The applicant for judicial review and appellant in this proceeding, CPAWS, is a national environmental group with a sizeable membership across Canada. It is active in the promotion and protection of parks and wilderness areas in Canada and has opposed the proposal to construct a road in Wood Buffalo National Park by participating in the public consultative processes held in connection with it.]

EVANS J.A.: —

Introduction

Wood Buffalo National Park is the biggest national park in Canada and one of the world's largest. Situated mainly in northern Alberta, and partly in the Northwest Territories, the Park measures nearly 45,000 square kilometres. It was established in 1922 especially to protect the resident bison and today remains home to the largest herd of free-roaming bison in the world. The Park also contains the last known nesting area of the endangered whooping crane, the finest example of gypsum karst landforms in North America, and vast undisturbed boreal forests. In recognition of its ecological importance, Wood Buffalo National Park was declared a UNESCO world heritage site in 1987.

These proceedings arise from the approval of a proposal to establish a winter road in the Park. The road would occupy less than 1% of the park's total area. The Canadian Parks and Wilderness Society ("CPAWS") applied for judicial review of the approval of the road by the Minister of Canadian Heritage, acting through her delegate, the Director General, Western and Northern, Parks Canada Agency. The Minister made the decision to approve the road after considering an environmental screening assessment report and concluding that the proposed road was "not likely to cause significant adverse environmental effects". [...]

Factual Background

The Parties

[...] The Minister of Canadian Heritage is a respondent to the application. The Minister is responsible for the direction of the Parks Canada Agency and for the management of national parks. The other respondent is the Thebacha Road Society. The Society is a non-profit group established by residents in and adjacent to the Park to promote the development of the road. Its members include the town of Fort Smith (population 2,500), which is located just outside the Park, Fort Smith Métis, the Salt River First Nation who live in Fort Smith, Smith's Landing First Nation, and the Little Red River Cree. If the road goes ahead, the Society, not Parks Canada, will be responsible for financing, constructing and maintaining it.

The Proposed Road

The construction of a road along the route of a previous winter road, which was built in 1958 and abandoned in 1960, has been contemplated since the early 1980s, and was accepted in principle in 1984 by the Wood Buffalo National Park Management Plan. The present road proposal emerged from meetings in 1999 at Fort Smith between the Minister and supporters of a road.

The road will be for winter use only and is unlikely to be open for more than about four months each year. It will be constructed mostly of compacted snow and ice and, except for two one-lane bailey bridges, ice bridges will be constructed to take the road across rivers in the Park. The road will be 118 kilometres in length, with a right-of-way of 10 metres in width. The road itself will be 8.4 metres wide, which will allow two vehicles to pass and snow to be stored on each side of the road. [...]

The Concerns

The road proposal has proved to be very controversial. Opposition has come from environmental groups and some local residents, including Aboriginal people who are concerned that the road may adversely affect their traplines in the Park. Indeed, the Mikisew Cree First Nation, some of whose members live on the Peace Point Reserve, has successfully challenged the approval of the road on the ground that, in the absence of adequate consultation, the decision will unjustifiably interfere with their treaty rights to trap and hunt in the Park: *Mikisew Cree First Nation v. Canada (Minister of Canadian Heritage)* (2001), 214 F.T.R. 48, 2001 FCT 1426. [**Ed. Note:** Later in this chapter we consider the decision of the Supreme Court of Canada, which upheld this decision.] [...]

CPAWS' objections to the road are pitched at different levels. First is what I would term the "in principle" objection to any development in a national park that is not demonstrably required either for reasons of sound ecological management or for increasing public access to the wilderness without endangering it. In CPAWS' view, the proposal to construct a road does not meet these criteria because it is not required for any of the purposes for which the Park was created, but is merely a means of satisfying a perceived regional transportation need.

Second, CPAWS' opposition to the road is driven by a fear that incremental degradation poses a major threat to the integrity of the ecology of Canada's parks. That is, while an individual project may in itself cause no great environmental damage, the approval of one project makes others more difficult to resist. A park may thus be more vulnerable to death from a thousand small blows than from a single lethal attack. [...]

The Decision-making Process

In accordance with the *Canadian Environmental Assessment Act*, S.C. 1992, c. 37, section 18 ("CEAA"), Parks Canada developed terms of reference for independent consultants to subject the road proposal to an environmental screening assessment. In addition, Parks Canada initiated public hearings, surveys and workshops to consider the proposal. Reports from the screening assessment process became available in April and August 2000. They indicated that, because it was proposed to construct a narrow road mostly within the route of the previous road, little clearance would be required. Thus, re-establishing a winter road would cause minimal loss of habitat and fragmentation of the existing boreal forest. CPAWS no longer challenges the validity of the environmental assessment process.

On the basis of these reports, the Minister's approval of the winter road was announced on May 25, 2001. The decision stated that any adverse environmental impact of the road would be insignificant, both because of its design and limited use, and because of the measures that would be taken to monitor and mitigate any unforeseen problems through "adaptive management" techniques. [...]

The decision to approve the road was purportedly made pursuant to subsection 8(1) of the CNPA, which confers on the Minister responsibility for the administration, management and control of the Park, including the administration of the public lands within it. [...]

One other component of the administrative process should also be mentioned. In 1998, the Minister established a Panel on Ecological Integrity to advise on the development of new legislation, which ultimately became the CNPA. After the Act was passed, the Panel was disbanded. Before its demise, the Panel listed the road as one of the environmental stressors on national parks that it had visited.

The Panel's particular achievement with respect to the CNPA appears to have been securing the expansion of the application of the principle of ecological integrity in subsection 8(2) of the Act, a provision that assumes considerable importance in this litigation. Under subsection 5(1.2) of the previous statute, the *National Parks Act*, R.S.C. 1985, c. N-14 ("NPA"), "the maintenance of ecological integrity" was "the first priority ... when considering park zoning and visitor use in a management plan". The Panel was of the view that the scope of this provision was too narrow and that Parks Canada had not always been sufficiently committed to implementing a policy of maintaining and restoring ecological integrity. In an attempt to ensure the necessary change in the Agency's culture, subsection 8(2) was added to the CNPA and provides that the maintenance or restoration of ecological integrity shall be the first priority of the Minister when considering "all aspects of the management of parks".

The Decision of the Trial Division

[...] Gibson J. held that the approval of the road was not inconsistent with the duty imposed on the Minister by subsection 8(2) of the CNPA to give "the first priority" to the "maintenance or restoration of ecological integrity" of the Park "when considering all aspects of the management of parks". He observed that ecological integrity is not the only statutory priority of the Minister and that the Minister is required to engage in a "delicate balancing of conflicting interests" identified in the purposes provisions in subsection 4(1) of the CNPA. [...]

Issues and Analysis

[...]

Was the Minister's Approval of the Road in Breach of the Statutory Requirement That "Ecological Integrity" Shall Be the "First Priority" of the Minister When Considering All Aspects of Park Management?

The duty in question is contained in subsection 8(2) of the CNPA which, for convenience, I set out again.

> 8(2) Maintenance or restoration of ecological integrity, through the protection of natural resources and natural processes, shall be the first priority of the Minister when considering all aspects of the management of parks.

Also relevant is the definition of "ecological integrity" provided in subsection 2(1), which reads as follows:

> "ecological integrity" means, with respect to a park, a condition that is determined to be characteristic of its natural region and likely to persist, including abiotic components and the composition and abundance of native species and biological communities, rates of change and supporting processes.

The Standard of Review

The first question to be decided is the standard of review that the Court should apply to determining if the Minister complied with subsection 8(2). As Gibson J. noted (at para. 53), since subsection 8(2) provides that ecological integrity is the first priority, there must be other priorities to which the Minister may also have regard when considering the administration and management of the parks.

Hence, if the Minister has had regard to ecological integrity, her decision to approve the road is reviewable on the ground that she failed to treat ecological integrity as the first priority. However, it is not the function of a reviewing court to determine whether, giving the maintenance of ecological integrity the first priority, it would have approved the road. That would be to subject the Minister's exercise of discretion with respect to competing priorities to a standard of correctness which, counsel agreed, was not the appropriate standard of review. Whether the relevant standard of review is patent unreasonableness or simple unreasonableness is the question. A pragmatic or functional analysis leads me to conclude that patent unreasonableness is the applicable standard of review.

The exercise of discretion involved in this case is properly characterized as bearing on issues of a polycentric nature: weighing competing and conflicting interests, and determining the public interest from among the claims and perspectives of different groups and individuals, on the understanding that first priority must be given to restoring or maintaining ecological integrity. This is not a zero sum game.

Thus, on the one hand, residents in the Park believe that a winter road will reduce the isolation, which is particularly burdensome in the long northern winters by enabling them to visit, and be visited by, family and friends who live in or near the Park. Others support the road because it will significantly shorten the travelling time to destinations south of the Park region.

On the other hand, the road comes at a price: the difficult-to-quantify risks that it poses to wildlife and vegetation in the Park and the integrity of the Park's ecology, as well as to the livelihoods of those whose traditional traplines may be adversely affected by the road.

In addition, the fact that Parliament has conferred on the Minister broad responsibility for the administration, management and control of national parks, along with the powers necessary for its discharge, is another indication of a legislative intent that the standard of review should be at the most deferential end of the range. The duty of the Minister to justify her conduct to Parliament is the primary mechanism for holding the Minister accountable for the way that she balances competing interests and claims with respect to the use of park lands. While political accountability is often dismissed as an inadequate check on the abuse of power, in my opinion this view is not compelling in the context of the present case for at least three reasons.

First, as counsel for CPAWS argued, Parliament has always taken a close interest in the creation and protection of Canada's national parks. The establishment of a winter road in Canada's largest national park, a scheme that has been the subject of a vigorous public debate, is therefore very likely to register on the political radar.

Second, the political accountability of ministers to the public, both through Parliament and more directly, tends to be more effective when a minister's action engages with competing public interests than when it primarily concerns the interests of an individual.

Third, the decision-making processes employed in the consideration of the road proposal and its approval by the Minister render the decision transparent, in the sense that the bases of the decision and the countervailing arguments and evidence are part of the public record. This, too, is a factor that tends to enhance ministerial accountability through the political process. [...]

Thus, in reviewing the Minister's approval of the road on the ground that it was in breach of her duty under subsection 8(2), the Court must ask whether, on the basis of both the factors that the Minister had to consider and the material before her, it was patently unreasonable to have concluded that the road proposal was incompatible with maintaining as the first priority the ecological integrity of the Park through the protection of natural resources and natural processes. [...]

Failure to Consider a Relevant Consideration

Counsel for CPAWS submitted that, in exercising her discretion, the Minister failed to take into account a relevant consideration. The reasons for decision do not state that, in deciding whether to approve the road, the Minister had as her first priority the restoration or maintenance of the ecological integrity of the Park. [...]

[...] I agree that the Minister ought to have referred explicitly to the "ecological integrity" test, which had become applicable to decisions made under subsection 8(1) only three months before the date of the decision, and after the preparation of the environmental screening assessment report on which the decision relied.

The failure of a decision-maker to consider a factor that she or he was required in law to consider in the exercise of discretion is an indication that the decision was patently unreasonable: *Suresh v. Canada (Minister of Citizenship and Immigration)*, [2002] 1 S.C.R. 3 at paras. 37-38. However, I am not persuaded that the Minister committed a reviewable error when she failed to refer specifically to the need to ensure that the maintenance of ecological integrity was the first priority when exercising her power to approve the road under subsection 8(1).

That a decision-maker does not expressly mention a relevant consideration in the reasons for decision does not necessarily mean that it was not in fact considered. [...]

In the present case, it is difficult to believe that both the Minister and Parks Canada had overlooked the very recent and much heralded enactment of the expanded duty to ensure as the first priority in all aspects of decision-making relating to national parks the restoration or maintenance of the ecological integrity of the Park.

Indeed, the environmental assessment report, on which the Minister relied in making her decision, quoted as follows from the report of the Panel on Ecological Integrity:

> The overriding objective behind every recommendation in our report is to firmly and unequivocally establish ecological integrity as the core of Parks Canada's mandate.

The environmental assessment report went on to observe:

> although it is not yet clear how, and to what extent, Parks Canada will implement the panel's recommendation, it is likely that the panel's findings will significantly influence Parks Canada's approach to future human development within the national parks.

In addition, the Minister acknowledged the receipt of a letter from the Chair of the Panel raising the issue of ecological integrity prior to the screening process. By the time that the Minister made her decision, of course, the Panel's recommendation respecting the pre-eminence of the principle of ecological integrity in decision-making had received the enthusiastic support of the Minister and had become law. And, even before subsection 8(2) was added to the legislation, paragraph 3.1.2 of *Parks Canada Guiding Principles and Operational Policies* stated:

> Human activities within a national park that threatens the integrity of park ecosystems will not be permitted.

Moreover, counsel for CPAWS was unable to identify items that would be pertinent to the restoration or maintenance of ecological integrity through the protection of natural resources and natural processes that were not considered in the Minister's reasons for decision or in the environmental screening assessment report prepared by independent consultants that the Minister had before her when deciding to approve the road. Rather, his argument was that the "restoration or maintenance of ecological integrity" was a higher standard than "significant adverse environmental effects". However, he could not explain in what respects, or by how much, the standard was higher.

Since, in this case, the same facts are relevant to both statutory standards, and the standards seem not call for very different kinds of assessment, the Court can review the Minister's exercise of discretion by asking whether the material before her was sufficient in law to support her decision. On the basis of the statutory definition in subsection 2(1) of the CNPA, failure to maintain the "ecological integrity" of a park seems to be simply a sub-set of "significant adverse environmental effects", but one to which first priority must be given in the making of decisions.

Moreover, as explained below, I am satisfied that, on the material before her, the Minister's carefully considered and fully reasoned decision was not patently unreasonable. Indeed, in my opinion it would also survive review on the more demanding standard of reasonableness *simpliciter*. [...]

Conclusion

For these reasons, I would dismiss the appeal and award the Thebacha Road Society its costs as against CPAWS. The Minister did not seek costs and none are awarded.

Notes and Questions

1. Consider the discussion of "standard of review" in this case in light of the subsequent judgment (discussed in Chapter 6) of the Supreme Court of Canada in *Dunsmuir v. New Brunswick*, 2008 SCC 9. Would the principles and new approach set out in *Dunsmuir* have led to the same conclusion?

2. On what basis does the Federal Court conclude that the Minister gave appropriate priority to "ecological integrity" as required by section 8 of the CNPA? Do you agree with this conclusion?

3. The Federal Court seems to equate the determination of whether a proposed project fails to give priority to "restoration or maintenance of ecological integrity", as required by the CNPA, with a legal standard employed under the *Canadian Environmental Assessment Act* (CEAA 1995), namely,

whether the project would create "significant adverse environmental effects". Recalling the material covered in Chapter 7, do you agree?

4. Further reflections on the implications of the *CPAWS* case are offered in the commentary by Professor Fluker excerpted below. Do you agree with his critique and prescription?

Shaun Fluker,
" 'Maintaining Ecological Integrity Is Our First Priority' —
Policy Rhetoric or Practical Reality in Canada's National
Parks? A case comment on *Canadian Parks & Wilderness*
***Society v. Canada (Minister of Canadian Heritage)*"**
(2003) 13 J. Envtl. L. & Prac. 131

Both Federal Court [the FCA and FCTD] judgments significantly undermine the *Parks Act* s. 8(2). They interpret ecological integrity as simply another factor for parks management consideration, despite the language of s. 8(2) and the Ecological Integrity Panel Report proposal that ecological integrity be an "overriding" priority. The Court of Appeal, without any analysis, interprets the ecological integrity standard as equivalent to that of a federal environmental assessment screening. Finally, both judgments suggest that the Minister's parks management decisions, despite *Parks Act* s. 8(2), need not make any explicit reference to ecological integrity at all.

Why did the Court of Appeal go to such lengths to defend the Minister's decision, undermining the *Parks Act* s. 8(2) in the process? The obvious reason is that the Court applied the established policy of judicial deference to administrative or discretionary decisions. Unfortunately in this instance, the Minister made it very awkward for the Court to be deferential simply because she failed to expressly consider ecological integrity in her decision. The question remains as to why the Minister failed to reference ecological integrity in her decision.

Arguably, the *Parks Act* ecological integrity definition was the source of trouble for both the Minister and the Court. For the Minister, the definition makes s. 4(1) and s. 8(2) incompatible: that is, the *Parks Act* ecological integrity definition renders the s. 8(2) ecological integrity "first priority" incompatible with the s. 4(1) national parks dedication to the enjoyment of Canadians. In this case, the Minister chose to avoid discussing "ecological integrity". For the Court, the definition allows for a conceptual separation between humans and *nature*: that is, the Trial Division separated human community concerns from "ecological integrity" and the Court of Appeal interpreted "ecological integrity" as another way of describing "environmental effects". Accordingly, both the Minister and the Court asked themselves how to resolve a conflict between the needs of humans and those of *nature* (understood as non-humans). Viewing a decision as conflict resolution may be familiar territory for the law, however it is an impediment towards solving difficult value-based problems concerning Canada's national parks.

There are various perspectives on ecological integrity which debate whether ecological integrity and humans can co-exist. Some commentators, represented by the work of James Karr, Stephen Woodley, and Laura Westra, believe ecological integrity can exist only in the absence of human influence. Ecological integrity is independent from humans — (*natural ecological integrity*). In contrast, others such as James Kay, Henry Regier, and Eric Schneider, reject the hypothesis that human activity and ecological integrity are mutually exclusive. From their perspective, ecological integrity represents a desirable socio-ecological relationship wherein social and ecological systems are understood as mutually dependent self-organizing entities — (*socio-ecological integrity*).

The *Parks Act* ecological integrity definition refers to natural ecological integrity. In fact the Ecological Integrity Panel Report which led to this statutory definition explicitly associated ecological integrity with a natural state "... where humans do not dominate the ecosystem". Together, natural ecological integrity and its place as the first priority in management decisions should significantly restrict or eliminate human activity within national parks. Management decisions consistent with *Parks Act* s. 8(2) require national parks to be managed as core preservation areas within the larger context of a core/buffer land conservation strategy. The parks are a place where the preservation of *nature* is the first priority, with human interests of secondary concern. The effect of s. 8(2) is to elevate ecological integrity, as a *natural* condition, to a position of dominance over humans. This is the troublesome underlying rationale of the *Parks Act* s. 8(2), one that breeds a false perception of conflict between humans and the rest of nature.

Critics suggest natural ecological integrity, by failing to acknowledge that nature means different things to different persons, will remain an unpersuasive policy goal: "Tempting as it may be to play nature as a trump card in this way, it quickly becomes a self-defeating strategy: adversaries simply refuse to recognize each other's" trump and then go off to play by themselves". Moreover, why should public decision-makers take natural ecological integrity seriously? Human society inevitably alters its ecological context. As William Rees notes, humans are "patch disturbers" like many other species. "Human ecology begins with recognition that the mere existence of people in a given habitat implies significant effects on local ecosystems' structure and function". Accordingly some commentators reject the preservation of natural ecological integrity as a desirable public policy goal generally.

The mandate to maintain or restore *natural* ecological integrity is particularly troublesome for the Minister because the *Parks Act* s. 4(1) dedicates the parks to the use and enjoyment by people. The preservation of natural ecological integrity, where humans are *not* understood as natural, inevitably places decisions that conform with s. 8(2) in conflict with the s. 4(1) dedication. Natural ecological integrity, as a management priority, is simply too rigid for the majority of Canada's national parks.

Natural ecological integrity, and the underlying rationale of the *Parks Act* s. 8(2), will necessarily exclude humans from places where they want to be. Furthermore it promotes language of conflict rather than relationship between humans and the rest of nature. In this case, it led the Minister and the Federal Court to ask how to balance "competing" social and ecological interests, rather than ask the more difficult value-laden question of what socio-ecological relationship is desirable for the park. Decisions concerned with maintaining ecological integrity (in this case "socio-ecological integrity") should seek to answer the latter question.

Social and ecological interests co-exist rather than compete. Human social systems rely upon the energy and components of their surrounding ecological systems for sustenance. In the process of sustaining themselves, social systems alter the structure and processes of ecological systems. In turn, these alterations influence the structure and processes of social systems in desirable or undesirable ways. Feedback loops are created and eliminated as social and ecological systems self-organize and influence each other. Socio-ecological integrity represents a desirable relationship between these systems.

The primary policy attribute of socio-ecological integrity is that it requires decision-makers to seriously consider the *mutual* influences between social and ecological systems. Within the outer bounds of limiting human activity to leave our ecological context unchanged, and fostering human activity which results in ecological collapse, is a range of socio-ecological relationships both desirable and undesirable. Our management challenge is to implement the desirable relationships by making inclusive, value-based decisions. The maintenance of socio-ecological integrity, achieved by meeting this challenge, can lead the way as a policy goal in public decision-making. Socio-ecological integrity must, however, govern our decisions rather than simply be taken into account. Given the presence of "ecological integrity" in the *Parks Act*, Canada's national parks represent an ideal starting point for this form of decision-making in today's society.

Parliament made a choice in selecting natural ecological integrity to lead the way in Canada's national parks. Parliament chose a decision-making tool that, as presently interpreted, separates humans from the rest of *nature* and leads to park management decisions that exclude people from national parks. As it currently stands, the *Parks Act* s. 4(1) dual mandate simply cannot co-exist with the rationale of s. 8(2). Accordingly in this case, it seems that s. 8(2) was overlooked by the Minister.

To overcome this problem, either the *Parks Act* definition of ecological integrity should be amended to represent socio-ecological integrity (for example, by including humans and their values as important components of ecological integrity), or the *Parks Act* s. 4(1) should be amended to assert that parks are a place where the preservation of natural ecological integrity is the first priority, with human interests of secondary concern.

Reconciling Parks and Protected Areas Policy with Aboriginal Rights and Title

The implications of recognizing and respecting Aboriginal rights and title as guaranteed by section 35 of the *Constitution Act, 1982* is, as we have seen, an overarching concern for Canadian environmental law and policy. While this issue frequently arises out of Crown resource allocation decisions, particularly in the forestry and mining contexts, it is also an important consideration in the context of parks and protected areas. Many of Canada's parks and protected areas were created without consultation with First Nations. The Supreme Court of Canada's decisions in *Haida Nation v. British Columbia (Minister of Forests)*, 2004 SCC 73, and *Taku River Tlingit First Nation v. British Columbia (Project*

Assessment Director), (sub nom. Taku River Tlingit First Nation v. Tulsequah Chief Mine Project (Project Assessment Director)) 2004 SCC 74, underscore the Crown's duty to consult and accommodate where a proposed decision or action might infringe a section 35 protected right: see Chapter 3. As we shall see, this principle has important implications not only for future designation decisions but also, more generally, for parks and protected areas management. Among them is recognition of the need, where park conservation objectives overlap with traditional territories of First Nations, to develop new management structures and policies that ensure First Nations' community economic development goals are accommodated.

Philip Dearden & Steve Langdon, "Aboriginal Peoples and National Parks"

in P. Dearden & R. Rollins, eds., *Parks and Protected Areas in Canada: Planning and Management*, 3rd ed. (Oxford University Press, 2009)

[...] On 1 March 1872 over 810,000 ha of north-western Wyoming were designated as the world's first national park — Yellowstone. The park was set aside during an effort to subdue Plains Indian tribes, and the traditional inhabitants of the park moved to reservations or were forced out by the United States Army. In 1885, Banff National Park was established in Alberta, seven years after the Siksika (Blackfoot) and Nakoda (Stoney) tribes ceded much of southwestern Alberta to the Crown. The treaty allowed the tribes to continue hunting in the region, but the federal government decided these rights would not apply to Banff National Park. Since the establishment of these early national parks, thousands of new protected areas have been created throughout the world. Many of these protected areas have been designated on lands traditionally used by Aboriginal peoples. Often, they have been established without the participation of Aboriginal peoples living in the regions affected. In many instances, the Aboriginal people have been forcibly removed from regions in which protected areas were established. Early establishment of national parks in Canada followed the same pattern, but in more recent times (post-1982) rights have been recognized and traditional activities have been allowed to continue.

The practice of establishing protected areas without regard for the needs of Aboriginal people has sometimes adversely affected both Aboriginal societies and protected area conservation initiatives. In effect, 'indigenous people have borne the costs of protecting natural areas, through the loss of access for hunting, trapping or other harvesting activities'. Displacement of Aboriginal people often disrupts traditional social and economic systems and results in serious social problems, such as malnutrition and loss of cultural identity. At the very least, such negative impacts may reduce popular support among Aboriginal peoples for protected areas. Consequently, the effectiveness of conservation in protected areas has been compromised because of poaching, clandestine exploitation of resources, or other forms of non-compliance with regulations governing protected areas.

In response to these problems, it became clear there was a need to understand Aboriginal perspectives on parks, involve Aboriginal peoples in protected-area planning and management, and further, to allow exploitation of resources in protected areas for subsistence purposes.

The role of Aboriginal people in national parks has become an important area of concern globally for Aboriginal organizations, as well as for protected area managers and social scientists. In the last 30 years, the relationship between Aboriginal people and national parks in Canada has changed fundamentally, although these changes are uneven across the country. Aboriginal peoples in northern Canada have played a significant role in national park planning and development, while in southern Canada their role has varied from park to park. In general, national parks established since the Constitution Act, 1982, with its entrenchment of Aboriginal and treaty rights have working relationships with Aboriginal people. Steady progress is being made in parks established before that date, as the value of strong working relationships is recognized by Parks Canada in its corporate plan. A number of northern national parks have been established in conjunction with Aboriginal land claim [...] settlements, while park reserves await claims settlement before attaining full park status. Overall, more than 50 per cent of the land area in Canada's national park system has been protected as a result of Aboriginal peoples' support for conservation of their lands and 17 formal co-operative management agreements exist in addition to numerous informal agreements. Dearden and Berg (1993) suggest that First Nations have emerged as the most dominant force influencing the establishment of national parks in Canada over the years since the 1982 *Constitution Act* [...]

Many of Canada's national protected parks were designated at a time when both the federal and provincial governments did not acknowledge Aboriginal rights and title. Aboriginal peoples utilizing traditional lands or occupying reserves encompassed by newly designated parks were given little, if any, input in park planning and management. Indeed, when Riding Mountain National Park was established in 1933, the Keeseekoowenen Band was evicted and their houses burned (Morrison, 1995). Aboriginal people with reserves in proposed park areas were encouraged by Parks Canada to sell or trade their reserves for lands outside proposed parks, and were prevented from hunting and trapping within them. There was little appreciation within government that parks could be used to support and maintain the land uses of Aboriginal peoples, and hence protect their land-based cultures. Instead, Parks Canada stressed the need for the parks system to represent biophysically defined natural areas. Adherence to the natural areas framework may have contributed to the estrangement of parks from Aboriginal peoples. Parks identified through the framework might have been excellent choices to represent natural areas, but were sometimes irrelevant to protecting vital wildlife habitat, the element of parks legislation that interested many Aboriginal groups. To Aboriginal peoples dependent on hunting, fishing, and trapping, the location of a park was the key to its utility and political acceptability.

The attitude of Parks Canada began to change in the 1970s as the aspirations of Aboriginal peoples became better known and appreciated by the Canadian public and political leaders. This process was aided by public hearings into oil and gas megaprojects, which brought representatives of Aboriginal peoples and environmental and other groups into the same camp. The Berger inquiry of 1974-7 into a proposed gas pipeline from the Mackenzie Delta and northern Alaska, for example, noted the need for parks and conservation areas to be planned simultaneously with non-renewable resource development. In addition, Justice Thomas Berger, who earlier had acted as chief counsel to the Nisga'a, proposed a new type of park, a 'wilderness park', to preserve wildlife, wildlife habitat, and natural landscapes in northern Yukon, and to under-pin the still-vibrant renewable resource economy of Inuvialuit and Dene. This recommendation is now an acknowledged milestone in the debate that connects Aboriginal peoples with national parks. [...]

In 1994, Parks Canada revised its policies, with a new and strong emphasis on ecological integrity, improved regional integration through co-operation with other jurisdictions, and a more comprehensive approach to working with Aboriginal peoples. The 1994 *Guiding Principles and Operational Policies* sets out several polices with respect to Aboriginal interests:

- negotiation of comprehensive claims based on traditional uses and occupancy of land;

- rights and benefits in relation to wildlife management and the use of water and land, and the opportunity for participation on advisory or public government bodies;

- respect for the principles set out in court decisions, such as *Sparrow v. The Queen*, where existing Aboriginal or treaty rights occur within protected areas;

- at the time of new park establishment, respect for Canada's legal and policy framework regarding Aboriginal rights as affirmed by section 35 of the *Constitution Act*, and consultation with affected Aboriginal communities. [...]

While Parks Canada still faces many legal situations related to the interpretation of legal rights, the organization is recognized as a national and international leader in cooperative management of protected areas.

The most recent *National Parks System Plan* reflects implementation of Parks Canada's policies with respect to Aboriginal people by endorsing, 'a new type of national park where traditional subsistence resource harvesting by Aboriginal people [...] continues and where cooperative management approaches are designed to reflect Aboriginal rights and regional circumstances' (Parks Canada, 1997b).

Amendments to the *National Parks Act* in 1988 and 2000 also recognize the importance of traditional resource harvesting to Aboriginal peoples. The 1988 amendments allowed specific Aboriginal groups to carry out such harvesting in certain parks. It also extended, at the minister's discretion, traditional renewable resource harvesting rights in wilderness areas of national parks to Aboriginal peoples with land claim settlements, and allowed for regulation of traditional renewable resource harvesting in national parks by Order-in-Council.

The Canada *National Parks Act* of 2000 extend harvesting rights to a larger number of parks, including all those established by agreement. Section 10(1) of the Act also supports co-operative agreements with a wide range of organizations, including Aboriginal governments, for carrying out the purposes of the Act. The Act specifies that the federal cabinet may 'make regulations respecting the exercise of traditional renewable resource harvesting activities' in Wood Buffalo, Wapusk, and Gros Morne national parks, any park established in the District of Thunder Bay in the Province of Ontario; and 'any park established in an area where the continuation of such activities is provided for by an agreement between the

Government of Canada and the government of a province respecting the establishment of the park' (s. 17(1)). For the first time, the *National Parks Act* also provides for the removal of non-renewable resources in the form of carving stone, in order to support traditional economies.

The new *National Parks Act* does not guarantee co-operative management for Aboriginal peoples whose traditional lands fall within national parks; however, on a policy basis, Parks Canada has been very active in developing not only a formalized consultative process but also co-operative management arrangements as well. The Gulf Islands National Park Reserve is a good example of how Parks Canada, in advance of treaty settlements, has developed three cooperative management arrangements with Aboriginal groups to ensure consultation and input into major park decisions that affect them. In the case of Gwaii Haanas, the *National Parks Act* specifies in Section 41(1), that, 'the Governor in Council may authorize the Minister to enter into an agreement with the Council of the Haida Nation respecting the management and operation of Gwaii Haanas National Park Reserve of Canada'. Section 41(2), further allows for 'regulations, applicable in the Gwaii Haanas National Park Reserve of Canada, respecting the continuance of traditional renewable resource harvesting activities and Haida cultural activities by people of the Haida Nation to whom subsection 35(1) of the *Constitution Act, 1982* applies.

Aboriginal people are permitted to harvest plants and animals in many national parks based on land claim settlements or on other policy-related arrangements. All national parks in the North have harvesting regimes, as do several in southern Canada. Some examples are Pukaskwa in Ontario, Gulf Islands, Gwaii Haanas, and Pacific Rim in BC. Animals that are harvested range from large mammals such as moose to fur bearers such as mink. Harvesting activities happen primarily in the northern parks, although exact records of harvest activities are not kept. Although rights or granted access may exist, the level of harvest is relatively low. This may reflect the Aboriginal perspective that these jointly protected areas are special and, therefore, that harvesting should be minimized. It is also known that, in some situations, access to resources is easier in areas outside of national parks.

Perhaps the most important accommodation the *National Parks Act* makes to Aboriginal peoples lies in the term 'national park reserve', introduced through amendment to the statute in 1972. This designation applies, for example, to Nahanni, and Pacific Rim, which are to become full national parks upon settlement of comprehensive land claims. The 'reserve' designation allowed Parks Canada to treat and manage the areas in question as national parkland, but did not extinguish any Aboriginal rights or title to the areas. Importantly, this designation does not prejudice the ability of Aboriginal peoples to select parkland in the course of land claim negotiations.

Canadian legislators seem to have chosen an ad hoc approach to accommodating the needs of Aboriginal peoples in national parks. Wood Buffalo National Park and Auyuittuq National Park Reserve provide examples of this ad hoc approach. The area around Wood Buffalo National Park was a favoured hunting ground of Aboriginal people for many years prior to its establishment as a park in 1922 (Lothian, 1976). When the park was established, Aboriginal people who had previously hunted and trapped in the area continued these activities under permit. In 1949, special district game regulations for Wood Buffalo National Park were instituted, which superseded the National Parks Game Regulations and allowed for traditional hunting, trapping, and fishing by Aboriginal people (*ibid.*). The *National Parks Act* also enables the appointment of a Wildlife Advisory Board for the traditional hunting grounds of Wood Buffalo National Park, and this Board has a role, for example in bison management and hunting, fishing, and trapping regulations (*Canada National Parks Act*, s. 37). Auyuittuq National Park Reserve, located on Baffin Island, was established in 1972 long before the Nunavut Agreement. Public park planning meetings in the early 1970s resolved that the Inuit, who had inhabited the region for almost 4,000 years, would retain traditional resource extraction rights within the park. When Auyuittuq National Park Reserve was established there was provision for a "park advisory committee". This represented one of the first co-operative efforts by Parks Canada. All of the national parks found in Nunavut currently have park advisory committees, and they have evolved into an effective means for the Inuit people to participate in the planning and management of the national parks found in their traditional territories.

The interaction between Aboriginal peoples and National Parks in Canada is not as clear as might be suggested by National Park Policy and legislation. Land claim settlements, in addition to Parks Canada policy and legislation and legal precedent, determine the role of Aboriginal peoples in planning for, and managing, national parks. This has given rise to subtly different kinds of parks in northern and southern Canada, for a significant park planning and management role is accorded Aboriginal peoples in northern Canada where parks are tied to settlement of land claims. Land claims in northern Canada will likely be completed sooner than many of those, for example, in British Columbia. In addition, many Aboriginal peoples in the south must look to treaties, legal precedent and the *National Parks Act* and Parks Canada's *Guiding Principles and Operating Policies*, rather than to comprehensive land claim settlements, to protect their interests.

In response to this variation in approaches to working with Aboriginal organizations, the Panel on the Ecological Integrity of Canada's National Parks recommended that, 'Parks Canada adopt clear policies to encourage and support the development and maintenance of genuine partnerships with Aboriginal peoples in Canada'. The Panel also outlined key steps to foster trust and respect between Parks Canada and Aboriginal peoples, such as initiating a process of healing; providing adequate resources to maintain genuine partnerships; integrating Aboriginal culture, knowledge, and experience into education and interpretation programs; and ensuring protection of cultural sites, sacred areas, and artifacts. In an effort to move beyond the constraints of strict government legal positions, Parks Canada established an Aboriginal Secretariat in 1999, with the task of improving relationships with Aboriginal organizations throughout the national park system. Under the direction of the chief executive officer of the day, the Parks Canada corporate plan was also modified to better reflect the need for strong relationships with Aboriginal people and the important role they play in delivery of the Parks Canada mandate of protection, memorable experiences and educational opportunities.

The following article is based on an interview by Carol Linnitt with Valérie Courtois, director of Indigenous Leadership Initiative, in March 2018 following the announcement of the federal Nature Legacy initiative and its focus on Indigenous participation in conservation efforts. The interview explores the relationship between nature protection from a western perspective and the way Indigenous peoples connect with the natural world.

Carol Linnitt,
"How Indigenous Peoples Are Changing the Way
Canada Thinks About Conservation"

The Narwhal, March 10, 2018,
online: < https://thenarwhal.ca/how-indigenous-peoples-
are-changing-way-canada-thinks-about-conservation >

From the historic agreement that created the Great Bear Rainforest to B.C.'s Dasiqox Tribal Park to uniquely co-managed forest resources in Labrador, Indigenous-led conservation efforts are transforming the way Canadians understand and practice conservation. Far from the colonial idea of preserving natural landscapes from human incursion, Indigenous land use plans put sustainable human-nature relationships that seek to revitalize traditional cultural practices at the centre. It's a vision of conservation and land use planning that can help Canada deliver on its promise of reconciliation and a renewed nation to nation relationship, according to Valérie Courtois, director of Indigenous Leadership Initiative. In the recent federal budget, the Trudeau government committed $1.3 billion towards the creation of protected areas in Canada and some of those dollars are specially earmarked to support Indigenous participation. We asked Courtois [...] about Indigenous-led conservation, why it's important and how it could transform Canada from the ground up. [...]

In the federal government's most recent budget there was a big emphasis on support for Indigenous participation in conservation. Does this represent a changing tide when it comes to the way we view the creation of protected areas in Canada?

Yes. Certainly the courts have been pretty clear on these things and — to government's credit — it feels like they're not just doing the bare minimum of what the courts have asked them to do in this reconciliation process. This is really about resetting and renewing the relationship between crown governments and Indigenous peoples. At the same time as that's happening there's also a real nationhood movement within Indigenous peoples — we have a population that is more educated, getting more sophisticated in terms of its political strategies and voices and certainly has never had more capacity to manage lands within a modern land management context. I'm not dismissing exciting governance systems of lands that were there for thousands of years, but this movement towards nationhood and the seriousness of being nations is happening at this same time as this recognition is happening. We not only have the ability to fill that space but be very creative and provide leaders in that space because of this movement that's happening in our communities too.

Do you see conservation as pathway to nationhood and community revitalization?

For me it's hard to talk about Indigenous nations outside the context of my own but when we think about nationhood it's all about who you are where you are — who you are within the land that is your home. And conservation is one of the tools that allows us to fulfill a responsibility to our land within the reality of it being the central core of who we are as nations. Much of our nationhood over time has been undermined because of the impacts on that relationship, whether that's residential schools that took us away from the land or crazy development projects. So, for example, if you're a member of West Moberly First Nation in northeastern B.C., it's very tough to be who you are on that landscape, especially if you consider the community's historic relationship with caribou. You can now count the remaining number of caribou there on two hands. That free-for-all mentality of "the land is open," has really had a huge impact on the cultural survival on our nations. So any tool that allows us to protect that land we need to be who we are and to be a part of decision-making on scale, pace and scope of development — especially if that develop is done to our benefit — then that will create some good scenarios. I'm Innu. We're caribou people. Our whole lifestyle revolves around following migratory and woodland caribou herds, which means we need a lot of space to be who are as a people. When we talk about protecting lands in the east we're not just talking about the forest, we're talking about huge caribou landscapes. Our elders say all the time: for us as Innu, if the caribou disappear we won't be Innu anymore. It's a fundamental thing and the caribou situation right across this country is very worrisome.

Most non-Indigenous Canadians don't have a meaningful relationship with caribou. And yet caribou are so significant for conservation in Canada. Someone recently said to me if we lose the caribou we lose all the protections that have come in the fight for their survival. Do you see caribou as a sort of conservation gateway?

Absolutely. Also a gateway in terms of getting people to see beyond the evident value that touches them. So, for example, I used to do this all the time, when I would host meetings in the community. When I'd tell people it's about the forest management plan, we'd get two people. If we said it was about caribou, the whole community was there. They're the same issue — it's all about habitat management and the amount of forest that is available. But that species and that relationship compels people more and that's something we use to improve our community based processes as well. Right now if you're in central Manitoba and you['re] First Nations I can guarantee you're worried about moose. There's a decline generally with moose there and you've got a declining forest industry. To me that would be a great opportunity to think about, "okay shouldn't we take this opportunity to think about other values forest has to save the moose and perhaps eventually create a context for a more sustainable forestry industry?"

What kinds of conversations are happening in Indigenous conservation circles about the non-Indigenous community and non-Indigenous conservation efforts?

There's always this effort of finding ways of a parallel recognition of Indigenous science and western science in what we do. When we were leading the Innu Nation our Elders said, it's important to know Innu science but your job is to use the best information you have to make decisions — no matter where that comes from. We hear that more and more with from communities who are looking at science not so much as a barrier anymore but as a body of knowledge in itself that is separate than their own but to be acknowledged and to be valued. In terms of the conservation community generally, it has been and can be another form of colonialism, another way for other people to put a value on your land that isn't your own. There is a risk for conservation organizations if they push things based on their own values. And that's why a lot of conservation organizations have had trouble in the past working with First Nations. You see this in the media every once in a while — this idea of conservation being a new colonial frontier. But there are ways to avoid that and ways for First Nations to make sure they choose the right partners. Some are developing partnership protocols which state what they look for in partners, state what they are looking for in organizations that want to work on their land and what the processes should be. When those protocols exist relationships tend to be much more fulsome. There's a risk in that but there are things organizations can do to create the right space. The thing I worry about with conservation organizations is this idea that Indigenous people cannot be a means to the conservation organizations' ends. So if they're looking at this budget and saying "we need to protect areas by 17 per cent" and they look at a map and say it needs to be areas A, B, and C, then they're going to say we need to talk to First Nations [in] Area A. That's a problem. That is not the right place to start a relationship. The relationship needs to start with the goal of having Indigenous leadership and nations make decision[s] on their lands. That needs to be the end goal itself as opposed to a means to an end.

On that note there's an interesting difference in worldviews when it comes to land use planning. From a white, Western perspective we have this idea of creating protected areas that are so-called pristine preservations. What I've heard from some Indigenous communities is they want to live on the land, they want their hands in the ground, they want to hunt the animals that live there and gather medicines. They see themselves as part of that landscape. Can you talk about how an emphasis on Indigenous-led conservation is maybe inviting white communities to re-envision what conservation means?

I can't think of one landscape in Canada that hasn't been affected in some way by humans. It's a false premise to think that landscapes are at their best without us. It's not the natural state in much of North America. And we've seen that whether it's the use of fire to create berry areas or to manage large wildlife species. When I was working on the forestry plan out here in the east and talking with the elders about fires, I was looking on a map where the fires were and elders were saying, 'yeah, I lit that because I wanted a berry area 10 years later." This idea of absence is totally artificial. We've been living with that balance or with that relationship as humans in nature for 10,000 plus years — in some places on the coast 13,000 plus years. Obviously that's a sustainable model! To me, this deep ecology where people have to be separate from nature is completely artificial. If I could use an expression from Trudeau: "that's so 1970." We're so far beyond that. The other thing is that ecosystems, they're not just for nature, they're for us, they are our habitat. As Indigenous peoples we are a part of that biodiversity. Article 8(j) on the Convention on Biological Diversity actually says that: Indigenous peoples are part of biodiversity of nature. It's false to think you can separate those things. Conservation and any management of land is the way we're going to preserve cultures and have them flourish and really achieve their aspiration as a society. We have that responsibility as a nation, we've affected over 50 different cultures through colonialism. It's the right thing to do — to encourage that link.

When it comes to Indigenous rights in Canada, do you see conservation as a way of Indigenous peoples asserting those rights?

Yes, for sure. I guess the best way for me to answer that question is to speak about an example here in Labrador. Innus have been in negotiations for a treaty for over 30 years. In that 30 years there's been one of the world's largest hydro projects and a second one is in development now. We've seen the world's largest nickel mine and the expansion of the world's largest iron facilities. Development has really progressed at quite a pace. If you're the Innu Nation and you're looking at your lands 30 years ago when you started negotiations and looking at them now you have less opportunity as a nation to think about sustainable revenue streams, to think about what you're going to do on your land base and how you're going to draw your revenue sources out of your land base. Those opportunities diminish as things get taken off the land whether that's trees, minerals or water or whatever. So conservation in the Innu Nation case as they were negotiating the treaty, they're said look we've got this forestry issue where we can really test out what co-management and our relationship over the long term could look like on these forest resources. So the Innu Nation and the province signed a unique co-management agreement that doesn't involve a third party.

Do you see Indigenous land use leadership as a benefit to all Canadians?

This is another interesting thing about Indigenous leadership: it can also help out with non-Indigenous communities. Here in Goose Bay, when the government first started talking about doing forestry, the community didn't want anything to do with it. There was a settler group here in town who didn't trust government at all. They created a group that was essentially a protest group to the forest process. When the Innu came on, they cooled their jets. They were like, "oh, the Innu Nation cares about the environment. We know because they blocked NATO, blocked Inco, they intervened on these processes that could have been devastating to the environment." The fact that we were there brought them enough comfort that they were no longer going to protest the process. It was fascinating. We could really see it. I was there for the consultation process and I witnessed that shift from going from "we don't trust anyone in government" and a very aggressive approach to seeing Innu guys there in their guardian uniforms talking about their values saying "we trust this plan."

Looking forward, when it comes to Indigenous participation in conservation in Canada, what are you looking forward to? Or even beyond that, what are your hopes for what you're seeing taking place in Canada right now?

I'm a generally optimistic person, generally hopeful person. I think there's never been a moment in time like we're in now for a) the Indigenous empowerment movement to be where it is and b) of our awareness of environmental risk and the importance to conservation. That's the key moment in time and it's important for us who work on these issues to think about that moment in time and advance things as much as possible. The reconciliation movement in this country will only become truly real when we figure out the land jurisdiction question. When we think about respecting Indigenous peoples on their lands while balancing the reality that we are a federation and the settler population is here. So what does that look like? What does our shared future look like? It['s] this, that [our] shared future is one where nations are strengthened and jurisdiction is figured out. When that happens, when Indigenous people have their relationship with land fully restored and cultures are strengthened and that responsibility and sense of stewardship is re-fostered I think we're going to have the best managed ecosystems in the world, we're going to be global leaders in that reality. We're going to have Indigenous peoples that are coming into who they're supposed to be, which are strong nations who care for the land. I feel like it's essentially the fulfillment of the eighth fire prophecy. The prophecy tells about how Indigenous people are going to rise up from the ashes of colonialism and this dark period we were in over the last 200 plus years and really rise up to finally become who we are meant to be: these leading land carers that others look to for inspiration and leadership on those issues. I very much feel like we're in the moment of that happening.

The following article provides a brief overview of the terms of the first Indigenous protected area in Canada announced in October 2018 under Canada's Nature Legacy program. As you learn about this initiative, consider how effective it is in integrating nature conservation with reconciliation with Indigenous communities.

Environment and Climate Change Canada,
"First New Indigenous Protected Area in
Canada: Edéhzhíe Protected Area"
Backgrounder (October 11, 2018),
online: < https://www.canada.ca/en/environment-climate-
change/news/2018/10/first-new-indigenous-protected-area-
in-canada-edehzhie-protected-area.html >

Located in the traditional Dehcho territory in the southwestern part of the Northwest Territories, Edéhzhíe is a spiritual place that is ecologically and physically unique. Its lands, waters, and wildlife are integral to the Dehcho Dene culture, language, and way of life. Edéhzhíe protects the headwaters of much of the watershed of the Dehcho region. Its diverse habitat — from wetlands to forests — is home to a wide variety of northern plants and animals. Edéhzhíe encompasses the Horn Plateau, a 600-metre escarpment rising above the Mackenzie Valley, and the surrounding area of boreal forest drained by the Horn and Willowlake rivers. Edéhzhíe provides important habitat for boreal woodland caribou and wood bison: two threatened species listed under the federal Species at Risk Act. It also contains a portion of Mills Lake, a key habitat site hosting significant portions of the national population of migratory birds, including 12 per cent of Canada's eastern population of Tundra swans and 14 per cent of our mid-continent population of greater white-fronted geese. By designating Edéhzhíe as an Indigenous protected area and national wildlife area, the Dehcho First Nations and the Government of Canada will work together to protect the area's ecological integrity from impacts of future development and ensure that the Dehcho Dene way of life is maintained for present and future generations.

The Edéhzhíe Protected Area is the first Indigenous protected area designated in Canada under Budget 2018's Nature Legacy, and it is an important step toward reconciliation with Indigenous Peoples. Support for Indigenous protected areas was a key recommendation of the Indigenous Circle of Experts' report released in March 2018 and a commitment made in Budget 2018. Protection of this area was achieved through a collaborative process between the Dehcho First Nations and the Government of Canada. This new protection will ensure that the relationships between the Dehcho Dene peoples and the lands of Edéhzhíe are maintained for present and future generations. The Indigenous protected area will encourage Dehcho Dene presence on the land and continuance of language, harvesting, and other aspects of Dehcho Dene culture. Furthermore, the lands that make up the Edéhzhíe Protected Area will make a significant contribution to Canada's international commitment to protecting 17 per cent of land and fresh water by 2020. The Edéhzhíe Protected Area is 14,218 square kilometres, covering an area more than twice the size of Banff National Park.

Environment and Climate Change Canada is also working in collaboration with the Dehcho First Nations to formally designate the area as a national wildlife area by 2020. Establishing Edéhzhíe as a national wildlife area will complement the objectives of the Indigenous protected area by providing additional protection and stewardship measures. By joining the national network of national wildlife areas, Edéhzhíe will have even greater support to achieve results for the conservation of wildlife and wildlife habitat.

A key part of the establishment of Edéhzhíe is the expansion of Dehcho K'éhodi. The Dehcho K'éhodi Stewardship Program is a regional on-the-land program for stewardship activities. Dehcho K'éhodi means "taking care of the Dehcho" in the language of the Dehcho Dene. Resourcing this program to operate in the protected area is a core element of the Edéhzhíe establishment agreement and an essential part of the Indigenous protected area management. The guardians will be responsible for much of the monitoring and management of Edéhzhíe. The Dehcho K'éhodi will undertake on-the-land stewardship activities including patrols, research projects, and youth mentoring in the Indigenous protected area. Local Dene guardians will be the eyes and ears of Edéhzhíe. Along with Dene laws and values, their work will be guided by a management plan developed by the Edéhzhíe management board. The board will be made up of representatives from the Dehcho First Nations and Environment and Climate Change Canada, and it will make its decisions by consensus.

Notes and Questions

1. How much potential do Indigenous parks offer as a means of addressing the broad suite of purposes that parks and protected areas have been traditionally called upon to serve? What points of friction might exist

between the interests that traditionally have been asserted to support parks and protected areas and those that support the recognition of tribal parks?

2. The *Mikisew* decision, below, arose in litigation that was pursued in parallel with the *CPAWS* case discussed above. Consider what lessons can be drawn from the *Mikisew* case in terms of the evolution of Parks Canada policy with respect to First Nations' rights and interests.

Mikisew Cree First Nation v.
Canada (Minister of Canadian Heritage)
2005 SCC 69

BINNIE J.: — The fundamental objective of the modern law of aboriginal and treaty rights is the reconciliation of aboriginal peoples and non-aboriginal peoples and their respective claims, interests and ambitions. The management of these relationships takes place in the shadow of a long history of grievances and misunderstanding. The multitude of smaller grievances created by the indifference of some government officials to aboriginal people's concerns, and the lack of respect inherent in that indifference has been as destructive of the process of reconciliation as some of the larger and more explosive controversies. And so it is in this case.

Treaty 8 is one of the most important of the post-Confederation treaties. Made in 1899, the First Nations who lived in the area surrendered to the Crown 840,000 square kilometres of what is now northern Alberta, northeastern British Columbia, northwestern Saskatchewan and the southern portion of the Northwest Territories. Some idea of the size of this surrender is given by the fact that it dwarfs France (543,998 square kilometres), exceeds the size of Manitoba (650,087 square kilometres), Saskatchewan (651,900 square kilometres) and Alberta (661,185 square kilometres) and approaches the size of British Columbia (948,596 square kilometres). In exchange for this surrender, the First Nations were promised reserves and some other benefits including, most importantly to them, the following rights of hunting, trapping, and fishing:

[In 2001], the federal government approved a 118-kilometre winter road that, as originally conceived, ran through the new Mikisew First Nation Reserve at Peace Point. The government did not think it necessary to engage in consultation directly with the Mikisew before making this decision. After the Mikisew protested, the winter road alignment was changed to track the boundary of the Peace Point reserve instead of running through it, again without consultation with the Mikisew. The modified road alignment traversed the traplines of approximately 14 Mikisew families who reside in the area near the proposed road, and others who may trap in that area although they do not live there, and the hunting grounds of as many as 100 Mikisew people whose hunt (mainly of moose), the Mikisew say, would be adversely affected. The fact the proposed winter road directly affects only about 14 Mikisew trappers and perhaps 100 hunters may not seem very dramatic (unless you happen to be one of the trappers or hunters in question) but, in the context of a remote northern community of relatively few families, it is significant. Beyond that, however, the principle of consultation in advance of interference with existing treaty rights is a matter of broad general importance to the relations between aboriginal and non-aboriginal peoples. It goes to the heart of the relationship and concerns not only the Mikisew but other First Nations and non-aboriginal governments as well.

In this case, the relationship was not properly managed. Adequate consultation in advance of the Minister's approval did not take place. The government's approach did not advance the process of reconciliation but undermined it. The duty of consultation which flows from the honour of the Crown, and its obligation to respect the existing treaty rights of aboriginal peoples (now entrenched in s. 35 of the *Constitution Act, 1982*), was breached.

The Mikisew appeal should be allowed, the Minister's approval quashed, and the matter returned to the Minister for further consultation and consideration.

Facts

About 5 percent of the territory surrendered under Treaty 8 was set aside in 1922 as Wood Buffalo National Park. The Park was created principally to protect the last remaining herds of wood bison (or buffalo) in northern Canada and covers 44,807 square kilometres of land straddling the boundary between northern Alberta and southerly parts of the Northwest Territories. It is designated a UNESCO World Heritage Site. The Park itself is larger than Switzerland.

At present, it contains the largest free-roaming, self-regulating bison herd in the world, the last remaining natural nesting area for the endangered whooping crane, and vast undisturbed natural boreal forests. More to the point, it was been inhabited by First Nation peoples for more than over 8,000 years, some of whom still earn a subsistence living hunting, fishing and commercial trapping within the Park boundaries. The Park includes the traditional lands of the Mikisew. As a result of the *Treaty Land Entitlement Agreement*, the Peace Point Reserve was formally excluded from the Park in 1988 but of course is surrounded by it.

The members of the Mikisew Cree First Nation are descendants of the Crees of Fort Chipewyan who signed Treaty 8 on June 21, 1899. It is common ground that its members are entitled to the benefits of Treaty 8.

The Winter Road Project

The proponent of the winter road is the respondent Thebacha Road Society, whose members include the Town of Fort Smith (located in the Northwest Territories on the northeastern boundary of Wood Buffalo National Park, where the Park headquarters is located), the Fort Smith Métis Council, the Salt River First Nation, and Little Red River Cree First Nation. The advantage of the winter road for these people is that it would provide direct winter access among a number of isolated northern communities and to the Alberta highway system to the south. The trial judge accepted that the government's objective was to meet "regional transportation needs".

The Consultation Process

According to the trial judge, most of the communications relied on by the Minister to demonstrate appropriate consultation were instances of the Mikisew's being provided with standard information about the proposed road in the same form and substance as the communications being distributed to the general public of interested stakeholders. Thus Parks Canada acting for the Minister, provided the Mikisew with the Terms of Reference for the environmental assessment on January 19, 2000. The Mikisew were advised that open house sessions would take place over the summer of 2000. The Minister says that the first formal response from the Mikisew did not come until October 10, 2000, some two months after the deadline she had imposed for "public" comment. Chief Poitras stated that the Mikisew did not formally participate in the open houses, because "... an open house is not a forum for us to be consulted adequately".

On May 25, 2001, the Minister announced on the Parks Canada website that the Thebacha Road Society was authorised to build a winter road 10 metres wide with posted speed limits ranging from 10 to 40 kilometres per hour. The approval was said to be in accordance with "Parks Canada plans and policy" and "other federal laws and regulations". No reference was made to any obligations to the Mikisew.

The Minister now says the Mikisew ought not to be heard to complain, about the process of consultation because they declined to participate in the public process that took place. Consultation is a two-way street, she says. It was up to the Mikisew to take advantage of what was on offer. They failed to do so. In the Minister's view, she did her duty.

The proposed winter road is wide enough to allow two vehicles to pass. Pursuant to s. 36(5) of the *Wood Buffalo National Park Game Regulations*, SOR/78-830, creation of the road would trigger a 200-metre wide corridor within which the use of firearms would be prohibited. The total area of this corridor would be approximately 23 square kilometres.

The Mikisew objection goes beyond the direct impact of closure of the area covered by the winter road to hunting and trapping. The surrounding area would be, the trial judge found, injuriously affected. Maintaining a traditional lifestyle, which the Mikisew say is central to their culture, depends on keeping the land around the Peace Point reserve in its natural condition and this, they contend, is essential to allow them to pass their culture and skills onto the next generation of Mikisew. The detrimental impact of the road on hunting and trapping, they argue, may simply prove to be one more incentive for their young people to abandon a traditional lifestyle and turn to other modes of living in the south.

Analysis

The post-Confederation numbered treaties were designed to open up the Canadian west and northwest to settlement and development. Treaty 8 itself recites that "the said Indians have been notified and informed by Her Majesty's said commission that it is Her desire to open for settlement, immigration, trade, travel, mining, lumbering and such other purposes as to Her Majesty may seem meet". This stated purpose is reflected in a corresponding limitation on the Treaty 8 hunting, fishing and trapping rights to exclude such "tracts as may be required or taken up from time to time for settlement, mining, lumbering, trading or other purposes". The "other purposes" would be at least as broad as the purposes listed in the recital, mentioned above, including "travel".

There was thus from the outset an uneasy tension between the First Nations' essential demand that they continue to be as free to live off the land after the treaty as before and the Crown's expectation of increasing numbers of non-aboriginal people moving into the surrendered territory.

As Cory J. explained in *Badger*, at para. 57, "[t]he Indians understood that land would be taken up for homesteads, farming, prospecting and mining and that they would not be able to hunt in these areas or to shoot at the settlers' farm animals or buildings".

The Process of Treaty Implementation

Both the historical context and the inevitable tensions underlying implementation of Treaty 8 demand a *process* by which lands may be transferred from the one category (where the First Nations retain rights to hunt, fish and trap) to the other category (where they do not). The content of the process is dictated by the duty of the Crown to act honourably. Although *Haida Nation* was not a treaty case, McLachlin C.J. pointed out, at paras. 19 and 35:

> The honour of the Crown also infuses the processes of treaty making and treaty interpretation. In making and applying treaties, the Crown must act with honour and integrity, avoiding even the appearance of "sharp dealing" (*Badger*, at para. 41). Thus in *Marshall*, *supra*, at para. 4, the majority of this Court supported its interpretation of a treaty by stating that "nothing less would uphold the honour and integrity of the Crown in its dealings with the Mi'kmaq people to secure their peace and friendship".

> But, when precisely does a duty to consult arise? The foundation of the duty in the Crown's honour and the goal of reconciliation suggest that the duty arises when the Crown has knowledge, real or constructive, of the potential existence of the Aboriginal right or title and contemplates conduct that might adversely affect it.

The Mikisew Legal Submission

The appellant, the Mikisew, essentially reminded the Court of what was said in *Haida Nation* and *Taku River*. This case, the Mikisew say, is stronger. In those cases, unlike here, the aboriginal interest to the lands was asserted but not yet proven. In this case, the aboriginal interests are protected by Treaty 8. They are established legal facts. As in *Haida Nation*, the trial judge found the aboriginal interest was threatened by the proposed development. If a duty to consult was found to exist in *Haida Nation* and *Taku River* then *a fortiori*, the Mikisew argue, it must arise here and the majority judgment of the Federal Court of Appeal was quite wrong to characterise consultation between governments and aboriginal peoples as nothing more than a "good practice".

The Minister's Response

The respondent Minister seeks to distinguish *Haida Nation* and *Taku River*. Her counsel advances three broad propositions in support of the Minister's approval of the proposed winter road.

1. In "taking up" the 23 square kilometres for the winter road the Crown was doing no more than Treaty 8 entitled it to do. The Crown as well as First Nations have rights under Treaty 8. The exercise by the Crown of *its*

Treaty right to "take up" land is not an infringement of the Treaty but the performance of it.

2. The Crown went through extensive consultations with First Nations in 1899 at the time Treaty 8 was negotiated. Whatever duty of accommodation was owed to First Nations was discharged at that time. The terms of the Treaty do not contemplate further consultations whenever a "taking up" occurs.

3. In the event further consultation was required, the process followed by the Minister through Parks Canada in this case was sufficient.

For the reasons that follow, I believe that each of these propositions must be rejected.

In "Taking Up" Land for the Win[t]er Road the Crown Was Doing No More Than It Was Entitled to Do under the Treaty

The Minister [...] assert[s] [...] that the test ought to be "whether, after the taking up, it still remains reasonably practicable, within the Province as a whole, for the Indians to hunt, fish and trap for food [to] the extent that they choose to do so" (emphasis added). This cannot be correct. It suggests that a prohibition on hunting at Peace Point would be acceptable so long as decent hunting was still available in the Treaty 8 area north of Jasper, about 800 kilometres distant across the province, equivalent to a commute between Toronto and Quebec City (809 kilometres) or Edmonton and Regina (785 kilometres). One might as plausibly invite the truffle diggers of southern France to try their luck in the Austrian Alps, about the same distance as the journey across Alberta deemed by the Minister to be an acceptable fulfilment of the promises of Treaty 8.

The "meaningful right to hunt" is not ascertained on a treaty-wide basis (all 840,000 square kilometres of it) but in relation to the territories over which a First Nation traditionally hunted, fished and trapped, and continues to do so today. If the time comes that in the case of a particular Treaty 8 First Nation "no meaningful right to hunt" remains over *its* traditional territories, the significance of the oral promise that "the same means of earning a livelihood would continue after the treaty as existed before it" would clearly be in question, and a potential action for treaty infringement, including the demand for a *Sparrow* justification, would be a legitimate First Nation response.

Did the Extensive Consultations with First Nations Undertaken in 1899 at the Time Treaty 8 Was Negotiated Discharge the Crown's Duty of Consultation and Accommodation?

The Crown's second broad answer to the Mikisew claim is that whatever had to be done was done in 1899. The Minister contends:

> While the government should consider the impact on the treaty right, there is no duty to accommodate in this context. The treaty itself constitutes the accommodation of the aboriginal interest; taking up lands, as defined above, leaves intact the essential ability of the Indians to continue to hunt, fish and trap. As long as that promise is honoured, the treaty is not breached and no separate duty to accommodate arises. [Emphasis added]

This is not correct. Consultation that excludes from the outset any form of accommodation would be meaningless. The contemplated process is not simply one of giving the Mikisew an opportunity to blow off steam before the Minister proceeds to do what she intended to do all along. Treaty making is an important stage in the long process of reconciliation, but it is only a stage. What occurred at Fort Chipewyan in 1899 was not the complete discharge of the duty arising from the honour of the Crown, but a rededication of it.

The Crown has a treaty right to "take up" surrendered lands for regional transportation purposes, but the Crown is nevertheless under an obligation to inform itself of the impact its project will have on the exercise by the Mikisew of their hunting and trapping rights, and to communicate its findings to the Mikisew. The Crown must then attempt to deal with the Mikisew "in good faith, and with the intention of substantially addressing" Mikisew concerns (*Delgamuukw*, at para. 168). This does not mean that whenever a government proposes to do anything in the Treaty 8 surrendered lands it must consult with all signatory First Nations, no matter how remote or unsubstantial the impact. The duty to consult is, as stated in *Haida Nation*, triggered at a low threshold, but adverse impact is a matter of degree, as is the extent of the Crown's duty. Here the impacts were clear, established and demonstrably adverse to the continued exercise of the Mikisew hunting and trapping rights over the lands in question.

In summary, the 1899 negotiations were the first step in a long journey that is unlikely to end any time soon. [...]

Was the Process Followed by the Minister Through Parks Canada in This Case Sufficient?

I should state at the outset that the winter road proposed by the Minister was a permissible purpose for "taking up" lands under Treaty 8. It is obvious that the listed purposes of "settlement, mining, lumbering" and "trading" all require suitable transportation. The treaty does not spell out permissible "other purposes" but the term should not be read restrictively.

The question is whether the Minister and her staff pursued the permitted purpose of regional transportation needs in accordance with the Crown's duty to consult. The answer turns on the particulars of that duty shaped by the circumstances here. In *Delgamuukw*, the Court considered the duty to consult and accommodate in the context of an infringement of aboriginal title (at para. 168).

In *Haida Nation*, the Court pursued the kinds of duties that may arise in pre-proof claim situations, and McLachlin C.J. used the concept of a spectrum to frame her analysis (at paras. 43—45).

The determination of the content of the duty to consult will, as *Haida* suggests, be governed by the context. One variable will be the specificity of the promises made. Where, for example, a treaty calls for certain supplies, or Crown payment of treaty monies, or a modern land claims settlement imposes specific obligations on aboriginal peoples with respect to identified resources, the role of consultation may be quite limited. If the respective obligations are clear the parties should get on with performance. Another contextual factor will be the seriousness of the impact on the aboriginal people of the Crown's proposed course of action. The more serious the impact the more important will be the role of consultation.

Another factor in a non-treaty case, as *Haida* points out, will be the strength of the aboriginal claim. The history of dealings between the Crown and a particular First Nation may also be significant. Here, the most important contextual factor is that Treaty 8 provides a framework within which to manage the continuing changes in land use already foreseen in 1899 and expected, even now, to continue well into the future. In that context, consultation is key to achievement of the overall objective of the modern law of treaty and aboriginal rights, namely reconciliation.

The duty here has both informational and response components. In this case, given that the Crown is proposing to build a fairly minor winter road on *surrendered* lands where the Mikisew hunting, fishing and trapping rights are expressly subject to the "taking up" limitation, I believe the Crown's duty lies at the lower end of the spectrum. The Crown was required to provide notice to the Mikisew and to engage directly with them (and not, as seems to have been the case here, as an afterthought to a general public consultation with Park users). This engagement ought to have included the provision of information about the project addressing what the Crown knew to be Mikisew interests and what the Crown anticipated might be the potential adverse impact on those interests. The Crown was required to solicit and to listen carefully to the Mikisew concerns, and to attempt to minimize adverse impacts on the Mikisew hunting, fishing and trapping rights. The Crown did not discharge this obligation when it unilaterally declared the road realignment would be shifted from the reserve itself to a track along its boundary.

Had the consultation process gone ahead, it would not have given the Mikisew a veto over the alignment of the road. As emphasized in *Haida Nation*, consultation will not always lead to accommodation, and accommodation may or may not result in an agreement. There could, however, be changes in the road alignment or construction that would go a long way towards satisfying the Mikisew objections. We do not know, and the Minister cannot know in the absence of consultation, what such changes might be.

In the result I would allow the appeal, quash the Minister's approval order, and remit the winter road project to the Minister to be dealt with in accordance with these reasons.

Notes and Questions

1. The importance of *Mikisew* extends far beyond the interactions between First Nations with treaty rights in Canadian parks and the federal government. In many ways, the decision sheds new light on the obligations of government generally when making land or resource use decisions that potentially affect treaty rights. In this vein, Professor Bankes argues that three features of *Mikisew* are especially important:

   > First, it confirms that the First Nation signatories to the numbered treaties have a continuing interest in their traditional territories and that the provincial Crown cannot ignore this interest. Although expressed in formal terms as a hunting right, the Court protects this interest by imposing on the Crown a duty to consult in

relation to any disposition or regulatory decision that may affect the quality or quantity of that right. The case will have implications not only for Crown disposition policies but also, and perhaps more importantly, for the regulatory activities of government departments and regulatory tribunals such as the Energy and Utilities Board. Second, the case confirms that the treaty right to hunt is not exhausted by its use as a defence to a charge of illegal harvesting of wildlife or other natural resources. *Mikisew* therefore adds to the body of case law in which First Nations have used the treaty right to hunt as a sword to contest competing land use policies. Third, by severing the source of the duty to consult from a rights infringement, and by locating that duty in the honour of the Crown rather than the particular language of the treaty, the court has indicated its willingness to develop a body of constitutional common law to apply to the intersocietal relationship between indigenous and settler societies in order to further the objective of reconciliation enshrined in s. 35 of the *Constitution Act, 1982.*

(N. Bankes, "Mikisew Cree and the Lands Taken Up Clause of the Numbered Treaties" (2005-2006) 92 Resources 1, at 7.)

2. In many provinces, an emerging issue is balancing the goals of promoting biodiversity protection and conservation with the Crown's constitutional obligation to recognize and respect Aboriginal rights and title. This is particularly true in British Columbia, where much of the land base with high conservation values currently facing resource development pressures is subject to unresolved Aboriginal rights and title claims.

A key venue in which this challenge has played out is BC's Central and North Coast, the future of which, for much of the last decade, has been the subject of intense negotiations involving provincial government, First Nations and conservation organizations. The size of the area in question is approximately 6.4 million hectares, or more than twice the size of Vancouver Island. Included in the area is a large intact coastal old-growth area, dubbed by conservationists as the "Great Bear Rainforest". Ultimately, as a result of a collaborative process that involved First Nations, industry, environmentalists, local governments and other stakeholders, a comprehensive plan for the management of the area was developed. One of the prerequisites to implementing this plan was amending BC's *Park Act*, R.S.B.C. 1996, c. 344, to create a new protected area designation known as "conservancies": see the *Park (Conservancy Enabling) Amendment Act, 2006*, S.B.C. 2006, c. 25 (Bill 28).

This new designation addresses First Nations' concerns about their traditional territories being designated for protection under predecessor provincial legislation. These concerns included the need to maintain and protect Aboriginal food, social and ceremonial rights and the need to ensure that opportunities for low impact compatible economic activities were not lost. As the result of government-to-government negotiations between First Nations and the provincial government on the Central and North Coast, the amendments explicitly recognize the importance of maintaining and protecting First Nations values related to social, ceremonial and cultural uses. At the same time, a wider range of low impact, compatible economic opportunities may be permitted in a conservancy than in a Class A park. In a Class A park, economic activities are limited to those related to recreation and tourism. Compatible economic activities in conservancies must be consistent with the legislation and are determined through a management planning process. Commercial logging, mining, and hydro-electric power generation (other than run-of-river/"micro-hydro" projects) are prohibited in conservancies. A park use permit may be issued for local run-of-river projects within conservancies, for the purposes of supplying power for approved uses in a conservancy or to nearby communities that do not have access to the power grid.

Currently, North and Central Coast First Nations are developing Collabora-tive Management Agreements with the province, which specify how the conservancies in each First Nations' territory will be managed collaboratively in a government-to-government relationship.

**Katherine Turner & Christopher Bitonti,
"Conservancies in British Columbia, Canada: Bringing
Together Protected Areas and First Nations' Interests"**
(2011) 2 Int'l. Indigenous Pol'y J. 1

The new protected area (PA) designation of Conservancy in British Columbia, Canada, is a positive addition to the provincial PA system because it marks a shift in government policy concerning PAs and the role of First Nations in land and resource management and conservation. Until recent decades, many parks and other protected areas in British Columbia, across Canada, and elsewhere were regularly established with little to no recognition of Indigenous People's interests, traditional ecological knowledge, or territorial rights and title. Consequently, ecological conservation through PAs has often resulted in negative impacts for Aboriginal Peoples in Canada and other local and Indigenous Peoples around the world. The legal mandate of parks and other PAs, as well as the assumptions surrounding them, however, appear to be changing in ways that better reflect, acknowledge and incorporate the resource and territorial rights of local and Indigenous Peoples. The incorporation of Conservancies into the BC Parks System, in 2006, is the first substantive evidence of a new approach to PAs at the Provincial-level in Canada. Unlike other designations under the BC Park Act, Conservancies were created "expressly to recognize the importance of some natural areas to First Nations for food, social and ceremonial purposes". Individual First Nations and the Provincial Government are enacting this objective through collaborative planning and management. This paper presents a review of Conservancies within a political ecology and legal context, and offers a preliminary assessment of some of the opportunities and challenges presented by this new designation.

The New Arrival: An Overview of British Columbia Conservancies

In 2006, the Government of British Columbia amended the province's Park Act (the Act) to establish Conservancies as a new designation of provincial protected area. It is the first and only provincial-level PA designation in Canada to explicitly incorporate First Nations' interests into its legal framework. Pursuant to section 5(3.1) of the Act, Conservancies are set-aside for four distinct purposes:

1. "[...] the protection and maintenance of their biological diversity and natural environments";

2. "[...] the preservation and maintenance of social, ceremonial and cultural uses of First Nations";

3. "[...] the protection and maintenance of their recreational values"; and

4. "[...] to ensure that development or use of their natural resources occurs in a sustainable manner consistent with the" first three purposes.

The Minister of Environment has expressly stated that these four purposes (local ecological integrity, Aboriginal use, recreation, and sustainable resource development) are intended to complement each other, with each being given equal priority in decision-making surrounding the use and management of a Conservancy.

Conservancies are distinguished from other PA designations under the Act by two main features that reflect their purposes. First is the explicit recognition of First Nations' social, cultural and ceremonial uses within the PA. Secondly, the test for issuing Park Use Permits (PUPs) explicitly restricts commercial logging, mining, or commercial hydro-electricity, but allows local First Nations on a priority basis and others, to pursue a wider diversity of low-impact economic development activities within a Conservancy than is possible within Class A parks.

There is also a procedural difference that distinguishes Conservancies from other provincial PAs: the identification of areas for Conservancy classification is undertaken in conjunction between individual First Nations and the Province. In this way, First Nations are partners in selecting locations within their traditional territories that could benefit from the protection and land use agreements afforded by a Conservancy designation. It is important to remember, however, that aboriginal title has not been extinguished in British Columbia (*Delgamuukw v. BC*, 1997) and therefore Conservancies may still be subject to Aboriginal land claims despite the cooperative model for establishing and managing these PAs. Any party, including First Nations, must apply for a PUP permit, which will only be granted if the proposed economic use fits within the framework of the purposes of laid out in s. 5(3.1) of the Act, the specific Conservancy management plan, if there is one, as well as BC's Parks Impact Assessment. Permissible economic activities include, wildlife viewing, guided hiking and fishing, shellfish aquaculture, and small-scale, run-of-the-river hydro projects for local and tourism needs (BC, 2011; Turning Point, 2009).

The new Conservancy designation has been widely implemented since its inception in 2006. By March 2011, 144 Conservancies, covering 2,119,131 ha of the provinces, were established in BC through inclusion in schedules to the *Protected Areas of British Columbia Act*. Conservancies now comprise approximately 16% of the BC's total 13,142,123 ha of protected areas and are second in their contribution to this total only to Class A Parks (at 10,418,083 ha). Though originally created specifically for implementation in the North and Central Coast regions of the province (Bill 28, 2006), the Conservancy designation has since been extended to other regions, including Haida Gwaii, Morice, and Sea-to-Sky. [...]

Conservancies within Canadian Protected Areas: Policy and Practice

Conservancies are an international PA designation and one that is gaining currency in Pas that are designated for local, sustainable resource use in many parts of the world, as in the Conservancies of Namibia. In Canada and the United States, the designation of Land Trust has been a more common category than Conservancy to denote areas of combined human use and ecological conservation, but these trusts often refer to private lands and therefore are not appropriate for First Nations' lands. The search for a new category of PA within BC, in many respects mirrors a search in recent decades at international, national and regional levels for PA categories that provide for livelihood needs and "conservation with a human face", which includes respect for and recognition of the Rights of Indigenous Peoples. This search has resulted in new types of Pas that provide more pluralistic options for conservation that recognizes humans as a part of, and not separated from, natural systems.

At the federal level within Canada, changes to national parks policy and practice are fledging, but apparent. The shift in federal policy to recognize the rights and perspectives of Aboriginal Peoples in parks and PA policy has been significantly influenced by a series of legal challenges by Aboriginal Peoples against the Canadian government. The Inuit initiated the first such case during the 1970s. They argued successfully that the Federal Government's plans to expand the National Parks System through the establishment of a number of new northern parks was tantamount to unilateral expropriation of Aboriginal lands and, therefore, in contravention of the Canadian Bill of Rights (McNamee, 2009). The result was an amendment to the National Parks Act that allowed for the creation of National Park Reserves, in which, "the Native People were not giving up their claim to lands to which they asserted Aboriginal title; they simply agreed to allow the federal government to administer parks on their land until such time as their land claims agreement was ratified by both Parliament and the Inuit" (McNamee, 2009, p. 43).

This process set a precedent for other National Parks Reserves in both northern and southern Canada as well as for Federal Government negotiation with both affected Aboriginal Peoples and Provincial or Territorial Governments during the creation of new National Parks (McNamee, 2009). The growing recognition of Aboriginal rights within Canadian PA policy has also been enhanced by a series of other court cases that are accumulating a growing body of law supporting Aboriginal rights and title, including: The *Calder* Case, The *Sparrow* Case, The *Delgamuukw* Case (*Delgamuukw v. BC*, 1997), and more recently *Haida* and *Tuke* and *Sappier* and *Polchies*, as well as lobbying efforts that led to changes in the Constitution Act, 1982. These cases have established the legally constituted existence of Aboriginal rights, as well as the duty of governments and industry to consult with Aboriginal groups prior to land and resource use decisions affecting Aboriginal peoples and territories.

Changes to Parks Canada policy to recognize Aboriginal interests in ecological protection alongside those of the Government and other stakeholders also have implications for the stability of conservation through parks and other PAs. Boyd argues, "The strongest legal protection that can be given to a park in Canada is inclusion in treaty and land claims settlements with Aboriginal people". Indeed, it has been suggested that Canadian parks have entered a new era — the

Aboriginal Period — in which Aboriginal people are gaining a paramount influence in Canadian conservation policy.

In spite of these successes, access by Aboriginal peoples to lands and natural resources in Canadian parks and PAs can depend on a variety of factors, including the particular statutory framework of a park or other PA, treaty rights held by an Aboriginal group4, as well as how, where and when Aboriginal rights and title are established.[5] Resultantly, levels of access vary significantly across the country.

Furthermore, changes in federal policy and practice have not been paralleled by substantive changes at the provincial and territorial level. Provincial and territorial PAs constitute approximately two-thirds of Canada's total PA system (Boyd, 2003, p.169). Although there is a diversity of classifications for parks and other PAs at the provincial-level, our review of provincial parks and PA categories across Canada [...] found the designation of Conservancy in BC to be the only provincial designation that explicitly incorporates First Nations peoples into planning and management, and enshrines the "preservation and maintenance of social, ceremonial and cultural uses of First Nations" (Act, s. 5(3.1)), alongside the need for low-impact economic activities, as central features of a PA.

Momentum for a New Approach to PAs in British Columbia

BC's new Conservancy designation emerged as part of a twenty-year shift in Government-First Nations relations in the province. Prompted by intense conflict between industry, First Nations, environmentalists and other stakeholders over land and resource use during the 1980s and early 1990s, the government committed to establishing what it termed a "New Relationship" with British Columbian First Nations. These New Relationship commitments with First Nations emerged alongside other commitments by the Province to develop a new collaborative land use approach for BC.

The first steps in bridging these commitments focused on land use decisions on the Central and North Coast, which resulted in sub-regional land use plans containing recommendations to the Province with respect to managing public land and resources. These Land and Resource Management Plans (LRMPs) were initiated by the Ministry of Sustainable Resource Management in consultation with a broad set of stakeholders, including governments, conservation groups, industry, and First Nations (BC, 2001). Although Coastal First Nations were represented, they abstained from the decision-making process at the LRMP stage (Coastal First Nations, n.d.b), choosing instead to create their own land and resource management plans designed for their specific territories.

Discrepancies between the LRMPs and the local land use plans were resolved first by Coastal First Nations and the Province) and the Province entering into the Land and Resource Protocol Agreements (LRPAs) to structure decision-making and next through Strategic Land Use Planning Agreements (SLUPAs), negotiated on a government-to-government basis between individual First Nations and the Province. SLUPAs include demarcations of specific land-use zones in the territory, what those zones are intended for, as well as specific management objectives.

The idea for Conservancies emerged during the LRMPs, LRPAs, and SLUPAs negotiations when it was recognized that a new PA designation was needed to support the LRMPs and the New Relationship (BC, 2011). Areas within

First Nations' traditional territory that First Nations and the government felt could benefit from Conservancy status were identified during the creation of Land Use Plans. [...]

Conclusions

BC's Conservancy designation is a positive addition to the BC PAs system, because of the unique combination of local ecological conservation, Aboriginal use, recreation, and allowance for sustainable resource development intertwined in the Conservancy mandate. Furthermore, Conservancies are significant because of the joint-management conditions under which new areas are identified, established and managed. As such, Conservancies are an integrated response to the interlocking challenges facing many parts of the province: pressures for resource development, the need for job creation, and the imperatives of conservation and respect for First Nations rights.

The creation of Conservancies seems to demonstrate a substantive shift in planning and management of parks and other PAs in BC with respect to First Nations-Government relations. However, as Berkes cautions, there are no panacea approaches to conservation. Rather, plurality and inclusivity in the tools and approaches to conservation should be sought. In this way, Conservancies are a positive addition to the BC Protected Areas System, since they increase the diversity and scope of PAs within the province.

Whether or not other provincial park authorities in Canada will adopt similar designations in the future will likely depend on the continued successful implementation and management of BC Conservancies. Likely the success of individual Conservancies in meeting their broad set of objectives will vary, reflecting a range in the effectiveness of capacity building, management plan implementation and evaluation, as well as other local and institutional contexts. An ongoing commitment by both the provincial government and First Nations to work together and to invest time and resources in the management of BC's new PAs is vital in order to ensure that the spirit of the Conservancy legislation, related government-to-government agreements and land management plans continue to be upheld in both the short and long term.

Notes and Questions

1. The preceding article suggests that "Canadian parks have entered a new era — the Aboriginal Period — in which Aboriginal people are gaining a paramount influence in Canadian conservation policy". Do you agree? What *indicia* support this conclusion?

2. In the not-too-distant past, as set out in several of the articles excerpted in this Part, governments created many parks and protected areas without consulting affected First Nations. This has resulted in areas being set aside for "protection" that First Nations have traditionally relied upon for various forms of subsistence. Revisiting these designations to ensure that they do not preclude traditional hunting and gathering activities, and ensuring that future designations occur only after appropriate consultations with First

Nations organizations and communities are critical issues for many working in this area.

Given the foregoing, where and how do you see the "conservancy" designation discussed above playing a role in future parks and protected areas discussions? What features of the conservancy designation might allow it to gain traction and support with First Nations (and potentially others) as opposed to other designations?

Part IV — Emerging Issues in Parks and Protected Areas Law

In this concluding Part, we offer some prospective thoughts on the future of protected areas law in Canada. Two themes, in our view, are especially deserving of attention in this regard. The first theme concerns the potential for citizens to secure greater protection for protected areas using the public trust doctrine. In Chapter 2, we provided an overview of the doctrine and discussed the implications of *British Columbia v. Canadian Forest Products Ltd.*, 2004 SCC 38 ("*Canfor*"), a decision that observers suggest may portend a more robust role for the doctrine in Canadian law in the years ahead. This is especially true, we would argue, in the context of securing enhanced protection for protected areas. The second theme concerns the potential and options for law reform. To manage our expanding protected areas network, both provincially and nationally, many have argued that we need to enhance the legal regimes under which they are governed. In order to consider some of the law reform options that present themselves, we examine the key features of Ontario's *Provincial Parks and Conservation Reserves Act, 2006*, S.O. 2006, c. 12.

The Public Trust Doctrine

Chapter 2 introduced the public trust doctrine as a common law principle, vesting in the Crown a trust-like duty to protect public resources for the benefit of the public at large. In its common law guise, the doctrine has ancient roots. And in more modern times, especially in the United States, it has proven to be a powerful tool to advance the goals of environmental stewardship. In contrast, in Canada until recently, the doctrine has been relatively quiescent. Academic commentators, however, believe that the decision in *Canfor* may create an opportunity for the doctrine to blossom.

One realm in which the doctrine could play a particularly important role is in the context of public resources that are governed by parks legislation. In this setting, it is argued that such resources are protected by not only a common law public trust but also a statutory one. The argument that the Crown is under a statutory public trust in managing parks derives from the dedication language that is frequently present in parks legislation. For example, as discussed below, the CNPA states that:

4(1) The national parks of Canada are hereby dedicated to the people of Canada for their benefit, education and enjoyment, subject to this Act and the regulations, and the parks shall be maintained and made use of so as to leave them unimpaired for the enjoyment of future generations.

Comparable, although in some instances less unequivocal, language is contained in most provincial parks laws.

Both in the United States and in Canada, environmental organizations have sought to compel governments to take action to protect public resources within parks, contending that analogous dedication provisions create an actionable right to enforce a statutory public trust. Below we offer excerpts from two early cases where this argument was mounted. The differing analyses and outcomes are illustrative of the general trajectory of the public trust doctrine to date.

Sierra Club v. Department of Interior
376 F. Supp. 90 (N.D. Cal., 1974)

SWEIGERT D.J.: — This is an action by plaintiff, Sierra Club, against the Department of the Interior, and officials of the Department, to obtain judgment of this court directing defendants to use certain of their powers to protect Redwood National Park from damage allegedly caused or threatened by certain logging operations on peripheral privately-owned lands.

[The] complaint alleges in substance and effect as follows:

> That subsequent to the establishment of the Redwood National Park in 1968 plaintiff learned that logging operations on slopes surrounding and upstream from the park were seriously endangering the park's resources, and that these dangers were reported to defendants

> That on September 24, 1971, plaintiff formally petitioned the Secretary of the Interior to take immediate action pursuant to his authority under the *Redwood National Park Act* to prevent further harm to the park's resources, and that a task force was then created by the Department of the Interior to make intensive field investigations of the threatened and actual damage to the Redwood National Park and to prepare a report of its findings;

> That defendants have taken no action to prevent damage to the park from the consequences of logging on lands surrounding or upstream from the park, except to request the voluntary cooperation of timber companies to reform their operations on minor portions upstream and upslope from the park; that the timber companies have not effectively cooperated with this request and that defendants manifest no intent to protect the park from further damage to the park's trees, soil, scenery and streams; That past and present logging operations on privately-owned steep slopes on the periphery of the park leave the park vulnerable to high winds, landslides, mudslides and siltation in the streams which endangers tree roots and aquatic life.

Plaintiff, citing the *National Park System Act* and the *Redwood National Park Act* contends that defendants have a judicially-enforceable duty to exercise certain powers granted by these provisions to prevent or to mitigate such actual or potential damage to the park and its redwoods as is alleged in the complaint.

The *National Park System Act* provides for the creation of the National Park Service in the Department of the Interior which Service shall:

promote and regulate the use of Federal areas known as national parks, monuments, and reservations ... by such means and measures as conform to the fundamental purpose of said parks, monuments, and reservations, which purpose is to conserve the scenery and the natural and historic objects and the wild life therein and *to provide for the enjoyment of the same in such manner and by such means as will leave them unimpaired for the enjoyment of future generations* (emphasis added)

In addition to these general fiduciary obligations of the Secretary of the Interior, the Secretary has been invested with certain specific powers and obligations in connection with the unique situation of the Redwood National Park.

The Redwood National Park was created on October 2, 1968 by the *Redwood National Park Act*,

to preserve significant examples of the primeval coastal redwood (Sequoia sempervirens) forests and the streams and seashores with which they are associated for purposes of public inspiration, enjoyment, and scientific study [...]

Congress limited the park to an area of 58,000 acres; appropriated 92 million dollars to implement the Act, of which, according to the Second Claim of the Amended Complaint, 20 million dollars remain unspent; and conferred upon the Secretary specific powers expressly designed to prevent damage to the park by logging on peripheral areas.

The question presented is whether on the allegations of the amended complaint, considered in the light of these statutory provisions, this court can direct the Secretary to exercise the powers granted under [the *National Parks Systems Act*].

Good sense suggests that the existence, nature and extent of potentially damaging conditions on neighboring lands and the effect thereof on the park, and the need for action to prevent such damage are matters that rest, primarily at least, within the judgment of the Secretary. However, neither the terms nor the legislative history of the *Redwood National Park Act* are such as to preclude judicial review of the Secretary's action or inaction.

In *Rockbridge v. Lincoln*, 449 F.2d 567 (9th Cir. 1971) our Circuit [...] held that, in view of the trust relationship of the Secretary toward the Indians [...] such discretion as was vested in the Secretary was not an unbridled discretion to refuse to regulate but only a discretion to decide what specific regulations to promulgate and, therefore, a cause for judicial relief [...] was stated [...]

In view of the analogous trust responsibility of the Secretary of the Interior with respect to public lands [...] and the analogous legislative history indicating a specific set of objectives which the provisions of the *Redwood National Park Act* were designed to accomplish, we consider *Rockbridge, supra,* to be strongly persuasive to the point that a case for judicial relief has been made out by plaintiff.

We are of the opinion that the terms of the statute [...] impose a legal duty on the Secretary to utilize the specific powers given to him whenever reasonably necessary for the protection of the park and that any discretion vested in the Secretary concerning time, place and specifics of the exercise of such powers is subordinate to his paramount legal duty imposed, not only under his trust obligation but by the statute itself, to protect the park.

Notes and Questions

1. Litigation aimed at protecting Redwood National Park from the impacts of adjacent logging continued for several more years after this decision. In 1975, the court found that the Interior Secretary was in violation of his statutory public trust obligations even though, after the decision excerpted above, his Department had entered into various agreements with logging companies to mitigate impacts on the Park: *Sierra Club v. Department of Interior*, 398 F. Supp. 284 (US Dist. Crt., 1975). The Court criticized the adequacy of these agreements and ordered the Secretary to develop a protection plan for court approval. Ultimately, in the late 1970s, the controversy was resolved when the US government expanded the Park's boundaries by buying out affected logging interests.

2. The next case provides an interesting counterpoint. As you read *Green v. Ontario*, decided just as the Redwood litigation was gearing up, consider the factual and analytic differences between the two cases.

Green v. Ontario
(1972), [1973] 2 O.R. 396 (Ont. H.C.)

LERNER J.: — These reasons are the result of separate motions by each defendant [...] wherein they seek orders striking out the statement of claim as it relates to each of them and dismissing the action [...]

From the statement of claim it appears that the plaintiff, Larry Green, is a Canadian citizen residing in Metropolitan Toronto and a researcher in the employ of "Pollution Probe" at the University of Toronto. [...] Lake Ontario Cement Limited, entered into a written lease on January 12, 1968, with the Province of Ontario for a parcel of land containing 16.02 acres and forming part of the sand banks and some lands under the waters of West Lake in the Township of Hallowell, Prince Edward County [...] for 75 years [...] to remove and carry away, from time to time and without charge, sand in unlimited quantities from the lands [...]

Some two years and three months later, pursuant to the authority of the *Provincial Parks Act*, the Province of Ontario established the "Sandbanks Provincial Park" as a provincial park [...] consisting of 1,802 acres [...] adjacent to and adjoining the 16.02 acres previously leased to Lake Ontario Cement before any park was ever in existence. The 16.02 acres have never been nor are they now, part of the said park lands so dedicated.

The statement of claim sets out s. 2 of the *Provincial Parks Act* which states:

> All provincial parks are dedicated to the people of the Province of Ontario and others who may use them for their healthful enjoyment and education, and the provincial parks shall be maintained for the benefit of future generations in accordance with this Act and the regulations.

and on the basis of s. 2 alleges that it imposes a trust upon the Province of Ontario with regard to Sandbanks Provincial Park so designated, to maintain that park in keeping with the "spirit" of s. 2 and that by permitting the use of the adjoining lands which the Province of Ontario had legally conveyed by leasehold to the other defendant were in breach of the trust implicit in s. 2 set out above.

This plaintiff was careful not to frame the action in public nuisance. Counsel for the plaintiff conceded in argument that on the basis of a public nuisance, the action could not succeed because there is no suggestion of any damage or injury to the plaintiff, Larry Green, beyond that which might be alleged by any other member of the public [...]

The plaintiff, in fact, is seeking a declaration of breach of a statutory trust which is not open to him unless he has a special interest above that of the general public [...]

It was also admitted by counsel for the plaintiff that but for the existence of s. 2 of the *Provincial Parks Act* there would be no basis for bringing the action. Notwithstanding the philosophical and noble intentions (my expression) of the Legislature to express in the pertinent section an ideological concept, no statutory trust has been created. It becomes necessary to break down the wording thereof: "All provincial parks are dedicated to the people of the Province of Ontario and others who may use them [...]" [...] This simply makes it clear that all persons (and I presume that includes those lawfully in Canada) are entitled to make use of the parks without the inhibitions or restrictions of race, religion, creed or other prejudicial implications inimical to the welfare of society and particularly the people of Ontario. "[...] and the provincial parks shall be maintained for the benefit of future generations in accordance with this Act and the regulations" implies that the Province of Ontario is required to physically maintain the parks so dedicated. This view is confirmed and amplified by the provisions of s. 3(1) and all the subsections of s. 19 covering such things as the issuing of permits, the fees for the right to enter and use the parks, which are so complete as to make the power of the Province in the whole concept of park lands, absolute.

A reading of s. 2 together with s. 3(2) makes it clear that the subject-matter of the trust is not certain. Section 3(2) empowers the Province to increase, decrease or even put an end to or "close down" any park. There cannot be a trust as is alleged by the plaintiff herein unless the subject-matter of the trust is of certainty.

[...] considered in the light of s. 3(2) and when coupled with s. 2 should make it clear that the Province of Ontario cannot be held to be a trustee. Section 3(2) cannot be construed as compelling the Province to hold these lands or for that matter any park lands, for any certain period of time or forever for the purposes that are alleged by the respondent to be read into s. 2 of the *Provincial Parks Act*.

[...] [Moreover] s. 19 of the *Provincial Parks Act* [...] gives unfettered and wide ranging powers to the Province in the operation and use of its parks and their ancillary or collateral benefits not only for the public but it also permits the use of same for private business enterprises, other gainful activities for special "classes", e.g., amusement operators, tourist accommodation operators, retail and wholesale stores and all manner of trades and businesses all of which would depend upon the discretion of the government. The action therefore as framed for breach of trust discloses no reasonable cause of action.

No one can be critical of resort to the Courts to remedy social wrongs or injustices by way of interpretation of law, either statutory or by precedent. This is desirable in our rapidly changing society and preferable to the lawless or anarchi[c]al way of seeking rectification of real as well as unreal injustices, inequities and abuses as practised in other jurisdictions. Nevertheless, if resort to the Courts is to be had, care must be taken that such steps are from a sound base in law otherwise ill-founded actions for the sake of using the Courts as a vehicle for expounding philosophy are to be discouraged.

Having first concluded that the plaintiff has no status to maintain this action and that the statement of claim discloses no reasonable cause of action, on reflection, I do not think it improper for me to find also that the action is vexatious and frivolous. I say this because the plaintiff had to know of the existence and terms of the lease and that it pre-dated by a substantial period of time, the establishment of Sandbanks Provincial Park.

[...] the applications of both defendants are allowed and the action against all defendants is dismissed with costs [...]

Notes and Questions

1. Identify the factual and legal distinctions between the two preceding cases. Which of these distinctions are most important to explaining the differing legal results?

2. One key distinction between the cases is the level of judicial comfort with the public trust doctrine, particularly one that provides its beneficiaries with a right of action. In the *Canfor* decision, Binnie J. refers to American public trust case law, including the seminal decision of the US Supreme Court in *Illinois Central Railroad Co. v. Illinois*, 146 U.S. 387 (U.S., 1892), in the course of concluding that "there is no legal barrier to the Crown suing for compensation as well as injunctive relief in a proper case on account of public nuisance, or negligence causing environmental damage to public lands, and perhaps other torts such as trespass". Notably, however, Binnie J. stops short of recognizing a stand-alone Crown right to sue based on the public trust. And he deliberately leaves open what he refers to as some "important and novel policy questions". These questions, in his view, include:

   > [...] the Crown's potential liability for *inactivity* in the face of threats to the environment, the existence or non-existence of enforceable fiduciary duties owed to the public by the Crown in that regard, the limits to the role and function and remedies available to governments taking action on account of activity harmful to public enjoyment of public resources, and the spectre of imposing on private interests an indeterminate liability for an indeterminate amount of money for ecological or environmental damage.

   Clearly, then, while the door has been opened to renewed attempts by individual litigants to pursue relief akin to that sought in *Green*, the future of the public trust doctrine — whether in its common law or statutory forms — is by no means clear.

3. If the *Green* case was litigated today, in a Canadian court, what result would you expect? What if a case, with facts similar to those in *Sierra Club v. Department of the Interior*, was filed in response to duly authorized, private logging on provincial Crown lands adjacent to Pacific Rim National Park?

Reforming Ontario Parks Legislation:
The Ontario Experience

Christopher J.A. Wilkinson,
"Protected Areas Law in Ontario, Canada: Maintenance of
Ecological Integrity as the Management Priority"
(2008) 28 Natural Areas J. 180

[...] Ontario's system of protected areas includes 329 provincial parks, 292 conservation reserves, and 10 wilderness areas, all of which are managed by the Ministry of Natural Resources. These areas combine to cover approximately 9% of the province's land base, totalling 8.7 million hectares.

Provincial parks, formerly regulated under the *Provincial Parks Act*, R.S.O. 1990, account for 88% of the total land base of protected areas in Ontario (Ministry of Natural Resources 2004:4). Provincial parks range from small areas intended mainly for recreation, such as Devil's Glen Provincial Park covering just 61 hectares, to huge wilderness parks, such as Woodland Caribou Provincial Park encompassing more than 450,000 hectares. Many of these provincial parks are actively operated to provide recreational opportunities — 105 operating parks provide facilities or services on a formal basis. These operating parks offer 18,810 vehicle-accessible campsites and 7000 interior campsites accessible by foot or canoe. Ontario's provincial parks host more than 10 million visits each year and generate an economic impact of approximately 380 million a year. At the same time, these protected areas are meant to conserve habitat for many of Ontario's 2900 species of vascular plants, 160 species of fish, 80 species of amphibians and reptiles, 400 species of birds, and 85 species of mammals.

Conservation reserves make up about 12% of the protected areas network. This type of protected area was created in 1994 under the authority of the *Public Lands Act*. Conservation reserves were intended primarily to protect significant features and provide recreational opportunities. These areas had fewer restrictions on recreational and commercial uses than provincial parks, although they did exclude logging and mining. However, the Environmental Commissioner of Ontario (2004:46) previously reported that "the *Public Lands Act* was not intended or designed to protect natural heritage features such as sensitive habitats or important species, and thus it is not a good public policy mechanism for protecting these values in conservation reserves".

Wilderness areas, regulated under the *Wilderness Areas Act* of 1959, make up about 0.001% of the protected areas network. A total of 33 wilderness areas were established in Ontario, although no new wilderness areas have been established since the early 1960s and only 10 areas are located outside existing provincial parks or conservation reserves.

[...] The primary statute at issue, the *Provincial Parks Act* was introduced in 1954 when there were only eight provincial parks in Ontario. Indeed, many different stakeholders, independent experts, and government panels and agencies have called for such reforms over the years, stating that the law did not reflect modern science, planning, or environmental realities (Swaigen 1978, 1982, 2001;

Eagles 1984; Michels et al. 1998; Campbell 2000: Wilkinson and Eagles 2001; Environmental Commissioner of Ontario 2002; Wilkinson 2002; Bell 2002). As Bell (2002:19) observes,

> The legislative changes needed to set an unequivocal conservation mandate for the Provincial Parks system have been discussed for twenty years now, and there is general agreement that these must include, at the very least, a provision for public consultation, the prohibition of industrial activities and a clear statement of purpose and guiding principles. [...] The province should act now, in the public interest, to protect the ecological integrity of the Provincial Parks system.

Protected areas are the very foundation of any concerted effort to conserve biodiversity in Ontario (Campbell 2000; Wilkinson 2002). The loss of natural areas is one of the greatest threats to biodiversity worldwide, including within Ontario (Environmental Commissioner of Ontario 2002). Protected areas are places meant to maintain and restore ecological and natural heritage values. They should be havens for wild species, conserving the diversity among and within them. Ideally, these areas serve a crucial conservation role at a local level, but equally as important, they also should function as an interconnected network at a landscape level. The degree to which the law actually protects these areas is critical, marking the difference between them existing as simple lines on a map or places where biodiversity is truly safeguarded.

Wilkinson and Eagles examined the need for legislative reform of Ontario's protected area legislation, concluding that a new statute should contain: "(1) the recognition of biodiversity conservation as the primary goal; (2) the need for management plans for each park, and (3) the requirement for an open consultative process". This examination also raised the issues of better regulating appropriate and prohibited activities, the necessity of adequate funding and staffing for protected areas by the provincial government, and the need to address increasing recreational demands on the system (Wilkinson and Eagles 2001).

The Environmental Commissioner of Ontario (2004:46) has also noted that "only 38 out of 548 protected areas (7 per cent) in Ontario have approved plans that involved public consultation and that are not in need of review. Without sound planning and conscientious management, Ontario's protected areas are little more than "paper parks — simple lines on a map" A similar set of concerns previously was expressed by another independent officer of the Legislative Assembly of Ontario (Auditor General of Ontario 2002:208–225).

Discussion

All provincial parks, formerly regulated by the *Provincial Parks Act*, and all conservation reserves, formerly regulated under the *Public Lands Act*, will now be administered under the *Provincial Parks and Conservation Reserves Act, 2006*. The Ministry of Natural Resources will also evaluate the 10 wilderness areas, regulated under the *Wilderness Areas Act*, that are outside provincial parks and conservation reserves. Where natural values justify protection, the ministry will regulate these areas through a public consultation process as either provincial parks or conservation reserves.

This new legislation repeals the *Provincial Parks Act*, the *Wilderness Areas Act* and *the Algonquin Provincial Park Extension Act, 1960-61*. It also makes minor amendments to the *Algonquin Forestry Authority Act*, the *Crown Forest Sustainability Act, 1994*, the *Historical Parks Act*, the *Kawartha Highlands Signature Site Park Act, 2003*, the *Mining Act*, and the *Off-Road Vehicles Act*.

Principles to Guide the Management of Protected Areas

Section 1 of the *Provincial Parks and Conservation Reserves Act, 2006* states that the purpose of this statute is "to permanently protect a system of provincial parks and conservation reserves that includes ecosystems that are representative of all of Ontario's natural regions, protects provincially significant elements of Ontario's natural and cultural heritage, maintains biodiversity and provides opportunities for compatible, ecologically sustainable recreation". This purpose statement is notable because, for the first time, Ontario's protected areas are expressly mandated to maintain biodiversity. Further, it also recognizes that provincial parks and conservation reserves are intended to be managed as a system, rather than as isolated areas. Swaigen (2001:226) comments that such purpose sections within a statute are important in "setting the tone for those agencies that implement it and for the Courts that interpret it".

The most significant change to the governance of Ontario's protected areas is that ecological integrity is now the guiding purpose for planning and management. Subsection 3(1) of the statute states that the "maintenance of ecological integrity shall be the first priority and the restoration of ecological integrity shall be considered" for all provincial parks and conservation reserves. Unlike its legislative predecessor, the *Provincial Parks and Conservation Reserves Act, 2006* also explicitly recognizes in subsection 3(2) that opportunities for public consultation shall be provided in the planning and management of protected areas.

Importantly, the new statute defines ecological integrity in subsection 5(2) as "a condition in which biotic and abiotic components of ecosystems and the composition and abundance of native species and biological communities are characteristic of their natural regions and rates of change and ecosystem processes are unimpeded". The inclusion of a definition of ecological integrity is of fundamental importance, for both ministry staff in administering the Act and for the public to clearly understand the purpose of Ontario's protected areas (see Panel on the Ecological Integrity of Canada's National Parks 2000). The *Provincial Parks and Conservation Reserves Act, 2006* also further defines ecological integrity in subsection 5(3) as including "healthy and viable populations of native species, including species at risk, and maintenance of the habitat on which the species depend" and "levels of air and water quality consistent with protection of biodiversity and recreational enjoyment". This encompassing definition is similar to that contained in the *Canada National Parks Act*, which defines ecological integrity as "with respect to a park, a condition that is determined to be characteristic of its natural region and likely to persist, including abiotic components and the composition and abundance of native species and biological communities, rates of change and supporting processes".

In a similar fashion to the old *Provincial Parks Act*, the new statute contains relatively benign language that dedicates the parks to the people of Ontario and others for reasons such as their enjoyment and education. However, the *Provincial Parks and Conservation Reserves Act* significantly expands upon this dedication in section 6 by specifying that provincial parks and conservation reserves "shall be managed to maintain their ecological integrity and to leave them unimpaired for future generations". This language is important as it reinforces that the legal mandate of these areas is to maintain ecological integrity and that all other activities should be managed within that context.

It is noteworthy that the Ontario Parks branch of the Ministry of Natural Resources does not have an overall mandate to maintain ecological integrity, unlike its federal counterpart. The *Parks Canada Agency Act* firmly establishes in its preamble that the mandate of Parks Canada as an agency is "to maintain or restore the ecological integrity of national parks". The *Ministry of Natural Resources Act* solely directs in section 13(1) that "the Minister may establish programs to promote and stimulate the development and management of natural resources in Ontario". Arguably, the combination of the ecological integrity provisions within the *Canada National Parks Act* and the *Parks Canada Agency Act* provide for a stronger "presumption against developments and activities that would impair the ecological integrity" of protected areas than what now exists at the provincial level in Ontario (Swaigen 2001:230).

Goals and Objectives

The legal objective of both provincial parks and conservation reserves will now be "to permanently protect representative ecosystems, biodiversity and provincially significant elements of Ontario's natural and cultural heritage and to manage these areas to ensure that ecological integrity is maintained" as stated in subsection 2(1) of the new statute. This objective is a significant improvement as the old *Provincial Parks Act* was silent in this regard and those objectives for provincial parks that did exist were both weaker and relegated to non-binding policy. Indeed, prior to this new legislation, conservation reserves lacked many basic legal protections when they were regulated under the *Public Lands Act*.

Provincial parks also have the new legal objective, in subsection 2(1), to provide opportunities for "ecologically sustainable outdoor recreation", "in addition to providing opportunities for visitors to increase their knowledge of Ontario's natural and cultural heritage. These objectives vary slightly for conservation reserves in that they may be managed to provide ecologically sustainable land uses, including traditional outdoor heritage activities". as set out in subsection 2(2) of the new statute. Provincial parks and conservation reserves also both have the objective of facilitating scientific research and serving as benchmarks to monitor ecological change on the broader landscape.

Classification and Zoning

The *Provincial Parks and Conservation Reserves Act, 2006*, akin to its predecessor, recognizes six classes of provincial parks in subsection 8(1): wilderness, nature reserve, cultural heritage, natural environment, waterway, and recreational class. However, the new statute now states the specific objectives of each of these classes, whereas previously these directions were left to ministry policy. Further, the statute also creates a new aquatic class of provincial park at a date to be proclaimed later by the Lieutenant Governor.

The new statute allows for a system of zoning to be applied to both provincial parks and conservation reserves. This is a similar approach to that of the old *Provincial Parks Act*, in which detailed policies would then apply to specific areas within a given class of park. However, the *Provincial Parks and Conservation Reserves Act, 2006* states in subsection 12(3) that zoning shall not constrain hunting in conservation reserves.

Mandatory Management Direction and State of Protected Areas Reporting

The Ministry of Natural Resources now is required by section 10 of the new statute to prepare "management direction" for all provincial parks and conservation reserves. These directions may apply to one or more protected areas and shall identify site-specific management policies to cover a 20-year period. Management directions may take one of two forms, either a detailed management plan or a management statement, when addressing non-complex issues. Unlike the old *Provincial Parks Act*, the new legislation also explicitly requires in subsection 10(6) that public consultation occur when producing, reviewing, or amending management direction. The new legislation also contains language, similar to subsection 10(1) of the *Canada National Parks Act*, which would make it possible for the Ministry of Natural Resources to enter into co-management agreements with First Nations for specific provincial parks and conservation reserves.

The new statute does not expressly state that indicators of ecological integrity should be identified in the management plans or statements for each protected area. Ideally, the use of identified indicators and measurable objectives in each management direction would also form the basis of each protected area's ecological monitoring program. The Panel on the Ecological Integrity of Canada's National Parks (2000) has noted that the management direction should also contain a description of how visitor use stresses the protected area's ecological integrity and how such stresses arc being mitigated or eliminated.

The *Provincial Parks and Conservation Reserves Act, 2006* requires the preparation of a planning manual to replace the "Ontario Provincial Parks: Planning and Management Policies". Known as the Blue Book, it was last significantly updated in 1992, and it contains the detailed policy directions for provincial parks. Conservation reserves lacked similar detailed policies, and they will now be covered under the new manual.

The new statute requires in section 11 that the Ministry of Natural Resources produce a state-of-the-parks report every five years. This reporting requirement is similar to Parks Canada's system-wide reports for national parks as required in subsection 12(2) of the *Canada National Parks Act*. These reports will contain an assessment of the extent to which the objectives of provincial parks and conservation reserves are being achieved, including "ecological and socio-economic conditions and benefits, the degree of ecological representation, number and area of provincial parks and conservation reserves, known threats to ecological integrity of provincial parks and conservation reserves and their ecological health and socio-economic benefits" as stated in subsection 11(2). The new statute states that the Ministry of Natural Resources shall post these reports on the publicly accessible Environmental Registry, as established by section 5 and 6 of the *Environmental Bill of Rights, 1993*.

Major Industrial Uses

The *Provincial Parks and Conservation Reserves Act, 2006* explicitly prohibits in section 16 the following activities in protected areas: the commercial harvest of timber; the generation of electricity; prospecting, staking mining claims, developing mineral interests or working mines; and extracting aggregate, topsoil, or peat. The inclusion of these prohibitions is a dramatic improvement compared to the old legislative framework, as historically such details were often *left to the* discretion of non-binding policy (Swaigen 2001). However, the new statute does include numerous exceptions to these prohibitions, such as allowing for electricity generation facilities within protected areas for 'off-the-grid' communities.

The most environmentally significant exception to these prohibitions is that commercial timber operations are allowed to continue in Algonquin Provincial Park, as stated in section 17. The new statute essentially defers to subsection 11(1) of the *Algonquin Forestry Authority Act* that states that the management of this protected area be balanced between recreation and "the public interest in providing a flow of logs from Algonquin Provincial Park". The Environmental Commissioner of Ontario has urged the Ministry of Natural Resources to conduct a public review of the appropriateness of commercial logging in Algonquin and to address "how the proposed park management goal of ecological integrity would be achieved if this policy is allowed to continue".

The *Provincial Parks and Conservation Reserves Act, 2006* reasonably addresses the issue of resource access roads. In some instances, these roads are necessary as a protected area may entirely surround sites with mineral tenure, or timber operations on Crown land may be inaccessible without a road to cross a protected area. The new statute states in sub-section 21(1) that such resource access roads may only be constructed if there is no reasonable alternative (lower cost is not justification), and all reasonable measures will be under-taken to minimize harmful environmental impacts and to protect ecological integrity. Further, when the road is no longer required for the purpose for which it was approved or will not be used for a period of five years or more, it will be closed, effective measures will be taken to prevent its use, and the rehabilitation and removal of any infrastructure (i.e., bridges) will be undertaken.

Non-Industrial Uses

Human use is a part of the nature of protected areas, but some forms, levels, or timings of activities are incompatible with ecological integrity. Further, what may be an appropriate activity in one protected area may not be suitable in another area. Experts also recognize that any determination of what is an appropriate activity should not be based on the need for revenue generation. With few exceptions, almost all non industrial uses are not addressed in the new statute and are left to regulation or policy.

The *Provincial Parks and Conservation Reserves Act, 2006* does distinguish, in one specific instance, the differences between classes of provincial parks and which activities are appropriate. Borrowing from ministry policy, the new statute states in subsection 8(2) that visitors to Ontario's eight wilderness class parks may only travel by "non-mechanized means" or engage in "low-impact recreation". These terms are not defined, but the Ministry of Natural Resources will presumably provide further detail in the regulations that will accompany the new statute.

The new statute does not change the manner in which hunting is permitted in Ontario's protected areas, despite Swaigen's (2001:233) recommendation that it should be limited to "necessary aboriginal hunting". By default, recreational hunting is permitted in all conservation reserves. By exception, recreational hunting is permitted in provincial parks. However, that exception has been extended to allow recreational hunting in 132 provincial parks as prescribed in Part 3 of Ontario Regulation 663/98 under the *Fish and Wildlife Conservation Act*. Consequently recreational hunting is allowed in more than two-thirds of Ontario's protected areas However, as noted by the Panel on the Ecological Integrity of Canada's National Parks (2000), the recreational harvest of species can conflict with the maintenance of ecological integrity in a protected area and can impair their utility as true ecological benchmarks. The new statute does not explicitly address commercial trapping, but existing policy dictates that it will be phased out of all provincial parks by no later than January 2010. In contrast to the provincial approach, the *Canada National Parks Act* only allows aboriginal hunting and trapping in a limited number of national parks [...]

Deregulation and Disposition of Land

The *Provincial Parks and Conservation Reserves Act, 2006* establishes new conditions for the deregulation and alteration of boundaries of provincial parks and conservation reserves. The Lieutenant Governor in Council, effectively the Cabinet of the Government of Ontario, may dispose of an area of a provincial park or conservation reserve that is less than 50 hectares or less than 1% of the total area, whichever is the lesser as stated in subsection 9(3). For any larger disposition, the Minister of Natural Resources must table the disposition before the Legislative Assembly and obtain its endorsement. However, dispositions do not have to follow this process if they are part of a land claims settlement, an addition to a national park or marine conservation area, or part of a transaction that increases the size of the protected area and enhances ecological integrity as stated in subsection 9(5).

A long-standing criticism, voiced by many stakeholders over the past decade, is that protected areas may be used as floating reserves and that boundaries may be re-drawn to accommodate industrial activities such as mining. It is unfortunate that the new statute did not give the authority to the Minister to order the withdrawal of lands from mineral staking, under the *Mining Act*, for all candidate protected areas.

Conclusions

The *Provincial Parks and Conservation Reserves Act, 2006* is a significant improvement to the legislative framework governing Ontario's protected areas. While not flawless, this new legislation moves Ontario from the back of the pack to near the forefront of protected areas law in Canada. It is a promising beginning to the much-needed overhaul of how Ontario's provincial parks and conservation reserves are managed, and the new statute resolves many of the deficiencies of its legislative predecessor. As next steps, the Ministry of Natural Resources must now revise the regulations and policies that will provide many of the essential details and specific directions that will guide the planning and management of these protected areas. Further, the ministry also must begin to address the substantial backlog of protected areas that do not have a current management plan.

Despite this new statute, concerns still remain as to how Ontario's protected area system is managed overall by the Government of Ontario. These concerns serve as a valuable starring point to possible future research. Firstly, both the Environmental Commissioner of Ontario and the Auditor General of Ontario have expressed concern that the Ontario Parks branch of the Ministry of Natural Resources does not have sufficient resources to properly fulfil its mandate. Ontario is among the only jurisdictions in North America that is attempting to run its protected areas system on a cost recovery basis, and its funding is very low given the vast amount of land that is involved.

The Government of Ontario only allocates approximately $15 million (Cdn.) a year for the Ministry of Natural Resources to plan, manage, protect, and monitor approximately 94,000 km2 of protected areas in Ontario. Between 1992 and 2007, in inflation-adjusted terms, the Government of Ontario's funding for Ontario Parks decreased by 73%. Almost half of all operating provincial parks do not have sufficient staff or funding to meet existing minimum standards of operation. Further, the majority of non-operating parks are visited only once a year or not at all by ministry staff (Environmental Commissioner of Ontario 2004:43). Therefore, if a protected area is not paying for itself, there is no assurance that the law — maintaining ecological integrity — is being upheld. It will be a significant challenge for the Ministry of Natural Resources to adequately administer and enforce the *Provincial Parks and Conservation Reserves Act, 2006* unless there are significant increases to its budget.

Secondly, it is a common fallacy that protected areas are unimpaired swaths of wilderness with pristine natural conditions. In reality, Ontario's provincial parks and conservation reserves are threatened by numerous ecological stresses and threats, some of which originate beyond their boundaries. Indeed, in many cases, the boundaries of protected areas are political constructs and do not reflect natural boundaries. As such, there may be an issue of concern outside of a protected area that affects its management, but it is beyond an imaginary line and cannot be effectively addressed by Ontario Parks staff or even the Ministry of Natural Resources.

In contrast, section 48 of the federal *Canadian Environmental Assessment Act* can require that an environmental assessment be conducted for any project outside the boundaries of a national park that may adversely affect its ecological integrity. Ontario's provincial laws fail to contain any similar safeguards. Unlike national parks, the land inside and outside of most protected areas in Ontario has the benefit of being managed by the same entity; yet, the Government of Ontario has few mechanisms to restrict incompatible land uses, such as urbanization or commercial timber harvesting, near the boundaries of its own protected areas.

What is needed is an ecologically sensible landscape-level approach to the broader issue of Crown land management. Different branches or ministries — all part of the same government — should not be seen as threatening or competing against each other's interests. Protected areas should be given the priority and recognition that they deserve. Provincial parks and conservation reserves must be managed on a greater ecosystem basis in order to fulfil their mandate of protecting Ontario's ecological integrity. Wildlife and natural processes know no boundaries; therefore, failing to take this wider perspective imperils Ontario's protected areas.

Notes and Questions

1. The author concludes that the *Provincial Parks and Conservation Reserves Act, 2006* "moves Ontario from the back of the pack to near the forefront of protected areas law in Canada". What are the strengths of the new legislation? What weaknesses remain?

2. Compare and contrast the new Ontario legislation with the *Canadian National Parks Act* and, if you are from a province other than Ontario, with applicable parks legislation in your province. Applicable legislation for other provinces includes:

> British Columbia — *Park Act*, R.S.B.C. 1996, c. 344
> Alberta — *Provincial Parks Act*, R.S.A. 2000, c. P-35
> Saskatchewan — *Parks Act*, S.S. 1986, c. P-1.1
> Manitoba — *Provincial Parks Act*, R.S.M. 1993, c. 39 (C.C.S.M. c. P20)
> Quebec — *Parks Act*, R.S.Q. 1977, c. P-9 (C.Q.L.R., c. P-9)
> New Brunswick — *Parks Act*, R.S.N.B. 2011, c. 202
> Nova Scotia — *Provincial Parks Act*, R.S.N.S. 1989, c. 367
> Prince Edward Island — *Natural Areas Protection Act*,
>   R.S.P.E.I. 1988, c. N-2
> Newfoundland and Labrador — *Provincial Parks Act*,
>   R.S.N. 1990, c. P-32
> Yukon — *Parks and Land Certainty Act*, R.S.Y. 2002, c. 165
> Northwest Territories — *Territorial Parks Act*, R.S.N.W.T. 1988, c. T-4
> Nunavut — *Territorial Parks Act*, R.S.N.W.T. (Nu) 1988, c. T-4

In 2002, David Boyd created a report card for the laws governing Canada's parks. In that report, federal legislation scored a B, but only two of the provinces, Nova Scotia (B) and Newfoundland (D), passed. Using Boyd's criteria set out below (from *Wild by Law: A Report Card on Laws Governing Canada's Parks and Protected Areas* (Polis Project, University of Victoria, 2002) at p. 6-8), assess your province's current parks legislation. How does it fare?

> 1. Mandates conservation and ecological integrity as top priority;
> 2. Prohibits industrial resource use (logging, mining, etc.);
> 3. Protects permanently (boundaries legislated);
> 4. Incorporates dedication to future generations;
> 5. Ensures public participation in *mandatory* parks planning;
> 6. Requires reporting on the state of the parks;
> 7. Recognizes Aboriginal rights;
> 8. Enshrines minimum 12% protection of all ecosystems within jurisdiction;

9. Provides additional protection for ecological reserves and wilderness areas; and
10. Establishes regional management responsibility.

References and Further Readings

N. Bankes, "Mikisew Cree and the Lands Taken Up Clause of the Numbered Treaties" (2005-2006) 92 Resources 1

D.R. Boyd, *Unnatural Law: Rethinking Canadian Environmental Law and Policy* (Vancouver: UBC Press, 2003)

D.R. Boyd, *Wild by Law: A Report Card on Laws Governing Canada's Parks and Protected Areas* (Polis Project, University of Victoria, 2002)

Canadian Parks Council, *Canadian Protected Areas Status Report 2000– 2005*, Executive Summary, online: <http://www.parks-parcs.ca/english/cpc/status.php>

P. Dearden, "Progress and Problems in Canada's Protected Areas: Overview of Progress, Chronic Issues and Emerging Challenges in the Early 21st Century", Paper commissioned for the Canadian Parks for Tomorrow: 40th Anniversary Conference, University of Calgary, May 8 to 11, 2008, online: <http://parkscanadahistory.com/publications/2008-conference/dearden. pdf>

P. Dearden & R. Canessa, "Marine Protected Areas" in P. Dearden & R. Rollins, eds., *Parks and Protected Areas in Canada: Planning and Management*, 3rd ed. (Oxford University Press, 2009)

P. Dearden & J. Dempsey, "Protected Areas in Canada: Decade of Change" (2004) 48 Canadian Geographer 225–239. Copyright 2004, The Canadian Association of Geographers/L'Association canadienne des géographes. Reproduced with permission of Blackwell Publishing Ltd.

P. Dearden & S. Langdon, "Aboriginal Peoples and National Parks" in P. Dearden & R. Rollins, eds., *Parks and Protected Areas in Canada: Planning and Management*, 3rd ed. (Oxford University Press, 2009)

P. Dearden & R. Rollins, "Parks and Protected Areas in Canada" in P. Dearden & R. Rollins, eds., *Parks and Protected Areas in Canada: Planning and Management*, 3rd ed. (Oxford University Press, 2009)

Environment and Climate Change Canada, "First New Indigenous Protected Area in Canada: Edéhzhíe Protected Area", Backgrounder (October 11, 2018), online: <https://www.canada.ca/en/environment-climate-change/news/2018/10/first-new-indigenous-protected-area-in-canada-edehzhie-protected-area.html>

S. Fluker, " 'Maintaining Ecological Integrity Is Our First Priority' — Policy Rhetoric or Practical Reality in Canada's National Parks? A case comment on *Canadian Parks & Wilderness Society v. Canada (Minister of Canadian Heritage)*" (2003) 13 J. Envtl. L. & Prac. 131

C. Linnitt, "How Indigenous Peoples Are Changing the Way Canada Thinks About Conservation", The Narwhal, March 10, 2018, online: <https://thenarwhal.ca/how-indigenous-peoples-are-changing-way-canada-thinks-about-conservation>

C. Malcolm, "Protected Areas: The Provincial Story" in P. Dearden & R. Rollins, eds., *Parks and Protected Areas in Canada: Planning and Management*, 3rd ed. (Oxford University Press, 2009)

K. Turner & C. Bitonti, "Conservancies in British Columbia, Canada: Bringing Together Protected Areas and First Nations' Interests" (2011) 2 Int'l. Indigenous Pol'y J. 1

R.W. Turner, "Market Failures and the Rationale for National Parks", Journal of Economic Education, Vol. 33, No. 4, pp. 347–356, Autumn, 2002. Reprinted with permission of the Helen Dwight Reid Education Foundation. Published by Heldref Publications, 1319 Eighteenth St. NW, Washington DC 20036-1802. Copyright 2009

C.J.A. Wilkinson, "Protected Areas Law in Ontario, Canada: Maintenance of Ecological Integrity as the Management Priority" (2008) 28 Natural Areas J. 180

Chapter 9

Species at Risk

Introduction

Canada has long prided itself as a key global biodiversity storehouse. On the international stage, it has aspired to play a leading role in protecting biodiversity worldwide. This is evidenced by, among other things, Canada being the first signatory to the *Rio Convention on Biological Diversity*. But just how effectively has Canada protected its biodiversity legacy? Is our reputation for international leadership on biodiversity issues justified? By what measures can we assess these questions? With these issues in mind, in this chapter we explore the Canadian record with respect to species protection, a key dimension and indicator of the larger challenge of protecting biodiversity.

This chapter is in six parts. Part I provides an overview of the nature and magnitude of species at risk as a national and global public policy problem. It also provides an introduction to the history of Canada's *Species at Risk Act*, S.C. 2002, c. 29 (SARA) and some of the rationales that support using legislation to protect species at risk.

Parts II to IV review some of the key features and issues arising under SARA. Part II considers the procedures by which species are listed for protection and, more generally, the tension between science and politics in the listing process. Part III concerns the regime governing designation of critical habitat for listed species including recovery strategies and action plans. Much of the judicial consideration of SARA to date has arisen in connection with these provisions. Part IV then considers SARA provisions that seek to prevent harm to species and their habitat including provisions that prohibit such harm, as well as so-called "safety net" and "emergency" orders. We also consider administrative requirements relating to the permitting and assessment of projects that could harm species or their habitat, an issue addressed by the Federal Court of Appeal in relation to Southern Resident Orcas in its 2018 decision in *Tsleil-Waututh Nation v. Canada (Attorney General)*.

Building on this context, in Part V, we explore a variety of what might be termed governance-related themes in species protection. These include the challenges associated with promoting biodiversity in a federal state; the species protection record at the provincial and territorial levels, as measured against the aspirations of the 1996 *Accord for the Protection of Species at Risk*; and the legal relationship between the aspirations and principles set out in SARA and provincial land and resource-use decision-making. Finally, in Part VI, we offer some emerging and critical perspectives on species and biodiversity protection including Indigenous-led initiatives.

Part I — Overview of the Magnitude and Nature of the Problem

Paul M. Wood & Laurie Flahr,
"Taking Endangered Species Seriously?
British Columbia's Species-at-Risk Policies"
(2004) 30 Can. Pub. Pol'y 382

We are now in the beginning of the sixth major mass extinction event of all geological time. The major cause of the current event is well known: the alteration, fragmentation, or destruction of species' habitats by humans. Overexploitation of resource species and the introduction of destructive "exotic" species into ecosystems where they are not native are additional contributing factors. By 2050, global climate change is predicted to compete with habitat alteration as the leading cause of species extinctions.

At the current rate, "the loss of biodiversity ... has serious consequences for the human prospect in the future" (Royal Society in a joint statement with the US National Academy of Sciences 1992) because humanity in the long term is dependent on the maintenance of the world's biodiversity. Scientists recognized the beginning of the current extinction phenomenon approximately three decades ago. In response, the United Nations formulated the *World Charter for Nature* in 1982 followed by the more specific *Global Biodiversity Strategy* in 1992. The single most significant human response to date occurred in 1992 when most of the world's nations signed the *Convention on Biological Diversity* at the world's first Earth Summit in Rio de Janeiro. Canada was the first nation to sign this Convention.

A requirement of the Convention was for each signatory party (nation) to develop domestic legislation to protect biodiversity. Biodiversity conservation legislation can be classified into three broad categories. The first category encompasses legislation that authorizes governments to legally designate large protected areas in which species and natural processes may persist relatively undisturbed by human activities. The *Canada National Parks Act* and the several provincial equivalents are examples.

In the second category are those pieces of legislation that stipulate preventative measures to protect biodiversity and other specified environmental values on the matrix of public or private lands beyond the boundaries of protected areas. British Columbia's *Forest and Range Practices Act* is an example. Its purpose is to mitigate harmful environmental consequences that can result from forest harvesting operations on public lands.

The third category encompasses legislation aimed at protecting from further harm those species that are already at risk of extinction. In addition, this type of legislation usually requires the recovery of species at risk in order to rectify past harms. Recovery usually entails repopulating the number of individuals in a species' natural habitat and/or re-habilitating its habitat. The US *Endangered Species Act* was an early example and the recently passed Canadian federal *Species at Risk Act* is another.

Kate Smallwood,
A Guide to Canada's Species at Risk Act
(Vancouver: Sierra Legal Defence Fund, 2003)

Canada is internationally renowned for its natural beauty. One of the largest countries on the planet, Canada is home to about 20% of the Earth's wilderness, 24% of its wetlands, 20% of its freshwater and 10% of its forests.

This incredible biodiversity is under threat. Over 400 species have been identified as being at risk in Canada, although the number is in fact much higher. A report by the Canadian Endangered Species Council, *Wild Species 2000, The General Status of Species in Canada*, examined the status of over 1,600 Canadian species. Of these species, only 65% were considered to be secure, while 10% were considered to be at risk or potentially at risk. Canada's list of plants and animals at risk includes Canadian icons like the Grizzly Bear, Killer Whale, Polar Bear and Eastern Cougar, as well as species like the Burrowing Owl, the Salish Sucker, the Northern Leopard Frog and the Small White Lady's Slipper.

Species loss and decline is not limited to Canada. Globally, we are now experiencing an unprecedented loss of species and genetic diversity — the sixth major period of extinction in the history of the Earth. In 1992, the international community sought to address this problem by passing the United Nations *Convention on Biological Diversity* (the "Rio Convention"). Article 8 of the Convention, which addresses "in situ" or "on the ground" conservation, includes the specific commitment to pass legislation for the protection of species at risk. Although Canada was the first industrialized nation to ratify the Rio Convention, it has taken Canada nearly a decade to address this commitment. Bill C-5, the *Species at Risk Act* ("SARA"), was the government's fourth attempt at passing endangered species legislation. SARA passed through the Senate without amendment on December 12, 2002 [...]

SARA took nearly ten years to pass for a variety of reasons, including jurisdictional wrangling between the federal and provincial governments; major policy debates over how habitat should be protected and whether scientists or politicians should decide which species would be legally protected; fears about "U.S.-style" litigation over endangered species, concerns about private land issues and compensation, and two federal elections. SARA is clearly the product of these policy and jurisdictional debates. As a policy decision, the federal government has elected to protect species and habitat only within a very narrow interpretation of federal jurisdiction and leave the primary role for species and habitat protection in Canada to the provinces and territories. The federal government has also consciously chosen to rely on voluntary conservation and stewardship initiatives as the primary approach for habitat protection, especially on private land.

The end result is a law that is largely restricted to federal lands, aquatic species and migratory birds under the *Migratory Birds Convention Act*. The majority of species listed under the Act will only be protected if they are found on federal land — a mere 5% of Canada outside the territories. Elsewhere in Canada, species at risk will be subject to a patchwork of protection. Significant gaps exist in the legislative framework for species and habitat protection from East to West. Neither BC nor Alberta, for example, has their own species legislation. Other provinces that do have endangered species legislation have consistently failed to list and protect species at risk listed by COSEWIC (the Committee on the Status of Endangered Wildlife in Canada). None of the provinces or territories is meeting all the requirements for species and habitat protection outlined in the *National Accord for the Protection of Species at Risk*, the primary national policy document on species at risk in Canada.

John Charles Kunich,
"Preserving the Womb of the Unknown Species with Hotspots Legislation"
(2001) 52 Hastings L.J. 1149

Why Should We Care About Species We Have Never Identified?

In a world dominated by humans, in which the needs of humans are, not surprisingly, seen as preeminent by most members of that species, it is important to examine the question of why we should be concerned with the extinction of other life forms. The ESA certainly has been controversial, in part because of the perceived conflict it generates between people and other living things. If the ESA or other pieces of legislation are to be given a chance of making a difference, people will need to understand the benefits they can expect to derive from the bargain. The reasons for humans to attempt to prevent the extinction of other creatures can be bundled into four main groups: (1) present practical value; (2) potential future practical value; (3) intangible value; and (4) moral duty. I will summarize each of these briefly.

First, many species of plants and animals currently provide Homo sapiens with a variety of tangible, practical benefits of real value to people. A host of domesticated animals and crop plants are obvious examples, directly supplying nutrients for the human diet. People can derive this nutrition directly, by consuming all or part of the plant or animal itself, or indirectly, by eating substances produced by the plant or animal, such as eggs, milk, honey, fruit, grains, vegetables, and foods made therefrom. In addition to food, plants and animals are the producers of essentials such as cotton, wool, silk, leather, wood, paper, dyes, and their ancillary commodities. However, only twenty species provide ninety percent of the global food supply today, and three species (corn, wheat, and rice) contribute more than half of the total. Countless other species, currently known or unknown, could perhaps "be bred or provide genes to increase production in deserts, saline flats and other marginal habitats" to feed the world's expanding population in the future.

Plants are the source of many medicinal drugs, and about half of all prescription drugs in the United States come from wild organisms, of a total value estimated to exceed $14 billion per year. Our antibiotics, anti-cancer agents, pain killers, and blood thinners have been derived thus far from only a few hundred species, leaving the biochemistry and genetic components of millions of other species unexplored and untapped as a potentially colossal reservoir of new medicines and healing agents [...]

The role of animals in medical and other scientific research has been of inestimable worth, and largely the contribution of otherwise insignificant or despised creatures such as the common mouse, rat, and fruit fly. Less obvious but still practical benefits come from creatures that facilitate the production of other plants or animals which in turn are consumed or otherwise used. This includes a vast array of insects, which pollinate many flowering plants, including fruit-bearing varieties, and which are the primary food source for many birds; it also includes annelids (earthworms) and other burrowing organisms which similarly play an unobtrusive yet vital role in aerating soil, making it suitable for producing plant life.

Ecological benefits conferred by living things are sometimes overlooked by laypersons, but are of paramount importance. In addition to all of the human-centered practical reasons for preserving species as individual species, there are tangible synergistic benefits produced by species interactions on an ecosystem level. The concept of "ecosystem services" is fairly new, but several enormously significant examples have been identified. These include the decomposition and detoxification of organic matter and other wastes, which is mostly performed by the smallest, least charismatic organisms in any ecosystem. Without the microorganisms and insects that effectuate the decomposition process for organic material, the world would quickly be buried in its own waste. Other examples are generation and renewal of soil, mitigation of floods, purification of air and water, and partial stabilization of climate.

Among the most fundamental of ecosystem services is the photosynthetic process of most plants, which not only fixes, or converts, solar energy into usable nutrients, but also converts carbon dioxide into oxygen, literally the life-breath of our species. And the exquisitely intricate natural system of checks and balances by which various species keep one another's populations-including those of pest and disease-causing organisms-within manageable limits is far more effective and safe than any pesticide program.

Most previously-identified species that provide obvious, practical benefits to humans are not in danger of extinction. In fact, many are actively safeguarded, raised, cultivated, and otherwise managed to maximize their productivity. There have been some cases of over-harvesting of such species, but for the most part this type of species is safe, due to our own self-interest. Of course, this presupposes that humans have (1) discovered the species and (2) learned of the benefits the species has to offer. In the case of the myriad unidentified species inhabiting the world's hotspots, neither of these presuppositions obtains.

The species that are less ostentatious about their value to people, moreover, may be even less fortunate. In some cases, for example, it is not even known which species of insects pollinate which useful plants, or which species are depended on by birds, fish, and other creatures for their sustenance, so humans may destroy or allow the destruction of these insects without realizing the consequences.

A second basic reason for humans to preserve species is that they may have future practical value to people. New uses are continually being discovered for living things, often transforming apparently inconsequential species into valuable assets. By definition, of course, it is impossible to know which or how many species fall into this category at any point in time. But it should be evident that modem technology and research methods are powerful tools for unleashing the power of helpful genies from the most unassuming, unlikely magic lamps. Given some of the important benefits now being derived from uncharismatic and previously unimportant species, it would be wise to preserve as many as possible to provide future investigators with the raw material for their experiments.

Each living species can be viewed as the end product of countless years of research and development, the culmination of eons of experimentation in nature's laboratory. As Edward O. Wilson has stated, "each species of higher organism is richer in information than a Caravaggio painting, Bach fugue, or any other great work of art".

Each species represents a successful set of strategies for meeting some of life's challenges and threats. Much can be learned from the collective experience of these myriad generations in assisting people with their own problems. And with the advent of genetic engineering, wherein it is increasingly possible to transfer genetic material from one taxonomic group to another (even across the kingdom barrier) to confer previously lacking biological traits, each species is potentially a significant genetic, resource. This genetic wealth, in millions of different forms, could be as vital in tomorrow's society as wood and paper in today's.

It is possible, and even probable, that some currently "insignificant" species could take on a crucial role in the ecosystems of the future. Wild relatives of current crop species can be an invaluable source of genetic diversity in the event the monoculture cultivated plants fall prey to disease or other environmental conditions. And if environmental conditions change, through global warming, increased pollution, or other habitat alterations, some other species may possess traits that will prove pre-adapted to these new circumstances. Some species that occupy key positions in today's ecosystems may be unable to adapt, and unless other species are available to fill their niche, the ecosystems may suffer catastrophic degradation. The redundancy provided for by millions of years of natural selection cannot be fully understood and appreciated unless and until it is needed. It is not necessarily the large, obvious life forms that play these pivotal roles; in fact, the "lower" levels of the food web are the foundation upon which all other components of each ecosystem depend.

The biosphere that is the planet earth may be conceptualized as an exceedingly complex "computer program" with millions of parts, each of which is evolving. It would be foolish indeed to destroy, or to allow the destruction of, the program's codes, because we do not and cannot know their importance, whether at present or in some unforeseeably altered world of the future. Extinction shuts doors and deprives us forever of the option to discover value in that which we previously found valueless.

A corollary of this principle is that some species may be valuable precisely because they are endangered or threatened. A particularly vulnerable species within a given habitat may someday provide an early warning signal that there are problems that may eventually affect far more species. This has been termed the "canary in the mine" syndrome. For such species, their strength is in their weakness.

A third main reason to preserve species is their intangible value. Although less practical, and less susceptible to being reduced to monetary worth, there is real wealth in living things. Many people find great beauty in nature, and nowhere else is the maxim more true that beauty is in the eye of the beholder. Depending on one's individual preferences, species as diverse as a house cat, a fern, a goldfish, a beetle, and a paramecium can be works of art, supplying emotional sustenance. Entire industries are tailored for the loyal human aficionados of these living art forms.

Finally, fourth, and least pragmatic, is the moral duty not to exterminate our fellow passengers on this planet. With its origins at least as ancient as the biblical injunction to "replenish" the earth as its caretakers, this moral duty has strong precedential support. Although most people accept the propriety of human use of other species for food, clothing, and other purposes, they likely would draw the line at exploiting these species into extinction. The moral duty may be seen as an obligation to refrain from "murdering" another species, because that species has in some sense a right to exist. Additionally, people may want to preserve other species as a living legacy for their children and grandchildren, feeling it is wrong to deprive their posterity of a heritage their own ancestors had passed down for their enjoyment.

Notes and Questions

1. In most countries, legislation to protect species is fairly new. The world's first purpose-built species protection legislation was enacted by the United States in 1966. Dubbed the "pitbull" of American environmental law, the federal *Endangered Species Act* (ESA) remains one of that country's most powerful environmental laws. Substantially strengthened through amendments in 1973, it has weathered various attempts in Congress to scale back its potent protection provisions which include, among other things, well-used citizen suit enforcement provisions (see Chapter 5). Moreover, there is evidence showing that the ESA has been effective at promoting species recovery. According to a recent analysis of recovery trends for representative populations of marine mammal and sea turtle species that are listed under the ESA, the researchers found that 78% of marine mammal populations and 75% of sea turtle populations studied experienced significant population increases after listing: Abel Valdivia, Shaye Wolf and Kieran Suckling, "Marine Mammals and Sea Turtles listed under the U.S. *Endangered Species Act* Are Recovering" (2019), online: PLOS One <https://doi.org/10.1371/journal.pone.0210164>. A few of these species have been delisted as a result of successful conservation measures triggered under the ESA. While two Canadian provinces (Ontario and New Brunswick) also enacted species protection in this early period, these laws were considerably less rigorous than ESA. In 2007, Ontario enacted endangered species legislation that commentators have heralded as the strongest law of its kind in Canada.

2. At the federal level, Canada did not have species protection legislation until late 2002, when the *Species at Risk Act* received Royal Assent (SARA's provisions came into force in three stages, coming fully into force on June 1, 2004). The law reform process that preceded the enactment of SARA lasted almost a decade. In the early 1990s, environmental groups mounted a concerted campaign for a federal law. In 1994, the government committed to enacting federal legislation. The next eight years saw often-heated debates over the philosophy and content of the proposed law both in Ottawa and across the country. The issues we profile in Part II were central to the debate

over the design and operation of the legal regime that ultimately was
enacted as SARA.

Part II — Species Listing under SARA

A key legislative design issue in developing species protection legislation is
the listing process. During the negotiations leading up to enactment of SARA,
Canadian environmentalists urged the federal government to adopt an entirely
science-based approach to listing, akin to the one that exists under the US
Endangered Species Act. This position met with considerable political
resistance. In the end, as chronicled by Smallwood, SARA reflects a
compromise which, for species identified in need of protection after enactment
of the law, vests in Cabinet the power to veto a scientific listing recommendation.

Kate Smallwood,
A Guide to Canada's Species at Risk Act
(Vancouver: Sierra Legal Defence Fund, 2003)

Listing is the prerequisite to protection under SARA. [...] [a key] debate has
been whether the federal government should adopt a scientific listing process or a
political listing process. Under a *scientific listing process*, the national list of species
at risk prepared by the Committee on the Status of Wildlife in Canada
("COSEWIC") would become the legal list under the Act. Under a *political
listing process*, COSEWIC's role would be advisory only — federal Cabinet would
have the ultimate decision as to which species would be listed under the Act.
Political listing has been a proven failure provincially, as most species listed by
COSEWIC are not listed provincially.

At third reading, the government finally agreed to the compromise solution
supported by the House Standing Committee on Environment and Sustainable
Development — "negative option" or "reverse onus" listing. Under this approach,
the COSEWIC list becomes the legal list under the Act unless Cabinet takes
contrary action within nine months. This process will ensure that no species will be
ignored or indefinitely deferred through Cabinet inaction [...]

The Legal List

The List of Wildlife Species at Risk (the "legal list") is contained in
Schedule 1 of the Act and constitutes the legal list under the Act. Unless a species
is included in the legal list, it will not be protected under SARA. Under the listing
process [...], COSEWIC listing assessments will be included on the legal list in
Schedule 1 unless within nine months after receiving the assessment federal
Cabinet takes contrary action. [...] once federal Cabinet has received an assessment
from COSEWIC, it has nine months to review the assessment (s. 27). During that
time period, Cabinet may, on the recommendation of the Minister of the
Environment, take one of three courses of action:

(a) accept the assessment and add the species to the list;

(b) decide not to add the species to the List; or

(c) refer the matter back to COSEWIC for further information or consideration.

If federal Cabinet decides not to add the species to the legal list or decides to refer the matter back to COSEWIC, the Minister of Environment, after the approval of Cabinet, is required to include a statement in the public registry setting out the reasons for the decision. If Cabinet takes no action within nine months after receiving an assessment, the Minister of Environment is required to amend the legal list in accordance with COSEWIC's assessment. Before making a recommendation to Cabinet in respect of a wildlife species, the Minister of the Environment must take into account COSEWIC's assessment in respect of the species, and must consult with the competent minister or ministers (the Minister of Fisheries and Oceans and the Minister of Canadian Heritage). If the species is found in an area governed by a wildlife management board under a land claims agreement, the Minister of the Environment must consult with the wildlife management board before making a recommendation to Cabinet.

Listing Categories

There are four different listing categories under SARA (s. 2):

- *Extirpated species*: means a wildlife species that no longer exists in the wild in Canada, but exists elsewhere in the wild.
- *Endangered species*: means a wildlife species that is facing imminent extirpation or extinction.
- *Threatened species*: means a wildlife species that is likely to become an endangered species if nothing is done to reverse the factors leading to its extirpation or extinction.
- *Species of special concern*: means a wildlife species that may become a threatened or endangered species because of a combination of biological characteristics and identified threats.

The listing categories are important because the risk category under which a species is listed dictates the level of protection it will receive under the Act. In general, species of special concern receive a much lower level of protection under the Act and in certain circumstances, extirpated species will only be covered if a recovery strategy has recommended the reintroduction of the species into the wild in Canada.

The three key areas where the difference in listing category becomes important are:

- *Basic prohibitions* — There are two basic prohibitions in SARA. Section 32 prohibits killing, harming, harassing, capturing or taking a listed species as well as possession or trading of a listed species or any part of a listed species. Section 33 prohibits damaging or destroying a listed species' "residence". The basic prohibitions only apply to listed extirpated, endangered or threatened species. Species of special concern are not covered. Both sets of prohibitions are limited to federal jurisdiction only, i.e. federal lands, aquatic species and migratory birds under the *Migratory Birds Convention Act*.

- *Critical Habitat Prohibition* — Section 58 prohibits the destruction of critical habitat within federal jurisdiction (federal lands, federal waters, aquatic species and migratory birds under the *Migratory Birds Convention Act*). The critical habitat prohibition applies to listed endangered and listed threatened species. Listed extirpated species are only covered if a recovery strategy has recommended the reintroduction of the species into the wild in Canada. Species of special concern are not covered.

- *Recovery Process* — Recovery strategies must be prepared for all listed extirpated, endangered and threatened species. The recovery process for species of special concern is addressed through a separate and less prescriptive process involving management plans.

Arne O. Mooers *et al.*,
"Science, Policy, and Species at Risk in Canada"
(2010) 60 BioScience 843

For many aspects of policymaking, especially regarding environmental issues such as endangered species conservation, the use of sound and reliable scientific knowledge is required. In practice, the translation of scientific information into policy is difficult. Scientific evidence may be called mere scientific "claims" in a complex argument among people with different worldviews. However, it is necessary to understand and delineate the essential role of science in the policymaking realm to foster a constructive dialogue between competing interests and agendas and to form effective environmental policy.

Endangered species legislation is a major framework for the delivery of science advice to conservation policy. Much has been written of the 35-year-old US *Endangered Species Act* (ESA), but Canada's much more recent *Species at Risk Act* (SARA) is only now undergoing its first statutory review by the Canadian federal government. This review offers opportunities to draw lessons for creating or improving legal frameworks to protect biodiversity, particularly with regard to the role of independent scientific advice in the policymaking process.

Here, we evaluate the key elements of SARA; outline an important strength and several of its critical shortcomings, both in terms of the statute's design and implementation; and offer suggestions for addressing these shortcomings. Our main conclusion is that the implementation of environmental legislation such as SARA requires a very clear delineation between all natural and social-scientific inputs and the relevant political trade-offs.

The Current Process: Design and Intent

The SARA process [...] begins with assessment of species by the independent Committee on the Status of Endangered Wildlife in Canada (COSEWIC).

Assessment of Species

The committee uses biological criteria, aboriginal and traditional knowledge, and input from many stakeholders to assess Canadian wildlife species as extirpated, endangered, threatened, of special concern, or not at risk. The criteria for status assessment are patterned after the International Union for Conservation of Nature's (IUCN) scheme, and delineate legally defined "wildlife species" using the concept of a "designatable unit". These designatable units meet similar criteria of discreteness and evolutionary significance to those used to identify distinct population segments in the United States.

COSEWIC identifies wildlife species suspected of being at risk and commissions status reports for those given highest priority. Relevant jurisdictions (i.e., federal agencies or provinces and territories) review draft reports first; the reports are then reviewed by scientists in the relevant species specialist subcommittees of COSEWIC and holders of traditional aboriginal knowledge. The subcommittees' final draft recommendations are then discussed by all COSEWIC members before the committee makes a status recommendation for the species to the federal government. The government ultimately decides whether to add the species in question to the SARA registry. The classification process thus draws on broad input, with more than 100 people generally commenting on any one report. COSEWIC status assignments are made public on its Web site following wildlife species assessment meetings. Thus, SARA incorporates a science-based prioritization and assessment of wildlife species independent of legal listing decisions. It is important to note that COSEWIC considers neither the feasibility nor the cost of recovery, nor the social or political ramifications of its assessment decisions. At the time of this article's writing, 598 wildlife species were on COSEWIC's list of wildlife species at risk. Although COSEWIC's list of wildlife species at risk has grown steadily, the rate of growth is primarily a reflection of the rate at which COSEWIC can assess wildlife species requiring examination.

Under SARA, COSEWIC's recommendations impose no federal duty to list a wildlife species. The Canadian government has three options: It can (1) accept COSEWIC's recommendation to legally list a wildlife species; (2) decline the recommendation, in which case the responsible minister must provide reasons for such action; or (3) return the issue to COSEWIC for further clarification. In making listing decisions, the federal government considers input from public consultations and internal economic assessments, in addition to COSEWIC's scientific assessment.

After Listing

As soon as a wildlife species is listed as endangered or threatened, individuals of that species and their dwellings are automatically protected on federal land. SARA typically applies only to federally managed lands, waters, and species; the responsibility for protecting wildlife species on lands managed by provinces and territories usually falls to the province or territory, although aquatic species and migratory birds are managed by the federal government under pre-existing statutes.

Listing also initiates a two-step recovery planning process. The first step is the development of a recovery strategy. The recovery strategy identifies the needs of and threats to the wildlife species, as well as objectives for population and distribution recovery. Recovery strategies can be contentious because of their socioeconomic implications. The next step is development of a recovery action plan. These plans put the strategy into action by specifying concrete recovery measures and evaluating potential socioeconomic impacts of these actions. Both the recovery strategy and the recovery action plan must identify critical habitat — the habitat necessary for a listed species' survival or recovery (SARA, s. 2.1) — to the extent possible. Once defined, the federal government must protect critical habitat on federal land (which constitutes 4% of Canada's 10 southern provinces as well as most of the three northern territories), and SARA is clear that the government may move to protect critical habitat outside of federal lands should it so choose (though, notably, it has never done so). The government must report on recovery progress for each species every five years.

There is no separate process for delisting wildlife species under SARA; in Canada, wildlife species at risk are simply reassessed by COSEWIC at least every 10 years. Such reassessments offer one window into the trajectory of Canada's imperiled wildlife: Since the inception of COSEWIC in 1977 (predating SARA), wildlife species that have been assessed more than once have moved to a more imperiled status nearly twice as often as they have moved to a less imperiled status (52 versus 27) [...]

Listing issues

Here we outline several potential issues relating to current listing procedures under SARA.

Independent Assessment and Legal Listing

There are limits to administrative capacity, and SARA instructs that priority for assessment should be given to species that are more likely to go extinct. Candidate species for assessment are themselves prioritized by COSEWIC according to a combination of probable threat, taxonomic distinctiveness, geographic extent, and endemism; data are required for each criterion. However, a "data deficient" assessment ruling triggers neither more research under SARA nor automatic reassessment. Such designations may be more common for taxa for which there is less taxonomic expertise, and this taxonomic deficit may become a more acute problem in the future as attention turns to invertebrates.

The separation of assessment from legal listing has its own implications: It can give the government an opportunity to avoid or delay the costs and consequences of protecting imperiled wildlife species. As of December 2007, the Canadian federal government has chosen not to list a taxonomically and geographically non-random 23% (60 of 252) of wildlife species recommended by COSEWIC since SARA's enactment in 2002. However, the framework also allows a time window for stakeholders and civil society to become more involved in the legal listing process at the consultation stage. Most important, the framework allows for a transparent separation of science and policy, providing the opportunity for accurate and science-based assessments as well as an unequivocal government response. We see this as the primary strength of SARA. We describe significant weaknesses in later stages of listing and recovery below.

Incomplete Economic Considerations in Listing Decisions

Although SARA makes no mention of economic analyses at the listing stage, it is the Canadian government's policy to review the economic implications of any regulatory change (such as a listing). A key component of reviews under Canadian legislation is the regulatory impact assessment statement (RIAS). When developing a RIAS before making a listing decision, government policy analysts are directed to work with scientists and resource managers to develop plausible scenarios for economic costs and benefits and impact analyses on the basis of the best available information. The depth of analysis is dictated by the potential economic consequences of regulatory change. Government guidelines recognize the need to account for the economic value of public environmental goods. Economic impact analyses, which address short-term distributional issues regarding jobs and regional economic effects, may also be conducted when sufficient data are available. Thus there is a framework for making evidence-based, informed economic SARA decisions, and such economic concerns have been given as an explicit reason in 50% of the cases (10 out of 20) in which listing has been denied outright.

Despite the clear RIAS framework, there are several challenges to informed decision-making, all compounded by the nine-month legally mandated timeline for making a listing decision (SARA s. 27.3; note that this time line is often extended through an apparent loophole in the legislation; see Mooers 2004). The initial choice of plausible scenarios to analyze is unclear. There is also substantial uncertainty about the potential impacts of listing or not listing under any scenario, as well as significant technical challenges with economic cost-benefit analyses for RIASs. For species listings with potential impacts on industry or economic interests, there has been an emphasis on short-term, regional economic impacts (e.g., local jobs, effects on local businesses). As is typical in policy analyses focused on regional impacts, attention is diverted from long-term, national benefits to Canadian society as a whole.

This focus is evident in SARA listing decisions. In one egregious example, listing was denied for the porbeagle shark (*Lamna nasus*) in part because of (a) the costs to a single community that derived 2% of its total landings' value, and (b) the costs to two fishers who earned less than 25% of their gross revenue from the porbeagle shark fishery (DFO 2006). Preliminary data available at the time of the non-listing decision estimated the porbeagle shark's non-use value to Canadian society at tens of millions of dollars annually.

Although we see the explicit incorporation of economic analysis as a reasonable part of the SARA process, this approach has often failed to live up to its potential. This is perhaps because it comes too early, because of a lack of general policy analysis capacity within government, or perhaps because economic analysis is not supplied as independent science advice but rather is embedded in a non-scientific policy-based framework.

Notes and Questions

1. Ontario's species protection law adopts an approach to listing that is much closer to the ESA's science-based model than the SARA approach: see *infra*, this chapter.

2. There has been considerable controversy in the implementation of species listing since SARA's enactment. These controversies include the federal government's attempts to extend the nine-month time limit, and the Minister of the Environment's practice of referring out for consultation COSEWIC listing recommendations with the result that these recommendations are analyzed through a "socio-economic" lens: see Ecojustice Legal Defence Fund's SARA enforcement complaint to the CEC at 2-6 and see CEC Citizen Submission SEM-06-05 "Species at Risk" cited at end of this chapter.

3. Some commentators contend that listing decisions are often influenced by economic and other considerations that are not always well documented or justified. Some commentators have gone further, claiming that the listing process displays bias: see A. Mooers *et al.*, "Biases in Legal Listing under Canadian Endangered Species Legislation" (2007) 21 Conservation Biology 572. When SARA came into force in 2003, all 233 species previously assessed by COSEWIC as imperilled were automatically included on the legal list. Since then, the authors claim that Cabinet listing decisions made between 2003 and 2006 display a pronounced bias against listing marine and northern species. According to the authors:

    > ... two factors ... seem to have contributed to the taxonomic and geographic biases in legal listing decisions under Canada's endangered species legislation. The first is a reluctance by wildlife management boards and the Department of Fisheries and Oceans to accept the additional stewardship responsibilities required by SARA. The second pertains to deficiencies in the cost-benefit analyses that precede the legal listing decisions.

    > Wildlife management boards (WMBs), whose responsibilities are primarily in the north, are involved in the legal listing decisions for species in their jurisdictions. The stated governmental reason for not listing northern mammals is to allow for further consultation with WMBs, notably the Nunavut WMB. The SARA provides no timelines for such post-assessment consultations, and the WMBs are consulted by COSEWIC before each assessment. The resulting delays may elevate the extinction risk for some species. For example, Bourdages et al. (2002) estimated that current harvesting rates of the eastern Hudson Bay beluga whale population, which was denied listing, will lead to its extinction within 10-15 years. These consultations also affect populations outside Nunavut insofar as Nunavut-based delays have prevented the listing of the wolverine, grizzly bear, and polar bear elsewhere in Canada.

    > Although not made explicit in SARA, the legal listing process includes something called a regulatory impact analysis (RIAS). The RIASs are cost-benefit analyses undertaken by the federal government, promulgated under the *Financial Admin-istration Act*. A RIAS typically take place during the 9 months that immediately precede a listing decision, prior to the development of any form of recovery strategy or action plan. This timing is clearly problematic; A RIAS will be unable to provide a complete assessment of the costs and benefits of species recovery,

potentially biasing the perception of the socioeconomic impact of a listing decision. In addition, these cost-benefit analyses are not subject to external review.

A major deficiency of RIAS is that relatively little effort is expended in estimating benefits. By one estimate, half of all RIASs examined do not quantify benefits at all. Quantifying the benefits of recovering species is obviously critical if cost-benefit analyses are to be taken seriously. Globally, the loss of habitats and populations deprives humanity of goods and services with a net worth of perhaps US$250 billion annually. In Canada failure to take meaningful action to reduce fishing mortality on Newfoundland's northern Atlantic cod in the late 1980s led to a subsequent expenditure of C$2-C$3 billion for income support, buy outs of commercial fishing licenses, and training for alternative employment for displaced fishers and processors. Benefits to listing must also account for non-use economic values. These are the benefits of conservation that can be reflected in part by the value that society holds for the preservation of species.

Biodiversity conservation would be best served by strict, transparent, legislated timelines for all aspects of the listing process following receipt by the Minister of the Environment of the status assessments undertaken by COSEWIC. We also recommend that, within the RIAS framework, SARA require that the full costs of extinction and the full benefits of recovery be quantified in externally reviewed reports so that they can be fairly weighed against the impacts of legal protection.

Drawing on this research, the David Suzuki Foundation published "Left Off the List: A Profile of Marine and Northern Species Denied Listing under SARA" (2007). Among the species discussed in this report are the Peary caribou, polar bear, wolverine, grizzly bear, Beluga whale, Coho salmon, Atlantic cod and Porbeagle shark. The conclusions of Mooers *et al.* has since been confirmed and elaborated on in C. Scott Finlay, Stewart Elgie, Brian Giles & Linda Burr, "Species Listing under Canada's Species at Risk Act: A Follow-up to Mooers *et al.*" (2009) 23 Conservation Biology 1609.

Part III — Critical Habitat Designation, Recovery Strategies and Action Plans

Introduction

Ultimately, the efficacy of species protection legislation turns on the efficacy with which it succeeds in protecting critical habitat. Whether critical habitat will be designated is subject to a highly discretionary process that commences with the development of a *recovery strategy* and culminates in implementation of an *action plan*. "Critical habitat" is defined in SARA as "the habitat that is necessary for the survival or recovery of a listed wildlife species and that is identified as the species' critical habitat in the recovery strategy or in an action plan for the species": see section 2. Recovery strategies are intended to set out the overall scientific framework within which recovery is to be implemented, while action plans describe the specific actions to be taken to implement the recovery plan. Recovery strategies are intended to be exclusively science-based, while action plans may take socio-economic factors into account.

Upon species listing, SARA requires recovery planning to commence. Recovery strategies are the primary tool for mapping and bringing about the actions needed to reverse the decline of species at risk and lay the groundwork for their recovery. Newly listed species must have recovery strategies posted on the SARA public registry within one year of listing, whereas endangered species that were listed when the Act came into force must have recovery strategies posted within three years of the section coming into force, which was June 3, 2003.

As of April 2019, 297 recovery strategies have been completed, with approximately 31 currently overdue. In addition to delays in completing recovery strategies, environmentalists have criticized the adequacy of many of the completed plans. SARA provides that recovery plans must identify critical habitat "to the extent possible, based on the best information": see paragraph 41(1)(c). In a complaint filed with the NAFTA Commission for Environmental Cooperation in 2006, Ecojustice claimed that:

> ... to date (September 2006), of the 23 recovery strategies posted on the *SARA* registry, only 3 identify critical habitat, and 5 partially identify critical habitat. There is little certainty as to whether the prohibitions in the *SARA* apply where critical habitat has been identified only partially. Moreover, the 3 species where recovery plans identify critical habitat are located within protected areas (Aurora Trout and Horsetail Spike-rush), or have restricted distribution (Barrens Willow). Further, research into two of the plans indicates that where habitat was not identified, or only partially identified, science for full identification does exist but has not been incorporated into the strategy (see recovery plans for the Piping Plover and Spotted Owl).

Once a recovery strategy has been completed, SARA requires an action plan(s) to be developed, which specifies measures that are to be taken to carry out the proposed recovery strategy. The overall procedure for preparation of action plans is very similar to the procedure for preparation of recovery strategies. There are mandatory requirements for consultation and cooperation; the proposed plan must be filed in the public registry; there is a public comment period; existing plans may be used in whole or part; and the competent minister may amend the action plan or plans. Unlike recovery strategies, however, SARA does not prescribe a time period for the completion of actions and, as noted above, action plans may incorporate socio-economic factors.

One of the reasons for the apparent reluctance of federal officials to identify critical habitat in the recovery strategies issued to date are concerns about potential impacts on private landowners. The failure to identify critical habitat in recovery strategies is documented in an independent report commissioned by the federal government, which evaluated the federal government's implementation of SARA. According to this report, authored by the consulting firm of Stratos Inc.:

> Core departments have made very limited, and less than anticipated progress in identifying critical habitat through the recovery planning process ... Policy considerations are also a factor [in not identifying critical habitat]. Where provinces/territories are leading recovery planning efforts, they report a reluctance

to identify critical habitat on non-federal lands until the supporting policy framework is clarified. (2006)

Below is another extract from the article by Mooers *et al.* we looked at above. In this excerpt, the authors critique the SARA recovery strategy/action plan process.

Arne O. Mooers *et al.*,
"Science, Policy, and Species at Risk in Canada"
(2010) 60 BioScience 843

Recovery Strategies: Ineffective Meshing of Science and Policy

The production of recovery strategies has been slow and problematic. Issues may result from having science input that is too deeply embedded in a policy framework. Although a choice of minimal conservation goals may be a legitimate societal decision, there should be clarity about whether the goals are selected on the basis of scientific or socioeconomic considerations.

As mandated under SARA, population and distribution objectives are crucial goalposts for species recovery and must be specified in recovery strategies (SARA s. 41.1[d]). Transparent conservation decisions depend on the clarification of the biological meanings of key terms that are not defined in SARA, such as survival and recovery. Because critical habitat is defined as the habitat "necessary for the survival or recovery" of a listed wildlife species (SARA, s. 2.1), the quantity and location of critical habitat (and associated socioeconomic impacts) and permitting will be sensitive to the biological interpretation of survival and of recovery. Permitting for activities that affect listed species is allowed when regulators believe that such activities will not "jeopardize the survival or recovery of the species" (SARA, s. 73.3.[c]). A standard interpretation of survival from the scientific literature using minimum viable populations (which are widely viewed as the minimum unit for species conservation; see, e.g., Traill et al. 2007) would, following IUCN criteria, characterize survival as a greater than 90% chance of species persistence for at least 100 years. A species not meeting the definition of the minimum viable population for survival would trigger a listing of "at risk" in Canada, in the United States, and internationally. The Canadian federal government has suggested policy whereby survival would mean maintaining the current population in the "short term". It is therefore important to ask whether a benchmark of 100 years is considered "short term" in Canadian policy: For a species already listed as at risk of extinction, merely maintaining its current population size for some limited time (e.g., until the next COSEWIC reassessment in 10 or fewer years) would provide little assurance of continued survival.

Recovery has been defined in Canadian policy as "long-term persistence" or simply where decline is "arrested or reversed". The definition of "long term" must be clarified here. The "or" in the second definition is also potentially important, as the easier goal (arresting decline) could become the default policy. Arresting decline may be enough action for the few species with large population sizes that are still widely distributed but nonetheless considered imperilled. However, recovery as restoration, rather than merely an arrested decline, implies higher benchmarks with respect to population size and distribution.

Critical habitat designation has been hampered for several reasons. First, although the law is clear that the precautionary approach must be followed (SARA, s. 38), and that critical habitat must be identified to the extent possible using the best available information (SARA, s. 41.1[c]), such habitat has been identified for just 23 of the 104 species with finalized recovery strategies, and thus for only 23 of 447 (roughly 5%) of listed species.

Two species' recovery strategies (the greater sage grouse and the Nooksack dace) that omitted known critical habitat were successfully challenged in court in 2009 (*Alberta Wilderness Association v. Minister of the Environment*, 2009 FC 710; *Environmental Defense Canada v. Minister of Fisheries and Oceans*, 2009 FC 878). Although these precedent-setting lawsuits may lead to the official identification of some critical habitat in other recovery strategies, we wonder whether litigation or fear of it is the most efficient approach for identifying the critical habitat needed to achieve species recovery. Currently, the government oversees the preparation of recovery strategies, though it usually seeks outside scientific advice. However, the government ministries involved may have conflicting interests that could affect the final scientific content of these strategies. We suggest that the process of writing an official recovery strategy could benefit from something similar to the two-step listing process, using unbiased scientific proposals that meet clear goals that are followed by clear government responses.

Recovery Action Plans: Lost in the Fog

Recovery action plans detail the specific projects and activities that must be implemented to enable species recovery, in addition to analyzing potential costs and benefits. They are supposed to be developed and implemented by biologists, managers, economists, and stakeholders using scientific guidance from the recovery strategy. Although voluntary recovery activities have been initiated for many species, only a single wildlife species, the Banff Springs snail (Physella johnsoni), whose entire range is in a national park, has a legally accepted recovery action plan. It is important to note that if critical habitat is not described in the initial recovery strategy, there are no legal time lines for identifying and thus protecting such habitat because the recovery plans themselves have no legal time lines for completion. A lack of definition means that much effort can be expended in a legal process of identifying, listing, and strategizing for the eventual recovery of a species with no certainty that the process will ever lead to action on the ground.

Conclusions

To ensure accountability, environmental legislation must clearly delineate the role of independent science in the implementation of recovery actions. SARA is one of a widening net of endangered species protection laws that have slowly emerged around the world: By our count, at least 36 countries now have legislation to identify and protect species threatened with extirpation or extinction. To its credit, SARA was written to explicitly incorporate both scientific and economic concerns, and in a few places the law seems to limit consideration to purely scientific concerns when appropriate (e.g., listing assessments, critical habitat identification, and the determination of the feasibility of recovery). In many other cases SARA also allows for the quantification of economic costs and benefits. This emphasis on economic analysis and planning is arguably better embodied in SARA than in, for example, the US ESA.

In theory, more explicit and transparent consideration of competing governmental priorities might avoid the distorted implementations sometimes seen in environmental laws that are less realistic about competing agendas. Though the assessment process itself might be improved, it does offer a clear delineation between independent science and policy. Following COSEWIC's recommendations, however, the legal listing, recovery planning, and implementation phases of SARA do not offer this delineation. These phases have been identified as problematic, such that hard choices are simply being postponed indefinitely.

In particular, we suggest that both social and natural sciences must better inform independent social and economic analyses that are necessary to decide whether a wildlife species is listed. One simple improvement would be to subject the scenario choices and the resulting evaluations to independent, nongovernmental peer review. It is worth considering whether extra emphasis on this important stage would require longer mandated time lines in conjunction with interim legal protection, as is how these evaluations would flow into the recovery phase. In the same vein, we recommend timely independent peer review and oversight of both recovery strategies and recovery action plans, as is policy under, for example, the ESA.

In general, a structural separation of information gathering and interpretation (i.e., scientific advice) from strategic planning and action (i.e., policy and implementation) seems an excellent basis on which to proceed. This aim would be best served by extracting all of the science-based aspects of the conservation process — assessments of biological status, of critical habitat and threats, population and distribution objectives, and economic analysis — as discrete modules that would produce independent and transparent scientific advice to feed back into a political process, with attendant hard deadlines. The need for a mandated framework for the delivery of such independent scientific advice into subsequent political processes is a significant hurdle to improving SARA, and may be also be an important component for environmental legislation elsewhere.

Habitat Designation and Recovery Strategy Litigation

One aspect of SARA that has seen considerable litigation is its provisions governing critical habitat designation and recovery strategies. In this section, we provide excerpts from three important decisions arising from litigation resulting from delays and alleged inadequacies in the completion of federal recovery strategies. We present these decisions in the order in which they were decided. The first case in this emerging line of authority concerns a terrestrial species (*Greater Sage-Grouse*); it alleges that the federal Minister failed to designate all of the critical habitat to the extent possible. The following two cases involve federal/aquatic species: the Nooksack Dace and the Southern Resident Orcas. Like *Greater Sage-Grouse*, the *Nooksack Dace* case challenged the adequacy of the federally-issued recovery strategy in terms of habitat designation. The *Southern Resident Orcas* case arises in a somewhat different procedural context. It involves a challenge to a "protection statement" offered by a federal Minister claiming that orca habitat had been "legally protected" in compliance with SARA.

Alberta Wilderness Assn. v. Canada (Minister of Environment)
2009 FC 710,
additional reasons 2009 FC 882

ZINN J.: — This is an application for judicial review of the 'Recovery Strategy for the Greater Sage-Grouse (*Centrocercus urophasianus urophasianus*) in Canada' (the Recovery Strategy) posted by the Minister of the Environment under the *Species at Risk Act*, S.C. 2002, c. 29 ("SARA") on January 14, 2008.

The applicants are non-profit environmental and natural history organizations that are concerned about the survival and recovery of the Greater Sage-Grouse, and other species at risk. Their specific complaint concerning the Recovery Strategy is that it fails to identify any "critical habitat" for the Greater Sage-Grouse. They submit that the Minister erred in law in his interpretation of the relevant statutory provisions of the SARA. For the reasons that follow, I find that there has been no error of law by the respondent; however, this application for judicial review is allowed as the decision of the respondent, to the extent that it fails to identify any critical habitat, is unreasonable.

Background

There is little dispute between the parties with respect to the fundamental facts concerning the Greater Sage-Grouse, the SARA regime and the process that lead to the drafting and posting of the Recovery Strategy. Where the parties differ concerns the obligation of the Minister to identify the critical habitat of the Greater Sage-Grouse and whether, at the time the Recovery Strategy was prepared and posted, such identification was possible given known facts.

There are approximately 150,000 Greater Sage-Grouse in North America; less than one percent are in Canada. The Greater Sage-Grouse is located in southeastern Alberta and southwestern Saskatchewan as well as in a number of the northwestern States of the United States of America. The Greater Sage-Grouse is dependent on sagebrush for food and shelter.

Greater Sage-Grouse have specific habitat requirements for breeding, nesting, brood-rearing and wintering. The description of these is set out in the Recovery Strategy and may be briefly described as follows.

1. Breeding habitat, referred to as leks, is an open area of sparse vegetation, located slightly lower than surrounding areas and often near standing water. Leks range in size from 1.4 to 16 hectares.

2. Nesting habitat is a broad area of sagebrush with horizontal and vertical vegetative diversity. It is usually located near leks with average lek-to-nest distance in Alberta ranging from 0.42 to 15.4 kilometres.

3. Brood-rearing or summer habitat is usually located within 3 kilometres of nesting habitat.

4. Winter habitat has been little investigated in Canada. During the fall Greater Sage-Grouse congregate in gender segregated flocks. The Greater Sage-Grouse is listed as an endangered species under Schedule I of the SARA which means that it has been identified as facing imminent extirpation (i.e. no longer existing in the wild in Canada, but existing elsewhere in the wild) or extinction. Section 39 of the SARA provides that when a species is listed as endangered, the competent Minister, in this case the Minister of the Environment, must prepare a strategy for the recovery of that species.

The SARA prescribes a recovery planning process for endangered species. It is a two-step process. The first step is the preparation and posting of a recovery strategy and the second step is the development and posting of an action plan to implement the recovery strategy. The present application concerns only the recovery strategy step of the process.

Section 41 of the SARA sets out the content of a recovery strategy. Content is dependent on whether the Minister has determined that the recovery of the listed species is feasible or not. In this case, the Minister determined that recovery is feasible. Subsection 41(1) of the SARA stipulates the content of a recovery strategy when the Minister has determined that recovery of the species is feasible. In so doing the Minister is required, in many instances, to consider the information provided by COSEWIC (the Committee on the Status of Endangered Wildlife in Canada) that is established pursuant to the SARA. Subsection 41(1) of the SARA reads as follows:

> 41. (1) If the competent minister determines that the recovery of the listed wildlife species is feasible, the recovery strategy must address the threats to the survival of the species identified by COSEWIC, including any loss of habitat, and must include
>
> (a) a description of the species and its needs that is consistent with information provided by COSEWIC;
>
> (b) an identification of the threats to the survival of the species and threats to its habitat that is consistent with information provided by COSEWIC and a description of the broad strategy to be taken to address those threats;
>
> (c) an identification of the species' critical habitat, to the extent possible, based on the best available information, including the information provided by COSEWIC, and examples of activities that are likely to result in its destruction;
>
> (c.1) a schedule of studies to identify critical habitat, where available information is inadequate;
>
> (d) a statement of the population and distribution objectives that will assist the recovery and survival of the species, and a general description of the research and management activities needed to meet those objectives;
>
> (e) any other matters that are prescribed by the regulations;

(f) a statement about whether additional information is required about the species; and

(g) a statement of when one or more action plans in relation to the recovery strategy will be completed.

"Critical habitat" and "habitat" are both defined terms in the SARA:

"critical habitat" means the habitat that is necessary for the survival or recovery of a listed wildlife species and that is identified as the species' critical habitat in the recovery strategy or in an action plan for the species.

"habitat" means

(a) in respect of aquatic species, spawning grounds and nursery, rearing, food supply, migration and any other areas on which aquatic species depend directly or indirectly in order to carry out their life processes, or areas where aquatic species formerly occurred and have the potential to be reintroduced; and

(b) in respect of other wildlife species, the area or type of site where an individual or wildlife species naturally occurs or depends on directly or indirectly in order to carry out its life processes or formerly occurred and has the potential to be reintroduced.

In their memorandum of argument, the applicants state that the respondent "failed to perform a mandatory statutory duty as required by s. 41(1)(c) of the SARA, namely, to include an 'identification of the species' critical habitat, to the extent possible, based on the best available information.'"

The development of the Recovery Strategy occurred over many months and involved a number of parties. In June 2005 lead responsibility for the development of the Recovery Strategy was assigned to Parks Canada Agency ("PCA"). [...]

For the purposes of funding a recovery planning process, PCA requires that a project charter be prepared identifying the recovery planning to be undertaken and the approaches to it, including major recovery planning issues. The project charter for the Greater Sage-Grouse is dated July 5, 2006, and contains the following statement with respect to identifying critical habitat:

The strategy will **not** include the identification of critical habitat. Critical Habitat designation has been deferred due to lack of comprehensive information particularly in Saskatchewan but a schedule of studies is included in the Recovery Strategy. [bolded emphasis in original]

[...] There is no discretion vested in the Minister in identifying critical habitat under the SARA. Subsection 41(1)(c) requires that the Minister identify in a recovery strategy document as much critical habitat as it is possible to identify at that time, even if all of it cannot be identified, and to do so based on the best information then available. I note that this requirement reflects the precautionary principle that "where there are threats of serious or irreversible damage, lack of full scientific certainty should not be used as a reason for postponing measures to prevent environmental degradation," as it was put by the Supreme Court of Canada, citing the *Bergen Ministerial Declaration on Sustainable Development* in *114957 Canada Ltée (Spraytech, Société d'arrosage) v. Hudson (Town)*, 2001 SCC 40.

In light of this agreement on interpretation, the real issues in dispute, in my view, are the following:

1. What is the correct standard of review of the respondent's decision to not identify any critical habitat in the Greater Sage-Grouse Recovery Strategy?

2. Does the decision of the respondent to not identify any critical habitat meet that test and, if not, what is the appropriate remedy?

Analysis

What is the applicable standard of review?

Subsection 41(1)(c) of the SARA provides that the Minister must identify the species' critical habitat "to the extent possible". The applicants submit that this means that if all of the critical habitat cannot be identified then the Minister is required to identify as much of the critical habitat as is possible. It is only if it is impossible to identify any critical habitat that the Minister may issue a recovery strategy that defines no critical habitat. The applicants' submission on the standard of review was premised largely, if not entirely, on its view that because it was possible, based on the best information available, to identify some critical habitat for the Greater Sage-Grouse in the Recovery Strategy, and since the Minister did not do so, he must have misinterpreted subsection 41(1)(c). In fact, as previously noted, both parties interpret subsection 41(1)(c) in the same fashion; their disagreement is whether, based on the best information available, one could identify some critical habitat for the Greater Sage-Grouse in the Recovery Strategy. The applicants say it was possible to identify some critical habitat; the respondent says it was not. The issue for the Court's determination is whether the Minister's decision that no critical habitat could be identified, within the meaning of section 41(1) of the SARA, was reasonable; the question defines the proper standard of review.

Is the decision to not identify any critical habitat reasonable?

Subsection 41(1)(c) of the SARA requires the Minister to identify critical habitat, to the extent possible, "based on the best available information." The Minister submits that the critical habitat finding was a finding of fact and is entitled to the highest level of deference. It can only be interfered with by the Court if it was unreasonable in that it fell "outside a range of possible, acceptable outcomes which are defensible in respect of the facts and law": *Dunsmuir v. New Brunswick*, 2008 SCC 9 at para. 47.

The applicants submit that the best available information was such that the Minister could have identified some critical habitat for the Greater Sage-Grouse. Specifically, the applicants submit that:

- The location of most if not all active leks have been known for years. Greater Sage-Grouse population has been estimated from annual counts of strutting males at leks. In 2005, there were nine known active leks in Alberta and eight in Saskatchewan.

- Some of the Greater Sage-Grouse's brooding and nesting habitat has been identified by Dr. Aldridge in his 2005 Ph.D. thesis, namely the habitat near Manyberries, Alberta.

I agree with the respondent that the Court is not an academy of science and that the determination of what constitutes critical habitat is to be left to experts who have studied the Greater Sage-Grouse. The Court's limited role is to determine whether the Minister's decision to not identify any critical habitat was reasonable. That is to be assessed based on the record before the Court and, with great respect to counsel for the respondent who suggested otherwise, it does not require that the Court engage in any scientific examination. It merely requires an examination of the evidence that was available to the decision-maker — admittedly most of which has a scientific focus.

In examining whether the respondent's decision was reasonable, it is appropriate to examine the decision not to identify any critical habitat by looking at the Recovery Strategy itself to see whether there is anything in it that leads to a conclusion that the decision (being the Recovery Strategy) was based on an erroneous finding of fact (namely that critical habitat could not be identified) made in a capricious or perverse manner or without regard for the material before it, as described in subsection 18.1(4)(d).

As previously noted, the respondent in the Recovery Strategy identifies four habitat requirements of the Greater Sage-Grouse: breeding habitat, nesting habitat, brood-rearing habitat and winter habitat. In so doing the respondent concluded that each habitat is essential to the Greater Sage-Grouse. In determining that no critical habitat could be identified, the respondent concluded that it could identify no critical breeding habitat, no critical nesting habitat, no critical brood-rearing habitat and no critical winter habitat. Had it been able to identify a part of any one or more of these four habitat as critical, then it was required to identify that habitat pursuant to section 41(1)(c) of the SARA, as it is required to identify critical habitat "to the extent possible."

Breeding Habitat or Leks

The Recovery Strategy states that it is essential to the recovery of the Greater Sage-Grouse that there be no loss of active leks.

The following goals focus on the elimination of further losses to population numbers and habitat, while striving to improve availability of quality habitat for population increases via short and long-term targets:

- No loss of active Sage-Grouse leks or Sage-Grouse population numbers in any portion of the current Sage-Grouse range in Alberta and Saskatchewan, ...

The respondent determined that all active leks are to be maintained. Thus, the respondent effectively determined that they are "habitat that is necessary for the survival or recovery" of the Greater Sage-Grouse, within the definition of "critical habitat" in the SARA. There is evidence in the Recovery Strategy that these active leks can be identified, based on the best available information. In deciding that no critical habitat would be identified in the Recovery Strategy, I find that the respondent reached that decision without regard to the material before it. It is not a decision that "falls within a range of possible, acceptable outcomes which are defensible in respect of the facts and law."

Nesting Habitat and Brood Rearing Habitat

The Recovery Strategy endorses the model developed by Dr. Aldridge in his Ph.D. thesis to identify the nesting and brood-rearing habitat of the Greater Sage-Grouse. Dr. Aldridge applied his model to an area in Alberta, the Manyberries area, in order to prove that his model would accurately predict these habitats. The applicants acknowledge that the model has not been applied outside the Manyberries area and that this would have to be done in order to identify nesting and brood-rearing habitat outside the area of his study. However, they submit that as Dr. Aldridge had identified the nesting and brood-rearing habitat within the Manyberries area, this was known and identified habitat, and was also critical habitat.

The respondent has accepted Dr. Aldridge's model and proposes to use it to identify the other nesting and brood-rearing habitat in the remainder of Alberta and Saskatchewan. It may be that after that has been done, the scientific community will conclude that not all of the identified habitat is critical habitat. However, the SARA stipulates that the respondent must make the determination of critical habitat based on the best available information, which is to say the best information that exists at any one point in time. That information may change over time, but the identification of critical habitat cannot be postponed for that reason alone.

In this case, the respondent concluded that source habitat is to be protected, i.e. that it is "habitat that is necessary for the survival or recovery" of the Greater Sage-Grouse, within the definition of "critical habitat" in the SARA. The respondent also accepted Dr. Aldridge's identification of source nesting and broodrearing habitat for some of the geographic area where the Greater Sage-Grouse is found and stated that this model would be applied to other geographic areas. It is therefore unreasonable for the respondent to then conclude that no critical habitat can be identified now. The source habitat identified by Dr. Aldridge in the Manyberries area could have been and ought to have been identified by the respondent. It may be that after all of the geography of the Greater Sage-Grouse has been modeled, scientists will determine that not all of the source nesting and brood-rearing habitat is critical habitat. It may well be that some of this habitat in the Manyberries area will be identified as not being critical habitat. However, at the time the Recovery Strategy was drafted and posted, some critical habitat could be identified, namely that identified by Dr. Aldridge as source habitat. Failure to identify any habitat as critical is unreasonable in light of the conclusion that source habitat is to be maintained.

For these reasons the application for judicial review must be allowed.

Notes and Questions

1. This decision, and the others that we will be considering in this Part, was decided after the SCC's landmark 2008 decision in *Dunsmuir v. New Brunswick*, 2008 SCC 9. Explain how *Dunsmuir* is applied here. Do you agree with how Zinn J. applied *Dunsmuir* in this case?

2. An argument that is often mounted by government lawyers in SARA litigation is that courts must avoid becoming "academies of science". Zinn J. wastes little time discounting this concern. What is the underlying policy basis for this argument? Is it a valid concern? Can courts grapple with and apply science without becoming scientific academies?

3. Arguably, part of the reason that this was an "easier" case for Zinn J. to decide was because the Minister declined to identify any habitat whatsoever. Suppose the Minister had chosen to identify *some* critical habitat, but not enough to satisfy the applicant; how would that have affected Zinn J.'s analysis?

The next judgment we will look at was decided a few months after Zinn J. decided the *Greater Sage-Grouse* case. As with the *Greater Sage-Grouse* case, counsel for the applicant was Ecojustice Canada. As you read this next case, which involves a freshwater minnow known as the Nooksack Dace, consider the differences in judicial style and language between this case and *Greater Sage-Grouse*.

Environmental Defence Canada v.
Canada (Minister of Fisheries & Oceans)
2009 FC 878

CAMPBELL J.: — By these reasons, the Nooksack Dace, a small minnow whose habitat is four fresh water streams in the Lower Mainland of British Columbia, has the distinction of being the first endangered species in Canada to benefit by a comprehensive interpretation by this Court of key elements of its protective legislation: the *Species at Risk Act*, [S.C.] 2002, c. 29 (*SARA*).

A decision of the Minister of Fisheries and Oceans (Minister) pursuant to *SARA* has prompted the Applicants to bring the present Application as a "test case" respecting the Minister's interpretation of *SARA* as displayed in the decision under review. The Applicants argue that the Minister knowingly failed to follow the mandatory requirements of s. 41(1)(c) and (c.1) of *SARA* with respect to the Final Recovery Strategy for the Nooksack Dace. However, during the course of the hearing, Counsel for the Applicants stressed that no allegation of bad faith is being made respecting this conduct.

Nevertheless, in my opinion, the story that gave rise to the present litigation and the conduct of the litigation itself is important to be told. This is so because a review of the Minister's decision-making under *SARA* applied to the Nooksack Dace provides ample proof that the bringing of the present Application was absolutely necessary. This is a story about the creation and application of policy by the Minister in clear contravention of the law, and a reluctance to be held accountable for failure to follow the law. Therefore, this is a case about the rule of law described by Justices Bastarache and LeBel at paragraph 28 of *Dunsmuir v. New Brunswick*, 2008 SCC 9, [2008] 1 S.C.R. 190 [...]

In the end result, the Applicants' judicial review argument concerning the Minister's failure in decision-making is limited to a question of statutory interpretation. For the reasons which follow, I find that the Minister acted contrary to the law intended by Parliament to protect the Nooksack Dace.

Overview of the Present Dispute

The Applicants' purpose in launching the present Application is stated in the following paragraphs of the Notice of Application:

> [...] The Applicants are "public interest groups" in that they are charities that work or environmental protection and have no personal, proprietary or pecuniary interest in the outcome of the Application.

> [...] The Applicants believe that they need to bring this Application to address federal failure to implement the SARA, which failure is further endangering Canada's at risk species. They believe that an order requiring SARA to be complied with is in the public interest because the viability of Canada's wildlife populations is a matter affecting all Canadians.

> The grounds for the application are: [...]

> 3. The Nooksack dace is a small (<15 cm) stream-dwelling minnow. Within Canada it is known from four lowland streams in British Columbia's Fraser Valley. The global distribution includes approximately 20 additional streams in north-west Washington.

> 4. The Nooksack dace is "listed" pursuant to the SARA as an "endangered" species, meaning that it on the List of endangered Wildlife Species set out in Schedule 1 to the SARA. The dace's status as "endangered" means that it is "a wildlife species that is facing imminent extirpation." "Extirpated" means no longer existing in the wild in Canada, but existing elsewhere in the wild. (s. 2). The Nooksack dace is extirpated from some tributaries in Canadian watersheds where it was abundant in the 1960s.

> 5. Listing triggers SARA's provisions to prevent extirpation and provide for recovery of species. These include prohibitions against harm (s. 32), protections for residence (s. 33) and the requirement of the Minister to undertake recovery planning (ss. 37-46) and recovery plan implementation ("action planning") (ss. 47-64). [...]

> 9. The Nooksack dace was a species listed on Schedule 1 of the SARA when the Act came into force, therefore the Recovery Strategy was due June 5th, 2006 (ss. 42(2)).

> 10. The SARA requires a proposed recovery strategy to be placed on a SARA Public Registry where, for 60 days, the public may file written comments with the Minister (s. 43(1)). 30 days after this, the Minister must include the final recovery strategy on the Public Registry (s. 43(2)).

> 11. A draft [proposed] Nooksack Dace Recovery Strategy was posted to the Public Registry on or about September 25th, 2006. Comments were submitted on

behalf of the Applicants which noted, *inter alia*, the failure of the Recovery Strategy to identify critical habitat notwithstanding that its location is known. On July 23, 2007, one year after it was due, the final Nooksack Dace Recovery Strategy was posted to the Public Registry.

12. The Recovery Strategy does not identify critical habitat while identifying loss of habitat as one of the main threats to the Nooksack dace's survival, and recommending habitat protection in ensuring the species' survival and recovery.

13. The Recovery Team, formed to provide the minister with advice on the Recovery Strategy and comprised of leading experts regarding the Nooksack dace, could and did identify critical habitat and wished to include that identification of critical habitat in the Nooksack Dace Recovery Strategy.

14. But, at the direction of the Minister and/or his delegate, the Recovery Team removed the identification of critical habitat from the Recovery Strategy and inserted it into a separate document which was not posted to the Public Registry. [...]

Thus, the present Application primarily concerns the recovery strategy provisions of *SARA* as applied to the Nooksack Dace and, in particular, the correct interpretation of s. 41(1)(c) and (c.1) [...]

Of primary concern with respect to s. 41(1)(c) and (c.1) is the definitions of "habitat" for aquatic species and "critical habitat" provided in s. 2 of *SARA*. The issue is whether the term "habitat" includes two features: a defined geographic area capable of being located on a map and the physical and biological attributes of that area that allow a species to use it for the function of carrying out its life processes. [...]

The Minister's Final Recovery Strategy Decision

The process leading to the posting of the Final Recovery Strategy of the Nooksack Dace involved the preparation of a Draft Proposed Recovery Strategy, the posting of the Proposed Recovery Strategy, public consultation, and then the posting of the Final Recovery Strategy.

The Recovery Team's Draft Proposed Recovery Strategy

Recovery strategies under *SARA* in British Columbia for freshwater fish are developed by a Recovery Team composed of a core group of experts and others added to assist with individual species as needed. With respect to the Nooksack Dace, a subcommittee of such a team was formed in December 2003 to begin assessment of the Nooksack Dace and to continue assessment of the Salish Sucker; one of the members of the sub-working group was Dr. Mike Pearson, a self-employed professional biologist who is the lead authority in Canada on the ecology, conservation, and habitat needs of freshwater fish generally and, in particular, the Nooksack Dace and Salish Sucker. Dr. Pearson has provided his expertise to DFO under contract since 2003.

Dr. Pearson was requested to prepare a preliminary draft of a recovery st[r]ategy for both the Nooksack Dace and Salish Sucker for the consideration of the Recovery Team with an eye towards placing a final draft before the Minister as the Proposed Recovery Strategy required to be posted pursuant to s. 42(1) of *SARA* [...] Pearson provided his draft to the Recovery Team in June 2004, and a second draft in January 2005. The Recovery Team then provided its final "Draft Recovery Strategy" to DFO in June 2005.

Ms. Webb's Direction

With respect to the Recovery Team's Draft Recovery Strategy, and with respect to compliance with s. 41(1)(c) of *SARA*, Ms. Webb made the critical decision to direct the altering of all draft recovery strategies then in progress in the Pacific Region of DFO, including the Nooksack Dace Draft Recovery Strategy; the altered document was proposed three months later as the Proposed Recovery Strategy.

The details of "critical habitat" that Ms. Webb decided to remove are described by Dr. Pearson as follows:

> In September 2006, the Proposed Recovery Strategy was posted on the SARA public registry with some of the information related to the critical habitat removed. Specifically, our map of Nooksack Dace critical habitat (Figure 4, page 13 of Exhibit "D"), and a table listing activities likely to result in destruction of critical habitat (page 14) were removed, and the description of critical habitat altered to remove references to its length and the specific definition. For example, the sentence "The combined length of proposed critical habitat in the three watersheds where it has been surveyed is 21.3 km (of 36.4 km of surveyed stream channel)" was removed.

Mr. Murray was asked to approve Ms. Webb's direction. It appears that a legal opinion from the Department of Justice regarding the interpretation of s. 41(1)(c) of *SARA* played a role in the development of the recommendation [...] Mr. Murray concurred to the recommendation on July 18, 2007. As a result of Mr. Murray's concurrence, the Final Recovery Strategy contains the following statement with respect to the critical habitat of the Nooksack Dace:

Critical Habitat

Identification of Critical Habitat

The Recovery Team has developed biologically-based recommendations for defining critical habitat for Nooksack dace. These recommendations have been prepared as a separate document (Pearson 2007), which is available to the public upon request to the Recovery Team. The proposed critical habitat document will be submitted for external scientific peer review through the Pacific Science Advisory Review Committee. After the peer review process, a final version will form the biological recommendations for designating critical habitat. To conform with current policy on species at risk and recovery strategy content, the following discussion on critical habitat presents general habitat features that should be considered when defining and designating critical habitat, but does not make specific geospatial recommendations.

Critical habitat is defined in SARA as "the habitat that is necessary for the survival or recovery of a listed wildlife species and that is identified as the species' critical habitat in the recovery strategy or in an action plan for the species." [SARA s. 2(1)]. Attributes of critical habitat for Nooksack dace have been defined but not mapped or designated in this recovery strategy. A quantity of proposed critical habitat sufficient to ensure the survival and recovery of Nooksack dace will be designated through the action planning process, which will include socioeconomic analysis and consultation with affected interests. The Recovery Team has compiled scientific data that will provide the basis for an official designation of critical habitat (Pearson 2007). Further studies are required to confirm the presence of other Nooksack dace populations and their critical habitats, and to characterize specific threats. Designating critical habitat will contribute to the refinement of recovery objectives and the management of activities that impact the species.

The Applicants' Position on the Interpretation of s. 41(1)(c) and (c.1) of SARA

In support of the present Application, Counsel for the Applicants supplied a detailed argument that the statement of the critical habitat of the Nooksack Dace in the Final Recovery strategy resulting from Mr. Murray's decision is contrary to law. The basic features of this argument are as follows:

1. It is mandatory that each of the requirements listed in s. 41(1)(a) to (g) be met, including those specified in s. 41(1)(c) and (c.1);

2. Sections 41(1)(c) and (c.1) impose conjunctive duties;

3. The mandatory requirement in s. 41(1)(c) to identify a species' critical habitat is met by determining and stating its features and providing a geospatial delineation of its location in a Final Recovery Strategy because only after critical habitat is so identified can an important object of *SARA* be met; providing legal protection for a species at risk;

4. The mandatory requirement in s. 41(1)(c) to identify a species' critical habitat "to the extent possible" means identifying as much critical habitat as possible, and in as much detail as possible, even if it is not possible to identify all critical habitat areas or features;

5. The mandatory requirement in s. 41(1)(c) to identify a species' critical habitat to the extent possible "based on the best available information" means that the identification of a species critical habitat to the extent possible must be based on the information in existence not the best possible information that can be acquired in the future.

The Correct Interpretation of s. 41(1)(c) and (c.1)

Points of Agreement

The Standard of Review Is Correctness

In the present Application the Applicants question the Minister's authority to alter the terms of *SARA* by government policy. As authority is a question of law, it is agreed that the Minister's decision must be considered on the standard of correctness (*Dunsmuir v. New Brunswick*, 2008 SCC 9, [2008] 1 S.C.R. 190).

Interpretation of SARA Requires a Textual, Contextual, and Purposive Analysis

The correct interpretation of *SARA* must be found in the approach to modern statutory interpretation.

Section 38 Is a Codification of the Precautionary Principle

Canada has ratified the *United Nations Convention on the Conservation of Biological Diversity* (the *Convention*) and, therefore, is committed to apply its principles. An important feature of the *Convention* is the "precautionary principle" which is stated by the Supreme Court of Canada as follows:

> In order to achieve sustainable development, policies must be based on the precautionary principle. Environmental measures must anticipate, prevent and attack the causes of environmental degradation. Where there are threats of serious or irreversible damage, lack of full scientific certainty should not be used as a reason for postponing measures to prevent environmental degradation.

> (*114957 Canada Ltée (Spraytech, Société d'arrosage) v. Hudson (Town)*, 2001 SCC 40, [2001] 2 S.C.R. 241 at para. 31)

It is agreed that s. 38 of *SARA* is a codification of the precautionary principle which, as stated in the Preamble, in part, meets Canada's commitments under the *Convention*:

> Commitments to be considered

> 38. In preparing a recovery strategy, action plan or management plan, the competent minister must consider the commitment of the Government of Canada to conserving biological diversity and to the principle that, if there are threats of serious or irreversible damage to the listed wildlife species, cost-effective measures to prevent the reduction or loss of the species should not be postponed for a lack of full scientific certainty.

Therefore, s. 38 is a mandatory interpretative principle that applies during the preparation of recovery strategies. However, in this respect, Counsel for the Minister emphasizes two factors: the codification in s. 38 introduces the factor of "cost effective" measures to Canada's commitment and, as stated in the Preamble, community knowledge and interests, including "socio-economic interests", should be considered in "developing and implementing recovery measures". It is important to clarify the precise role that each of these factors plays in the recovery strategy process composed of, first, preparing a recovery strategy, and, second, acting on it.

The use of "cost effective measures" is understandable in a situation of scarce economic resources, but, nevertheless, the words in the provision are precise and unequivocal: the measures required to "prevent the reduction or loss of the species" must still be taken and "should not be postponed for a lack of full scientific certainty".

The words in the Preamble are also precise and unequivocal; the "development and implementation of recovery measures" is an action taken with respect to a final recovery strategy. Once a final recovery strategy is prepared, an action plan involving recovery measures is required to be developed and implemented; s. 49(1)(e) of *SARA* makes it clear that it is only at this stage of the process that "socio-economic costs" are considered.

For clarification with respect to their position on the application of the *Convention*, the Applicants make the following argument:

> The *Convention* is a binding treaty, and SARA was enacted in part to implement Canada's treaty commitments. Furthermore, the *Convention* is part of the "entire context" to be considered in interpreting the SARA. Therefore, not only must the SARA be construed to conform to the values and principles of the *Convention*, but

the Court must avoid any interpretation that could put Canada in breach of its *Convention* obligations.

As the Minister does not disagree with this argument, I find it is correct in law.

The Provisions of s. 41 of SARA

It is agreed that the provisions of s. 41 of *SARA* are mandatory. Most recently, Justice Zinn has made this point very clear in *Alberta Wilderness Association Assn. v. Canada (Minister of Environment)*, 2009 FC 710, [2009] F.C.J. No. 876 at paragraph 25:

> There is no discretion vested in the Minister in identifying critical habitat under the SARA. Subsection 41(1)(c) requires that the Minister identify in a recovery strategy document as much critical habitat as it is possible to identify at that time, even if all of it cannot be identified, and to do so based on the best information then available. I note that this requirement reflects the precautionary principle that "where there are threats of serious or irreversible damage, lack of full scientific certainty should not be used as a reason for postponing measures to prevent environmental degradation," as it was put by the Supreme Court of Canada, citing the *Bergen Ministerial Declaration on Sustainable Development* in *114957 Canada Ltée (Spraytech, Société d'arrosage) v. Hudson (Town)*, 2001 SCC 40 **are mandatory** [Emphasis added]

Therefore, as argued by the Applicants, I find that Ms. Webb's direction and Mr. Murray's approval of her direction are actions contrary to law. The result of these actions is that the Minister failed to meet the mandatory requirements of s. 41(1)(c) in the Final Recovery Strategy. The totality of this conduct is fundamentally inconsistent with the precautionary principle as codified in *SARA*.

With respect to the requirement on the Minister to identify critical habitat to the extent possible based on the best available information at the recovery strategy stage without political or socioeconomic considerations in play, as argued by the Applicants, I find that the following statement made in the Final Recovery Strategy as quoted above is an error in law:

> Attributes of critical habitat for Nooksack dace have been defined but not mapped or designated in this recovery strategy. A quantity of proposed critical habitat sufficient to ensure the survival and recovery of Nooksack dace will be designated through the action planning process, which will include socioeconomic analysis and consultation with affected interests.

Sections 41(1)(c) and (c.1) Impose Conjunctive Duties Based on the Best Available Information

It is agreed that with respect to a competent Minister making the determinations required under s. 41(1)(c), the phrase "best available information" comprises relevant scientific, community, and Aboriginal traditional knowledge, and requires a competent Minister to gather, review, and evaluate the available information during the preparation of a recovery strategy and not to disregard, ignore, or remove reliable information about a species' critical habitat. It is agreed that where the available information so evaluated is determined by the competent Minister to be inadequate, the recovery strategy must include a schedule of studies.

It is also agreed that the determinations made by a competent Minister under s. 41(1)(c) and (c.1) are subject to judicial review on the standard of reasonableness. This principle is confirmed by Justice Zinn's decision in *Alberta Wilderness Assn.*, above.

The Primary Point of Disagreement: The Definition of "habitat" and "critical habitat"

In the final result, after the full conduct of the decision-making and challenge that is the focus of the present Application, this is the primary question in dispute: what are the constituents that must be included in the identification of a species' critical habitat? The answer to the question lies in the correct interpretation of the definition of "habitat" because "critical habitat" is a sub-set of the definition of "habitat". The definitions found in s. 2 of *SARA* are worth repeating: [...]

The Applicants maintain that the constituents of the habitat, and accordingly the critical habitat, of a specific species are an identifiable location and the attributes of that location that meet the criteria of the statutory definition of both terms. When the present Application was commenced, there was no apparent dispute about location and attributes as the constituents. The Final Recovery Strategy for the Nooksack Dace makes it clear that, in the identification of critical habitat, location and attributes are inextricably linked. The bone of contention that fuelled the present Application was the Minister's removal of the location constituent from the Final Recovery Strategy.

It is important to note that in the preparation of the Draft Recovery Strategy the approach of citing both location and attributes was consistent with Canadian government policy statements and, indeed, the policy statements were followed in the Final Recovery Strategy but for the removal of location for the stated reason that a peer review of Dr. Pearson's findings was necessary [...]

[Ed. Note: The Court then sets out and considers the Minister's position that the identification of critical habitat is synonymous with a geographic place or location, and the applicants' response to this argument. This portion of the decision is omitted.]

Conclusion

I find the Minister's textual, contextual, and purposive argument to be weak. [...] I agree that the definition of "habitat" places a focus on a certain location but it is implicit that the location is only identifiable because special features exist at that location upon which the species depends to carry out its life processes. Therefore, in the definition of "habitat", a location is inextricably linked to its special identifiable features and includes its special identifiable features.

[...] the Minister's textual argument does not meaningfully address what I find to be the compelling logic of interpreting "habitat" to include its essential attributes; the argument is completely unresponsive to this important issue. As described by Dr. Pearson, for the Nooksack Dace, habitat is all about the "riffles". Thus, as a practical matter, the identification of the habitat of the

Nooksack Dace must include the identification of the riffles feature of its critical habitat; doing so is, in my opinion, also a legal matter.

[...] the Applicants effectively argue that little weight should be given to the Minister's textual interpretation on the meaning of "habitat" and "critical habitat" because it is contrary to the published expectations of the government of Canada with respect to the development of recovery strategies. Counsel for the Minister's response is essentially that the *Technical Guidelines* are irrelevant because the interpretation of *SARA* is required to be conducted according to the statute. In my opinion this submission neglects the critical point that a contextual and purposive analysis requires a broad approach.

As a result, I find that the Applicants are correct in their interpretation of the definition of "habitat" and "critical habitat".

The Meaning of "to the extent possible"

Any dispute about the meaning of this phrase is resolved by Justice Zinn in *Alberta Wilderness Assn.*, above, [...] he accepted an agreement between Counsel for the Minister of the Environment and the Applicants that "[s]ubsection 41(1)(c) requires that the Minister identify in a recovery strategy document as much critical habitat as it is possible to identify at that time, even if all of it cannot be identified, and to do so based on the best information then available". There is no question that this ruling applies to the Minister in the present case.

Conclusion

For the reasons provided, I find that, whether by agreement or by contest, the Applicants are wholly successful in the present Application.

Notes and Questions

1. The decision of Campbell J. in *Nooksack Dace* goes considerably farther than the decision in *Greater Sage-Grouse*. Identify the following: (1) the extent to which Campbell J. follows and applies Zinn J.'s decision in *Greater Sage-Grouse*; and (2) the extent to which Campbell J. takes the law further.

2. The applicant argues, "not only must the SARA be construed to conform to the values and principles of the *Convention*, but the Court must avoid any interpretation that could put Canada in breach of its *Convention* obligations". According to Campbell J., counsel for the federal Crown did not dispute this legal argument; accordingly, he takes the applicant's argument on this point to be legally valid. Consider and discuss the implications of this approach to interpreting treaty-based obligations in light of the principles elaborated in Chapter 1. Is this an example of a contextual interpretation of legislation, or is it based on the conformity principle? In light of the status of the ratification and implementation of the *Convention* through SARA, do you agree with Campbell J. that SARA has to be interpreted so as to avoid Canada breaching its *Convention* obligations?

3. The next decision is the only one considered in this section that was appealed to and decided by the Federal Court of Appeal. Both the trial and the appellate decisions in this case are worthy of close review. Ultimately, in a decision that builds on both the *Greater Sage-Grouse* and *Nooksack Dace* decisions, the Court of Appeal upholds the decision of Russell J. in the case below. Russell J.'s decision at first instance is a stinging rebuke to the Department of Fisheries and Oceans: *Georgia Strait Alliance v. Canada (Minister of Fisheries & Oceans)*, 2010 FC 1233, additional reasons (2011), 59 C.E.L.R. (3d) 103 (F.C.), reversed in part 2012 FCA 40. Indeed, after rendering the decision, he awarded costs to the applicants on a solicitor-and-client basis, describing the conduct of the Department as "unjustifiably evasive and obstructive" and concluding that its actions "unreasonably lengthened and complicated proceedings".

Georgia Strait Alliance v.
Canada (Minister of Fisheries & Oceans)
2012 FCA 40

MAINVILLE J.A.: — The Minister of Fisheries and Oceans ("Minister") is appealing a judgment of the Federal Court cited as 2010 FC 1233 ("Reasons") in which Russell J. ("Federal Court judge") declared that ministerial discretion does not "legally protect" critical habitat under section 58 of the *Species at Risk Act*, S.C. 2002, c. 29 ("SARA") and which further declared that it was unlawful for the Minister to have cited discretionary provisions of the *Fisheries Act*, R.S.C. 1985, c. F-14 in a protection statement concerning the critical habitat of the Northeast Pacific Northern and Southern populations of killer whales.

Subsection 58(5) of the SARA provides that the Minister must make an order under subsections 58(1) and (4) protecting the critical habitat of listed endangered or threatened aquatic species if such critical habitat "is not legally protected by provisions in, or measures under, this or any other Act of Parliament". The Minister had determined that the *Fisheries Act* legally protected some aspects of the critical habitat of killer whales and could thus be resorted to as a substitute to a protection order under the SARA.

The Federal Court judge ruled that the Minister may avoid issuing a critical habitat protection order under the SARA only where the legal protection offered that habitat under another Act of Parliament is the same as that provided under a protection order. He further ruled that the measures available to the Minister under the *Fisheries Act* could be diluted under the sweeping and largely unfettered discretions granted to the Minister under that statute. Consequently, he concluded that the *Fisheries Act* could not be resorted to as a substitute to a critical habitat protection order under the SARA.

Overview of Conclusions

The Minister is appealing to this Court on two main grounds.

The first ground of appeal concerns the standard of review. [**Ed. Note:** Discussion of this aspect of the case is omitted.]

The second ground of appeal concerns the interpretation of the SARA. The Minister does not dispute that the protection of critical habitat under the SARA is compulsory. However, the Minister submits that Parliament intended that there should be some flexibility as to the modalities of that compulsory protection. The Minister states that he does not wish to retain discretion under the *Fisheries Act* to undermine that protection or to provide protection which is inferior to that afforded under a SARA protection order. Rather, the Minister submits that certain measures under the *Fisheries Act* do protect critical habitat against destruction, and that he should therefore be able to resort to such measures as alternatives to a SARA protection order even though they might be subject to his discretion.

I do not accept the Minister's interpretation of the SARA on this point. When Parliament adopted section 58 of the SARA, its intent was to provide for compulsory and non-discretionary legal protection from destruction for the identified critical habitat of listed endangered or threatened aquatic species. This protection can be achieved through a provision or measure under an Act of Parliament which legally protects from destruction that habitat and which is not subject to dilution through discretionary ministerial action. In the absence of such a legally enforceable provision or measure, the Minister must make a protection order under subsections 58(1) and (4) of the SARA to ensure the protection of that habitat.

While the Minister submits that, by retaining his discretion under the *Fisheries Act*, he does not intend to undermine the protection provided under the SARA or to provide protection that is inferior to that available under a SARA protection order, he fails to explain how his discretion under the *Fisheries Act* would be legally fettered. Parliament adopted section 58 of the SARA precisely to avoid the destruction of the identified critical habitat of listed endangered and threatened aquatic species though any means. If the Minister's position were accepted, the compulsory and non-discretionary protection scheme set out by Parliament under the SARA would be transformed into a protection scheme largely subject to ministerial discretion. Such was not Parliament's intent in adopting the SARA.

However — and contrary to the conclusions of the Federal Court judge in this case — there may be circumstances in which the Minister may rely on section 36 of the *Fisheries Act* (which I take to include regulations made under that section) in a protection statement made under paragraph 58(5)(*b*) of the SARA. Section 36 of the *Fisheries Act* prohibits the deposit of deleterious substances in water frequented by fish, unless such deposit is authorized under regulations adopted by the Governor in Council. In a given case, the combined operation of section 36 of the *Fisheries Act* and of its regulations may afford a particular endangered or threatened species the legal protection mandated by section 58 of the SARA. In such a case, it may be appropriate for the Minister to rely on those provisions for the purposes of paragraph 58(5)(*b*) of the SARA.

However, in this case, the record contains no evidence as to the effect, if any, of section 36 and its regulations on the killer whale critical habitat at issue. Therefore, there was no basis in these proceedings upon which the Federal Court judge could have determined whether the Minister's reliance on section 36 could have been justified in light of the provisions of section 58 of the SARA.

Overview of the Provisions of the Species at Risk Act Relevant to This Appeal

The SARA was assented to in 2002 as the first comprehensive federal legislation seeking (a) to prevent wildlife species from being extirpated or becoming extinct and (b) to provide for the recovery of wildlife species that are extirpated, endangered or threatened as a result of human activity. That legislation was adopted partly to meet Canada's obligations under the United Nations Convention on the Conservation of Biological Diversity. [...]

The listing of an aquatic species in Schedule 1 of the SARA as endangered or threatened also requires the Minister to prepare a recovery strategy for that species within specified timelines: subsections 37(1) and 42(2) of the SARA. Such a recovery strategy must be prepared in cooperation with various stakeholders: section 39. If the Minister determines that the recovery of the endangered or threatened aquatic species is feasible, the recovery strategy must address the threats to the survival of the species identified by the COSEWIC, including any loss of habitat, and must include, *inter alia*, an identification of the species' critical habitat to the extent possible, based on the best available information, including information provided by COSEWIC, and examples of activities that are likely to result in its destruction: paragraph 41(1)(c).

The proposed recovery strategy is then subject to public consultations. The Minister must consider any comments received, and make the changes he considers appropriate. Finally, the Minister must finalize the recovery strategy by including a copy in the public registry established for the purposes of the SARA: section 43. The Minister must also publicly report every five years on the implementation of the recovery strategy and the progress towards meeting its objectives: section 46.

The Minister must prepare one or more action plans based on the recovery strategy, and such plans must include, *inter alia*: an identification of the aquatic species critical habitat and examples of activities which are likely to result in its destruction; a statement of measures which are proposed to be taken to protect the species critical habitat; an identification of any portions of the species critical habitat that have not been protected; and a statement of the measures that are to be taken to implement the recovery strategy: section 47 and paragraphs 49(1) (a)(b)(c) and (d).

A final recovery strategy for a listed endangered or threatened aquatic species has important legal consequences under the SARA since the entire critical habitat identified in the recovery strategy must be protected: section 57 and subsections 58(1) to (5) of the SARA. This protection is achieved either,

   (a) through provisions in or measures under the SARA or any other Act of Parliament; in such case, the Minister must identify how the critical habitat is legally protected in a protection statement made pursuant to paragraph 58(5)(b); or

   (b) through a protection order made by the Minister under subsections 58(1) and (4) in respect of the critical habitat or portion of the critical habitat specified in the order.

Background to These Proceedings

Killer whales are the largest members of the dolphin family. They are long-lived animals with no natural predators. They are found in all three of Canada's oceans, as well as occasionally in Hudson Bay and the Gulf of St. Lawrence. In British Columbia, they have been recorded in almost all salt-water areas. Three distinct forms of killer whale inhabit Canadian Pacific waters: transient, offshore and resident. These forms are sympatric but socially isolated and differ in their dietary preferences, genetics, morphology and behaviour.

Resident killer whales are the best understood. Their social organization is highly structured and their fundamental unit is matrilineal, comprising all surviving members of a female lineage. A typical matrilineal unit comprises an adult female, her offspring, and the offspring of her daughters. Both sexes remain within their natal matrilineal unit.

There are two communities of resident killer whales in British Columbia: the northern resident population and the southern resident population. These resident killer whale populations are considered at risk because of their small population size, low reproductive rate, and the existence of a variety of man-made threats that have the potential to prevent recovery or to cause further declines. Principal among these threats are environmental contamination, reductions in the availability and quantity of prey, and both physical and acoustic disturbance. In 2003, the southern resident killer whale population counted 85 members, while the northern resident population counted 205 members.

In 2001, COSEWIC designated the southern population as endangered, and the northern population as threatened. These populations were listed accordingly in Schedule 1 of the SARA when that statute was adopted by Parliament. Consequently, under subsections 37(1) and 42(2) of the SARA, the Minister was required to prepare a recovery strategy for these killer whale populations within specified timelines. For this purpose, a Resident Killer Whale Recovery Team (the "Recovery Team") comprising independent and government experts was convened in 2004.

Following extensive study and review, a final draft recovery strategy was completed in May of 2006 for submission to the Minister. The manner in which critical habitat was described in this draft led to disputes between the Recovery Team and officials from the Department of Fisheries and Oceans. These disputes delayed the posting and approval of the recovery strategy, which was only included in the public registry established under the SARA in March of 2008.

Pursuant to subsection 58(5) of the SARA, the inclusion of the recovery strategy in the public registry required the Minister to ensure that the critical habitat identified in that strategy be protected within 180 days. That protection could be achieved either through a protection order made by the Minister under subsections 58(1) and (4) or through a statement by the Minister setting out how the critical habitat or portions of it, as the case may be, would be legally protected under an Act of Parliament. The Minister did not make a protection order under the SARA. Rather, he included in the public registry a statement setting out how the critical habitat of the concerned killer whale populations was legally protected (the "Killer Whales Protection Statement").

The Killer Whales Protection Statement restricted the concept of critical habitat for the purposes of the SARA to geophysical attributes. Consequently, the Killer Whales Protection Statement identified three types of human activity which could potentially destroy the geophysical attributes of the critical habitat of the concerned killer whale populations in the identified areas. It further identified various legislative provisions, including section 35 of the *Fisheries Act* and subsection 22(1) of the *Fishery (General) Regulations*, SOR/93-53 which were deemed to ensure the protection of these geophysical attributes. The pertinent paragraphs of the Killer Whales Protection Statement read as follows:

> Human activity which could potentially destroy the geophysical attributes of critical habitat for these species, as identified in the Final Recovery Strategy, and the federal legislations, regulations and/or policies which would be used to provide protection against such destruction are:
>
> — Industrial activities such as construction, drilling, pile driving, pipe-laying, and dredging, and construction of physical structures such as wharves and net pens for aquaculture
>> — Protected under provisions of the *Fisheries Act* s. 35 and the *Canadian Environmental Protection Act* (Part VII, Division 3). This protection is supported by processes under the *Canadian Environmental Assessment Act*.
>
> — Fishing vessels using gear that drags along the bottom
>> — Protected through provisions of the *Fisheries Act* or regulations made thereunder, in particular s. 22(1) of the *Fishery (General) Regulations*. This protection is supported by processes under the Fisheries and Oceans Canada policy on Managing the Impacts of Fishing on Sensitive Benthic Areas.
>
> — Use of vessel anchors which may permanently damage the seabed, or which may serve to destroy a rubbing beach
>> — Protected through provisions of the *Fisheries Act* s. 35, or of the *Oceans Act* s. 35 and/or s. 36. In addition, a Code of Conduct and outreach initiatives to inform and sensitise Canadians to the need to protect Resident Killer Whale habitat will continue to be developed and implemented.

The difficulty in defining critical habitat in terms of geophysical attributes was that some of the most important elements of the critical habitat which had been identified in the recovery strategy were left without protection. The recovery strategy had indeed identified acoustic degradation, chemical and biological contamination and diminished prey availability as key components of the critical habitat of killer whales. Yet the Killer Whales Protection Statement did not consider these components as part of "critical habitat" for the purposes of protection under the SARA. Rather, the Killer Whales Protection Statement treated these components as "ecosystem features" to be dealt with through "legislative and policy tools", and not under the SARA. The Killer Whales Protection Statement thus treated these components as follows:

> While the Recovery Strategy identifies the critical habitat as a defined geophysical area, Fisheries and Oceans Canada (DFO) recognizes that other ecosystem features such as the availability of prey for foraging and the quality of the environment are important to the survival and recovery of Northern and Southern Resident Killer

Whales. A variety of legislative and policy tools are available to manage and mitigate threats to these functions of the Resident Killer Whale critical habitat, to individuals and to populations.

— Disturbance
  — Threat management and mitigation is afforded under the *Marine Mammal Regulations* and the Whale Watching Guidelines developed cooperatively by industry and DFO.
— Degradation of the Acoustic Environment
  — Threat management and mitigation is afforded under the *Marine Mammal Regulations*, the Statement of Practice with Respect to the Mitigation of Seismic Sound in the Marine Environment, and protocols for military sonar use.
— Marine Environmental Quality
  — Threat management and mitigation is afforded under provisions of the *Fisheries Act*, or regulations made thereunder, and the *Canadian Environmental Protection Act* or regulations made thereunder.
— Availability of Prey
  — Threat management and mitigation is afforded under the *Fisheries Act* or regulations made thereunder, supported by the Wild Salmon Policy and use of Integrated Fisheries Management Plans.

History of the Litigation

The respondents in this appeal challenged the lawfulness of the Killer Whales Protection Statement by initiating a judicial review application before the Federal Court in October of 2008, wherein they asked that Court to make various declarations, set aside the Killer Whales Protection Statement, and a refer the matter back to the Minister for a new decision under section 58 of the SARA.

In their application, the respondents argued that the critical habitat of the concerned killer whale populations included not only the geophysical elements of that habitat, but also all the other components identified in the recovery strategy. They further argued that, in a protection statement, the Minister could not resort to non-binding policy, prospective legislation or on ministerial discretion.

Before this judicial review application could be heard, the Minister reversed himself. Both he and the Minister of the Environment jointly issued a protection order under subsections 58(1) and (4) of the SARA, which order was registered on February 19, 2009 as the *Critical Habitats of the Northeast Pacific Northern and Southern Resident Populations of Killer Whale (Orcinus orca) Order*, SOR/2009-68 (the "Killer Whales Protection Order"). Maps identifying the critical habitat areas contemplated by that order are attached in a schedule to these reasons. These are the same critical habitat areas as identified in the recovery strategy.

The Reasons and Judgment of the Federal Court

The Federal Court judge hearing both applications on their merits granted most of the declarations sought and provided detailed reasons in support thereof.

Turning his attention to the standard of review, the Federal Court judge found that since the issues raised were essentially questions of statutory interpretation, the correctness standard applied.

As to the scope of "critical habitat" under the SARA, the Federal Court judge concluded that the issue had been conclusively decided by Campbell J. of the Federal Court in *Environmental Defence Canada v. Canada (Fisheries and Oceans)*, 2009 FC 878, 349 F.T.R. 225 ("*Environmental Defence*").

The issue in *Environmental Defence* mainly concerned the scope of the expression "critical habitat" for the purposes of inclusion in a recovery strategy under paragraphs 41(1)(c) and (c.1) of the SARA. The applicants in *Environmental Defence* submitted that the constituents of habitat — and by implication of critical habitat — for specified species "are an identifiable location and the attributes of that location": *Environmental Defence* at para. 46. Campbell J. agreed, and ruled that for the purposes of the SARA, the word "areas" in the definition of "habitat" set out in the SARA did not just connote a location, "but a location that includes its special identifiable features": *Environmental Defence* at para. 58. The order of Campbell J. in *Environmental Defence* was not appealed from by the Minister, who now accepts that both the location and the components of critical habitat are contemplated by the SARA.

Since, in this case, the recovery strategy identified reduced availability of prey, environmental contaminants and physical and acoustic disturbance as components of the critical habitat of the concerned killer whale populations, the Federal Court judge found that the Killer Whales Protection Order had to apply to all these components: Reasons at paras. 163-164 and 337 to 339. Moreover, in light of *Environmental Defence*, the Minister had in fact conceded this point before the Federal Court judge: Reasons at paras. 159 and 163. By necessary implication, the Killer Whales Protection Statement was also flawed since it did not include these elements as critical habitat: Reasons at paras. 337 to 339.

The Federal Court judge then went on to reject the Minister's contention that the declarations sought in regard to the Killer Whales Protection Order were beyond the jurisdiction of the Federal Court. The Minister had indeed submitted that the Killer Whales Protection Order was not a "decision" subject to judicial review; he argued that the order was rather a "regulation" within the meaning of the *Statutory Instruments Act*, R.S.C., 1985, c. S-22, and that it was thus immune from judicial review. The Federal Court judge was not persuaded, ruling instead that Parliament had not shielded decisions under subsection 58(5) of the SARA from judicial review through the use of a privative clause or otherwise. In his view, the SARA was clearly a justiciable statute that imposed duties on the Minister, and whose actions under that statute were subject to review before the Federal Court: Reasons at paras 183-184.

The Federal Court judge also decided to hear the application concerning the Killer Whales Protection Statement even if the Killer Whales Protection Order had made that application moot. Applying the factors established in *Borowski v. Canada (Attorney General)*, [1989] 1 S.C.R. 342, the Federal Court judge concluded that, in view of the fundamental points of law raised by the proceedings, a quite live controversy between the parties did remain: Reasons at paras. 242 to 245. He also concluded that these points were of general importance for the interpretation and application of the SARA: Reasons at paras. 250-251.

The Federal Court judge then ruled that a competent minister may not resort to another federal statute as a substitute for a protection order unless that statute provides an equal level of legal protection for critical habitat as would be engaged through a protection order: Reasons at paras. 257 and 272. The Federal Court judge made that ruling on the basis of a purposive reading of the pertinent provisions of the SARA; he concluded that Parliament had sought to limit ministerial discretion where the protection of critical habitat of endangered and threatened species was at issue: Reasons at paras. 277 to 280.

The Federal Court judge then went on to conclude that the *Fisheries Act*, and the regulations adopted under that statute, could not be used as a substitute for a protection order. His conclusion was based on the highly discretionary nature of the broad powers afforded to the Minister under the scheme of the *Fisheries Act*, including a broad discretion to authorize the destruction of fish habitat under subsection 35(2) and to attach conditions to a fishing licence under section 22 of the *Fishery (General) Regulations*: Reasons paras. 320-321.

The Federal Court judge also discarded section 36 of the *Fisheries Act* — which prohibits the deposit of a deleterious substance into waters frequented by fish — on the basis that such deposits may nevertheless be authorized through regulations adopted "at the Cabinet's discretion": Reasons at para. 325.

The Issues in This Appeal

[...]

Did the Minister err by relying on the provisions of the Fisheries Act and of its regulations in making the Killer Whales Protection Statement?

The Minister concedes that the protection of the critical habitat of endangered and threatened aquatic species under the SARA is not discretionary. However, the Minister submits that Parliament intended that he be allowed some flexibility as to how to provide that compulsory protection. The Minister further submits that such flexibility would not exist if the conclusions of the Federal Court judge are upheld by this Court. The Minister adds that not every instrument relied on in a protection statement need be a "legal provision" which provides mandatory, enforceable protection against the destruction of critical habitat. This alternative approach would give him a large degree of flexibility in determining how that protection should be best provided. This, the Minister submits, is what Parliament intended. Had Parliament intended only a legal prohibition from destruction to protect critical habitat — as it has done for residences and the killing, harming or harassing of individuals — it would not have provided the alternative of a protection statement. Consequently, protection measures relied upon in a protection statement need not be prohibitions from destruction.

The difficulty I have with the Minister's position is that it is not compatible with the provisions of the SARA, which clearly require compulsory "legal protection" for all identified critical habitat of listed endangered or threatened aquatic species. If I were to accept the Minister's position, the compulsory non-discretionary critical habitat **protection** scheme under the SARA would be effectively replaced by the discretionary **management** scheme of the *Fisheries Act*. That is not what the SARA provides for.

Interpretation of the Pertinent Provisions of the SARA

The preamble of the SARA recognizes that "the habitat of species at risk is key to their conservation". In this respect, section 57 of the SARA — which is an interpretative provision — provides that all critical habitat identified in a recovery strategy must be protected within 180 days after the recovery plan is included in the public registry:

> 57. *The purpose of section 58 is to ensure that,* within 180 days after the recovery strategy or action plan that identified the critical habitat referred to in subsection 58(1) is included in the public registry, *all of the critical habitat is protected* by
>
> (*a*) provisions in, or measures under, this or any other Act of Parliament, including agreements under section 11; or
>
> (*b*) the application of subsection 58(1)
>
> [emphasis added]

Section 58 of the SARA adds that this protection must be achieved through legally enforceable measures. The pertinent provisions of section 58 read as follows:

> 58. (1) Subject to this section, no person shall destroy any part of the critical habitat of any listed endangered species or of any listed threatened species — or of any listed extirpated species if a recovery strategy has recommended the reintroduction of the species into the wild in Canada — if [...]
>
> (*b*) the listed species is an aquatic species; [...]
>
> (4) [...] subsection (1) applies in respect of the critical habitat or portion of the critical habitat, as the case may be, specified in an order made by the competent minister.
>
> (5) Within 180 days after the recovery strategy or action plan that identified the critical habitat is included in the public registry, the competent minister must, [...] with respect to all of the critical habitat or any portion of the critical habitat [...]
>
> (*a*) make the order referred to in subsection (4) if the critical habitat or any portion of the critical habitat is not legally protected by provisions in, or measures under, this or any other Act of Parliament, including agreements under section 11; or
>
> (*b*) if the competent minister does not make the order, he or she must include in the public registry a statement setting out how the critical habitat or portions of it, as the case may be, are legally protected.

[...] A legal protection scheme is not a regulatory management scheme. Had Parliament's intent been to authorize the Minister to regulate critical habitat of aquatic species through existing regulatory schemes — such as the *Fisheries Act* — it would not have adopted a provision requiring the compulsory non-discretionary legal protection of that habitat. This textual analysis is reinforced by a contextual and purposive analysis.

Section 57 of the SARA provides in no uncertain language that the purpose of section 58 is to ensure that all the critical habitat is protected by provisions in, or measures under, an Act of Parliament or by a protection order issued under subsections 58(1) and (4) of the SARA. Surely this is an indication that there must be some equivalence between the two contemplated means of protection. They need not be the same, but surely they must have the same objective. Pursuant to subsection 58(1), the objective of a protection order is to ensure that "no person [...] destroy any part of the critical habitat of any listed endangered species or of any listed threatened species [...] if the listed species is an aquatic species". Provisions in, or measures under, an Act of Parliament should thus — in principle — achieve the same objective if they are to be resorted to as a substitute to a protection order.

In conclusion, a textual, contextual and purposive analysis of section 58 of the SARA shows that Parliament is precisely seeking to avoid the destruction of identified critical habitat of listed endangered and threatened aquatic species though any means, including through activities authorized under discretionary permits or licences. Consequently, a provision in, or a measure under, an Act of Parliament only legally protects critical habitat for the purposes of section 58 if that provision or measure prevents the destruction of critical habitat through legally enforceable means which are not subject to ministerial discretion.

Section 35 of the Fisheries Act

I will now turn to the *Fisheries Act* to ascertain if the provisions of that statute may be relied upon by the Minister for the purposes of section 58 of the SARA.

Subsection 35(1) of the *Fisheries Act* prohibits any work or undertaking that results in the harmful alteration, disruption or destruction of fish habitat. However, subsection 35(2) allows the Minister to authorize the alteration, disruption or destruction of fish habitat under any conditions he deems appropriate. The prohibitions set out in subsection 35(1), when read in conjunction with subsection 35(2), thus constitute a legal means whereby the Minister is enabled to manage and control the alteration, disruption or destruction of fish habitat. In other words, subsection 35(2) allows the Minister to issue a permit to a person to engage in conduct harmful to fish habitat that would otherwise contravene subsection 35(1).

[**Ed. Note:** See discussion and analysis of subsection 35(1) and section 36 of the *Fisheries Act* in Chapter 4.]

In the Minister's submission, it "is irrelevant" that subsection 35(2) allows for the alteration, disruption or destruction of fish habitat, since "the mere possibility of a future authorization cannot negate the fact that s. 35(1) provides habitat protection". He adds that "[a]lthough the Minister's discretion under the *Fisheries Act* is generally very broad, where the Minister has relied on the protections provided by the *Fisheries Act* to meet the requirements of the SARA, that reliance will guide the exercise of discretion to ensure that critical habitat remains protected".

The Minister reads subsection 35(1) in isolation from subsection 35(2). However, both subsections are closely related and interdependent; they must be read and understood together. There is no dispute that the protection offered fish habitat under subsection 35(1) may be waived at the discretion of the Minister acting under subsection 35(2). Consequently, this provision cannot ensure that the critical habitat of endangered or threatened aquatic species is "legally protected" under the meaning of section 58 of the SARA.

The Minister — through his counsel — states that he intends not to use his discretion under subsection 35(2) of the *Fisheries Act* to authorize the destruction of critical habitat. However, he does not explain how his intent can be legally enforced should he change his mind in the future for some presumably good reason; nor does he explain how his current intent would bind his successors. Intent not to use discretion is not legally enforceable. A mere intent does not ensure that critical habitat is "legally protected" under the meaning of section 58 of the SARA.

Section 36 of the Fisheries Act

Section 36 of the *Fisheries Act* is meant to prevent the pollution of water frequented by fish — which includes marine animals — by prohibiting any person from depositing deleterious substances of any type in such water or in any place under any conditions where the deleterious substances may enter such water. However, subsection 36(4) of the *Fisheries Act* allows for the deposit of wastes, pollutants and deleterious substances in such waters or places in a quantity or concentration and under the conditions authorized by regulation made by the Governor in Council under any Act of Parliament or under subsection 36(5) of the *Fisheries Act* [...]

The principal regulations made under subsection 36(5) of the *Fisheries Act* are the *Metal Mining Effluent Regulations*, SOR/2002-222, and the *Pulp and Paper Effluent Regulations*, SOR/92-269.

The *Metal Mining Effluent Regulations* allow the deposit of mining effluent that contain deleterious substances into waters frequented by fish insofar as (a) the concentration of the deleterious substance in the effluent does not exceed the authorized limits set out in the regulations; (b) the pH of the effluent is equal to or greater than 6.0 but is not greater than 9.5; and (c) the deleterious substance is not an acutely lethal effluent. The authorization is subject to numerous conditions set out in the regulations and which concern in particular environmental effects monitoring, effluent monitoring, and reporting. The *Pulp and Paper Effluent Regulations* allow, for the purpose of paragraph 36(4)(*b*) of the *Fisheries Act*, the deposit in any water or place — up to certain prescribed maxima — of any matter that consumes oxygen dissolved in water and of suspended solids [...]

The Federal Court judge ruled that section 36 of the *Fisheries Act* could not be relied on by the Minister for the purposes of a protection statement under section 58 of the SARA. He based this ruling on his conclusion that though this section "prohibits the deposit of a deleterious substance into water frequented by fish [it] allows for the authorization of such deposits through regulation at Cabinet's discretion"; Reasons at para. 325. I am unable to agree with that ruling.

Compliance with subsection 36(3) of the *Fisheries Act* may not be waived by the Minister through a licence, permit or other authorization, nor may the Minister authorize derogations from the *Metal Mining Effluent Regulations* or the *Pulp and Paper Effluent Regulations*. Measures under this section and these regulations are legally enforceable and are not subject to ministerial discretion.

This section and the regulations made under it thus provide for compulsory, non-discretionary and legally enforceable measures.

Like most other regulatory provisions, regulations made under section 36 of the *Fisheries Act* may be adopted or amended from time to time. The fact a statutory provision or a regulatory provision may be eventually modified does not entail that it may not be relied upon by the Minister for the purposes of subsection 58(5) of the SARA. Where it otherwise, the Minister could rely on no statutory or regulatory provision. This is not what subsection 58(5) of the SARA provides. There is a fundamental difference between a non-discretionary and legally enforceable regulation and a discretionary ministerial licencing scheme.

In a given case, the combined operation of section 36 of the *Fisheries Act* and of the regulations made under that section may afford protection from destruction for critical habitat. Indeed, the limits set out in the *Metal Mining Effluent Regulations* and the *Pulp and Paper Effluent Regulations* are legally enforceable and may, in appropriate circumstances, be viewed as protecting critical habitat. Where this is the case, section 36 and its regulations may afford a particular endangered or threatened species the legal protection mandated by section 58 of the SARA. In such appropriate cases, these provisions may be relied upon as ensuring that critical habitat is "legally protected" under section 58 of the SARA. Consequently, in appropriate circumstances, section 36 of the *Fisheries Act* and its regulations may be relied upon in a protection statement made under paragraph 58(5)(*b*) of the SARA.

However, in this case, there is no evidence in the record before this Court showing whether the pollution controls set out in these regulations protect from destruction the critical habitat of the concerned killer whale populations. Therefore, there was no basis in these proceedings upon which the Federal Court judge could have determined whether the Minister's reliance on section 36 of the *Fisheries Act* could have been justified in light of the provisions of section 58 of the SARA.

Consequently, to the extent that the Federal Court judge's declaration impedes the Minister from relying, in appropriate cases, on section 36 of the *Fisheries Act* and its regulations for the purposes of a protection statement made under paragraph 58(1)(*b*) of the SARA, it cannot stand. However, in light of the evidentiary record before us and the nature of these proceedings, we need not decide if the Minister's reliance on this provision met the requirements of section 58 of the SARA in this case.

Conclusions

For the reasons set out above, declaration 1(d) found in the judgment of the Federal Court judge should be upheld save insofar as, for the purposes of section 58 of the SARA, it impedes the Minister from relying, in appropriate cases, on section 36 of the *Fisheries Act* and the regulations adopted under that section. I would therefore allow this appeal to that extent only, and consequently quash in part declaration 1(d) of the Federal Court's judgment.

Notes and Questions

1. Consider how and to what extent the *Southern Resident Orcas* decision builds on the *Greater Sage-Grouse* and *Nooksack Dace* decisions. Would the FCA have decided this case in the same way had these other decisions not been made?

2. What meaning and significance does the FCA give to the concepts of "discretion" and "enforceability" in this judgment?

Part IV — Harm Prohibitions, Safety Net & Emergency Orders, and Permitting & Assessment Requirements

---

Introduction

SARA contains a variety of provisions that are intended to ensure that listed species and designated habitat receive legal protection. The statute contemplates that threats to species or their habitat can come from both governmental action and inaction, as well as from various private sector activities. Accordingly, SARA contains a variety of protection mechanisms that are intended to respond both proactively and reactively to situations where species or their habitat are or may be harmed.

These protective measures fall into four categories:

- Prohibitions on harming species or their habitat (sections 32-33);
- Safety net orders (subsection 34(2) and section 61);
- Emergency protection orders (section 80); and
- Administrative requirements binding decision-makers before issuing permits that could harm species or their habitat (sections 73-79).

In understanding the availability of these options, it is first important to consider whether the species is a "federal" one, and whether the habitat or residence of that species is on "federal lands". Federal species are generally considered to be aquatic species or migratory birds as defined in the *Migratory Birds Convention Act, 1994*, S.C. 1994, c. 22. Under SARA, "federal lands" include federal Crown land and the internal waters and territorial sea of Canada, as well as lands "reserved for Indians" under that federal head of power.

All so-called "federal" species listed under SARA receive automatic protection against "takings": they cannot be killed, harmed or traded (section 32), nor can their "residences" be damaged or destroyed (section 33). It is worth noting, parenthetically, that SARA uses the concept of "residence" as opposed to "critical habitat", the former being a much more limited (and politically palatable) aspect of the latter.

Non-federal species and their "residences" are likewise protected on federal lands under sections 32 and 33. However non-federal species on non-federal lands ordinarily do not enjoy SARA protection under these sections: see subsection 34(1). A non-federal species can gain SARA protection from section 32 takings that would be otherwise illegal under sections 32 and 33 if it is the beneficiary of a so-called "safety net order" under subsection 34(2). The Governor in Council may make an order extending the protections of sections 32 and 33 upon Ministerial recommendation. The Minister must make such a recommendation if she believes that the laws of the province do not effectively protect the species or the residences of its individuals. The relevant provisions of SARA are set out below:

> 32. (1) No person shall kill, harm, harass, capture or take an *individual* of a wildlife species that is listed as an extirpated species, an endangered species or a threatened species.

> 33. No person shall damage or destroy the *residence* of one or more individuals of a wildlife species that is listed as an endangered species or a threatened species, or that is listed as an extirpated species if a recovery strategy has recommended the reintroduction of the species into the wild in Canada.

> 34. (1) With respect to individuals of a listed wildlife species that is not an aquatic species or a species of birds that are migratory birds protected by the *Migratory Birds Convention Act, 1994*, sections 32 and 33 do not apply in lands in a province that are not federal lands unless an order is made under subsection (2) to provide that they apply.

> (2) The Governor in Council may, on the recommendation of the Minister, by order, provide that sections 32 and 33, or either of them, apply in lands in a province that are not federal lands with respect to individuals of a listed wildlife species that is not an aquatic species or a species of birds that are migratory birds protected by the *Migratory Birds Convention Act, 1994*.

> (3) The Minister must recommend that the order be made if the Minister is of the opinion that the laws of the province do not effectively protect the species or the residences of its individuals.

There is also a secondary safety net order power that is available to protect the critical habitat of non-federal species on non-federal lands: see section 61. As with the subsection 34(2) order power, the subsection 61(2) order power is vested in the Governor in Council. It may only act on recommendation of the Minister. In turn, the Minister is only obliged to make such a recommendation if she believes that the laws of the province do not provide effective protection, in this context, for the species' "critical habitat". The relevant provisions state:

> 61. (1) No person shall destroy any part of the critical habitat of a listed endangered species or a listed threatened species that is in a province or territory and that is not part of federal lands.

> (2) Subsection (1) applies only to the portions of the critical habitat that the Governor in Council may, on the recommendation of the Minister, by order, specify.

> (4) The Minister must make a recommendation if he or she is of the opinion, after consultation with the appropriate provincial or territorial minister, that

> (a)   there are no provisions in, or other measures under, this or any other Act of Parliament that protect the particular portion of the critical habitat, including agreements under section 11; and
>
> (b)   the laws of the province or territory do not effectively protect the critical habitat.

A third means of protecting species and their habitat is by way of an emergency order. Emergency orders can be made in relation to both federal and non-federal species, and can apply on federal and non-federal lands. As with safety net orders, power to make the order rests with the Governor in Council. It may only act on the recommendation of the Minister. The Minister has discretion whether to make such an order; however, she must make such a recommendation if she is of the opinion that the species faces imminent threats to its survival or recovery. The key provisions are as follows:

> 80. (1) The Governor in Council may, on the recommendation of the competent minister, make an emergency order to provide for the protection of a listed wildlife species.
>
> (2) The competent minister must make the recommendation if he or she is of the opinion that the species faces imminent threats to its survival or recovery.

Finally, SARA also contains provisions to protect species and habitat that are more proactive in nature. While safety net and emergency orders are designed to respond to situations where a species is at serious risk, often due to governments failing to take timely steps to protect it or its habitat, sections 73-79 are intended to operate in a more prophylactic manner. The provisions require that competent ministers (defined in SARA as the Minister of Environment, the Minister of Fisheries and Oceans, and the Minister responsible for Parks), and to a lesser extent other federal ministers, to exercise special scrutiny before approving activities which could affect a listed species, its residence or its critical habitat. Section 73 deals with permits issued by competent ministers, and section 77 deals with permits, licences and authorizations under other federal legislation. Interestingly, one federal agency — the National Energy Board (NEB) — is specifically exempted from these SARA requirements in the exercise of its duties under the *National Energy Board Act*, R.S.C. 1985, c. N-7 (though not when it is carrying out duties under other statutes including CEAA 2012): see subsection 77(1.1) SARA.

The relevant SARA provisions are as follows:

> 73. (1) The competent minister may enter into an agreement with a person, or issue a permit to a person, authorizing the person to engage in an activity affecting a listed wildlife species, any part of its critical habitat or the residences of its individuals.
>
> (3) The agreement may be entered into, or the permit issued, only if the competent minister is of the opinion that
>
> (a)   all reasonable alternatives to the activity that would reduce the impact on the species have been considered and the best solution has been adopted;

(b)   all feasible measures will be taken to minimize the impact of the activity on the species or its critical habitat or the residences of its individuals; and

(c)   the activity will not jeopardize the survival or recovery of the species.

77. (1) Despite any other Act of Parliament, any person or body, other than a competent minister, authorized under any Act of Parliament, other than this Act, to issue or approve a licence, a permit or any other authorization that authorizes an activity that may result in the destruction of any part of the critical habitat of a listed wildlife species may enter into, issue, approve or make the authorization only if the person or body has consulted with the competent minister, has considered the impact on the species' critical habitat and is of the opinion that

(a)   all reasonable alternatives to the activity that would reduce the impact on the species' critical habitat have been considered and the best solution has been adopted; and

(b)   all feasible measures will be taken to minimize the impact of the activity on the species' critical habitat.

(1.1) Subsection (1) does not apply to the National Energy Board when it issues a certificate under an order made under subsection 54(1) of the *National Energy Board Act.*

Clustered in this part of the SARA are also some important requirements arising in the context of projects that are undergoing federal environmental assessments. Any person or federal authority that is required to carry out such as assessment or make a determination under CEAA 2012 is required to notify the competent minister or ministers without delay if a project is likely to affect a listed species or its critical habitat: subsection 79(1). Such a person must also identify the adverse effects of the project on the listed species and its critical habitat, and ensure that measures, consistent with any recovery strategies or action plans, are taken to mitigate and monitor those effects.

79. (1) Every person who is required by or under an Act of Parliament to ensure that an assessment of the environmental effects of a project is conducted, and every authority who makes a determination under paragraph 67(a) or (b) of the *Canadian Environmental Assessment Act, 2012* in relation to a project, must, without delay, notify the competent minister or ministers in writing of the project if it is likely to affect a listed wildlife species or its critical habitat.

(2) The person must identify the adverse effects of the project on the listed wildlife species and its critical habitat and, if the project is carried out, must ensure that measures are taken to avoid or lessen those effects and to monitor them. The measures must be taken in a way that is consistent with any applicable recovery strategy and action plans.

In the balance of this Part, we consider in more detail the case law and policy surrounding the taking prohibitions and safety net order provisions (sections 32, 33 and 61), the emergency order power (section 81) and the administrative permitting and assessment-related requirements (sections 73-79).

Harm Prohibitions and Safety Net Order Provisions: Sections 32, 33 and 61

Prior to the expiry of the six-month time limit prescribed by subsection 58(5), the federal government must issue either a "protection statement" or a "protection order" confirming that the critical habitat identified in the relevant strategy or plan is indeed protected. As will be recalled, in *Georgia Strait Alliance v. Canada (Minister of Fisheries & Oceans)*, 2012 FCA 40, this was the situation in which the Minister of Fisheries and Oceans found himself when the Recovery Strategy for Southern Resident Orcas was released. In response, at first he issued a protection statement; he then later replaced the statement with a protection order. In the end, however, the courts determined neither the Minister's Protection Statement nor his Protection Order complied with the requirements of section 58.

Ordinarily, as noted below, section 58 protection only applies to areas within federal jurisdiction. Its application can, however, be extended to areas within provincial or territorial jurisdiction but only where the Governor in Council, at its discretion, upon the recommendation of the Minister of the Environment, makes an order to that effect. This is known as a "safety net" order: see section 61.

The Minister of the Environment *must* make the recommendation if the Minister is of the opinion, after consultation with the appropriate provincial or territorial minister, that:

- There are no provisions in or measures under SARA, including conservation agreements under section 11, that protect the particular critical habitat;
- There are no provisions in or measures under other federal legislation that protect the particular critical habitat; and
- The *laws of the province or territory do not effectively protect the critical habitat*. (emphasis added)

It is unclear at this stage how the federal government will assess whether the laws of a province or territory do provide effective protection for critical habitat. To date there is no jurisprudence interpreting the "safety net" provisions either under subsection 34(3) or subsection 61(2).

An order made under subsection 61(2) lasts for five years, unless the Governor in Council, by order, renews it (subsection 61(5)). If the Minister of the Environment is of the opinion that an order made under subsection 61(2) is no longer necessary to protect the critical habitat to which the order relates or that the province or territory has brought laws into force which protect that critical habitat, the Minister *must* recommend that the order be repealed.

To date, there has been no definitive judicial interpretation of the meaning of the "take" prohibition in subsection 32(1) of SARA. The provision reads as follows:

> 32. (1) No person shall kill, harm, harass, capture or take an individual of a wildlife species that is listed as an extirpated species, an endangered species or a threatened species.

The first-ever conviction in Canada under this provision occurred in 2012, in a case arising in the waters off the northeast coast of Vancouver Island. The case involves the harassment of a pod of orcas by a recreational boater. The defendant was fined $7,500 (to be paid to the Environment Canada's Environmental Damages Fund) and ordered to write a newspaper article acknowledging his wrongdoing.

The following excerpt analyzes these provisions in more detail, describing their political and legislative history.

Kate Smallwood,
A Guide to Canada's Species at Risk Act
(Vancouver: Sierra Legal Defence Fund, 2003)

Most species listed at risk under SARA will not be protected by the basic prohibitions unless they are found at national parks, federal agricultural lands, Indian reserves, military bases, airports, post offices, coast guard stations or other federal land [unless the federal government invokes its "safety net" order power discussed *infra*].

Section 32 prohibits two broad categories of activity — harm to a listed species, and possession or trade in a listed species or parts of a listed species:

> (1) No person shall kill, harm, harass, capture or take an individual of a wildlife species that is listed as an extirpated species, an endangered species or a threatened species.

> (2) No person shall possess, collect, buy, sell or trade an individual of a wildlife species that is listed as an extirpated species, an endangered species or a threatened species, or any part or derivative of such an individual.

Section 33 prohibits damage or destruction of a species' "residence". The prohibition applies to listed endangered and threatened species, and listed extirpated species provided a recovery strategy has recommended the reintroduction of the species into the wild in Canada. The term "residence" is not a biological or scientific concept. It is an artificial tool to minimize the automatic consequences of listing a species under SARA by restricting legal protection to a minimal portion of the species' critical habitat.

As originally drafted in Bill C-5, "residence" was defined to mean:

> [...] a dwelling-place, such as a den, nest or other similar area, place or structure, that is occupied or habitually occupied by one or more individuals during all or part of their life cycles, including breeding, rearing or hibernating.

Various stakeholders [...] objected to this definition because it was too narrow, rendering it biologically inapplicable to many species. By restricting the definition to "den, nest or other similar area", many species such as caribou that do not have a den or nest or "similar" area, would not be eligible for protection.

In response to these concerns, the House Standing Committee on Environment and Sustainable Development expanded the definition to include areas used for feeding, staging and wintering, but failed to delete the word "similar". The amended definition was then somewhat contradictory — areas used for wintering and feeding, for example, are not "similar" to a den, nest or other dwelling area.

Aside from one minor amendment, the government retained the Committee's definition. The definition — which remains somewhat contradictory, although it is clear that broader areas are meant to be covered — now reads:

> a dwelling place, such as a den, nest or other similar area or place, that is occupied or habitually occupied by one or more individuals during all or part of their life cycles, including breeding, rearing, staging, wintering, feeding or hibernating

Section 58 is the primary section under SARA for protection of critical habitat. "Critical habitat" as defined in the Act means:

> habitat that is necessary for the survival or recovery of a listed wildlife species and that is identified as the species' critical habitat in the recovery strategy or action plan for the species.

Unlike the basic prohibitions therefore, protection of critical habitat does not apply automatically upon listing a species, but is delayed until the recovery process.

Section 58 contains an outright prohibition against the destruction of any part of the critical habitat of a listed endangered, threatened or extirpated species, if a recovery strategy has recommended the reintroduction of the species into the wild in Canada. Protection under the section is limited to species within areas of federal jurisdiction i.e. federal lands, federal waters (exclusive economic zone of Canada and continental shelf of Canada), aquatic species and migratory birds under the *Migratory Birds Convention Act*.

The stated purpose of section 58 [as set out in section 57] is to ensure that within six months after critical habitat has been identified in a recovery strategy or action plan that has been filed in the public registry, that critical habitat is protected by:

- provisions in or measures under SARA, including conservation agreements under section 11;
- provisions in or measures under other federal legislation; or
- the critical habitat prohibition under section 58(1) of SARA (i.e. critical habitat within federal jurisdiction).

In contrast, in the United States, a significant body of law has developed that interprets the ambit of the protection against "takings" under the federal *Endangered Species Act* (ESA). For the most part, courts have interpreted the analogous ESA provision (section 9) in a broad, purposive fashion. The decision of the US Supreme Court excerpted below, which arose in connection the long-standing controversy over protection of spotted owl habitat in the US Pacific Northwest, is illustrative of the dominant judicial approach to this issue.

Babbitt v. Sweet Home Chapter of Communities for a Great Oregon
515 U.S. 687 (1995)

STEVENS J.: — Section 9 of the Act makes it unlawful for any person to "take" any endangered or threatened species. The Secretary has promulgated a regulation that defines the statute's prohibition on takings to include "significant habitat modification or degradation where it actually kills or injures wildlife". This case presents the question whether the Secretary exceeded his authority under the Act by promulgating that regulation.

Section 3(19) of the Act defines the statutory term "take": "The term 'take' means to harass, harm, pursue, hunt, shoot, wound, kill, trap, capture, or collect, or to attempt to engage in any such conduct".

The Act does not further define the terms it uses to define "take". The Interior Department regulations that implement the statute, however, define the statutory term "harm":

> Harm in the definition of "take" in the Act means an act which actually kills or injures wildlife. Such act may include significant habitat modification or degradation where it actually kills or injures wildlife by significantly impairing essential behavioral patterns, including breeding, feeding, or sheltering.

Respondents in this action are small landowners, logging companies, and families dependent on the forest products industries in the Pacific Northwest and in the Southeast, and organizations that represent their interests [...] Respondents [argued] [...] that Congress did not intend the word "take" in s. 9 to include habitat modification, as the Secretary's "harm" regulation provides.

The text of the Act provides three reasons for concluding that the Secretary's interpretation is reasonable. First, an ordinary understanding of the word "harm" supports it. The dictionary definition of the verb form of "harm" is "to cause hurt or damage to: injure". In the context of the ESA, that definition naturally encompasses habitat modification that results in actual injury or death to members of an endangered or threatened species.

Second, the broad purpose of the ESA supports the Secretary's decision to extend protection against activities that cause the precise harms Congress enacted the statute to avoid [...] As stated in s. 2 of the Act, among its central purposes is "to provide a means whereby the ecosystems upon which endangered species and threatened species depend may be conserved" [...]

Third, the fact that Congress in 1982 authorized the Secretary to issue permits for takings that s. 9 would otherwise prohibit, "if such taking is incidental to, and not the purpose of, the carrying out of an otherwise lawful activity" strongly suggests that Congress understood s. 9 to prohibit indirect as well as deliberate takings [...] This reference to the foreseeability of incidental takings undermines respondents' argument that [the 1982 amendment] covered only accidental killings of endangered and threatened animals that might occur in the course of hunting or trapping other animals. Indeed, Congress had habitat modification directly in mind [...]

Notes and Questions

1. Canadian courts are often reluctant to give much weight to precedents arising from the domestic interpretation of legislation in foreign jurisdictions. It is rare, for example, for decisions interpreting SARA, CEAA or CEPA to cite judgments that interpret analogous federal US laws. With this caveat, to what extent is the *Babbitt* decision useful or instructive in terms of interpreting the meaning of subsection 32(1) of SARA? Could an argument be made in Canada that the term "take" in subsection 32(1) prohibits not only harm to the species itself but also other actions (such as habitat degradation or destruction) that indirectly can cause harm to the species?

2. In section 9 of ESA, the prohibition is against the "take" of listed species. The term "take" is defined elsewhere in the ESA as including a long list of activities: see subsection 3(19). The SARA takes a somewhat different approach. Subsection 32(1) of SARA also employs the term "take" but as part of a list of prohibited actions. As a matter of statutory interpretation, leaving aside other jurisdictional and jurisprudential differences between Canada and the United States, does this distinction in drafting suggest a distinction in meaning?

Emergency Orders: Section 80

A new area of SARA litigation is developing in relation to the federal power to order that a species be given emergency protection where it faces "imminent threats to its survival or recovery" under subsection 80(2) of SARA. In 2018, prompted by the federal government's approval of the Trans Mountain pipeline extension project and the likely impacts it would have on the declining Southern Resident Orca population, conservation groups filed a lawsuit seeking to compel the Minister of Environment and Climate Change to recommend to her Cabinet colleagues that they issue an emergency order under SARA. While this emergency order case was still pending before the courts, in the summer of 2018, the Southern Resident Orca population enjoyed another SARA legal victory arising in relation to this same project, which we consider shortly when we look at section 79 of SARA.

Emergency order applications are rare. To date, emergency orders have been made in relation to the Greater Sage-Grouse in southern Alberta and Saskatchewan and the Western Chorus Frog in Quebec: see Nicolas Rehberg-Besler & Cameron S.G. Jefferies, "The Case for a Southern Resident Killer Whale Emergency Protection Order under Canada's *Species at Risk Act*" (2019) 32(2) J. Envtl. L. & Prac. 137. An emergency protection order was also unsuccessfully sought for Boreal caribou in *Adam v. Canada (Minister of the Environment)*, excerpted below. *Adam* remains an important decision on the interpretation of the scope and meaning of subsection 80(2) of SARA and nicely illustrates how this order power fits within the SARA architecture. We then consider the Federal Court's 2015 decision in the *Western Chorus Frog* case, the first instance in which a court has ordered that a Minister reconsider her decision not to recommend a species for emergency protection.

Adam v. Canada (Minister of the Environment)
2011 FC 962

CRAMPTON J.: — The Applicants are First Nation bands, members of those bands and environmental organizations who have been attempting to persuade the Minister of the Environment to: (i) finalize a recovery strategy for boreal caribou located in Northeastern Alberta; and (ii) recommend, pursuant to subsection 80(2) of the *Species at Risk Act*, SC 2002, c 29 (SARA), that the Governor in Council make an emergency Order providing for the protection of those caribou.

Having been unsuccessful to date in those attempts, they filed applications with this Court seeking, among other things:

1. An Order declaring that the Minister has failed to prepare a recovery strategy for the caribou within the time period mandated by subsection 42(2) of SARA;

2. an Order in the nature of *mandamus* compelling the Minister to comply with his duties under subsection 80(2) of SARA, as described above; and

3. in addition or in the alternative to the foregoing, an Order declaring that the Minister's failure to recommend that the Governor in Council make an emergency Order to provide for the protection of the boreal caribou in north eastern Alberta is unlawful or unreasonable.

Subsequent to filing their applications, the Minister explicitly declined to make a recommendation under subsection 80(2), when he accepted a recommendation of the Deputy Minister, Environment Canada, that he conclude that "there are no imminent threats to the national survival or recovery of boreal caribou in Canada," as contemplated by that provision.

It is common ground between the parties that even if the Minister had made a recommendation to the Governor in Council pursuant to subsection 80(2), the Governor in Council may have declined to issue the requested emergency Order, after weighing and balancing relevant public-interest considerations.

For the reasons set forth below, I have decided to:

(i) set aside the Minister's decision and remit the matter back to him for reconsideration in accordance with these reasons;

(ii) defer, until September 1, 2011, ruling on the Applicants' request for the above-described declaratory relief; and

(iii) reject the Applicants' request for an Order in the nature of *mandamus*.

Background

There are two main groups of Applicants in these proceedings. The first group, (collectively, the First Nations), consists of three individuals representing themselves, the other members of their respective First Nations bands, and the bands themselves, namely: Athabasca Chipewyan First Nation, Beaver Lake Cree

Nation, and Enoch Cree Nation. All three of these First Nations have traditionally hunted boreal caribou. The other group of Applicants consists of the Alberta Wilderness Association and the Pembina Institute for Appropriate Development (the ENGOs), which are not-for-profit environmental associations that have a genuine interest in the survival and recovery of the boreal caribou.

On July 15, 2010, the First Nations wrote to the Minister of the Environment requesting that he recommend, within 45 days, that the Governor in Council make an emergency Order under section 80 of the SARA for the protection of the seven herds (the Seven Herds) of boreal caribou that roam in north eastern Alberta.

On August 17, 2010, the ENGOs wrote to the Minister in support of the First Nations, and essentially repeated their request that he recommend that an emergency Order be made to protect the Seven Herds.

After failing to receive a response from the Minister, the First Nations and the ENGOs filed their respective applications for relief from this Court, on September 8, 2010. The applications were consolidated by Prothonotary Tabib on October 21, 2010.

The Relevant Legislation

[...] To supplement the various provisions in SARA regarding the protection and recovery of species, subsections 80(1) and (2) provide for the issuance of emergency protective Orders as follows:

Emergency order

80. (1) The Governor in Council may, on the recommendation of the competent minister, make an emergency order to provide for the protection of a listed wildlife species.

Obligation to make recommendation

(2) The competent minister must make the recommendation if he or she is of the opinion that the species faces imminent threats to its survival or recovery.

[...]

The Decision under Review

After summarizing the procedural history in this matter, the recommendation that was endorsed by the Minister (the Decision) addressed the current status of the boreal caribou. Among other things, this part of the Decision noted the following: Boreal caribou is one of six different populations that make up the population of "woodland caribou." There are approximately 39,000 boreal caribou in Canada, distributed across 57 herds that live in the boreal forest region of seven provinces and two territories. In order to thrive, those caribou need large areas of suitable habitat, low levels of human disturbance, and low numbers of predators. In 2002, COSEWIC assessed the general population of boreal caribou in Canada to be threatened, within the meaning of the SARA. The basis for that assessment was that sub-populations had decreased throughout most of the boreal caribou's range, the distribution of boreal caribou had contracted, and boreal caribou was threatened by habitat loss and increased predation. In 2008, a scientific review conducted by Environment Canada (the 2008 Scientific Review) concluded that 30 of 57 herds, also known as local populations, across Canada are not currently self-sustaining, meaning that they are not stable or growing and are not sufficiently large enough to withstand random events and human-caused pressures. Of those 30 herds, 21 were considered to be the subject of high levels of disturbance, indicating that their habitat conditions need to be improved to restore the herds to self-sustaining levels and reduce their risk of extirpation. Those 21 herds include all 13 herds in Alberta, which face an elevated risk of extirpation. With respect to the Seven Herds in particular, their numbers are "insufficient for these populations to be self-sustaining."

The Decision then addressed the emergency powers in section 80 of SARA. In this regard, it noted that the 2009 draft *Species At Risk Policies* issued by Environment Canada (the Draft Policies) "describe factors that the Minister will consider in forming his opinion" under subsection 80(2) as to whether "a species faces imminent threats to its survival or recovery." The Decision stated that these factors [...] include whether:

i.   a serious, sudden decline in the species' population and/or habitat that jeopardizes the survival or recovery of the species is in progress and is anticipated to continue unless immediate protective actions are taken;

ii. there is a strong indication of impending danger or harm to the species or its habitat, with inadequate or no mitigation measures in place to address the threat, such that the survival or recovery of the species is at risk; or

iii. one or more gaps have been identified in the existing suite of protection measures for the species that will jeopardize its survival or recovery, and it is not possible to achieve protection by other means in a timely fashion.

Based on the premise that the current range and conditions are sufficient for 27 of the 57 herds of boreal caribou in Canada, the Decision stated that "there are no imminent threats to the survival of boreal caribou" and thus a section 80 order is not warranted at this time to protect the survival of boreal caribou. [...]

It was then observed that the provinces and territories are responsible for managing terrestrial species on provincial and territorial land, and that Alberta and other jurisdictions have developed their own recovery plans for their caribou that include population and distribution objectives. [...]

With respect to the Seven Herds in particular, it was noted that the existing gap in national boreal caribou distribution will widen. It was acknowledged that this would: (i) have potential negative consequences, due to disruption of genetic and demographic processes that would further increase the risk to the recovery of boreal caribou in Canada; and (ii) represent a range retraction for boreal caribou in Canada. It was also observed that the extirpation of the Seven Herds would impact the boreal caribou populations in the Northwest Territories, British Colombia and especially Saskatchewan. Moreover, it was recognized that the ability of those jurisdictions to recover their portion of the shared populations of boreal caribou would be constrained by Alberta's approach to recovery.

Notwithstanding all of the foregoing, it was then concluded that the boreal caribou population in Manitoba and eastern Canada, which appear to be healthy, widespread and with ample gene flow among them, could allow Canada to maintain a self-sustaining population of boreal caribou.

In this regard, the Board noted that Alberta's local populations comprise only 6% of the total number of boreal caribou in Canada, and that the Seven Herds only represent 3% of the national boreal caribou population. The Board added that while the extirpation of the Seven Herds would result in further range retraction in the middle of the range of boreal caribou and would constrain national recovery objectives: (i) it is possible to maintain a self-sustaining population of boreal caribou in eastern Canada; and (ii) the eastern Canadian local populations could provide the basis for achieving a national recovery objective.

Issues

The [...] issues that have been raised by the Applicants can be grouped as follows:

  i.   Did the Minister err in interpreting subsection 80(2)?
  ii. Should an Order of *mandamus* be granted compelling the Minister to make a recommendation under subsection 80(2)?
  iii. Did the Minister err in failing or refusing to recommend an emergency Order under subsection 80(2), by failing to consider relevant factors?
  iv. Should the Court declare that the Minister has contravened subsection 42(2) by failing to post a proposed Recovery Strategy for woodland caribou in the public registry?

Standard of Review

The interpretation of a decision-maker's enabling (or home) statute, or "statutes closely connected to its function, with which it will have particular familiarity" (Closely Related Statute), is usually accorded deference and subjected to review on a reasonableness standard: see *Dunsmuir v. New Brunswick*, 2008 SCC 9 at paragraph 54, [2008] 1 SCR 190 (*Dunsmuir*); *Celgene Corp v. Canada (Attorney General)*, 2011 SCC 1 at paragraph 34, [2011] 1 SCR 3; *Smith v. Alliance Pipeline Ltd*, 2011 SCC 7 at paragraph 26, [2011] 1 SCR 160 (*Smith*). However, where there are constitutional considerations at play, no such deference is warranted, at least insofar as those considerations are concerned (*Dunsmuir*, above, at paragraph 58; *Smith*, above, at paragraph 37). [...]

The First Nations Applicants have raised serious issues with respect to the impact of the Minister's interpretation of subsection 80(2) on their treaty rights and the honour of the Crown. Accordingly, in my view, the standard of review applicable to the Minister's interpretation of subsection 80(2) is correctness, at least insofar as his interpretation implicates those issues. As discussed at paragraph 40 below, there are good reasons why the "usual" approach of applying a reasonableness standard of review to the Minister's interpretation of his statutory mandate should apply to other aspects of his interpretation of the language in subsection 80(2).

The issue of whether the Minister erred in failing or refusing to recommend an emergency order under subsection 80(2), by failing to consider relevant factors, is an issue of mixed fact and law that is reviewable on a standard of reasonableness (*Dunsmuir*, above, at paragraphs 51-55).

With respect to the Minister's alleged contravention of subsection 42(2) of the SARA, the Respondents conceded in their submissions that the Minister did not prepare a Recovery Strategy for the boreal caribou within the time limit provided for in SARA. Accordingly, it is not necessary to address the standard of review applicable to this issue.

Analysis

Did the Minister err in interpreting subsection 80(2)?

In the course of reviewing the Applicants' submissions, the Decision noted that the First Nations Applicants had submitted that "the Minister erred in law or acted unreasonably, or both, by failing to consider certain factors adequately or at all, including the Applicants' Treaty Rights and the honour of the Crown."

In the latter regard, the Decision stated, among other things, that:

> [f]actors such as the potential impact of the decline of the boreal caribou on the applicants' Treaty Rights and the Crown's obligation to act honourably in all of its dealings with Aboriginal peoples are not relevant in considering whether or not the species' survival or recovery is imminently threatened under section 80.

The Respondents did not contest that the members of the Applicant Athabasca Chipewan First Nation band are beneficiaries of Treaty No. 8 and that the members of the Applicants Beaver Lake Cree Nation and Enoch Cree Nation are beneficiaries of Treaty No. 6. [...] They also did not contest the evidence that:

i. Treaties No. 8 and No. 6 protect the First Nations Applicants' right to pursue their "avocations" or "usual vocations" of hunting and fishing, subject to certain limitations;

ii. the Report of the Commissioners who negotiated Treaty No. 8 on behalf of the Government of Canada confirmed that hunting and fishing rights were of particular concern to the First Nations and that the Commissioners "assured them that the treaty would not lead to any forced interference with their mode of life" (*R v. Horseman*, [1990] 1 SCR 901 at paragraphs 12 and 63 (available on CanLII));

iii. the First Nations Applicants have traditionally hunted boreal caribou as an integral part of their traditional way of life and have a spiritual connection and relationship with the caribou;

iv. the First Nations Applicants have traditionally relied on caribou meat as a critical source of food, and also rely on caribou for a broad range of other purposes; and

v. the First Nations Applicants have voluntarily stopped hunting boreal caribou, in an attempt to address the current threat to the caribou's survival and recovery.

[...] Considering all of the foregoing, and keeping in mind that "[i]nterpretations of treaties and statutory provisions which have an impact upon treaty or aboriginal rights must be approached in a manner which maintains the integrity of the Crown" (*Badger*, above), the Minister clearly erred in reaching his decision by failing to take into account the First Nations Applicants' Treaty Rights and the honour of the Crown in interpreting his mandate under subsection 80(2). The Decision therefore warrants being set aside on that basis alone (*Little Salmon*, above). Additional support for this conclusion arguably is provided by the established principles that: (i) "any ambiguities or doubtful expressions in the wording of the treaty or document must be resolved in favour of the Indians"; and (ii) "any limitations which restrict the rights of Indians under treaties must be narrowly construed" [...]

In reconsidering his decision, the Minister should not confine his consideration of the honour of the Crown to an assessment of whether any active course of conduct may negatively affect treaty rights of the First Nations. I agree with the Applicants that such an approach would present an impoverished view of the honour of the Crown. A broader view is required to be taken. This includes assessing the extent to which the ongoing violation of the SARA (by failing to post a Recovery Strategy) and continued inaction with respect to the boreal caribou would, in all of the circumstances discussed in this decision and in the more detailed Certified Record pertaining to the Decision, would be consistent with the honour of the Crown (*R v. Marshall*, [1999] 3 SCR 456 at paragraphs 49-52 (available on CanLII); *West Moberly First Nations v. British Columbia (Ministry of Energy, Mines and Petroleum Resources)*, 2010 BCSC 359, [2010] BCJ No 488 (QL), at paragraphs 51-55, 59 and 63).

The foregoing should not be interpreted as suggesting that a proper consideration of the First Nations Applicants' Treaty Rights and the honour of the Crown would necessarily have led the Minister to reach a particular opinion in exercising his mandate under subsection 80(2) (see, for example, *Badger*, above, at paragraph 58). Rather, my conclusion is simply that the Minister erred in deciding that these matters were not relevant to his interpretation of subsection 80(2).

With respect to the specific language in subsection 80(2), the Applicants requested the Court to endorse the following propositions:

i.   Subsection 80(2) imposes a mandatory duty;

ii. subsection 80(2) is triggered by threats to recovery or survival, or both;

iii. a key purpose of section 80 is to protect habitat while awaiting a recovery strategy;

iv. subsection 80(2) requires an objective inquiry based on the best available scientific information;

v.   inaction is not permitted due to a lack of full scientific certainty;

vi. section 80 orders can be made for only part of the range of the species;

vii. imminent threats need not be guaranteed to materialize;

viii. the impact of threats must be considered over a biologically appropriate timescale; and

ix. timely decision-making is required.

Generally speaking, these propositions are supported either by the plain meaning of the language in the statute, including the preamble thereto, or the legislative history of the SARA (see, for example, *House of Commons Debates*,

37th Parl, 1st Sess, No 149 (26 February 2002) at 1150 (Hon Karen Redman); Standing Committee on Environment and Sustainable Development, *Minutes/ Evidence*, March 22, 2001, at 09:35-09:40). That said, in my view, the following is equally clear:

i.   The mandatory duty contemplated in subsection 80(2) is only triggered when the Minister reaches the "opinion" referred to in that provision.

ii.   The language in subsection 80(1) is sufficiently broad to permit the Governor in Council to make an emergency order on recommendation of the competent minister in situations other than those contemplated by subsection 80(2), however, the competent minister would not have any statutory duty to make a recommendation in such other situations.

iii.   In reaching an opinion under subsection 80(2), the Minister is not confined to considering the best available scientific information — for example, the Minister may also consider legal advice with respect to the meaning of the language in subsection 80(2).

iv.   Keeping in mind the "emergency" nature of the power contemplated in section 80, it may nevertheless be legitimate for the Minister to take a short period of time, following a request such as was made by the Applicants to: (a) obtain information necessary to make an informed opinion under subsection 80(2); or (b) obtain receipt of scientific or other information that is in the process of being prepared.

v.   The fact that an Order may be made (under subsection 80(4)(c)) for only part of the range of a listed species, and the fact that the term "wildlife species" is defined in subsection 2(1) to include a "subspecies, variety or geographically or genetically distinct population," do not imply that an Order must always be made whenever the listed species faces threats to its survival or recovery in only a part of its habitat. The Minister's decision will properly depend on the nature of the scientific information, legal advice and other information that he receives and that is relevant to the determination to be made under subsection 80(2), including with respect to the biologically appropriate timescale within which to assess a particular threat.

vi.   Conversely, I agree with the Applicants' submission that there is nothing in the plain language of subsection 80(2) which limits the mandatory duty imposed on the Minister to situations in which a species faces imminent threats to its survival or recovery on a national basis.

vii.   The less likely the threats are, the less weight that they may merit in the Minister's assessment of the imminency of the threats.

[...] the First Nations Applicants submitted that any interpretation of the words "survival" or "recovery" that would allow for the extirpation of one or more of the Seven Herds would violate the basic purposes of the SARA. They added that a threat to the survival or recovery of any of the Seven Herds is by definition a threat to the survival or recovery of boreal caribou generally. The ENGO Applicants went further by submitting that "[t]he only reasonable interpretation of 'survival' or 'recovery' in subsection 80(2) is therefore one that aims to conserve and recover all of the Herds to self-sustaining levels." In their joint Reply submissions, the Applicants added the words "throughout their current ranges" to the latter assertion.

To the extent that the Applicants are suggesting that any time the survival or recovery of any herd or particular group of any listed species, or a sub-species or individual population thereof, is threatened in any area of its range or habitat, the Minister is required to make a recommendation for an emergency protective order under subsection 80(2), I respectfully disagree. In my view, this interpretation of subsection 80(2) is not supported by the plain language of that provision.

The operative words in that provision are "is of the opinion that *the species* faces imminent threats to *its* survival or recovery" (emphasis added). The species in question is the "listed wildlife species" referred to in subsection 80(1). There is no mention of herds or other local populations of species or subspecies in subsection 80(2). The logical extension of the Applicants' position on this point would require the Minister to make a recommendation for an emergency Order under subsection 80(2) even where only a small herd, group or local population of a species or a subspecies is facing a threat to its ability to be self-sustaining in a small area of a particular province. A plain reading of the above quoted words in subsection 80(2) does not support such an interpretation of that provision. Such an interpretation would also be inconsistent with Parliament's decision to grant some scope for the exercise of subjective discretion by the Minister, as evidenced by the words "if he or she is of the opinion that ...".

In short, the Minister is not required to make a recommendation for an emergency Order under subsection 80(2) in the circumstances described immediately above, unless he or she comes to the opinion that the listed species in question (in this case, woodland caribou, boreal population) faces imminent threats to its survival or recovery.

The Applicants further submitted that, based on the facts which appear to have been accepted by the Minister, it was not reasonably open to the Minister to reach the opinion that "there are no imminent threats to the national survival or recovery of boreal caribou in Canada." Those facts, as set forth in the Decision, include the following:

i.   In 2002, COSEWIC assessed the population of boreal caribou in Canada to be threatened because populations have decreased throughout most of its range, the distribution of boreal caribou has contracted and boreal caribou are threatened by habitat loss and increased predation.

ii. Environment Canada's 2008 Scientific Review concluded that 30 of 57 local populations across Canada are not currently self-sustaining.

iii. All 13 local populations of boreal caribou in Alberta are at an elevated risk of extirpation, and the current population and habitat conditions of the Seven Herds are insufficient for those herds to be self-sustaining.

iv. Extirpation of Alberta herds or even just the Seven Herds would not be consistent with Alberta's plans. However, achieving recovery of many of those caribou populations will be extremely challenging given the current status and trend.

v.   The scientific subcommittee of Alberta's Endangered Species Conservation Committee recommended in 2010 that woodland caribou be up-
listed from threatened to endangered in that province.

vi. Maps of the current boreal caribou distribution show a developing gap
centered on north eastern Alberta/north eastern Saskatchewan.

vii. If the Seven Herds are extirpated (i.e., no longer existing in Alberta), the
existing gap in national boreal caribou distribution will widen. This
would have potential negative consequences due to disruption of genetic
and demographic processes that would further increase the risk to
recovery of boreal caribou in Canada. This would also represent a further
range retraction for caribou in Canada. If all Alberta herds were
extirpated, the challenge to recovery would be exacerbated. Given that
there is some migration between local populations, this situation with
respect to the herds in Alberta has implications beyond the boundaries of
that province. Specifically, the ability of Saskatchewan, the Northwest
Territories and British Columbia to recover their portion of shared
populations will be constrained by the approach that is taken with respect
to the recovery of the herds in Alberta.

I acknowledge that it is not immediately apparent how, given the foregoing
facts, the Minister reasonably could have concluded that there are no imminent
threats to the national recovery of boreal caribou.

However, in the absence of any meaningful discussion in the Decision of the
basis upon which the Minister's conclusion was reached, I am not prepared to
agree with the Applicants' position that it was not reasonably open to the Minister
to reach that conclusion.

In my view, the better approach is to set aside the Minister's Decision on the
basis that it did not "fit comfortably with the principles of justification,
transparency and intelligibility" (*Canada (Minister of Citizenship and
Immigration) v. Khosa*, 2009 SCC 12, [2009] 1 SCR 339, at paragraph 59),
because it failed to adequately explain the basis for the decision. This is discussed
in part VI.C of these reasons below.

In the absence of additional submissions from the parties regarding the
specific meaning of the words "imminent threats to its survival or recovery," I am
reluctant to make any further determinations in that regard, particularly given my
finding that the Decision should be set aside for the reasons discussed above and
below. In my view, it would be better to defer any such further determinations to
another day, when the meaning of those words has been the subject of more
fulsome submissions. My conclusion in this regard is reinforced by the fact that
counsel to the respondent was unable, during the oral hearing in this matter, to
articulate the specific interpretation of subsection 80(2) that was or even may have
been adopted by the Minister in reaching his Decision.

Should an Order of mandamus be granted compelling the Minister to make a recommendation under subsection 80(2)?

The Applicants submitted that the scientific evidence that was acknowledged
in the Minister's Decision was such that the only reasonable decision available to

the Minister was to: (i) conclude that there are imminent threats to the recovery of boreal caribou; and (ii) make a recommendation to the Governor in Council, as contemplated by subsection 80(2). Based on this proposition, the Applicants assert that this Court should compel the Minister to make the recommendation that he should have made under subsection 80(2).

In the case at bar, the Applicants concede that subsection 80(2) contemplates the making of the decision by the Minister that is discretionary in nature. This is clear from the words "if he or she *is of the opinion* that" (emphasis added). Accordingly, the well established principle that *mandamus* is not available to compel the exercise of discretion in a particular way applies (*Canada (Chief Electoral Officer) v. Callaghan*, 2011 FCA 74, at paragraph 126; *St Brieux (Town) v. Canada (Minister of Fisheries & Oceans)*, 2010 FC 427, at paragraph 57).

In an attempt to avoid that principle, the Applicants state that they "do not seek to compel the Minister to form a certain opinion." Rather, they assert that "they seek to compel him to recommend an emergency Order based on concessions he has made about the status of the [Seven] Herds and about the threat this poses to the survival or recovery of Boreal Caribou." In this regard, they rely on *Trinity Western University v. British Columbia College of Teachers*, [2001] 1 SCR 772, at paragraphs 41 and 43. However, that case is distinguishable on the basis that the only reason given by the British Columbia College of Teachers (BCCT) for refusing certification of the appellant was the latter's adoption of discriminatory practices, a matter that was found to be beyond the jurisdiction of the BCCT to consider.

In my view, the factual "concessions" made by the Minister, which are summarized at paragraph 48 above, together with the other evidence in the Certified Record, are not such that the only reasonable conclusion available to the Minister was that there are imminent threats to the recovery of boreal caribou.

As discussed at paragraphs 48-51 of these reasons, I acknowledge that it is not immediately apparent how the Minister could have reasonably reached his conclusion that "eastern local populations could provide the basis for achieving a national recovery objective." This is because, as explained in the next section below, the Minister's decision did not explain the basis for that conclusion. In these circumstances, and given the other errors made by the Minister, the appropriate remedy is to set aside the Minister's decision and to remit it back to him for reconsideration in accordance with these reasons.

Did the Minister err in failing or refusing to recommend an emergency Order under subsection 80(2), by failing to consider relevant factors?

In the alternative to an Order of *mandamus*, the Applicants seek a declaration that, in refusing to make an affirmative recommendation under subsection 80(2), the Minister erred in law or acted unreasonably, or both, by failing to consider various relevant factors, including:

i.   The First Nations Applicants' treaty rights and the honour of the Crown;

ii.   The Minister's ongoing breach of his mandatory obligation to prepare a Recovery Strategy for boreal caribou and post it on the public registry within the time period mandated by subsection 42(2) of the SARA;

   iii. The purposes of the SARA;

   iv. The draft recovery objectives for boreal caribou set forth in the Draft Policies; and

   v. The best available science.

Given my determinations in Part VI.A above with respect to the Minister's position regarding First Nations Applicants' treaty rights and the honour of the Crown, it is not necessary to revisit those issues again.

With respect to the remaining considerations that the Applicants allege were not taken into account by the Minister, I am satisfied that all but the purposes of the SARA were in fact considered by the Minister.

As to the overdue Recovery Strategy, this was addressed near the outset of the Decision and again when the Decision addressed whether an Order under section 80 should be recommended based on whether there are imminent threats to the recovery of boreal caribou. In this regard, it was specifically recognized that "given that the draft recovery strategy will only be posted [in] summer 2011, assessing the requirement for a Section 80 order based on imminent threats to recovery is less straightforward than it is for survival." The Decision proceeded to recognize that "[t]he department has publicly acknowledged that the recovery strategy for boreal caribou was due in 2007." Then, in the pen-ultimate paragraph of the Decision, the following was stated: "[t]he proposed national recovery strategy to be posted in the summer of 2011 will set out boreal caribou population and distribution objectives. Once these recovery objectives are formulated, it may be necessary to re-examine whether a section 80 order is warranted for the species, or any population." Additional discussion of the status of the Recovery Strategy was provided in the Background appendix to the Decision. Based on all the foregoing, I am satisfied that the Minister did not err by failing to consider the ongoing breach of his obligation to prepare a Recovery Strategy for boreal caribou and post it on the public registry within the time period mandated by subsection 42(2) of the SARA.

With respect to the draft recovery objectives for boreal caribou set forth in the Draft Policies, once again, these were adequately addressed in the Decision [...] In my view, what was missing in the Decision was not a consideration of the recovery objectives set forth in the Draft Policies, but rather a meaningful explanation for how the Minister reached his overall conclusion, notwithstanding all of the contrary evidence that was addressed in the Decision with respect to the threats faced by boreal caribou in Alberta. This is addressed below.

With respect to the best available science, I am satisfied that the decision reasonably addressed the scientific information that was included in the Certified Record which was before the Minister when he made the Decision. That Certified Record included extensive information that was reasonably addressed in the Decision (including the Background appendix that was attached thereto).

Although the Decision did not specifically address certain other scientific information that was submitted to Environment Canada by the Applicants prior to the Minister's Decision, I am satisfied that such information was consistent with the information that was addressed in the Decision, and that therefore the Minister did not err by failing to specifically address such information, including reports authored by Dr. Stan Boutin and by the Athabasca Landscape Team, respectively. [...]

Given all of the information that was specifically addressed in the Decision, it was not a reviewable error for the Minister to have failed to have specifically addressed the objectives of the SARA in his Decision. In my view, the manner in which the Decision addressed the relevant scientific and other information in the Certified Record was not inconsistent with the purposes of the SARA, which are "to prevent wildlife species from being extirpated or becoming extinct, to provide for the recovery of wildlife species that are extirpated, endangered or threatened as a result of human activity and to manage species of special concern to prevent them from becoming endangered or threatened" (s. 6).

Instead, where the Minister erred was in failing to provide a meaningful explanation for how he reached his conclusion not to recommend an emergency Order, given (i) the scientific and other information that was reviewed over the course of several pages in the Decision, (ii) the recovery objectives for boreal caribou set forth in the Draft Policies, and (iii) the language of subsection 80(2), the purposes of the SARA, as set forth in section 6, and the overall scheme of that legislation.

Notwithstanding the substantial scientific and other evidence that was discussed and that contradicted the overall conclusion reached by the Minister in the Decision, the Minister concluded that there are no imminent threats to the national recovery of boreal caribou in Canada. The sole basis that was provided in the Decision for that conclusion was the following:

> Although the extirpation of even the [Seven Herds] would result in further range retraction in the middle of the range of boreal caribou, it is possible to maintain a self sustaining population of boreal caribou in eastern Canada. As such, even though national recovery objectives and approaches would be constrained by the extirpation of even the 7 Alberta herds in question, the Eastern local populations could provide the basis for achieving a national recovery objective.

In my view, these very short reasons provided for the conclusion reached by the Minister do not enable me to conduct a meaningful review of the Decision (*Canada (Minister of Citizenship and Immigration) v. Ragupathy*, 2006 FCA 151, at paragraph 14). This is because the basis for the overall conclusion reached by the Minister, particularly the evidentiary basis, was not meaningfully discussed (*Law Society of Upper Canada v. Neinstein*, 2010 ONCA 193, at paragraph 61; *Clifford v. Ontario Municipal Employees Retirement System*, 2009 ONCA 670, at paragraph 40; *Khosa*, above), and the record does not otherwise explain the Minister's decision in a satisfactory manner (*R v. Sheppard*, 2002 SCC 26, at paragraphs 15, 24 and 28, [2002] 1 SCR; *R v. REM*, 2008 SCC 51 at paragraph 37, [2008] 3 SCR). In the context of the Decision as a whole, this conclusion essentially came "out of the blue". The Applicants, the public and the Court are left to speculate as to:

i.   the scientific basis for the conclusion that it is possible to maintain a self sustaining population of boreal caribou in eastern Canada;

ii.   the content of "the national recovery objectives and approaches that would be constrained by the extirpation of" the Seven Herds;

iii. the basis upon which it was concluded that the eastern local populations
could provide the basis for achieving a national recovery objective;

iv. the likelihood of achieving such national recovery objective if the Seven
Herds become extirpated; and

v. the basis upon which this conclusion was considered to be consistent with
the language of subsection 80(2), the purposes of the SARA, as set forth
in section 6, and the SARA as a whole (Elmer Dredger, *Construction of
Statutes*, 2nd ed. (Toronto: Butterworths Ltd., 1983) at page 87; *Rizzo &
Rizzo Shoes Ltd. (Re)*, [1998] 1 SCR 27 at paragraph 21).

Accordingly, the Decision cannot stand and must be set aside.

Should the Court declare that the Minister has contravened subsection 42(2) by failing to include a proposed Recovery Strategy for woodland caribou in the public registry?

The Respondents have conceded that the Minister failed to prepare a
Recovery Strategy within the three year time limit set forth in subsection 42(2),
namely, by June 5, 2007. The Respondents explained that the posting of a recovery
strategy to the public registry "was delayed to allow for further scientific studies
and to work with aboriginal organizations and stakeholders affected by the
recovery strategy, because it was found that there was not enough information to
identify critical habitat for the boreal caribou," presumably in the draft Recovery
Strategy. The Applicants have not alleged any bad faith on the part of the Minister
with respect to his desire to further consult with aboriginal organizations and
stakeholders.

That said, the Applicants note that they made clear, in their initial request for
an emergency Order under subsection 80(2), their view that no such further
consultation is required. [...]

With the foregoing in mind, and considering that the Minister was required to
post the Recovery Strategy to the public registry approximately four years ago, the
Applicants urged the Court to declare that the Minister has breached his
obligation under subsection 42(2) of the SARA, to "send a clear message to the
federal government and to the Canadian public that it is not acceptable for
responsible ministers to continue to miss mandatory deadlines established by
Parliament."

Given that there has been no suggestion, let alone a demonstration, that the
Minister's delay in posting a Recovery Strategy is attributable to bad faith on his
part, and particularly given that the Minister has publicly committed to posting
the Recovery Strategy "in the summer of 2011", i.e. sometime in the next five
weeks, I have decided to defer making a decision with respect to the requested
declaration, until September 1, 2011. This will give the Minister the opportunity to
meet his previously announced commitment.

Conclusion

The application is granted in part. The Minister's Decision will be set aside.
The matter is remitted to the Minister for reconsideration in accordance with these
reasons. The Applicants' request for an Order in the nature of *mandamus* is

denied. The Applicants' request for an Order declaring that the Minister has failed to prepare a Recovery Strategy for the listed species of woodland caribou (boreal population) within the time period established in the SARA, is deferred until September 1, 2011.

Notes and Questions

1. Crampton J. held that the appropriate standard of review in this case was correctness for the issues relating to the honour of the Crown in relation to First Nations rights, and reasonableness for all other issues. More recently, the Federal Court of Appeal held that while the existence and extent of the duty to consult is a question of law reviewable on a correctness standard, the adequacy of the consultation is a question of mixed law and fact reviewable on a reasonableness standard: *Tsleil-Waututh Nation v. Canada (Attorney General)*, 2018 FCA 153 at para. 225, citing *Haida Nation v. British Columbia (Minister of Forests)*, 2004 SCC 73 at paras. 61-63. Do you prefer the conclusion of Crampton J. in this case or that of the Federal Court of Appeal in *Tsleil-Waututh*? Why?

2. Crampton J. rests his decision to set aside the Minister's decision on the basis not that the decision was wrong, but rather that the Minister failed to provide reasons for the decision that allowed for "meaningful review". What, in your view, attracted Crampton J. to this approach? Is there a parallel between his ruling and the ruling of the reviewing judge in the *Kearl Oil Sands* case (*Pembina Institute for Appropriate Development v. Canada (Attorney General)*, 2008 FC 302) discussed in Chapter 6? The Supreme Court of Canada in *Newfoundland & Labrador Nurses' Union v. Newfoundland & Labrador (Treasury Board)*, 2011 SCC 62 ("*NLNU*"), released after the *Adam* decision, rejected the proposition that inadequacy of reasons can be a stand-alone basis for quashing a decision; rather, "the reasons must be read together with the outcome and serve the purpose of showing whether the result falls within a range of possible outcomes" (para. 14). How, if at all, would Crampton J.'s decision in *Adam* have been different if he followed *NLNU*?

3. Environment Canada finally released the Recovery Strategy for the Boreal population of Woodland Caribou in October 2012. Among other things, the Recovery Strategy contains descriptions of critical habitat and recovery objectives for Boreal caribou. One of the objectives is to stabilize and achieve self-sustaining status for the "Not Self-Sustaining" local populations of Boreal caribou. For populations with a small or declining size, recovery to a minimum of 100 animals will be necessary. Also, for populations with less than 65% undisturbed habitat, efforts to restore disturbed habitat to a minimum of 65% undisturbed habitat will be needed. The Recovery Strategy identifies 14 existing self-sustaining populations, while 37 others are deemed not self-sustaining. For example, the Recovery Strategy identifies the Little Smoky population as a "Not Self-Sustaining" population (population size 78 and declining) and only 5% of its habitat as undisturbed. Therefore,

the appropriate management response should be to avoid further disturbance to their habitat and restore disturbed habitat of the Little Smoky
population back to a minimum of 65% undisturbed habitat. Does the release
of this strategy enhance or detract from the potential to refile an application
seeking an emergency order for the protection of this population?
Conversely, does the fact that Environment Canada has still not released
a Recovery Strategy for the Southern Mountain Caribou population make
that population a better candidate for an emergency order at this point?

4. Following the release of a federal Recovery Strategy for Boreal caribou in
    2012, provinces were given three to five years to complete their own caribou
    range plans. Several provinces, including Alberta, missed this deadline,
    prompting speculation that environmental groups will renew their efforts to
    secure protection for caribou under both the federal emergency order power
    and the safety net order power.

The Court's decision in *Adam* to order the Minister to reconsider her opinion
as to whether caribou were under "imminent threat" turned on its conclusion that
the Minister's reasons for forming this opinion were legally inadequate. Going
forward, this may be a hard argument to make based on the case law as it has
evolved post-*Adam*: see Chapter 6. Nonetheless, subsequent jurisprudence on
the emergency power suggests that litigation opportunities to compel Ministerial
reconsideration remain.

Centre québécois du droit de l'environnement c.
Canada (Ministre de l'Environnement)

2015 FC 773

[The applicants sought judicial review of a refusal by the Minister to
recommend to Cabinet an emergency order for the Western Chorus Frog. The
Minister claimed the frog was not facing an "imminent threat". The Court held
that the Minister's opinion was unreasonable given the evidentiary record, and
ordered the Minister to reconsider the matter.]

MARTINEAU J.: — The applicants, the Centre québécois du droit de
l'environnement and Nature Québec, are two non-profit organizations working in
the field of protection of the environment and of species at risk. They are
challenging the legality of a decision dated March 27, 2014, by which the Minister
of the Environment refused to recommend to the Governor in Council that an
emergency order be made under section 80 of the *Species at Risk Act*, SC 2002,
c 29 (federal Act), to provide for the protection of the Western Chorus Frog
(*Pseudacris triseriata*), a threatened wildlife species that is likely to become an
endangered species if nothing is done to reverse the factors leading to its
extirpation or extinction.

For the reasons that follow, this application for judicial review should be
allowed.

Legal Environment

To understand the real issues in this case and the nature of the specific questions that arise, it seems necessary to situate the Minister's refusal within the legal environment — international and domestic — for the protection of species at risk. [...]

Cruelty to animals is inflicted by exceptionally ill-intentioned individuals whose actions are severely punished by society, and is a crime. Its suppression is therefore within the power of Parliament under subsection 91(27) of the *Constitution Act, 1867*, 30 & 31 Victoria, c 3. But humans are also gregarious beings who themselves live in society in an environment inhabited by all kinds of animal and plant species. What happens when humans, as supreme creatures pursuing their civilizing mission, settle in places where, just yesterday, the American eastern cougar or the Prairie grizzly bear reigned supreme over vast areas of land with the wolverine feared by our forebears? And when human activity destroys in its wake the natural habitat of all these wildlife species — animals and varieties of plants — that cannot tolerate urban life or agriculture, to the point that their survival is threatened in the relatively short to medium term? Have we collectively imposed on ourselves a rule of civilization by which we must prevent the annihilation of individuals of a threatened wildlife species and the destruction of their natural habitat?

This does seem to be the case, for otherwise the *United Nations Convention on Biological Diversity*, June 5, 1992, 1760 UNTS 79 (CBD), which entered into force on December 29, 1993, would not have been ratified by 196 states parties, including Canada. The otherness between humans and animals, between owners and their property, between people and things without an owner, has given way to a universal legal concept whereby wildlife species and ecosystems are part of the world's heritage and it has become necessary to preserve the natural habitat of species at risk. The *Species at Risk Act*, SC 2002, c 29 (federal Act), which was assented to on December 12, 2002, is in fact intended to implement Canada's obligations under the CBD. This is reflected in the fact that, in the preamble to the federal Act, the Government of Canada formally sets out its commitment to conserving biological diversity and to the principle that, if there are threats of serious or irreversible damage to a wildlife species, cost-effective measures to prevent the reduction or loss of the species should not be postponed for a lack of full scientific certainty (precautionary principle). [...]

In addition to the federal Act, account should be taken of the *Act respecting threatened or vulnerable species*, CQLR, c E-12.01 (Quebec Act), and the *Endangered Species Act, 2007*, SO 2007, c 6 (Ontario Act). These two statutes in turn incorporate the CBD's general principles in the provincial sphere and supplement the federal scheme for the protection and recovery of species at risk from a sustainable development perspective. The Quebec Act (1999) makes the Minister of Sustainable Development, Environment and Parks responsible for proposing to the province's government a policy of protection and management of designated threatened or vulnerable species or of species likely to be so designated, while the *Act respecting the conservation and development of wildlife*, CQLR, c C-61.1, establishes various prohibitions that relate to the conservation of wildlife resources. The Ontario Act, which is more recent (2007), is a complete code dealing with extinct, extirpated, endangered, threatened and special concern species. Indeed, the following is noted in the preamble to the Ontario Act: "Biological diversity is among the great treasures of our planet. It has ecological, social, economic, cultural and intrinsic value. Biological diversity makes many essential contributions to human life, including foods, clothing and medicines, and is an important part of sustainable social and economic development. Unfortunately, throughout the world, species of animals, plants and other organisms are being lost forever at an alarming rate. The loss of these species is most often due to human activities, especially activities that damage the habitats of these species. Global action is required ... In Ontario, our native species are a vital component of our precious natural heritage ..." [...]

Factual Context

The Western Chorus Frog is a small amphibian (a category that includes frogs, toads and bullfrogs) approximately 2.5 centimetres in length that lives and breeds in wetlands. Because it is a species that does not move around much, its home range lies within a small radius (approximately 250 metres) of its breeding habitat. The wetland (pool of water, swamp or flooded woodland clearing) initially serves as a breeding habitat and must be close to open land (field, clearing or woodland). The breeding season takes place during the spring. The majority of adults generally breed only once, and in most cases their life span is no more than one year, although it sometimes reaches two or three years.

The Western Chorus Frog's range extends from south-western to north-eastern North America. Approximately nine percent of the Western Chorus Frog's global range is in Canada, where it occupies the lowlands of southern Ontario and Quebec. Suburban sprawl and changes in farming practices are contributing to the ongoing destruction of Western Chorus Frog habitats and are thereby threatening the species' survival in Canada and elsewhere in the world. Populations and metapopulations (composed of separate population groups that interact to some degree) found along the Great Lakes/St. Lawrence and Canadian Shield are particularly exposed to the human threat, which makes them highly vulnerable.

In Quebec, the Western Chorus Frog was historically present in the south of the province, from the Ottawa Valley to the foothills of the Appalachians and west of the Richelieu River. Today it is thought to occupy only 10% of this historical range. In Montérégie, the species has been reduced to just over 800 highly fragmented sites over a narrow 20-kilometre strip between the municipalities of Beauharnois to the south and Contrecoeur to the north. Its presence has also been confirmed in just over 220 sites in the Outaouais region on a strip approximately 10 kilometres wide that extends over a distance of approximately 100 kilometres from east to west along the Ottawa River between the city of Gatineau and Île-du-Grand-Calumet. In 2010, scientists estimated that the species occupied at least 102 square kilometres of habitat: 60 square kilometres in Montérégie and 42 square kilometres in the Outaouais. It is estimated that the Western Chorus Frog has already lost close to 90% of its historic range in Montérégie, and it can now be found only on Île Perrot and on Montréal's South Shore between Saint-Stanislas-de-Kostka and Varennes, along a small strip of land approximately 20 kilometres wide. Within this area only nine metapopulations and seven small isolated populations survive, occupying a total area of approximately 50 square kilometres. [...]

The foregoing is a general factual overview. I now come to the specific facts on which this case is based. On May 15, 2013, the applicant Nature Québec served a letter on the then Environment Minister, the Honourable Peter Kent, asking him to recommend the making of an emergency order under section 80 of the federal Act and invoking an "imminent threat" to what may have remained of the Western Chorus Frog metapopulation in La Prairie, namely that of the "Bois de la Commune", as a result of the deforestation and alteration of the wetlands surrounding the completion of a housing project called "Domaine de la nature".

Nature Québec indicates that this metapopulation has already undergone losses of more than 50% since the early 1990s and that the species' recovery is compromised. Nature Québec alleges that it recently obtained a copy of the minutes (dated February 20, 2013, final version April 2, 2013) of a meeting of the species recovery team in Quebec, composed of experts including an Environment Canada representative. It is expressly acknowledged that the current protection and compensation measures planned for what remains of the Bois de la Commune metapopulation do not offer the necessary safeguards to ensure the survival of the species and jeopardize its recovery. Protection of the Bois de la Commune metapopulation had already been identified as a critical habitat in the provincial recovery plan.

Nature Québec therefore submitted a formal request to the Minister of the Environment asking that he exercise his power to make a recommendation under section 80 of the federal Act and to (TRANSLATION) "quickly prepare an order to be adopted on an emergency basis by the Governor in Council and to provide for designation of the habitat necessary to the survival or recovery of the species in the area targeted by the order, i.e. La Prairie, and to include in this order *provisions prohibiting activities that may adversely affect the species and its habitat*" (emphasis added). No immediate action was taken by the Minister of the Environment, who was slow to reply to the letter of May 15, 2013.

On October 16, 2013, Nature Québec's counsel sent to the Honourable Peter Kent's successor, the Honourable Leona Aglukkaq (the Minister of the Environment), a formal demand that reiterated the arguments made in their previous letter. On November 14, 2013, the Director General of the Canadian Wildlife Service at Environment Canada responded, indicating that the Department was seeking additional information from the other jurisdictions on the situation of the Western Chorus Frog and on the measures taken to ensure the conservation of this species, in order to ensure that the Minister would be able to make a fully informed decision.

On December 13, 2013, Environment Canada's Canadian Wildlife Service an internal scientific report looking at the issue of whether there were imminent threats: "Threat and protection assessment of the Western Chorus Frog (Great Lakes/St. Lawrence–Canadian Shield Protection) following petitions for an emergency order to protect the species in Bois de la Commune, La Prairie, Quebec" (the internal expert report). The purpose of the internal expert report was to provide the Minister of the Environment with a science-based, credible and objective assessment in order to help her make an informed decision.

The internal expert report noted that 260 habitats of the threatened species in Canada had been identified as critical habitats in Quebec and 211 in Ontario. Over the previous 10 years there had been a 37% decline in the species in Quebec and a 42.6% decline in Ontario, while over the previous 60 years the Chorus Frog had disappeared from 90% of the area it had historically occupied in Montérégie. The species' critical habitat included habitats for breeding, feeding and overwintering that had been inhabited by populations at least twice during the previous 20 years, including at least once during the previous 10 years. The Bois de la Commune metapopulation was part of the nine Montérégie metapopulations whose habitats had to be protected. According to the internal expert report, however, the problem was that there were no appropriate protective measures under Quebec law at that point, while the conservation area proposed by the municipality of La Prairie was not sufficient to ensure the survival of the Bois de la Commune metapopulation. Although the *survival* of the species in Canada was not directly compromised, the housing project represented an imminent threat *to the recovery* of the species in Canada. According to the detailed analysis carried out by the scientists, all of the factors previously identified in the Draft Policy for the making of an emergency order had been met in this case.

On February 5, 2014, the Western Chorus Frog recovery team sent to the competent authorities an additional scientific opinion concluding that the Bois de la Commune housing project constituted an imminent threat to the recovery of the species and that the location of the conservation area identified in the agreement with the municipality of La Prairie should be amended to bring it more in line with the zone recommended in the provincial conservation plan.

Minister's Refusal

On March 27, 2014, the Minister of the Environment decided not to recommend the adoption of an emergency order because, in her opinion, the Western Chorus Frog was not facing an imminent threat to its survival or recovery. The letter of refusal signed by Mr. Beale, Assistant Deputy Minister of the Environmental Stewardship Branch at Environment Canada (the Minister's delegate), provided the following explanation:

(TRANSLATION)

Environment Canada representatives have considered your request. The threat the species is currently experiencing is related to habitat destruction in the species' range in Quebec and Ontario owing to suburban sprawl and changes in farming practices. Although the decline in the Western Chorus Frog throughout southern Quebec and Ontario can be described as serious from a biological point of view, Environment Canada considers that the scope of the project proposed for the La Prairie site does not threaten the possibility of the species' presence elsewhere in Ontario and Quebec. Accordingly, the Western Chorus Frog is not facing an imminent threat with regard to its survival or its recovery.

The only relevant documents that were before the Minister or her delegate were those identified by the delegate in the file transmission notice, filed on June 9, 2014, under rule 318 of the *Federal Courts Rules*, SOR/98-106 (Rules). The internal expert report of December 13, 2013, was not submitted to the decision-maker. However, some of the information it contained is summarized in a draft memorandum to the Minister (MIN-175318) attached to the correspondence dated February 9, 2014, from the Director General of the Wildlife Service to the delegate (point 6b). A draft of a proposed species recovery strategy (2013) was also brought to the attention of the Minister or her delegate (point 4a). [...]

Analysis

[...] This has been an oft-repeated refrain of the courts since *Dunsmuir*: the review of a decision on a reasonableness standard concerns the outcome of the decision as well as its transparency and intelligibility (*Dunsmuir*, at paragraph 47). Referring to this new general principle, the Supreme Court took pains to explain in *Newfoundland Nurses*, above, at paragraph 16, that "if the reasons allow the reviewing court to understand why the tribunal made its decision and permit it to determine whether the conclusion is within the range of acceptable outcomes, the *Dunsmuir* criteria are met".

There is cause to intervene herein. The arguments submitted by the applicants in favour of setting aside the disputed decision seem valid. In the case at hand, if one refers to the review of the documents submitted to the Court by the federal office under rule 318, the Minister seems to have "put the cart before the horse", to coin a popular 16th-century saying, as her reasoning in the letter dated March 27, 2014 seems to have been shaped by the specific outcome sought. Otherwise, I fail to understand why the logic and the analytical checklist specified in the Draft Policy discussed earlier at paragraphs 21 and 22 were ignored. Granted, the Minister is not bound by departmental policy. However, the specific reasons for deviating from such policies should be made clear.

The Minister's succinct reasons for the refusal are stated in the delegate's letter. They are stated plainly enough. They come down to the fact that despite the biological severity of the threats currently confronting the Western Chorus Frog, (TRANSLATION) "the scope of the project proposed for the La Prairie site does not threaten the possibility of the species' presence elsewhere in Ontario and Quebec". However, the problem is that the evidence in the certified file compiled under rule 318 does not logically support the Minister's finding that (TRANSLATION) "[a]ccordingly, the Western Chorus Frog is not facing an imminent threat with regard to its survival *or* its recovery" (emphasis added). The species' "survival" and "recovery" are two quite distinct notions (see paragraph 23, above). In terms of "recovery", the Minister's logic is seriously flawed.

The internal procedure by which the Minister's decision was made was by no means transparent. This opacity is evident in the documentation that the applicants were able to obtain under rule 318. The respective roles of the various interveners on issues of scientific, political and legal interest remain unknowable to the Court. However, what is clear is a reversal in the public servants' position. Their final position, however, is not based on any scientific analysis. In the matter at bar, I do not believe that the Minister's refusal constitutes an acceptable outcome based on the evidentiary record and the applicable law. Therefore, the Minister's refusal is unreasonable.

The Minister is required to act in accordance with the federal Act. The precautionary principle applies to material determinations made under the federal Act. This principle stands in contrast to administrative or ministerial *laissez-faire*.

Where no provincial measure exists to sufficiently protect a wild species registered on the federal List, an imminent threat to the survival or recovery of the species can obviously be expected in the relatively short term. The reasoning applied must conform to the spirit and intent of the federal Act, as well as any rational, objective criteria previously used within the Department to judge the imminence of a threat.

The Court has already rejected the restrictive interpretation suggested by the respondents — whereby the mandatory requirement provided in subsection 80(2) is limited to cases where a species is exposed to imminent threats to its survival or recovery on a *national basis* — in *Adam*, above, at para 39. Not only did the Minister arbitrarily and capriciously ignore the scientific opinion of her own Department's experts and the Chorus Frog recovery team, but the Minister's logic leads to an absurd outcome, in contradiction of the Act: as long as individuals of the species are threatened by human activity locally, an imminent threat cannot exist since other individuals elsewhere in the country are not under threat nationally.

Through the lens of its complex mechanics, the federal Act perceives critical habitat as a single unit, each part contributing to the species' survival and recovery across Canada. The two major threats to the Western Chorus Frog are urbanization and agricultural development. These threats are present across Canada. According to the evidentiary record, these two threats are extreme, serious, continuous and ongoing, and jeopardize the survival and recovery of the Western Chorus Frog in Canada. If we rely on the information that was available at the time of the disputed decision, the work included in the Domaine de la nature project will destroy a portion of the species' critical habitat. The result is the brutal and sudden disappearance of the Bois de la Commune metapopulation in La Prairie — unless, of course, mitigation measures are taken to allow the species to recover in the area identified by the possible recovery program.

The Minister's reasoning ignores that the species' recovery in Canada is currently in danger, based on the evidentiary record. A decimated metapopulation cannot recover after its critical habitat is destroyed. The delegate offers no explanation in the disputed decision of how the absence of an imminent threat to other populations might offset the disappearance or decline of a metapopulation facing an imminent threat. Ample and uncontroverted evidence shows that the species has experienced a severe and irreversible decline in Canada over the past few years, while experts investigating the issue have identified various shortfalls arising from inadequate protection in Ontario and Quebec to counter urbanization and intensified farming. Based on the internal report of December 2013, the prohibition against destroying the residences of individuals and the critical habitat of the species seems to be the only effective means of preventing the early demise of the metapopulations identified in the Montérégie area.

According to Environment Canada's definition of the term "recovery", which means halting or reversing the decline of a species, the disappearance of a metapopulation obviously threatens the species' recovery, in the absence of offsetting measures targeting other populations of the species. The fact that other populations are not directly under threat is not sufficient to show that the recovery is not threatened, particularly when documents on record prove that protection of the metapopulation in question is an important strategic objective in the recovery plan proposed for the species.

During the hearing, the respondents explained that the Western Chorus Frog recovery plan would be implemented in future years. However, at the risk of repeating myself, this recovery plan is not currently in force and nothing in the record indicates that tangible protection measures to assist the recovery of the species in the Montérégie area were in place at the time of the disputed decision, hence the importance for the Minister to determine whether an emergency order should have been made to protect metapopulations whose survival or recovery were under imminent threat.

Conclusion and Remedies

The applicants are asking the Court to set aside the disputed decision and issue a *mandamus* or a declaratory judgment compelling the Minister to recommend that an order be made. In the alternative, the applicants are asking the Court to set aside the disputed decision and return the case for a new review by the Minister, with specific instructions concerning their right of participation and the time-frame in which the new decision is to be made.

In light of all of the evidence and submissions presented by the parties, from the time this matter was taken under deliberation, the Court considers it inappropriate to issue a *mandamus* compelling the Minister to recommend an emergency order. It is similarly inappropriate to reach a declaratory judgment of law. It is sufficient to set aside the disputed decision, which in my view is unreasonable, and to ask the Minister to examine the matter again, with the stipulation that the reasons for judgment and any intervening developments shall be taken into account.

Further, although the Court decided to allow this application for judicial review while limiting its review of the reasonableness of the Minister's refusal to items directly brought to the final decision-maker's attention in March 2014, it is plainly evident that we are dealing with an ongoing situation. The practical problem in this case is that we cannot turn back the clock. The department must study the request for a recommendation again in light of any new, ensuing developments of relevance. In this regard, the upcoming publication of a final version of the recovery program, and compliance or non-compliance with the protective measures imposed by provincial or municipal authorities — as conditions for issuing work permits to the developer — are some of the new factors that the Minister must consider when she decides for a second time on the appropriateness of recommending that the Governor General issue an emergency order under section 80 of the federal Act.

It is also clear that the Minister's fresh determination must include a consultative component that in my humble opinion should not be limited to consideration of the applicants' evidence and submissions. However, rather than give the Minister specific instructions in the Court's judgment, it seems advisable that the existing shortfalls in the current decision-making process be corrected by the Department internally, to account for the opinions of scientists, provincial and municipal authorities, public stakeholders such as the applicants herein and any other interested party.

Considering the lengthy delays already encountered, it is also appropriate to determine the time-frame in which a new decision shall be made by the Minister or her delegate. A period of six months following this judgment seems reasonable in the circumstances.

For these reasons, the application for judicial review is allowed. The decision given on March 27, 2014, is set aside and the case is referred back to the Minister of the Environment for redetermination to be made within six months following this Court's judgment. The Minister shall consider the reasons for the judgment and any intervening developments. The Minister shall allow the applicants and any other interested individuals or organizations, including the intervener, to submit evidence and make representations before a new decision is reached in this case. Given the outcome, the applicants are awarded costs against the respondents. The intervener is not awarded costs.

Notes and Questions

1. The resulting emergency order, issued in 2016, is one of only two emergency orders that have been made to date under the *Species at Risk Act* since it was enacted in 2002. The other was made in relation to the Greater Sage-Grouse: Environment Canada, *Amended Recovery Strategy for the Greater Sage-Grouse (Centrocercus urophasianus urophasianus) in Canada*, Species at Risk Act Recovery Strategy Series (Ottawa: Environment Canada, 2014).

2. A notable follow-up case is *Groupe Maison Candiac inc. c. Canada (Procureur général)*, 2018 FC 643. In this case, a private developer challenged the constitutional validity of clause 80(4)(c)(ii) of the *Species at Risk Act*. The Federal Court upheld the provision on the basis of criminal law power and POGG. It also rejected the argument that the provision illegally allowed for the expropriation of private property rights without compensation.

Permitting and Assessment Requirements:
Sections 73-79

While SARA is designed to equip decision-makers with tools to respond when species face imminent threats or where their interests are not being effectively protected by provincial laws, it is also designed to ensure that decision-makers consider the interests of species in a more proactive manner. The components of SARA that are intended to fulfill this role are largely untested in court, with one very notable exception: in the Trans Mountain litigation, a key issue was whether the NEB's environmental assessment under CEAA 2012 and, subsequently, the Governor in Council's decision to approve the project, complied with sections 77 and 79 of SARA. In an historic decision, the Federal Court of Appeal held that the NEB's assessment of the project violated these

SARA provisions and on that basis concluded that the Governor in Council's subsequent approval of the project was unlawful. How did this happen?
Let us first, once again, reproduce the relevant SARA provisions.

Licences, permits, etc., under other Acts of Parliament

77. (1) Despite any other Act of Parliament, any person or body, other than a competent minister, authorized under any Act of Parliament, other than this Act, to issue or approve a licence, a permit or any other authorization that authorizes an activity that may result in the destruction of any part of the critical habitat of a listed wildlife species may enter into, issue, approve or make the authorization only if the person or body has consulted with the competent minister, has considered the impact on the species' critical habitat and is of the opinion that

(a)   all reasonable alternatives to the activity that would reduce the impact on the species' critical habitat have been considered and the best solution has been adopted; and

(b)   all feasible measures will be taken to minimize the impact of the activity on the species' critical habitat.

Notification of Minister

79. (1) Every person who is required by or under an Act of Parliament to ensure that an assessment of the environmental effects of a project is conducted, and every authority who makes a determination under paragraph 67(a) or (b) of the *Canadian Environmental Assessment Act, 2012* in relation to a project, must, without delay, notify the competent minister or ministers in writing of the project if it is likely to affect a listed wildlife species or its critical habitat.

(2) The person must identify the adverse effects of the project on the listed wildlife species and its critical habitat and, if the project is carried out, must ensure that measures are taken to avoid or lessen those effects and to monitor them. The measures must be taken in a way that is consistent with any applicable recovery strategy and action plans.

Consider now this extract from an article authored by the lawyers who challenged the federal approval of the Trans Mountain pipeline, alleging that the NEB and the Governor in Council had failed to comply with sections 77 and 79 of SARA.

Dyna Tuytel & Margot Venton,
Challenges in Receiving SARA Protections:
A Killer (Whale) Case Study

Paper delivered at the Symposium on Environment in the Courtroom:
Enforcement Issues in Canadian Wildlife Protection, Canadian
Institute of Resources Law, University of Calgary, March 2 & 3, 2018

The Trans Mountain Expansion Project would triple the capacity of the existing Trans Mountain oil pipeline from Alberta to British Columbia, and increase the number of oil tankers departing the Westridge Marine Terminal in Burnaby, and travelling through SRKW [southern resident killer whale] critical habitat to the open ocean, from approximately five to approximately 34 Aframax class tankers per month. This will adversely affect SRKW by exacerbating one of the three main threats, physical and acoustic disturbance, in critical habitat, and by increasing the risk of an oil spill in critical habitat.

The National Energy Board conducted the review and environmental assessment of the project and concluded that project-related marine shipping "is likely to result in significant adverse effects to the Southern resident killer whale", will "further contribute to cumulative effects that are already jeopardizing the survival and recovery of [SRKW]", will "impact numerous individuals of the [SRKW] population in a habitat identified as critical to [their] recovery", and will result in vessel noise that is "a threat to the acoustic integrity of ... critical habitat." It found that the project-related death of an individual SRKW could "result in population level impacts and could jeopardize recovery". It cited the Recovery Strategy statement that "while the probability of [SRKW] being exposed to an oil spill is low, the impact of such an event is potentially catastrophic."

Nevertheless, the NEB recommended, and the Governor in Council approved, the project, and did so without conditions to mitigate these effects. The result is that Project-related shipping, which the NEB found will have significant adverse effects on the SRKW and their critical habitat and will jeopardize their recovery, will proceed absent any measures to mitigate those effects.

Two conservation organizations brought applications for judicial review of the NEB's recommendation and the Governor in Council's approval, arguing that both decision-makers failed to comply with s. 79(2) of SARA, and that the Governor in Council failed to comply with additional obligations under s. 77(1).

As stated above, the express purposes of SARA include preventing wildlife species from becoming extinct and providing for the recovery of species that are endangered due to human activity. In support of these purposes, SARA's protective provisions, including ss. 77 and 79, work together to protect endangered species from existing threats and ensure that the effects of new activities are addressed before they begin in order to prevent extinction and to allow for recovery. To give effect to sections 79 and 77 of SARA, the NEB and the GIC had to consider the Project in a way that fulfilled these broad statutory purposes.

Section 77 of SARA is intended to protect critical habitat from potential harm that may result from activities authorized under other Acts of Parliament. Subsection 77(1) applies to any person or body other than a competent minister who is authorized under any other Act to "issue or approve ... any ... authorization that authorizes an activity that may result in the destruction of any part of the critical habitat" of a SARA-listed species. Before issuing any authorization, this person must consider the impact on critical habitat and be of the opinion that "all feasible measures will be taken to minimize the impact of the activity on the species' critical habitat."

The applicants in the judicial review argued that the Governor in Council erred in authorizing the project because, when faced with the NEB's factual findings indicating that project-related shipping may destroy critical habitat, the Governor in Council either failed to form an opinion that all feasible measures would be taken, or, if it did, that opinion was unreasonable in the absence of any conditions to mitigate the effects of marine shipping on SRKW critical habitat identified by the NEB.

Section 79 of SARA is intended to protect endangered species and their critical habitat from the effects of new projects. It ensures that the harmful effects of proposed projects and activities are mitigated as part of the review and approval process. Section 79(2) of SARA is triggered by the *Canadian Environmental Assessment Act, 2012* ("CEAA 2012") and applies when a proposed project that is subject to either a full environmental assessment or a determination under s. 67 is likely to affect a listed species or its critical habitat. Subsection 79(1) requires the person conducting the environmental assessment or making the determination to notify the competent minister(s) if the project is likely to affect a SARA-listed species or its critical habitat. Subsection 79(2) further requires that person to identify the project's effects on the listed species and its critical habitat and to "ensure that measures are taken to avoid or lessen" them. The measures must be taken in a way that is consistent with any applicable recovery strategy or action plan.

The applicants argued that s. 79(2) should have applied either because shipping is part of the "designated project" as defined in s. 2(1) of CEAA 2012 (being "incidental" to it), or, alternatively, because it is a "project" under s. 67. Despite its factual conclusions about the effects of marine shipping on SRKW, the NEB took the position that s. 79(2) of SARA did not apply to its assessment of shipping, on the basis that the project for the purposes of CEAA 2012 included only the pipeline and facilities, up to the Westridge Marine Terminal. The NEB conceded that it had not ensured any measures to avoid or lessen effects of shipping on SRKW on its recommended conditions. The Governor in Council approved the NEB's recommendations and adopted its recommended conditions without changes.

This example illustrates difficulties in receiving SARA protections because such a narrow reading of the law severely limits SARA's ability to protect species and their critical habitat, and undermines SARA's purposes. This is a case of, depending on one's perspective, a technicality or an unlawfully narrow interpretation of the law standing in the way of meaningful protection.

Sections 79 and 77 play an integral role in the purposes of preventing extinction and providing for recovery. Circumventing these provisions defeated the purpose of these provisions and of SARA as a whole, which is intended to prevent extinction and provide for recovery of listed species, including by addressing the effects of new activities that might further imperil species at risk before those new activities occur. Activities causing new (and significant) adverse effects that contribute to cumulative effects on SRKW and their critical habitat will continue to proceed unabated, even in a case when there were decision points where these effects could have been addressed. [...]

This example further illustrates that a critical habitat protection order does not protect critical habitat in and of itself. This project was approved despite involving activities identified in the Recovery Strategy as likely to result in destruction of critical habitat.

The Federal Court of Appeal ultimately concluded that the process by which the Trans Mountain pipeline secured Cabinet approval violated section 79 of SARA.

According to the Court, the NEB's failure to comply with section 79 stemmed originally from the NEB's erroneous decision to scope out project-related marine shipping from its CEAA 2012 assessment. This error, in turn, arose due to the NEB's erroneous conclusion that it could not assess a subject matter over which it did not have regulatory authority. This was incorrect on two grounds. First, the NEB had jurisdiction to assess subject matters within the *legislative authority* of Parliament; the scope of its own *regulatory authority* was irrelevant. Second, the NEB's conclusion did not take into account its jurisdiction to assess physical activities "incidental to" the assessed project.

The Court concluded, however, that section 77 did not apply to a determination made by the Governor in Council in these circumstances. The excerpt below has been edited to focus on the Court's analysis of the NEB's failure to comply with section 79 of SARA.

Tsleil-Waututh Nation v. Canada (Attorney General)
2018 FCA 153,
additional reasons 2018 FCA 155

[This challenge to Cabinet's decision to approve the Trans Mountain pipeline expansion project is considered in various other chapters including Chapter 3 (jurisdiction) and Chapter 6 (judicial review). This extract concerns the relationship between the validity of the report completed by the NEB as mandated under CEAA 2012 and its obligations under sections 77 and 79 of SARA.]

DAWSON J.A.: —

Did the Board err in its treatment of the Species at Risk Act?

The purposes of the *Species at Risk Act* are: to prevent wildlife species from being extirpated or becoming extinct; to provide for the recovery of wildlife species that are extirpated, endangered or threatened as a result of human activity; and, to manage species of special concern to prevent them from becoming endangered or threatened (section 6).

Important protections are found in section 77 of the Act, which is intended to protect the critical habitat of listed wildlife species, and section 79, which is intended to protect listed wildlife species and their critical habitat from new projects. Listed wildlife species are those species listed in Schedule 1 of the Act, a list of wildlife species at risk. Sections 77 and 79 are set out in the Appendix to these reasons.

Raincoast and Living Oceans argue that as a result of unreasonably defining the designated project not to include Project-related marine shipping, the Board failed to meet the requirement of subsection 79(2) of the *Species at Risk Act*. As a result of this error they say it was unreasonable for the Governor in Council to rely upon the Board's report without first ensuring that the Board had complied with subsection 79(2) of the Act with respect to Southern resident killer whales.

They also argue that it was unreasonable for the Governor in Council not to comply with its additional, independent obligations under subsection 77(1) of the *Species at Risk Act.* [...]

Did the Board err by concluding that section 79 of the Species at Risk Act did not apply to its consideration of the effects of Project-related marine shipping?

Section 79 obligates every person required "to ensure that an assessment of the environmental effects of a project is conducted" to:

i. promptly notify the competent minister or ministers if the project "is likely to affect a listed wildlife species or its critical habitat." (subsection 79(1));

ii. identify the adverse effects of the project on the listed wildlife species and its critical habitat (subsection 79(2)); and,

iii. if the project is carried out, ensure that measures are taken "to avoid or lessen those effects and to monitor them." The measures taken must be taken in a way that is consistent with any applicable recovery strategy and action plans (subsection 79(2)).

Subsection 79(3) defines a "project" to mean, among other things, a designated project as defined in subsection 2(1) of the *Canadian Environmental Assessment Act, 2012.*

The Board acknowledged its obligations under section 79 of the *Species at Risk Act* in the course of its environmental assessment (Chapter 10, page 161). However, because it had not defined the designated project to include Project-related marine shipping, the Board rejected Living Oceans' submission that the Board's obligations under section 79 of the *Species at Risk Act* applied to its consideration of the effects of Project-related marine shipping on the Southern resident killer whale (Chapter 14, page 332). Notwithstanding this conclusion that section 79 did not apply, for reasons that are not explained in its report, the Board did comply with the obligation under subsection 79(1) to notify the responsible ministers that the Project might affect Southern resident killer whales and their habitat. The Board did this by letter dated April 23, 2014 (a letter sent approximately three weeks after the Board made its scoping decision).

I have found that the Board unjustifiably excluded Project-related marine shipping from the Project's description. It follows that the failure to apply section 79 of the *Species at Risk Act* to its consideration of the effects of Project-related marine shipping on the Southern resident killer whale was also unjustified.

Both Canada and Trans Mountain argue that, nonetheless, the Board substantially complied with its obligations under section 79 of the *Species at Risk Act.* Therefore, as with the issue of Project-related marine shipping, the next question is whether the Board substantially complied with its obligations under section 79.

Did the Board substantially comply with its obligations under section 79 of the Species at Risk Act?

The respondents argue that, in addition to complying with the notification requirement found in subsection 79(1), the Board considered:

- the adverse impacts of marine shipping on listed wildlife species and their critical habitat;
- all reasonable alternatives to marine shipping that would reduce impact on listed species' critical habitat; and
- measures, consistent with the applicable recovery strategies or action plans, to avoid or lessen any adverse impacts of the Project.

Canada and Trans Mountain submit that as a result the Board met its requirements "where possible." (Trans Mountain's memorandum of fact and law, paragraph 120). On this last point, Trans Mountain submits that the Board lacked authority to impose conditions or otherwise ensure that measures were taken to avoid or lessen the effects of marine shipping on species at risk. Thus, while the Board could identify potential mitigation measures, and encourage the appropriate regulatory authorities to take further action, it could not ensure compliance with subsection 79(2) of the *Species at Risk Act*.

Canada and Trans Mountain have accurately summarized the Board's findings that are relevant to its consideration of Project-related shipping in the context of the *Species at Risk Act*. However, I do not accept their submission that the Board's consideration of the Project's impact on the Southern resident killer whale substantially complied with its obligation under section 79 of the *Species at Risk Act*. I reach this conclusion for the following reason.

By defining the Project not to include Project-related marine shipping, the Board failed to consider its obligations under the *Species at Risk Act* when it considered the Project's impact on the Southern resident killer whale. Had it done so, in light of its recommendation that the Project be approved, subsection 79(2) of the *Species at Risk Act* required the Board to ensure, if the Project was carried out, that "measures are taken to avoid or lessen" the Project's effects on the Southern resident killer whale and to monitor those measures.

While I recognize the Board could not regulate shipping, it was nonetheless obliged to consider the consequences at law of its inability to "ensure" that measures were taken to ameliorate the Project's impact on the Southern resident killer whale. However, the Board gave no consideration in its report to the fact that it recommended approval of the Project without any measures being imposed to avoid or lessen the Project's significant adverse effects upon the Southern resident killer whale.

Because marine shipping was beyond the Board's regulatory authority, it assessed the effects of marine shipping in the absence of mitigation measures and did not recommend any specific mitigation measures. Instead it encouraged other regulatory authorities "to explore any such initiatives" (report, page 349). While the Board lacked authority to regulate marine shipping, the final decision-maker was not so limited. In my view, in order to substantially comply with section 79 of the *Species at Risk Act* the Governor in Council required the Board's exposition of all technically and economically feasible measures that are available to avoid or lessen the Project's effects on the Southern resident killer whale. Armed with this information the Governor in Council would be in a position to see that, if approved, the Project was not approved until all technically and economically feasible mitigation measures within the authority of the federal government were in place. Without this information the Governor in Council lacked the necessary information to make the decision required of it. [...]

[**Ed. Note:** The portion of the Court's judgment dealing with the inapplicability of section 77 in these circumstances is omitted.]

Conclusion: the Governor in Council erred by relying upon the Board's report as a proper condition precedent to the Governor in Council's decision

Trans Mountain's application was complex, raising challenging issues on matters as diverse as Indigenous rights and concerns, pipeline integrity, the fate and behaviours of spilled hydrocarbons in aquatic environments, emergency prevention, preparedness and response, the need for the Project and its economic feasibility and the effects of Project-related shipping activities.

The approval process was long and demanding for all participants; after the hearing the Board was left to review tens of thousands of pages of evidence.

Many aspects of the Board's report are not challenged in this proceeding.

This said, I have found that the Board erred by unjustifiably excluding Project-related marine shipping from the Project's definition. While the Board's assessment of Project-related shipping was adequate for the purpose of informing the Governor in Council about the effects of such shipping on the Southern resident killer whale, the Board's report was also sufficient to put the Governor in Council on notice that the Board had unjustifiably excluded Project-related shipping from the Project's definition.

It was this exclusion that permitted the Board to conclude that section 79 of the *Species at Risk Act* did not apply to its consideration of the effects of Project-related marine shipping. This exclusion then permitted the Board to conclude that, notwithstanding its conclusion that the operation of Project-related marine vessels is likely to result in significant adverse effects to the Southern resident killer whale, the Project (as defined by the Board) was not likely to cause significant adverse environmental effects. The Board could only reach this conclusion by defining the Project not to include Project-related shipping.

The unjustified exclusion of Project-related marine shipping from the definition of the Project thus resulted in successive deficiencies such that the Board's report was not the kind of "report" that would arm the Governor in Council with the information and assessments it required to make its public interest determination and its decision about environmental effects and their justification. In the language of *Gitxaala* this resulted in a report so deficient that it could not qualify as a "report" within the meaning of the legislation and it was unreasonable for the Governor in Council to rely upon it. The Board's finding that the Project was not likely to cause significant adverse environmental effects was central to its report. The unjustified failure to assess the effects of marine shipping under the *Canadian Environmental Assessment Act, 2012* and the resulting flawed conclusion about the effects of the Project was so critical that the Governor in Council could not functionally make the kind of assessment of the Project's environmental effects and the public interest that the legislation requires.

I have considered the reference in the Explanatory Note to the Order in Council to the government's commitment to the proposed Action Plan for the Southern resident killer whale and the then recently announced Oceans Protection

Plan. These inchoate initiatives, while laudable and to be encouraged, are by themselves insufficient to overcome the material deficiencies in the Board's report because the "report" did not permit the Governor in Council to make an informed decision about the public interest and whether the Project is likely to cause significant adverse environmental effects as the legislation requires.

Notes and Questions

1. Dawson J.A. notes that "[b]ecause marine shipping was beyond the NEB's regulatory authority, it assessed the effects of marine shipping in the absence of mitigation measures and did not recommend any specific mitigation measures." She goes on to opine that it was only by excluding the effects of project-related marine shipping on orcas that the Project (as defined by the NEB) was not likely to cause significant adverse environmental effects. As she put it, the NEB "could only reach this conclusion by defining the Project not to include Project-related shipping".

2. What caused the NEB to commit the error in scoping discussed in *Tsleil-Waututh*? What was the nature of the error, and how did it compound over time? Having made the error, what steps could the NEB have taken to fix it before the matter proceeded to decision by Cabinet? What do you think of the argument made by Canada and Trans Mountain that the NEB substantially complied with its obligations under section 79 of SARA?

3. What lessons can be learned from *Tsleil-Waututh* about the relationship between SARA and federal environmental assessment? What lessons can be learned from *Tsleil-Waututh* and the other cases considered in this part as to the significance of SARA as a platform for public interest litigation?

Part V — Species Protection as a Governance Issue

Introduction

Biodiversity protection, and more particularly species protection, poses especially difficult challenges in federal states, where jurisdiction over key powers is divided between national and sub-national levels of government.

In this respect, as we have seen, the debates and tensions chronicled above in developing a federal endangered species law in Canada have parallels not only in the United States, but also in other federal states, such as Australia. While, on paper and in practice, our constitutional arrangements differ from those in the United States and elsewhere, our federal endangered species law departs (in many ways quite deliberately) from its US counterpart, SARA and ESA represent attempts to grapple with analogous governance-related issues.

This Part commences with some ruminations on the tensions between federalism and biodiversity from a leading American environmental law scholar.

We offer this excerpt to provoke discussion about the extent to which species protection may be inherently more difficult in a federation and, as such, must be viewed as a governance issue.

We then provide a brief overview of the state of endangered species protection at the provincial level. In this vein, we will canvass one of the founding principles of SARA, namely, its commitment to promoting species protection through a cooperative approach in which the federal, provincial and territorial governments are partners. Whether the commitment to cooperation, embodied in the 1996 *Accord for the Protection of Species at Risk* and reflected in bilateral agreements (that have been concluded between the federal government and most of its provincial and territorial counterparts pursuant to section 10 of SARA), is showing results is one of the key questions addressed in this section. We also consider the interaction between SARA and provincial land use decision-making processes, and examine the role, both in theory and in practice, of the SARA federal safety net power.

Federalism and Biodiversity

A. Dan Tarlock,
"Biodiversity Federalism"
(1995) 54 Md. L. Rev. 1315

Environmental protection policy is subdividing into two branches: risk minimization and biodiversity protection. Risk reduction is a difficult, if problematic, objective to accomplish because we have no reliable way to measure the magnitude of the risks that we are trying to minimize. However, this objective has been widely accepted as a legitimate public policy for the past twenty-five years. Risk prevention is consistent with the Western legal tradition because it seeks to prevent or redress human injury. Biodiversity protection on the other hand presents much more difficult problems of legitimacy and implementation within this tradition because it partially collapses the ethical dichotomy between humans and nature. As a result of scientific and popular alarm over species declines, the maintenance of biological diversity has rapidly emerged as a primary objective of both international and United States environmental law, because it provides a reasonably coherent and general principle of natural resources management.

However, the achievement of this objective remains highly contingent because biodiversity protection strategies pose greater challenges to existing legal institutions as compared with the reduction of air, water and land pollution risks. At bottom, the achievement of effective biodiversity protection is difficult because the very idea of biodiversity protection is antithetical to the Western idea of human economic progress through science, technology and the encouragement of individual initiative. These challenges vividly manifest themselves in the efforts to fit biodiversity protection into a federal system which seeks to promote values associated with economic progress.

This Article explores ongoing efforts to implement biodiversity protection programs within the United States federal system, although the problems are the same in analogous political systems such as Australia and Canada. Federalism problems are a subset of the much noticed fragmentation of biodiversity protection efforts both in the United States and other countries.

Biodiversity protection programs reflect the tension between the universality of the abstract justifications for the exercise of national power to promote this objective, and the inherently local or site-specific nature of the problems. Universal biodiversity protection goals may be easily articulated, but they cannot be applied across the board. The chief threat to biodiversity protection is habitat loss. Thus, the objective of any protection program is habitat conservation and restoration, rather than the regulation of industrial activities through the application of standard technology. As Edward O. Wilson has written, "[t]he primary tactic in conservation must be to locate the world's hot spots and to protect the entire environment they contain". In short, biodiversity protection requires strong land-use regulation and incentive schemes to induce the dedication of protected habitat, both of which are among the most difficult natural resources management or environmental objectives to achieve in a federal system.

None of the dominant models of federalism are suited to protect biodiversity or to describe the protection experiments underway. In fact, federalism principles are as likely to frustrate biodiversity protection as to promote it for three principal reasons. First, federalism is premised on the search for the optimum exclusive regulatory balance, and this can often frustrate necessary intergovernmental cooperation. Second, the maintenance of national protection floors supplemented by states is unworkable because in contrast to air and water pollution control, there are no uniform standards that one can realistically apply to biodiversity in states as different as Alaska, Arizona and Florida. Third, the national government must rely on powers [...] that are traditionally and firmly lodged within state and local governments.

This misfit is critically important to biodiversity protection because the main threat to achieving this objective is local resistance that may undermine national efforts. This statement simply reflects the long standing tension between national articulation of resource management goals and local efforts to promote unrestricted access to natural resources for economic exploitation. Although the tradition of local resistance to national conservation is well into its second century, the current manifestation of this tension is the wise-use movement which seeks to tie all regulation to statutory compensation in excess of that required under federal or state constitutional law. Innovative state and local attempts to promote biodiversity are driven by the need to comply with federal mandates, primarily the *Endangered Species Act*. But, despite the constitutional power of the national government to achieve this objective, federal mandates are perceived as intrusions on state and local sovereignty [...]

Biodiversity protection [...] does not mesh well with federalism for a number of reasons. The most important are: (1) federalism often impedes the protection of biodiversity because the political boundaries of the federal system do not match ecosystem boundaries; (2) many of the implementation problems involve conflicts among different federal agency mandates [...] (3) many of the constitutional values sought to be protected by federalism, specifically those protecting private property and individual liberty interests, are difficult to adapt to biodiversity protection; (4) federalism jurisprudence is neutral with respect to biodiversity maintenance and thus Supreme Court decisions and doctrines are as likely to hinder as promote it; and (5) the demands of biodiversity protection exceed the effective ability, as opposed to the constitutional authority, of the national government to achieve effective protection without state and local cooperation in the experiment.

Notes and Questions

1. To what extent, if at all, do you find Professor Tarlock's observations about the relationship between biodiversity and federalism relevant to the Canadian experience? If his arguments are generalizable beyond the US context, are some models of federalism (centralized vs. decentralized; various modes of allocating heads of power) more functional than others from a biodiversity protection perspective?

2. We return to some of these issues in Chapter 10, when we look at biodiversity in the context of climate change. Unmitigated climate change is expected to result in the extinction of a third of the species on the planet. A particular focus of Part IV of Chapter 10 is whether current species at risk legislation provides the necessary tools to protect species from the effects of climate change. The debate around the listing of the polar bear as an endangered species in Canada and the US illustrates some of the challenges: see Part IV of Chapter 10.

Species Protection Initiatives at the Provincial Level

Seven years before SARA came into force, the federal, provincial and territorial governments jointly committed to enhancing their respective efforts to protect endangered species under the auspices of the 1996 *Accord for the Protection of Species at Risk* (the "Accord"). Rhetorically, at least, it was on the faith that the provinces and territories were adhering to these commitments that the federal government took the position that a cooperative approach to species protection (with the provinces and territories taking the lead role subject only to federal intervention via the "emergency" and "safety net" order powers) should inform the design and operation of SARA.

Under the Accord, each government committed to implement 14 principles to ensure the survival of Canadian species at risk (SAR):

1. All non-domestic species covered.
2. Independent assessment of SAR status.
3. Legal designation of species as endangered/threatened.
4. Immediate legal protection for SAR.
5. Protection for habitat of SAR.

6. Time limits for completion of recovery plans that address threats to SAR and habitat.

7. Interjurisdictional cooperation for cross-border SAR recovery plans.

8. Consideration of needs of SAR as part of environmental assessment process.

9. Timely implementation of recovery plans.

10. Monitoring, assessing and reporting on status of all wild species.

11. Emphasis on preventative measures.

12. Improved awareness of needs of SAR.

13. Support for citizen conservation/protection.

14. Effective enforcement.

How effectively have the provinces and territories lived up to the expectations associated with this Accord? Environmental organizations claim that, by and large, the record has been bleak. In a 2012 report, extracted below, Ecojustice Canada undertook the task of grading Canadian governments in terms of species protection. The Government of Canada was assigned a grade of C-. Ontario received a C+; all of the other provinces and territories had lower marks and BC, Alberta and Saskatchewan all received failing grades. The report derived these grades based on the efficacy of four elements of the regimes being analyzed: the listing process, "take" protection, habitat protection, and recovery planning.

Ecojustice Canada,
Failure to Protect: Grading Canada' Species at Risk Laws
(Ecojustice, 2012)

Across the board, the provinces and territories are doing a poor job of protecting at-risk species

- Provinces like B.C. and Alberta, which do not have any dedicated species at risk legislation, failed outright while other provinces lost marks for failing to strengthen weak laws and implement on-the-ground protections.

- The end result is a patchwork of weak, inconsistent laws that do not have the jurisdiction to adequately protect species whose natural ranges stretch across borders (ex. boreal woodland caribou).

- Even governments that once set the bar for strong species laws — like Ontario — have fallen behind. In some cases, governments (Government of Canada, Ontario) are making moves to weaken existing laws, clearing the way for major industrial projects that will irreparably alter the forests and rivers endangered animals and plants need to survive.

The current conditions represent an opportunity for the federal government to provide leadership on the issue of protecting species at risk

- The federal government can lead by example, starting with fulfilling its responsibilities under SARA, namely its duty to produce recovery strategies that clearly identify the critical habitat it must protect to help endangered species survive and recover.

- Species protection cannot be left to the provinces and territories because they do not have the necessary tools to recover a species on their own.

- Without a national plan and strong federal legislation to coordinate conservation efforts, species with populations distributed across more than one province or territory will continue to fall through the cracks.

Notes and Questions

1. Review what the Ecojustice report says about species protection in your home province or territory. Do you agree with the analysis set out and the grade assessed?

SARA and Provincial Land and Resource Use Decision-making

Another intriguing question is the extent to which SARA is having a direct or indirect impact on the many decisions made each day by provincial resource and environmental permitting and licencing agencies. Has SARA, the Accord or provincial species protection legislation made any difference to these processes? Consider the following cases: the first from British Columbia (which has no provincial species protection law), and a second decision from Ontario (which enacted a new species protection law in 2007).

0707814 BC Ltd. v. British Columbia
(Assistant Regional Water Manager)
(2008), 34 C.E.L.R. (3d) 163 (B.C. Environmental App. Bd.)

[A provincial water approvals manager refused an application by a developer to infill a wetland in a ravine near a suburban area on the basis that it would negatively impact the habitat for several species at risk, including the Redlegged Frog (a SARA-listed species of concern) and the Oregon Forestsnail (a SARA-listed endangered species). The developer revised and resubmitted the application, which was again refused. Under both applications, the habitat of the species, and the species occupying the ravine, would be destroyed.]

The Revised Application proposes to infill the ravine which means that the habitat, and the species there at the time, will be eliminated. In terms of gravity and magnitude of harm, there are few things that could be worse: the magnitude and gravity of the harm is at the most severe end of the scale. The Appellant argues, however, that the answer is really not this simple. It submits that there is a bigger question to be answered first. That is, would the species at issue in this case persist if the ravine and Ravine Pond were left in their current state? More specifically, if the Revised Application is not granted, would those species survive in any event? If they would not persist on the property, the Appellant argues that this should change the amount of weight they are to be given in the context of the application. If they will not survive anyway, why should the Revised Application not be granted?

The Appellant submits that, based on the most credible evidence, those species at issue in this case will not persist. It maintains that the evidence shows that there are too many threats to their habitat already. It submits that the only way to ensure the species have some reasonable chance of survival is to grant its application and impose conditions to protect the most suitable habitat for them: the Ravine Pond [...]

This has been a very difficult question for the Panel. The Panel's findings were particularly difficult in relation to the Oregon Forestsnail, already listed as endangered federally, as well as the Red-legged Frog. While there was some discussion about attempting to capture and relocate some of these species to other locations, the Panel finds that this is not a feasible option for most of the species involved, although salvage on the property may be feasible for some.

Like many areas of science, predicting whether a species will persist is not an exercise in certainties. When considering the ravine and Ravine Pond in their current state, and predicting what will happen to those habitats in the future, the Panel is relying on "best guesses", based on the best available evidence.

Regarding the need for further study, the Panel finds that this is not the appropriate case to make such an order. Even assuming that good habitat exists in the ravine and the Ravine Pond there is no question that threats to these species' survival already exist at the site:

- the site is not pristine,
- it is surrounded by developments,
- further development directly north of the property may occur, and more are planned up the mountain, and
- there is already evidence that at least part of the subject property is used regularly by the public.

The property is an oasis in an urban landscape.

The Panel finds that the presence of threats to the persistence of these species does not mean that they will not, or cannot, persist despite these pressures. However, in the present case, the pressures are simply too overwhelming for the Panel to have any confidence that, without the protection proposed by the Appellant, any of the species, except for the Pacific Waterleaf, is reasonably likely to persist. With the protection around the Ravine Pond, at least some will have a better chance of persisting on the property.

Unfortunately, the *Water Act* is not meant to deal with land use issues. The Participants submit that what is needed in this case is to actively protect the ravine and the Ravine Pond. The Participants state:

> Once a species is listed nationally as endangered, threatened, or special concern, or provincially as red or blue, trends need to be reversed if its path on the road to extinction (from special concern to threatened to endangered to extirpated to extinct) is to be stopped and eventually reversed. Further, it is important to implement protections as early as possible on this path, namely at the special concern (or blue) stage, rather than waiting for the problem to approach crisis proportions, namely threatened and beyond.

The Panel agrees with this statement. However, the *Water Act* is an inadequate tool to address the problems for the species on this property. Unfortunately, the protection of these species in this area needed to have occurred some time ago in order to ensure the continued survival of a viable population.

In this regard, the Panel finds that although the site is a functioning ecosystem now, [...] it is no longer one of "high value". The Participants are correct that, despite the surrounding development, the species are still on the property. However, the Panel finds that the property is too cut-off from other viable populations and natural habitat. All of the experts agree generally that isolation of the site affects the quality of the habitat for the species resident there, and that development of portions of the site and surrounding area would further fragment and isolate this habitat. Thus, the species' habitat is being degraded, and more is expected.

Therefore, based on all of the evidence, the Panel finds that, with the exception of the Pacific Waterleaf, the species identified are not likely to persist in the ravine and Ravine Pond without help. That help is not coming from the City, as it is the City that is making the road a condition of development approval. As the City states in its closing submissions, "ironically, the way to protect the environment of this compromised site is to allow the application and protect the wetland and adjacent area through a covenant".

Given all of the evidence, the Panel finds that the Revised Application will not have an irreparable impact on the species at risk identified in this case.

[**Ed. Note:** In the result, the appeals were allowed and the development was permitted to proceed with conditions.]

Guelph (City) v. Soltys
(2009), 45 C.E.L.R. (3d) 26 (Ont. S.C.J.)

GRAY J.: — It is likely that most citizens will not have heard of the Jefferson Salamander. As it happens, the Jefferson Salamander is a "threatened species", within the meaning of the *Endangered Species Act, 2007*. The issue before me is what effect, if any, this has on the right of the City of Guelph to proceed with the development of a project known as the Hanlon Creek Business Park.

Background

The City of Guelph and Belmont Equity (HCBP) Holdings Ltd. are the owners of about 271 hectares of land, bordered, in part, by Downey Road, Forestell Road and Hanlon Parkway, in the City of Guelph. It is bisected, from east to west, by Laird Road. The plaintiffs intend to develop these lands as a corporate and industrial business park. [...] All necessary assessments, approvals, certificates and permits to develop Phase 1 of the park have been obtained. An environment impact study was completed in August, 2000. Further environmental impact studies have been done. Approximately $20 million has been spent on the project so far.

In the past, the lands had been used for agricultural purposes. There are areas of uncleared forest and wetlands, and a tributary of Hanlon Creek runs through the property. As part of the approved draft plan of subdivision, a roadway will be built that crosses the creek. The creek crossing will be by way of a culvert that crosses the creek in an east-west direction. Due to time constraints, the culvert must be built first, with the rest of the infrastructure for Phase 1 of the project to follow. The culvert is likely to take six weeks to build, and the plaintiffs suggest that it must be completed on or before September 15, 2009. It is said that if this date is missed the entire project must be delayed at least one year.

In early 2009, the City was contacted by individuals who expressed concern about environmental issues regarding development of the park. Some of these people belonged to a group called Land Is More Important Than Sprawl (LIMITS). One of the main supporters of LIMITS is the defendant Matthew Soltys. Representatives of the City had a number of discussions with Mr. Soltys about environmental issues relating to the park. The City has had other meetings, including participation in a public forum.

On April 20, 2009, a dead hybrid salamander was discovered along Laird Road, within the park. This specimen was collected and provided to Dr. James Bogart at the University of Guelph. Dr. Bogart has provided an affidavit in these proceedings. There is no doubt that he is eminently qualified to discuss issues surrounding the Jefferson Salamander; indeed, from 2002 to the present, he has been Chair of the Jefferson Salamander Recovery Team (Canadian Species at Risk).

In the spring of 2009, the City retained Natural Resource Solutions Inc. (NRSI) to provide an opinion on the existence of the Jefferson Salamander on the property. NRSI performed various tests, and, in substance, has concluded that it is likely that the habitat of the Jefferson Salamander does not exist within the vicinity of the location where it is proposed that the culvert be installed.

The information regarding the finding of the dead salamander, and other information in the City's possession, has been shared with the Ministry of Natural Resources. The Ministry's recommendation has been that development of the road that will cross the creek, and the building of the culvert, be postponed due to the unknown location of Jefferson Salamander breeding points on the property. Dr. Bogart identified the dead salamander as an LJJ unisexual salamander, that exists with Jefferson Salamander and uses that species for reproduction. Dr. Bogart has expressed the view that it is very difficult to document the absence of breeding in particular ponds, especially when the individual salamanders are few in number. Because the majority of LJJ females remain within 800 metres of a breeding pond, the particular breeding pond is expected to be within an 800 metre circumference of the collected specimen [...]

With leave, Dan Hagman was called to give *viva voce* evidence. He is the Guelph District Manager of the Ministry of Natural Resources. He is familiar with the project, has visited the site, and is familiar with the issue involving the Jefferson Salamander. He testified that no formal approval of the MNR is required to proceed with the work, and that the MNR has taken no formal steps to prevent the work being done. He testified that the City has been working with the MNR in an attempt to address the Jefferson Salamander issue. The MNR's preference is that work on the culvert, and the road leading up to it, be suspended until further study has been done regarding the habitat of the Jefferson Salamander in the area. However, he recently attended a meeting in which it apparently was acknowledged that the City would proceed with the culvert work. When asked how this is consistent with the MNR's view that the work should be suspended, he said the MNR did not have the power to issue a stop work order under s. 27 of the *Act* because a regulation had not been promulgated defining the area of habitat of the Jefferson Salamander.

Commencing on or about July 27, 2009, a number of individuals, including the defendants, entered the property and shut down construction of the culvert. Some of these people wore bandanas and sunglasses that hid their facial features. Demands that they leave the property have been ignored. Since that date, the blockading has continued, so that the contractor retained by the City has been unable to do any work on the culvert and the roadway leading to it.

The plaintiffs bring this motion for an injunction, effectively to restrain the defendants from trespassing on the lands and impeding the construction activities. In opposition to the plaintiffs' injunction, the defendants have filed a number of affidavits, including one from Mr. Soltys. It is fair to observe that in many of the affidavits complaint is made about the development itself, and the overall impact on the environment, rather than any specific complaint about the impact on the Jefferson Salamander. However, by the time the matter was argued before me, counsel for the defendants had narrowed his argument to the impact that the proposed development, and specifically the creek crossing, may have on the habitat of the Jefferson Salamander. Shortly before the argument of the plaintiffs' motion, counsel for the defendants served a separate motion for an injunction, to restrain the plaintiffs from continuing construction activities, based on the potential impact of those activities on the habitat of the Jefferson Salamander.

Submissions

Counsel for the plaintiffs submits that an injunction should issue, restraining the defendants from trespassing on lands owned by the plaintiffs, and from impeding lawful construction activities on those lands. Counsel for the plaintiffs submits that the well-known tests for an interlocutory injunction, discussed in *R.J.R. MacDonald Inc. v. Canada (Attorney General)*, [1994] 1 S.C.R. 311, have been satisfied. Under those tests, the plaintiffs must show:

(a) that there is a serious issue to be tried;

(b) that the plaintiffs will suffer irreparable harm if the injunction is not granted; and

(c) the balance of convenience favours the plaintiffs.

Counsel for the plaintiffs submits that where the conduct complained of consists of trespass to property owned by the plaintiff, the tests in (b) and (c) are less important. In essence, a property owner is *prima facie* entitled to an injunction where trespass occurs, even if the plaintiff cannot demonstrate irreparable harm. Reliance is placed on Sharpe J.A.'s text, *Injunctions and Specific Performance* (Canada Law Book, 2001), Chapter 4, and *Hamilton (City) v. Loucks* (2003), 232 D.L.R. (4th) 362 (Ont. S.C.J.).

Counsel for the defendants asserts that the defendants do not intend to continue their occupation of the property. However, counsel submits that if I determine that an injunction in favour of the plaintiffs is appropriate, I should only issue such an injunction, prohibiting the defendants from trespassing or blocking construction, on condition that the plaintiffs are themselves enjoined from engaging in any construction activities, for a reasonable period, that may interfere with the habitat of the Jefferson Salamander, and specifically suspend construction of the culvert over the creek. A reasonable period, in counsel's submission, would be for the duration of the anticipated breeding season, which would run until mid to late fall, 2009. Mr. Gillespie submits, in the alternative, that if I am not persuaded that I should enjoin the plaintiffs in the context of their injunction motion, I should grant the defendants an injunction in the same terms, based on the motion for an injunction that they have brought themselves.

Counsel for the defendants submits that I should have regard for the "precautionary principle", which, simply put, contemplates that where there is a threat of a significant reduction or loss of biological diversity, lack of full scientific certainty should not be used as a reason for postponing measures to avoid or minimize such a threat. Reliance in this respect is placed on *114957 Canada Ltée (Spraytech, Société d'arrosage) v. Hudson (Town)*, [2001] 2 S.C.R. 241, at paras. 31 and 32. In this case, the Jefferson Salamander is clearly recognized as a threatened species, as contemplated in the *Endangered Spec[ies] Act, 2007*. Since a dead salamander was discovered within the lands slated for development, and close to the location of the creek crossing, it is a virtual certainty that breeding grounds for the salamander are somewhere within the park. Just because it is presently unknown where those breeding grounds are is not sufficient reason to decline to take steps to avoid the potential destruction or interference with the habitat of the Jefferson Salamander. To fail to do so would be directly contrary to the precautionary principle. Mr. Gillespie notes that Dr. Bogart is of the view that up to three years may be required in order to adequately investigate the matter, and he asserts that an injunction lasting until the end of the breeding season in 2009 would be entirely reasonable in the circumstances.

Mr. Gillespie submits that if construction is allowed to continue, and it develops that breeding grounds have been destroyed as a result, that consequence is irreversible. Any delay in pursuing the construction of the works is, in the circumstances, a small price to pay.

Mr. Gillespie acknowledges that, in the context of the motion for an injunction brought by the defendants, it will be necessary for the defendants to persuade me that they should be granted standing to pursue their injunction as public interest litigants, since they have no personal interest in the matter above that of any other member of the public. However, Mr. Gillespie asserts that, in the circumstances, the defendants satisfy the requirements for granting them standing as public interest litigants.

In reply, counsel for the plaintiff submits that, whether it is done as a condition to the plaintiffs' injunction, or as a separate injunction granted to the defendants, the plaintiffs should not be restrained in continuing their construction activities, specifically the construction of the culvert at the creek crossing. Mr. Bordin submits that the defendants do not qualify as public interest litigants. Further, it is submitted that the Minister of Natural Resources, and her Ministry, are charged with the responsibility of enforcing the *Endangered Species Act, 2007*. The plaintiffs have cooperated with the Ministry, and are continuing to work with the Ministry to proceed carefully with the construction activities, so that any habitat of the salamander can be discovered at the earliest opportunity, and means can be taken to ameliorate any potential damage. While it is the Ministry's preference that construction of the culvert be postponed until further study can be done, most recently the Ministry has signalled its acceptance of the construction of the culvert, provided it is done carefully and in consultation with the Ministry.

Mr. Bordin submits that the enforcement mechanisms conferred on the Ministry and the Minister under the *Act* are exclusive, and accordingly the Court is deprived of jurisdiction to grant an injunction to the defendants, even if they are granted standing as public interest litigants. Since the Minister and/or the Ministry have not issued orders under the *Act*, the Court should not do so.

Analysis

I will consider the matter in two stages. First, I will consider whether the plaintiffs should be granted the injunction they seek, to prevent trespassing and interference with the construction activities in the park. Second, I will consider the defendants' request for an injunction to restrain the plaintiffs from continuing construction activities, at least for some period. In my view, the plaintiffs must be granted an injunction to restrain trespassing and interference with construction activities. Fundamentally, the defendants have no right to take the law into their own hands. If the defendants believe that they have the right, either on their own behalf or as public interest litigants, to stop the plaintiffs from developing the park or any aspect of it, their proper course is to apply to the Court for relief. Belief in the rightness of one's cause does not confer any right to bypass the courts and do what one pleases. The courts look with disfavour on self-help of this nature [...]

For the foregoing reasons, an Order will issue, restraining the defendants and any person having notice of the order, until trial or other final disposition of the action, from engaging in the conduct described in paragraphs 4(a), (b) (c), (d) and (e) of the plaintiffs' Notice of Motion. In addition to the named defendants, it is best to specifically make the order applicable to "any person having notice of the Order". Because contempt proceedings can be brought against non-parties in any event, it is better to add this sort of terminology to avoid confusion: see *MacMillan Bloedel Ltd. v. Simpson*, [1996] 2 S.C.R. 1048.

That brings me to the defendants' motion for an injunction. I do not intend to entertain the defendants' request for injunctive relief within the context of the plaintiffs' motion. I doubt that, as a condition of granting an injunction to the plaintiffs, I could grant a corresponding injunction to the defendants. However, even if I could, I am not prepared to allow the defendants to do so as a convenient way of allowing them to sidestep the requirement that they establish their right to pursue an injunction as public interest litigants. If the defendants are entitled to injunctive relief, they must persuade me that they are entitled to such relief in the context of their own motion. As part of the analysis, I must consider whether they should be granted standing as public interest litigants.

In order to succeed in obtaining an interlocutory injunction, the defendants must satisfy the three-part test discussed in *R.J.R. MacDonald, supra*. I do not see why the issue of public interest standing cannot be considered as part of the requirement to show that there is a serious issue to be tried. If the moving parties can show that there is a serious issue to be tried as to whether they qualify as public interest litigants, that may be sufficient to justify an interlocutory injunction, depending on the circumstances. If it is necessary for me to make a final determination as to whether the defendants qualify as public interest litigants in this case, for the reasons discussed hereafter I conclude that they do, at least for the purpose of the very limited injunction that I will be granting, and having regard to the reasons I will be granting it.

Fundamentally, the defendants argue that it is necessary to grant an injunction in order to preserve the ability to determine whether the construction activities will adversely impact on the habitat of the Jefferson Salamander. In order to appreciate the defendants' submissions, it is necessary to have regard for certain of the provisions of the *Endangered Species Act, 2007* [...] Certain of the provisions of the *Act* require comment.

First, it is apparent from the Preamble to the *Act*, and from the purposes of the *Act* described in s. 1, that the policy reflected in the *Act* is considered, by the legislators, to be of importance. The balance of the *Act*'s provisions are considered to be those that are necessary to carry the important principles of the *Act* into effect.

Second, the term "habitat" has both a geographical and non-geographical · component. Where a regulation has been made defining a specific area, that area is deemed to be the habitat of the species in question. However, where no such regulation is made, the area is undefined, and is simply defined as "an area on which the species depends, directly or indirectly, to carry on its life processes, including life processes such as reproduction, rearing, hibernation, migration or feeding."

Third, the Jefferson Salamander is specifically defined, by statute, as a threatened species.

Fourth, it is clear that, while the destruction or damage of habitat of an endangered or threatened species is prohibited, wherever it may occur, the treatment of habitat for enforcement purposes before the making of a regulation defining the habitat's area is different. The combined effect of s. 10(1) and (3) of the *Act* is to create a prohibition on the damaging or destruction of habitat, but to suspend that prohibition until a regulation defining the area is made, subject only to the power of the Minister of Natural Resources to make a stop work order in some circumstances. That becomes clear when one examines the enforcement provisions [...]

To paraphrase, these provisions authorize the Minister to make an order requiring a person to stop engaging in an activity if that person is about to engage in an activity that is destroying or is about to destroy or seriously damage an important feature of an area used as habitat, even if s. 10(3) would otherwise neutralize the prohibition in s. 10(1). Thus, the statutory scheme of enforcement is complete: an enforcement officer can make a stop work order if a regulation defining the area of habitat is in force, and if there is no such regulation, the Minister can make an order pursuant to the terms of s. 28. Section 30 of the *Act* provides an opportunity for the holding of a hearing, but it is noteworthy that the requirement for the hearing does not stay the order.

Where the Legislature has specified a tribunal having jurisdiction to adjudicate matters of a specified nature, it is generally understood that the jurisdiction of such a tribunal is exclusive, and the jurisdiction of the ordinary courts is ousted. This is particularly so where the jurisdiction of the tribunal is defined under the specific statute under which the rights being adjudicated are created or governed: see *Seneca College v. Bhadauria*, [1981] 2 S.C.R. 181; and *Weber v. Ontario Hydro*, [1995] 2 S.C.R. 929.

In this case, as part of the public policy considerations reflected in the substantive provisions of the *Act* itself, the Legislature has chosen to confer enforcement powers on the Ministry of Natural Resources and, in some respects, on the Minister. Specifically, the Minister has power to determine the very matter in issue in the defendants' motion for an injunction: namely, whether work on the project should be stopped, and if so, to what degree and for how long, because of some anticipated negative impact on the habitat of the Jefferson Salamander.

The Minister can make that assessment on an ongoing basis, and is in a much better position to assess the competing policy considerations, as well as legal considerations, than is the Court. Thus, in my view, the Court is deprived of jurisdiction to grant an injunction.

An exception to the general principle exists where it is sought to enjoin an activity until the statutory tribunal can exercise the statutory decision-making power: see *Brotherhood of Maintenance of Way Employees Canadian Pacific System Federation v. Canadian Pacific Ltd.*, [1996] 2 S.C.R. 495.

In this case, Mr. Hagman testified that the Ministry's preference is that work on the culvert, and the road leading up to it, be suspended until further investigation can be done as to the habitat of the Jefferson Salamander. When asked why a stop work order has not been made, he testified that one could not be issued because a regulation defining the area of habitat has not yet been made. To this extent, Mr. Hagman's evidence is consistent with s. 27(1), which limits the power of an enforcement officer to make an order to those circumstances where a regulation defining the area of habitat has been made.

There is no evidence before me, however, that the Minister has even considered making an order under s. 28 of the *Act*. If the construction activity commences immediately, it may prevent, or at least seriously limit, any opportunity for the Minister to consider making such an order.

In this context, the defendants have satisfied the three-part test for an injunction, at least to allow the Minister to make a decision one way or the other. If necessary, I will grant standing to the defendants as public interest litigants for this purpose: see *Finlay v. Canada (Minister of Finance)*, [1986] 2 S.C.R. 607. There is obviously a serious question to be tried, at least by the Minister, as to whether a stop work order should be issued. If the injunction is not granted, the work is commenced, and habitat is destroyed, the harm will be irreparable. I am persuaded that the balance of convenience favours an injunction of short duration.

It is for the Minister to decide whether the circumstances are such that an order under s. 28(1) of the *Act* is justified, and if so, whether her discretion should be exercised to grant one. She may decide that the informal monitoring by the MNR is sufficient. These considerations are for the Minister, and it is not for the Court to usurp the Minister's authority. The residual jurisdiction of the Court to grant injunctive relief should be sparingly exercised, and should be exercised in aid of, rather than in substitution for, the jurisdiction of the Minister.

I will grant an injunction to prevent any further work on the culvert and the road leading up to it for a period of up to 30 days. That will give the Minister enough time to decide whether she will make an order pursuant to s. 28 of the *Act*. If the Minister issues an order under s. 28, or if she signifies, in writing, that she does not intend to issue such an order, my order will terminate. If the Minister does nothing, my order will expire 30 days from today.

I am not persuaded that the deadline for finishing the culvert work, said to be September 15, 2009, is immutable. I expect that, if necessary, the work can be speeded up, or the City can live with an extension of the deadline, or both. If that is not the case, and it turns out that the project must be delayed for a year, so be it. The policies enshrined in the *Endangered Species Act, 2007* must prevail in these circumstances.

Part VI — Emerging Perspectives on Species and Biodiversity Protection

In this concluding section we canvass three issues that are relevant to charting the course ahead. The first issue is one that is increasingly taking centre stage in species at risk discussions: the relationship between Indigenous rights and species protection. To this end, we have extracted from submissions prepared by the Maritime Aboriginal Peoples Council. This publication, offered as a critique of SARA, identifies some gaps in Canada's species at risk legislation, and proposes a new approach(es) to ensure Indigenous perspectives are considered alongside western science.

A second set of issues concerns whether, and to what extent, a focus on protecting species, particularly "special species", may need to be rethought. Doremus argues that the dominance of this approach, particularly in the US context, has had a variety of unintended and unfortunate consequences for biodiversity protection. In an innovative and provocative article, she argues that governments need to tackle biodiversity protection using a much broader suite of regulatory instruments and approaches than have been deployed to date.

A third set of issues pertain to the relationship between protected areas and enhancing species protection. A key assumption of the traditional approach to species protection is that, in large measure, the solution lies in setting aside habitat areas as protected reserves. But just how effectively is our current network of protected reserves functioning to protect species? New research into this question, by Deguise and Kerr, has generated some interesting conclusions, which suggest that the relationship between protecting areas and protecting species may not be as straightforward as might be assumed. Like Doremus, they conclude that while establishing protected areas is part of the answer, securing long-term species protection on a national scale will require a broader, more integrated conservation strategy that incorporates agricultural and urban land-use planning outside of formally protected areas.

Joshua E. McNeely & Roger J. Hunka,
Policy Critique of the Draft Species at Risk Act Overarching Policy Framework: Perspectives for the Improvement of the Government of Canada's Implementation of the Species at Risk Act
(Truro Heights, NS: Maritime Aboriginal Peoples Council, 2011)

Foundational Elements & Guiding Principles

[...]

SARA and Aboriginal Peoples

Specifically for the relationship between the Government of Canada and the Aboriginal Peoples of Canada, SARA's legal requirements can be considerably complex. Compounding the issue is the continued reluctance by the Government of Canada to grasp and adopt a paradigm shift as called for by the CBD [*Convention on Biodiversity*], and especially those articles of international law requiring recognition and reconciliation with Indigenous Peoples, respecting the diversity of Indigenous Peoples within UN member States.

During the Bill C-5 discussions, the Aboriginal Working Group realized that full SARA implementation would be difficult, if not impossible, without a specific Aboriginal Peoples and Government of Canada collaborative working accord. Bill C-5 readings in the House of Commons intermittently included elements of consultations and Aboriginal advisory groups, but did not elaborate. The Aboriginal Working Group expressed a lot of concern with the Bill C-5 text. The language did not fully grasp the needs or requirements of Aboriginal Peoples or the responsibilities of Canada under Treaties, the Constitution, and court dicta to recognize, consult, accommodate, and reconcile with the Aboriginal Peoples of Canada. It was evident, given Canada's track record and the mistrust between Aboriginal Peoples and governments, that an additional national framework agreement or accord was needed, beyond SARA, which could be used to implement SARA with the Aboriginal Peoples of Canada — an accord similar to the federal/provincial/territorial National Accord, which eases the ability for those governments to work together, as the Government of Canada, on species at risk.

In 2001, before SARA became law, the Aboriginal Working Group agreed that a national accord between Aboriginal Peoples and the Government of

Canada was necessary as an umbrella document to clarify, find common ground, and set requirements and priorities for each of the parties. Through consultations, five National Aboriginal Organizations agreed upon a draft "national Aboriginal accord" under the CBD, CBS [*Canadian Biodiversity Strategy*], and the soon to be passed SARA.

The draft Aboriginal accord was founded on guiding principles which reflected the growing international call for governments to make available to Aboriginal Peoples mechanisms and tools to allow Aboriginal Peoples to meaningfully participate in national decision-making and at the same time to protect their knowledge, innovations, practices, cultures, languages, etc.

Under the draft Aboriginal accord the Government of Canada and Aboriginal Peoples would have adopted guiding principles and commitments to:

- fully engage the governments of Aboriginal Peoples in decision-making,
- assist Aboriginal Peoples to build capacity,
- actively cooperate with Aboriginal Peoples,
- give full and equal consideration to scientific knowledge and ATK [Aboriginal Traditional Knowledge], and
- provide sufficient funding to fully enable such commitments.

The draft Aboriginal accord also raised three key administrative and implementation requirements, as fundamental and a point of departure, for the meaningful involvement of Aboriginal Peoples in the implementation of SARA:

- ongoing consultation with affected Aboriginal Peoples throughout the SARA cycle,
- establishment of a national council of Aboriginal Peoples to advise governments on SARA implementation and administration, and
- establishment of a committee of ATK-holders to ensure ATK was considered and accepted in SARA.

If these five guiding principles and three implementation requirements could have been embodied in an Aboriginal accord between Aboriginal Peoples and the Government of Canada, Aboriginal Peoples would have been assured a comprehensive mechanism, with tools, guidance, support, and requisite Government of Canada and Aboriginal leadership, to allow for the meaningful interchange and relevant input to support the many aspects of SARA. Sadly, the draft Aboriginal accord was rejected by the federal government; which puts into question Canada's ability to fully implement SARA with the meaningful involvement and participation of the Aboriginal Peoples of Canada.

Although the suggested elements of: consultation with Aboriginal Peoples, the establishment of an Aboriginal Peoples ministerial advisory body on the implementation of SARA, and the inclusion of ATK were accepted into SARA, they are extremely limited, when considering that there are over seventy-three Aboriginal Nations of Aboriginal Peoples throughout Canada. A few members of an advisory committee, at best can only speak on behalf of their respective Aboriginal Nation or from the knowledge they have acquired from their respective traditional homeland. Likewise, ATK is not a homogenous, all inclusive knowledge — it is as specific and diverse as the people who hold the ATK.

Even so, these elements are a beginning step. Unfortunately, many obstacles have slowed, confused, or even halted the implementation of these. For example, NACOSAR [National Aboriginal Council on Species at Risk] does not have control over its own administrative budget or, frequently, its own agenda. It does not even have an office or telephone. Administration of NACOSAR is controlled by EC [Environment Canada] public servants, and thus the Minister of Environment (he[re]after referred to as "the Minister") is sheltered through several layers of bureaucracy, preventing NACOSAR from gaining direct access to advise the Minister. NACOSAR contracts a coordinator from time to time who is left to try to operate out of any office they can find. The role of NACOSAR is not respected or understood by Government of Canada officials. NACOSAR members (NACOSARians) are viewed to be persons who can provide answers on the minutia of all things Aboriginal, even to provide opinions on ATK, proposed species listings under SARA, and much more. NACOSAR does not have the funds and is not allowed the flexibility to undertake the vital work it needs to accomplish so that it can advise the Minister and provide advice and recommendations to Canadian Endangered Species Conservation Council (CESCC), such as undertaking studies and submitting independent findings directly to EC, DFO [Department of Fisheries and Oceans Canada], PCA [Parks Canada Agency], or CESCC on the obvious problems with the implementation of SARA.

The ATK-SC [Aboriginal Traditional Knowledge Subcommittee established under s. 18(1) of the SARA], instead of being a body to provide advice on the use of ATK throughout the SARA process, is instead a body of COSEWIC [Committee on the Status of Endangered Wildlife in Canada]. This restricts or requires the ATK-SC to conform to certain COSEWIC scientific independence norms and processes. While these norms are necessary for COSEWIC to maintain credibility among the rigorous scientific community, they have proved problematic for the ATK-SC in maintaining credibility among some authoritative ATK-holders. It has been shown that COSEWIC western scientific norms cannot effectively bridge the two sciences of western science and Aboriginal science. There is a need for a *Two-Eyed Seeing Approach** to be allowed to grow and advance to bridge the two sciences and consider the two sciences, for a fuller understanding of the true nature of biodiversity.

---

* The advancement of the *Two-Eyed Seeing Approach* is largely accredited to Mi'kmaq Elder Albert Marshall to advance our collective (Aboriginal Peoples and non-Aboriginal Peoples) understanding about the natural world. *Two-Eyed Seeing* recognizes that both ATK and western science have valuable insights and contributions toward understanding the natural world. However, each is also limited in certain aspects. For example, benefits include: for ATK, a long-term and eco-system based knowledge; and for western science, an ability to conduct controlled testing to achieve repeatable results. Drawbacks include: for ATK, a subjectivity of the ATK-holder to time and place; and for western science, the inability to grasp many cause and effect relationships existing simultaneously within a large living eco-system. The approach of *Two-Eyed Seeing* is to recognize that each "science" is different and cannot be directly compared to the other; but a person who understands both "sciences" has a more holistic and more realistic view, better than what either "science" can capture on its own.

One good measure to begin the path toward a *Two-Eyed Seeing Approach* is to allow the ATK-SC full independence from COSEWIC norms and procedures; and at the end bring both ATK findings from the ATK-SC and scientific findings from COSEWIC together, with equal consideration, to formulate decisions about species at risk. Currently, lack of full ATK-SC independence from COSEWIC has the result of again subjugating ATK to be less than western knowledge.

As for SARA consultation, it has occurred at different levels within different regions, at different times. For example, some Aboriginal organizations or groups that have pre-existing relationships with the federal government, such as through the DFO Aboriginal Aquatic Resources and Oceans Management initiative or PCA park programs, there is evidence that SARA consultation has improved between some Aboriginal organizations and some federal government departments over the years. There is also some evidence of more detailed consultation with some Aboriginal Peoples on SARA proposed listings, recovery strategies, action plans, and management plans. However, for many Aboriginal Peoples across Canada, SARA is still something of an unknown and far from their sights, even after eight years since SARA was assented. There are many reasons for this. Most noticeably looming is that, to date, there is no overarching federal policy as to consultation, accommodation, reconciliation, and compensation for Aboriginal Peoples. There is no federal policy on consultation with Aboriginal Peoples about SARA, despite the explicit requirements in SARA for the federal government to undertake extensive ongoing consultations with Aboriginal Peoples throughout the SARA cycle.

Aboriginal Peoples continue to bring up the deficiencies that hinder or block their involvement in the many aspects of the administration or implementation of SARA. Without a framework agreement to advance fundamental principles like: *engender direct action, responsibility, multi-jurisdictional recovery, multi-party involvement, key role of teams, adaptive management, retain process flexibility, time frame for actions, focus on appropriate scale, socio-economic values, optimize resource use, and evaluate success* toward reaching *the conservation of biological diversity, the sustainable use of its components, and the fair and equitable sharing of benefits arising from the use of genetic resources*, Aboriginal Peoples have found over the past few years that their participation in SARA has been very fragmented, misunderstood, a passing thought, and in many cases limited to some small one-time projects, which are heavily impeded, scrutinized, and subject to the focused priorities of the responsible authority's funding system.[...]

Closing Views

With the release of the Canadian Biodiversity Strategy in 1995, Canada proclaimed that

> We are no longer planning and making decisions based exclusively on a species-by-species or sector-by-sector basis, but are practising ecological management.

The Aboriginal Peoples of Canada know what it means to "practice ecological management" — ultimately it is to recognize that humankind is an interconnected and interdependent part of the natural world, not a conqueror of nature. "Ecological management" is about managing human practices, as a part of the surrounding natural ecology, so that the natural world is respected and preserved. Under the eco-centric worldview humankind receives the gifts of life; it does not take for profit and power.

For a new governance model in Canada, proposed by the CBS, that requires changes in thinking, changes in values, and changes in practices. Those can only be achieved by all Canadians coming together to share and learn with the Aboriginal Peoples of Canada (the holders of traditional knowledge about Canada's vast biodiversity), and together plan for a better future for biodiversity and for Canadians, as part of that biodiversity.

Unfortunately, we still do not see any evidence that Canada is in a new era of ecological management or governance. The necessary invitation is not extended to include Canadians and Aboriginal Peoples to protect and become involved in saving an integral part of their "national identity and heritage" — i.e., wildlife in all its forms and all its habitats throughout the vast diverse eco-systems of Canada, where each and every single animal and plant has value in and of itself and is valued by all Canadians. How can there be "ecological management" when the single largest management element, the work and ethics of people, is left out?

SARA recognizes that the machinery of government cannot or has not accepted the value of considering the conservation and sustainable use of biodiversity to be equal or greater than exploration and exploitation for profit. For this reason, SARA specifically requires certain legal actions, as the minimum, to assess, protect, and recover species at risk and critical habitats.

SARA also includes many opportunities to look at and address the deeper and more important issues in Canada that ultimately result in destruction of habitat and endangerment of species. If the opportunities presented in SARA are utilized, to advance SARA as Canada's flagship for the implementation of the CBD, then Canada can use SARA to weave a fabric of protection and respect for our natural world and Canadian[s'] place within, a much greater protection than afforded through the legal measures of SARA.

Unfortunately, we see the federal government obsessed with the former and not active or even addressing the possibilities of the latter, as evidence[d] by the draft Policy Framework. SARA struggles alone, crawling inch-by-inch, against an overwhelming tide of "Business as Usual".

Notes and Questions

1. What do you think about the "two-eyed seeing" approach? Will this always be possible? How is Aboriginal traditional knowledge recognized in SARA decision-making, or how can it be?

2. To what extent are SARA decision-makers under an obligation to consider or prioritize Indigenous understandings of species at risk? Can western science and Indigenous knowledge systems work in synergy? What is the role of law in this context?

3. Recent analysis conducted by researchers at Carleton University corroborates the submissions of the Maritime Aboriginal Peoples Council that the

involvement of Indigenous peoples in the administration and implementation of the SARA has been severely limited and deficient. In a study published in 2019, Hill *et al.* examined recovery strategies and management plans on the SARA registry published between 2006 and 2017, and assigned a score to each document based on the extent of Indigenous involvement that took place as part of the process culminating in the document's formation. The researchers excluded documents pertaining to species that are not present on Indigenous lands and where Indigenous involvement was declined by the affected Indigenous groups themselves. Troublingly, the researchers found that 52% of the approximately 250 documents examined contained no indication of any Indigenous involvement at all, despite a legal requirement to do so: see SARA paragraphs 66(1)(d) and 39(1)(d). Documents pertaining to species in central Canada and Quebec showed significantly lower involvement than in other regions. Documents pertaining to mammals and marine species tended to include more Indigenous involvement than those involving reptiles, amphibians and plants. Finally, Indigenous involvement was demonstrably less for documents coordinated by Environment and Climate Change Canada than those coordinated by Parks Canada and by Fisheries and Oceans Canada. These findings suggest systemic failure by federal agencies to properly cooperate with affected Indigenous communities in the preparation of recovery strategies and management plans despite the express legislative requirement under the SARA. See also Cassandra J. Hill, Richard Schustera and Joseph R. Bennett, "Indigenous Involvement in the Canadian Species at Risk Recovery Process" (2019) 94 Envt'l Sci. & Pol'y 220.

Holly Doremus,
"Biodiversity and the Challenge of Saving the Ordinary"
(2002) 38 Idaho L. Rev. 325

Both scientists and policymakers today tout the goal of protecting biodiversity, understood to encompass the range of biotic resources. Ecologists and conservation biologists wholeheartedly endorse biodiversity protection. It is enshrined [in the mandates and policies of many federal agencies]. The protection of biodiversity has even been enshrined as a goal of international law, through the adoption of the *Convention on Biological Diversity*. Of course, as a society we are still arguing vociferously about how much biodiversity to protect, what costs we are willing to bear in the name of biodiversity, and how to divide those costs. My point is only that we seem, at least on the surface, to have a strong consensus at the policymaking level that biodiversity protection is an important goal.

Unfortunately, our dominant strategy for achieving that goal remains one developed in another era for different purposes. As we did in the earliest days of conscious nature protection, we continue to concentrate on setting aside special places and protecting dwindling special resources against exhaustion. Given today's conditions, that strategy is not likely to achieve our current goal of protecting a wide range of biotic resources over a long period of time. If we are to succeed in protecting biodiversity, we must find ways to focus the law and the public on ordinary nature rather than merely the obviously special or unique aspects of nature.

Conventional Criticisms of Current Strategies for Biodiversity Protection

We have recognized for some time that our current strategies for nature protection are not well suited to saving biodiversity. We have not yet acknowledged, however, that the root problem is our focus on the special. Instead, critics have focused on the way we identify the special elements of nature on which our strategies concentrate. Two frequently repeated criticisms of the ESA illustrate this point. The first is that biodiversity protection could be accomplished more efficiently and effectively if we emphasized the protection of ecosystems, biodiversity hot spots, or more carefully selected focal species. The second is that we delay taking protective action until it is nearly, and perhaps entirely, too late.

Protection of individual endangered species through the ESA is not effectively protecting the range of biodiversity. At first, this may seem surprising. The ESA, which is framed as a safety net for all plant and wildlife species, should in theory be capable of protecting biodiversity which, after all, equates at least roughly to the sum of all species. Indeed, the ESA should be a very sensible mechanism for biodiversity protection, covering all plant and animal species but concentrating our efforts on those in most dire need of our immediate attention. In reality, however, as the critics point out, only the most extraordinarily special species, and only those special in a very particular way, are actually helped by the ESA. Only those species with significant public appeal or tenacious human advocates are able to run the gauntlet of the ESA's listing process. Of those species that do make it to listing, a handful of the most charismatic, not necessarily the most threatened or ecologically critical, receive the bulk of the resources put into species recovery.

By interpreting specialness differently, perhaps we could use individual species more effectively as surrogates for biodiversity. It has been suggested that by setting our species protection priorities carefully, concentrating on indicator, keystone, and umbrella species, we might wind up protecting far more than the relatively small number of species that become listed. Indicator species are supposed to reflect the health of the larger ecosystem, so that by ensuring their health we ensure that of the ecosystem. Keystone species are thought to be especially important contributors to community structure, so saving them should keep the community intact. Umbrella species are those that require extremely large ranges; their protection, it is hoped, will guarantee that of many smaller-range species. Alternatively, critics suggest that we should shift our focus to protecting key ecosystems, or "hotspots" — locations that harbor unusually high levels of biodiversity.

Conservation advocates have deliberately chosen the strategy of the special for its political appeal. Threats to special places and special things attract attention and can motivate people to action. Even those who seek much more than protection of individual charismatic species have concentrated on that strategy, expecting, or at least hoping, that the political appeal of the most special places and species could be leveraged to achieve the larger goal of biodiversity protection. Our experience so far under the ESA, though, counsels to the contrary. Protection of the special has not proven an effective strategy for saving the ordinary.

Indeed, it may not be possible to use special locations or species as effective surrogates for larger systems. Ecologists have found it difficult to define the keystone concept or identify species that fit it, and umbrella species now appear far less useful than we once thought.

Even if it were possible to leverage conservation of the right set of individual species or the right collection of reserves to protect biodiversity, by adopting the strategy of the special we almost ensure that we will not choose our protected set to achieve that particular goal. Our experience to date validates this claim. We have shown little or no inclination to set our species protection priorities with a view toward biodiversity protection. When we demand that entities qualify for protection by being sufficiently special, we should not be surprised that the most charismatic or symbolically appealing species end up first in line. For species to be chosen on the basis of their ability to stand in for biodiversity protection, we would need to convince the public that biodiversity itself is special.

That is difficult to do because biodiversity is so abstract, and so ordinary. Human beings simply are not wired to care about, or even to notice, the ordinary. We cannot attend to everything that competes for our attention. We have therefore developed a variety of filtering mechanisms to help us focus effectively on some things by more or less shutting out others [...]

It is therefore much easier to convince people to take action to save whales, wolves, or other specific, eye and imagination-catching creatures, than it is to persuade them that they must act to save nature as a whole, or biodiversity, which is nearly the same thing [...]

The strategy of the special predisposes us, perhaps even unconsciously, to focus our efforts on government-owned lands in particular and on setting aside nature reserves in general. It almost inevitably leads us to see nature as something apart from our daily lives. That, in turn, is likely to doom our efforts to save a broad range of nature [...]

The strategy of the special sends us to the public lands because those lands, and only those lands, are already special in our cultural understanding. Unlike privately-owned lands, public lands are supposed to be dedicated to some vision of the public good.

The importance of private lands for biodiversity protection poses a challenge for biodiversity advocates because our background assumption is that private lands are not particularly special. We seem culturally ingrained to assume that landowners are entitled to control their lands in most respects, including the extent of accommodation they choose to make for nature. Of course some landowners choose to dedicate their land to nature protection, and even seek out and acquire lands for the express purpose of biodiversity protection. [...] Landowners assume that they are or should be free to use their land in virtually any way they please, so long as other people are not directly injured by that use. Because that assumption is widespread and politically powerful, the effort to impose the kinds of regulatory controls on land use that are essential to biodiversity protection faces particularly formidable institutional barriers. That kind of change to the legal status quo must be supported by an appealing focal point, something special enough to rally the needed political support.

The law also needs focal points for effective implementation [...] [these] focal points need not be the places or things we are protecting. Instead of trying to craft a single "magic bullet" biodiversity law, we might be better off with a patchwork of federal, state, and local law focusing on things, places, and activities that affect biodiversity. We might well find that the sum of those disparate parts is greater protection than we could hope to get from any one law.

Our portfolio of biodiversity protection should include regulation that proscribes, limits, or establishes prerequisites to those activities that predictably pose a threat to biodiversity. Habitat degradation, for example, results from: air and water pollution; water diversion and storage; residential, commercial and industrial construction; extractive industries such as mining, silviculture, and agriculture; and recreation, among other activities. Regulating all of those activities seems like a tall order, but in fact many of them already are subject to some kind of federal, state, or local regulation. The trick with respect to those activities is to ensure that biodiversity considerations are adequately factored into existing regulatory schemes. That is a political problem, not an institutional one. We can take biodiversity into account if we are sufficiently motivated to do so.

Broad geographic regions can also provide useful focal points for the law [...] Protecting biodiversity means keeping nature ordinary, and for that we need planning efforts that cover most of the landscape, not just isolated hotspots.

Local land use regulation, which has developed institutions for long-range area-wide planning applicable to a wide range of activities, has an important role to play in our biodiversity protection efforts. However, because of the need for coordination and a broader vision, balkanized local regulation is not likely to be effective. Multi-jurisdictional regional plans are needed.

In addition to regulations applicable to specific activities that pose special threats to biodiversity, effective biodiversity policy probably requires implementation of a large-scale planning approach applicable to all or nearly all lands. Our planning efforts should be devoted to protecting biodiversity, or as I would prefer to say, protecting nature, broadly, not just in limited locations.

The biodiversity problem sharply highlights the challenge of saving the ordinary. We are naturally drawn to the strategy of the special, but that strategy does not work to protect biodiversity, which is the entire tapestry of nature. In order to save biodiversity, we must find institutional focal points other than special places and special creatures. That is not trivial, but it can be done with some creativity.

We can use human activities and geographic regions, for example, as focal points for law. The tougher challenge is building the political support to limit human actions, saving some room on the planet for nature. That requires the development and maintenance of emotional connections to ordinary nature.

Notes and Questions

1. To what extent does Doremus's argument resonate in the Canadian context? Do we tend to value "charismatic mega-fauna" over more humble and anonymous creatures and, if so, has this skewed public policy? Or do the sagas of the Spotted Owl and Nooksack Dace suggest other conclusions?

2. The following article, like the preceding one, speaks powerfully to the need for a more integrated and holistic approach to biodiversity protection.

**Isabelle Deguise & Jeremy Kerr,
"Protected Areas and Prospects for Endangered
Species Conservation in Canada"**
(2006) 20 Conservation Biology 48

To be effective, reserve networks must be able to ameliorate the effects of factors that threaten species with extinction, which have been well studied. In the United States, habitat loss is a primary cause of species endangerment. Similarly [...] land-use conversion to agriculture was the best predictor of numbers of endangered species in Canada. Introduced species and urbanization have also caused the decline of many species. Overhunting, even in the absence of serious land-use changes, is believed to be the primary threat to more than one-third of World Conservation Union (IUCN) red-listed mammals and birds. These and other threats can act additively, act synergistically, or interact unexpectedly to deplete biodiversity.

Reserve networks represent one of the leading strategies for reducing extinction rates. The gap between the potential utility of reserves and their actual contribution, however, is sometimes substantial, largely because relatively few reserves have been designated specifically to conserve biodiversity. Many species cannot maintain viable populations even within some of the largest reserves ever established [...]

As human activities continue to expand into remaining wilderness areas, the need to establish protected areas in areas where they are most needed becomes progressively more acute. In Canada, where permanent land use changes are still relatively concentrated and extensive wilderness areas persist, protected-areas networks are considered critical to the protection and recovery of endangered species and are integrated into new endangered species legislation (*Species at Risk Act 2002*). Many of Canada's endangered species are also threatened in the United States, and conserving peripheral populations of these species is particularly important for their long-term survival.

We used new data on endangered species and protected areas in Canada to address two questions. First, given the distribution of terrestrial endangered species within each of Canada's fifteen ecozones, how effectively does the existing reserve system include endangered species relative to randomly situated reserves? Second, we tested for a relationship between patterns of species endangerment and the extent of protected areas across Canada. A significant proportion of the world's remaining wilderness is in Canada, so measurements of the effectiveness of biodiversity conservation strategies there could inform conservation planning for the world's remaining wilderness frontiers. [...] [**Ed. Note:** More information about Canada's ecozones can be found online: <https://ccea.org/ecozones-maps/>.]

Among Canada's ecozones, existing reserve networks most commonly included no more endangered species than expected by chance. In the most seriously degraded ecozone, the Mixed Wood Plains, randomly generated reserve networks included more endangered species than expected by chance. This area is the most densely populated in Canada, includes extensive urban and agricultural land uses, has the greatest concentration of endangered species, and is for many taxa the most diverse region in the country. There were also many endangered species in the Montane Cordillera, where the existing reserve network included fewer endangered species than any randomly generated network. Land uses that inhibit reserve establishment in this ecozone include extensive forestry activities and agriculture, which are concentrated in the south.

The benefits of reserves in the most threatened regions of Canada are limited by their small size: mean reserve size in Canada declined sharply as numbers of endangered species per ecozone increased.

Areas with the highest diversity are now dominated by agricultural land uses, which makes it difficult to establish new reserves or expand existing, small reserves. Similar patterns of skewed reserve distributions have been found across the Western Hemisphere. Canada's *Species at Risk Act* provides little additional habitat protection in areas with the largest numbers of endangered species (and therefore the smallest reserves), although it promotes cooperative conservation measures in these areas of mostly privately owned land. These efforts have not yet been widely implemented and their effects cannot yet be evaluated.

Species in some northern ecozones (e.g., Taiga Shield and Boreal Cordillera) were included in existing reserves relatively completely, although there were few endangered species in these areas and low species richness overall [...] Even in Canada's wilderness areas, however, reserve systems in three ecozones (Arctic Cordillera, Taiga Plains, and Hudson Plains) included significantly fewer endangered species than expected by chance.

Reserve networks in Canada might include unexpectedly few endangered species for two reasons. First, endangered species are concentrated in areas with extensive human land use, clearly inhibiting reserve establishment or expansion. This cannot explain why reserve networks in ecozones consisting predominantly of wilderness include fewer endangered species than expected by chance (although land claims and traditional land uses by aboriginal Canadians influence reserve placement). A second reason for poor reserve performance, however, is that protected areas have simply not been established to protect biodiversity. National parks, for example, are intended to maintain areas for the "benefit, education and enjoyment" of Canadians (*National Parks Act 2000*). It is only in the later *Species at Risk Act* that an endangered species protection role is firmly established for national parks.

Cordillera, and even some ecozones that lack extensive permanent human land uses, protected areas networks alone are unlikely to provide effective endangered species protection in Canada.

Conservation activities outside reserves, especially efforts that involve private landowners, should be a high priority. Tax incentives and conservation easements may prove effective in this respect and would reduce the land-use conflicts that would arise from — and probably scuttle — efforts to establish large protected areas in the midst of privately held lands. Even had existing reserve networks included more endangered species than expected by chance, reserve area is far smaller in areas with many endangered species. Thus, we emphasize the importance of distinguishing between inclusiveness and effectiveness. The small reserves in ecozones with many endangered species are unlikely to maintain viable populations of most endangered species. Even species that can reach high population densities (e.g., invertebrates) in small reserves cannot be reliably conserved in such areas [...] Integrating conservation into agricultural and urban land-use practices will be critical for reducing the loss of species in Canada given the wide gap between the effectiveness of reserves and the needs of endangered species.

Notes and Questions

1. Do the findings reported above surprise you? What implications or lessons do they offer for species protection policy-makers? What about for policy-makers working in the realm of parks and protected areas?

2. See Chapter 8 for excerpts from an article that discusses the concept of tribal parks and similar initiatives aimed at providing Indigenous communities with the means to protect species at risk and their habitats as well as culturally significant sites: Carol Linnitt, "How Indigenous Peoples Are Changing the Way Canada Thinks About Conservation", The Narwhal, 10 March 2018, online: <https://thenarwhal.ca/how-indigenous-peoples-are-changing-way-canada-thinks-about-conservation/>.

References and Further Readings

J. Benidickson, *Environmental Law*, 5th ed. (Irwin Law, 2019)

D.R. Boyd, *Unnatural Law: Rethinking Canadian Environmental Law and Policy* (UBC Press, 2003)

David Suzuki Foundation, "Left Off the List: A Profile of Marine and Northern Species Denied Listing under SARA" (Vancouver, 2007)

I. Deguise & J. Kerr, "Protected Areas and Prospects for Endangered Species Conservation in Canada" (2006) 20 Conservation Biology 48–55. Copyright 2006, Society for Conservation Biology. Reproduced with permission of Blackwell Publishing Ltd.

H. Doremus, "Biodiversity and the Challenge of Saving the Ordinary" (2002) 38 Idaho L. Rev. 325

Ecojustice Canada, *Failure to Protect: Grading Canada's Species at Risk Laws* (Ecojustice, 2012)

Ecojustice Legal Defence Fund, "Species at Risk" (2006), Citizen Submission SEM-06-05 to the Secretariat of the Commission on Environmental Cooperation, online: <http://www.cec.org/citizen/submissions/details/index.cfm?varlan=english&ID=114>.

S. Elgie, "The Politics of Extinction: The Birth of Canada's Species at Risk Act" in D. Van Nijnatten & R. Boardman, eds., *Canadian Environmental Law and Policy*, 3rd ed. (Oxford University Press, 2009)

S. Elgie, "Statutory Structure and Species Survival: How Constraints on Cabinet Discretion Affect Endangered Species Listing Decisions" (2009) 19 J. Envtl. L. & Prac.

C.S. Finlay, S. Elgie, B. Giles & L. Burr, "Species Listing under Canada's Species at Risk Act: A Follow-up to Mooers *et al.*" (2009) 23 Conservation Biology 1609

C.J. Hill, R. Schustera and J.R. Bennett, "Indigenous Involvement in the Canadian Species at Risk Recovery Process" (2019) 94 Envt'l Sci. & Pol'y 220

J. Kunich, "Preserving the Womb of the Unknown Species with Hotspots Legislation" (2001) 52 Hastings L.J. 1149. Copyright 2001 by University of California, Hastings College of the Law. Reprinted from Hastings Law Journal, Volume 52, Number 6, 2001, by permission.

J.E. McNeely & R.J. Hunka, *Policy Critique of the Draft Species at Risk Act Overarching Policy Framework: Perspectives for the Improvement of the Government of Canada's Implementation of the Species at Risk Act* (Truro Heights, NS: Maritime Aboriginal Peoples Council, 2011)

A. Mooers *et al.*, "Biases in Legal Listing under Canadian Endangered Species Legislation" (2007) 21 Conservation Biology 572

A.O. Mooers *et al.*, "Science, Policy, and Species at Risk in Canada" (2010) 60 BioScience 843

B.H. Powell, "A Comment by the Environmental Law Centre on the Use of Compensation under the Proposed *Species at Risk Act*" (2000) 10 J. Envtl. L. & Prac. 283

H.I. Rounthwaite, "A Theory of Compensation under the *Species at Risk Act* Bill C-5" (2000) 10 J. Envtl. L. & Prac. 259

K. Smallwood, *A Guide to Canada's Species at Risk Act* (Vancouver: Sierra Legal Defence Fund, 2003)

A.D. Tarlock, "Biodiversity Federalism" (1995) 54 Md. L. Rev. 1315

D. Tuytel & M. Venton, *Challenges in Receiving SARA Protections: A Killer (Whale) Case Study*, Symposium on Environment in the Courtroom: Enforcement Issues in Canadian Wildlife Protection (Calgary: Canadian Institute of Resources Law, University of Calgary, 2018)

P. Wood & L. Flahr, "Taking Endangered Species Seriously? British Columbia's Species-at-Risk Policies" (2004) 30 Can. Pub. Pol'y 382

Chapter 10

Climate Change

Introduction

This chapter serves a dual role. It provides an opportunity to review some of the key themes explored in the previous chapters and to apply them to what is arguably the greatest environmental, economic, social and political challenge of our time: climate change. It also explores, in a preliminary way, the future of environmental law through the example of climate change.

The chapter is divided into five Parts. We start in Part I with the international realm, offering a review of the evolution of international initiatives dating back from the negotiation of the *United Nations Framework Convention on Climate Change* (UNFCCC) in 1992 to the most recent report of the Intergovernmental Panel on Climate Change (IPCC) in 2018. In Part II we consider how constitutional division of powers shapes governmental options for responding to climate change as a policy issue. To this end, we first consider the federal and provincial heads of power that are relevant to this question, then analyze some existing federal and provincial climate law and policy regimes, and finally compare the pros and cons of two key climate policy instruments: cap-and-trade and carbon taxes. In Part III, we consider the interplay between climate law and litigation processes. Increasingly, climate issues are ending up in court. In this Part we look at recent and pending cases arising in four distinct litigation settings: (a) judicial review and statutory appeals, (b) challenges relating to the division of powers, (c) tort litigation and other common law claims, and (d) climate litigation under the *Canadian Charter of Rights and Freedoms*. In Part IV, we consider how climate change is influencing and reshaping environmental law in other ways: in particular, by driving the law reform agenda in relation to environmental assessment and species at risk. We conclude in Part V by exploring the future of environmental law in light of the challenges that climate change will present in the years ahead.

Part I — The International Context: United Nations Efforts on Climate Change

The global human imprint on the climate is increasing. This trend appears doomed to continue, as global efforts to curb emissions show few signs of coming into line with scientific observations and predictions, which, in turn, have become more alarming with every passing year. As global greenhouse gas (GHG) emissions and resulting concentrations in the atmosphere continue to increase, polar regions are feeling the effects first. Canada, therefore, has reason to be particularly concerned about the impacts of climate change.

In every comprehensive assessment since 2007, the Intergovernmental Panel on Climate Change (IPCC) has concluded that deep emission reductions by all countries will be needed to have a reasonable chance of avoiding the runaway climate change scenarios that are associated with increases of global temperature of 2°C or higher. In order to keep the door open to preventing runaway climate change, the IPCC suggested emission reductions in the range of 25-40% below 1990 levels by 2020 by developed countries in combination with reductions of about 15% below business as usual from key developing countries in the same timeframe. The proposed total effort is based on the best science available in 2007, whereas the allocation of effort between developed and developing countries and within each group of countries is based on certain assumptions of what is an equitable burden sharing. Much deeper cuts would have to follow between 2020 and 2050.

As briefly discussed in Chapter 1, global efforts to address climate change have been under way since 1988. Major steps in the United Nations efforts on climate change include the following:

- establishment of the IPCC in 1988, with full assessment reports on the science released in 1990, 1995, 2001, and 2007;
- negotiation of the *United Nations Framework Convention on Climate Change* (UNFCCC) in 1992;
- entry into force of the UNFCCC in 1994;
- negotiation of the *Kyoto Protocol* in 1997;
- entry into force of the *Kyoto Protocol* in 2005;
- the first commitment period of the *Kyoto Protocol* from 2008 to 2012;
- agreement to a second commitment period under the *Kyoto Protocol* to run from 2013 to 2020;
- negotiation of the *Paris Agreement* in 2015;
- entry into force of the *Paris Agreement* in 2016.

The origins of the international climate change regime can be traced back to a series of United Nations General Assembly resolutions adopted in the late 1980s. These resolutions, signed at the UN Earth Summit at Rio de Janeiro in 1992, resulted in the negotiation of the UNFCCC, which entered into force in 1994, establishing the architecture for subsequent climate change agreements. The General Assembly resolutions also resulted in the establishment of the IPCC to give scientific and technical advice to negotiators and policy makers. Since 1990, the IPCC has prepared five comprehensive assessment reports on the state of the science of climate change, each at critical junctures of the development of the climate change regime as well as, on request, more focused reports on issues ranging from land use change and forestry issues to carbon capture and storage, and, in 2018, on the 1.5°C target.

Kyoto Protocol

The first substantive agreement following the UNFCCC was the *Kyoto Protocol*, negotiated in 1997. Upon its entry into force in 2005, it became the heart of the international climate change regime. It established the first binding emission reduction targets for each of the "developed countries" listed in Annex 1 of the UNFCCC from 2008 to 2012, the first commitment period.

At the heart of the *Kyoto Protocol* are greenhouse gas emission reduction targets for developed states. Each Annex I country is given a combined emission reduction target for the six gases covered in the *Kyoto Protocol*. The target is relative to emissions in that country in 1990 and is presented in tons of carbon dioxide equivalent (CO_2e) emissions. This emission reduction target is then translated into emissions permits assigned to each Annex I country for the commitment period. The first commitment period ran from 2008 to 2012, and the second commitment period from 2013 to 2020. The permits issued in line with the emission reduction targets for each commitment period are called assigned amount units (AAUs).

Paris Agreement

In 2015, after a decade of complex and often divisive negotiations, the global community agreed to a successor to the *Kyoto Protocol* in the form of the *Paris Agreement*. The *Kyoto Protocol* is not expected to continue after 2020. The *Paris Agreement*, initially expected to come into force in 2020, entered into force in record time in 2016 with the speedy ratification of many key Parties including the US, Canada and the European Union. However, US President Trump has since announced his intention to withdraw from the *Paris Agreement*.

Among the key elements of the *Paris Agreement* are collective long-term goals, nationally determined contributions to the collective goals to be set by each Party, five-year review cycles of progress in implementing individual efforts toward the collective goals, reporting, compliance and support, and a commitment to increase ambition as part of the five-year review cycles to ensure the collective long-term goals are met. This section offers a brief overview of these elements.

The first of the key elements of the *Paris Agreement* is its set of long-term goals. The objective of keeping global average temperature increase to "well below" 2°C, and the aspiration to limit this increase to 1.5°C, are at the heart of the *Paris Agreement*. The temperature goal is supplemented with a commitment to ensure emissions peak as soon as possible and decline rapidly thereafter to reach a balance of emissions and removals in the second half of the century. Arguably, 1.5°C has now become the ultimate standard against which the success of collective mitigation efforts under the UNFCCC will be measured, and it seems clear that GHG emission neutrality will have to be reached in most countries well before 2050 to meet the temperature goal. This ambitious set of long-term goals provides an important foundation for each State's future nationally determined contributions (NDCs), their justification on the grounds of equity, and the five-year cycles of NDC communication and the Global Stocktake (the requirement for Parties to periodically "take stock" of the *Paris Agreement's* implementation). Over time, as the IPCC completes its scenario work, the "well below 2°C" and "1.5°C" goals can be expected to shape further discussions on elements of the long-term ambition, such as specific time frames for the expressed need for global emissions to peak as soon as possible, the rate of decline in emissions thereafter, and a clear date for reaching a balance of emissions and removals.

The long-term temperature goal also provides important context for other key elements of the *Paris Agreement*, particularly adaptation and finance.

Meeting the long-term mitigation goal is an essential precondition for successful adaptation efforts, and finance in turn is critical for meeting both the mitigation and adaptation goals of the *Paris Agreement*. Important connections are made to poverty eradication, human rights and sustainable development. Through the process for the Global Stocktake under Article 14, the long-term goal articulated in Article 2 is expected to become the ultimate guide for the implementation of the *Paris Agreement*.

The starting point in the *Paris Agreement* is the overall effort on mitigation, adaptation and finance, largely represented by the individual NDCs measured against the long-term temperature goal but supplemented by efforts outside the UN climate regime, such as efforts of the International Maritime Organization (IMO), the International Civil Aviation Organization (ICAO) and initiatives under the ozone regime to eliminate the use of hydrofluorocarbons (HFCs). Parties recognized in Paris that the initial NDCs would not add up to an adequate collective effort in light of the long-term goal. NDCs are therefore to be strengthened every five years starting in 2020, informed by the 2018 Talanoa Dialogue (the facilitative dialogue under the UNFCCC on ways to increase ambition), and then every five years starting in 2025, following a global stocktaking exercise carried out two years before each updated NDC is due. The *Paris Agreement* offers guidance on how Parties are to determine the adequacy of their NDCs with respect to mitigation.

Article 4.1 of the *Paris Agreement* provides that Parties will aim to reach global peaking of emissions as soon as possible, and to undertake rapid reductions thereafter on the basis of science and equity. Parties recognize that it will take longer for developing country emissions to peak, putting pressure on developed countries to accelerate their emission reductions to achieve a global peaking as soon as possible. Parties are to achieve a collective balance between emissions and removals of GHG from the atmosphere in the second half of the century, suggesting that GHG concentrations should stabilize and start to decline sometime after 2050.

These provisions offer some clarity on the scale and allocation of mitigation efforts and create a number of procedural obligations, but they provide neither a method for determining appropriate NDCs for individual Parties, nor a legal obligation to fully implement NDCs and meet targets set. Notably, the long-term mitigation goals are framed in technology-neutral language and thereby leave open how much specific technologies, from renewable energy to carbon capture and storage and the enhancement of sinks, should contribute to the effort. The additional guidance for Parties on what is expected of them takes on added significance as the Paris Outcome (*i.e.*, the *Paris Agreement* and accompanying UNFCCC decision) explicitly recognizes that there is an ambition gap between commitments made by Parties to date and the long-term goal. The ambition gap is quantified in Decision 1/CP.21 to be upward of 15 gigatonnes by 2030.

The *Paris Agreement* affirms the importance of the enhancement and conservation of sinks, and specifically mentions forests in this context. The *Paris Agreement* confirms that international emissions trading and other market mechanisms are acceptable tools for Parties to meet their emission reduction goals, as long as they serve to increase the level of ambition. The *Paris Agreement* sets out general principles for the use of market mechanisms, such as the avoidance of double-counting, environmental integrity, robust accounting and transparency. The *Paris Agreement* also makes provision for non-market approaches to assist Parties with the implementation of their NDCs.

The transparency rules apply to all Parties, with some modest differentiation, mainly through a commitment to flexibility and support for developing countries. For all Parties, the information they submit will be subject to a technical expert review and a multilateral, facilitative consideration of progress. Importantly, flexibility with respect to transparency is specifically linked to capacity, not to the broader concept of Common But Differentiated Responsibilities and Respective Capabilities (CBDR-RC). Special accommodations are included for the Least Developed Countries (LDCs) and Small Island Developing States (SIDS). Transparency is a focus of capacity-building efforts under the *Paris Agreement*, a signal that developed State Parties are motivated to help build capacity in developing countries in order to minimize differentiation on transparency.

The *Paris Agreement* signals the intention to build on and enhance transparency arrangements under the UNFCCC, including national communications, biennial reports and update reports, international assessment and review, and international consultation and analysis. It specifically calls for more regular and comprehensive reporting, a more harmonized verification process, and common modalities, procedures and guidelines. The *Paris Agreement* offers a surprising level of detail on accounting and reporting in the 15 paragraphs of Article 13. This is further supplemented with specific references to transparency in key provisions on mitigation, adaptation, finance and capacity-building.

The establishment of a five-year review and ambition cycle, including the Talanoa Dialogue in 2018 and the Global Stocktake process starting in 2023, constitutes another core element of the overall effort to ensure the goals of the *Paris Agreement* are met through the collective efforts of Parties in cooperation with other regimes. The Global Stocktake set out in Article 14 covers mitigation, adaptation, means of implementation and support. The first Global Stocktake is to take place in 2023, in time for the revision of Parties' NDCs by 2025. The goal of the Global Stocktake is to enhance both national action and international cooperation. The Talanoa Dialogue, an initial stocktaking process among Parties initially called the "facilitative dialogue", took place in 2018 and served as a first experiment with this review and ambition cycle under the *Paris Agreement*.

The compliance mechanism is to be facilitative, non-adversarial and non-punitive in nature and applies to all Parties. The compliance committee is to consist of 12 members with relevant technical expertise, with membership determined in a manner similar to the facilitative branch of the compliance committee under the *Kyoto Protocol*. The committee is directed to be sensitive to national capabilities and circumstances of Parties in carrying out its work.

The transparency provisions with respect to Parties' implementation of their NDCs, in combination with the Global Stocktake and the compliance system, are at the heart of the process put in place under the *Paris Agreement* to ensure progression of individual and collective ambition toward the long-term goal. The basic elements are in place in the form of Articles 13 to 15, and they appear sound. However, at the time of writing, the rules had yet to be implemented. The success of the transparency, review, stocktaking and compliance approach in the *Paris Agreement* in increasing ambition sufficiently to meet the long-term goal will ultimately depend on many factors outside the purview of the new climate regime, most notably the economic, political and social circumstances in key State Parties.

"Rapid and Far-reaching Transitions"

On October 8, 2018, the IPCC released a special report on the impacts of global warming of 1.5°C above pre-industrial levels, and efforts that the international community must make in order to avert such warming. Under the *Paris Agreement*, Parties commit to an aspirational goal of limiting the increase in global temperatures to within 1.5°C. The report presents a sobering picture of the state of the climate change impacts and an urgency with which we must act to avoid runaway climate impacts.

According to the IPCC, there is a high confidence that human activities have caused approximately 0.8°C to 1.2°C of global warming from pre-industrial levels, and that global warming is likely to reach 1.5°C between 2030 and 2052 if the current trend continues. Anthropogenic emissions since pre-industrial times to the present already in the atmosphere will continue to cause warming and other long-term impacts for centuries to millennia.

The report compiles the latest scientific information and predicts adverse impacts on human and environmental systems that may be avoided if the world can limit global warming to 1.5°C rather than 2°C. For example, extreme weather conditions such as heavy precipitation or drought are predicted to be more serious and intense at 2°C of warming than at 1.5°C. Global mean sea level rise by 2100 is predicted to be lower with warming of 1.5°C compared to 2°C. Adverse impacts on biodiversity and ecosystems are also predicted to be lower at 1.5°C of warming. Climate-related risks to health, livelihoods, food security, water supply, human security and economic growth are predicted to be more severe at 2°C of warming. Finally, the IPCC predicts that most adaptation needs will be lower at 1.5°C of warming.

Perhaps the most crucial data in the report are the IPCC's conclusions regarding emissions pathways. In order to avoid global warming of more than 1.5°C, carbon dioxide emissions in particular must decline by about 45% below 2010 levels by 2030, and reach net zero around 2050. This means that the global community must achieve sharp emissions reductions within the next decade, and that by 2050 any remaining carbon dioxide emissions must be balanced globally with carbon dioxide removal technology. The IPCC recognizes that achieving the goal of limiting global warming to 1.5°C requires "rapid and far-reaching transitions in energy, land, urban and infrastructure (including transport and buildings), and industrial systems." This transition would have to be "unprecedented" in scale and would require "deep emissions reductions" across all sectors.

So far, the global community has not stepped up to the task. According to the IPCC report, the NDCs that Parties have submitted under the *Paris Agreement* would not be sufficient to avoid global warming of 1.5°C. In fact, based on the current NDCs, the world is heading towards warming of over 3°C by 2100.

_____

With this background, we can now consider the jurisdictional, political and policy issues that arise in connection with the potential steps that Canada — as well as provinces and territories — may take to implement our international climate commitments.

_____

Part II — Jurisdictional, Political and Policy Issues in Climate Law

In this Part, we review how the constitutional division of powers shapes governmental options for responding to climate change as a policy issue. To this end, we first consider the federal and provincial heads of power that are relevant to this question. Next, we explore existing legal and policy responses, focusing on developments at the federal level. In the notes following that section, we also briefly touch on policy responses in BC and Ontario as examples of what provinces have been doing. Finally, we consider the pros and cons of two key climate policy instruments: cap-and-trade and carbon taxes.

_____

Climate Change and Division of Powers

Recall in Chapter 3 that we discussed the topic of jurisdiction over the environment through the lens of division of powers. As a federal system, the federal and provincial governments share and divide jurisdiction among them over various subject-matters in accordance with the Canadian Constitution. Both levels of government have a role in regulating in relation to climate change. What is less clear is how these overlapping jurisdictions can be reconciled.

In the excerpt that follows, Professor Chalifour analyzes the scope of federal jurisdiction in this area. It is followed by an article by Professors Hsu and Elliot that considers provincial jurisdiction.

_____

Nathalie J. Chalifour,
"Canadian Climate Federalism: Parliament's Ample Constitutional
Authority to Legislate GHG Emissions through Regulations, a
National Cap and Trade Program, or a National Carbon Tax"

(2016) Nat'l J. Const. L. 331

[Before discussing federal constitutional powers, the author introduced three federal policy options that the article will examine: (a) federal spending and investments, (b) carbon pricing such as carbon tax or a cap-and-trade program, and (c) GHG regulations.]

[...] Readers of this journal will know that the environment is not an enumerated subject assigned to either the federal or provincial government in the

Constitution. Authority to legislate on environmental issues is shared between both levels of government, depending on the dominant purpose of particular legislation. For instance, under their authority over property and civil rights, provincial land, natural resources, and other powers, the provinces legislate in respect to the water, air, waste and wildlife within their boundaries. Under its powers over fisheries, international borders, trade, navigation and shipping, criminal law and the Peace Order and Good Government [POGG] power, the federal government legislates on matters such as fisheries, species at risk, toxic substances and the transportation of dangerous goods.

The federal government's current GHG regulations are enacted under the rubric of the *Canadian Environmental Protection Act (CEPA)*, which essentially regulates pollution. GHGs were added to Schedule I of *CEPA* in 2005, thereby enabling the government to pass regulations pertaining to GHG emissions under *CEPA*'s authority. In the 1997 *Hydro-Québec* case, the Supreme Court upheld provisions of *CEPA* as being valid federal legislation under the criminal law power. This makes it quite likely that additional regulations restricting GHGs under *CEPA* would be constitutionally valid under the criminal law power, though constitutionality will always depend on the dominant purpose of a given provision. It is also not a foregone conclusion that the federal government would choose to enact further climate policies under the rubric of *CEPA*. It may wish to enact a national climate law incorporating a number of provisions, or enact provisions under other existing statutes (such as tax legislation). Whatever the federal government chooses to do will be influenced by the way in which it plans to justify its legislative authority constitutionally.

In this section, I examine the five federal powers which are most relevant in an analysis of the constitutionality of the federal policy options identified in Section 2. These are: POGG (including the National Concern and Emergency doctrines), criminal law, taxation, trade and commerce and the declaratory power. I begin with a brief discussion of the spending power. This is followed by a discussion of two powers which would authorize any type of climate policy, whether or not they intrude on provincial jurisdiction, as long as they were within the confines of the appropriate power: the emergency branch of POGG and the declaratory power. These two powers are interesting in that they do not require a colourability analysis. Next, I discuss the four powers that could authorize federal climate legislation: the National Concern branch of POGG, criminal law, taxation and trade and commerce.

Spending Power

There is no explicit power to spend within the Constitution. However, the Courts have confirmed that the federal and provincial governments are free to spend the money they raise (whether through taxation or their property) on matters even if they fall outside of their legislative authority, provided they do not, in so doing, seek to regulate provincial matters. As explained by the Supreme Court in *YMHA Jewish Community Centre of Winnipeg Inc. v. Brown* (accepting Peter Hogg's explanation), the federal spending power "must be inferred from the power to levy taxes (s. 91(3)), to legislate in relation to public property (s. 91(1A)), and to appropriate federal funds (s. 106)". While the act of spending itself falls within the jurisdiction of the executive branch, such spending must always be approved by Parliament (as per the notion of responsible government). Consequently, Parliament can either approve the amount and give the federal government full discretion to impose any conditions to such transfers or it can approve the amount and legislate certain conditions other parties must fulfill in order to receive such transfers.

[**Ed. Note:** The author's discussion of the use of federal spending power on health and social programs is omitted.]

The climate funding that the federal government has announced to date is not of the same genre as the national health care programme, which is more of a cost-shared programme. However, the federal government indicated in the 2016 Budget that it may attach some conditions to climate-related spending to ensure that the funding goes to carbon reductions that are the lowest cost. The federal government is in a position to freely fund climate-related initiatives in the provinces and territories, and may even attach conditions to such funding to ensure that it leads to GHG reductions. The only legal caveat is that the spending must not be a disguised attempt to regulate in areas not within federal competence. The jurisprudence clearly shows that this is a high threshold, which means that climate spending made conditional upon performance standards (such as actual emissions reductions or cost-effectiveness of those reductions) is unlikely to be successfully challenged. While there is no formal requirement for a national consensus, the *Vancouver Declaration* signed by all First Ministers is evidence of consensus on a number of key issues relating to climate change and clean energy.

Federal Powers That Eclipse Provincial Jurisdiction

This section discusses two federal powers that authorize Parliament to pass legislation that intrudes on provincial jurisdiction. Not surprisingly, these powers are rarely used, since they upset the balance of powers in our federalist state. Indeed, Parliament would be unlikely to use them in the context of climate change, as it would undoubtedly anger many of the provinces and territories. However, they are discussed as they are legally relevant and, if anything, provide a potential bargaining chip for Parliament's negotiations with provinces and territories in the development of the pan-Canadian climate policy framework.

The Emergency Branch of POGG

The emergency branch of POGG allows federal incursion into areas of provincial control on a temporary and extraordinary basis in times of emergency. The emergency branch of POGG has been fairly narrowly construed in the past, being used to justify legislative measures in times of war and to deal with inflation. For instance, the *War Measures Act* authorized the federal government's use of price controls, rent control and even the deportation of Japanese Canadians during and shortly after the first and second world wars. The *War Measures Act* was also used to justify policing powers in the October crisis of 1970. When Parliament enacted the *Anti-Inflation Act*, the Court found that the emergency power justified federal wage and price controls. The Supreme Court held that twenty months of double-digit inflation and relatively high rates of unemployment constituted an emergency, holding that the federal measures were "temporarily necessary to meet a situation of economic crisis imperiling the well-being of Canada as a whole and requiring Parliament's stern intervention in the interest of the country as a whole".

Importantly, the emergency branch will only justify temporary legislation. This is logical, since emergencies are understood to be temporary situations. However, in contrast to the National Concern doctrine, where the matter must be found to be an appropriate federal power, the emergency doctrine allows the federal government to legislate on matters that would normally be part of provincial jurisdiction, but for the emergency. As such, it is very powerful.

Is Climate Change an Emergency?

[**Ed. Note:** The author's summary of climate change impacts on environmental and economic systems is omitted.]

Is this situation an emergency in the context of POGG? If high rates of inflation combined with relatively high levels of unemployment constituted an emergency in the court's view, the urgent need to decarbonize a carbon-dependent economy in order to safeguard humans and ecosystems against further warming would seem to qualify as an emergency. World leaders have repeatedly characterized this as an urgent challenge, and it is widely understood that delayed action is problematic for the climate and the economy. The Supreme Court's words about the anti-inflation measures being "temporarily necessary to meet a situation of economic crisis imperiling the well-being of Canada as a whole and requiring Parliament's stern intervention in the interest of the country as a whole" could be just as appropriate to the climate context: national measures are urgently needed to set the Canadian economy on a path of decarbonization in order to address the climate crisis imperiling the well-being of Canadians and indeed the world, and Parliament's stern intervention in the interest of the country as a whole is required.

The emergency branch offers certain advantages for Parliament. The first is its breadth. As noted earlier, the emergency power authorizes Parliament to intrude in areas of provincial jurisdiction for the duration of the emergency. This means that Parliament would not have to be concerned (at least legally and within the confines of the emergency) with designing the legislation to avoid subjects within provincial control. The power would authorize any form of carbon pricing, whether in the form of a tax or cap and trade system, as well as GHG regulations of any nature.

A second advantage relates to the burden of proof. As readers will know, the burden of proving that a given provision is unconstitutional lies with the challenger. [...] If federal emergency legislation to address GHG emissions was challenged, the challenging party would bear the burden of proving that there is no rational basis for the federal law. In the case of climate legislation, that rational basis would be grounded in facts relating to the economic condition of the country, the international context, consumer and producer behaviour, and a range of other social and economic factors, not to mention evolving science. Since this is not a subject that is susceptible to black and white findings, it would be difficult to prove that there was no rational basis for the determination. This would make it difficult to challenge the federal government's finding of an emergency.

One could argue that many of the impacts of climate change are yet to be felt, suggesting it is not yet an emergency. This raises the question of whether the emergency power could justify legislation designed to prevent future emergencies. The answer seems to be yes, since the anti-inflation measures were meant to stem a growing crisis, thus addressing not only current harms but also future risks. As such, this may not be a significant hurdle, as it would seem fair to allow climate legislation that deals with the current and future risks posed by the climate emergency. [...]

[Ed. Note: The author's discussion of the potential for Parliament to use its power under section 92(10)(c) of the *Constitution Act, 1867* to declare power-generating works and infrastructure to be for the general advantage of Canada and impose GHG restrictions on them is omitted.]

Federal Powers That Do Not Eclipse Provincial Jurisdiction

The two preceding powers discussed were unusual in that they allow Parliament to intrude into provincial jurisdiction. The rest of the article focuses on the more traditional federal powers that must coexist with provincial powers in related areas.

The National Concern Branch of POGG

[Ed. Note: The author's canvassing of the case law on the national concern branch of POGG such as *Crown Zellerbach* is omitted. We addressed this topic in Chapter 3.]

Could Federal GHG Regulations Be Justified as a National Concern?

GHGs are the quintessential global pollutants, impacting the atmosphere regardless of where they are emitted. The Court in *Crown Zellerbach* was unanimous in holding that Parliament has jurisdiction over extra-provincial pollution. In fact, La Forest J.'s dissent states unequivocally that Parliament can, as an aspect of its international sovereignty, exercise jurisdiction over the control of pollution beyond its borders. The *Interprovincial Cooperatives* judgment is similarly supportive of the federal role in regulating interprovincial pollution. However, the sheer breadth of GHG emissions and their intimate links to virtually all kinds of economic activity mean that federal GHG regulations will inevitably impact several spheres of provincial authority, including property and civil rights (s. 92(13)), natural resources (s. 92A), local works and undertakings (92(10)) and matters of a local or private nature (s. 92(16)). Not surprisingly, provinces are leery about Parliament's intrusion (especially if they already have GHG policies in place). While overlapping jurisdiction within the context of cooperative federalism has become the norm rather than the exception, federal authority must still be clearly justifiable under POGG and limited to what is essentially a national subject matter.

Existing GHG regulations have been designed to fall under the criminal law power given the decision in *Hydro-Québec* discussed below. Could expanded regulations, such as increased vehicle emissions standards or renewable fuel content, or new regulatory measures, such as methane emissions (whether under

CEPA or a new law), also be justifiable as criminal law or would they best be authorized by POGG? For justification under POGG, the key question would be whether such regulations have the singleness, distinctiveness and indivisibility that clearly distinguishes them from matters of provincial concern and a scale of impact on provincial jurisdiction that is reconcilable with the fundamental distribution of legislative power under the Constitution.

Let's assume that the dominant purpose of these regulations was to reduce GHG emissions in order to meet Canada's national Paris target. This is a matter of national concern to Canada as a whole, and an appropriate federal purpose. The international nature of the climate problem and the fact that the control of GHG emissions is the subject of an international agreement would help qualify it as a single and distinct matter. In *Crown Zellerbach*, Le Dain J. for the majority qualified marine pollution as a clear matter of concern to Canada as a whole, given its predominantly extra provincial and international character and implications. The *Ocean Dumping Act* was enacted pursuant to the international *Convention on the Prevention of Marine Pollution by Dumping of Wastes and other Matter* (1972), and the majority in *Crown Zellerbach* pointed to this fact in holding that marine pollution is of national concern. In *Ontario Hydro v. Ontario*, the Supreme Court had little difficulty finding that the "production, use and application of atomic energy constitute a matter of national concern," pointing to the predominantly extra-provincial and international implications of nuclear energy. One could say that GHG emissions are similarly extra-provincial and international (and thus of national concern) since GHG emissions affect the atmosphere at a global level, wherever they are released.

While action in Canada is not going to be sufficient to address the impacts of climate change, since Canada's GHG emissions represent only some 2% of global emissions, Canada is part of an internationally binding legal agreement to reduce global GHG emissions and Canada needs to do its part along with other jurisdictions. To argue that there is no point in reducing emissions in Canada, in case other jurisdictions do not do their part, is not only unethical (especially for a wealthy country such as ours), but the kind of thinking that could undermine action on just about any transboundary issue. The Dutch Court in the *Urgenda* decision (which found that there existed a government duty to mitigate GHG emissions) was unconvinced by such an argument, and the Canadian courts should be as well.

One of most compelling ways to justify authority for legislation with a GHG emissions reduction purpose under the National Concern branch would be to show that the failure of one province to deal with the problem could injure the residents of other provinces. For example, if a province, say Alberta or Saskatchewan, were to fail to reduce its GHG emissions, the effects on another province, say an Atlantic province or a Northern Territory, might be increased risks to human health, food security and/or economic harms from climate-related impacts. To make it even more concrete, consider that P.E.I. is losing an estimated 28 cm of shoreline every year, and that the winter road infrastructure of the three Territories is compromised due to melting permafrost. Saskatchewan's (or another province's) failure to effectively mitigate its GHG emissions could have serious effects on P.E.I.'s shoreline or the NWT's road infrastructure.

Provincial inaction would also impact the federal government, since Canada's ability to meet its own national targets, as well as international targets under the Paris Agreement, can be jeopardized by the inaction (or inadequate action) of even one province (especially one that has a high rate of emissions). To assess this effect, one only need consider the status quo. While some provinces and territories have enacted meaningful GHG reduction policies over the last decade, others have not (or have done so only recently), and Canada's GHG emissions have continued to rise. If one province does not do its fair share, other provinces and/or the federal government will have to do more to comply with Paris commitments, incurring the resulting costs and risking the economic and reputational consequences of non-compliance with an international agreement. In *Munro*, the Court justified federal legislation relating to the national capital region under POGG because the failure of either Québec or Ontario to cooperate would have denied Canadians the symbolic value of a suitable national capital. Surely, following this reasoning, federal climate legislation could be justified to ensure Canada meets its national and international GHG reduction targets in order to mitigate the devastating impacts of climate change.

As Hogg states, the "most important element of national concern is a need for one national law which cannot realistically be satisfied by cooperative provincial action because the failure of one province to cooperate would carry with it adverse consequences for the residents of other provinces". No single province or territory is able to deal effectively with reducing GHG emissions because of the significant sources of emissions in several provinces. Only the federal government has the ability to mandate reductions that ensure the country's overall GHG emissions are lowered.

The second element of justification under National Concern is that the impact on provincial jurisdiction must be reconcilable with the fundamental distribution of legislative power under the Constitution. Given the province's extensive powers over pollution, energy and resources, it would be important that federal regulatory measures be focused on the GHG content of activity, rather than regulating the activities of one or more industrial sectors more generally. Even with such a focus, the reality is that many provinces have existing regulatory measures relating to GHGs (such as energy efficiency standards). It is possible for such measures to peacefully co-exist with federal ones, as long as there is no genuine conflict and that each law is appropriately justified under a relevant provincial or federal head of power. As elaborated in section 5 below, several doctrines, such as double aspect and ancillary powers, are relevant here. The key is that the federal measure must not be a tricky (colourable) attempt to legislate in areas of provincial jurisdiction, and that it be focused on the matter of national concern — reducing GHG emissions — rather than regulating economic activity or a particular sector.

[**Ed. Note:** The author's continued discussion of the power of the federal government to impose a national cap on GHG emissions and to impose a national carbon levy under the national concern branch of POGG is omitted.]

Summary

In my view, there is ample scope within the National Concern branch of POGG to authorize Parliament to regulate GHGs, whether through regulations or a national carbon levy or cap and trade program. Given the evidence of widespread impacts of climate change in all parts of the country, dealing with climate change can only reasonably be described as being the concern of the Dominion as a whole. The reality that inaction in one province can have implications for other provinces, Territories and the federal government is further evidence of the national dimensions of this issue. The fact that there is still room for provincial legislation to address aspects of the same subject as far as it affects that province is not a roadblock to federal authority. The provinces would maintain jurisdiction over economic activities within their boundaries, subject to federal requirements that affect the nature of the GHG emissions from those activities. Federal legislation would need to be carefully drafted to focus on the GHG component of emissions, rather than applying to industrial activity more generally, and be aimed at achieving national (and international) climate targets. It is quite possible that such policies may be justified under other heads of power, as discussed elsewhere in this paper. Much will depend on the specific design and language of legislation and related policy documents. In any event, having multiple spheres of authority can only be helpful for Parliament.

Notes and Questions

1. In this article, the author continues on to discuss and analyze the federal government's constitutional authority to enact and adopt various GHG measures under different federal heads of power. She concludes that, if designed appropriately, GHG regulations, a national cap-and-trade program and a carbon tax are likely justifiable under the criminal law power. A federal carbon tax could be supported under the taxation power. Moreover, the trade aspects of a national cap-and-trade program can be justified under the trade and commerce power. What arguments can you make in support of federal jurisdiction in respect of these policy instruments? What arguments can you make against using such instruments?

2. Recall in Part I that the UN Intergovernmental Panel on Climate Change released a report in October 2018 concluding that the global community must reduce carbon dioxide emissions rapidly by about 45% below 2010 levels by 2030 to avoid global warming of more than 1.5°C. What role, if any, can this report play in an argument that climate change is an emergency in the context of the emergency branch of POGG discussed in the previous article?

In the following extract from an article by Hsu and Elliot, the authors analyze the same three policy instruments (carbon tax, cap-and-trade and regulations) through the perspective of provincial jurisdiction.

Shi-Ling Hsu & Robin Elliot,
"Regulating Greenhouse Gases in Canada:
Constitutional and Policy Dimensions"
(2009) 54 McGill L.J. 463

The validity under sections 91 and 92 of the *Constitution Act, 1867* of legislation enacted by the federal and provincial orders of government to regulate greenhouse gas emissions will depend on a number of factors [...] We begin with three general observations about the manner in which the Supreme Court of Canada has tended to approach the task of reviewing on federalism grounds legislation designed to protect the environment.

The first is that the Court has made it clear that the power to protect the environment does not reside exclusively with either Parliament or the provincial legislatures. [...] The jurisprudence makes it clear that this connection to heads of power on both sides of the federal-provincial divide is present even if the word "environment" is understood in more limited terms to mean the physical environment alone. Hence, the courts have upheld as valid both federal and provincial legislation designed to protect the physical environment. They have been able to do that in part because they have shown a willingness to permit Parliament and the provincial legislatures to rely in support of such legislation on their respective jurisdictions over both some of the causes and some of the effects of polluting activities.

The second observation is that the Supreme Court has been willing to permit Parliament to regulate certain kinds of polluting activities under its POGG and criminal law (s. 91(27)) powers even though it has had to push the doctrinal envelopes governing those two heads of power in order to do so: see *R. v. Crown Zellerbach*, and *R. v. Hydro-Quebec*. Taken together, these two decisions can be said to reflect a willingness on the part of the Supreme Court of Canada to use the room to manoeuvre that the doctrine in this area leaves them with to afford the federal order of government broad authority to protect the physical environment. They also reflect a high degree of sympathy on the Court's part for the goal of environmental protection.

Thirdly, the law is clear that the power to enact legislation in implementation of obligations undertaken by the Government of Canada in an international treaty or convention does not fall to Parliament simply because the legislation has been enacted for that purpose: see the *Labour Conventions* case [...]. Jurisdiction to enact legislation to implement treaty obligations rests with the order of government that has jurisdiction to legislate in relation to the subject matter of those obligations. The federal order cannot therefore claim jurisdiction to enact legislation regulating greenhouse gas emissions on the basis that such legislation is being enacted in fulfillment of Canada's obligations under the Kyoto Protocol [...]. That said, there is support in the jurisprudence for the notion that the fact that federal legislation has been enacted to implement treaty obligations might assist the federal government's cause if that legislation were to be subjected to attack on federalism grounds, at least if the subject matter of the treaty can be said to relate to a matter of "predominantly extra-provincial as well as international character and implications".

Provincial Jurisdiction

We consider here the question of whether or not the provincial legislatures have the requisite constitutional authority to regulate greenhouse gas emissions through the vehicles of (a) a carbon tax, (b) a cap-and-trade/intensity-based trading regime, and (c) a command-and-control regime.

Carbon Taxes

The power of the provincial legislatures to tax is prescribed by s. 92(2) of the *Constitution Act, 1867* in the following terms: "Direct Taxation within the Province in order to the raising of a Revenue for Provincial Purposes". Those terms suggest that, in order for provincial legislation to be sustained on the basis of s. 92(2), the legislation must (a) impose a "tax", which tax must (b) be "direct", (c) be imposed "within the province", and (d) be imposed "in order to the raising of a revenue for provincial purposes".

Given the manner in which requirements (a), (b) and (c) have come to be understood, there is little doubt that provincial legislation imposing a carbon tax of the kind that we have discussed above would be held to impose a "tax", and that that "tax" would be held to be both "direct" and imposed "within the province". [...] This leaves us with requirement (d) — that the tax be levied "in order to the raising of a Revenue for Provincial Purposes". On the face of it, that language would appear to provide the basis for a challenge to a provincial carbon tax that is revenue neutral, like the tax imposed by the Legislature of British Columbia. Can it not be argued that a tax that is advertised as being, and is required by the legislation imposing it to be, revenue neutral has not been levied "in order to the raising of a revenue"? And if the tax has not been levied for that purpose, can it not be said that the legislation imposing it exceeds provincial jurisdiction under s. 92(2)?

In our view, while an argument that provincially imposed taxes that are designed to be, and are in fact, revenue neutral cannot be sustained by s. 92(2) is certainly plausible, it is likely that, if such an argument were to be advanced in a constitutional attack upon a carbon tax like that imposed by the Legislature of British Columbia, it would fail. We believe that the courts would find the weaknesses of that argument to outweigh its strengths, and moreover, that they would be right to do so. [...] In the result, then, it is our opinion that provincially created carbon taxes would be held to fall within the scope of s. 92(2) of the *Constitution Act, 1867*, and therefore be upheld as valid.

Cap-and-Trade/Intensity-Based Trading Regimes

The validity of a provincially created cap-and-trade or intensity-based trading regime would depend to a very considerable degree on the form it took, with the controlling factor being the entities to which the regime applied. If the regime were to be limited to business undertakings that the provincial legislatures have the authority to regulate qua businesses under any or all of s. 92(5), s. 92(10), s. 92(13) and s. 92A, there is good reason to believe that it would be upheld as valid. If, however, it were not to be so limited, and were made applicable by its terms to business undertakings that fall within federal legislative jurisdiction, there is good reason to believe that it would be held to be invalid, at least insofar as its application to those undertakings is concerned.

The industries that fall within [squarely within] provincial jurisdiction [...] are numerous, and include many of the industries that emit large amounts of carbon into the atmosphere and are therefore good candidates for a cap-and-trade/intensity-based trading regime — oil and gas, manufacturing, mining, forestry, construction, intraprovincial truck and bus lines, etc. Moreover, the power of the provincial legislatures to regulate the business activities of those industries has been understood broadly by the courts. In particular, it has been held to permit them to regulate those activities for a range of different purposes — to protect consumers from fraudulent dealings, to protect the health and safety of consumers, to establish quality standards, to ensure adequate supply and to protect the economic and other interests of employees. It has also been held to permit them to regulate those activities for the purpose of protecting the environment. There is every reason to believe, therefore, that provincial legislation establishing a cap-and-trade/intensity-based trading regime that is limited in its scope to such undertakings would be upheld as valid. [...]

Would it be open to a provincial legislature to extend the reach of a cap-and-trade/intensity-based trading regime to include industries that normally fall within federal legislative jurisdiction, such as aeronautics, international/interprovincial truck and bus lines and nuclear power generation? Given the nature of such regimes, extending their reach in this way could only be accomplished by specifically including such industries in the list of industries to which they apply. This means that companies doing business within one of the listed industries that objected to being included would have a target within the statute to attack — the specific reference to the industry in question. Such an attack would likely be analyzed by the courts on the basis of what is called the necessarily incidental doctrine. The current understanding of that doctrine requires consideration of three distinct questions within the following analytical framework: (1) to what extent does the impugned part of the statute — here the inclusion in the list of industries to which the cap-and-trade regime applies of the industry in question — encroach on the legislative jurisdiction of the federal order of government when that part is viewed in isolation? (2) is the rest of the statute valid? and (3) given the answer to (1), is the impugned part sufficiently integrated into the rest of the statute to profit from its validity and be considered valid itself?

[...] the answer to the first of these questions would likely be that provincial legislation that imposes legally enforceable constraints on the amount of carbon which companies within a federally regulated industry in question can emit in the course of conducting their normal business activities would be held to be a very serious encroachment on federal legislative jurisdiction over that industry.

[...] if the first question were to be answered in that manner, the courts would almost certainly hold that the inclusion of the federally regulated industry in the list of industries to which the regime is intended to apply is unconstitutional [...]

As noted above, the cap-and-trade regime proposed by the Legislature of British Columbia may be integrated into a regionally defined cap-and-trade system that will include at least one other Canadian province (Manitoba) and several of the states in the western United States. Would the fact that such a regime has that kind of regional character render it constitutionally suspect in the eyes of the courts? We do not believe that it would. While it is true, as noted above, that the regulation of international and interprovincial trade falls within exclusive federal legislative jurisdiction under s. 91(2) of the *Constitution Act, 1867*, a regime of this nature merely makes it possible for the undertakings governed by the British Columbia statute to engage in the interprovincial and international trading of emission allowances if they believe that it is in their interests to do so. It is not, as it would have to be in order to be vulnerable to attack on this ground, directed at the regulation of such trading.

Command-and-Control Regimes

The ability of provincial legislatures to regulate greenhouse gas emissions on the basis of a command-and-control approach turns on the same considerations as their ability to do so through the enactment of cap-and-trade/intensity-based trading regimes. If the legislation is limited in its reach to those industries that are considered to fall within provincial legislative jurisdiction, it will therefore likely be valid. If, by contrast, the legislation is also made applicable to industries that are considered to fall within federal jurisdiction, it will be vulnerable to attack, at least insofar as its application to those industries is concerned.

Notes and Questions

1. Based on the articles by Chalifour and by Hsu and Elliot excerpted above, both the federal and provincial levels of government seem to have constitutional jurisdiction to enact a similar suite of measures to address climate change. Considering the doctrines of double aspect, interjurisdictional immunity, and federal paramountcy, to what extent can federal and provincial regimes for a carbon tax co-exist? What about GHG regulations, or a cap-and-trade system?

2. Which level(s) of government has jurisdiction to implement energy efficiency and conservation measures? What about measures to promote renewable energy? Can the federal government pass legislation to restrict the consumption of fossil fuels across Canada? What about production?

Federal Policy Responses to Climate Change

Bearing in mind the division of powers issues set out above, consider now the federal government's policy response in addressing climate change over the past 30 years as discussed in the following excerpt of a blog article by Meinhard Doelle.

Meinhard Doelle,
adapted from "Decades of Climate Policy Failure
in Canada: Can We Break the Vicious Cycle?"

(2018), online: < https://blogs.dal.ca/melaw >

During the past three decades, Canada has shown varying levels of leadership on climate policy. At times, Canada is seen as a leader on the international stage, while at other times Canada has been criticized as a laggard both domestically and abroad. In recent years, Canada's climate policy has been put into question by its withdrawal from the *Kyoto Protocol* and the failure to effectively implement the *Paris Agreement*.

At the UN Earth Summit held in Rio de Janeiro in 1992, Canada made a non-binding commitment to reduce its greenhouse gas emissions to 1990 levels by 2000, a commitment that Canada failed to implement. Canada also signed onto the *United Nations Framework Convention on Climate Change* (UNFCCC) at the Rio Summit, a treaty that Canada ratified later that year.

Following its leadership role in 1997 in the Kyoto negotiations, Canada ratified the *Kyoto Protocol* in 2002. Canada's GHG emission target under the first commitment period of the *Kyoto Protocol* was to reduce its emissions to 6% below 1990 levels by the end of 2012. To achieve this, Canada must hold valid credits or permits to offset all of its emissions during the commitment period. Canada had the option meet this commitment in three ways. First, Canada could have actually reduced its emissions to 94% of 1990 levels and retain all its AAUs. Second, Canada could have obtained GHG emissions reduction credits by undertaking projects that remove GHGs from the atmosphere through a variety of approved processes commonly referred to as sinks — natural processes that take carbon dioxide out of the atmosphere and store it in soils, forests and other vegetation. Third, Canada could have purchased emissions credits to offset any excess between its emissions and its AAUs.

Canada pursued none of these options. Instead, it withdrew from the *Kyoto Protocol* in 2011 before it could be held accountable by the Protocol's compliance committee for its failure to comply, and in the process did very little to reduce domestic emissions compared to most developed and even some developing countries. Some provinces, such as British Columbia, Ontario, Quebec and Nova Scotia, stepped up from time to time to lead during this period of federal withdrawal, but Canada as a whole never achieved any leadership in its domestic mitigation efforts.

Canada has more recently made another effort at climate leadership, this time in the context of the *Paris Agreement* in December 2015. The Liberal Party under Justin Trudeau showed signs of leadership on climate change during the 2015 federal election. It beat out the NDP in part by appealing to traditional NDP and Green Party voters on issues such as climate change. Once elected, it continued to show leadership during the UN climate negotiations, by playing an important, constructive role in the final days of the Paris climate negotiations in December 2015. It was part of an 'ambition coalition' of over 100 countries that secured the inclusion of the global goals of keeping temperature increases to well below 2°C while striving for 1.5°C, and to aim to reach global carbon neutrality by the second half of the century. Canada continued to show leadership by ratifying the

Paris Agreement quickly to help bring it into force in record time by November 2016.

As the Trudeau government turned its attention to domestic implementation, the failure to turn international leadership into domestic action soon began to show. In spite of its criticism of the Harper government on its inadequate efforts on climate change, and in spite of its commitment to the *Paris Agreement*, the Trudeau government did not increase the ambition of Canada's Nationally Determined Contribution (NDC) from the inadequate draft NDC that the previous government had filed before the *Paris Agreement* was finalized. Despite agreeing to provisions in the *Paris Agreement* that recognize the gap between individual commitments and the collective goals and call for an increase of effort over time to meet the collective goals, Canada continues to show no willingness to increase its commitment by revising its NDC.

The Trudeau government took more encouraging steps in 2016, when it was able to negotiate a *Pan-Canadian Framework on Climate Change* with most of the provinces and all territories. Key elements of the agreement were a carbon price of $10 by 2018 (to increase to $50 by 2022), the phase-out of coal by 2030, and a number of federal measures to reduce emissions, including efforts to reduce methane emissions. The agreement was disappointing to some in that it did not bring all provinces on board, and its implementation would not get Canada all the way to its 2020 or 2030 emission reduction targets under Canada's NDC. Nevertheless, it had the potential to be an important breakthrough in overcoming the past divisions over effective climate mitigation in Canada, and to finally put Canada on the path to decarbonization.

Perhaps the biggest flaw of this effort was the federal government's failure to clearly position the *Pan-Canadian Framework*, from the start, as an initial step that needed to be strengthened over time. Instead, it has become a high-water mark to be attacked and whittled down by those who oppose the decarbonization of Canadian society out of self-interest and political opportunism, particularly those who benefit from the status quo. There is no credible evidence that Canada, as a whole, will benefit from resisting this transition. There are strong indications to the contrary even in the short to medium term, and the combination of the cost of inaction and the economic opportunities associated with action leaves little doubt about the net economic benefits of decarbonization in the long term. In response to such attacks, the federal government has made various compromises to the *Pan-Canadian Framework*, which include:

- Developing backstop legislation for a key element of the *Pan-Canadian Framework*, the carbon pricing element, that exempts 70% of emissions for some industry sectors from the carbon price. This essentially means that most emissions from these sectors are actually not subject to a carbon price at all.

- Announcing that exemption to some industries will be increased to 80% and 90%, further eroding the carbon pricing element of the framework, meaning that even more emissions from these sectors are not subject to a carbon price. Assuming modest efforts to reduce emissions, these sectors may now be exempt from the carbon price altogether, without a clear signal that the remainder will be priced in the future.

- Negotiating agreements with some provinces that will delay the 2030 coal phase-out under the *Pan-Canadian Framework* well past 2030.
- Significantly weakening its methane emission reduction initiative under the *Pan-Canadian Framework*, even though it is clear that reducing methane emissions in the short term is critical for meeting the collective goals in the *Paris Agreement*, given that methane is a much more potent GHG than CO_2 which has a shorter lifespan in the atmosphere.
- Indicating that it intends to exclude certain new fossil fuel projects (such as *in situ* oil sands projects) from the scrutiny of its reformed assessment process under the new *Impact Assessment Act*.
- Approving new fossil fuel infrastructure without imposing conditions on the approvals to ensure consistency with Canada's climate commitments (such as carbon offsetting or restricting project lifespans in line with a clear decarbonization timeframe consistent with Canada's climate commitments), and without demonstrating the economic viability of this infrastructure if it is to operate within the constraints of Canada's climate commitments.
- Releasing a discussion paper on a planned strategic assessment that signals a reluctance to carefully consider the climate implications of new projects, particularly infrastructure and industrial projects likely to lock in future GHG emissions and undermine Canada's ability to meet its current NDC, let alone meet Canada's commitment to increase the ambition of its NDC to make a fair contribution to the global effort to keep temperatures well below 2°C and decarbonize the global economy in time to achieve this temperature goal.

Whatever the reasons, Canada has failed to deal with the climate crisis for the past 20 years, even though the science is clear that the consequences of not doing so will come at an incredibly high price for humanity. What's more, the economics are clear that the sooner we act, and the more quickly we reduce emissions, the better off we will be economically, given that mitigation as a general rule is cheaper and more effective than adaptation, which in turn tends to be cheaper than dealing with the loss and damage of unabated climate change. Dealing with the economic and non-economic losses of climate change will be an incredible burden on societies for generations to come. While Canada has continued to fail to implement effective domestic action, other countries (such as China, Germany, the UK, Denmark and Sweden) have demonstrated that there are economic gains to be had from leading this transition. Canada is one of very few developed countries whose emissions are still on the rise, and among the countries with the highest per capita emissions in the world.

Understanding the federal government's ineffective policy response to climate change is far from straightforward. The climate crisis is complex, putting a full understanding of all its key elements beyond the understanding of any one scientist, any one politician, any one citizen. The debate about an effective response to the climate crisis has not paid adequate attention to facts, science, or the long-term best interests of Canada or the global community, and Canadians have not been well informed about the perils and opportunities involved. The discourse, instead, has been predominantly about selective short-term economic interests, about power and influence, about the manipulation of public opinion, and about myopic politics. While a detailed assessment of the federal's government's ineffectiveness, and that of the broader Canadian society, would not be possible for present purposes, the following are a few key contributors:

- We seem to live in an increasingly complex, post-fact society, where, for more and more citizens, facts appear to be indistinguishable from opinion. This means that on any given issue, including climate change, too many citizens are unable or unwilling to reach their own conclusion, and instead choose a side to "believe in".

- Few citizens seem to get their information from credible sources that seek to test the accuracy of claims being made by those with a vested interest in the issue.

- We seem to have a political system that overvalues selective social and economic benefits of the status quo, overemphasizes the cost of change, and underemphasizes the benefits of change and the cost of standing still.

- Those with a stake in preserving the status quo have effectively utilized the complexity of the issue of climate change to undermine governments who have tried to take effective steps to facilitate the decarbonization of our society.

- Those who stand to benefit from the status quo have more resources, power and influence than those who stand to benefit from the decarbonization of our society.

- We have, over the past two decades, increasingly allowed concerns about environmental harm of human activity to be marginalized as anti-development and anti-business, rather than make rational decisions informed by science and fact, and in the interest of society as a whole.

- In trying to make a transition from fossil fuels to renewable energy, we encounter governments who listen to the fossil fuel industry more than the renewable energy industry. That is the equivalent of listening to the horse and buggy industry in dealing with the transition to mechanized transportation, or letting the commercial fishing industry decide whether to reduce fishing quotas to save the cod or to change fishing practices to save the right whale.

- Governments have reacted by either appearing almost ideologically opposed to action on climate change, or, if they are willing to act, becoming facilitators of stakeholders and their lobbyists, rather than leaders that drive policy. With the relentless and powerful lobby from the industry sectors trying to prevent or slow down the decarbonization of the economy, this has inevitably resulted in domestic inaction on this critical issue in Canada.

- As individuals, we have not adequately connected with the climate crisis in our capacities as investors, as employees, as parents, as voters and as citizens.

Studying the history of federal climate policy allows us to better understand the state of democracy in Canada. What can we say about Canada's democratic institutions, at least at the federal level, when the goalposts keep moving in response to pressure from industry sectors? The experience with the development of climate mitigation policy in Canada points to a failure to draw an appropriate line between the legitimate role of affected industries and their undue influence over policy. Affected industries have an important role to play in helping to find effective, efficient and fair ways to reach a given policy goal, such as the decarbonization of our society. However, we cross a line when those industries are given a role in deciding whether we will even work toward critical societal goals at all, and at what pace. The lessons of the past 20 years go well beyond climate change. They demonstrate that the way we govern our society is not well suited to respond to change, to deal quickly, effectively and fairly with challenges, or to take advantage of opportunities ahead. This is troubling in a world of accelerated change — change in environmental impact of human activities, change in technology, and change in the globalization of human societies. If we cannot respond effectively to a crisis as serious as climate change, we need to recognize that we likely have a fundamental and systemic problem. It seems that the way we govern ourselves in Canada does not allow us to respond effectively and swiftly to changing circumstances in a transparent and accountable manner. This should be a tremendous concern in a world of accelerating change that shows no signs of letting up. We need to find ways to govern ourselves so that those who resist change for personal short-term gain do not have a disproportionate voice, a voice that is the product of their current power and influence in our society rather than their role in the future we strive for.

Of course, it is not too late to turn things around on climate change. We have to recognize, however, that until the underlying problems are addressed, the cards are stacked against such efforts, and those who persist in spite of these challenges do so at the risk of paying the price at the ballot box. In this difficult time, what we need are politicians with the courage to persist on critical issues such as climate change in spite of the odds, and politicians with the courage to address the serious structural problems with our system of government and our democracy.

Notes and Questions

1. As alluded to in the above extract, various provinces have stepped up with their own policy responses during periods of federal withdrawal. In British Columbia, the BC Liberal government introduced a carbon tax in 2008 that covers most types of fuel use and carbon emissions. This was the first carbon tax of its kind in North America. Under the *Carbon Tax Act*, S.B.C. 2008, c. 40, the initial tax was set at $10 per tonne of carbon dioxide equivalents (CO_2e), rising each year until it reached $30/tonne CO_2e by 2012. When it was first enacted, the *Carbon Tax Act* contained "tax neutrality" provisions that required the government to offset the revenue generated by the carbon tax with tax reductions in other areas. While these tax cuts were initially equally distributed among low income tax cuts, personal income tax cuts and corporate tax cuts, the share of the carbon tax revenue going into corporate tax cuts has grown over the years of the tax's

implementation. In the 2013 provincial elections, the incumbent Liberal government was returned to power and followed through with their campaign promise to freeze the tax for five years or until other jurisdictions also implement carbon taxes. This freeze ended in 2018 when the newly elected BC NDP government amended the *Carbon Tax Act* to establish a $35/tonne CO_2e tax, rising each year until it reaches $50/tonne CO_2e by 2021. However, with this renewed increase, the government also repealed the tax neutrality provisions of the Act.

In Ontario, the provincial Liberal government introduced the *Climate Change Mitigation and Low-carbon Economy Act, 2016*, S.O. 2016, c. 7, which came into effect on January 1, 2017. The centrepiece of this legislation was a framework for a cap-and-trade program for CO_2e. The Act required facilities that emit over 25,000 tonnes of CO_2e per year to register as mandatory participants in the program. Facilities that emit less than that amount may voluntarily register as participants as well. Registered participants must quantify and report their greenhouse gas emissions. For each compliance period, a participant must submit allowances and credits equal to the reported emissions for that period. Regulations made under the Act provided the cap for emission allowances, which decreased over time. The Act also provided an offset program that allowed participants to meet their compliance requirements through emissions reduction, avoidance and removal. The first compliance period was to run from 2017 to 2020, with subsequent compliance periods that followed. However, with the election of a new Progressive Conservative government, the provincial government tabled legislation in 2018 to cancel the cap-and-trade program, claiming that it would save the average family $260 per year. In response, the federal government has imposed a carbon tax on Ontario, which the province is challenging in court as an unconstitutional exercise of federal power. Environmental groups have also filed a lawsuit against the provincial government, arguing that the lack of public consultation over the cancelling of the cap-and-trade program was an unlawful breach of Ontario's *Environmental Bill of Rights* legislation.

2. What programs have been implemented by your provincial government to address greenhouse gas emissions and the impacts of climate change? Recall the article by William R. MacKay reproduced in Chapter 3 regarding the patterns of intergovernmental relations in Canadian environmental policy. Would you characterize the pattern of intergovernmental relations between the federal government and that of your province as an example of collaborative or competitive federalism?

Finally, we take a closer look at the two policy instruments governments typically use to price carbon: carbon taxes and cap-and-trade. As mentioned above, British Columbia has opted to impose a carbon tax, whereas Ontario (prior to the Ford government) elected to create a cap-and-trade regime. In the article that follows, Avi-Yonah and Uhlmann compare and contrast these two systems, ultimately arguing that a carbon tax is a better instrument than cap-and-trade.

Reuven S. Avi-Yonah & David M. Uhlmann,
"Combating Global Climate Change: Why a Carbon Tax Is a
Better Response to Global Warming Than Cap and Trade"
(2009) 28 Stan. Envtl. L.J. 3

Key Features of a Carbon Tax and Cap and Trade

An upstream carbon tax arguably is the most straightforward approach to the global climate change problem. A carbon tax would be imposed on all oil, coal, and natural gas production in the United States, as well as all imports. The tax rate would be based on the marginal cost of carbon dioxide emissions (also referred to as the "social cost of carbon") and would be increased annually to reflect the increase in the harmful effects of carbon dioxide emissions. A carbon tax thereby would provide a price signal that captures what is now an externality, namely the harmful effects of carbon dioxide emissions. Tax credits would be provided for carbon sequestration programs, which eliminate or reduce carbon dioxide emissions (and, in some circumstances, could be used to generate energy). Tax revenues would be used to expand tax credits for development of alternative energy and to address any regressive effects of the carbon tax.

If the carbon tax did not produce the desired reduction in carbon dioxide emissions, the tax would be increased; if the tax "overcorrected" and produced greater than anticipated reductions, it could be decreased. Implementation and enforcement of a carbon tax would occur through existing programs within the Internal Revenue Service and the Energy Department. Moreover, by establishing a carbon tax in advance of any international agreement on global carbon dioxide emissions, the United States would meet its obligation to begin reducing its carbon dioxide emissions and establish much-needed credibility in the ensuing international negotiations.

An upstream cap and trade system would establish a cap on the carbon content of fuels in much the same way that an upstream carbon tax would impose a tax on those fuels. The cap would decline over time to achieve the desired level of carbon dioxide emission reductions. Where a cap and trade system becomes more complicated and, as Part III discusses, potentially unwieldy, is in the setting of baselines for the distribution of allowances and in the monitoring and enforcement of a complex allowance system.

Under an upstream cap and trade system, all producers and importers of fossil fuels would be required to have allowances to "cover" the carbon content of the fuels they produce. The number of those allowances would be limited by the overall "cap" imposed by the system. Allowances could be distributed either for free, through an auction system, or some combination. The leading cap and trade proposal in Congress, the *Lieberman-Warner Climate Security Act of 2008*, would distribute the majority of allowances for free in the early years of the cap and trade system, with increasing percentages distributed by auction in subsequent years. Absent an auction, no revenue would be generated by cap and trade to support the development of alternative energy or carbon sequestration technologies. But, theoretically, market forces would provide a substitute for government subsidies: companies that developed alternative energy and otherwise found ways to limit their carbon dioxide emissions would have "surplus" allowances that they could sell to companies that needed more allowances.

The best example of a cap and trade system on a national level in the United States is the cap and trade program under Title IV of the *Clean Air Act*, which was implemented under the *Clean Air Act* Amendments of 1990 to curtail acid rain. The acid rain program is widely viewed as an overwhelming success, both in terms of the environmental protection it provided and the degree to which change occurred without significant economic dislocation. Because the acid rain problem focused on 111 facilities in the Midwest (the so-called "Big Dirties"), however, we do not have experience in the United States — or the rest of the world — with an economy-wide cap and trade system.

In contrast to the limited experience in the U.S. with cap and trade, carbon taxes have been successfully implemented in a growing number of countries. Carbon taxes have been implemented in Quebec and British Columbia as part of Canadian efforts to meet the requirements of the Kyoto Protocol. In addition, Denmark, Finland, Italy, the Netherlands, Norway, and Sweden have introduced carbon taxes in combination with energy taxes. The existing carbon taxes are too new to draw meaningful conclusions about their long-term benefits, but many economists believe that a carbon tax would be the most effective method of reducing carbon dioxide emissions. Cap and trade systems for carbon dioxide emissions have been implemented by the European Union and on a regional basis in New England; in addition, seven Western states and four Canadian provinces have taken steps to develop a cap and trade system. As discussed in Part III, the European Union system has not been particularly successful to date, but that has not diminished enthusiasm in the United States and abroad for relying on cap and trade systems as the principal method of reducing carbon dioxide emissions.

The Case for a Carbon Tax

Given the urgency of the global climate change problem, and the increasing acceptance of a cap and trade system as a desirable alternative, the argument could be made that a cap and trade system should be implemented in the United States (and abroad) without further delay. This Part provides a comparison between a carbon tax and a cap and trade system and concludes that a carbon tax is preferable to cap and trade.

Advantages of a Carbon Tax

Simplicity

[...] A carbon tax is inherently simple: a tax is imposed at X dollars per ton of carbon content on the main sources of carbon dioxide emissions in the economy, namely coal, oil, and natural gas. (Other greenhouse gas sources, such as methane, are not included because energy accounts for nearly eighty-five percent of the 7147 million metric tons of greenhouse gases in the U.S. economy.) The tax is imposed "upstream", *i.e.*, at the point of extraction or importation, which means than it can be imposed on only about 2000 taxpayers (500 coal miners and importers, 750 oil producers and importers, and 750 natural gas producers and importers). Credits can be given to carbon sequestration projects and to other projects that reduce greenhouse gas emissions (although this would need to be addressed in a way that does not dilute the price signal or create undue complexity), and exports are exempted. Beyond that, the main question is what to do with the revenue, which will be discussed below.

Cap and trade, on the other hand, is inherently more complicated. While the cap can also be imposed "upstream", it has several features that require complexity. First, baselines need to be set for purposes of establishing the emissions cap. Second, the proposal needs to determine how allowances will be created and distributed, either for free or by auction. Free distribution requires deciding which industries receive allowances, while an auction requires a complex monitoring system to prevent cheating. Third, the trading in allowances needs to be set up and monitored: a system needs to be devised to prevent the same allowance from being used twice, and penalties need to be established for polluters who exceed their allowances. Fourth, if allowances are to be traded with other countries, the international trading of allowances would need to be monitored as well. Fifth, to prevent Cost Uncertainty, cap and trade proposals typically have complex provisions for banking and borrowing allowances, and some of them provide for safety valves. Sixth, offsets are needed for carbon sequestration and similar projects, and those are more complicated than credits against a carbon tax liability. Finally, most cap and trade proposals involve provisions for coordinating with the cap and trade policies of other countries, and for punishing countries that do not have a greenhouse gas emissions control policy.

It is important to note that this difference in complexity is inherent in the two policies as initially proposed, before any legislative amendments and before any implementation and enforcement issues. A pure cap and trade system is inevitably more complex than any carbon tax.

Cap and trade is also relatively untried: we have never had an economy-wide cap and trade system, while we have extensive experience with economy-wide excise taxes on a wide variety of products, including gasoline. This is why Congressman Larson's carbon tax bill can simply envisage adding three new relatively short sections to the existing excise tax part of the *Internal Revenue Code*. Cap and trade, on the other hand, is a major new and separate piece of legislation. A new administration determined to implement cap and trade would probably have to take at least two years to get the program passed in Congress and set up for implementation, even with swift Congressional action, because of the inherent delays in the rulemaking process. A carbon tax can be enacted and enforced practically tomorrow. Given that we have already delayed action for decades, and that every year that passes makes the climate change problem more difficult to solve, a carbon tax may be preferable to cap and trade — as well as traditional regulatory approaches — based on timing concerns alone.

In addition to its inherent complexity, cap and trade also is more difficult to enforce. Under cap and trade, an elaborate mechanism would need to be set up to distribute and collect allowances and to ensure that allowances are real (a difficult task, especially if allowances from non-United States programs are permitted) and that polluters are penalized if they emit greenhouses gases without an allowance. A new administrative body would need to be set up for this purpose, or at least a new office within EPA, and new employees with the relevant expertise would need to be hired. A carbon tax, on the other hand, could be enforced by the IRS with its existing staff, which has the relevant expertise in enforcing other excise taxes.

Cap and trade also raises collateral issues that are not present in a carbon tax, such as the need for the Securities and Exchange Commission to enforce rules regarding futures trading in allowances. A good example is the tax implications of both policies. A carbon tax, as a federal tax, has no tax implications: it is simply collected and is not deductible. Allowances under cap and trade, on the other hand, raise a multitude of tax issues: What are the tax implications of distributing allowances for free? What are the tax implications of trading in allowances? Should allowance exchanges be permitted to avoid the tax on selling allowances? What amount of the purchase price of a business should be allocated to its allowances? If borrowing and banking occur, what are the tax consequences? Can allowances be amortized? None of these issues arise under a carbon tax.

Revenue

A carbon tax by definition generates revenue. A relatively modest tax of $10 per ton of carbon content is estimated to generate $50 billion per year; the *America's Energy Security Trust Fund Act* envisages a tax of $16.50 per ton and generates correspondingly more revenue. While the current federal budget deficit and even larger actuarial deficit may justify revenue raising measures in general, revenues from a carbon tax should be segregated and devoted to addressing any regressive effects of the tax and reducing greenhouse gas emissions. Some carbon tax proposals promise "revenue neutrality" and focus on eliminating regressive effects.

We agree that regressive effects must be addressed but otherwise would use revenues from the carbon tax to provide tax credits for alternative energy development and more energy-efficient motor vehicles, since the positive externalities that result from such research and development means that funding is likely to be undersupplied by the private sector even with a carbon tax in place. Revenues could also be used to support carbon sequestration projects and other projects that reduce greenhouse gas emissions, like mass transit and green building.

Segregating the revenue from a carbon tax and using the proceeds to support further greenhouse gas reductions is justified because it reduces Benefit Uncertainty, which is the most serious drawback of a carbon tax compared to cap and trade. In addition, segregating the revenue is likely to reduce some political opposition to raising taxes in general, at least to the extent that such opposition is based on the perception that government is wasteful.

In theory, cap and trade can be used to generate the same amount of revenue as a carbon tax, if all the allowances are auctioned. In practice, however, all cap and trade proposals introduced in Congress, as well as most academic proposals and existing cap and trade programs in the United States and abroad, include some free distribution of allowances. For example, the EU cap and trade regime distributed ninety-five percent of the allowances for free, and most Congressional proposals distribute over half of the allowances for free. The reason is obvious: for politicians, a significant attraction of cap and trade is that it creates from nothing a new, scarce resource that they can use to reward their constituents and donors. But if allowances are distributed for free, cap and trade generates less revenue than a carbon tax, and this means less potential to support research and development, carbon sequestration, and other greenhouse-gas-reducing efforts.

Moreover, it seems unlikely that free allocation of allowances would produce the optimal reduction in greenhouse gas emissions. Some polluting industries are likely to get too many allowances, and that would affect the trading price of allowances. At the extreme, the result would be what occurred in Europe, where politicians created so many free allowances that no reduction from business as usual was required at all, the price of allowances collapsed, and the EU failed to meet its goals under the Kyoto Protocol. A similar risk to free distribution of allowances under a carbon tax would be pressure from affected industries for tax exemptions. The process of enacting tax exemptions is more visible than the process of distributing free allowances, however, and any exemption to one of the three industries affected (coal, natural gas, and oil) would be met by resistance from the other two, hopefully resulting in no exemptions at all.

Cost Certainty

A carbon tax ensures Cost Certainty: the cost is the amount of the tax, and whatever the incidence of the tax (*i.e.*, whether it can be passed on to consumers or not), the cost cannot rise above the tax rate. This enables businesses to plan ahead, secure in the knowledge that raising the tax rate beyond any automatic adjustment, which can be planned for, requires another vote in Congress that they can hope to influence.

A cap and trade regime, on the other hand, suffers from inherent Cost Uncertainty. While allowances may be initially distributed for free, the key question for polluting businesses that need to acquire allowances to address a reduction in the cap is what would be the future price of allowances. Existing cap and trade programs like the Southern California RECLAIM system for nitrogen oxide emissions, in which the allowance prices spiked in 2000 to more than twenty times their historical level, and the EU Emission Trading Scheme (ETS), in which the price of allowances collapsed when it became clear that too many allowances had been distributed, illustrate the problem of Cost Uncertainty in cap and trade programs. Cost Uncertainty makes it inherently difficult for businesses to plan ahead. The fundamental problem is that the reduction in the cap that is built into cap and trade would necessarily make allowances more expensive. How much more expensive depends on the development of future technologies, which cannot be predicted with any accuracy over the longer time period (fifty years or more) required for a cap and trade program to achieve its environmental goals.

Cap and trade proponents argue that Cost Uncertainty can be mitigated by provisions for banking extra allowances for use in future years, and borrowing allowances from future years to use in the present. These provisions add complexity, and it is unclear whether they will be effective: in the early years of the program, there are few allowances to bank, while borrowing risks leaving the business with insufficient allowances in the future when the cap is lower.

Ultimately, the only sure way of preventing Cost Uncertainty in a cap and trade regime is to build in a "safety valve", which would permit businesses to receive or purchase at a fixed price additional allowances if the market price of allowances becomes too high. Several of the current proposals in Congress have such built-in safety valves. However, the problem with safety valves is that they sacrifice Benefit Certainty, which is the main advantage of cap and trade: by definition, providing extra allowances when the cap is lowered means raising the cap.

Even if a cap and trade program has no safety valve built into it from the start, the commitment to Benefit Certainty may be misleading. If the lowered cap begins to seriously hurt businesses and the price of allowances spikes, one should expect strong pressure on politicians to stop lowering the cap. Benefit Certainty under cap and trade as implemented may therefore be an illusion, while Cost Uncertainty is very real.

Signaling

A carbon tax sends a clear signal to polluters: pollution imposes a negative externality on others, and you should be forced to internalize that cost by paying the tax. There is no ambiguity about the message that is intended to be conveyed. Greenhouse gas emissions are costly, and even if people are willing to pay the price, they should be aware of the societal cost they are imposing.

A cap and trade system, however, sends a different and more ambiguous message. On the one hand, its goal is to reduce greenhouse gas emissions. On the other hand, it achieves that goal by either allowing polluters to purchase the right to pollute (from the government or from each other), or to receive permits to pollute for free. The underlying message is that the government permits you to pollute as long as you are willing to pay. Of course, the message (and the cost imposed) may be the same, regardless of whether a tax is paid or whether an allowance is purchased, although it is not the same if allowances are distributed for free. Labels are important, however, and calling the cost a tax sends a different signal than calling it the purchase price for a right to pollute.

Admittedly, most of the activities that give rise to greenhouse gases were until recently considered perfectly legitimate and even positive. Driving a car or riding an airplane has no inherent moral value, and operating an industrial plant creates jobs. But we now know that these activities involve an additional collective cost, and taxing them directly or indirectly forces us to acknowledge this cost in an unambiguous way. Permitting polluters to purchase the right to pollute does not send the same signal.

Disadvantages of a Carbon Tax

Political Resistance

A primary reason that both presidential candidates supported cap and trade during the 2008 election, and that other political leaders and many academics support cap and trade, rather than a carbon tax, reflects concern that a carbon tax cannot get enacted because it is a tax. Politicians vividly remember the fate of the Clinton-Gore BTU tax proposal in 1993, and "to be BTU'd" has become the shorthand among Clinton Administration veterans for what happens to supporters of politically unpopular proposals.

However, 2009 is not 1993. The public has shown overwhelming support in the United States for decisive action to curb greenhouse gas emissions. When asked, Americans express just as much willingness to support a carbon tax as a cap and trade regime (which is more difficult to explain). If a new administration were to propose a carbon tax in 2009, the political consequences might be less than past experience suggests, especially if the revenue is segregated and used to reduce greenhouse gas emissions, although this clearly is the most significant practical challenge facing a carbon tax.

Moreover, opponents of cap and trade inevitably liken it to a carbon tax. If allowances are auctioned, or even if they have to be purchased from private parties, the resulting cost is likely to be passed on to consumers. Thus, cap and trade is not just more complicated, it is also subject to the same criticism as a carbon tax: it will "increase gas prices at the pump" — an argument every voter understands. If we are to mitigate greenhouse gas emissions, politicians will need to face down inevitable resistance whether they propose a carbon tax or cap and trade.

Much of the opposition to a carbon tax is likely to come from organized groups that stand to benefit from cap and trade. These include industry groups that can easily reduce their emissions and can therefore expect to derive income from selling excess allowances (which they envisage receiving for free), and Wall Street, which can imagine the hefty fees it will charge for arranging trades in allowances and futures trading to hedge against Cost Uncertainty. However, the carbon tax will also have its supporters, primarily industry groups that will suffer from Cost Uncertainty under cap and trade and would prefer the Cost Certainty provided under the carbon tax.

Benefit Uncertainty

The main substantive disadvantage of a carbon tax compared to cap and trade is Benefit Uncertainty. There can be no assurance that any given tax level will result in the desired reduction in greenhouse gas emissions. If the desired benefit is not achieved, the tax may have to be raised, resulting in renewed political opposition, which could defeat the tax increase and thereby limit the environmental benefits of the tax.

However, there are several reasons not to reject the carbon tax because of Benefit Uncertainty. First, as pointed out above, cap and trade may in fact be subject to similar Benefit Uncertainty, because if costs rise too high one can expect pressure to adjust the cap, even if there is no built-in safety valve.

Second, the tax rate can in fact be adjusted. General experience with other taxes has shown that once a tax is in place, it is usually not as hard to raise its rate despite political opposition to tax hikes; this is why people say that "an old tax is a good tax". The United States income tax began in 1913 with a rate of one percent, and has been raised (and lowered) many times since then (although Americans have become increasingly unwilling to accept tax increases). The Value Added Tax (VAT), which is now the most important tax in the world, was typically introduced in over 100 countries at a much lower rate than the current one. If it becomes clear that the carbon tax rate needs to be raised to achieve the necessary reduction in emissions, and if voters remain convinced of the need to reduce emissions, historical experience suggests that the rate could be raised, notwithstanding the political challenges.

Finally, neither cap and trade (without a safety valve) nor a carbon tax can truly achieve Benefit Certainty, because the desired level of emissions (450 ppm) is based on *worldwide* emissions, not United States emissions. We can have the strictest cap and trade regime and suffer the full cost, but if China and India do nothing, we will not have Benefit Certainty. From this perspective, in addition to reducing greenhouse gas emissions in the United States, both a carbon tax and a cap and trade system serve the essential function of persuading the rest of the world that we are serious, and therefore that they should cooperate in a global policy to curb greenhouse gas emissions. Both cap and trade and a carbon tax are equally useful from that perspective, but for the reasons explained above, a carbon tax can be implemented much faster than cap and trade and, therefore, is preferable from the stand-point of international leadership. Stated differently, Benefit Certainty requires bringing large developing countries to the bargaining table, and a carbon tax is better and faster in doing so than cap and trade.

Tax Exemptions

Proponents of cap and trade argue that it is better than a carbon tax because the political bargain over which industries will get relief from its cost has to be reached up front as part of the decision of how to allocate allowances. They also argue that a carbon tax will be subject to pressure to enact permanent exemptions for affected industries, which will permanently weaken its effect and exacerbate its Benefit Uncertainty.

However, it is not clear that a carbon tax would necessarily be weakened by any exemptions. This Article supports a proposal that would apply the tax upstream to only three industries: coal, oil, and natural gas producers and importers. None of these three industries is in a particularly good position to argue for exemptions vis-a-vis the other two, and the ultimate incidence of the tax is too unclear for other industries to effectively argue for exemptions.

The choice between free allocation of allowances under cap and trade and exemptions under a carbon tax is similar to the familiar debate in the tax literature over whether direct subsidies or tax expenditures are superior. Tax expenditures are indirect subsidies delivered through tax reductions or exemptions. While the traditional view has favored direct subsidies because they are arguably more transparent and easier to administer, recently the consensus has shifted to view both types of programs as equally transparent, and so the choice between them comes down to administrative considerations, which generally favor tax expenditures that can be administered by the IRS.

In the cap and trade versus carbon tax debate, the choice between free allowances and tax exemptions is simpler. Tax exemptions are not necessary at all, but if they are enacted they will be quite transparent and subject to criticism as giveaways to unpopular industries. They will also be relatively easy to administer by the IRS. Free allowances, on the other hand, are inherently more complicated to distribute and monitor, for the reasons given above. This debate therefore favors the carbon tax.

Coordination

Another alleged advantage of cap and trade and disadvantage of the carbon tax is that it is easier to coordinate with the regimes implemented by other countries, and especially the EU ETS. Proponents of cap and trade envisage direct transfers of allowances between the United States cap and trade and the EU ETS, as well as other potential cap and trade regimes in, for example, Canada.

Coordination issues may become more significant over time, if cap and trade emerges as the dominant global approach to climate change mitigation. However, this advantage is largely illusory at present. The initial EU ETS has not been successful because too many allowances were distributed, and it is unclear whether its replacement will be more successful. Canada is still debating between cap and trade and a carbon tax. As a result, there currently is no global cap and trade regime for the United States to join.

Moreover, exchanging allowances with foreign cap and trade regimes exponentially increases the enforcement difficulties inherent in cap and trade. Foreign allowances would have to be carefully monitored and verified to prevent widespread cheating. This problem is exacerbated under the EU ETS because allowances are distributed "downstream" to many different polluters. A carbon tax, on the other hand, can easily be collected on imports and rebated on exports, and as long as it is also imposed on domestic production, it does not pose significant World Trade Organization compliance issues.

If, as a result of enacting a United States carbon tax, the United States is able to participate in negotiating a worldwide accord on curbing greenhouse gases, and if that accord is built on a global cap and trade regime, then we can consider adopting a United States cap and trade system to match with that regime. In the absence of such a regime, it would be unwise to enact cap and trade just because the EU has adopted a flawed cap and trade system.

Conclusion

The global climate change crisis will not be resolved simply by implementing a carbon tax or a cap and trade system — or by any other legislative approach. Fundamental changes in energy production, development, and conservation, as well as changes in transportation, land use, and natural resource policies, must be pursued alongside efforts to reduce carbon dioxide emissions.

An effective carbon mitigation strategy, however, will be the centerpiece of any successful program to combat global climate change. While the widespread embrace of cap and trade is a positive development after decades of inaction, before we move forward we should pause to consider whether a cap and trade system is the best approach to combating global climate change. This Article demonstrates that a better response to global climate change would be a carbon tax that is adjusted over time to achieve the necessary reductions in carbon dioxide emissions, as well as the corresponding improvements in alternative energy sources and land and resource management practices that are essential to conserving our planet for future generations.

Notes and Questions

1. Do the authors overstate the case for carbon taxes over cap-and-trade? Do you agree with their analysis? Compare and contrast the various approaches different Canadian jurisdictions have taken to deal with climate change. What factors might explain why some have adopted carbon taxes while most have resisted this approach?

2. Consider the current federal approach to mitigating climate change. How does it compare to the approach in your province? Do you see any policy inconsistencies that may pose problems in the future?

3. The European Union, in 2005, was the first jurisdiction to implement a cap-and-trade system. For a detailed analysis of the EU experience, see M. Rodi, ed., *Emissions Trading in Europe: Initial Experiences and Lessons for the Future* (Berlin: Lexxion, 2008). For a detailed discussion of subsidies and social norms, see Andrew Green, "You Can't Pay Them Enough: Subsidies, Environmental Law, and Social Norms" (2005) 30 Harv. Envtl. L. Rev. 407. In this article, the author considered the role of subsidies in mitigating climate change. He concluded that subsidies are of limited use for a number of reasons: besides draining government resources, subsidies have limited potential to cause a shift in societal norm towards one in which we find it inappropriate to engage in activities that unnecessarily contribute to greenhouse gas emissions. Why do you think subsidies have nevertheless been a tool of choice in Canada with respect to climate change?

Part III — Climate Change Litigation

International efforts to ensure an effective global response to climate change have been underway for at least three decades. Similarly, domestic efforts in many countries including Canada have been ongoing since the entry into force of the UNFCCC in 1994. With the passage of time, it is becoming increasingly likely that these efforts will be inadequate to prevent serious and perhaps even catastrophic climate change related loss and damage. In these circumstances, it is not surprising that the issue of climate change has found its way into the judicial realm. Sometimes these lawsuits appear to have been brought as a last-ditch effort to compel action to reduce greenhouse gas emissions. In other instances, these suits have more modest goals including creating clarity as to who will be liable for the loss and damage caused by human-induced climate change. American-based plaintiffs have led the way in pursuing litigation either seeking redress for the impacts of climate change or pushing for government action. A number of lawsuits commenced to date have targeted large corporations in the energy and automotive sectors seeking damages and injunctive relief with respect to past and present greenhouse gas emissions. In this Part, we offer an overview of climate litigation in four distinct litigation settings: (a) judicial review and statutory appeals, (b) challenges related to the division of powers, (c) tort litigation and other common law claims, and (d) climate litigation under the *Canadian Charter of Rights and Freedoms*.

Judicial Review and Statutory Appeals

Judicial review and statutory appeals are two major avenues for challenging government decisions and actions in court. As we introduced in Chapter 6, judicial review can be a powerful avenue to hold government decision-makers to account in many areas of environmental decision-making. While judicial review originates at common law from the inherent supervisory function of the judiciary over Crown delegates, the availability and mechanism of judicial review has been codified in statute in federal legislation (see *Federal Courts Act*, R.S.C. 1985, c. F-7, section 18.1) and in various provincial statutes and Rules of Court. Legislation may also provide a statutory right of appeal from a government decision to a court. For example, section 22 of the *National Energy Board Act*, R.S.C. 1985, c. N-7, provides that a statutory right of appeal lies from a decision or order of the National Energy Board to the Federal Court of Appeal under certain circumstances.

In the field of climate litigation, judicial review and statutory appeals may be used as a way to challenge government decisions that hinder our ability to meet our greenhouse gas reduction commitments and transition to a carbon neutral economy. For example, as alluded to in the notes under the previous section, Ecojustice on behalf of Greenpeace Canada has applied to the Ontario Superior Court of Justice for judicial review over the Ontario government's cancelling of the provincial cap-and-trade legislation. In particular, the applicant challenges the government's decision to exempt Regulation 386/18 and Bill 4 from the public consultation requirements under Ontario's *Environmental Bill of Rights, 1993*, S.O. 1993, c. 28 (EBR). Regulation 386/18 revoked the operational elements of the cap-and-trade program under the *Climate Change Mitigation and Low-carbon Economy Act, 2016*, S.O. 2016, c. 7, and prohibits the trading of emission allowances and credits. Bill 4 would enact the *Cap and Trade Cancellation Act, 2018*, S.O. 2018, c. 13, which would repeal Ontario's cap-and-trade legislation. The applicant seeks, among other things, declarations that the government's failure to comply with the EBR was unlawful and to quash the Regulation.

As an avenue for climate litigation, judicial review can be very versatile because so many different government decisions from all levels of government influence Canada's greenhouse gas emissions and Canada's ability to meet its climate change obligations. These decisions range from discrete regulatory approvals of projects or facilities that may emit greenhouse gases to broad policy instruments such as a carbon tax or cap-and-trade program. However, judicial review as an avenue for climate litigation becomes more challenging when the target of the judicial review is decision-making at the highest levels. One of the key reasons for this is the courts' tendency to eschew polycentric policy decisions and to defer to the executive or legislative branches of government in these instances. Courts are more comfortable when the legal dispute is a "justiciable" issue of law rather than the appropriateness of government policy.

Consider the case below, in which an environmental not-for-profit organization was challenging the federal government's failure to comply with the *Kyoto Protocol Implementation Act*, S.C. 2007, c. 30 (KPIA). In dismissing the applications for judicial review, the Federal Court discussed the issue of justiciability and the proper role of a court in a judicial review.

Friends of the Earth–Les Ami(e)s de la Terre v.
Canada (Governor in Council)

2008 FC 1183,
affirmed 2009 FCA 297, leave to appeal
refused 2010 CarswellNat 666 (S.C.C.)

BARNES J.: — The Applicant, Friends of the Earth–Les Ami(e)s de la Terre (FOTE), is a Canadian not-for-profit organization with a mission to protect the national and global environment. It has 3,500 Canadian members and is part of an international federation representing 70 countries.

FOTE brings three applications for judicial review before the Court each seeking declaratory and mandatory relief in connection with a succession of alleged breaches of duties said to arise under the *Kyoto Protocol Implementation Act*, S.C. 2007, c. 30 (KPIA). All three of the applications are closely related and they were ordered to be heard consecutively by an Order of Justice Anne Mactavish dated April 17, 2008. Because these applications are all based on common material facts and involve interrelated issues of statutory interpretation, it is appropriate to issue a single set of reasons.

In its first application for judicial review (T-1683-07) FOTE alleges that the Minister of the Environment (Minister) failed to comply with the duty imposed upon him under s. 5 of the KPIA to prepare an initial Climate Change Plan that fulfilled Canada's obligations under Article 3.1 of the Kyoto Protocol [...] its second application for judicial review (T-2013-07) FOTE alleges that the Governor In Council (GIC) failed to comply with s. 8 and 9 of the KPIA by failing to publish proposed regulations in the Canada Gazette with accompanying statements and by failing to prepare a statement within 120 days setting out the greenhouse gas emission reductions reasonably expected to result from each proposed regulatory change and from other proposed mitigation measures [...] its third application (T-78-08) concerns s. 7 of the KPIA. It alleges that the GIC failed in its duty within 180 days to make, amend or repeal regulations necessary to ensure that Canada meets its obligations under Article 3.1 of the Kyoto Protocol.

FOTE argues that the language of s. 5, 7, 8 and 9 of the KPIA is unambiguous and mandatory. It says that the Respondents have refused to carry out the legal duties imposed upon them by Parliament and they have each thereby acted outside of the rule of law.

The Respondents assert that the statutory duties that are the subject of these applications are not justiciable because they are not properly suited or amenable to judicial review. In particular, the Respondents say that the KPIA creates a system of Parliamentary accountability involving scientific, public policy and legislative choices that the Court cannot and should not assess. In short, they assert that their accountability for their failure to fulfill Canada's Kyoto obligations will be at the ballot box and cannot be in the courtroom.

Legislative History and Background

Following its introduction to Parliament as a private member's bill (Bill C-288), the KPIA became law on June 22, 2007. The KPIA was not supported by the government which had earlier stated that Canada would not comply with the Kyoto Protocol targets. The KPIA thus embodies a legislative policy which is inconsistent with stated government policy. This also explains why the KPIA does not authorize the expenditure of public funds to achieve its objectives. A money bill cannot be introduced to Parliament unless it is presented by the government.

The KPIA imposes a number of responsibilities upon the Minister and upon the GIC. A central element of the legislation requires the Minister to prepare an annual Climate Change Plan which describes "the measures to be taken [by the federal government] to ensure that Canada meets its [Kyoto] obligations". Each Plan must be tabled in Parliament and referred to an appropriate standing Committee. The KPIA also directs the GIC to make, amend or repeal environmental regulations to ensure, as well, that Canada complies with its Kyoto obligations; this provision is tied to others which create additional reporting functions all tied to various timelines for action.

The Minister's initial Climate Change Plan was released on August 21, 2007. The Plan, on its face, acknowledges the responsibilities imposed by the KPIA upon the Minister and the GIC although, at least implicitly, it characterizes some of those responsibilities as discretionary. For instance, in describing the provisions of the KPIA dealing with regulatory change, the Plan states:

> With regard to Sections 6 through 8 of the Act, these call for the Government to regulate compliance with the Kyoto Protocol, but are silent on what types of regulation are expected and which sectors of society should shoulder the burden. The Governor-in-Council has discretion on whether and how best to regulate to meet legislative objectives, in order that the Government may pursue a balanced approach that protects both the environment and the economy. The Government is taking aggressive action to reduce greenhouse gases and will therefore continue to fulfil its proper role in Canada's parliamentary system by regulating where appropriate and in a balanced and responsible manner. In that context, this document elaborates on the Government's existing plan to regulate greenhouse gas emissions and air pollution, *Turning the Corner*.

The Climate Change Plan also makes it very clear that the Government of Canada has no present intention to meet its Kyoto Protocol commitments. The Climate Change Plan does confirm Canada's ratification of the Kyoto Protocol, which requires a reduction of greenhouse gas emissions between 2008 and 2012 to levels below 1990 (base year) levels. The Climate Change Plan indicates that Canada's Kyoto target for emission reduction is 6% below 1990 levels. In March 2007 Canada declared its base year emissions to be 599 Mt CO_2 equivalent. For Canada to meet its Kyoto reduction targets its average annual greenhouse gas emissions between 2008 and 2012 are thus limited to 563 Mt CO_2 equivalent.

Canada's greenhouse gas emissions have not declined. In fact, they have steadily increased since 1990 including during the period following Canada's ratification of the Kyoto Protocol. According to the Climate Change Plan that growth, if not constrained, is projected to lead to average annual emissions levels between 2008 and 2012 of 825 Mt CO_2 equivalent. Because of Canada's increasing post-Kyoto reliance on fossil fuels, the Climate Change Plan states that Canada would have to achieve an average 33% reduction in emissions each year for five years to meet the promise of 6% below base year levels. The Climate Change Plan also describes the government's position on the challenges it faces in complying with the Kyoto Protocol. [...]

The evidence is uncontradicted that at the point of commencement of FOTE's second and third applications the GIC had not carried out any regulatory action as contemplated by s. 7, 8 and 9 of the KPIA. [...]

The Principles of Statutory Interpretation and Justiciability

The issues raised by these applications concern the interpretation of a number of the provisions of the KPIA to determine whether the responsibilities imposed respectively upon the Minister and the GIC are justiciable. Before examining the specific language of the KPIA relied upon by FOTE, it is helpful to recall some of the general principles of statutory interpretation and justiciability.

Statutory Interpretation

One of the guiding principles of statutory interpretation is that the search for the meaning of specific words or phrases is informed by the context of the entire statutory text. Words should not be construed in isolation from other surrounding language. Wherever possible the exercise is one of looking for internal consistency and harmony of the language used with the ultimate goal of advancing the intention of Parliament. A useful general statement of these points can be found in the following passage from *Ontario (Minister of Transport) v. Ryder Truck Rental Canada Ltd.* (2000), 47 O.R. (3d) 171, [2000] O.J. No. 297 (Ont. C.A.):

> The modern approach to statutory interpretation calls on the court to interpret a legislative provision in its total context. The court should consider and take into account all relevant and admissible indicators of legislative meaning. The court's interpretation should comply with the legislative text, promote the legislative purpose, reflect the legislature's intent, and produce a reasonable and just meaning. The Supreme Court has repeatedly affirmed this approach to statutory interpretation, most recently in *R. v. Gladue*, [1999] 1 S.C.R. 688 at p. 704, 171 D.L.R. (4th) 385, where Cory and Iacobucci JJ. wrote:
>
> > "As this Court has frequently stated, the proper construction of a statutory provision flows from reading the words of the provision in their grammatical and ordinary sense and in their entire context, harmoniously with the scheme of the statute as a whole, the purpose of the statute, and the intention of Parliament. The purpose of the statute and the intention of Parliament, in particular, are to be determined on the basis of intrinsic and admissible extrinsic sources regarding the Act's legislative history and the context of its enactment [...]"

Justiciability

The parties do not disagree about the principles of justiciability but only in their application in these proceedings. They agree, for instance, that even a largely political question can be judicially reviewed if it "possesses a sufficient legal component to warrant a decision by a court": see *Reference Re Canada Assistance Plan (B.C.)*, [1991] 2 S.C.R. 525 at para. 27, 83 D.L.R. (4th) 297. The disagreement here is whether the questions raised by these applications contain a sufficient legal component to permit judicial review. The problem, of course, is that "few share any precise sense of where the boundary between political and legal questions should be drawn": see Lorne M. Sossin, *Boundaries of Judicial Review: The Law of Justiciability in Canada* (Scarborough: Carswell, 1999) at p. 133.

One of the guiding principles of justiciability is that all of the branches of government must be sensitive to the separation of function within Canada's constitutional matrix so as not to inappropriately intrude into the spheres reserved to the other branches [...] Generally a court will not involve itself in the review of the actions or decisions of the executive or legislative branches where the subject matter of the dispute is either inappropriate for judicial involvement or where the court lacks the capacity to properly resolved it [...]

Appropriateness not only includes both normative and positive elements, but also reflects an appreciation for both the capacities and legitimacy of judicial decision-making. Tom Cromwell (now Mr. Justice Cromwell of the Nova Scotia of Appeal) summarized this approach to justiciability in the following terms:

> The justiciability of a matter refers to its being suitable for determination by a court. Justiciability involves the subject matter of the question, the manner of its presentation and the appropriateness of judicial adjudication in light of these factors. This appropriateness may be determined according to both institutional and constitutional standards. It includes both the question of the adequacy of judicial machinery for the task as well as the legitimacy of using it.

While it is helpful to develop the criteria for a determination of justiciability, including factors such as institutional capacity and institutional legitimacy, it is necessary to leave the content of justiciability open-ended. We cannot state all the reasons why a matter may be non-justiciable. While justiciability will contain a diverse and shifting set of issues, in the final analysis, all one can assert with confidence is that there will always be, and always should be, a boundary between what courts should and should not decide, and further, that this boundary should correspond to predictable and coherent principles. As Galligan concludes, "Non-justiciability means no more and no less than that a matter is unsuitable for adjudication".

While the courts fulfill an obvious role in the interpretation and enforcement of statutory obligations, Parliament can, within the limits of the constitution, reserve to itself the sole enforcement role: see *Canada (Auditor General) v. Canada (Minister of Energy, Mines and Resources)*, [1989] 2 S.C.R. 49, [1989] S.C.J. No. 80, ¶68 to 70. Such a Parliamentary intent must be derived from an interpretation of the statutory provisions in issue — a task which may be informed, in part, by considering the appropriateness of judicial decision-making in the context of policy choices or conflicting scientific predictions.

Are the Issues Raised by These Applications Justiciable?

The question presented by FOTE's first application is whether, under s. 5 of the KPIA, the Minister is permitted as a matter of law to tender a Climate Change Plan that, on its face, is non-compliant with Canada's Kyoto obligations. In other words, does the KPIA contemplate judicial review in a situation like this where the government declares to Parliament and to Canadians that it will not, for reasons of public policy, meet or attempt to meet the emissions targets established by the Kyoto Protocol.

The question posed by FOTE's second and third applications concerns the right of the Court to involve itself in the regulatory business of the executive branch of government.

Section 5 of the KPIA deals with the Minister's duty to prepare an annual Climate Change Plan. FOTE relies heavily on the opening language of s. 5 which speaks to a Climate Change Plan that ensures that Canada meets its Kyoto obligations. FOTE says quite simply that the Minister's Climate Change Plan does not ensure Kyoto compliance because it expressly acknowledges noncompliance.

FOTE advances much the same argument with respect to s. 7 and 9 of the KPIA. Those provisions similarly impose responsibilities on the GIC and on the Minister to ensure, by various means, that Canada meets its Kyoto obligations. Section 8 of the KPIA requires the GIC to pre-publish for consultation any proposed environmental regulations made pursuant to s. 7 with accompanying efficacy statements. Section 9 is also linked to s. 7 because it requires the Minister to prepare a statement concerning the emission reductions anticipated from any regulation created under s. 7. The justiciability of the s. 8 and 9 obligations is, therefore, dependent upon the authority of the Court to order the GIC to make, amend, or repeal the environmental regulations referenced in s. 7.

The justiciability of all of these issues is a matter of statutory interpretation directed at identifying Parliamentary intent: in particular, whether Parliament intended that the statutory duties imposed upon the Minister and upon the GIC by the KPIA be subjected to judicial scrutiny and remediation.

All of the statutory provisions which are the subject of FOTE's applications are linked to one another and, in order to construe any one of them, it is necessary to consider all of them [...]

Section 5

If the intent of s. 5 of the Act was to ensure that the Government of Canada strictly complied with Canada's Kyoto obligations, the approach taken was unduly cumbersome. Indeed, a simple and unequivocal statement of such an intent would not have been difficult to draft. Instead s. 5 couples the responsibility of ensuring Kyoto compliance with a series of stated measures some of which are well outside of the proper realm of judicial review. For instance, s. 5(1)(a)(iii.1) requires that a Climate Change Plan provide for a *just transition* for workers affected by greenhouse gas emission reductions and s. 5(1)(d) requires an *equitable distribution* of reduction levels among the sectors of the economy that contribute to greenhouse gas emissions. These are policy-laden considerations which are not the proper subject matter for judicial review. That is so because there are no objective legal criteria which can be applied and no facts to be determined which would allow a Court to decide whether compliance had been achieved: see *Chiasson v. Canada*, 2003 FCA 155 [...]

It is not appropriate for the Court to parse the language of s. 5 into justiciable and non-justiciable components, at least, insofar as that language deals with the content of a Climate Change Plan. This provision must be read as a whole and it cannot be judicially enforced on a piecemeal basis. While the failure of the Minister to prepare a Climate Change Plan may well be justiciable, an evaluation of its content is not [...]

There are other reasons for not construing the words in s. 5 "to ensure that Canada meets its [Kyoto] obligations" as creating justiciable duties. The Act contemplates an ongoing process of review and adjustment within a continuously evolving scientific and political environment. It refers to cooperative initiatives with third parties including provincial authorities and industry. These are not matters that can be completely controlled by the Government of Canada such that it could unilaterally ensure Kyoto compliance within any particular timeframe. The Act also recognizes that the implementation of any given Climate Change Plan may not be fully accomplished in any given year. This is the obvious purpose of ss. 5(1)(f), which allows for a failure to implement any of the required remedial measures for ensuring Kyoto compliance in a given year. Any such failure must be explained by the Minister in the succeeding Climate Change Plan to be tabled in Parliament, but it is implicit in this provision that strict compliance with the Kyoto emission obligations in the context of any particular Climate Change Plan is not required by s. 5.

Furthermore, if the Court is not permitted by the principles of justiciability to examine the substantive merits of a Climate Change Plan that dubiously claimed Kyoto compliance, it would be incongruous for the Court to be able to order the Minister to prepare a compliant plan where he has deliberately and transparently declined to do so for reasons of public policy.

Section 7

That the words "to ensure" used in s. 5 of the Act reflect only a permissive intent is also indicated by the use of those words in s. 7 of the Act dealing with the authority of the GIC to pass, repeal or amend environmental regulations.

An isolated and strictly literal interpretation of ss. 7(1) would suggest that the GIC had a duty to make all of the regulatory changes required to ensure Kyoto compliance within 180 days of the Act coming into force. Such a construction is, however, incompatible with the practical realities of making such regulatory changes, and is also inconsistent with the language of ss. 7(2) which allows the GIC at any time after the passage of the Act to make further regulatory changes to also "ensure" that Canada meets its Kyoto obligations [...]

The argument that ss. 7(1) creates a justiciable duty is further weakened by the problem facing the Court for crafting a meaningful remedy. FOTE concedes that the Court cannot dictate what it was that the GIC must have done to regulate compliance with Kyoto. Nevertheless, it argues that the GIC had a residual duty to do something of a regulatory nature within 180 days of the KPIA becoming law. It is undeniable that an attempt by the Court to dictate the content of the proposed regulatory arrangements would be an inappropriate interference with the executive role. The idea that the Court should declare that the GIC had a legal duty to make some sort of regulatory adjustment within 180 days, however insignificant that response might have been, has very little appeal and seems to me to pose an unsatisfactory role for the Court. In *R. v. Secretary of State*, above, Lord Nicholls declined to recognize as justiciable a statutory duty requiring the

Secretary of State to appoint a date for the commencement of certain statutory provisions. Lord Nicholls was concerned about the judicial enforcement of a duty that was "substantially empty of content" and where the Minister's substantive decision involved consideration of a "wide range of circumstances".

Given that the Court is in no position to consider or to dictate the substance of the regulatory scheme anticipated by the Act, it seems to me to be highly unlikely that Parliament intended that the 180-day timeframe be mandatory and justiciable. Indeed, I question whether, outside of the constitutional context, the Court has any role to play in controlling or directing the other branches of government in the conduct of their legislative and regulatory functions. This was the view of Justice Barry Strayer in *Alexander Band No. 134 v. Canada (Minister of Indian Affairs and Northern Development)*, [1991] 2 F.C. 3, [1990] F.C.J. No. 1085, where he observed that the enactment of regulations must be seen as primarily the performance of a political duty which is not judicially enforceable [...]

Sections 8 and 9

If s. 7 of the KPIA does not create a mandatory duty to regulate, it necessarily follows that all of the regulatory and related duties described in s. 8 and s. 9 of the KPIA are not justiciable if the GIC declines to act. If the government cannot be compelled to regulate, it cannot be required to carry out the ancillary duties of publishing, reporting or consulting on the efficacy of such measures — unless and until there is a proposed KPIA regulatory change.

Parliamentary Accountability

The issue of justiciability must also be assessed in the context of the other mechanisms adopted by the Act for ensuring Kyoto compliance. In this case, the Act creates rather elaborate reporting and review mechanisms within the Parliamentary sphere. On this point I agree with the counsel for the Respondents that, with respect to matters of substantive compliance with Kyoto, the Act clearly contemplates Parliamentary and public accountability. While such a scheme will not always displace an enforcement role for the Court, in the overall context of this case, I think it does. If Parliament had intended to impose a justiciable duty upon the government to comply with Canada's Kyoto commitments, it could easily have said so in clear and simple language [...]

All of the above measures are directed at ensuring compliance with Canada's substantive Kyoto commitments through public, scientific and political discourse, the subject matter of which is mostly not amenable or suited to judicial scrutiny.

Considering the scope of the review mechanisms established by the Act alongside of the statutory construction issues noted above, the statutory scheme must be interpreted as excluding judicial review over issues of substantive Kyoto compliance including the regulatory function. Parliament has, with the KPIA, created a comprehensive system of public and Parliamentary accountability as a substitute for judicial review. The practical significance of Parliamentary oversight and political accountability should not, however, be underestimated, particularly in the context of a minority government: see *Canada (Auditor General) v. Canada (Minister of Energy, Mines and Resources)*, above, at para. 71 [...]

As stated by Chief Justice Dickson in *Canada (Auditor General) v. Canada (Minister of Energy, Mines & Resources)*, *supra* at pp. 90-91, a determination of whether a matter is justiciable is:

> [...] first and foremost, a normative inquiry into the appropriateness as a matter of constitutional judicial policy of the courts deciding a given issue, or instead, deferring to other decision-making institutions of the polity [...] There is an array of issues which calls for the exercise of judicial judgment on whether the questions are properly cognizable by the courts. Ultimately, such judgment depends on the appreciation by the judiciary of its own position in the constitutional scheme.

In the view of this member of the judiciary, while this application raises important questions, they are of an inherently political nature and should be addressed in a political forum rather than in the courts.

The Act requires that the annual report tabled by the Minister be laid before each House of Parliament, thus indicating that Parliament's intention in creating this obligation was to provide for review and debate on the content of the reports by Parliament itself. Allegations of informational deficiencies with such reports are, therefore, to be addressed and dealt with by that branch of government, and not, in my view, by the judiciary. It is not for the courts to usurp the role of Parliament in determining the nature and quality of the information it has deemed necessary to conduct its functions. As stated by Justice McLachlin, as she then was, in *New Brunswick Broadcasting Co. v. Nova Scotia (Speaker of the House of Assembly)*, [1993] 1 S.C.R. 319 at p. 389:

> [...] Our democratic government consists of several branches: the Crown, as represented by the Governor General and the provincial counterparts of that office; the legislative body; the executive; and the courts. It is fundamental to the working of government as a whole that all these parts play their proper role. It is equally fundamental that no one of them overstep its bounds, that each show proper deference for the legitimate sphere of activity of the other.

The Minister's duty to report to Parliament on an annual basis as to provincial compliance with the Act's criteria and conditions is clear. The determination of what constitutes "all relevant information" for the purpose of the reporting requirement is appropriately determined by the Minister, in consultation with the provinces, and is subject to policy and political concerns, the parameters of which it is not for this Court to determine. The Minister is accountable to Parliament for the scope and accuracy of the information the report contains. I agree with the respondent that the section 23 obligation is one owed to Parliament and not to the applicants or the public at large although requiring production of an annual report will necessarily inform public debate on the subject. Any remedy, therefore, with regards to fulfilling the section 23 obligation lies within Parliament and not with the courts.

Conclusion

I have concluded that the Court has no role to play reviewing the reasonableness of the government's response to Canada's Kyoto commitments within the four corners of the KPIA. While there may be a limited role for the Court in the enforcement of the clearly mandatory elements of the Act such as those requiring the preparation and publication of Climate Change Plans, statements and reports, those are not matters which are at issue in these applications.

Even if I am wrong about the issue of justiciability, I would, as a matter of discretion, still decline to make a mandatory order against the Respondents. Such an order would be so devoid of meaningful content and the nature of any response to it so legally intangible that the exercise would be meaningless in practical terms.

In the result, these applications must be dismissed. I will deal with the issue of costs in writing.

Notes and Questions

1. Do you agree with the Federal Court that the application raises issues that are not justiciable? Compare the Court's approach to justiciability to the principles raised successfully in defence to lawsuits related to climate change in the US, including the *Kivalina* decision discussed later in this Part. How do these cases compare to the approach to justiciability in the *Urgenda* case of the Hague District Court reproduced below?

2. Does it matter that the *Kyoto Protocol* includes three flexibility mechanisms, which would have allowed Canada to meet its emission reduction obligations without making domestic emission reductions?

3. The Court seems to be influenced by the fact that the legal obligations arose out of a private member's bill that was passed by opposition parties in a minority parliament. What relevance do these factors have in determining whether to require the government to comply with the provisions of the KPIA? Is the judgment consistent with the notion of parliamentary sovereignty?

4. What if the government had filed a plan that experts concluded was inadequate to meet Canada's emissions reduction obligations? What if the plan had simply stated that the government intended to purchase credits to make up for any emissions above the target? Do you think it would have affected the Court's decision?

5. Do you agree that granting the relief sought would have been meaningless in practical terms?

Another issue pertinent to judicial review of governmental decisions affecting climate change is the role of science in the courtroom. Recall in Chapter 6 we discussed the courts' reluctance to act as "academies of science" in judicial reviews, particularly in the area of environmental law. In that chapter, we reproduced parts of an article by Jason MacLean and Chris Tollefson critiquing the Federal Court of Appeal's usage of that concept. In the excerpt that follows, MacLean and Tollefson apply their critique to two examples of judicial review arising in the energy context.

Jason MacLean & Chris Tollefson,
"Climate-Proofing Judicial Review After
Paris: Judicial Competence and Courage"
(2018) 31 J. Envtl. L. & Prac. 245

[After providing general critique of the argument that courts should eschew tackling legal issues that turn on complex scientific or technical evidence so as to avoid becoming "academies of science" (see excerpt in Chapter 6), the authors survey the jurisprudence in patent law, public procurement law and competition law to illustrate the fact that courts do not shy away from grappling with scientific and technical information, which at times can be very complex, in areas outside environmental law.]

[...] the increasingly tenuous presumption of superior administrative expertise and independence in Canada more generally argues in favour of a more robust regime of judicial review across the spectrum of administrative decision-making, including administrative decision-making in respect of environmental protection and natural resources development. There is no more reason to simply presume superior substantive expertise on the part of key environmental and natural resources administrative agencies in Canada than there is regarding the Competition Tribunal. A brief discussion of two recent and ongoing cases illustrates our point.

Consider first the Canadian Environmental Assessment Agency's (Agency) assessment of the Pacific NorthWest liquefied natural gas (LNG) terminal project in British Columbia. The federal government approved the $36 billion project proposed by Malaysia's state-owned energy company Petronas in the fall of 2016 following the Agency's environmental assessment, which noted that the project "would be one of the largest greenhouse gas emitters in Canada." On this basis, the Agency concluded that effects associated with the cumulative GHG emissions from the project would be significant and adverse.

In reaching this determination, however, the Agency considered only the project's annual GHG emissions, and ignored altogether its *cumulative* GHG emissions and contribution to Canada's share of the total global carbon budget. In so doing it violated a mandatory assessment requirement set out in its own home statute, the *Canadian Environmental Assessment Act, 2012*. This statute obliges all federal environmental assessments to "... take into account the following factors: [...] any *cumulative environmental effects* that are likely to result from the designated project." An expert analysis of the project's cumulative GHG emissions found that, depending on how Canada's share of the total global carbon budget is calculated, the project will in and of itself consume between 3% and 10% of Canada's total, all-time carbon budget. The Agency, however, failed to give any consideration at all to these cumulative GHG emissions, and the federal government approved the project in the absence of the statutorily-required cumulative effects analysis.

Consider next the National Energy Board's recent review of TransCanada's Prince Rupert Gas Transmission pipeline, a 900-kilometer natural gas pipeline that would move gas from hydraulic fracturing operations in northeastern British Columbia to the Pacific NorthWest LNG terminal (discussed above) near Prince Rupert, British Columbia. Following the B.C. Oil and Gas Commission's approval of the pipeline, a B.C. resident concerned about the pipeline's environmental impacts formally requested the National Energy Board to consider whether the pipeline requires federal approval. The Board refused, however, to afford the question a full hearing. According to the Federal Court of Appeal in *Sawyer v. Transcanada Pipeline Limited*, the National Energy Board erred in failing to consider whether the gas transmission pipeline project is within its jurisdiction under its home statute, the *National Energy Board Act*. The federal courts have only rarely overturned decisions made by the Board, whose presumptive substantive expertise is reflected in ss. 12(1) of the *Act*, which gives the Board "full and exclusive jurisdiction" to determine whether an inquiry would be in the "public interest." In *Sawyer*, however, the court noted that the Board "erred in its appreciation and application of the *prima facie* test in determining its mandate, and in respect of the legal analysis of the constitutional question."

The cause of the Board's error, however, was not a deficient understanding of Canadian constitutional law, for which it might otherwise be forgiven. Rather, the Board's error arose squarely within its presumed realm of expertise. The Federal Court of Appeal put it this way:

> [T]he Board did not direct its mind to the nature of the enterprise or undertaking in issue. There was considerable evidence before the Board, none of which was in dispute, that the purpose of the PRGT [the gas transmission line] was to move gas from the WCSB [Western Canadian Sedimentary Basin] for export to international markets. *The Board looked at where the pipeline was, and did not ask what it did.*

Notes and Questions

1. The federal government's environmental assessment and approval of the Pacific NorthWest LNG Project mentioned in the article by MacLean and Tollefson above was subject to applications for judicial review filed by Indigenous groups and an environmental organization at the Federal Court. One of the preliminary issues that the Federal Court was called upon to deal with was the admissibility of expert reports relating to climate science and climate change impacts that were not before the original decision-maker (also known as "extra-record" evidence).

    SkeenaWild Conservation Trust, the organization that filed the judicial review, challenged the validity of the environmental assessment, alleging that the Canadian Environmental Assessment Agency had failed to conduct a legally required cumulative effects assessment of greenhouse gas emissions. It also claimed that the Agency's assessment of project alternatives was deficient. In support of these arguments, SkeenaWild filed two expert reports. One expert report addressed the nature and role of greenhouse gas emissions as a cumulative environmental effect and elaborated on how the Agency could have conducted a cumulative effects assessment of project-related greenhouse gas emissions using a carbon budget approach. Using a carbon budget approach, the expert concluded that the project itself could consume between 3% and 10% of Canada's total, all-time carbon budget for meeting the 2°C temperature target under the

Paris Agreement. The other report addressed cumulative project-related greenhouse gas emissions that could be achieved if the project were powered from the grid rather than by burning natural gas.

Both the project proponent and the Attorney General of Canada, who were respondents in the judicial review, filed motions to strike these expert reports. They argued that a court in a judicial review is only permitted to review documents that were part of the record before the original decision-maker. The admissibility of "extra-record" evidence such as these expert reports is governed by the Federal Court of Appeal's authority in *Assn. of Universities & Colleges of Canada v. Canadian Copyright Licensing Agency*, 2012 FCA 22 ("*Access Copyright*"). In *Access Copyright,* the Court identified three exceptions to the bar against extra-record evidence: (a) evidence to provide general background that helps orient the court to the record, (b) evidence to show a procedural defect, and (c) evidence to highlight complete absence of relevant consideration. The moving parties argued that the expert reports did not fall into any of these three categories.

In response, SkeenaWild argued that the two expert reports did fall under the exceptions articulated in *Access Copyright.* More importantly, Skeena-Wild also argued that the Court in *Access Copyright* held that the list of exceptions is not closed. SkeenaWild argued that the Federal Court's decision in *Save Halkett Bay Marine Park Society v. Canada (Minister of the Environment),* 2015 FC 302, provided a fourth exception.

Halkett Bay was a judicial review of a Disposal at Sea Permit granted by the federal Minister of the Environment to the Artificial Reef Society of British Columbia. Save Halkett Bay Marine Park Society challenged the permit and tendered expert affidavits that claimed the hull of the vessel that the Artificial Reef Society of BC wanted to sink contained a banned anti-fouling chemical harmful to the environment. In finding that the expert affidavits were admissible, Crampton C.J. applied *Access Copyright* and recognized an additional exception:

> An important issue before the Minister was the nature of the 'risk to the marine environment or human health'. In my view, this is an exceptional public interest issue that warrants a relaxation of the typical rules of evidence pertaining to a judicial review of a decision made by a Minister or other public official in respect of such an issue. If there is evidence to demonstrate an *unacceptable risk to human health or the environment,* that evidence should be admissible on a judicial review of a decision that focussed on that issue. That is particularly so if the evidence was not before the Minister or other public official. The public would be justified in demanding nothing less.

> [emphasis added]

SkeenaWild argued that the expert reports in question showed an unacceptable risk to the environment, particularly in light of the expert's finding that the project alone, if approved, would consume 3-10% of Canada's all-time carbon budget for limiting global temperature increase to within 2°C.

The parties argued the motion before the Federal Court in July 2017, and the Court reserved judgment. However, before the Court rendered its decision, the project proponent decided to cancel the project. The judicial reviews were stayed without the Court ruling on the admissibility of these expert reports and the applicability of *Halkett Bay*.

2. So far, Crampton C.J.'s decision in *Halkett Bay* has not received consideration by other courts for its recognition of a fourth "unacceptable risk" exception to the rule barring admissibility of extra-record evidence in judicial review. Do you agree with Crampton C.J. that "extra-record" evidence showing unacceptable risk to human health or the environment ought to be admissible in judicial review? How would you use *Halkett Bay* in judicial review proceedings challenging government decisions and actions over greenhouse gases and climate change? Does *Halkett Bay* make it easier for applicants to successfully challenge a government's climate-related decision or action on judicial review, or does the exception only serve to make judicial review more complicated? How does *Halkett Bay* fit into the broader discussion about courts in judicial review acting as "academies of science"?

We now turn to exploring examples of climate-related judicial reviews and statutory appeals abroad. In the United States, the Keystone XL Pipeline is a project proposal to provide additional pipeline capacity connecting the existing Keystone Pipeline System to the oil sands in Canada. The project is proposed by TransCanada Corporation, which owns and operates the existing pipeline system. Environmentalists are concerned about this pipeline extension for the risk of oil spills and for the increase in greenhouse gas emissions associated with oil sands extraction. The National Energy Board approved the Canadian portion of the pipeline extension back in 2007, but the project is stalled in the United States by controversy and legal action.

In 2015, the Obama administration determined that Keystone XL was not in the public interest and rejected the project. However, shortly after President Donald Trump was elected into office in 2017, he and the State Department granted a Presidential Permit allowing TransCanada to construct the pipeline. In response, several groups sued the State Department and various governmental agencies on the ground that the government's decision violated a number of federal statutes. In the decision that follows, U.S. District Judge Brian Morris ruled on a motion for summary judgment brought by the plaintiffs.

Indigenous Envtl. Network v. US Dep't of State
(8 November 2018), Great Falls 4:17-cv-00029-BMM (D. Mont.)

[In this lawsuit, the Indigenous Environmental Network, River Alliance and Northern Plains Resource Council sued the State Department and various governmental agencies on the ground that the Presidential Permit and the accompanying Record of Decision (ROD) and National Interest Determination (NID) in relation to the approval of the Keystone XL Pipeline violated the *National*

Environmental Policy Act (NEPA), the Endangered Species Act (ESA) and the Administrative Procedure Act (APA).]

MORRIS J.: —

[...] A court should grant summary judgment where the movant demonstrates that no genuine dispute exists "as to any material fact" and the movant is "entitled to judgment as a matter of law." Summary judgment remains appropriate for resolving a challenge to a federal agency's actions when review will be based primarily on the administrative record.

The APA standard of review governs Plaintiffs' claims. The APA instructs a reviewing court to "hold unlawful and set aside" agency action deemed "arbitrary, capricious, an abuse of discretion, or otherwise not in accordance with law." A rational connection must exist between the facts found and the conclusions made in support of the agency's action. The Court reviews the Department's compliance with NEPA and the ESA under the arbitrary and capricious standard pursuant to the APA.

Discussion

Did the Department Violate NEPA When It Approved Keystone?

[...] Plaintiffs next allege that the Department violated NEPA by failing to evaluate the cumulative climate impacts of Keystone in combination with other pipelines. Plaintiffs argue that the 2014 SEIS [supplemental environmental impact statement] viewed Keystone in isolation. Plaintiffs allege that this isolated view failed to account for the expansion of the Alberta Clipper pipeline from 450,000 bpd to 880,000 bpd, and failed to use updated emissions modeling.

The Department announced in 2013 that it would prepare an EIS for the Alberta Clipper pipeline expansion. The Department issued a permit for the Alberta Clipper expansion in 2017. When Keystone was proposed, Plaintiffs urged the Department to evaluate the cumulative climate impacts of Keystone and the Alberta Clipper expansion in the Keystone 2014 SEIS. The Department acknowledged the proposed expansion of the Alberta Clipper in the Keystone 2014 SEIS. The Department failed, however, to analyze the cumulative greenhouse gas emissions impacts of both pipelines. The Department instead limited its analysis of emissions to the capacity of Keystone alone.

The Department analyzed the cumulative emissions of Keystone and the Alberta Clipper in the Alberta Clipper EIS. The Alberta Clipper EIS also used the updated Greenhouse Gas, Regulated Emissions, and Energy Use in Transportation ("GREET") model to analyze greenhouse gas emissions. The GREET model results in estimates of greenhouse gas emissions that are up to 20% higher than the model used in the 2014 SEIS. Plaintiffs argue that the development of the Alberta Clipper expansion, and the new GREET model constitute new and relevant information that warrants supplement.

NEPA requires that an EIS consider the cumulative impacts of the proposed action. "Cumulative impact is the impact on the environment which results from the incremental impact of the action when added to other past, present, and reasonably foreseeable future actions regardless of what agency (federal or non-

Federal) or person undertakes such other actions." The cumulative impacts analysis must do more than merely catalogue relevant projects in the area.

Cumulative impacts instead must give sufficiently detailed analysis about these projects and the differences between them. This provision requires an agency to discuss and analyze in sufficient detail to assist "the decisionmaker in deciding whether, or how, to alter the program to lessen cumulative impacts." Further, the environmental consequences must be considered together when several projects that may have cumulative environmental impacts are pending concurrently.

Defendants failed to analyze cumulative climate impacts along with the pending Alberta Clipper expansion. The Court considers the Department's analysis of Keystone in the Alberta Clipper EIS as a cumulative action. The Department similarly should have analyzed the Alberta Clipper pipeline's emissions in the Keystone SEIS. The Department argues that the Keystone SEIS obtained a full picture of the pipeline's climate change impacts. The Department also admits, however, that the 2014 SEIS failed to analyze greenhouse gas emissions associated with the Alberta Clipper. The Department thus failed to paint a full picture of emissions for these connected actions, and, therefore, ignored its duty to take a "hard look."

The Department argues that the cumulative analysis in the Alberta Clipper EIS obviated the need for it to conduct a separate cumulative analysis for Keystone. The Department equates this omission to harmless error. In determining whether a NEPA violation proves harmless, a court considers "whether the error 'materially impeded NEPA's goals — that is, whether the error caused the agency not to be fully aware of the environmental consequences of the proposed action, thereby precluding informed decisionmaking and public participation, or otherwise materially affected the substance of the agency's decision.' "

The Keystone SEIS indicated that greenhouse gas emissions associated with the pipeline would range annually from 1.3 to 27.4 $MMTCO_2e$. The Alberta Clipper EIS determined that combined greenhouse gas emissions associated with both pipelines would range annually from 2.1 to 49.9 $MMTCO_2e$. A difference of this magnitude cannot be dismissed simply as harmless error. The error left out significant information from the climate analysis in the Department's possession. The Department should have considered the cumulative impacts of both projects. The Court recognizes the Department's decision to issue the permit regarding the Alberta Clipper expansion. The Court cannot assume without reasoned analysis, however, that the Department would reach the same conclusion for the Keystone permit. The Department must supplement this analysis to include the same information. Further, the Department must supplement the environmental analysis to include the same updated GREET model analysis used in the Alberta Clipper EIS. [...]

An agency must provide a detailed justification for reversing course and adopting a policy that "rests upon factual findings that contradict those which underlay its prior policy." Agency action qualifies as "arbitrary and capricious if the agency has ... offered an explanation for its decision that runs counter to the evidence before the agency, or is so implausible that it could not be ascribed to a difference in view or the product of agency expertise."

[...] The Department denied the permit in its 2015 ROD. The Department relied heavily on the United States's role in climate leadership. The Department issued a new ROD in 2017. The new ROD noted that "there have been numerous developments related to global action to address climate change, including announcements by many countries of their plans to do so" since the 2015 ROD. Moreover, the new ROD suggested that "a decision to approve [the] proposed Project would support U.S. priorities relating to energy security, economic development, and infrastructure." The Department argues that this about-face constitutes a mere policy shift, and that on its own, cannot be found arbitrary and capricious.

The Department possesses the authority to give more weight to energy security in 2017 than it had in 2015. *Kake* and *State Farm* make clear, however, that "even when reversing a policy after an election, an agency may not simply discard prior factual findings without a reasoned explanation." The Department did not merely make a policy shift in its stance on the United States's role on climate change. It simultaneously ignored the 2015 ROD's Section 6.3 titled "Climate Change-Related Foreign Policy Considerations."

Section 6.3 of the 2015 ROD determined that the United States's climate change leadership provided a significant basis for denying the permit. The Department acknowledged science supporting a need to keep global temperature below two degrees Celsius above pre-industrial levels. The Department further recognized the scientific evidence that human activity represents a dominant cause of climate change. The Department cited transboundary impacts including storm surges and intense droughts. And finally, the Department accepted the United States's impact as the world's largest economy and second-largest greenhouse gas emitter.

The 2017 ROD initially tracked the 2015 ROD nearly word-for-word. The 2017 ROD, without explanation or acknowledgment, omitted entirely a parallel section discussing "Climate Change-Related Foreign Policy Considerations." The 2017 ROD ignores the 2015 ROD's conclusion that 2015 represented a critical time for action on climate change. The 2017 ROD avoids this conclusion with a single paragraph. The 2017 ROD simply states that since 2015, there have been "numerous developments related to global action to address climate change, including announcements by many countries of their plans to do so." Once again, this conclusory statement falls short of a factually based determination, let alone a reasoned explanation, for the course reversal. "An agency cannot simply disregard contrary or inconvenient factual determinations that it made in the past, any more than it can ignore inconvenient facts when it writes on a blank slate."

The Department's 2017 conclusory analysis that climate-related impacts from Keystone subsequently would prove inconsequential and its corresponding reliance on this conclusion as a centerpiece of its policy change required the Department to provide a "reasoned explanation." The Department instead simply discarded prior factual findings related to climate change to support its course reversal.

[**Ed. Note:** District Judge Morris's further analysis of whether the government's decisions in approving Keystone XL violated the *Endangered Species Act* and *Administrative Procedure Act* is omitted.]

Conclusions and Remedies

[...] The Department's analysis of the following issues fell short of a "hard look" and requires a supplement to the 2014 SEIS in order to comply with its obligations under NEPA:

- The effects of current oil prices on the viability of Keystone;
- The cumulative effects of greenhouse gas emissions from the Alberta Clipper expansion and Keystone;
- A survey of potential cultural resources contained in the 1,038 acres not addressed in the 2014 SEIS; and
- An updated modeling of potential oil spills and recommended mitigation measures.

These omissions require a remand with instructions to the Department to satisfy its obligations under NEPA to take a "hard look" at the issues through a supplement to the 2014 SEIS.

[...] The Department failed to comply with NEPA and the APA when it disregarded prior factual findings related to climate change and reversed course. The Court vacates the 2017 ROD and remands with instructions to provide a reasoned explanation for the 2017 ROD's change in course.

[...] It is further ordered that the Department's ROD issued on March 23, 2017, is vacated.

Plaintiffs' request for injunctive relief is granted. The Court enjoins Federal Defendants and TransCanada from engaging in any activity in furtherance of the construction or operation of Keystone and associated facilities until the Department has completed a supplement to the 2014 SEIS that complies with the requirements of NEPA and the APA.

This matter is remanded to the Department for further consideration consistent with this order.

Notes and Questions

1. As Morris J. indicated in his reasons, administrative decisions in the United States may be quashed if they are found to be "arbitrary, capricious, an abuse of discretion, or otherwise not in accordance with law." Further, there must be a "rational connection ... between the facts found and the conclusions made in support of the agency's action." How is the legal test in the United States similar or different from *Dunsmuir* and subsequent case law in Canada governing judicial review? Would a reviewing court in Canada have approached this case differently on an equivalent set of facts? How do you think a court in Canada would rule on this case?

Further abroad, the District Court of The Hague made international headlines in 2015 when it ruled in favour of the non-profit Urgenda Foundation along with 900 co-plaintiffs that the government of The Netherlands must do more to reduce the country's greenhouse gas emissions in order to protect its citizens from the adverse effects of climate change. The case is precedent-setting as the first time that the tort law of negligence has been successfully used to hold a government liable for failing to adequately implement measures to address climate change. As such, we will return to this case in the later section dealing with climate litigation using tort law. However, the District Court also dealt with alleged contraventions of constitutional and legislative obligations that would ordinarily be raised in a judicial review in Canadian courts. Of course, given that The Netherlands uses a civil law system, we need to be cautious about analogizing Dutch jurisprudence to a Canadian common law context. However, the District Court's discussion of separation of powers and "judicial review" reproduced in the excerpt below offers an interesting comparison to Canadian jurisprudence.

Urgenda Foundation v. The State of the Netherlands

(24 June 2015), C/09/456689/HA ZA 13-1396 (Hague District Court)
English Translation from Dutch available on website of the
Dutch judiciary: < http://uitspraken.rechtspraak.nl/
inziendocument?id = ECLI:NL:RBDHA:2015:7196 >

mr. H.F.M. HOFHUIS, *mr.* J.W. BOCKWINKEL and *mr.* I. BRAND: —

The System of Separation of Powers

The main point of this dispute concerns if allowing Urgenda's main claim — an order for the State to limit greenhouse gas emissions further than it has currently planned — would constitute an interference with the distribution of powers in our democratic system. Urgenda has answered this question in the negative and the State, relying on the *trias politica*, has arrived at an opposing viewpoint.

The court states first and foremost that Dutch law does not have a full separation of state powers, in this case, between the executive and judiciary. The distribution of powers between these powers (and the legislature) is rather intended to establish a balance between these state powers. This does not mean that the one power in a general sense has primacy over the other power. It does mean that each state power has its own task and responsibilities. The court provides legal protection and settles legal disputes, which it *must* [do] if requested to do so. It is an essential feature of the rule of law that the actions of (independent, democratic, legitimised and controlled) political bodies, such as the government and parliament can — and sometimes must — be assessed by an independent court. This constitutes a review of lawfulness. The court does not enter the political domain with the associated considerations and choices. Separate from any political agenda, the court has to limit itself to *its own* domain, which is the application of law. Depending on the issues and claims submitted to it, the court will review them with more or less caution. Great restraint or even abstinence is required when it concerns policy-related considerations of ranging interests which impact the structure or organisation of society. The court has to be aware that it only plays one of the roles in a legal dispute between two or more parties. Government authorities, such as the State (with bodies such as the government and the States-General), have to make a general consideration, with due regard for possibly many more positions and interests.

This distinctive difference between these state powers does not automatically provide an answer to the question how the court should decide if it finds that allowing a claim in a dispute between two parties has substantial consequences for third parties which are not part of the proceedings. A decision between two private parties in itself does not have consequences for the position of third parties, so that the position of these third parties does not need to be considered in principle. However, a claim seeking an order such as is the case here, in a case against central government, could have direct or indirect consequences for third parties. This prompts the court to exercise restraint in allowing such claims, all the more if the court does not have a clear picture of the magnitude and meaning of these consequences.

It is worthwhile noting that a judge, although not elected and therefore has no democratic legitimacy, has democratic legitimacy in another — but vital — respect. His authority and ensuing "power" are based on democratically established legislation, whether national or international, which has assigned him the task of settling legal disputes. This task also extends to cases in which citizens, individually or collectively, have turned against government authorities. The task of providing legal protection from government authorities, such as the State, pre-eminently belong[s] to the domain of a judge. This task is also enshrined in legislation.

In a general sense, given the grounds put forward by Urgenda, the claim does not fall outside the scope of the court's domain. The claim essentially concerns legal protection and therefore requires a "judicial review". This does not mean that allowing one or more components of the claim can also have political consequences and in that respect can affect political decision-making. However, this is inherent in the role of the court with respect to government authorities in a state under the rule of law. The possibility — and in this case even certainty — that the issue is also and mainly the subject of political decision-making is no reason for curbing the judge in his task and authority to settle disputes. Whether or not there is a "political support base" for the outcome is not relevant in the court's decision-making process. This does not mean that the requirement of restraint referred to above applies in full to judgments with unforeseeable or difficult to assess consequences for third parties.

The court has also established that the State has failed to argue that it does not have the possibility, at law or effectively, to take measures that go further than those in the current national climate policy. Th[is] follows from the fact that the EU is willing to pursue further-reaching targets if other countries do more than currently can be expected. Nor has the State argued that the court should apply equally Book 6, Section 168, subsection 1 of the Dutch Civil Code, which offers the court the option to reject a claim intended to prohibit a wrongful conduct based on the fact that this conduct should be tolerated due to compelling social interests. The court is of the opinion that the opposite has occurred in this case, namely that based on the facts agreed between the Parties the State must take further-reaching measures to realise the 2° target.

It deserves separate discussion that climate policy is to a great extent adopted in an international context, although it can also be established at state level. The State has put forward that allowing the claim regarding the reduction order would damage the Netherlands' negotiation position at, for instance, the conference in Paris in late 2015. In the opinion of the court, this does not have independent significance in the sense that — if the court rules that the law obliges the State towards Urgenda to realise a certain target — the government is not free to disregard that obligation in the context of international negotiations. However, it applies here too that the court should exercise restraint given the possibility that the consequences of the court's intervention are difficult to assess.

In this, it is relevant to note that the claim discussed here is not intended to order or prohibit the State from taking certain legislative measures or adopting a certain policy. If the claim is allowed, the State will retain full freedom, which is pre-eminently vested in it, to determine how to comply with the order concerned. The court has also taken into account here that the State has failed to argue that [it] is actually incapable of executing the order. The State has also failed to argue here that other, fundamental interests it is expected to promote would be damaged.

The court has arrived at the conclusion regarding the issue discussed here that the aspects associated with the *trias politica* in general do not constitute an obstacle to allowing one or more components of the claim, particularly those related to ordering the reduction concerned. The restraint which the court should exercise does not result in a further limitation than that ensuing from the State's discretionary power, discussed previously.

Notes and Questions

1. Compare and contrast the decision of the Hague District Court in *Urgenda* with the decision of our Federal Court in *Friends of the Earth* reproduced earlier in this section. To what extent do the two courts share or not share a concern for maintaining the proper role of the judiciary? In *Urgenda*, the District Court characterized the case as one concerning "legal protection and therefore requires a 'judicial review'". In contrast, the Federal Court in *Friends of the Earth* held that the questions raised in that case were of an "inherently political nature and should be addressed in a political forum rather than in the courts." What do you think accounts for the differences in approach taken by the two courts even though both cases dealt with the state's implementation of measures to meet its international climate change commitments?

2. The Government unsuccessfully appealed the decision of the Hague District Court to the Hague Court of Appeal. The appeal decision was released on October 9, 2018. A translation of the decision is available online: <https://uitspraken.rechtspraak.nl/inziendocument?id=ECLI:NL:GHDHA:2018:

2610>. How does the reasoning of the Court of Appeal compare to that of the District Court?

The final case we will explore in this section is another landmark case arising out of the New South Wales Land and Environment Court in Australia. This court was established by statute in 1980 as the world's first specialist environmental superior court with a mandate to hear appeals with respect to various environmental and land planning matters in the state of New South Wales. This case is precedent-setting for being the first time that a superior court in Australia (and quite possibly in any American or Commonwealth legal jurisdiction) has rejected a development project on the basis of its impact on climate change using a "carbon budget" analysis.

In this case, Gloucester Resources Limited (GRL) proposed a new open cut coal mine called the Rocky Hill Coal Project. GRL unsuccessfully applied to the Minister for Planning for "development consent" and GRL appealed to the Land and Environment Court. In this statutory appeal, the Court exercised the function of the Minister as the "consent authority" and heard GRL's application afresh on its merits. Such a statutory appeal stands in contrast to judicial reviews that we have explored so far in this section, where the court reviews an administrative decision only on the basis of the "record of the decision" and does not allow the admission of fresh evidence save on certain exceptional circumstances (see discussion of "extra-record evidence" in Note 1 following the excerpt of the article by Jason MacLean and Chris Tollefson earlier in this section). Moreover, unlike in a judicial review, the Court in this statutory appeal owed no deference to the Minister.

The local community group Groundswell Gloucester Inc., which successfully obtained party status from the Court as a respondent in the appeal, tendered expert evidence on the mine's adverse impacts not only on the local community but also critically on climate change. As you will see in the excerpt below, in turning down the mine proposal, Chief Judge Brian Preston accepted and relied heavily on the expert report of Emeritus Professor Will Steffen, who provided a carbon budget analysis of the proposal's impact on the world's ability to meet its greenhouse gas reduction targets under the *Paris Agreement*.

Gloucester Resources Limited v. Minister of Planning

[2019] NSWLEC 7 (New South Wales Land and Environment Court), online: < https://www.caselaw.nsw.gov.au/decision/5c59012ce4b02a5a800be47f >

PRESTON C.J.: —

The Impacts of the Mine on Climate Change

Gloucester Groundswell's Argument for Refusal of the Mine

Gloucester Groundswell contended that the Rocky Hill Coal Project should be refused because the greenhouse gas (GHG) emissions from the Project would adversely impact upon measures to limit dangerous anthropogenic climate change. The effects of carbon in the atmosphere arising from activities in the Project site, and the burning of the coal extracted from the mine, are inconsistent with existing carbon budget and policy intentions to keep global temperature increases to below 1.5° to 2° Celsius (C) above pre-industrial levels and would have a cumulative effect on climate change effects in the long term. Gloucester Groundswell submitted, "in light of that substantial planning harm, and the critical importance of combatting climate change now, the Project should be refused". Gloucester Groundswell developed this argument as follows.

The Rocky Hill Coal Project will cause, directly and indirectly, emissions of greenhouse gases (GHGs). The most significant GHGs will be carbon dioxide (CO_2) and methane (CH_4). Different gases have different greenhouse warming effects (referred to as global warming potentials) and emission factors take into account the global warming potentials of the gases. The estimated emissions are referred to in terms of CO_2 equivalent (CO_2-e) emissions by applying the relevant global warming potential [...].

Project-related GHG emissions can be direct or indirect.

Direct GHG emissions are emissions that occur from sources that are owned or controlled by the reporting entity. [...]

Direct GHG sources for the Rocky Hill Coal Project include emissions from undertaking mining operations, including vegetation stripping, release of fugitive methane during open cut mining and combustion of fuels by vehicles, plant and equipment during mining operations (referred to as Scope 1 Emissions) [...].

Indirect GHG emissions are emissions from the generation of purchased energy products (principally electricity) by the entity (referred to as Scope 2 emissions). In relation to coal mines, Scope 2 emissions typically cover electricity that is purchased or otherwise brought into the organisational boundary of the entity. For the Rocky Hill Coal Project, the principal Scope 2 emissions will be indirect emissions associated with on-site electricity [...]. Scope 2 emissions physically occur outside the boundary of the coal mine, such as at the power station that generates the electricity that is purchased. These are "upstream" indirect emissions.

Other indirect GHG emissions are emissions that are a consequence of the activities of an entity, but which arise from sources not owned or controlled by that entity (referred to as Scope 3 emissions). Examples of Scope 3 emissions are emissions from the extraction and production of purchased materials, transportation of purchased fuels and use of sold products and services. In the case of the Rocky Hill Coal Project, Scope 3 emissions will include emissions associated with the extraction, processing and transportation of diesel and the transportation and combustion of product coals. Emissions from the combustion of product coal are "downstream" emissions as they physically occur at the power stations or steel mills combusting product coal from the mine [...].

[Ed. Note: Preston C.J.'s overview of the scientific consensus on climate change, drawing chiefly from IPCC reports, is omitted.]

Professor Will Steffen, an earth systems scientist who is an Emeritus Professor at the Australian National University, Senior Fellow of the Stockholm Resilience Centre and Member of the Climate Council of Australia, called by Gloucester Groundswell, summarised the impacts of climate change that are already being experienced [...].

Professor Steffen also predicted the likely future changes in the climate of Australia and the mid NSW north coast region and adjacent inland region: [...].

To address these impacts of GHG emissions on the climate system, the terrestrial and oceanic environment and the people of the planet, governments around the world have not only agreed the United Nations Framework Convention on Climate Change in 1992 but in 2015 agreed in the Paris Agreement [...].

[**Ed. Note:** Preston C.J.'s discussion of the *Paris Agreement* and Australia's NDC is omitted.]

A commonly used approach to determine whether the NDCs of the parties to the Paris Agreement cumulatively will be sufficient to meet the long term temperature goal of keeping the global temperature rise to between 1.5°C and 2°C is the carbon budget approach. The carbon budget approach is based on the well-proven relationship between the cumulative anthropogenic emissions of GHGs and the increase in global average surface temperature. The carbon budget approach "is a conceptually simple, yet scientifically robust, approach to estimating the level of greenhouse gas emission reductions required to meet a desired temperature target", such as the Paris Agreement targets of 1.5°C or 2°C (Steffen report [38]). The approach is based on the approximately linear relationship between the cumulative amount of CO_2 emitted from all human sources since the beginning of industrialisation (often taken as 1870) and the increase in global average surface temperature (Figure 2 in IPCC (2013) Summary for Policy Makers, cited in Steffen report, [39]). Once the carbon budget has been spent (emitted), emissions need to become "net zero" to avoid exceeding the temperature target. "Net zero" emissions means the magnitude of CO_2 emissions to the atmosphere is matched by the magnitude of CO_2 removal from the atmosphere (Steffen report, [40]). [...]

Professor Steffen demonstrated how the carbon budget approach can be used for the 2°C temperature target in the Paris Agreement:

> Applying the carbon budget for a 2°C target demonstrates how it can be used. The IPCC estimates that for a greater than 66% probability of limiting global average temperature rise to no more than 2°C, cumulative human emissions since 1870 must be less than 1,000 Gt C (emitted as CO_2) [...]. If non-CO_2 greenhouse gases are not reduced at the same rate, the carbon budget must be reduced by up to a further 210 Gt C to 790 Gt C [...]. From 1870 through 2017 cumulative human emissions have been about 575 Gt C [...]. The remaining budget then becomes 215 Gt C.
>
> The current rate of human emissions of CO_2 is about 10 Gt C per year [...], so at these present rates of emissions, the carbon budget would be consumed in little more than two decades (at about 2040). [...]
>
> The conclusion is that the world has 21-22 years of emissions (at current rates) remaining before the world's economy must reach net zero emissions (215 Gt C divided by 10 Gt C per year = 21.5 years).
>
> (Steffen report, [42]-[45]).

[**Ed. Note:** Preston C.J. further set out in detail the expert evidence of Professor Steffen regarding the need to abstain from new fossil fuel developments if the *Paris Agreement* targets are to be met. This portion of the decision is omitted.]

Professor Steffen concluded from this analysis of the carbon budget that:

> The conclusions from this — or any other analysis based on a carbon budget — are:
>
> – Australia's existing fossil fuel industries must be phased out as quickly as possible, with most of the Australian fossil fuel reserves (and nearly all of Australia's coal reserves) left in the ground.
>
> – Development of new fossil fuel reserves, no matter how small, is incompatible with any carbon budget assuming a 50% or better chance of the budget meeting the temperature target [...] and with Australia's commitments to the Paris accord.
>
> – Based on this analysis, approval of the development of the Rocky Hill Coal Mine is inconsistent with the carbon budget approach towards climate stabilisation.
>
> (Steffen report, [55]).

Professor Steffen contended that the refusal of the Rocky Hill Coal Project is justified on this carbon budget approach regardless of the fact that the total GHG emissions of the Project would be a small fraction of total global emissions. Professor Steffen noted that:

> [...] global greenhouse gas emissions are made up of millions, and probably hundreds of millions of individual emissions around the globe. All emissions are important because cumulatively they constitute the global total of greenhouse gas emissions, which are destabilising the global climate system at a rapid rate. Just as many emitters are contributing to the problem, so many emission reduction activities are required to solve the problem.
>
> (Steffen Report, [57]).

GRL's Argument for Approval of the Mine

[**Ed. Note:** Preston C.J. summary of GRL's arguments here is omitted. Preston C.J. discussed GRL's arguments in his analysis in the following section reproduced below.]

The GHG Emissions of the Project Support Refusal of the Project

Both Direct and Indirect GHG Emissions Should Be Considered

[**Ed. Note:** Preston C.J., having canvassed the applicable legislations and reviewed relevant Australian and U.S. jurisprudence, held that a consent authority ought to consider both direct and indirect GHG emissions, which were set out as Scope 1, 2, and 3 emissions in the Project's environmental impact statement. This portion of the decision is omitted.]

All GHG Emissions Contribute to Climate Change

All of the direct and indirect GHG emissions of the Rocky Hill Coal Project will impact on the environment. All anthropogenic GHG emissions contribute to climate change. As the IPCC found, most of the observed increase in global average temperatures is due to the observed increase in anthropogenic GHG concentrations in the atmosphere. The increased GHG concentrations in the atmosphere have already affected, and will continue to affect, the climate system.

The current and future impacts of climate change were summarised by Professor Steffen and have been set out earlier in the judgment.

The direct and indirect GHG emissions of the Rocky Hill Coal Project will contribute cumulatively to the global total GHG emissions. In aggregate, the Scope 1, 2 and 3 emissions over the life of the Project will be at least 37.8Mt CO_2-e, a sizeable individual source of GHG emissions. It matters not that this aggregate of the Project's GHG emissions may represent a small fraction of the global total of GHG emissions. The global problem of climate change needs to be addressed by multiple local actions to mitigate emissions by sources and remove GHGs by sinks. As Professor Steffen pointed out, "global greenhouse gas emissions are made up of millions, and probably hundreds of millions, of individual emissions around the globe. All emissions are important because cumulatively they constitute the global total of greenhouse gas emissions, which are destabilising the global climate system at a rapid rate. Just as many emitters are contributing to the problem, so many emission reduction activities are required to solve the problem" (Steffen report, [57]).

Many courts have recognised this point that climate change is caused by cumulative emissions from a myriad of individual sources, each proportionally small relative to the global total of GHG emissions, and will be solved by abatement of the GHG emissions from these myriad of individual sources.

[**Ed. Note:** Preston C.J.'s overview of Australian and U.S. jurisprudence and the decision of the Hague District Court and Hague Court of Appeal in *Urgenda* is omitted.]

The Project's Emissions Will Contribute to Climate Change

There is a causal link between the Project's cumulative GHG emissions and climate change and its consequences. The Project's cumulative GHG emissions will contribute to the global total of GHG concentrations in the atmosphere. The global total of GHG concentrations will affect the climate system and cause climate change impacts. The Project's cumulative GHG emissions are therefore likely to contribute to the future changes to the climate system and the impacts of climate change. In this way, the Project is likely to have indirect impacts on the environment, including the climate system, the oceanic and terrestrial environment, and people.

The approval of the Project (which will be a new source of GHG emissions) is also likely to run counter to the actions that are required to achieve peaking of global GHG emissions as soon as possible and to undertake rapid reductions thereafter in order to achieve net zero emissions (a balance between anthropogenic emissions by sources and removals by sinks) in the second half of this century. [...]

Nevertheless, the exploitation and burning of a new fossil fuel reserve, which will increase GHG emissions, cannot assist in achieving the rapid and deep reductions in GHG emissions that are necessary in order to achieve "a balance between anthropogenic emissions by sources and removals by sinks of greenhouse gases in the second half of this century" (Article 4(1) of the Paris Agreement) or the long term temperature goal of limiting the increase in global average temperature to between 1.5°C and 2°C above pre-industrial levels (Article 2 of the Paris Agreement). As Professor Steffen explained, achieving these goals implies phasing out fossil fuel use within that time frame. He contended that one of the implications of the carbon budget approach is that most fossil fuel reserves will need to be left in the ground, unburned, to remain within the carbon budget and achieve the long term temperature goal. The phase out of fossil fuel use by the second half of this century might permit a minority of fossil fuel reserves to be burned in the short term. From a scientific perspective, it matters not which fossil fuel reserves are burned or not burned, only that, in total, most of the fossil fuel reserves are not burned. Professor Steffen explained, however, that the existing and already approved but not yet operational mines/wells will more than account for the fossil fuel reserves that can be exploited and burned and still remain within the carbon budget. This is the reason he considered that no new fossil fuel developments should be allowed.

GRL contended that nevertheless the Rocky Hill Coal Project should be one of the fossil fuel reserves that should be allowed to be exploited and burned for four reasons.

No Specific Proposal to Offset the Project's Emissions

The first reason GRL gave was that the increase in GHG emissions associated with the Project would not necessarily cause the carbon budget to be exceeded, because, as Dr Fisher had argued, reductions in GHG emissions by other sources (such as in the electricity generation and transport sectors) or increases in removals of GHGs by sinks (in the oceans or terrestrial vegetation or soils) could balance the increase in GHG emissions associated with the Project.

I do not accept this reason. It is speculative and hypothetical. There is no evidence before the Court of any specific and certain action to "net out" the GHG emissions of the Project. A consent authority cannot rationally approve a development that is likely to have some identified environmental impact on the theoretical possibility that the environmental impact will be mitigated or offset by some unspecified and uncertain action at some unspecified and uncertain time in the future. This is not a case where the applicant for development consent commits to taking specific and certain action to mitigate and offset the environmental impact of the proposed development. In the climate change context, for example, an applicant for development consent could commit to reducing the GHG emissions of the development by deploying emission reduction technologies, such as carbon capture and storage, or offsetting the GHG emissions of the development by increasing the removal of GHGs in the atmosphere by establishing sinks, such as by reafforestation or afforestation of land. The Rocky Hill Coal Project, however, is not proposed to be carbon neutral. GRL has not proposed to balance the emissions by sources with removals by sinks.

Possibility of Abatement Unrelated to the Project Not Relevant

The second reason given by GRL was based on Dr Fisher's argument that "the size of the global abatement task calls for making emissions reductions where they count most and generate the least economic and social harm." (Fisher report [13]). Dr Fisher considered that refusing approval to individual coal mines, such as the Rocky Hill Coal Project, would not achieve this abatement at least cost.

I do not accept this second reason. A consent authority, in determining an application for consent for a coal mine, is not formulating policy as to how best to make emissions reductions to achieve the global abatement task. The consent authority's task is to determine the particular development application and determine whether to grant or refuse consent to the particular development the subject of that development application. Where the development will result in GHG emissions, the consent authority must determine the acceptability of those emissions and the likely impacts on the climate system, the environment and people. The consent authority cannot avoid this task by speculating on how to achieve "meaningful emissions reductions from large sources where it is cost-effective and alternative technologies can be brought to bear" (Fisher Report, [13]). Such emissions reductions from other sources are unrelated to the development that is the subject of the development application that the consent authority is required to determine.

If the consent authority considers that the GHG emissions of the development for which consent is sought, and the impacts of those emissions, are unacceptable, and as a consequence determines that the development should be refused in order to avoid the emissions and their impacts, it would not be rational to nevertheless approve the development because greater emissions reductions could be achieved from other sources at lower cost by other persons or bodies. [...]

Assumptions of Market Substitution and Carbon Leakage Unproven

The third reason GRL advanced for approving the Project was that the GHG emissions of the Project will occur regardless of whether the Project was approved or not, because of market substitution and carbon leakage. On market substitution, Dr Fisher suggested that having regard to the limited substitutes for coking coal in steel making and the strong projected demand for coking coal as large countries such as India industrialise and intensify their steel use, "if demand is not met from Australian coal mines, investment will flow to other large coal producers and mines will be developed in countries such as India and Indonesia" (Fisher report, [67]). There will therefore be at least the same amount of GHG emissions, merely coming from those other mines rather than from the Project.

On carbon leakage, Dr Fisher argued that GHG emissions could actually increase if coal mining were to be moved from Australia to other countries. Dr Fisher said that Australian coal mines operate to some of the highest environmental standards in the world and regulations ensure a strict recognition and accounting of GHG emissions, but this is not the case in all countries where coal mining occurs (Fisher report, [65]). This situation is sometimes referred to as "carbon leakage" where, as a result of more stringent climate policies or more stringent application of climate policies in a country, businesses move their production from that country to other countries with less ambitious climate policies or less ambitious application of climate policies, which can lead to a rise in global GHG emissions.

I reject this third reason. On carbon leakage, GRL has failed to substantiate, in the evidence before the Court, that this risk of carbon leakage will actually occur if approval for the Rocky Hill Coal Project were not to be granted. Although there was some disagreement between the experts on coal demand,

Mr Buckley and Mr Manley, they did agree that there were other coking coal mines, both existing and approved, in Australia that could meet current and likely future demand for coking coal, including coking coal with the properties of the coal from the Project. This would mean that the demand for coking coal would be met by Australian coking coal of the highest quality in the world from Australian coal mines operating to the highest environmental standards in the world. There is, therefore, unlikely to be a moving of coal mining abroad or carbon leakage.

A similar carbon leakage argument was rejected by the Hague Court of Appeal in *The State of Netherlands v Urgenda Foundation*. The Court of Appeal held that the State had failed to substantiate that the risk of carbon leakage — the risk that companies will move their production to other companies with less strict greenhouse gas reduction obligations — will actually occur if the Netherlands were to increase its efforts to reduce greenhouse gas emissions before 2020 (at [57]).

The market substitution argument is also flawed. There is no certainty that there will be market substitution by new coking coal mines in India or Indonesia or any other country supplying the coal that would have been produced by the Project. As both Professor Steffen and Mr Buckley explained, countries around the world are increasingly taking action to reduce greenhouse gas emissions in their countries, not only to meet their nationally determined contributions but also to reduce air pollution. [...]

If approval for the Project in the developed country of Australia were to be refused, on grounds including the adverse effects of the mine's GHG emissions on climate change, there is no inevitability that developing countries such as India or Indonesia will instead approve a new coking coal mine instead of the Project, rather than following Australia's lead to refuse a new coal mine. [...]

Developing countries might consider that domestic mitigation measures to achieve their nationally determined contributions for reducing GHG emissions should include not approving new development for the exploitation or burning of fossil fuel reserves. Developing countries may be encouraged to take such mitigation measures by developed countries taking the lead in doing so in their countries. Hence, there is no certainty that refusal of consent to the Project will cause a new coal mine in another country to substitute coking coal for the volume lost in the open market by refusal of the Project.

Thirdly, the ability of a new coking coal mine in another country to substitute for any volume of coal lost by refusal of the Project will depend on the market, including the demand and supply of substitute sources of coal and any difference in price between coal from the Project and from other substitute sources, which price difference might affect substitutability. Without any evidence about the existence and effect of these market forces on substitutability, no assumption can be made that there would be market substitution by coal from new coal mines in other countries if the Project were to be refused. [...]

There is also a logical flaw in the market substitution assumption. If a development will cause an environmental impact that is found to be unacceptable, the environmental impact does not become acceptable because a hypothetical and uncertain alternative development might also cause the same unacceptable environmental impact. The environmental impact remains unacceptable regardless of where it is caused. The potential for a hypothetical but uncertain alternative development to cause the same unacceptable environmental impact is not a reason to approve a definite development that will certainly cause the unacceptable environmental impacts. In this case, the potential that if the Project were not to be approved and therefore not cause the unacceptable GHG emissions and climate change impacts, some other coal mine would do so, is not a reason for approving the Project and its unacceptable GHG emissions and climate change impacts [...].

Producing Coking Coal Not a Justification for GHG Emissions

The fourth reason GRL advanced for approving the Project is that the GHG emissions associated with the Project are justifiable. GRL contended that the Project will produce high quality coking coal, not thermal coal, which is needed for the main way of producing steel, by the BOF process; steel is critical to our society; and there are limited substitutes for coking coal in steel production.

I find that GRL overstates this argument. It may be true that currently most of the world's steel (around 74%) is produced using the BOF process, which depends on coking coal, and although technological innovations might reduce the proportion of steel produced using the BOF process, for the reasons given by Mr Buckley, there is still likely to be demand for coking coal for steel production during the life of the Project.

The current and likely future demand for coking coal for use in steel production can be met, however, by other coking coal mines, both existing and approved, in Australia. [...] Hence, demand for coking coal for use in steel production will be able to be met by supply from other Australian mines if the Project is not approved.

On this basis, it is not necessary to approve the Project in order to maintain steel production worldwide. The GHG emissions of the Project cannot therefore be justified on the basis that the Project is needed in order to supply the demand for coking coal for steel production.

The Project's Poor Environmental and Social Performance Justifies Refusal

I return to the point made by Professor Steffen that, in order to remain within the carbon budget and achieve the long term temperature goal of holding the increase in global average temperatures to between 1.5°C and 2°C above pre-industrial levels, most fossil fuel reserves will need to remain in the ground unburned.

This admits that some fossil fuel reserves can be exploited and burned in the short-term. The question is which fossil fuel reserves should be allowed to be exploited and burned. Professor Steffen accepted that already approved and operational fossil fuel mines/wells could continue, although he considered that they also will need to be rapidly phased-out. He considered that these existing and approved fossil fuel developments already account for the GHG emissions that could be allowed and still keep within the carbon budget.

While this argument is logical, it does assume that all existing and approved fossil fuel developments will continue and there will be no reduction in GHG emissions from these sources. It gives priority to existing and approved fossil fuel developments, along the lines of "first in, best dressed." It also frames the decision as a policy decision that no fossil fuel development should ever be approved.

I consider the better approach is to evaluate the merits of the particular fossil fuel development that is the subject of the development application to be determined. Should this fossil fuel development be approved or refused? Answering this question involves consideration of the GHG emissions of the development and their likely contribution to climate change and its consequences, as well as the other impacts of the development. The consideration can be in absolute terms or relative terms.

In absolute terms, a particular fossil fuel development may itself be a sufficiently large source of GHG emissions that refusal of the development could be seen to make a meaningful contribution to remaining within the carbon budget and achieving the long term temperature goal. In short, refusing larger fossil fuel developments prevents greater increases in GHG emissions than refusing smaller fossil fuel developments.

In relative terms, similar size fossil fuel developments, with similar GHG emissions, may have different environmental, social and economic impacts. Other things being equal, it would be rational to refuse fossil fuel developments with greater environmental, social and economic impacts than fossil fuel developments with lesser environmental, social and economic impacts. To do so not only achieves the goal of not increasing GHG emissions by source, but also achieves the collateral benefit of preventing those greater environmental, social and economic impacts.

In the case of the Rocky Hill Coal Project, the aggregate GHG emissions over the life of the Project are sizeable, although the Project is not one of the largest coal mines in Australia. The Minister noted that the proposed production of the Rocky Hill mine appears to be about a third of the production of the average coal mine in NSW [...]. Refusal of consent to the Project would prevent a meaningful amount of GHG emissions, although not the greater GHG emissions that would come from refusal of a larger coal mine. However, the better reason for refusal is the Project's poor environmental and social performance in relative terms. As I have found elsewhere in the judgment, the Project will have significant and unacceptable planning, visual and social impacts, which cannot be satisfactorily mitigated. The Project should be refused for these reasons alone. The GHG emissions of the Project and their likely contribution to adverse impacts on the climate system, environment and people adds a further reason for refusal. Refusal of the Project will not only prevent the unacceptable planning, visual and social impacts, it will also prevent a new source of GHG emissions. I do not consider the justifications advanced by GRL for approving the Project, notwithstanding its GHG emissions, are made out for the reasons I have given earlier.

Notes and Questions

1. This case shows the importance of complex scientific evidence in climate litigation. Preston C.J.'s findings and conclusions were heavily influenced as much by the expert report of Professor Steffen as by the absence of

evidence from the proponent. Preston C.J. rejected many of GRL's arguments, such as greenhouse gas offsetting, market substitution and carbon leakage, on the basis that GRL failed to adduce evidence in support of those arguments. Such arguments are often made by industry proponents. For example, supporters of oil sands development in Alberta argue that Albertan oil is "cleaner" due to stronger environmental laws in Canada than in other developing countries, and supporters of liquified natural gas development in British Columbia argue that BC's natural gas would displace dirtier fossil fuels in overseas markets. How do you think Preston C.J. would have ruled in this case if GRL did adduce evidence in support of those arguments? Would evidentiary support for those arguments be sufficient to change the outcome of this case?

2. As we discussed in Chapter 1, international law plays a role in Canadian jurisprudence by, at the very least, being an aid to statutory interpretation, particularly in the environmental context. In this case, Preston C.J. referred to and relied upon the climate targets set under the *Paris Agreement*. What role does this international treaty play in Preston C.J.'s reasons? As we will explore later in this Part, the Hague District Court also considered and relied upon the *Paris Agreement* in the landmark ruling in *Urgenda Foundation v. The State of the Netherlands*. What role does the treaty play in that case?

3. Both in Chapter 6 and earlier in this Part, we discussed the role that deference plays in limiting the scope of judicial review of government's environmental decision-making. As illustrated by this case, the NSW Land and Environment Court has *de novo* jurisdiction in certain statutory appeals to hear a matter afresh, stepping into the shoes of the original administrative decision-maker without owing any deference. As a superior court, its decisions have precedential value in the Australian legal system and serve as persuasive precedents in Commonwealth jurisdictions. Therefore, the NSW Land and Environment Court exhibits an interesting amalgamation of the judicial and executive branches of government. Do you think that it would be useful to have a similar specialist superior court for environmental matters in Canada? In this country, the National Energy Board (NEB) is an expert quasi-judicial tribunal regulating international and interprovincial pipelines and energy development and trade. The NEB has the powers of a "court of record" (*National Energy Board Act*, R.S.C. 1985, c. N-7, s. 11(1)); however, it is not a superior court, so its decisions are not binding precedents. What would your arguments be, both for and against, elevating the NEB to a superior court, much like the NSW Land and Environment Court, for matters within its regulatory jurisdiction?

4. The carbon budget is a powerful tool for planning and decision-making in the context of meeting our climate commitments under the *Paris Agreement*. Outside the context of litigation, what role can carbon budget analysis play in environmental decision-making? In considering this question, think about, among other things, the role that carbon budgets can play in environmental regulation (see Chapter 4) and in environmental assessments (see Chapter 7).

5. Preston C.J. also wrote the leading decision in *Telstra Corporation Ltd. v. Hornsby Shire Council*, [2006] NSWLEC 133, which provided a working legal framework for the application of the precautionary principle in Australian jurisprudence: see discussion of the principle and the *Telstra* case in Chapter 1, Part III.

Division of Powers Litigation

As our discussion in Chapter 3 makes clear, legislative jurisdiction over the environment is shared between the federal and provincial levels of government under Canada's constitutional scheme. Earlier in this chapter, we also canvassed in particular the federal and provincial governments' constitutional authority to enact and implement various measures to address climate change. As with other areas of environmental jurisdiction discussed in Chapter 3, litigation over legislative competence of particular environmental law regimes clarifies the boundaries in the division of powers in respect of the environment. At the time of writing, the extent to which the federal government is able to impose a carbon tax and a cap-and-trade system is being tested in the courts through legal challenges.

As mentioned in Meinhard Doelle's article above, the federal government under Prime Minister Justin Trudeau negotiated the *Pan-Canadian Framework on Clean Growth and Climate Change* with provinces and territories as part of the federal government's efforts to meet its commitments under the *United Nations Framework Convention on Climate Change* and the *Paris Agreement*. One of the elements of this *Pan-Canadian Framework* is a piece of "backstop" legislation which would empower the federal government to impose a carbon tax or a cap-and-trade system on any province or territory that the federal government deems not to have a sufficient carbon pricing system in place. This legislation, the *Greenhouse Gas Pollution Pricing Act*, S.C. 2018, c. 12, s. 186, came into force and was enacted as part of the omnibus budget legislation in 2018.

The preamble to the Act makes clear that the legislation is intended to support Canada's commitments in the UNFCCC, the *Paris Agreement*, Canada's Nationally Determined Contributions under the *Paris Agreement*, and the *Pan-Canadian Framework*. The preamble also affirms the "broad scientific consensus" on climate change impacts from anthropogenic greenhouse gas emissions and that climate change is an intergenerational issue with no geographic boundaries.

The Act consists of two instruments: a levy on fossil fuels (carbon tax) and an "output-based pricing system" (cap-and-trade scheme). The Act is a "backstop" legislation because the Act will only apply in provinces and territories listed in a schedule, which the federal government can amend to add or remove provinces and territories based on whether they have a sufficient carbon pricing system in place. The federal carbon tax will be levied on certain fuel users, distributors and importers in an applicable province or territory beginning with \$10 per tonne of CO_2e in 2018, rising annually to \$50/tonne CO_2e

in 2022. The federal cap-and-trade scheme will only apply to facilities in a listed province or territory that emit over 50,000 tonnes of greenhouse gases per year. Facilities that are subject to the cap-and-trade scheme will be exempt from the federal carbon tax. Facilities that emit over their emissions limit in a compliance period must pay a charge equivalent to the applicable carbon tax for the excess emissions, submit surplus credits, or provide other eligible offsets. The federal government is expected to finalize the list of initially applicable provinces and territories by 2019. Since British Columbia, Alberta and Quebec have their own carbon pricing schemes, the federal Act is not expected to apply in these provinces, although the situation in Alberta may change depending on the outcome of the provincial election in 2019.

Several other provinces have criticized and challenged the federal government's ability to impose a federal carbon pricing scheme. In New Brunswick, the provincial Liberal government was resistant to enacting a provincial carbon tax and in early 2018 proposed instead a plan to divert gas tax revenue to climate change projects. The federal government in response indicated that such a plan was insufficient and announced its intention to impose the federal carbon tax on New Brunswick. The carbon tax became an election issue later that year. The Progressive Conservatives won the election in November 2018 partly on the promise to oppose the carbon tax. New Brunswick has since joined the effort to challenge the federal carbon pricing scheme in court.

Two other provinces have launched legal challenges against the *Greenhouse Gas Pollution Pricing Act*. Saskatchewan was a staunch opponent of the *Pan-Canadian Framework* and was a hold-out on signing the agreement. In April 2018, the Government of Saskatchewan launched a reference case in the Saskatchewan Court of Appeal questioning the constitutional validity of the Act. The province argues that carbon emissions fall under provincial, rather than federal, jurisdiction and therefore the Act is *ultra vires* Parliament. Moreover, the province argues that the unequal treatment of provinces under the Act is constitutional.

With the election of a Progressive Conservative government in June 2018, the Ontario government joined Saskatchewan in the legal battle against the federal carbon pricing scheme. In August 2018, the Government of Ontario also filed a reference case in the Ontario Court of Appeal. Ontario has two main arguments. Firstly, Ontario argues that the federal carbon tax is unconstitutional because the revenue from the tax does not have to be used for greenhouse gas reductions under the Act and therefore there is no connection between the imposition of the tax and the stated statutory purpose. More importantly for our purposes in this section, Ontario also argues that the federal carbon tax violates division of powers, though in a different approach than that taken by Saskatchewan.

Review the following Statement of Particulars filed by the Government of Ontario in the reference case in respect of Ontario's division of powers arguments.

Attorney General of Ontario,
"In the Matter of a Reference to the Court of Appeal pursuant to section 8 of the
Courts of Justice Act, **R.S.O. 1990, c. C.34, by Order-in-Council 1014/2018**
respecting the constitutionality of the *Greenhouse Gas Pollution Pricing Act*,
Part 5 of the *Budget Implementation Act, 2018, No. 1*, **S.C. 2018, c. 12"**
Statement of Particulars (13 September 2018)

The Attorney General of Ontario submits that the *Greenhouse Gas Pollution Pricing Act*, enacted by s. 186 of S.C. 2018, c. 12 ("the Act") is unconstitutional and of no force and effect for the following reasons [...]

Counsel for the Attorney General of Canada has stated that the Act is intended to impose a regulatory charge supported by the national concern branch of the federal peace, order and good government ("POGG") power, which originates in the opening words of section 91 of the *Constitution Act, 1867* (UK), 30&31 Vict., c. 3.

The Attorney General for Ontario, however, submits that the Act cannot be supported by the national concern branch of POGG. The provinces are capable of regulating greenhouse gas emissions themselves and there is no need to expand the scope of federal jurisdiction to impose a one-size-fits-all federal carbon price. Nor do the wide variety of activities that give rise to greenhouse gas emissions have the singleness, distinctiveness and indivisibility that must be present before the national concern branch can apply. [...]

The POGG power, and in particular the national concern branch of that power, is a residuary power that only applies to matters that do not otherwise fall within the heads of power allocated between Parliament and the provincial legislatures by sections 91 to 95 of the *Constitution Act, 1867*.

Expanding the scope of the national concern branch to permit Parliament to regulate the nearly limitless swath of human activity which can result in greenhouse gas emissions would represent an unprecedented and unwarranted intrusion into provincial jurisdiction that is irreconcilable with the fundamental distribution of legislative power under the Constitution. The Act is therefore *ultra vires* and unconstitutional in its entirety.

The mere fact that greenhouse gas emissions can have extra-provincial effects is insufficient to justify resort to the national concern branch of POGG. The provincial legislatures have ample ability to regulate greenhouse gas emissions under the enumerated heads of power set out in section 92 of the *Constitution Act, 1867*. Acting separately or in concert, the provinces are well equipped to effectively combat climate change in a manner that takes into account each province's unique circumstances.

The regulation of greenhouse gases does not become a matter of "national concern" just because different provinces take different views as to the most effective method to regulate them. The provinces are able to decide how best to regulate greenhouse gas emissions themselves without any need for a one-size-fits-all federal carbon price.

Even if the provinces were unable to do so, resort to the national concern branch would still be unwarranted. Greenhouse gas emissions lack the singleness, distinctiveness and indivisibility required for the national concern branch of POGG to apply.

The Act attempts to regulate emissions of 33 different greenhouse gases (a list that can be amended by the Governor in Council at any time). Those greenhouse gases are produced by an incredibly broad range of diverse activities, including home and office heating, electricity generation, transportation, industrial processes, manufacturing, agriculture, and waste management. Such a varied range of activities do not share the single, distinctive, and indivisible nature of the other matters that have been found to be subject to federal regulation under the national concern branch.

Finding the regulation of the wide variety of greenhouse gases emitted by all of these disconnected activities to be a single, distinctive, and indivisible matter of national concern would greatly expand the scope of federal jurisdiction beyond the specific matters enumerated in section 91 of the *Constitution Act, 1867*. Granting Parliament an amorphous and ill-defined jurisdiction over such a wide range of matters traditionally regulated by the provinces would distort the existing division of powers, unduly expand the scope of federal jurisdiction, and erode the constitutional balance inherent in the Canadian federal state.

Notes and Questions

1. Compare and contrast the legal arguments raised by Saskatchewan and Ontario over the *Greenhouse Gas Pollution Pricing Act* with the Supreme Court of Canada's decision in *R. v. Crown Zellerbach Canada Ltd.*, [1988] 1 S.C.R. 401, which was a case involving a constitutional challenge of Parliament's authority to legislate in respect of marine pollution under the *Ocean Dumping Control Act*, S.C. 1974-75-76, c. 55, and the Supreme Court's decision in *Canada (Procureure générale) c. Hydro-Québec*, [1997] 3 S.C.R. 213, involving a constitutional challenge of Parliament's ability to control toxic substances under the *Canadian Environmental Protection Act*, R.S.C. 1985, c. 16. Relevant excerpts from both cases are reproduced in Chapter 3. Do you think that the federal carbon pricing scheme under the *Greenhouse Gas Pollution Pricing Act* can be justified under the National Doctrine branch of POGG?

2. Recall the discussion by Nathalie J. Chalifour of federal jurisdiction to impose a carbon tax or a cap-and-trade scheme and the discussion by Shi-Ling Hsu and Robin Elliot of provincial jurisdiction do likewise, whose articles are reproduced earlier in this chapter. How would you characterize the pith and substance of the *Greenhouse Gas Pollution Pricing Act*? Which heads of power would you invoke were you to argue that the Act is a valid piece of federal legislation?

Saskatchewan argues that the differential treatment of provinces under the *Greenhouse Gas Pollution Pricing Act* violates federalism and is unconstitutional. In 2017, the Government of Manitoba commissioned a legal opinion on the constitutionality of the Act, which at that point was still a bill tabled before the House of Commons. The legal opinion, authored by Dr. Bryan Schwartz of the University of Manitoba, was made publicly available by the

Government of Manitoba in October 2017. In the excerpt reproduced below, Dr. Schwartz offers his expert opinion on the constitutional legality of the differential treatment under the Act.

Bryan P. Schwartz,
"Legal Opinion on the Constitutionality of the Federal Carbon Pricing Benchmark & Backstop Proposals"

Prepared for the Government of Manitoba (2017),
online: < http://www.gov.mb.ca/asset_library/en/climatechange/
federal_carbon_pricing_benchmark_backstop_proposals.pdf >

[Dr. Schwartz analyzed the constitutional validity of the *Greenhouse Gas Pollution Pricing Act*, which at that time was only a proposed measure. In his view, there was a strong likelihood that the Supreme Court of Canada would uphold the carbon tax on the basis of the federal taxation power or some other federal heads of power. Moreover, in his view, the Court would also likely uphold the cap-and-trade regime as a necessary "add-on" to the carbon tax.]

The Proposed Selective Backstop

This opinion has expressed the view that the federal government probably can enact the proposed carbon tax/levy, apart from its "selective application/ backstop" features. What remains to be discussed is whether those selective backstop features are themselves enforceable, or otherwise affect the integrity of the proposed carbon tax/levy.

To recap, the selective backstop feature of the proposed federal carbon tax/ levy would provide that the law would apply in any province that has not put in place measures that satisfy federal benchmarks. In other words, provinces can effectively "opt out" of the federal legislation, but only by enacting compliant legislation of their own. The tightly constrained flexibility (or lack thereof) given to the provinces likely does not enhance the case that the subject matter of the law is within federal jurisdiction. If the Supreme Court of Canada decides the proposed carbon tax/levy would ordinarily be outside of federal authority, its selective backstop feature will almost certainly not rescue it.

In the *Securities Reference*, the Supreme Court of Canada struck down a proposed federal scheme to create a national securities regulator. That federal scheme involved an "opt in" feature — the scheme would have operated only in provinces whose governments affirmatively chose to accept its operation. But this "opt in" feature did not, in the Supreme Court of Canada's view, excuse the enactment of legislation that otherwise intruded into provincial jurisdiction. By contrast, the proposed federal legislation which is being examined in this case, the carbon tax/levy and carbon trading add-on, provides far less consideration to provincial government preferences.

Having considered whether the backstop feature would validate otherwise invalid federal legislation (it would not), the opposite question must now be asked: if the proposed carbon tax/levy and carbon trading add-on would ordinarily be within federal authority, would its selective backstop feature render it invalid?

The answer is essentially no. The mere fact that federal legislation will be inactive in compliant provinces would not by itself make the law unconstitutional. It seems consistent with the theme of "cooperative federalism", as stated by the Supreme Court of Canada, that innovative means of coordinating federal and provincial authority are welcomed, from a legal perspective.

A precedent for the selective backstop feature of proposed carbon tax/levy is the *Personal Information Protection and Electronic Documents Act*, the federal private sector privacy law. It only applies to the provincially-regulated private sector in provinces that have not enacted their own laws which are "substantially similar" to PIPEDA. In an article commenting upon the *Securities Reference*, however, former Supreme Court of Canada Justice Michel Bastarache questioned whether the federal government is in fact constitutionally competent to impose PIPEDA upon the provinces by way of a selective backstop measure. According to former Justice Bastarache, the federal government's stated justification for the law — its power over trade and commerce arising from Subsection 91(2) of the *Constitution* — may be inapplicable, following the Court's comments in the *Securities Reference*. [...]

Assuming, then, that the carbon tax/levy is within the federal government's authority to implement, is there a reason why a selective backstop feature would invalidate what was an otherwise valid law? This opinion now examines two untested (with respect to Canadian federalism) arguments that might be used to argue that a selective backstop feature might place the carbon tax/levy outside government's authority.

Federal Power Cannot Be Exercised "Coercively"?

The Supreme Court of Canada might eventually develop a doctrine whereby "coerciveness" with respect to the provinces provides a basis for striking down certain federal legislation.

According to the Supreme Court of the United States, the use of the federal spending power in that country must not go beyond attaching incentives for the states to access federal money, thereby in practice reaching the point of being coercive. In the so-called "Obamacare case", Chief Justice Roberts — with the concurrence of two of the more liberal members of the Court — found that Congress could not strip states of their existing Medicaid funding, merely because the states did not participate in a program to expand Medicaid. The Court concluded that to strip the states of their funds would have been coercive; essentially, forcing the states onto one particular policy path that had been chosen by the federal government.

The Supreme Court of Canada has not to date developed any comparable doctrine with respect to the use of the federal spending power. In practice, the Government of Canada has reduced the extent to which it attaches conditions to federal transfers to the provinces. The Meech Lake Accord and Charlottetown Accord (in a manner consistent with Québec's five demands for approving the 1982 amendments to the Constitution) would have placed restrictions on new federal cost-shared programs. Under these restrictions, provinces could opt out of such cost-shared programs, yet still receive the same funding as participating provinces, as long as the opting out provinces created programs that were compatible with the federal programs. In the 2007 federal budget, the federal government promised to honour the same principle.

To be clear, the Supreme Court of Canada has not yet recognized any anti-coercive limits on the federal spending power. If such limits are recognized, they will likely operate notwithstanding that the federal spending power is otherwise unlimited, and because the Court is instead looking for an avenue to provide structure and moderation to broadly-stated federal powers that might otherwise upset the federal-provincial balance of power in the particular case before the Court.

There does not appear to be any realistic possibility that the Supreme Court of Canada would use this carbon/tax levy case — which does not involve questions about the federal government's spending power — to suddenly create an anti-coercion doctrine with respect to the use of federal authority, in general. In this case, the heads of authority upon which the federal government would likely rely already have structure and limits imposed by established doctrine. The Supreme Court of Canada might clarify or revise these doctrines, but it is unlikely that it would suddenly insert an anti-coercion principle into them. It will be a challenge to define the nature of an anti-coercion principle, and in any event, it would likely not be necessary to do so in order to achieve a result that the Supreme Court of Canada views as being consistent with the federal-provincial balance of powers. On these facts, it is far from self-evident that the selective backstop feature actually is coercive. If the federal government could enact a carbon tax/levy in any event, then leaving space for substantially compliant provinces can instead be viewed as an exercise in cooperative federalism.

Exercises of Federal Power and Equality among the Provinces

There is another argument against the selective backstop feature of the carbon tax/levy — again, without any Canadian judicial precedent — that might nonetheless be considered as being credible, and which would have at least a chance of being accepted by the Supreme Court of Canada. This argument would concern the selective application of federal law to some provinces, but not others, which, depending on the facts, could be framed as a denial of the legal equality of the provinces. [...]

The selective application of federal laws has been tested from the point of the individual right to non-discrimination under the *Charter*. The Supreme Court of Canada has held that federal legislation that discriminates on the basis of provincial residence cannot be the basis for an equality claim under the *Charter*. The *Charter* is concerned with protecting individuals against discrimination based on hostility and stereotyping, on grounds such as ethnicity or gender. The claim here would be based on the juridical equality of provinces within the federation, which is a fundamentally different matter than the grounds which have to date been recognized in *Charter* equality claims.

The strength of this "juridical equality" argument would depend on the extent to which Manitoba could show that its made-in-Manitoba plan would accomplish federal objectives at least as well as the proposed carbon tax/levy and carbon trading add-on. The more likely it is that Manitoba's measures would provide a carbon reduction outcome which would be similar to the proposed federal regime, the easier it would be to argue that the proposed carbon tax/levy and carbon trading add-on constitute arbitrary discrimination which unduly denies Manitoba's ability to pursue its own course. [...]

This argument would require the Supreme Court of Canada to recognize a fundamental principle it has not adopted before, and to apply this new principle in the context of a case that is both legally and politically controversial. There can be no assurance that it would do so, even if Manitoba could demonstrate a strong factual foundation for its case of arbitrary discrimination.

It is an argument, however, that would likely be considered by the Court as being worthy of serious contemplation. The argument should not be expected to fail merely because it would only be advanced by one or two smaller provinces. Instead, the Supreme Court of Canada might be expected to give this argument fair consideration and deliberation, even though those who may support it would not have anywhere near the political or economic clout within the federation as the four largest provinces.

In summary, then, if the Supreme Court of Canada found that the federal government had authority to implement the proposed carbon tax/levy and carbon trading add-on, the inclusion of a backstop feature would probably not in and of itself render the law unconstitutional. If the backstop feature effectively discriminates against some provinces, however, there is a credible but untested argument to be made that the federal law would be inconsistent with the binding legal principle that the equal legislative authority of the provinces must be respected.

In these circumstances, the model for "equivalency" or "substitution" agreements (which has been previously adopted by federal and provincial laws concerning environmental protection) may present a solution which accommodates all parties' interests.

In an equivalency agreement, federal and provincial governments may agree that one level will use the other's environmental assessment process as the basis for its own decision about whether a project may proceed, or that the other level will both assess and decide upon the project.

Laws which provide for equivalency agreements sometimes stipulate conditions that must be met when a government accepts the other level's processes or decisions. These laws also in some cases appear to leave room for the exercise of discretion, by the other level of government.

Notes and Questions

1. In his legal opinion, Dr. Schwartz makes reference to "cooperative federalism", a concept that we have discussed in Chapter 3 and elsewhere in this chapter. According to Dr. Schwartz, it would be consistent with cooperative federalism to allow for federal-provincial coordination in the implementation of carbon pricing across the country. Do you agree with his assessment? To what extent can the backstop measures in the *Greenhouse Gas Pollution Pricing Act* be characterized as an "innovative means of coordinating federal and provincial authority" when the Act empowers the

federal government to unilaterally impose a federal carbon pricing scheme on provinces and territories that do not live up to the federal government's standards?

2. Dr. Schwartz proposes "equivalency" or "substitution" agreements as a way to coordinate federal and provincial carbon pricing schemes. Recall from Chapter 7 that equivalency and substitution are features under the *Canadian Environmental Assessment Act, 2012*, S.C. 2012, c. 19, s. 52. Under the CEAA 2012, the Minister must, on request of a province, approve the substitution of the federal environmental assessment process with a provincial one if the Minister is of the opinion that the provincial process in question "would be an appropriate substitute". Furthermore, where there is substitution with a provincial process, the CEAA 2012 empowers the Governor in Council to enter into an equivalency agreement with that province to fully exempt designated projects from application of the CEAA 2012. Given that the basis for substitution and equivalency is the Minister's opinion that the provincial process would be an appropriate substitute, the federal government retains the discretion to harmonize the federal process with provincial ones. How does the substitution and equivalency provisions under the CEAA 2012 compare with the selective backstop mechanism under the *Greenhouse Gas Pollution Pricing Act* in terms of the scope that they provide the federal government to maintain a certain level of harmonization across the country? Do you see one mechanism as better than the other in both constitutional validity and practical effect? If the *Greenhouse Gas Pollution Pricing Act* were to use a mechanism similar to the CEAA 2012 for harmonization, would it increase the likelihood that the Act would be upheld by the courts, or would it stay the same?

Tort Litigation and Other Common Law Claims

In Chapter 2, we discussed the many challenges in utilizing the common law to address environmental issues. Climate change is showing signs of becoming the testing ground for many of the issues we explored. The efforts to make use of the common law to force governments and private entities to address climate change will likely intensify as governments continue to struggle to implement effective legislative and regulatory measures to deal with this global challenge. Tort claims that can be raised in an action against governments or private entities for harm that they may have caused a plaintiff through their actions or inactions in relation to greenhouse gas emissions include negligence, nuisance, the tort in *Rylands v. Fletcher* (1868), L.R. 3 H.L. 330 (U.K. H.L.), trespass and battery. Besides these tradtional tort claims, another common law principle that is gaining traction in the United States as a way to recognize a common law right to the environment is the public trust doctrine. These common law and tort-like claims play a growing role in climate litigation all over the world in both common law and civil law jurisdictions. The US-based Sabin Center for Climate Change Law and the law firm Arnold &

Porter Kaye Scholer LLP jointly maintain climate change litigation databases for both US and non-US climate litigation, which show a growing number of tort-based climate claims in and outside the United States: <http://climatecasechart.com/>.

For a more detailed discussion of opportunities to use the common law to pursue liability claims for climate change, see the Canada chapter in Lord *et al.*, eds., *Climate Change Liability: Transnational Law and Practice* (Cambridge University Press, 2012). The chapter explores negligence, conspiracy, private nuisance, strict liability and public nuisance. It identifies the issue of causation as a particular challenge in bringing climate liability cases under tort law. The chapter also explores opportunities to pursue climate litigation under the public trust doctrine discussed in Chapters 2 and 8.

In the excerpts that follow, we canvass some of the issues surrounding the use of tort and other common law claims in climate litigation. We will begin with a look at two major hurdles in climate litigation using private claims: justiciability and causation. Then, we will revisit the Hague District Court's decision in *Urgenda Foundation v. The State of the Netherlands* as a precedent-setting example of using a negligence claim in climate litigation. Lastly, we will review Aiken J.'s decision in *Juliana v. United States* for the use of the public trust doctrine as a potential common law principle to be used for climate litigation.

Native Village of Kivalina v. ExxonMobil Corp.
663 F. Supp. 2d 863 (N.D. Cal., 2009)

[In 2008, the Native Village of Kivalina and the City of Kivalina, which are located in Alaska, filed a complaint at the US District Court (N.D. Cal.) for monetary damages against a number of companies in the fossil fuel and energy industry for their role in causing climate change, which was having devastating effects upon their lands and people. In 2009, the District Court granted a motion to dismiss the lawsuit for lack of subject-matter jurisdiction. This decision was upheld by the Ninth Circuit in 2012, and an appeal to the US Supreme Court was dismissed without reasons in 2013. In her reasons reproduced below, District Judge Saundra Brown Armstrong reviews the background to the case and the claims made by the plaintiffs, before turning her mind to the issue of justiciability.]

ARMSTRONG J.: —

Overview

The Village is a self-governing, federally-recognized Tribe of Inupiat Eskimos established pursuant to the provisions of the Indian Reorganization Act of 1934, as amended in 1936. Members of the Village reside in Kivalina, which is a unified municipality incorporated under Alaska law in 1969 with a population of approximately 400 persons. Kivalina is located at the tip of a six-mile long barrier reef, approximately seventy miles north of the Arctic Circle, between the Chukchi Sea and the Kivalina and Wulik Rivers on the Northwest coast of Alaska. The Kivalina coast is protected by Arctic sea ice that is present during the fall, winter and spring. The sea ice, which attaches to the Kivalina coast, acts as a barrier against the coastal storms and waves that affect the coast of the Chukchi Sea. As a result of global warming, however, the sea ice now attaches to the Kivalina coast later in the year and breaks up earlier and is thinner and less extensive than before, thus subjecting Kivalina to coastal storm waves and surges. The resulting erosion has now reached the point where Kivalina is becoming uninhabitable. Plaintiffs allege that as a result, the Village will have to be relocated, at a cost estimated to range from $95 to $400 million.

Procedural History

Plaintiffs filed their Complaint on February 26, 2008. The Complaint alleges four claims for relief: (1) Federal Common Law: Public Nuisance; (2) State Law: Private and Public Nuisance; (3) Civil Conspiracy; and (4) Concert of Action. Compl. ¶¶ 249-282. As Defendants, Plaintiffs have named various oil companies, power companies and utility providers, all of whom are alleged to be jointly and severally liable for causing damage to Plaintiffs. The Complaint does not seek injunctive relief nor does it specify a particular amount of monetary damages. However, Plaintiffs claim that the effects of global warming mean that they will have to relocate the inhabitants of Kivalina at an estimated cost of $95 million to $400 million. [...]

Utility Defendants' Motion to Dismiss

The threshold question presented by Defendants' motions is whether the Court has subject matter jurisdiction over Plaintiffs' federal claim for common law nuisance. In particular, Defendants argue that under the political question doctrine, the Court lacks jurisdiction to consider the merits of Plaintiffs' nuisance claim because its resolution will require the Court to make policy determinations relating to the use of fossil fuels and other energy sources and consider their value in relation to the environmental, economic and social consequences of such use. Defendants argue that such questions are inherently political and that there are no judicially manageable standards available to adjudicate these issues. [...]

The Political Question Doctrine

[...] The political question doctrine is a species of the separation of powers doctrine and provides that certain questions are political as opposed to legal, and thus, must be resolved by the political branches rather than by the judiciary. "The political question doctrine serves to prevent the federal courts from intruding unduly on certain policy choices and value judgments that are constitutionally committed to Congress or the executive branch." *Koohi v. United States*, 976 F.2d 1328, 1331 (9th Cir. 1992). "A nonjusticiable political question exists when, to resolve a dispute, the court must make a policy judgment of a legislative nature, rather than resolving the dispute through legal and factual analysis."

In *Baker v. Carr*, 369 U.S. 186, 210 (1962), the Supreme Court set forth six independent factors. [...] The six Baker factors have been grouped into three general inquiries: "(i) Does the issue involve resolution of questions committed by the text of the Constitution to a coordinate branch of Government? (ii) Would resolution of the question demand that a court move beyond areas of judicial expertise? (iii) Do prudential considerations counsel against judicial intervention?" [...]

Scope of Judicial Expertise

Judicially Discoverable and Manageable Standards

In Alperin, the Ninth Circuit explained that focus of the second Baker factor is "not whether the case is unmanageable in the sense of being large, complicated, or otherwise difficult to tackle from a logistical standpoint. Rather, courts must ask whether they have the legal tools to reach a ruling that is 'principled, rational, and based upon reasoned distinctions.'" Thus, "[i]nstead of focusing on the logistical obstacles," the relevant inquiry is whether the judiciary is granting relief in a reasoned fashion versus allowing the claims to proceed such that they "merely provide 'hope' without a substantive legal basis for a ruling."

Plaintiffs contend that "[t]he judicially discoverable and manageable standards here are the same as they are in all nuisance cases." They assert that the salient inquiry underlying their federal nuisance claim is whether Defendants contributed to "an unreasonable interference with public rights[.]" Resolution of what is "reasonable," Plaintiffs assert, is to be determined by examining whether the conduct involves a "significant interference with the public health, the public safety, the public peace, the public comfort or the public convenience" and whether the conduct is "of a continuing nature" or has produced a "permanent or long lasting effect[.]" However, the flaw in Plaintiffs' argument is that it overlooks that the evaluation of a nuisance claim is not focused entirely on the unreasonableness of the harm. Rather, the factfinder must also balance the utility and benefit of the alleged nuisance against the harm caused.

A public nuisance is defined as an "unreasonable interference with a right common to the general public." Restatement (Second) of Torts § 821(b)(1) (1979). Whether the interference is unreasonable turns on weighing "the gravity of the harm against the utility of the conduct." "The unreasonableness of a given interference represents a judgment reached by comparing the social utility of an activity against the gravity of the harm it inflicts, taking into account a handful of relevant factors."

Stated another way, resolution of a nuisance claim is not based on whether the plaintiff finds the invasion unreasonable, but rather, "whether reasonable persons generally, looking at the whole situation impartially and objectively, would consider it unreasonable." ("In every case, the court must make a comparative evaluation of the conflicting interests according to objective legal standards, and the gravity of harm to the plaintiff must be weighed against the utility of the defendant's conduct.")

Applying the above-discussed principles here, the factfinder will have to weigh, inter alia, the energy-producing alternatives that were available in the past and consider their respective impact on far ranging issues such as their reliability as an energy source, safety considerations and the impact of the different alternatives on consumers and business at every level. See *People of the State of Calif. v. Gen. Motors Corp.*, 2007 WL 2726871 (N.D. Cal., Sept. 17, 2007) ("Plaintiff's claim would require the Court to balance the competing interests of reducing global warming emissions and the interests of advancing and preserving economic and industrial development"); ("To assess the utility of Defendants' conduct, the jury must consider several factors, including the primary purpose of Defendants' conduct and the social value of that purpose") (citing Restatement (Second) of Torts § 828 & cmt. e). The factfinder would then have to weigh the benefits derived from those choices against the risk that increasing greenhouse gases would in turn increase the risk of causing flooding along the coast of a remote Alaskan locale. Plaintiffs ignore this aspect of their claim and otherwise fail to articulate any particular judicially discoverable and manageable standards that would guide a factfinder in rendering a decision that is principled, rational, and based upon reasoned distinctions.

Plaintiffs next argue that the existence of judicially discoverable or manageable standards is exemplified by the long, prior history of air and water pollution cases. The *Second Circuit in Connecticut v. Am. Elec. Power Co. Inc.*, – F.3d –, 2009 WL 2996729 (2d Cir. Sept. 21, 2009) (AEP) agreed with this reasoning in holding that the political question doctrine did not bar a nuisance lawsuit brought by eight states, a city and three land trusts against six electric power corporations "to cap and then reduce their carbon monoxide emissions." With regard to the second Baker factor, the AEP court rejected the defendants' reliance on "uncertainties" regarding the precise effect of greenhouse gas emissions and noted that "federal courts have successfully adjudicated complex common law nuisance cases for over a century." Based on the judiciary's history of addressing "new and complex problems," including those concerning environmental pollution, the court concluded that "[w]ell-settled principles of tort and public nuisance law provide appropriate guidance to the district court in assessing Plaintiffs' claims and federal courts are competent to deal with these issues" such that their global warming concerns can "be addressed through principled adjudication." This Court is not so sanguine. While such principles may provide sufficient guidance in some novel cases, this is not one of them.

The cases cited by Plaintiffs as well as the AEP court involved nuisance claims founded on environmental injuries far different than those alleged in the instant case. The common thread running through each of those cases is that they involved a discrete number of "polluters" that were identified as causing a specific injury to a specific area. Yet, Plaintiffs themselves concede that considerations involved in the emission of greenhouse gases and the resulting effects of global warming are "entirely different" than those germane to water or air pollution cases. While a water pollution claim typically involves a discrete, geographically definable waterway, Plaintiffs' global warming claim is based on the emission of greenhouse gases from innumerable sources located throughout the world and affecting the entire planet and its atmosphere. Notably, Plaintiffs acknowledge that the global warming process involves "common pollutants that are mixed together in the atmosphere [that] cannot be similarly geographically circumscribed."

Despite the admitted and significant distinctions between a nuisance claim based on water or air pollution and one, such as the present, based on global warming, neither Plaintiffs nor AEP offers any guidance as to precisely what judicially discoverable and manageable standards are to be employed in resolving the claims at issue. Although federal courts undoubtedly are well suited to resolve new and complex issues and cases, the Court is not persuaded that this is such a case. Plaintiffs' global warming nuisance claim seeks to impose liability and damages on a scale unlike any prior environmental pollution case cited by Plaintiffs. Those cases do not provide guidance that would enable the Court to reach a resolution of this case in any "reasoned" manner. Consequently, the Court concludes that application of the second Baker factor precludes judicial consideration of Plaintiff's federal nuisance claim.

Initial Policy Determination

Equally problematic for Plaintiffs is the third Baker factor, which requires the Court to determine whether it would be impossible for the judiciary to decide the case "without an initial policy determination of a kind clearly for nonjudicial discretion." A political question under this factor "exists when, to resolve a dispute, the court must make a policy judgment of a legislative nature, rather than resolving the dispute through legal and factual analysis." This factor is aimed at preventing a court from "removing an important policy determination from the Legislature." Plaintiffs emphasize that because they are not seeking injunctive relief, there is no need for the Court to delve into the task of retroactively determining what emission limits should have been imposed. This argument rests on the same faulty logic discussed above; to wit, that Plaintiffs' nuisance claim can be resolved solely by examining the reasonableness of the harm, while avoiding any consideration of the conduct causing the nuisance. As noted, Plaintiffs' federal nuisance claim inherently requires the factfinder to consider both the harm experienced by Plaintiff as well as the utility or value of Defendants' actions. The fact that Plaintiff is seeking damages as opposed to injunctive relief does not counsel a different result. Regardless of the relief sought, the resolution of Plaintiffs' nuisance claim requires balancing the social utility of Defendants' conduct with the harm it inflicts.

That process, by definition, entails a determination of what would have been an acceptable limit on the level of greenhouse gases emitted by Defendants. ("[R]egardless of the relief sought, the Court is left to make an initial decision as to what is unreasonable in the context of carbon dioxide emissions.")

Plaintiffs also fail to confront the fact that resolution of their nuisance claim requires the judiciary to make a policy decision about who should bear the cost of global warming. Though alleging that Defendants are responsible for a "substantial portion" of greenhouse gas emissions, Plaintiffs also acknowledge that virtually everyone on Earth is responsible on some level for contributing to such emissions. Yet, by pressing this lawsuit, Plaintiffs are in effect asking this Court to make a political judgment that the two dozen Defendants named in this action should be the only ones to bear the cost of contributing to global warming. Plaintiffs respond that Defendants should be the ones held responsible for damaging Kivalina allegedly because "they are responsible for more of the problem than anyone else in the nation ...". But even if that were true, Plaintiffs ignore that the allocation of fault — and cost — of global warming is a matter appropriately left for determination by the executive or legislative branch in the first instance. The Court thus concludes that the third Baker factor also militates in favor of dismissal.

Notes and Questions

1. Compare the Canadian principle of justiciability discussed in the *Friends of the Earth* case above with the principles that guided the Court in the *Kivalina* case. What are some of the similarities and differences in the courts' approaches?

2. Armstrong J. held that the plaintiffs in *Kivalina* failed to show that their claims provided "judicially discoverable or manageable standards". Recall the article by Jason MacLean and Chris Tollefson reproduced in Chapter 6 in which the authors discussed the unwillingness of Canadian courts to become "academies of science" in judicial reviews of environmental matters. To what extent do you think the US District Court was animated by similar concerns?

As tort-based climate litigation continues to grow in popularity, a key legal hurdle that plaintiffs must overcome is demonstrating causation between the impugned actions and the harm suffered by the plaintiffs. In the article that follows, the authors canvass international cases against private corporations responsible for greenhouse gas emissions and the trend in the jurisprudence on causation in these private claims.

Geetanjali Ganguly, Joana Setzer & Veerle Heyvaert,
"If at First You Don't Succeed: Suing Corporations for Climate Change"

(2018) 38 Oxford J. Leg. Stud. 841,
online: DOI < https://doi.org/10.1093/ojls/gqy029 >

Introduction

In recent talks, former NASA scientist James Hansen called for a wave of lawsuits against governments and fossil fuel companies that are delaying action on climate change. For Hansen, a pioneer of climate science, the key is to sue corporations like ExxonMobil, BP and Shell for the damage they are doing to the environment, those affected and future generations. Hansen is currently involved in a lawsuit against the US federal government, brought by his granddaughter and 20 others. Similarly, Jeffrey Sachs, economist, director of the Earth Institute at Columbia University and a UN special adviser, now urges citizens to pursue major polluters and negligent governments for liability and damages, and 'flood the courts' with legal cases demanding the right to a safe and clean environment.

This article contributes to the burgeoning literature on climate litigation by examining recent developments in climate litigation launched against corporations. We argue that, notwithstanding the failure of a past generation of climate litigation to hold private actors to account, the second wave of pending court challenges is by no means doomed to failure. The second wave is characterised by a broader range of arguments and litigation strategies than its predecessor, and unfolds within a rapidly evolving scientific, discursive and constitutional context. We argue that this evolving context generates new opportunities for judges to rethink the interpretation of existing legal and evidentiary thresholds for claimants to meet the burden of proof and apply them in a way that will enhance the accountability of private greenhouse gas (GHG) emitters. Although the judicial enforcement of corporate accountability for climate change has proved elusive thus far, future cases may fare better. Moreover, even unsuccessful cases may help to guide climate change-responsive adjudication in the longer term. [...]

The First Wave of Private Climate Litigation

The first wave of private climate litigation spanned 2005 to 2015 and was mainly concentrated in the United States. Several lawsuits filed in state district courts were dismissed on the grounds of non-justiciability of a political question. The most salient examples are *Comer v Murphy Oil* and *Kivalina v ExxonMobil*. In both cases, the plaintiffs argued that the defendants (energy producers) engaged in emitting activities which contributed substantially to climate change and were therefore responsible for climate change-related injuries suffered by them. In *Comer*, the plaintiffs (residents of Louisiana) alleged that the emitting activities of the defendant energy companies contributed to climate change and had intensified the destructive capacity of Hurricane Katrina. Similarly, in the *Kivalina* case, the plaintiffs (Inupiat Eskimo peoples from Alaska) alleged that the activities of a group of energy companies, including ExxonMobil, were responsible for the transboundary release of GHGs, which had produced a series of adverse climate impacts in *Kivalina*, such as coastal erosion and the melting of Arctic sea ice and permafrost. These impacts threatened the existence of their village and way of life, and ultimately resulted in their displacement and relocation.

Common allegations in the first wave of private climate litigation were built around the argument that the carbon-emitting behaviour of corporations causes damage to legally protected interests, and that this damage should be remedied. Consequently, most cases revolved around (i) procedural questions of standing and jurisdiction, and (ii) substantive issues of causation and damage. The sections below further explore the court's reasoning on these matters, with specific reference to *Comer* and *Kivalina*.

[**Ed. Note:** The authors' discussion of standing and jurisdiction is omitted.]

The difficulty of proving causation — the link between an actor's behaviour and subsequent harm to another — has also been an obstacle to successful private climate litigation. Causation requires that a plaintiff demonstrate a causal connection between an injury and the defendant's action to satisfy the proposition that remedies for injury should come from those responsible. Yet, pinpointing the actor(s) responsible for an injury can be factually and conceptually difficult, if not impossible, in cases where the damage is a result of climate change. The difficulties for plaintiffs to persuasively pinpoint the cause of climate change-related harm is, again, beautifully illustrated in *Kivalina*. The district court held that the plaintiffs could not demonstrate either a 'substantial likelihood' that ExxonMobil's activities had caused the plaintiffs' injuries or that the 'seed' of their injuries was 'fairly traceable' to the defendant's GHG emissions. Specifically, the court concluded that the plaintiffs could not establish causation because there was 'no realistic possibility of tracing any particular alleged effect of global warming to any particular emissions by any specific person, entity, [or] group at any particular point in time'. The Ninth Circuit affirmed the decision of the district court, although it did so without revisiting the issues raised by the political question doctrine and standing. The Ninth Circuit held, instead, that federal legislation pre-empted the plaintiffs' federal common law claims, explaining that any solution for the alleged effects of global warming 'must rest in the hands of the legislative and executive branches of our government, not the federal common law'. Similarly, the district court in the *Comer* case ruled that the plaintiffs could not demonstrate proximate causation.

The Second Wave of Private Climate Litigation

Although so far no precedents exist of successful private climate litigation, future private climate lawsuits are by no means doomed to failure. A rapidly evolving scientific, discursive and constitutional context has cleared the path for a second wave of strategic private litigation cases, which have a better chance of overcoming the judicial hurdles of standing, proof of harm and causation that scuppered earlier attempts. This 'new wave' of private climate litigation was motivated by the publication of the Carbon Majors study in 2013 and has spread beyond the United States into new jurisdictions. It gathered momentum in 2015, with a petition filed with the Commission on Human Rights of the Philippines by typhoon survivors, advocates, NGOs including Greenpeace Southeast Asia, and thousands of online supporters. This initiative was followed by cases such as *Lliuya v RWE*, also filed in 2015; the cases filed by two Californian counties (San Mateo and Marin County) and the city of Imperial Beach against 37 oil, natural gas and coal companies and trade groups in 2017; *Guy Abrahams v Commonwealth Bank of Australia*, which was filed in the Federal Court of Australia, again in 2017; and a lawsuit filed by New York City against the world's five largest Carbon Majors (ExxonMobil, Shell, BP, Chevron and Conoco-Phillips) in January 2018. At the time of writing, the second wave of strategic private climate litigation shows no sign of cresting, as news alerts regarding new or planned litigation continue to be filed on a regular basis. [...]

Scientific Context

The first factor propelling a new wave of strategic private climate litigation — and the likelihood of courts upholding claims in damages against large emitters — is the scientific context in which the litigation evolves. Strategic private climate litigation today looks significantly different from private climate litigation 10 years ago as a result of (i) the growth and consolidation of climate science released by the Intergovernmental Panel on Climate Change (IPCC), and better and up-to-date localised data; (ii) the increased possibility of quantifying the proportional contribution of the world's largest emitters to climate change; and (iii) developments in attribution science.

[**Ed. Note:** The authors discuss each of these three points in turn. They argue that new developments in climate science and research are delivering new evidence that can strengthen assertions of a causal link between climate change-related harm and a private company's behaviour. This portion of the article is omitted.]

Legal Discourse

The developments discussed in the preceding paragraphs involve changes in scientific knowledge which may make it easier for claimants in private climate cases to meet evidentiary thresholds. Through a combination of advances in climate science, quantification and attribution science, claimants may now argue with some credibility that, 'but for' the emissions of company X, they would not have suffered a particular, measurable harm. The proliferation of such argumentation could result in climate change no longer being represented before the court as a diffuse and general problem caused by myriad unknown and unidentifiable sources, but instead as the consequence of a specific set of choices and actions, undertaken by a discrete group of well-informed actors, which causes particular and measurable damage. This conceptualisation could trigger a shift in the judicial mindset and recast climate change from a political question into an individual concern. Recent litigation already shows signs of subtle shifts in the narrative. Two prominent emanations of this shift are (i) the resurgence of interest in exploiting the precedential value of tobacco and asbestos litigation and (ii) recent changes in the discourse around directors' liability and disclosure requirements.

[...] The challenges surrounding private climate litigation have a number of similarities with those affecting asbestos and tobacco litigation. In all cases, liability involves the manufacture of products (asbestos, tobacco and fossil fuels, respectively) initially considered harmless but later understood to create severe health and environmental risks. In all cases, attribution of harm is complicated by the existence of multiple sources of causation. Moreover, in all cases the government, as a provider of public services, incurs major public costs in dealing with the consequences of, respectively, asbestos exposure, tobacco use and climate change. But the success of private asbestos and tobacco litigation was not replicated in the first wave of strategic private climate litigation. The main reason was the relatively greater challenge in establishing a causal chain in climate cases. Whereas tobacco and asbestos victims could at least pinpoint the group of potential culprits, plaintiffs in first-generation climate change lawsuits could not.

However, in light of the changing context of causation in the field of climate change, tobacco and asbestos precedents might be more instructive for future tort-based climate litigation. Developments in attribution science are likely to bring private climate litigation into closer alignment with asbestos and tobacco litigation, particularly since the cohort of potential defendants in climate litigation has become easier to identify and narrow down to a key set of players, the Carbon Majors. Moreover, there has been an ongoing effort to demonstrate that, much like 'big tobacco', major carbon emitters have long had knowledge and awareness of climate change, yet took actions to confound or mislead the public. In the landmark tobacco case of *USA v Philip Morris*, DC District Court Judge Kessler famously ruled that the Department of Justice had presented overwhelming evidence of Philip Morris's participation in a conspiracy to defraud the public. The US experience thus showed that it was not only possible for directly affected private parties to sue for damage, but that governments, too, could sue corporations to recover health and environmental damage-related costs. ExxonMobil has been at the centre of a similar controversy in the context of climate change, being accused of suppressing climate change research, as well as spreading doubt in advertorials.

Recent attempts to build on the legacy of tobacco and asbestos litigation and use it as a relevant precedent for climate litigation are the Californian lawsuits filed in July 2017 by San Mateo County, Marin County and the City of Imperial Beach. In a manner analogous to the tobacco and asbestos litigation of the 1990s, the plaintiffs in the California climate lawsuits accuse oil companies of knowing that their emitting activities are causing catastrophic climate change. The emergence of governments as claimants in private climate litigation moreover helps to overcome some of the legal obstacles that thwarted the claimants in *Kivalina* and *Comer*. Rather than relying on federal common law, which the courts decided could not be applied because the common law on these issues was displaced by the Clean Air Act, these cases are grounded instead in state common law, which is unaffected by the prior rulings.

Notes and Questions

1. The "but for" test for causation in private claims mentioned in the article above remains the prevailing causation test in negligence claims in Canada. However, the Supreme Court of Canada has held that, in rare circumstances, a plaintiff can prove causation using a "material contribution" test: *Hanke v. Resurfice Corp.*, 2007 SCC 7. In cases where it is impossible for the plaintiff to prove "but for" causation due to factors outside the plaintiff's control (*e.g.*, the limits of scientific knowledge) *and* the injury suffered by the plaintiff fell within ambit of risk created by defendant's breach of the duty of care, then the plaintiff need only show that the defendant's negligent action materially contributed to an increase in the risk that the plaintiff would suffer that harm. Consider the difficulties in demonstrating direct causation in a climate change case. How could a "material contribution" test be used to ground a negligence claim against "carbon major" companies?

2. The authors mentioned *Lliuya v. RWE AG* (2015), 2-O-285/15 (Essen Regional Court), in their article above. In this case, a farmer in Peru filed a complaint in German court against RWE, the largest electricity producer in Germany. The plaintiff alleged that RWE knowingly contributed to climate change by emitting substantial volumes of greenhouse gases, which in turn contributed to the melting of glaciers near a town in Peru that caused him and his town to incur costs for flood prevention. The plaintiff asserted that the defendant was responsible for 0.47% of global historic greenhouse gas emissions, and so should be liable for 0.47% of the costs of remediation. This type of "market-share liability" can be found in American jurisprudence: *Sindell v. Abbott Laboratories*, 26 Cal. 3d 588 (Cal. S.C. 1980). Canadian courts have yet to adopt "market-share liability". Instead, Canadian case law on multiple tortfeasors in an action for negligence allows more than one defendant to be held liable where they all participated in the negligent action, but where the plaintiff cannot show which defendant caused the actual injury: *Lewis v. Cook*, [1951] S.C.R. 830. At common law, this principle may

be unavailable if the plaintiff also committed contributory negligence: *Lange v. Bennett* (1963), 41 D.L.R. (2d) 691 (Ont. H.C.). What arguments would you make to a court to find multiple greenhouse gas emitters liable for climate change damages even though the plaintiff is also in all likelihood a greenhouse gas contributor in their daily lives?

We introduced *Urgenda* earlier in this chapter for its discussion on justiciability. We now return to this decision of the Hague District Court for its precedent-setting value. This was the first time that the tort law of negligence has been successfully used to hold a government liable for failing to adequately implement measures to address climate change. As you read through this decision, consider how a Canadian court may deal with the same issues of duty of care, standard of care, and causation on these facts.

Urgenda Foundation v. The State of the Netherlands

(24 June 2015), C/09/456689/HA ZA 13-1396 (Hague District Court)
English Translation from Dutch available on website of the
Dutch judiciary: < http://uitspraken.rechtspraak.nl/
inziendocument?id = ECLI:NL:RBDHA:2015:7196 >

[The Court first canvassed the science behind climate change, relying heavily on the reports by the Intergovernmental Panel on Climate Change. The Dutch Government did not contest the findings in the IPCC reports. The Court then reviewed applicable international and domestic law, including the Dutch Constitution, to find that none could lead to a conclusion that the State was under a legal obligation to the plaintiffs to reduce greenhouse gas emissions.]

mr. H.F.M. HOFHUIS, *mr.* J.W. BOCKWINKEL and *mr.* I. BRAND: —

Intermediate Conclusion About the Duty of Care

The foregoing leads the court to conclude that a legal obligation of the State towards Urgenda cannot be derived from Article 21 of the Dutch Constitution, the "no harm" principle, the UN Climate Change Convention, with associated protocols, and Article 191 TFEU [Treaty on the Functioning of the European Union] with the ETS [European Union Emission Trading System] Directive and Effort Sharing Decision based on TFEU. Although Urgenda cannot directly derive rights from these rules and Articles 2 and 8 ECHR [European Convention on Human Rights], these regulations still hold meaning, namely in the question discussed below whether the State has failed to meet its duty of care towards Urgenda. First of all, it can be derived from these rules what degree of discretionary power the State is entitled to in how it exercises the tasks and authorities given to it. Secondly, the objectives laid down in these regulations are relevant in determining the minimum degree of care the State is expected to observe. In order to determine the scope of the State's duty of care and the discretionary power it is entitled to, the court will therefore also consider the objectives of international and European climate policy as well as the principles on which the policies are based.

Breach of Standard of Due Care Observed in Society, Discretionary Power

The question whether the State is in breach of its duty of care for taking insufficient measures to prevent dangerous climate change, is a legal issue which has never before been answered in Dutch proceedings and for which jurisprudence does not provide a ready-made framework. The answer to the question whether or not the State is taking sufficient mitigation measures depends on many factors, with two aspects having particular relevance. In the first place, it has to be assessed whether there is an unlawful hazardous negligence on the part of the State. Secondly, the State's discretionary power is relevant in assessing the government's actions. From case law about government liability it follows that the court has to assess fully whether or not the State has exercised or exercises sufficient care, but that this does not alter the fact that the State has the discretion to determine how it fulfils its duty of care. However, this discretionary power vested in the State is not unlimited: the State's care may not be below standard. However, the test of due care required here and the discretionary power of the State are not wholly distinguishable. After all, the detailing of the duty of care of the person called to account will also have been included in his specific position in view of the special nature of his duty or authority. The standard of care has been attuned to this accordingly.

Factors to Determine Duty of Care

Urgenda has relied on the "Kelderluik" ruling of the Supreme Court [...] and on jurisprudence on the doctrine of hazardous negligence developed later to detail the requirement of acting with due care towards society. Understandably, the State has pointed out the relevant differences between this jurisprudence and this case. This case is different in that the central focus is on dealing with a hazardous global development, of which it is uncertain when, where and to what extent exactly this hazard will materialise. Nevertheless, the doctrine of hazardous negligence, as explained in the literature, bears a resemblance to the theme of hazardous climate change, so that several criteria stated below can be derived from hazardous negligence jurisprudence in order to detail the concept of acting negligently towards society.

In principle, the extent to which the State is entitled to a scope for policymaking is determined by the statutory duties and powers vested in the State. As has been stated above, under Article 21 of the Constitution, the State has a wide discretion of power to organise the national climate policy in the manner it deems fit. However, the court is of the opinion that due to the nature of the hazard (a global cause) and the task to be realised accordingly (shared risk management of a global hazard that could result in an impaired living climate in the Netherlands), the objectives and principles, such as those laid down in the UN Climate Change Convention and the TFEU, should also be considered in determining the scope for policymaking and duty of care.

[**Ed. Note:** The Court's canvassing of the objectives and principles in the *United Nations Framework Convention on Climate Change* and the European climate policy set out in the *Treaty on the Functioning of the European Union* is omitted.]

The objectives and principles stated here do not have a direct effect due to their international and private-law nature, as has been considered above.

However, they do determine to a great extent the framework for and the manner in which the State exercises its powers. Therefore, these objectives and principles constitute an important viewpoint in assessing whether or not the State acts wrongfully towards Urgenda. With due regard for all the above, the answer to the question whether or not the State is exercising due care with its current climate policy depends on whether according to objective standards the reduction measures taken by the State to prevent hazardous climate change for man and the environment are sufficient, also in view of the State's discretionary power. In determining the scope of the duty of care of the State, the court will therefore take account of:

   (i)   the nature and extent of the damage ensuing from climate change;
   (ii) the knowledge and foreseeability of this damage;
   (iii) the chance that hazardous climate change will occur;
   (iv) the nature of the acts (or omissions) of the State;
   (v)   the onerousness of taking precautionary measures;
   (vi) the discretion of the State to execute its public duties — with due regard
         for the public-law principles, all this in light of:
         –   the latest scientific knowledge;
         –   the available (technical) option to take security measures, and
         –   the cost-benefit ratio of the security measures to be taken.

[...]

Conclusion About the Duty of Care and Determining the Reduction Target

Due to the severity of the consequences of climate change and the great risk of hazardous climate change occurring — without mitigating measures — the court concludes that the State has a duty of care to take mitigation measures. The circumstance that the Dutch contribution to the present global greenhouse gas emissions is currently small does not affect this. Now that at least the 450 scenario is required to prevent hazardous climate change, the Netherlands must take reduction measures in support of this scenario. [**Ed. Note:** Here the court was referencing the conclusion by the IPCC, which the court accepted, that in order to maintain global temperature increase to within 2°C, atmospheric concentration of greenhouse gases must be stabilized at about 450 ppm.]

It is an established fact that with the current emission reduction policy of 20% at most in an EU context (about 17% in the Netherlands) for the year 2020, the State does not meet the standard which according to the latest scientific knowledge and in the international climate policy is required for Annex I countries to meet the 2°C target.

Urgenda is correct in arguing that the postponement of mitigation efforts, as currently supported by the State (less strict reduction between the present day and 2030 and a significant reduction as of 2030), will cause a cumulation effect, which will result in higher levels of CO_2 in the atmosphere in comparison to a more even procentual [*sic*] or linear decrease of emissions starting today. A higher reduction target for 2020 (40%, 30% or 25%) will cause lower total, cumulated greenhouse gas emissions across a longer period of time in comparison with the target of less than 20% chosen by the State. The court agrees with Urgenda that by choosing this reduction path, even though it is also aimed at realising the 2°C target, [it] will in fact make significant contributions to the risk of hazardous climate change and can therefore not be deemed as a sufficient and acceptable alternative to the scientifically proven and acknowledged higher reduction path of 25-40% in 2020.

This would only be different if the reduction target of 25-40% was so disproportionately burdensome for the Netherlands (economically) or for the State (due to its limited financial means) that this target should be deviated from to prevent a great potential danger. However, the State did not argue that this is the case. On the contrary: the State also argues that a higher reduction target is one of the possibilities. This leads the court to the conclusion regarding this issue of the dispute that the State, given the limitation of its discretionary power discussed here, in case of a reduction below 25-40% fails to fulfil its duty of care and therefore acts unlawfully. Although it has been established that the State in the past committed to a 30% reduction target and it has not been established that this higher reduction target is not feasible, the court sees insufficient grounds to compel the State to adopt a higher level than the minimum level of 25%. According to the scientific standard, a reduction target of this magnitude is the absolute minimum and sufficiently effective, for the Netherlands, to avert the danger of hazardous climate change, but the obligation to adhere to a higher percentage clashes with the discretionary power vested in the State, also with due regard for the limitation discussed here.

Attributability

From the aforementioned considerations regarding the nature of the act (which includes the omission) of the government it ensues that the excess greenhouse gas emission in the Netherlands that will occur between the present time and 2020 without further measures, can be attributed to the State. After all, the State has the power to issue rules or other measures, including community information, to promote the transition to a sustainable society and to reduce greenhouse gas emission in the Netherlands.

Damages

The State has argued that an allowance of one of Urgenda's claims, although it requests preventative legal protection, there is at least the *possibility* of damages in the form of a decrease in assets or loss of benefits. Although the State acknowledges that it is not required for damages to actually have been *incurred*, the State believes that it has to be established that Urgenda's interests are concretely at risk of being affected. The State also argues that it is insufficient that there is a risk in abstract terms or that there is a chance that anywhere in the world a risk of loss will occur for anyone. Urgenda has responded by stating that it has a sufficiently concrete interest.

The court finds as follows. It is an established fact that climate change is occurring partly due to the Dutch greenhouse gas emissions. It is also an established fact that the negative consequences are currently being experienced in the Netherlands, such as heavy precipitation, and that adaptation measures are already being taken to make the Netherlands "climate-proof". Moreover, it is established that if the global emissions, partly caused by the Netherlands, do not decrease substantially, hazardous climate change will probably occur. In the opinion of the court, the possibility of damages for those whose interests Urgenda represents, including current and future generations of Dutch nationals, is so great and concrete that given its duty of care, the State must make an adequate contribution, greater than its current contribution, to prevent hazardous climate change.

Causal Link

From the above considerations [...], it follows that a sufficient causal link can be assumed to exist between the Dutch greenhouse gas emissions, global climate change and the effects (now and in the future) on the Dutch living climate. The fact that the current Dutch greenhouse gas emissions are limited on a global scale does not alter the fact that these emission[s] contribute to climate change. The court has taken into consideration in this respect as well that the Dutch greenhouse emissions have contributed to climate change and by their nature will also continue to contribute to climate change. [...]

Conclusion Regarding the State's Legal Obligation

Based on the foregoing, the court concludes that the State [...] has acted negligently and therefore unlawfully towards Urgenda by starting from a reduction target for 2020 of less than 25% compared to the year 1990.

Notes and Questions

1. Having found that the Dutch Government acted negligently, the Hague District Court ordered the government "to limit the joint volume of Dutch annual greenhouse gas emissions, or have them limited, so that this volume will have reduced by at least 25% at the end of 2020 compared to the level of the year 1990, as claimed by Urgenda, in so far as acting on its own behalf."

2. The Dutch Government appealed the decision of the District Court. In October 2018, the Hague Court of Appeal upheld the lower court's decision and agreed with the lower court's finding that the State should reduce its emissions by at least 25% by the end of 2020. A translation of the Court of Appeal decision is available online: <https://uitspraken.rechtspraak.nl/inziendocument?id=ECLI:NL:GHDHA:2018:2610>. On November 16, 2018, the Dutch government announced that it would appeal the Court of Appeal's decision to the Supreme Court of the Netherlands.

3. Given that the *Urgenda* decision was based on an inquisitorial civil law system, we should be cautious about its usefulness in a Canadian adversarial common law context. In addition, though not reproduced in the excerpt above, the Hague District Court canvassed at length the science behind climate change and the scientific linkage between greenhouse gas emissions and adverse impacts, based largely on analyses and conclusions of the IPCC. Given that the Dutch Government did not contest the IPCC's findings, the Court accepted that scientific evidence. In their 2018 article reproduced earlier in this section, Ganguly *et al.* mentioned *Comer v.*

Murphy Oil USA Inc., 607 F.3d 1049 (5th Cir. 2010), as a key example of first wave private climate litigation in the United States. In that case, the US District Court characterized the state of climate science as a matter of scientific debate. Compare the approach taken by the Hague District Court and that taken by the US District Court. What do you think accounts for the difference in findings?

4. Consider the potential to deal with climate change liability under negligence in Canada. How would you define the duty of care of a possible defendant? Would it be based on a per capita allocation of emission rights? Would it be based on "reasonable efforts" to reduce GHG emissions, and if so, from what point forward? One of the challenges with common law actions on climate change is how to apportion liability for climate impacts, such as those experienced by the Village of Kivalina. Would you hold anyone who breaches your proposed standard of care to be jointly and severally liable? The issue of apportionment of liability has been the subject of debate in the context of contaminated property for some time. For a good overview of the state of the Canadian law in this area see: Nova Scotia Law Reform Commission, *Contaminated Sites in Nova Scotia — Final Report* (2009) at pp. 23-28.

In Chapter 2, we introduced the public trust doctrine, which is a legal principle found in American common law jurisprudence. In short, the public trust doctrine stipulates that the government holds the legal title over certain public resources in trust for its citizens, and that the government must maintain these resources for public use and benefit. The public trust doctrine originated in American case law involving public right to access navigable waters, but there have been growing attempts to expand the "trust asset" to include other components of the environment. In Canada, aside from a brief mention of the public trust doctrine in *British Columbia v. Canadian Forest Products Ltd.*, 2004 SCC 38, the doctrine has gained little traction in Canadian courts. However, in the United States, the public trust doctrine features prominently in *Juliana v. United States*. There have been various attempts by the defendants to delay the case or to have it dismissed altogether. In this ongoing legal proceeding, a group of young plaintiffs represented by lawyers with the non-profit organization Our Children's Trust are suing the United States government for deliberately allowing greenhouse gas emissions to continue, while knowing the climate change impacts that these emissions would cause, and thereby violating the plaintiffs' constitutional rights to life, liberty and property, as well as failing to protect essential public trust resources.

In the excerpt that follows, US District Judge Ann Aiken upheld the recommendation of Magistrate Judge Thomas Coffin to dismiss motions by the defendants to have the case dismissed before trial. In her decision, Aiken J. discussed the public trust claim advanced by the plaintiffs.

Juliana v. United States
217 F. Supp. 3d 1224 (D. Or. 2016)

AIKEN J.: — Plaintiffs in this civil rights action are a group of young people between the ages of eight and nineteen ("youth plaintiffs"); Earth Guardians, an association of young environmental activists; and Dr. James Hansen, acting as guardian for future generations. Plaintiffs filed this action against defendants the United States, President Barack Obama, and numerous executive agencies. Plaintiffs allege defendants have known for more than fifty years that the carbon dioxide ("CO_2") produced by burning fossil fuels was destabilizing the climate system in a way that would "significantly endanger plaintiffs, with the damage persisting for millen[n]ia." Despite that knowledge, plaintiffs assert defendants, "[b]y their exercise of sovereign authority over our country's atmosphere and fossil fuel resources, ... permitted, encouraged, and otherwise enabled continued exploitation, production, and combustion of fossil fuels, ... deliberately allow[ing] atmospheric CO_2 concentrations to escalate to levels unprecedented in human history[.]" Although many different entities contribute to greenhouse gas emissions, plaintiffs aver defendants bear "a higher degree of responsibility than any other individual, entity, or country" for exposing plaintiffs to the dangers of climate change. Plaintiffs argue defendants' actions violate their substantive due process rights to life, liberty, and property, and that defendants have violated their obligation to hold certain natural resources in trust for the people and for future generations.

Plaintiffs assert there is a very short window in which defendants could act to phase out fossil fuel exploitation and avert environmental catastrophe. They seek (1) a declaration their constitutional and public trust rights have been violated and (2) an order enjoining defendants from violating those rights and directing defendants to develop a plan to reduce CO_2 emissions.

Defendants moved to dismiss this action for lack of subject matter jurisdiction and failure to state a claim. Intervenors the National Association of Manufacturers, the American Fuel & Petrochemical Manufacturers, and the American Petroleum Institute moved to dismiss on the same grounds. After oral argument, Magistrate Judge Coffin issued his Findings and Recommendation ("F&R") and recommended denying the motions to dismiss. Judge Coffin then referred the matter to me for review pursuant to 28 U.S.C. § 636 and Federal Rule of Civil Procedure 72. Defendants and intervenors filed objections, and on September 13, 2016, this Court heard oral argument.

For the reasons set forth below, I adopt Judge Coffin's F&R as elaborated in this opinion and deny the motions to dismiss.

Background

This is no ordinary lawsuit. Plaintiffs challenge the policies, acts, and omissions of the President of the United States, the Council on Environmental Quality, the Office of Management and Budget, the Office of Science and Technology Policy, the Department of Energy, the Department of the Interior, the Department of Transportation ("DOT"), the Department of Agriculture, the Department of Commerce, the Department of Defense, the Department of State, and the Environmental Protection Agency ("EPA"). This lawsuit challenges decisions defendants have made across a vast set of topics — decisions like whether and to what extent to regulate CO_2 emissions from power plants and vehicles, whether to permit fossil fuel extraction and development to take place on federal lands, how much to charge for use of those lands, whether to give tax breaks to the fossil fuel industry, whether to subsidize or directly fund that industry, whether to fund the construction of fossil fuel infrastructure such as natural gas pipelines at home and abroad, whether to permit the export and import of fossil fuels from and to the United States, and whether to authorize new marine coal terminal projects. Plaintiffs assert defendants' decisions on these topics have substantially caused the planet to warm and the oceans to rise. They draw a direct causal line between defendants' policy choices and floods, food shortages, destruction of property, species extinction, and a host of other harms.

This lawsuit is not about proving that climate change is happening or that human activity is driving it. For the purposes of this motion, those facts are undisputed. The questions before the Court are whether defendants are responsible for some of the harm caused by climate change, whether plaintiffs may challenge defendants' climate change policy in court, and whether this Court can direct defendants to change their policy without running afoul of the separation of powers doctrine. [...]

Public Trust Claims

In its broadest sense, the term "public trust" refers to the fundamental understanding that no government can legitimately abdicate its core sovereign powers. See *Stone v. Mississippi*, 101 U.S. 814, 820 (1879) ("[T]he power of governing is a trust committed by the people to the government, no part of which can be granted away.") The public trust doctrine rests on the fundamental principle that "[e]very succeeding legislature possesses the same jurisdiction and power with respect to [the public interest] as its predecessors." *Newton v. Mahoning Cnty. Comm'rs*, 100 U.S. 548, 559 (1879). The doctrine conceives of certain powers and obligations — for example, the police power — as inherent aspects of sovereignty. Permitting the government to permanently give one of these powers to another entity runs afoul of the public trust doctrine because it diminishes the power of future legislatures to promote the general welfare.

Plaintiffs' public trust claims arise from the particular application of the public trust doctrine to essential natural resources. With respect to these core resources, the sovereign's public trust obligations prevent it from "depriving a future legislature of the natural resources necessary to provide for the well-being and survival of its citizens." *Br. of Amici Curiae Global Catholic Climate Movement and Leadership Council of Women Religious* at 3. Application of the public trust doctrine to natural resources predates the United States of America. Its roots are in the Institutes of Justinian, part of the Corpus Juris Civilis, the body of Roman law that is the "foundation for modern civil law systems." Timothy G. Kearley, *Justice Fred Blume and the Translation of Justinian's Code*, 99 Law Libr. J. 525, ¶1 (2007). The Institutes of Justinian declared "the following things are by natural law common to all — the air, running water, the sea, and consequently the seashore." J. Inst. 2.1.1 (J.B. Moyle trans.). The doctrine made its way to the United States through the English common law. See *Idaho v. Coeur d'Alene Tribe of Idaho*, 521 U.S. 261, 284 (1997) ("American law adopted as its own much of the English law respecting navigable waters, including the principle that submerged lands are held for a public purpose."); *Phillips Petroleum Co. v. Mississippi*, 484 U.S. 469, 473 (1988) ("At common law, the title and dominion in lands flowed by the tide water were in the King for the benefit of the nation ... Upon the American Revolution, these rights, charged with a like trust, were vested in the original States within their respective borders[.]" (quoting *Shively v. Bowlby*, 152 U.S. 1, 57 (1894)); Joseph L. Sax, *The Public Trust Doctrine in Natural Resource Law: Effective Judicial Intervention*, 68 Mich. L. Rev. 471, 475-76 (1970) (discussing the history of the public trust doctrine in the United States).

The first court in this country to address the applicability of the public trust doctrine to natural resources was the New Jersey Supreme Court, in 1821. The court explained that public trust assets were part of a taxonomy of property:

> Every thing susceptible of property is considered as belonging to the nation that possesses the country, as forming the entire mass of its wealth. But the nation does not possess all those things in the same manner. By very far the greater part of them are divided among the individuals of the nation, and become private property. Those things not divided among the individuals still belong to the nation, and are called public property. Of these, again, some are reserved for the necessities of the state, and are used for the public benefit, and those are called "the domain of the crown or of the republic," others remain common to all the citizens, who take of them and use them, each according to his necessities, and according to the laws which regulate their use, and are called common property. Of this latter kind, according to the writers upon the law of nature and of nations, and upon the civil law, are the air, the running water, the sea, the fish, and the wild beasts.

Arnold v. Mundy, 6 N.J.L. 1, 71 (N.J. 1821) (emphasis in original).

The seminal United States Supreme Court case on the public trust is *Illinois Central Railroad Company v. Illinois*, 146 U.S. 387 (1892). The Illinois legislature had conveyed to the Illinois Central Railroad Company title to part of the submerged lands beneath the harbor of Chicago, with the intent to give the company control over the waters above the submerged lands "against any future exercise of power over them by the state." *Id.* at 452. The Supreme Court held the legislature's attempt to give up its title to lands submerged beneath navigable waters was either void on its face or always subject to revocation. *Id.* at 453. "The state can no more abdicate its trust over property in which the whole people are interested, like navigable waters and soils under them ... than it can abdicate its police powers in the administration of government and the preservation of the peace." *Id.* In light of the "immense value" the harbor of Chicago carried for the people of Illinois, the "idea that its legislature can deprive the state of control over its bed and waters, and place the same in the hands of a private corporation" could not "be defended." *Id.* at 454.

The natural resources trust operates according to basic trust principles, which impose upon the trustee a fiduciary duty to "protect the trust property against damage or destruction." George G. Bogert et al., *Bogert's Trusts and Trustees*, § 582 (2016). The trustee owes this duty equally to both current and future beneficiaries of the trust. Restatement (Second) of Trusts § 183 (1959). In natural resources cases, the trust property consists of a set of resources important enough to the people to warrant public trust protection. *See* Mary C. Wood, *A Nature's*

Trust: Environmental Law for a New Ecological Age 167-75 (2014). The government, as trustee, has a fiduciary duty to protect the trust assets from damage so that current and future trust beneficiaries will be able to enjoy the benefits of the trust. *Id.* The public trust doctrine is generally thought to impose three types of restrictions on governmental authority:

> [F]irst, the property subject to the trust must not only be used for a public purpose, but it must be held available for use by the general public; second, the property may not be sold, even for a fair cash equivalent; and third, the property must be maintained for particular types of uses.

> Joseph L. Sax, *The Public Trust Doctrine in Natural Resource Law: Effective Judicial Intervention*, 68 Mich. L. Rev. 471, 477 (1970).

This lawsuit is part of a wave of recent environmental cases asserting state and national governments have abdicated their responsibilities under the public trust doctrine. *See, e.g., Alec L. v. Jackson*, 863 F. Supp. 2d 11 (D.D.C. 2012); *Sanders-Reed ex rel. Sanders-Reed v. Martinez*, 350 P.3d 1221 (N.M. Ct. App. 2015); *Kanuk ex rel. Kanuk v. State, Dep't of Natural Res.*, 335 P.3d 1088 (Alaska 2014); *Chernaik v. Kitzhaber*, 328 P.3d 799 (Or. Ct. App. 2014). These lawsuits depart from the "traditional" public trust litigation model, which generally centers on the second restriction, the prohibition against alienation of a public trust asset. Instead, plaintiffs assert defendants have violated their duties as trustees by nominally retaining control over trust assets while actually allowing their depletion and destruction, effectively violating the first and third restrictions by excluding the public from use and enjoyment of public resources.

Defendants and intervenors argue the public trust doctrine has no application in this case. They advance four arguments: (1) the atmosphere, the central natural resource at issue in this lawsuit, is not a public trust asset; (2) the federal government, unlike the states, has no public trust obligations; (3) any common-law public trust claims have been displaced by federal statutes; and (4) even if there is a federal public trust, plaintiffs lack a right of action to enforce it. I address each contention in turn.

Scope of the Public Trust Asset

The complaint alleges defendants violated their duties as trustees by failing to protect the atmosphere, water, seas, seashores, and wildlife. Defendants and intervenors argue plaintiffs' public trust claims fail because the complaint focuses on harm to the atmosphere, which is not a public trust asset. I conclude that it is not necessary at this stage to determine whether the atmosphere is a public trust asset because plaintiffs have alleged violations of the public trust doctrine in connection with the territorial sea.

The federal government holds title to the submerged lands between three and twelve miles from the coastlines of the United States. *See* Restatement (Third) of The Foreign Relations Law of the United States § 51 l(a) (1987) (international law permits a nation to claim as its territorial sea an area up to twelve miles from its coast); Presidential Proclamation of Dec. 27, 1988, No. 5928, 3 C.F.R. § 547 (1989) (President Reagan expanding United States' claim from three-mile territorial sea to twelve-mile territorial sea); 43 U.S.C. § 1312 (seaward boundary of a coastal state is "a line three geographical miles distant from its coast line"). Time and again, the Supreme Court has held that the public trust doctrine applies to "lands beneath tidal waters." *See Phillips Petroleum Co.*, 484 U.S. at 474 (discussing *Shively*, 152 U.S. at 57 and *Knight v. US. Land Ass'n*, 142 U.S. 161, 183 (1891)); *Alabama v. Texas*, 347 U.S. 272, 278 (1954) (Black, J., dissenting) ("In ocean waters bordering our country, if nowhere else, day-to-day national power — complete, undivided, flexible, and immediately available — is an essential attribute of federal sovereignty."); id. at 282 (Douglas, J., dissenting) ("Thus we are dealing here with incidents of national sovereignty. ... The authority over [the sea] can no more be abdicated than any of the other great powers of the Federal Government. It is to be exercised for the benefit of the whole."); *see also* Joseph L. Sax, *The Public Trust Doctrine in Natural Resource Law: Effective Judicial Intervention*, 68 Mich. L. Rev. 471, 556 (1970) (public trust law covers "that aspect of the public domain below the low-water mark on the margin of the sea and the great lakes, the waters over those lands, and the waters within rivers and streams of any consequence"). Because a number of plaintiffs' injuries relate to the effects of ocean acidification and rising ocean temperatures, they have adequately alleged harm to public trust assets. [...]

Conclusion

[...] A deep resistance to change runs through defendants' and intervenors' arguments for dismissal: they contend a decision recognizing plaintiffs' standing to sue, deeming the controversy justiciable, and recognizing a federal public trust and a fundamental right to climate system capable of sustaining human life would be unprecedented, as though that alone requires its dismissal. This lawsuit may be groundbreaking, but that fact does not alter the legal standards governing the motions to dismiss. Indeed, the seriousness of plaintiffs' allegations underscores how vitally important it is for this Court to apply those standards carefully and correctly. [...]

Judge Goodwin is no stranger to highly politicized legal disputes. Nearly fifty years ago, he authored the landmark opinion that secured Oregon's ocean beaches for public use. Private landowners wanted to construct fences and otherwise keep private the beaches in front of their properties; they brought suit to challenge an Oregon state law requiring public access to all dry sand beaches. *State ex rel. Thornton v. Hay*, 462 P.2d 671, 672-73 (Or. 1969). Writing for five of the six members of the Oregon Supreme Court, then-Justice Goodwin rooted his determination the beaches were public property in a concept from English common law:

> Because so much of our law is the product of legislation, we sometimes lose sight of the importance of custom as a source of law in our society. It seems particularly appropriate in the case at bar to look to an ancient and accepted custom in this state as the source of a rule of law. The rule in this case, based upon custom, is salutary in confirming a public right, and at the same time it takes from no man anything which he has a legitimate reason to regard as exclusively his.

> *Id.* at 678.

In an argument with strong echoes in defendants' and intervenors' objections here, the plaintiff private property owner contended it was "constitutionally impermissible ... to dredge up an inapplicable, ancient English doctrine that has been universally rejected in modern America." Kathryn A. Straton, *Oregon's Beaches: A Birthright Preserved* 65 (Or. State Parks & Recreation 1977). The Oregon Supreme Court was not persuaded by this call to judicial conservatism. Because of the application of an ancient doctrine, Oregon's beaches remain open to the public now and forever.

Notes and Questions

1. Since Aiken J.'s ruling, the Trump Administration has tried on multiple occasions to either obtain a stay of the proceedings or to have the case be dismissed, all unsuccessful. The trial on the merits was originally set to begin on October 29, 2018. However, due to further procedural efforts by the Trump Administration to resist having the matter proceed to trial, that trial date was missed. On November 8, 2018, in response to another motion for stay, the Ninth Circuit Court of Appeals ordered a temporary stay of the District Court proceedings pending consideration of the government's petition for a writ of *mandamus*. In the American legal system, a petition for a writ of *mandamus* can be used to seek an order from an appellate court directing a subordinate court to take certain actions. Here, the government is asking the Ninth Circuit to direct the District Court to dismiss the case. In early 2019, the Ninth Circuit granted the plaintiffs' request to expedite the interlocutory appeal, which at the time of writing is scheduled for June 2019.

2. Consider Aiken J.'s discussion of the history and derivation of the public trust doctrine in American common law. How viable do you think the public trust doctrine can be imported into Canadian jurisprudence? How would you structure a public trust claim in a piece of climate change litigation in Canada?

Climate Litigation under the Charter

The last topic we will cover regarding climate litigation is the potential of using the *Canadian Charter of Rights and Freedoms* to frame a climate change case. Increasingly, public interest litigants in Canada are turning to the *Charter*, in particular section 7, as a way to entrench a constitutional right to a healthy environment. In their article below, Nathalie J. Chalifour and Jessica Earle offer their views on issues around bringing a section 7 *Charter* claim in climate litigation. The authors discussed the challenges regarding justiciability and causation that we have already canvassed above. We will focus on the authors' discussion of the principles of fundamental justice.

Nathalie J. Chalifour & Jessica Earle,
"Feeling the Heat: Climate Litigation under the Canadian
Charter's Right to Life, Liberty, and Security of the Person",
(2018) 42 Vt. L. Rev. 689

Is the Infringement in Accordance with the Principles of Fundamental Justice?

Section 7 only allows the right to life, liberty, and security of the person to be infringed upon if in accordance with the principles of fundamental justice. The purpose and requirements of fundamental justice remain somewhat foggy despite their importance and the number of applicable judgments from the Supreme Court. This is perhaps not surprising because, as Hogg notes, the principles of fundamental justice "did not have a firmly established meaning in Anglo-Canadian law" when the *Charter* was adopted in 1982. In accounting for the wide variety of outcomes in section 7 cases, Hogg points to the "enormous discretion that the Supreme Court of Canada has assumed for itself under the rubric of fundamental justice."

In spite of this variation, a common thread that ties the case law together is the treatment of fundamental justice as a normative concept. Professor Hamish Stewart compellingly argues that fundamental justice is ultimately a normative inquiry about the function of law, requiring the courts to engage in "a process of determining the values that are sufficiently fundamental to restrain the exercise of state power when the subject's most vital interests — life, liberty, and security of the person — are at stake." He argues, rightly in our view, that this stage of the section 7 inquiry, instead of being empirical or historical, is deeply principled in nature because "the decisive question is what role the principle plays in a legal order that is committed to the values expressed in the Charter."

Each time the courts accept — or are asked to accept — a new principle of fundamental justice, they are adjudicating whether a proposition is sufficiently foundational to the core values enshrined in the *Charter* to warrant restraining or directing the actions of government.

In *Malmo-Levine*, the Court articulated three defining characteristics for principles of fundamental justice, noting that: (1) they must be legal in nature (thereby ensuring courts avoid adjudication of policy matters); (2) there must be "significant societal consensus that [the principle] is fundamental to the way in which the legal system ought fairly to operate"; and (3) they must be capable of being "identified with sufficient precision to yield a manageable standard ..." The Court in *Bedford* emphasized that principles of fundamental justice ensure the means the state uses to attain its objectives are not fundamentally flawed, e.g., "arbitrary, overbroad, or ... grossly disproportionate to the legislative goal." In 2015, the Court in *Carter* added that principles of fundamental justice are "the minimum constitutional requirements that a law that trenches on life, liberty or security of the person must meet."

To determine whether any of these three principles have been violated, the courts must clearly define the objective of the challenged state conduct. The objective of deterring prostitution, for instance, was held in *Bedford* to be insufficiently precise. Similarly, in *Carter*, the Court found the objective of preserving life to be too broad, as compared to the goal of "preventing vulnerable persons from being induced to commit suicide at a time of weakness," which is sufficiently precise. Importantly, the inquiry is specific to the violations of the claimants' rights in a given case, and not a broader inquiry. In other words, "[t]he question under [section] 7 is whether anyone's life, liberty or security of the person has been denied" and the "effect on one person is sufficient to establish a breach of [section] 7."

The Supreme Court also made it clear in *Carter* that courts are not to consider the competing social interests or public benefits that the government might confer when assessing whether a deprivation of rights is in accordance with principles of fundamental justice. These broader issues are more appropriately considered in the section 1 analysis. To do otherwise would be to impose the section 1 burden on section 7 claimants.

Over the course of the *Charter*'s existence, three central principles have emerged: arbitrariness, overbreadth, and gross disproportionality. Analyzing each of these principles requires first identifying the goal of the government action that causes harm under section 7. The principles-of-fundamental-justice (PFJ) analysis will thus vary based on how the decision is framed. However, in cases where the courts considered whether the combined effects of multiple legislative provisions created an infringement, they treated the combined effect of the legislative acts as one prohibition or decision for the purposes of the PFJ analysis. As such, in the case of a climate *Charter* challenge framed around a set of decisions that lead to harmful levels of GHG emissions, the Courts would likely seek to identify the overall policy goal driving the decisions, which might be to provide convenient and inexpensive sources of energy. While the government might be tempted to underline the economic and social benefits of facilitating production of fossil-fuel energy, the jurisprudence is clear that these benefits are not part of the PFJ analysis, but must be reserved for section 1. The question would then be whether the state's conduct in authorizing, enabling, and investing in activities that lead to harmful levels of GHG emissions is arbitrary, overbroad, or grossly disproportionate relative to the purpose of such authorizations and investments. If the case was framed around the government's failure to reduce emissions in accordance with its target, the PFJ analysis would need to be applied flexibly, as elaborated in the following discussion.

Arbitrariness

A law is considered to be arbitrary if it affects section 7 interests for no valid reason. In other words, an arbitrary law is one that undermines its own purpose or where there is no rational connection between its purpose and the limit it imposes on rights. The government thus breaches section 7 when it "exacts a constitutional price in terms of rights, without furthering the public good that is said to be the object of the law." As Hogg and Stewart note, *Carter*'s conception of fundamental justice requires first looking to ensure that the chosen means of policy is capable of achieving the statutory goal ("instrumental rationality").

If climate claimants targeted decisions that authorize and enable fossil-fuel extraction and development, the question would be whether the purpose of these decisions — presumably to promote the development of fossil-fuel energy, a resource of economic and social utility — is rationally connected to the harms they cause to the plaintiffs. Framed in this way, it would be possible to argue convincingly that there is no rational connection between the purpose of promoting fossil-fuel activities and the harms caused by GHG emissions. How can a government justify loss of life, liberty, and security of the person to promote an already pampered industry whose assets are increasingly stranded because the market knows we are headed into a decarbonized future?

The argument of arbitrariness would be even stronger, however, if the lawsuit was framed around the overall GHG-reduction target. Claimants could point to Canada's goal of reducing GHG emissions to the level required to avoid 2°C warming: action it has characterized as urgent and critical to avoid the dire consequences of failing to reduce emissions. Claimants would need only to point to the irrationality of continuing to approve major fossil-fuel infrastructure, like pipelines and liquefied natural gas terminals that will lead to significant increases in GHG emissions to demonstrate the arbitrariness of such government decisions. As noted earlier, Environment Canada's own models show that, even with full implementation of the policies in the Pan-Canadian Framework, Canada's emissions will still be 44 Mt over its 2030 target. Ongoing decisions to approve fossil-fuel infrastructure that will lead to long-lasting and significant GHG emissions are therefore not only arbitrary, but patently foolish.

Another way claimants could frame their argument would be to point to evidence that the Canadian government's decisions and policies are fundamentally incompatible with the goal of meeting the IPCC 2020 emissions benchmark, which would require Canadian emissions to be 367-458 Mt CO_2e in 2020, or the Canadian government's own 2020 GHG emissions-reduction targets of 622 Mt CO_2e. Once again, the government's decisions to enable GHG emissions could be seen as arbitrary relative to its own GHG-reduction commitments.

As such, there is considerable merit to the argument that the government's conduct in continuing to authorize and subsidize GHG emissions is, relative to its objective of reducing GHG emissions, arbitrary in a way that offends fundamental justice.

Gross Disproportionality

The principle of gross disproportionality is "infringed if the impact of the restriction on the individual's life, liberty or security of the person is grossly disproportionate to the object of the measure." Climate litigants could argue that the violation of their rights to life, liberty, and security of the person as a result of climate change is grossly disproportionate to the government's conduct in making decisions that lead to harmful levels of GHG emissions. This argument would be especially compelling for a group of youth indigenous claimants since the deprivation undermines all section 7 interests for an entire generation and likely multiple future generations.

If we consider (1) the government's statement that taking strong action to address climate change is critical and urgent and (2) its 2020 goal of reducing GHG emissions by 17% and 2030 goal of reducing emissions by 30%, the state's conduct in authorizing, enabling, and investing in activities that lead to harmful levels of GHG emissions certainly appears grossly disproportionate to the violations of section 7 rights. The government explicitly acknowledges that "the costs of inaction are much greater than the costs of addressing climate change," meaning it recognizes the repercussions of delaying action to reduce GHG emissions. To continue to make decisions that undercut the national commitment to GHG reductions is to say that the individual section 7 rights of Canadians are less important than the economic rights of fossil-fuel companies, many of which are foreign owned. Even if the government raised the social benefits of fossil-fuel development (something that is meant to be part of the section 1 analysis, rather than PFJ), the claimants could argue that, although energy development is important to Canadians, fossil fuels are not the only means of producing energy. In fact, the growth in renewable energy is so great that countries that fail to transition to clean forms of energy in a timely manner risk being left in a cloud of (fossil-fuel) dust. If we boil down the issue to its core — that the government is prioritizing short-term economic interests over the future of human life as we know it — the only rational conclusion is that it is a grossly disproportionate choice.

Overbreadth

A law will be considered overbroad if it "goes too far by denying the rights of some individuals in a way that bears no relation to the object" of the law. In other words, a law is overbroad if it has the effect of targeting conduct that bears no relation to its purpose. The Supreme Court in *Carter* found the prohibition on assisted suicide was too broad since it applied to all people, not just those who were vulnerable (the group of people the law was designed to protect). Similarly, in *Bedford*, the Supreme Court held that the prohibition against living on the avails of prostitution was overbroad since it had the effect of punishing anyone who earned a living through a relationship with a prostitute, such as drivers and bodyguards, rather than just those who might exploit them. Even though it can be challenging to define the target group (such as those vulnerable to assisted suicide or prostitutes who might be exploited), that does not justify overly broad legislation.

The overbreadth argument is more cumbersome to make in the context of climate change, since claimants would need to find some conduct that bears relation to the government's purpose of reducing GHG emissions. Given that the stated purpose of the Pan-Canadian Framework is to "develo[p] a concrete plan which, when implemented, will allow [the government] to achieve Canada's international commitments," climate litigants could argue that the effect of the Canadian government's decisions to authorize and subsidize fossil-fuel extraction are too broad in relation to the goal of reducing emissions. However, this is a more awkward argument than those under arbitrariness and gross disproportionality.

Perhaps it would be more interesting for courts to attenuate the overbreadth principle, which addresses laws that go too far, to consider laws or state conduct that do not go far enough and thereby infringe on section 7 rights. In this way, courts could squarely address a claim of infringement due to inadequate government action: inadequate action would not be in accordance with the principles of fundamental justice because it bears no relation to the government's goal of reducing GHG emissions.

Notes and Questions

1. How would you construct a section 7 climate case? What kind(s) of government action or legislation would you target? Who would have standing to bring such a case? Would it be an alleged deprivation of the right to life, to liberty, to security of the person, or to a combination of these?

2. Chalifour and Earle believe that, of the three principles of fundamental justice discussed, an argument regarding overbreadth is the most cumbersome to make. Do you agree? Instead of challenging state conduct that bears relation to the government's goal of reducing greenhouse gas emissions as the authors suggest, a claimant may also attack state conduct that furthers the purpose of economic development. Would an overbreadth argument be easier to make if the state conduct furthering economic development also has the side effect of causing climate-related injury to the plaintiff? Which principle(s) of fundamental justice would you say is violated by the deprivation of a claimant's section 7 right?

3. While not a piece of climate litigation, *Grassy Narrows First Nation v. Ontario (Attorney General)* is an example of how section 7 of the *Charter* is being used to advance environmental justice. The Grassy Narrows First Nation is situated in northwestern Ontario. For decades, members of this Nation have suffered adverse health effects from mercury contamination due to clearcut logging activities, which release mercury into streams frequented by fish that the Nation consumes. In 2015, they applied to the Ontario Divisional Court for judicial review of a provincial government decision approving clearcut logging activities on their territories and refusing to order an environmental assessment regarding potential mercury contamination. They argue that mercury contamination in their food caused by the government's decisions deprives them of their right to life, liberty and security of the person. They further argue that the deprivation violated the following principles of fundamental justice: (a) respect for the sanctity of human life, (b) procedural fairness, (c) gross disproportionality and (d) equality rights under subsection 15(1) of the *Charter*. After the application was filed, the Ontario government agreed not to authorize any clearcutting in the Grassy Narrows area until 2022. In the meantime, the judicial review proceeding has been put on hold.

Next, as a comparison to Canadian *Charter* law, we briefly revisit Aiken J.'s decision in *Juliana v. United States* for her discussion on the plaintiffs' argument that the government's actions in allowing greenhouse gas emissions to continue violated their fundamental rights guaranteed under the Fifth Amendment of the United States Constitution. Among other things, the Fifth Amendment provides that no one shall be "deprived of life, liberty, or property, without due process of law."

Juliana v. United States
217 F. Supp. 3d 1224 (D. Or. 2016)

AIKEN J.: —

Due Process Claims

The Due Process Clause of the Fifth Amendment to the United States Constitution bars the federal government from depriving a person of "life, liberty, or property" without "due process of law." Plaintiffs allege defendants have violated their due process rights by "directly caus[ing] atmospheric CO_2 to rise to levels that dangerously interfere with a stable climate system required alike by our nation and Plaintiffs[,]"; "knowingly endanger[ing] Plaintiffs' health and welfare by approving and promoting fossil fuel development, including exploration, extraction, production, transportation, importation, exportation, and combustion"; and, "[a]fter knowingly creating this dangerous situation for Plaintiffs, ... continu[ing] to knowingly enhance that danger by allowing fossil fuel production, consumption, and combustion at dangerous levels".

Defendants and intervenors challenge plaintiffs' due process claims on two grounds. First, they assert any challenge to defendants' affirmative actions (i.e. leasing land, issuing permits) cannot proceed because plaintiffs have failed to identify infringement of a fundamental right or discrimination against a suspect class of persons. Second, they argue plaintiffs cannot challenge defendants' inaction (i.e., failure to prevent third parties from emitting CO_2 at dangerous levels) because defendants have no affirmative duty to protect plaintiffs from climate change.

Infringement of a Fundamental Right

When a plaintiff challenges affirmative government action under the due process clause, the threshold inquiry is the applicable level of judicial scrutiny. The default level of scrutiny is rational basis, which requires a reviewing court to uphold the challenged governmental action so long as it "implements a rational means of achieving a legitimate governmental end[.]" When the government infringes a "fundamental right," however, a reviewing court applies strict scrutiny. Substantive due process "forbids the government to infringe certain 'fundamental' liberty interests at all, no matter what process is provided, unless the infringement is narrowly tailored to serve a compelling state interest." It appears undisputed by plaintiffs, and in any event is clear to this Court, that defendants' affirmative actions would survive rational basis review. Resolution of this part of the motions to dismiss therefore hinges on whether plaintiffs have alleged infringement of a fundamental right.

Fundamental liberty rights include both rights enumerated elsewhere in the Constitution and rights and liberties which are either (1) "deeply rooted in this Nation's history and tradition" or (2) "fundamental to our scheme of ordered liberty[.]" The Supreme Court has cautioned that federal courts must "exercise the utmost care whenever we are asked to break new ground in this field, lest the liberty protected by the Due Process Clause be subtly transformed into" judicial policy preferences.

This does not mean that "new" fundamental rights are out of bounds, though. When the Supreme Court broke new legal ground by recognizing a constitutional right to same-sex marriage, Justice Kennedy wrote that

> The nature of injustice is that we may not always see it in our own times. The generations that wrote and ratified the Bill of Rights ... did not presume to know the extent of freedom in all its dimensions, and so they entrusted to future generations a charter protecting the right of all persons to enjoy liberty as we learn its meaning. When new insight reveals discord between the Constitution's central protections and a received legal stricture, a claim to liberty must be addressed.

Thus, "[t]he identification and protection of fundamental rights is an enduring part of the judicial duty to interpret the Constitution ... [that] has not been reduced to any formula." In determining whether a right is fundamental, courts must exercise "reasoned judgment," keeping in mind that "[h]istory and tradition guide and discipline this inquiry but do not set its outer boundaries." The genius of the Constitution is that its text allows "future generations [to] protect ... the right of all persons to enjoy liberty as we learn its meaning."

Often, an unenumerated fundamental right draws on more than one Constitutional source. The idea is that certain rights may be necessary to enable the exercise of other rights, whether enumerated or unenumerated. In *Roe v. Wade*, [...] the Court exhaustively chronicled the jurisprudential history of the fundamental right to privacy — another right not mentioned in the text of the Constitution. *Roe*'s central holding rests on the Due Process Clause of the Fourteenth Amendment. But the Court also found "roots" of the right to privacy in the First Amendment, the Fourth Amendment, the Fifth Amendment, the penumbras of the Bill of Rights, and the Ninth Amendment. Similarly, in *Obergefell*, the Court's recognition of a fundamental right to marry was grounded in an understanding of marriage as a right underlying and supporting other vital liberties. [...]

Exercising my "reasoned judgment," I have no doubt that the right to a climate system capable of sustaining human life is fundamental to a free and ordered society. Just as marriage is the "foundation of the family," a stable climate system is quite literally the foundation "of society, without which there would be neither civilization nor progress." [...]

Defendants and intervenors contend plaintiffs are asserting a right to be free from pollution or climate change, and that courts have consistently rejected attempts to define such rights as fundamental. Defendants and intervenors mischaracterize the right plaintiffs assert. Plaintiffs do not object to the government's role in producing any pollution or in causing any climate change; rather, they assert the government has caused pollution and climate change on a catastrophic level, and that if the government's actions continue unchecked, they will permanently and irreversibly damage plaintiffs' property, their economic livelihood, their recreational opportunities, their health, and ultimately their (and their children's) ability to live long, healthy lives. Echoing *Obergefell*'s reasoning, plaintiffs allege a stable climate system is a necessary condition to exercising other rights to life, liberty, and property.

In framing the fundamental right at issue as the right to a climate system capable of sustaining human life, I intend to strike a balance and to provide some protection against the constitutionalization of all environmental claims. On the one hand, the phrase "capable of sustaining human life" should not be read to require a plaintiff to allege that governmental action will result in the extinction of humans as a species. On the other hand, acknowledgment of this fundamental right does not transform any minor or even moderate act that contributes to the warming of the planet into a constitutional violation. In this opinion, this Court simply holds that where a complaint alleges governmental action is affirmatively and substantially damaging the climate system in a way that will cause human deaths, shorten human lifespans, result in widespread damage to property, threaten human food sources, and dramatically alter the planet's ecosystem, it states a claim for a due process violation. To hold otherwise would be to say that the Constitution affords no protection against a government's knowing decision to poison the air its citizens breathe or the water its citizens drink. Plaintiffs have adequately alleged infringement of a fundamental right.

Notes and Questions

1. Aiken J. held that "the right to a climate system capable of sustaining human life is fundamental to a free and ordered society." Consider the factors for recognizing a principle of fundamental justice discussed by Chalifour and Earle in their article above. What is your assessment of the likelihood that "a climate system capable of sustaining human life" could be recognized as a principle of fundamental justice? What about "sustainable development" as a principle of fundamental justice? If these concepts are not capable of being a principle of fundamental justice, how would you develop them so that they may be recognized as principles of fundamental justice (PFJs)?

2. In framing the due process violation, Aiken J. held that governments are not required to refrain from pollution, simply that governmental action cannot affirmatively and substantially damage the climate system in a way that threatens its capacity to sustain human life. What parallels can you draw from this framework to a possible gross disproportionality argument under section 7 of the *Charter*?

Part IV — Climate Change, Environmental Assessments and Species at Risk

In recent years, the focus of the regulatory debate with respect to climate change has changed from "whether" to "how" to respond to the challenge. In other words, most Canadian governments are now in the midst of either developing or implementing regulatory responses to climate change. In this setting, lawyers can play an important role, both in assisting policy makers in weighing the pros and cons of various policy options and in designing policy regimes that are effective and consistent with regulatory initiatives in other jurisdictions. In Part II, we reviewed the policy instruments adopted by the federal government (and a few provinces) to address climate change, particularly carbon taxes and cap-and-trade. In this Part, we explore how governments can take climate considerations into account in other regulatory spheres. We first explore issues in how to incorporate climate change considerations in the context of environmental or impact assessments. Then, we will examine climate change issues in protecting species and biodiversity.

Climate Change and Assessment Law

Efforts to utilize environmental assessment processes in Canada to address climate change impacts of new proposals, most notably energy projects such as oil sands developments, oil refineries and pipeline infrastructure, have met with very limited success to date. With recent developments to reform environmental assessment law, which we canvassed in Chapter 7, there are renewed efforts to examine how we can integrate considerations of climate impacts within the architecture of federal environmental assessment law. Professors Meinhard Doelle, Robert Gibson and others have written on this topic. Extracts from their recent work follows. We begin with Professor Doelle's article, which deals with the following elements of the assessment process and how they should consider climate change: triggering, information needs, analysis, decision-making and follow-up. The extract of the article by Professor Gibson *et al.* focuses more squarely on how to integrate a climate test into environmental or impact assessments.

Meinhard Doelle,
"Integrating Climate Change into Environmental
Impact Assessments: Key Design Elements"
(2018), online: SSRN < https://ssrn.com/abstract = 3273499 >

Introduction

With the successful conclusion of the UN climate negotiations in Paris in December, 2015, and its entry into force on November 4, 2016, most UN member states have committed to making all reasonable efforts to reduce and eliminate GHG emissions and to fully decarbonize within the next few decades. Impact assessment (IA) is a critical tool for meeting these commitments for a number of reasons. IA has become a key decision-making tool for proposed new activities in many countries, and often provides the main public forum for dialogue seeking common ground among proponents, government, and the public on whether and under what conditions to approve proposed projects. Even though its potential as a decision making tool has yet to be fully realized, it offers perhaps the best hope of ensuring that proposed new activities are consistent with long-term biophysical, social and economic aspirations and commitments generally and those related to decarbonization specifically.

Integrating climate change into IA requires consideration of both mitigation and adaptation, as well as any adverse impacts not prevented through effective mitigation and adaptation efforts (sometimes referred to as loss and damage, or impacts and vulnerability to climate change). While these areas are connected, each brings its unique challenges. The focus here is on the mitigation element (which is defined to include GHG emissions as well as impacts on natural sinks such as forests, soils, grasslands and oceans). The focus is on the consideration of the GHG emission and sinks impacts of a proposed project at five critical stages of IA: triggering, information gathering, analysis, the project decision, and post-approval follow-up. [...]

Climate change is unlike other adverse environmental impacts traditionally assessed, and a challenge to incorporate into traditional IA methodologies and processes. This is due in part to three key characteristics:

(i) the effects of releasing GHG emissions are felt globally, with regional variations in the nature and scale of the effects,

(ii) the effects are delayed, and

(iii) the emissions and effects on sinks are cumulative, with the result that a given effect cannot be traced back to a specific project.

The resulting dilemma is that the climate impacts of proposed projects are distributed globally and over time, including to future generations, while the benefits of projects tend to be more local and immediate. It is perhaps understandable that IA practitioners and project decision makers have in the past, preferred to ignore climate change altogether, or have tended to summarily dismiss the climate change effects of individual projects as insignificant. This approach, however, has contributed to the neglect of climate change, and the resulting ever-growing urgency of full decarbonization. [...]

Climate Change and IA Triggers

[...] From a climate mitigation perspective, triggering should be designed to ensure that all proposed projects not likely to assist with full decarbonization are assessed. Arbitrary annual GHG emission thresholds alone do not serve this purpose effectively, as they ignore the duration of the activity and the alternatives its approval displaces. Life-cycle emission thresholds alone are similarly ineffective as they tend to ignore the distribution of the emissions over time, indirect emissions, cumulative impacts, and the resulting effect on decarbonization efforts. Some projects with significant short term GHG emissions may be quite compatible with a transition to GHG neutrality. Other projects, even though the direct GHG emissions are small, may nevertheless put jurisdictions on a track that is incompatible with decarbonization. This is not to suggest that annual and life-cycle thresholds cannot be used, but they are a crude tool that risks missing many important projects.

The goal of ensuring that activities with the potential to hinder the decarbonization of affected jurisdictions are assessed can only be met through the use of a combination of tools. First, from a project IA perspective, a project list could be developed in each of the key sectors involved in the transition to GHG emission neutrality, including electricity, resource extraction, transportation, manufacturing, forestry, and agriculture. For each of these sectors, projects that warrant an assessment in light of their potential to hinder the transition could be listed. The lists could be developed with a reverse onus approach, so that all activities in identified climate risk categories get assessed unless they are demonstrated to be consistent with the transition without the need for an IA.

Strategic impact assessments (SIAs) of the key emitting sectors can serve to offer more specific guidance to prospective proponents to encourage innovation in project selection and design to help with this transition rather than propose projects that will hinder it. With appropriate policy signals in the key sectors, project proponents will know that projects that contribute to decarbonization will be welcome. Depending on the outcome of the SIAs, they can also serve to shorten the list of activities to be assessed at the project level. SIAs should therefore be carried out in each sector identified. In some cases, where conditions within the sector warrant, they can be carried out at a national level. In other cases, a regional approach may be required in light of different regional circumstances. [...]

Climate Mitigation Information Needs

As an underlying principle for information gathering, it is important to err on the side of gathering as much information as reasonably possible about the implications of the proposed project for decarbonization efforts. There may be a tendency to work back from the decision-making stage, to first decide how to determine whether the project is acceptable from a climate perspective, and to gather only information that is needed for that determination, however conceived. Given the seriousness and complexity of the issue, and the limited experience, it would be a mistake to limit the information gathered. Instead, it will be important to gather and publicly share as much information as possible about the potential implications of a proposed project on decarbonization efforts in affected jurisdictions. This will offer the best opportunities for innovative approaches during the course of the assessment, and will maximize learning opportunities after the project decision.

The starting point for any assessment is that it needs to be able to quantify the direct GHG emissions and any sinks impairment of the proposed activity over its life cycle. The more difficult question becomes what else is needed to be able to properly inform the analysis of the climate mitigation implications of the project, and to ultimately inform decision makers on whether the project will contribute to or hinder decarbonization efforts. These questions in turn can help identify the minimum information needs. [...]

It would seem that a good starting point for determining information needs would be a rebuttable presumption that the GHG emissions from a proposed activity are additional. In other words, the default conclusion would be that the life cycle direct emissions from a proposed activity are solely attributable to the proposed activity as a negative environmental effect. This would then raise the question whether there is a case to be made that the proposed activity will offset emissions under likely and reasonable alternative scenarios including the no project alternative. If the proponent intends to make the case that the project will displace emissions elsewhere, additional information would be needed on the GHG emissions associated with alternatives, and with the upstream and downstream GHG emissions associated with the proposed activity. Under this scenario a credible assessment of societal needs, alternative ways of meeting those needs and cumulative effect will be particularly critical. The burden of making the argument would be on the proponent. [...]

Climate Mitigation Analysis

As already explored in a preliminary way in the previous section, the analysis needed will depend, at least to some extent, on the climate mitigation claims made by proponents. They will also depend on national and subnational policies and commitments to reduce emissions. [...] If the proponent accepts that the life cycle direct emissions are additional and constitute a negative effect of the project, then the GHG emissions analysis beyond the prediction of the direct emissions associated with the project may be limited to considering whether the project should be held responsible as a catalyst for indirect emissions. If, however, the proponent takes the position that some or all of the project emissions are justified on the basis that they will result in emission reductions elsewhere, then a comprehensive analysis on the overall GHG emissions impact of the proposed project will have to be carried out.

For example, a proponent of a hydro-electric project may accept the GHG emissions from the construction and operation of its project as additional. In this case, no detailed analysis of the impact of the additional hydro power into existing markets may be required. However, the proponent may argue that the GHG emissions from the construction of the dam and the flooding of the reservoir are offset by the coal burning power plants that currently generate the power to be provided by the dam once in operat[ion]. In this case, a detailed analysis to determine whether the power from the dam will displace coal, gas, wind, solar, or conservation and efficiency measures in the markets it will enter will have to be carried out to determine to what extent the GHG emissions from the construction and operation of the dam are in fact offset by the displacement of higher emitting sources of electricity.

An important design question is how the information gathered about the proposed activity's GHG emissions is to be used during the assessment phase of the IA. The default assumption should be that GHG emission levels that would hinder the transition to full decarbonization would preclude approval of a proposed project, and the burden should be on the proponent to demonstrate that the proposed activity actually contributes to this transition in spite of its life cycle emissions. [...]

A related issue that will require more work is the methodology for determining whether the proposed initiative will have a positive, negative or neutral effect on a jurisdiction's global commitments. So far, I have expressed this determination in terms of Canada's transition to full decarbonization. Of course, there is no clear date for full decarbonization in the Paris Agreement itself or in Canada's nationally determined contributions (NDCs). [...] In short, more work is needed to turn these basic elements into a standard against which the GHG emission implications of individual projects can be measured. Federal-provincial negotiations can assist with this process, as can SIAs of key sectors that need to lead the transition to GHG emissions neutrality. In the end, there will be some basic options on how to develop the standard against which projects can be measured. One approach would be to develop national, provincial and sectoral carbon budgets (possibly with a domestic trading mechanism for provinces and sectors) for key stages in the transition, such as 2020, 2030, and 2040. Projects would then essentially have to compete against other existing and possible future activities for the limited carbon budget, and should be expected to pay for the privilege of having some of that budget allocated to them.

An alternative or complement to a carbon budget approach would be to use best available information to set prices for a ton of GHG emissions at 5 or ten year intervals for the life of the project that would include the social cost of carbon, and require projects to internalize this cost in demonstrating the project's economic viability. A third option would be to require project proponents to purchase offsets from sources that are transformational in their contribution to full decarbonization (within Canada, on the assumption that the goal is still to achieve GHG emission neutrality in Canada), either for all emissions, or for any that are deemed to be in excess of the budget allocation granted. Performance standards for sectors, or based on the social need being served would be further alternatives to explore.

Decision-making in Light of Climate Mitigation Analysis

The next stage of the IA process is the decision-making process. It is here that the information gathered and the analysis carried out is translated into decisions about whether specific proposed activities are permitted to proceed, and, if so, under what conditions. The focus remains on project IA, as the general assumption is that regional and strategic assessments serve to inform project IAs, and that while certain types of activities might get eliminated by policies and plans adopted on the basis of regional or strategic assessments (which should include early policy decisions not to proceed with categories of projects that are clearly not consistent with Canada's climate goals), it is at the project IA stage that project decisions ultimately are made.

To make a project decision in light of the analysis carried out in accordance with the approach discussed in the previous section, a number of key choices and determinations will have to be made:

- What emissions will be attributed to the proposed project for purposes of the project decision based on a clear and defensible rationale?
- Which alternatives to the project factor into the project decision based on a clear and defensible rationale, and how will decision makers determine whether they are better or worse from a climate mitigation perspective?
- Have all reasonable efforts been made to avoid negative climate impacts and contribute to decarbonization?
- Does the project help or hinder Canada's climate mitigation efforts in light of its Paris commitments?
- How should any remaining climate impacts be weighed against other adverse impacts, benefits, risks and uncertainties to determine whether the impacts are justified, whether the project makes an overall contribution to sustainability and whether the project is in the public interest?

Of course, these questions can only be adequately addressed at the decision making stage if the information gathering and analysis provides an appropriate basis for their consideration. To be clear, all questions would have to be answered before a project decision is made. The result would be a range of possible scenarios at the decision making stage of the project IA, resulting in a range of possible conclusions about the proposed project's contribution to Canada's climate mitigation [...]. In addition to identifying whether the project is predicted to help or hinder Canada's efforts to mitigate climate change, it will be important to quantify the positive or negative contribution the project is predicted to make, and the risks and uncertainties associated with the predictions made in the IA. [...]

Post Approval Considerations

For approved projects, the post approval (or follow-up) phase is critical for a number of reasons. It provides an opportunity to learn, particularly with respect to the accuracy of the predictions made about the GHG emissions of the project. This will be important for future assessments, so that prediction errors can be reduced over time. The follow-up phase is also important for compliance and adaptive management purposes. [...]

Conclusion

Ultimately, there are many difficult choices that will have to be made at a political level, and for which decision makers will have to be accountable as part of the democratic process. The role of IA is to minimize the need for political choices by seeking mutually supportive solutions. Where difficult choices are unavoidable, assessments must identify these political choices clearly and provide transparency and clarity about the decisions being made and the implications for climate change commitments and for a jurisdiction's contribution to the global effort.

More thought will have to be given to how best to guide those responsible for the process and ultimate project decisions to ensure progress towards climate commitments is facilitated and not hindered. Sound climate policy, rigorous and transparent SIAs and project IAs with clear guidance for decision makers are all critical elements in this regard. Only through a coordinated approach can we hope to redirect innovation towards integrated solutions that meet societal needs for energy, employment, health, education, and general wellbeing, while accelerating our transition to GHG neutrality.

Robert B. Gibson et al.,
"From Paris to Projects: Clarifying the Implications of Canada's
Climate Change Mitigation Commitments for the Planning and
Assessment of Projects and Strategic Undertakings — Summary Report"

(2018), online: < https://uwaterloo.ca/paris-to-projects/sites/ca.paris-to-projects/
files/uploads/files/p2p_summary_report_0.pdf >

Specifying Requirements for Assessments of Climate-Significant Undertakings

The federal *Impact Assessment Act* that is currently before Parliament has considerable potential as a vehicle for progress on climate change mitigation. **[Ed. Note:** see Chapter 7 for our overview of the IAA.] As noted above, assessment decisions on individual projects and other undertakings can do much to facilitate or frustrate progress towards climate responsibility. The forthcoming law's sustainability-based design and climate test (whether proposed undertakings would "hinder or contribute to" meeting Canada's climate change commitments), give it a strong foundation for climate-responsible results. However, the Act's promising basic requirements are unlikely to be understood reliably or applied predictably unless accompanied by specific regulatory directions and policy guidance for application and compliance.

For assessment applications, the central requirement is for a clear and explicit set of climate-centred tests in decision making. Elaboration and application of these tests are needed to clarify how to evaluate the extent to which assessed undertakings would "hinder or contribute to" meeting Canada's climate change commitments, as required under section 63(e) of the new law. While that clarification is most obviously needed for decision makers, the rules for decision makers will also guide proponents, assessment reviewers and other participants in assessment deliberations.

The major basic tests are summarized below [...]. The tests mobilize the several categories of tools outlined above to meet Canada's *Paris Agreement* commitments. Because those tools have different strengths and roles, the tests should be taken as a package of requirements, each of which should be met. All of the tests need some elaboration for practical application. Many specifics are open to debate and initial applications are likely to be primitive. However, the details are likely to be best informed by experience and, in any event, the tests will have to be adjusted as pathways, pricing and carbon budget allocations evolve, and as global requirements are tightened and climate science evolves.

Tests to Be Applied to Determine Whether a Proposed Undertaking Would or Would Not Contribute to Meeting Canada's International Climate Change Mitigation commitments

The core test is that all projects and other proposed undertakings that may be GHG significant over their lifetime must

- contribute to meeting Canada's international climate change mitigation commitments, and not hinder Canada's transition to GHG neutrality in time to meet those commitments.

The international commitments currently established chiefly under the *Paris Agreement* require Canada to do its fair share

- to keep overall climate warming "well below 2°C" and to pursue efforts to limit the increase to 1.5°C above pre-industrial levels" (Article 2.1);

- to achieve global peaking of GHG emissions as soon as possible and to reach GHG neutrality in the second half of this century at the latest, "on the basis of equity, and in the context of sustainable development and efforts to eradicate poverty" (Article 4.1.); and

- to anticipate regular review and revision of signatories' commitments to reflect progressively increasing nationally determined contributions that represent each signatory's "highest possible ambition" (Article 4.3, Article 14).

These commitments are to be met while also ensuring respect for human rights, including Indigenous rights, and pursuing other sustainability objectives such as biodiversity.

More specific tests that elaborate on the core test can be based on analyses using a suite of complementary available tools for determining whether a proposed undertaking will contribute to or hinder meeting our international commitments. The following list includes analyses that can be used in an elementary way now but need be developed and specified further for Canadian application.

Tests based on particular analyses using a range of tools would, for example, require a proposed undertaking

- to contribute to the major transformations that are needed in key sectors — including energy, transportation, buildings, manufacturing, resources, agriculture, and possibly forestry — to achieve GHG neutrality in Canada in time to meet our international commitments;

- to avoid any direct or indirect effects that would hinder timely transition to GHG neutrality;

- to fit on a credible sectoral or regional pathway to meeting Canada's international commitments;

- to be consistent with staying within an equitable GHG budget for Canada (and within the global GHG budget consistent with meeting international objectives), as further specified for a sector or region;

- to be viable if the proponents of the undertaking had to pay the full costs associated with all GHG emissions and sink impairments properly attributable to the undertaking over its lifespan and lifecycle, with these full costs determined by the GHG price needed to achieve timely transition to a GHG-neutral economy or the full social cost of associated climate change (the share of overall anticipated global damages attributable to the undertaking's GHGs);

- to avoid, or compensate for, any addition to the costs of making a timely transition to GHG neutrality;

- to avoid any properly attributable GHG emissions and sink impairments past the Canadian deadline for GHG neutrality entailed by Canada's current international commitments, or provide legitimate new domestic offsets to neutralize any such emissions or sink impairments; and

- to be consistent with ensuring that Canadian GHG mitigation and sink enhancement initiatives reflect "highest possible ambition" and best efforts, while not impeding or delaying more promising options.

Tests based on existing domestic policy guidance can also be used, if that guidance is adjusted to reflect our current and anticipated international commitments. Such tests would need to favour transparently developed and credible policies. In every case, the guidance would have to be consistent with meeting Canada's international commitments.

For illustration, given current domestic policy guidance, a proposed undertaking would be required

- to be consistent with meeting Canada's current Nationally Determined Contribution (NDC), plus additional requirements to address the gap between the current NDC and the more demanding commitments of the

Paris Agreement, and to anticipate needs for increasing ambitions in future national commitments under that Agreement; and

- to be consistent with the requirements implied by the *Pan-Canadian Framework on Clean Growth and Climate Change* and its implementing legislation, plus additional requirements to address the gap between the Framework components and the current NDC, as well as the gap between the current NDC and the *Paris Agreement*.

Specifying these tests through open and meaningfully participative strategic policy making, including application of legislated strategic assessment requirements, would be preferable to relying on case-by-case debates on the test requirements and implications. Also, these tests would need to be applied to all existing and proposed activities and undertakings affecting prospects for meeting Canada's climate change mitigation commitments, including those that would not be subject to legislated assessment requirements.

All climate tests will need to be updated regularly in light of tightening international commitments, the evolution of climate science and learning from application experience.

Notes and Questions

1. Compare the recommendations made in the two excerpts above to the provisions of the *Impact Assessment Act* discussed in Chapter 7. Do the changes to the federal assessment process discussed in Chapter 7 make the implementation of the recommendations in these articles easier or more difficult?

2. The *Kearl Oil Sands* case (*Pembina Institute for Appropriate Development v. Canada (Attorney General)*, 2008 FC 302) was one of the first successful judicial review cases in the climate change context: see discussion in Chapter 6. This judicial review application succeeded in forcing the Panel to justify its conclusion that the greenhouse gas emissions from the oil sands project were not likely to be significant. The success was, of course, limited by the Court's reluctance to engage in the substantive debate on what is a significant effect, allowing the Panel to still consider one of the largest single sources of GHG emissions in Canada to be insignificant. Based on the recommendations set out in the two articles above, how should a reviewing body go about assessing the climate impacts of that oil sands project?

Climate Change and Biodiversity

It is impossible to do justice to the links between climate change and biodiversity in this section. Any mitigation strategy, other than scaling back human activities responsible for GHG emissions, involves some risk to biodiversity. Notably, the use of natural and human processes to increase the recapture of greenhouse gases out of the atmosphere is a use of natural systems that at least has the potential to compete with biodiversity. Another climate change mitigation strategy that has clear implications for biodiversity is the replacement of fossil fuels with biofuels. These issues are not covered here. Instead, we propose in this Part to focus our attention on the interactions between a central dimension of biodiversity — endangered species — and climate change.

The focus of much of Chapter 9 was an assessment of the *Species at Risk Act* (SARA). To that end, we considered various elements of the SARA including (1) the listing process, (2) critical habitat designation and recovery strategies, and (3) prohibitions on species takings.

With the emergence of climate change and a growing appreciation of its present and future impact on species, as noted American ecologist Jane Lubchenco has put it, "we've entered a new territory". In the balance of this Part, we embark on an initial consideration of what this means for species and for law and policy makers in both Canada and the United States. The legal literature addressing this topic is in its infancy; to provide a focal point for this discussion, we offer excerpts from two early attempts to grapple with the topic.

In the first piece, Kostyack and Rohlf conclude in large measure that the US *Endangered Species Act* (ESA) provides a legal framework — in terms of listing, habitat protection, prohibitions on "takings" and so on — that is adequate: in their words, "no radical changes to the law are needed to ensure that the ESA addresses the effects of global warming". In their view, the real challenges lie elsewhere, including significant regulatory and economic policy reforms aiming at capping and reducing GHG emissions, ensuring that the agencies responsible for administering ESA are properly resourced, and the need for these agencies to revisit their approach to species protection by adopting approaches that emphasize adaptive management and ecosystem integrity. This will necessitate, in their view, a departure from the prevailing "species by species" approach to listing and recovery.

The second article, authored by Professor J.B. Ruhl, comes to many of the same conclusions but, in the final analysis, advocates for even more sweeping changes in the way responsible federal agencies (most notably, the US Fish and Wildlife Service or "FWS") discharge their duties under the ESA.

As you read the excerpts, consider the applicability of their analysis and conclusions to the Canadian context. In Canada, is the interaction between climate change and species protection more of an environmental *policy* than an environmental *law* challenge?

John Kostyack & Dan Rohlf,
"Conserving Endangered Species in an Era of Global Warming"
(2008) 38 Envtl. L. Rep. 10,203

Global warming is the single most urgent threat to the future of wildlife and wildlife habitat. The 2007 reports of the Intergovernmental Panel on Climate Change (IPCC) conclude that human activity is "very likely" causing the world to warm. These reports also note that the average surface temperature of the earth increased 0.76 degrees Celsius in the 20th century and predict that this temperature will likely increase by another 1.8 to 4.0 degrees C in the 21st century, depending on pollution levels. The IPCC also finds that 20-30% of species worldwide are likely to be at increased risk of extinction if increases in average global temperatures exceed 2 to 3 degrees C above pre-industrial levels.

Unless governments and people around the world take action quickly to curtail global warming pollution, we will face rapid warming and other climatic and physical changes, including disappearing polar ice caps, large rises in sea levels, and extreme floods and droughts. If this scenario unfolds, society would increasingly turn its focus to providing for the countless climate refugees fleeing sea-level rise and drought, developing new supplies of food and drinking water, and otherwise rebuilding the infrastructure of civilization. The ESA, and most other traditional wildlife conservation programs would likely face drastic curtailments in the face of these competing priorities.

Even as work proceeds to reduce global warming pollution, we must recognize that reducing GHGs alone will not be enough to prevent widespread extinctions of species with which we share the planet. Even with significant reductions in global warming pollution from human sources, at least another 0.6 degree C increase will inevitably occur (over and above the increase of 0.76 degree C in the 20th century) in the coming decades due to GHGs already released into the atmosphere. Therefore, even if we immediately act to curb warming pollution, wildlife will still face threats from altered climates and major ecosystem disruptions. [...]

At the domestic level, the ESA can play a significant role in conserving U.S. wildlife threatened by global warming. When Congress enacted the ESA in 1973 and amended the statute in the 1970s and 1980s, lawmakers did not see global warming as a significant threat to wildlife. However, policymakers designed the ESA to address all threats to wildlife, no matter what their origin. Thus, no radical changes to the law are needed to ensure that the ESA addresses the effects of global warming. On the other hand, climate change greatly increases extinction risks of species already imperiled for other reasons and thereby greatly reduces the margin for error in implementing the ESA's protections and recovery programs. Policymakers therefore will need to consider significantly strengthening ESA programs — as well as increasing ESA funding — to help fulfill the nation's commitment to conserve abundant wildlife and healthy ecosystems for future generations.

Global warming is exactly that: global. No ecosystem on earth is immune to its effects. Herein, we review the impacts of global warming by major habitat types. But it is important to note that across all habitat types, two serious problems have surfaced at the species level: (1) changes in phenology (timing of seasonal events); and (2) changes in distribution of wildlife (most notably, the disappearance of northern hemisphere wildlife species from the southern portions of their ranges and from lower elevations). An example of the former phenomenon is the shift in the time of springtime peak insect abundance, which affects the reproductive success of songbirds that depend on high insect levels during the critical nestling phase. The 90% decline of the northwestern Minnesota moose population in the past 20 years, which biologists have attributed to excessive heat, provides an example of the latter. Another example is the decline of the American pika, a small rabbit-like mammal that inhabits talus fields in the mountains of the western United States. One study of Great Basin pikas finds that their range has shifted upslope by 900 feet and 36% of populations have been extirpated.

Just as climate change poses encompassing threats to the planet's ecosystems, it raises fundamental challenges to our government's ability to stem and ameliorate these threats. Though the U.S. Supreme Court labeled the ESA "the most comprehensive legislation for the preservation of endangered species ever enacted by any nation", the federal agencies charged with implementing the statute are only now beginning to consider how it can remain an effective conservation tool in light of global warming's tremendous threats to biodiversity. It is obvious that climate change will demand more of everything — more species listed as threatened or endangered, more resources devoted to assessing and reducing biological risks and to restoration efforts, and more agency personnel for implementation. In this section, we go beyond the obvious need to devote greater resources to saving threatened and endangered species in a warming world to explore the difficulties and questions that the central environmental threat of the 21st century will raise for a law enacted 35 years ago at the dawn of the modern environmental era.

[**Ed. Note:** Portions of the article where the authors address the implications of climate change for the application of ESA's listing, critical habitat, recovery and take provisions are omitted.]

Conserving Wildlife in a Changing Climate: Policy Recommendations

We have already begun to see the initial effects of climate change, and we must now act quickly to put in place new legal mechanisms to deal with its pervasive threats to biodiversity. At a broad level, it is crucial that Congress include within any climate change legislation specific provisions — and specific funding — to conserve biodiversity in a warming world. At the same time, policymakers must reaffirm the ESA's role as a primary legal tool for protecting the nation's at-risk species and their habitats. As noted above, the statute's comprehensive provisions and inherent flexibility enable it to deal with climate-based threats without major modifications to the law itself. However, within the framework of the existing statute, we recommend new policies and implementation schemes to ensure that agencies meaningfully confront threats to biodiversity posed by climate change.

Addressing Endangered Species in Federal Climate Change Legislation

While lawmakers do not appear poised to make fundamental changes to the ESA itself anytime in the near future, it seems likely that Congress will soon enact legislation with consequences for endangered species that are much more far-reaching than any ESA overhaul. As of this writing, lawmakers in the 110th Congress have introduced nearly a dozen bills that would place caps on emissions of global warming pollution, allow trading of emissions credits, i.e., permits, and generate substantial public funds (tens of billions of dollars) through an auction of emissions credits. Most of these bills contemplate that a portion of the auction proceeds would be devoted to programs to conserve wildlife threatened by global warming. The U.S. Senate Committee on Environment and Public Works has passed a bill with strong emissions caps and substantial funding for conservation of wildlife and other natural resources threatened by global warming, and the leaders of both the U.S. House of Representatives and Senate have indicated a strong desire to enact this or a measure of similar breadth and strength into law.

This is encouraging news for wildlife. As noted above, Congress can take no more important step to help wildlife and ecosystems than to legislate substantial, economy wide reductions in global warming pollution. It is also crucial that auctions of emissions credits be used to generate billions of dollars of dedicated funding annually to enable federal and state natural resource agencies to confront inevitable global warming. Although some may consider dedicating a substantial sum of such new annual funding for wildlife (say, $5 billion) a steep price to pay for biodiversity protection given the other urgent priorities for addressing global warming, it is in fact a necessary investment to maintain and restore the natural systems that serve as the foundation of our economy and quality of life.

Making Adaptive Management a Central Focus of the ESA

Although each year scientists are able to identify and project the ecosystem changes attributable to global warming with increasing degrees of precision, the exact consequences of global warming will always defy prediction. The average surface temperatures around the globe already exceed levels ever experienced since modern wildlife management began roughly a century ago, and they will soon exceed levels experienced since the beginning of human civilization approximately 13,000 years ago. This means that careful observation and the flexibility to change course in response to new information will be especially important components of ESA implementation in the coming years.

The concept of adaptive management is not new. In recent years, natural resource agencies have often touted the use of adaptive management in implementing the ESA and other wildlife programs. Unfortunately, however, agencies' use of this term has often proven to be more in the way of lip service than actual implementation. In order to practice adaptive management, the Services should enact regulations that insist upon a high degree of rigor in carrying out adaptive management programs. Key elements of any adaptive management program promulgated by the Services would be:

- Systematic observations of the impacts of global warming on wildlife and wildlife habitats;
- Projections and conservation planning based on these observations and on models of future climate conditions;
- Conservation actions pursuant to such projections and plans;
- Monitoring and evaluation; and
- Adjustments to projections, plans, and conservation actions based on monitoring and evaluation.

Ecosystem-Based Approaches

Given the overwhelming numbers of individual species likely to be put at risk due to climate change, it will be vital for the Services to develop methods of identifying species at risk and planning for the conservation of listed species that are more efficient than the current species-by-species approach to listing and recovery planning. Though largely ignored for the past few years, the FWS in 1994 adopted a policy statement calling for an ecosystem approach to implementing the ESA; the policy specifically mentions making listing decisions and developing recovery plans on an ecosystem basis when possible. The Services should update this policy statement to address how ecosystems will be defined and managed in light of changes in species distribution, disassembly of ecological communities, and other disruptions caused by global warming. Regardless of how these difficult definitional issues are resolved, it will remain essential to pursue ecosystem-based listing and recovery planning strategies. In places where climate change affects a large number of species — in Arctic and coral reef ecosystems, for example — such strategies would advance conservation with much less cost and much greater speed than carrying out listing and recovery planning actions on an individual species basis.

Applying the ESA to the Causes of Global Warming Pollution

As noted in the previous section, the ESA will increasingly intersect with a broad array of activities whose only connection to risks to listed species is emissions of GHGs. The trigger for application of section 7's substantive and procedural obligations is a federal action that may affect listed species. Rather than denying the impact of global warming pollution on listed species, the Services should construe any action that results in non-trivial net increases of GHGs as meeting this threshold. Similarly, the Services should interpret section 9's prohibition against take of protected species as covering the actions of non-federal GHG emitters.

Conclusion

Congress took a bold and decisive step in 1973 when it enacted the ESA in response to its recognition of the significant cant threats to biodiversity. Today, similarly bold and decisive action is imperative to reduce global warming pollution and to ensure that the impacts of inevitable global warming do not wipe out the conservation gains of the past 35 years. Although the United States must commit to significant additional research on global warming impacts and potential management responses, we already have substantial scientific information on steps needed to protect species and their habitat in a warming world. First and most urgently, Congress must put in place a national cap on global warming pollution, with aggressive annual reductions in pollution levels, and the United States must work at the international level to achieve similar commitments from other nations. Second, policymakers and natural resource managers must design and apply adaptive management strategies so that both projected and unanticipated changes on the landscape can be addressed. Ultimately, we must integrate biodiversity protection and necessary funding into a comprehensive federal regulatory response to climate change.

While the ESA in its present form will provide an effective tool for conserving species and habitats in the face of global warming, legislative and administrative changes will be needed to strengthen its ability to deal with the dangers and uncertainties of climate change. The most important variable in determining the success of species protection efforts, however, is both simple and enormously challenging: our continued resolve to ensure the secure future of all life on earth.

J.B. Ruhl,
"Climate Change and the *Endangered Species Act*:
Building Bridges to the No-Analog Future"
(2008) 88 B.U.L. Rev. 1

The task ahead of the Fish and Wildlife Service (FWS) is daunting, and it must use the discretion outlined [above] to develop a plan soon, lest climate change sweep away its mission along with its charges. [...] manifestations of climate change already are well underway and already have had adverse impacts on some species. More can be expected. Indeed, the FWS must assume that more climate change impacts will unfold even if the global community takes measures to mitigate greenhouse gas emissions [...] this assumption poses complex policy questions for the FWS, though [...] the agency has considerable flexibility in how it answers them. It has the discretion, within bounds, to adopt passive or aggressive policies for how to integrate climate change in ESA programs.

With that foundation established, what should define the agency's set of operating assumptions about how the global community responds generally to climate change — pessimism or optimism? A worst case scenario would have the global community utterly fail to contain greenhouse gas emissions and, as a result, climate change spiraling into chaos for centuries. In that scenario, the FWS might as well pack up its bags and close shop, as climate change will become an unassailable force in ecological reshuffling, overwhelming any management of ecosystems or species. Exercising the ESA, in other words, is pointless in this scenario.

On the other hand, the agency also cannot afford to assume a Pollyanna future in which the global community comes together tomorrow, drastically reduces emissions, somehow sucks carbon dioxide out of the troposphere, and reaches 1990 overall levels by the end of this decade. The message of *Massachusetts v. EPA* is that a regulatory agency can't assume someone else will address the climate change problem. Each agency must "whittle away" with whatever knife Congress has provided it.

The ESA will be best served if the FWS adopts a cautious optimism that recognizes the limits of the ESA but keeps the statute relevant. Conceding that some human-induced climate change is inevitable even in the best of circumstances does not concede that it will be perpetual and chaotic. Rather, the FWS can reasonably assume that the global community will eventually arrest greenhouse gas emissions to a benchmark level and that, as a consequence, climate regimes will eventually settle into a new "natural" pattern of variation. We have no analog for what that pattern will be, and the transition from the present to that future will be, by all appearances, a rocky ride, but in all probability we will get there. The job of the ESA is to help as many species as is reasonably possible get there with us — to serve as their bridge across the climate change transition into the no-analog future.

Ironically, to do this will take some humility and restraint. Going for the jugular by regulating greenhouse gas emissions is not where the ESA can be of most help to imperilled species. There is little to be gained for the FWS or for climate-threatened species by having the agency go down this road. The agency has no explicit authority to do so, does not have the expertise to do so, and would risk undermining the political viability of the ESA by doing so. Rather, the FWS can provide expert assistance to the agencies more appropriately charged with regulating greenhouse gas emissions, such as the EPA, by advising them about the effects of climate change on species.

As for its direct role in addressing climate change, the FWS can employ the ESA most effectively by identifying species threatened by climate change, identifying which of those can be helped through the ESA's habitat-based programs, and devising a management plan — one that uses regulatory action as well as recovery planning — to build each such species its bridge. Indeed, this strategy allows the FWS to dispense with the distinction between human-induced and natural climate variation. Climate change is climate change — it does not matter to the species what is causing it. What does matter to them is whether and in what shape they survive it.

This brings us to the six policy choice pressure points raised in Part II. To implement the proposed bridge policy, I suggest the FWS approach the policy choices as follows:

Identifying Climate-Threatened Species

The agency's objective should be to use the ESA to define and monitor the ecological reshuffling effects of climate change. The agency should aggressively identify species threatened by climate change. Early identification of species threatened by climate change and of the critical habitat they require for survival through climate change transition will help in defining the extent of ecological reshuffling and guide human adaptation programs. Early identification also will provide the basis for listing species as threatened, which provides more flexibility in terms of regulatory effects and recovery efforts.

Regulating Greenhouse Gas Emissions

The agency's objective should be to not squander agency resources in a futile effort for which the ESA is simply not equipped. The FWS should not attempt to use its Section 7 and Section 9 regulatory programs in an effort to regulate greenhouse gas emissions. As for the take prohibition, listing species as threatened early will allow the agency to remove greenhouse gas emissions from consideration under Section 9 while keeping the take prohibition active with respect to other contributing threats. If an animal species is in endangered status, meaning Section 9 necessarily applies in full force, difficulties in establishing the burden of proof would support the exercise of prosecutorial discretion not to attempt to regulate greenhouse gas emissions. Under the Section 7 consultation program, project-specific jeopardy analyses should promote other federal agencies to consider ways of reducing greenhouse gas emissions, but should not lead to jeopardy findings.

Regulating Non-Climate Effects to Protect Climate-Threatened Species

The agency's objective should be to support the bridge function of the ESA and to reduce the adverse impacts on species from human adaptation to climate change. Where a species weakened by climate change is also threatened by other anthropogenic sources, such as loss of habitat, and where the agency reasonably believes addressing the non-climate threats will help carry the species through the climate change transition, the agency should use [its] regulatory powers to the extent necessary. In particular, where human adaptation to climate change exacerbates threats to a species, the agency should aggressively employ its regulatory presence through Section 7 consultations and enforcement of the Section 9 take prohibition. The agency also must monitor the impacts of human adaptation on species that face no direct or secondary ecological threat from climate change and employ Section 7 and Section 9 powers accordingly. Clearly, however, innovative approaches will be needed, such as market-based incentives and regional planning efforts, to facilitate human adaptation measures as much as species can tolerate.

Designing Conservation and Recovery Initiatives

The agency's objective should be to get as many species with a long-term chance at survival and recovery through the transition to the other side of climate change as is realistically possible. The agency must initially differentiate between species that are unlikely to survive climate change under any circumstances and those that are likely to benefit from assistance in their home ecosystems. Agency resources should not be wasted in developing recovery plans or other conservation measures for non-recoverable species. For species that appear likely to withstand climate change under the ESA's protection, recovery plans should identify the expected intensity of assistance required to manage or respond to primary and secondary ecological effects. Conservation measures for species that require intensive assistance [...] should be designed around adaptive management techniques that involve ample monitoring and considerable room for adjustment of management actions in order to account for the possibility that continuing climate change will alter the effectiveness of those actions.

Species Trade-Offs

The agency's objective should be to not contribute to ecological reshuffling through its species management efforts. Where the measures described above are complicated by species trade-offs — when helping one may harm another — the agency should adopt an ecosystem-based management approach modeled on promoting long-term species diversity and ecosystem multi-functionality. When ecological models do not point to a particular management action to serve those goals, general default priorities, such as assisting top-level predators and resisting induced invasions, may help mediate between species in conflict.

Dealing with the Doomed

The agency's objective should be to avoid accelerating the decline of species who stand no chance of surviving climate change, but not to take measures on their behalf which could pose threats to other species. Under this standard, assisted migration should be employed for such a species only if the FWS has assembled conclusive evidence of the extinction threat, a quantitative model showing the likely success of assisted migration for the species with de minimis anticipated effects on other species, and an assisted migration management plan including long term monitoring and active adaptive management. Human adaptation measures that could accelerate the extinction of the species, which could cascade to affect other species, should be regulated under Section 7 and Section 9 as for any other listed species.

Conclusion

The "pit-bull" has met its match, but sometimes old dogs can learn new tricks. It is sobering to find that ecological reshuffling is inevitable and to realize that the ESA can't do anything about it. Yet this is precisely what leads me to my proposal that the statute be employed in a more focused manner in the decades leading to our no-analog future. What the statute has done best is stop the decline of imperilled species brought under its protective wings, and it has done so in the face of problems as intractable as urbanization and invasive species. The ESA has not solved urban sprawl or invasive species — it has helped species deal with them. Likewise, we must find a way for the ESA to help species deal with the effects of climate change, not its causes. The statute provides this flexibility — the means to proactively identify the threat of climate change and focus on helping those species that can be helped.

My proposal is unlikely to satisfy strong supporters of the ESA or its strong critics. The former are likely to believe the "pit bull" has found its ultimate calling in climate change. If there is any statute that can wrestle greenhouse gas emissions to the ground (i.e., to 1990 levels), they might think it is the ESA and its unrelenting biocentric mission, whereas my proposal keeps the statute at bay. The latter will object to my proposal's aggressive call for species listings, which is based on wholesale adoption of the premise of human-induced climate change, and to its continued use of the statute as a regulatory weapon against habitat loss and other non-climate threats to climate-threatened species.

Both views doom the ESA. Of course, that may be the intent and hope of the statute's critics, with or without climate change. But adopting the strong version of the ESA in the climate change era, in which the FWS charges hard after greenhouse gas emissions, would play right into the critics' hands — the statute is neither designed to regulate something so ubiquitous as greenhouse gas emissions nor so sacrosanct as to survive the political battle attempting to do so would ignite. Support for the ESA, therefore, must be tempered by practical and political reality if the ESA itself is to survive climate change. The trade-off I propose — standing back from greenhouse gas emissions but staying fully engaged in regulating non-climate threats, particularly those stemming from human adaptation to climate change — is the plan the ESA needs in order to build the bridge for species into the no-analog future.

Notes and Questions

1. One indication that the FWS is beginning to appreciate the need to approach its role in a new way given climate change is its landmark 2008 decision to list the polar bear as endangered: see Federal Register Vol. 73, No. 5. Professor Ruhl takes this decision as a positive sign, though he notes that it also reflects growing external pressure on the agency around climate change issues. As he puts it:

   ... although clearly not enthusiastic about the prospect, the FWS appears ready to carry the ESA into the climate change era, having recently proposed to extend ESA protection to the polar bear because of the diminishing ice habitat that the species depends upon for survival. The agency is getting strong nudges from the outside as well, as members of Congress have urged the agency to evaluate the effects of climate change on species generally, environmental advocacy groups have petitioned the agency to promulgate rules to address climate change, and one court has admonished the agency for failing to take climate change into account in its regulatory programs.

2. While the polar bear was listed as threatened under the ESA in 2008, it does not have a comparable listing in Canada. Currently it is listed as a SARA "species of special concern" which means that it is still subject to commercial hunting. As a result, a US-based environmental group has filed a petition with the Commission for Environmental Cooperation that alleges the Canadian government has failed to effectively enforce its domestic environmental laws. In late 2012, the CEC announced that it had accepted this "citizen submission", filed by the Center for Biological Diversity, for investigation: see SEM-11-003, online: <www.cec.org>. However, the CEC Council voted in 2014 not to instruct the Secretariat to prepare a factual record, and so the matter never proceeded any further.

3. Compare the features of the ESA with those of SARA canvassed in Chapter 9. Do the key differences between ESA and SARA dictate a Canadian approach to responding to the impacts of climate change on endangered species that is different from what is argued for in the articles above? In other words, can the federal government mount an effective response to this challenge without amending SARA? What suggestions, offered in the excerpts above, have the most relevance and importance in the Canadian context?

Part V — Perspectives on the Future of Climate Law and Policy

Many would argue that we are now in a period where the prospects for preventing catastrophic, global climate change are bleaker and more remote than ever before. Still, many are hopeful about what the future holds, and of the opportunities that the fight against climate change creates for democratic change. A case in point is the following article.

Jedediah Purdy,
"The Politics of Nature: Climate Change,
Environmental Law, and Democracy"

(2010) 119 Yale L.J. 1122

[...] This Article began by challenging two claims about environmental public language. One is that "environmentalism" is unsuited to the nature and scale of today's problems, especially climate change, because environmental values are negative and defensive on the one hand, and, on the other, reliant on a naÿve and untenable contrast between humanity and nature. The second challenged claim is that, whatever its more specific defects, such language is vague, motivationally weak, and thus a presumptively poor resource for addressing the next generation of environmental challenges.

The first claim depends on simplistic accounts of environmental politics, which are belied by the history of environmental public language.

[**Ed. Note:** The author proceeds with a detailed account of the performance of the US environmental movement to make the point that it has and can play a constructive role in identifying a sustainable path forward. This portion of the article is omitted.]

In answer to the second challenge, that environmental public language has negligible practical relevance, this Article recasts the problem. The question is not simply whether a static and discrete set of concerns called "environmentalism" has more or less force. Environmental public language has been thoroughly interwoven with other era-defining themes, around which citizens have sought to persuade one another of the content of their values and interests. To be a little too schematic about it, the persuasion has generally aimed at two kinds of changes. One has been to recognize substantively new purposes. The kind of aesthetic encounter with nature that the Sierra Club and Wilderness Society pioneered and moved from eccentricity to a cornerstone of environmental public language is exemplary of this sort of substantive innovation. The other kind of change involves the scope of interests outside one's self that one takes into account, rather than their content. An exemplar is Gifford Pinchot's case for utilitarian management of forests, which required not just empirical recognition of the remote effects of deforestation, but also an ethical and, perhaps, imaginative identification with the interests of Americans far away in space and time. In both kinds of changes, environmental public language has been inseparable from broader contests about national purpose, civic dignity, and the role and scale of government.

The Politics of Anomaly

These contests continue, which is one reason that the narrow view of climate politics that this Article challenges is inadequate. Consider one example that makes little sense through the lens of narrow self-interest, much more as part of an on-going debate over environmental values: the organizing project that, at the time of writing, has led 1015 city governments, representing nearly eighty-two million Americans, to adopt the goals of the Kyoto Protocol (a seven percent reduction in greenhouse-gas emissions from 1990 levels by 2012) through an instrument called the Mayors Climate Protection Agreement. Originally an initiative of the Seattle mayor's office, the Agreement is now managed through the United States Conference of Mayors and overlaps substantially with the Sierra Club's "Cool Cities" campaign. A 2007 survey (with serious selection-bias problems) of then-participating cities found most assuming some costs to pursue the (admittedly unrealistic) Kyoto goal. Seattle claims to have reduced the greenhouse gas emissions of city operations by sixty percent since 2005. While most efforts are similarly concentrated in city-government actions, Austin Energy, in Texas's capital city, has set a goal of securing twenty percent renewable energy sources and fifteen percent of net supply from efficiency efforts by 2020, and cities from Fort Collins, Colorado, to Burlington, Vermont, have been investing in wind energy and other renewables. Residents of Marin County, California, are seeking permission to give utility customers the option of paying a higher rate to tap into a renewable and local set of energy sources, and forty-one percent of San Francisco voters in November supported a ballot initiative requiring that all city energy come from renewable sources by 2040.

Anomaly as Persuasion

Is this behavior merely trivial or silly? To be sure, it is fair to describe some of the efforts just sketched as low-hanging fruit and, in cases, cheap talk. But since the costs are not zero, and the benefits, in theory, are almost exactly that, the question of motivation is still fairly sharply presented. (If one says the benefits are to the politicians, then one must restate the problem for the voters who support them, who pay taxes and utility bills.) No one, of course, really doubts that those involved are acting from some combination of moral motive and self-interest as they understand it. The aim here is to make their action more intelligible by treating it as part of the same kind of public debate treated throughout this Article, an integral part of a story about democratic self-interpretation, rather than an anomaly in a story about self-interest. In private interviews and public statements, city officials and activists explain their efforts in several ways. They are quick to cite the advantage certain regions, such as California, hope to enjoy from early adoption and manufacture of technologies that may later become standard (a calculation that predicts effective political action on climate in the future, meaning that it is not really consistent with a larger pessimistic view of the problem). They embrace a simple public-choice motive: city governments hope to benefit from green-development block grants and, in the longer term, density-friendly economic development, and early efforts may position them to do both. They also regard themselves as engaged in political persuasion that they hope will induce others to take similar action. Whether this is plausible is partly endogenous to the politics itself. This politics seeks to affect the reasons — specifically those grounded in environmental values — that people understand themselves to have for joining collective undertakings. Rather than a specimen of an independently established logic of collective action, it is an engagement with that logic itself.

What is the nature of the persuasion? In addressing this question, I am mainly concerned with how the leaders I spoke with understood their own participation and that of the people they recruited. Their opponents offered familiar arguments that local climate action can only be futile, and in their advocacy, the leaders developed a concrete sense of how to engage those arguments.

First, local climate activists appreciate that they are engaged in a symbolic politics made possible by the country's adoption of environmental commitments in the 1970s and earlier. Before the 2008 presidential election, which brought a new emphasis on climate change to the White House, their actions invoked those commitments when the national government was seen as neglecting them. The activists sought to announce that the commitments remained vital, and, in doing so, contribute to the truth of the assertion. These symbolic actions reflect the existence of environmental commitments as national values; by adopting nominal emission limits, cities make a public argument that the federal government should do the same.

Second, these initiatives are intended as existence proofs that coordinated action can succeed in reducing greenhouse gas emissions, at least within a locality (ignoring for the moment the prospect of emitting activities fleeing to other jurisdictions). A successful experiment is a powerful form of persuasion, establishing a concrete option for others with salience that a merely hypothetical alternative is unlikely to command.

Third, local climate initiatives are attempts to reframe the cultural valence of climate change from an ideological flashpoint associated with left-liberal attitudes to a rallying point of pragmatic effort. Studies of public opinion on climate change show that views of both the severity of the problem and the human power to address it conform to the hypothesis that people assess facts based on whether the truth or falsehood of those facts would confirm or undercut the bases of their social status and moral vision of the world. Those who regard the problem as serious and profess to believe that people can do something about it are also pro regulatory economic and political egalitarians.

Those who profess to think that the threat is negligible and beyond human influence in any case (two views that would not seem inherently aligned but for their affinity in the cultural-meaning register) fall on the other side of those larger markers of world view. Strategists for local initiatives emphasize practical local vulnerability to climate change. The paradigm case is Seattle's dependence on the Cascade snowpack for water and hydroelectric power, which figured importantly in the local argument for leading the conference of Mayors Agreement initiative. This argument is available across the snowpack-dependent West, as is the danger of drought for already water-stressed regions in the Southwest and, in some recent droughts, the Southeast. If it succeeds, like nineteenth-century arguments tying forest conservation to erosion prevention and future timber harvests, this effort will have made climate change a different kind of problem. This sort of change relies on both empirical knowledge and democratic self-interpretation.

Finally, the activists aim to create new norms of climate regulation within small and rather insular populations at a time when such norms have little purchase in the larger society. Ultimately, local initiatives aim to make low carbon conduct conventional — part of a practice of membership and mutual respect. As a starting place, the initiatives take advantage of small and dense networks, such as mayors, city officials, and environmental activists. This is an attempt to create a practice among members of a limited public, rather as the Sierra Club once created a limited public in which the Romantic experience of nature was widely shared and explored as a public language.

The unifying aim of this activism is persuasion: to give a broader class of people reasons to believe climate change is both real and susceptible to action. Local climate initiatives engage the questions of: (1) what reasons exist to address climate change; (2) who has those reasons; and (3) what reasons would be sufficient to spur collective action. At least for their activist core of proponents, local initiatives are acts of defiance against the idea that politics is finite — against the pessimistic account of climate change and collective action sketched earlier. If they were merely defiant, they would count only as expressive, in just the vein of a chanted slogan. The burden of the argument here is that local climate initiatives are intended rather as efforts at persuasive politics, bearing on the reasons for action that operate in the political community and its subcommunities. Those who work for local climate initiatives understand the argument that their action is necessarily futile. Proving otherwise is a project motivated precisely by an understanding of the argument and a wish to change the terms on which it rests.

Community, Politics, Thresholds

We have seen that throughout the history of American environmental law, intrinsically satisfying ways of interacting with the natural world have spurred instrumental political action, such as calls for conservation laws. The Sierra Club's members moved into advocacy powered by a way of experiencing the Sierra Nevada and the California redwoods. The struggle to develop and express a similarly potent experience of wilderness shaped the early work of the Wilderness Society. These motives are particularly important because politically relevant communities and movements can form around them for the sake of a satisfying shared experience, whether or not participants expect to achieve political goals. As these groups grow, they become more likely to be politically effective, even if political efficacy is not what attracts their growing membership. In this way, intrinsic motives can carry communities of conviction across thresholds of political relevance.

Implicit in pessimistic analyses of climate politics is a seldom-expressed idea that climate change presents no opportunities for intrinsic satisfactions of this sort — that carbon reduction, mitigation, and the rest are all cost and no reward, and that therefore no one would rationally undertake them without first solving the collective-action problems that dog climate politics. As Sarah Krakoff has recently argued, this may not be true. Local carbon-reduction efforts seem to be, among other things, some citizens' effort to (1) do the ecologically right thing and (2) form and participate in communities that do the same. This development resembles both the shared aesthetic and spiritual experience that drove the early Sierra Club and the "new nationalist" strand of Progressivism, with its insistence that a share of personal meaning and worth comes from the goodness or greatness of one's polity. This development differs from early Sierra culture, though, in being less ecstatic than deliberate, closer to an atmospheric land ethic than to John Muir's aesthetic rapture. It differs from many Progressive predecessors in being, for the moment, a matter of local rather than national or global politics; but that may be momentary. [...]

Conclusion

Ideas about the value of the natural world are, and have always been, integral to the repertoire of arguments that Americans use to try to persuade one another of the character and implications of common commitments. How we understand nature is part of civic identity. It has developed by interacting with other, better-trodden themes of American public language: national purpose, civic dignity, and the role and appropriate scale of government, to name those that have figured most prominently in this Article. This understanding of the natural world is anything but monolithic: it is one of the common terms that Americans interpret differently in battling over their disagreements. The natural world has stood at various times, and for various constituencies, for the idea of infinite material progress, the possibility of rational resource management in the public interest, and the need to redefine human flourishing beyond material mastery of nature toward a heightened aesthetic awareness and spiritual response to it. The politics of nature has contributed to the civic dignity of the free labor idea, in which the public domain must be open to citizens' settlement and exploitation; to that of progressive reformers, in which the citizen should do her part in maintaining a social order that manages its complex and interdependent systems for health and mutual benefit; and to that of the Romantic, whose loyalty to the political community is paradoxically conditioned on its enabling him to leave its constraints from time to time, escaping into solitude, reflection, and perhaps mystical ecstasy.

More than a century of development in these themes contributed to the rise of modern environmentalism, sometimes inaptly described as an event without a history. These themes contributed mightily to the specific shape that early environmentalism gave to the anxieties of the 1960s and early 1970s. Environmentalism, in turn, gave ideas of nature's intrinsic value and moral instructiveness new reach in American public language. Understanding that era as one in which legislators joined movements and commentators in adopting this new account of the natural world casts light on the peculiarities and limits of their landmark legislation. In turn, understanding today's politics as a continuation of the politics of nature casts light on a signal anomaly of climate politics, the proliferation of local initiatives to control greenhouse-gas emissions. In a broader spirit, it also suggests the value of imaginative forecasting like that attempted in Part V, which connects today's emerging environmental problems with the themes of environmental public language.

The developments that this Article explores were acts of democratic self-interpretation. Social movements, political leaders, and public commentators repeatedly adapted ideas of the natural world to the needs of their times, and in turn recast those needs in light of new understandings of the meaning and value of nature. The philosophical and literary canon of American conservationism — Thoreau, Muir, Leopold — is badly miscast when taken as a line of prophets or an intergenerational seminar in environmental ethics. These touchstone expositors were, rather, parts of their respective worlds and times, and their intelligibility to us is partly a product of the politics of nature between then and now. Thoreau and Muir were sources of material for the self-interpretation of individuals and movements, Thoreau perhaps diffidently, Muir deliberately, as he turned his role as publicist of Romantic aesthetics into that of social-movement impresario.

Leopold, for his part, was a product of the intensely practical, public-oriented argument-making of a movement culture, and his work was a response to the challenges of justifying wilderness in the terms available in the 1920s through the 1940s. None of this makes their conviction less real or reduces their literary or theoretical interest. But it does set their meaning for environmental law and politics just where it belongs: in relation to the self-interpreting democratic community that they addressed and to which they belonged — along with millions of mostly forgotten people who gave their ideas form and life, from the weekend sojourners of the Sierra Club and the uncharismatic Wilderness Society editor, Howard Zahniser, to the federal legislators of the 1960s and mayors in the last decade. That larger community and the limited publics within it are the ultimate actors in this story.

They — we — will choose which strands of the inheritance set out here will remain a living tradition in the environmental politics of our time. Climate change comes draped in claims of apocalypse, national mission, and market-friendly technological optimism — a culturally over-determined phenomenon if ever we have faced one. Which accounts will prevail is partly a political choice, one made of old materials in new circumstances. The choice will be the work of the next generation of the cultural innovation, political argument, and social movements that have produced American environmental public language so far.

The fight against climate change can be seen as closely aligned with the struggle for recognition of Indigenous peoples' rights. The following article offers a critique of the global climate regime and its evolution through the lens of Indigenous rights. A critical point made in the article is that Indigenous interests are not formally represented in the UN-based nation-to-nation negotiation process. Influential nations with significant Indigenous populations, such as Canada, the United States, Australia and New Zealand, have failed to represent those interests. As you will see, this leads the author to advocate for a human rights-based approach as a way forward.

Paul Havemann,
"Ignoring the Mercury in the Climate Change
Barometer: Denying Indigenous Peoples' Rights"

(2009) 13 Austl. Indigenous L. Rev. 1

UN Secretary-General Ban Ki-Moon recently declared that those least responsible for climate change bear the greatest burden:

> Our earth is more fragile than we might think. Whole ecosystems that support millions of lives face significant disruption. In some cases, whole countries and peoples — not only animal species — are at risk of disappearing. And the effects are being felt most acutely by those least able to cope and least responsible for the problem. This is a moral issue. Our responses must be guided by the principles of common responsibility and the common good.

Indigenous peoples are amongst the groups most vulnerable to climate change and yet are the least responsible for the unnatural (ie, anthropogenic, human-induced) carbon cycle that is causing it. The absence of a human rights-based approach to climate change governance, which would recognise Indigenous rights to participation and other human rights, constitutes a major flaw in the processes, policies and measures of the entire climate change regime. Denial of these rights permeates processes under the 1992 United Nations *Framework Convention on Climate Change* ('UNFCCC') and its 1997 *Kyoto Protocol*, as well as the policies, measures, rules and procedures promulgated annually by Conferences of the Parties for determining how to break the unnatural carbon cycle. Participation is defined here as the right to contribute to the deliberations and decisions of decision-making bodies, in contrast to the mere opportunity to be consulted or to be an observer of proceedings at the behest of the state parties. Indigenous peoples' organisations are only able to obtain observer status in UNFCCC proceedings. Despite the unique impact of climate change on Indigenous peoples, their organisations are among the groups least likely to have their substantive and procedural rights recognised. As a consequence, Indigenous peoples' rights are abrogated both by climate change itself and by the current measures to mitigate and adapt to it, including carbon trading. Both the 'clean development mechanism' defined in art 12 of the *Kyoto Protocol* and UN Collaborative Programme on Reducing Emissions from Deforestation and Forest Degradation in Developing Countries ('REDD') are intended to reduce greenhouse gas emissions through the creation of a carbon market; thus far neither Indigenous peoples nor other global civil society actors have had the option of assessing the merits of carbon trading. At present, neither the human rights of Indigenous peoples nor respect for the governance principle of free, prior and informed consent is intrinsic to the climate change governance regime and the resulting carbon market.

This commentary stresses the urgent need to fill the human rights gap in climate change governance. The human rights-based approach imposes a threefold obligation upon states and the intergovernmental organisations through which they work internationally. In accordance with what was declared by the 1993 Vienna World Conference on Human Rights, this threefold obligation is to:

- respect rights by refraining from interfering with the enjoyment of people's rights;
- protect rights by preventing these from being violated by third parties such as corporations and other states as well as individuals;
- fulfil rights by taking action towards the full realisation of people's human rights though legislation, enforcement and expenditure.

The process of implementing human rights imposes upon states a further set of obligations to:

- ensure a core minimum of rights is enjoyed by every citizen whatever the state's resource constraints;
- give priority to the rights of those most vulnerable and at risk;
- ensure the participation of people in designing and implementing measures which will affect their rights;

- establish mechanisms to respond to the violation of human rights and to monitor and report on the status of respect for human rights; and
- cooperate internationally in the realisation of human rights.

The human rights-based approach to climate change governance must explicitly incorporate the substantive and the procedural human rights of Indigenous peoples (and of other highly vulnerable groups). As an intrinsic element of climate change governance, the human rights-based approach must be proactively integrated into the design, redesign, development and implementation of all climate change abatement measures, including regulation of the carbon markets.

The right to a healthy, bio-diverse and sustainable environment is not expressly articulated in the 'International Bill of Rights' — that is, collectively, the *Universal Declaration of Human Rights* ('UDHR'), the *International Covenant on Economic, Social and Cultural Rights* ('JCESCR') and the *International Covenant on Civil and Political Rights* ('ICCPR') and its protocols — or elsewhere. As yet, no 'grundnorm' in international law specifies a human right to a healthy, bio-diverse and sustainable environment; therefore, the human rights-based approach to climate change mitigation and adaptation has to be assembled from the whole body of international law. Some experts suggest that such a right is evolving, as an inferential step, from the recognition of the rights to health, life and other basic human rights, coupled with the duty of states not to commit trans-boundary environmental harm against other states. Two regional human rights treaties, the 1981 *African Charter on Human and Peoples' Rights* and the 1988 *Additional Protocol to the American Convention on Human Rights in the Area of Economic, Social and Cultural Rights*, while not enforceable by individuals or peoples, do recognise a right to an environment of a certain quality. They suggest that a possible avenue of recognition for environmental human rights comes by way of a corollary from the duties states have accepted in relation to international environmental law under the 1994 UN *Convention on the Law of the Sea*, UNFCCC, and *Kyoto Protocol*. Nevertheless, the lack of an express right to a sustainable environment illustrates the urgency of the need to articulate and implement a human rights-based approach to climate change governance, as well as in response to climate change-induced disasters.

Climate change litigation at the international and national levels is an important, though limited, dimension to a human rights-based approach. Litigation is often a reactive response that is costly, time consuming and always hostage to the caprice of courts, human rights tribunals, other complaints mechanisms and, of course, governments. For example, in 2005 the Inuit peoples petitioned the Inter-American Commission on Human Rights to obtain recognition of their claim that United States greenhouse gas emissions have violated their human rights by adversely impacting upon every facet of fruit life. The Inter-American Commission initially responded to the Inuit petition by stating that 'the information provided does not enable us to determine whether the alleged facts would tend to characterize a violation of the rights protected by the American Declaration [of the Rights and Duties of Man]', declining even to try to make the causal link between climate change impacts and human rights; however, in 2007 the Commission agreed to the request for a further hearing. To the author's knowledge the matter is still pending. [**Ed. Note: The petition has since been denied without reasons.**] Litigation in the climate change context has an important function in the 'politics of rights', where human rights do provide a valuable resource for articulating claims and critiquing the rupture between the rhetoric and the reality of 'rights-talk'. That being said, climate change litigation *per se* is not the focus of this commentary.

Since 2007, at least, there are clear and positive indications that the building blocks for a human rights-based approach are being assembled. The UN finally started to explore how human rights can be integrated into the climate change regime at the December 2007 Bali Conference of the Parties to the UNFCCC. There the UN Deputy High Commissioner for Human Rights called for recognition of human rights and sustainable development in the context of the treat that climate change posed to the Millennium Development Goals. In March 2008, the UN Human Rights Council stated that it was 'concerned that climate change poses an immediate and far reaching threat to peoples and communities around the world and has implications for the full enjoyment of human rights'. At the same time the Council requested the Office of the UN High Commissioner for Human Rights ('OHCHR') conduct a detailed study of the relationship between human rights and climate change.

In April-May 2008, the Seventh Session of the UN Permanent Forum on Indigenous Issues devoted several days of deliberation to Indigenous peoples' rights and climate change, and issued a statement requesting participation in UNFCCC's Conferences of Parties. By mid-2009, the OHCHR had received a substantial number of submissions on climate change and human rights from states as well as nongovernmental organisations ('NGOs'). Notably, Oxfam International's briefing paper advocates a human rights-based approach, and is grounded in a rigorous critique of the political economy of the carbon market-based approach to mitigation and adaptation.

Amongst national human rights bodies, the Australian Human Rights Commission (formerly the Australian Human Rights and Equal Opportunity Commission) has shown leadership by identifying climate change as a human rights issue; and in this regard, the rights of Indigenous peoples are high on its agenda. Excellent submissions made to the OHCHR by the Environmental Defenders' Office NSW and by the Sydney Centre for International Law also reflect recognition of the specific treat climate change poses to Indigenous peoples' human rights.

The UN High Commissioner for Refugees has also been working with other agencies on a human rights-based approach to humanitarian relief in the aftermath of climate-induced disasters, jointly producing comprehensive operational guidelines in 2008. Also in 2008, the Secretariat of the 1994 UN *Convention to Combat Desertification* published a report that links vulnerability and climate change to desertification, drought and land degradation, and advocates a human rights-based approach for Indigenous and tribal peoples, and the peoples of small island developing states. The right to water is a key focus.

Unless a human rights-based approach becomes integral to climate change regime governance, there is a danger that recognition of such rights will be addressed retrospectively and reactively or neglected altogether. Integration of a human rights-based approach ought, therefore, to be a basic agenda item for the

15th UNFCCC Conference of Parties at Copenhagen in 2009, when it deliberates on the shape of the post-2012 climate change regime. Further, justiciable Indigenous peoples' rights, as well as environmental, substantive and procedural human rights, ought to form the basis of a possible Australian bill or charter of rights, which is currently under review. The coming years will be critical in addressing the problems of climate change and in attempting to alter the current trajectory to avert ecocide, and the consequential disastrous impacts on Indigenous people and their way of life. [...]

Conclusion

At the Poznan UNFCCC Conference of the Parties Victoria Tauli-Corpuz felt compelled to state:

> Witnessing the way indigenous peoples rights are undermined by the very States who took the lead in formulating and adopting the UN Declaration on Human Rights, 60 years ago, is a tragic thing. These States are very keen to include REDD as part of the agreement on mitigation which will be agreed upon during the 15th Conference of Parties in Copenhagen which will be held in 2009. However, they obstinately refuse to recognize the rights of indigenous peoples and other forest peoples, who are the ones who sacrificed life and limb to keep the world's remaining tropical and sub-tropical rainforests.

The human rights/governance gap in the climate change regime is presently very wide. The gap is at its widest for Indigenous peoples, and other vulnerable minority groups, whose rights to exist, to self-determination and to basic individual freedoms are not high priorities for states. States must embrace the human rights-based approach as an expression of their sovereignty and duty to citizens, not as a restriction upon this anachronistic expression of international legal personality. States must ensure that their actions in the international arena reflect tis necessary shift, away from the mutually assured destruction that is likely under the present market-based regime, to an ecologically sustainable global governance regime based upon human rights.

The present trajectory of current solutions to the gross overproduction of greenhouse gas emissions is to commodify rights in the carbon dump, and to trade these between low and high emitters. Carbon trading is a dangerous shell game that distracts everyone from mainstream emissions reduction measures. This has particularly pernicious consequences for Indigenous people, and other people whose lives and cultures are intimately bound to the health and sustainable biodiversity of the Earth. Their territory is likely to be the target of yet another land grab by 'carbon baggers' who will trample their rights.

The next phase of development of the climate change regime must be grounded in human rights, not carbon rights, and based fundamentally on real emission reduction strategies. As it presently operates at the international level, where the governance gap is most conspicuous, as well as at the national level, where one can speculate that the chasm between states and civil society is even greater, the climate change regime has not served Indigenous peoples well. As expressed by the Chair of the Permanent Forum on Indigenous Issues at the closing of its Seventh Session:

> while having the smallest ecological footprints themselves, indigenous peoples [have] suffered not only from the effects of climate change, but also from some of the 'solutions' imposed on them, such as biofuel plantations and large renewable energy projects, including hydroelectric dams. Emission trading schemes [do] not bring direct benefits to many indigenous peoples.

Acknowledging Indigenous peoples' rights can be justified on the grounds of morality or legality altruism or self-interest. The absence of a human rights-based approach represents an ethical, as well as legal, deficit that the global economic crisis must not be allowed to overshadow. Climate change governance internationally, regionally and nationally must be founded upon a human rights-based approach that includes as a fundamental principle free, prior and informed consent. The human rights-based approach will assist in bridging the governance gap, and will benefit all of global civil society. Ultimately, no one will be exempt from the impacts of global warming. Unabated climate change will radically degrade life on Earth as we know it, for present as well as future generations. The present plight of Indigenous peoples, without a human rights-based approach to climate governance, will be the future for all of humankind. Indigenous people are the miner's canary, the mercury in the global warming barometer.

Notes and Questions

1. It is clear that many Indigenous communities are particularly vulnerable to climate change, and it is equally clear that they have done little to contribute to the problem. At the same time, many Indigenous communities find themselves within nations, such as the United States and Canada, that are among the biggest contributors to climate change, and among the most reluctant participants in global efforts to address the problem. In your view, should these issues be left to individual nations to resolve internally, or does the international community have a role to play in addressing this issue? What role should Indigenous communities play in the global climate negotiations? How should human rights regimes deal with this issue? Consider the Indigenous platform currently being designed under the UN Climate Regime. Does it constitute an effective response to the problems identified in the article?

2. The article was written some time ago. There have been important developments since, including Canada's commitment to *United Nations Declaration on the Rights of Indigenous Peoples* (UNDRIP) (see Chapter 1), the development of an Indigenous platform under the UNFCCC to give Indigenous peoples a voice in the regime, and the Trudeau Government's commitment to a Nation-to-Nation relationship with Indigenous peoples in Canada. At the same time, as explored earlier in this chapter, Canada continues to struggle to implement policies to effectively reduce its GHG emissions. How much progress have we made?

References and Further Readings

Randall S. Abate, "Public Nuisance Suits for the Climate Justice Movement: The Right Things and the Right Time" (2010) 85 Wash. L. Rev. 197

Reuven S. Avi-Yonah & David M. Uhlmann, "Combating Global Climate Change: Why a Carbon Tax Is a Better Response to Global Warming than Cap and Trade" (2009) 28 Stan. Envtl. L.J. 3

Alexis Bélanger, "Canadian Federalism in the Context of Combating Climate Change" (2011) 20 Const. Forum 21

Jutta Brunnee, Meinhard Doelle & Lavanya Rajamani, *Promoting Compliance in an Evolving Climate Change Regime* (Cambridge University Press, 2012)

Karen Bubna-Litic & Nathalie Chalifour, "Are Climate Change Policies Fair to Vulnerable Communities — The Impact of British Columbia's Carbon Tax and Australia's Carbon Pricing Policy on Indigenous Communities" (2012) 35 Dalhousie L.J. 127

Rowena Cantley-Smith, "Climate Change and the Copenhagen Legacy: Where to from Here?" (2010) 36 Monash U.L. Rev. 278

Nathalie Chalifour, "Canadian Climate Federalism: Parliament's Ample Constitutional Authority to Legislate GHG Emissions through Regulations, a National Cap and Trade Program, or a National Carbon Tax" (2016) 36 Nat'l J. Const. L. 331

Nathalie Chalifour, "Making Federalism Work for Climate Change: Canada's Division of Powers over Carbon Taxes" (2009) 22 N.J.C.L. 119

Nathalie J. Chalifour & Jessica Earle, "Feeling the Heat: Climate Litigation under the Canadian Charter's Right to Life, Liberty, and Security of the Person" (2018) 42 Vt. L. Rev. 689

J. Scott Childs, "Continental Cap-and-Trade: Canada, the United States, and Climate Change Partnership in North America" (2010) 32 Hous. J. Int'l. L. 393

Thomas Claridge, "Federal Court Rejects Kyoto Protocol Lawsuit" (2009) 28 The Lawyers Weekly 33

Julia Dehm, "Carbon Colonialism or Climate Justice? Interrogating the International Climate Regime from a TWAIL Perspective" (2016) 33 Windsor Y.B. Access to Just. 129

Meinhard Doelle, "Arctic Climate Governance: Can the Canary in the Coal Mine Lift Canada's Head out of the Sand(s)?" (2012), online: SSRN <http://ssrn.com/ abstract=2106157>

Meinhard Doelle, "Decades of Climate Policy Failure in Canada: Can We Break the Vicious Cycle?" (2018), online: <https://blogs.dal.ca/melaw>

Meinhard Doelle, "Integrating Climate Change into Environmental Impact Assessments: Key Design Elements" (2018), online: SSRN <https://ssrn.com/abstract=3273499>

Stewart Elgie, "Kyoto, the Constitution and Carbon Trading: Waking a Sleeping BNA Bear (or Two)" (2007) 13 Queen's L.J. 67

James D. Ford *et al.*, "Climate Change in the Arctic: Current and Future Vulnerability in Two Inuit Communities in Canada" (2008) 174 The Geographical Journal 45

Andrew Gage, "Climate Change Litigation and the Public Right to a Healthy Atmosphere" (2013) 24 J. Envtl. L. & Prac. 257

Geetanjali Ganguly, Joana Setzer & Veerle Heyvaert, "If at First You Don't Succeed: Suing Corporations for Climate Change" (2018) 38 Oxford J. Leg. Stud. 841, online: DOI <https://doi.org/10.1093/ojls/gqy029>

Robert B. Gibson *et al.*, "From Paris to Projects: Clarifying the Implications of Canada's Climate Change Mitigation Commitments for the Planning and Assessment of Projects and Strategic Undertakings — Summary Report" (2018), online: <https://uwaterloo.ca/paris-to-projects/sites/ca.paris-to-projects/files/uploads/files/p2p_summary_report_0.pdf>

John C. Goetz, Morella M. De Castro, Gray Taylor & Karen Haugen-Kozyra, "Development of Carbon Emissions Trading in Canada" (2009) 46 Alta. L. Rev. 377

Andrew Green, "You Can't Pay Them Enough: Subsidies, Environmental Law, and Social Norms" (2005) 30 Harv. Envtl. L. Rev. 407

Ryan Hackney, "Flipping *Daubert*: Putting Climate Change Defendants in the Hot Seat" (2010) 40 Envtl. L. 255

Jarrad Harvey, "Old Habits Die Hard — Reflections on the Scope of the Royal Prerogative following Turp v. Canada (Minister of Justice)" (2013) 22 Const. Forum 13

Paul Havemann, "Ignoring the Mercury in the Climate Change Barometer: Denying Indigenous Peoples' Rights" (2009) 13 Austl. Indigenous L. Rev. 1

Anthony Ho & Chris Tollefson, "Sustainability-based Assessment of Project-related Climate Change Impacts: A Next Generation EA Policy Conundrum" (2016) 30 J. Envtl. L. & Prac. 67

Erkki Hollo, Kati Kulovesi & Michael Mehling, eds., *Climate Change and the Law* (Berlin: Springer, 2012)

Shi-Ling Hsu, "Carbon Tax: The Only Way Forward" (2010) 29 The Lawyers Weekly 48

Shi-Ling Hsu & Robin Elliot, "Regulating Greenhouse Gases in Canada: Constitutional and Policy Dimensions" (2009) 54 McGill L.J. 463

Indian and Northern Affairs Canada, *Report on Adaptation to Climate Change Activities in Arctic Canada* (Ottawa: Government of Canada, 2007)

Cameron Jefferies, "Filling the Gaps in Canada's Climate Change Strategy: All Litigation, All the Time" (2015) 38 Fordham Int'l L.J. 1371

Christie J. Kneteman, "Building an Effective North American Emissions Trading System: Key Considerations and Canada's Role" (2010) 20 J. Envtl. L. & Prac. 127

Albert Koehl, "EA and Climate Change Mitigation" (2010) 21 J Envtl. L. & Prac. 181

John Kostyack & Dan Rohlf, "Conserving Endangered Species in an Era of Global Warming" (2008) 38 Envtl. L. Rep. 10,203

Douglas A. Kysar, "What Climate Change Can Do about Tort Law" (2011) 41 Envtl. L. 1

D.S. Lemmen *et al.*, eds., *From Impacts to Adaptation: Canada in a Changing Climate 2007* (Ottawa: Government of Canada, 2008)

Richard Lord *et al.*, eds., *Climate Change Liability: Transnational Law and Practice* (Cambridge University Press, 2012)

Jason MacLean, "Will We Ever Have Paris? Canada's Climate Change Policy and Federalism 3.0" (2018) 55 Alberta L. Rev. 889, online: SSRN <https://ssrn.com/abstract=3080710>

Jason MacLean & Chris Tollefson, "Climate-Proofing Judicial Review after Paris: Judicial Competence and Courage" (2018) 31 J. Envtl. L. & Prac. 245

Dennis Mahony, ed., *Climate Change Law in Canada* (Aurora: Canada Law Book, 2011)

Sharon Mascher, "Neglected Sovereignty: Filling Canada's Climate Change Gap with Unilateral Measures" (2016) 29 J. Envtl. L. & Prac. 361

Lynn McDonald, "Constitutional Change to Address Climate Change and Nonrenewable Energy Use" (2008) 17 Const. Forum 113

Karin Mickelson, "Beyond a Politics of the Possible? South-North Relations and Climate Justice" (2009) 10 Melbourne J. Int'l. L. 411

Ava Murphy & Shi-Ling Hsu, *Climate Change Litigation: Inuit v. the U.S. Electricity Generation Industry* (Vancouver: University of British Columbia Faculty of Law, 2008)

Martin Olszynski, Sharon Mascher & Meinhard Doelle, "From Smokes to Smokestacks: Lessons from Tobacco for the Future of Climate Change Liability" (2017) 30 Georgetown Envtl. L. Rev. 1

Jedediah Purdy, "The Politics of Nature: Climate Change, Environmental Law, and Democracy" (2010) 119 Yale L.J. 1122

Benjamin J. Richardson, ed., *Local Climate Change Law: Environmental Regulation in Cities and Other Localities* (Edward Elgar Publishing, 2012)

J.B. Ruhl, "Climate Change Adaptation and the Structural Transformation of Environmental Law" (2010) 40 Envtl. L. 343

J.B. Ruhl, "Climate Change and the *Endangered Species Act:* Building Bridges to the No-Analog Future" (2008) 88 Boston U.L. Rev. 1

Bryan P. Schwartz, "Legal Opinion on the Constitutionality of the Federal Carbon Pricing Benchmark & Backstop Proposals" Prepared for the Government of Manitoba (2017), online: <http://www.gov.mb.ca/asset_library/en/climatechange/federal_carbon_pricing_benchmark_backstop_proposals.pdf>

Sara Seck, "Revisiting Transnational Corporations and Extractive Industries: Climate Justice, Feminism, and State Sovereignty" (2017) 26 Transnat'l L. & Contemp. Probs. 383

Michael Slattery, "Pathways from Paris: Does Urgenda Lead to Canada?" (2017) 30 J. Envtl. L. & Prac. 241

R. Trent Taylor, "The Death of Environmental Common Law?: The Ninth Circuit's Decision in *Native Village of Kivalina v. ExxonMobil Corp.*" (2012), online: McGuireWoods <http://www.mcguirewoods.com/Client-Resources/Alerts/2012/10/Death-Environmental-Common-Law.aspx>

Chris Tollefson & Anthony Ho, "Understanding Canada's Responses to Citizen Submissions under the NAAEC" (2014) 7 Golden Gate U. Envtl. L.J. 55